THE POEMS OF
ALEXANDER POPE

THE POEMS OF
ALEXANDER POPE

A one-volume edition of
the Twickenham text
with selected annotations

EDITED BY JOHN BUTT

ROUTLEDGE
LONDON AND NEW YORK

This edition first published 1963
Reprinted 1965

© *1963 by John Butt*

First published as a University Paperback in 1965
Reprinted with corrections 1968
Reprinted seven times

Reprinted 1989 by
Routledge
11 New Fetter Lane, London EC4P 4EE

ISBN 0 415 04000 0

Printed in Great Britain by
Richard Clay Ltd, Bungay, Suffolk

Preface

The completion of the first stage of the Twickenham Edition in six volumes has provided an opportunity of making a new one-volume edition of Pope's entire poetical work, except for the translation of Homer. Such an edition would have been a formidable undertaking without the labours of the Twickenham editors, whose work upon the text, canon, chronology, and elucidation of Pope's poetry has been put to use at every stage. This edition is in a real sense a reduced version of the Twickenham edition. The text is the Twickenham text but without the variant readings, without the Latin original of the *Imitations of Horace*, without the mock indexes to each version of *The Dunciad*, without the poems of doubtful authenticity, the 1712 version of *The Rape of the Lock*, and a few small pieces in volume VI that were subsequently incorporated in longer poems. The annotation is derived with few exceptions from the Twickenham annotation. All Pope's notes are reprinted here in full, but without variant readings and without indication of the editions in which they are to be found. They are designated by the Letter P within square brackets, except in *The Dunciad* where the commentary is largely Pope's. When editorial addition has been required within his notes (or in *The Dunciad*, has been appended to them), it has been placed within diagonal brackets.

The arrangement of the poems posed a problem. Pope himself never attempted to collect all his verse in a single volume. The octavo editions of his works published in the last years of his life extend to three volumes of poems, the first two of which were issued in two parts each. In these editions he grouped his poems under the following headings: 'Original Poems written under 25 years of age', 'Translations done at the same time', 'Imitations of English Poets', 'Epistles', 'Epitaphs', 'Epigrams', and 'Imitations of Horace and Dr. Donne'. Thus he abandoned the category of 'Miscellanies on Several Occasions', which he had used in the *Works* of 1717, since all that he chose to reprint could be found without much difficulty in one or other of these new groups.

With only a few minor poems selected for inclusion, Pope's problem was relatively simple. But when Warburton set himself to prepare the first collected edition after Pope's death and decided that several more of the shorter pieces should be included, he was constrained to restore the category of 'Miscellanies'. Every

subsequent editor has followed this practice; and since this category has grown in size in each edition, it has meant that more
and more poems have been loosely and illogically associated in
positions where they are most easily overlooked and least easily
found.

In the Twickenham edition, volume VI, an attempt was made to
arrange the minor poems in chronological order of composition,
and the titles of the major poems were inserted in their proper
years. Though this arrangement enabled the student to see both
the whole range of Pope's poetical career in perspective and the
development of his style from 1700 to 1744, besides presenting an
intermittent but progressive record of his activities, thoughts, and
feelings, it was an arrangement which could not be adopted for an
edition of the poems in a single volume. To follow the chronological
order entails separating the four ethical *Epistles to Several Persons*
which Warburton re-named *Moral Essays* and abandoning the
order which Pope prescribed for them in 1735 and to which readers
have accordingly grown accustomed. Pope also devised what he
called a 'proper Order' for the *Imitations of Horace*, and this was not
the chronological order.

The order adopted for this volume preserves some features of
Pope's categories, yet does not depart so far from chronological
order as to mislead the reader and to destroy all sense of a develop-
ing career.

In the first section are found all poems written between 1700
and 1717, the year of Pope's first collected edition. The 'Imitations
of English Poets' and the 'Translations and Paraphrases done in
Youth' are Pope's categories, but they have been extended to contain other authentic poems of this period; together they indicate
the sort of prentice work he undertook. They are succeeded by the
Pastorals and later poems written in this period, and a group called
'Minor Verse: 1700–1717'. What constitutes a 'major' poem is a
decision that has given the editor delight to exercise; and an opportunity has been taken in this and the following two sections of
'promoting' a few poems which have not yet received the critical
attention they deserve.

The second section covers the years 1718–1729 and ends with
The Dunciad Variorum. The relative scarceness of major poems
in this section is owing to Pope's long labours on the translation
of Homer. The minor verse of the period contains several epistles,

epitaphs, and epigrams, categories which, on a balance of considerations, were not thought to deserve retaining.

The major poems of the last section contain the two completed parts of what Pope designed as an 'ethic work in four books', that is to say, the *Essay on Man* and the *Moral Essays*. These are followed by the *Imitations of Horace*, and of Donne, 'in proper Order', a few 'promoted' poems, and *The Dunciad in Four Books*.

The date of composition and of publication of each poem is briefly indicated below its title. For more precise information on this and on other details the reader is referred to the Twickenham edition, where he will also find full references to passages quoted in the notes. An asterisk added to the title of a poem in the list of contents indicates that the poem was never acknowledged by Pope either publicly or tacitly, but that its credentials rest on evidence set out in the Twickenham edition.

JOHN BUTT

Edinburgh, 1961

Contents

PREFACE   *page* vii

CHRONOLOGICAL TABLE   xix

LIST OF ABBREVIATIONS   xxiii

THE PREFACE OF 1717   xxv

POEMS: 1700–1717

IMITATIONS OF ENGLISH POETS

Verses in imitation of Waller   3

   i Of a Lady singing to her Lute   3

   ii Of the Lady who could not sleep in a stormy
     Night   3

   iii Of her Picture   4

   iv Of her Sickness   4

   v Of her walking in a Garden after a Shower   4

   vi Of her Sighing   5

Verses in imitation of Cowley   5

   i Weeping   5

   ii Presenting a Lark   6

   iii The River   6

To the Author of a Poem, intitled, Successio   7

On Silence   8

Chaucer   9

Spenser: The Alley   10

Waller: On a Fan of the Author's design   12

Cowley: The Garden   12

E. of Dorset: i Artimesia   13

       ii Phryne   14

The Happy Life of a Country Parson   15

TRANSLATIONS AND PARAPHRASES DONE IN YOUTH

A Paraphrase on Thomas a Kempis; L. 3, C. 2   17

Polyphemus and Acis   18

The Fable of Vertumnus and Pomona   22

Translations and Paraphrases done in Youth (continued)

The Fable of Dryope	*page* 26
Sapho to Phaon	29
The First Book of Statius His Thebais	35
The Gardens of Alcinous	59
The Episode of Sarpedon	60
The Arrival of Ulysses in Ithaca	69
Argus	75
January and May; or, the Merchant's Tale: from Chaucer	76
The Wife of Bath her Prologue, from Chaucer	98
Rondeau	111
*On the Statue of Cleopatra	111
*Psalm XCI	113
*Stanza's. From the french of Malherbe	114
*From Boetius, de cons. Philos.	115
*Hymn of St. Francis Xavier	115
Adaptations of the Emperor Hadrian:	
i Adriani morientis ad Animam	116
ii The Dying Christian to his Soul	116
Imitation of Tibullus, (Lib. i. Eleg. IV)	117
Imitation of Martial, Book 10, Epig. 23	117
Written over a Study; out of Maynard	118
The Prayer of Brutus	118
PASTORALS, WITH A DISCOURSE ON PASTORAL	119
ODE FOR MUSICK, ON ST. CECILIA'S DAY	139
AN ESSAY ON CRITICISM	143
EPISTLE TO MISS BLOUNT, With the Works of Voiture	169
THE TEMPLE OF FAME	172
MESSIAH	189
WINDSOR-FOREST	195
THREE THEATRICAL PIECES	
Prologue to Mr. Addison's Tragedy of *Cato*	211
*Prologue, Design'd for Mr. Durfy's last Play	212
Epilogue to Jane Shore	213

TO MR. ADDISON, Occasioned by his Dialogues
    on Medals   *page* 215
THE RAPE OF THE LOCK   217
EPISTLE TO MISS BLOUNT, on her leaving the
    Town, after the Coronation   243
A FAREWELL TO LONDON   245
THE UNIVERSAL PRAYER   247
EPISTLE TO MR. JERVAS   249
ELOISA TO ABELARD   252
ELEGY TO THE MEMORY OF AN UNFORTUNATE
    LADY   262

MINOR VERSE: 1700–1717

    Ode on Solitude   265
    Lines from Alcander   265
    *An Epistle to Henry Cromwell, Esq;   267
    Epigram. Occasion'd by Ozell's Translation of
        Boileau's Lutrin   271
    Letter to Cromwell   271
    Lines added to Wycherley's Poems   272
        i On Dulness   272
        ii Similitudes (*a*) Of the Byass of a Bowl,
                    (*b*) Of the Weights of a Clock   273
        iii Similitudes   273
        iv Lines on Solitude and Retirement   274
        v Conclusion of The Bill of Fare   275
    Epigrams from Private Letters, 1708–10   276
    *Lines from The Critical Specimen   277
    Fragments from Private Letters   278
    *Epitaph. On John Lord Caryll   278
    The Balance of Europe   279
    *Verses to be prefix'd before Bernard Lintot's
        New Miscellany   279
    *Verses Occasion'd by an &c. at the End of
        Mr. D'Urfy's Name   280
    Fragments, 1712   283
    *On a Lady who P—st at the Tragedy of Cato   283

Minor Verse: 1700–1717 (continued)

*Two or Three; or a Receipt to make a Cuckold *page* 283

*Upon a Girl of Seven Years Old 284

*To Belinda on the Rape of the Lock 284

*The Three gentle Shepherds 285

Verses in the Scriblerian Manner 285

*Impromptu, To Lady Winchelsea 288

To Eustace Budgell, Esq. on his Translation of the
　　Characters of Theophrastus 288

To a Lady with the Temple of Fame 289

*Four Poems from A Key to the Lock 289

Characters:

　　i Macer 292

　　*ii Umbra 293

　　iii Atticus 293

Epitaph on P. P. Clerk of the Parish 294

Couplets on Wit 295

Two Chorus's to the Tragedy of Brutus 296

Lines on Curll 298

*To Mr. John Moore, Author of the Celebrated
　　Worm-Powder 298

A Roman Catholick Version of the First Psalm 300

Epitaph. On Sir William Trumbull 300

*Sandys's Ghost 301

*Epigram. On the Toasts of the Kit-Cat Club 304

*Prologue to The Three Hours after Marriage 304

The Court Ballad 305

*Epigrams, Occasion'd by an Invitation to Court 307

*Epistle to a Lady 308

Occasion'd by some Verses of his Grace the Duke
　　of Buckingham 308

*Verses sent to Mrs. T. B. with his Works 309

A Hymn written in Windsor Forest 310

POEMS: 1718–1729

Epistle to Robert Earl of Oxford 313

To Mrs. M. B. on her Birth-day *page* 315
THE DUNCIAD VARIORUM 317

MINOR VERSE: 1718–1729

Lines on Mr. Hatton's Clocks 461
Lines to Lord Bathurst 461
Verses in the Scriblerian Manner 462
Three Epitaphs on John Hewet and Sarah Drew 462
*Answer to Mrs. Howe 463
Epitaph. Intended for Mr. Rowe 464
Epitaph. Designed for Mr. Dryden's Monument 464
Epistle to James Craggs, Esq; 465
*A Dialogue 465
On Lady Mary Wortley Montagu's Portrait 465
*To Sir Godfrey Kneller, On his painting for me the
    Statues of Apollo, Venus, and Hercules 466
*In behalf of Mr. Southerne. To the Duke of
    Argyle 466
*Lines from Acis and Galatea 466
*Duke upon Duke 467
*An Inscription upon a Punch-Bowl 472
*To Mr. Gay 472
Epitaph. On the Honble. Simon Harcourt 473
Verses to Mrs. Judith Cowper 473
Lines to Bolingbroke 473
Inscription 474
Epitaph On Lady Kneller 474
*On a certain Lady at Court 474
*Lines on Swift's Ancestors 475
*Receipt to make Soup. For the Use of Dean Swift 475
Presentation Verses to Nathaniel Pigott 476
*The Capon's Tale 477
*The Discovery: or, The Squire turn'd Ferret 478
*Epigram, in a Maid of Honour's Prayer-Book 481
*Verses on Gulliver's Travels 481
Epitaph On James Craggs, Esq.; 490

Minor Verse: 1718–1729 (continued)

Fragment of a Satire   *page* 490

Sylvia, a fragment   492

*Lines from The Art of Sinking   493

*Verses to be placed under the Picture of England's
   Arch-Poet   494

To the Right Honourable the Earl of Oxford.
   Upon a piece of News in Mist   495

*Epitaph. On G——   496

*Epitaphs from the Latin on the Count of
   Mirandula   496

Lines: i in Conclusion of a Satire; ii Inscriptio   497

Epitaph On Sir Godfrey Kneller   497

Epitaph On the Monument of the Honble. Robert
   Digby, and of his sister Mary   498

POEMS: 1730–1744

AN ESSAY ON MAN   501

MORAL ESSAYS
   i To Richard Temple, Viscount Cobham. Of the
      Knowledge and Characters of Men   549
   ii To a Lady. Of the Characters of Women   559
   iii To Allen Lord Bathurst. Of the Use of Riches   570
   iv To Richard Boyle, Earl of Burlington. Of the Use
      of Riches   586

AN EPISTLE TO DR. ARBUTHNOT   597

IMITATIONS OF HORACE
   The First Satire of the Second Book of Horace
      Imitated   613
   The Second Satire of the Second Book of Horace
      Paraphrased   619
   The First Epistle of the First Book of Horace
      Imitated   624
   The Sixth Epistle of the First Book of Horace
      Imitated   630

Imitations of Horace (continued)

The First Epistle of the Second Book of Horace
Imitated *page* 634

The Second Epistle of the Second Book of Horace
Imitated 650

An Imitation of the Sixth Satire of the Second
Book of Horace 659

The Seventh Epistle of the First Book of Horace
Imitated in the Manner of Dr. Swift 664

Sober Advice from Horace 667

The First Ode of the Fourth Book of Horace 673

Part of the Ninth Ode of the Fourth Book 674

The Second Satire of Dr. John Donne Versifyed 676

The Fourth Satire of Dr. John Donne Versifyed 679

Epilogue to the Satires 688

*On receiving from the Right Hon. the Lady Frances
Shirley a Standish and two Pens 704

*On lying in the Earl of Rochester's Bed at Atterbury 706

Verses on a Grotto by the River Thames at
Twickenham 707

THE DUNCIAD in Four Books 709

MINOR VERSE: 1730–1744

*Prologue to Sophonisba 807

Epigram: When other Ladies 808

Epitaph. Intended for Sir Isaac Newton 808

Epitaph. On Mr. Elijah Fenton 808

Epitaph. On General Henry Withers 809

Epitaph. On Mrs. Corbet 809

To Mr. C. 810

Epigrams from The Grub-Street Journal 810

Lines to a Friend 812

Epitaph. On Charles Earl of Dorset 813

On the Countess of Burlington cutting Paper 813

Horace, Satyr 4. Lib. I. Paraphrased 814

Wrote by Mr. P. in a Volume of Evelyn on Coins 815

The Six Maidens 815

Minor Verse: 1730–1744 (continued)

Epitaph. For Dr. Francis Atterbury	*page* 816
Poems from Miscellanies, 1732	817
Epitaph. On Mr. Gay	818
The Crux-Easton Epigrams	818
Prologue, for the Benefit of Mr. Dennis	819
To the Earl of Burlington asking who writ the Libels against him	820
To Lord Hervey & Lady Mary Wortley	820
A Character	820
Epigrams Occasion'd by Cibber's Verses in Praise of Nash	821
Epigram. On One who made long Epitaphs	822
Epitaph. On Edmund Duke of Buckingham	822
Epitaph. On John Knight	823
Bounce to Fop	823
Epigram. Engraved on the Collar of a Dog which I gave to his Royal Highness	826
Sonnet Written upon Occasion of the Plague	826
Epitaph. For one who would not be buried in Westminster-Abbey	827
Epitaph. On Himself	827
One Thousand Seven Hundred and Forty	827
Epigram. On lopping Trees in his Garden	831
Verbatim from Boileau	832
On the Benefactions in the late Frost	832
Epigrams 1738–1741	832
Epigram. On Cibber's Declaration that he will have the Last Word with Mr. Pope	835
Tom Southerne's Birth-day Dinner at Ld. Orrery's	835
Epigram. On Bishop Hough	835
Epitaph on Mr. Rowe	836
Fragment of Brutus, an Epic	836
Lines on Bounce	837
INDEX OF TITLES	839
INDEX OF FIRST LINES	844

Chronological Table

1688 (May 21) Alexander Pope born in London of elderly parents.

c. 1700 Pope's family moved to Binfield, in Windsor Forest, [?] to comply with anti-Catholic regulations. Some ten miles away at Mapledurham lived Martha Blount.
Death of Dryden.

c. 1705 Pope began to make acquaintance with the literary society of London.

1709 (May) The *Pastorals* published in the sixth part of Tonson's *Miscellanies*.

1711 (May) *An Essay on Criticism* published; praised in *The Spectator* by Addison, and damned by Dennis.

1712 (May) The *Messiah* published by Steele in *The Spectator*. Lintot's *Miscellany* published, containing the first version of *The Rape of the Lock*, and other poems by Pope. Pope was becoming acquainted with Swift, Gay, Parnell, and Arbuthnot, who together formed the Scriblerus Club.

1713 (March) *Windsor-Forest.*
(April) Addison's *Cato* first acted, with a prologue by Pope. Pope was contributing to Steele's *Guardian*.
(October) Proposals issued for a translation of the *Iliad*. Began to take lessons in painting from Jervas.

1714 (March) The enlarged version of *The Rape of the Lock.*

1715 (February) *The Temple of Fame.*
(June 6) The *Iliad*, Books I–IV, published; followed two days later by Tickell's translation of *Iliad* I and by numerous attacks on Pope's *Iliad*. During this year [?], Pope wrote his character of Addison, and became acquainted with Lady Mary Wortley Montagu.

1716 (March) *Iliad*, vol. II.
(April) Pope's family sold the house at Binfield, and

xix

settled at Chiswick, where their neighbour was Lord
Burlington.

1717 (January) *Three Hours after Marriage* by Pope, Gay, and
Arbuthnot, first acted; ridiculed by Cibber.
(June) *Iliad*, vol. III.
The collected volume of Pope's *Works*, containing *Verses
to the Memory of an Unfortunate Lady* and *Eloisa to
Abelard*.
(October) Pope's father died.

1718 (June) *Iliad*, vol. IV.
Death of Parnell. Pope and his mother moved to Twickenham late in the year.

1719 Death of Addison.

1720 (May) *Iliad*, vols. V and VI.

1721 (September) The *Epistle to Addison* prefixed to Tickell's
edition of Addison's *Works*.
(December) The *Epistle to Oxford* prefixed to Pope's edition of Parnell's *Poems*.

1723 (January) Pope's edition of John Sheffield, Duke of Buckingham's *Works* published, and seized by the Government
on suspicion of Jacobitish passages.
(May) Pope called before the House of Lords as a witness
at Atterbury's trial.

1725 (March) Pope's edition of Shakespeare published in six
volumes.
(April) *Odyssey*, vols. I–III. Grub Street taunts Pope as a
'poetical undertaker'.
Bolingbroke returned from exile, and settled near Pope at
Dawley Farm, Uxbridge.

1726 (March) Theobald's *Shakespeare Restored: or, a Specimen
of the Many Errors . . . Committed . . . by Mr. Pope*.
(June) *Odyssey*, vols. IV–V.
Pope visited by Swift. *Gulliver's Travels* published in
October.

1727 (June) Pope-Swift *Miscellanies*, vols. I and II.
Swift's second visit to Pope.

1728 (March) Pope-Swift *Miscellanies*, 'last' volume. The
Peri Bathous arouses angry comment.
(May) *The Dunciad*, in three books, with Theobald as hero.
Numerous attacks on Pope follow.

1729 (April) *The Dunciad Variorum*.

1731 (December) *Epistle to Burlington* [Moral Essay IV].

1732 (October) Pope-Swift *Miscellanies*, 'third' volume.
(December) Death of Gay.

1733 (January) *Epistle to Bathurst* [Moral Essay III].
(February) The first *Imitation of Horace* [Sat. II i].
(February-May) *An Essay on Man*, Epistles I-III.
(June) Death of Pope's mother.

1734 (January) *Epistle to Cobham* [Moral Essay I].
An Essay on Man, Epistle IV.
(July) *Imitation of Horace* [Sat. II ii].
(December) *Sober Advice from Horace*.

1735 (January) *Epistle to Dr. Arbuthnot*.
(February) *Of the Characters of Women* [Moral Essay II].
Death of Arbuthnot.
(April) The *Works*, vol. II.
(May) Curll's edition of Pope's letters.
Bolingbroke returned to France.

1737 (April) *Imitation of Horace* [Ep. II ii].
(May) Pope's edition of his letters.
Imitation of Horace [Ep. II i].
An Essay on Man attacked by Crousaz, Professor of Mathematics and Philosophy at Lausanne.

1738 (January-March) *Imitations of Horace* [Eps. I vi and I i].
(May-July) *Epilogue to the Satires*.
Warburton began his replies to Crousaz.
Pope visited by Bolingbroke.

1740 (April) Pope's first meeting with Warburton.

1742 (March) *The New Dunciad* [i.e. Book IV].

1743 (October) *The Dunciad* in four books with Cibber enthroned in the place of Theobald.

1744 (May 30) Death of Pope.

List of Abbreviations

Dia = *Epilogue to the Satires* (p. 688)

Dunciad A = *The Dunciad Variorum* (p. 317)

Dunciad B = *The Dunciad in Four Books* (p. 709)

E. on C. = *Essay on Criticism* (p. 143)

Ep. I i = *First Epistle of the First Book
of Horace Imitated* (p. 624)

Ep. I vi = *Sixth Epistle of the First Book
of Horace Imitated* (p. 630)

Ep. II i = *First Epistle of the Second Book
of Horace Imitated* (p. 634)

Ep. II ii = *Second Epistle of the Second Book
of Horace Imitated* (p. 650)

OED = *Oxford English Dictionary*

PSM = *Pope-Swift Miscellanies*

PSO = *Poems on Several Occasions*

PW = *Note written jointly by Pope and
Warburton*

Sat. II i = *First Satire of the Second Book
of Horace Imitated* (p. 613)

Sat. II ii = *Second Satire of the Second Book
of Horace Paraphrased* (p. 619)

Sob. Adv. = *Sober Advice from Horace* (p. 667)

The Preface of 1717

I am inclined to think that both the writers of books, and the readers of them, are generally not a little unreasonable in their expectations. The first seem to fancy that the world must approve whatever they produce, and the latter to imagine that authors are obliged to please them at any rate. Methinks as on the one hand, no single man is born with a right of controuling the opinions of all the rest; so on the other, the world has no title to demand, that the whole care and time of any particular person should be sacrificed to its entertainment. Therefore I cannot but believe that writers and readers are under equal obligations, for as much fame, or pleasure, as each affords the other.

Every one acknowledges, it would be a wild notion to expect perfection in any work of man; and yet one would think the contrary was taken for granted, by the judgment commonly past upon Poems. A Critic supposes he has done his part, if he proves a writer to have fail'd in an expression, or err'd in any particular point: and can it then be wonder'd at, if the Poets in general seem resolv'd not to own themselves in any error? For as long as one side will make no allowances, the other will be brought to no acknowledgements.

I am afraid this extreme zeal on both sides is ill-plac'd; Poetry and Criticism being by no means the universal concern of the world, but only the affair of idle men who write in their closets, and of idle men who read there.

Yet sure upon the whole, a bad Author deserves better usage than a bad Critic: for a Writer's endeavour, for the most part, is to please his Readers, and he fails merely through the misfortune of an ill judgment; but such a Critic's is to put them out of humor; a design he could never go upon without both that and an ill temper.

I think a good deal may be said to extenuate the fault of bad Poets. What we call a Genius, is hard to be distinguish'd by a man himself, from a strong inclination: and if his genius be ever so great, he can not at first discover it any other way, than by giving way to that prevalent propensity which renders him the more liable to be mistaken. The only method he has, is to make the experiment by writing, and appealing to the judgment of others: now if he happens to write ill (which is certainly no sin in itself) he is immediately made an object of ridicule. I wish we had the humanity to reflect that even the worst authors might, in their endeavour to please us, deserve something at our hands. We have no cause to quarrel with them but for their obstinacy in persisting to write; and this too may admit of alleviating circumstances. Their particular friends may be either ignorant, or insincere; and the rest of the world in general is too well bred to shock them with a truth, which generally their Booksellers are the first that inform them of. This happens not till they have spent too much of their time, to apply to any profession which might better fit their talents; and till such talents as they have are so far discredited, as to be but of small service to them. For (what is the hardest case imaginable) the reputation of a man generally depends upon the first steps he makes in the world, and people will establish their opinion of us, from what we do at that season when we have least judgment to direct us.

On the other hand, a good Poet no sooner communicates his works with the same desire of information, but it is imagin'd he is a vain young creature given up to the ambition of fame; when perhaps the poor man is all the while trembling with the fear of being ridiculous. If he is made to hope he may please the world, he falls under very unlucky circumstances; for from the moment he prints, he must expect to hear no more truth, than if he were a Prince, or a Beauty. If he has not very good sense (and indeed there are twenty men of wit, for one man of sense) his living thus in a course of flattery may put him in no small danger of becoming a Coxcomb: If he has, he will consequently have so much diffidence, as not to reap any great satisfaction from his praise; since if it be given to his face, it can scarce be distinguish'd from flattery, and if in his absence, it is hard to be certain of it. Were he sure to be commended by the best and most knowing, he is as sure of being envy'd by the worst and most ignorant, which are the majority; for it is with a fine Genius as with a fine fashion, all those are displeas'd at it who are not able to follow it: And 'tis to be fear'd that esteem will seldom do any man so much good, as ill-will does him harm. Then there is a third class of people who make the largest part of mankind, those of ordinary or indifferent capacities; and these (to a man) will hate, or suspect him: a hundred honest gentlemen will dread him as a wit, and a hundred innocent women as a satyrist. In a word, whatever be his fate in Poetry, it is ten to one but he must give up all the reasonable aims of life for it. There are indeed some advantages accruing from a Genius to Poetry, and they are all I can think of: the agreeable power of self-amusement when a man is idle or alone; the privilege of being admitted into the best company; and the freedom of saying as many careless things as other people, without being so severely remark'd upon.

I believe, if any one, early in his life should contemplate the dangerous fate of authors, he would scarce be of their number on any consideration. The life of a Wit is a warfare upon earth; and the present spirit of the learned world is such, that to attempt to serve it (any way) one must have the constancy of a martyr, and a resolution to suffer for its sake. I could wish people would believe what I am pretty certain they will not, that I have been less concern'd about Fame than I durst declare till this occasion, when methinks I should find more credit than I could heretofore: since my writings have had their fate already, and 'tis too late to think of prepossessing the reader in their favour. I would plead it as some merit in me, that the world has never been prepared for these Trifles by Prefaces, byast by recommendations, dazled with the names of great Patrons, wheedled with fine reasons and pretences, or troubled with excuses. I confess it was want of consideration that made me an author; I writ because it amused me; I corrected because it was as pleasant to me to correct as to write; and I publish'd because I was told I might please such as it was a credit to please. To what degree I have done this, I am really ignorant; I had too much fondness for my productions to judge of them at first, and too much judgment to be pleas'd with them at last. But I have reason to think they can have no reputation which will continue long, or which deserves to do so: for they have always fallen short not only of what I read of others, but even of my own Ideas of Poetry.

If any one should imagine I am not in earnest, I desire him to reflect, that the Ancients (to say the least of them) had as much Genius as we; and that to take more pains, and employ more time, cannot fail to produce more complete pieces. They constantly apply'd themselves not only to that art, but to that single branch of an art, to which their talent was most powerfully bent; and it was the business of their lives to correct and finish their works for posterity. If we can pretend to have used the same industry, let us expect the same immortality: Tho' if we took the same care, we should still lie under a farther misfortune: they writ in languages that became universal and everlasting, while ours are extremely limited both in extent, and in duration. A mighty foundation for our pride! when the utmost we can hope, is but to be read in one Island, and to be thrown aside at the end of one Age.

All that is left us is to recommend our productions by the imitation of the Ancients: and it will be found true, that in every age, the highest character for sense and learning has been obtain'd by those who have been most indebted to them. For to say truth, whatever is very good sense must have been common sense in all times; and what we call Learning, is but the knowledge of the sense of our predecessors. Therefore they who say our thoughts are not our own because they resemble the Ancients, may as well say our faces are not our own, because they are like our Fathers: And indeed it is very unreasonable, that people should expect us to be Scholars, and yet be angry to find us so.

I fairly confess that I have serv'd my self all I could by reaaing; that I made use of the judgment of authors dead and living; that I omitted no means in my power to be inform'd of my errors, both by my friends and enemies. But the true reason these pieces are not more correct, is owing to the consideration how short a time they, and I, have to live: One may be ashamed to consume half one's days in bringing sense and rhyme together; and what Critic can be so unreasonable as not to leave a man time enough for any more serious employment, or more agreeable amusement?

The only plea I shall use for the favour of the publick, is, that I have as great a respect for it, as most authors have for themselves; and that I have sacrificed much of my own self-love for its sake, in preventing not only many mean things from seeing the light, but many which I thought tolerable. I would not be like those Authors, who forgive themselves some particular lines for the sake of a whole Poem, and *vice versa* a whole Poem for the sake of some particular lines. I believe no one qualification is so likely to make a good writer, as the power of rejecting his own thoughts; and it must be this (if any thing) that can give me a chance to be one. For what I have publish'd, I can only hope to be pardon'd; but for what I have burn'd, I deserve to be prais'd. On this account the world is under some obligation to me, and owes me the justice in return, to look upon no verses as mine that are not inserted in this collection. And perhaps nothing could make it worth my while to own what are really so, but to avoid the imputation of so many dull and immoral things, as partly by malice, and partly by ignorance, have been ascribed to me. I must farther acquit my self of the presumption of having lent my name[1] to recommend any Miscellanies, or works of other men, a thing I never thought becoming a person who has hardly credit enough to answer for his own.

In this office of collecting my pieces, I am altogether uncertain, whether to look upon my self as a man building a monument, or burying the dead?

If time shall make it the former, may these Poems (as long as they last) remain as a testimony, that their Author never made his talents subservient to the mean and unworthy ends of Party or self-interest; the gratification of publick prejudices, or private passions; the flattery of the undeserving, or the insult of the unfortunate. If I have written well, let it be consider'd that 'tis what no man can do

---

[1] Pope had not 'lent his name' to a Miscellany, but he was engaged at this time in editing, anonymously, a volume entitled *Poems on Several Occasions*.

without good sense, a quality that not only renders one capable of being a good writer, but a good man. And if I have made any acquisition in the opinion of any one under the notion of the former, let it be continued to me under no other title than that of the latter.

But if this publication be only a more solemn funeral of my Remains, I desire it may be known that I die in charity, and in my senses; without any murmurs against the justice of this age, or any mad appeals to posterity. I declare I shall think the world in the right, and quietly submit to every truth which time shall discover to the prejudice of these writings; not so much as wishing so irrational a thing, as that every body should be deceiv'd, meerly for my credit. However, I desire it may then be consider'd, that there are very few things in this collection which were not written under the age of five and twenty[1]; so that my youth may be made (as it never fails to be in Executions) a case of compassion. That I was never so concern'd about my works as to vindicate them in print, believing if any thing was good it would defend itself, and what was bad could never be defended. That I used no artifice to raise or continue a reputation, depreciated no dead author I was oblig'd to, brib'd no living one with unjust praise, insulted no adversary with ill language, or when I could not attack a Rival's works, encourag'd reports against his Morals. To conclude, if this volume perish, let it serve as a warning to the Critics, not to take too much pains for the future to destroy such things as will die of themselves; and a *Memento mori* to some of my vain co-temporaries the Poets, to teach them that when real merit is wanting, it avails nothing to have been encourag'd by the great, commended by the eminent, and favour'd by the publick in general.

Nov. 10,
1716.

[1] Pope was twenty-five in 1713; by that time he had published the *Pastorals* (1709), *An Essay on Criticism* (1711), *The Rape of the Lock* (original version) and *Messiah* (1712), *Windsor-Forest* (1713).

Poems 1700-1717

Imitations of English Poets

Verses in imitation of Waller, by a Youth of thirteen

[written c. 1701; published, *PSO* 1717]

I. OF A LADY SINGING TO HER LUTE

Fair charmer cease, nor make your voice's prize
A heart resign'd the conquest of your eyes:
Well might, alas! that threaten'd vessel fail,
Which winds and lightning both at once assail.
We were too blest with these inchanting lays,   5
Which must be heav'nly when an angel plays;
But killing charms your lover's death contrive,
Lest heav'nly musick should be heard alive.
Orpheus could charm the trees, but thus a tree
Taught by your hand, can charm no less than he;   10
A poet made the silent wood pursue;
This vocal wood had drawn the poet too.

II. OF THE LADY WHO COULD NOT SLEEP IN A STORMY NIGHT

As gods sometimes descend from heav'n and deign
On earth a while with mortals to remain,
So gentle sleep from *Serenissa* flies,
To dwell at last upon her lover's eyes.
That god's indulgence can she justly crave,   5
Who flies the tyrant to relieve the slave?
Or should those eyes alone that rest enjoy,
Which in all others they themselves destroy?
Let her whom fear denies repose to take,
Think for her love what crowds of wretches wake.   10
So us'd to sighs, so long inur'd to tears,
Are winds and tempests dreadful to her ears?
Jove with a nod may bid the world to rest,
But *Serenissa* must becalm the breast.

3

III. OF HER PICTURE

The nymph her graces here express'd may find,
And by this picture learn to dress her mind;
For here no frowns make tender love afraid,
Soft looks of mercy grace the flatt'ring shade,
And, while we gaze, the gracious form appears   5
T'approve our passion and forbid our fears.
Narcissus here a different fate had prov'd,
Whose bright resemblance by himself was lov'd;
Had he but once this fairer shade descry'd,
Not for his own, but hers, the youth had dy'd.   10

IV. OF HER SICKNESS

Ah *Serenissa*, from our arms
Did you for death's preserve your charms;
From us that serv'd so long in vain,
Shall heav'n so soon the prize obtain?
Sickness, its courtship, makes the fair   5
As pale as her own lovers are.
    Sure you, the goddess we adore,
Who all cœlestial seem'd before,
While vows and service nothing gain'd,
Which, were you woman, had obtain'd;   10
At last in pity, for our sake,
Descend an human form to take,
And by this sickness chuse to tell
You are not now invincible.

V. OF HER WALKING IN A GARDEN
AFTER A SHOWER

See how the sun in dusky skies
Veils his fair glories, while he spies
Th' unclouded lustre of her eyes!
    Her bashful beauties once descry'd,
The vanquish'd roses lose their pride,   5
And in their buds their blushes hide.
    Myrtles have lost their balmy smell,
And drooping lillies seem to tell
How much her sweets their own excel.
    See! She retires: Nor can we say   10
If light breaks out or goes away,

For *Sol's* is now the only ray.
  Lo how their heads the lillies rear,
  And with fresh sweets perfume the air,
  When their bright rival is not there.   15
    Again grown proud, the spreading rose
  Its bloomy beauties does disclose,
  And to the skies its incense throws.
    Her glorious charms eclipse the day;
  Nature itself is only gay,   20
  When *Serenissa* is away.
    Like, yet unlike these flow'rs am I;
  I languish when her charms draw nigh,
  But if she disappears, I dye.

VI. OF HER SIGHING

When love would strike th' offending fair,
This incense bribes the god to spare;
And *Cytheræa* now does prize
No sweets but *Serenissa*'s sighs.
The yielding nymph by these confest,   5
Encourag'd lovers seek her breast:
So spicy gales at once betray
Th' *Arabian* coast, and waft us on our way.

Verses in imitation of Cowley. By a Youth of thirteen
[written c. 1701; published, *PSO*, 1717]

I. WEEPING

While *Celia*'s tears make sorrow bright,
Proud grief sits swelling in her eyes:
The sun (next those the fairest light)
  Thus from the ocean first did rise.
And thus thro' mists we see the sun,   5
Which else we durst not gaze upon.

These silver drops, like morning dew,
  Foretell the fervour of the day;
So from one cloud soft show'rs we view,
  And blasting lightnings burst away.   10

The stars that fall from *Celia*'s eye,
Declare our doom in drawing nigh.

The baby, in that sunny sphere
    So like a *Phaëton* appears,
That heav'n, the threaten'd world to spare,   15
    Thought fit to drown him in her tears:
Else might th' ambitious nymph aspire,
To set, like him, heav'n too on fire.

II. PRESENTING A LARK

Go tuneful bird, forbear to soar,
And the bright sun admire no more;
Go bask in *Serenissa*'s eyes,
And turn a bird of paradise.

In those fair beams thy wings display,   5
Take shorter journies to the day,
And at an humbler pitch prefer
Thy musick to an angel's ear.

Nor, tho' her slave, thy lot deplore;
The god of love himself's no more: 10
Ev'n him to constancy she brings,
And clips, like thine, his wav'ring wings.

She gains from us, as now from thee,
Our songs by our captivity;
But happier you attention gain,   15
While wretched lovers sing in vain.

III. THE RIVER

Hail sacred spring, whose fruitful stream
    Fattens the flocks, and cloaths the plain;
The melancholy poets theme,
    And solace of the thirsty swain.

Thou fly'st, like time, with eager haste;   5
    Behind thy self thou still dost stay;
Thy stream, like his, is never past,
    And yet is ever on the way.

While mankind boasts superior sight,
　With eyes erect the heav'ns to see;　　　　10
The starry eyes of heav'n delight
　To gaze upon themselves in thee.

A second sun thou dost present,
　And bring new heav'ns before our eyes;
We view a milder firmament,　　　　　　　15
　And pleas'd, look downward to the skies.

Thy streams were once th' impartial test
　Of untaught nature's humble pride,
When by thy glass the nymphs were drest,
　In flow'rs, the honours of thy side.　　　20

Of thee they drank, till blushing fruit
　Was ravisht from the tender vine;
And man, like thee, was impollute,
　Till mischief learn'd to mix with wine.

To the Author of a Poem, intitled, Successio

[written c. 1702; published, Lintot's
Miscellany, 1712]

Begone ye Criticks, and restrain your Spite,
Codrus writes on, and will for ever write;
The heaviest Muse the swiftest Course has gone,
As Clocks run fastest when most Lead is on.
What tho' no Bees around your Cradle flew,　　5
Nor on your Lips distill'd their golden Dew?
Yet have we oft discover'd in their stead,
A Swarm of Drones, that buzz'd about your Head.
When you, like Orpheus, strike the warbling Lyre,
Attentive Blocks stand round you, and admire.　　10
Wit, past thro' thee, no longer is the same,

The person addressed as the Author of . . . Successio was Elkanah
Settle, whose poem in praise of the Hanoverian succession, Eusebia
Triumphans, was published in 1702. Pope stated that his poem was
written in imitation of the style of the Earl of Dorset.
　2. Codrus] A Latin poet, temp. Domitian, whose poverty became
proverbial.

As Meat digested takes a diff'rent Name;
But Sense must sure thy safest Plunder be,
Since no Reprizals can be made on thee.
Thus thou may'st Rise, and in thy daring Flight   15
(Tho' ne'er so weighty) reach a wondrous height;
So, forc'd from Engines, Lead it self can fly,
And pondrous Slugs move nimbly thro' the Sky.
Sure *Bavius* copy'd *Mævius* to the full,
And *Chærilus* taught *Codrus* to be dull;   20
Therefore, dear Friend, at my Advice give o'er
This needless Labour, and contend no more,
To prove a dull *Succession* to be true,
Since 'tis enough we find it so in You.

17f. Inserted later in *The Dunciad* A, I 177–80, with a revision of l. 4.
19. *Bavius . . . Mævius*] Two stupid and malevolent poets of the
Augustan age.
20. *Chærilus*] A type of blundering poet who occasionally writes a good
line.

On Silence

[IN IMITATION OF THE EARL OF ROCHESTER]

[written c. 1702; published, Lintot's
Miscellany, 1712]

Silence! Cœval with Eternity;
Thou wert e'er Nature's self began to be,
'Twas one vast Nothing, All, and All slept fast in thee.

Thine was the Sway, e'er Heav'n was form'd or Earth,
E'er fruitful *Thought* conceiv'd Creation's Birth,   5
Or Midwife *Word* gave Aid, and spoke the Infant forth.

Then various Elements against thee join'd,
In one more various Animal combin'd,
And fram'd the clam'rous Race of busie Human-kind.

The tongue mov'd gently first, and Speech was low,   10
'Till wrangling *Science* taught it Noise and Show,
And wicked *Wit* arose, thy most abusive Foe.

But Rebel Wit deserts thee oft in vain;
Lost in the Maze of Words, he turns again,
And seeks a surer State, and courts thy gentle Reign.   15

Afflicted *Sense* thou kindly dost set free,
Oppress'd with Argumental Tyranny,
And routed *Reason* finds a safe Retreat in thee.

With thee in private modest *Dulness* lies,
And in thy Bosom lurks in *Thought*'s Disguise;   20
Thou Varnisher of *Fools*, and Cheat of all the *Wise*.

Yet thy Indulgence is by both confest;
Folly by thee lies sleeping in the Breast,
And 'tis in thee at last that *Wisdom* seeks for Rest.

Silence, the Knave's Repute, the Whore's good Name,   25
The only Honour of the wishing Dame;
Thy very want of Tongue makes thee a kind of Fame.

But could'st thou seize some Tongues that now are free,
How Church and State should be oblig'd to thee!
At Senate, and at Bar, how welcome would'st thou be!   30

Yet *Speech*, ev'n there, submissively withdraws
From *Rights* of *Subjects*, and the *Poor Man's Cause*;
Then pompous *Silence* reigns, and stills the noisie Laws.

Past Services of Friends, good Deeds of Foes,
What Fav'rites gain, and what the Nation owes,   35
Fly the forgetful World, and in thy Arms repose.

The Country Wit, Religion of the Town,
The Courtier's Learning, Policy o' th' Gown,
Are best by thee express'd, and shine in thee alone.

The Parson's Cant, the Lawyer's Sophistry,   40
Lord's Quibble, Critick's Jest; all end in thee,
All rest in Peace at last, and sleep eternally.

Chaucer

[written before 1709; published, *PSM*, 1727]

Women ben full of Ragerie,
Yet swinken nat sans Secresie.
Thilke moral shall ye understond,
From Schole-boy's Tale of fayre *Irelond*:

Which to the Fennes hath him betake,   5
To filch the gray Ducke fro the Lake.
Right then, there passen by the Way,
His Aunt, and eke her Daughters tway:
Ducke in his Trowzes hath he hent,
Not to be spied of Ladies gent.   10
'But ho! our Nephew,' (crieth one,)
'Ho!' quoth another, 'Cozen *John*!'
And stoppen, and lough, and callen out,—
This sely Clerk full low doth lout:
They asken that, and talken this,   15
'Lo here is *Coz*, and here is *Miss*.'
But, as he glozeth with Speeches soote,
The Ducke sore tickleth his Erse Roote:
Fore-piece and Buttons all-to-brest,
Forth thrust a white Neck, and red Crest.   20
Te-he cry'd Ladies; Clerke nought spake:
Miss star'd; and gray Ducke crieth *Quaake*.
'O Moder, Moder,' (quoth the Daughter,)
'Be thilke same Thing Maids longen a'ter?
Bette is to pyne on Coals and Chalke,   25
Then trust on Mon, whose yerde can *talke*.'

Spenser: The Alley

[written before 1709; published, *PSM*, 1727]

In ev'ry Town, where *Thamis* rolls his Tyde,
A narrow Pass there is, with Houses low;
Where ever and anon, the Stream is ey'd,
And many a Boat soft sliding to and fro.
There oft' are heard the Notes of Infant Woe,   5
The short thick Sob, loud Scream, and shriller Squawl:
How can ye, Mothers, vex your Children so?
Some play, some eat, some cack against the Wall,
And as they crouchen low, for Bread and Butter call.

And on the broken Pavement here and there,   10
Doth many a stinking Sprat and Herring lie;
A Brandy and Tobacco Shop is near,
And Hens, and Dogs, and Hogs are feeding by:
And here a Sailor's Jacket hangs to dry:
At ev'ry Door are Sun-burnt Matrons seen,   15
Mending old Nets to catch the scaly Fry;

Now singing shrill, and scolding eft between,
Scolds answer foul-mouth'd Scolds; bad Neighbourhood
    I ween.

The snappish Cur, (the Passengers annoy)
Close at my Heel with yelping Treble flies;   20
The whimp'ring Girl, and hoarser-screaming Boy,
Join to the yelping Treble shrilling Cries;
The scolding Quean to louder Notes doth rise,
And her full Pipes those shrilling Cries confound:
To her full Pipes the grunting Hog replies;   25
The grunting Hogs alarm the Neighbours round,
And Curs, Girls, Boys, and Scolds, in the deep Base are
    drown'd.

Hard by a Sty, beneath a Roof of Thatch,
Dwelt *Obloquy*, who in her early Days
Baskets of Fish at *Billingsgate* did watch,   30
Cod, Whiting, Oyster, Mackrel, Sprat, or Plaice:
There learn'd she Speech from Tongues that never cease.
Slander beside her, like a Magpye, chatters,
With *Envy*, (spitting Cat,) dread Foe to Peace:
Like a curs'd Cur, *Malice* before her clatters,   35
And vexing ev'ry Wight, tears Cloaths and all to Tatters.

Her Dugs were mark'd by ev'ry Collier's Hand,
Her Mouth was black as Bull-Dogs at the Stall:
She scratched, bit, and spar'd ne Lace ne Band,
And Bitch and Rogue her Answer was to all;   40
Nay, e'en the Parts of Shame by Name would call:
Yea when she passed by or Lane or Nook,
Would greet the Man who turn'd him to the Wall,
And by his Hand obscene the Porter took,
Nor ever did askance like modest Virgin look.   45

Such place hath *Deptford*, Navy-building Town,
Woolwich and *Wapping*, smelling strong of Pitch;
Such *Lambeth*, Envy of each Band and Gown,
And *Twick'nam* such, which fairer Scenes enrich,
Grots, Statues, Urns, and *Jo—n*'s *Dog* and *Bitch*:   50

50. *Jo—n's Dog and Bitch*] James Johnston (1655–1737), one-time
Secretary of State for Scotland, and responsible for the inquiry into the
Glencoe massacre; in retirement he was a near neighbour of Pope's at
Twickenham, and displayed on his garden wall 'two miserable little leaden
figures of a dog and a bitch'.

Ne Village is without, on either side,
All up the silver *Thames*, or all a down;
Ne *Richmond*'s self, from whose tall Front are ey'd
Vales, Spires, meandring Streams, and *Windsor*'s tow'ry
    Pride.

Waller: On a Fan of the Author's design, in which was painted the story of Cephalus and Procris with the Motto, Aura Veni

[written before 1709; published,
Spectator, 1712]

Come, gentle Air! th' *Æolian* Shepherd said,
While *Procris* panted in the secret shade;
Come, gentle Air, the fairer *Delia* cries,
While at her feet her swain expiring lies.
Lo the glad gales o'er all her beauties stray,   5
Breathe on her lips, and in her bosom play!
In *Delia*'s hand this toy is fatal found,
Nor could that fabled dart more surely wound:
Both gifts destructive to the givers prove;
Alike both lovers fall by those they love.   10
Yet guiltless too this bright destroyer lives,
At random wounds, nor knows the wound she gives:
She views the story with attentive eyes,
And pities *Procris*, while her lover dies.

Cowley: The Garden

[written before 1709; published, *Works*, 1736]

Fain would my Muse the flow'ry Treasures sing,
And humble glories of the youthful Spring;
Where opening *Roses* breathing sweets diffuse,
And soft *Carnations* show'r their balmy dews;
Where *Lillies* smile in virgin robes of white,   5
The thin Undress of superficial Light,
And vary'd *Tulips* show so dazling gay,
Blushing in bright diversities of day.
Each painted flouret in the lake below
Surveys its beauties, whence its beauties grow;   **10**

And pale *Narcissus* on the bank, in vain
Transformed, gazes on himself again.
Here aged trees Cathedral walks compose,
And mount the Hill in venerable rows:
There the green Infants in their beds are laid,   15
The Garden's Hope, and its expected shade.
Here *Orange*-trees with blooms and pendants shine,
And vernal honours to their autumn join;
Exceed their promise in the ripen'd store,
Yet in the rising blossom promise more.   20
There in bright drops the crystal Fountains play,
By *Laurels* shielded from the piercing Day:
Where *Daphne*, now a tree as once a maid,
Still from *Apollo* vindicates her shade,
Still turns her beauties from th' invading beam,   25
Nor seeks in vain for succour to the Stream.
The stream at once preserves her virgin leaves,
At once a shelter from her boughs receives,
Where *Summer*'s beauty midst of *Winter* stays,
And *Winter*'s Coolness spite of *Summer*'s rays.   30

E. of Dorset

[written before 1709; published, *PSM*, 1727]

I. ARTIMESIA

Tho' *Artimesia* talks, by Fits,
Of Councils, Classicks, Fathers, Wits;
   Reads *Malbranche*, *Boyle*, and *Locke*:
Yet in some Things methinks she fails,
'Twere well if she would pare her Nails,   5
   And wear a cleaner Smock.

Haughty and huge as *High-Dutch* Bride,
Such Nastiness and so much Pride
   Are odly join'd by Fate:

It is unnecessary to search, with earlier commentators, for prototypes
of these two type-characters.
   (i) 3. Nicole Malebranche (1638–1715), French philosopher. *Recherche
de la Vérité* (1674), translated into English 1694. Robert Boyle (1627–91),
author of numerous books on chemistry, physics, and philosophy. John
Locke (1632–1704). *An Essay concerning Humane Understanding* (1690)
had reached a seventh edition by 1716.

On her large Squab you find her spread,   10
Like a fat Corpse upon a Bed,
   That lies and stinks in State.

She wears no Colours (sign of Grace)
On any Part except her Face;
   All white and black beside: 15
Dauntless her Look, her Gesture proud,
Her Voice theatrically loud,
   And masculine her Stride.

So have I seen, in black and white
A prating Thing, a Magpy height,   20
   Majestically stalk;
A stately, worthless Animal,
That plies the Tongue, and wags the Tail,
   All Flutter, Pride, and Talk.

II. PHRYNE

Phryne had Talents for Mankind,
Open she was, and unconfin'd,
   Like some free Port of Trade:
Merchants unloaded here their Freight,
And Agents from each foreign State,   5
   Here first their Entry made.

Her Learning and good Breeding such,
Whether th' *Italian* or the *Dutch*,
   Spaniard or *French* came to her;
To all obliging she'd appear: 10
'Twas *Si Signior*, 'twas *Yaw Mynheer*,
   'Twas *S'il vous plaist, Monsieur*.

Obscure by Birth, renown'd by Crimes,
Still changing Names, Religions, Climes,
   At length she turns a Bride: 15
In Di'monds, Pearls, and rich Brocades,
She shines the first of batter'd Jades,
   And flutters in her Pride.

10. *Squab*] A sofa or couch.
  (*ii*) *Phryne*] *Grk.* φρύνη, a toad. The nickname of several Athenian courtesans.

So have I known those Insects fair,
(Which curious *Germans* hold so rare,)   20
    Still vary Shapes and Dyes;
Still gain new Titles with new Forms;
First Grubs obscene, then wriggling Worms,
    Then painted Butterflies.

The Happy Life of a Country Parson

[written c. 1713; published, *PSM*, 1727]

Parson, these Things in thy possessing
Are better than the Bishop's Blessing.
A *Wife* that makes Conserves; a *Steed*
That carries double when there's need:
October, store, and best *Virginia*,   5
Tythe-Pig, and mortuary *Guinea*:
Gazettes sent Gratis down, and frank'd,
For which thy Patron's weekly thank'd:
A large Concordance, (bound long since,)
Sermons to *Charles* the First, when Prince;   10
A Chronicle of antient standing;
A *Chrysostom* to smooth thy Band in:
The *Polygott*—three Parts,—my *Text*,
Howbeit,—likewise—now to my next,
Lo here the *Septuagint*,—and *Paul*,   15
To *sum the whole*,—the *Close of all*.
    He that has these, may pass his Life,
Drink with the 'Squire, and kiss his Wife;
On Sundays preach, and eat, his Fill;
And fast on Fridays, if he will;   20
Toast Church and Queen, explain the News,
Talk with Church-Wardens about Pews,
Pray heartily for some new Gift,
And shake his Head at Doctor *S——t*.

This poem was first entitled *The Happy Life of a Country Parson. In Imitation of Martial*, but was later called an imitation of Swift, and placed in the *Imitations of English Poets. Done by the Author in his Youth*.

5. *October*] i.e. ale brewed in October.

6. *Tythe-Pig*] A pig due to the parson in payment of tithe.

mortuary Guinea] A customary gift formerly claimed by the incumbent of a parish from the estate of a deceased parishioner.

7. *frank'd*] Superscribed with a privileged signature, e.g. of a Member of Parliament, and so free from postage dues.

13. *Polyglot*] Brian Walton's *Biblia Sacra Polyglotta*, 1657.

Translations and Paraphrases
DONE IN YOUTH

———————————❁———————————

A Paraphrase on Thomas a Kempis;
L. 3, C. 2

DONE BY THE AUTHOR AT 12 YEARS OLD
[written, c. 1700; published, 1854]

Speak, Gracious Lord, oh speak; thy Servant hears:
  For I'm thy Servant, and I'l still be so:
Speak words of Comfort in my willing Ears;
  And since my Tongue is in thy praises slow,
And since that thine all Rhetorick exceeds;   5
Speak thou in words, but let me speak in deeds!

Nor speak alone, but give me grace to hear
  What thy cælestïal Sweetness does impart;
Let it not stop when entred at the Ear
  But sink, and take deep rooting in my heart.   10
As the parch'd Earth drinks Rain (but grace afford)
With such a Gust will I receive thy word.

Nor with the Israelites shall I desire
  Thy heav'nly word by Moses to receive,
Lest I should die: but Thou who didst inspire   15
  Moses himself, speak thou, that I may live.
Rather with Samuel I beseech with tears
Speak, gracious Lord, oh speak; thy Servant hears.

Moses indeed may say the words but Thou
  Must give the Spirit, and the Life inspire;   20
Our Love to thee his fervent Breath may blow,
  But 'tis thy self alone can give the fire:
Thou without them may'st speak and profit too;
But without thee, what could the Prophets do?

They preach the Doctrine, but thou mak'st us do't;   25
  They teach the Misteries thou dost open lay;

17

The Trees they water, but thou giv'st the fruit;
  They to Salvation shew the arduous way,
But none but you can give us Strength to walk;
You give the Practise, they but give the Talk.   30

Let them be silent then; and thou alone
  (My God) speak comfort to my ravish'd Ears;
Light of my eyes, my Consolation,
  Speak when thou wilt, for still thy Servant hears.
What-ere thou speak'st, let this be understood;   35
Thy greater Glory, and my greater Good!

Polyphemus and Acis

OUT OF THE THIRTEENTH BOOK OF
OVID'S METAMORPHOSES

[written c. 1702; published 1749]

CONNEXION OF THE FABLE

On occasion of Æneas's Passage by Scylla and Charybdis, the Poet introduces an Account of the former; who was, before her Transformation, an Attendant of Galatea. As she is employed in dressing her
Mistress, she relates to her the following Story of her Amours with
Acis, and the Love of Polyphemus.

From fair Symæthis and her Faunus came
A lovely youth, and Acis was his name;
His parents joy, who did a comfort prove
To them by nature, but to me by love:
To me the boy did an affection bear,   5
His only pleasure, and his early care.
E'er sixteen passing years had overlaid
His downy cheeks with a beginning shade,
Acis I lov'd, and Polyphemus too
With equal ardour did my love pursue;   10
Nor knew I then which passion greater prov'd,
If most I hated, or if most I lov'd.
Great queen of love! how boundless is thy sway;
Which monsters wild, and savages obey!
Thy force the barb'rous Polyphemus try'd,   15
The proud despiser of all heav'n beside;
Ev'n, he, the terror of his native grove,

Dismiss'd his fierceness, and cou'd learn to love!
  Now all neglected, he forgets his home,
His flocks at random round the forest roam: 20
While nice, and anxious in his new disease,
He vainly studies every art to please:
To trim his beard, th'unweildy scythe prepares;
And combs with rakes, his rough, disorder'd hairs:
Adjusts his shapes; while in the crystal brook   25
He views and practises a milder look.
Love makes him all his cruelty forego,
And ships, in safety, wander to and fro.
  It chanc'd prophetick Telemus, who knew
The flight of birds, and thence presages drew,   30
Arriving then by Ætna's steepy height,
Foretold the Cyclops he shou'd lose his sight.
The laughing Cyclops gave the bard the lye,
And said, a charming female stole that eye.
Thus scorning prophecy, and warn'd in vain,   35
With heavy steps he sinks the sandy plain;
Then weary grown, to shady grotts retires,
But finds no shelter from his raging fires.
  Far in the main a promontory grows,
Around whose rocky sides the water flows: 40
High in the midst, upon this airy steep
He sate, pursu'd by all his flocks of sheep.
Before his feet his pondrous staff he cast;
A pine which ships might challenge for a mast:
His whistle (which a hundred reeds compose)   45
With all his strength the giant-lover blows;
The neighbouring mountains, and resounding main
Shook, and return'd the dreadful blast again.
Hid in a rock, and by my Acis laid,
The boist'rous musick did my ears invade;   50
While to his reeds he sung his amorous pains,
In words like these, which still my mind retains.
  Oh! lovely nymph, and more than lilies fair,
More sweet than winter's sun, or summer's air,
And smooth as shells that gliding waters wear;   55
Not ice or crystal equal splendor yield,
O far more pleasing than the flow'ry field!
Wanton as kids; and more delicious far,
Than grapes mature, or blushing apples are;
More strait than alders, taller than the planes;   60

25. *shapes*] Appearance, perhaps, or attitude and dress.

And soft as down upon the breast of swans:
As gardens fresh, where running rivers stray,
But, ah! like rivers, swift to glide away;
And what alone must all my hopes remove,
Swift as the wind before pursuing love;   65
   Yet know, coy maid, and curse your long delay,
Know from whose arms you fly so fast away.
Behold the rocky caverns where I dwell,
Which summer suns, and winter frosts expel.
See how my fruits the loaded branches bend,   70
And grapes in clusters from the vine depend;
These bright, like gold, and those with purple shine;
And these and those, my dearest, shall be thine.
Here cornels rise, and in the shady grove
Grow scarlet strawberries to feast my love: 75
The chesnut, wilding, plum, and every tree,
For thee shall bear their fruits, and offer all to thee!
   These flocks are mine, and more are pen'd at home,
Range in the woods, and in the vallies roam:
So great the tale, I scarce can count them o'er;   80
The poorest shepherd best may tell his store.
Believe not me, but come and witness here,
How, scarce, my ewes their strutting udders bear;
What tender lambkins here my folds contain,
And there what kids of equal age remain.   85
Nor boast we only common dainties here,
But roes and lev'rets, and the fallow deer;
The goat, the hare, with ev'ry forest beast;
And turtles taken from their airy nest.
Two cubs I have, as like as twins can be;   90
And these, dear nymph, are kept to play with thee:
Two little bears, I found them, and did please
Myself to think, my mistress shou'd have these.
   Come Galatea, from the sea arise,
And see my presents, nor the gifts despise.   95
I'm not so monst'rous; I my face did view
In yon clear lake, and thought it handsome too:
How great I look'd! of what a godlike size!
Not Jove himself (your Jove that sways the skies)
Is half so mighty, half so large, my love;   100
Your beauty charms a greater man than Jove.
Hairs, like a wood, my head and shoulders grace,
And cast a majesty on all my face:
The comely steeds are grac'd with flowing manes;

With fleeces sheep, and birds with plumy trains; 105
Leaves deck the stately trees; and man is fair,
By bearded cheeks, and members rough with hair.
With one large eye my ample front is grac'd,
Round like a shield, and in the middle plac'd:
The sun all objects views beneath the sky, 110
And yet, like me, has but a single eye.
My father o'er your seas presides; and he
Will be your father by your wedding me.
Oh! yeild at last, nor still remain severe;
I worship you, and you alone I fear! 115
Jove's harmless lightning unregarded flies;
No lightning wounds me but your angry eyes.
Nor thy contempt cou'd cause me thus to mourn,
If thou all others didst despise and scorn:
But Acis, Acis is thy dear delight; 120
For his embraces you the Cyclops slight.
Well, he may please himself, and you may share
His pleasures too (tho' that I scarce can bear)
Yet he shall find, wou'd time th'occasion shew,
The strength and fury of a giant foe. 125
I'll from his bleeding breast his entrails tear,
And hurl his mangled carcass in the air;
Or cast his limbs into thy guilty flood,
And mix thy waters with his reeking blood!
For oh! I burn, nor you my flames asswage; 130
And love disdain'd revives with fiercer rage.

Two lines here wanting

This said, he rose, and frantick with his pain,
Roar'd out for rage, and hurried o'er the plain:
So bulls in forests hunt their absent loves,
And stung with anguish bellow through the groves. 135
But as around his rowling orb he cast,
Myself and Acis he descry'd at last.
These thefts, false nymph, thou shalt enjoy no more,
He cry'd, and Ætna trembled with the roar!
Frighted, beneath my native deeps I fled; 140
Acis too run, and help, oh help! he said,
A wretch undone: O parents help, and deign
T'admit your offspring in your watry reign!
The Cyclops follow'd, and a stone he threw,
Torn from the rock, which threatned as it flew; 145
No further speech the thundering rock affords,

O'ertakes the flying boy, and smothers half his words.
Yet what we cou'd, and what no fates deny'd, ⎫
We soon perform'd, and Acis deify'd,   ⎬
To rule in streams to which he was ally'd: ⎭   150
His body press'd beneath the stone, the blood
Flow'd from the marble in a crimson flood;
Which lost its native red; and first appear'd
A troubled stream; the troubled stream was clear'd;
The rock asunder cleav'd, and thro' the chink   155
Long reeds sprung up as on a fountain's brink:
Strait from the hollow cliff, and yawning ground,
Insulting waters yield a murmuring sound:
At last a youth above the waist arose,
Whose horned temples reedy wreaths inclose;   160
And, but he seem'd a larger bulk to bear,
With looks more azure, Acis might appear;
And Acis was; who now transform'd became
A crystal fountain, and preserv'd the name.

Memorandum. Done at 14 years old.

158. *insulting*] Assaulting.

The Fable of Vertumnus and Pomona

FROM
THE FOURTEENTH BOOK OF OVID'S
METAMORPHOSES

[written c. 1702; published, Lintot's
Miscellany, 1712]

Rege sub hoc Pomona fuit———&c.

The fair *Pomona* flourish'd in his Reign;
Of all the Virgins of the Sylvan Train,
None taught the Trees a nobler Race to bear,
Or more improv'd the Vegetable Care.
To her the shady Grove, the flow'ry Field,   5
The Streams and Fountains, no Delights cou'd yield;
'Twas all her Joy the ripening Fruits to tend,
And see the Boughs with happy Burthens bend.
The Hook she bore, instead of *Cynthia*'s Spear,

1. *his Reign*] The reign of Procas, legendary king of Alba Longa.

To lop the Growth of the luxuriant Year, 10
To decent Form the lawless Shoots to bring,
And teach th'obedient Branches where to spring.
Now the cleft Rind inserted Graffs receives,
And yields an Off-spring more than Nature gives;
Now sliding Streams the thirsty Plants renew, 15
And feed their Fibres with reviving Dew.
　These Cares alone her Virgin Breast imploy,
Averse from *Venus* and the Nuptial Joy;
Her private Orchards wall'd on ev'ry side,
To lawless Sylvans all Access deny'd. 20
How oft the *Satyrs* and the wanton *Fawns*,
Who haunt the Forests or frequent the Lawns,
The *God* whose Ensign scares the Birds of Prey,
And old *Silenus*, youthful in Decay,
Imploy'd their Wiles and unavailing Care, 25
To pass the Fences, and surprize the Fair?
Like these, *Vertumnus* own'd his faithful Flame,
Like these, rejected by the scornful Dame.
To gain her Sight, a thousand Forms he wears,
And first a Reaper from the Field appears, 30
Sweating he walks, while Loads of golden Grain
O'ercharge the Shoulders of the seeming Swain.
Oft o'er his Back a crooked Scythe is laid,
And Wreaths of Hay his Sun-burnt Temples shade;
Oft in his harden'd Hand a Goad he bears, 35
Like one who late unyok'd the sweating Steers.
Sometimes his Pruning-hook corrects the Vines,
And the loose Straglers to their Ranks confines.
Now gath'ring what the bounteous Year allows,
He pulls ripe Apples from the bending Boughs. 40
A Soldier now, he with his Sword appears;
A Fisher next, his trembling Angle bears.
Each Shape he varies, and each Art he tries,
On her bright Charms to feast his longing Eyes.
　A Female Form at last *Vertumnus* wears, ⎫ 45
With all the Marks of rev'rend Age appears, ⎬
His Temples thinly spread with silver Hairs: ⎭
Prop'd on his Staff, and stooping as he goes,

23. *The God*] Priapus, the god of fertility in vegetable and animal life.
Images of Priapus were placed in gardens as protection against robbers
and birds.
27. *Vertumnus*] A deity thought to preside over the seasons and their
various productions in the vegetable world. To him gardeners offered their
first fruits (cf. l. 96).

A painted Mitre shades his furrow'd Brows.
The God, in this decrepit Form array'd,   50
The Gardens enter'd, and the Fruits survey'd,
And *happy You*! (he thus address'd the Maid)
Whose Charms as far all other Nymphs out-shine,
As other Gardens are excell'd by thine!
Then kiss'd the Fair; (his Kisses warmer grow   55
Than such as Women on their Sex bestow.)
Then plac'd beside her on the flow'ry Ground,
Beheld the Trees with Autumn's Bounty crown'd;
An Elm was near, to whose Embraces led,
The curling Vine her swelling Clusters spread;   60
He view'd their twining Branches with Delight,
And prais'd the Beauty of the pleasing Sight.
    Yet this tall Elm, but for his Vine (he said)
Had stood neglected and a barren shade;
And this fair Vine, but that her Arms surround   65
Her marry'd Elm, had crept along the Ground.
Ah beauteous Maid, let this Example move
Your Mind, averse from all the Joys of Love.
Deign to be lov'd, and ev'ry Heart subdue!
What Nymph cou'd e'er attract such Crowds as you?   70
Not she whose Beauty urg'd the *Centaur*'s Arms,
Ulysses' Queen, nor *Helen*'s fatal Charms.
Ev'n now, when silent Scorn is all they gain,
A thousand court you, tho' they court in vain,
A thousand Sylvans, Demigods, and Gods,   75
That haunt our Mountains and our *Alban* Woods.
But if you'll prosper, mark what I advise,
Whom Age and long Experience render wise,
And one whose tender Care is far above
All that these Lovers ever felt of Love,   80
(Far more than e'er can by your self be guest)
Fix on *Vertumnus*, and reject the rest.
For his firm Faith I dare ingage my own,
Scarce to himself, himself is better known.
To distant Lands *Vertumnus* never roves;   85
Like you, contented with his Native Groves;
Nor at first sight, like most, admires the Fair;
For you he lives; and you alone shall share
His last Affection, as his early Care.
Besides, he's lovely far above the rest,   90

49. *painted Mitre*] The *mitra* was a head-dress worn by women; it was
probably embroidered.

With Youth Immortal and with Beauty blest.
Add, that he varies ev'ry Shape with ease,
And tries all Forms, that may *Pomona* please.
But what shou'd most excite a mutual Flame,
Your Rural Cares, and Pleasures, are the same.   95
To him your Orchards early Fruits are due,
(A pleasing Off'ring when 'tis made by you;)
He values these; but yet (alas) complains,
That still the best and dearest Gift remains.
Not the fair Fruit that on yon' Branches glows   100
With that ripe red th'Autumnal Sun bestows,
Nor tastful Herbs that in these Gardens rise,
Which the kind Soil with milky Sap supplies;
You, only you, can move the God's Desire:
Oh crown so constant and so pure a Fire!   105
Let soft Compassion touch your gentle Mind;
Think, 'tis *Vertumnus* begs you to be kind!
So may no Frost, when early Buds appear,
Destroy the Promise of the youthful Year;
Nor Winds, when first your florid Orchard blows,   110
Shake the light Blossoms from their blasted Boughs!
    This when the various God had urg'd in vain,
He strait assum'd his Native Form again;
Such, and so bright an Aspect now he bears,
As when thro' Clouds th'emerging Sun appears,   115
And thence exerting his refulgent Ray,
Dispels the Darkness and reveals the Day.
Force he prepar'd, but check'd the rash Design;
For when, appearing in a Form Divine,
The Nymph surveys him, and beholds the Grace   120
Of charming Features and a youthful Face,
In her soft Breast consenting Passions move,
And the warm Maid confess'd a mutual Love.

112. *various*] Appearing in a variety of forms.

The Fable of Dryope

FROM THE NINTH BOOK OF
OVID'S METAMORPHOSES

[written c. 1702; published, *Works*, 1717]

Upon occasion of the death of Hercules, *his mother* Alcmena *recounts
her misfortunes to* Iole, *who answers with a relation of those of her
own family, in particular the transformation of her sister* Dryope,
which is the subject of the ensuing Fable.

She said, and for her lost *Galanthis* sighs,
When the fair Consort of her son replies.
Since you a servant's ravish'd form bemoan,
And kindly sigh for sorrows not your own;
Let me (if tears and grief permit) relate   5
A nearer woe, a sister's stranger fate.
    No nymph of all *Oechalia* could compare
For beauteous form with *Dryope* the fair,
Her tender mother's only hope and pride,
(My self the offspring of a second bride.)   10
This nymph compress'd by him who rules the day,
Whom *Delphi* and the *Delian* isle obey,
Andræmon lov'd; and bless'd in all those charms
That pleas'd a God, succeeded to her arms.
    A Lake there was, with shelving banks around,   15
Whose verdant summit fragrant myrtles crown'd.
These shades, unknowing of the fates, she sought,
And to the *Naiads* flow'ry garlands brought,
Her smiling babe (a pleasing charge) she prest
Within her arms, and nourish'd at her breast.   20
Not distant far a watry *Lotos* grows;

1. *She said*] Alcmena has just told the story of Galanthis, one of her
maids. Juno sent Lucina, goddess of childbirth, to cause the death of
Alcmena by delaying the birth of Hercules, her son by Zeus. Galanthis
brought about the delivery of Hercules by outwitting Lucina, but as
punishment she was turned into a weasel.

2. *Consort of her son*] Iole, who was the wife not of Hercules but of
Hyllus, his son. The Latin *nurus* applies not only to the wife of a son,
but to the wife of a grandson.

7. *nymph*] The Latin *nympha* can mean either a young woman or a
demi-goddess. In this line the word has the former sense, though there is
nothing in Ovid to which it corresponds. Elsewhere (ll. 31, 37) Pope uses
it to imply semi-divine status.

21. *watry Lotos*] Not the well-known Egyptian lotus, a water-lily, but
probably the *Zizyphus lotus*, a jujube tree, the fruit of which was esteemed
by the ancients.

The spring was new, and all the verdant boughs
Adorn'd with blossoms, promis'd fruits that vie
In glowing colours with the *Tyrian* dye.
Of these she crop'd, to please her infant son;   25
And I my self the same rash act had done,
But lo! I saw, (as near her side I stood)
The violated blossoms drop with blood;
Upon the tree I cast a frightful look;
The trembling tree with sudden horror shook.   30
Lotis the nymph (if rural tales be true)
As from *Priapus'* lawless lust she flew,
Forsook her form; and fixing here, became
A flow'ry plant, which still preserves her name.
    This change unknown, astonish'd at the sight   35
My trembling sister strove to urge her flight,
And first the pardon of the nymphs implor'd,
And those offended sylvan pow'rs ador'd:
But when she backward wou'd have fled, she found
Her stiff'ning feet were rooted in the ground: 40
In vain to free her fasten'd feet she strove,
And as she struggles, only moves above;
She feels th'encroaching bark around her grow
By quick degrees, and cover all below:
Surpriz'd at this, her trembling hand she heaves   45
To rend her hair; her hand is fill'd with leaves;
Where late was hair, the shooting leaves are seen
To rise, and shade her with a sudden green.
The child *Amphisus*, to her bosom prest,
Perceiv'd a colder and a harder breast,   50
And found the springs that ne'er till then deny'd
Their milky moisture, on a sudden dry'd.
I saw, unhappy! what I now relate,
And stood the helpless witness of thy fate;
Embrac'd thy boughs, the rising bark delay'd,   55
There wish'd to grow, and mingle shade with shade.
    Behold, *Andræmon* and th' unhappy Sire
Appear, and for their *Dryope* enquire;
A springing tree for *Dryope* they find,
And print warm kisses on the panting rind,   60
Prostrate, with tears their kindred plant bedew,
And close embrace, as to the roots they grew.
The face was all that now remain'd of thee;

32. *Priapus*] See *Vertumnus and Pomona*, l. 23*n* (p. 23, above)
57. *th'unhappy Sire*] Eurytus, Dryope's father.

No more a woman, nor yet quite a tree:
Thy branches hung with humid pearls appear,   65
From ev'ry leaf distills a trickling tear,
And strait a voice, while yet a voice remains,
Thus thro' the trembling boughs in sighs complains.
  If to the wretched any faith be giv'n,
I swear by all th'unpitying pow'rs of heav'n,   70
No wilful crime this heavy vengeance bred,
In mutual innocence our lives we led:
If this be false, let these new greens decay,
Let sounding axes lop my limbs away,
And crackling flames on all my honours prey.   75
But from my branching arms this infant bear,
Let some kind nurse supply a mother's care:
And to his mother let him oft' be led,
Sport in her shades, and in her shades be fed;
Teach him, when first his infant voice shall frame   80
Imperfect words, and lisp his mother's name,
To hail this tree; and say, with weeping eyes,
Within this plant my hapless parent lies:
And when in youth he seeks the shady woods,
Oh, let him fly the crystal lakes and floods,   85
Nor touch the fatal flow'rs; but, warn'd by me,
Believe a Goddess shrin'd in ev'ry tree.
My sire, my sister, and my spouse farewell!
If in your breasts or love or pity dwell,
Protect your plant, not let my branches feel   90
The browzing cattel, or the piercing steel.
Farewell! and since I cannot bend to join
My lips to yours, advance at least to mine.
My son, thy mother's parting kiss receive,
While yet thy mother has a kiss to give.   95
I can no more; the creeping rind invades
My closing lips, and hides my head in shades:
Remove your hands, the bark shall soon suffice
Without their aid, to seal these dying eyes.
  She ceas'd at once to speak, and ceas'd to be;   100
And all the nymph was lost within the tree;
Yet latent life thro' her new branches reign'd,
And long the plant a human heat retain'd.

75. *honours*] Her foliage. The word was frequently used of trees in this
sense.

Sapho to Phaon

WHOLLY TRANSLATED

[written c. 1707; published,
Ovid's Epistles, 1712]

Say, lovely Youth, that dost my Heart command,
Can *Phaon*'s Eyes forget his *Sapho*'s Hand?
Must then her Name the wretched Writer prove?
To thy Remembrance lost, as to thy Love!
Ask not the cause that I new Numbers chuse,   5
The Lute neglected, and the Lyric Muse;
Love taught my Tears in sadder Notes to flow,
And tun'd my Heart to Elegies of Woe.
I burn, I burn, as when thro' ripen'd Corn
By driving Winds the spreading Flames are born!   10
Phaon to *Ætna*'s scorching Fields retires,
While I consume with more than *Ætna*'s Fires!
No more my Soul a Charm in Musick finds,
Musick has Charms alone for peaceful Minds:
Soft Scenes of Solitude no more can please,   15
Love enters there, and I'm my own Disease:
No more the *Lesbian* Dames my Passion move,
Once the dear Objects of my guilty Love;
All other Loves are lost in only thine,
Ah Youth ungrateful to a Flame like mine!   20
Whom wou'd not all those blooming Charms surprize,
Those heav'nly Looks, and dear deluding Eyes?
The Harp and Bow wou'd you like *Phœbus* bear,
A brighter *Phœbus*, *Phaon* might appear;
Wou'd you with Ivy wreath your flowing Hair,   25
Not *Bacchus*' self with *Phaon* cou'd compare:
Yet *Phœbus* lov'd, and *Bacchus* felt the Flame,
One *Daphne* warm'd, and one the *Cretan* Dame;

5. *new Numbers*] An allusion to the elegiac distichs used by Ovid,
which differ from the Sapphic metre used by Sappho and named after
her.
11. To avoid Sappho's love, Phaon had fled to Sicily, where Mount
Aetna is situated.
28. *warm'd*] Inspired with love.
the Cretan Dame] Ariadne, daughter of Minos, king of Crete. She was
abandoned by Theseus on the island of Naxos, where Bacchus discovered
her on his return from India. Ovid tells the story of Apollo and Daphne
in *Met.* 1.

Nymphs that in Verse no more cou'd rival me,
Than ev'n those Gods contend in Charms with thee.   30
The Muses teach me all their softest Lays,
And the wide World resounds with *Sapho*'s Praise.
Tho' great *Alcæus* more sublimely sings,
And strikes with bolder Rage the sounding Strings,
No less Renown attends the moving Lyre,   35
Which *Venus* tunes, and all her Loves inspire.
To me what Nature has in Charms deny'd
Is well by Wit's more lasting Flames supply'd.
Tho' short my Stature, yet my Name extends
To Heav'n it self, and Earth's remotest Ends.   40
Brown as I am, an *Æthiopian* Dame
Inspir'd young *Perseus* with a gen'rous Flame.
Turtles and Doves of diff'ring Hues, unite,
And glossy Jett is pair'd with shining White.
If to no Charms thou wilt thy Heart resign,   45
But such as merit, such as equal thine,
By none alas! by none thou can'st be mov'd,
Phaon alone by *Phaon* must be lov'd!
Yet once thy *Sapho* cou'd thy Cares employ,
Once in her Arms you center'd all your Joy: 50
No Time the dear Remembrance can remove,
For oh! how vast a Memory has Love?
My Musick, then, you cou'd for ever hear,
And all my Words were Musick to your Ear.
You stop'd with Kisses my inchanting Tongue,   55
And found my Kisses sweeter than my Song.
In all I pleas'd, but most in what was best;
And the last Joy was dearer than the rest.
Then with each Word, each Glance, each Motion fir'd,
You still enjoy'd, and yet you still desir'd,   60
Till all dissolving in the Trance we lay,
And in tumultuous Raptures dy'd away.
The fair *Sicilians* now thy Soul inflame;
Why was I born, ye Gods, a *Lesbian* Dame?

29. *Nymphs*] Daphne was a nymph, but Ariadne was not. Here, as in
l. 65, the word describes a young and lovely woman. Cf. *Dryope*, l. 7*n*
(p. 26, above).

33. *Alcæus*] An older contemporary of Sappho, he was also a native of
Lesbos. Love and wine, satire and politics, were subjects of his odes,
written in the alcaic metre, so called after him.

38. *Wit*] Genius, Latin *ingenium*.

41. *Æthiopian Dame*] Andromeda, daughter of Cepheus and Cas-
siopeia king and queen of Ethiopia.

But ah beware, *Sicilian* Nymphs! nor boast   65
That wandring Heart which I so lately lost;
Nor be with all those tempting Words abus'd,
Those tempting Words were all to *Sapho* us'd.
And you that rule *Sicilia*'s happy Plains,
Have pity, *Venus*, on your Poet's Pains!   70
Shall Fortune still in one sad Tenor run,
And still increase the Woes so soon begun?
Enur'd to Sorrow from my tender Years,

My Parent's Ashes drank my early Tears.
My Brother next, neglecting Wealth and Fame,   75
Ignobly burn'd in a destructive Flame.
An Infant Daughter late my Griefs increast,
And all a Mother's Cares distract my Breast.
Alas, what more could Fate it self impose,
But Thee, the last and greatest of my Woes?   80
No more my Robes in waving Purple flow,
Nor on my Hand the sparkling Diamonds glow,
No more my Locks in Ringlets curl'd diffuse
The costly Sweetness of *Arabian* Dews,
Nor Braids of Gold the vary'd Tresses bind,   85
That fly disorder'd with the wanton Wind:
For whom shou'd *Sapho* use such Arts as these?
He's gone, whom only she desir'd to please!
Cupid's light Darts my tender Bosom move,
Still is there cause for *Sapho* still to love: 90
So from my Birth the *Sisters* fix'd my Doom,
And gave to *Venus* all my Life to come;
Or while my Muse in melting Notes complains,
My yielding Heart keeps Measure to my Strains.
By Charms like thine which all my Soul have won,   95
Who might not—ah! who wou'd not be undone?
For those, *Aurora Cephalus* might scorn,
And with fresh Blushes paint the conscious Morn.
For those might *Cynthia* lengthen *Phaon*'s Sleep,
And bid *Endymion* nightly tend his Sheep.   100
Venus for those had rapt thee to the Skies,
But *Mars* on thee might look with *Venus*' Eyes.
O scarce a Youth, yet scarce a tender Boy!

70. *Venus*] Erycina, a surname of Aphrodite, in the original. There was a temple dedicated to Venus on Mount Eryx in Sicily.

84. *Arabian Dews*] Perfumes, reputed to come from Arabia.

97. The hunter Cephalus, faithful husband of Procris, was loved in vain by Aurora.

98. *conscious*] Sensible of wrong-doing, guilty.

O useful Time for Lovers to employ!
Pride of thy Age, and Glory of thy Race,   105
Come to these Arms, and melt in this Embrace!
The Vows you never will return, receive;
And take at least the Love you will not give.
See, while I write, my Words are lost in Tears;
The less my Sense, the more my Love appears.   110
Sure 'twas not much to bid one kind Adieu,
(At least to feign was never hard to you.)
Farewel my Lesbian *Love!* you might have said,
Or coldly thus, *Farewel oh* Lesbian *Maid!*
No Tear did you, no parting Kiss receive,   115
Nor knew I then how much I was to grieve.
No Lover's Gift your *Sapho* cou'd confer,
And Wrongs and Woes were all you left with her.
No Charge I gave you, and no Charge cou'd give,
But this; *Be mindful of our Loves, and live.*   120
Now by the Nine, those Pow'rs ador'd by me,
And Love, the God that ever waits on thee,
When first I heard (from whom I hardly knew)
That you were fled, and all my Joys with you,
Like some sad Statue, speechless, pale, I stood;   125
Grief chill'd my Breast, and stop'd my freezing Blood;
No Sigh to rise, no Tear had pow'r to flow;
Fix'd in a stupid Lethargy of Woe.
But when its way th'impetuous Passion found,
I rend my Tresses, and my Breast I wound,   130
I rave, then weep, I curse, and then complain,
Now swell to Rage, now melt in Tears again.
Not fiercer Pangs distract the mournful Dame,
Whose first-born Infant feeds the Fun'ral Flame.
My scornful Brother with a Smile appears,   135
Insults my Woes, and triumphs in my Tears,
His hated Image ever haunts my Eyes,
And *why this Grief? thy Daughter lives*; he cries.
Stung with my Love, and furious with Despair,
All torn my Garments, and my Bosom bare,   140
My Woes, thy Crimes, I to the World proclaim;
Such inconsistent things are Love and Shame!

'Tis thou art all my Care and my Delight,
My daily Longing, and my Dream by Night:
O Night more pleasing than the brightest Day,   145
When Fancy gives what Absence takes away,
And drest in all its visionary Charms,

Restores my fair Deserter to my Arms!
Then round your Neck in wanton Wreaths I twine,
Then you, methinks, as fondly circle mine: 150
A thousand tender Words, I hear and speak;
A thousand melting Kisses, give, and take:
Then fiercer Joys—I blush to mention these,
Yet while I blush, confess how much they please!
But when with Day the sweet Delusions fly,   155
And all things wake to Life and Joy, but I,
As if once more forsaken, I complain,
And close my Eyes, to dream of you again.
Then frantick rise, and like some Fury rove
Thro' lonely Plains, and thro' the silent Grove,   160
As if the silent Grove, and lonely Plains
That knew my Pleasures, cou'd relieve my Pains.
I view the *Grotto*, once the Scene of Love,
The Rocks around, the hanging Roofs above,
That charm'd me more, with Native Moss o'ergrown, 165
Than *Phrygian* Marble or the *Parian* Stone.
I find the Shades that veil'd our Joys before,
But, *Phaon* gone, those Shades delight no more.
Here the prest Herbs with bending Tops betray
Where oft entwin'd in am'rous Folds we lay;   170
I kiss that Earth which once was prest by you,
And all with Tears the with'ring Herbs bedew.
For thee the fading Trees appear to mourn,
And Birds defer their Songs till thy Return:
Night shades the Groves, and all in Silence lye,   175
All, but the mournful *Philomel* and I:
With mournful *Philomel* I join my Strain,
Of *Tereus* she, of *Phaon* I complain.
   A Spring there is, whose Silver Waters show,
Clear as a Glass, the shining Sands below;   180
A flow'ry *Lotos* spreads its Arms above,
Shades all the Banks, and seems it self a Grove;
Eternal Greens the mossie Margin grace,
Watch'd by the Sylvan *Genius* of the Place.
Here as I lay, and swell'd with Tears the Flood,   185
Before my Sight a Watry Virgin stood,
She stood and cry'd, 'O you that love in vain!
Fly hence; and seek the fair *Leucadian* Main;
There stands a Rock from whose impending Steep

181. *flow'ry Lotos*] Cf. *The Fable of Dryope*, l. 21*n* (p. 26, above).
188. *Leucadian Main*] Leucadia, now called Leucas, is one of the

Apollo's Fane surveys the rolling Deep;   190
There injur'd Lovers, leaping from above,
Their Flames extinguish, and forget to love.
Deucalion once with hopeless Fury burn'd,
In vain he lov'd, relentless *Pyrrha* scorn'd;
But when from hence he plung'd into the Main,   195
Deucalion scorn'd, and *Pyrrha* lov'd in vain.
Haste *Sapho*, haste from high *Leucadia* throw
Thy wretched Weight, nor dread the Deeps below!'
She spoke, and vanish'd with the Voice—I rise,
And silent Tears fall trickling from my Eyes.   200
I go, ye Nymphs! those Rocks and Seas to prove;
How much I fear, but ah! how much I love?
I go, ye Nymphs! where furious Love inspires:
Let Female Fears submit to Female Fires!
To Rocks and Seas I fly from *Phaon*'s Hate,   205
And hope from Seas and Rocks a milder Fate.
Ye gentle Gales, beneath my Body blow,
And softly lay me on the Waves below!
And thou, kind *Love*, my sinking Limbs sustain, ⎫
Spread thy soft Wings, and waft me o'er the Main, ⎬ 210
Nor let a Lover's Death the guiltless Flood profane! ⎭
On *Phœbus*' Shrine my Harp I'll then bestow,
And this Inscription shall be plac'd below.
'Here She who sung, to Him that did inspire,
Sapho to *Phœbus* consecrates her Lyre,   215
What suits with *Sapho*, *Phœbus*, suits with thee;
The Gift, the Giver, and the God agree.'
  But why alas, relentless Youth! ah why
To distant Seas must tender *Sapho* fly?
Thy Charms than those may far more pow'rful be,   220
And *Phœbus*' self is less a God to me.
Ah! canst thou doom me to the Rocks and Sea,
O far more faithless and more hard than they?
Ah! canst thou rather see this tender Breast
Dash'd on these Rocks, than to thy Bosom prest?   225
This Breast which once, in vain! you lik'd so well;
Where the *Loves* play'd and where the *Muses* dwell.—
Alas! the *Muses* now no more inspire,
Untun'd my Lute, and silent is my Lyre,

Ionian islands, off the west coast of Greece. It terminates in a promontory
2,000 feet in height, on which can still be seen the remains of the temple
of Apollo to which Ovid alludes. It was said that lovers who threw themselves from this headland into the sea might be cured of their infatuation.

My languid Numbers have forgot to flow,   230
And Fancy sinks beneath a Weight of Woe.
Ye *Lesbian* Virgins, and ye *Lesbian* Dames,
Themes of my Verse, and Objects of my Flames,
No more your Groves with my glad Songs shall ring,
No more these Hands shall touch the trembling String: 235
My *Phaon*'s fled, and I those Arts resign,
(Wretch that I am, to call that *Phaon* mine!)
Return fair Youth, return, and bring along
Joy to my Soul, and Vigour to my Song:
Absent from thee, the Poet's Flame expires,   240
But ah! how fiercely burn the Lover's Fires?
Gods! can no Pray'rs, no Sighs, no Numbers move
One savage Heart, or teach it how to love?
The Winds my Pray'rs, my Sighs, my Numbers bear,
The flying Winds have lost them all in Air!   245
Oh when, alas! shall more auspicious Gales
To these fond Eyes restore thy welcome Sails?
If you return—ah why these long Delays?
Poor *Sapho* dies while careless *Phaon* stays.
O launch thy Bark, nor fear the watry Plain,   250
Venus for thee shall smooth her native Main.
O launch thy Bark, secure of prosp'rous Gales,
Cupid for thee shall spread the swelling Sails.
If you will fly—(yet ah! what Cause can be,
Too cruel Youth, that you shou'd fly from me?)   255
If not from *Phaon* I must hope for Ease,
Ah let me seek it from the raging Seas:
To raging Seas unpity'd I'll remove,
And either cease to live, or cease to love!

The First Book of Statius his Thebais

[written c. 1703; published, Lintot's
Miscellany, 1712]

THE ARGUMENT

OEdipus *King of* Thebes *having by mistake slain his Father* Laius,
and marry'd his Mother Jocasta, *put out his own Eyes, and resign'd
the Realm to his Sons,* Etheocles *and* Polynices. *Being neglected by
them, he makes his Prayer to the Fury* Tisiphone, *to sow Debate betwixt the Brothers. They agree at last to Reign singly, each a Year by
turns, and the first Lot is obtain'd by* Etheocles. Jupiter, *in a Council*

of the Gods, declares his Resolution of punishing the Thebans, *and* Argives *also, by means of a Marriage betwixt* Polynices *and one of the Daughters of* Adrastus *King of* Argos. Juno *opposes, but to no effect; and* Mercury *is sent on a Message to the Shades, to the Ghost of* Laius, *who is to appear to* Etheocles, *and provoke him to break the Agreement.* Polynices *in the mean time departs from* Thebes *by Night, is overtaken by a Storm, and arrives at* Argos; *where he meets with* Tydeus, *who had fled from* Calydon, *having kill'd his Brother.* Adrastus *entertains them, having receiv'd an Oracle from* Apollo *that his Daughters shou'd be marry'd to a Boar and a Lion, which he understands to be meant of these Strangers by whom the Hydes of those Beasts were worn, and who arriv'd at the time when he kept an annual Feast in honour of that God. The Rise of this Solemnity he relates to his Guests, the Loves of* Phœbus *and* Psamathe, *and the Story of* Chorœbus. *He enquires, and is made acquainted with, their Descent and Quality; The Sacrifice is renew'd, and the Book concludes with a Hymn to* Apollo.

The Translator hopes he needs not apologize for his Choice of this Piece, which was made almost in his Childhood. But finding the Version better than he expected, he gave it some Correction a few Years afterwards.

> Fraternal Rage, the guilty *Thebes* Alarms,
> Th' Alternate Reign destroy'd by Impious Arms,
> Demand our Song; a sacred Fury fires
> My ravish'd Breast, and All the Muse inspires.
> O Goddess, say, shall I deduce my Rhimes   5
> From the dire Nation in its early Times,
> *Europa*'s Rape, *Agenor*'s stern Decree,
> And *Cadmus* searching round the spacious Sea?
> How with the Serpent's Teeth he sow'd the Soil,
> And reap'd an Iron Harvest of his Toil;   10
> Or how from joyning Stones the City sprung,

5. *deduce*] To trace the course of, treat, deal with.
6. *dire*] A Latinism: ill-omened, unfortunate.
7. *Agenor's stern Decree*] Agenor, king of Phoenicia, sent his son Cadmus to search for Europa, forbidding him to return should he fail.
8. Cadmus's search proved vain. In obedience to the oracle of Delphi he went into Boeotia, where his followers were killed by a dragon. Cadmus slew the dragon and sowed its teeth in the earth, whence sprang up armed warriors whom Cadmus caused to fight amongst themselves till only five remained. With their help he founded the city of Thebes and fulfilled the oracle.
11. *from joyning Stones*] Another legend attributed the foundation of Thebes to Amphion and Zethus, twin sons of Jupiter and Antiope.

While to his Harp Divine *Amphion* sung?
Or shall I *Juno*'s Hate to *Thebes* resound,
Whose fatal Rage th'unhappy Monarch found;
The Sire against the Son his Arrows drew, 15
O'er the wide Fields the furious Mother flew,
And while her Arms her Second Hope contain,
Sprung from the Rocks, and plung'd into the Main.
  But wave whate'er to *Cadmus* may belong,
And fix, O Muse! the Barrier of thy Song, 20
At *Oedipus*—from his Disasters trace
The long Confusions of his guilty Race.
Nor yet attempt to stretch thy bolder Wing,
And mighty *Cæsar*'s conqu'ring Eagles sing;
How twice he tam'd proud *Ister*'s rapid Flood, 25
While *Dacian* Mountains stream'd with barb'rous Blood;
Twice taught the *Rhine* beneath his Laws to roll,
And stretch'd his Empire to the frozen Pole;
Or long before, with early Valour strove
In youthful Arms t'assert the Cause of *Jove*. 30
And Thou, great Heir of all thy Father's Fame,
Encrease of Glory to the *Latian* Name;
Oh bless thy *Rome* with an Eternal Reign,
Nor let desiring Worlds intreat in vain!
What tho' the Stars contract their Heav'nly Space, 35

13. *Juno's Hate*] Juno's jealous hatred of Europa extended to all her family and descendants, the house of Thebes.

14. *unhappy Monarch*] Athamas, who was married to Nephele, but fell in love with Ino, daughter of Cadmus, by whom he had two sons. At Juno's instigation the fury Tisiphone caused Athamas and Ino to go mad. Athamas slew one of his sons, and Ino, with the other son, Melicertes, in her arms, flung herself into the sea. Ino and Melicertes were changed into sea deities, under the names of Leucothea and Palaemon. Cf. ll. 167–8, below.

19. *wave*] Waive.

20. *Barrier*] Either the boundary line, or perhaps an allusion to the 'carcer', or starting-place, in the ancient race-course.

22. *long Confusions*] The troubled histories of Polynices, Eteocles, Antigone.

24. *mighty Cæsar*] Domitian, emperor of Rome, A.D. 81–96.

25. *proud Ister*] The Danube. Far from 'taming' Dacia, the Romans, owing to Domitian's defeat by the Marcomanni, were obliged to make peace with the Dacian general, Decebalus, and pay tribute for the first time in Roman history.

27. Domitian annexed the Taunus district between the Rhine and the Main.

31. *thy Father*] Vespasian, emperor A.D. 69–79.

35 ff. Members of the imperial family were deified, and as divinities were placed among the constellations. See l. 46 below.

And crowd their shining Ranks to yield thee place;
Tho' all the Skies, ambitious of thy Sway,
Conspire to court thee from our World away;
Tho' *Phœbus* longs to mix his Rays with thine,
And in thy Glories more serenely shine;   40
Tho' *Jove* himself no less content wou'd be,
To part his Throne and share his Heav'n with thee;
Yet stay, great *Cæsar*! and vouchsafe to reign
O'er the wide Earth, and o'er the watry Main,
Resign to *Jove* his Empire of the Skies,   45
And People Heav'n with *Roman* Deities.
      The Time will come, when a diviner Flame
Shall warm my Breast to sing of *Cæsar*'s Fame:
Mean while permit that my preluding Muse
In *Theban* Wars an humbler Theme may chuse: 50
Of furious Hate surviving Death, she sings,
A fatal Throne to two contending Kings,
And Fun'ral Flames, that parting wide in Air,
Express the Discord of the Souls they bear:
Of Towns dispeopled, and the wandring Ghosts   55
Of Kings unbury'd, on the wasted Coasts;
When *Dirce*'s Fountain blush'd with *Grecian* Blood,
And *Thetis*, near *Ismenos*' swelling Flood,
With Dread beheld the rolling Surges sweep
In Heaps his slaughter'd Sons into the Deep.   60
      What Hero, *Clio*! wilt thou first relate?
The Rage of *Tydeus*, or the Prophet's Fate?
Or how with Hills of slain on ev'ry side,

39–40. The suggestion is that Phoebus would like to mix the rays from
his nimbus with those from the nimbus Domitian will acquire when he is
divinized. In ancient art emperors and consuls are occasionally represented
with a nimbus.

51–4. The smoke from the bodies of Eteocles and Polynices, who were
placed on the same funeral pyre, did not mingle.

58. *Thetis*] Daughter of Nereus, and chief of the fifty Nereids.

60. *his slaughter'd Sons*] The Thebans, descendants of Cadmus.

61. *What Hero*] Which one, that is, of the famous seven who fought
against Thebes. They were Polynices, Adrastus (king of Argos), Tydeus,
Amphiaraus, Hippomedon, Parthenopaeus, and Capaneus.

62. *The Rage of Tydeus*] An allusion to the horrible episode related later
in the *Thebais*, VIII 751–62, in which the dying Tydeus gnaws the head of
his dead adversary Melanippus in a frenzy of hatred.

the Prophet's Fate] Amphiaraus, who prophesied the destruction of all
the leaders except Adrastus. Jupiter saved him from the spear of the
Theban Periclymenus by causing the earth to swallow him with his
chariot and horses.

Hippomedon repell'd the hostile Tyde?
Or how the Youth with ev'ry Grace adorn'd,   65
Untimely fell, to be for ever mourn'd?
Then to fierce *Capaneus* thy Verse extend,
And sing, with Horror, his prodigious End.
    Now wretched *Oedipus*, depriv'd of Sight,
Led a long Death in everlasting Night;   70
But while he dwells where not a chearful Ray
Can pierce the Darkness, and abhors the Day;
The clear, reflecting Mind, presents his Sin
In frightful Views, and makes it Day within;
Returning Thoughts in endless Circles roll,   75
And thousand Furies haunt his guilty Soul.
The Wretch then lifted to th'unpitying Skies
Those empty Orbs, from whence he tore his Eyes,
Whose Wounds yet fresh, with bloody Hands he strook,
While from his Breast these dreadful Accents broke.   80
    Ye Gods that o'er the gloomy Regions reign
Where guilty Spirits feel Eternal Pain;
Thou, sable *Styx!* whose livid Streams are roll'd
Thro' dreary Coasts which I, tho' Blind, behold:
Tisiphone! that oft hast heard my Pray'r,   85
Assist, if *Oedipus* deserve thy Care!
If you receiv'd me from *Jocasta*'s Womb,
And nurst the Hope of Mischiefs yet to come:
If leaving *Polybus*, I took my Way
To *Cyrrha*'s Temple on that fatal Day,   90
When by the Son the trembling Father dy'd,
Where the three Roads the *Phocian* Fields divide:
If I the *Sphynxe*'s Riddles durst explain,
Taught by thy self to win the promis'd Reign:
If wretched I, by baleful Furies led,   95
With monstrous Mixture stain'd my Mother's Bed,
For Hell and Thee begot an impious Brood,
And with full Lust those horrid Joys renew'd:
Then self-condemn'd to Shades of endless Night,

64. *Hippomedon*] The bodies of the enemy slain by Hippomedon dammed the Ismenos.
65. *Parthenopæus.* [P]. He was the son of Atalanta of Calydon.
67. *Capaneus*] He defied Jupiter, who slew him with a thunderbolt as he was scaling the walls of Thebes.
85. *Tisiphone*] One of the three Furies, the avenger of murder. Cf. l. 14*n*.
89. *Polybus*] King of Corinth, who raised Oedipus as his son.
90. *Cyrrha's Temple*] The spring at Delphi, beneath the peaks of Parnassus, where Oedipus went to consult the oracle.

Forc'd from these Orbs the bleeding Balls of Sight.   100
Oh hear, and aid the Vengeance I require;
If worthy Thee, and what Thou might'st inspire!
My Sons their old, unhappy Sire despise,
Spoil'd of his Kingdom, and depriv'd of Eyes;
Guideless I wander, unreguarded mourn,   105
While These exalt their Scepters o'er my Urn;
These Sons, ye Gods! who with flagitious Pride
Insult my Darkness, and my Groans deride.
Art thou a Father, unregarding *Jove!*
And sleeps thy Thunder in the Realms above?   110
Thou *Fury*, then, some lasting Curse entail,
Which o'er their Childrens Children shall prevail:
Place on their Heads that Crown distain'd with Gore,
Which these dire Hands from my slain Father tore;
Go, and a Parent's heavy Curses bear;   115
Break all the Bonds of Nature, and prepare
Their kindred Souls to mutual Hate and War.
Give them to dare, what I might wish to see,
Blind as I am, some glorious Villany!
Soon shalt thou find, if thou but arm their Hands,   120
Their ready Guilt preventing thy Commands:
Cou'dst thou some great, proportion'd Mischief frame,
They'd prove the Father from whose Loins they came.
    The Fury heard, while on *Cocytus*' Brink
Her Snakes, unty'd, Sulphureous Waters drink;   125
But at the Summons, roll'd her Eyes around,
And snatch'd the starting Serpents from the Ground.
Not half so swiftly shoots along in Air
The gliding Lightning, or descending Star.
Thro' Crouds of Airy Shades she wing'd her Flight,   130
And dark Dominions of the silent Night;
Swift as she past, the flitting Ghosts withdrew,
And the pale Spectres trembled at her View:
To th'Iron Gates of *Tænarus* she flies,
There spreads her dusky Pinions to the Skies.   135
The Day beheld, and sick'ning at the Sight,
Veil'd her fair Glories in the Shades of Night.
Affrighted *Atlas*, on the distant Shore,
Trembl'd, and shook the Heav'ns and Gods he bore.
Now from beneath *Malea*'s airy Height   140

134. *Tænarus*] The southernmost promontory of the Peloponnesus,
considered to be one of the gates of Hades.
140. *Malea*] Promontory at the south-eastern point of the Peloponnesus.

Aloft she sprung, and steer'd to *Thebes* her Flight;
With eager Speed the well-known Journey took,
Nor here regrets the Hell she late forsook.
A hundred Snakes her gloomy Visage shade,
A hundred Serpents guard her horrid Head,   145
In her sunk Eye-balls dreadful Meteors glow,
Such Rays from *Phœbe*'s bloody Circle flow,
When lab'ring with strong Charms, she shoots from high
A fiery Gleam, and reddens all the Sky.
Blood stain'd her Cheeks, and from her Mouth there came
Blue steaming Poisons, and a Length of Flame;   151
From ev'ry Blast of her contagious Breath,
Famine and Drought proceed, and Plagues, and Death:
A Robe obscene was o'er her Shoulders thrown,
A Dress by Fates and Furies worn alone: 155
She tost her meagre Arms; her better Hand
In waving Circles whirl'd a Fun'ral Brand;
A Serpent from her left was seen to rear
His flaming Crest, and lash the yielding Air.
But when the Fury took her Stand on high,   160
Where vast *Cythæron*'s Top salutes the Sky,
A Hiss from all the Snaky Tire went round; ⎫
The dreadful Signal all the Rocks rebound, ⎬
And thro' th' *Achaian* Cities send the Sound. ⎭
Oete, with high *Parnassus*, heard the Voice;   165
Eurota's Banks remurmur'd to the Noise;
Again *Leucothoë* shook at these Alarms,
And press'd *Palæmon* closer in her Arms.
Headlong from thence the glowing Fury springs,
And o'er the *Theban* Palace spreads her Wings,   170
Once more invades the guilty Dome, and shrouds
Its bright Pavilions in a Veil of Clouds.
Strait with the Rage of all their Race possest, ⎫
Stung to the Soul, the Brothers start from Rest, ⎬
And all the Furies wake within their Breast. ⎭   175

142. *well-known Journey*] Tisiphone had had occasion to visit Thebes
before. Cf. l. 14*n*.
161. *Cythæron's Top*] The mountain range between Athens and
Thebes, from which the Fury looked down on her goal.
165. *Oete*] A mountain south of Thessaly, a land famous for spells and
witches.
166. *Eurota*] The Eurotas, a river in Sparta.
167–8. See l. 14*n*.
173. Gentilisque animos subit furor, *seems a better reading than*
Gentilesque. [P]

Their tortur'd Minds repining Envy tears,
And Hate, engender'd by suspicious Fears;
And sacred Thirst of Sway; and all the Ties
Of Nature broke; and Royal Perjuries;
And impotent Desire to Reign alone,   180
That scorns the dull Reversion of a Throne;
Each wou'd the sweets of Sovereign Rule devour,
While Discord waits upon divided Pow'r.
    As stubborn Steers by brawny Plowmen broke,
And join'd reluctant to the galling Yoke,   185
Alike disdain with servile Necks to bear
Th' unwonted Weight, or drag the crooked Share,
But rend the Reins, and bound a diff'rent way,
And all the Furrows in Confusion lay:
Such was the Discord of the Royal Pair,   190
Whom Fury drove precipitate to War.
In vain the Chiefs contriv'd a specious way,
To govern *Thebes* by their Alternate Sway;
Unjust Decree! while This enjoys the State,
That mourns in Exile his unequal Fate;   195
And the short Monarch of a hasty Year
Foresees with Anguish his returning Heir.
Thus did the League their impious Arms restrain,
But scarce subsisted to the Second Reign.
    Yet then no proud aspiring Piles were rais'd,   200
No fretted Roofs with polish'd Metals blaz'd,
No labour'd Columns in long Order plac'd,
No *Grecian* Stone the pompous Arches grac'd;
No nightly Bands in glitt'ring Armour wait
Before the sleepless Tyrant's guarded Gate;   205
No Chargers then were wrought in burnish'd Gold,
Nor Silver Vases took the forming Mold,
Nor Gems on Bowls emboss'd were seen to shine,
Blaze on the Brims, and sparkle in the Wine—
Say, wretched Rivals! what provokes your Rage?   210
Say to what End your impious Arms engage?
Now All bright *Phœbus* views in early Morn,
Or when his Evening Beams the West adorn,
When the South glows with his Meridian Ray,
And the cold North receives a fainter Day;   215

178. *sacred Thirst*] *Sacred* here means *accursed* (Latin *sacer*), and alludes
to Virgil's famous phrase, *Aen.*, III 56-7: 'auri sacra fames'.
    181. *Reversion*] The right of succession to an office or place of emolu-
ment, after the death or retirement of the holder.

For Crimes like these, not all those Realms suffice,
Were all those Realms the guilty Victor's Prize!
  But Fortune now (the Lots of Empire thrown)
Decrees to proud *Etheocles* the Crown:
What Joys, oh Tyrant! swell'd thy Soul that Day,   220
When all were Slaves thou cou'dst around survey,
Pleas'd to behold unbounded Pow'r thy own,
And singly fill a fear'd and envy'd Throne!
  But the vile Vulgar, ever discontent,
Their growing Fears in secret Murmurs vent,   225
Still prone to change, tho' still the Slaves of State,
And sure the Monarch whom they have, to hate;
New Lords they madly make, then tamely bear,
And softly curse the Tyrants whom they fear.
And one of those who groan beneath the Sway   230
Of Kings impos'd, and grudgingly obey,
(Whom Envy to the Great, and vulgar Spight
With Scandal arm'd, th' Ignoble Mind's Delight,)
Exclaim'd—O *Thebes*! for thee what Fates remain,
What Woes attend this inauspicious Reign?   235
Must we, alas! our doubtful Necks prepare,
Each haughty Master's Yoke by turns to bear,
And still to change whom chang'd we still must fear?
These now controul a wretched People's Fate,
These can divide, and these reverse the State;   240
Ev'n Fortune rules no more:—Oh servile Land,
Where exil'd Tyrants still by turns command!
Thou Sire of Gods and Men, Imperial *Jove!*
Is this th'Eternal Doom decreed above?
On thy own Offspring hast thou fix'd this Fate,   245
From the first Birth of our unhappy State;
When banish'd *Cadmus* wandring o'er the Main,
For lost *Europa* search'd the World in vain,
And fated in *Bœotian* Fields to found
A rising Empire on a foreign Ground,   250
First rais'd our Walls on that ill-omen'd Plain
Where Earth-born Brothers were by Brothers slain?
What lofty Looks th'unrival'd Monarch bears!
How all the Tyrant in his Face appears!
What sullen Fury clowds his scornful Brow!   255
Gods! how his Eyes with threatning Ardour glow!
Can this Imperious Lord forget to Reign,

236. *doubtful*] Full of fear or apprehension.
252. Cf. l. 8*n*.

Quit all his State, descend, and serve again?
Yet who, before, more popularly bow'd,
Who more propitious to the suppliant Crowd,   260
Patient of Right, familiar in the Throne?
What Wonder then? he was not then Alone.
Oh wretched we, a vile submissive Train,
Fortune's tame Fools, and Slaves in ev'ry Reign!
  As when two Winds with Rival Force contend,   265
This way and that, the wav'ring Sails they bend,
While freezing *Boreas* and black *Eurus* blow,
Now here, now there, the reeling Vessel throw:
Thus on each side, alas! our tott'ring State
Feels all the Fury of resistless Fate,   270
And doubtful still, and still distracted stands,
While that Prince Threatens, and while this Commands.
  And now th'Almighty Father of the Gods
Convenes a Council in the blest Abodes:
Far in the bright Recesses of the Skies,   275
High o'er the rowling Heav'ns, a Mansion lyes,
Whence, far below, the Gods at once survey
The Realms of rising and declining Day,
And all th'extended Space of Earth, and Air, and Sea.
Full in the midst, and on a Starry Throne,   280
The Majesty of Heav'n superior shone;
Serene he look'd, and gave an awful Nod,
And all the trembling Spheres confess'd the God.
At *Jove*'s Assent, the Deities around
In solemn State the Consistory crown'd: 285
Next a long Order of Inferior Pow'rs
Ascend from Hills, and Plains, and shady Bow'rs;
Those from whose Urns the rowling Rivers flow,
And those that give the wandring Winds to blow,
Here all their Rage, and ev'n their Murmurs cease,   290
And sacred Silence reigns, and universal Peace.
A shining Synod of Majestick Gods
Gilds with new Lustre the divine Abodes,
Heav'n seems improv'd with a superior Ray,
And the bright Arch reflects a double Day.   295
The Monarch then his solemn Silence broke,
The still Creation listen'd while he spoke,
Each sacred Accent bears eternal Weight,

267. *Eurus*] The east wind.
282. Placido quatiens tamen omnia Vultu, *is the common reading; I believe it should be* Nutu, *with reference to the word* quatiens. [P]

And each irrevocable Word is Fate.
   How long shall Man the Wrath of Heav'n defy,   300
And force unwilling Vengeance from the Sky?
Oh Race confed'rate into Crimes, that prove
Triumphant o'er th'eluded Rage of *Jove* !
This weary'd Arm can scarce the Bolt sustain,
And unregarded Thunder rolls in vain: 305
Th' o'erlabour'd *Cyclop* from his Task retires;
Th' *Æolian* Forge exhausted of its Fires.
For this, I suffer'd *Phœbus'* Steeds to stray,
And the mad Ruler to misguide the Day,
When the wide Earth to Heaps of Ashes turn'd,   310
And Heav'n it self the wandring Chariot burn'd.
For this, my Brother of the watry Reign   ⎫
Releas'd th'impetuous Sluices of the Main,— ⎬
But Flames consum'd, and Billows rag'd in vain. ⎭
Two Races now, ally'd to *Jove*, offend;   315
To punish these, see *Jove* himself descend!
The *Theban* Kings their Line from *Cadmus* trace,
From God-like *Perseus* those of *Argive* Race.
Unhappy *Cadmus'* Fate who does not know?
And the long Series of succeeding Woe: 320
How oft the Furies from the deeps of Night
Arose, and mix'd with Men in Mortal Fight:
Th'exulting Mother stain'd with Filial Blood;
The Savage Hunter, and the haunted Wood;
The direful Banquet why shou'd I proclaim,   325
And Crimes that grieve the trembling Gods to name?
E'er I recount the Sins of these Profane,   ⎫
The Sun wou'd sink into the Western Main, ⎬
And rising gild the radiant East again.   ⎭
Have we not seen (the Blood of *Laius* shed)   330
The murd'ring Son ascend his Parent's Bed,
Thro' violated Nature force his way,
And stain the sacred Womb where once he lay?

307. *Th' Æolian Forge*] Vulcan's forge, where he worked with the Cyclopes, was supposed to be on Hiera, one of the Æolian islands, off Sicily.

309. *mad Ruler*] Phaethon.

312–14. An allusion to the deluge.

323. *Th'exulting Mother*] Agave, daughter of Cadmus, who, blinded by bacchic fury, tore to pieces her own son, Pentheus.

324. *The Savage Hunter*] Athamas. Cf. l. 14*n.*

325. *direful Banquet*] An allusion to the story of Tantalus, the king of Argos who served up his own son as meat for the gods.

Yet now in Darkness and Despair he groans,
And for the Crimes of guilty Fate attones;   335
His Sons with Scorn their Eyeless Father view,
Insult his Wounds, and make them bleed anew.
Thy Curse, oh *Oedipus*, just Heav'n alarms,
And sets th'avenging Thunderer in Arms.
I from the Root thy guilty Race will tear,   340
And give the Nations to the Waste of War.
Adrastus soon, with Gods averse, shall join
In dire Alliance with the *Theban* Line;
Hence Strife shall rise, and mortal War succeed;
The guilty Realms of *Tantalus* shall bleed;   345
Fix'd is their Doom; this all-remembring Breast
Yet Harbours Vengeance for the Tyrant's Feast.
    He said; and thus the Queen of Heav'n return'd;
(With sudden Grief her lab'ring Bosom burn'd)
Must I whose Cares *Phoroneus*' Tow'rs defend,   350
Must I, oh *Jove !* in bloody Wars contend ?
Thou know'st those Regions my Protection claim,
Glorious in Arms, in Riches, and in Fame:
Tho' there the fair *Ægyptian* Heifer fed,
And there deluded *Argus* slept and bled;   355
Tho' there the Brazen Tow'r was storm'd of old,
When *Jove* descended in Almighty Gold.
Yet I can pardon those obscurer Rapes,
Those bashful Crimes disguis'd in borrow'd Shapes;
But *Thebes*, where shining in Cœlestial Charms   360
Thou cam'st Triumphant to a Mortal's Arms,
When all my Glories o'er her Limbs were spread,
And blazing Lightnings danc'd around her Bed;
Curs'd *Thebes* the Vengeance it deserves, may prove,—
Ah why shou'd *Argos* feel the Rage of *Jove* ?   365
Yet since thou wilt thy Sister-Queen controul,
Since still the Lust of Discord fires thy Soul,
Go, rase my *Samos*, let *Mycenè* fall,
And level with the Dust the *Spartan* Wall:
No more let Mortals *Juno*'s Pow'r invoke,   ⎫   370
Her Fanes no more with Eastern Incense smoke, ⎬
Nor Victims sink beneath the Sacred Stroke;   ⎭

345–7. Cf. l. 325*n*.
350. *Phoroneus' Tow'rs*] Argos, of which Phoroneus was reputed
founder.
354. *Ægyptian Heifer*] Io.
361. *a Mortal's Arms*] Semele's.
368–9. Mycenae and Sparta were Juno's favourite cities.

But to your *Isis* all my Rites transfer,
Let Altars blaze and Temples smoke for her;
For her, thro' *Ægypt*'s fruitful Clime renown'd,   375
Let weeping *Nilus* hear the Timbrel sound.
But if thou must reform the stubborn Times,
Avenging on the Sons the Father's Crimes,
And from the long Records of distant Age
Derive Incitements to renew thy Rage;   380
Say, from what Period then has *Jove* design'd
To date his Vengeance; to what Bounds confin'd?
Begin from thence, where first *Alphëus* hides
His wandring Stream, and thro' the briny Tydes,
Unmix'd, to his *Sicilian* River glides.   385
Thy own *Arcadians* there the Thunder claim,
Whose impious Rites disgrace thy mighty Name,
Who raise thy Temples where the Chariot stood
Of fierce *Oenomäus*, defil'd with Blood;
Where once his Steeds their savage Banquet found,   390
And Human Bones yet whiten all the Ground.
Say, can those Honours please? and canst thou love
Presumptuous *Crete*, that boasts the Tomb of *Jove*?
And shall not *Tantalus* his Kingdoms share
Thy Wife and Sister's Tutelary Care?   395
Reverse, O *Jove*, thy too severe Decree,
Nor doom to War a Race deriv'd from thee;
On Impious Realms, and barb'rous Kings, impose
Thy Plagues, and curse 'em with such Sons as those.
    Thus, in Reproach and Pray'r, the Queen exprest   400
The Rage and Grief contending in her Breast;
Unmov'd remain'd the Ruler of the Sky,
And from his Throne return'd this stern Reply.

373. *Isis*] Io, with whom Isis, worshipped by the Egyptians, was sometimes identified.

387. *impious Rites*] Perhaps a reference to the worship of Jupiter with
human sacrifices. The original seems to refer merely to the establish-
ment of temples to Jupiter on the ground defiled by Oenomaus (cf.
389*n*).

389. *fierce Oenomäus*] King of Pisa. Warned that he would die by the
hand of his son-in-law, he challenged all suitors for his daughter Hippo-
damia to a chariot race against his own horses. The defeated suitors were
fed to these man-eating horses.

393. The Cretan Zeus, born on Mount Ida, was thought to die and to
be reborn at certain periods.

394. Cf. 325*n*.

399. *Etheocles* and *Polynices*. [P]

'Twas thus I deem'd thy haughty Soul wou'd bear⎤
The dire, tho' just, Revenge which I prepare   ⎬ 405
Against a Nation thy peculiar Care: ⎦
No less *Dione* might for *Thebes* contend,
Nor *Bacchus* less his Native Town defend,

Yet these in Silence see the Fates fulfil
Their Work, and rev'rence our Superior Will.   410
For by the black infernal *Styx* I swear,
(That dreadful Oath which binds the Thunderer)
'Tis fix'd; th'irrevocable Doom of *Jove*;
No Force can bend me, no Persuasion move.
Haste then, *Cyllenius*, thro' the liquid Air,   415
Go mount the Winds, and to the Shades repair;
Bid Hell's black Monarch my Commands obey,
And give up *Laius* to the Realms of Day,
Whose Ghost yet shiv'ring on *Cocytus*' Sand
Expects its Passage to the farther Strand: 420
Let the pale Sire revisit *Thebes*, and bear
These pleasing Orders to the Tyrant's Ear;
That, from his exil'd Brother, swell'd with Pride
Of foreign Forces, and his *Argive* Bride,
Almighty *Jove* commands him to detain   425
The promis'd Empire, and Alternate Reign:
Be this the Cause of more than mortal Hate;
The rest, succeeding Times shall ripen into Fate.
    The God obeys, and to his Feet applies
Those golden Wings that cut the yielding Skies;   430
His ample Hat his beamy Locks o'erspread,
And veil'd the Starry Glories of his Head:
He seiz'd the Wand that causes Sleep to fly,
Or in soft Slumbers seals the wakeful Eye;
That drives the Dead to dark *Tartarean* Coasts,   435
Or back to Life compells the wondring Ghosts.
Thus, thro' the parting Clouds the Son of *May*
Wings on the whistling Winds his rapid way,
Now smoothly steers through Air his equal Flight,
Now springs aloft, and tow'rs th'Ethereal Height,   440
Then wheeling down the Steep of Heav'n he flies,

---

407. *Dione*] Venus was occasionally referred to by the name of her
mother, Dione.
  408. Bacchus was the son of Semele, a daughter of Cadmus, founder
of Thebes.
  415. *Cyllenius*] Mercury, born on Mount Cyllene.
  419. *yet shiv'ring*] Because he had been killed by his own son.
  437. Mercury was the son of Jupiter and Maia, daughter of Atlas.

And draws a radiant Circle o'er the Skies.
  Mean time the banish'd *Polynices* roves
(His *Thebes* abandon'd) thro' th'*Aonian* Groves,
While future Realms his wandring Thoughts delight, 445
His daily Vision, and his Dream by Night;
Forbidden *Thebes* appears before his Eye,
From whence he sees his absent Brother fly,
With Transport views the airy Rule his own,
And swells on an imaginary Throne. 450
Fain wou'd he cast a tedious Age away,
And live out all in one triumphant Day.
He chides the lazy Progress of the Sun,
And bids the Year with swifter Motion run.
With anxious Hopes his craving Mind is tost, 455
And all his Joys in length of Wishes lost.
  The Hero then resolves his Course to bend⎫
Where ancient *Danaus*' fruitful Fields extend, ⎬
And fam'd *Mycene*'s lofty Tow'rs ascend, ⎭
(Where late the Sun did *Atreus*' Crimes detest 460
And disappear'd, in Horrour of the Feast.)
And now by Chance, by Fate, or Furies led,
From *Bacchus*' consecrated Caves he fled,
Where the shrill Cries of frantick Matrons sound,
And *Pentheus*' Blood enrich'd the rising Ground, 465
Then sees *Cythæron* towring o'er the Plain,
And thence declining gently to the Main.
Next to the Bounds of *Nisus*' Realm repairs,
Where treach'rous *Scylla* cut the Purple Hairs:
The hanging Cliffs of *Scyron*'s Rock explores, 470
And hears the Murmurs of the diff'rent Shores:
Passes the Strait that parts the foaming Seas,
And stately *Corinth*'s pleasing Site surveys.
  'Twas now the Time when *Phœbus* yields to Night,
And rising *Cynthia* sheds her silver Light, 475
Wide o'er the World in solemn Pomp she drew
Her airy Chariot, hung with Pearly Dew;
All Birds and Beasts lye hush'd; Sleep steals away

449. *airy*] Unsubstantial; imaginary.
458. Danaus was a former king of Argos.
460–1. The sky was darkened when Atreus, son of Pelops, served up the sons of his brother Thyestes as a meal for their father.
463–5. Cf. 323*n*.
468–9. Scylla, daughter of Nisus, king of Megara, fell in love with Minos when he besieged Megara, and pulled out the purple hair on which her father's life depended.

The wild Desires of Men, and Toils of Day,
And brings, descending thro' the silent Air,   480
A sweet Forgetfulness of Human Care.
Yet no red Clouds, with golden Borders gay,
Promise the Skies the bright Return of Day;
No faint Reflections of the distant Light
Streak with long Gleams the scatt'ring Shades of Night;
From the damp Earth impervious Vapours rise,   486
Encrease the Darkness and involve the Skies.
At once the rushing Winds with roaring Sound
Burst from th'*Æolian* Caves, and rend the Ground,
With equal Rage their airy Quarrel try,   490
And win by turns the Kingdom of the Sky:
But with a thicker Night black *Auster* shrouds
The Heav'ns, and drives on heaps the rowling Clouds,
From whose dark Womb a ratling Tempest pours,
Which the cold North congeals to haily Show'rs.   495
From Pole to Pole the Thunder roars aloud,
And broken Lightnings flash from ev'ry Cloud.
Now Smoaks with Show'rs the misty Mountain-Ground,
And floated Fields lye undistinguish'd round:
Th' *Inachian* Streams with headlong Fury run,   500
And *Erasinus* rowls a Deluge on:
The foaming *Lerna* swells above its Bounds,
And spreads its ancient Poysons o'er the Grounds:
Where late was Dust, now rapid Torrents play,
Rush thro' the Mounds, and bear the Dams away: 505
Old Limbs of Trees from crackling Forests torn,
Are whirl'd in Air, and on the Winds are born;
The Storm the dark *Lycean* Groves display'd,
And first to Light expos'd the Sacred Shade.
Th'intrepid *Theban* hears the bursting Sky,   510
Sees yawning Rocks in massy Fragments fly,
And views astonish'd from the Hills afar
The Floods descending and the watry War,
That driv'n by Storms, and pouring o'er the Plain,
Swept Herds, and Hinds, and Houses to the Main.   515
Thro' the brown Horrors of the Night he fled,
Nor knows, amaz'd, what doubtful Path to tread,

492. *Auster*] The south wind.
500-1. Inachus and Erasinus were rivers in Argos.
503. *ancient Poysons*] Those of the Hydra killed by Hercules in the marshes of Lerna.
508. *dark Lycean Groves*] The groves on Mount Lycaeus, which the sun did not penetrate, were sacred to Jupiter.

His Brother's Image to his Mind appears,
Inflames his Heart with Rage, and wings his Feet with Fears.
    So fares a Sailor on the stormy Main,   520
When Clouds conceal *Boötes*' golden Wain,
When not a Star its friendly Lustre keeps,
Nor trembling *Cynthia* glimmers on the Deeps;
He dreads the Rocks, and Shoals, and Seas, and Skies,
While Thunder roars, and Lightning round him flies. 525
    Thus strove the Chief on ev'ry side distress'd,
Thus still his Courage, with his Toils, encreas'd;
With his broad Shield oppos'd, he forc'd his way
Thro' thickest Woods, and rouz'd the Beasts of Prey.
Till he beheld, where from *Larissa*'s Height   530
The shelving Walls reflect a glancing Light;
Thither with haste the *Theban* Hero flies;
On this side *Lerna*'s pois'nous Water lies,
On that, *Prosymna*'s Grove and Temple rise:
He pass'd the Gates which then unguarded lay,   535
And to the Regal Palace bent his way;
On the cold Marble spent with Toil he lies,
And waits 'till pleasing Slumbers seal his Eyes.
    Adrastus here his happy People sways,
Blest with calm Peace in his declining Days,   540
By both his Parents of Descent divine,
Great *Jove* and *Phœbus* grac'd his noble Line;
Heav'n had not crown'd his Wishes with a Son,
But two fair Daughters heir'd his State and Throne.
To him *Apollo* (wondrous to relate!   545
But who can pierce into the Depths of Fate?)
Had sung—'Expect thy Sons on *Argos*' Shore,
A Yellow Lyon and a bristly Boar.'
This, long revolv'd in his Paternal Breast,
Sate heavy on his Heart, and broke his Rest;   550
This, great *Amphiaraus*, lay hid from thee,
Tho' skill'd in Fate and dark Futurity.
The Father's Care and Prophet's Art were vain,
For thus did the Predicting God ordain.
    Lo hapless *Tydeus*, whose ill-fated Hand   555
Had slain his Brother, leaves his Native Land,

530. *Larissa*] The citadel of Argos.
534. *Prosymna's Grove*] Part of the temple of Juno (Heraeum) was situated near Prosymna.
551. *Amphiaraus*] Cf. l. 62n.
555. *Tydeus*] Son of Oeneus, king of Calydon. He is called Oenides at l. 572.

And seiz'd with Horror, in the Shades of Night,
Thro' the thick Desarts headlong urg'd his Flight:
Now by the Fury of the Tempest driv'n,
He seeks a Shelter from th'inclement Heav'n,   560
Till led by Fate, the *Theban*'s Steps he treads,
And to fair *Argos*' open Court succeeds.
   When thus the Chiefs from diff'rent Lands resort
T'*Adrastus*' Realms and Hospitable Court,
The King surveys his Guests with curious Eyes,   565
And views their Arms and Habit with Surprize.
A Lyon's yellow Skin the *Theban* wears,
Horrid his Mane, and rough with curling Hairs;
Such once employ'd *Alcides*' youthful Toils,
E're yet adorn'd with *Nemea*'s dreadful Spoils.   570
A Boar's stiff Hyde, of *Calydonian* Breed,
Oenides' manly Shoulders overspread,
Oblique his Tusks, erect his Bristles stood,
Alive, the Pride and Terror of the Wood.
   Struck with the Sight, and fix'd in deep Amaze,   575
The King th'accomplish'd Oracle surveys,
Reveres *Apollo*'s vocal Caves, and owns
The guiding Godhead, and his future Sons.
O'er all his Bosom secret Transports reign,
And a glad Horror shoots through ev'ry Vein: 580
To Heav'n he lifts his Hands, erects his Sight,
And thus invokes the silent *Queen* of *Night*.
   Goddess of Shades, beneath whose gloomy Reign
Yon spangled Arch glows with the starry Train,
You who the Cares of Heav'n and Earth allay,   585
Till Nature quicken'd by th'Inspiring Ray,
Wakes to new Vigor with the rising Day.
Oh thou who freest me from my doubtful State,
Long lost and wilder'd in the Maze of Fate!
Be present still, oh Goddess! in our Aid;   590
Proceed, and firm those Omens thou hast made!
We to thy Name our Annual Rites will pay,
And on thy Altars Sacrifices lay;
The Sable Flock shall fall beneath the Stroke,
And fill thy Temples with a grateful Smoke: 595
Hail faithful *Tripos*! Hail ye dark Abodes
Of awful *Phœbus*: I confess the Gods!

591. *firm*] A Latinism, for *confirm*.
596. *faithful Tripos*] The tripod on which the Pythoness seated herself
when prophesying.

Thus, seiz'd with Sacred Fear, the Monarch pray'd;
Then to his Inner Court the Guests convey'd;
Where yet thin Fumes from dying Sparks arise,⎫ 600
And Dust yet white upon each Altar lies,   ⎬
The Relicks of a former Sacrifice.   ⎭
The King once more the solemn Rites requires,
And bids renew the Feasts, and wake the Fires.
His Train obey; while all the Courts around   605
With noisie Care and various Tumult sound.
Embroider'd Purple cloaths the Golden Beds;
This Slave the Floor, and That the Table spreads;
A Third dispels the Darkness of the Night,
And fills depending Lamps with Beams of Light;   610
Here Loaves in Canisters are pil'd on high,
And there, in Flames the slaughter'd Victims fry.
Sublime in Regal State, *Adrastus* shone,
Stretch'd on rich Carpets, on his Iv'ry Throne;
A lofty Couch receives each Princely Guest;   615
Around, at awful Distance, wait the rest.
  And now the King, his Royal Feast to grace,
Acestis calls, the Guardian of his Race,
Who first their Youth in Arts of Virtue train'd,
And their ripe Years in modest Grace maintain'd.   620
Then softly whisper'd in her faithful Ear,
And bad his Daughters at the Rites appear.
When from the close Apartments of the Night,
The Royal Nymphs approach divinely bright,
Such was *Diana*'s, such *Minerva*'s Face;   625
Nor shine their Beauties with superior Grace,
But that in these a milder Charm indears,
And less of Terror in their Looks appears.
As on the Heroes first they cast their Eyes,
O'er their fair Cheeks the glowing Blushes rise,   630
Their down cast looks a decent Shame confest,
Then, on their Father's rev'rend Features rest.
  The Banquet done, the Monarch gives the Sign
To fill the Goblet high with sparkling Wine,
Which *Danaus* us'd in sacred Rites of old,   635
With Sculpture grac'd, and rough with rising Gold.
Here to the Clouds victorious *Perseus* flies;⎫
Medusa seems to move her languid Eyes,   ⎬
And, ev'n in Gold, turns paler as she dies. ⎭
There from the Chace *Jove*'s tow'ring Eagle bears   640

618. *the Guardian*] The nurse of his two daughters.

On golden Wings, the *Phrygian* to the Stars;
Still as he rises in th'Æthereal Height,
His native Mountains lessen to his Sight;
While all his sad Companions upward gaze,
Fix'd on the Glorious Scene in wild Amaze,   645
And the swift Hounds, affrighted as he flies,
Run to the Shade, and bark against the Skies.

This Golden Bowl with gen'rous Juice was crown'd,
The first Libations sprinkled on the Ground;
By turns on each Celestial Pow'r they call;   650
With *Phœbus'* Name resounds the vaulted Hall.
The Courtly Train, the Strangers, and the rest,
Crown'd with chast Laurel, and with Garlands drest,
(While with rich Gums the fuming Altars blaze)
Salute the God in num'rous Hymns of Praise.   655

Then thus the King: Perhaps, my Noble Guests,
These honour'd Altars, and these annual Feasts,
To bright *Apollo*'s awful Name design'd,
Unknown, with Wonder may perplex your Mind.
Great was the Cause; our old Solemnities   660
From no blind Zeal or fond Tradition rise;
But sav'd from Death, our *Argives* yearly pay
These grateful Honours to the God of Day.

When by a thousand Darts the *Python* slain
With Orbs unroll'd lay covering all the Plain,   665
(Transfix'd as o'er *Castalia*'s Streams he hung,
And suck'd new Poisons with his triple Tongue)
To *Argos'* Realms the Victor God resorts,
And enters old *Crotopus'* humble Courts.
This rural Prince one only Daughter blest,   670
That all the Charms of blooming Youth possest;
Fair was her Face, and spotless was her Mind,
Where Filial Love with Virgin Sweetness join'd.
Happy! and happy still She might have prov'd,
Were she less beautiful, or less belov'd!   675
But *Phœbus* lov'd, and on the Flow'ry Side
Of *Nemea*'s Stream the yielding Fair enjoy'd:
Now, e'er ten Moons their Orb with Light adorn,
Th'illustrious Off-spring of the God was born.

641. *the Phrygian*] Ganymede, carried off to be the cup-bearer of the gods.
655. *num'rous*] Measured, rhythmic, harmonious.
664 ff. Python was the dragon who guarded the oracle of Delphi. He was killed by Apollo, who then took possession of the oracle.
669. *Crotopus*] Former king of Argos.

The Nymph, her Father's Anger to evade, 680
Retires from *Argos* to the Sylvan Shade,
To Woods and Wilds the pleasing Burden bears,
And trusts her Infant to a Shepherd's Cares.
   How mean a Fate, unhappy Child! is thine?
Ah how unworthy those of Race divine? 685
On flow'ry Herbs in some green Covert laid,
His Bed the Ground, his Canopy the Shade,
He mixes with the bleating Lambs his Cries,⎫
While the rude Swain his rural Musick tries,⎬
To call soft Slumbers on his infant Eyes. ⎭ 690
Yet ev'n in those obscure Abodes to live,
Was more, alas! than cruel Fate wou'd give!
For on the grassie Verdure as he lay,
And breath'd the Freshness of the early Day,
Devouring Dogs the helpless Infant tore, 695
Fed on his trembling Limbs, and lapt the Gore.
Th'astonish'd Mother when the Rumour came,
Forgets her Father, and neglects her Fame,
With loud Complaints she fills the yielding Air,
And beats her Breast, and rends her flowing Hair; 700
Then wild with Anguish, to her Sire she flies;
Demands the Sentence, and contented dies.
   But touch'd with Sorrow for the Dead, too late,
The raging God prepares t'avenge her Fate.
He sends a Monster, horrible and fell, 705
Begot by Furies in the Depths of Hell;
The Pest a Virgin's Face and Bosom bears; ⎫
High on her Crown a rising Snake appears, ⎬
Guards her black Front, and hisses in her Hairs:⎭
About the Realm she walks her dreadful Round, 710
When Night with sable Wings o'erspreads the Ground,
Devours young Babes before their Parents' Eyes,
And feeds and thrives on Publick Miseries.
   But gen'rous Rage the bold *Chorœbus* warms,
Chorœbus, fam'd for Virtue as for Arms; 715
Some few like him, inspir'd with Martial flame,
Thought a short Life well lost for endless Fame.
These, where two Ways in equal Parts divide,⎫
The direful Monster from afar descry'd; ⎬
Two bleeding Babes depending at her Side; ⎭ 720
Whose panting Vitals, warm with Life, she draws,
And in their Hearts embrues her cruel Claws.
The Youth surround her with extended Spears;

But brave *Chorœbus* in the Front appears,
Deep in her Breast he plung'd his shining Sword,   725
And Hell's dire Monster back to Hell restor'd.
Th'*Inachians* view the Slain with vast Surprize,
Her twisting Volumes, and her rowling Eyes,
Her spotted Breast, and gaping Womb imbru'd
With livid Poyson and our Children's Blood.   730
The Crowd in stupid Wonder fix'd appear,
Pale ev'n in Joy, nor yet forget to fear.
Some with vast Beams the squallid Corps engage,
And weary all the wild Efforts of Rage.
The Birds obscene, that nightly flock'd to Tast,   735
With hollow Screeches fled the dire Repast;
And ravenous Dogs, allur'd by scented Blood,
And starving Wolves, ran howling to the Wood.
   But fir'd with Rage, from cleft *Parnassus'* Brow
Avenging *Phœbus* bent his deadly Bow,   740
And hissing flew the feather'd Fates below;
A Night of sultry Clouds involv'd around
The Tow'rs, the Fields, and the devoted Ground:
And now a thousand Lives together fled,
Death with his Scythe cut off the fatal Thread,   745
And a whole Province in his Triumph led.
   But *Phœbus*, ask'd why noxious Fires appear,
And raging *Sirius* blasts the sickly Year,
Demands their Lives by whom his Monster fell,
And dooms a dreadful Sacrifice to Hell.   750
   Blest be thy Dust, and let Eternal Fame
Attend thy *Manes*, and preserve thy Name;
Undaunted Hero! who, divinely brave,
In such a Cause disdain'd thy Life to save;
But view'd the Shrine with a superior Look,   755
And its upbraided Godhead thus bespoke.
   With Piety, the Soul's securest Guard,
And conscious Virtue, still its own Reward,
Willing I come; unknowing how to fear;
Nor shalt thou, *Phœbus*, find a Suppliant here: 760
Thy Monster's Death to me was ow'd alone,
And 'tis a Deed too glorious to disown.

727. *Th'Inachians*] Descendants of Inachus, founder of Argos.
728. *Volumes*] Coils.
743. *devoted*] Consigned to evil or destruction, doomed.
752. *Manes*] Here probably the soul or spirit of Choroebus.
753. *Undaunted Hero*] Choroebus.

Behold him here, for whom, so many Days,
Impervious Clouds conceal'd thy sullen Rays;
For whom, as Man no longer claim'd thy Care,   765
Such Numbers fell by Pestilential Air!
But if th'abandon'd Race of Human-kind
From Gods above no more Compassion find;
If such Inclemency in Heav'n can dwell; ⎫
Yet why must un-offending *Argos* feel   ⎬ 770
The Vengeance due to this unlucky Steel? ⎭
On me, on me, let all thy Fury fall,
Nor err from me, since I deserve it all:
Unless our Desart Cities please thy Sight,
Our Fun'ral Flames reflect a grateful Light.   775
Discharge thy Shafts, this ready Bosom rend,
And to the Shades a Ghost Triumphant send;
But for my Country let my Fate attone,
Be mine the Vengeance, as the Crime my own.
   Merit distress'd impartial Heav'n relieves;   780
Unwelcome Life relenting *Phœbus* gives;
For not the vengeful Pow'r, that glow'd with Rage,
With such amazing Virtue durst engage.
The Clouds dispers'd, *Apollo*'s Wrath expir'd,
And from the wondring God th'unwilling Youth retir'd.
Thence we these Altars in his Temple raise,   786
And offer Annual Honours, Feasts, and Praise;
These solemn Feasts propitious *Phœbus* please,
These Honours, still renew'd, his antient Wrath appease.
   But say, Illustrious Guest (adjoin'd the King)   790
What Name you bear, from what high Race you spring?
The noble *Tydeus* stands confess'd, and known
Our Neighbour Prince, and Heir of *Calydon*:
Relate your Fortunes, while the friendly Night
And silent Hours to various Talk invite.   795
   The *Theban* bends on Earth his gloomy Eyes,
Confus'd, and sadly thus at length replies:
Before these Altars how shall I proclaim
(Oh gen'rous Prince) my Nation or my name,
Or thro' what Veins our ancient Blood has roll'd?   800
Let the sad Tale for ever rest untold!
Yet if propitious to a Wretch unknown,
You seek to share in Sorrows not your own;
Know then, from *Cadmus* I derive my Race,
Jocasta's Son, and *Thebes* my Native Place.   805
To whom the King, (who felt his gen'rous Breast

Touch'd with Concern for his unhappy Guest)
Replies—Ah why forbears the Son to Name
His wretched Father, known too well by Fame?
Fame, that delights around the World to stray,   810
Scorns not to take our *Argos* in her Way.
Ev'n those who dwell where Suns at distance roll,
In *Northern* Wilds, and freeze beneath the Pole;
And those who tread the burning *Lybian* Lands,
The faithless *Syrtes* and the moving Sands;   815
Who view the *Western* Sea's extreamest Bounds,
Or drink of *Ganges* in their *Eastern* Grounds;
All these the Woes of *Oedipus* have known,
Your Fates, your Furies, and your haunted Town.
If on the Sons the Parents' Crimes descend,   820
What Prince from those his Lineage can defend?
Be this thy Comfort, that 'tis thine t'efface ⎫
With Virtuous Acts thy Ancestor's Disgrace,   ⎬
And be thy self the Honour of thy Race.   ⎭
But see! the Stars begin to steal away,   825
And shine more faintly at approaching Day;
Now pour the Wine; and in your tuneful Lays,
Once more resound the Great *Apollo*'s Praise.
    Oh Father *Phœbus!* whether *Lycia*'s Coast
And snowy Mountains thy bright Presence boast;   830
Whether to sweet *Castalia* thou repair,
And bathe in silver Dews thy yellow Hair;
Or pleas'd to find fair *Delos* float no more,
Delight in *Cynthus* and the Shady Shore;
Or chuse thy Seat in *Ilion*'s proud Abodes,   835
The shining Structures rais'd by lab'ring Gods!
By thee the Bow and mortal Shafts are born,
Eternal Charms thy blooming Youth adorn:
Skill'd in the Laws of Secret Fate above,
And the dark Counsels of Almighty *Jove*,   840
'Tis thine the Seeds of future War to know,

815. *Syrtes*] Quicksands off the northern coast of Africa.
829. *Lycia*] A state in Asia Minor where the worship of Apollo was active.
833. *float no more*] Delos supposedly drifted through the Aegean until Jupiter moored it as a refuge for Latona. There she gave birth to Apollo and Diana.
834. *Shady Shore*] The shadow cast by Mount Cynthus, the mountain in Delos on the Aegean shore.
836 *lab'ring Gods*] According to legend, the walls of Troy were built by Apollo and Neptune.

The Change of Scepters, and impending Woe;
When direful Meteors spread thro' glowing Air
Long Trails of Light, and shake their blazing Hair.
Thy Rage the *Phrygian* felt, who durst aspire   845
T'excel the Musick of thy Heav'nly Lyre;
Thy Shafts aveng'd lewd *Tityus*' guilty Flame,
Th'Immortal Victim of thy Mother's Fame;
Thy Hand slew *Python*; and the Dame who lost
Her num'rous Off-spring for a fatal Boast.   850
In *Phlegias*' Doom thy just Revenge appears,
Condemn'd to Furies and Eternal Fears;
He views his Food, but dreads, with lifted Eye,
The mouldring Rock that trembles from on high.
   Propitious hear our Pray'r, O Pow'r Divine!   855
And on thy Hospitable *Argos* shine.
Whether the Style of *Titan* please thee more,
Whose Purple Rays th' *Achæmenes* adore;
Or great *Osyris*, who first taught the Swain
In *Pharian* Fields to sow the Golden Grain;   860
Or *Mitra*, to whose Beams the *Persian* bows,
And pays in hollow Rocks his awful Vows,
Mitra, whose Head the Blaze of Light adorns,
Who grasps the strugling Heifer's Lunar Horns.

845. *the Phrygian*] Marsyas, a river god who competed with his flute
against Apollo and his lyre. He was defeated and flayed alive by the god.
   847. *Tityus' guilty Flame*] Tityus, a giant, attempted to violate Latona.
He was killed by Apollo and Diana and hurled by them into Tartarus,
where two vultures fed perpetually on his liver.
   849. *the Dame*] Niobe.
   851-4. Phlegyas set fire to Apollo's temple at Delphi because the god
had seduced his daughter Coronis.
   858. *Achæmenes*] The people of Achaemenes, the legendary ancestor of
the Persian kings.
   860. *Pharian*] Egyptian.
   861. *Mitra*] Mithras, the Persian god of light. He was identified by the
Greeks with Apollo and introduced later into Roman mythology. Statius
alludes to the famous relief representing Mithras slaying a bull.

The Gardens of Alcinous

FROM THE SEVENTH BOOK OF HOMER'S ODYSSES

[written c. 1713; published, *Guardian*, 1713]

Close to the gates a spacious garden lies,
From storms defended, and inclement skies:
Four acres was th' allotted space of ground,

Fenc'd with a green enclosure all around.
Tall thriving trees confess'd the fruitful mold;   5
The red'ning apple ripens here to gold,
Here the blue fig with luscious juice o'erflows,
With deeper red the full pomegranate glows,
The branch here bends beneath the weighty pear,
And verdant olives flourish round the year.   10
The balmy spirit of the western gale
Eternal breathes on fruits untaught to fail:
Each dropping pear a following pear supplies,
On apples apples, figs on figs arise:
The same mild season gives the blooms to blow,   15
The buds to harden, and the fruits to grow.
  Here order'd vines in equal ranks appear
With all th' united labours of the year,
Some to unload the fertile branches run,
Some dry the black'ning clusters in the sun,   20
Others to tread the liquid harvest join,
The groaning presses foam with floods of wine.
Here are the vines in early flow'r descry'd, ⎫
Here grapes discolour'd on the sunny side, ⎬
And there in autumn's richest purple dy'd. ⎭   25
  Beds of all various herbs, for ever green,
In beauteous order terminate the scene.
  Two plenteous fountains the whole prospect ⎫
      crown'd; ⎪
This thro' the gardens leads its streams around, ⎬
Visits each plant, and waters all the ground: ⎭   30
While that in pipes beneath the palace flows,
And thence its current on the town bestows;
To various use their various streams they bring,
The People one, and one supplies the King.

The Episode of Sarpedon

TRANSLATED FROM THE TWELFTH AND SIXTEENTH
BOOKS OF HOMER'S ILIADS

[written c. 1707; published, Tonson's
Miscellanies, 1709]

THE ARGUMENT

Sarpedon, *the Son of* Jupiter, *commanded the* Lycians *who came to
the Aid of* Troy. *In the first Battel when* Diomed *had put the*
Trojans *to flight, he encourag'd* Hector *to rally, and signaliz'd*

himself by the Death of Tlepolemus. *Afterwards when the* Greeks *had rais'd a Fortification to cover their Fleet, which the* Trojans *endeavour'd to overthrow, this Prince was the Occasion of effecting it. He incites* Glaucus *to second him in this Action by an admirable Speech, which has been render'd in English by* Sir John Denham; *after whom the Translator had not the Vanity to attempt it for any other reason, than that the Episode must have been very imperfect without so Noble a part of it.*

Thus *Hector*, great in Arms, contends in vain
To fix the Fortune of the fatal Plain,
Nor *Troy* cou'd conquer, nor the *Greeks* wou'd yield,
'Till bold *Sarpedon* rush'd into the Field;
For Mighty *Jove* inspir'd with Martial Flame   5
His God-like Son, and urg'd him on to Fame.
In Arms he shines, conspicuous from afar,
And bears aloft his ample Shield in Air,
Within whose Orb the thick Bull-hides were roll'd,
Pondrous with Brass, and bound with ductile Gold;   10
And while two pointed Jav'lins arm his Hands,
Majestick moves along, and leads his *Lycian* Bands.
    So prest with Hunger, from the Mountain's Brow,
Descends a Lion on the Flocks below;
So stalks the Lordly Savage o'er the Plain,   15
In sullen Majesty, and stern Disdain:
In vain loud Mastives bay him from afar,
And Shepherds gaul him with an Iron War;
Regardless, furious, he pursues his way;
He foams, he roars, he rends the panting Prey.   20
    Resolv'd alike, Divine *Sarpedon* glows
With gen'rous Rage, that drives him on the Foes.
He views the Tow'rs, and meditates their Fall;
To sure Destruction dooms the *Grecian* Wall;
Then casting on his Friend an ardent Look,   25
Fir'd with the Thirst of Glory, thus he spoke.
    Why boast we, *Glaucus*, our extended Reign,
Where *Xanthus*' Streams enrich the *Lycian* Plain?
Our num'rous Herds that range each fruitful Field,
And Hills where Vines their Purple Harvest yield?   30
Our foaming Bowls with gen'rous *Nectar* crown'd,
Our Feasts enhanc'd with Musick's sprightly Sound?
Why on those Shores are we with Joy survey'd,

15. *Lordly Savage*] Cf. *Windsor-Forest*, l. 57*n* (p. 197).
23. *meditates*] Cf. *Windsor-Forest*, l. 102*n* (p. 199).

Admir'd as Heroes, and as Gods obey'd?
Unless great Acts superior Merit prove,   35
And Vindicate the bounteous Pow'rs above:
'Tis ours, the Dignity They give, to grace;
The first in Valour, as the first in Place:
That while with wondring Eyes our Martial Bands
Behold our Deeds transcending our Commands,   40
Such, they may cry, deserve the Sov'reign State,
Whom those that Envy dare not Imitate!
Cou'd all our Care elude the greedy Grave,
Which claims no less the Fearful than the Brave,
For Lust of Fame I shou'd not vainly dare   45
In fighting Fields, nor urge thy Soul to War.
But since, alas, ignoble Age must come,
Disease, and Death's inexorable Doom;
The Life which others pay, let Us bestow,
And give to Fame what we to Nature owe;   50
Brave, tho' we fall; and honour'd, if we live;
Or let us Glory gain, or Glory give!
   He said, his Words the list'ning Chief inspire
With equal Warmth, and rouze the Warrior's Fire;
The Troops pursue their Leaders with Delight,   55
Rush to the Foe, and claim the promis'd Fight.
Menestheus from on high the Storm beheld,
Threat'ning the Fort, and black'ning in the Field;
Around the Walls he gaz'd, to view from far
What Aid appear'd t'avert th'approaching War,   60
And saw where *Teucer* with th'*Ajaces* stood,
Insatiate of the Fight, and prodigal of Blood.
In vain he calls, the Din of Helms and Shields
Rings to the Skies, and ecchoes thro' the Fields,
The Gates resound, the Brazen Hinges fly,   65
While each is bent to conquer or to die.
Then thus to *Thoos*;—Hence with speed (he said)
And urge the bold *Ajaces* to our Aid;
Their Strength united best may help to bear
The bloody Labours of the doubtful War: 70
Hither the *Lycian* Princes bend their Course,
The best and bravest of the *Trojan* Force.
But if too fiercely, there, the Foes contend,
Let *Telamon* at least our Tow'rs defend,
And *Teucer* haste, with his unerring Bow,   75
To share the Danger, and repel the Foe.

60. *War*] Soldiers in fighting array. Cf. l. 134, below.

Swift as the Word, the Herald speeds along
The lofty Ramparts, through the Warlike Throng,
And finds the Heroes, bath'd in Sweat and Gore,
Oppos'd in Combate on the dusty Shore. 80
Strait to the Fort great *Ajax* turn'd his Care,
And thus bespoke his Brothers of the War:
Now valiant *Lycomede*, exert your Might,
And Brave *Oïleus*, prove your Force in Fight:
To you I trust the Fortune of the Field, 85
'Till by this Arm the Foe shall be repell'd;
That done, expect me to compleat the Day;
Then, with his Sev'nfold Shield, he strode away.
With equal Steps bold *Teucer* prest the Shore,
Whose fatal Bow the strong *Pandion* bore. 90
High on the Walls appear'd the *Lycian* Pow'rs,
Like some black Tempest gath'ring round the Tow'rs:
The *Greeks* oppress'd, their utmost Force unite,
Prepar'd to labour in th' unequal Fight;
The War begins; mix'd Shouts and Groans arise; 95
Tumultuous Clamour mounts, and thickens in the Skies.
Fierce *Ajax* first th'advancing Host invades,
And sends the brave *Epicles* to the Shades,
Sarpedon's Friend; Across the Warrior's Way,
Rent from the Walls, a Rocky Fragment lay; 100
In modern Ages not the strongest Swain
Cou'd heave th'unwieldy Burthen from the Plain:
He poiz'd, and swung it round; then tost on high,
It flew with Force, and labour'd up the Sky;
Full on the *Lycian*'s Helmet thundring down, 105
The pondrous Ruin crush'd his batter'd Crown.
As skilful Divers from some Airy Steep
Headlong descend, and shoot into the Deep,
So falls *Epicles*; then in Groans expires,
And murm'ring from the Corps th'unwilling Soul retires. 110
While to the Ramparts daring *Glaucus* drew,
From *Teucer*'s Hand a winged Arrow flew,
The bearded Shaft the destin'd Passage found,
And on his naked Arm inflicts a Wound.
The Chief who fear'd some Foe's insulting Boast 115
Might stop the Progress of his warlike Host,
Conceal'd the Wound, and leaping from his Height,
Retir'd reluctant from th'unfinish'd Fight.
Divine *Sarpedon* with Regret beheld
Disabl'd *Glaucus* slowly quit the Field; 120

His beating Breast with gen'rous Ardour glows,
He springs to Fight, and flies upon the Foes.
Alcmaon first was doom'd his Force to feel,
Deep in his Breast he plung'd the pointed Steel,
Then from the yawning Wound with Fury tore   125
The Spear, pursu'd by gushing Streams of Gore;
Down sinks the Warrior, with a thundring Sound,
His Brazen Armour rings against the Ground.
     Swift to the Battlement the Victor flies,
Tugs with full Force, and ev'ry Nerve applies;   130
It shakes; the pondrous Stones disjoynted yield;
The rowling Ruins smoak along the Field.
A mighty Breach appears, the Walls lye bare,
And like a Deluge rushes in the War.
At once bold *Teucer* draws the twanging Bow,   135
And *Ajax* sends his Jav'lin at the Foe;
Fix'd in his Belt the feather'd Weapon stood,
And thro' his Buckler drove the trembling Wood;
But *Jove* was present in the dire Debate,
To shield his Off-spring, and avert his Fate.   140
The Prince gave back; not meditating Flight,
But urging Vengeance and severer Fight;
Then rais'd with Hope, and fir'd with Glory's Charms,
His fainting Squadrons to new Fury warms.
O where, ye *Lycians*, is the Strength you boast,   145
Your former Fame, and ancient Virtue lost?
The Breach lyes open, but your Chief in vain
Attempts alone the guarded Pass to gain:
Unite, and soon that Hostile Fleet shall fall,
The Force of pow'rful Union conquers All.   150
     This just Rebuke inflam'd the *Lycian* Crew,
They join, they thicken, and th'Assault renew;
Unmov'd, th'embody'd *Greeks* their Fury dare,
And fix'd support the Weight of all the War:
Nor cou'd the *Greeks* repell the *Lycian* Pow'rs,   155
Nor the bold *Lycians* force the *Grecian* Tow'rs.
As on the Confines of adjoyning Grounds,
Two stubborn Swains with Blows dispute their Bounds;
They tugg, they sweat; but neither gain, nor yield,
One Foot, one Inch, of the contended Field: 160
 Thus obstinate to Death, they fight, they fall;
 Nor these can keep, nor those can win the Wall:
 Their Manly Breasts are pierc'd with many a Wound,
 Loud Strokes are heard, and ratling Arms resound,

The copious Slaughter covers all the Shore,   165
And the high Ramparts drop with Human Gore.
   As when two Scales are charg'd with doubtful Loads,
From side to side the trembling Balance nods,
'Till poiz'd aloft, the resting Beam suspends
Each equal Weight, nor this, nor that descends.   170
So Conquest loth for either to declare,
Levels her Wings, and hov'ring hangs in Air.
'Till *Hector* came, to whose Superior Might
Jove ow'd the Glory of the destin'd Fight.
Fierce as a Whirlwind, up the Walls he flies,   175
And fires his Host with loud repeated Cries:
Advance ye *Trojans*, lend your valiant Hands,
Haste to the Fleet, and toss the blazing Brands!
They hear, they run, and gath'ring at his Call,
Raise scaling Engines, and ascend the Wall: 180
Around the Works a Wood of glitt'ring Spears
Shoots up, and All the rising Host appears.
A pondrous Stone bold *Hector* heav'd to throw,
Pointed above, and rough and gross below:
Not two strong Men th'enormous Weight cou'd raise,   185
Such Men as live in these degen'rate Days.
Yet this, as easie as a Swain wou'd bear
The snowy Fleece; he tost, and shook in Air:
For *Jove* upheld, and lighten'd of its Load
Th'unwieldy Rock, the Labour of a God.   190
Thus arm'd, before the folded Gates he came,
Of massy Substance and stupendous Frame,
With Iron Bars and brazen Hinges strong,
On lofty Beams of solid Timber hung.
Then thundring thro' the Planks, with forceful Sway,   195
Drives the sharp Rock; the solid Beams give way,
The Folds are shatter'd, from the crackling Door
Leap the resounding Bars, the flying Hinges roar.
Now rushing in the furious Chief appears,
Gloomy as Night, and shakes two shining Spears;   200
A dreadful Gleam from his bright Armour came,
And from his Eye-balls flash'd the living Flame:
He moves a God, resistless in his Course,
And seems a Match for more than Mortal Force.
Then pouring after, thro' the gaping Space   205
A Tide of *Trojans* flows, and fills the Place;
The *Greeks* behold, they tremble, and they fly,
The Shore is heap'd with Death, and Tumult rends the Sky.

Connection of the foregoing
with the following Part

The Wall being forc'd by Hector, *an obstinate Battel was fought before
the Ships, one of which was set on fire by the* Trojans. Patroclus
thereupon obtaining of Achilles *to lead out the* Myrmidons *to the
Assistance of the* Greeks, *made a great Slaughter of the Enemy,
'till he was oppos'd by* Sarpedon. *The Combate betwixt these Two,
and the Death of the latter, with the Grief of* Jupiter *for his Son,
are describ'd in the ensuing Translation, from the Sixteenth Book
of the* Iliads.

When now the Chief his valiant Friends beheld
Grov'ling in Dust, and gasping on the Field,   210
With this Reproach his flying Host he warms,
Oh Stain to Honour! oh Disgrace of Arms!
Forsake, inglorious, the contended Plain;
This Hand unaided shall the War sustain:
The Task be mine the Hero's Strength to try,   215
Who mows whole Troops, and makes whole Armies fly.
　He said, and leap'd from off his lofty Car;
Patroclus lights, and sternly waits the War.
As when two Vulturs on the Mountain's Height
Stoop with their sounding Pinions to the Fight;   220
They cuff, they tear, they raise a screaming Cry;
The Desart ecchoes, and the Rocks reply;
The Warriors thus oppos'd in Arms engage,
With equal Valour, and with equal Rage.
　Jove view'd the Combate, whose Event foreseen,   225
He thus bespoke his Sister and his Queen.
The Hour draws on; the Destinies ordain,
My God-like Son shall press the *Phrygian* Plain:
Already on the Verge of Death he stands,
His Life is ow'd to fierce *Patroclus'* Hands.   230
What Passions in a Parent's Breast debate!
Say, shall I snatch him from Impending Fate;
And send him safe to *Lycia*, distant far
From all the Dangers and the Toils of War;
Or to his Doom my bravest Off-spring yield,   235
And fatten, with Celestial Blood, the Field?
　Then thus the Goddess with the radiant Eyes:
What Words are these, O Sov'reign of the Skies?

220. *Stoop*] See *Ep. to Arbuthnot*, 341n (p. 608).

Short is the Date prescrib'd to Mortal Man;
Shall *Jove*, for one, extend the narrow Span,   240
Whose Bounds, were fix'd before his Race began?
How many Sons of Gods, foredoom'd to Death,
Before proud *Ilion* must resign their Breath!
Were thine exempt, Debate wou'd rise above,
And murm'ring Pow'rs condemn their partial *Jove*.   245
Give the bold Chief a glorious Fate in Fight;
And when th'ascending Soul has wing'd her Flight,
Let *Sleep* and *Death* convey, by thy Command,
The breathless Body to his Native Land.
His Friends and People, to his future Praise,   250
A Marble Tomb and Pyramid shall raise,
And lasting Honours to his Ashes give;
His Fame ('tis all the Dead can have!) shall live.
    She said; the Cloud-Compeller overcome,
Assents to Fate, and ratifies the Doom.   255
Then, touch'd with Grief, the weeping Heav'ns distill'd
A Show'r of Blood o'er all the fatal Field.
The God, his Eyes averting from the Plain,
Laments his Son, predestin'd to be slain,
Far from the *Lycian* Shores, his happy Native Reign.   260
    Now met in Arms the Combatants appear,
Each heav'd the Shield, and pois'd the lifted Spear:
From strong *Patroclus*' Hand the Jav'lin fled,
And pass'd the Groin of valiant *Thrasymed*,
The Nerves unbrac'd no more his Bulk sustain,   265
He falls, and falling, bites the bloody Plain.
Two sounding Darts the *Lycian* Leader threw,
The first aloof with erring Fury flew,
The next more fatal pierc'd *Achilles*' Steed,
The gen'rous *Pedasus*, of *Theban* Breed;   270
Fix'd in the Shoulder's Joint, he reel'd around;
Rowl'd in the bloody Dust, and paw'd the slipp'ry Ground.
His sudden Fall the entangled Harness broke;
Each Axle groan'd; the bounding Chariot shook;
When bold *Automedon*, to disengage   275
The starting Coursers, and restrain their Rage,
Divides the Traces with his Sword, and freed
Th'incumber'd Chariot from the dying Steed:
The rest move on, obedient to the Rein;
The Car rowls slowly o'er the dusty Plain.   280
    The towring Chiefs to fiercer Fight advance,
And first *Sarpedon* tost his weighty Lance,

Which o'er the Warrior's Shoulder took its Course,
And spent, in empty Air, its dying Force.
Not so *Patroclus* never-erring Dart;   285
Aim'd at his Breast, it pierc'd the mortal Part
Where the strong Fibres bind the solid Heart.
Then as the stately Pine, or Poplar tall,
Hewn for the Mast of some great Admiral,
Nods, groans, and reels, 'till with a crackling Sound   290
It sinks, and spreads its Honours on the Ground;
Thus fell the King; and laid on Earth Supine,
Before his Chariot stretch'd his Form divine:
He grasp'd the Dust, distain'd with streaming Gore,
And, pale in Death, lay groaning on the Shore.   295
So lyes a Bull beneath the Lion's Paws,
While the grim Savage grinds with foamy Jaws
The trembling Limbs, and sucks the smoking Blood;
Deep Groans and hollow Roars rebellow thro' the Wood.
    Then to the Leader of the *Lycian* Band,   300
The dying Chief address'd his last Command.
Glaucus, be bold, Thy Task be first to dare
The glorious Dangers of destructive War,
To lead my Troops, to combate at their Head,
Incite the Living, and supply the Dead.   305
Tell 'em, I charg'd them with my latest Breath,
Not unreveng'd to bear *Sarpedon*'s Death.
What Grief, what Shame must *Glaucus* undergo,
If these spoil'd Arms adorn a *Grecian* Foe?
Then as a Friend, and as a Warrior, fight;   310
Defend my Corps, and conquer in my Right;
That taught by great Examples, All may try
Like thee to vanquish, or like me to die.
    He ceas'd; the Fates supprest his lab'ring Breath,
And his Eyes darken'd with the Shades of Death: 315
Th'insulting Victor with Disdain bestrode
The prostrate Prince, and on his Bosom trod;
Then drew the Weapon from his panting Heart,
The reeking Fibres clinging to the Dart;
From the wide Wound gush'd out a Stream of Blood,   320
And the Soul issu'd in the Purple Flood.
    Then thus to *Phœbus*, in the Realms above,
Spoke from his Throne the Cloud-compelling *Jove*:
Descend my *Phœbus*, on the *Phrygian* Plain,
And from the Fight convey *Sarpedon* slain;   325

291. *Honours*] The foliage of the tree.

Then bathe his Body in the crystal Flood,
With Dust dishonour'd, and deform'd with Blood:
O'er all his Limbs *Ambrosial* Odours shed,
And with Celestial Robes adorn the mighty Dead.
Those Honours paid, his sacred Corps bequeath   330
To the soft Arms of silent *Sleep* and *Death*;
They to his Friends the mournful Charge shall bear;
His Friends a Tomb and Pyramid shall rear;
These unavailing Rites he may receive,
These, after Death, are All a God can give!   335
   Apollo bows, and from Mount *Ida*'s Height
Swift to the Field precipitates his Flight;
Thence, from the War, the breathless Hero bore,
Veil'd in a Cloud, to silver *Simois* Shore:
There bath'd his honourable Wounds, and drest   340
His Manly Members in th'Immortal Vest,
And with Perfumes of sweet *Ambrosial* Dews,
Restores his Freshness, and his Form renews.
Then *Sleep* and *Death*, two Twins of winged Race,
Of matchless Swiftness, but of silent Pace,   345
Receiv'd *Sarpedon*, at the God's Command,
And in a Moment reach'd the *Lycian* Land;
The Corps amidst his weeping Friends they laid,
Where endless Honours wait the Sacred Shade.

The Arrival of Ulysses in Ithaca

BEING PART OF THE XIIITH BOOK OF
HOMER'S ODYSSES

[written c. 1707; published, Steele's
Miscellanies, 1713]

The Beginning of this Book describes the Parting of Ulysses *from* Phæacia; *with the Gifts of* Alcinous *to his Guest; and his taking Ship for his Native Country* Ithaca.

    The Sun descending, the *Phæacian* Train
Spread their broad Sails, and launch into the Main:
At once they bend, and strike their equal Oars,
And leave the sinking Hills, and less'ning Shores.
While on the Deck the Chief in Silence lies,   5
And pleasing Slumbers steal upon his Eyes.

1. Pope translated Homer's ll. 78 to 125, and 187 to 360.

As fiery Coursers in the rapid Race,
Urg'd by fierce Drivers thro' the dusty Space,
Toss their high Heads, and scour along the Plain;
So mounts the bounding Vessel o'er the Main: 10
Back to the Stern the parted Billows flow,
And the black Ocean foams and roars below.
    Thus with spread Sails the winged Gally flies;
Less swift, an Eagle cuts the liquid Skies:
Divine *Ulysses* was her Sacred Load,   15
A Man, in Wisdom equal to a God.
Much Danger long, and mighty Toils he bore,
In Storms by Sea, and Combats on the Shore:
All which soft Sleep now banish'd from his Breast;
Wrapt in a pleasing, deep, and death-like Rest.   20
    But when the morning Star with early Ray
Flam'd in the Front of Heav'n, and promis'd Day,
Like distant Clouds the Mariner descries
Fair *Ithaca*'s emerging Hills arise.
Far from the Town, a spacious Port appears,   25
Sacred to *Phorcys*' Pow'r, whose Name it bears;
Two craggy Rocks, projecting to the Main,
The roaring Winds tempestuous Rage restrain;
Within, the Waves in softer Murmurs glide,
And Ships secure without their Haulsers ride.   30
High at the Head a branching Olive grows,
And crowns the pointed Cliffs with shady Boughs.
Beneath, a gloomy *Grotto*'s cool Recess
Delights the *Nereids* of the neighb'ring Seas;
Where Bowls and Urns were form'd of living Stone,   35
And massie Beams in native Marble shone,
On which the Labours of the Nymphs were roll'd,
Their Webs Divine of Purple mix'd with Gold.
Within the Cave, the clustring Bees attend
Their Waxen Works, or from the Roof depend.   40
Perpetual Waters o'er the Pavement glide;
Two Marble Doors unfold on either side;
Sacred the South, by which the Gods descend,
But Mortals enter at the Northern End.
    Thither they bent, and haul'd their Ship to Land,   45
(The crooked Keel divides the yellow Sand)
Ulysses sleeping, on his Couch they bore,

35. *living Stone*] In its native condition and site.
36. *Beams*] The wooden rollers or cylinders in a loom, on which the warp is wound before weaving.

And gently plac'd him on the Rocky Shore:
His Treasures next, *Alcinous*' Gifts, they laid
In the wild Olive's unfrequented Shade; 50
Secure from Theft: Then launch'd the Bark again,
And tugg'd their Oars, and measur'd back the Main.
 Mean while *Ulysses* in his Country lay,
Releas'd from Sleep; and round him might survey
The solitary Shore, and rowling Sea. 55
Yet had his Mind, thro' tedious Absence, lost
The dear Remembrance of his Native Coast;
Besides *Minerva* to secure her Care,
Diffus'd around a Veil of thicken'd Air:
For so the Gods ordain'd, to keep unseen 60
His Royal Person from his Friends and Queen,
Till the proud Suitors, for their Crimes, afford
An ample Vengeance to her injur'd Lord.
 Now all the Land another Prospect bore,
Another Port appear'd, another Shore, 65
And long-continu'd Ways, and winding Floods,
And unknown Mountains, crown'd with unknown Woods.
Pensive and slow, with sudden Grief opprest,
The King arose, and beat his careful Breast,
Cast a long Look o'er all the Coast and Main, 70
And sought around his Native Realm in vain;
Then with erected Eyes stood fix'd in Woe,
And, as he spoke, the Tears began to flow.
 Ye Gods (he cry'd) upon what barren Coast,
In what new Region is *Ulysses* tost? 75
Possest by wild Barbarians fierce in Arms?
Or Men, whose Bosom tender Pity warms?
Where shall this Treasure now in Safety lie?
And whither, whither its sad Owner flie?
Ah why did I *Alcinous*' Grace implore? 80
Ah why forsake *Phæacia*'s happy Shore?
Some juster Prince perhaps had entertain'd,
And safe restor'd me to my Native Land.
Is this the promis'd, long expected Coast;
And this the Faith *Phæacia*'s Rulers boast? 85
Oh righteous Gods! of all the Great, how few
Are just to Heav'n, and to their Promise true!
But He the Pow'r, to whose All-seeing Eyes
The Deeds of Men appear without Disguise,
'Tis his alone, t'avenge the Wrongs I bear; 90

67. *unknown*] Cf. *Windsor-Forest*, l. 87*n* (p. 198).

For still th'Opprest are his peculiar Care:
To count these *Presents*, and from thence to prove
Their Faith, is mine; the rest belongs to *Jove*.
   Then on the Sands he rang'd his wealthy Store,
The Gold, the Vests, the Tripods number'd o'er;   95
All these he found, but still, in Error lost,
Disconsolate he wanders on the Coast:
Sighs for his Country; and laments again
To the deaf Rocks, and hoarse-resounding Main.
When lo! the Guardian Goddess of the Wise,   100
Celestial *Pallas*, stood before his Eyes;
In show a youthful Swain, of Form divine,
Who seem'd descended from some Princely Line:

A graceful Robe her slender Body drest,
Around her Shoulders flew the waving Vest.   105
Her decent Hand a shining Jav'lin bore,
And painted Sandals on her Feet she wore:
To whom the King: Whoe'er of Human Race
Thou art, that wander'st in this desart Place,
With Joy to thee, as to some God, I bend,   110
To thee my Treasures and my self commend.
O tell a Wretch, in Exile doom'd to stray,
What Air I breath, what Country I survey?
The fruitful Continent's extreamest Bound,
Or some fair Isle which *Neptune*'s Arms surround?   115
   From what far Clime (said she) remote from Fame,
Arriv'st thou here, a Stranger to our Name?
Thou seest an Island, not to those unknown,
Whose Hills are brighten'd by the rising Sun.
Nor those, that plac'd beneath his utmost Reign,   120
Behold him sinking in the Western Main.
The rugged Soil allows no level Space
For flying Chariots, or the rapid Race;
Yet not ungrateful to the Peasant's Pain,
Suffices Fulness to the swelling Grain;   125
The loaded Trees their various Fruits produce,
And clustring Grapes afford a gen'rous Juice;
Woods crown our Mountains, and in ev'ry Grove
The bounding Goats and frisking Heyfers rove;
Soft Rains and kindly Dews refresh the Field,   130
And rising Springs Eternal Verdure yield.
Ev'n to those Shores is *Ithaca* renown'd,
Where *Troy*'s Majestic Ruins strow the Ground.
   At this, the Chief with Transport was possest,

His panting Heart exulted in his Breast: 135
Yet well dissembling his untimely Joys,
And veiling Truth in plausible Disguise;
Thus, with an Air sincere, in Fiction bold,
His ready Tale th'inventive Hero told.

  Oft have I heard, in *Crete*, this Island's Name,   140
For 'twas from *Crete*, my Native Soil, I came;
Self-banish'd thence, I sail'd before the Wind,
And left my Children and my Friends behind.
From fierce *Idomeneus'* Revenge I flew,
Whose Son, the swift *Orsilochus*, I slew,   145
(With Brutal Force he seiz'd my *Trojan* Prey,
Due to the Toils of many a bloody Day.)
Unseen I scap'd; and favour'd by the Night,
In a *Phœnician* Vessel took my Flight;
For *Pyle* or *Elis* bound; but Tempests tost,   150
And raging Billows drove us on your Coast:
In dead of Night an unknown Port we gain'd,
Spent with Fatigue, and slept secure on Land;
But ere the Rosie Morn renew'd the Day,
While in th'Embrace of pleasing Sleep I lay,   155
Sudden, invited by auspicious Gales,
They land my Goods, and hoist their flying Sails.
Abandon'd here, my Fortune I deplore,
A hapless Exile on a Foreign Shore.

  Thus while he spoke, the blue-ey'd Maid began   160
With pleasing Smiles to view the God-like Man;
Then chang'd her Form, and now divinely bright
Jove's heav'nly Daughter stood confess'd to Sight,
Like a fair Virgin in her Beauty's Bloom,
Skill'd in th'illustrious Labours of the Loom.   165

  O still the same *Ulysses !* she rejoin'd,   ⎫
In useful Craft successfully refin'd;   ⎬
Artful in Speech, in Action, and in Mind!   ⎭
Suffic'd it not, that thy long Labours past
Secure thou seest thy Native Shore at last ?   170
But this to me ? who, like thy self, excel
In Arts of Counsel, and Dissembling well:
To me, whose Wit exceeds the Pow'rs Divine,
No less, than Mortals are surpass'd by thine:
Know'st thou not me, who made thy Life my Care,   175
Thro' ten Years Wand'ring, and thro' ten Years War;
Who taught thee Arts, *Alcinous* to persuade,
To raise his Wonder, and ingage his Aid ?

And now appear, thy Treasures to protect, ⎫
Conceal thy Person, thy Designs direct,   ⎬   180
And tell what more thou must from Fate expect; ⎭
Domestick Woes, far heavier to be born,
The Pride of Fools, and Slaves insulting Scorn.
But thou be Silent, nor reveal thy State,
Yield to the Force of unresisted Fate,   185
And bear unmov'd the Wrongs of base Mankind,
The last and hardest Conquest of the Mind.
    Goddess of Wisdom! (*Ithacus* replies) ⎫
He who discerns thee must be truly wise,   ⎬
So seldom view'd, and ever in Disguise.   ⎭   190
When the bold *Argives* led their warring Pow'rs
Against proud *Ilion*'s well-defended Tow'rs,
Ulysses was thy Care, Celestial Maid,
Grac'd with thy Sight, and favour'd with thy Aid:
But when the *Trojan* Piles in Ashes lay,   195
And, bound for *Greece*, we plow'd the Watry way;
Our Fleet dispers'd, and driv'n from Coast to Coast;
Thy sacred Presence from that Hour I lost;
Till I beheld thy radiant Form once more,
And heard thy Counsels on *Phæacia*'s Shore.   200
But by th'Almighty Author of thy Race,
Tell me, oh tell, is this my Native Place?
For much I fear, long Tracts of Land and Sea
Divide this Coast from distant *Ithaca*.
The sweet Delusion kindly you impose,   205
To sooth my Hopes and mitigate my Woes.
    Thus he: The blue-ey'd Goddess thus replies:
How prone to Doubt, how cautious are the Wise?
Who vers'd in Fortune, fear the flatt'ring Show,
And taste not half the Bliss the Gods bestow.   210
The more shall *Pallas* aid thy just Desires,
And guard the Wisdom which her self inspires.
Others, long absent from their Native Place,   ⎫
Strait seek their Home, and fly with eager Pace, ⎬
To their Wives Arms, and Childrens dear Embrace. ⎭ 215
Not thus *Ulysses*; he decrees to prove
His Subjects Faith, and Queen's suspected Love,
Who mourn'd her Lord twice ten revolving Years,
And wastes the Days in Grief, the Nights in Tears.
But *Pallas* knew (thy Friends and Navy lost)   220
Once more 'twas giv'n thee to behold thy Coast:
Yet how cou'd I with adverse Fate engage,

And Mighty *Neptune*'s unrelenting Rage ?—
Now lift thy longing Eyes, while I restore
The pleasing Prospect of thy Native Shore!   225
Behold the Port of *Phorcys* fenc'd around
With Rocky Mountains, and with Olives crown'd!
Behold the gloomy *Grot*, whose cool Recess
Delights the *Nereids* of the neighb'ring Seas;
Whose now neglected Altars, in thy Reign   230
Blush'd with the Blood of Sheep and Oxen slain.
Behold where *Neritus* the Clouds divides,
And shakes the waving Forests on his Sides!
  So spake the Goddess, and the Prospect clear'd,
The Mists dispers'd, and all the Coast appear'd: 235
The King with Joy confess'd his Place of Birth,
And, on his Knees, salutes his Mother Earth;
Then, with his suppliant Hands upheld in Air,
Thus to the Sea-green Sisters sends his Pray'r.
  All hail! Ye Virgin Daughters of the Main;   240
Ye Streams, beyond my Hopes beheld again!
To you once more your own *Ulysses* bows,
Attend his Transports, and receive his Vows.
If *Jove* prolong my Days, and *Pallas* crown
The growing Virtues of my youthful Son,   245
To you shall Rites Divine be ever paid,
And grateful Off'rings on your Altars laid.

Argus

[written 1709; published, *Miscellanea*, 1727]

When wise *Ulysses*, from his native coast
Long kept by wars, and long by tempests tost,
Arriv'd at last, poor, old, disguis'd, alone,
To all his friends, and ev'n his Queen, unknown,
Chang'd as he was, with age, and toils, and cares,   5
Furrow'd his rev'rend face, and white his hairs,
In his own Palace forc'd to ask his bread,
Scorn'd by those slaves his former bounty fed
Forgot of all his own domestic crew;
The faithful Dog alone his rightful Master knew!   10

These lines were sent to Henry Cromwell in a letter dated 19 October
1709. No more than ll. 10–12, 15–16 were used, in amended form, in
Pope's translation of the *Odyssey*.

Unfed, unhous'd, neglected, on the clay,
Like an old servant now cashier'd, he lay;
Touch'd with resentment of ungrateful Man,
And longing to behold his ancient Lord again.
Him when he saw—he rose, and crawl'd to meet,   15
('Twas all he cou'd) and fawn'd, and lick'd his feet,
Seiz'd with dumb joy—then falling by his side,
Own'd his returning Lord, look'd up, and dy'd!

*January and May; or, the Merchant's Tale:
from Chaucer*

[written c. 1704; published, Tonson's
Miscellanies, 1709]

There liv'd in *Lombardy*, as Authors write,
In Days of old, a wise and worthy Knight;
Of gentle Manners, as of gen'rous Race,
Blest with much Sense, more Riches, and some Grace.
Yet led astray by *Venus'* soft Delights,   5
He scarce cou'd rule some Idle Appetites;
For long ago, let Priests say what they cou'd,
Weak, sinful Laymen were but Flesh and Blood.
    But in due Time, when Sixty Years were o'er,
He vow'd to lead this Vicious Life no more.   10
Whether pure Holiness inspir'd his Mind,
Or Dotage turn'd his Brain, is hard to find;
But his high Courage prick'd him forth to wed,
And try the Pleasures of a lawful Bed.
This was his nightly Dream, his daily Care,   15
And to the Heav'nly Pow'rs his constant Pray'r,
Once, ere he dy'd, to taste the blissful Life
Of a kind Husband, and a loving Wife.
    These Thoughts he fortify'd with Reasons still,
(For none want Reasons to confirm their Will)   20

Title] *This Translation was done at sixteen or seventeen Years of
Age.* [P]
    1-18. Chaucer 1-22.
    3 f. Pope.
    7. Pope.
    18. After this line Pope omits Chaucer 17-22 as 'redundant'.
    19-50. Chaucer 23-66.
    19 f. Pope.

Grave Authors say, and witty Poets sing,
That honest Wedlock is a glorious Thing:
But Depth of Judgment most in him appears,
Who wisely weds in his maturer Years.
Then let him chuse a Damsel young and fair,   25
To bless his Age, and bring a worthy Heir;
To sooth his Cares, and free from Noise and Strife
Conduct him gently to the Verge of Life.
Let sinful Batchelors their Woes deplore,
Full well they merit all they feel, and more: 30
Unaw'd by Precepts, Human or Divine,
Like Birds and Beasts, promiscuously they join:
Nor know to make the present Blessing last,
To hope the future, or esteem the past;
But vainly boast the Joys they never try'd,   35
And find divulg'd the Secrets they wou'd hide.
The marry'd Man may bear his Yoke with Ease,
Secure at once himself and Heav'n to please;
And pass his inoffensive Hours away,
In Bliss all Night, and Innocence all Day: 40
Tho' Fortune change, his constant Spouse remains,
Augments his Joys, or mitigates his Pains.
   But what so pure, which envious Tongues will spare?
Some wicked Wits have libell'd all the Fair:
With matchless Impudence they stile a Wife   45
The dear-bought Curse and lawful Plague of Life:
A Bosome Serpent, a Domestick Evil,
A Night-Invasion, and a Mid-day-Devil.
Let not the Wise these slandrous Words regard,
But curse the Bones of ev'ry lying Bard.   50
   All other Goods by Fortune's Hand are giv'n,
A Wife is the peculiar Gift of Heav'n:
Vain Fortune's Favours, never at a Stay,
Like empty Shadows, pass, and glide away;
One solid Comfort, our Eternal Wife,   55
Abundantly supplies us all our Life:
This Blessing lasts, (if those who try, say true)
As long as Heart can wish—and longer too.
   Our Grandsire *Adam*, ere of *Eve* possest,
Alone, and ev'n in Paradise, unblest,   60

31, 33–5. Pope.
39 f. Pope.
51–8. Chaucer 67–74.
59–64. Chaucer 75–92.

With mournful Looks the blissful Scenes survey'd,
And wander'd in the solitary Shade:
The Maker saw, took pity, and bestow'd
Woman, the last, the best reserv'd of God.

   A Wife! ah gentle Deities, can he   65
That has a Wife, e'er feel Adversity?
Wou'd Men but follow what the Sex advise,
All things wou'd prosper, all the World grow wise.
'Twas by *Rebecca*'s Aid that *Jacob* won
His Father's Blessing from an Elder Son: 70
Abusive *Nabal* ow'd his forfeit Life
To the wise Conduct of a prudent Wife:
Heroick *Judeth*, as old *Hebrews* show,
Preserv'd the *Jews*, and slew th' *Assyrian* Foe:
At *Hester*'s Suit, the Persecuting Sword   75
Was sheath'd, and *Israel* liv'd to bless the Lord.

   These weighty Motives *January* the Sage
Maturely ponder'd in his riper Age;
And charm'd with virtuous Joys, and sober Life,
Wou'd try that Christian Comfort, call'd a Wife: 80
His Friends were summon'd, on a Point so nice,
To pass their Judgment, and to give Advice;
But fix'd before, and well resolv'd was he,
(As Men that ask Advice are wont to be.)

   My Friends, he cry'd, (and cast a mournful Look   85
Around the Room, and sigh'd before he spoke:)
Beneath the Weight of threescore Years I bend,
And worn with Cares, am hastning to my End;
How I have liv'd, alas you know too well,
In worldly Follies, which I blush to tell;   90
But gracious Heav'n has op'd my Eyes at last,
With due Regret I view my Vices past,
And as the Precept of the Church decrees,
Will take a Wife, and live in Holy Ease.
But since by Counsel all things shou'd be done,   95
And many Heads are wiser still than one;
Chuse you for me, who best shall be content
When my Desire's approv'd by your Consent.

64. Pope.
65-8. Chaucer 93-117.
69-76. Chaucer 118-30.
77-84. Chaucer 149-54.
85-98. Chaucer 155-70.
93 f. Pope. He omits Chaucer 164 f.

　　One Caution yet is needful to be told,
To guide your Choice; This Wife must not be old:　100
There goes a Saying, and 'twas shrewdly said,
Old Fish at Table, but young Flesh in Bed.
My Soul abhors the tastless, dry Embrace,
Of a stale Virgin with a Winter Face;
In that cold Season Love but treats his Guest　105
With Beanstraw, and tough Forage, at the best.
No crafty Widows shall approach my Bed,
Those are too wise for Batchelors to wed;
As subtle Clerks by many Schools are made,
Twice-marry'd Dames are Mistresses o' th' Trade:　110
But young and tender Virgins, rul'd with Ease,
We form like Wax, and mold them as we please.
　　Conceive me Sirs, nor take my Sense amiss,
'Tis what concerns my Soul's Eternal Bliss;
Since if I found no Pleasure in my Spouse,　115
As Flesh is frail, and who (God help me) knows?
Then shou'd I live in lewd Adultery,
And sink downright to *Satan* when I die.
Or were I curst with an unfruitful Bed,
The righteous End were lost for which I wed,　120
To raise up Seed to bless the Pow'rs above,
And not for Pleasure only, or for Love.
Think not I dote; 'tis Time to take a Wife,
When vig'rous Blood forbids a chaster Life:
Those that are blest with Store of Grace Divine　125
May live like Saints, by Heav'ns Consent, and mine.
　　And since I speak of Wedlock, let me say,
As, thank my Stars, in modest Truth I may,
My Limbs are active, still I'm sound at Heart,
And a new Vigour springs in ev'ry Part.　130
Think not my Virtue lost, tho' Time has shed
These rev'rend Honours on my Hoary Head;
Thus Trees are crown'd with Blossoms white as Snow,
The Vital Sap then rising from below:
Old as I am, my lusty Limbs appear　135
Like Winter Greens, that flourish all the Year.
Now Sirs you know to what I stand inclin'd,
Let ev'ry Friend with Freedom speak his Mind.

99–112. Chaucer 171–86.
113–26. Chaucer 187–212.
127–38. Chaucer 213–24.
129–36. Chaucer 214–22.

He said; the rest in diff'rent Parts divide,
The knotty Point was urg'd on either Side;   140
Marriage, the Theme on which they all declaim'd,
Some prais'd with Wit, and some with Reason blam'd.
'Till, what with Proofs, Objections, and Replies,
Each wondrous positive, and wondrous wise;
There fell between his Brothers a Debate,   145
Placebo This was call'd, and *Justin* That.
  First to the Knight *Placebo* thus begun,
(Mild were his Looks, and pleasing was his Tone)
Such Prudence, Sir, in all your Words appears,
As plainly proves, Experience dwells with Years: 150
Yet you pursue sage *Solomon*'s Advice,
To Work by Counsel when Affairs are nice:
But, with the Wiseman's Leave, I must protest, ⎫
So may my Soul arrive at Ease and Rest, ⎬
As still I hold your own Advice the best. ⎭   155
  Sir, I have liv'd a Courtier all my Days,
And study'd Men, their Manners, and their Ways;
And have observ'd this useful Maxim still,
To let my Betters always have their Will.
Nay, if my Lord affirm'd that Black was White,   160
My Word was this; *Your Honour's in the right.*
Th'assuming Wit, who deems himself so wise
As his mistaken Patron to advise,
Let him not dare to vent his dang'rous Thought;
A Noble Fool was never in a Fault.   165
This Sir affects not you, whose ev'ry Word
Is weigh'd with Judgment, and befits a Lord:
Your Will is mine; and is (I will maintain)
Pleasing to God, and shou'd be so to Man;
At least, your Courage all the World must praise,   170
Who dare to wed in your declining Days.
Indulge the Vigour of your mounting Blood,
And let grey Fools be Indolently good;
Who past all Pleasure, damn the Joys of Sense,
With rev'rend Dulness, and grave Impotence.   175
  Justin, who silent sate, and heard the Man,
Thus, with a Philosophick Frown, began.

139–46. Chaucer 225–33.
144. Pope.
147–55. Chaucer 234–46.
156–75. Chaucer 247–74.
176–215. Chaucer 275–321.

A Heathen Author, of the first Degree,
(Who, tho' not *Faith*, had *Sense* as well as We)
Bids us be certain our Concerns to trust   180
To those of gen'rous Principles, and just.
The Venture's greater, I'll presume to say,
To give your Person than your Goods away:
And therefore, Sir, as you regard your Rest,
First learn your Lady's Qualities at least: 185
Whether she's chast or rampant, proud or civil;
Meek as a Saint, or haughty as the Devil;
Whether an easie, fond, familiar *Fool*,
Or such a *Wit* as no Man e'er can rule?
'Tis true, Perfection none must hope to find   190
In all this World, much less in Womankind;
But if her Virtues prove the larger Share,
Bless the kind Fates, and think your Fortune rare.
Ah gentle Sir, take Warning of a Friend,
Who knows too well the State you thus commend   195
And, spight of all its Praises, must declare,
All he can find is Bondage, Cost, and Care.
Heav'n knows, I shed full many a private Tear,
And sigh in Silence, Lest the World shou'd hear:
While all my Friends applaud my blissful Life,   200
And swear no Mortal's happier in a Wife;
Demure and chast as any Vestal Nun,
The meekest Creature that beholds the Sun!
But, by th' Immortal Pow'rs, I feel the Pain,
And he that smarts has Reason to complain.   205
Do what you list, for me; you must be sage,
And cautious sure; for Wisdom is in Age:
But, at these Years, to venture on the Fair!
By him, who made the Ocean, Earth, and Air,
To please a Wife when her Occasions call,   210
Wou'd busie the most Vig'rous of us all.
And trust me, Sir, the chastest you can chuse
Will ask Observance, and exact her Dues.
If what I speak my noble Lord offend,
My tedious Sermon here is at an End   215
    'Tis well, 'tis wondrous well, the Knight replies,

179. Pope.
186–93. Chaucer 289–99.
199. Pope.
202. Pope.
216–21. Chaucer 322–7. Pope's January speaks ironical, Chaucer's
direct, scorn.

Most worthy Kinsman, faith, you're mighty wise!
We, Sirs, are Fools; and must resign the Cause
To heathnish Authors, Proverbs, and old Saws.
He spoke with Scorn, and turn'd another way—   220
What does my Friend, my dear *Placebo* say?
    I say, quoth he, by Heav'n the Man's to blame,
To slander Wives, and Wedlock's holy Name.
At this, the Council rose, without Delay;
Each, in his own Opinion, went his Way;   225
With full Consent, that all Disputes appeas'd,
The Knight should marry, when and where he pleas'd.
    Who now but *January* exults with Joy?
The Charms of Wedlock all his Soul imploy:
Each Nymph by turns his wav'ring Mind possest,   230
And reign'd the short-liv'd Tyrant of his Breast;

While Fancy pictur'd ev'ry lively Part,
And each bright Image wander'd o'er his Heart.
Thus, in some publick *Forum* fix'd on high,
A Mirrour shows the Figures moving by;   235
Still one by one, in swift Succession, pass
The gliding Shadows o'er the polish'd Glass.
This Lady's Charms the Nicest cou'd not blame,
But vile Suspicions had aspers'd her Fame;
That was with Sense, but not with Virtue blest;   240
And one had Grace, that wanted all the rest.
Thus doubting long what Nymph he shou'd obey
He fix'd at last upon the youthful *May*.
Her Faults he knew not, Love is always blind,
But ev'ry Charm revolv'd within his Mind: 245
Her tender Age, her Form divinely Fair,
Her easie Motion, her attractive Air,
Her sweet Behaviour, her enchanting Face,
Her moving Softness, and majestick Grace.
    Much in his Prudence did our Knight rejoice,   250
And thought no Mortal cou'd dispute his Choice:
Once more in haste he summon'd ev'ry Friend,
And told them all, their Pains were at an End.

222 f. Chaucer 328 f.
224–7. Chaucer 330–2.
228–49. Chaucer 333–60.
234–7. Chaucer 338–41.
238–41. Chaucer 345–9.
244. After this line Pope omits Chaucer 355.
246–9. Chaucer 357–60.
250–75. Chaucer 361–410.

Heav'n that (said he) inspir'd me first to wed,
Provides a Consort worthy of my Bed;   255
Let none oppose th'Election, since on this
Depends my Quiet, and my future Bliss.
   A Dame there is, the Darling of my Eyes,
Young, beauteous, artless, innocent and wise;
Chast tho' not rich; and tho' not nobly born,   260
Of honest Parents, and may serve my Turn.
Her will I wed, if gracious Heav'n so please;
To pass my Age in Sanctity and Ease:
And thank the Pow'rs, I may possess alone
The lovely Prize, and share my Bliss with none!   265
If you, my Friends, this Virgin can procure,
My Joys are full, my Happiness is sure.
   One only Doubt remains; Full oft I've heard
By Casuists grave, and deep Divines averr'd;
That 'tis too much for Human Race to know   270
The Bliss of Heav'n above, and Earth below.
Now shou'd the Nuptial Pleasures prove so great,
To match the Blessings of the future State,
Those endless Joys were ill exchanged for these;
Then clear this Doubt, and set my Mind at ease.   275
   This *Justin* heard, nor cou'd his Spleen controul,
Touch'd to the Quick, and tickl'd at the Soul.
Sir Knight, he cry'd, if this be all you dread,
Heav'n put it past your Doubt whene'er you wed,
And to my fervent Pray'rs so far consent,   280
That ere the Rites are o'er, you may repent!
Good Heav'n no doubt the nuptial State approves,
Since it chastises still what best it loves.
Then be not, Sir, abandon'd to Despair; ⎫
Seek, and perhaps you'll find, among the Fair, ⎬   285
One, that may do your Business to a Hair; ⎭
Not ev'n in Wish, your Happiness delay,
But prove the Scourge to lash you on your Way:
Then to the Skies your mounting Soul shall go,
Swift as an Arrow soaring from the Bow!   290
Provided still, you moderate your Joy,
Nor in your Pleasures all your Might imploy,
Let Reason's Rule your strong Desires abate,
Nor please too lavishly your gentle Mate.

269. Pope.
276–98. Chaucer 411–44.
282 f. Pope.

Old Wives there are, of Judgment most acute,   529
Who solve these Questions beyond all Dispute;
Consult with those, and be of better Chear;
Marry, do Penance, and dismiss your Fear.
    So said they rose, nor more the Work delay'd;
The Match was offer'd, the Proposals made: 300
The Parents, you may think, wou'd soon comply;
The Old have Int'rest ever in their Eye:
Nor was it hard to move the Lady's Mind;
When Fortune favours still the Fair are kind.
    I pass each previous Settlement and Deed,   305
Too long for me to write, or you to read;
Nor will with quaint Impertinence display
The Pomp, the Pageantry, the proud Array.
The Time approach'd, to Church the Parties went,
At once with carnal and devout Intent: 310
Forth came the Priest, and bade th'obedient Wife
Like *Sarah* or *Rebecca* lead her Life:
Then pray'd the Pow'rs the fruitful Bed to bless,
And made all sure enough with Holiness.
    And now the Palace Gates are open'd wide,   ⎫ 315
The Guests appear in Order, Side by Side,   ⎬
And, plac'd in State, the Bridegroom and the Bride. ⎭
The breathing Flute's soft Notes are heard around,
And the shrill Trumpets mix their Silver Sound;
The vaulted Roofs with ecchoing Musick ring,   320
These touch the vocal Stops, and those the trembling
    String.
Not thus *Amphion* tun'd the warbling Lyre,
Nor *Joab* the sounding Clarion cou'd inspire,
Nor fierce *Theodamas*, whose sprightly Strain   324
Cou'd swell the Soul to Rage, and fire the Martial Train.

295 f. Chaucer 440–3:
        But wade we fro this matter to another.
        The wife of Bathe, if ye vnderstand
        Of mariage, which ye now haue in hand,
        Declareth full well in a litle space.
Pope wishes his story to be independent of its context in the *Canterbury Tales*.
298. Pope.
299–304. Chaucer 445–51.
305–14. Chaucer 452–64.
306 f. Pope.
310. Pope.
315–40. Chaucer 465–97.

Bacchus himself, the Nuptial Feast to grace,
(So Poets sing) was present on the Place;
And lovely *Venus*, Goddess of Delight,
Shook high her flaming Torch, in open Sight,
And danc'd around, and smil'd on ev'ry Knight: 330
Pleas'd her best Servant wou'd his Courage try,
No less in Wedlock than in Liberty.
Full many an Age old *Hymen* had not spy'd
So kind a Bridegroom, or so bright a Bride.
Ye Bards! renown'd among the tuneful Throng   335
For gentle Lays, and joyous Nuptial Song;
Think not your softest Numbers can display
The matchless Glories of this blissful Day;
The Joys are such as far transcend your Rage,
When tender Youth has wedded stooping Age.   340
   The beauteous Dame sate smiling at the Board,
And darted am'rous Glances at her Lord;
Not *Hester*'s self, whose Charms the *Hebrews* sing,
E're look'd so lovely on her *Persian* King:
Bright as the rising Sun, in Summer's Day,   345
And fresh and blooming as the Month of *May*!
The joyful Knight survey'd her by his Side,
Nor envy'd *Paris* with the *Spartan* Bride:
Still as his Mind revolv'd with vast Delight
Th'entrancing Raptures of th'approaching Night;   350
Restless he sate, invoking ev'ry Pow'r
To speed his Bliss, and haste the happy Hour.
Mean time the vig'rous Dancers beat the Ground,
And Songs were sung, and flowing Bowls went round;
With od'rous Spices they perfum'd the Place,   355
And Mirth and Pleasure shone in ev'ry Face.
   Damian alone, of all the Menial Train,
Sad in the midst of Triumphs, sigh'd for Pain;
Damian alone, the Knight's obsequious Squire,
Consum'd at Heart, and fed a secret Fire.   360
His lovely Mistress all his Soul possest,
He look'd, he languish'd, and cou'd take no Rest:
His Task perform'd, he sadly went his Way,
Fell on his Bed, and loath'd the Light of Day.

340. Chaucer 494.
After this line Pope omits Chaucer 495–7.
  341–56. Chaucer 498–527.
  348. After this line Pope omits Chaucer 511–17.
  357–66. Chaucer 528–38.
  362. Chaucer 533 f.

There let him lye, 'till his relenting Dame   365
Weep in her turn, and waste in equal Flame.
  The weary Sun, as Learned Poets write,
Forsook th' *Horizon*, and roll'd down the Light;
While glitt'ring Stars his absent Beams supply,
And Night's dark Mantle overspread the Sky.   370
Then rose the Guests; and as the time requir'd,
Each paid his Thanks, and decently retir'd.
  The Foe once gone, our Knight prepar'd t'undress,
So keen he was, and eager to possess:
But first thought fit th'Assistance to receive,   375
Which grave Physicians scruple not to give;
Satyrion near, with hot *Eringo*'s stood,
Cantharides, to fire the lazy Blood,
Whose Use old Bards describe in luscious Rhymes,
And Criticks learn'd explain to Modern Times.   380
  By this the Sheets were spread, the Bride undrest,
The Room was sprinkled, and the Bed was blest.
What next ensu'd beseems not me to say;
'Tis sung, he labour'd 'till the dawning Day,
Then briskly sprung from Bed, with Heart so light, ⎫   385
As all were nothing he had done by Night;   ⎬
And sipt his Cordial as he sate upright: ⎭
He kiss'd his balmy Spouse, with wanton Play,
And feebly sung a lusty Roundelay:
Then on the Couch his weary Limbs he cast;   390
For ev'ry Labour must have Rest at last.
  But anxious Cares the pensive Squire opprest,

366. After this line Pope omits Chaucer 539-50, an invocation of the
'auctor'.
  367-72. Chaucer 551-60.
  367. *as . . . write*] Pope.
  369. Pope.
  373-80. Chaucer 561-8.
  375 f. Pope.
  377 f. Chaucer 563 f. Satyrion (a kind of orchis), eringo (sea holly), and
cantharides (a particular kind of dried beetle) were all held to have
aphrodisiac properties.
  379 f. Pope may refer principally to the Paris edition (1660) of Ovid's
Ars Amandi 'Cum notis & interpretatione Gallica'.
  380. After this line Pope omits Chaucer 569-73 in which the house is
cleared of 'priuie friends . . . Men drinken, and the trauers drew anon'.
  381-91. Chaucer 574-621.
  385. Pope adds the briskness.
  386. Pope.
  392-9. Chaucer 631-40. Pope omits Chaucer 622-30, a transitional
passage.

Sleep fled his Eyes, and Peace forsook his Breast;
The raging Flames that in his Bosome dwell,
He wanted Art to hide, and Means to tell.   395
Yet hoping Time th'Occasion might betray,
Compos'd a Sonnet to the lovely *May*;
Which writ and folded, with the nicest Art,
He wrapt in Silk, and laid upon his Heart.

    When now the fourth revolving Day was run,   400
('Twas *June*, and *Cancer* had receiv'd the Sun)
Forth from her Chamber came the beauteous Bride,
The good old Knight mov'd slowly by her Side.
High Mass was sung; they feasted in the Hall;
The Servants round stood ready at their Call.   405
The Squire alone was absent from the Board,
And much his Sickness griev'd his worthy Lord,
Who pray'd his Spouse, attended by her Train,
To visit *Damian*, and divert his Pain.
Th'obliging Dames obey'd with one Consent;   410
They left the Hall, and to his Lodging went;
The Female Tribe surround him as he lay,
And close beside him sate the gentle *May*:
Where, as she try'd his Pulse, he softly drew
A speaking Sigh, and cast a mournful View;   415
Then gave his Bill, and brib'd the Powr's Divine
With secret Vows, to favour his Design.

    Who studies now but discontented *May*?
On her soft Couch uneasily she lay:
The lumpish Husband snor'd away the Night,   420
'Till Coughs awak'd him near the Morning Light.
What then he did, I'll not presume to tell,
Nor if she thought her self in Heav'n or Hell.
Honest and dull, in Nuptial Bed they lay,
'Till the Bell toll'd, and All arose to Pray.   425
    Were it by forceful Destiny decreed,

395. Pope.
397. *Sonnet*] Chaucer 637: 'a complaint or a lay'.
400–17. Chaucer 641–710. Pope cuts out the direct speech.
400 f. Chaucer 641–3.
403. Pope, stating what Chaucer implies.
414. as . . . *Pulse*] Chaucer 691: Comforting him as goodly as she may.
416. *Bill*] So Chaucer 693.
416 f. *and brib'd . . . Design*] Pope. After this line Pope omits Chaucer 697–710.
418–25. Chaucer 711–22.
425. Chaucer 722: 'Till evensong ring'.
426–39. Chaucer 723–50. Pope preserves some of Chaucer's irony.

Or did from Chance, or Nature's Pow'r proceed,
Or that some Star, with Aspect kind to Love,
Shed its selectest Influence from above;
Whatever was the Cause, the tender Dame   430
Felt the first Motions of an infant Flame;
Receiv'd th'Impressions of the Love-sick Squire,
And wasted in the soft, infectious Fire.

　　Ye Fair draw near, let *May*'s Example move
Your gentle Minds to pity those who love!   435
Had some fierce Tyrant in her stead been found,
The poor Adorer sure had hang'd, or drown'd:
But she, your Sexe's Mirrour, free from Pride,
Was much too meek to prove a Homicide.

　　But to my Tale: Some Sages have defin'd   440
Pleasure the Sov'reign Bliss of Humankind:
Our Knight (who study'd much, we may suppose)
Deriv'd his high Philosophy from Those;
For, like a Prince, he bore the vast Expence
Of lavish Pomp, and proud Magnificence: 445
His House was stately, his Retinue gay,
Large was his Train, and gorgeous his Array.
His spacious Garden, made to yield to none,
Was compass'd round with Walls of solid Stone;
Priapus cou'd not half describe the Grace   450
(Tho' God of Gardens) of this charming Place:
A Place to tire the rambling Wits of *France*
In long Descriptions, and exceed *Romance*;
Enough to shame the gentlest Bard that sings
Of painted Meadows, and of purling Springs.   455
　　Full in the Center of the flow'ry Ground,
A Crystal Fountain spread its Streams around, 　}
The fruitful Banks with verdant Lawrels crown'd: 　}
About this Spring (if ancient Fame say true)
The dapper Elves their Moonlight Sports pursue;   460
Their Pigmy King, and little Fairy Queen,
In circling Dances gambol'd on the Green,
While tuneful Sprights a merry Consort made,

432. *Impressions*] Chaucer's word [734].
435. Chaucer 742: Lo pittie renneth sone in gentle hert.
439. After this line Pope omits Chaucer 751–6.
440–64. Chaucer 777–97.
450–3. Pope generalizes Chaucer's reference to the author of the
Romant of the Rose [788] and by so doing hits at the seventeenth-century
French romances.
463 f. Chaucer 796: Disporten hem and maken melodie.

And Airy Musick warbled thro' the Shade.
Hither the Noble Knight wou'd oft repair   465
(His Scene of Pleasure, and peculiar Care)
For this, he held it dear, and always bore
The Silver Key that lock'd the Garden Door.
To this Sweet Place, in Summer's sultry Heat,
He us'd from Noise and Business to retreat;   470
And here in Dalliance spend the livelong Day,
Solus cum Sola, with his sprightly *May*.
For whate'er Work was undischarg'd a-bed,
The duteous Knight in this fair Garden sped.
But ah! what Mortal lives of Bliss secure,   475
How short a Space our Worldly Joys endure?
O Fortune fair, like all thy treach'rous Kind,
But faithless still, and wav'ring as the Wind!
O painted Monster form'd Mankind to cheat
With pleasing Poison, and with soft Deceit!   480
This rich, this am'rous, venerable Knight,
Amidst his Ease, his Solace and Delight,
Struck blind by thee, resigns his Days to Grief,
And calls on Death, the Wretch's last Relief.
The Rage of Jealousie then seiz'd his Mind,   485
For much he fear'd the Faith of Womankind.
His Wife, not suffer'd from his Side to Stray, ⎫
Was Captive kept; he watch'd her Night and Day, ⎬
Abridg'd her Pleasures, and confin'd her Sway. ⎭
Full oft in Tears did hapless *May* complain,   490
And sigh'd full oft, but sigh'd and wept in vain;
She look'd on *Damian* with a Lover's Eye,
For oh, 'twas fix'd, she must possess or die!
Nor less Impatience vex'd her Am'rous Squire,
Wild with Delay, and burning with Desire.   495
Watch'd as she was, yet cou'd He not refrain
By secret Writing to disclose his Pain,
The Dame by Signs reveal'd her kind Intent,
'Till both were conscious what each other meant.
Ah gentle Knight, what wou'd thy Eyes avail,   500

465–74. Chaucer 798–812.
472. Chaucer 806: And Maie his wife, & no wight but they two.
475–84. Chaucer 813–28.
475–80. Chaucer 813–20.
485–99. Chaucer 829–62.
493. Chaucer 850–2.
495. Pope.
500–3. Chaucer 863–6.

Tho' they cou'd see as far as Ships can sail?
'Tis better sure, when Blind, deceiv'd to be,
Than be deluded when a Man can see!
   Argus himself, so cautious and so wise,
Was overwatch'd, for all his hundred Eyes: 505
So many an honest Husband may, 'tis known,
Who, wisely, never thinks the Case his own.
   The Dame at last, by Diligence and Care,
Procur'd the Key her Knight was wont to bear;
She took the Wards in Wax before the Fire,   510
And gave th'Impression to the trusty Squire.
By means of this, some Wonder shall appear,
Which in due Place and Season, you may hear.
   Well sung sweet *Ovid*, in the Days of yore,
What Sleight is that, which Love will not explore?   515
And *Pyramus* and *Thisbe* plainly show
The Feats, true Lovers when they list, can do:
Tho' watch'd, and captive, yet in spight of all,
They found the Art of Kissing thro' a Wall.
   But now no longer from our Tale to stray;   520
It happ'd, that once upon a Summer's Day,
Our rev'rend Knight was urg'd to Am'rous Play:
He rais'd his Spouse ere Matin Bell was rung,
And thus his Morning Canticle he sung.
   Awake my Love, disclose thy radiant Eyes;   525
Arise my Wife, my beauteous Lady rise!
Hear how the Doves with pensive Notes complain,
And in soft Murmurs tell the Trees their Pain;
The Winter's past, the Clouds and Tempests fly,
The Sun adorns the Fields, and brightens all the Sky. 530
Fair without Spot, whose ev'ry charming Part
My Bosome wounds, and captivates my Heart,
Come, and in mutual Pleasures let's engage,
Joy of my Life, and Comfort of my Age!
   This heard, to *Damian* strait a Sign she made   535
To haste before; the gentle Squire obey'd:
Secret, and undescry'd, he took his Way,
And ambush'd close behind an Arbour lay.
   It was not long ere *January* came,
And Hand in Hand, with him, his lovely Dame;   540
Blind as he was, not doubting All was sure,

504-19. Chaucer 867-87.
535-74. Chaucer 905-40.

He turn'd the Key, and made the Gate secure.
  Here let us walk, he said, observ'd by none,
Conscious of Pleasures to the World unknown:
So may my Soul have Joy, as thou, my Wife,   545
Art far the dearest Solace of my Life;
And rather wou'd I chuse, by Heav'n above,
To die this Instant, than to lose thy Love.
Reflect what Truth was in my Passion shown, ⎫
When Un-endow'd, I took thee for my own,   ⎬   550
And sought no Treasure but thy Heart alone. ⎭
Old as I am, and now depriv'd of Sight,   ⎫
While thou art faithful to thy own true Knight, ⎬
Nor Age, nor Blindness, rob me of Delight. ⎭
Each other Loss with Patience I can bear,   555
The Loss of thee is what I only fear.
  Consider then, my Lady and my Wife,
The solid Comforts of a virtuous Life.
As first, the Love of Christ himself you gain;
Next, your own Honour undefil'd maintain;   560
And lastly that which sure your Mind must move,
My whole Estate shall gratifie your Love:
Make your own Terms; and ere to-morrow's Sun
Displays his Light, by Heav'n it shall be done.
I seal the Contract with a holy Kiss,   565
And will perform, by this—my Dear, and this.—
Have Comfort, Spouse, nor think thy Lord unkind;
'Tis Love, not Jealousie, that fires my Mind.
For when thy Charms my sober Thoughts engage,
And join'd to them, my own unequal Age;   570
From thy dear Side I have no Pow'r to part,
Such secret Transports warm my melting Heart.
For who that once possest those Heav'nly Charms,
Cou'd live one Moment, absent from thy Arms?
  He ceas'd, and *May* with modest Grace reply'd;   575
Weak was her Voice, as while she spoke she cry'd.
Heav'n knows, (with that a tender Sigh she drew)
I have a Soul to save as well as You;
And, what no less you to my Charge commend,
My dearest Honour, will to Death defend.   580

542. Chaucer 915: And clapt to the wicket suddainly.
548. *die*] Chaucer 919: 'dien on a knife'.
553–6. Pope.
568. In Chaucer January admits his jealousy [933].
575–608. Chaucer 941–74.

To you in holy Church I gave my Hand,
And join'd my Heart, in Wedlock's sacred Band:
Yet after this, if you distrust my Care,
Then hear, my Lord, and witness what I swear.
  First may the yawning Earth her Bosome rend,   585
And let me hence to Hell alive descend;
Or die the Death I dread no less than Hell,
Sow'd in a Sack, and plung'd into a Well;
Ere I my Fame by one lewd Act disgrace,
Or once renounce the Honour of my Race.   590
For know, Sir Knight, of gentle Blood I came,
I loath a Whore, and startle at the Name.
But jealous Men on their own Crimes reflect,
And learn from thence their Ladies to suspect:
Else why these needless Cautions, Sir, to me?   595
These Doubts and Fears of Female Constancy?
This Chime still rings in ev'ry Lady's Ear,
The only Strain a Wife must hope to hear.
  Thus while she spoke, a sidelong Glance she cast,
Where *Damian* kneeling, worshipp'd as she past.   600
She saw him watch the Motions of her Eye,
And singled out a Pear-Tree planted nigh:
'Twas charg'd with Fruit that made a goodly Show,
And hung with dangling Pears was ev'ry Bough.
Thither th'obsequious Squire address'd his Pace,   605
And climbing, in the Summit took his Place:
The Knight and Lady walk'd beneath in View,
Where let us leave them, and our Tale pursue.
  'Twas now the Season when the glorious Sun
His Heav'nly Progress thro' the *Twins* had run;   610
And *Jove*, Exalted, his mild Influence yields,
To glad the Glebe, and paint the flow'ry Fields.
Clear was the Day, and *Phœbus* rising bright,
Had streak'd the Azure Firmament with Light;
He pierc'd the glitt'ring Clouds with golden Streams,   615
And warm'd the Womb of Earth with Genial Beams.
  It so befel, in that fair Morning-tide,
The Fairies sported on the Garden's Side,
And, in the midst, their Monarch and his Bride.   619

585 f. Pope.
592. Chaucer 958: I am a gentlewoman, and no wench.
597 f. Chaucer 960: And women haue reproofe of you, aye new.
599–601. Chaucer 963–5.
609–16. Chaucer 975–80.
617–25. Chaucer 981–92.

So featly tripp'd the light-foot Ladies round,
The Knights so nimbly o'er the Greensword bound,
That scarce they bent the Flow'rs, or touch'd the Ground.
The Dances ended, all the Fairy Train
For Pinks and Daisies search'd the flow'ry Plain;
While on a Bank reclin'd of rising Green, 625
Thus, with a Frown, the King bespoke his Queen.
   'Tis too apparent, argue what you can,
The Treachery you Women use to Man:
A thousand Authors have this Truth made out,
And sad Experience leaves no room for Doubt. 630
   Heav'n rest thy Spirit, noble *Solomon*,
A wiser Monarch never saw the Sun:
All Wealth, all Honours, the supreme Degree
Of Earthly Bliss, was well bestow'd on thee!
For sagely hast thou said; Of all Mankind, 635
One only just, and righteous, hope to find:
But shoud'st thou search the spacious World around,
Yet one good Woman is not to be found.
   Thus says the King who knew your Wickedness;
The Son of *Sirach* testifies no less. 640
So may some Wildfire on your Bodies fall,
Or some devouring Plague consume you all,
As well you view the Leacher in the Tree,
And well this Honourable Knight you see;
But since he's blind and old, (a helpless Case) 645
His Squire shall cuckold him before your Face.
   Now, by my own dread Majesty I swear,
And by this awful Scepter which I bear,
No impious Wretch shall 'scape unpunish'd long,
That in my Presence offers such a Wrong. 650
I will this Instant undeceive the Knight,
And, in the very Act, restore his Sight:
And set the Strumpet here in open View,
A Warning to these Ladies, and to You,
And all the faithless Sex, for ever to be true. 655
   And will you so, reply'd the Queen, indeed?
Now, by my Mother's Soul, it is decreed,
She shall not want an Answer at her Need.

620–2. Pope.
627–55. Chaucer 993–1019.
631–4. Chaucer 998–1000.
641. *some Wildfire*] Chaucer 1008: 'A wild fire'. 'In imprecations [=]
A name for erysipelas and various inflammatory eruptive diseases' (*OED*).
648 f. Pope.   656–99. Chaucer 1020–66.   656. Chaucer 1020.

For her, and for her Daughters I'll ingage,
And all the Sex in each succeeding Age,   660
Art shall be theirs to varnish an Offence,
And fortify their Crimes with Confidence.
Nay, were they taken in a strict Embrace,
Seen with both Eyes, and pinion'd on the Place,
All they shall need is to protest, and swear,   665
Breathe a soft Sigh, and drop a tender Tear;
'Till their wise Husbands, gull'd by Arts like these,
Grow gentle, tractable, and tame as Geese.
    What tho' this sland'rous *Jew*, this *Solomon*,
Call'd Women Fools, and knew full many a one?   670
The wiser Wits of later Times declare
How constant, chast, and virtuous, Women are.
Witness the Martyrs, who resign'd their Breath,
Serene in Torments, unconcern'd in Death;
And witness next what *Roman* Authors tell,   675
How *Arria*, *Portia*, and *Lucretia* fell.
    But since the Sacred Leaves to All are free,
And Men interpret *Texts*, why shou'd not We?
By this no more was meant, than to have shown, ⎫
That Sovereign Goodness dwells in *Him* alone   ⎬   680
Who only *Is*, and is but only *One*.   ⎭
But grant the worst; shall Women then be weigh'd
By ev'ry Word that *Solomon* has said?
What tho' this King (as ancient Story boasts)
Built a fair Temple to the Lord of Hosts;   685
He ceas'd at last his Maker to adore,
And did as much for Idol-Gods, or more.
Beware what lavish Praises you confer
On a rank Leacher, and Idolater,
Whose Reign Indulgent God, says Holy Writ,   690
Did but for *David*'s Righteous Sake permit;
David, the Monarch after Heav'ns' own Mind,
Who lov'd our Sex, and honour'd all our Kind.
    Well, I'm a Woman, and as such must speak;
Silence wou'd swell me, and my Heart wou'd break.   695
Know then, I scorn your dull Authorities,
Your idle Wits, and all their Learned Lies.

661-8. Chaucer 1024-31.
669 f. Chaucer 1033 f.
674. Pope.
676. Pope gives instances of what Chaucer [1040] leaves as 'Romain jests' [i.e. *gesta*].
677 f. Pope.

By Heav'n, those Authors are our Sexe's Foes,
Whom, in our Right, I must, and will oppose.
   Nay, (quoth the King) dear Madam be not wroth;   700
I yield it up; but since I gave my Oath,
That this much-injur'd Knight again shou'd see;
It must be done—I am a King, said he,
And one, whose Faith has ever sacred been.
   And so has mine, (she said)—I am a Queen!   705
Her Answer she shall have, I undertake;
And thus an End of all Dispute I make:
Try when you list; and you shall find, my Lord,
It is not in our Sex to break our Word.
   We leave them here in this Heroick Strain,   710
And to the Knight our Story turns again,
Who in the Garden, with his lovely *May*
Sung merrier than the Cuckow or the Jay:
This was his Song; Oh kind and constant be,
Constant and kind I'll ever prove to thee.   715
   Thus singing as he went, at last he drew
By easie Steps, to where the Pear-Tree grew:
The longing Dame look'd up, and spy'd her Love
Full fairly perch'd among the Boughs above.
She stopp'd, and sighing, Oh good Gods, she cry'd,   720
What Pangs, what sudden Shoots distend my Side?
O for that tempting Fruit, so fresh, so green;
Help, for the Love of Heav'ns' immortal Queen!
Help dearest Lord, and save at once the Life
Of thy poor Infant, and thy longing Wife!   725
   Sore sigh'd the Knight, to hear his Lady's Cry,
But cou'd not climb, and had no Servant nigh,
Old as he was, and void of Eye-sight too,
What cou'd, alas, the helpless Husband do?
And must I languish then (she said) and die,   730
Yet view the lovely Fruit before my Eye?

698. *By Heav'n*] Chaucer 1064: As euer mote I hole broke my tresses.
700–9. Chaucer 1067–75.
703–5. Chaucer 1070–2.
706. Chaucer 1073: Her answere she shall haue I vndertake.
707. Chaucer 1075: Forsooth I will no longer you contrary.
710–39. Chaucer 1076–1105.
713. *Cuckow or the Jay*] Chaucer 1078: 'the Popingay'.
714 f. Chaucer 1079: You loue I best, and shall, and other non.
718. Pope.
724 f. Chaucer 1091–3.
730 f. Pope.

At least, kind Sir, for Charity's sweet sake,
Vouchsafe the Trunk between your Arms to take;
Then from your Back I might ascend the Tree;
Do you but stoop, and leave the rest to me.   735
   With all my Soul, he thus reply'd again;
I'd spend my dearest Blood to ease thy Pain.
With that, his Back against the Trunk he bent;
She seiz'd a Twig, and up the Tree she went.

   Now prove your Patience, gentle Ladies all,   740
Nor let on me your heavy Anger fall:
'Tis Truth I tell, tho' not in Phrase refin'd;
Tho' blunt my Tale, yet honest is my Mind.
What Feats the Lady in the Tree might do,
I pass, as Gambols never known to you: 745
But sure it was a merrier Fit, she swore,
Than in her Life she ever felt before.

   In that nice Moment, lo! the wondring Knight
Look'd out, and stood restor'd to sudden Sight.
Strait on the Tree his eager Eyes he bent,   750
As one whose Thoughts were on his Spouse intent;
But when he saw his Bosome-Wife so drest,
His Rage was such, as cannot be exprest:
Not frantick Mothers when their Infants die,
With louder Clamours rend the vaulted Skie: 755
He cry'd, he roar'd, he storm'd, he tore his Hair;
Death! Hell! and Furies! what dost Thou do there?

   What ails my Lord? the trembling Dame reply'd;
I thought your Patience had been better try'd:
Is this your Love, ungrateful and unkind,   760
This my Reward, for having cur'd the Blind?
Why was I taught to make my Husband see,
By Strugling with a Man upon a Tree?
Did I for this the Pow'r of Magick prove?
Unhappy Wife, whose Crime was too much Love!   765
   If this be Strugling, by this holy Light,

732-5. Chaucer 1097-1101.
738 f. Chaucer 1104 f.
740-7. Chaucer 1106 ff.
748-57. Chaucer 1110-23.
748 f. After this line Pope omits Chaucer 1113 f.
753. In Chaucer it is the sight that 'may not be expressed' [1118].
754 f. Chaucer 1120 f.
756 f. Chaucer 1122-4.
758-816. Chaucer 1124-71.
764 f. Pope.
766 f. Chaucer 1132: Strogle (qd. he) ye algate in it went.

'Tis Strugling with a Vengeance, (quoth the Knight:)
So Heav'n preserve the Sight it has restor'd,
As with these Eyes I plainly saw thee whor'd;
Whor'd by my Slave—Perfidious Wretch! may Hell   770
As surely seize thee, as I saw too well.

  Guard me, good Angels! cry'd the gentle *May*,
Pray Heav'n, this Magick work the proper Way:
Alas, my Love, 'tis certain, cou'd you see,
You ne'er had us'd these killing Words to me.   775
So help me Fates, as 'tis no perfect Sight,
But some faint Glimm'ring of a doubtful Light.

  What I have said, quoth he, I must maintain;
For, by th'Immortal Pow'rs, it *seem'd* too plain—
  By all those Pow'rs, some Frenzy seiz'd your Mind, ⎫ 780
(Reply'd the Dame:) Are these the Thanks I find? ⎬
Wretch that I am, that e'er I was so Kind! ⎭
She said; a rising Sigh express'd her Woe,
The ready Tears apace began to flow,
And as they fell, she wip'd from either Eye   785
The Drops, (for Women when they list, can cry.)

  The Knight was touch'd, and in his Looks appear'd
Signs of Remorse, while thus his Spouse he chear'd:
Madam, 'tis past, and my short Anger o'er;
Come down, and vex your tender Heart no more: 790
Excuse me, Dear, if ought amiss was said,
For, on my Soul, amends shall soon be made:
Let my Repentance your Forgiveness draw,
By Heav'n, I swore but what I *thought* I saw.

  Ah my lov'd Lord! 'twas much unkind (she cry'd)   795
On bare *Suspicion* thus to treat your Bride;
But 'till your Sight's establish'd, for a while,
Imperfect Objects may your Sense beguile:
Thus when from Sleep we first our Eyes display, ⎫
The Balls are wounded with the piercing Ray, ⎬ 800
And dusky Vapors rise, and intercept the Day: ⎭
So just recov'ring from the Shades of Night, ⎫
Your swimming Eyes are drunk with sudden Light, ⎬
Strange Phantoms dance around, and skim before ⎭
    your Sight.

768. Pope.
777. Chaucer 1139: Ye haue some glimsing, and no perfit sight.
780. Chaucer 1143: Ye mase ye mase, good sir (quoth she).
783–6. Pope.
797–806. Chaucer 1153–66.

Then Sir be cautious, nor too rashly deem;   805
Heav'n knows, how seldom things are what they seem!
Consult your Reason, and you soon shall find,
'Twas You were jealous, not your Wife unkind:
Jove ne'er spoke Oracle more true than this,
None judge so wrong as those who think amiss.   810
   With that, she leap'd into her Lord's Embrace,
With well-dissembl'd Virtue in her Face:
He hugg'd her close, and kiss'd her o'er and o'er,
Disturb'd with Doubts and Jealousies no more:
Both, pleas'd and blest, renew'd their mutual Vows,   815
A fruitful Wife, and a believing Spouse.
   Thus ends our Tale, whose Moral next to make,
Let all wise Husbands hence Example take;
And pray, to crown the Pleasure of their Lives,
To be so well deluded by their Wives.   820

807–10. Pope.
813. Chaucer 1170 f.
814–16. Pope.
817–20. Pope.

The Wife of Bath her Prologue, from Chaucer

[written c. 1704; published, Steele's
Miscellanies, 1713]

Behold the Woes of Matrimonial Life,
And hear with Rev'rence an experienc'd Wife!
To dear-bought Wisdom give the Credit due,
And think, for once, a Woman tells you true.
In all these Trials I have born a Part;   5
I was my self the Scourge that caus'd the Smart;
For, since Fifteen, in Triumph have I led
Five Captive Husbands from the Church to Bed.
   Christ saw a Wedding once, the Scripture says,
And saw but one, 'tis thought, in all his Days;   10
Whence some infer, whose Conscience is too nice,
No pious Christian ought to marry twice.
   But let them read, and solve me, if they can,
The Words addrest to the *Samaritan*:

1–8. Pope combines Chaucer 1–8 with Chaucer 172–5.
9–16. Chaucer 9–25.

Five times in lawful Wedlock she was join'd;   15
And sure the certain Stint was ne'er defin'd.
    Encrease and multiply was Heav'ns' Command,
And that's a Text I clearly understand.
This too, *Let Men their Sires and Mothers leave,*
And to their dearer Wives for ever cleave.   20
More Wives than One by *Solomon* were try'd,
Or else the Wisest of Mankind's bely'd.
I've had, my self, full many a merry Fit,
And trust in Heav'n I may have many yet.
For when my transitory Spouse; unkind,   25
Shall die, and leave his woful Wife behind,
I'll take the next good Christian I can find.
    Paul, knowing One cou'd never serve our Turn,
Declar'd 'twas better far to Wed, than Burn.
There's Danger in assembling Fire and Tow,   30
I grant 'em that, and what it means you know.
The same Apostle too has elsewhere own'd
No Precept for Virginity he found:
'Tis but a Counsel—and we Women still
Take which we like, the Counsel, or our Will.   35
    I envy not their Bliss, if He or She
Think fit to live in perfect Chastity,
Pure let them be, and free from Taint of Vice;
I, for a few slight Spots, am not so nice.
Heav'n calls us different Ways, on these bestows   40
One proper Gift, another grants to those:
Not ev'ry Man's oblig'd to sell his Store,
And give up all his Substance to the Poor;
Such as are perfect, may, I can't deny;
But by your Leave, Divines, so am not I.   45
    Full many a Saint, since first the World began,
Liv'd an unspotted Maid in spite of Man:
Let such (a God's Name) with fine Wheat be fed,
And let us honest Wives eat Barley Bread.
For me, I'll keep the Post assign'd by Heav'n,   50

17–20. Pope omits the Wife's hit at glosers of texts [26 f.].
22. *bely'd*] = 'misrepresented,' perhaps suggesting that he was wisest
because most polygamous.
23. *merry Fit*] Chaucer 42.
28. Pope, on a hint from Chaucer 66.
30 f. Chaucer 89 f.
32–5. Chaucer 59–76.
36–45. Chaucer 77–112. Pope omits Chaucer 113 f.
46–55. Chaucer 139–62. Pope omits the mention of Christ.

And use the copious Talent it has giv'n;
Let my good Spouse pay Tribute, do me Right,
And keep an equal Reck'ning ev'ry Night;
His proper Body is not his, but mine;
For so said *Paul*, and *Paul*'s a sound Divine.   55
   Know then, of those five Husbands I have had,
Three were just tolerable, two were bad.
The three were Old, but rich and fond beside,
And toil'd most piteously to please their Bride:
But since their Wealth (the best they had) was mine,   60
The rest, without much Loss, I cou'd resign.
Sure to be lov'd, I took no Pains to please,
Yet had more Pleasure far then they had Ease.
   Presents flow'd in apace: With Show'rs of Gold,
They made their Court, like *Jupiter* of old.   65
If I but smil'd, a sudden Youth they found,
And a new Palsie seiz'd them when I frown'd.
   Ye Sov'reign Wives! give Ear, and understand;
Thus shall ye speak, and exercise Command.
For never was it giv'n to Mortal Man,   70
To lye so boldly as we Women can.
Forswear the Fact, tho' seen with both his Eyes,
And call *your Maids* to Witness how he lies.
   Hark old Sir *Paul* ('twas thus I us'd to say)
Whence is our Neighbour's Wife so rich and gay?   75
Treated, caress'd, where-e'er she's pleas'd to roam—
I sit in Tatters, and immur'd at home!
Why to her House do'st thou so oft repair?
Art thou so Am'rous? and is she so fair?
If I but see a Cousin or a Friend,   80
Lord! how you swell, and rage like any Fiend!
But you reel home, a drunken beastly Bear,
Then preach till Midnight in your easie Chair;
Cry Wives are false, and ev'ry Woman evil,

55. *and . . . Divine.*] Pope.
56–63. Pope tones down Chaucer 193–216.
57. Cf. Chaucer 196: Three of hem were good, and two were bad.
59. *piteously*] Chaucer 202.
63. After this line Chaucer refers to the Dunmow flitch.
64–7. Cf. Chaucer 219–23.
68–73. Chaucer 224–34.
74–85. Chaucer 235–47.
77. Cf. Chaucer 238: I sit at home, and haue no thriftie cloth.
79. Cf. Chaucer 240: Is she so faire? art thou so amorous?
After this line Pope omits Chaucer 241 f.
82. Chaucer 246: 'as drunken as Mouse'.

And give up all that's Female to the Devil. 85
   If poor (you say) she drains her Husband's Purse;
If rich, she keeps her Priest, or something worse;
If highly born, intolerably vain;
Vapours and Pride by turns possess her Brain:
Now gayly Mad, now sow'rly Splenatick, 90
Freakish when well, and fretful when she's Sick.
If fair, then Chast she cannot long abide,
By pressing Youth attack'd on ev'ry side.
If foul, her Wealth the lusty Lover lures,
Or else her Wit some Fool-Gallant procures, 95
Or else she Dances with becoming Grace,
Or Shape excuses the Defects of Face.
There swims no Goose so gray, but, soon or late,
She finds some honest Gander for her Mate.
   Horses (thou say'st) and Asses, Men may try, 100
And ring suspected Vessels ere they buy,
But Wives, a random Choice, untry'd they take;
They dream in Courtship, but in Wedlock wake.
Then, nor 'till then, the Veil's remov'd away,
And all the Woman glares in open Day. 105
   You tell me, to preserve your Wife's good Grace,
Your Eyes must always languish on my Face,
Your Tongue with constant Flatt'ries feed my Ear,
And tag each Sentence with, *My Life! my Dear!*
If, by strange Chance, a modest Blush be rais'd, 110
Be sure my fine Complexion must be prais'd:
My Garments always must be new and gay,
And Feasts still kept upon my Wedding-Day:
Then must my Nurse be pleas'd, and Fav'rite Maid;
And endless Treats, and endless Visits paid, 115
To a long Train of Kindred, Friends, Allies;

All this thou say'st, and all thou say'st are Lies.
   On *Jenkin* too you cast a squinting Eye;
What? can your Prentice raise your Jealousie?
Fresh are his ruddy Cheeks, his Forehead fair, 120
And like the burnish'd Gold his curling Hair.

86–99. Chaucer 248–70.
99. After this line Pope omits Chaucer 271–84 as 'redundant'.
100–2. Chaucer 285–91.
103–5. Chaucer 292.
106–17. Chaucer 293–302.
110–12. Pope.   115. Pope.
117. Chaucer 302: Thus saiest thou old barell full of lies.
118–23. Chaucer 303–7.

But clear thy wrinkled Brow, and quit thy Sorrow,
I'd scorn your Prentice, shou'd you die to-morrow.
  Why are thy Chests all lockt? On what Design?
Are not thy Worldly Goods and Treasure mine?   125
Sir, I'm no Fool: Nor shall you, by St. *John*,
Have Goods and Body to your self alone.
One you shall quit—in spight of both your Eyes—
I heed not, I, the Bolts, the Locks, the Spies.
If you had Wit, you'd say, 'Go where you will,   130
Dear Spouse, I credit not the Tales they tell.
Take all the Freedoms of a married Life;
I know thee for a virtuous, faithful Wife.'
  Lord! When you have enough, what need you care
How merrily soever others fare?   135
Tho' all the Day I give and take Delight,
Doubt not, sufficient will be left at Night.
'Tis but a just and rational Desire,
To light a Taper at a Neighbour's Fire.
  There's Danger too, you think, in rich Array,   140
And none can long be modest that are gay.
The Cat, if you but singe her Tabby Skin,
The Chimney keeps, and sits content within;
But once grown sleek, will from her Corner run,
Sport with her Tail, and wanton in the Sun;   145
She licks her fair round Face, and frisks abroad
To show her Furr, and to be *Catterwaw'd*.
  Lo thus, my Friends, I wrought to my Desires
These three right Ancient Venerable Sires.
I told 'em, *Thus you say*, and *thus you do*—   150
And told 'em false, but *Jenkin* swore 'twas true.
I, like a Dog, cou'd bite as well as whine;
And first complain'd, whene'er the Guilt was mine.
I tax'd them oft with Wenching and Amours,

124–33. Chaucer 308–20.
126. *by St. John*] Chaucer 312.   132. Pope.
133. After this line Pope omits Chaucer 321 f. as 'redundant'.
134–9. Chaucer 323–34.
138 f. Chaucer 333 f.
140–7. Chaucer 337–54.
140 f. Chaucer 337–47.
142–7. Chaucer 348–54.
Pope omits 355 f., and 357–78.
148–51. Chaucer 379–83.
151. After this line Pope omits an exclamatory couplet [384 f.].
152 f. Chaucer 386–92.
154–65. Chaucer 393–408.   154 f. Chaucer 393 f.

When their weak Legs scarce dragg'd 'em out of Doors;
And swore the Rambles that I took by Night,   156
Were all to spy what Damsels they bedight.
That Colour brought me many Hours of Mirth;
For all this Wit is giv'n us from our Birth:
Heav'n gave to woman the peculiar Grace   160
To spin, to weep, and cully Human Race.
By this nice Conduct and this prudent Course,
By Murmuring, Wheedling, Stratagem and Force,
I still prevail'd, and wou'd be in the right,
Or Curtain-Lectures made a restless Night.   165
If once my Husband's Arm was o'er my Side,
What? so familiar with your Spouse? I cry'd:
I levied first a Tax upon his Need,
Then let him—'twas a *Nicety* indeed!
Let all Mankind this certain Maxim hold,   170
Marry who will, our *Sex* is to be Sold!
With empty Hands no Tassels you can lure,
But fulsom Love for Gain we can endure:
For Gold we love the Impotent and Old,
And heave, and pant, and kiss, and cling, for Gold.   175
Yet with Embraces, Curses oft I mixt,
Then kist again, and chid and rail'd betwixt.
Well, I may make my Will in Peace, and die,
For not one Word in Man's Arrears am I.
To drop a dear Dispute I was unable,   180
Ev'n tho' the Pope himself had sate at Table.
But when my Point was gain'd, then thus I spoke,
'*Billy*, my dear! how sheepishly you look!
Approach my Spouse, and let me kiss thy Cheek!
Thou should'st be always thus, resign'd and meek!   185
Of *Job*'s great Patience since so oft you preach,
Well shou'd you practise, who so well can teach.
'Tis difficult to do, I must allow,
But I, my dearest, will instruct you how.
Great is the Blessing of a prudent Wife,   190

161. *cully*] = to make a fool of.
165. Pope.
166–82. Chaucer 409–31.
168 f. Chaucer 411 f.
172 *Tassels*] = tercels, peregrine falcons.
174 f. Chaucer 417 f.
183–204. Chaucer 431–50.
183. Chaucer 432: How meekly looketh wilken our sheep.
190 f. Pope.

Who puts a Period to Domestick Strife!
One of us two must rule, and one obey,
And since in Man right Reason bears the Sway,
Let that frail Thing, weak Woman, have her way.
The Wives of all my Family have rul'd   195
Their tender Husbands, and their Passions cool'd.
Fye, 'tis unmanly thus to sigh and groan;
What? wou'd you have me to your self alone?
Why take me Love! take all and ev'ry part!
Here's your Revenge! you love it at your Heart.   200
Wou'd I vouchsafe to sell what Nature gave,
You little think what Custom I cou'd have!
But see! I'm all your own—nay hold—for Shame!
What means my Dear—indeed—you are to blame.'
    Thus with my first three Lords I past my Life;   205
A very Woman, and a very Wife!
What Sums from these old Spouses I cou'd raise,
Procur'd young Husbands in my riper Days.
Tho' past my Bloom, not yet decay'd was I,
Wanton and wild, and chatter'd like a Pye.   210
In Country Dances still I bore the Bell,
And sung as sweet as Evening *Philomel*.
To clear my Quail-pipe, and refresh my Soul,
Full oft I drain'd the Spicy Nut-brown Bowl;
Rich luscious Wines, that youthful Blood improve,   215
And warm the swelling Veins to Feats of Love:
For 'tis as sure as Cold ingenders Hail,
A Liqu'rish Mouth must have a Lech'rous Tail;
Wine lets no Lover unrewarded go,
As all true Gamesters by Experience know.   220
    But oh good Gods! whene'er a Thought I cast
On all the Joys of Youth and Beauty past,
To find in Pleasures I have had my Part,

192–4. Chaucer 440–2.
195 f. Pope.
201–4. Chaucer 447–50.
205–20. Chaucer 451–68.
205 f. Pope.
207–30. Chaucer 453–82.
207 f. Pope, authorized by Chaucer's general meaning.
213. *Quail-pipe*] = 'a pipe or whistle on which the note of a quail can
be imitated, in order to lure the birds into a net' (*OED*).
215 f. Pope.
218. Chaucer 466: A licorus mouth must haue a lecherous taile.
219 f.: Chaucer 467 f.
221–8. A poor equivalent for Chaucer 469–79.

Still warms me to the Bottom of my Heart.
This wicked World was once my dear Delight;   225
Now all my Conquests, all my Charms good night!
The Flour consum'd, the best that now I can
Is e'en to make my Market of the Bran.
   My fourth dear Spouse was not exceeding true;
He kept, 'twas thought, a private Miss or two;   230
But all that Score I paid—As how? you'll say,
Not with my Body, in a filthy way—
But I so drest, and danc'd, and drank, and din'd;
And view'd a Friend, with Eyes so very kind,
As stung his Heart, and made his Marrow fry   235
With burning Rage, and frantic Jealousie.
His Soul, I hope, enjoys eternal Glory,
For here on Earth I was his Purgatory.
Oft, when his Shoe the most severely wrung,
He put on careless Airs, and sat and sung.   240
How sore I gall'd him, only Heav'n cou'd know,
And he that felt, and I that caus'd the Woe.
He dy'd when last from Pilgrimage I came,
With other Gossips, from *Jerusalem*,
And now lies buried underneath a Rood,   245
Fair to be seen, and rear'd of honest Wood.
A Tomb, indeed, with fewer Sculptures grac'd,
Than that *Mausolus*' Pious Widow plac'd,
Or where inshrin'd the great *Darius* lay;
But Cost on Graves is meerly thrown away.   250
The Pit fill'd up, with Turf we cover'd o'er,
So bless the good Man's Soul, I say no more.
   Now for my fifth lov'd Lord, the last and best;
(Kind Heav'n afford him everlasting Rest)
Full hearty was his Love, and I can shew   255
The Tokens on my Ribs, in Black and Blue:

231–52. Chaucer 483–502.
235 f. Chaucer 487 f.
237 f. Chaucer 489 f.
241 f. Chaucer 493 f.
   248 f. Artemisia, the widow of the Carian prince Mausolus, was incon-
solable; to perpetuate his memory she built at Halicarnassus the celebrated monument, Mausoleum, which was regarded as one of the seven
wonders of the world. Darius I, of Persia, caused his sepulchre to be built
during his life.
   253–62. Chaucer 503–23.
   255. *hearty*] Pope misunderstood Chaucer's 'dangerous' [514] which
means 'holding off', 'stand-offish', and so gives a different slant to the
whole passage.

Yet, with a Knack, my Heart he cou'd have won,
While yet the Smart was shooting in the Bone.
How quaint an Appetite in Women reigns!
Free Gifts we scorn, and love what costs us Pains: 260
Let Men avoid us, and on them we leap;
A glutted Market makes Provision cheap.
   In pure good Will I took this jovial Spark,
Of *Oxford* he, a most egregious Clerk:
He boarded with a Widow in the Town,   265
A trusty Gossip, one dame *Alison*.
Full well the Secrets of my Soul she knew,
Better than e'er our Parish Priest cou'd do.
To her I told whatever cou'd befal;
Had but my Husband Pist against a Wall,   270
Or done a thing that might have cost his Life,
She—and my Neice—and one more worthy Wife
Had known it all: What most he wou'd conceal,
To these I made no Scruple to reveal.
Oft has he blush'd from Ear to Ear for Shame,   275
That e'er he told a Secret to his Dame.
   It so befell, in Holy Time of *Lent*,
That oft a Day I to this Gossip went;
(My Husband, thank my Stars, was out of Town)
From House to House we rambled up and down,   280
This Clerk, my self, and my good Neighbour *Alce*,
To see, be seen, to tell, and gather Tales;
Visits to ev'ry Church we daily paid,
And march'd in ev'ry holy Masquerade,
The Stations duly, and the Vigils kept;   285
Not much we fasted, but scarce ever slept.
At Sermons too I shone in Scarlet gay;   ⎫
The wasting Moth ne'er spoil'd my best Array;   ⎬
The Cause was this; I wore it ev'ry Day.   ⎭
   'Twas when fresh *May* her early Blossoms yields,   290
This Clerk and I were walking in the Fields.

263–76. A straightforward version of Chaucer 525–42.
277–89. Chaucer 543–62.
278. After this line Chaucer has a 'redundant' couplet [545 f.] naming
March, April, and May; Pope reinstates May at l. 290 below.
279. Chaucer 550: 'thank my Stars' is Pope's inadequate version of
Chaucer 553 f.
283 f. Pope translates Chaucer's 'visitations' [555] by 'visits' and so
points the contemporary satire.
285 *Stations*] Pope. Here used in the sense of a bi-weekly fast.
290–9. Chaucer 563–74.

We grew so intimate, I can't tell how,
I pawn'd my Honour and ingag'd my Vow,
If e'er I laid my Husband in his Urn,
That he, and only he, shou'd serve my Turn.   295
We strait struck Hands; the Bargain was agreed;
I still have shifts against a Time of Need:
The Mouse that always trusts to one poor Hole,
Can never be a Mouse of any Soul.

 I vow'd, I scarce cou'd sleep since first I knew him, 300
And durst be sworn he had Bewitch'd me to him:
If e'er I slept, I dream'd of him alone,
And Dreams foretel, as Learned Men have shown:
All this I said; but Dreams, Sirs, I had none.
I followed but my crafty Crony's Lore,   305
Who bid me tell this Lye—and twenty more.

 Thus Day by Day, and Month by Month we past;
It pleas'd the Lord to take my Spouse at last!
I tore my Gown, I soil'd my Locks with Dust,
And beat my Breasts, as wretched Widows—must.   310
Before my Face my Handkerchief I spread,
To hide the Flood of Tears I did *not* shed.
The good Man's Coffin to the Church was born;
Around, the Neighbours, and my Clerk too, mourn.
But as he march'd, good Gods! he show'd a Pair   315
Of Legs and Feet, so clean, so strong, so fair!
Of twenty Winters' Age he seem'd to be;
I (to say truth) was twenty more than he:
But vig'rous still, a lively buxom Dame,
And had a wond'rous Gift to quench a Flame.   320
A Conjurer once that deeply cou'd divine,
Assur'd me, *Mars* in *Taurus* was my Sign.
As the Stars order'd, such my Life has been:
Alas, alas, that ever Love was Sin!
Fair *Venus* gave me Fire and sprightly Grace,   325
And *Mars* Assurance, and a dauntless Face.
By Vertue of this pow'rful Constellation,
I follow'd always my own Inclination.

299. *Soul*] Intellectual or spiritual power.
300–6. Chaucer 575–84.
308–28. Chaucer 587–623.
309–12. Chaucer 588–92.
320. Chaucer 600–8.   321. Pope.
324. Chaucer 614 verbatim.
325 f. Chaucer 611 f. and 619.
327 f. Chaucer 615 f.

But to my Tale: A Month scarce past away,
With Dance and Song we kept the Nuptial Day.   330
All I possess'd I gave to his Command,
My Goods and Chattels, Mony, House, and Land:
But oft repented, and repent it still;
He prov'd a Rebel to my Sov'reign Will:
Nay once by Heav'n he struck me on the Face: 335
Hear but the Fact, and judge your selves the Case.
    Stubborn as any Lionness was I:
And knew full well to raise my Voice on high;
As true a Rambler as I was before,
And wou'd be so, in spight of all he swore.   340
He, against this, right sagely wou'd advise,
And old Examples set before my Eyes;
Tell how the *Roman* Matrons led their Life,
Of *Gracchus'* Mother, and *Duilius'* Wife;
And close the Sermon, as beseem'd his Wit,   345
With some grave Sentence out of Holy Writ.
Oft wou'd he say, Who builds his House on Sands,
Pricks his blind Horse across the Fallow Lands,
Or lets his Wife abroad with Pilgrims roam,
Deserves a Fool's-Cap and long Ears at home.   350
All this avail'd not; for whoe'er he be
That tells my Faults, I hate him mortally:
And so do Numbers more, I'll boldly say,
Men, Women, Clergy, Regular and Lay.
    My Spouse (who was, you know, to Learning bred)   355
A certain Treatise oft at Evening read,
Where divers Authors (whom the Dev'l confound
For all their Lies) were in one Volume bound.
Valerius, whole; and of St. *Jerome*, Part;
Chrysippus and *Tertullian; Ovid*'s Art;   360
Solomon's Proverbs, *Eloïsa*'s Loves;
And many more than sure the Church approves.
More Legends were there here, of wicked Wives,
Than good, in all the *Bible* and *Saints'-Lives.*
Who drew the *Lion Vanquish'd*? 'Twas a *Man.*   365
But cou'd we Women write as Scholars can,
Men shou'd stand mark'd with far more Wickedness,

329-36. Chaucer 627-36.
337-54. Chaucer 637-63.
347-50. Chaucer 655-8.
351. Chaucer 659 f.
355-76. Chaucer 669-712.
363 f. Chaucer 686-91.

Than all the Sons of *Adam* cou'd redress.
Love seldom haunts the Breast where Learning lies,
And *Venus* sets ere *Mercury* can rise: 370
Those play the Scholars who can't play the Men;
And use that Weapon which they have, their Pen;
When old, and past the Relish of Delight,
Then down they sit, and in their Dotage write,
That not one Woman keeps her Marriage Vow.   375
(This by the Way, but to my Purpose now.)
   It chanc'd my Husband on a Winter's Night
Read in this Book, aloud, with strange Delight,
How the first Female (as the Scriptures show)
Brought her own Spouse and all his Race to Woe;   380
How *Samson* fell; and he whom *Dejanire*
Wrapt in th' envenom'd Shirt, and set on Fire.
How curst *Eryphile* her Lord betray'd,
And the dire Ambush *Clytemnestra* laid.
But what most pleas'd him was the *Cretan* Dame,   385
And Husband-Bull—Oh monstrous! fie, for Shame!
   He had by Heart the whole Detail of Woe
Xantippe made her good Man undergo;
How oft she scolded in a Day, he knew,
How many Pisspots on the Sage she threw;   390
Who took it patiently, and wip'd his Head;
Rain follows Thunder, that was all he said.
   He read how *Arius* to his Friend complain'd
A fatal *Tree* was growing in his Land,
On which three Wives successively had twin'd   395
A sliding Noose, and waver'd in the Wind.
Where grows this Plant (reply'd the Friend) oh where?
For better Fruit did never Orchard bear:
Give me some Slip of this most blissful Tree,
And in my Garden planted shall it be!   400
   Then how two Wives their Lord's Destruction prove,
Thro' Hatred one, and one thro' too much Love;
That for her Husband mix'd a Poys'nous Draught;
And this for Lust an am'rous Philtre bought,
The nimble Juice soon seiz'd his giddy Head,   405
Frantic at Night, and in the Morning dead.
How some with Swords their sleeping Lords have slain,

369 f. Chaucer 697–705.
377–410. Chaucer 713–85.
385 f. Chaucer 733–6.
407–10. Chaucer 765–85.

And some have hammer'd Nails into their Brain,
And some have drench'd them with a deadly Potion;
All this he read, and read with great Devotion.   410
    Long time I heard, and swell'd, and blush'd, and
        frown'd,
But when no End of these vile Tales I found,
When still he read, and laugh'd, and read again,
And half the Night was thus consum'd in vain;
Provok'd to Vengeance, three large Leaves I tore,   415
And with one Buffet fell'd him on the Floor.
With that my Husband in a Fury rose,
And down he settled me with hearty Blows:
I groan'd, and lay extended on my Side;
Oh thou hast slain me for my Wealth (I cry'd)   420
Yet I forgive thee—Take my last Embrace.
He wept, kind Soul! and stoop'd to kiss my Face;
I took him such a Box as turn'd him blue,
Then sigh'd and cry'd, *Adieu my Dear, adieu!*
    But after many a hearty Struggle past,   425
I condescended to be pleas'd at last.
Soon as he said, My Mistress and my Wife,
Do what you list the Term of all your Life:
I took to Heart the Merits of the Cause,
And stood content to rule by wholsome Laws;   430
Receiv'd the Reins of Absolute Command, ⎫
With all the Government of House and Land; ⎬
And Empire o'er his Tongue, and o'er his Hand. ⎭
As for the Volume that revil'd the Dames,
'Twas torn to Fragments, and condemn'd to Flames. 435
    Now Heav'n on all my Husbands gone, bestow
Pleasures above, for Tortures felt below:
That Rest they wish'd for, grant them in the Grave,
And bless those Souls my Conduct help'd to save!

411–24. Chaucer 786–810.
411. Chaucer 486 f.
412–14. Chaucer 788 f.
423 f. Chaucer 808–10.
425–35. Chaucer 811–22.

Rondeau

[written 1710; published, *Mist's Weekly
Journal*, 1726]

You know where you did despise
(T'other day) my little eyes,
Little legs, and little thighs,
And some things of little size,
                  You know where.   5

You, 'tis true, have fine black eyes,
Taper legs, and tempting thighs,
Yet what more than all we prize
Is a thing of little size,
                  You know where.   10

A paraphrase of Voiture's 'Ou vous sçavez tromper bien finement'.

On the Statue of Cleopatra, made into
a Fountain by Leo the Tenth

TRANSLATED FROM THE LATIN OF
COUNT CASTIGLIONE

[written c. 1710; published, *PSO*, 1717]

CLEOPATRA SPEAKS

Whoe're thou art whom this fair statue charms,
These curling aspicks, and these wounded arms,
Who view'st these eyes for ever fixt in death,
Think not unwilling I resign'd my breath.
What, shou'd a *Queen*, so long the boast of fame,   5
Have stoop'd to serve an haughty *Roman* dame?
Shou'd I have liv'd, in *Cæsar*'s triumph born,
To grace his conquests and his pomp adorn?
I, whom the blest *Ægyptian* climate bore
To the soft joys of *Nile*'s delightful shore.   10
Whom prostrate Kings beheld unrival'd shine,
And the wide *East* ador'd with rites divine!
Deny'd to reign, I stood resolv'd to die,
Such charms has death when join'd with liberty.

Title] Baldassare Castiglione (1478–1529), Italian diplomat. His *Libro
del Cortegiano* (1528) translated by Sir Thomas Hoby (1561).

Let future times of *Cleopatra* tell,   15
Howe're she liv'd none ever dy'd so well.
No chains I felt, but went a glorious ghost,
Free, and a Princess, to the *Stygian* coast.
Th' eluded victor, envious of my fate,
Vex'd with vain rage, and impotently great,   20
To *Jove*'s high Capitol ignobly led
The mournful image of a Princess dead.
Yet not content with this to feast his eyes,
Lest kinder time shou'd hide our miseries,
Lest the last age our fortunes shou'd not know,   25
This breathing stone immortaliz'd my woe:
This with the noblest force of sculpture grac'd,
In *Rome*'s proud *Forum* young *Octavius* plac'd,
And in the midst of that majestic band
Of Gods and heroes, made a Woman stand;   30
But in the rock my flowing tears supprest,
Those tears, which only cou'd have have eas'd my breast.
Not that I'd ask a single drop to mourn
A fate so glorious, and so nobly born,
(Not death it self from me cou'd force a tear,   35
Or teach the soul of *Cleopatra* fear)
But for my *Antony*—to whom these eyes
Give all his rites, and all his obsequies!
To his dear ashes and his honour'd shade,
My tears eternal tribute shou'd be paid: 40
My tears the want of off'rings had supply'd;
But these, ev'n these, remorseless *Rome* deny'd!
　　But thou great *Leo !* in whose *golden* days
Revive the honours of *Rome*'s ancient praise;
If Heav'n, to pity human woes inclin'd,   ⎫   45
Has sent thee down in mercy to mankind,   ⎬
And boundless pow'r with boundless virtue join'd; ⎭
If all the Gods entrust thee to bestow
With bounteous hands their blessings here below;
Let not a suppliant Queen entreat in vain,   50
The only wretch beneath thy happy reign!
Sure just and modest this request appears,
Nor is it much to give me back my tears;
Release my eyes, and let them freely flow;
'Tis all the comfort fate has left me now!   55
The haughty *Niobe* whose impious pride
Scorn'd Heaven it self, and durst the Gods deride,
Still, tho' a rock, can thus relieve her woe,

And tears eternal from the marble flow.
No guilt of mine the rage of Heav'n cou'd move;   60
I knew no crime, if 'tis no crime to love.

Then as a lover give me leave to weep;
Lull'd by these fountains the distrest may sleep;
And while the Dogstar burns the thirsty field,
These to the birds refreshing streams may yield;   65
The birds shall sport amidst the bending sprays,
And fill the shade with never ceasing lays;
New greens shall spring, new flow'rs around me grow,
And on each tree the golden apples glow;
Here, where the fragrant Orange groves arise,   70
Whose shining scene with rich *Hesperia* vies.

Psalm XCI

[written c. 1710; published, *PSO*, 1717]

He who beneath thy shelt'ring wing resides,
Whom thy hand leads, and whom thy glory guides
To Heav'n familiar his bold vows shall send,
And fearless say to God—*Thou* art my friend!
'Tis Thou shalt save him from insidious wrongs,   5
And the sharp arrows of censorious tongues.
When gath'ring tempests swell the raging main,
When thunder roars, and lightning blasts the plain,
Amidst the wrack of nature undismay'd,
Safe shall he lye, and hope beneath thy shade.   10
By day no perils shall the just affright,
No dismal dreams or groaning ghosts by night.
His God shall guard him in the fighting field,
And o'er his breast extend his saving shield:
The whistling darts shall turn their points away,   15
And fires around him innocently play.
Thousands on ev'ry side shall yield their breath;
And twice ten thousand bite the ground in death;
While he, serene in thought, shall calm survey
The sinners fall, and bless the vengeful day!   20
  Heav'n is thy hope: thy refuge fix'd above;
No harms can reach thee, and no force shall move.
I see protecting Myriads round thee fly,
And all the bright *Militia* of the sky.
These in thy dangers timely aid shall bring,   25
Raise in their arms, and waft thee on their wing,

These shall perform th' almighty orders given,
Direct each step, and smooth the path to Heaven.
Thou on the fiery Basilisk shalt tread,
And fearless crush the swelling Aspick's head,   30
Rouze the huge Dragon, with a spurn, from rest,
And fix thy foot upon the Lion's crest.
Lo *I*, his *God!* in all his toils am near:
I see him ever, and will ever hear:
When he the rage of sinners shall sustain,   35
I share his griefs, and feel my self his pain:
When foes conspiring rise against his rest,
I'll stretch my arm, and snatch him to my breast.
Him will I heap with honours, and with praise,
And glutt with full satiety of days;   40
Him with my glories crown; and when he dies,
To him reveal my joys, and open all my skies.

Stanza's. From the french of Malherbe

[written c. 1710; published, *PSO*, 1717]

At length, my soul! thy fruitless hopes give o'er,
Believe, believe the treach'rous world no more.
Shallow, yet swift, the stream of fortune flows,
Which some rude wind will always discompose;
As children birds, so men their bliss pursue,   5
Still out of reach, tho' ever in their view.

In vain, for all that empty greatness brings,
We lose our lives amidst the courts of kings,
And suffer scorn, and bend the supple knee;
The monarch dies—one moment's turn destroys   10
Long future prospects, and short present joys:
Oh unperforming, false mortality!

All is but *dust*, when once their breath is fled;
The fierce, the pompous majesty lyes dead!
The world no longer trembles at their pow'r!   15
Ev'n in those tombs where their proud names survive,
Where still in breathing brass they seem to live,
Th' impartial worms that very *dust* devour.

Title: *Malherbe*] François de Malherbe (1555-1628); French poet.
This is a translation of his 'Paraphrase du Psaume CXLV' (1627).

The lofty styles of happy, glorious great,
The Lords of fortune, Arbiters of fate,   20
And Gods of war, lye lost within the grave!
Their mighty minions then come tumbling down,
They lose their flatt'rers as they lose their crown,
Forgot of ev'ry friend, and ev'ry slave!

From Boetius, de cons. Philos.

O qui perpetua mundum ratione gubernas.

[written c. 1710; published, *PSO*, 1717]

O thou, whose all-creating hands sustain
The radiant Heav'ns, and Earth, and ambient main!
Eternal Reason! whose presiding soul
Informs great nature and directs the whole!
Who wert, e're time his rapid race begun,   5
And bad'st the years in long procession run:
Who fix't thy self amidst the rowling frame,
Gav'st all things to be chang'd, yet ever art the same!
Oh teach the mind t' ætherial heights to rise,
And view familiar, in its native skies,   10
The source of good; thy splendor to descry,
And on thy self, undazled, fix her eye.
Oh quicken this dull mass of mortal clay;
Shine through the soul, and drive its clouds away!
For thou art Light. In thee the righteous find   15
Calm rest, and soft serenity of mind;
Thee they regard alone; to thee they tend;
At once our great original and end,
At once our means, our end, our guide, our way,
Our utmost bound, and our eternal stay!   20

Title] A translation of *De Consolatione Philosophiæ*, lib. 3, metrum, I,
the work of a sixth-century Roman philosopher.

Hymn of St. Francis Xavier

[written c. 1711; published 1791]

Thou art my God, sole object of my love;
Not for the hope of endless joys above;

Title: *St. Francis Xavier*] Jesuit missionary (1506–52), whose labours
in the East and sanctity of life procured him the title of 'Apostle of the
Indies'. A translation of his 'O Deus! ego amo te'.

Not for the fear of endless pains below,
Which they who love thee not must undergo.

For me, and such as me, thou deign'st to bear   5
An ignominious cross, the nails, the spear:
A thorny crown transpierc'd thy sacred brow,
While bloody sweats from ev'ry member flow.

For me in tortures thou resign'd'st thy breath,
Embrac'd me on the cross, and sav'd me by thy death.   10
And can these suff'rings fail my heart to move?
What but thyself can now deserve my love?

Such as then was, and is, thy love to me,
Such is, and shall be still, my love to thee—
To thee, Redeemer! mercy's sacred spring!   15
My God, my Father, Maker, and my King!

Adaptations of the Emperor Hadrian

[written 1712; published Lewis's
Miscellany, 1730]

I. ADRIANI MORIENTIS AD ANIMAM, OR, THE HEATHEN TO HIS DEPARTING SOUL

Ah fleeting Spirit! wand'ring Fire,
  That long hast warm'd my tender Breast,
Must thou no more this Frame inspire?
  No more a pleasing, chearful Guest?

Whither, ah whither art thou flying!   5
  To what dark, undiscover'd Shore?
Thou seem'st all trembling, shivr'ing, dying,
  And Wit and Humour are no more!

II. THE DYING CHRISTIAN TO HIS SOUL, ODE

Vital spark of heav'nly flame!
Quit, oh quit this mortal frame:
Trembling, hoping, ling'ring, flying,
Oh the pain, the bliss of dying!

Title] Attributed to Hadrian by Aelius Spartianus in his *De Vita Hadriani*, § xxv.

Cease, fond Nature, cease thy strife, 5
And let me languish into life.

Hark! they whisper; Angels say,
Sister Spirit, come away.
What is this absorbs me quite?
Steals my senses, shuts my sight, 10
Drowns my spirits, draws my breath?
Tell me, my Soul, can this be Death?

The world recedes; it disappears!
Heav'n opens on my eyes! my ears
    With sounds seraphic ring: 15
Lend, lend your wings! I mount! I fly!
O Grave! where is thy Victory?
    O Death! where is thy Sting?

Imitation of Tibullus (*Lib. 1 Eleg. iv*)

Here stopt by hasty Death, Alexis lies,
Who crost half Europe, led by Wortley's eyes!

Found in a letter (10 November 1716) written to Lady Mary W.
Montagu when she was travelling across Europe to Constantinople.

Imitation of Martial, Book 10, Epig. 23
[written c. 1716; published, *PSO*, 1717]

Jam numerat placido felix Antonius ævo, &c.

At length my Friend (while Time, with still career,
Wafts on his gentle wing his eightieth year)
Sees his past days safe out of fortune's pow'r,
Nor dreads approaching fate's uncertain hour;
Reviews his life, and in the strict survey ⎫ 5
Finds not one moment he cou'd wish away, ⎬
Pleas'd with the series of each happy day. ⎭
Such, such a man extends his life's short space,
And from the goal again renews the race;
For he lives twice, who can at once employ 10
The present well, and ev'n the past enjoy.

Written over a Study; out of Maynard

IN ENGLISH FOR SIR W. TRUMBULL

[written c. 1716; published, *PSO*, 1717]

Tir'd with vain hopes, and with complaints as vain,
Of anxious love's alternate joy and pain,
Inconstant fortune's favour and her hate,
And unperforming friendships of the great;
Here both contented and resign'd, I lye;   5
Here learn to live; nor wish, nor fear to die.

Title: *Maynard*] François Maynard (1582–1646), French poet. A translation of his 'Las d'esperer, et de me plaindre'.

The Prayer of Brutus

[written 1717; published 1718]

Goddess of Woods, tremendous in the chace,
To Mountain-wolves and all the Savage race,
Wide o'er th' aerial Vault extends thy sway,
And o'er th' infernal Regions void of day,
On thy third Reign look down; disclose our Fate,   5
In what new Nation shall we fix our Seat?
When shall we next thy hallow'd Altars raise,
And Quires of Virgins celebrate thy praise?

A translation of Brutus' prayer made for Aaron Thompson's translation of Geoffrey of Monmouth's *British History*, 1718; 'Diva potens nemorum, terror silvestribus apris.'

Pastorals

WITH A DISCOURSE ON PASTORAL

Written in the Year 1704
[published, Tonson's *Miscellanies*, 1709]

Rura mihi & rigui placeant in vallibus amnes,
Flumina amem, ſylvaſque, inglorius!

VIRG.

❁

A Discourse on Pastoral Poetry [1]

There are not, I believe, a greater number of any sort of verses than of those which are called Pastorals, nor a smaller, than of those which are truly so. It therefore seems necessary to give some account of this kind of Poem, and it is my design to comprize in this short paper the substance of those numerous dissertations the Criticks have made on the subject, without omitting any of their rules in my own favour. You will also find some points reconciled, about which they seem to differ, and a few remarks which I think have escaped their observation.

The original of Poetry is ascribed to that age which succeeded the creation of the world: And as the keeping of flocks seems to have been the first employment of mankind, the most ancient sort of poetry was probably pastoral. [2] 'Tis natural to imagine, that the leisure of those ancient shepherds admitting and inviting some diversion, none was so proper to that solitary and sedentary life as singing; and that in their songs they took occasion to celebrate their own felicity. From hence a Poem was invented, and afterwards improv'd to a perfect image of that happy time; which by giving us an esteem for the virtues of a former age, might recommend them to the present. And since the life of shepherds was attended with more tranquillity than any other rural employment, the Poets chose to introduce their Persons, from whom it receiv'd the name of Pastoral.

A Pastoral is an imitation of the action of a shepherd, or one considered under that character. The form of this imitation is

[1] *Written at sixteen years of age.* [P]
[2] *pastoral*] *Fontenelle's Disc. on Pastorals.* [P]

119

dramatic, or narrative, or mix'd of both[1]; the fable simple, the
manners not too polite nor too rustic: The thoughts are plain, yet
admit a little quickness and passion, but that short and flowing: The
expression humble, yet as pure as the language will afford; neat, but
not florid; easy, and yet lively. In short, the fable, manners,
thoughts, and expressions, are full of the greatest simplicity in
nature.

The complete character of this poem consists in simplicity,[2]
brevity, and delicacy; the two first of which render an eclogue
natural, and the last delightful.

If we would copy Nature, it may be useful to take this Idea along
with us, that pastoral is an image of what they call the Golden age.
So that we are not to describe our shepherds as shepherds at this
day really are, but as they may be conceiv'd then to have been;
when the best of men follow'd the employment. To carry this
resemblance yet farther, it would not be amiss to give these shepherds some skill in astronomy, as far as it may be useful to that sort
of life. And an Air of piety to the Gods should shine thro' the
Poem, which so visibly appears in all the works of antiquity: And
it ought to preserve some relish of the old way of writing; the connections should be loose, the narrations and descriptions short,[3] and
the periods concise. Yet it is not sufficient that the sentences only be
brief, the whole Eclogue should be so too. For we cannot suppose
Poetry in those days to have been the business of men, but their
recreation at vacant hours.

But with a respect to the present age, nothing more conduces to
make these composures[4] natural, than when some Knowledge in
rural affairs is discover'd.[5] This may be made to appear rather done
by chance than on design, and sometimes is best shewn by infer-
ence; lest by too much study to seem natural, we destroy that easy
simplicity from whence arises the delight. For what is inviting in
this sort of poetry proceeds not so much from the Idea of that
business, as of the tranquillity of a country life.

We must therefore use some illusion to render a Pastoral delightful; and this consists in exposing the best side only of a shepherd's
life, and in concealing its miseries.[6] Nor is it enough to introduce
shepherds discoursing together in a natural way; but a regard must
be had to the subject; that it contain some particular beauty in itself,

[1] *mix'd of both*] *Heinsius in Theocr.* [P]
[2] *simplicity*] *Rapin de Carm. Past. p. 2.* [P]
[3] *descriptions short*] *Rapin, Reflex. sur l'Art Poet. d'Arist. p. 2. Refl.*
xxvii. [P]
[4] *composures*] Compositions.
[5] *discover'd*] *Pref. to Virg. Past. in Dryd. Virg.* [P]
[6] *its miseries*] *Fontenelle's Disc. of Pastorals.* [P]

and that it be different in every Eclogue. Besides, in each of them a
design'd scene or prospect is to be presented to our view, which
should likewise have its variety.[1] This Variety is obtain'd in a great
degree by frequent comparisons, drawn from the most agreeable
objects of the country; by interrogations to things inanimate; by
beautiful digressions, but those short; sometimes by insisting a
little on circumstances; and lastly by elegant turns on the words,
which render the numbers extremely sweet and pleasing. As for the
numbers themselves, tho' they are properly of the heroic measure,
they should be the smoothest, the most easy and flowing imaginable.

It is by rules like these that we ought to judge of Pastoral. And
since the instructions given for any art are to be deliver'd as that art
is in perfection, they must of necessity be deriv'd from those in
whom it is acknowledg'd so to be. 'Tis therefore from the practice
of *Theocritus* and *Virgil*, (the only undisputed authors of Pastoral)
that the Criticks have drawn the foregoing notions concerning it.

Theocritus excells all others in nature and simplicity. The subjects of his *Idyllia* are purely pastoral, but he is not so exact in his
persons, having introduced Reapers[2] and fishermen as well as
shepherds. He is apt to be too long in his descriptions, of which that
of the Cup in the first pastoral is a remarkable instance. In the
manners he seems a little defective, for his swains are sometimes
abusive and immodest, and perhaps too much inclining to rusticity;
for instance, in his fourth and fifth *Idyllia*. But 'tis enough that all
others learn'd their excellencies from him, and that his Dialect
alone has a secret charm in it which no other could ever attain.

Virgil who copies *Theocritus*, refines upon his original: and in all
points where Judgment is principally concerned, he is much
superior to his master. Tho' some of his subjects are not pastoral in
themselves, but only seem to be such; they have a wonderful
variety in them which the *Greek* was a stranger to.[3] He exceeds him
in regularity and brevity, and falls short of him n nothing but
simplicity and propriety of style; the first of which perhaps was the
fault of his age, and the last of his language.

Among the moderns, their success has been greatest who have
most endeavour'd to make these ancients their pattern. The most
considerable Genius appears in the famous *Tasso*, and our *Spenser*.
Tasso in his *Aminta* has as far excell'd all the Pastoral writers, as in
his *Gierusalemme* he has outdone the Epic Poets of his country. But
as this piece seems to have been the original of a new sort of poem,

[1] *its variety*] *See the forementioned Preface.* [P]
[2] *Reapers*] ΘΕΡΙΣΤΑΙ *Idyl.* x. *and* ΑΛΙΕΙΣ *Idyl.* xxi. [P]
[3] *a stranger to.*] *Rapin Refl. on Arist. part* ii. *refl.* xxvii.—*Pref. to the Ecl.
in Dryden's Virg.* [P]

the Pastoral Comedy, in *Italy*, it cannot so well be consider'd as a copy of the ancients. *Spenser's Calender*, in Mr. *Dryden's* opinion, is the most complete work of this kind which any Nation has produc'd ever since the time of *Virgil*.[1] Not but that he may be thought imperfect in some few points. His Eclogues are somewhat too long, if we compare them with the ancients. He is sometimes too allegorical, and treats of matters of religion in a pastoral style as *Mantuan*[2] had done before him. He has employ'd the Lyric measure, which is contrary to the practice of the old Poets. His Stanza is not still the same, nor always well chosen. This last may be the reason his expression is sometimes not concise enough: for the Tetrastic has oblig'd him to extend his sense to the length of four lines, which would have been more closely confin'd in the Couplet.

In the manners, thoughts, and characters, he comes near to *Theocritus* himself; tho' notwithstanding all the care he has taken, he is certainly inferior in his Dialect: For the *Doric* had its beauty and propriety in the time of *Theocritus*; it was used in part of *Greece*, and frequent in the mouths of many of the greatest persons; whereas the old *English* and country phrases of *Spenser* were either entirely obsolete, or spoken only by people of the lowest condition. As there is a difference between simplicity and rusticity, so the expression of simple thoughts should be plain, but not clownish. The addition he has made of a Calendar to his Eclogues is very beautiful: since by this, besides the general moral of innocence and simplicity, which is common to other authors of pastoral, he has one peculiar to himself; he compares human Life to the several Seasons, and at once exposes to his readers a view of the great and little worlds, in their various changes and aspects. Yet the scrupulous division of his Pastorals into Months, has oblig'd him either to repeat the same description, in other words, for three months together; or when it was exhausted before, entirely to omit it: whence it comes to pass that some of his Eclogues (as the sixth, eighth, and tenth for example) have nothing but their Titles to distinguish them. The reason is evident, because the year has not that variety in it to furnish every month with a particular description, as it may every season.

Of the following Eclogues I shall only say, that these four comprehend all the subjects which the Critics upon *Theocritus* and *Virgil* will allow to be fit for pastoral: That they have as much variety of description, in respect of the several seasons, as *Spenser's*: That in order to add to this variety, the several times of the day are

[1] *Virgil*] Dedication to *Virg. Ecl.* [P]
[2] *Mantuan*] Baptista Mantuanus (1448–1516), the 'Christian Virgil', whose Latin eclogues enjoyed great popularity during the Renaissance.

observ'd, the rural employments in each season or time of day, and the rural scenes or places proper to such employments; not without some regard to the several ages of man, and the different passions proper to each age.

But after all, if they have any merit, it is to be attributed to some good old Authors, whose works as I had leisure to study, so I hope I have not wanted care to imitate.

Spring. The First Pastoral, or Damon

TO SIR WILLIAM TRUMBULL

First in these Fields I try the Sylvan Strains,
Nor blush to sport on *Windsor*'s blissful Plains:

These Pastorals were written at the age of sixteen, and then past thro' the hands of Mr. *Walsh*, Mr. *Wycherley*, G. *Granville*, afterwards Lord *Lansdown*, Sir *William Trumbal*, Dr. *Garth*, Lord *Halifax*, Lord *Somers*, Mr. *Mainwaring*, and others. All these gave our Author the greatest encouragement, and particularly Mr. *Walsh*, (whom Mr. Dryden, in his Postscript to Virgil, calls the best critic of his age.) 'The Author (says he) seems to have a particular genius for this kind of Poetry, and a judgment that much exceeds his years. He has taken very freely from the Ancients. But what he has mixed of his own with theirs is no way inferior to what he has taken from them. It is not flattery at all to say that Virgil had written nothing so good at his Age. His Preface is very judicious and learned.' *Letter to Mr. Wycherley, Ap.* 1705. The Lord Lansdown about the same time, mentioning the youth of our Poet, says (in a printed Letter of the Character of Mr. Wycherley) 'that if he goes on as he has begun in the Pastoral way, as Virgil first tried his strength, we may hope to see English Poetry vie with the Roman,' etc. Notwithstanding the early time of their production, the Author esteem'd these as the most correct in the versification, and musical in the numbers, of all his works. The reason for his labouring them into so much softness, was, doubtless, that this sort of poetry derives almost its whole beauty from a natural ease of thought and smoothness of verse; whereas that of most other kinds consists in the Strength and fulness of both. In a Letter of his to Mr. *Walsh* about this time, we find an enumeration of several Niceties in Versification, which perhaps have never been strictly observ'd in any *English* poem, except in these Pastorals. They were not printed till 1709. [P]

Sir *William Trumbal*] Our Author's friendship with this gentleman commenced at very unequal years; he was under sixteen, but Sir William above sixty, and had lately resign'd his employment of Secretary of State to King William. [P]

1.   *Prima Syracosio dignata est ludere versu,*
             Nostra nec erubuit sylvas habitare Thalia.

This is the general Exordium and opening of the Pastorals, in imitation of the 6th of *Virgil*, which some have therefore not improbably thought

Fair *Thames* flow gently from thy sacred Spring,
While on thy Banks *Sicilian* Muses sing;
Let Vernal Airs thro' trembling Osiers play, 5
And *Albion*'s Cliffs resound the Rural Lay.
  You, that too Wise for Pride, too Good for Pow'r,
Enjoy the Glory to be Great no more,
And carrying with you all the World can boast,
To all the World Illustriously are lost! 10
O let my Muse her slender Reed inspire,
'Till in your Native Shades You tune the Lyre:
So when the Nightingale to Rest removes,
The Thrush may chant to the forsaken Groves,
But, charm'd to Silence, listens while She sings, 15
And all th' Aerial Audience clap their Wings.
  Soon as the Flocks shook off the nightly Dews,
Two Swains, whom Love kept wakeful, and the Muse,
Pour'd o'er the whitening Vale their fleecy Care,
Fresh as the Morn, and as the Season fair: 20
The Dawn now blushing on the Mountain's Side,
Thus *Daphnis* spoke, and *Strephon* thus reply'd.

---

to have been the first originally. In the beginnings of the other three Pastorals, he imitates expressly those which now stand first of the three chief Poets in this kind, *Spenser, Virgil, Theocritus,*

> *A Shepherd's Boy (he seeks no better name)—*
> *Beneath the shade a spreading Beech displays,—*
> Thyrsis, *the Music of that murm'ring Spring,—*

are manifestly imitations of

> *A Shepherd's Boy (no better do him call)—*
> *Tityre, tu patulæ recubans sub tegmine fagi.—*
> 'Aδύ τι τὸ ψιθύρισμα καὶ ἁ πίτυς, αἰπόλε, τήνα.—* [P]

Cf. respectively Spenser, *Januarye,* 1; Virgil, *Ecl.* 1 1; Theocritus, *Idyll* 1, 1.

4. *Sicilian Muses*] The pastoral Muses, so called because, Theocritus the first writer of pastoral, was Sicilian.

11. *inspire*] Breathe into.

12. *in your Native Shades*] Sir *W. Trumbal* ⟨1639–1716⟩ was born in *Windsor*-Forest, to which he retreated after he had resign'd the post of Secretary of State to King *William* III. [P]

17 ff. The Scene of this Pastoral a Vally, the Time the Morning. It stood originally thus; ⟨Pope here quotes the *1709–17* variant.⟩

19. *whitening*] happily describes a *progressive* effect.

21. *Mountain*] Often applied at this time to elevations of moderate altitude.

28. *Purple*] Here used in the Latin sense of the most vivid colouring in general, not of a peculiar tint.

DAPHNIS

Hear how the Birds, on ev'ry bloomy Spray,
With joyous Musick wake the dawning Day!
Why sit we mute, when early Linnets sing,   25
When warbling *Philomel* salutes the Spring?
Why sit we sad, when *Phosphor* shines so clear,
And lavish Nature paints the Purple Year?

STREPHON

Sing then, and *Damon* shall attend the Strain,
While yon slow Oxen turn the furrow'd Plain.   30
Here the bright Crocus and blue Vi'let glow;
Here Western Winds on breathing Roses blow.
I'll stake yon' Lamb that near the Fountain plays,
And from the Brink his dancing Shade surveys.

DAPHNIS

And I this Bowl, where wanton Ivy twines,   35
And swelling Clusters bend the curling Vines:
Four Figures rising from the Work appear,
The various Seasons of the rowling Year;
And what is That, which binds the Radiant Sky,
Where twelve fair Signs in beauteous Order lye?   40

DAMON

Then sing by turns, by turns the Muses sing,
Now Hawthorns blossom, now the Daisies spring,
Now Leaves the Trees, and Flow'rs adorn the Ground;
Begin, the Vales shall ev'ry Note rebound.

32. *breathing*] Emitting fragrance. Cf. *Messiah*, 24 (p. 190); *Rape of the Lock*, I 134 (p. 222).
34. The first reading was, *And his own Image from the bank surveys*. [P]
35 f.   *Lenta quibus torno facili superaddita vitis,*
         Diffusos edera vestit pallente corymbos.
                 Virg. ⟨*Ecl.* III 38–9⟩ [P]
36. *And clusters lurk beneath the curling vines.* [P]
37. *rising*] The word refers to the figures carved in relief on the bowl.
38. *The various Seasons*] The Subject of these Pastorals engraven on the bowl is not without its propriety. The Shepherd's hesitation at the name of the *Zodiac*, imitates that in *Virgil* ⟨*Ecl.* III 40–1⟩,
               ————————*Et quis fuit alter?*
       Descripsit radio totum qui gentibus orbem. [P]
41. *Then sing by turns.*] Literally from *Virgil* ⟨*Ecl.* III 59, 56–7⟩,
       Alternis dicetis, amant alterna Camœnæ:
       Et nunc omnis ager, nunc omnis parturit arbos,
       Nunc frondent sylvæ, nunc formosissimus annus. [P]

STREPHON

Inspire me *Phœbus*, in my *Delia*'s Praise,   45
With *Waller*'s Strains, or *Granville*'s moving Lays!
A Milk-white Bull shall at your Altars stand,
That threats a Fight, and spurns the rising Sand.

DAPHNIS

O Love! for *Sylvia* let me gain the Prize,
And make my Tongue victorious as her Eyes;   50
No Lambs or Sheep for Victims I'll impart,
Thy Victim, Love, shall be the Shepherd's Heart.

STREPHON

Me gentle *Delia* beckons from the Plain,
Then hid in Shades, eludes her eager Swain;
But feigns a Laugh, to see me search around,   55
And by that Laugh the willing Fair is found.

DAPHNIS

The sprightly *Sylvia* trips along the Green,
She runs, but hopes she does not run unseen,
While a kind Glance at her Pursuer flies,
How much at variance are her Feet and Eyes!   60

STREPHON

O'er Golden Sands let rich *Pactolus* flow,
And Trees weep Amber on the Banks of *Po*;
Blest *Thames*'s Shores the brightest Beauties yield,
Feed here my Lambs, I'll seek no distant Field.

46. *Granville*—] *George Granville*, afterwards Lord *Lansdown*, known for his Poems, most of which he compos'd very young, and propos'd *Waller* as his model. [P]

47. *A Milk-white Bull*] Virg. ⟨*Ecl.* III 86–7⟩

——*Pascite taurum,*
Qui cornu petat, & pedibus jam spargat arenam. [P]

58. *She runs, but hopes*] Imitation of *Virgil* ⟨Ecl. III 64–5⟩,
Malo me Galatea petit, lasciva puella,
Et fugit ad salices, sed se cupit ante videri. [P]

61. It stood thus at first,
Let rich Iberia *golden fleeces boast,*
Her purple wool the proud Assyrian *coast,*
Blest Thames's *shores,* &c. [P]

Pactolus] A river in Lydia, in Asia Minor, famous for the gold dust once carried in its waters.

62. In Ovid, *Met.*, II, Phaethon, having been hurled down from the sky, fell on to the banks of the Po (Eridanus); his sisters, the Heliades, were transformed into poplars weeping tears of amber (ll. 364–5).

DAPHNIS

Celestial *Venus* haunts *Idalia*'s Groves,   65
Diana Cynthus, Ceres Hybla loves;
If *Windsor*-Shades delight the matchless Maid,
Cynthus and *Hybla* yield to *Windsor*-Shade.

STREPHON

All Nature mourns, the Skies relent in Show'rs,
Hush'd are the Birds, and clos'd the drooping Flow'rs;
If *Delia* smile, the Flow'rs begin to spring,   71
The Skies to brighten, and the Birds to sing.

DAPHNIS

All Nature laughs, the Groves are fresh and fair,
The Sun's mild Lustre warms the vital Air;
If *Sylvia* smiles, new Glories gild the Shore,   75
And vanquish'd Nature seems to charm no more.

STREPHON

In Spring the Fields, in Autumn Hills I love,
At Morn the Plains, at Noon the shady Grove;
But *Delia* always; absent from her Sight,
Nor Plains at Morn, nor Groves at Noon delight.   80

DAPHNIS

Sylvia's like Autumn ripe, yet mild as *May*,
More bright than Noon, yet fresh as early Day,
Ev'n Spring displeases, when she shines not here,
But blest with her, 'tis Spring throughout the Year.

65. *Celestial Venus*] Aphrodite Urania, the 'heavenly' Aphrodite, to
distinguish her from Aphrodite Pandemos, the common, or sensual,
Aphrodite.
  Idalia] A town in Cyprus consecrated to Aphrodite.
66. *Cynthus*] Diana was said to have been born on Mt. Cynthus, in
Delos.
  Hybla] A mountain in Sicily, famous for its thyme and honey.
69. *All nature mourns.*] Virg. ⟨VII 57, 59⟩

> *Aret ager, vitio moriens sitit aëris herba*, &c.
> *Phyllidis adventu nostræ nemus omne virebit*—[P]

relent] To 'assume a liquid form; to dissolve into water' (*OED*).
69 ff. These verses were thus at first;

> *All nature mourns, the birds their songs deny,*
> *Nor wasted brooks the thirsty flow'rs supply;*
> *If* Delia *smile, the flow'rs begin to spring,*
> *The brooks to murmur, and the birds to sing.* [P]

STREPHON

Say, *Daphnis*, say, in what glad Soil appears   85
A wondrous *Tree* that Sacred *Monarchs* bears ?
Tell me but this, and I'll disclaim the Prize,
And give the Conquest to thy *Sylvia*'s Eyes.

DAPHNIS

Nay tell me first, in what more happy Fields
The *Thistle* springs, to which the *Lilly* yields ?   90
And then a nobler Prize I will resign,
For *Sylvia*, charming *Sylvia* shall be thine.

DAMON

Cease to contend, for (*Daphnis*) I decree
The Bowl to *Strephon*, and the Lamb to thee:
Blest Swains, whose Nymphs in ev'ry Grace excell;   95
Blest Nymphs, whose Swains those Graces sing so well!
Now rise, and haste to yonder Woodbine Bow'rs,
A soft Retreat from sudden vernal Show'rs;
The Turf with rural Dainties shall be Crown'd,
While opening Blooms diffuse their Sweets around.   100
For see! the gath'ring Flocks to Shelter tend,
And from the *Pleiads* fruitful Show'rs descend.

86. *A wondrous Tree that Sacred Monarchs bears*] An allusion to the
Royal Oak, in which *Charles* the second had been hid from the pursuit
after the battle of *Worcester*. [P]

90. *The Thistle springs, to which the Lilly yields*] alludes to the Device
of the *Scots* Monarchs, the *Thistle*, worn by Queen *Anne*; and to the
Arms of *France*, the *Fleur de Lys*. The two Riddles are in imitation of
those in *Virg. Ecl.* 3 ⟨106–7⟩.

> *Dic quibus in terris inscripti nomina* Regum
> *Nascantur* Flores, & *Phyllida solus habebis.*   [P]

99. Was originally,

> *The turf with country dainties shall be spread,*
> *And trees with twining branches shade your head.* [P]

102. *from the Pleiads*] The Pleiades were the mythical daughters of
Atlas. Because of their sorrow at the burden imposed on their father they
were changed into a small group of stars in the constellation Taurus and
rose with the sun in April. They were associated with the vernal equinox
and the westerly rains of spring.

Summer. The Second Pastoral, or Alexis

TO DR. GARTH

A Shepherd's Boy (he seeks no better Name)
Let forth his Flocks along the silver *Thame*,
Where dancing Sun-beams on the Waters play'd,
And verdant Alders form'd a quiv'ring Shade.
Soft as he mourn'd, the Streams forgot to flow,   5
The Flocks around a dumb Compassion show,
The *Naiads* wept in ev'ry Watry Bow'r,
And *Jove* consented in a silent Show'r.

   Accept, O *Garth*, the Muse's early Lays,
That adds this Wreath of Ivy to thy Bays;   10
Hear what from Love unpractis'd Hearts endure,
From Love, the sole Disease thou canst not cure!

   Ye shady Beeches, and ye cooling Streams,
Defence from *Phœbus*', not from *Cupid*'s Beams;
To you I mourn; nor to the Deaf I sing,   15
The Woods shall answer, and their Echo ring.
The Hills and Rocks attend my doleful Lay,
Why art thou prouder and more hard than they?
The bleating Sheep with my Complaints agree,
They parch'd with Heat, and I inflam'd by thee.   20
The sultry *Sirius* burns the thirsty Plains,
While in thy Heart Eternal Winter reigns.

   Where stray ye Muses, in what Lawn or Grove,

Ver. 1, 2, 3, 4 were thus printed in the first edition; ⟨Pope here cites the *1709–17* variant.⟩

3. The Scene of this Pastoral by the River's side; suitable to the heat of the season; the Time, Noon. [P]

8. *And* Jove *consented*] Virg. ⟨*Ecl.* VII 60⟩

     Jupiter & læto descendet plurimus imbri. [P]

9. Dr. *Samuel Garth*, Author of the *Dispensary*, was one of the first friends of the author, whose acquaintance with him began at fourteen or fifteen. Their friendship continu'd from the year 1703, to 1718, which was that of his death. [P]

10. *Ivy to thy Bays*] For discussion of this image, see *Ess. on Crit.*, 706*n* (p. 167).

15. *nor to the Deaf I sing*] *Non canimus surdis, respondent omnia sylvæ.* Virg. ⟨*Ecl.* x 8⟩ [P]

16. *The woods shall answer, and their Echo ring*, is a line out of *Spenser's Epithalamion*. [P]

21. The Dog-star was regarded as the source of the sultry heat of summer and of the maladies which prevailed at that time.

23. *Where stray ye Muses*, &c.]

     Quæ nemora, aut qui vos saltus habuere, puellæ

While your *Alexis* pines in hopeless Love?
In those fair Fields where Sacred *Isis* glides,   25
Or else where *Cam* his winding Vales divides?
As in the Crystal Spring I view my Face,
Fresh rising Blushes paint the watry Glass;
But since those Graces please thy Eyes no more,
I shun the Fountains which I sought before.   30
Once I was skill'd in ev'ry Herb that grew,
And ev'ry Plant that drinks the Morning Dew;
Ah wretched Shepherd, what avails thy Art,
To cure thy Lambs, but not to heal thy Heart!
  Let other Swains attend the Rural Care,   35
Feed fairer Flocks, or richer Fleeces share;
But nigh yon' Mountain let me tune my Lays,
Embrace my Love, and bind my Brows with Bays.
That Flute is mine which *Colin*'s tuneful Breath
Inspir'd when living, and bequeath'd in Death;   40
He said; *Alexis*, take this Pipe, the same
That taught the Groves my *Rosalinda*'s Name—
But now the Reeds shall hang on yonder Tree,
For ever silent, since despis'd by thee.
O were I made by some transforming Pow'r,   45
The Captive Bird that sings within thy Bow'r!

Naiades, indigno cum Gallus amore periret?
Nam neque Parnassi vobis juga, nam neque Pindi
Ulla moram fecere, neque Aonia Aganippe.
        Virg. ⟨*Ecl.* x 9-12⟩ out of *Theoc.* ⟨*Idyll* 1 65-7.⟩ [P]

25. *Isis*] Name given to the Thames about Oxford.

27.   *Oft in the crystal spring I cast a view,*
            And equal'd Hylas, *if the glass be true;*
            But since those graces meet my eyes no more,
            I shun, &c.

Virgil ⟨*Ecl.* II 25-7⟩ again from the *Cyclops* ⟨*Idyll* XI⟩ of *Theocritus,*
            ————————*nuper me in littore vidi*
    Cum placidum ventis staret mare, non ego Daphnim,
    Judice te, metuam, si nunquam fallit imago. [P]

39. *Colin*] The name taken by *Spenser* in his Eclogues, where his
mistress is celebrated under that of *Rosalinda.* [P]
  Note that Pope claims here to be the successor of Spenser. *Alexis*
suggests Pope's Christian name, *Alexander.*

40. *Virg. Ecl.* 2. ⟨36-8⟩
            Est mihi disparibus septem compacta cicutis
            Fistula, Damœtas dono mihi quam dedit olim
            Et dixit moriens, Te nunc habet ista secundum. [P]

Then might my Voice thy list'ning Ears employ,
And I those Kisses he receives, enjoy.
　　And yet my Numbers please the rural Throng,
Rough *Satyrs* dance, and *Pan* applauds the Song:　　50
The Nymphs forsaking ev'ry Cave and Spring,
Their early Fruit, and milk-white Turtles bring;
Each am'rous Nymph prefers her Gifts in vain,
On you their Gifts are all bestow'd again!
For you the Swains the fairest Flow'rs design,　　55
And in one Garland all their Beauties join;
Accept the Wreath which You deserve alone,
In whom all Beauties are compriz'd in One.
　　See what Delights in Sylvan Scenes appear!
Descending Gods have found *Elysium* here.　　60
In Woods bright *Venus* with *Adonis* stray'd,
And chast *Diana* haunts the Forest Shade.
Come lovely Nymph, and bless the silent Hours,
When Swains from Sheering seek their nightly Bow'rs;
When weary Reapers quit the sultry Field,　　65
And crown'd with Corn, their Thanks to *Ceres* yield.
This harmless Grove no lurking Viper hides,
But in my Breast the Serpent Love abides.
Here Bees from Blossoms sip the rosie Dew,
But your *Alexis* knows no Sweets but you.　　70
Oh deign to visit our forsaken Seats,
The mossie Fountains, and the Green Retreats!
Where-e'er you walk, cool Gales shall fan the Glade,
Trees, where you sit, shall crowd into a Shade,
Where-e'er you tread, the blushing Flow'rs shall rise,　75
And all things flourish where you turn your Eyes.
Oh! how I long with you to pass my Days,
Invoke the Muses, and resound your Praise;
Your Praise the Birds shall chant in ev'ry Grove,

60. *Descending Gods have found* Elysium *here.*] ——*Habitarunt Di quoque sylvas*—Virg. ⟨*Ecl.* 11 60⟩
　　Et formosus oves ad flumina pavit Adonis. Idem. ⟨x 18⟩ [P]

79 ff.　　*Your praise the tuneful birds to heav'n shall bear,*
　　　　And list'ning wolves grow milder as they hear.

So the verses were originally written. But the author, young as he was, soon found the absurdity which *Spenser* himself overlooked, of introducing Wolves into England. [P]
　　But see Spenser's *September*, 151–3.
Wolves are said to have disappeared from England in the reign of Henry VII.

And Winds shall waft it to the Pow'rs above.   80
But wou'd you sing, and rival *Orpheus'* Strain,
The wondring Forests soon shou'd dance again,
The moving Mountains hear the pow'rful Call,
And headlong Streams hang list'ning in their Fall!
　　But see, the Shepherds shun the Noon-day Heat,   85
The lowing Herds to murm'ring Brooks retreat,
To closer Shades the panting Flocks remove,
Ye Gods! and is there no Relief for Love?
But soon the Sun with milder Rays descends
To the cool Ocean, where his Journey ends;   90
On me Love's fiercer Flames for ever prey,
By Night he scorches, as he burns by Day.

80. *And Winds shall waft*] *Partem aliquam, venti, divum referatis ad aures!* Virg. ⟨*Ecl.* III 73⟩ [P]
　88. *Me tamen urit amor, quis enim modus adsit amori?* Id. ⟨Virgil, *Ecl.* II 68⟩ [P]
　91. *Me love inflames, nor will his fires allay.* [P]

Autumn. The Third Pastoral,
or Hylas and Ægon

TO MR. WYCHERLEY

Beneath the Shade a spreading Beech displays,
Hylas and *Ægon* sung their Rural Lays;
This mourn'd a faithless, that an absent Love,
And *Delia*'s Name and *Doris* fill'd the Grove.
Ye *Mantuan* Nymphs, your sacred Succour bring;   5
Hylas and *Ægon*'s Rural Lays I sing.
　　Thou, whom the Nine with *Plautus'* Wit inspire,
The Art of *Terence*, and *Menander*'s Fire;
Whose Sense instructs us, and whose Humour charms,
Whose Judgment sways us, and whose Spirit warms!   10

This Pastoral consists of two parts, like the 8th of *Virgil*: The Scene
a Hill; the Time, at Sun-set. [P]
　7. *Thou, whom the Nine,*] Mr. Wycherley, a famous Author of Comedies;
of which the most celebrated were the *Plain-Dealer* and *Country-Wife.*
He was a writer of infinite spirit, satire, and wit. The only objection made
to him was that he had too much. However he was followed in the same
way by Mr. Congreve; tho' with a little more correctness. [P]

Oh, skill'd in Nature! see the Hearts of Swains,
Their artless Passions, and their tender Pains.
  Now setting *Phœbus* shone serenely bright,
And fleecy Clouds were streak'd with Purple Light;
When tuneful *Hylas* with melodious Moan   15
Taught Rocks to weep, and made the *Mountains* groan.
  Go gentle Gales, and bear my Sighs away!
To *Delia*'s Ear the tender Notes convey!
As some sad Turtle his lost Love deplores,
And with deep Murmurs fills the sounding Shores;   20
Thus, far from *Delia*, to the Winds I mourn,
Alike unheard, unpity'd, and forlorn.
  Go gentle Gales, and bear my Sighs along!
For her, the feather'd Quires neglect their Song;
For her, the Lymes their pleasing Shades deny;   25
For her, the Lillies hang their heads and dye.
Ye Flow'rs that droop, forsaken by the Spring,
Ye Birds, that left by Summer, cease to sing,
Ye Trees that fade when Autumn-Heats remove,
Say, is not Absence Death to those who love?   30
  Go gentle Gales, and bear my Sighs away!
Curs'd be the Fields that cause my *Delia*'s Stay:
Fade ev'ry Blossom, wither ev'ry Tree,
Dye ev'ry Flow'r, and perish, All but She.
What have I said?—where-e'er my *Delia* flies,   35
Let Spring attend, and sudden Flow'rs arise;
Let opening Roses knotted Oaks adorn,
And liquid Amber drop from ev'ry Thorn.
  Go gentle Gales, and bear my Sighs along!
The Birds shall cease to tune their Ev'ning Song,   40
The Winds to breathe, the waving Woods to move,
And Streams to murmur, e'er I cease to love.
Not bubling Fountains to the thirsty Swain,
Not balmy Sleep to Lab'rers faint with Pain,
Not Show'rs to Larks, or Sunshine to the Bee,   45

11. *skill'd in Nature*] I.e. Wycherley knew *human nature*; hence
interest he could take in the passions and pains of Pope's shepherds.

37.   ————*Aurea duræ*
           Mala ferant quercus, narcisso floreat alnus,
           Pinguia corticibus sudent electra myricæ.
                   Virg. Ecl. 8 ⟨52–4⟩ [P]

43 ff.   *Quale sopor fessis in gramine, quale per æstum*
           Dulcis aquæ saliente sitim restinguere rivo.
               ⟨Virgil⟩ Ecl. 5. ⟨46–7⟩

44. *Pain*] Labour, toil.

Are half so charming as thy Sight to me.
  Go gentle Gales, and bear my Sighs away!
Come, *Delia*, come; ah why this long Delay?
Thro' Rocks and Caves the Name of *Delia* sounds,
Delia, each Cave and ecchoing Rock rebounds.   50
Ye Pow'rs, what pleasing Frensie sooths my Mind!
Do Lovers dream, or is my *Delia* kind?
She comes, my *Delia* comes!—Now cease my Lay,
And cease ye Gales to bear my Sighs away!
  Next *Ægon* sung, while *Windsor* Groves admir'd;   55
Rehearse, ye Muses, what your selves inspir'd.
  Resound ye Hills, resound my mournful Strain!
Of perjur'd *Doris*, dying I complain:
Here where the *Mountains* less'ning as they rise,
Lose the low Vales, and steal into the Skies.   60
While lab'ring Oxen, spent with Toil and Heat,
In their loose Traces from the Field retreat;
While curling Smokes from Village-Tops are seen,
And the fleet Shades glide o'er the dusky Green.
  Resound ye Hills, resound my mournful Lay!   65
Beneath yon Poplar oft we past the Day:
Oft on the Rind I carv'd her Am'rous Vows,
While She with Garlands hung the bending Boughs:
The Garlands fade, the Vows are worn away;
So dies her Love, and so my Hopes decay.   70
  Resound ye Hills, resound my mournful Strain!
Now bright *Arcturus* glads the teeming Grain,
Now Golden Fruits on loaded Branches shine,
And grateful Clusters swell with floods of Wine;
Now blushing Berries paint the yellow Grove;   75
Just Gods! shall all things yield Returns but Love?
  Resound ye Hills, resound my mournful Lay!
The Shepherds cry, 'Thy Flocks are left a Prey—'
Ah! what avails it me, the Flocks to keep,
Who lost my Heart while I preserv'd my Sheep.   80

52. *An qui amant, ipsi sibi somnia fingunt?* Ecl. 8. ⟨108⟩ [P]
64. *And the fleet shades fly gliding o'er the green.* [P]
72. According to the ancients, the weather was stormy for a few days when Arcturus rose with the sun, which took place in September, and Pope apparently means that rain at this crisis was beneficial to the standing corn.
74. *grateful Clusters*] Grapes were successfully cultivated in England. Pope planted a vineyard in his garden at Twickenham, and Sir William Temple in his essay *Of Gardening* had described his own success with various kinds of grapes.

Pan came, and ask'd, what Magick caus'd my Smart,
Or what *Ill Eyes* malignant Glances dart?
What Eyes but hers, alas, have Pow'r to move!
And is there Magick but what dwells in Love?
Resound ye Hills, resound my mournful Strains!   85
I'll fly from Shepherds, Flocks, and flow'ry Plains.—
From Shepherds, Flocks, and Plains, I may remove,
Forsake Mankind, and all the World—but Love!
I know thee Love! on foreign Mountains bred,
Wolves gave thee suck, and savage Tygers fed.   90
Thou wert from *Ætna*'s burning Entrails torn,
Got by fierce Whirlwinds, and in Thunder born!
Resound ye Hills, resound my mournful Lay!
Farewell ye Woods! adieu the Light of Day!
One Leap from yonder Cliff shall end my Pains.   95
No more ye Hills, no more resound my Strains!
Thus sung the Shepherds till th' Approach of Night,
The Skies yet blushing with departing Light,
When falling Dews with Spangles deck'd the Glade,
And the low Sun had lengthen'd ev'ry Shade.   100

82. *Or what Ill Eyes*] *Nescio quis teneros oculus mihi fascinat agnos.*
⟨Virgil, *Ecl.* III 103⟩ [P]
83.   *What eyes but hers, alas, have pow'r on me!*
          Oh mighty Love! what magic is like thee! [P]

89. *Nunc scio quid sit amor, duris in cotibus illum,* &c. ⟨Virgil, *Ecl.*
VIII 43⟩ [P]

Winter. The Fourth Pastoral, or Daphne

TO THE MEMORY OF MRS. TEMPEST

LYCIDAS

Thyrsis, the Musick of that murm'ring Spring
Is not so mournful as the Strains you sing,

Mrs. Tempest] This Lady was of an ancient family in Yorkshire, and
particularly admired by the Author's friend Mr. *Walsh*, who having
celebrated her in a Pastoral Elegy, desired his friend to do the same, as
appears from one of his Letters, dated Sept. 9, 1706. 'Your last Eclogue
being on the same subject with mine on Mrs. Tempest's death, I should
take it very kindly in you to give it a little turn as if it were to the memory
of the same lady.' Her death having happened on the night of the great
storm in 1703, gave a propriety to this eclogue, which in its general turn
alludes to it. The Scene of the Pastoral lies in a grove, the Time at
midnight. [P]

Nor Rivers winding thro' the Vales below,
So sweetly warble, or so smoothly flow.
Now sleeping Flocks on their soft Fleeces lye,   5
The Moon, serene in Glory, mounts the Sky,
While silent Birds forget their tuneful Lays,
Oh sing of *Daphne*'s Fate, and *Daphne*'s Praise!

THYRSIS

Behold the *Groves* that shine with silver Frost,
Their Beauty wither'd, and their Verdure lost.   10
Here shall I try the sweet *Alexis*' Strain,
That call'd the list'ning *Dryads* to the Plain?
Thames heard the Numbers as he flow'd along,
And bade his Willows learn the moving Song.

LYCIDAS

So may kind Rains their vital Moisture yield,   15
And swell the future Harvest of the Field!
Begin; this Charge the dying *Daphne* gave,
And said; 'Ye Shepherds, sing around my Grave!'
Sing, while beside the shaded Tomb I mourn,
And with fresh Bays her Rural Shrine adorn.   20

THYRSIS

Ye gentle *Muses* leave your Crystal Spring,
Let *Nymphs* and *Sylvans* Cypress Garlands bring;
Ye weeping *Loves*, the Stream with Myrtles hide,
And break your Bows, as when *Adonis* dy'd;
And with your Golden Darts, now useless grown,   25
Inscribe a Verse on this relenting Stone:
'Let Nature change, let Heav'n and Earth deplore,
Fair *Daphne*'s dead, and Love is now no more!'
'Tis done, and Nature's various Charms decay;
See gloomy Clouds obscure the chearful Day!   30
Now hung with Pearls the dropping Trees appear,

5 f.   *In the warm folds the tender flocks remain,*
          The cattle slumber on the silent plain,
          While silent birds neglect their tuneful lays,
          Let us, dear Thyrsis, *sing of* Daphne's *praise.* [P]
13. Thames *heard*] *Audiit Eurotas, jussitque ediscere lauros.* Virg. ⟨*Ecl.*
VI 83⟩ [P]
Pope used the willows of England (the symbol of grief) instead of the
laurels of the Greek Eurotas.
23 ff.   ——*Inducite fontibus umbras*——
          Et tumulum facite, & tumulo superaddite carmen.
⟨Virgil, *Ecl.* V 40, 42⟩ [P]

Their faded Honours scatter'd on her Bier.
See, where on Earth the flow'ry Glories lye,
With her they flourish'd, and with her they dye.
Ah what avail the Beauties Nature wore?   35
Fair *Daphne*'s dead, and Beauty is no more!
  For her, the Flocks refuse their verdant Food,
The thirsty Heifers shun the gliding Flood.
The silver Swans her hapless Fate bemoan,
In Notes more sad than when they sing their own.   40
In hollow Caves sweet *Echo* silent lies,
Silent, or only to her Name replies,
Her Name with Pleasure once she taught the Shore,
Now *Daphne*'s dead, and Pleasure is no more!
  No grateful Dews descend from Ev'ning Skies,   45
Nor Morning Odours from the Flow'rs arise.
No rich Perfumes refresh the fruitful Field,
Nor fragrant Herbs their native Incense yield.
The balmy *Zephyrs*, silent since her Death,
Lament the Ceasing of a sweeter Breath.   50
Th' industrious Bees neglect their Golden Store;
Fair *Daphne*'s dead, and Sweetness is no more!
  No more the mounting Larks, while *Daphne* sings,
Shall list'ning in mid Air suspend their Wings;
No more the Birds shall imitate her Lays,   55
Or hush'd with Wonder, hearken from the Sprays:
No more the Streams their Murmurs shall forbear,
A sweeter Musick than their own to hear,
But tell the Reeds, and tell the vocal Shore,
Fair *Daphne*'s dead, and Musick is no more!   60
  Her Fate is whisper'd by the gentle Breeze,
And told in Sighs to all the trembling Trees;
The trembling Trees, in ev'ry Plain and Wood,
Her Fate remurmur to the silver Flood;
The silver Flood, so lately calm, appears   65
Swell'd with new Passion, and o'erflows with Tears;
The Winds and Trees and Floods her Death deplore,
Daphne, our Grief! our Glory now no more!
  But see! where *Daphne* wondring mounts on high,
Above the Clouds, above the Starry Sky.   70

38.   For her the flocks the dewy herbs disdain,
       Nor hungry heifers graze the tender plain. [P]
69 ff.   ——*miratur limen Olympi,*
      Sub pedibusque vidit nubes & sydera Daphnis.
                Virg. ⟨*Ecl.* v 56–7⟩ [P]

Eternal Beauties grace the shining Scene,
Fields ever fresh, and Groves for ever green!
There, while You rest in *Amaranthine* Bow'rs,
Or from those Meads select unfading Flow'rs,
Behold us kindly who your Name implore,   75
Daphne, our Goddess, and our Grief no more!

LYCIDAS

How all things listen, while thy Muse complains!
Such Silence waits on *Philomela*'s Strains,
In some still Ev'ning, when the whisp'ring Breeze
Pants on the Leaves, and dies upon the Trees.   80
To thee, bright Goddess, oft a Lamb shall bleed,
If teeming Ewes encrease my fleecy Breed.
While Plants their Shade, or Flow'rs their Odours give,
Thy Name, thy Honour, and thy Praise shall live!

THYRSIS

But see, *Orion* sheds unwholsome Dews,   85
Arise, the Pines a noxious Shade diffuse;
Sharp *Boreas* blows, and Nature feels Decay,
Time conquers All, and We must Time obey.
Adieu ye *Vales*, ye *Mountains*, *Streams* and *Groves*,
Adieu ye Shepherd's rural *Lays* and *Loves*,   90
Adieu my Flocks, farewell ye *Sylvan* Crew,
Daphne farewell, and all the World adieu!

73 f. The amaranth flower was reputed never to fade.
81.   ————————*illius aram*
              Sæpe tener nostris ab ovilibus imbuet agnus.
                                    Virg. ⟨*Ecl.* 1 7–8⟩ [P]
85. The rising and setting of the constellation Orion was thought to
bring storm and rain.
86.   ——*solet esse gravis cantantibus umbra,*
              Juniperi gravis umbra————
                                    Virg. ⟨*Ecl.* x 75–6⟩ [P]
89 ff. These four last lines allude to the several *Subjects* of the four
Pastorals, and to the several *Scenes* of them, particularized before in
each. [P]

Ode for Musick, on St. Cecilia's Day

[written c. 1708; published 1713]

Descend ye Nine! descend and sing;
    The breathing Instruments inspire,
Wake into Voice each silent String,
    And sweep the sounding Lyre!
In a sadly-pleasing Strain   5
    Let the warbling Lute complain:
    Let the loud Trumpet sound,
    Till the Roofs all around
    The shrill Ecchos rebound:
While in more lengthen'd Notes and slow,   10
The deep, majestick, solemn Organs blow.
    Hark! the Numbers, soft and clear,
    Gently steal upon the Ear;
    Now louder, and yet louder rise,
    And fill with spreading Sounds the Skies;   15
Exulting in Triumph now swell the bold Notes,
In broken Air, trembling, the wild Musick floats;
    Till, by degrees, remote and small,
        The Strains decay,
        And melt away   20
    In a dying, dying Fall.

By Musick, Minds an equal Temper know,
    Nor swell too high, nor sink too low.
If in the Breast tumultuous Joys arise,
Music her soft, assuasive Voice applies;   25
    Or when the Soul is press'd with Cares
    Exalts her in enlivening Airs.
Warriors she fires with animated Sounds;
Pours Balm into the bleeding *Lover*'s Wounds:
    Melancholy lifts her Head;   30
    Morpheus rowzes from his Bed;

St. Cecilia's Day (22 November) had been observed as an annual festival by musicians in London since 1683, and many poets, including Oldham, Dryden (twice), Addison (twice), and Congreve, were called on to provide the odes, songs, or hymns which were set to music for performance on that day. The custom was falling into disuse by about 1708, though sporadic attempts were later made to revive it. Pope's *Ode* was probably never set to music, nor performed on St. Cecilia's Day. In 1730 he rewrote it for Dr. Greene, whose musical setting was performed at 'Publick Commencement' at Cambridge on 6 July of that year.

Sloath unfolds her Arms and wakes;
List'ning *Envy* drops her Snakes;
Intestine War no more our *Passions* wage,
And giddy *Factions* hear away their Rage.   35

But when our Country's Cause provokes to Arms,
How martial Musick every Bosom warms!
So when the first bold Vessel dar'd the Seas,
High on the Stern the *Thracian* rais'd his Strain,
   While *Argo* saw her kindred Trees   40
   Descend from *Pelion* to the Main.
Transported Demi-Gods stood round,
And Men grew Heroes at the Sound,
   Enflam'd with Glory's Charms:
Each Chief his sevenfold Shield display'd,   45
And half unsheath'd the shining Blade;
And Seas, and Rocks, and Skies rebound
   To Arms, to Arms, to Arms!

But when thro' all th' Infernal Bounds
Which flaming *Phlegeton* surrounds,   50
Love, strong as Death, the Poet led
To the pale Nations of the Dead,
What Sounds were heard,
What Scenes appear'd,
   O'er all the dreary Coasts!   55
      Dreadful Gleams,
      Dismal screams,
      Fires that glow,
      Shrieks of Woe,
      Sullen Moans,   60
      Hollow Groans,
   And Cries of tortur'd Ghosts.
But hark! he strikes the golden Lyre;
And see! the tortur'd Ghosts respire,
   See shady Forms advance!   65
Thy stone, O *Sysiphus*, stands still;
Ixion rests upon his Wheel,
   And the pale Spectres dance!
The Furies sink upon their Iron Beds,
And Snakes uncurl'd hang list'ning round their Heads.   70

   By the Streams that ever flow,
   By the fragrant Winds that blow

O'er th' *Elysian* Flowers,
By those happy Souls who dwell
In Yellow Meads of *Asphodel*,   75
    Or *Amaranthine* Bowers:
By the Heroe's armed Shades,
Glitt'ring thro' the gloomy Glades,
By the Youths that dy'd for Love,
Wandring in the Myrtle Grove,   80
Restore, restore *Eurydice* to Life;
Oh take the Husband, or return the Wife!

He sung, and Hell consented
    To hear the Poet's Pray'r;
Stern *Proserpine* relented,   85
    And gave him back the Fair.
    Thus Song could prevail
    O'er Death and o'er Hell,
A Conquest how hard and how glorious?
    Tho' Fate had fast bound her   90
    With *Styx* nine times round her,
Yet Musick and Love were Victorious.

But soon, too soon, the Lover turns his Eyes:
Again she falls, again she dies, she dies!
How wilt thou now the fatal Sisters move?   95
No Crime was thine, if 'tis no Crime to love.
    Now under hanging Mountains,
    Beside the Falls of Fountains,
    Or where *Hebrus* wanders,
    Rolling in *Mæanders*,   100
        All alone,
        Unheard, unknown,
    He makes his Moan;
    And calls her Ghost
For ever, ever, ever lost!   105
Now with Furies surrounded,
Despairing, confounded,
He trembles, he glows,
Amidst *Rhodope*'s Snows:
See, wild as the Winds, o'er the Desart he flies;   110
Hark! *Hæmus* resounds with the *Bacchanals*' Cries—
        —Ah see, he dies!
Yet ev'n in Death *Eurydice* he sung,
Eurydice still trembled on his Tongue,

Eurydice the Woods,   115
Eurydice the Floods,
Eurydice the Rocks, and hollow Mountains rung.

Musick the fiercest Grief can charm,
And Fate's severest Rage disarm:
Musick can soften Pain to Ease,   120
And make Despair and Madness please:
Our Joys below it can improve,
And antedate the Bliss above.
    This the divine *Cecilia* found,
And to her Maker's Praise confin'd the Sound.   125
When the full Organ joins the tuneful Quire,
    Th' Immortal Pow'rs incline their Ear;
Born on the swelling Notes our Souls aspire,
While solemn Airs improve the sacred Fire;
    And Angels lean from Heav'n to hear!   130
Of *Orpheus* now no more let Poets tell,
To bright *Cecilia* greater Pow'r is giv'n;
    His Numbers rais'd a Shade from Hell,
        Hers lift the Soul to Heav'n.

An Essay on Criticism

[written c. 1709; published 1711]

—————————*Si quid novisti rectius istis,*
Candidus imperti; si non, his utere mecum.
HORAT.

THE CONTENTS OF THE ESSAY ON CRITICISM

PART I

*Introduction. That 'tis as great a fault to judge ill, as to write ill, and
a more dangerous one to the public,* V I.
That a true Taste *is as rare to be found, as a* true Genius, V 9 *to* 18.
That most men are born with some Taste, but spoil'd by false Educa-
tion, V 19 *to* 25.
The Multitude of Critics, *and causes of them,* V 26 *to* 45.
That we are to study our own Taste, *and know the* Limits *of it,* V 46
to 67.
Nature *the best guide of Judgment,* V 68 *to* 87.
Improv'd by Art *and* Rules, *which are but* methodis'd Nature, V 88.
Rules *deriv'd from the Practice of the* Ancient Poets, V *id. to* 110.
That therefore the Ancients *are necessary to be study'd by a* Critic,
particularly Homer *and* Virgil, V 120 *to* 138.
Of Licenses, *and the use of them by the Ancients,* V 140 *to* 180.
Reverence due to the Ancients, *and praise of them,* V 181, *&c.*

PART II. VER. 203, ETC.

Causes hindering a true Judgment. I Pride, V 208. 2. Imperfect
Learning, V 215. 3. *Judging by* parts, *and not by the* whole, V 233
to 288. Critics *in* Wit, Language, Versification, *only,* V 288. 305.
339, *&c.* 4. *Being too hard to please, or too apt to admire,* V 384.
5. Partiality—*too much Love to a* Sect,—*to the* Ancients *or*
Moderns, V 394. 6. Prejudice *or* Prevention, V 408. 7. Singularity,
V 424. 8. Inconstancy, V 430. 9. Party Spirit, V 452, *&c.* 10. Envy,
V 466. *Against* Envy, *and in praise of Good-nature,* V 508, *&c.*
When Severity is chiefly to be used by Critics, V 526, *&c.*

PART III. VER. 560, ETC.

Rules for the Conduct *of* Manners *in a Critic,* I. Candour, V 563.
Modesty, V 566. Good-breeding, V 572. Sincerity, *and* Freedom
of Advice, V 578. 2. *When one's Counsel is to be restrained,* V 584.
Character of an incorrigible Poet, V 600. *And of an* impertinent
Critic, V 610, *&c. Character of a* good Critic, V 629. *The* History

of Criticism, *and Characters of the best Critics,* Aristotle, v 645. Horace, v 653. Dionysius, v 665. Petronius, v 667. Quintilian, v 670. Longinus, v 675. *Of the Decay of Criticism, and its Revival.* Erasmus, v 693. Vida, v 705. Boileau, v 714. *Lord* Roscommon, *&c.* v 725. *Conclusion.*

An Essay on Criticism

'Tis hard to say, if greater Want of Skill
Appear in *Writing* or in *Judging* ill;
But, of the two, less dang'rous is th' Offence,
To tire our *Patience,* than mis-lead our *Sense:*
Some few in *that,* but Numbers err in *this,*   5
Ten Censure wrong for one who Writes amiss;
A *Fool* might once *himself* alone expose,
Now *One* in *Verse* makes many more in *Prose.*
   'Tis with our *Judgments* as our *Watches,* none
Go just *alike,* yet each believes his own.   10
In *Poets* as true *Genius* is but rare,
True *Taste* as seldom is the *Critick*'s Share;
Both must alike from Heav'n derive their Light,
These *born* to Judge, as well as those to Write.
Let such teach others who themselves excell,   15
And *censure freely* who have *written well.*
Authors are partial to their *Wit,* 'tis true,
But are not *Criticks* to their *Judgment* too?
   Yet if we look more closely, we shall find
Most have the *Seeds* of Judgment in their Mind;   20
Nature affords at least a *glimm'ring Light*;
The *Lines,* tho' touch'd but faintly, are drawn right.
But as the slightest Sketch, if justly trac'd,⎫
Is by ill *Colouring* but the more disgrac'd, ⎬
So by *false Learning* is *good Sense* defac'd; ⎭   25

15. *Qui scribit artificiosè ab aliis commodè scripta facile intelligere poterit.* Cic. ad Herenn. lib. 4 ⟨cap. 4⟩. [P]
   De Pictore, Sculptore, Fictore, nisi Artifex judicare non potest. Pliny ⟨*Ep.* 1 10⟩. [P]
   20. *Omnes tacito quodam sensu, sine ulla arte, aut ratione, quæ sint in artibus ac rationibus recta ac prava dijudicant.* Cic. de ⟨Orat. lib. 3 ⟨50⟩. [P]
   25. *Plus sine doctrina prudentia, quam sine prudentia valet doctrina.* Quint. ⟨*Inst. Orat.,* VI v 11⟩. [P]
   25. Between Verse 25 and 26 were these lines,

         Many are spoil'd by that pedantic *throng,*
         Who with great pains teach youth to reason wrong.

Some are bewilder'd in the Maze of Schools,
And some made *Coxcombs* Nature meant but *Fools*.
In search of *Wit* these lose their *common Sense*,
And then turn Criticks in their own Defence.
Each burns alike, who can, or cannot write,   30
Or with a *Rival*'s or an *Eunuch*'s spite.
All *Fools* have still an Itching to deride,
And fain *wou'd* be upon the *Laughing Side:*
If *Mævius* Scribble in *Apollo*'s spight,
There are, who *judge* still *worse* than he can *write*.   35
   Some have at first for *Wits*, then *Poets* past,
Turn'd *Criticks* next, and prov'd plain *Fools* at last;
Some neither can for *Wits* nor *Criticks* pass,
As heavy Mules are neither *Horse* nor *Ass*.
Those half-learn'd Witlings, num'rous in our Isle,   40
As half-form'd Insects on the Banks of *Nile*;

Unfinish'd Things, one knows not what to call,
Their Generation's so *equivocal*:
To tell 'em, wou'd a *hundred Tongues* require,
Or *one vain Wit*'s, that might a hundred tire.   45

  But *you* who seek to *give* and *merit* Fame,
And justly bear a Critick's noble Name,
Be sure *your self* and your own *Reach* to know,
How far your *Genius, Taste,* and *Learning* go;
Launch not beyond your Depth, but be discreet,   50
And mark *that Point* where Sense and Dulness *meet*.
   Nature to all things fix'd the Limits fit,
And wisely curb'd proud Man's pretending Wit:
As on the *Land* while *here* the *Ocean* gains,
In *other Parts* it leaves wide sandy Plains;   55
Thus in the *Soul* while *Memory* prevails,
The solid Pow'r of *Understanding* fails;

    Tutors, *like* Virtuoso's, *oft inclin'd*
    By strange transfusion *to improve the mind,*
    Draw off the sense we have, to pour in new;
    Which yet, with all their skill, they ne'er could do.
                                  [P]

34. *Maevius*] See p. 8, l. 19*n*.
36 f. Perhaps a hit at Dennis.
39. *heavy Mules*] The simile has a double import: the 'witlings' are neither one thing nor the other, and besides, like mules, they are barren.
41. *Insects*] The word was applied to earth-worms, snails, and even rogs, and also to insignificant and despicable persons.
43. *equivocal*] The (supposed) production of plants and animals without parents; spontaneous generation.

Where Beams of warm *Imagination* play,
The *Memory*'s soft Figures melt away.
One *Science* only will one *Genius* fit;   60
So *vast* is Art, so *narrow* Human Wit;
Not only bounded to *peculiar Arts*,
But oft in *those*, confin'd to *single Parts*.
Like Kings we lose the Conquests gain'd before,
By vain Ambition still to make them more: 65
Each might his *sev'ral Province* well command,
Wou'd all but *stoop* to what they *understand*.
     First follow N A T U R E, and your Judgment frame
By her just Standard, which is still the same:
Unerring Nature, still divinely bright,   70
One *clear*, *unchang'd*, and *Universal* Light,
Life, Force, and Beauty, must to all impart,
At once the *Source*, and *End*, and *Test* of *Art*.
Art from that Fund each *just Supply* provides,
Works *without Show*, and *without Pomp* presides: 75
In some fair Body thus th' informing Soul
With Spirits feeds, with Vigour fills the whole,
Each Motion guides, and ev'ry Nerve sustains;
It self unseen, but in th' *Effects*, remains.
Some, to whom Heav'n in Wit has been profuse,   80
Want as much more, to turn it to its use;
For *Wit* and *Judgment* often are at strife,
Tho' meant each other's Aid, like *Man* and *Wife*.
'Tis more to *guide* than *spur* the Muse's Steed;
Restrain his Fury, than provoke his Speed;   85
The winged Courser, like a gen'rous Horse,
Shows most true Mettle when you *check* his Course.
     Those R U L E S of old *discover'd*, not *devis'd*,
Are *Nature* still, but *Nature Methodiz'd*;
Nature, like *Liberty*, is but restrain'd   90
By the same Laws which first *herself* ordain'd.
     Hear how learn'd *Greece* her useful Rules indites,
When to repress, and when indulge our Flights:

59. *soft*] The metaphor seems to be taken from waxen figures melting
in the sunshine.
61. *Art*] Scholarship, learning, science.
68. NATURE] The cosmos, which in its order, regularity, and harmony,
reflects the order and harmony in the Divine Mind of its Creator.
76. *informing*] Endowing with a form, or essential character.
80-4. An assertion of the complementary relationship of wit and
judgment against those who set them apart as opposed faculties.
86. *gen'rous*] Applied to animals means *spirited*.

High on *Parnassus'* Top her Sons she show'd,
And pointed out those arduous Paths they trod,   95
Held from afar, aloft, th' Immortal Prize,
And urg'd the rest by equal Steps to rise;
Just *Precepts* thus from great *Examples* giv'n,
She drew from *them* what they deriv'd from *Heav'n.*
The gen'rous Critick *fann'd* the *Poet's Fire*,   100
And taught the World, *with Reason* to *Admire.*
Then Criticism the Muse's Handmaid prov'd,
To dress her Charms, and make her more belov'd;
But following Wits from that Intention stray'd;
Who cou'd not win the Mistress, woo'd the Maid;   105
Against the Poets *their own Arms* they turn'd,
Sure to hate most the Men from whom they *learn'd.*
So modern *Pothecaries,* taught the Art
By *Doctor's Bills* to play the *Doctor's Part,*
Bold in the Practice of *mistaken Rules,*   110
Prescribe, apply, and call their *Masters Fools.*
Some on the Leaves of ancient Authors prey,
Nor Time nor Moths e'er spoil'd so much as they:
Some dryly plain, without Invention's Aid,
Write dull *Receits* how Poems may be made: 115
These leave the Sense, their Learning to display,
And those explain the Meaning quite away.
    You then whose Judgment the right Course wou'd steer,
Know well each ANCIENT'S proper *Character,*
His *Fable, Subject, Scope* in ev'ry Page,   120
Religion, Country, Genius of his *Age:*
Without all these at once before your Eyes,
Cavil you may, but never *Criticize.*

98. *Nec enim artibus editis factum est ut argumenta inveniremus, sed dicta sunt omnia antequam præciperentur, mox ea scriptores observata & collecta ediderunt.* Quintil. ⟨*Inst. Orat.* v x 120⟩. [P]

108–11. A reference to the controversy between the apothecary and the physician. Though they lacked formal medical training, the apothecaries had learned enough to usurp, especially among the poor, the doctor's role. Because of high fees charged for drugs, many apothecaries prospered exceedingly. The College of Physicians proposed a plan for giving free medical advice to the poor, and opened a dispensary in 1696, where drugs were sold at cost. The apothecaries charged that this was a mere device to get the profits of the drug trade into the physicians' hands.

109. *Bills*] Medical prescriptions or recipes.

119. *proper Character*] Pope here reflects the increasing interest in the historical method in criticism.

123. *Cavil you may but never criticise*] The author after this verse

Be *Homer's* Works your *Study*, and *Delight*,
Read them by Day, and meditate by Night,   125
Thence form your Judgment, thence your Maxims bring,
And trace the Muses *upward* to their *Spring*;
Still with *It self compar'd*, his *Text* peruse;
And let your *Comment* be the *Mantuan Muse*.
    When first young *Maro* in his boundless Mind   130
A Work t' outlast Immortal *Rome* design'd,
Perhaps he seem'd *above* the Critick's Law,
And but from *Nature's Fountains* scorn'd to draw:
But when t'examine ev'ry Part he came,
Nature and *Homer* were, he found, the *same*:   135
Convinc'd, amaz'd, he checks the bold Design,⎫
And Rules as strict his labour'd Work confine, ⎬
As if the *Stagyrite* o'erlook'd each Line.   ⎭
Learn hence for Ancient *Rules* a just Esteem;
To copy *Nature* is to copy *Them*.   140
    Some Beauties yet, no Precepts can declare,
For there's a *Happiness* as well as *Care*.

---

originally inserted the following, which he has however omitted in all
the editions:

> Zoilus, *had these been known, without a name*
> *Had dy'd, and* Perault *ne'er been damn'd to fame;*
> *The sense of sound Antiquity had reign'd,*
> *And sacred* Homer *yet been unprophan'd.*
> *None e'er had thought his comprehensive mind*⎫
> *To modern Customs, modern Rules confin'd;*   ⎬
> *Who for all Ages writ and all Mankind.*   ⎭

                                                         [P]
An allusion to the *Parallèle des Anciens et des Modernes*, in which
Perrault put the modern writers above the ancient and criticized Homer
severely.

129. *Mantuan Muse*] Virgil, born near Mantua.

130 f. Virgil, Eclog, 6. *Cum canerem Reges & Prœlia, Cynthius aurem
Vellit——*

It is a tradition preserved by *Servius*, that *Virgil* began with writing a
poem of the *Alban* and *Roman* affairs; which he found above his years,
and descended first to imitate *Theocritus* on rural subjects, and afterwards
to copy *Homer* in Heroic poetry. [P]

138. *Stagyrite*] Aristotle, born at Stagira in 384 B.C.

141–80. The influence of Longinus and the School of Taste is apparent
throughout. The belief that irregular genius is preferable to a cold and
flat correctness, that there is a criticism by *taste* as well as by *rules*, that
the success of a work of art may depend upon a quality difficult to define,
a *je ne sais quoi*, that a criticism of *beauties* is preferable to a criticism of
faults, that departures from poetic rules are like irregular but pleasing
objects in the natural world, is emphatic in the lines, and declares the lack
of rigour with which Pope adhered to the 'Rules'.

Musick resembles *Poetry*, in each
Are *nameless Graces* which no Methods teach,
And which a *Master-Hand* alone can reach.   145
If, where the *Rules* not far enough extend,
(Since Rules were made but to promote their End)
Some Lucky L I C E N C E answers to the full
Th' Intent propos'd, *that Licence is a Rule*.
Thus *Pegasus*, a nearer way to take,   150
May boldly deviate from the common Track.
Great Wits sometimes may *gloriously offend*,
And *rise* to *Faults* true Criticks *dare not mend*;
From *vulgar Bounds* with *brave Disorder* part,
And *snatch* a *Grace* beyond the Reach of Art,   155
Which, without passing thro' the *Judgment*, gains
The *Heart*, and all its End *at once* attains.
In *Prospects*, thus, some *Objects* please our Eyes,
Which *out of* Nature's *common Order* rise,
The shapeless *Rock*, or hanging *Precipice*.   160
But tho' the *Ancients* thus their *Rules* invade,
(As *Kings* dispense with *Laws* Themselves have made)
Moderns, beware! Or if you must offend
Against the *Precept*, ne'er transgress its *End*,
Let it be *seldom*, and *compell'd by Need*,   165
And have, at least, *Their Precedent* to plead.
The Critick else proceeds without Remorse,
Seizes your Fame, and puts his Laws in force.
   I know there are, to whose presumptuous Thoughts
Those *Freer Beauties*, ev'n in *Them*, seem Faults: 170
Some Figures *monstrous* and *mis-shap'd* appear,
Consider'd *singly*, or beheld too *near*,
Which, but *proportion'd* to their *Light*, or *Place*,
Due Distance *reconciles* to Form and Grace.
A prudent Chief not always must display   175
His Pow'rs in *equal Ranks*, and *fair Array*,
But with th' *Occasion* and the *Place* comply,
Conceal his Force, nay seem sometimes to *Fly*.

146. *If, where the rules, &c.*] *Neque enim rogationibus plebisue scitis sancta sunt ista Præcepta, sed hoc quicquid est, Utilitas excogitavit; Non negabo autem sic utile esse plerumque; verum si eadem illa nobis aliud suadebit utilitas, hanc, relictis magistrorum autoritatibus* [sic], *sequemur.* Quintil. lib. ii. cap. 13 ⟨6–7⟩. [P]

158–60. The approval of the wilder and more irregular aspects of nature suggests the influence of Longinus.

168. *Seizes*] Here used probably in the legal sense: 'to take possession of . . . in pursuance of a judicial order' (*OED*).

Those oft are *Stratagems* which *Errors* seem,
Nor is it *Homer Nods*, but *We* that *Dream*.   180
  Still green with Bays each *ancient* Altar stands,
Above the reach of *Sacrilegious* Hands,
Secure from *Flames*, from *Envy's* fiercer Rage,
Destructive *War*, and all-involving *Age*.
See, from *each Clime* the Learn'd their Incense bring; 185
Hear, in *all Tongues* consenting *Pæans* ring!
In Praise so just, let ev'ry Voice be join'd,
And fill the *Gen'ral Chorus* of *Mankind*!
Hail *Bards Triumphant*! born in *happier Days*;
Immortal Heirs of *Universal* Praise!   190
Whose Honours with Increase of Ages *grow*,
As Streams roll down, *enlarging* as they flow!
Nations *unborn* your mighty Names shall sound,
And Worlds applaud that must not yet be *found*!
Oh may some Spark of *your* Cœlestial Fire   195
The last, the meanest of your Sons inspire,
(That on weak Wings, from far, pursues your Flights;
Glows while he *reads*, but *trembles* as he *writes*)
To teach vain Wits a Science *little known*,
T' *admire* Superior Sense, and *doubt* their own!   200

  Of all the Causes which conspire to blind
Man's erring Judgment, and misguide the Mind,
What the weak Head with strongest Byass rules,
Is *Pride*, the *never-failing Vice of Fools*.
Whatever Nature has in *Worth* deny'd,   205
She gives in large Recruits of *needful Pride*;
For as in *Bodies*, thus in *Souls*, we find
What wants in *Blood* and *Spirits*, swell'd with *Wind*;
Pride, where Wit fails, steps in to our Defence,
And fills up all the *mighty Void* of *Sense*!   210

180. *Modeste, & circumspecto judicio de tantis viris pronunciandum est, ne quod (quod plerisque accidit) damnent quod non intelligunt. Ac si necesse est in alteram errare partem, omnia eorum legentibus placere, quam multa displicere maluerim.* Quintil. ⟨lib. x i 26.⟩ [P]

184. *all-involving Age*] The four great causes of the ravage amongst ancient writings are here alluded to: The destruction of the *Alexandrine* and *Palatine* libraries by fire; the fiercer rage of *Zoilus* and *Mævius* and their followers against Wit; the irruption of the *Barbarians* into the empire; and the long reign of Ignorance and Superstition in the cloisters.

186. *consenting*] In harmony, in concord; unanimous.

203. *Byass*] A term in bowls: the construction of a bowl which imparts an oblique motion.

206. *Recruits*] Additional supplies.

If once right Reason drives *that Cloud* away,
Truth breaks upon us with *resistless Day*;
Trust not your self; but your Defects to know,
Make use of ev'ry *Friend*—and ev'ry *Foe*.
   A *little Learning* is a dang'rous Thing;   215
Drink deep, or taste not the *Pierian* Spring:
There *shallow Draughts* intoxicate the Brain,
And drinking *largely* sobers us again.
Fir'd at first Sight with what the *Muse* imparts,
In *fearless Youth* we tempt the Heights of Arts,   220
While from the bounded *Level* of our Mind,
Short Views we take, nor see the *Lengths behind*,
But *more advanc'd*, behold with strange Surprize
New, distant Scenes of *endless* Science rise!
So pleas'd at first, the towring *Alps* we try,   225
Mount o'er the Vales, and seem to tread the Sky;
Th' Eternal Snows appear already past,
And the first *Clouds* and *Mountains* seem the last:
But *those attain'd*, we tremble to survey
The growing Labours of the lengthen'd Way,   230
Th' *increasing* Prospect *tires* our wandring Eyes,
Hills peep o'er Hills, and *Alps* on *Alps* arise!
   A perfect Judge will *read* each Work of Wit
With the same Spirit that its Author *writ*,
Survey the *Whole*, nor seek slight Faults to find,   235
Where *Nature moves*, and *Rapture warms* the Mind;
Nor lose, for that malignant dull Delight,
The *gen'rous Pleasure* to be charm'd with Wit.
But in such Lays as neither *ebb*, nor *flow*,
Correctly cold, and *regularly low*,   240
That shunning Faults, one quiet *Tenour* keep;
We cannot *blame* indeed—but we may *sleep*.
In Wit, as Nature, what affects our Hearts
Is not th' Exactness of peculiar Parts;
'Tis not a *Lip*, or *Eye*, we Beauty call,   245
But the joint Force and full *Result* of *all*.
Thus when we view some well-proportion'd Dome,
(The *World*'s just Wonder, and ev'n *thine* O *Rome*!)

216. *Pierian Spring*] A spring sacred to the Pierides, a surname of the
Muses.
   220. *tempt*] Attempt.
   233 ff. *Diligenter legendum est, ac pæne ad scribendi sollicitudinem: Nec
per partes modo scrutanda sunt omnia, sed perlectus liber utique ex integro
resumendus.* Quintilian. ⟨*Inst. Orat.*, x i 20.⟩ [P]

No single Parts unequally surprize;
All comes *united* to th' admiring Eyes;   250
No monstrous Height, or Breadth, or Length appear;
The *Whole* at once is *Bold*, and *Regular*.
    Whoever thinks a faultless Piece to see,
Thinks what ne'er was, nor is, nor e'er shall be.
In ev'ry Work regard the *Writer's End*,   255
Since none can compass more than they *Intend*;
And if the *Means* be just, the *Conduct* true,
Applause, in spite of trivial Faults, is due.
As Men of Breeding, sometimes Men of Wit,
T' avoid *great Errors*, must the *less* commit,   260
Neglect the Rules each *Verbal Critick* lays,
For *not* to know some Trifles, is a Praise.
Most Criticks, fond of some subservient Art,
Still make the *Whole* depend upon a *Part*,
They talk of *Principles*, but Notions prize,   265
And All to one lov'd Folly Sacrifice.
    Once on a time, *La Mancha*'s Knight, they say,
A certain *Bard* encountring on the Way,
Discours'd in Terms as just, with Looks as Sage,
As e'er cou'd *Dennis*, of the *Grecian* Stage;   270
Concluding all were desp'rate Sots and Fools,
Who durst depart from *Aristotle*'s Rules.
Our Author, happy in a Judge so nice,
Produc'd his Play, and beg'd the Knight's Advice,
Made him observe the *Subject* and the *Plot*,   275
The *Manners*, *Passions*, *Unities*, what not?
All which, exact to *Rule* were brought about,
Were but a *Combate in the Lists* left out.
What! Leave the Combate out? Exclaims the Knight;
Yes, or we must renounce the *Stagyrite*.   280
Not so by Heav'n (he answers in a Rage)
Knights, Squires, and Steeds, must enter on the Stage.
So vast a Throng the Stage can ne'er contain.
Then build a New, or act it in a Plain.
    Thus Criticks, of less *Judgment* than *Caprice*,   285
Curious, not *Knowing*, not *exact*, but *nice*,
Form *short Ideas*; and offend in *Arts*

261. *Verbal Critick*] One who pays too much attention to detail, and
sacrifices the spirit to the letter of the rules.
267. Pope found the episode in *A Continuation of the Comical History
Of the most Ingenious Knight, Don Quixote De la Mancha*, chap. x, bk III
(1705).

(As most in *Manners*) by a *Love to Parts*.
  Some to *Conceit* alone their Taste confine,
And glitt'ring Thoughts struck out at ev'ry Line;   290
Pleas'd with a Work where nothing's just or fit;
One *glaring Chaos* and *wild Heap* of *Wit:*
Poets like Painters, thus, unskill'd to trace
The *naked Nature* and the *living Grace*,
With *Gold* and *Jewels* cover ev'ry Part,   295
And hide with *Ornaments* their *Want of Art*.
True Wit is *Nature* to Advantage drest,
What oft was *Thought*, but ne'er so well *Exprest*,
Something, whose Truth convinc'd at Sight we find,
That gives us back the Image of our Mind: 300
As Shades more sweetly recommend the Light,
So modest Plainness sets off sprightly Wit:
For *Works* may have more *Wit* than does 'em good,
As *Bodies* perish through Excess of *Blood*.
  Others for *Language* all their Care express,   305
And value *Books*, as Women *Men*, for *Dress*:
Their Praise is still—*The Stile is excellent*:
The *Sense*, they humbly take upon Content.
Words are like *Leaves*; and where they most abound,
Much *Fruit* of *Sense* beneath is rarely found.   310
False Eloquence, like the *Prismatic Glass*,
Its gawdy Colours spreads on *ev'ry place*;
The Face of Nature we no more Survey,
All glares *alike*, without *Distinction* gay:
But true *Expression*, like th' unchanging *Sun,*⎫   315
Clears, and *improves* whate'er it shines upon,⎬
It *gilds* all Objects, but it *alters* none.⎭
Expression is the *Dress* of *Thought*, and still
Appears more *decent* as more *suitable*;
A vile Conceit in pompous Words exprest,   320
Is like a Clown in regal Purple drest;
For diff'rent *Styles* with diff'rent *Subjects* sort,
As several Garbs with Country, Town, and Court.
Some by *Old Words* to Fame have made Pretence;

297 ff. *True Wit*] *Naturam intueamur, hanc sequamur: id facillimè*
accipiunt animi quod agnoscunt. Quintil. lib. viii c. 3 ⟨71⟩. [P]
  308. *take upon Content*] To accept without question or examination.
  322 f. The subjects appropriate to 'Country, Town, and Court' are
perhaps, respectively, pastoral, satire or comedy, and epic.
  324. *Abolita & abrogata retinere, insolentiæ cujusdam est, & frivolæ in*
parvis jactantiæ. Quintil. lib. i. c. 6 ⟨20⟩.
  Opus est ut verba à vetustate repetita neque crebra sint, neque manifesta

Ancients in *Phrase,* meer Moderns in their *Sense!*   325
Such *labour'd Nothings,* in so *strange* a Style,
Amaze th'unlearn'd, and make the Learned *Smile.*
Unlucky, as *Fungoso* in the Play,
These Sparks with aukward Vanity display
What the Fine Gentleman wore *Yesterday!*   330
And but so mimick ancient Wits at best,
As Apes our Grandsires in their *Doublets drest.*
In *Words,* as *Fashions,* the same Rule will hold;
Alike Fantastick, if *too New,* or *Old;*
Be not the *first* by whom the *New* are try'd,   335
Nor yet the *last* to lay the *Old* aside.
　　But most by *Numbers* judge a Poet's Song,
And *smooth* or *rough,* with them, is *right* or *wrong;*
In the bright *Muse* tho' thousand *Charms* conspire,
Her *Voice* is all these tuneful Fools admire,   340
Who haunt *Parnassus* but to please their Ear,
Not mend their Minds; as some to *Church* repair,
Not for the *Doctrine,* but the *Musick* there.
These *Equal Syllables* alone require,
Tho' oft the Ear the *open Vowels* tire,   345
While *Expletives* their feeble Aid *do* join,
And ten low Words oft creep in one dull Line,
While they ring round the same *unvary'd Chimes,*
With sure *Returns* of still *expected Rhymes.*
Where-e'er you find *the cooling Western Breeze,*   350
In the next Line, it *whispers thro' the Trees;*
If *Chrystal Streams with pleasing Murmurs creep,*
The Reader's threaten'd (not in vain) with *Sleep.*
Then, at the *last,* and *only* Couplet fraught

---

quia nil est odiosius affectatione, nec utique ab ultimis repetita temporibus.
Oratio cujus summa virtus est perspicuitas, quam sit vitiosa, si egeat inter-
prete? Ergo ut novorum optima erunt maximè vetera, ita veterum maximè
nova. Idem ⟨39–41⟩. [P]
　　328.—*unlucky as* Fungoso] *See* Ben. Johnson's *Every Man in his*
Humour. [P]
　　The allusion is to *Every Man out of his Humour.*
　　337.　　*Quis populi sermo est? quis enim? nisi carmina molli*
　　　　　　Nunc demum numero fluere, ut per læve severos
　　　　　　Effundat junctura ungues: scit tendere versum,
　　　　　　Non secus ac si oculo rubricam dirigat uno.
　　　　　　　　　　　　　　　　Persius, Sat. 1 ⟨63–6⟩. [P]
　　345. *Fugiemus crebras vocalium concursiones, quæ vastam atque hiantem*
orationem reddunt. Cic. ad Heren. lib. iv ⟨12⟩. *Vide etiam* Quintil. lib.
ix. c. 4 ⟨33⟩. [P]

With some *unmeaning* Thing they call a *Thought*,   355
A *needless Alexandrine* ends the Song,
That like a wounded Snake, drags its slow length along.
Leave such to tune their own dull Rhimes, and know
What's *roundly smooth*, or *languishingly slow*;
And praise the *Easie Vigor* of a Line,   360
Where *Denham*'s Strength, and *Waller*'s Sweetness join.
True Ease in Writing comes from Art, not Chance,
As those move easiest who have learn'd to dance.
'Tis not enough no Harshness gives Offence,
The *Sound* must seem an *Eccho* to the *Sense*.   365
Soft is the Strain when *Zephyr* gently blows,
And the *smooth Stream* in *smoother Numbers* flows;
But when loud Surges lash the sounding Shore,
The *hoarse, rough Verse* shou'd like the *Torrent* roar.

When *Ajax* strives, some Rock's vast Weight to throw,
The Line too *labours*, and the Words move *slow*;   371
Not so, when swift *Camilla* scours the Plain,
Flies o'er th'unbending Corn, and skims along the Main.
Hear how *Timotheus*' vary'd Lays surprize,
And bid Alternate Passions fall and rise!   375
While, at each Change, the Son of *Lybian Jove*
Now *burns* with Glory, and then *melts* with Love;
Now his *fierce Eyes* with *sparkling Fury* glow;
Now *Sighs* steal out, and *Tears begin to flow*:
Persians and *Greeks* like *Turns of Nature* found,   380
And the *World's Victor* stood subdu'd by *Sound!*
The Pow'r of Musick all our Hearts allow;
And what *Timotheus* was, is *Dryden* now.

361. *Denham's Strength*] Cf. Dryden, *Epistle Dedicatory of the Rival Ladies* (*Essays*, I 7): 'This sweetness of Mr. Waller's lyric poesy was afterwards followed in the epic by Sir John Denham, in his *Cooper's Hill*, a poem which your Lordship knows for the majesty of the style.'

Waller's Sweetness] Pope told Spence, p. 24: 'In versification there is a sensible difference between softness and sweetness that I could distinguish from a boy. Thus on the same points, Dryden will be found to be softer, and Waller sweeter.'

374. *See* Alexander's Feast, *or* the Power of Music; *an Ode by Mr. Dryden*. [P]
Dryden introduces into his ode the Theban musician Timotheus, who
to his breathing Flute,
And sounding Lyre,
Cou'd swell the Soul to rage, or kindle soft Desire.

376. *Libyan Jove*] When Alexander visited the oracle of Zeus Ammon in the oasis of Siwah in Libya, he was proclaimed son of the god.

Avoid *Extreams*; and shun the Fault of such,
Who still are pleas'd *too little*, or *too much*.   385
At ev'ry Trifle scorn to take Offence,
That always shows *Great Pride*, or *Little Sense*;
Those *Heads* as *Stomachs* are not sure the best
Which nauseate all, and nothing can digest.
Yet let not each gay *Turn* thy Rapture move,   390
For Fools *Admire*, but Men of Sense *Approve*;
As things seem *large* which we thro' *Mists* descry,
Dulness is ever apt to *Magnify*.
       Some *foreign* Writers, some our *own* despise;
The *Ancients* only, or the *Moderns* prize: 395
(Thus *Wit*, like *Faith*, by each Man is apply'd
To *one small Sect*, and All are *damn'd beside*.)
Meanly they seek the Blessing to confine,
And force *that Sun* but on a *Part* to Shine;
Which not alone the *Southern Wit* sublimes,   400
But ripens Spirits in cold *Northern Climes*;
Which from the first has shone on *Ages past*,
Enlights the *present*, and shall warm the *last*:
(Tho' *each* may feel *Increases* and *Decays*,
And see now *clearer* and now *darker Days*)   405
Regard not then if Wit be *Old* or *New*,
But blame the *False*, and value still the *True*.
       Some ne'er advance a Judgment of their own,
But *catch* the *spreading Notion* of the Town;
They reason and conclude by *Precedent*,   410
And own *stale Nonsense* which they ne'er invent.
Some judge of Authors' *Names*, not *Works*, and then
Nor praise nor blame the *Writings*, but the *Men*.
Of all this *Servile Herd* the worst is He
That in *proud Dulness* joins with *Quality*,   415
A constant Critick at the Great-man's Board,
To *fetch and carry* Nonsense for my Lord.
What *woful stuff* this Madrigal wou'd be,
In some starv'd Hackny Sonneteer, or me?
But let a *Lord* once own the *happy Lines*,   420
How the *Wit brightens*! How the *Style refines*!

390. *Turn*] An iterative or echoing pattern of words.
400. *sublimes*] To exalt, but also perhaps, in the context of 'ripens' in the next line, to 'cause (the juices of a plant) to rise, and thereby rarefy and purify them' (*OED*).
419. *Hackny*] 'Doing or ready to do work for hire' (*OED*).
Sonneteer] Not a writer of sonnets, but a 'minor or indifferent poet' (*OED*).

Before *his* sacred Name flies ev'ry Fault,
And each *exalted* Stanza *teems* with *Thought*!
   The *Vulgar* thus through *Imitation* err;
As oft the *Learn'd* by being *Singular*;   425
So much they scorn the Crowd, that if the Throng
By *Chance* go right, they *purposely* go wrong;
So Schismatics the *plain Believers* quit,
And are but damn'd for having *too much Wit*.
   Some praise at Morning what they blame at Night; 430
But always think the *last* Opinion *right*.
A Muse by these is like a Mistress us'd,
This hour she's *idoliz'd*, the next *abus'd*,
While their weak Heads, like Towns unfortify'd,
'Twixt Sense and Nonsense daily change their Side.   435
Ask them the Cause; *They're wiser still*, they say;
And still to Morrow's wiser than to Day.
We think our *Fathers* Fools, so *wise* we grow;
Our *wiser Sons*, no doubt, will think *us* so.
Once *School-Divines* this zealous Isle o'erspread;   440
Who knew most *Sentences* was *deepest read*;
Faith, Gospel, All, seem'd made to be *disputed*,
And none had *Sense enough to be Confuted*.
Scotists and *Thomists*, now, in Peace remain,
Amidst their *kindred Cobwebs* in *Duck-Lane*.   445
If *Faith* it self has *diff'rent Dresses* worn,
What wonder *Modes* in *Wit* shou'd take their Turn?

441. *Sentences*] An allusion to such works as Peter Lombard's *Libri quattuor sententiarum*, designed 'to place before the student, in as strictly logical a form as practicable, the views (*sententiae*) of the fathers and all the great doctors of the church upon the chief and most difficult points in the Christian belief. Conceived with the purpose of allaying and preventing, it really stimulated, controversy'.

444. *Scotists and Thomists*] Conflicts between followers of the Franciscan Duns Scotus (1265 or 1275–1308), Doctor Subtilis, and the Dominican Thomas Aquinas (c. 1227–1274), Doctor Angelicus, dominated the intellectual life of the 14th century. In the Renaissance Duns Scotus became for humanists the symbol of an utter misuse of the human reason. From his name derives the word *dunce*.

445. *Cobwebs in Duck-Lane*] A place where old and second-hand books were sold formerly, near *Smithfield*. [P]

447. Between Verse 449 and 450 ⟨447 and 448⟩:

> *The rhyming Clowns that gladded* Shakespear's *age,*
> *No more with crambo entertain the stage.*
> *Who now in Anagrams their Patron praise,*
> *Or sing their Mistress in Acrostic lays?*
> *Ev'n pulpits pleas'd with merry puns of yore;*
> *Now all are banish'd to the* Hibernian *shore!*

Oft, leaving what is Natural and fit,
The *current Folly* proves the *ready Wit*,
And Authors think their Reputation safe,   450
Which lives as long as *Fools* are pleas'd to *Laugh*.
  Some valuing those of their own *Side*, or *Mind*,
Still make themselves the measure of Mankind;
Fondly we think we honour Merit then,
When we but praise *Our selves* in *Other Men*.   455
Parties in *Wit* attend on those of *State*,
And publick Faction doubles private Hate.
Pride, *Malice*, *Folly*, against *Dryden* rose,
In various Shapes of *Parsons*, *Criticks*, *Beaus*;
But *Sense* surviv'd, when *merry Jests* were past;   460
For rising Merit will *buoy up* at last.
Might he return, and bless once more our Eyes,
New *Blackmores* and new *Milbourns* must arise;
Nay shou'd great *Homer* lift his awful Head,
Zoilus again would start up from the Dead.   465
Envy will *Merit* as its *Shade* pursue,
But like a Shadow, proves the *Substance* true;
For envy'd Wit, like *Sol* Eclips'd, makes known
Th' *opposing Body's* Grossness, not its *own*.
When first that Sun too powerful Beams displays,   470
It draws up Vapours which obscure its Rays;

> *Thus leaving what was natural and fit,*
> *The current folly prov'd their ready wit;*
> *And authors thought their reputation safe,*
> *Which liv'd as long as fools were pleas'd to laugh.* [P]

'Crambo' is a game 'in which one player gives a word or line of verse to which each of the others has to find a rime'.

459. *Parsons, Criticks, Beaus*] The parsons were the Rev. Jeremy Collier who, in his *A Short View of the Profaneness and Immorality of the English Stage* (1698), accused Dryden of profanity, lewdness, and blasphemy, and the Rev. Luke Milbourne, whose *Notes on Dryden's Virgil* (1698) was full of tedious and carping criticisms against Dryden's tr. of Virgil's *Eclogues* and *Georgics*. Among the more important contemporary 'critics' were Thomas Shadwell, who engaged in a bitter feud with Dryden in the 1680's; Elkanah Settle, who initiated an attack on Dryden in 1674; Sir Richard Blackmore, who attacked Dryden in his *A Satyr Against Wit* and in *Prince Arthur*, bk VI; Gerard Langbaine, who was hostile to Dryden in his *An Account of the English Dramatic Poets*. The 'beaus' included George Villiers, Duke of Buckingham, one of the authors of *The Rehearsal* (1671), and John Wilmot, Earl of Rochester, who satirized Dryden in his *An Allusion to Horace The 10th Satyr of the 1st Book*.

465. Zoilus, a Greek grammarian of the third or fourth century B.C., known for his severe and captious criticisms of Homer.

But ev'n those Clouds at last adorn its Way,
Reflect new Glories, and augment the Day.
    Be thou the *first* true Merit to befriend;
His Praise is lost, who stays till *All* commend;   475
Short is the Date, alas, of *Modern Rhymes*;
And 'tis but just to let 'em live *betimes*.
No longer now that Golden Age appears,
When *Patriarch-Wits* surviv'd a *thousand Years*;
Now Length of *Fame* (our *second* Life) is lost,   480
And bare Threescore is all ev'n That can boast:
Our Sons their Fathers' *failing Language* see,
And such as *Chaucer* is, shall *Dryden* be.
So when the faithful *Pencil* has design'd
Some *bright Idea* of the Master's Mind,   485
Where a *new World* leaps out at his command,
And ready Nature waits upon his Hand;
When the ripe Colours *soften* and *unite*,
And sweetly *melt* into just Shade and Light,
When mellowing Years their full Perfection give,   490
And each Bold Figure just begins to *Live*;
The *treach'rous Colours* the fair Art betray,
And all the bright Creation fades away!
    Unhappy *Wit*, like most mistaken Things,
Attones not for that *Envy* which it brings.   495
In *Youth* alone its empty Praise we boast,
But soon the Short-liv'd Vanity is lost!
Like some fair *Flow'r* the early *Spring* supplies,
That gaily Blooms, but ev'n in blooming *Dies*.
What is this *Wit* which must our Cares employ?   500
The *Owner's Wife*, that *other Men* enjoy,
Then most our *Trouble* still when most *admir'd*,
And still the more we *give*, the more *requir'd*;
Whose Fame with *Pains* we guard, but lose with *Ease*,
Sure *some* to *vex*, but never *all* to *please*;   505
'Tis what the *Vicious fear*, the *Virtuous shun*;
By *Fools* 'tis *hated*, and by *Knaves undone*!
    If *Wit* so much from *Ign'rance* undergo,
Ah let not *Learning* too commence its Foe!
Of old, those met *Rewards* who cou'd *excel*,   510
And such were *Prais'd* who but *endeavour'd well*:

480 f. The impermanent nature of the English language was a common
complaint in Pope's time.
    509. In his *Satyr against Wit* Sir R. Blackmore tried to set learning in
opposition to wit.

Tho' *Triumphs* were to *Gen'rals* only due,
Crowns were reserv'd to grace the *Soldiers* too.
Now, they who reach *Parnassus'* lofty Crown,
Employ their Pains to spurn some others down;   515
And while Self-Love each jealous Writer rules,
Contending Wits become the *Sport of Fools:*

But still the *Worst* with most Regret commend,
For each *Ill Author* is as bad a *Friend.*
To what base Ends, and by what abject Ways,   520
Are Mortals urg'd thro' *Sacred Lust of Praise!*
Ah ne'er so *dire* a *Thirst of Glory* boast,
Nor in the *Critick* let the *Man* be lost!
Good-Nature and *Good-Sense* must ever join;
To Err is *Humane*; to Forgive, *Divine.*   525
  But if in Noble Minds some Dregs remain,
Not yet purg'd off, of Spleen and sow'r Disdain,
Discharge that Rage on more Provoking Crimes,
Nor fear a Dearth in these Flagitious Times.
No Pardon vile *Obscenity* should find,   530
Tho' *Wit* and *Art* conspire to move your Mind;
But *Dulness* with *Obscenity* must prove
As Shameful sure as *Impotence* in *Love.*
In the fat Age of Pleasure, Wealth, and Ease,
Sprung the rank Weed, and thriv'd with large Increase;
When *Love* was all an easie Monarch's Care;   536
Seldom at *Council*, never in a *War:*
Jilts rul'd the State, and Statesmen *Farces* writ;
Nay *Wits* had *Pensions*, and *young Lords* had *Wit:*

513-15. *Crowns*] Crowns of various kinds were awarded, at the time of a general's triumph, to soldiers who had distinguished themselves in the field: the *corona civica* to one who had saved a fellow-soldier's life, the golden *corona muralis* to the first man to storm an enemy wall. Pope seems to apply the ideas of both the *corona civica* and the *corona muralis* to poets in an almost literal (and highly ironic) way in ll. 514 f.: those poets who scale the heights of Parnassus gain its 'crown'; but then, instead of saving or aiding (like soldiers in an assault) those behind them, they rather kick them down the heights.

521. *Sacred*] The latinism *sacred* means *accursed*.

525. *Humane*] A common earlier spelling of 'human'.

536. *easie Monarch's*] Charles II.

537. *never in a War*] Charles commanded an army which was defeated at the Battle of Worcester, Sept. 3, 1651.

538. *Jilts rul'd the State*] A 'jilt' here means a 'kept mistress' (*OED*). Alluding to Lady Castlemaine, and the Duchess of Portsmouth.

  Statesmen Farces writ] The allusion is to the Duke of Buckingham's part in the writing of *The Rehearsal* (1671).

539. *Wits had Pensions*] The contrary was nearer the truth.

The Fair sate panting at a *Courtier's Play*,   540
And not a Mask went *un-improv'd* away:
The modest Fan was lifted up no more,
And Virgins *smil'd* at what they *blush'd* before—
The following Licence of a Foreign Reign
Did all the Dregs of bold *Socinus* drain;   545
Then Unbelieving Priests reform'd the Nation,
And taught more *Pleasant* Methods of Salvation;
Where Heav'ns Free Subjects might their *Rights* dispute,
Lest God himself shou'd seem too *Absolute*.
Pulpits their *Sacred Satire* learn'd to spare,   550
And Vice *admir'd* to find a *Flatt'rer there* !
Encourag'd thus, Witt's *Titans* brav'd the Skies,
And the Press groan'd with Licenc'd *Blasphemies*—
These Monsters, Criticks! with your Darts engage,
Here point your Thunder, and exhaust your Rage!   555
Yet shun their Fault, who, *Scandalously nice*,
Will needs *mistake* an Author *into Vice*;
All seems Infected that th' Infected spy,
As all looks yellow to the Jaundic'd Eye.

LEARN then what MORALS Criticks ought to show,
For 'tis but *half* a *Judge's Task*, to *Know*.   561

540. *a Courtier's Play*] A reference to such courtiers as Sir Charles
Sedley, the undoubted author of at least three plays.

541. While the mask was worn by ladies of quality immediately after
the Restoration, a few years later it apparently was given over, owing to
its convenience for intrigue, to women of the town. The use of masks by
theatre-audiences was forbidden in 1704.

544. Possibly a reference to the policy of increased toleration, especially
toward the Nonconformists, which characterized William III's reign, and
to the lapsing of the Licensing Act of 1663, thereby permitting the
publication of books Pope and others would regard as heretical and
blasphemous.

545. *bold Socinus*] Laelius Socinus (Lelio Sozzini, 1525–62) rejected
the doctrines of the divinity of Christ and of the atonement or satisfaction for sin by Christ. Socinianism developed in England into
Unitarianism.

545. *The Author has omitted two lines which stood here, as containing a*
National Reflection, *which in his stricter judgment he could not but dis-
approve, on any People whatever.* [P]

546 f. Bishops Burnet, Kennett, and other 'unbelieving priests',
usually Whigs in their politics, taught that the government of God, like
that of the king, was a limited, not an absolute monarchy, and that men
were free to yield or to withhold their allegiance. The passage thus
bears directly on contemporary disputes over the doctrines of divine
right and of non-resistance and passive obedience to the 'Supreme
Power'.

552. *Witt's Titans*] The deistic writers.

'Tis not enough, Taste, Judgment, Learning, join;
In all you speak, let Truth and Candor shine:
That not alone what to your *Sense* is due,
All may allow; but seek your *Friendship* too.   565
   Be *silent* always when you *doubt* your Sense;
And *speak,* tho' *sure,* with *seeming Diffidence*:
Some positive persisting Fops we know,
Who, if *once wrong,* will needs be *always so*;
But you, with Pleasure own your Errors past,   570
And make each Day a *Critick* on the last.
   'Tis not enough your Counsel still be *true,*
Blunt Truths more Mischief than *nice Falshoods* do;
Men must be *taught* as if you taught them *not*;
And Things *unknown* propos'd as Things *forgot*:   575
Without *Good Breeding,* *Truth* is disapprov'd;
That only makes *Superior* Sense *belov'd.*
   Be Niggards of Advice on no Pretence;
For the *worst Avarice* is that of *Sense*:
With mean Complacence ne'er betray your Trust,   580
Nor be so *Civil* as to prove *Unjust*;
Fear not the Anger of the Wise to raise;
Those best can *bear Reproof,* who *merit Praise.*
   'Twere well, might Criticks still this Freedom take;
But *Appius* reddens at each Word you speak,   585
And *stares, Tremendous*! with a *threatning Eye,*
Like some *fierce Tyrant* in *Old Tapestry*!
Fear most to tax an *Honourable* Fool,
Whose Right it is, *uncensur'd* to be dull;
Such without *Wit* are Poets when they please,   590
As without *Learning* they can take *Degrees.*

563. *Candor*] Sweetness of temper, openness or kindness of mind.
571. *a Critick on the last*] That is, a *criticism.*
586. *This picture was taken to himself by* John Dennis, *a furious old Critic by profession, who, upon no other provocation, wrote against this Essay and its author, in a manner perfectly lunatic: For, as to the mention made of him in ver. 270, he took it as a Compliment, and said it was treacherously meant to cause him to overlook this Abuse of his Person.* [P]
Pope applied to Dennis the name of one of the characters in his tragedy *Appius and Virginia* (Drury Lane, Feb. 5, 1709), who was as sensitive to criticism as his creator. The play was withdrawn after a run of four nights, a failure which made Pope's allusion to Appius all the more stinging.
586. *stares, Tremendous*] The stare was one of Dennis's characteristics, and 'tremendous' a favourite epithet.
588-91. *Honourable . . . Degrees*] Degrees could be conferred upon privy councillors and others without requiring them to fulfil any of the conditions imposed upon other candidates.

Leave dang'rous *Truths* to unsuccessful *Satyrs*,
And *Flattery* to fulsome *Dedicators*,
Whom, when they *Praise*, the World believes no more,
Than when they promise to give *Scribling* o'er.   595
'Tis best sometimes your Censure to restrain,
And *charitably* let the Dull be *vain*:
Your Silence there is better than your *Spite*,
For who can *rail* so long as they can *write*?
Still humming on, their drowzy Course they keep,   600
And *lash'd* so long, like *Tops*, are lash'd *asleep*.
False Steps but help them to renew the Race,
As after *Stumbling*, Jades will *mend* their Pace.
What Crouds of these, impenitently bold,
In *Sounds* and jingling *Syllables* grown old,   605
Still *run on* Poets in a raging Vein,
Ev'n to the Dregs and *Squeezings* of the *Brain*;
Strain out the last, dull droppings of their Sense,
And Rhyme with all the *Rage* of *Impotence*!
    Such shameless *Bards* we have; and yet 'tis true,   610
There are as mad, abandon'd *Criticks* too.
The Bookful Blockhead, ignorantly read,
With *Loads* of *Learned Lumber* in his Head,
With his own Tongue still edifies his Ears,
And always *List'ning to Himself* appears.   615
All Books he reads, and all he reads assails,
From *Dryden*'s *Fables* down to *Durfey*'s *Tales*.
With *him*, most Authors steal their Works, or buy;
Garth did not write his own *Dispensary*.
Name a new *Play*, and *he's* the Poet's *Friend*,   620
Nay show'd his Faults—but when wou'd Poets mend?
No Place so Sacred from such Fops is barr'd,
Nor is *Paul's Church* more safe than *Paul's Church-yard*:
Nay, fly to *Altars*; *there* they'll talk you dead;
For *Fools* rush in where *Angels* fear to tread.   625

612. *The Bookful Blockhead*] *Nihil pejus est iis, qui paullum aliquid ultra
primas litteras progressi, falsam sibi scientiæ persuasionem induerunt: Nam
& cedere præcipiendi peritis indignantur, & velut jure quodam potestatis, quo
ferè hoc hominum genus intumescit, imperiosi, atque interim sævientes,
Stultitiam suam perdocent.* Quintil. lib. i. ch. i ⟨8⟩. [P]

619. A common slander at that time in prejudice of that deserving
author. Our poet did him this justice, when that slander most prevail'd;
and it is now (perhaps the sooner for this very verse) dead and forgotten.
[P]

623. Between Verse 625 and 626 ⟨623 and 624⟩;
          In vain you shrug, and sweat, and strive to fly,
          These know no Manners, but in Poetry:

Distrustful *Sense* with modest Caution speaks;
It still *looks home*, and *short Excursions* makes;
But *ratling Nonsense* in full *Vollies* breaks;
And never shock'd, and never turn'd aside,
Bursts out, resistless, with a thundring Tyde!   630
   But where's the Man, who Counsel *can* bestow,
Still *pleas'd* to *teach*, and yet not *proud* to *know*?
Unbiass'd, or by *Favour* or by *Spite*;
Not *dully prepossest*, nor *blindly right*;
Tho' Learn'd, well-bred; and tho' well-bred, sincere; 635
Modestly bold, and Humanly severe?
Who to a *Friend* his Faults can freely show,
And gladly praise the Merit of a *Foe*?
Blest with a *Taste* exact, yet unconfin'd;
A *Knowledge* both of *Books* and *Humankind*;   640
Gen'rous Converse; a *Soul* exempt from *Pride*;
And *Love to Praise*, with *Reason* on his Side?
   Such once were *Criticks*, such the Happy *Few*,
Athens and *Rome* in better Ages knew.
The mighty *Stagyrite* first left the Shore,   645
Spread all his Sails, and durst the Deeps explore;
He steer'd securely, and discover'd far,
Led by the Light of the *Mæonian Star*.
Poets, a *Race* long unconfin'd and free,
Still fond and proud of *Savage Liberty*,   650
Receiv'd his Laws, and stood convinc'd 'twas fit
Who conquer'd *Nature*, shou'd preside o'er *Wit*.

They'll stop a hungry Chaplain in his Grace,
To treat of Unities *of* Time *and* Place.   [P]

623. Pope's statement is literally true, for in the seventeenth century
St. Paul's Cathedral was used regularly as a meeting-place to transact
business. The aisles were the recognized haunts of loiterers, needy
adventurers, and broken-down gallants.

640. *and Humankind*] Pope's conception of the ideal critic is closely
related to that of the 'poète honnête homme' in Boileau, *L'Art Poét.*, IV
121-4.

641. *Gen'rous Converse*] Well-bred intercourse.

648. Between Verse 650 and 651 ⟨648 and 649⟩;

    He when all Nature was subdu'd before,
    Like his great pupil, sigh'd, and long'd for more:
    Fancy's wild regions yet unvanquish'd lay,
    A boundless empire, and that own'd no sway.
    Poets, &c.   [P]

Mæonian Star] Homer. Maeonia was the name often given to Lydia,
where Homer was supposed to have been born.

Horace still charms with graceful Negligence,
And without Method *talks* us into Sense,
Will like a *Friend* familiarly convey   655

The *truest Notions* in the *easiest way*.
He, who Supream in Judgment, as in Wit,
Might boldly censure, as he boldly writ,
Yet *judg'd* with *Coolness* tho' he sung with *Fire*;
His *Precepts* teach but what his *Works* inspire.   660
Our *Criticks* take a contrary Extream,
They *judge* with *Fury*, but they *write* with *Fle'me*:
Nor suffers *Horace* more in wrong *Translations*
By *Wits*, than *Criticks* in as wrong *Quotations*.
  See *Dionysius Homer*'s Thoughts refine,   665
And call new Beauties forth from ev'ry Line!
  Fancy and Art in gay *Petronius* please,
The *Scholar's Learning*, with the *Courtier's Ease*.
  In grave *Quintilian*'s copious Work we find
The justest *Rules*, and clearest *Method* join'd;   670
Thus *useful Arms* in Magazines we place,
All rang'd in *Order*, and dispos'd with *Grace*,
But less to please the Eye, than arm the Hand,
Still fit for Use, and ready at Command.
  Thee, bold *Longinus*! all the Nine inspire,   675
And bless *their Critick* with a *Poet's Fire*.
An ardent *Judge*, who Zealous in his Trust,
With *Warmth* gives Sentence, yet is always *Just*;
Whose *own Example* strengthens all his Laws,
And *Is himself* that great *Sublime* he draws.   680
  Thus long succeeding Criticks justly reign'd,
Licence repress'd, and *useful Laws* ordain'd;
Learning and *Rome* alike in Empire grew,
And *Arts* still *follow'd* where her *Eagles flew*;
From the same Foes, at last, both felt their Doom,   685
And the same Age saw *Learning* fall, and *Rome*.
With *Tyranny*, then *Superstition* join'd,

656. *easiest*] In the smoothest and most flowing style.
664. *than Criticks*] Than by critics.
665. Dionysius *of* Halicarnassus. [P]
671 ff. Here Pope applies to Quintilian one of that writer's own favourite
comparisons. See *Inst. Orat.*, II i 12; VII x 14.
684. *Eagles flew*] The Eagles carried as standards by the Roman armies.
686. *Rome*] Pope here uses an older pronunciation. The modern pronunciation of the word derives from the French, but it had been used by
Dryden and Cowley, and elsewhere in the *Essay* by Pope himself (see
l. 248).

As that the *Body*, this enslav'd the *Mind*;
Much was *Believ'd*, but little *understood*,
And to be *dull* was constru'd to be *good*;   690
A *second* Deluge Learning thus o'er-run,
And the *Monks* finish'd what the *Goths* begun.
  At length, *Erasmus*, that *great*, *injur'd* Name,
(The *Glory* of the Priesthood, and the *Shame*!)
Stemm'd the *wild Torrent* of a *barb'rous Age*,   695
And drove those *Holy Vandals* off the Stage.
  But see! each *Muse*, in *Leo*'s Golden Days,
Starts from her Trance, and trims her wither'd Bays!
Rome's ancient *Genius*, o'er its *Ruins* spread,
Shakes off the *Dust*, and rears his rev'rend Head!   700
Then *Sculpture* and her *Sister-Arts* revive;
Stones leap'd to *Form*, and *Rocks* began to *live*;
With *sweeter Notes* each *rising Temple* rung;
A *Raphael* painted, and a *Vida* sung!
Immortal *Vida*! on whose honour'd Brow   705

690. Between Verse 690 and 691 the author omitted these two:
    Vain Wits and Critics were no more allow'd,
    When none but Saints had Licence to be proud. [P]

693. Erasmus (1466–1536) traditionally has occupied an ambiguous
position in the history of religious controversy. Although ordained a
priest, he attacked the abuses of the clergy and influenced in important
respects the course of the Reformation. Congenial as he was to the Protestant and humanist spirit of his time, he yet remained loyal to the
Roman Catholic Church.

694. Erasmus was the 'glory' of the priesthood because of his learning,
and its 'shame' because of the treatment he received at its hands.

697. *Leo's Golden Days*] *Saecla Leonis, Saecla Aurea.* The election of
Leo X to the Papal throne (1513) was hailed by humanists on all sides as
the end of an iron age and as a return to a Golden Age of art and learning.
He was patron to such scholars, poets, and artists as Lascaris, Bembo,
Raphael, Michelangelo, Bramante. The humanist tradition in which Pope
wrote exaggerated heavily the very real praise due to Leo X's patronage
of art. Much that his predecessors initiated and accomplished was
credited to Leo's reign.

698. *trims*] Perhaps here means *restores*.

702 ff. This whole paragraph recalls the myth of Amphion, who moved
the stones of Thebes into place by the music of his lyre. Pope is imitating
the passage in Ovid (*Met.*, xv 418–35) which recalls Amphion and also
describes the transfer of glory from ancient city to ancient city, and finally
suggests that Rome is to be the capital of the world.

704. *Raphael*] For many in Pope's age Raphael Santi (1483–1520) was
pre-eminently 'sublime' in his genius.

705. *Immortal Vida*] M. Hieronymus Vida, *an excellent* Latin *Poet,
who writ an Art of Poetry in Verse. He flourish'd in the time of* Leo *the
Tenth.* [P]

Vida (1490?–1566) wrote didactic poems in Latin, and Pope had care-

The Poet's *Bays* and Critick's *Ivy* grow:
Cremona now shall ever boast thy Name,
As next in Place to *Mantua*, next in Fame!
 But soon by Impious Arms from *Latium* chas'd,
Their *ancient Bounds* the banish'd Muses past;   710
Thence Arts o'er all the *Northern World* advance;
But *Critic Learning* flourish'd most in *France*.
The *Rules*, a Nation born to serve, obeys,
And *Boileau* still in Right of *Horace* sways.
But *we*, brave *Britons*, *Foreign Laws* despis'd,   715
And kept *unconquer'd*, and *unciviliz'd*,
Fierce for the *Liberties of Wit*, and bold,
We still defy'd the *Romans*, as *of old*.
Yet *some* there were, among the *sounder Few*
Of those who *less presum'd*, and *better knew*,   720
Who durst assert the *juster Ancient Cause*,
And here *restor'd* Wit's *Fundamental Laws*.
Such was the Muse, whose Rules and Practice tell,
Nature's chief Master-piece is writing well.

---

fully studied his *Poetica*. The game of Ombre in *The Rape of the Lock*
had a measure of debt to Vida's *Game of Chess*.
 706. *Critick's Ivy*] Pope seems to have been the first to crown a critic
with ivy, normally associated not only with poets but with learned men.
 709. *Impious Arms*] The reference is to the Sack of Rome in 1527 by
the troops of the Emperor Charles V under the leadership of the Duke
of Bourbon.
 713. A reflexion on the servility of the French, who submitted to the
despotic government of Louis XIV., as contrasted with the independence
of the 'brave Britons', who had within the limits of half-a-century cut off
the head of one king and expelled another.
 724. *Essay on Poetry, by the Duke of* Buckingham. Our Poet is not the
only one of his time who complimented this *Essay*, and its noble Author.
Mr. Dryden had done it very largely in the Dedication to his translation
of the Æneid; and Dr. Garth in the first Edition of his Dispensary says,
 The Tyber now no courtly Gallus sees,
 But smiling Thames enjoys his Normanbys.
Tho' afterwards omitted, when parties were carried so high in the reign of
Queen Anne, as to allow no commendation to an opposite in Politics.
The Duke was all his life a steady adherent to the Church of England-
Party, yet an enemy to the extravagant measures of the Court in the
reign of Charles II. On which account after having strongly patronized
Mr. Dryden, a coolness succeeded between them on that poet's absolute
attachment to the Court, which carried him some lengths beyond what
the Duke could approve of. This Nobleman's true character had been
very well marked by Mr. Dryden before,
                                  the Muse's friend,
 Himself a Muse. In Sanadrin's debate
 True to his prince, but not a slave of state.
               Abs. and Achit. ⟨1 877–9⟩

Such was *Roscomon*—not more *learn'd* than *good*,   725
With Manners gen'rous as his Noble Blood;
To him the Wit of *Greece* and *Rome* was known,
And ev'ry Author's *Merit*, but his own.
Such late was *Walsh*,—the Muse's Judge and Friend,
Who justly knew to blame or to commend;   730
To Failings *mild*, but *zealous* for Desert;
The *clearest Head*, and the *sincerest Heart*.
This humble Praise, lamented *Shade*! receive,
This Praise at least a grateful Muse may give!
The Muse, whose early Voice you taught to Sing,   735
Prescrib'd her Heights, and prun'd her tender Wing,
(Her Guide now lost) no more attempts to *rise*,
But in low Numbers short Excursions tries:
Content, if hence th' Unlearn'd their Wants may view,
The Learn'd reflect on what before they knew: 740
Careless of *Censure*, nor too fond of *Fame*,
Still pleas'd to *praise*, yet not afraid to *blame*,
Averse alike to *Flatter*, or *Offend*,
Not *free* from Faults, nor yet too vain to *mend*.

Our Author was more happy, he was honour'd very young with his
friendship, and it continued till his death in all the circumstances of a
familiar esteem. [P]

725. *Roscomon*] Wentworth Dillon, fourth Earl of Roscommon (1633?–
1685), translated Horace's *Art of Poetry* (1680) and wrote *An Essay on
Translated Verse* (1684), in the second edn (1685) of which he was one of
the first publicly to praise Milton's *Par. Lost*.

734 f. *Muse*] Pope himself.

prun'd] To trim or dress the feathers with the beak.

Epistle to Miss Blount, With the Works of Voiture

[written c. 1710; published, Lintot's
Miscellany, 1712]

In these gay Thoughts the Loves and Graces shine,
And all the Writer lives in ev'ry Line;
His easie Art may happy Nature seem,
Trifles themselves are Elegant in him.
Sure to charm all was his peculiar Fate,   5
Who without Flatt'ry pleas'd the Fair and Great;
Still with Esteem no less convers'd than read;
With Wit well-natur'd, and with Books well-bred;
His Heart, his Mistress and his Friend did share;
His Time, the Muse, the Witty, and the Fair.   10
Thus wisely careless, innocently gay,
Chearful, he play'd the Trifle, Life, away,
'Til Fate scarce felt his gentle Breath supprest,
As smiling Infants sport themselves to Rest:
Ev'n Rival Wits did *Voiture*'s Death deplore,   15
And the Gay mourn'd who never mourn'd before;
The truest Hearts for *Voiture* heav'd with Sighs;
Voiture was wept by all the brightest Eyes;
The *Smiles* and *Loves* had dy'd in *Voiture*'s Death,
But that for ever in his Lines they breath.   20

   Let the strict Life of graver Mortals be
A long, exact, and serious Comedy,
In ev'ry Scene some Moral let it teach,
And, if it can, at once both Please and Preach:
Let mine, an innocent gay Farce appear,   25
And more Diverting still than Regular,
Have Humour, Wit, a native Ease and Grace;
Tho' not too strictly bound to Time and Place:
Criticks in Wit, or Life, are hard to please,
Few write to those, and none can live to these.   30

   Too much *your Sex* is by their Forms confin'd,
Severe to all, but most to Womankind;
Custom, grown blind with Age, must be your Guide
Your Pleasure is a Vice, but not your Pride;

Title: *Voiture*] Vincent de Voiture (1598–1648), French poet and
letter-writer.

By nature yielding, stubborn but for Fame;   35
Made Slaves by Honour, and made Fools by Shame.
Marriage may all those petty Tyrants chace,
But sets up One, a greater, in their Place;
Well might you wish for Change, by those accurst,
But the last Tyrant ever proves the worst.   40
Still in Constraint your suff'ring Sex remains,
Or bound in formal, or in real Chains;
Whole Years neglected for some Months ador'd,
The fawning Servant turns a haughty Lord;
Ah quit not the free Innocence of Life!   45
For the dull Glory of a virtuous Wife!
Nor let false Shows, or empty Titles please:
Aim not at Joy, but rest content with Ease.
    The Gods, to curse *Pamela* with her Pray'rs,
Gave the gilt Coach and dappled *Flanders* Mares,   50
The shining Robes, rich Jewels, Beds of State,
And to compleat her Bliss, a Fool for Mate.
She glares in *Balls*, *Front-boxes*, and the *Ring*,
A vain, unquiet, glitt'ring, wretched Thing!
Pride, Pomp, and State but reach her outward Part,   55
She sighs, and is no *Dutchess* at her Heart.
    But, Madam, if the Fates withstand, and you
Are destin'd *Hymen*'s willing Victim too,
Trust not too much your now resistless Charms,
Those, Age or Sickness, soon or late, disarms;   60
Good Humour only teaches Charms to last,
Still makes new Conquests, and maintains the past:
Love, rais'd on Beauty, will like That decay,
Our Hearts may bear its slender Chain a Day,
As flow'ry Bands in Wantonness are worn;   65
A Morning's Pleasure, and at Evening torn:
This binds in Ties more easie, yet more strong,
The willing Heart, and only holds it long.
    Thus *Voiture*'s early Care still shone the same,
And *Monthausier* was only chang'd in Name: 70
By this, ev'n now they live, ev'n now they charm,

53. *The Ring*] Where the carriages of fashionable society drove in Hyde Park.

61. cf. p. 238, l. 30; p. 569, l. 292.

69. *Voiture's early care*] Madamoiselle Paulet [P]. Daughter of Charles Paulet, Secretary of the King's Bed-Chamber.

70. *Monthausier*] Julie Lucine d'Angennes, duchesse de Monthausier (1607–71), eldest daughter of the Marquise de Rambouillet, one of Voiture's principal correspondents.

Their Wit still sparkling and their Flames still warm.
  Now crown'd with Myrtle, on th' *Elysian* Coast,
Amid those Lovers, joys his gentle Ghost,
Pleas'd while with Smiles his happy Lines you view,   75
And finds a fairer *Rambouïllet* in you.
The brightest Eyes of *France* inspir'd his Muse,
The brightest Eyes of *Britain* now peruse,
And dead as living, 'tis our Author's Pride,
Still to charm those who charm the World beside.   80

The Temple of Fame
Written in the Year 1711 [published 1715]

ADVERTISEMENT

The Hint of the following Piece was taken from Chaucer's House of Fame. *The Design is in a manner entirely alter'd, the Descriptions and most of the particular Thoughts*[1] *my own: Yet I could not suffer it to be printed without this Acknowledgement, or think a Concealment of this Nature the less unfair for being common. The Reader who would compare this with* Chaucer, *may begin with his Third Book of* Fame, *there being nothing in the Two first Books that answers to their Title.*[2]

[NOTE]

Some modern Criticks, from a pretended Refinement of Taste, have declar'd themselves unable to relish allegorical Poems. 'Tis not easy to penetrate into the meaning of this Criticism; for if Fable be allow'd one of the chief Beauties, or as Aristotle *calls it, the very Soul of Poetry, 'tis hard to comprehend how that Fable should be the less valuable for having a Moral. The Ancients constantly made use of Allegories: My Lord* Bacon *has compos'd an express Treatise in proof of this, entitled,* The Wisdom of the Antients; *where the Reader may see several particular Fictions exemplify'd and explain'd with great Clearness, Judgment and Learning. The Incidents indeed, by which the Allegory is convey'd, must be vary'd, according to the different Genius or Manners of different Times: and they should never be spun too long, or too much clog'd with trivial Circumstances, or little Particularities. We find an uncommon Charm in Truth, when it is convey'd by this Side-way to our Understanding; and 'tis observable, that even in the most ignorant Ages this way of Writing has found Reception. Almost all the Poems in the old* Provençal *had this Turn; and from these it was that* Petrarch *took the Idea of his Poetry. We have his* Trionfi *in this kind; and* Boccace[3] *pursu'd in the same Track. Soon after* Chaucer *introduc'd it here, whose* Romaunt of the Rose, Court of Love, Flower and the Leaf,[4] House of Fame, *and some others of his Writings are Master-pieces of this sort. In Epick Poetry, 'tis true, too nice and exact a Pursuit of the Allegory is justly esteem'd*

---

[1] *particular Thoughts*] thoughts on particular heroes.
[2] *The Reader . . . Title*] Pope takes a few details from Book ii, and specifies two of them in his notes on 11 ff. and 428 ff.
[3] *Boccace*] Canto vi of Boccaccio's *Amorosa Visione* includes a *Triumpho di Gloria*.
[4] *Flower and the Leaf*] First suspected as apocryphal by Tyrwhitt.

a fault; and Chaucer *had the Discernment to avoid it in his* Knight's Tale, *which was an Attempt towards an Epick Poem.* Ariosto, *with less judgment, gave intirely into it in his* Orlando; *which tho carry'd to an Excess, had yet so much Reputation in* Italy, *that* Tasso *(who reduc'd Heroick Poetry to the juster Standard of the Antients) was forc'd to prefix to his Work a scrupulous Explanation of the Allegory of it, to which the Fable it-self could scarce have directed his Readers. Our Countryman* Spencer *follow'd, whose Poem is almost intirely allegorical, and imitates the manner of* Ariosto *rather than that of* Tasso. *Upon the whole, one may observe this sort of Writing (however discontinu'd of late) was in all Times so far from being rejected by the best Poets, that some of them have rather err'd by insisting on it too closely, and carrying it too far: And that to infer from thence that the Allegory it-self is vicious, is a presumptuous Contradiction to the Judgment and Practice of the greatest Genius's, both antient and modern.* [P]

In that soft Season when descending Showers
Call forth the Greens, and wake the rising Flowers;
When opening Buds salute the welcome Day,
And Earth relenting feels the Genial Ray;
As balmy Sleep had charm'd my Cares to Rest,   5
And Love it self was banish'd from my Breast,
(What Time the Morn mysterious Visions brings,
While purer Slumbers spread their golden Wings)
A Train of Phantoms in wild Order rose,
And, join'd, this Intellectual Scene compose.   10
   I stood, methought, betwixt Earth, Seas, and Skies;
The whole Creation open to my Eyes:
In Air self-ballanc'd hung the Globe below,
Where Mountains rise, and circling Oceans flow;
Here naked Rocks, and empty Wastes were seen,   15
There Tow'ry Cities, and the Forests green:
Here sailing Ships delight the wand'ring Eyes;
There Trees, and intermingl'd Temples rise:
Now a clear Sun the shining Scene displays,
The transient Landscape now in Clouds decays.   20
   O'er the wide Prospect as I gaz'd around,
Sudden I heard a wild promiscuous Sound,

4. *relenting*] 'melt[ing] under the influence of heat' (*OED*).
10. *Intellectual*] Ideal; perceived by the intellect, not the senses.
11 ff. Pope's note quotes Chaucer ii 389 ff.

Like broken Thunders that at distance roar,
Or Billows murm'ring on the hollow Shoar:
Then gazing up, a glorious Pile beheld,   25
Whose tow'ring Summit ambient Clouds conceal'd.
High on a Rock of Ice the Structure lay,
Steep its Ascent, and slipp'ry was the Way;
The wond'rous Rock like *Parian* Marble shone,
And seem'd to distant Sight of solid Stone.   30
Inscriptions here of various Names I view'd,
The greater Part by hostile Time subdu'd;
Yet wide was spread their Fame in Ages past,
And Poets once had promis'd they should last.
Some fresh ingrav'd appear'd of Wits renown'd;   35
I look'd again, nor cou'd their Trace be found.
Criticks I saw, that other Names deface,
And fix their own with Labour in their place:
Their own like others soon their Place resign'd,
Or disappear'd, and left the first behind.   40
Nor was the Work impair'd by Storms alone,
But felt th'Approaches of too warm a Sun;
For Fame, impatient of Extreams, decays
Not more by Envy than Excess of Praise.
Yet Part no Injuries of Heav'n cou'd feel,   45
Like Crystal faithful to the graving Steel:
The Rock's high Summit, in the Temple's Shade,
Nor Heat could melt, nor beating Storm invade.
There Names inscrib'd unnumber'd Ages past
From Time's first Birth, with Time it self shall last;   50
These ever new, nor subject to Decays,
Spread, and grow brighter with the Length of Days.
    So *Zembla*'s Rocks (the beauteous Work of Frost)
Rise white in Air, and glitter o'er the Coast;

26. *ambient*] 'surrounding as a fluid; circumfused' (*OED*).
27 ff. Pope's note quotes Chaucer iii 26 ff.
31 ff. Pope's note quotes Chaucer iii 46 ff.
41 ff. Pope's notes quote Chaucer iii 58 ff. 61 ff.
53–60. *Tho a strict Verisimilitude be not requir'd in the Descriptions of
this visionary and allegorical kind of Poetry, which admits of every wild
Object that Fancy may present in a Dream, and where it is sufficient if the
moral Meaning atone for the Improbability: Yet Men are naturally so
desirous of Truth, that a Reader is generally pleas'd, in such a Case, with
some Excuse or Allusion that seems to reconcile the Description to Probability
and Nature. The Simile here is of that sort, and renders it not wholly unlikely
that a Rock of Ice should remain for ever, by mentioning something like it
in the Northern Regions, agreeing with the Accounts of our modern Travellers.*
[P]

Pale Suns, unfelt, at distance roll away,   55
And on th' impassive Ice the Lightnings play:
Eternal Snows the growing Mass supply,
Till the bright Mountains prop th' incumbent Sky:
As *Atlas* fix'd, each hoary Pile appears,
The gather'd Winter of a thousand Years.   60
   On this Foundation *Fame*'s high Temple stands;
Stupendous Pile! not rear'd by mortal Hands.
Whate'er proud *Rome*, or artful *Greece* beheld,
Or elder *Babylon*, its Frame excell'd.
Four Faces had the Dome, and ev'ry Face   65
Of various Structure, but of equal Grace:
Four brazen Gates, on Columns lifted high,
Salute the diff'rent Quarters of the Sky.
Here fabled Chiefs in darker Ages born,
Or Worthys old, whom Arms or Arts adorn,   70
Who Cities rais'd, or tam'd a monstrous Race;
The Walls in venerable Order grace:
Heroes in animated Marble frown,
And Legislators seem to think in Stone.
   Westward, a sumptuous Frontispiece appear'd,   75
On Doric Pillars of white Marble rear'd,
Crown'd with an Architrave of antique Mold,
And Sculpture rising on the roughen'd Gold.
In shaggy Spoils here *Theseus* was beheld,
And *Perseus* dreadful with *Minerva*'s Shield: 80
There great *Alcides* stooping with his Toil,
Rests on his Club, and holds th' *Hesperian* Spoil.
Here *Orpheus* sings; Trees moving to the Sound
Start from their Roots, and form a Shade around:

---

65. *Dome*] in its meaning of (dignified) *building* (Latin, *domus*). Contrast l. 90 below.

65 ff. *The Temple is describ'd to be square, the four Fronts with open Gates facing the different Quarters of the World, as an Intimation that all Nations of the Earth may alike be receiv'd into it. The Western Front is of* Grecian *Architecture: the Dorick Order was peculiarly sacred to Heroes and Worthies. Those whose Statues are after mention'd, were the first Names of old* Greece *in Arms and Arts.* [P]

75. *Frontispiece*] 'The principal face or front of a building; "but the term is more usually applied to the decorated entrance of a building" ' (*OED*).

81 f. *This Figure of* Hercules *is drawn with an eye to the Position* [= posture] *of the famous Statue of* Farnese. [P]

83 ff. Orpheus and Amphion symbolize the civilizing virtues of poetry in primitive times.

Amphion there the loud creating Lyre   85
Strikes, and behold a sudden *Thebes* aspire!
Cythæron's Ecchoes answer to his Call,
And half the Mountain rolls into a Wall:
There might you see the length'ning Spires ascend,
The Domes swell up, the widening Arches bend,   90
The growing Tow'rs like Exhalations rise,
And the huge Columns heave into the Skies.
  The Eastern Front was glorious to behold,
With Diamond flaming, and *Barbaric* Gold.
There *Ninus* shone, who spread th' *Assyrian* Fame,   95
And the Great Founder of the *Persian* Name:
There in long Robes the Royal *Magi* stand,
Grave *Zoroaster* waves the circling Wand:
The Sage *Chaldæans* rob'd in White appear'd,
And *Brachmans* deep in desert Woods rever'd.   100
These stop'd the Moon, and call'd th' unbody'd Shades
To Midnight Banquets in the glimmering Glades;
Made visionary Fabricks round them rise,
And airy Spectres skim before their Eyes;
Of *Talismans* and *Sigils* knew the Pow'r,   105
And careful watch'd the Planetary Hour.
Superior, and alone, *Confucius* stood,
Who taught that useful Science, to be *good*.
  But on the South a long Majestic Race
Of *Ægypt*'s Priests the gilded Niches grace,   110
Who measur'd Earth, describ'd the Starry Spheres,
And trac'd the long Records of Lunar Years,
High on his Car *Sesostris* struck my View,
Whom scepter'd Slaves in golden Harness drew:

93–108. Cyrus *was the Beginning of the* Persian, *as* Ninus *was of the*
Assyrian *Monarchy. The* Magi *and* Chaldeans (*the chief of whom was*
Zoroaster) *employ'd their Studies upon Magick and Astrology, which was in
a manner almost all the Learning of the antient* Asian *People. We have scarce
any Account of a moral Philosopher except* Confucius, *the great Lawgiver
of the* Chinese, *who liv'd about two thousand Years ago.* [P]

104 f. A sigil was 'an occult sign or device supposed to have mysterious
powers' (*OED*); at a 'Planetary Hour' the planets stood in significant
conjunctions.

109–18. *The Learning of the old* Egyptian *Priests consisted for the most
part in Geometry and Astronomy: They also preserv'd the History of their
Nation. Their greatest Hero upon Record is* Sesostris, *whose Actions and
Conquests may be seen at large in* Diodorus, *&c. He is said to have caus'd the
Kings he vanquish'd to draw him in his Chariot. The Posture of his Statue,
in these Verses, is correspondent to the Description which* Herodotus *gives of
one of them remaining in his own time.* [P]

His Hands a Bow and pointed Jav'lin hold,   115
His Giant Limbs are arm'd in Scales of Gold.
Between the Statues Obelisks were plac'd,
And the Learn'd Walls with Hieroglyphics grac'd.
  Of *Gothic* Structure was the Northern Side,
O'er-wrought with Ornaments of barb'rous Pride.   120
There huge Colosses rose, with Trophies crown'd,
And *Runic* Characters were grav'd around:
There sate *Zamolxis* with erected Eyes,
And *Odin* here in mimick Trances dies.
There, on rude Iron Columns smear'd with Blood,   125
The horrid Forms of *Scythian* Heroes stood,
Druids and *Bards* (their once loud Harps unstrung)
And Youths that dy'd to be by Poets sung.
These and a Thousand more of doubtful Fame,
To whom old Fables gave a lasting Name,   130
In Ranks adorn'd the Temple's outward Face;
The Wall in Lustre and Effect like Glass,
Which o'er each Object casting various Dies,
Enlarges some, and others multiplies.
Nor void of Emblem was the mystic Wall,   135
For thus Romantick Fame increases all.
  The Temple shakes, the sounding Gates unfold,
Wide Vaults appear, and Roofs of fretted Gold:
Rais'd on a thousand Pillars, wreath'd around
With Lawrel-Foliage, and with Eagles crown'd: 140
Of bright, transparent Beryl were the Walls,
The Freezes Gold, and Gold the Capitals:
As Heaven with Stars, the Roof with Jewels glows,
And ever-living Lamps depend in Rows.
Full in the Passage of each spacious Gate   145
The sage Historians in white Garments wait;

119 ff. *The Architecture is agreeable to that part of the World. The Learning of the* Northern *Nations lay more obscure than that of the rest.* Zamolxis *was the Disciple of* Pythagoras, *who taught the Immortality of the Soul to the* Scythians. Odin, *or* Woden, *was the great Legislator and Hero of the* Goths. *They tell us of him that being subject to Fits, he persuaded his Followers, that during those Trances he receiv'd Inspirations from whence he dictated his Laws. He is said to have been the Inventor of the* Runic *Characters.* [P]

127 ff. *These were the Priests and Poets of those People, so celebrated for their savage Virtue. Those heroick Barbarians accounted it a Dishonour to die in their Beds, and rush'd on to certain Death in the Prospect of an After-Life, and for the Glory of a Song from their Bards in Praise of their Actions.* [P]

132 ff. Pope's note quotes Chaucer iii 199 ff.

Grav'd o'er their Seats the Form of *Time* was found,
His Scythe revers'd, and both his Pinions bound.
Within, stood Heroes who thro' loud Alarms
In bloody Fields pursu'd Renown in Arms.   150
High on a Throne with Trophies charg'd, I view'd
The *Youth* that all things but himself subdu'd;
His Feet on Sceptres and *Tiara's* trod,
And his horn'd Head bely'd the *Lybian* God.
There *Cæsar*, grac'd with both *Minerva's*, shone;   155
Cæsar, the World's great Master, and his own;
Unmov'd, superior still in every State;
And scarce detested in his Country's Fate.
But chief were those who not for Empire fought,
But with their Toils their People's Safety bought: 160
High o'er the rest *Epaminondas* stood;
Timoleon, glorious in his Brother's Blood;
Bold *Scipio*, Saviour of the *Roman* State,
Great in his Triumphs, in Retirement great.
And wise *Aurelius*, in whose well-taught Mind ⎫   165
With boundless Pow'r unbounded Virtue join'd, ⎬
His own strict Judge, and Patron of Mankind. ⎭
    Much-suff'ring Heroes next their Honours claim,
Those of less noisy, and less guilty Fame,
Fair Virtue's silent Train: Supreme of these   170
Here ever shines the Godlike *Socrates*:
He whom ungrateful *Athens* cou'd expel,
At all times Just, but when he sign'd the Shell.
Here his Abode the martyr'd *Phocion* claims,
With *Agis*, not the last of *Spartan* Names: 175
Unconquer'd *Cato* shews the Wound he tore,
And *Brutus* his ill Genius meets no more.

147 f. The reversing of insignia or emblems indicated dishonour in heraldry.

152. Alexander *the Great: The* Tiara *was the Crown peculiar to the* Asian *Princes: His Desire to be thought the Son of* Jupiter Ammon *caus'd him to wear the Horns of that God, and to represent the same upon his Coins, which was continu'd by several of his Successors.* [P]

154. *bely*] = to counterfeit.

162. Timoleon *had sav'd the Life of his Brother* Timophanes *in the Battel between the* Argives *and* Corinthians; *but afterwards kill'd him when he affected the Tyranny, preferring his Duty to his Country to all the Obligations of Blood.* [P]

172-5. Aristides, *who for his great Integrity was distinguish'd by the Appellation of the* Just. *When his Countrymen would have banish'd him by the* Ostracism, *where it was the Custom for every Man to sign the Name of the Person he voted to Exile in an Oysters Shell; a Peasant, who could not write, came to* Aristides *to do it for him, who readily sign'd his own Name.* [P]

But in the Centre of the hallow'd Quire
Six pompous Columns o'er the rest aspire;
Around the Shrine it self of *Fame* they stand,   180
Hold the chief Honours, and the Fane command.
High on the first, the mighty *Homer* shone;
Eternal Adamant compos'd his Throne;
Father of Verse! in holy Fillets drest,
His Silver Beard wav'd gently o'er his Breast;   185
Tho' blind, a Boldness in his Looks appears,
In Years he seem'd, but not impair'd by Years.
The Wars of *Troy* were round the Pillar seen:
Here fierce *Tydides* wounds the *Cyprian* Queen;
Here *Hector* glorious from *Patroclus*' Fall,   190
Here dragg'd in Triumph round the *Trojan* Wall.
Motion and Life did ev'ry Part inspire,
Bold was the Work, and prov'd the Master's Fire;
A strong Expression most he seem'd t'affect,
And here and there disclos'd a brave Neglect.   195
A Golden Column next in Rank appear'd,
On which a Shrine of purest Gold was rear'd;
Finish'd the whole, and labour'd ev'ry Part,
With patient Touches of unweary'd Art:
The *Mantuan* there in sober Triumph sate,   200
Compos'd his Posture, and his Look sedate;
On *Homer* still he fix'd a reverend Eye,
Great without Pride, in modest Majesty.
In living Sculpture on the Sides were spread
The *Latian* Wars, and haughty *Turnus* dead;   205
Eliza stretch'd upon the fun'ral Pyre,
Æneas bending with his aged Sire:
Troy flam'd in burning Gold, and o'er the Throne
Arms and the Man in Golden Cyphers shone.
Four Swans sustain a Carr of Silver bright,   210

178–243. *In the midst of the Temple, nearest the Throne of* Fame, *are plac'd the greatest Names in Learning of all Antiquity. These are describ'd in such Attitudes as express their different Characters. The Columns on which they are rais'd are adorn'd with Sculptures, taken from the most striking Subjects of their Works; which Sculpture bears a Resemblance in its Manner and Character, to the Manner and Character of their Writings.* [P]

179 ff. Pope's notes quote Chaucer iii 331 ff., 375 ff.

196. Pope's note quotes Chaucer iii 391 ff.

198. *labour'd*] having had great pains expended on its decoration.

210–21. Pindar *being seated in a Chariot, alludes to the Chariot-Races he celebrated in the* Grecian *Games. The Swans are Emblems of* Poetry, *their soaring Posture intimates the Sublimity and Activity of his Genius.* Neptune *presided over the* Isthmian, *and* Jupiter *over the* Olympian *Games.* [P]

With Heads advanc'd, and Pinions stretch'd for Flight:
Here, like some furious Prophet, *Pindar* rode,
And seem'd to labour with th' inspiring God.
A-cross the Harp a careless Hand he flings,
And boldly sinks into the sounding Strings,   215
The figur'd Games of *Greece* the Column grace,
Neptune and *Jove* survey the rapid Race:
The Youths hang o'er their Chariots as they run;
The fiery Steeds seem starting from the Stone;
The Champions in distorted Postures threat,   220
And all appear'd Irregularly great.
    Here happy *Horace* tun'd th' *Ausonian* Lyre
To sweeter Sounds, and temper'd *Pindar*'s Fire:
Pleas'd with *Alcæus*' manly Rage t'infuse
The softer Spirit of the *Sapphick* Muse.   225
The polish'd Pillar diff'rent Sculptures grace;
A Work outlasting Monumental Brass.
Here smiling *Loves* and *Bacchanals* appear,
The *Julian* Star, and Great *Augustus* here.
The Doves that round the Infant Poet spread   230
Myrtles and Bays, hung hov'ring o'er his Head.

222. *Horace*] *This expresses the mixt Character of the Odes of* Horace.
The second of these Verses alludes to that Line of his:
        Spiritum Graiæ tenuem Camœnæ. [*Odes*, II xvi 38.]
As another which follows, to
        Exegi Monumentum ære perennius. [*Odes*, III xxx 1.]
    The Action of the Doves *hints at a passage in the 4th Ode of his third*
Book,
                Me fabulosæ Vulture in Appulo,
                Altricis extra limen Apuliæ,
                    Ludo fatigatumque somno,
                    Fronde nova puerum Palumbes
                Texêre; mirum quod foret omnibus—
                Ut tuto ab atris corpore viperis
                Dormirem & ursis: ut premerer sacra
                    Lauroque, collataque myrto,
                    Non sine Dis animosus infans.
Which may be thus english'd;
                While yet a Child, I chanc'd to stray,
                And in a Desart sleeping lay;
                The savage Race withdrew, nor dar'd
                To touch the Muses future Bard:
                But Cytheræa's *gentle Dove*
                    Myrtles *and* Bays *around me spread,*
                And crown'd your Infant Poet's Head,
                Sacred to Musick *and to* Love. [P]

Ausonian] = Italian.

Here in a Shrine that cast a dazling Light,
Sate fix'd in Thought the mighty *Stagyrite*;
His Sacred Head a radiant Zodiack crown'd,
And various Animals his Sides surround;   235
His piercing Eyes, erect, appear to view
Superior Worlds, and look all Nature thro'.
    With equal Rays immortal *Tully* shone,
The *Roman Rostra* deck'd the Consul's Throne:
Gath'ring his flowing Robe, he seem'd to stand,   240
In Act to speak, and graceful, stretch'd his Hand:
Behind, *Rome*'s *Genius* waits with *Civic* Crowns,
And the Great Father of his Country owns.
    These massie Columns in a Circle rise,
O'er which a pompous Dome invades the Skies: 245
Scarce to·the Top I stretch'd my aking Sight,
So large it spread, and swell'd to such a Height.
Full in the midst, proud *Fame*'s Imperial Seat
With Jewels blaz'd, magnificently great;
The vivid Em'ralds there revive the Eye;   250
The flaming Rubies shew their sanguine Dye;
Bright azure Rays from lively Saphirs stream,
And lucid Amber casts a Golden Gleam.
With various-colour'd Light the Pavement shone,
And all on fire appear'd the glowing Throne;   255
The Dome's high Arch reflects the mingled Blaze,

And forms a Rainbow of alternate Rays.
When on the *Goddess* first I cast my Sight,
Scarce seem'd her Stature of a Cubit's height,

But swell'd to larger Size, the more I gaz'd,   260
Till to the Roof her tow'ring Front she rais'd.
With her, the Temple ev'ry Moment grew,
And ampler *Vista's* open'd to my View,
Upward the Columns shoot, the Roofs ascend,
And Arches widen, and long Iles extend.   265
Such was her Form, as antient Bards have told,
Wings raise her Arms, and Wings her Feet infold;
A Thousand busy Tongues the Goddess bears,
And Thousand open Eyes, and Thousand list'ning Ears.
Beneath, in Order rang'd, the tuneful Nine   270
(Her Virgin Handmaids) still attend the Shrine:

238. *equal*] Combining the meanings (a) equal to the rays cast around
Aristotle, (b) even, equable.
259 ff. Pope's note quotes Chaucer iii 279 ff.
270 ff. Pope's notes quote Chaucer iii 307 ff., 431 ff.

With Eyes on Fame for ever fix'd, they sing;
For Fame they raise the Voice, and tune the String.
With Time's first Birth began the Heav'nly Lays,
And last Eternal thro' the Length of Days.   275
    Around these Wonders as I cast a Look,
The Trumpet sounded, and the Temple shook,
And all the Nations, summon'd at the Call,
From diff'rent Quarters fill the crowded Hall:
Of various Tongues the mingled Sounds were heard;   280
In various Garbs promiscuous Throngs appear'd;
Thick as the Bees, that with the Spring renew
Their flow'ry Toils, and sip the fragrant Dew,
When the wing'd Colonies first tempt the Sky,
O'er dusky Fields and shaded Waters fly,   285
Or settling, seize the Sweets the Blossoms yield,
And a low Murmur runs along the Field.
Millions of suppliant Crowds the Shrine attend,
And all Degrees before the Goddess bend;
The Poor, the Rich, the Valiant, and the Sage,   290
And boasting Youth, and Narrative old Age.
Their Pleas were diff'rent, their Request the same;
For Good and Bad alike are fond of Fame.
Some she disgrac'd, and some with Honours crown'd;
Unlike Successes equal Merits found.   295
Thus her blind Sister, fickle *Fortune* reigns,
And undiscerning, scatters Crowns and Chains.
    First at the Shrine the Learned World appear,
And to the Goddess thus prefer their Prayer:
Long have we sought t'instruct and please Mankind,   300
With Studies pale, with Midnight Vigils blind;
But thank'd by few, rewarded yet by none,
We here appeal to thy superior Throne:
On Wit and Learning the just Prize bestow,
For *Fame* is all we must expect below.   305
    The Goddess heard, and bade the Muses raise
The Golden Trumpet of eternal Praise:
From Pole to Pole the Winds diffuse the Sound,
That fills the Circuit of the World around:
Not all at once, as Thunder breaks the Cloud;   310
The Notes at first were rather sweet than loud:
By just degrees they ev'ry moment rise,
Fill the wide Earth, and gain upon the Skies.

284. *tempt*] Cf. *Windsor-Forest*, l. 389*n* (p. 209).
294 ff. Pope's note quotes Chaucer iii 448 ff.

At ev'ry Breath were balmy Odours shed,
Which still grew sweeter as they wider spread: 315
Less fragrant Scents th' unfolding Rose exhales,
Or Spices breathing in *Arabian* Gales.
  Next these the Good and Just, an awful Train,
Thus on their Knees address the sacred Fane.
Since living Virtue is with Envy curst, 320
And the best Men are treated like the worst,
Do thou, just Goddess, call our Merits forth,
And give each Deed th' exact intrinsic Worth.
Not with bare Justice shall your Act be crown'd,
(Said Fame) but high above Desert renown'd: 325
Let fuller Notes th' applauding World amaze,
And the loud Clarion labour in your Praise.
  This Band dismiss'd, behold another Crowd

Prefer'd the same Request, and lowly bow'd,
The constant Tenour of whose well-spent Days 330
No less deserv'd a just Return of Praise.
But strait the direful Trump of Slander sounds,
Thro' the big Dome the doubling Thunder bounds:

Loud as the Burst of Cannon rends the Skies,
The dire Report thro' ev'ry Region flies: 335
In ev'ry Ear incessant Rumours rung,
And gath'ring Scandals grew on ev'ry Tongue.
From the black Trumpet's rusty Concave broke
Sulphureous Flames, and Clouds of rolling Smoke:
The pois'nous Vapor blots the purple Skies, 340
And withers all before it as it flies.
  A Troop came next, who Crowns and Armour wore,
And proud Defiance in their Looks they bore:
For thee (they cry'd) amidst Alarms and Strife,
We sail'd in Tempests down the Stream of Life; 345
For thee whole Nations fill'd with Flames and Blood,
And swam to Empire thro' the purple Flood.
Those Ills we dar'd thy Inspiration own,
What Virtue seem'd, was done for thee alone.
Ambitious Fools! (the Queen reply'd, and frown'd) 350
Be all your Acts in dark Oblivion drown'd;
There sleep forgot, with mighty Tyrants gone,
Your Statues moulder'd, and your Names unknown.

318 ff. Pope's note quotes Chaucer iii 567 ff.
328 ff. Pope's note quotes Chaucer iii 516 ff.
340. *purple*] brilliant &c. (*OED*, sense 3 a).

A sudden Cloud strait snatch'd them from my Sight,
And each Majestic Phantom sunk in Night.   355
   Then came the smallest Tribe I yet had seen,
Plain was their Dress, and modest was their Mein.
Great Idol of Mankind! we neither claim
The Praise of Merit, nor aspire to Fame;
But safe in Desarts from th' Applause of Men,   360
Would die unheard of, as we liv'd unseen.
'Tis all we beg thee, to conceal from Sight
Those Acts of Goodness, which themselves requite.
O let us still the secret Joy partake,
To follow Virtue ev'n for Virtue's sake.   365
   And live there Men who slight immortal Fame?
Who then with Incense shall adore our Name?
But Mortals! know, 'tis still our greatest Pride,
To blaze those Virtues which the Good would hide.
Rise! Muses, rise! add all your tuneful Breath,   370
These must not sleep in Darkness and in Death.
She said: in Air the trembling Musick floats,
And on the Winds triumphant swell the Notes;
So soft, tho high, so loud, and yet so clear,
Ev'n list'ning Angels lean'd from Heaven to hear: 375
To farthest Shores th' Ambrosial Spirit flies,
Sweet to the World, and grateful to the Skies.
   Next these a youthful Train their Vows exprest,
With Feathers crown'd, with gay Embroid'ry drest;
Hither, they cry'd, direct your Eyes, and see   380
The Men of Pleasure, Dress, and Gallantry:
Ours is the Place at Banquets, Balls and Plays;
Sprightly our Nights, polite are all our Days;
Courts we frequent, where 'tis our pleasing Care
To pay due Visits, and address the Fair: 385
In fact, 'tis true, no Nymph we cou'd persuade,
But still in Fancy vanquish'd ev'ry Maid;
Of unknown Dutchesses leud Tales we tell,
Yet would the World believe us, all were well.
The Joy let others have, and we the Name,   390
And what we want in Pleasure, grant in Fame.

356 ff. Pope's note quotes Chaucer iii 613 ff.
376. *Spirit*] 'a breath (of wind or air)' (*OED*, sense iv 15).
377. This line is repeated at *Epil. to Satires*, Dial. ii 245 (p. 703).
378 ff. Pope's note quotes Chaucer iii 637 ff.
388. *unknown*] in a double sense of social and sexual knowledge.

The Queen assents, the Trumpet rends the Skies,
And at each Blast a Lady's Honour dies.
  Pleas'd with the strange Success, vast Numbers prest
Around the Shrine, and made the same Request: 395
What you (she cry'd) unlearn'd in Arts to please,
Slaves to your selves, and ev'n fatigu'd with Ease,
Who lose a Length of undeserving Days;
Wou'd you usurp the Lover's dear-bought Praise?
To just Contempt, ye vain Pretenders, fall,   400
The People's Fable, and the Scorn of all.
Strait the black Clarion sends a horrid Sound,
Loud Laughs burst out, and bitter Scoffs fly round,
Whispers are heard, with Taunts reviling loud,
And scornful Hisses run thro all the Croud.   405
  Last, those who boast of mighty Mischiefs done,
Enslave their Country, or usurp a Throne;
Or who their Glory's dire Foundation laid,
On Sovereigns ruin'd, or on Friends betray'd,
Calm, thinking Villains, whom no Faith cou'd fix,   410
Of crooked Counsels and dark Politicks;
Of these a gloomy Tribe surround the Throne,
And beg to make th' immortal Treasons known.
The Trumpet roars, long flaky Flames expire,
With Sparks, that seem'd to set the World on fire.   415
At the dread Sound, pale Mortals stood aghast,
And startled Nature trembled with the Blast.
  This having heard and seen, some Pow'r unknown
Strait chang'd the Scene, and snatch'd me from the Throne.
Before my View appear'd a Structure fair,   420
Its Site uncertain, if in Earth or Air;
With rapid Motion turn'd the Mansion round;
With ceaseless Noise the ringing Walls resound:
Not less in Number were the spacious Doors,
Than Leaves on Trees, or Sands upon the Shores;   425
Which still unfolded stand, by Night, by Day,
Pervious to Winds, and open ev'ry way.
As Flames by Nature to the Skies ascend,
As weighty Bodies to the Center tend,
As to the Sea returning Rivers roll,   430

---

406 ff. Pope's note quotes Chaucer iii 721 ff.
414. *Flake* = 'a detached portion of flame' (*OED*).
418 ff. Pope's note quotes Chaucer iii 828 ff.
428 ff. Pope's note quotes Chaucer ii 221 ff.

And the touch'd Needle trembles to the Pole:
Hither, as to their proper Place, arise
All various Sounds from Earth, and Seas, and Skies,
Or spoke aloud, or whisper'd in the Ear;
Nor ever Silence, Rest or Peace is here.   435

As on the smooth Expanse of Chrystal Lakes,
The sinking Stone at first a Circle makes;
The trembling Surface, by the Motion stir'd,
Spreads in a second Circle, then a third;
Wide, and more wide, the floating Rings advance,   440
Fill all the wat'ry Plain, and to the Margin dance.
Thus ev'ry Voice and Sound, when first they break,
On neighb'ring Air a soft Impression make;
Another ambient Circle then they move,
That, in its turn, impels the next above;   445
Thro undulating Air the Sounds are sent,
And spread o'er all the fluid Element.
   There various News I heard, of Love and Strife,
Of Peace and War, Health, Sickness, Death, and Life;
Of Loss and Gain, of Famine and of Store,   450
Of Storms at Sea, and Travels on the Shore,
Of Prodigies, and Portents seen in Air,
Of Fires and Plagues, and Stars with blazing Hair,
Of Turns of Fortune, Changes in the State,
The Falls of Fav'rites, Projects of the Great,   455
Of old Mismanagements, Taxations new—
All neither wholly false, nor wholly true.
   Above, below, without, within, around,
Confus'd, unnumber'd Multitudes are found,
Who pass, repass, advance, and glide away;   460
Hosts rais'd by Fear, and Phantoms of a Day.
Astrologers, that future Fates foreshew,
Projectors, Quacks, and Lawyers not a few;
And Priests and Party-Zealots, num'rous Bands
With home-born Lyes, or Tales from foreign Lands;   465
Each talk'd aloud, or in some secret Place,
And wild Impatience star'd in ev'ry Face:
The flying Rumours gather'd as they roll'd,

448 ff. Pope's note quotes Chaucer iii 871 ff.
453. *Stars . . . Hair*] = comets.
458 ff. Pope's note quotes Chaucer iii 944 ff.
463. *Projectors*] = 'promotor of bubble companies; a speculator'
(*OED*).

Scarce any Tale was sooner heard than told;
And all who told it, added something new, ⎫ 470
And all who heard it, made Enlargements too, ⎬
In ev'ry Ear it spread, on ev'ry Tongue it grew. ⎭
Thus flying East and West, and North and South,
News travel'd with Increase from Mouth to Mouth;
So from a Spark that kindled first by Chance, 475
With gath'ring Force the quick'ning Flames advance;
Till to the Clouds their curling Heads aspire,
And Tow'rs and Temples sink in Floods of Fire.
   When thus ripe Lyes are to perfection sprung,
Full grown, and fit to grace a mortal Tongue, 480
Thro thousand Vents, impatient forth they flow,
And rush in Millions on the World below.
Fame sits aloft, and points them out their Course,
Their Date determines, and prescribes their Force:
Some to remain, and some to perish soon, 485
Or wane and wax alternate like the Moon.
Around, a thousand winged Wonders fly,
Born by the Trumpet's Blast, and scatter'd thro the Sky.
   There, at one Passage, oft you might survey
A Lye and Truth contending for the way; 490
And long 'twas doubtful, both so closely pent,
Which first should issue thro the narrow Vent:
At last agreed, together out they fly,
Inseparable now, the Truth and Lye;
The strict Companions are for ever join'd, 495
And this or that unmix'd, no Mortal e'er shall find.
   While thus I stood, intent to see and hear,
One came, methought, and whisper'd in my Ear;
What cou'd thus high thy rash Ambition raise?
Art thou, fond Youth, a Candidate for Praise? 500
   'Tis true, said I, not void of Hopes I came,
For who so fond as youthful Bards of Fame?
But few, alas! the casual Blessing boast,
So hard to gain, so easy to be lost:
How vain that second Life in others' Breath, 505
Th' Estate which Wits inherit after Death!

---

489 ff. Pope's note quotes Chaucer iii 998 ff.
  497 ff.] *The hint is taken from a passage in another part of the third book* ⟨778 ff.⟩, *but here more naturally made the conclusion, with the addition of a* Moral *to the whole. In* Chaucer, *he only answers 'he came to see the place*⟨'⟩; *and the book ends abruptly, with his being surprized at the sight of a* Man of great authority, *and awaking in a fright.* [P]

Ease, Health, and Life, for this they must resign,
(Unsure the Tenure, but how vast the Fine!)
The Great Man's Curse without the Gains endure,
Be envy'd, wretched, and be flatter'd, poor;   510
All luckless Wits their Enemies profest,
And all successful, jealous Friends at best.
Nor Fame I slight, nor for her Favours call;
She comes unlook'd for, if she comes at all:
But if the Purchase costs so dear a Price,   515
As soothing Folly, or exalting Vice:
Oh! if the Muse must flatter lawless Sway,
And follow still where Fortune leads the way;
Or if no Basis bear my rising Name,
But the fall'n Ruins of Another's Fame: 520
Then teach me, Heaven! to scorn the guilty Bays;
Drive from my Breast that wretched Lust of Praise;
Unblemish'd let me live, or die unknown,
Oh grant an honest Fame, or grant me none!

Messiah

A SACRED ECLOGUE, IN IMITATION OF
VIRGIL'S POLLIO

[written c. 1712; published, *Spectator*, 1712]

ADVERTISEMENT

In reading several passages of the Prophet *Isaiah*, which foretell the coming of Christ and the felicities attending it, I could not but observe a remarkable parity between many of the thoughts, and those in the *Pollio* of *Virgil*. This will not seem surprizing when we reflect, that the Eclogue was taken from a *Sybilline* prophecy on the same subject. One may judge that *Virgil* did not copy it line by line, but selected such Ideas as best agreed with the nature of pastoral poetry, and disposed them in that manner which serv'd most to beautify his piece. I have endeavour'd the same in this imitation of him, tho' without admitting any thing of my own; since it was written with this particular view, that the reader by comparing the several thoughts might see how far the images and descriptions of the Prophet are superior to those of the Poet. But as I fear I have prejudiced them by my management, I shall subjoin the passages of *Isaiah*, and those of *Virgil*, under the same disadvantage of a literal translation. [P]

> Ye Nymphs of *Solyma* ! begin the Song:
> To heav'nly Themes sublimer Strains belong.
> The Mossie Fountains and the Sylvan Shades,
> The Dreams of *Pindus* and th' *Aonian* Maids,
> Delight no more—O Thou my Voice inspire   5
> Who touch'd *Isaiah*'s hallow'd Lips with Fire!
> Rapt into future Times, the Bard begun;
> A *Virgin* shall conceive, a *Virgin* bear a Son!

---

1. *Solyma*] The latter part of the Greek name for Jerusalem, Ἱεροσόλυμα.
4. *Pindus*] A mountain in Thessaly regarded as a seat of the Muses.
Aonian Maids] Aonia was another name for Boeotia. The Muses, who frequented Mt. Helicon in Boeotia, were called Aonides, the Aonian Maidens.
7. *Rapt*] Carried away *in spirit*, without bodily removal.
begun] The form was common in Pope's time.
8. *A Virgin shall conceive———All Crimes shall cease, &c.*] V I R G. E. 4.
v. 6.

> Jam redit & Virgo, redeunt Saturnia regna,
> Jam nova progenies cælo demittitur alto——
> Te duce, si qua manent sceleris vestigia nostri,

189

From *Jesse*'s Root behold a Branch arise,
Whose sacred Flow'r with Fragrance fills the Skies.   10
Th' Æthereal Spirit o'er its Leaves shall move,
And on its Top descends the Mystic Dove.
Ye Heav'ns! from high the dewy Nectar pour,
And in soft Silence shed the kindly Show'r!
The Sick and Weak the healing Plant shall aid;   15
From Storms a Shelter, and from Heat a Shade.
All Crimes shall cease, and ancient Fraud shall fail;
Returning Justice lift aloft her Scale;
Peace o'er the World her Olive-Wand extend,
And white-roab'd Innocence from Heav'n descend.   20
Swift fly the Years, and rise th'expected Morn!
Oh spring to Light, Auspicious Babe, be born!
See Nature hasts her earliest Wreaths to bring,
With all the Incence of the breathing Spring:

> Irrita perpetua solvent formidine terras——
> Pacatumque reget patriis virtutibus orbem.

Now the Virgin returns, now the kingdom of Saturn *returns, now a new Progeny is sent down from high heaven. By means of thee, whatever reliques of our crimes remain, shall be wip'd away, and free the world from perpetual fears. He shall govern the earth in peace, with the virtues of his Father.*

ISAIAH, Ch. 7. v. 14. *Behold a Virgin shall conceive, and bear a Son*—Ch. 9. v. 6, 7. *Unto us a Child is born, unto us a Son is given; The Prince of Peace: of the increase of his government, and of his Peace, there shall be no end: Upon the Throne of* David, *and upon his Kingdom, to order and to stablish it, with judgment, and with justice, for ever and ever.* [P]

In classical mythology Astraea, or Justice, left the earth at the end of the Golden Age and was placed in the Zodiac as the constellation called the Virgin.

9. *Jesse's Root*] Isaiah, Ch. 11. v. 1. [P]
13. *dewy Nectar*] Ch. 45. v. 8. [P]
15. *The Sick and Weak*] Ch. 25. v. 4. [P]
18. *Returning Justice*] Ch. 9. v. 7. [P]
23. *See Nature hasts,* &c.] VIRG. E. 4. v. 18.

> At tibi prima, puer, nullo munuscula cultu,
> Errantes hedæras passim cum baccare tellus,
> Mixtaque ridenti colocasia fundet acantho——
> Ipsa tibi blandos fundent cunabula flores.

For thee, O Child, shall the earth, without being tilled, produce her early offerings; winding Ivy, mixed with Baccar, *and* Colocasia *with smiling* Acanthus. *Thy Cradle shall pour forth pleasing flowers about thee.*

ISAIAH, Ch. 35. v. 1. *The wilderness and the solitary place shall be glad, and the desert shall rejoice and blossom as the rose.* Ch. 60. v. 13. *The glory of* Lebanon *shall come unto thee, the firr-tree, the pine-tree, and the box together, to beautify the place of thy Sanctuary.* [P]

24. *Incence*] Pope seems to combine the suggestions of a flower's perfume and those of religious homage.

See lofty *Lebanon* his Head advance,   25
See nodding Forests on the Mountains dance,
See spicy Clouds from lowly *Saron* rise,
And *Carmel*'s flow'ry Top perfumes the Skies!
Hark! a glad Voice the lonely Desert chears:
Prepare the Way! a God, a God appears.   30
A God, a God! the vocal Hills reply,
The Rocks proclaim th'approaching Deity.
Lo Earth receives him from the bending Skies!
Sink down ye Mountains, and ye Vallies rise:
With Heads declin'd, ye Cedars, Homage pay;   35
Be smooth ye Rocks, ye rapid Floods give way!
The SAVIOR comes! by ancient Bards foretold:
Hear him ye Deaf, and all ye Blind behold!
He from thick Films shall purge the visual Ray,
And on the sightless Eye-ball pour the Day.   40
'Tis he th'obstructed Paths of Sound shall clear,
And bid new Musick charm th'unfolding Ear.
The Dumb shall sing, the Lame his Crutch foregoe,
And leap exulting like the bounding Roe.
No Sigh, no Murmur the wide World shall hear,   45
From ev'ry Face he wipes off ev'ry Tear.
In adamantine Chains shall Death be bound,
And Hell's grim Tyrant feel th'eternal Wound.
As the good Shepherd tends his fleecy Care,
Seeks freshest Pasture and the purest Air,   50
Explores the lost, the wand'ring Sheep directs,

25. *lofty Lebanon*] Ch. 35. v 2. [P]
29. *Hark! a glad Voice*, &c] VIRG. E. 4. v. 46 ⟨48–9⟩.

> Aggredere ô magnos, aderit jam tempus, honores,
> Cara deûm soboles, magnum Jovis incrementum——
> Ipsi lætitia voces ad sydera jactant
> Intonsi montes, ipsæ jam carmina rupes,
> Ipsa sonant arbusta, Deus, deus ille Menalca!
>   E. 5. V. 62.

Oh come and receive the mighty honours: The time draws nigh, O beloved
offspring of the Gods, O great encrease of Jove! *The uncultivated mountains*
send shouts of joy to the stars, the very rocks sing in verse, the very shrubs cry
out, A God, a God!
ISAIAH, Ch. 40. V. 3, 4. *The voice of him that crieth in the wilderness,*
Prepare ye the way of the Lord! make strait in the desert a high way for our
God! Every valley shall be exalted, and every mountain and hill shall be
made low, and the crooked shall be made strait, and the rough places plain.
Ch. 44. V. 23. *Break forth into singing, ye mountains! O forest, and every*
tree therein! for the Lord hath redeemed Israel. [P]
38 ff. Ch. 42. v. 18. Ch. 35. v. 5, 6. [P]   47. Ch. 25. v. 8. [P]
   51. *Explores*] To search for; to find by searching.

By Day o'ersees them, and by Night protects;
The tender Lambs he raises in his Arms,
Feeds from his Hand, and in his Bosom warms:
Thus shall Mankind his Guardian Care ingage,   55
The promis'd Father of the future Age.
No more shall Nation against Nation rise,
Nor ardent Warriors meet with hateful Eyes,
Nor Fields with gleaming Steel be cover'd o'er;
The Brazen Trumpets kindle Rage no more: 60
But useless Lances into Scythes shall bend,
And the broad Faulchion in a Plow-share end.
Then Palaces shall rise; the joyful Son
Shall finish what his short-liv'd Sire begun;
Their Vines a Shadow to their Race shall yield;   65
And the Same Hand that sow'd, shall reap the Field.
The Swain in barren Desarts with surprize
See Lillies spring, and sudden Verdure rise;
And Starts, amidst the thirsty Wilds, to hear
New Falls of Water murm'ring in his Ear: 70
On rifted Rocks, the Dragon's late Abodes,
The green Reed trembles, and the Bulrush nods.
Waste sandy Vallies, once perplex'd with Thorn,
The spiry Firr and shapely Box adorn;
To leaf-less Shrubs the flow'ring Palms succeed,   75
And od'rous Myrtle to the noisome Weed.
The Lambs with Wolves shall graze the verdant Mead,

53. Ch. 40. v. 11. [P]
56. *The promis'd Father*] Ch. 9. v. 6. [P]
57. Ch. 2. v. 4. [P]
63. *the joyful Son*] Ch. 65. v. 21, 22. [P]
67. *The Swain in barren Desarts*, &c.] VIRG. E. 4. v. 28.

> Molli paulatim flavescet campus arista,
> Incultisque rubens pendebit sentibus uva,
> Et duræ quercus sudabunt roscida mella.

The field shall grow yellow with ripen'd ears, and the red grape shall hang upon the wild brambles, and the hard Oaks shall distill honey like dew.

ISAIAH, Ch. 35. v. 7. *The parched ground shall become a pool, and the thirsty land springs of water: In the habitations where dragons lay, shall be grass, and reeds and rushes. Ch. 55. v. 13. Instead of the thorn shall come up the firr-tree, and instead of the briar shall come up the myrtle-tree.* [P]

67 ff. Ch. 35. v. 1, 7. [P]
73. *sandy Vallies*] Ch. 41. v. 19, *and* Ch. 55. v. 13. [P]
perplex'd] Intricate, entangled.
77. *The Lambs with Wolves*, &c.] VIRG. E. 4. v. 21.

> Ipsæ lacte domum referent distenta capellæ
> Ubera, nec magnos metuent armenta leones——

And Boys in flow'ry Bands the Tyger lead;
The Steer and Lion at one Crib shall meet;
And harmless Serpents lick the Pilgrim's Feet.   80
The smiling Infant in his Hand shall take
The crested Basilisk and speckled Snake;
Pleas'd, the green Lustre of the Scales survey,
And with their forky Tongue shall innocently play.
Rise, crown'd with Light, Imperial *Salem* rise!   85
Exalt thy Tow'ry Head, and lift thy Eyes!
See, a long Race thy spatious Courts adorn;
See future Sons, and Daughters yet unborn
In crowding Ranks on ev'ry Side arise,
Demanding Life, impatient for the Skies!   90
See barb'rous Nations at thy Gates attend,
Walk in thy Light, and in thy Temple bend.
See thy bright Altars throng'd with prostrate Kings,
And heap'd with Products of *Sabæan* Springs!

Occidet & serpens, & fallax herba veneni
Occidet.————

The goats shall bear to the fold their udders distended with milk: nor shall the herds be afraid of the greatest lions. The serpents shall die, and the herb that conceals poison shall die.
ISAIAH, Ch. II. v. 6 &c. *The wolf shall dwell with the lamb, and the leopard shall lie down with the kid, and the calf and the young lion and the fatling together; and a little child shall lead them—And the lion shall eat straw like the ox. And the sucking child shall play on the hole of the asp, and the weaned child shall put his hand on the den of the cockatrice.* [P]

77. *The Lambs*] Ch. II. v. 6, 7, 8. [P]
80. Ch. 65, v. 25. [P]
82. *Basilisk*] A fabulous reptile (Lat. *basiliscus*) characterized by a crest on its head.
85. *Rise, crown'd with Light, &c.*] The thoughts of *Isaiah*, which compose the latter part of the Poem, are wonderfully elevated, and much above those general exclamations of *Virgil* which make the loftiest parts of his *Pollio.*

Magnus ab integro sæclorum nascitur ordo!
————toto surget gens aurea mundo!
————incipient magni procedere menses!
Aspice, venturo lætentur ut omnia sæclo! &c.
⟨ll. 5, 9, 12, 52⟩

The reader needs only turn to the passages of *Isaiah*, here cited. [P]
85. *Rise, crown'd*] Ch. 60. v. 1. [P]
Salem] Σαλήμ was thought to be an ancient name of Jerusalem.
87. *a long Race*] Ch. 60. v. 4. [P]
91 f. Ch. 60. v. 3. [P]
94. *Sabæan Springs*] Ch. 60. v. 6. [P]
Saba (Sheba in AV) was famous for its gold and incense.

For thee, *Idume*'s spicy Forests blow;   95
And Seeds of Gold in *Ophyr*'s Mountains glow.
See Heav'n its sparkling Portals wide display,
And break upon thee in a Flood of Day!
No more the rising *Sun* shall gild the Morn,
Nor Evening *Cynthia* fill her silver Horn,   100
But lost, dissolv'd in thy superior Rays;
One Tyde of Glory, one unclouded Blaze,
O'erflow thy Courts: The LIGHT HIMSELF shall shine
Reveal'd; and *God*'s eternal Day be thine!
The Seas shall waste; the Skies in Smoke decay;   105
Rocks fall to Dust, and Mountains melt away;
But fix'd *His* Word, *His* saving Pow'r remains:
Thy *Realm* for ever lasts! thy own *Messiah* reigns!

95. *Idume*] The Greek equivalent of Edom, a region to the south of Palestine.

96. *Ophyr*] A place celebrated in antiquity for its gold, but whether it was in Africa, Arabia, or the Far East remains uncertain. Gold was popularly believed to ripen, plant-like, within the earth.

99. *No more the rising Sun*] Ch. 60. v. 19, 20. [P]

106. *melt away*] Ch. 51. v. 6. *and* Ch. 54. v. 10. [P]

Windsor-Forest

TO THE RIGHT HONOURABLE
GEORGE LORD LANSDOWN

[written 1704–13; published 1713]

Non injuſſa cano: Te noſtræ, Vare, Myricæ
Te Nemus omne canet; nec Phœbo gratior ulla eſt
Quam ſibi quæ Vari præſcripſit Pagina nomen.
                                                    VIRG.

Thy Forests, *Windsor*! and thy green Retreats,
At once the Monarch's and the Muse's Seats,
Invite my Lays. Be present, Sylvan Maids!
Unlock your Springs, and open all your Shades.
Granville commands: Your Aid O Muses bring!   5
What Muse for *Granville* can refuse to sing?
  The Groves of *Eden*, vanish'd now so long,
Live in Description, and look green in Song:
These, were my Breast inspir'd with equal Flame,
Like them in Beauty, should be like in Fame.   10
Here Hills and Vales, the Woodland and the Plain,
Here Earth and Water seem to strive again,
Not *Chaos*-like together crush'd and bruis'd,
But as the World, harmoniously confus'd:
Where Order in Variety we see,   15
And where, tho' all things differ, all agree.
Here waving Groves a checquer'd Scene display,
And part admit and part exclude the Day;
As some coy Nymph her Lover's warm Address
Nor quite indulges, nor can quite repress.   20
There, interspers'd in Lawns and opening Glades,
Thin Trees arise that shun each others Shades.

---

1. This poem was written at two different times: the first part of it
which relates to the country, in the year 1704, at the same time with the
Pastorals: the latter part was not added till the year 1713, in which it was
publish'd. [P]
  The 'first part' ended at l. 290 (see 290*n*).
  3, &c. originally thus,

> ————*Chaste Goddess of the woods,*
> *Nymphs of the Vales, and Naiads of the floods,*
> *Lead me thro' arching bow'rs, and glimm'ring glades.* [P]

7 ff. Alluding to the 'Eden' re-created in *Par. Lost.*
21. *Lawns*] An open space between woods; a glade. Cf. ll. 81, 149.

Here in full Light the russet Plains extend;
There wrapt in Clouds the blueish Hills ascend:
Ev'n the wild Heath displays her Purple Dies,   25
And 'midst the Desart fruitful Fields arise,
That crown'd with tufted Trees and springing Corn,
Like verdant Isles the sable Waste adorn.
Let *India* boast her Plants, nor envy we
The weeping Amber or the balmy Tree,   30
While by our Oaks the precious Loads are born,
And Realms commanded which those Trees adorn.
Not proud *Olympus* yields a nobler Sight,
Tho' Gods assembled grace his tow'ring Height,
Than what more humble Mountains offer here,   35
Where, in their Blessings, all those Gods appear.
See *Pan* with Flocks, with Fruits *Pomona* crown'd,
Here blushing *Flora* paints th'enamel'd Ground,
Here *Ceres*' Gifts in waving Prospect stand,
And nodding tempt the joyful Reaper's Hand,   40
Rich Industry sits smiling on the Plains,
And Peace and Plenty tell, a S T U A R T reigns.
    Not thus the Land appear'd in Ages past,
A dreary Desart and a gloomy Waste,
To Savage Beasts and Savage Laws a Prey,   45

23. *russet*] Of a reddish-brown colour.
25.   *Why should I sing our better suns or air,*
            Whose vital draughts prevent the leach's care,
            While thro' fresh fields th'enliv'ning odours breathe,
            Or spread with vernal blooms the purple heath. [P]
27. *tufted Trees*] OED defines *tuft* as a 'small group of trees or bushes;
a clump'.
31. *Oaks*] Alluding to the ships built of English oak which 'bore'
valuable spices to England and enabled her to rule over the lands whence
they came.
38. *enamel'd Ground*] A technical phrase, referring to the process 'of
entirely covering metals with enamel, to form a ground for painting in
vitrifiable colours . . .'. The *ground* is in painting the 'main surface or first
coating of colour, serving as a support for other colours or a background
for designs . . .'
43 ff. This portion of the poem re-creates the traditional view of the
tyrannies exercised by the Norman kings, especially as they were
illustrated in the formation of the New Forest as a royal hunting ground
by William I. The fact that so many members of the Conqueror's family
met their death in the New Forest led commentators into the mythical
view that these deaths were examples of divine vengeance, taken because
of the wickedness involved in the creation of the royal preserve. This is
an essential element in Pope's version.
45. *Savage Laws*] *The Forest Laws*. [P]
'With the Norman Conquest, the forest law and the forest courts of

And Kings more furious and severe than they:
Who claim'd the Skies, dispeopled Air and Floods,
The lonely Lords of empty Wilds and Woods.
Cities laid waste, they storm'd the Dens and Caves,
(For wiser Brutes were backward to be Slaves).   50
What could be free, when lawless Beasts obey'd,
And ev'n the Elements a Tyrant sway'd?
In vain kind Seasons swell'd the teeming Grain,
Soft Show'rs distill'd, and Suns grew warm in vain;
The Swain with Tears his frustrate Labour yields,   55
And famish'd dies amidst his ripen'd Fields.
What wonder then, a Beast or Subject slain
Were equal Crimes in a Despotick Reign;
Both doom'd alike for sportive Tyrants bled,
But while the Subject starv'd, the Beast was fed.   60
Proud *Nimrod* first the bloody Chace began,
A mighty Hunter, and his Prey was Man.
Our haughty *Norman* boasts that barb'rous Name,
And makes his trembling Slaves the Royal Game.
The Fields are ravish'd from th'industrious Swains,   65
From Men their Cities, and from Gods their Fanes:
The levell'd Towns with Weeds lie cover'd o'er,
The hollow Winds thro' naked Temples roar;
Round broken Columns clasping Ivy twin'd;
O'er Heaps of Ruin stalk'd the stately Hind;   70

Normandy were introduced into England, and they resulted in a rapid
and violent extension of "forest" land—that is, land outside (*foris*) the
common law and subject to a special law, whose object was the preservation of the king's hunting. The word "forest" was thus a legal and not a
geographical term.' See *An Historical Geography of England Before A.D.
1800* (1936), ed. H. C. Darby.

57, &c.   *No wonder savages or subjects slain—*
                But subjects starv'd while savages were fed.

It was originally thus, but the word Savages is not properly apply'd to
beasts but to men; which occasion'd the alteration. [P]

    61 f. The text of Genesis speaks of Nimrod only as a hunter, but com-
mentators make it clear that he was regarded as the type of the despot.

    65. *The fields are ravish'd etc.*] *Alluding to the destruction made in the*
New Forest, *and the Tyrannies exercis'd there by* William I. [P]

    65. *The Fields . . . Fanes*] Translated from,

                Templa adimit divis, fora civibus, arva colonis,

an old monkish writer, I forget who. [P]

Pope's forgotten source was *Camden's Britannia* (*Newly Translated into
English: With Large Additions and Improvements* . . . London, 1695, p.
115), where it is said of the New Forest '. . . there are extant some Verses
of *John White* [1510–1560] Bishop of Winchester; which . . . falsely
attribute the making of this Forest to William Rufus.'

The Fox obscene to gaping Tombs retires,
And savage Howlings fill the sacred Quires.
Aw'd by his Nobles, by his Commons curst,
Th' Oppressor rul'd Tyrannick where he *durst*,
Stretch'd o'er the Poor, and Church, his Iron Rod,   75
And serv'd alike his Vassals and his God.
Whom ev'n the *Saxon* spar'd, and bloody *Dane*,
The wanton Victims of his *Sport* remain.
But see the Man who spacious Regions gave
A Waste for Beasts, himself deny'd a Grave!   80
Stretch'd on the Lawn his second Hope survey,
At once the Chaser and at once the Prey.
Lo *Rufus*, tugging at the deadly Dart,
Bleeds in the Forest, like a wounded Hart.
Succeeding Monarchs heard the Subjects Cries,   85
Nor saw displeas'd the peaceful Cottage rise.
Then gath'ring Flocks on unknown Mountains fed,
O'er sandy Wilds were yellow Harvests spread,
The Forests wonder'd at th'unusual Grain,
And secret Transport touch'd the conscious Swain.   90
Fair *Liberty*, *Britannia*'s Goddess, rears
Her chearful Head, and leads the golden Years.

   Ye vig'rous Swains! while Youth ferments your Blood,
And purer Spirits swell the sprightly Flood,
Now range the Hills, the gameful Woods beset,   95
Wind the shrill Horn, or spread the waving Net.
When milder Autumn Summer's Heat succeeds,

72 var. *And wolves with howling fill, &c.*] The Author thought this an error, wolves not being common in *England* at the time of the Conqueror. [P]
   Cf. *Summer*, l. 79n.
79-84. The deaths of both William I and William III were hastened by falls from horses while hunting, and an element of divine justice was attributed to both accidents by opponents of William III. Throughout this whole passage Pope seems to imply a parallel between the reigns of the two kings.
81. *second Hope*] Richard, *second Son of* William *the Conqueror*. [P]
87. *on unknown Mountains fed*] Mountains hitherto unknown to the flocks, now for the first time permitted to feed there.
91.   *Oh may no more a foreign master's rage*
              With wrongs yet legal, curse a future age!
              Still spread, fair Liberty! thy heav'nly wings,
              Breath plenty on the fields, and fragrance on the springs. [P]
   94. The allusion is to the animal spirits which were supposed to move in the blood.
97.   *When yellow autumn summer's heat succeeds,*
              And into wine the purple harvest bleeds,

And in the new-shorn Field the Partridge feeds,
Before his Lord the ready Spaniel bounds,
Panting with Hope, he tries the furrow'd Grounds,   100
But when the tainted Gales the Game betray,
Couch'd close he lyes, and meditates the Prey;
Secure they trust th'unfaithful Field, beset,
Till hov'ring o'er 'em sweeps the swelling Net.
Thus (if small Things we may with great compare)   105
When *Albion* sends her eager Sons to War,
Some thoughtless Town, with Ease and Plenty blest,
Near, and more near, the closing Lines invest;
Sudden they seize th'amaz'd, defenceless Prize,
And high in Air *Britannia*'s Standard flies.   110
    See! from the Brake the whirring Pheasant springs,
And mounts exulting on triumphant Wings;
Short is his Joy! he feels the fiery Wound,
Flutters in Blood, and panting beats the Ground.
Ah! what avail his glossie, varying Dyes,   115
His Purple Crest, and Scarlet-circled Eyes,
The vivid Green his shining Plumes unfold;
His painted Wings, and Breast that flames with Gold?
    Nor yet, when moist *Arcturus* clouds the Sky,
The Woods and Fields their pleasing Toils deny.   120
To Plains with well-breath'd Beagles we repair,
And trace the Mazes of the circling Hare.
(Beasts, urg'd by us, their Fellow Beasts pursue,
And learn of Man each other to undo.)
With slaught'ring Guns th'unweary'd Fowler roves,   125
When Frosts have whiten'd all the naked Groves;
Where Doves in Flocks the leafless Trees o'ershade,
And lonely Woodcocks haunt the watry Glade.
He lifts the Tube, and levels with his Eye;
Strait a short Thunder breaks the frozen Sky.   130

The partridge feeding in the new-shorn fields
Both morning sports and ev'ning pleasures yields.
Perhaps the Author thought it not allowable to describe the season by
a circumstance not proper to our climate, the vintage. [P]. But see
Autumn, 74*n* (p. 134).
    101. *tainted*] Imbued with the scent of an animal.
    102. *meditates*] To fix one's attention upon, to observe with interest or
intentness.
    105 ff. Perhaps inspired by the capture of Gibraltar in 1704.
    119.   *When hoary winter cloaths the year in white,*
                The woods and fields to pleasing toils invite. [P]
    119. See *Autumn*, 72*n* (p. 134).
    129. *The fowler lifts his level'd tube on high.* [P]

Oft, as in Airy Rings they skim the Heath,
The clam'rous Lapwings feel the Leaden Death:
Oft as the mounting Larks their Notes prepare,
They fall, and leave their little Lives in Air.
    In genial Spring, beneath the quiv'ring Shade   135
Where cooling Vapours breathe along the Mead,
The patient Fisher takes his silent Stand
Intent, his Angle trembling in his Hand;
With Looks unmov'd, he hopes the Scaly Breed,
And eyes the dancing Cork and bending Reed.   140
Our plenteous Streams a various Race supply;
The bright-ey'd Perch with Fins of *Tyrian* Dye,
The silver Eel, in shining Volumes roll'd,
The yellow Carp, in Scales bedrop'd with Gold,
Swift Trouts, diversify'd with Crimson Stains,   145
And Pykes, the Tyrants of the watry Plains.
    Now *Cancer* glows with *Phœbus*' fiery Car;
The Youth rush eager to the Sylvan War;
Swarm o'er the Lawns, the Forest Walks surround,
Rowze the fleet Hart, and chear the opening Hound.   150
Th'impatient Courser pants in ev'ry Vein,
And pawing, seems to beat the distant Plain,
Hills, Vales, and Floods appear already crost,
And ere he starts, a thousand Steps are lost.
See! the bold Youth strain up the threatning Steep,   155
Rush thro' the Thickets, down the Vallies sweep,
Hang o'er their Coursers Heads with eager Speed,
And Earth rolls back beneath the flying Steed.
Let old *Arcadia* boast her ample Plain,
Th' Immortal Huntress, and her Virgin Train;   160
Nor envy *Windsor*! since thy Shades have seen
As bright a Goddess, and as chast a Queen;
Whose Care, like hers, protects the Sylvan Reign,
The Earth's fair Light, and Empress of the Main.

143. *Volumes*] Coils, folds, convolutions, especially of a serpent.
147.   *But when bright* Phœbus *from the twins invites*
             Our active genius to more free delights,
             With springing day we range the lawns around. [P]
The sun (Phoebus's car) is in the constellation of the Twins (the
zodiacal sign of Gemini) from about May 21 to June 22. It enters the
constellation of the Crab (the zodiacal sign of Cancer) at the summer
solstice, June 22.
   150. *Rowze*] A technical hunting term: 'to rouse a hart, is to raise him
from his harbour'.
opening] Giving tongue.
   163. An allusion to the interest taken by Anne in hunting.

Here too, 'tis sung, of old *Diana* stray'd,   165
And *Cynthus*' Top forsook for *Windsor* Shade;
Here was she seen o'er Airy Wastes to rove,
Seek the clear Spring, or haunt the pathless Grove;
Here arm'd with Silver Bows, in early Dawn,
Her buskin'd Virgins trac'd the Dewy Lawn.   170
   Above the rest a rural Nymph was fam'd,
Thy Offspring, *Thames*! the fair *Lodona* nam'd,
(*Lodona*'s Fate, in long Oblivion cast,
The Muse shall sing, and what she sings shall last)
Scarce could the Goddess from her Nymph be known, 175
But by the Crescent and the golden Zone,
She scorn'd the Praise of Beauty, and the Care;
A Belt her Waste, a Fillet binds her Hair,
A painted Quiver on her Shoulder sounds,
And with her Dart the flying Deer she wounds.   180
It chanc'd, as eager of the Chace the Maid
Beyond the Forest's verdant Limits stray'd,
Pan saw and lov'd, and burning with Desire
Pursu'd her Flight; her Flight increas'd his Fire.
Not half so swift the trembling Doves can fly,   185
When the fierce Eagle cleaves the liquid Sky;
Not half so swiftly the fierce Eagle moves,
When thro' the Clouds he drives the trembling Doves;
As from the God she flew with furious Pace,
Or as the God, more furious, urg'd the Chace.   190
Now fainting, sinking, pale, the Nymph appears;
Now close behind his sounding Steps she hears;
And now his Shadow reach'd her as she run,
(His Shadow lengthen'd by the setting Sun)
And now his shorter Breath with sultry Air   195
Pants on her Neck, and fans her parting Hair.
In vain on Father *Thames* she calls for Aid,
Nor could *Diana* help her injur'd Maid.
Faint, breathless, thus she pray'd, nor pray'd in vain;
'Ah *Cynthia*! ah—tho' banish'd from thy Train,   200
Let me, O let me, to the Shades repair,
My native Shades—there weep, and murmur there.'
She said, and melting as in Tears she lay,
In a soft, silver Stream dissolv'd away.

170. *trac'd*] I.e. trod or traversed.
176. *Crescent*] The crescent moon, emblem of Diana.
Zone] A girdle or belt.
186. *liquid Sky*] Latin *liquidus*, i.e. clear, transparent.

The silver Stream her Virgin Coldness keeps,   205
For ever murmurs, and for ever weeps;
Still bears the Name the hapless Virgin bore,
And bathes the Forest where she rang'd before.
In her chast Current oft the Goddess laves,
And with Celestial Tears augments the Waves.   210
Oft in her Glass the musing Shepherd spies
The headlong Mountains and the downward Skies,
The watry Landskip of the pendant Woods,
And absent Trees that tremble in the Floods;
In the clear azure Gleam the Flocks are seen,   215
And floating Forests paint the Waves with Green.
Thro' the fair Scene rowl slow the lingring Streams,
Then foaming pour along, and rush into the *Thames*.
   Thou too, great Father of the *British* Floods!
With joyful Pride survey'st our lofty Woods,   220
Where tow'ring Oaks their growing Honours rear,
And future Navies on thy Shores appear.
Not *Neptune*'s self from all his Streams receives
A wealthier Tribute, than to thine he gives.
No Seas so rich, so gay no Banks appear,   225
No Lake so gentle, and no Spring so clear.
Nor *Po* so swells the fabling Poet's Lays,
While led along the Skies his Current strays,
As thine, which visits *Windsor*'s fam'd Abodes,
To grace the Mansion of our earthly Gods.   230
Nor all his Stars above a Lustre show,
Like the bright Beauties on thy Banks below;
Where *Jove*, subdu'd by mortal Passion still,
Might change *Olympus* for a nobler Hill.
   Happy the Man whom this bright Court approves,   235

207. *Still bears the Name*] *The River* Loddon. [P]
   As the river Loddon flows into the Thames near Binfield, Pope perhaps
knew it better than the other tributaries he mentions later. The idea of
using the Loddon may have been suggested by the fact that the river in
Arcadia where Syrinx met her fate (Ovid, *Met.*, I 702) was called the
Ladon.
   211–16. These six lines were added after the first writing of this poem.
[P]
   228. Virgil (*Georgics* I 482, IV 372) and Ovid (*Met.*, II 372) gave to the
river Po the name of Eridanus, a constellation of the southern hemisphere
which has the form of a winding river.
   235.   *Happy the man who to the shades retires,*
                 But doubly happy, if the Muse inspires!
                 Blest whom the sweets of home-felt quiet please;
                 But far more blest, who study joins with ease. [P]

His Sov'reign favours, and his Country loves;
Happy next him who to these Shades retires,
Whom Nature charms, and whom the Muse inspires,
Whom humbler Joys of home-felt Quiet please,
Successive Study, Exercise and Ease.   240
He gathers Health from Herbs the Forest yields,
And of their fragrant Physick spoils the Fields:
With Chymic Art exalts the Min'ral Pow'rs,
And draws the Aromatick Souls of Flow'rs.
Now marks the Course of rolling Orbs on high;   245
O'er figur'd Worlds now travels with his Eye.
Of ancient Writ unlocks the learned Store,
Consults the Dead, and lives past Ages o'er.
Or wandring thoughtful in the silent Wood,
Attends the Duties of the Wise and Good,   250
T'observe a Mean, be to himself a Friend,
To follow Nature, and regard his End.
Or looks on Heav'n with more than mortal Eyes,
Bids his free Soul expatiate in the Skies,
Amid her Kindred Stars familiar roam,   255
Survey the Region, and confess her Home!
Such was the Life great *Scipio* once admir'd,
Thus *Atticus*, and *Trumbal* thus retir'd.
    Ye sacred Nine! that all my Soul possess,
Whose Raptures fire me, and whose Visions bless,   260
Bear me, oh bear me to sequester'd Scenes,
The Bow'ry Mazes and surrounding Greens;
To *Thames*'s Banks which fragrant Breezes fill,
Or where ye Muses sport on *Cooper*'s Hill.

243. *exalts*] In Alchemy and early Chemistry: To raise (a substance or its qualities) to a higher 'degree' . . . to intensify, render more powerful.

244. *draws*] To inhale, or perhaps to extract by suction or distillation.

246. *figur'd Worlds*] Perhaps the Zodiac, or a globe of the world. To figure is to portray or represent.

257. After his victory over Hannibal in the second Punic War, Scipio Africanus declined political distinctions offered him. When, many years later, his enemies brought him to trial on charges of misconduct, he reminded the Romans of his past services, set the laws at defiance, and retired to his country seat at Liternum. He never returned to Rome, but passed his life cultivating his estate.

258. *Atticus*] Titus Pomponius, the friend and correspondent of Cicero, refused to sue for public honour or to become engaged in political controversy. Instead he withdrew from Rome to Athens and devoted himself to a life of study. He was called Atticus because of his long residence in Athens.

(On *Cooper*'s Hill eternal Wreaths shall grow,   265
While lasts the Mountain, or while *Thames* shall flow)
I seem thro' consecrated Walks to rove,
I hear soft Musick dye along the Grove;
Led by the Sound I roam from Shade to Shade,
By God-like Poets Venerable made: 270
Here his first Lays Majestick *Denham* sung;
There the last Numbers flow'd from *Cowley*'s Tongue.
O early lost! what Tears the River shed
When the sad Pomp along his Banks was led?
His drooping Swans on ev'ry Note expire,   275
And on his Willows hung each Muse's Lyre.
  Since Fate relentless stop'd their Heav'nly Voice,
No more the Forests ring, or Groves rejoice;
Who now shall charm the Shades where *Cowley* strung
His living Harp, and lofty *Denham* sung?   280
But hark! the Groves rejoice, the Forest rings!
Are these reviv'd? or is it *Granville* sings?
'Tis yours, my Lord, to bless our soft Retreats,
And call the Muses to their ancient Seats,
To paint anew the flow'ry Sylvan Scenes,   285
To crown the Forests with Immortal Greens,
Make *Windsor* Hills in lofty Numbers rise,
And lift her Turrets nearer to the Skies;
To sing those Honours you deserve to wear,
And add new Lustre to her Silver *Star*.   290

266. *Mountain*] Cooper's Hill. See *Spring*, 21n (p. 124).

271. *first Lays*] Before the opening of the Civil War in 1642, Denham had written *The Destruction of Troy* (a translation of *Aeneid* II), the first draft of *Cooper's Hill*, and *The Sophy*. His house in Egham, near Windsor, was confiscated by the Parliamentary forces in 1643.

272. *Mr.* Cowley *died at* Chertsey, *on the Borders of the Forest, and was from thence convey'd to* Westminster. [P]

273. *O early lost*] Cowley died in 1667, at the age of 49. His body was floated down the river from Chertsey to London.

275.   *What sighs, what murmurs fill'd the vocal shore!*
            His tuneful swans were heard to sing no more. [P]

276. *each Muse's Lyre*] Cowley attempted many poetical genres. In his epitaph in Westminster Abbey, he is called *Anglorum Pindarus, Flaccus, Maro*.

290. All the lines that follow were not added to the poem till the year 1710. What immediately followed this, and made the Conclusion, were these,

            My humble Muse in unambitious strains
            Paints the green forests and the flow'ry plains;
            Where I obscurely pass my careless days,
            Pleas'd in the silent shade with empty praise,

Here noble *Surrey* felt the sacred Rage,
Surrey, the *Granville* of a former Age:
Matchless his Pen, victorious was his Lance;
Bold in the Lists, and graceful in the Dance:
In the same Shades the *Cupids* tun'd his Lyre,   295
To the same Notes, of Love, and soft Desire:
Fair *Geraldine*, bright Object of his Vow,
Then fill'd the Groves, as heav'nly *Myra* now.
 Oh wou'dst thou sing what Heroes *Windsor* bore,
What Kings first breath'd upon her winding Shore,   300
Or raise old Warriors whose ador'd Remains
In weeping Vaults her hallow'd Earth contains!
With *Edward*'s Acts adorn the shining Page,
Stretch his long Triumphs down thro' ev'ry Age,
Draw Monarchs chain'd, and *Cressi*'s glorious Field,   305
The Lillies blazing on the Regal Shield.
Then, from her Roofs when *Verrio*'s Colours fall,
And leave inanimate the naked Wall;

Enough for me that to the list'ning swains
First in these fields I sung the sylvan strains. [P]
 290. *Silver Star*] The Star of the Order of the Garter, instituted at
Windsor Castle by Edward III. It was to provide a meeting-place for the
Order that Edward reconstructed Windsor Castle.
 291. *Surrey*] Henry Howard, *Earl of* Surrey, *one of the first Refiners of
the* English *Poetry*; *who flourish'd in the time of* Henry *the* VIIIth. [P]
 297. *Fair Geraldine*] Lady Elizabeth Fitzgerald (1528?-89), youngest
daughter of the Earl of Kildare. Surrey's love poems were long supposed
to have been addressed to her.
 298. *Myra*] The name Granville bestowed in his songs, first upon Mary
of Modena, then upon Frances Brudenal, Countess of Newburgh, when
the latter became his mistress.
 300. Edward III (1312) and Henry VI (1421) were born at Windsor.
Edward IV, Henry VIII, and Charles I were buried there.
 winding Shore] Perhaps Pope knew the etymological meaning of the
word *Windsor* as given in *Camden's Britannia* (1695), p. 151: 'Next, the
Thames goes to *Windsor*, call'd in Saxon Windesoure, Windlesora, and
also Windlesofra, from the *winding banks*, ofre in that language signifying
a *bank* or *shore*.' But compare Dryden, *Æn.*, 1 809: 'The Ports and Creeks
of ev'ry winding Shore'.
 303. Edward III, *born here.* [P]
 303-10. Antonio Verrio (1639-1707) had represented in St. George's
Hall at Windsor the triumphal procession in which King John of France
was led captive by the Black Prince. See *Ep. to Burlington*, 146 (p. 593).
 305. *Monarch's chain'd*] An allusion to David II, King of Scotland,
taken prisoner at the battle of Neville's Cross in 1346 and released in
1357; and to Jean le Bon, King of France, whom the Black Prince
defeated and captured at Poitiers in 1356.
 306. On Jan. 26, 1340, Edward III assumed the title of king of France,
and quartered the lilies of France with the leopards of England.
 307. Verrio's painted ceilings had begun to deteriorate.

Still in thy Song shou'd vanquish'd *France* appear,
And bleed for ever under *Britain*'s Spear.   310
   Let softer Strains Ill-fated *Henry* mourn,
And Palms Eternal flourish round his Urn.
Here o'er the Martyr-King the Marble weeps,
And fast beside him, once-fear'd *Edward* sleeps:
Whom not th'extended *Albion* could contain,   315
From old *Belerium* to the *Northern* Main,
The Grave unites; where ev'n the Great find Rest,
And blended lie th' Oppressor and th' Opprest!
   Make sacred *Charles*'s Tomb for ever known,
(Obscure the Place, and uninscrib'd the Stone)   320
Oh Fact accurst! What Tears has *Albion* shed,
Heav'ns! what new Wounds, and how her old have bled?
She saw her Sons with purple Deaths expire,
Her sacred Domes involv'd in rolling Fire,
A dreadful Series of Intestine Wars,   325
Inglorious Triumphs, and dishonest Scars.
At length great *ANNA* said—Let Discord cease!
She said, the World obey'd, and all was *Peace*!
   In that blest Moment, from his Oozy Bed
Old Father *Thames* advanc'd his rev'rend Head.   330

311. *Henry*] Henry VI. [P]
Edward, duke of York, proclaimed himself king under the title of
Edward IV in 1461. Henry VI was a fugitive in the North until he was
taken prisoner in 1465. From October, 1470, to April, 1471, Henry was
restored to the throne, and Edward took flight. Henry's allies were
defeated at Barnet, April 14, 1471, and Henry was probably murdered on
May 21. His body was transferred from its grave in Chertsey Abbey to
Windsor in 1484. He was buried in St. George's Chapel, not far from
Edward IV, who had been buried there in 1483. The *palms eternal* are
not those of victory, but of martyrdom.
314. *Edward*] Edward IV. [P]
316. *old Belerium*] *Belerium* (or *Bolerium*) *promontorium* was the Latin
name for Land's End.
319. *Charles's Tomb*] The body of Charles I was buried in St. George's
Chapel, in the same tomb as Henry VIII, and without any service.
323 ff. The Great Plague (1665), the Great Fire (1666), and the
Revolution of 1688: evil effects of Charles I's execution.
324. *Domes*] A stately building, a mansion.
326. *dishonest*] Shameful.
330. Between Verse 330 and 331 originally stood these lines,
       From shore to shore exulting shouts he heard,
       O'er all his banks a lambent light appear'd,
       With sparkling flames heav'ns glowing concave shone,
       Fictitious stars, and glories not her own.
       He saw, and gently rose above the stream;
       His shining horns diffus'd a golden gleam:

His Tresses dropt with Dews, and o'er the Stream
His shining Horns diffus'd a golden Gleam:
Grav'd on his Urn appear'd the Moon, that guides
His swelling Waters, and alternate Tydes;
The figur'd Streams in Waves of Silver roll'd,   335
And on their Banks *Augusta* rose in Gold.
Around his Throne the Sea-born Brothers stood,
Who swell with Tributary Urns his Flood.
First the fam'd Authors of his ancient Name,
The winding *Isis*, and the fruitful *Tame*:   340
The *Kennet* swift, for silver Eels renown'd;
The *Loddon* slow, with verdant Alders crown'd:
Cole, whose dark Streams his flow'ry Islands lave;
And chalky *Wey*, that rolls a milky Wave:
The blue, transparent *Vandalis* appears;   345
The gulphy *Lee* his sedgy Tresses rears;
And sullen *Mole*, that hides his diving Flood;
And silent *Darent*, stain'd with *Danish* Blood.
   High in the midst, upon his Urn reclin'd,
(His Sea-green Mantle waving with the Wind)   350
The God appear'd; he turn'd his azure Eyes
Where *Windsor*-Domes and pompous Turrets rise,

With pearl and gold his tow'ry front was drest,
   The tributes of the distant East and West. [P]
332. *shining Horns*] 'The River-gods were often given the head or horns
of a bull, indicative of their roaring or winding, of their strength or of
their influence on agriculture.'

335. *figur'd*] Shaped into a figure, represented by figures.
336. *Augusta*] The name given at one time to London by the Romans.
337. *Sea-born Brothers*] The legend was that all rivers were born of
Oceanus and Tethys.

339-48. Pope's catalogue of rivers resembles closely that found in
Ausonius, *Mosella*, 349-74. The lines are also indebted to Spenser, *F.Q.*,
IV xi; to Milton, *At a Vacation Exercise*; and to Drayton, *Poly-Olbion*,
Song XVII.

339. *fam'd Authors*] The Thames (Tamesis) was thought to be the off-
spring of the Thame and the Isis.

345. *transparent Vandalis*] The Wandle.

347. *sullen Mole*] In *A Tour Thro' the whole Island of Great Britain*,
Defoe says that this river is 'called the *Mole*, from its remarkable sinking
into the Earth, *at the Foot of* Box-Hill, *near a Village call'd* Mickleham,
and working its way under Ground like a *Mole*, rising again at or near this
Town of *Leatherhead*'.

348. *silent Darent*] Pope perhaps read in *Camden's Britannia* that 'The
Thames afterwards growing narrower, is met by the river *Darent*, which
coming out of Surrey, flows with a gentle chanel nor far from *Seven-oke*
. . . and so to . . . *Otford*, famous for a bloody defeat of the Danes in the
year 1016.'

Then bow'd and spoke; the Winds forget to roar,
And the hush'd Waves glide softly to the Shore.
    Hail Sacred *Peace*! hail long-expected Days,   355
That *Thames*'s Glory to the Stars shall raise!
Tho' *Tyber*'s Streams immortal *Rome* behold,
Tho' foaming *Hermus* swells with Tydes of Gold,
From Heav'n it self tho' sev'nfold *Nilus* flows,
And Harvests on a hundred Realms bestows;   360
These now no more shall be the Muse's Themes,
Lost in my Fame, as in the Sea their Streams.
Let *Volga*'s Banks with Iron Squadrons shine,
And Groves of Lances glitter on the *Rhine*,
Let barb'rous *Ganges* arm a servile Train;   365
Be mine the Blessings of a peaceful Reign.
No more my Sons shall dye with *British* Blood
Red *Iber*'s Sands, or *Ister*'s foaming Flood;
Safe on my Shore each unmolested Swain
Shall tend the Flocks, or reap the bearded Grain;   370
The shady Empire shall retain no Trace
Of War or Blood, but in the Sylvan Chace,
The Trumpets sleep, while chearful Horns are blown,
And Arms employ'd on Birds and Beasts alone.
Behold! th'ascending *Villa*'s on my Side   375
Project long Shadows o'er the Chrystal Tyde.
Behold! *Augusta*'s glitt'ring Spires increase,
And Temples rise, the beauteous Works of Peace.
I see, I see where two fair Cities bend
Their ample Bow, a new *White-Hall* ascend!   380

355. The preliminaries to the Treaty of Utrecht were signed in London
in October, 1711.

363. *Volga's Banks*] An allusion to the war of Charles XII of Sweden
against Russia.

365. *Ganges*] An allusion to the wars waged by the Moghul Emperor
Aurangzeb against the rising Maratha powers. He died in 1707.

366. 'This fine panegyric on *peace*, in opposition to the horrors and
devastations of war, was in part occasioned, I presume, by our author's
politics; by his hostility to the name of *Marlborough*, and an uneasiness
at the glory of his victories.'

368 *Iber's Sands*] The modern Ebro. An allusion to the Allies' campaign in Spain in 1710 and to the victory gained at Saragossa.

Ister's foaming Flood] The Danube. An allusion to Marlborough's
victory at Blenheim (1704).

378. *Temples rise*] The fifty new Churches. [P] See *Sat.* II ii 119 (p.
622), *Moral Es.* IV 195n (p. 595).

379. *two fair Cities bend*] London and Westminster, at that time two
distinct towns.

380. *a new White-Hall*] Whitehall Palace was at various times the

There mighty Nations shall inquire their Doom,
The World's great Oracle in Times to come;
There Kings shall sue, and suppliant States be seen
Once more to bend before a *British* QUEEN.
  Thy Trees, fair *Windsor*! now shall leave their Woods,
And half thy Forests rush into my Floods,   386
Bear *Britain*'s Thunder, and her Cross display,
To the bright Regions of the rising Day;
Tempt Icy Seas, where scarce the Waters roll,
Where clearer Flames glow round the frozen Pole;   390
Or under Southern Skies exalt their Sails,
Led by new Stars, and born by spicy Gales!
For me the Balm shall bleed, and Amber flow,
The Coral redden, and the Ruby glow,
The Pearly Shell its lucid Globe infold,   395
And *Phœbus* warm the ripening Ore to Gold.
The Time shall come, when free as Seas or Wind
Unbounded *Thames* shall flow for all Mankind,
Whole Nations enter with each swelling Tyde,
And Seas but join the Regions they divide;   400

---

residence of English monarchs till it was burned down in 1698. Inigo
Jones's Banqueting Hall alone survived. Cf. *Sat.* II ii 120*n* (p. 622),
Dunciad A, III 324 (p. 423), and Pope's note.

381–422. The pervasive influence of Isaiah, chap. 60, is discernible
throughout.

Ver. 383, &c. were originally thus:

> *Now shall our fleets the bloody Cross display*
> *To the rich regions of the rising day,*
> *Or those green isles, where headlong* Titan *steeps*
> *His hissing axle in th'*Atlantic *deeps.*
> *Tempt icy seas,* &c. [P]

384. *Once more*] The aliusion is to those occasions, in 1575 and 1585,
when the sovereignty of the United Provinces was offered to Queen
Elizabeth and her aid was solicited in the struggles of the Dutch against
Philip of Spain.

386. The trees of Windsor Forest, turned into ships, will carry British
power and commerce all over the world.

387. *her Cross*] The red cross of St George on the Union Jack.

389. *Tempt*] To adventure oneself in; to risk the perils of.

393. *Balm shall bleed*] From the wound inflicted on the bark to draw off
the juices of the tree.

396. *ripening Ore*] An allusion to the belief that gold and precious stones
were 'ripened' into maturity by the sun.

398. *Unbounded Thames*] A wish that London may be made a FREE
PORT. [P]
Cf. the name given by Addison to the representative of moneyed
interests, Sir Andrew Freeport (*Spectator*, March 2, 1711).

Earth's distant Ends our Glory shall behold,
And the new World launch forth to seek the Old.
Then Ships of uncouth Form shall stem the Tyde,
And Feather'd People crowd my wealthy Side,
And naked Youths and painted Chiefs admire   405
Our Speech, our Colour, and our strange Attire!
Oh stretch thy Reign, fair *Peace!* from Shore to Shore,
Till Conquest cease, and Slav'ry be no more:
Till the freed *Indians* in their native Groves
Reap their own Fruits, and woo their Sable Loves,   410
Peru once more a Race of Kings behold,
And other *Mexico's* be roof'd with Gold.
Exil'd by Thee from Earth to deepest Hell,
In Brazen Bonds shall barb'rous *Discord* dwell:
Gigantick *Pride*, pale *Terror*, gloomy *Care*,   415
And mad *Ambition*, shall attend her there.
There purple *Vengeance* bath'd in Gore retires,
Her Weapons blunted, and extinct her Fires:
There hateful *Envy* her own Snakes shall feel,
And *Persecution* mourn her broken Wheel: 420
There *Faction* roar, *Rebellion* bite her Chain,
And gasping Furies thirst for Blood in vain.
　　Here cease thy Flight, nor with unhallow'd Lays
Touch the fair Fame of *Albion's* Golden Days.
The Thoughts of Gods let *Granville's* Verse recite, 425
And bring the Scenes of opening Fate to Light.
My humble Muse, in unambitious Strains,
Paints the green Forests and the flow'ry Plains,
Where Peace descending bids her Olives spring,
And scatters Blessings from her Dove-like Wing.   430
Ev'n I more sweetly pass my careless Days,
Pleas'd in the silent Shade with empty Praise;
Enough for me, that to the listning Swains
First in these Fields I sung the Sylvan Strains.

404 ff. Apparently an allusion to the four Iroquois Indian chiefs who
visited England in April, 1710, and who were granted a public audience
with Queen Anne.

409. *freed Indians*] From the tyranny of Spain.

413 ff. Discord was expelled from Heaven by Jupiter.

420. *broken Wheel*] Persons bound to the wheel for torture had their
arms and legs broken by blows from an iron bar. Pope suggests an
appropriate fate for the wheel itself.

431 ff. Pope's conclusion was modelled on that of the *Georgics*. As
Virgil closed his *Georgics* with the first line of his *Eclogues*, so Pope's final
couplet echoes the opening line of *Spring*.

Three Theatrical Pieces

To wake the soul by tender strokes of art,
To raise the genius, and to mend the heart;
To make mankind, in conscious virtue bold,
Live o'er each scene, and be what they behold:
For this the Tragic Muse first trod the stage, 5
Commanding tears to stream thro' ev'ry age;
Tyrants no more their savage nature kept,
And foes to virtue wonder'd how they wept.
Our author shuns by vulgar springs to move,
The hero's glory, or the virgin's love; 10
In pitying love we but our weakness show,
And wild ambition well deserves its woe.
Here tears shall flow from a more gen'rous cause,
Such tears, as Patriots shed for dying Laws:
He bids your breasts with ancient ardour rise, 15
And calls forth *Roman* drops from *British* eyes.
Virtue confess'd in human shape he draws,
What *Plato* thought, and godlike *Cato* was:
No common object to your sight displays,
But what with pleasure heav'n itself surveys; 20
A brave man struggling in the storms of fate,
And greatly falling with a falling state!
While *Cato* gives his little senate laws,
What bosom beats not in his Country's cause?
Who sees him act, but envies ev'ry deed? 25
Who hears him groan, and does not wish to bleed?
Ev'n when proud *Cæsar* 'midst triumphal cars,
The spoils of nations, and the pomp of wars,
Ignobly vain and impotently great,
Show'd *Rome* her *Cato*'s figure drawn in state; 30
As her dead Father's rev'rend image past,
The pomp was darken'd, and the day o'ercast,
The triumph ceas'd—Tears gush'd from ev'ry eye;
The World's great Victor pass'd unheeded by;
Her last good man dejected *Rome* ador'd, 35
And honour'd *Cæsar*'s less than *Cato*'s sword.
 Britons attend: Be worth like this approv'd,

Cato was first performed on 14 April 1713.

And show, you have the virtue to be mov'd.
With honest scorn the first fam'd *Cato* view'd
Rome learning arts from *Greece,* whom she subdu'd;   40
Our scene precariously subsists too long
On *French* translation, and *Italian* song.
Dare to have sense your selves; assert the stage,
Be justly warm'd with your own native rage.
Such Plays alone should please a *British* ear,   45
As *Cato*'s self had not disdain'd to hear.

PROLOGUE

DESIGN'D FOR MR. DURFY'S LAST PLAY

[written 1713; published, Steele's
Miscellanies, 1713]

Grown old in Rhyme, 'twere barbarous to discard
Your persevering, unexhausted Bard:
Damnation follows Death in other Men,
But your damn'd Poet lives and writes again.
Th' advent'rous Lover is successful still,   5
Who strives to please the Fair *against her Will:*
Be kind, and make him in his Wishes easy,
Who in your own *Despite* has strove to please ye.
He scorn'd to borrow from the Wits of yore;
But ever writ, as none e'er writ before.   10
You modern Wits, should each Man bring his Claim,
Have desperate Debentures on your Fame;
And little wou'd be left you, I'm afraid,
If all your Debts to *Greece* and *Rome* were paid.
From his deep Fund our Author largely draws;   15
Nor sinks his Credit lower than it was.
Tho' Plays for Honour in old Time he made,
'Tis now for better Reasons——to be paid.
Believe him, he has known the World too long,
And seen the Death of much Immortal Song.   20
He says, poor Poets lost, while Players won,
As Pimps grow rich, while Gallants are undone.
Tho' *Tom* the Poet writ with Ease and Pleasure,
The Comick *Tom* abounds in other Treasure.
Fame is at best an unperforming Cheat;   25
But 'tis substantial Happiness to *eat*—
Let Ease, his last Request, be of your giving,
Nor force him to be damn'd, to get his Living.

Written for a benefit performance of D'Urfey's *A Fond Husband* (1713).

EPILOGUE TO JANE SHORE
DESIGN'D FOR MRS. OLDFIELD

[written 1713; published, *Works*, 1717]

Prodigious this! the Frail one of our Play
From her own sex should mercy find to day!
You might have held the pretty head aside,
Peep'd in your fans, been serious, thus, and cry'd,
The Play may pass—but that strange creature, *Shore*,   5
I can't—indeed now—I so hate a whore—
Just as a blockhead rubs his thoughtless skull,
And thanks his stars he was not born a fool;
So from a sister sinner you shall hear,
'How strangely you expose your self, my dear!'   10
But let me die, all raillery apart,
Our sex are still forgiving at their heart;
And did not wicked custom so contrive,
We'd be the best, good-natur'd things alive.
    There are, 'tis true, who tell another tale,   15
That virtuous ladies envy while they rail;
Such rage without betrays the fire within;
In some close corner of the soul, they sin:
Still hoarding up, most scandalously nice,
Amidst their virtues, a reserve of vice.   20
The godly dame who fleshly failings damns,
Scolds with her maid, or with her chaplain crams.
Wou'd you enjoy soft nights and solid dinners?
Faith, gallants, board with saints, and bed with sinners.
    Well, if our author in the Wife offends,   25
He has a Husband that will make amends.
He draws him gentle, tender, and forgiving,
And sure such kind good creatures may be living.
In days of old they pardon'd breach of vows,
Stern *Cato*'s self was no relentless spouse: 30
Plu—*Plutarch*, what's his name that writes his life?
Tells us, that *Cato* dearly lovd his wife:
Yet if a friend a night, or so, should need her,
He'd recommend her, as a special breeder.
To lend a wife, few here would scruple make,   35
But pray which of you all would take her back?
Tho' with the Stoick chief our stage may ring,
The Stoick husband was the glorious thing.

Rowe's *Jane Shore* was first performed on 2 February 1713
Title: *Mrs. Oldfield*] Anne Oldfield (1683–1730), actress.

The man had courage, was a sage, 'tis true,
And lov'd his country—but what's that to you?   40
Those strange examples ne'er were made to fit ye,
But the kind cuckold might instruct the City:
There, many an honest man may copy *Cato*,
Who ne'er saw naked Sword, or look'd in *Plato*.
  If, after all, you think it a disgrace,   45
That *Edward*'s Miss thus perks it in your face,
To see a piece of failing flesh and blood,
In all the rest so impudently good:
Faith, let the modest matrons of the town,
Come here in crowds, and stare the strumpet down.   50

46. *Edward's Miss*] Jane Shore was Edward IV's mistress.

To Mr. Addison, Occasioned by
his Dialogues on Medals

[written ?1713; revised, 1719; published,
Works 1720]

See the wild Waste of all-devouring years!
How Rome her own sad Sepulchre appears,
With nodding arches, broken temples spread!
The very Tombs now vanish'd like their dead!
Imperial wonders rais'd on Nations spoil'd,   5
Where mix'd with Slaves the groaning Martyr toil'd;
Huge Theatres, that now unpeopled Woods,
Now drain'd a distant country of her Floods;
Fanes, which admiring Gods with pride survey,
Statues of Men, scarce less alive than they;   10
Some felt the silent stroke of mould'ring age,
Some hostile fury, some religious rage;
Barbarian blindness, Christian zeal conspire,
And Papal piety, and Gothic fire.
Perhaps, by its own ruins sav'd from flame,   15
Some bury'd marble half preserves a name;
That Name the learn'd with fierce disputes pursue,
And give to Titus old Vespasian's due.
   Ambition sigh'd; She found it vain to trust
The faithless Column and the crumbling Bust;   20
Huge moles, whose shadow stretch'd from shore to shore,
Their ruins ruin'd, and their place no more!
Convinc'd, she now contracts her vast design,
And all her Triumphs shrink into a Coin:
A narrow orb each crouded conquest keeps,   25
Beneath her Palm here sad Judæa weeps,
Here scantier limits the proud Arch confine,
And scarce are seen the prostrate Nile or Rhine,
A small Euphrates thro' the piece is roll'd,
And little Eagles wave their wings in gold.   30
   The Medal, faithful to its charge of fame,
Thro' climes and ages bears each form and name:
In one short view subjected to your eye
Gods, Emp'rors, Heroes, Sages, Beauties, lie.

26 ff. Descriptions of coins commemorating conquests of various
Cæsars.
   39. *Pescennius*] Coins of the pretender Pescennius Niger are the rarest
any ordinary collector hopes to possess.

With sharpen'd sight pale Antiquaries pore,   35
Th' inscription value, but the rust adore;
This the blue varnish, that the green endears,
The sacred rust of twice ten hundred years!
To gain Pescennius one employs his schemes,
One grasps a Cecrops in ecstatic dreams;   40
Poor Vadius, long with learned spleen devour'd,
Can taste no pleasure since his Shield was scour'd;
And Curio, restless by the Fair-one's side,
Sighs for an Otho, and neglects his bride.
   Theirs is the Vanity, the Learning thine: 45
Touch'd by thy hand, again Rome's glories shine,
Her Gods, and god-like Heroes rise to view,
And all her faded garlands bloom a-new.
Nor blush, these studies thy regard engage;
These pleas'd the Fathers of poetic rage;   50
The verse and sculpture bore an equal part,
And Art reflected images to Art.
   Oh when shall Britain, conscious of her claim,
Stand emulous of Greek and Roman fame?
In living medals see her wars enroll'd,   55
And vanquish'd realms supply recording gold?
Here, rising bold, the Patriot's honest face;
There Warriors frowning in historic brass:
Then future ages with delight shall see
How Plato's, Bacon's, Newton's looks agree;   60
Or in fair series laurell'd Bards be shown,
A Virgil there, and here an Addison.
Then shall thy CRAGS (and let me call him mine)
On the cast ore, another Pollio, shine;
With aspect open, shall erect his head,   65
And round the orb in lasting notes be read,
'Statesman, yet friend to Truth! of soul sincere,
In action faithful, and in honour clear;
Who broke no promise, serv'd no private end,
Who gain'd no title, and who lost no friend,   70
Ennobled by himself, by all approv'd,
And prais'd, unenvy'd, by the Muse he lov'd.'

44. Coins of Otho are the rarest in the popular series of the twelve
Cæsars.
64. *Pollio*] Asinius Pollio, friend of Virgil, to whom he addressed his
Fourth Eclogue.

The Rape of the Lock

AN HEROI-COMICAL POEM
IN FIVE CANTO'S

[two-Canto version 1712; five-Canto
version 1714]

Nolueram, Belinda, tuos violare capillos,
Sed juvat hoc precibus me tribuisse tuis.

MARTIAL

TO MRS. ARABELLA FERMOR

MADAM,

It will be in vain to deny that I have some Regard for this Piece,
since I Dedicate it to You. Yet You may bear me Witness, it was
intended only to divert a few young Ladies, who have good Sense
and good Humour enough, to laugh not only at their Sex's little
unguarded Follies, but at their own. But as it was communicated
with the Air of a Secret, it soon found its Way into the World.
An imperfect Copy having been offer'd to a Bookseller, You had
the Good-Nature for my Sake to consent to the Publication of one
more correct: This I was forc'd to before I had executed half my
Design, for the *Machinery* was entirely wanting to compleat it.

The *Machinery*, Madam, is a Term invented by the Criticks, to
signify that Part which the Deities, Angels, or Dæmons, are made
to act in a Poem: For the ancient Poets are in one respect like many
modern Ladies; Let an Action be never so trivial in it self, they
always make it appear of the utmost Importance. These Machines
I determin'd to raise on a very new and odd Foundation, the
Rosicrucian Doctrine of Spirits.

I know how disagreeable it is to make use of hard Words before a
Lady; but 'tis so much the Concern of a Poet to have his Works
understood, and particularly by your Sex, that You must give me
leave to explain two or three difficult Terms.

The *Rosicrucians* are a People I must bring You acquainted with.
The best Account I know of them is in a French Book call'd *Le
Comte de Gabalis*, which both in its Title and Size is so like a *Novel*,
that many of the Fair Sex have read it for one by Mistake. According to these Gentlemen, the four Elements are inhabited by Spirits,
which they call *Sylphs*, *Gnomes*, *Nymphs*, and *Salamanders*. The
Gnomes, or Dæmons of Earth, delight in Mischief; but the *Sylphs*,

217

whose Habitation is in the Air, are the best-condition'd Creatures
imaginable. For they say, any Mortals may enjoy the most intimate
Familiarities with these gentle Spirits, upon a Condition very easie
to all true *Adepts*, an inviolate Preservation of Chastity.

As to the following Canto's, all the Passages of them are as Fabulous, as the Vision at the Beginning, or the Transformation at the
End; (except the Loss of your Hair, which I always mention with
Reverence.) The Human Persons are as Fictitious as the Airy ones;
and the Character of *Belinda*, as it is now manag'd, resembles You
in nothing but in Beauty.

If this Poem had as many Graces as there are in Your Person, or
in Your Mind, yet I could never hope it should pass thro' the World
half so Uncensured as You have done. But let its Fortune be what
it will, mine is happy enough, to have given me this Occasion of
assuring You that I am, with the truest Esteem,

> *Madam*,
> > *Your Most Obedient*
> > *Humble Servant.*
> > > A. POPE.

CANTO I

What dire Offence from am'rous Causes springs,
What mighty Contests rise from trivial Things,
I sing—This Verse to *Caryll*, Muse! is due;
This, ev'n *Belinda* may vouchsafe to view:
Slight is the Subject, but not so the Praise,   5
If She inspire, and He approve my Lays.
  Say what strange Motive, Goddess! cou'd compel
A well-bred *Lord* t'assault a gentle *Belle*?
Oh say what stranger Cause, yet unexplor'd,
Cou'd make a gentle *Belle* reject a *Lord*?   10
In Tasks so bold, can Little Men engage,
And in soft Bosoms dwells such mighty Rage?
  Sol thro' white Curtains shot a tim'rous Ray,
And op'd those Eyes that must eclipse the Day;
Now Lapdogs give themselves the rowzing Shake,   15
And sleepless Lovers, just at Twelve, awake:

*The first sketch of this Poem was written in less than a fortnight's time,
in* 1711, *in two Canto's, and so printed in a Miscellany, without the name of
the Author. The Machines were not inserted till a year after, when he
publish'd it, and annex'd the foregoing Dedication.* [P]
  3. *Caryll*] A close friend of Pope and Gay.
  11 Cf. *Æneid*, i 11: . . . Tantaene animis caelestibus irae?

Thrice rung the Bell, the Slipper knock'd the Ground,
And the press'd Watch return'd a silver Sound.
Belinda still her downy Pillow prest,
Her Guardian *Sylph* prolong'd the balmy Rest.   20
'Twas he had summon'd to her silent Bed
The Morning-Dream that hover'd o'er her Head.
A Youth more glitt'ring than a *Birth-night Beau,*
(That ev'n in Slumber caus'd her Cheek to glow)
Seem'd to her Ear his winning Lips to lay,   25
And thus in Whispers said, or seem'd to say.
   Fairest of Mortals, thou distinguish'd Care
Of thousand bright Inhabitants of Air!
If e'er one Vision touch'd thy infant Thought,
Of all the Nurse and all the Priest have taught,   30
Of airy Elves by Moonlight Shadows seen,
The silver Token, and the circled Green,
Or Virgins visited by Angel-Pow'rs,
With Golden Crowns and Wreaths of heavn'ly Flow'rs,
Hear and believe! thy own Importance know,   35
Nor bound thy narrow Views to Things below.
Some secret Truths from Learned Pride conceal'd,
To Maids alone and Children are reveal'd:
What tho' no Credit doubting Wits may give?
The Fair and Innocent shall still believe.   40
Know then, unnumber'd Spirits round thee fly,
The light *Militia* of the lower Sky;
These, tho' unseen, are ever on the Wing,
Hang o'er the *Box,* and hover round the *Ring.*
Think what an Equipage thou hast in Air,   45
And view with scorn *Two Pages* and a *Chair.*
As now your own, our Beings were of old,
And once inclos'd in Woman's beauteous Mold;

17. The triple repetition is common in epic poetry.
Belinda's hand-bell not being answered, she knocked with her slipper.
Bell-hanging was not introduced into domestic apartments till much later.
   18. The 'repeater' watch sounded the hour and the quarters when
pressure was applied to the pin which projected from the case near the
pendant. The difficulty of striking a light made repeaters popular.
   21 ff. The gods sometimes communicate with the epic hero by means
of apparitions during sleep, e.g. *Æneid,* iii 147 ff.
   23. The dresses worn for the royal birthday celebrations were excep-
tionally splendid.
   33. Carrying a reference to the Annunciation and to the experiences of
virgin saints.
   44. *the Ring*] a fashionable parade for coaches in Hyde Park.
   46. *a Chair*] a sedan chair.

Thence, by a soft Transition, we repair
From earthly Vehicles to these of Air.					50
Think not, when Woman's transient Breath is fled,
That all her Vanities at once are dead:
Succeeding Vanities she still regards,
And tho' she plays no more, o'erlooks the Cards.
Her Joy in gilded Chariots, when alive,					55
And Love of *Ombre*, after Death survive.
For when the Fair in all their Pride expire,
To their first Elements their Souls retire:
The Sprights of fiery Termagants in Flame
Mount up, and take a *Salamander*'s Name.					60
Soft yielding Minds to Water glide away,
And sip with *Nymphs*, their Elemental Tea.
The graver Prude sinks downward to a *Gnome*,
In search of Mischief still on Earth to roam.
The light Coquettes in *Sylphs* aloft repair,					65
And sport and flutter in the Fields of Air.
    Know farther yet; Whoever fair and chaste
Rejects Mankind, is by some *Sylph* embrac'd:
For Spirits, freed from mortal Laws, with ease
Assume what Sexes and what Shapes they please.					70
What guards the Purity of melting Maids,
In Courtly Balls, and Midnight Masquerades,
Safe from the treach'rous Friend, the daring Spark,
The Glance by Day, the Whisper in the Dark;
When kind Occasion prompts their warm Desires,					75
When Musick softens, and when Dancing fires?

---

50. *Vehicles*] 'The *Platonists* doe chiefly take notice of *Three* Kindes of
Vehicles, Æthereal, Aereal, and *Terrestrial*' (Henry More, *Immortality of
the Soul,* ii 14, §1).
    55 f.					—*Quæ gratia currûm*
					Armorumque fuit vivis, quæ cura nitentes
					Pascere equos, eadem sequitur tellure repostos.
Virg. Æn. 6. ⟨653 ff.⟩ [P]
    Ombre] See III 27–104.
    58. *first*] = preponderating. A person's nature was supposed to depend
on the relative proportions of the four elements in the composition of his
body.
    59. 'Termagant . . . A scold; a bawling turbulent woman' (Johnson's
Dictionary, which cites this couplet).
    fiery] Pope puns on the two meanings (a) bad-tempered, (b) having a
preponderating amount of fire in one's constitution.
    62. *Tea*] Then a perfect rhyme with *away.* Cf. iii 7 f. below.
    73. *Spark*] 'A lively, showy, splendid, gay man. It is commonly used in
contempt' (Johnson's *Dictionary*).

'Tis but their *Sylph*, the wise Celestials know,
Tho' *Honour* is the Word with Men below.

   Some Nymphs there are, too conscious of their Face,
For Life predestin'd to the *Gnomes*' Embrace.   80
These swell their Prospects and exalt their Pride,
When Offers are disdain'd, and Love deny'd.
Then gay Ideas crowd the vacant Brain;
While Peers and Dukes, and all their sweeping Train,
And Garters, Stars and Coronets appear,   85
And in soft Sounds, *Your Grace* salutes their Ear.
'Tis these that early taint the Female Soul,
Instruct the Eyes of young *Coquettes* to roll,
Teach Infant-Cheeks a bidden Blush to know,
And little Hearts to flutter at a *Beau*.   90
   Oft when the World imagine Women stray,
The *Sylphs* thro' mystick Mazes guide their Way,
Thro' all the giddy Circle they pursue,
And old Impertinence expel by new.
What tender Maid but must a Victim fall   95
To one Man's Treat, but for another's Ball?
When *Florio* speaks, what Virgin could withstand,
If gentle *Damon* did not squeeze her Hand?
With varying Vanities, from ev'ry Part,
They shift the moving Toyshop of their Heart;   100
Where Wigs with Wigs, with Sword-knots Sword-knots
    strive,
Beaus banish Beaus, and Coaches Coaches drive.
This erring Mortals Levity may call,
Oh blind to Truth! the *Sylphs* contrive it all.
   Of these am I, who thy Protection claim,   105
A watchful Sprite, and *Ariel* is my Name.
Late, as I rang'd the Crystal Wilds of Air,
In the clear Mirror of thy ruling *Star*
I saw, alas! some dread Event impend,
Ere to the Main this Morning Sun descend.   110

79. too sensible of their beauty.
89. i.e. with rouge.
94. *Impertinence*] 'Trifle: thing of no value' (Johnson's *Dictionary*).
96. *Treat*] 'An entertainment of food and drink' (*OED*).
101. *Sword-knots*] Johnson defines as 'Ribband tied to the hilt of the sword', and quotes these lines.
102. *drive*] Another pun.
108. *In the clear Mirror*] *The Language of the Platonists, the writers of the intelligible world of Spirits, etc.* [P]

But Heav'n reveals not what, or how, or where:
Warn'd by thy *Sylph*, oh Pious Maid beware!
This to disclose is all thy Guardian can.
Beware of all, but most beware of Man!
   He said; when *Shock*, who thought she slept
      too long,   115
Leapt up, and wak'd his Mistress with his Tongue.
'Twas then *Belinda*! if Report say true,
Thy Eyes first open'd on a *Billet-doux*;
Wounds, Charms, and *Ardors*, were no sooner read,
But all the Vision vanish'd from thy Head.   120
   And now, unveil'd, the *Toilet* stands display'd,
Each Silver Vase in mystic Order laid.
First, rob'd in White, the Nymph intent adores
With. Head uncover'd, the *Cosmetic* Pow'rs.
A heav'nly Image in the Glass appears,   125
To that she bends, to that her Eyes she rears;
Th'inferior Priestess, at her Altar's side,
Trembling, begins the sacred Rites of Pride.
Unnumber'd Treasures ope at once, and here
The various Off'rings of the World appear;   130
From each she nicely culls with curious Toil,
And decks the Goddess with the glitt'ring Spoil.
This Casket *India*'s glowing Gems unlocks,
And all *Arabia* breathes from yonder Box.
The Tortoise here and Elephant unite,   135
Transform'd to *Combs*, the speckled and the white.
Here Files of Pins extend their shining Rows,
Puffs, Powders, Patches, Bibles, Billet-doux.
Now awful Beauty puts on all its Arms;
The Fair each moment rises in her Charms,   140
Repairs her Smiles, awakens ev'ry Grace,
And calls forth all the Wonders of her Face;
Sees by Degrees a purer Blush arise,
And keener Lightnings quicken in her Eyes.

112 ff. Warnings are common in the epics: cf., e.g., *Æneid*, ii 270 ff.
where the ghost of Hector appears to Æneas on the night of the sack of
Troy warning him to escape.
   115. The shock or shough was a kind of lap-dog.
   123 ff. Belinda is adoring her 'heavn'ly Image' in the mirror; her
image is the 'Goddess', she is the chief priestess.
   137 f. The rhyme is imperfect; cf. i 117 f. above.
   139 ff. Pope is parodying the arming of the epic hero.
   144. Belinda employs the juice of belladonna (deadly night-shade),
which enlarges the pupil of the eye, or else she darkens the surrounding
skin.

The busy *Sylphs* surround their darling Care;   145
These set the Head, and those divide the Hair,
Some fold the Sleeve, whilst others plait the Gown;
And *Betty's* prais'd for Labours not her own.

145. *Antient Traditions of the* Rabbi's *relate, that several of the fallen Angels became amorous of Women, and particularize some; among the rest* Asael, *who lay with* Naamah, *the wife of* Noah, *or of* Ham; *and who continuing impenitent, still presides over the Women's Toilets.* Bereshi Rabbi *in* Genes. 6. 2. [P]
148. *Betty*] At this time 'Betty' was a generic name for lady's maids.

CANTO II

Not with more Glories, in th' Etherial Plain,
The Sun first rises o'er the purpled Main,
Than issuing forth, the Rival of his Beams
Lanch'd on the Bosom of the Silver *Thames.*
Fair Nymphs, and well-drest Youths around her shone, 5
But ev'ry Eye was fix'd on her alone.
On her white Breast a sparkling *Cross* she wore,
Which *Jews* might kiss, and Infidels adore.
Her lively Looks a sprightly Mind disclose,
Quick as her Eyes, and as unfix'd as those: 10
Favours to none, to all she Smiles extends,
Oft she rejects, but never once offends.
Bright as the Sun, her Eyes the Gazers strike,
And, like the Sun, they shine on all alike.
Yet graceful Ease, and Sweetness void of Pride,   15
Might hide her Faults, if *Belles* had Faults to hide:
If to her share some Female Errors fall,
Look on her Face, and you'll forget 'em all.
  This Nymph, to the Destruction of Mankind,
Nourish'd two Locks, which graceful hung behind   20
In equal Curls, and well conspir'd to deck
With shining Ringlets the smooth Iv'ry Neck.
Love in these Labyrinths his Slaves detains,
And mighty Hearts are held in slender Chains.
With hairy Sprindges we the Birds betray,   25
Slight Lines of Hair surprize the Finny Prey,
Fair Tresses Man's Imperial Race insnare,
And Beauty draws us with a single Hair.
  Th' Adventrous *Baron* the bright Locks admir'd,
He saw, he wish'd, and to the Prize aspir'd: 30

1 ff. Cf. Æneas's voyage up the Tiber (*Æneid*, vii).

Resolv'd to win, he meditates the way,
By Force to ravish, or by Fraud betray;
For when Success a Lover's Toil attends,
Few ask, if Fraud or Force attain'd his Ends.
   For this, ere *Phœbus* rose, he had implor'd   35
Propitious Heav'n, and ev'ry Pow'r ador'd,
But chiefly *Love*—to *Love* an Altar built,
Of twelve vast *French* Romances, neatly gilt.
There lay three Garters, half a Pair of Gloves;
And all the Trophies of his former Loves.   40
With tender *Billet-doux* he lights the Pyre,
And breathes three am'rous Sighs to raise the Fire.
Then prostrate falls, and begs with ardent Eyes
Soon to obtain, and long possess the Prize:
The Pow'rs gave Ear, and granted half his Pray'r,   45
The rest, the Winds dispers'd in empty Air.
   But now secure the painted Vessel glides,
The Sun-beams trembling on the floating Tydes,
While melting Musick steals upon the Sky,
And soften'd Sounds along the Waters die.   50
Smooth flow the Waves, the Zephyrs gently play,
Belinda smil'd, and all the World was gay.
All but the *Sylph*—With careful Thoughts opprest,
Th'impending Woe sate heavy on his Breast.
He summons strait his Denizens of Air;   55
The lucid Squadrons round the Sails repair:
Soft o'er the Shrouds Aerial Whispers breathe,
That seem'd but *Zephyrs* to the Train beneath.
Some to the Sun their Insect-Wings unfold,
Waft on the Breeze, or sink in Clouds of Gold.   60
Transparent Forms, too fine for mortal Sight,
Their fluid Bodies half dissolv'd in Light.
Loose to the Wind their airy Garments flew,
Thin glitt'ring Textures of the filmy Dew;
Dipt in the richest Tincture of the Skies,   65
Where Light disports in ever-mingling Dies,
While ev'ry Beam new transient Colours flings,
Colours that change whene'er they wave their Wings.

32. *By Force . . . or by Fraud*] A common antithesis in the epics. Cf.
Dryden's *Æneid*, i 942, ii 62.
   45 f. Virg. Æn. 11 [794 f.] [P] Dryden's translation (1165 f.) reads:
        Apollo heard, and granting half his Pray'r,
      Shuffled in Winds the rest, and toss'd in empty Air.
   55. *Denizens*] Used in its proper sense of 'naturalized aliens'.

Amid the Circle, on the gilded Mast,
Superior by the Head, was *Ariel* plac'd;   70
His Purple Pinions opening to the Sun,
He rais'd his Azure Wand, and thus begun.
      Ye *Sylphs* and *Sylphids*, to your Chief give Ear,
Fays, Fairies, Genii, Elves, and *Dæmons* hear!
Ye know the Spheres and various Tasks assign'd,   75
By Laws Eternal, to th' Aerial Kind.
Some in the Fields of purest *Æther* play,
And bask and whiten in the Blaze of Day.
Some guide the Course of wandring Orbs on high,
Or roll the Planets thro' the boundless Sky.   80
Some less refin'd, beneath the Moon's pale Light
Pursue the Stars that shoot athwart the Night,
Or suck the Mists in grosser Air below,
Or dip their Pinions in the painted Bow,
Or brew fierce Tempests on the wintry Main,   85
Or o'er the Glebe distill the kindly Rain.
Others on Earth o'er human Race preside,
Watch all their Ways, and all their Actions guide:
Of these the Chief the Care of Nations own,
And guard with Arms Divine the *British Throne.*   90
      Our humbler Province is to tend the Fair,
Not a less pleasing, tho' less glorious Care.
To save the Powder from too rude a Gale,
Nor let th' imprison'd Essences exhale,
To draw fresh Colours from the vernal Flow'rs,   95
To steal from Rainbows ere they drop in Show'rs
A brighter Wash; to curl their waving Hairs,
Assist their Blushes, and inspire their Airs;
Nay oft, in Dreams, Invention we bestow,
To change a *Flounce,* or add a *Furbelo.*   100
      This Day, black Omens threat the brightest Fair
That e'er deserv'd a watchful Spirit's Care;
Some dire Disaster, or by Force, or Slight,
But what, or where, the Fates have wrapt in Night.
Whether the Nymph shall break *Diana*'s Law,   105
Or some frail *China* Jar receive a Flaw,
Or stain her Honour, or her new Brocade,
Forget her Pray'rs, or miss a Masquerade,
Or lose her Heart, or Necklace, at a Ball;
Or whether Heav'n has doom'd that *Shock* must fall.   110

100. *Furbelo*] 'A piece of stuff plaited and puckered together, either below or above, on the petticoats or gowns of women' [Johnson].

Haste then ye Spirits! to your Charge repair;
The flutt'ring Fan be *Zephyretta*'s Care;
The Drops to thee, *Brillante*, we consign;
And, *Momentilla*, let the Watch be thine;
Do thou, *Crispissa*, tend her fav'rite Lock;   115
Ariel himself shall be the Guard of *Shock*.
    To Fifty chosen *Sylphs*, of special Note,
We trust th' important Charge, the *Petticoat*:
Oft have we known that sev'nfold Fence to fail,
Tho' stiff with Hoops, and arm'd with Ribs of Whale. 120
Form a strong Line about the Silver Bound,
And guard the wide Circumference around.
    Whatever Spirit, careless of his Charge,
His Post neglects, or leaves the Fair at large,
Shall feel sharp Vengeance soon o'ertake his Sins,   125
Be stopt in *Vials*, or transfixt with *Pins*;
Or plung'd in Lakes of bitter *Washes* lie,
Or wedg'd whole Ages in a *Bodkin*'s Eye:
Gums and *Pomatums* shall his Flight restrain,
While clog'd he beats his silken Wings in vain;   130
Or Alom-*Stypticks* with contracting Power
Shrink his thin Essence like a rivell'd Flower.
Or as *Ixion* fix'd, the Wretch shall feel
The giddy Motion of the whirling Mill,
In Fumes of burning Chocolate shall glow,   135
And tremble at the Sea that froaths below!
    He spoke; the Spirits from the Sails descend;
Some, Orb in Orb, around the Nymph extend,
Some thrid the mazy Ringlets of her Hair,
Some hang upon the Pendants of her Ear;   140
With beating Hearts the dire Event they wait,
Anxious, and trembling for the Birth of Fate.

113. *Drops*] 'Diamond(s) hanging in the ear' [Johnson].
    116. The reason for Ariel's special post is hinted at iii 158 and iv 75 f.
    117 ff. Pope mimics the epic shield; cf. *Iliad*, vii 295 ff., xviii 551 ff.,
especially 701 ff. (where Vulcan, making the shield of Achilles, binds the
circumference with silver), and *Æneid*, viii 447 ff.
    123 ff. Cf. Jove's threats, *Iliad*, viii 11 ff. and 'the various Penances
enjoyn'd' before a soul in Hades can be made ready for human life again
(*Æneid*, vi 739 ff.).
    128. Pope plays on the various meanings of *bodkin*: (1) here it means a
blunt-pointed needle; (2) at iv 98 and v 95, a hair ornament; (3) at v 55
and 88 a dagger (with a pun on (2)).
    132. *rivell'd*] 'contract[ed] into wrinkles and corrugations' [Johnson].

CANTO III

Close by those Meads for ever crown'd with Flow'rs,
Where *Thames* with Pride surveys his rising Tow'rs,
There stands a Structure of Majestick Frame,
Which from the neighb'ring *Hampton* takes its Name.
Here *Britain*'s Statesmen oft the Fall foredoom   5
Of Foreign Tyrants, and of Nymphs at home;
Here Thou, Great *Anna*! whom three Realms obey,
Dost sometimes Counsel take—and sometimes *Tea*.
  Hither the Heroes and the Nymphs resort,
To taste awhile the Pleasures of a Court;   10
In various Talk th' instructive hours they past,
Who gave the *Ball*, or paid the *Visit* last:
One speaks the Glory of the *British Queen*,
And one describes a charming *Indian Screen*;
A third interprets Motions, Looks, and Eyes;   15
At ev'ry Word a Reputation dies.
Snuff, or the *Fan*, supply each Pause of Chat,
With singing, laughing, ogling, and all that.
  Mean while declining from the Noon of Day,
The Sun obliquely shoots his burning Ray;   20
The hungry Judges soon the Sentence sign,
And Wretches hang that Jury-men may Dine;
The Merchant from th' *Exchange* returns in Peace,
And the long Labours of the *Toilette* cease—
Belinda now, whom Thirst of Fame invites,   25
Burns to encounter two adventrous Knights,
At *Ombre* singly to decide their Doom;
And swells her Breast with Conquests yet to come.
Strait the three Bands prepare in Arms to join,
Each Band the number of the Sacred Nine.   30
Soon as she spreads her Hand, th' Aerial Guard
Descend, and sit on each important Card:

7. The English crown still kept up its absurd claim to rule France as
well as Great Britain and Ireland.

11 ff. 'At this Assembly [the Court of King William at Kensington],
the only diversion is playing at Cards: For which purpose there are two
Tables for *Basset* and three or four more for *Picket* and *Ombre*, but
generally the Basset-Tables are only fill'd while the rest of the Company
either sit or stand, talking on various Subjects, or justle about from one
end of the Gallery [of pictures] to the other, some to admire, and most to
find fault' (*Letters of Wit*, p. 214).

12. *Visit*] See note on iii 167 below.

17. The singular growth of the practice of taking snuff was a special
feature of the reign of Queen Anne: before 1702 it was comparatively
unknown.

First *Ariel* perch'd upon a *Matadore*,
Then each, according to the Rank they bore;
For *Sylphs*, yet mindful of their ancient Race,   35
Are, as when Women, wondrous fond of Place.
   Behold, four *Kings* in Majesty rever'd,
With hoary Whiskers and a forky Beard;
And four fair *Queens* whose hands sustain a Flow'r,
Th' expressive Emblem of their softer Pow'r;   40
Four *Knaves* in Garbs succinct, a trusty Band,
Caps on their heads, and Halberds in their hand;
And Particolour'd Troops, a shining Train,
Draw forth to Combat on the Velvet Plain.
   The skilful Nymph reviews her Force with Care;   45
Let Spades be Trumps! she said, and Trumps they were.
   Now move to War her Sable *Matadores*,
In Show like Leaders of the swarthy *Moors*.
Spadillio first, unconquerable Lord!
Led off two captive Trumps, and swept the Board.   50
As many more *Manillio* forc'd to yield,
And march'd a Victor from the verdant Field.
Him *Basto* follow'd, but his Fate more hard
Gain'd but one Trump and one *Plebeian* Card.
With his broad Sabre next, a Chief in Years,   55
The hoary Majesty of *Spades* appears;
Puts forth one manly Leg, to sight reveal'd;
The rest his many-colour'd Robe conceal'd.
The Rebel-*Knave*, who dares his Prince engage,
Proves the just Victim of his Royal Rage.   60
Ev'n mighty *Pam* that Kings and Queens o'erthrew,
And mow'd down Armies in the Fights of *Lu*,
Sad Chance of War! now, destitute of Aid,
Falls undistinguish'd by the Victor *Spade*!
   Thus far both Armies to *Belinda* yield;   65
Now to the *Baron* Fate inclines the Field.
His warlike *Amazon* her Host invades,
Th' Imperial Consort of the Crown of *Spades*.
The *Club*'s black Tyrant first her Victim dy'd,
Spite of his haughty Mien, and barb'rous Pride: 70

37 ff. This review of the forces is epical in all but length: cf. *Iliad*, iii
175 ff.
   46. Cf. Genesis i 3: 'And God said, "Let there be light:" and there was
light', which on the authority of Longinus (*De Sublimitate*, ix) became the
most famous of all instances of the sublime.

What boots the Regal Circle on his Head,
His Giant Limbs in State unwieldy spread?
That long behind he trails his pompous Robe,
And of all Monarchs only grasps the Globe?
   The *Baron* now his *Diamonds* pours apace;   75
Th' embroider'd *King* who shows but half his Face,
And his refulgent *Queen*, with Pow'rs combin'd,
Of broken Troops an easie Conquest find.
Clubs, *Diamonds*, *Hearts*, in wild Disorder seen,
With Throngs promiscuous strow the level Green.   80
Thus when dispers'd a routed Army runs,
Of *Asia*'s Troops, and *Africk*'s Sable Sons,
With like Confusion different Nations fly,
Of various Habit and of various Dye,
The pierc'd Battalions dis-united fall,   85
In Heaps on Heaps; one Fate o'erwhelms them all.
   The *Knave of Diamonds* tries his wily Arts,
And wins (oh shameful Chance!) the *Queen of Hearts*.
At this, the Blood the Virgin's Cheek forsook,
A livid Paleness spreads o'er all her Look;   90
She sees, and trembles at th' approaching Ill,
Just in the Jaws of Ruin, and *Codille*.
And now, (as oft in some distemper'd State)
On one nice *Trick* depends the gen'ral Fate.
An *Ace* of Hearts steps forth: The *King* unseen   95
Lurk'd in her Hand, and mourn'd his captive *Queen*.
He springs to Vengeance with an eager pace,
And falls like Thunder on the prostrate *Ace*.
The Nymph exulting fills with Shouts the Sky,
The Walls, the Woods, and long Canals reply.   100
  Oh thoughtless Mortals! ever blind to Fate,
Too soon dejected, and too soon elate!
Sudden these Honours shall be snatch'd away,
And curs'd for ever this Victorious Day.
   For lo! the Board with Cups and Spoons is crown'd,
The Berries crackle, and the Mill turns round.   106
On shining Altars of *Japan* they raise
The silver Lamp; the fiery Spirits blaze.
From silver Spouts the grateful Liquors glide,
While *China*'s Earth receives the smoking Tyde.   110

94. *Trick*] in two senses.
105 ff. Pope's version of the hearty meals in the epic.
107. *shining Altars of Japan*] = lacquered tables.

At once they gratify their Scent and Taste,
And frequent Cups prolong the rich Repast.
Strait hover round the Fair her Airy Band;
Some, as she sip'd, the fuming Liquor fann'd,
Some o'er her Lap their careful Plumes display'd,   115
Trembling, and conscious of the rich Brocade.
Coffee, (which makes the Politician wise,
And see thro' all things with his half-shut Eyes)
Sent up in Vapours to the *Baron*'s Brain
New Stratagems, the radiant Lock to gain.   120
Ah cease rash Youth! desist ere 'tis too late,
Fear the just Gods, and think of *Scylla*'s Fate!
Chang'd to a Bird, and sent to flit in Air,
She dearly pays for *Nisus*' injur'd Hair!
   But when to Mischief Mortals bend their Will,   125
How soon they find fit Instruments of Ill!
Just then, *Clarissa* drew with tempting Grace
A two-edg'd Weapon from her shining Case;
So Ladies in Romance assist their Knight,
Present the Spear, and arm him for the Fight.   130
He takes the Gift with rev'rence, and extends
The little Engine on his Fingers' Ends,
This just behind *Belinda*'s Neck he spread,
As o'er the fragrant Steams she bends her Head:
Swift to the Lock a thousand Sprights repair,   135
A thousand Wings, by turns, blow back the Hair,
And thrice they twitch'd the Diamond in her Ear,
Thrice she look'd back, and thrice the Foe drew near.
Just in that instant, anxious *Ariel* sought
The close Recesses of the Virgin's Thought;   140
As on the Nosegay in her Breast reclin'd,
He watch'd th' Ideas rising in her Mind,

117 f. The coffee houses had long been the chief haunt of amateur
politicians: they are satirized in *Tatlers* 155, 160, 178; *Spectator* 403.
   122 ff. *Vide* Ovid. Metam. 8. ⟨1 ff.⟩ [P]
   King Nisus, besieged in Megara by Minos, had a daughter Scylla who,
seeing Minos from a watch tower, fell in love with him. The safety of
Nisus and his kingdom was known to depend on a purple hair which,
among 'those of honourable silver', grew on his head. Scylla plucked out
this hair and took it to Minos but met with nothing but abhorrence for her
impiety. After his victory he sailed away; whereupon Scylla attempted to
cling to his ship till, beaten off by Nisus, who had become an osprey, she
also became a bird.
   128. *shining Case*] See note on v 116 below.
   132. *Engine*] The word being applicable to a large military object or
small domestic one is exactly appropriate for mock-heroic.

Sudden he view'd, in spite of all her Art,
An Earthly Lover lurking at her Heart.
Amaz'd, confus'd, he found his Pow'r expir'd,   145
Resign'd to Fate, and with a Sigh retir'd.
    The Peer now spreads the glitt'ring *Forfex* wide,
T'inclose the Lock; now joins it, to divide.
Ev'n then, before the fatal Engine clos'd,
A wretched *Sylph* too fondly interpos'd;   150
Fate urg'd the Sheers, and cut the *Sylph* in twain,
(But Airy Substance soon unites again)
The meeting Points the sacred Hair dissever
From the fair Head, for ever and for ever!
    Then flash'd the living Lightning from her Eyes,   155
And Screams of Horror rend th' affrighted Skies.
Not louder Shrieks to pitying Heav'n are cast,
When Husbands or when Lap-dogs breathe their last,
Or when rich *China* Vessels, fal'n from high,
In glittring Dust and painted Fragments lie!   160
    Let Wreaths of Triumph now my Temples twine,
(The Victor cry'd) the glorious Prize is mine!
While Fish in Streams, or Birds delight in Air,
Or in a Coach and Six the *British* Fair,
As long as *Atalantis* shall be read,   165
Or the small Pillow grace a Lady's Bed,
While *Visits* shall be paid on solemn Days,
When numerous Wax-lights in bright Order blaze,
While Nymphs take Treats, or Assignations give,
So long my Honour, Name, and Praise shall live!   170
    What Time wou'd spare, from Steel receives its date,
And Monuments, like Men, submit to Fate!
Steel cou'd the Labour of the Gods destroy,

149 f. The sylph is trying to imitate the angel (*Davideis*, p. 15) who puts by the spear which Saul flings at David.

149. The wooden horse is called 'the fatal Engine' in Dryden's *Æneid*, ii 345.

152. *See* Milton, *lib.* 6 ⟨330 f.⟩ [P]

165. Mrs. Manley's *Secret Memoirs and Manners of several Persons of Quality, of Both Sexes. From the New Atalantis, an Island in the Mediterranean*, had appeared in 1709 (2 vols.).

167 f. Visits were an essential part of the day's routine for a fashionable woman. They took place in the evening, and the lady was attended by servants bearing lights. An essential point of the visit was its appointed day; 'solemn' is therefore a pun; it includes the sense of *solemnis*, 'marked by the celebration of special observances or rites (especially of a religious character)'.

173 f. Troy was supposed to have been built by Apollo and Poseidon.

And strike to Dust th' Imperial Tow'rs of *Troy*;
Steel cou'd the Works of mortal Pride confound,   175
And hew Triumphal Arches to the Ground.
What Wonder then, fair Nymph! thy Hairs shou'd feel
The conqu'ring Force of unresisted Steel?

CANTO IV

But anxious Cares the pensive Nymph opprest,
And secret Passions labour'd in her Breast.
Not youthful Kings in Battel seiz'd alive,
Not scornful Virgins who their Charms survive,
Not ardent Lovers robb'd of all their Bliss,   5
Not ancient Ladies when refus'd a Kiss,
Not Tyrants fierce that unrepenting die,
Not *Cynthia* when her *Manteau*'s pinn'd awry,
E'er felt such Rage, Resentment and Despair,
As Thou, sad Virgin! for thy ravish'd Hair.   10
    For, that sad moment, when the *Sylphs* withdrew,
And *Ariel* weeping from *Belinda* flew,
Umbriel, a dusky melancholy Spright,
As ever sully'd the fair face of Light,
Down to the Central Earth, his proper Scene,   15
Repair'd to search the gloomy Cave of *Spleen*.
    Swift on his sooty Pinions flitts the *Gnome*,
And in a Vapour reach'd the dismal Dome.
No cheerful Breeze this sullen Region knows,
The dreaded *East* is all the Wind that blows.   20
Here, in a Grotto, sheltred close from Air,
And screen'd in Shades from Day's detested Glare,
She sighs for ever on her pensive Bed,

---

1. Virg. Æn. 4. ⟨1⟩ *At regina gravi, &c.* [P]
    8. *Manteau*] 'a loose upper Garment, now generally worn by Women,
instead of a straight-body'd Gown'.
    13 ff. The journey to the underworld is an epic commonplace. The
subsidiary horrors in the 'antre' of Chicane (Boileau, *Lutrin*, v 39 ff.), and
in the lairs of Envy and Death (Garth, *Dispensary*, pp. 15 f. and 105) are
like Pope's, fantastically allegorical. The source of all these is the cave
which Ovid invented for Envy, *Metam.*, ii 760 ff.
    16. *Spleen*] The fashionable name for an ancient malady, the incidence
of which was jealously confined to the idle rich.
    18. *Vapour*] Pope puns on vapour(s) again at ll. 39 and 59 below. The
spleen was also called the vapours and a misty climate was supposed to
induce it.
    20. The east wind was considered to provoke spleen.

Pain at her Side, and *Megrim* at her Head.
 Two Handmaids wait the Throne: Alike in Place, 25
But diff'ring far in Figure and in Face.
Here stood *Ill-nature* like an *ancient Maid*,
Her wrinkled Form in *Black* and *White* array'd;
With store of Pray'rs, for Mornings, Nights, and Noons,
Her Hand is fill'd; her Bosom with Lampoons. 30
 There *Affectation* with a sickly Mien
Shows in her Cheek the Roses of Eighteen,
Practis'd to Lisp, and hang the Head aside,
Faints into Airs, and languishes with Pride,
On the rich Quilt sinks with becoming Woe, 35
Wrapt in a Gown, for Sickness, and for Show.
The Fair-ones feel such Maladies as these,
When each new Night-Dress gives a new Disease.
 A constant *Vapour* o'er the Palace flies;
Strange Phantoms rising as the Mists arise; 40
Dreadful, as Hermit's Dreams in haunted Shades,
Or bright as Visions of expiring Maids.
Now glaring Fiends, and Snakes on rolling Spires,
Pale Spectres, gaping Tombs, and Purple Fires:
Now Lakes of liquid Gold, *Elysian* Scenes, 45
And Crystal Domes, and Angels in Machines.
 Unnumber'd Throngs on ev'ry side are seen
Of Bodies chang'd to various Forms by *Spleen*.
Here living *Teapots* stand, one Arm held out,
One bent; the Handle this, and that the Spout: 50
A Pipkin there like *Homer*'s *Tripod* walks;
Here sighs a Jar, and there a Goose-pye talks;

24. The organ called the spleen is at the left side of the body; megrim, or migraine, is a 'Disorder of the head' (Johnson's *Dictionary*), a severe headache: Pope places his allegorical figures accordingly.
 25. *wait*] = wait on, 'to be in readiness to receive orders'.
 33. *Tatler* 77, an essay on affectation (mainly that of men), notes lisping and carrying the head on one side as two marks of affectation, the former a recent fashion, the latter a fashion at the court of Alexander.
 43 ff. Starting from the usual hallucinatory symptoms of the spleen, Pope leads on to a satiric catalogue of the scenic effects of contemporary opera and pantomime.
 43. *Spires*] coils.
 47–54. These metamorphoses represent illusions commonly suffered by the splenetic.
 51 *See* Hom. *Iliad*. 18 439 ⟨ff.⟩, *of* Vulcan's *Walking tripods*. [P]
 Pipkin] a small earthen boiler.
 52. *Goose-pye*] *Alludes to a real fact, a Lady of distinction imagin'd herself in this condition*. [P]

Men prove with Child, as pow'rful Fancy works,
And Maids turn'd Bottels, call aloud for Corks.
  Safe past the *Gnome* thro' this fantastick Band,   55
A Branch of healing *Spleenwort* in his hand.
Then thus addrest the Pow'r—Hail wayward Queen!
Who rule the Sex to Fifty from Fifteen,
Parent of Vapours and of Female Wit,
Who give th' *Hysteric* or *Poetic* Fit,   60
On various Tempers act by various ways,
Make some take Physick, others scribble Plays;
Who cause the Proud their Visits to delay,
And send the Godly in a Pett, to pray.
A Nymph there is, that all thy Pow'r disdains,   65
And thousands more in equal Mirth maintains.
But oh! if e'er thy *Gnome* could spoil a Grace,
Or raise a Pimple on a beauteous Face,
Like Citron-Waters Matrons' Cheeks inflame,
Or change Complexions at a losing Game;   70
If e'er with airy Horns I planted Heads,
Or rumpled Petticoats, or tumbled Beds,
Or caus'd Suspicion when no Soul was rude,
Or discompos'd the Head-dress of a Prude,
Or e'er to costive Lap-Dog gave Disease,   75
Which not the Tears of brightest Eyes could ease:
Hear me, and touch *Belinda* with Chagrin;
That single Act gives half the World the Spleen.
  The Goddess with a discontented Air
Seems to reject him, tho' she grants his Pray'r.   80
A wondrous Bag with both her Hands she binds,
Like that where once *Ulysses* held the Winds;
There she collects the Force of Female Lungs,
Sighs, Sobs, and Passions, and the War of Tongues.
A Vial next she fills with fainting Fears,   85
Soft Sorrows, melting Griefs, and flowing Tears.
The *Gnome* rejoicing bears her Gifts away,
Spreads his black Wings, and slowly mounts to Day.

---

57 ff. This speech, which embodies common symptoms of the spleen, is built on the model of Nisus' speech to Luna (*Æneid*, ix 404 ff.), Sidrac's to Chicane (*Lutrin*, v 63 ff.), and Horoscope's to Disease (*Dispensary*, p. 37).

59–62. Melancholy was supposed to accompany creative genius.

The *Tatler* and *Spectator* always treated the spleen as a malady of both sexes. Pope restricts it entirely to women (except for l. 53).

69. *Citron-Waters*] Brandy distilled with the rind of citrons.

Sunk in *Thalestris'* Arms the Nymph he found,
Her Eyes dejected and her Hair unbound.   90
Full o'er their Heads the swelling Bag he rent,
And all the Furies issued at the Vent.
Belinda burns with more than mortal Ire,
And fierce *Thalestris* fans the rising Fire.
O wretched Maid! she spread her Hands, and cry'd,   95
(While *Hampton*'s Ecchos, wretched Maid! reply'd)
Was it for this you took such constant Care
The *Bodkin, Comb,* and *Essence* to prepare;
For this your Locks in Paper-Durance bound,
For this with tort'ring Irons wreath'd around?   100
For this with Fillets strain'd your tender Head,
And bravely bore the double Loads of Lead?
Gods! shall the Ravisher display your Hair,
While the Fops envy, and the Ladies stare!
Honour forbid! at whose unrival'd Shrine   105
Ease, Pleasure, Virtue, All, our Sex resign.
Methinks already I your Tears survey,
Already hear the horrid things they say,
Already see you a degraded Toast,
And all your Honour in a Whisper lost!   110
How shall I, then, your helpless Fame defend?
'Twill then be Infamy to seem your Friend!
And shall this Prize, th' inestimable Prize,
Expos'd thro' Crystal to the gazing Eyes,
And heighten'd by the Diamond's circling Rays,   115
On that Rapacious Hand for ever blaze?
Sooner shall Grass in *Hide*-Park *Circus* grow,
And Wits take Lodgings in the Sound of *Bow*;
Sooner let Earth, Air, Sea, to *Chaos* fall,
Men, Monkies, Lap-dogs, Parrots, perish all!   120
    She said; then raging to *Sir Plume* repairs,

89. Thalestris was the Queen of the Amazons.

98. Cf. note on ii 128 above.

99 ff. The imagery is from incarceration and torture. The curl papers of ladies' hair used to be fastened with strips of pliant lead.

101. *Fillets*] With a reference to the epic: e.g., priestesses wear fillets in the *Æneid.*

109. *toast*] a celebrated woman whose health is often drunk.

117. *Hide-Park Circus*] a fashionable place for coach-driving, destroyed when the Serpentine was created in 1736.

118. The City with its solid brick citizens' houses had become almost wholly mercantile.

121. *Sir Plume*] Sir George Browne, cousin of Arabella Fermor's mother.

And bids her *Beau* demand the precious Hairs:
(*Sir Plume*, of *Amber Snuff-box* justly vain,
And the nice Conduct of a *clouded Cane*)
With earnest Eyes, and round unthinking Face,   125
He first the Snuff-box open'd, then the Case,
And thus broke out— 'My Lord, why, what the Devil?
Z—ds! damn the Lock! 'fore Gad, you must be civil!
Plague on't! 'tis past a Jest—nay prithee, Pox!
Give her the Hair'—he spoke, and rapp'd his Box.   130
  It grieves me much (reply'd the Peer again)
Who speaks so well shou'd ever speak in vain.
But by this Lock, this sacred Lock I swear,
(Which never more shall join its parted Hair,
Which never more its Honours shall renew,   135
Clipt from the lovely Head where late it grew)
That while my Nostrils draw the vital Air,
This Hand, which won it, shall for ever wear.
He spoke, and speaking, in proud Triumph spread
The long-contended Honours of her Head.   140
  But *Umbriel*, hateful *Gnome*! forbears not so;
He breaks the Vial whence the Sorrows flow.
Then see! the *Nymph* in beauteous Grief appears,
Her Eyes half-languishing, half-drown'd in Tears;
On her heav'd Bosom hung her drooping Head,   145
Which, with a Sigh, she rais'd; and thus she said.
  For ever curs'd be this detested Day,
Which snatch'd my best, my fav'rite Curl away!
Happy! ah ten times happy, had I been,
If *Hampton-Court* these Eyes had never seen!   150
Yet am not I the first mistaken Maid,
By Love of *Courts* to num'rous Ills betray'd.
Oh had I rather un-admir'd remain'd
In some lone Isle, or distant *Northern* Land;
Where the gilt *Chariot* never marks the Way,   155

124. *clouded*] variegated with dark veins.
   127 ff. Sir Plume speaks the language of the 'common Swearer' in
Tatler 13, and the fop in *Tatler* 110.
   133 ff. *In allusion to* Achilles's *Oath in* Homer. *Il. i* ⟨309 ff.⟩. [P]
   141 f. *These two lines are additional; and assign the cause of the different
operation of the Passions of the two Ladies. The poem went on before without that distinction, as without any Machinery to the end of the Canto.*
[P]
   147 ff. This speech is modelled on Achilles' lament for Patroclus, *Iliad*,
xviii 107 ff.
   149 f. An adaptation of Dido's cry, *Æneid*, iv 657 f.

Where none learn *Ombre*, none e'er taste *Bohea*!
There kept my Charms conceal'd from mortal Eye,
Like Roses that in Desarts bloom and die.
What mov'd my Mind with youthful Lords to rome?
O had I stay'd, and said my Pray'rs at home!   160
'Twas this, the Morning *Omens* seem'd to tell;
Thrice from my trembling hand the *Patch-box* fell;
The tott'ring *China* shook without a Wind,
Nay, *Poll* sate mute, and *Shock* was most Unkind!
A *Sylph* too warn'd me of the Threats of Fate,   165
In mystic Visions, now believ'd too late!
See the poor Remnants of these slighted Hairs!
My hands shall rend what ev'n thy Rapine spares:
These, in two sable Ringlets taught to break,
Once gave new Beauties to the snowie Neck.   170
The Sister-Lock now sits uncouth, alone,
And in its Fellow's Fate foresees its own;
Uncurl'd it hangs, the fatal Sheers demands;
And tempts once more thy sacrilegious Hands.
Oh hadst thou, Cruel! been content to seize   175
Hairs less in sight, or any Hairs but these!

156. *Bohea*] A species of tea, of higher colour, and more astringent
taste, than green tea.
158. Cf. Waller, *Go lovely rose*, ll. 6 ff.

CANTO V

She said: the pitying Audience melt in Tears,
But *Fate* and *Jove* had stopp'd the *Baron*'s Ears.
In vain *Thalestris* with Reproach assails,
For who can move when fair *Belinda* fails?
Not half so fixt the *Trojan* cou'd remain,   5
While *Anna* begg'd and *Dido* rag'd in vain.
Then grave *Clarissa* graceful wav'd her Fan;
Silence ensu'd, and thus the Nymph began.
    Say, why are Beauties prais'd and honour'd most,
The wise Man's Passion, and the vain Man's Toast?   10
Why deck'd with all that Land and Sea afford,
Why Angels call'd, and Angel-like ador'd?
Why round our Coaches crowd the white-glov'd Beaus,
Why bows the Side-box from its inmost Rows?

7. *Clarissa*] *A new Character introduced in the subsequent Editions, to
open more clearly the* MORAL *of the Poem, in a parody of the speech of
Sarpedon to Glaucus in Homer.* [P] See pp. 60–62; 170, 568.

How vain are all these Glories, all our Pains,   15
Unless good Sense preserve what Beauty gains:
That Men may say, when we the Front-box grace,
Behold the first in Virtue, as in Face!
Oh! if to dance all Night, and dress all Day,
Charm'd the Small-pox, or chas'd old Age away;   20
Who would not scorn what Huswife's Cares produce,
Or who would learn one earthly Thing of Use?
To patch, nay ogle, might become a Saint,
Nor could it sure be such a Sin to paint.
But since, alas! frail Beauty must decay,   25
Curl'd or uncurl'd, since Locks will turn to grey,
Since painted, or not painted, all shall fade,
And she who scorns a Man, must die a Maid;
What then remains, but well our Pow'r to use,
And keep good Humour still whate'er we lose?   30
And trust me, Dear! good Humour can prevail,
When Airs, and Flights, and Screams, and Scolding fail.
Beauties in vain their pretty Eyes may roll;
Charms strike the Sight, but Merit wins the Soul.

  So spoke the Dame, but no Applause ensu'd;   35
Belinda frown'd, *Thalestris* call'd her Prude.
To Arms, to Arms! the fierce Virago cries,
And swift as Lightning to the Combate flies.
All side in Parties, and begin th' Attack;
Fans clap, Silks russle, and tough Whalebones crack;   40
Heroes' and Heroins' Shouts confus'dly rise,
And base, and treble Voices strike the Skies.
No common Weapons in their Hands are found,
Like Gods they fight, nor dread a mortal Wound.

  So when bold *Homer* makes the Gods engage,   45
And heav'nly Breasts with human Passions rage;
'Gainst *Pallas*, *Mars*; *Latona*, *Hermes* arms;
And all *Olympus* rings with loud Alarms.
Jove's Thunder roars, Heav'n trembles all around;
Blue *Neptune* storms, the bellowing Deeps resound;   50
Earth shakes her nodding Tow'rs, the Ground gives way;
And the pale Ghosts start at the Flash of Day!

35. *It is a verse frequently repeated in* Homer *after any speech,*
    So spoke—and all the Heroes applauded. [P]
  37. *From hence the first Edition goes on to the Conclusion, except a very few short insertions added, to keep the Machinery in view to the end of the poem.* [P]
  37. *Virago*] A female warrior, a woman with the qualities of a man.
  45. Homer *Il.* 20 ⟨91 ff.⟩. [P]

Triumphant *Umbriel* on a Sconce's Height
Clapt his glad Wings, and sate to view the Fight:
Propt on their Bodkin Spears, the Sprights survey   55
The growing Combat, or assist the Fray.
 While thro' the Press enrag'd *Thalestris* flies,
And scatters Deaths around from both her Eyes,
A *Beau* and *Witling* perish'd in the Throng,
One dy'd in *Metaphor*, and one in *Song*.   60
O cruel Nymph! a living Death I bear,
Cry'd *Dapperwit*, and sunk beside his Chair.
A mournful Glance Sir *Fopling* upwards cast,
Those Eyes are made so killing—was his last:
Thus on *Meander*'s flow'ry Margin lies   65
Th' expiring Swan, and as he sings he dies.
 When bold Sir *Plume* had drawn *Clarissa* down,
Chloe stept in, and kill'd him with a Frown;
She smil'd to see the doughty Hero slain,
But at her Smile, the Beau reviv'd again.   70
 Now *Jove* suspends his golden Scales in Air,
Weighs the Men's Wits against the Lady's Hair;
The doubtful Beam long nods from side to side;
At length the Wits mount up, the Hairs subside.
 See fierce *Belinda* on the *Baron* flies,   75
With more than usual Lightning in her Eyes;
Nor fear'd the Chief th' unequal Fight to try,
Who sought no more than on his Foe to die.
But this bold Lord, with manly Strength indu'd,
She with one Finger and a Thumb subdu'd: 80
Just where the Breath of Life his Nostrils drew,

53–6. *These four lines added, for the reason before* ⟨37n⟩ *mentioned*. [P]
 53 f. Minerva *in like manner, during the Battle of* Ulysses *with the Suitors in* Odyss. ⟨xxii 261 f.⟩ *perches on a beam of the roof to behold it*. [P]
Sconce] A pensile candlestick.
 62. Dapperwit is living up to his character in Wycherley's *Love in a Wood*; see, e.g., II i.
 63. *Sir Fopling*] The chief character in Etherege's *Man of Mode, or Sir Fopling Flutter*, one of 'our most applauded plays' (*Spectator*, 65).
 64. *The Words in a Song in the Opera of* Camilla. [P] *Camilla*, the most famous opera of Marc' Antonio Buononcini, brother of Handel's rival, was first performed in England on 30 April 1706. It was performed fifty-four times during 1706–9.
 65 f. Ov. Ep. ⟨vii 1 f.⟩
  Sic ubi fata vocant, udis abjectus in herbis,
   Ad vada Mæandri concinit albus olor. [P]
 71 ff. *Vid*. Homer. *Il*. 8 ⟨87 ff.⟩. & Virg. *Æn*. 12 ⟨725 ff.⟩. [P]
 81. Pope may intend a cross reference to iv 137: the wheel has come full circle for the Baron.

A Charge of *Snuff* the wily Virgin threw;
The *Gnomes* direct, to ev'ry Atome just,
The pungent Grains of titillating Dust.
Sudden, with starting Tears each Eye o'erflows,   85
And the high Dome re-ecchoes to his Nose.
    Now meet thy Fate, incens'd *Belinda* cry'd,
And drew a deadly *Bodkin* from her Side.
(The same, his ancient Personage to deck,
Her great great Grandsire wore about his Neck   90
In three *Seal-Rings*; which after, melted down,
Form'd a vast *Buckle* for his Widow's Gown:
Her infant Grandame's *Whistle* next it grew,
The *Bells* she gingled, and the *Whistle* blew;
Then in a *Bodkin* grac'd her Mother's Hairs,   95
Which long she wore, and now *Belinda* wears.)
    Boast not my Fall (he cry'd) insulting Foe!
Thou by some other shalt be laid as low.
Nor think, to die dejects my lofty Mind;
All that I dread, is leaving you behind!   100
Rather than so, ah let me still survive,
And burn in *Cupid*'s Flames,—but burn alive.
    Restore the Lock ! she cries; and all around
Restore the Lock ! the vaulted Roofs rebound.
Not fierce *Othello* in so loud a Strain   105
Roar'd for the Handkerchief that caus'd his Pain.
But see how oft Ambitious Aims are cross'd,
And Chiefs contend 'till all the Prize is lost!
The Lock, obtain'd with Guilt, and kept with Pain,
In ev'ry place is sought, but sought in vain: 110
With such a Prize no Mortal must be blest,
So Heav'n decrees! with Heav'n who can contest ?
    Some thought it mounted to the Lunar Sphere,
Since all things lost on Earth, are treasur'd there.

83 f. *These two lines added for the above reason.* [P]: see l. 37n above.
    89 ff. *In Imitation of the Progress of* Agamemnon's *Scepter in* Homer,
Il. 2. ⟨129 ff.⟩ [P]
    114 ff. *Vid.* Ariosto. Canto 34. ⟨stanzas 68 ff.⟩ [P]
Astolfo journeys to the moon in search of Orlando's lost wits, and finds
        A mighty masse of things strangely confus'd,
        Things that on earth were lost, or were abus'd.
Among these are 'The vowes that sinners make, and never pay,' gifts
given to princes, 'fond loves',
        Large promises that Lords make, and forget . . .
        The fruitlesse almes that men give when they die.
Here 'mans wit' is kept in jars after having been lost on earth through

There Heroes' Wits are kept in pondrous Vases,   115
And Beaus' in *Snuff-boxes* and *Tweezer-Cases*.
There broken Vows, and Death-bed Alms are found,
And Lovers' Hearts with Ends of Riband bound;
The Courtier's Promises, and Sick Man's Pray'rs,
The Smiles of Harlots, and the Tears of Heirs,   120
Cages for Gnats, and Chains to Yoak a Flea;
Dry'd Butterflies, and Tomes of Casuistry.
   But trust the Muse—she saw it upward rise,
Tho' mark'd by none but quick Poetic Eyes:
(So *Rome*'s great Founder to the Heav'ns withdrew,   125
To *Proculus* alone confess'd in view.)
A sudden Star, it shot thro' liquid Air,
And drew behind a radiant *Trail of Hair*.
Not *Berenice*'s Locks first rose so bright,
The Heav'ns bespangling with dishevel'd Light.   130
The *Sylphs* behold it kindling as it flies,
And pleas'd pursue its Progress thro' the Skies.
   This the *Beau-monde* shall from the *Mall* survey,
And hail with Musick its propitious Ray.
This, the blest Lover shall for *Venus* take,   135
And send up Vows from *Rosamonda*'s Lake.
This *Partridge* soon shall view in cloudless Skies,
When next he looks thro' *Galilæo*'s Eyes;
And hence th' Egregious Wizard shall foredoom
The Fate of *Louis*, and the Fall of *Rome*.   140
   Then cease, bright Nymph! to mourn thy ravish'd Hair
Which adds new Glory to the shining Sphere!

---

love, ambition, trade, service of lords, aspiration after powers magical,
alchemistical or poetical.
   116. *Tweezer-Cases*] Cf. *Tatler* 142: 'his Tweezer-Cases are incomparable: You shall have one not much bigger than your Finger, with seventeen several Instruments in it, all necessary every Hour of the Day, during
the whole Course of a Man's Life.'
   122. *Casuistry*] The minutely argued adaptation of ethical rules to
individual cases which the Counter-Reformation had encouraged, and in
England such churchmen as Jeremy Taylor, was now discredited.
   127. *liquid*] in the Latin sense of clear.
   131 f. *These two lines added for the same reason to keep in view the
Machinery of the Poem.* [P]
   133. *the Mall*] An enclosed walk in St. James's Park.
   136. *Rosamonda's Lake*] A pond in St. James's Park.
   137. John Partridge *was a ridiculous Star-gazer, who in his Almanacks
every year, never fail'd to predict the downfall of the Pope, and the King of
France, then at war with the* English. [P]
   138. Galileo improved the newly invented telescope and by its aid
inaugurated a new era in the history of astronomy.

Not all the Tresses that fair Head can boast
Shall draw such Envy as the Lock you lost.
For, after all the Murders of your Eye,   145
When, after Millions slain, your self shall die;
When those fair Suns shall sett, as sett they must,
And all those Tresses shall be laid in Dust;
This Lock, the Muse shall consecrate to Fame,
And mid'st the Stars inscribe *Belinda*'s Name!   150

Epistle To Miss Blount, on her leaving the Town, after the Coronation

[written 1714; published, *Works*, 1717]

As some fond virgin, whom her mother's care
Drags from the town to wholsom country air,
Just when she learns to roll a melting eye,
And hear a spark, yet think no danger nigh;
From the dear man unwilling she must sever,   5
Yet takes one kiss before she parts for ever:
Thus from the world fair *Zephalinda* flew,
Saw others happy, and with sighs withdrew;
Not that their pleasures caus'd her discontent,
She sigh'd not that They stay'd, but that She went.   10
    She went, to plain-work, and to purling brooks,
Old-fashion'd halls, dull aunts, and croaking rooks,
She went from Op'ra, park, assembly, play,
To morning walks, and pray'rs three hours a day;
To pass her time 'twixt reading and Bohea,   15
To muse, and spill her solitary Tea,
Or o'er cold coffee trifle with the spoon,
Count the slow clock, and dine exact at noon;
Divert her eyes with pictures in the fire,
Hum half a tune, tell stories to the squire;   20
Up to her godly garret after sev'n,
There starve and pray, for that's the way to heav'n,
    Some Squire, perhaps, you take delight to rack;
Whose game is Whisk, whose treat a toast in sack,
Who visits with a gun, presents you birds,   25
Then gives a smacking buss, and cries—No words!
Or with his hound comes hollowing from the stable,
Makes love with nods, and knees beneath a table;
Whose laughs are hearty, tho' his jests are coarse,
And loves you best of all things—but his horse.   30
    In some fair evening, on your elbow laid,
You dream of triumphs in the rural shade;
In pensive thought recall the fancy'd scene,
See Coronations rise on ev'ry green;
Before you pass th' imaginary sights   35
Of Lords, and Earls, and Dukes, and garter'd Knights;

15. *Bohea*] see p. 237, l. 156*n.*
24. *whisk*] whist.

While the spread Fan o'ershades your closing eyes;
Then give one flirt, and all the vision flies.
Thus vanish sceptres, coronets, and balls,
And leave you in lone woods, or empty walls.   40
   So when your slave, at some dear, idle time,
(Not plagu'd with headachs, or the want of rhime)
Stands in the streets, abstracted from the crew,
And while he seems to study, thinks of you:
Just when his fancy points your sprightly eyes,   45
Or sees the blush of soft *Parthenia* rise,
Gay pats my shoulder, and you vanish quite;
Streets, chairs, and coxcombs rush upon my sight;
Vext to be still in town, I knit my brow,
Look sow'r, and hum a tune—as you may now.   50

38. *flirt*] a sudden movement of the fan.
48. *chairs*] sedan-chairs.

A Farewell to London. In the Year 1715

[published 1775]

Dear, damn'd, distracting Town, farewell!
　Thy Fools no more I'll teize:
This Year in Peace, ye Critics, dwell,
　Ye Harlots, sleep at Ease!

Soft *B——* and rough *C———s*, adieu!　　　　5
　Earl *Warwick* make your Moan,
The lively *H————k* and you
　May knock up Whores alone.

To drink and droll be *Rowe* allow'd
　Till the third watchman toll;　　　　10
Let *Jervase* gratis paint, and *Frowd*
　Save Three-pence, and his Soul.

Farewell *Arbuthnot*'s Raillery
　On every learned Sot;
And *Garth*, the best good Christian he,　　　　15
　Altho' he knows it not.

Lintot, farewell! thy Bard must go;
　Farewell, unhappy *Tonson*!
Heaven gives thee for thy Loss of *Rowe*,
　Lean *Philips*, and fat *Johnson*.　　　　20

Why should I stay? Both Parties rage;
　My vixen Mistress squalls;
The Wits in envious Feuds engage;
　And *Homer* (damn him!) calls.

The Love of Arts lies cold and dead　　　　25
　In *Hallifax*'s Urn;

5. *B———*] Perhaps Bethel; see p. 540, ll. 125–6*n*.
C———s] Generally, but not certainly, identified as Craggs the younger.
6. *Warwick*] Son-in-law to Addison.
7. *H————k*] Doubtless Edward Richard, Viscount Hinchinbroke.
11. Philip Frowde (d. 1738), poet and friend of Swift, had suffered from his father's improvidence.
17. *Lintot*] Pope's bookseller, who had undertaken to publish the *Iliad*.
18. *Tonson*] 1656?–1736. The leading publisher of his generation.
26. *Hallifax*] Charles Montagu, Earl of Halifax (1661–1715). Politician, poet, and patron of poets.

And not one Muse of all he fed,
   Has yet the Grace to mourn.

My Friends, by Turns, my Friends confound,
   Betray, and are betray'd: 30
Poor *Y--r*'s sold for Fifty Pound,
   And *B----ll* is a Jade.

Why make I Friendships with the Great,
   When I no Favour seek?
Or follow Girls Seven Hours in Eight?—   35
   I need but once a Week.

Still idle, with a busy Air,
   Deep Whimsies to contrive;
The gayest Valetudinaire,
   Most thinking Rake alive.   40

Solicitous for others Ends,
   Tho' fond of dear Repose;
Careless or drowsy with my Friends,
   And frolick with my Foes.

Laborious Lobster-nights, farewell!   45
   For sober, studious Days;
And *Burlington*'s delicious Meal,
   For Sallads, Tarts, and Pease!

Adieu to all but *Gay* alone,
   Whose Soul, sincere and free,
Loves all Mankind, but flatters none,   50
   And so may starve with me.

31. *Y--r*] Mrs. Elizabeth Younger (1699?-1762), actress.
32. *B----ll*] Mrs. M. Bicknell (1695?-1723), actress, sister of Mrs.
Younger.

The Universal Prayer

DEO OPT. MAX.

[written c. 1715; published 1738]

Father of All! in every Age,
   In every Clime ador'd,
By Saint, by Savage, and by Sage,
   Jehovah, Jove, or Lord!

Thou Great First Cause, least Understood!   5
   Who all my Sense confin'd
To know but this,—that Thou art Good,
   And that my self am blind:

Yet gave me, in this dark Estate,
   To see the Good from Ill;   10
And binding Nature fast in Fate,
   Left free the Human Will.

What Conscience dictates to be done,
   Or warns me not to doe,
This, teach me more than Hell to shun,   15
   That, more than Heav'n pursue.

What Blessings thy free Bounty gives,
   Let me not cast away;
For God is pay'd when Man receives,
   T' enjoy, is to obey.   20

Yet not to Earth's contracted Span,
   Thy Goodness let me bound;
Or think Thee Lord alone of Man,
   When thousand Worlds are round.

Let not this weak, unknowing hand   25
   Presume Thy Bolts to throw,
And deal Damnation round the land,
   On each I judge thy Foe.

If I am right, oh teach my heart
   Still in the right to stay;   30

Composed in 1715, and subsequently revised for use as a pendant to the *Essay on Man*.

If I am wrong, Thy Grace impart
 To find that better Way.

Save me alike from foolish Pride,
 Or impious Discontent,
At ought thy Wisdom has deny'd,   35
 Or ought thy Goodness lent.

Teach me to feel another's Woe;
 To hide the Fault I see;
That Mercy I to others show,
 That Mercy show to me.   40

Mean tho' I am, not wholly so
 Since quicken'd by thy Breath,
O lead me wheresoe'er I go,
 Thro' this day's Life, or Death:

This day, be Bread and Peace my Lot;   45
 All else beneath the Sun,
Thou know'st if best bestow'd, or not;
 And let Thy Will be done.

To Thee, whose Temple is all Space,
 Whose Altar, Earth, Sea, Skies;   50
One Chorus let all Being raise!
 All Nature's Incence rise!

Epistle to Mr. Jervas

WITH DRYDEN'S TRANSLATION OF FRESNOY'S
ART OF PAINTING

[written c. 1715; published 1716]

This verse be thine, my friend, nor thou refuse
This, from no venal or ungrateful Muse.
Whether thy hand strike out some free design,
Where life awakes, and dawns at ev'ry line;
Or blend in beauteous tints the colour'd mass,   5
And from the canvas call the mimic face:
Read these instructive leaves, in which conspire
Fresnoy's close art, and *Dryden*'s native fire:
And reading wish, like theirs, our fate and fame,
So mix'd our studies, and so join'd our name,   10
Like them to shine thro' long succeeding age,
So just thy skill, so regular my rage.
  Smit with the love of Sister-arts we came,
And met congenial, mingling flame with flame;
Like friendly colours found them both unite,   15
And each from each contract new strength and light.
How oft' in pleasing tasks we wear the day,
While summer suns roll unperceiv'd away?
How oft' our slowly-growing works impart,
While images reflect from art to art?   20
How oft' review; each finding like a friend
Something to blame, and something to commend?
What flatt'ring scenes our wand'ring fancy wrought,
Rome's pompous glories rising to our thought!
Together o'er the *Alps* methinks we fly,   25
Fir'd with ideas of fair *Italy*.
With thee, on *Raphael*'s Monument I mourn,
Or wait inspiring dreams at *Maro*'s Urn:
With thee repose, where *Tully* once was laid,
Or seek some ruin's formidable shade;   30
While fancy brings the vanish'd piles to view,
And builds imaginary *Rome* a-new.
Here thy well-study'd Marbles fix our eye;
A fading Fresco here demands a sigh:

Title: *Mr. Jervas*] See p. 285, l. 28*n*.
Fresnoy] Charles Alphonse Dufresnoy (1611–65), painter and poet. *De arte graphica* (1668) translated by Dryden, 1695.

Each heav'nly piece unweary'd we compare,   35
Match *Raphael's* grace, with thy lov'd *Guido's* air,
Caracci's strength, *Correggio's* softer line,
Paulo's free stroke, and *Titian's* warmth divine.
    How finish'd with illustrious toil appears
This small, well-polish'd gem, the work of years!   40
Yet still how faint by precept is exprest
The living image in the Painter's breast?
Thence endless streams of fair ideas flow,
Strike in the sketch, or in the picture glow;
Thence beauty, waking all her forms, supplies   45
An Angel's sweetness, or *Bridgewater's* eyes.
    Muse! at that name thy sacred sorrows shed,
Those tears eternal, that embalm the dead:
Call round her tomb each object of desire,
Each purer frame inform'd with purer fire: 50
Bid her be all that chears or softens life,
The tender sister, daughter, friend and wife;
Bid her be all that makes mankind adore;
Then view this marble, and be vain no more!
    Yet still her charms in breathing paint engage; 55
Her modest cheek shall warm a future age.
Beauty, frail flow'r that ev'ry season fears,
Blooms in thy colours for a thousand years.
Thus *Churchill's* race shall other hearts surprize,
And other Beauties envy *Worsley's* eyes,   60
Each pleasing *Blount* shall endless smiles bestow,
And soft *Belinda's* blush for ever glow.
    Oh lasting as those colours may they shine,
Free as thy stroke, yet faultless as thy line!
New graces yearly, like thy works, display;   65
Soft without weakness, without glaring gay;
Led by some rule, that guides, but not constrains;
And finish'd more thro' happiness than pains!

---

46. *Bridgewater*] Elizabeth, Countess of Bridgewater, was the third of the four beautiful daughters of the Duke of Marlborough, who are alluded to in l. 59.

60. *Worsley's* eyes] Wife of Sir Robert Worsley. Nevertheless, in the early versions it was Lady Mary Wortley Montagu whose eyes Pope praised and whose name, after his quarrel with her, he changed to Worsley by the alteration of one letter.

61. *Blount*] Martha and Teresa Blount, a double portrait of whom Jervas was then painting.

62. *Belinda*] Arabella Fermor, the heroine of *The Rape of the Lock*.

The kindred arts shall in their praise conspire,
One dip the pencil, and one string the lyre.   70
Yet should the Graces all thy figures place,
And breathe an air divine on ev'ry face;
Yet should the Muses bid my numbers roll,
Strong as their charms, and gentle as their soul;
With *Zeuxis' Helen* thy *Bridgewater* vie,   75
And these be sung 'till *Granville*'s *Myra* die;
Alas! how little from the grave we claim?
Thou but preserv'st a Face and I a Name.

76. *Granville's Myra*] George Granville Lord Lansdowne (1667–1735),
who in his poems frequently celebrated the Countess of Newburgh under
the name of Myra.

Eloisa to Abelard

[written c. 1716; published, *Works*, 1717]

THE ARGUMENT

Abelard *and* Eloisa *flourish'd in the twelfth Century; they were two of the most distinguish'd persons of their age in learning and beauty, but for nothing more famous than for their unfortunate passion. After a long course of Calamities, they retired each to a several Convent, and consecrated the remainder of their days to religion. It was many years after this separation, that a letter of* Abelard's *to a Friend which contain'd the history of his misfortune, fell into the hands of* Eloisa. *This awakening all her tenderness, occasion'd those celebrated letters (out of which the following is partly extracted) which give so lively a picture of the struggles of grace and nature, virtue and passion.*

> In these deep solitudes and awful cells,
> Where heav'nly-pensive, contemplation dwells,
> And ever-musing melancholy reigns;
> What means this tumult in a Vestal's veins?
> Why rove my thoughts beyond this last retreat? 5
> Why feels my heart its long-forgotten heat?
> Yet, yet I love!—From *Abelard* it came,
> And *Eloisa* yet must kiss the name.
>   Dear fatal name! rest ever unreveal'd,
> Nor pass these lips in holy silence seal'd. 10
> Hide it, my heart, within that close disguise,
> Where, mix'd with God's, his lov'd Idea lies.
> Oh write it not, my hand—The name appears
> Already written—wash it out, my tears!
> In vain lost *Eloisa* weeps and prays, 15
> Her heart still dictates, and her hand obeys.
>   Relentless walls! whose darksom round contains
> Repentant sighs, and voluntary pains;
> Ye rugged rocks! which holy knees have worn;
> Ye grots and caverns shagg'd with horrid thorn! 20
> Shrines! where their vigils pale-ey'd virgins keep,
> And pitying saints, whose statues learn to weep!

1 ff. To show the writer as treasuring her lover's letter and as struggling with tears and emotion in her attempts to answer it, is a recognized opening for a heroic epistle.

20. Cf. *Comus*, l. 429:
       By grots, and caverns shag'd with horrid shades.
Pope's change emphasizes the Latin connotation of Milton's *horrid*; *horridus* = bristling.

Tho' cold like you, unmov'd, and silent grown,
I have not yet forgot my self to stone.
All is not Heav'n's while *Abelard* has part,   25
Still rebel nature holds out half my heart;
Nor pray'rs nor fasts its stubborn pulse restrain,
Nor tears, for ages, taught to flow in vain.
  Soon as thy letters trembling I unclose,
That well-known name awakens all my woes.   30
Oh name for ever sad! for ever dear!
Still breath'd in sighs, still usher'd with a tear.
I tremble too where-e'er my own I find,
Some dire misfortune follows close behind.
Line after line my gushing eyes o'erflow,   35
Led thro' a sad variety of woe:
Now warm in love, now with'ring in thy bloom,
Lost in a convent's solitary gloom!
There stern religion quench'd th' unwilling flame,
There dy'd the best of passions, Love and Fame.   40
  Yet write, or write me all, that I may join
Griefs to thy griefs, and eccho sighs to thine.
Nor foes nor fortune take this pow'r away.
And is my *Abelard* less kind than they?
Tears still are mine, and those I need not spare,   45
Love but demands what else were shed in pray'r;
No happier task these faded eyes pursue,
To read and weep is all they now can do.
  Then share thy pain, allow that sad relief;
Ah more than share it! give me all thy grief.   50
Heav'n first taught letters for some wretch's aid,
Some banish'd lover, or some captive maid;
They live, they speak, they breathe what love inspires,
Warm from the soul, and faithful to its fires,
The virgin's wish without her fears impart,   55
Excuse the blush, and pour out all the heart,
Speed the soft intercourse from soul to soul,
And waft a sigh from *Indus* to the *Pole*.
  Thou know'st how guiltless first I met thy flame,
When Love approach'd me under Friendship's name;   60

24. Cf. *Letters of Abelard and Heloise*, trs. Hughes, 129: 'O Vows! O Convent! I have not lost my Humanity under your inexorable Discipline! You have not made me Marble by changing my Habit'; and Milton, *Il Pens.*, 42: 'Forget thy self to Marble'.

51 ff. Cf. Hughes, 106: 'Letters were first invented for comforting such solitary Wretches as my self'.

56 *Excuse*] in the sense of 'exempt from the need of'.

My fancy form'd thee of Angelick kind,
Some emanation of th' all-beauteous Mind.
Those smiling eyes, attemp'ring ev'ry ray,
Shone sweetly lambent with celestial day:
Guiltless I gaz'd; heav'n listen'd while you sung;   65
And truths divine came mended from that tongue.
From lips like those what precept fail'd to move?
Too soon they taught me 'twas no sin to love.
Back thro' the paths of pleasing sense I ran,
Nor wish'd an Angel whom I lov'd a Man.   70
Dim and remote the joys of saints I see,
Nor envy them, that heav'n I lose for thee.
   How oft', when press'd to marriage, have I said,
Curse on all laws but those which love has made!
Love, free as air, at sight of human ties,   75
Spreads his light wings, and in a moment flies.
Let wealth, let honour, wait the wedded dame,
August her deed, and sacred be her fame;
Before true passion all those views remove,
Fame, wealth, and honour! what are you to Love?   80
The jealous God, when we profane his fires,
Those restless passions in revenge inspires;
And bids them make mistaken mortals groan,
Who seek in love for ought but love alone.
Should at my feet the world's great master fall,   85
Himself, his throne, his world, I'd scorn 'em all:
Not *Cæsar*'s empress wou'd I deign to prove;
No, make me mistress to the man I love;
If there be yet another name more free,
More fond than mistress, make me that to thee!   90
Oh happy state! when souls each other draw,
When love is liberty, and nature, law:
All then is full, possessing, and possest,
No craving Void left aking in the breast:
Ev'n thought meets thought ere from the lips it part,   95

66. *He was her Preceptor in Philosophy and Divinity.* [P]
   69 f. Wakefield paraphrases: 'Thy holy precepts and the sanctity of thy character had made me conceive of thee as a being more venerable than man. . . . But thy personal allurements soon inspired those tender feelings, which gradually conducted me from a *veneration* of the *angel* to a . . . *love* for the *man.*'
   75 ff.   *Love will not be confin'd by Maisterie:*
                 When Maisterie comes, the Lord of Love anon
                 Flutters his wings, and forthwith he is gone.
Chaucer ⟨*Franklin's Tale*, 36 ff.⟩. [P]

And each warm wish springs mutual from the heart.
This sure is bliss (if bliss on earth there be)
And once the lot of *Abelard* and me.
    Alas how chang'd! what sudden horrors rise!
A naked Lover bound and bleeding lies!   100
Where, where was *Eloise*? her voice, her hand,
Her ponyard, had oppos'd the dire command.
Barbarian stay! that bloody stroke restrain;
The crime was common, common be the pain.
I can no more; by shame, by rage supprest,   105
Let tears, and burning blushes speak the rest.
    Canst thou forget that sad, that solemn day,
When victims at yon' altar's foot we lay?
Canst thou forget what tears that moment fell,
When, warm in youth, I bade the world farewell?   110
As with cold lips I kiss'd the sacred veil,
The shrines all trembled, and the lamps grew pale:
Heav'n scarce believ'd the conquest it survey'd,
And Saints with wonder heard the vows I made.
Yet then, to those dread altars as I drew,   115
Not on the Cross my eyes were fix'd, but you;
Not grace, or zeal, love only was my call,
And if I lose thy love, I lose my all.
Come! with thy looks, thy words, relieve my woe;
Those still at least are left thee to bestow.   120
Still on that breast enamour'd let me lie,
Still drink delicious poison from thy eye,
Pant on thy lip, and to thy heart be prest;
Give all thou canst—and let me dream the rest.
Ah no! instruct me other joys to prize,   125
With other beauties charm my partial eyes,
Full in my view set all the bright abode,
And make my soul quit *Abelard* for God.
    Ah think at least thy flock deserves thy care,
Plants of thy hand, and children of thy pray'r.   130
From the false world in early youth they fled,
By thee to mountains, wilds, and deserts led.
You rais'd these hallow'd walls; the desert smil'd,
And Paradise was open'd in the Wild.

104. *pain*] = punishment (Latin *pœna*) as well as the common English meaning.

133. *He founded the Monastery*. [P]

134. The sudden oasis—'beauty lying in the lap of horror'—had been strongly presented in *Par. Lost*, iv 131 ff. (cf. Isaiah, li 3) and was to endear itself to all eighteenth-century aestheticians.

No weeping orphan saw his father's stores   135
Our shrines irradiate, or emblaze the floors;
No silver saints, by dying misers giv'n,
Here brib'd the rage of ill-requited heav'n:
But such plain roofs as piety could raise,
And only vocal with the Maker's praise.   140
In these lone walls (their day's eternal bound)
These moss-grown domes with spiry turrets crown'd,
Where awful arches make a noon-day night,
And the dim windows shed a solemn light;
Thy eyes diffus'd a reconciling ray,   145
And gleams of glory brighten'd all the day.
But now no face divine contentment wears,
'Tis all blank sadness, or continual tears.
See how the force of others' pray'rs I try,
(Oh pious fraud of am'rous charity!)   150
But why should I on others' pray'rs depend?
Come thou, my father, brother, husband, friend!
Ah let thy handmaid, sister, daughter, move,
And, all those tender names in one, thy love!
The darksom pines that o'er yon' rocks reclin'd   155
Wave high, and murmur to the hollow wind,
The wandring streams that shine between the hills,
The grots that eccho to the tinkling rills,
The dying gales that pant upon the trees,
The lakes that quiver to the curling breeze;   160
No more these scenes my meditation aid,
Or lull to rest the visionary maid:
But o'er the twilight groves, and dusky caves,
Long-sounding isles, and intermingled graves,
Black Melancholy sits, and round her throws   165
A death-like silence, and a dread repose:
Her gloomy presence saddens all the scene,
Shades ev'ry flow'r, and darkens ev'ry green,
Deepens the murmur of the falling floods,
And breathes a browner horror on the woods.   170

142. *domes*] See p. 175, l. 65*n.*
152 f. The superscription of Eloisa's first letter begins '*To her Lord, her Father, her Husband, her Brother; his Servant, his Child, his Wife, his Sister*'.
162. 'visionary' has two meanings at this time: Dryden's 'Visionary Maid' (*Æneid*, iii 576) = 'maid seeing visions' (as here), but at *Theodore and Honoria*, l. 280, the same phrase = 'maid seen in a vision' (cf. his *Æneid*, ii 365).
170. *Brown* shadows are found in English poetry as early as Fairfax's *Tasso*, xx 123, l. 1.

Yet here for ever, ever must I stay;
Sad proof how well a lover can obey!
Death, only death, can break the lasting chain;
And here ev'n then, shall my cold dust remain,
Here all its frailties, all its flames resign, 175
And wait, till 'tis no sin to mix with thine.
Ah wretch! believ'd the spouse of God in vain,
Confess'd within the slave of love and man.
Assist me heav'n! but whence arose that pray'r?
Sprung it from piety, or from despair? 180
Ev'n here, where frozen chastity retires,
Love finds an altar for forbidden fires.
I ought to grieve, but cannot what I ought;
I mourn the lover, not lament the fault;
I view my crime, but kindle at the view, 185
Repent old pleasures, and sollicit new:
Now turn'd to heav'n, I weep my past offence,
Now think of thee, and curse my innocence.
Of all affliction taught a lover yet,
'Tis sure the hardest science to forget! 190
How shall I lose the sin, yet keep the sense,
And love th' offender, yet detest th' offence?
How the dear object from the crime remove,
Or how distinguish penitence from love?
Unequal task! a passion to resign, 195
For hearts so touch'd, so pierc'd, so lost as mine.
Ere such a soul regains its peaceful state,
How often must it love, how often hate!
How often, hope, despair, resent, regret,
Conceal, disdain—do all things but forget. 200
But let heav'n seize it, all at once 'tis fir'd,
Not touch'd, but rapt, not waken'd, but inspir'd!
Oh come! oh teach me nature to subdue,
Renounce my love, my life, my self—and you.
Fill my fond heart with God alone, for he 205
Alone can rival, can succeed to thee.
How happy is the blameless Vestal's lot!
The world forgetting, by the world forgot.
Eternal sun-shine of the spotless mind!
Each pray'r accepted, and each wish resign'd; 210

177 ff. There are several parallels to this in the letters, since it is their
central conflict.
191. *sense*] in both meanings of 'faculty of perception' and 'faculty of
sensation'.

Labour and rest, that equal periods keep;
'Obedient slumbers that can wake and weep';
Desires compos'd, affections ever ev'n,
Tears that delight, and sighs that waft to heav'n.
Grace shines around her with serenest beams,   215
And whisp'ring Angels prompt her golden dreams.
For her th' unfading rose of *Eden* blooms,
And wings of Seraphs shed divine perfumes;
For her the Spouse prepares the bridal ring,
For her white virgins *Hymenæals* sing;   220
To sounds of heav'nly harps, she dies away,
And melts in visions of eternal day.
   Far other dreams my erring soul employ,
Far other raptures, of unholy joy:
When at the close of each sad, sorrowing day,   225
Fancy restores what vengeance snatch'd away,
Then conscience sleeps, and leaving nature free,
All my loose soul unbounded springs to thee.
O curst, dear horrors of all-conscious night!
How glowing guilt exalts the keen delight!   230
Provoking Dæmons all restraint remove,
And stir within me ev'ry source of love.
I hear thee, view thee, gaze o'er all thy charms,
And round thy phantom glue my clasping arms.
I wake—no more I hear, no more I view,   235
The phantom flies me, as unkind as you,
I call aloud; it hears not what I say;
I stretch my empty arms; it glides away:
To dream once more I close my willing eyes;
Ye soft illusions, dear deceits, arise!   240
Alas no more!—methinks we wandring go
Thro' dreary wastes, and weep each other's woe,
Where round some mould'ring tow'r pale ivy creeps,
And low-brow'd rocks hang nodding o'er the deeps.
Sudden you mount! you becken from the skies;   245
Clouds interpose, waves roar, and winds arise.
I shriek, start up, the same sad prospect find,
And wake to all the griefs I left behind.
   For thee the fates, severely kind, ordain
A cool suspense from pleasure and from pain;   250
Thy life a long, dead calm of fix'd repose;
No pulse that riots, and no blood that glows.
Still as the sea, ere winds were taught to blow,

212. *Taken from Crashaw ⟨Description of a Religious House,* l. 16⟩. [P]

Or moving spirit bade the waters flow;
Soft as the slumbers of a saint forgiv'n, 255
And mild as opening gleams of promis'd heav'n.
   Come *Abelard*! for what hast thou to dread?
The torch of *Venus* burns not for the dead;
Nature stands check'd; Religion disapproves;
Ev'n thou art cold—yet *Eloisa* loves. 260
Ah hopeless, lasting flames! like those that burn
To light the dead, and warm th' unfruitful urn.
   What scenes appear where-e'er I turn my view!
The dear Ideas, where I fly, pursue,
Rise in the grove, before the altar rise, 265
Stain all my soul, and wanton in my eyes!
I waste the Matin lamp in sighs for thee,
Thy image steals between my God and me,
Thy voice I seem in ev'ry hymn to hear,
With ev'ry bead I drop too soft a tear. 270
When from the Censer clouds of fragrance roll,
And swelling organs lift the rising soul;
One thought of thee puts all the pomp to flight,
Priests, Tapers, Temples, swim before my sight:
In seas of flame my plunging soul is drown'd, 275
While Altars blaze, and Angels tremble round.
   While prostrate here in humble grief I lie,
Kind, virtuous drops just gath'ring in my eye,
While praying, trembling, in the dust I roll,
And dawning grace is opening on my soul: 280
Come, if thou dar'st, all charming as thou art!
Oppose thy self to heav'n; dispute my heart;
Come, with one glance of those deluding eyes,
Blot out each bright Idea of the skies.
Take back that grace, those sorrows, and those tears, 285
Take back my fruitless penitence and pray'rs,
Snatch me, just mounting, from the blest abode,
Assist the Fiends and tear me from my God!
   No, fly me, fly me! far as Pole from Pole;
Rise *Alps* between us! and whole oceans roll! 290
Ah come not, write not, think not once of me,
Nor share one pang of all I felt for thee.
Thy oaths I quit, thy memory resign,
Forget, renounce me, hate whate'er was mine.

270. *too soft*] because tears of love, not of repentance.
282. *dispute*] 'To contend with opposing arguments or assertions . . .
to debate in a vehement manner' (*OED*).

Fair eyes, and tempting looks (which yet I view!)   295
Long lov'd, ador'd ideas! all adieu!
O grace serene! oh virtue heav'nly fair!
Divine oblivion of low-thoughted care!
Fresh blooming hope, gay daughter of the sky!
And faith, our early immortality!   300
Enter each mild, each amicable guest;
Receive, and wrap me in eternal rest!
   See in her Cell sad *Eloisa* spread,
Propt on some tomb, a neighbour of the dead!
In each low wind methinks a Spirit calls,   305
And more than Echoes talk along the walls.
Here, as I watch'd the dying lamps around,
From yonder shrine I heard a hollow sound.
Come, sister come! (it said, or seem'd to say)
Thy place is here, sad sister come away!   310
Once like thy self, I trembled, wept, and pray'd,
Love's victim then, tho' now a sainted maid:
But all is calm in this eternal sleep;
Here grief forgets to groan, and love to weep,
Ev'n superstition loses ev'ry fear: 315
For God, not man, absolves our frailties here.
   I come, I come! prepare your roseate bow'rs,
Celestial palms, and ever-blooming flow'rs.
Thither, where sinners may have rest, I go,
Where flames refin'd in breasts seraphic glow.   320
Thou, *Abelard*! the last sad office pay,
And smooth my passage to the realms of day:
See my lips tremble, and my eye-balls roll,
Suck my last breath, and catch my flying soul!
Ah no—in sacred vestments may'st thou stand,   325
The hallow'd taper trembling in thy hand,
Present the Cross before my lifted eye,
Teach me at once, and learn of me to die.
Ah then, thy once-lov'd *Eloisa* see!
It will be then no crime to gaze on me.   330
See from my cheek the transient roses fly!
See the last sparkle languish in my eye!
Till ev'ry motion, pulse, and breath, be o'er;
And ev'n my *Abelard* be lov'd no more.
O death all-eloquent! you only prove   335
What dust we doat on, when 'tis man we love.
   Then too, when fate shall thy fair frame destroy,
(That cause of all my guilt, and all my joy)

In trance extatic may thy pangs be drown'd,
Bright clouds descend, and Angels watch thee round,   340
From opening skies may streaming glories shine,
And Saints embrace thee with a love like mine.
    May one kind grave unite each hapless name,
And graft my love immortal on thy fame.
Then, ages hence, when all my woes are o'er,   345
When this rebellious heart shall beat no more;
If ever chance two wandring lovers brings
To *Paraclete*'s white walls, and silver springs,
O'er the pale marble shall they join their heads,
And drink the falling tears each other sheds,   350
Then sadly say, with mutual pity mov'd,
Oh may we never love as these have lov'd!
From the full quire when loud *Hosanna*'s rise,
And swell the pomp of dreadful sacrifice,
Amid that scene, if some relenting eye   355
Glance on the stone where our cold reliques lie,
Devotion's self shall steal a thought from heav'n,
One human tear shall drop, and be forgiv'n.
And sure if fate some future Bard shall join
In sad similitude of griefs to mine,   360
Condemn'd whole years in absence to deplore,
And image charms he must behold no more,
Such if there be, who loves so long, so well;
Let him our sad, our tender story tell;
The well-sung woes will sooth my pensive ghost;   365
He best can paint 'em, who shall feel 'em most.

343. Abelard *and* Eloisa *were interr'd in the same grave, or in monuments adjoining, in the Monastery of the* Paraclete: *He died in the year* 1142, *she* in 1163. [P]
    name] for *person*, as in Revel. iii 4.
354. *dreadful sacrifice*] the technical term for the celebration of the Eucharist.

Elegy to the Memory of an Unfortunate Lady

[written c. 1717; published, *Works*, 1717]

What beck'ning ghost, along the moonlight shade
Invites my step, and points to yonder glade?
'Tis she!—but why that bleeding bosom gor'd,
Why dimly gleams the visionary sword?
Oh ever beauteous, ever friendly! tell,   5
Is it, in heav'n, a crime to love too well?
To bear too tender, or too firm a heart,
To act a Lover's or a *Roman*'s part?
Is there no bright reversion in the sky,
For those who greatly think, or bravely die?   10
    Why bade ye else, ye Pow'rs! her soul aspire
Above the vulgar flight of low desire?
Ambition first sprung from your blest abodes;
The glorious fault of Angels and of Gods:
Thence to their Images on earth it flows,   15
And in the breasts of Kings and Heroes glows!
Most souls, 'tis true, but peep out once an age,
Dull sullen pris'ners in the body's cage:
Dim lights of life that burn a length of years,
Useless, unseen, as lamps in sepulchres;   20
Like Eastern Kings a lazy state they keep,
And close confin'd to their own palace sleep.
    From these perhaps (ere nature bade her die)
Fate snatch'd her early to the pitying sky.
As into air the purer spirits flow,   25
And sep'rate from their kindred dregs below;
So flew the soul to its congenial place,
Nor left one virtue to redeem her Race.
    But thou, false guardian of a charge too good,
Thou, mean deserter of thy brother's blood!   30
See on these ruby lips the trembling breath,
These cheeks, now fading at the blast of death:
Cold is that breast which warm'd the world before,
And those love-darting eyes must roll no more.

Title] *See the Duke of Buckingham's verses to a Lady designing to retire into a Monastery compared with Mr. Pope's Letters to several Ladies, p. 206. She seems to be the same person whose unfortunate death is the subject of this poem.* [P]

8. *To act a . . . Roman's part*] to commit suicide.
25 f. The image is from chemistry.

Thus, if eternal justice rules the ball, 35
Thus shall your wives, and thus your children fall:
On all the line a sudden vengeance waits,
And frequent herses shall besiege your gates.
There passengers shall stand, and pointing say,
(While the long fun'rals blacken all the way) 40
Lo these were they, whose souls the Furies steel'd,
And curs'd with hearts unknowing how to yield.
Thus unlamented pass the proud away,
The gaze of fools, and pageant of a day!
So perish all, whose breast ne'er learn'd to glow 45
For others' good, or melt at others' woe.
    What can atone (oh ever-injur'd shade!)
Thy fate unpity'd, and thy rites unpaid?
No friend's complaint, no kind domestic tear
Pleas'd thy pale ghost, or grac'd thy mournful bier; 50
By foreign hands thy dying eyes were clos'd,
By foreign hands thy decent limbs compos'd,
By foreign hands thy humble grave adorn'd,
By strangers honour'd, and by strangers mourn'd!
What tho' no friends in sable weeds appear, 55
Grieve for an hour, perhaps, then mourn a year,
And bear about the mockery of woe
To midnight dances, and the publick show?
What tho' no weeping Loves thy ashes grace,
Nor polish'd marble emulate thy face? 60
What tho' no sacred earth allow thee room,
Nor hallow'd dirge be mutter'd o'er thy tomb?
Yet shall thy grave with rising flow'rs be drest,
And the green turf lie lightly on thy breast:
There shall the morn her earliest tears bestow, 65
There the first roses of the year shall blow;
While Angels with their silver wings o'ershade
The ground, now sacred by thy reliques made.
    So peaceful rests, without a stone, a name,
What once had beauty, titles, wealth, and fame. 70

---

35. *ball*] the orb, the emblem of the world, often placed in the hand of statues of Justice.

64. *Sit tibi terra levis* was so common on Roman gravestones that it was often abbreviated to S.T.T.L. Pope is adding the final touches to his Roman elegy.

68. The expression has reference to ver. 61. 'No sacred earth allowed her room', but her remains have 'made sacred' the common earth in which she was buried.

How lov'd, how honour'd once, avails thee not,
To whom related, or by whom begot;
A heap of dust alone remains of thee;
'Tis all thou art, and all the proud shall be!
  Poets themselves must fall, like those they sung;   75
Deaf the prais'd ear, and mute the tuneful tongue.
Ev'n he, whose soul now melts in mournful lays,
Shall shortly want the gen'rous tear he pays;
Then from his closing eyes thy form shall part,
And the last pang shall tear thee from his heart,   80
Life's idle business at one gasp be o'er,
The Muse forgot, and thou belov'd no more!

74. Pope reverts to l. 43: the lady's proud persecutors will die as she has died.
  78. *want*] in the sense of 'lack' and also of 'need'.

Minor Verse 1700–1717

❋

Ode on Solitude
[written c. 1700; published *PSO*, 1717]

Happy the man, whose wish and care
A few paternal acres bound,
Content to breathe his native air,
           In his own ground.

Whose herds with milk, whose fields with bread,   5
Whose flocks supply him with attire,
Whose trees in summer yield him shade,
           In winter fire.

Blest! who can unconcern'dly find
Hours, days, and years slide soft away,   10
In health of body, peace of mind,
           Quiet by day,

Sound sleep by night; study and ease
Together mix'd; sweet recreation,
And innocence, which most does please,   15
           With meditation.

Thus let me live, unseen, unknown;
Thus unlamented let me dye;
Steal from the world, and not a stone
           Tell where I lye.   20

Pope stated that this poem was 'written at about twelve years old'; but the earliest extant draft dates from 1709.

Lines from Alcander

I

Shields, helms, and swords all jangle as they hang,
And sound formidinous with angry clang.

Alcander was an epic poem begun 'a little after the age of twelve', but burnt in the 1720's on the advice of Bishop Atterbury. Pope recalled four

265

II

Whose honours with increase of ages grow;
As streams roll down enlarging as they flow.

III

As man's meanders to the vital spring
Roll all their tides, then back their circles bring.

IV

So swift,—this moment here, the next 'tis gone,
So imperceptible the motion.

V

On a lady's drinking the Bath-waters

She drinks! She drinks! Behold the matchless Dame!
To her 'tis Water, but to us 'tis Flame:
Thus Fire is Water, Water Fire, by turns,
And the same Stream at once both cools and burns.

VI

The same lady goes into the Bath

Venus beheld her, 'midst her Crowd of Slaves,
And thought *Herself* just risen from the Waves.

VII

The Metonymy.

Lac'd in her *Cosins* new appear'd the Bride, ⎫
A *Bubble-boy* and *Tompion* at her Side,   ⎪
And with an Air divine her *Colmar* ply'd.   ⎬
Then oh! she cries, what Slaves I round me see? ⎪
Here a bright *Redcoat*, there a smart *Toupee*. ⎭

---

couplets in conversation with Spence (I–IV); the remainder were used to
illustrate types of extravagance in his prose treatise, *Peri Bathous*.

II. Incorporated in *Ess. on C.*, ll. 191–2.

III. Incorporated in *Dunciad* A, III 47–8.

VII. Illustrating the inversion of causes for effects, of inventors for
inventions.

1. *Cosins*] Stays, called after the famous maker of that day.

2. *Bubble-boy*] Tweezer-case.   *Tompion*] Watch, from the name
Thomas Tompion, a celebrated watchmaker, *temp*. Queen Anne.

3. *Colmar*] Fan (from Colmar, Alsace?).

5. *Toupee*] A sort of periwig.

VIII

An Eye-witness of things never yet beheld by Man

Thus Have I *seen*, in *Araby* the blest,
A *Phœnix* couch'd upon her Fun'ral Nest.

IX

How inimitably circumstantial is this [description]
of a War-Horse!

His Eye-Balls burn, he wounds the smoaking Plain,
And knots of scarlet Ribbond deck *his* Mane.

X

The Hyperbole
Of a Scene of Misery

Behold a Scene of Misery and Woe!
Here *Argus* soon might weep himself quite blind,
Ev'n tho' he had *Briareus'* hundred Hands
To wipe those hundred Eyes——

XI

The Periphrasis
A Country Prospect

I'd call them Mountains, but can't call them so,
For fear to wrong them with a Name too low;
While the fair Vales beneath so humbly lie,
That even humble seems a Term too high.

An Epistle to Henry Cromwell, Esq;

[written, 1707; published (piratically), 1727]

DEAR Mr. Cromwell,
                May it please ye!
Sit still a Moment; pray be easy—
Faith 'tis not five; no Play's begun;
No Game at *Ombre* lost or won.
Read something of a diff'rent Nature, 5
Than *Ev'ning Post,* or *Observator*;
And pardon me a little Fooling,
—Just while your Coffee stands a Cooling.

Since your Acquaintance with one *Brocas*,
Who needs will back the Muses Cock-horse,   10
I know you dread all those who write,
And both with Mouth and Hand recite;
Who slow, and leisurely rehearse,
As loath t' enrich you with their Verse;
Just as a Still, with Simples in it,   15
Betwixt each Drop stays half a Minute.
(That Simile is not my own,
But lawfully belongs to *Donne*)
(You see how well I can contrive a
Interpolatio Furtiva)   20
To *Brocas's* Lays no more you listen
Than to the wicked Works of *Whiston*;
In vain he strains to reach your Ear,
With what it wisely, will not hear:
You bless the Powers who made that Organ   25
Deaf to the Voice of such a *Gorgon*,
(For so one sure may call that Head,
Which does not Look, but Read Men dead.)

I hope, you think me none of those
Who shew their Parts as *Pentlow* does,   30
I but lug out to one or two
Such Friends, if such there are, as you,
Such, who read *Heinsius* and *Masson*,
And as you please their Doom to pass on,
(Who are to me both *Smith* and *Johnson*)   35
So seize them Flames, or take them *Tonson*.

But, Sir, from *Brocas*, *Fouler*, me,
In vain you think to 'scape Rhyme-free,
When was it known one Bard did follow
Whig Maxims, and abjure *Apollo*?   40
Sooner shall Major-General cease
To talk of War, and live in Peace;
Yourself for Goose reject Crow Quill,

22. *Whiston*] 1667–1752. Succeeded to Sir Isaac Newton's professor-
ship at Cambridge, 1701. His Boyle lectures (1707) were suspected of
heterodoxy.

30. *Pentlow*] A Gamester remarkable for his *Virile* Parts, which he us'd
to be fond of Shewing [Curll].

33. *Heinsius and Masson*] Heinsius was a Dutch and Masson a French
critic.

35. *Smith and Johnson*] Bays's two friends in the *Rehearsal*.

And for plain *Spanish* quit *Brasil*;
Sooner shall *Rowe* lampoon the UNION   45
Tydcombe take Oaths on the Communion;
The *Granvilles* write their Name plain *Greenfield*,
Nay, Mr. *Wycherley* see *Binfield*.

I'm told, you think to take a Step some
Ten Miles from Town, t' a Place call'd *Epsom*,   50
To treat those Nymphs like yours of *Drury*,
With—I protest, and I'll assure ye;—
But tho' from Flame to Flame you wander,
Beware; your Heart's no *Salamander*!
But burnt so long, may soon turn Tinder,   } 55
And so be fir'd by any Cinder-
(Wench, I'd have said did Rhyme not hinder)   }
Shou'd it so prove, yet who'd admire?
'Tis known, a Cook-maid roasted *Prior*,
Lardella fir'd a famous Author,   } 60
And for a Butcher's well-fed Daughter
Great *D—s* roar'd, like Ox at Slaughter.   }

(Now, if you're weary of my Style,
Take out your Box of right *Brasil*,
First lay this Paper under, then,   65
Snuff just three Times, and read again.)

I had to see you some Intent
But for a curst Impediment,
Which spoils full many a good Design,
That is to say, the Want of Coin.   70
For which, I had resolv'd almost,
To raise *Tiberius Gracchus* Ghost;
To get, by once more murd'ring *Caius*,
As much as did *Septimuleius*;
But who so dear will buy the Lead,   75
That lies within a Poet's Head,

44. *Spanish . . . Brasil*] Two kinds of snuff; see below, ll. 64–6.
45. *Rowe*] The great measure of the Union had just been passed, and the poet Rowe was a candidate for office.
46. *Tydcombe*] Lieutenant-General John Tidcombe (1642–1713), a member of the Kit-Cat club and an acquaintance of Pope's.
60. *Lardella*] a character in the *Rehearsal*.
62. *D—s*] Dennis.
73–8. Septimuleius, who cut off the head of Caius Gracchus, and was rewarded with its weight in gold, fraudulently filled the skull with lead.

As that which in the Hero's Pate
Deserv'd of Gold an equal Weight?

  Sir, you're so stiff in your Opinion,
I wish you do not turn *Socinian*;   80
Or prove Reviver of a Schism,
By modern Wits call'd *Quixotism*.
What mov'd you, pray, without compelling,
Like *Trojan* true, to draw for *Hellen*:
Quarrel with *Dryden* for a Strumpet,   85
(For so she was, as e'er show'd Rump yet,
Tho' I confess, she had much Grace,
Especially about the Face.)
Virgil, when call'd *Pasiphae Virgo*
(You say) he'd more good Breeding; *Ergo*—   90
Well argu'd, Faith! Your Point you urge
As home, as ever did *Panurge*:
And one may say of *Dryden* too,
(As once you said of you know who)
He had some Fancy, and cou'd write;   95
Was very learn'd, but not polite—
However from my Soul I judge
He ne'er (good Man) bore *Hellen* Grudge,
But lov'd her full as well it may be,
As e'er he did his own dear Lady.   100
You have no Cause to take Offence, Sir,
Z—ds, you're as sour as *Cato Censor*!
Ten times more like him, I profess,
Than I'm like *Aristophanes*.

  To end with News—the best I know,   105
Is, I've been well a Week, or so.
The Season of green Pease is fled,
And Artichoaks reign in their Stead.
Th' Allies to bomb *Toulon* prepare;
G—d save the pretty Lady's there!   110
One of our Dogs is dead and gone,
And I, unhappy! left alone.
  If you have any Consolation
T'administer on this Occasion,
Send it, I pray, by the next Post,   115
Before my Sorrow be quite lost.
  The twelfth or thirteenth Day of *July*,
But which, I cannot tell you truly.

Epigram. Occasion'd by Ozell's Translation of Boileau's Lutrin

PRINTED FOR E. SANGER, AND RECOMMENDED BY
MR. ROWE, IN WHICH MR. WYCHERLEY'S POEMS
PRINTED IN 1704, WERE REFLECTED ON
[written 1708; published (piratically) 1727]

Ozell, at *Sanger*'s Call, invok'd his Muse,
For who to sing for *Sanger* could refuse?
His numbers such, as *Sanger*'s self might use.
Reviving *Perault*, murd'ring *Boileau*, he
Slander'd the Ancients first, then *Wycherley*;   5
Not that it much that Author's Anger rais'd,
For those were slander'd most whom *Ozell* prais'd:
Nor had the toothless Satyr caus'd complaining,
Had not sage *Rowe* pronounc'd it *Entertaining*.
How great, how just, the Judgment of that Writer!   10
Who the *Plain-dealer* damns, and prints the *Biter*.

Title: *Boileau*] 1636–1711. His *Lutrin*, of which cantos I–IV were published in 1674, created a new kind of burlesque in French literature.

4. *Reviving Perault*] *Characters . . . of the Greatest Men . . . in France
. . . By Monsieur Perrault . . . Render'd into English, by J. Ozell.* Two
vols. Printed for Bernard Lintott. 1704–5.

9. *Rowe . . . Entertaining . . . how just*] In the foreword to Ozell's
Lutrin Rowe had praised the translation in these words.

11. *Plain-dealer . . . Biter*] Wycherley wrote the former play (and
was himself sometimes so designated) and Rowe the later, and inferior,
play. This line was used again the following year in the MS *Conclusion
to the Bill of Fare* (see p. 275, l. 14).

Letter to Cromwell

[published (piratically) 1727]

April ye 25. 1708.

Sir,

    This Letter greets you from the Shades;
(Not those which thin, unbody'd Shadows fill,
    That glide along th' Elysian Glades,
Or skim the flow'ry Meads of *Asphodill*:)
But those, in which a Learned Author said,   5
    Strong Drink was drunk, and Gambolls play'd,
And two substantial Meals a day were made.
    The Business of it is t' express,
    From me and from my Holiness,
    To you and to your Gentleness,   10

How much I wish you Health and Happiness;
And much good News, and little Spleen as may be;
    A hearty Stomach, and sound Lady;
And ev'ry Day a double Dose of Coffee,
To make you look as sage as any Sophy.   15

[*The letter is continued 'in plain prose' for a space, only
to resume verse with—*]

If Wit or Critick blame the tender Swain,   ⎫
Who stil'd the gentle Damsels in his Strain   ⎬
The Nymphs of *Drury*, not of *Drury*-Lane;   ⎭
Be this his Answer, and most just Excuse—   ⎫
'Far be it, Sirs, from my more civill Muse,   ⎬   20
Those Loving Ladies rudely to traduce.   ⎭
Allyes and Lanes are Terms too vile and base,
And give Idea's of a narrow Pass;
But the well-worn Paths of the Nymphs of Drury
Are large and wide; *Tydcomb* and I assure ye.'   25

[*After a further section in prose, the letter concludes thus—*]

    To *Baker* first my Service, pray;
        To *Tydcomb* eke,
        And Mr. *Cheek*;
    Last to *yourself* my best Respects I pay,
    And so remain, for ever and for ay,   30
                        Sir,
                    Yʳ Affectionate, humble Servᵗ:
                        A. Pope.

16. *the tender Swain*] i.e. Pope himself. The whole passage refers back
to his previous letter in rhyme (see p. 269, l. 51).
18. *Drury-Lane*] Notorious as the abode of loose women.
25. *Tydcomb*] See p. 269.
26. *Baker*] Possibly Thomas Baker, the dramatist (fl. 1700–09).

Lines added to Wycherley's Poems

[written, 1706–10; published, Wycherley's
Works 1728–9]

I. ON DULNESS

Thus Dulness, the safe Opiate of the Mind,
The last kind Refuge weary Wit can find,

Inserted in *A Panegyrick on Dulness.*

Fit for all Stations, and in each content
Is satisfy'd, secure, and innocent:
No Pains it takes, and no Offence it gives,　　　5
Un-fear'd, un-hated, un-disturb'd it lives.
—And if each writing Author's best pretence,
Be but to teach the Ignorant more Sense;
Then Dulness was the Cause they wrote before,
As 'tis at last the Cause they write no more;　　　10
So Wit, which most to scorn it does pretend,
With Dulness first began, in Dulness last must end.

II. SIMILITUDES

(a) Of the Byass of a Bowl

The Poize of Dulness to the heavy Skull,
Is like the Leaden Byass to the Bowl,
Which, as more pond'rous, makes its Aim more true,
And guides it surer to the Mark in view;
The more it seems to go about, to come　　　5
The nearer to its End, or Purpose, home.

(b) Of the Weights of a Clock

So Clocks to Lead their nimble Motions owe,
The Springs above urg'd by the Weight below;
The pond'rous Ballance keeps its Poize the same,
Actuates, maintains, and rules the moving Frame.

Inserted in *A Panegyrick on Dulness.*

III. SIMILITUDES

Thus either Men in private useless Ease
Lose a dull Length of undeserving Days;
Or Waste, for others Use, their restless Years
In busie Tumults, and in publick Cares,
And run precipitant, with Noise and Strife,　　　5
Into the vast Abyss of future Life;
Or others Ease and theirs alike destroy,
Their own Destruction by their Industry.

Inserted in *The Various Mix'd Life.* The 'similitudes' properly begin
with 'So Waters putrifie . . .'; but as that is in the middle of a paragraph,
and as the previous eight lines state the argument, it is possible that Pope
wrote the first part of the paragraph also. It is therefore printed here in
italic.

So Waters Putrifie with Rest, and lose
At once their Motion, Sweetness, and their Use;   10
Or haste in headlong Torrents to the Main,
To lose themselves by what shou'd them maintain,
And in th' impetuous Course themselves the sooner drain:
Neglect their Native Channel, Neighb'ring Coast,
Abroad in foreign Service to be lost;   15
Or else their Streams, when hinder'd in their Course,
Quite o'er the Banks to their own Ruin force.

The Stream of Life shou'd more securely flow
In constant Motion, nor too swift nor slow,
And neither swell too high, nor sink too low;   20
Not always glide thro' gloomy Vales, and rove
('Midst Flocks and Shepherds) in the silent Grove;
But more diffusive in its wand'ring Race;
Serve peopled Towns, and stately Cities grace;
Around in sweet Meanders wildly range,   25
Kept fresh by Motion, and unchang'd by Change.

IV. LINES ON SOLITUDE AND RETIREMENT

Honour and Wealth, the Joys we seek, deny
By their Encrease, and their Variety;
And more confound our Choice than satisfie:
Officious, bold Disturbances they grow,
That interrupt our Peace, and work our Woe: 5
Make Life a Scene of Pain, and constant Toil,
And all our Days in fresh Pursuits embroil.

But if to Solitude we turn our Eyes,
To View a thousand real Blessings rise;
Pleasures sincere, and unallay'd with Pain,   10
An easie Purchase, but an ample Gain!
There Censure, Envy, Malice, Scorn, or Hate,
Cannot affect Us in our tranquil State:
Those Cankers that on busie Honour prey,
And all their Spight on active Pomp display.   15

Alone, remov'd from Grandeur and from Strife,
And ev'ry Curse that loads a publick Life,
In Safety, Innocence, and full Repose,
Man the true Worth of his Creation knows.

Inserted in *For Solitude and Retirement against the Publick, Active Life.*

Luxurious Nature's Wealth in Thought surveys,   20
And meditates her Charms, and sings her Praise.
To him, with humble Privacy content,
Life is, in Courts, and gawdy Pride, mis-spent.
To him, the Rural Cottage does afford
What he prefers to the *Patrician* Board: 25
Such wholsome Foods as Nature's Wants supply,
And ne'er reproach him with his Luxury.
He traverses the blooming verdant Mead,
Nor envies those that on rich Carpets tread.
Basks in the Sun, then to the Shades retires,   30
And takes a Shelter from his pointed Fires.
Wak'd by the Morning-Cock, unseals his Eyes,
And sees the Rusticks to their Labours rise;
And in the Ev'ning, when those Labours cease,
Beholds them cheary eat the Bread of Peace: 35
Sees no foul Discords at their Banquets bred,
Nor Emulations, nor Disgusts succeed:
But all is quiet, jocund, and serene,
A Type of Paradise, the Rural Scene!

V. CONCLUSION OF THE BILL OF FARE

At length the Board, in loose disjointed Chat,
Descanted, some on this Thing, some on that;
Some, over each Orac'lous Glass, fore-doom
The Fate of Realms, and Conquests yet to come;
What Lawrels *Marlbro*' next shall reap, decree,   5
And swifter than *His* Arms, give *Victory*:
At the next Bottle, all their Schemes they cease,
Content at last to leave the World in Peace.
'Till having drown'd their Reason, they think fit
Railing at Men of Sense, to show their Wit;   10
Compare De Foe'*s Burlesque with* Dryden'*s Satyr,*
And Butler *with the* Lutrin'*s dull Translator,*
Decry'd each past, to raise each present Writer,
Damn'd the *Plain-dealer*, and admir'd the *Biter*.

These Censures o'er, to different Subjects next,   15
'Till rallying all, the Feast became the Text;

The half-dozen lines taken over more or less untouched from
Wycherley's conclusion are printed in italics.
12. *The Lutrin's dull Translator*] Ozell, who had just at that Time made
a poor Version of *Boileau*'s *Lutrin*, and in it reflected upon Mr. *Wycherley*
by Name. [P]

So to mine Host, the greatest Jest, they past,
And the Fool Treater grew the Treat at last.
Thus having eaten, drunk, laught, at his Cost,
To the next Day's Repentance, as they boast,   20
They left their senseless, treating, drunken Host.
   Soft be his Slumbers! But may this suffice
Our Friends the Wits and Poets to advise,
(Tho' Dinners oft they want and Suppers too)
Rather to starve, as they are us'd to do,   25
Than dine with Fools, that on their Guests will force
Mixt Wine, mixt Company, and mixt Discourse:
Since not much Wine, much Company, much Food,
Make Entertainments please us as they shou'd;
But 'tis of each, the *Little*, and the *Good*.   30

Epigrams from Private Letters, 1708–10

I. ON POETS

Damnation follows Death in other Men,
But your damn'd Poet lives and writes agen.

II. ON AUTHORS AND BOOKSELLERS

What Authors lose, their Booksellers have won,
So Pimps grow rich, while Gallants are undone.

III. LINES

i

Fatis agimur, cedite fatis!
Which, in our Tongue, as I translate is,
Fate rules us; then to Fate give way!
—Now, dreadful Critic! tell me pray,
What have you against this to say?

ii

My *Pylades*! what *Juv'nal* says, no Jest is;
Scriptus & in tergo, nec dum finitus Orestes.

Lines from The Critical Specimen
[written 1711; published, 1711]

I. A SIMILE

So on *Mæotis*' Marsh, (where Reeds and Rushes
Hide the deceitful Ground, whose waving Heads
Oft' bend to *Auster*'s blasts, or *Boreas*' Rage,
The Haunt of the voracious *Stork* or *Bittern*,
Where, or the *Crane*, Foe to *Pygmæan* Race,   5
Or Ravenous *Corm'rants* shake their flabby Wings,
And from soak'd Plumes disperse a briny Show'r,
Or spread their feather'd Sails against the Beams,
Or, of the Rising or *Meridian* Sun)
A baneful *Hunch-back'd Toad*, with look Maligne,   10
Glares on some Traveller's unwary steps,
Whether by Chance, or by Misfortune led
To tread those dark unwholesome, misty Fens,
Rage strait Collects his Venom all at once,
And swells his bloated Corps to largest size.   15

II. A RHAPSODY

Fly Pegasæan *Steed, thy Rider bear,*
To breath the Sweets of pure Parnassian *Air,*
Aloft I'm swiftly born, methinks I rise,
And with my Head Sublime *can reach the Sky.*
Large Gulps of Aganippe's *streams I'll draw,*   5
And give to Modern Writers Classic *Law;*
In Grecian Buskins *Tragedy shall Mourn,*
And to its Ancient *Mirth the* Comic Sock *return.*

A Simile pretends to be a fragment, too beautiful to lose, of a projected epic poem on the life of Dennis the Critic, and ridicules his trick of 'frowning and swelling with Anger and Resentment, as ready to burst with Passion'.

A Rhapsody occurs in a specimen chapter of a mock life of Dennis, where it is said to have been uttered by the small boy when astride his hobby-horse.

Fragments from Private Letters

[written 1711; published (piratically) 1727]

I. LINES ON COFFEE

As long as Moco's happy Tree shall grow,
While Berries crackle, or while Mills shall go;
While smoking Streams from Silver Spouts shall glide,
Or China's Earth receive the sable Tyde;
While Coffee shall to British Nymphs be dear;　　　　5
While fragrant Steams the bended Head shall chear;
Or grateful Bitters shall delight the Tast;
So long her Honour, Name, and Praise shall last!

II. LINES ON WRITING A TRAGEDY

[written 1711; published (piratically) 1727]

Tell me, by all the melting joys of Love,
By the warm Transports and entrancing Languors,
By the soft Fannings of the wafting Sheets,
By the dear Tremblings of the Bed of Bliss;
By all these tender Adjurations tell me,　　　　5
—Am I not fit to write a Tragedy?

III. COUPLET

[written 1711; published, *Lit. Corr.* 1735]

Jove was alike to *Latian* and to *Phrygian*,
For you well know, that Wit's of no Religion.

On being attacked by Dennis for his religion in *Reflections upon An Essay on Criticism.*

Epitaph. On John Lord Caryll

[written 1711; published 1854]

A manly Form; a bold, yet modest mind;
Sincere, tho' prudent; constant, yet resign'd;
Honour unchang'd; a Principle profest;
Fix'd to one side, but mod'rate to the rest;
An honest Courtier, and a Patriot too;　　　　5
Just to his Prince, and to his Country true:

Caryll, who withdrew to France in 1689 and became Secretary of State to the exiled dynasty, died in 1711.

All these were join'd in one, yet fail'd to save ⎫
The Wise, the Learn'd, the Virtuous, and the Brave; ⎬
Lost, like the common Plunder of the Grave! ⎭
   Ye Few, whom better Genius does inspire,   10
Exalted Souls, inform'd with purer Fire!
Go now, learn all vast Science can impart;
Go fathom Nature, take the Heights of Art!
Rise higher yet: learn ev'n yourselves to know;
Nay, to yourselves alone that knowledge owe.   15
Then, when you seem above mankind to soar,
Look on this marble, and be vain no more!

The Balance of Europe

[written 1711; published, *PSM*, 1727]

Now *Europe*'s balanc'd, neither Side prevails,
For nothing's left in either of the Scales.

Verses to be prefix'd before Bernard Lintot's New Miscellany

[written 1711; published, Lintot's
Miscellany, 1712]

Some *Colinæus* praise, some *Bleau*,
Others account 'em but so so;
Some *Plantin* to the rest prefer,
And some esteem *Old-Elzevir*;
Others with *Aldus* would besot us;   5
I, for my part, admire *Lintottus.*——
His Character's beyond Compare,
Like his own Person, large and fair.
They print their Names in Letters small,
But LINTOT stands in Capital: 10

1. *Colinæus*] Simon de Colines. French printer of Greek and Latin
books, at work between 1520 and 1546.
  Bleau] Willem Janszoon Blaeu (1571–1638), and his son Jan Blaeu
(d. 1679), Printers, at Amsterdam, of maps and books on geography.
  3. *Plantin*] Christophe Plantin (1514–89). A Belgian printer of Latin
and Greek classics, and a polyglot Bible in folio.
  4. *Old-Elzevir*] Louis Elzevier (1540–1617). Dutch printer of Latin
classics chiefly.
  5. *Aldus*] Aldus Manutius (c. 1450–1515). Venetian printer of Greek
and Latin classics.

Author and he, with equal Grace,
Appear, and stare you in the Face:
Stephens prints *Heathen Greek*, 'tis said,
Which some can't construe, some can't read:
But all that comes from *Lintot*'s Hand   15
Ev'n *Ra——son* might understand.
Oft in an *Aldus*, or a *Plantin*,
A Page is blotted, or Leaf wanting:
Of *Lintot*'s Books this can't be said,
All fair, and not so much as read.   20
Their Copy cost 'em not a Penny
To *Homer*, *Virgil*, or to any;
They ne'er gave *Sixpence* for *two Lines*,
To them, their Heirs, or their Assigns:
But *Lintot* is at vast Expence,   25
And pays prodigious dear for — Sense.
Their Books are useful but to few,
A Scholar, or a Wit or two:
Lintot's for gen'ral Use are fit;
For some Folks read, but all Folks sh—.   30

13. *Stephens*] Estienne, Robert (1503–59), and Henri (1528–98). French printers of Greek and Latin classics at Paris.
16. *Ra—son*] Thomas Rawlinson (1681–1725], barrister and bibliophile.

Verses Occasion'd by an &c. at the End of Mr. D'Urfy's Name in the Title to one of his Plays

[written c. 1712; published (piratically) 1726]

Jove call'd before him t'other Day
The *Vowels*, *U*, *O*, *I*, *E*, *A*,
All *Dipthongs*, and all *Consonants*,
Either of *England* or of *France*;
And all that were, or wish'd to be,   5
Rank'd in the Name of *Tom D'Urfy.*

Fierce in this Cause, the *Letters* spoke all,
Liquids grew rough, and *Mutes* turn'd vocal:

Title: *D'Urfy*] Tom Durfey (1653–1723), poet, dramatist, and a butt of the wits from Dryden's day.
Plays] This Accident happen'd by Mr. *D'Urfy*'s having made a Florish there, which the Printer mistook for a &c. [P]

Those four proud Syllables alone
Were silent, which by Fates Decree   10
Chim'd in so smoothly, one by one,
To the sweet Name of *Tom D'Urfy*.

   N, by whom Names subsist, declar'd,
To have no Place in this was hard:
And *Q* maintain'd 'twas but his Due   15
Still to keep Company with *U*;
So hop'd to stand no less than he
In the great Name of *Tom D'Urfy*.

   E shew'd, a *Comma* ne'er could claim
A Place in any *British* Name;   20
Yet making here a perfect Botch,
Thrusts your poor Vowell from his Notch:
Hiatus mî valde deflendus!
From which good *Jupiter* defend us!
Sooner I'd quit my Part in thee,   25
Than be no Part in *Tom D'Urfy*.

   P protested, puff'd, and swore,
He'd not be serv'd so like a Beast;
He was a Piece of Emperor,
And made up half a Pope at least.   30
C vow'd, he'd frankly have releas'd
His double Share in *Cæsar Caius*,
For only one in *Tom Durfeius*.

   I, Consonant and Vowel too,
To *Jupiter* did humbly sue,   35
That of his Grace he would proclaim
Durfeius his true *Latin* Name;
For tho' without them both, 'twas clear,
Himself could ne'er be *Jupiter*;
Yet they'd resign that Post so high,   40
To be the Genitive, *Durfei*.

   B and *L* swore Bl— and W—s
X and *Z* cry'd, P—x and Z—s
G swore, by G—d, it ne'er should be;
And *W* would not lose, not he,   45
An *English Letter*'s Property,
In the great Name of *Tom Durfy*.

In short, the rest were all in Fray,
From *Christcross* to *Et cætera*.
They, tho' but Standers-by too, mutter'd;   50
Dipthongs, and Tripthongs, swore and stutter'd,
That none had so much Right to be   ⎫
Part of the Name of stuttering *T*—   ⎬
T—*Tom*—*a*—*as*—*De*—*Dur*—*fe*—*fy*. ⎭

Then *Jove* thus spake: With Care and Pain   55
We form'd this Name, renown'd in Rhyme;
Not thine, Immortal *Neufgermain*!
Cost studious *Cabalists* more Time.
Yet now, as then, you all declare,   ⎫
Far hence to *Egypt* you'll repair,   ⎬   60
And turn strange Hieroglyphicks there;   ⎭
Rather than Letters longer be,
Unless i' th' Name of *Tom D'Urfy*.

Were you all pleas'd, yet what I pray,
To foreign Letters cou'd I say?   65
What if the *Hebrew* next should aim
To turn quite backward *D'Urfy*'s Name?
Should the *Greek* quarrel too, by *Styx*, I
Cou'd ne'er bring in *Psi* and *Xi*;
Omicron and *Omega* from us   70
Wou'd each hope to be *O* in *Thomas*;
And all th' ambitious Vowels vie,   ⎫
No less than *Pythagorick Y*,   ⎬
To have a Place in *Tom D'Urfy*.   ⎭

Then, well-belov'd and trusty Letters!   75
Cons'nants! and Vowels, (much their betters,)
WE, willing to repair this Breach,
And, all that in us lies, please each;
Et cæt'ra to our Aid must call,
Et cæt'ra represents ye all: 80
Et cæt'ra therefore, we decree,   ⎫
Henceforth for ever join'd shall be   ⎬
To the great Name of *Tom Durfy*.   ⎭

57. *Neufgermain*] A Poet, who used to make Verses ending with the last
Syllables of the Names of those Persons he praised: Which *Voiture* turn'd
against him in a Poem of the same kind. [P]

Fragments, 1712

I. INSCRIPTION. MARTHA BLOUNT; A: P:
[written 1712; published 1954]

Each pretty Carecter with pleasing Smart
Deepens the dear Idea in my heart.

In a copy of Lintot's *Miscellany*.

II. A WINTER PIECE
[written 1712; published 1871]

As when the freezing blasts of Boreas blow,
And scatter ore the Fields the driving Snow,
From dusky Clowds the fleecy Winter flyes,
Whose dazling Lustre whitens all the Skies.

On a Lady who P—st at the Tragedy of Cato

OCCASION'D BY AN EPIGRAM ON A LADY WHO WEPT AT IT
[written 1713; published, *PSM*, 1727]

While maudlin Whigs deplor'd their *Cato*'s Fate,
Still with dry Eyes the Tory *Celia* sate,
But while her Pride forbids her Tears to flow,
The gushing Waters find a Vent below:
Tho' secret, yet with copious Grief she mourns,   5
Like twenty River-Gods with all their Urns.
Let others screw their Hypocritick Face,
She shews her Grief in a sincerer Place;
There Nature reigns, and Passion void of Art,
For that Road leads directly to the Heart.   10

Two or Three; or A Receipt to make a Cuckold
[written 1713; published, Lintot's
Miscellany 1713]

Two or *Three* Visits, and *Two* or *Three* Bows,
Two or *Three* civil Things, *Two* or *Three* Vows,

Two or *Three* Kisses, with *Two* or *Three* Sighs,
Two or *Three* Jesus's—and let me dyes—
Two or *Three* Squeezes, and *Two* or *Three* Towses,
With *Two* or *Three* thousand Pound lost at their Houses,   } 5
Can never fail Cuckolding *Two* or *Three* Spouses.   }

Upon a Girl of Seven Years old
[written c. 1713; published, Lintot's *Miscellany*, 1714]

Wit's Queen, (if what the Poets sing be true)
And Beauty's Goddess Childhood never knew,
Pallas they say Sprung from the Head of *Jove*,
Full grown, and from the Sea the Queen of Love;
But had they, Miss, your Wit and Beauty seen,   5
Venus and *Pallas* both had Children been.
They, from the Sweetness of that Radiant Look,
A Copy of young *Venus* might have took:
And from those pretty Things you speak have told,
How *Pallas* talk'd when she was Seven Years old.   10

To Belinda on the Rape of the Lock
[written 1713; published, *PSO*, 1717]

Pleas'd in these lines, *Belinda*, you may view
How things are priz'd, which once belong'd to you:
If on some meaner head this Lock had grown,
The nymph despis'd, the Rape had been unknown.
But what concerns the valiant and the fair,   5
The Muse asserts as her peculiar care.
Thus *Helens* Rape and *Menelaus'* wrong
Became the Subject of great *Homer*'s song;
And, lost in ancient times, the golden fleece
Was rais'd to fame by all the wits of *Greece*.   10
    Had fate decreed, propitious to your pray'rs,
To give their utmost date to all your hairs;
This Lock, of which late ages now shall tell,
Had dropt like fruit, neglected, when it fell.
    Nature to your undoing arms mankind   15
With strength of body, artifice of mind;
But gives your feeble sex, made up of fears,
No guard but virtue, no redress but tears.

Yet custom (seldom to your favour gain'd)
Absolves the virgin when by force constrain'd.   20
Thus *Lucrece* lives unblemish'd in her fame,
A bright example of young *Tarquin*'s shame.
Such praise is yours—and such shall you possess,
Your virtue equal, tho' your loss be less.
Then smile Belinda at reproachful tongues,   25
Still warm our hearts, and still inspire our songs.
But would your charms to distant times extend,
Let *Jervas* paint them, and let *Pope* commend.
Who censure most, more precious hairs would lose,
To have the *Rape* recorded by his Muse.   30

28. *Jervas*] Charles Jervas (1675?–1739), portrait painter and translator
of *Don Quixote*. His house in Cleveland Court, St. James's, was Pope's
London residence from 1713 for several years, and there Pope took
lessons in painting.

The Three gentle Shepherds

[written c. 1713; published (piratically) 1726]

Of *gentle Philips* will I ever sing,
With *gentle Philips* shall the Vallies ring.
My Numbers too for ever will I vary,
With *gentle Budgell*, and with *gentle Carey*.
Or if in ranging of the Names I judge ill,   5
With *gentle Carey* and with *gentle Budgell*.
Oh! may all *gentle* Bards together place ye,
Men of good Hearts, and Men of Delicacy.
May *Satire* ne'er befool ye, or beknave ye,
And from all Wits that have a Knack Gad save ye.   10

1. *Philips*] Ambrose Philips (1675?–1749), a poet petted by the Whigs.
4. *Budgell*] Eustace Budgell (1686–1737), poet and miscellaneous writer.
Carey] Walter Carey (1686–1757), an Oxford wit.

Verses in the Scriblerian Manner

[written c. 1713; published posthumously]

In the winter of 1713–14 Pope and his friends formed themselves into
a society to which they gave the name of the 'Scriblerus Club', and where
they discussed and drafted schemes for books. Among the more frequent
visitors to the club was Robert Harley, Earl of Oxford, to whom invitations in rhyme were sent in the names of the members.

I

Tho the Dean has run from us in manner uncivil;
The Doctor, and He that's nam'd next to the Devil,
With Gay, who Petition'd you once on a time,
And Parnell, that would, if he had but a Rhyme.
(That Gay the poor Sec: and that arch Chaplain Parnell, 5
As Spiritual one, as the other is Carnal),
Forgetting their Interest, now humbly sollicit
You'd at present do nothing but give us a Visit.

	A. Pope.	
That all this true is	T. Parnell	10
Witness E. Lewis.	Jo: Arbuthnot	
	J. Gay.	

2. *The Doctor*] Arbuthnot.
He] Pope added an asterisk to 'He', and wrote in the margin 'Pope'.
5. *the poor Sec:*] Gay had been secretary to the Duchess of Monmouth.
10–11. *E. Lewis*] Harley's devoted secretary.

II

My Lord, forsake your Politick Utopians,
To sup, like Jove, with blameless Ethiopians

Pope.

2. *Jove . . . Ethiopians.*] Pope was then at work on the *Iliad*. See I 554,
556–7:
> The sire of gods, and all th' æthereal train . . .
> Now mix with mortals, nor disdain to grace
> The feast of Æthiopia's blameless race.

III

The Doctor and Dean, Pope, Parnell and Gay
In manner submissive most humbly do pray,
That your Lordship would once let your Cares all alone
And Climb the dark Stairs to your Friends who have none:
To your Friends who at least have no Cares but to please you
To a good honest Junta that never will teaze you.   6

From the Doctor's Chamber
past eight.

IV

A pox of all Senders
For any Pretenders
Who tell us these troublesome stories,
In their dull hum-drum key
Of Arma Virumque   5
Hannoniae qui primus ab oris.

A fig too for H——r
Who prates like his Grand mere
And all his old Friends would rebuke
In spite of the Carle   10
Give us but our Earle,
And the Devil may take their Duke.

Then come and take part in
The Memoirs of Martin,
Lay by your White Staff and gray Habit,   15
For trust us, friend Mortimer
Should you live years forty more
Haec olim meminisse juvabit.

by order of yᵉ Club
A. Pope
J. Gay
J. Swift
J. Arbuthnot
T. Parnel

6. *Hannoniae*] The duchy of Hainault, the scene of Marlborough's campaigns.

7. *H—r*] Hanmer, Sir Thomas (1677–1746). Chief of Hanoverian Tories; refused office from Lord Oxford, 1713; Speaker 1714–15.

12. *Duke*] The choice lies between Marlborough and Argyle.

14. *Martin*] Martinus Scriblerus.

16. *Mortimer*] Robert Harley, Earl of Oxford and Mortimer.

V

Let not the whigs our tory club rebuke;
Give us our earl, the devil take their duke.
Quaedam quae attinent ad Scriblerum,
Want your assistance now to clear 'em.
One day it will be no disgrace,   5
In scribbler to have had a place.
Come then, my lord, and take your part in
The important history of *Martin.*

VI

How foolish Men on Expeditions goe!
Unweeting Wantons of their wetting Woe!
For drizling Damps descend adown the Plain
And seem a thicker Dew, or thinner Rain;
Yet Dew or Rain may wett us to the Shift,   5
We'll not be slow to visit Dr. Swift.

Impromptu, To Lady Winchelsea

OCCASION'D BY FOUR SATYRICAL VERSES ON
WOMEN-WITS, IN THE RAPE OF THE LOCK

[written c. 1714; published, Bayle's *Dictionary*, 1741]

In vain you boast Poetic Names of yore,
And cite those *Sapho*'s we admire no more:
Fate doom'd the Fall of ev'ry Female Wit,
But doom'd it then when first *Ardelia* writ.
Of all Examples by the World confest,   5
I knew *Ardelia* could not quote the best;
Who, like her Mistress on *Britannia*'s Throne;
Fights, and subdues in Quarrels not her own.
To write their Praise you but in vain essay;
Ev'n while you write, you take that Praise away: 10
Light to the Stars the Sun does thus restore,
But shines himself till they are seen no more.

The 'four lines' which occasioned the dispute are canto IV, ll. 59-62.
4. *Ardelia*] The name under which the Countess occasionally wrote.

To Eustace Budgell, Esq. On his Translation of the Characters of Theophrastus

[written 1714; published 1954]

'Tis rumour'd, *Budgell* on a time
Writing a Sonnet, cou'd not rhyme;
Was he discouragd? no such matter;
He'd write in Prose—To the *Spectator*.
There too Invention faild of late: 5
What then? Gad damn him, he'd Translate,
Not Verse, to that he had a Pique—

Budgell's translation of *The Moral Characters of Theophrastus* was
dedicated to the Earl of Halifax and published in May 1714.

From *French*? He scornd it; no, from *Greek*.
He'd do't; and ne'r stand Shill—I Shall—I,
Ay, and inscribe to *Charles* Lord *Halli*——   10
Our *Gallo-Grecian* at the last
Has kept his word, Here's *Teophraste*.
How e're be not too vain, Friend *Budgell*!
Men of Ill Hearts, you know, will judge ill.
Some flatly say, the Book's as ill done,   15
As if by *Boyer*, or by *Gildon*;
Others opine you only chose ill,
And that this Piece was meant for *Ozell*.
For me, I think (in spite of Blunders)
You may, with *Addison*, do wonders.   20
But faith I fear, some Folks beside
These *smart, new Characters* supplyd.
The *honest Fellow out at Heels*
Pray between Friends, was not that *Steel*'s?
The *Rustic Lout* so like a Brute,   25
Was *Philips*'s beyond Dispute.
And the *fond Fop* so clean contrary,
Tis plain, tis very plain, was *Cary*.
Howe're, the *Coxcomb*'s thy own Merit,
That thou hast done, with *Life* and *Spirit*.   30

16. Abel Boyer (1667–1729), newswriter and compiler of a French-
English dictionary. Charles Gildon (1665–1724), critic and dramatist.
18. John Ozell, see p. 271.

To a Lady with the Temple of Fame
[written 1715; published, *PSM*, 1732]

What's Fame with Men, by Custom of the Nation,
Is call'd in Women only Reputation:
About them both why keep we such a pother?
Part you with one, and I'll renounce the other.

Four Poems from A Key to the Lock
[written 1715; published 1715]

I. TO MY MUCH HONOURED AND ESTEEMED
FRIEND, MR. E. BARNIVELT, AUTHOR OF THE
KEY TO THE LOCK. AN ANAGRAM AND ACROS-
TICK. BY N. CASTLETON, A WELL-WILLER TO
THE COALITION OF PARTIES

BARNIVELT

Anagram,

UN BAREL IT

B   arrels conceal the Liquor they contain,
A   nd Sculls are but the Barrels of the Brain.
R   ipe Politicks the Nation's Barrel fill,
N   one can like thee its Fermentation still.
I   ngenious Writer, lest thy Barrel split,   5
V   nbarrel thy just Sense, and broach thy Wit.
E   xtract from *Tory* Barrels all *French* Juice, ⎫
L   et not the *Whigs Geneva*'s Stumm infuse,   ⎬
T   hen shall thy Barrel be of gen'ral Use.   ⎭

                                    N. CASTLETON

N. Castleton] An obscure writer, whose penchant for 'the Mixture of
Inconsistent Metaphors' and 'the running of Metaphors into tedious
Allegories' was ridiculed in the *Spectator* (17 September 1714).

II. TO THE INGENIOUS MR. E. BARNIVELT

Hail, dear Collegiate, Fellow-Operator,
Censor of Tories, President of Satyr,
Whose fragrant Wit revives, as one may say,
The stupid World, like *Assa fetida.*
How safe must be the King upon his Throne,   5
When *Barnivelt* no Faction lets alone.
Of secret Jesuits swift shall be the Doom,
Thy Pestle braining all the Sons of *Rome.*
Before thy Pen vanish the Nation's Ills,
As all Diseases fly before thy Pills.   10
Such Sheets as these, whate'er be the Disaster,
Well spread with Sense, shall be the Nation's Plaister.

                            HIGH GERMAN DOCTOR

13. *High German Doctor*] Pseudonym of Philip Horneck (d. 1728), taken
from the title of his paper, which was scurrilously anti-Catholic.

III. TO MY INGENIOUS FRIEND, THE AUTHOR
OF THE KEY TO THE LOCK

Tho' many a Wit from time to time has rose
T' *inform* the World of what *it better knows,*
Yet 'tis a Praise that few their own can call,
To tell Men things they never *knew at all.*

This was reserv'd, Great *Barnivelt*, for Thee,   5
To save this Land from dangerous Mystery.
But thou too gently hast laid on thy Satyr;
What awes the World is Envy and ill Nature.
Can Popish Writings do the Nations good?
Each Drop of Ink demands a Drop of Blood.   10
A Papist wear the Lawrel! is it fit?
O *Button!* summon all thy Sons of Wit!
Join in the common Cause e'er 'tis too late;
Rack your Inventions some, and some *in time* translate.
If all this fail, let Faggot, Cart, and Rope,   15
Revenge our Wits and Statesmen on a *Pope*.

THE GRUMBLER

12. *Button*] Daniel Button, the manager of the coffee-house where Addison held his court.

13. *the common Cause*] i.e. the decrying, or suppression, of Pope's *Iliad*.

17. *The Grumbler*] Pseudonym of Thomas Burnet (1694–1753), pamphleteer, taken from the title of his paper.

IV. TO THE MOST LEARNED PHARMA-
COPOLITAN, AND EXCELLENT POLITICIAN,
MR. ESDRAS BARNIVELT

BY SIR JAMES BAKER, KNT.

The *Spaniard* hides his Ponyard in his Cloke,
The Papist masques his Treason in a Joke;
But ev'n as Coughs thy *Spanish* Liquorish heals,
So thy deep Knowledge dark Designs reveals.
Oh had I been Ambassador created,   5
Thy Works in *Spanish* shou'd have been translated,
Thy Politicks should ope the Eyes of *Spain*,
And, like true *Sevil* Snuff, awake the Brain.
Go on, Great Wit, contemn thy Foe's Bravado,
In thy defence I'll draw *Toledo*'s Spado.   10
Knighthoods on those have been conferr'd of late,
Who save our Eyesight, or wou'd save our State,
Unenvy'd Titles grace our mighty Names,
The learn'd Sir *William*, or the deep Sir *James*.
Still may those Honours be as justly dealt,   15
And thou be stil'd Sir *Esdras Barnivelt*.

JAMES BAKER, KNT.

14. *Sir William*] Sir William Read (d. 1715). An itinerant quack doctor.

Characters

I. MACER

[written c. 1715; published, *PSM*, 1728]

When simple *Macer*, now of high Renown,
First sought a Poet's Fortune in the Town:
'Twas all th' Ambition his great Soul could feel.
To wear red Stockings, and to dine with *St*——
Some Ends of Verse his Betters might afford,   5
And gave the harmless Fellow a good Word.
Set up with these, he ventur'd on the Town,
And in a borrow'd Play, out-did poor *Cr*——*n*.
There he stopt short, nor since has writ a tittle,
But has the Wit to make the most of little: 10
Like stunted hide-bound Trees, that just have got
Sufficient Sap, at once to bear and rot.
Now he begs Verse, and what he gets commends,
Not of the Wits his Foes, but Fools his Friends.

    So some coarse Country Wench, almost decay'd,   15
Trudges to Town, and first turns Chambermaid;
Aukward and supple, each Devoir to pay,
She flatters her good Lady twice a Day;
Thought wond'rous honest, tho' of mean Degree,
And strangely lik'd for her *Simplicity*:   20
In a translated Suit, then tries the Town,
With borrow'd Pins, and Patches not her own;
But just endur'd the Winter she began,
And in four Months, a batter'd Harridan.
Now nothing's left, but wither'd, pale, and shrunk,   25
To bawd for others, and go Shares with Punk.

A caricature of Ambrose Philips (see p. 285).
   1. *Macer*] Lat. *macer*, meagre; cf. *A Farewell to London*, l. 20, 'Lean
Philips' (p. 245).
   8. *a borrow'd Play*] *The Distrest Mother*, 1712, taken from Racine's
Andromaque.
   Cr—n] John Crowne (d. 1703?), dramatist; notorious for his borrowed
plays.
   13. *begs Verse*] He requested by publick Advertisements, the Aid of the
Ingenious, to make up a Miscellany in 1713. [P]
   20. *Simplicity*] An allusion to the laboured simplicity of Philips's
Pastorals.
   21. *a translated Suit*] Probably a fling at the *Persian Tales*, translated
by Philips.

II. UMBRA

[written c. 1714; published, *PSM*, 1728]

Close to the best known Author, *Umbra* sits,
The constant Index to all *Button*'s Wits.
Who's here? cries *Umbra:* 'Only *Johnson*'—*Oh!*
Your Slave, and *exit*; but returns with *Rowe*,
Dear Rowe, *lets sit and talk of Tragedies:*   5
Not long, *Pope* enters, and to *Pope* he flies.
Then up comes *Steele*; he turns upon his *Heel*,
And in a Moment fastens upon *Steele*.
But cries as soon, *Dear* Dick, *I must be gone*,
For, if I know his Tread, here's Addison.   10
Says *Addison* to *Steele*, 'Tis Time to go.
Pope to the Closet steps aside with *Rowe*.
Poor *Umbra*, left in this abandon'd Pickle,
E'en sits him down, and writes to honest *T*—.   15
    Fool! 'tis in vain from Wit to Wit to roam;
Know, Sense, like Charity, *begins at Home*.

Title] Possibly intended as a character of Budgell; see p. 288.
2. *Button's Wits*] The habitual Whig frequenters of Button's coffee-house.
14. *T*—] Thomas Tickell (1685–1740). Poet, Buttonian, and author of the rival translation of *Iliad* I.

III. ATTICUS

[written c. 1715; published (piratically) 1722]

Quod Te Roma legit, Rumpitur Invidia!

If meagre Gildon draws his venal quill,
I wish the Man a Dinner, and sit still;
If Dennis rhymes, and raves in furious Fret,
I'll answer Dennis, when I am in debt:
Hunger, not Malice, makes such Authors print,   5
And who'l wage War with Bedlam or the Mint?

This poem, provoked by the 'Battle of the Iliad', was originally sketched out about the time of the publication of the rival translation in the summer of 1715. It was first published in 1722. An expanded version (see p. 490) appeared in 1728, and in 1734 was incorporated after further revision in the *Epistle to Dr. Arbuthnot*, where it occupies lines 151–214 (see p. 603).
1–3. *Gildon . . . Dennis*] Charles Gildon (1665–1724), and John Dennis (1657–1734) critics, who had been attacking Pope since 1714 and 1709 respectively.
6. *the Mint*] A sanctuary for insolvent debtors in Southwark.

But were there One whom better Stars conspire
To bless, whom Titan touch'd with purer Fire,
Who born with Talents, bred in Arts to please,
Was form'd to write, converse, and live, with ease: 10
Should such a man, too fond to rule alone,
Bear, like the Turk, no Brother near the Throne;
View him with scornful, yet with jealous eyes,
And hate, for Arts that caus'd himself to rise;
Damn with faint praise, assent with civil Leer,   15
And without sneering, teach the rest to sneer;
Or pleas'd to wound, and yet afraid to strike,
Just hint a Fault, and hesitate Dislike;
Alike reserv'd to blame or to commend,
A tim'rous Foe and a suspitious Friend: 20
Fearing ev'n Fools, by Flatterers besieg'd;
And so obliging, that he ne'r oblig'd:
Who when two Wits on rival themes contest,
Approves them both, but likes the worst the best:
Like Cato, gives his little Senate Laws,   25
And sits attentive to his own Applause;
While Fops and Templars ev'ry Sentence raise,
And wonder with a foolish Face of Praise:
What pity, Heav'n! if such a Man there be?
Who would not weep, if Addison were He?   30

23 f. A reference to Tickell's rival translation of the *Iliad*, Bk. I, which
was published, with Addison's complicity and approval, within three or
four days of Pope's.
25. Cf. p. 211, l. 23.

Epitaph on P. P. Clerk of the Parish,

SAID TO BE WRITTEN BY HIMSELF

[written c. 1715, published, *PSM*, 1727]

O reader, if that thou canst read,
Look down upon this Stone;
Do all we can, Death is a Man
That never spareth none.

Appended to a skit on Bishop Burnet's *History of My Own Times*,
entitled 'Memoirs of P. P. Clerk of this Parish'.

Couplets on Wit

[written c. 1715; published 1776]

I

But our Great Turks in wit must reign alone
And ill can bear a Brother on the Throne.

II

Wit is like faith by such warm Fools profest
Who to be saved by one, must damn the rest.

III

Some who grow dull religious strait commence
And gain in morals what they lose in sence.

IV

Wits starve as useless to a Common weal
While Fools have places purely for their Zeal.

V

Now wits gain praise by copying other wits
As one Hog lives on what another sh——.

VI

Wou'd you your writings to some Palates fit
Purge all your verses from the sin of wit
For authors now are so conceited grown
They praise no works but what are like their own.

Preserved in the Homer MSS on the versos of rough drafts of lines
from his translation of *Iliad* VIII.

Two Chorus's to the Tragedy of Brutus
[written c. 1715; published, *Works* 1717]

I. CHORUS OF ATHENIANS

STROPHE I

Ye shades, where sacred truth is sought;
Groves, where immortal Sages taught;
Where heav'nly visions *Plato* fir'd,
And *Epicurus* lay inspir'd!
In vain your guiltless laurels stood,   5
Unspotted long with human blood.
War, horrid war, your thoughtful walks invades,
And steel now glitters in the Muses shades.

ANTISTROPHE I

Oh heav'n-born sisters! source of art!
Who charm the sense, or mend the heart;   10
Who lead fair Virtue's train along,
Moral *Truth*, and mystic *Song* !
To what new clime, what distant sky
Forsaken, friendless, shall ye fly ?
Say, will ye bless the bleak *Atlantic* shore ?   15
Or bid the furious *Gaul* be rude no more ?

STROPHE 2

When *Athens* sinks by fates unjust,
When wild *Barbarians* spurn her dust;
Perhaps ev'n *Britain*'s utmost shore
Shall cease to blush with stranger's gore,   20
See arts her savage sons controul,
And *Athens* rising near the pole!
'Till some new Tyrant lifts his purple hand,
And civil madness tears them from the land.

ANTISTROPHE 2

Ye Gods! what justice rules the ball ?   25
Freedom and Arts together fall;

Title] Altered from Shakespear by the Duke of Buckingham, at whose
desire these two Choruses were composed to supply as many wanting in
his play. They were set many years afterwards by the famous Bononcini,
and performed at Buckingham-house. [P]

Fools grant whate'er ambition craves,
And men, once ignorant, are slaves.
Oh curs'd effects of civil hate,
In every age, in every state!   30
Still, when the lust of tyrant pow'r succeeds,
Some *Athens* perishes, some *Tully* bleeds.

II. CHORUS OF YOUTHS AND VIRGINS

SEMICHORUS

Oh tyrant Love! hast thou possest
The prudent, learn'd, and virtuous breast?
Wisdom and wit in vain reclaim,
And arts but soften us to feel thy flame.
Love, soft intruder, enters here,   5
But entring learns to be sincere.
Marcus with blushes owns he loves,
And *Brutus* tenderly reproves.
   Why, virtue, doest thou blame desire,
     Which nature has imprest?   10
   Why, nature, dost thou soonest fire
     The mild and gen'rous breast?

CHORUS

Love's purer flames the Gods approve;
The Gods, and *Brutus* bend to love:
Brutus for absent *Portia* sighs,   15
And sterner *Cassius* melts at *Junia*'s eyes.
What is loose love? a transient gust,
Spent in a sudden storm of lust,
A vapour fed from wild desire,
A wandring, self-consuming fire.   20
   But *Hymen*'s kinder flames unite;
     And burn for ever one;
   Chaste as cold *Cynthia*'s virgin light,
     Productive as the Sun.

SEMICHORUS

Oh source of ev'ry social tye,   25
United wish, and mutual joy!
What various joys on one attend,
As son, as father, brother, husband, friend!

Whether his hoary sire he spies,
While thousand grateful thoughts arise;   30
Or meets his spouse's fonder eye;
Or views his smiling progeny;
    What tender passions take their turns,
      What home-felt raptures move!
    His heart now melts, now leaps, now burns,   35
      With rev'rence, hope, and love.

CHORUS

Hence guilty joys, distastes, surmizes,
Hence false tears, deceits, disguises,
Dangers, doubts, delays, surprizes;
    Fires that scorch, yet dare not shine: 40
Purest love's unwasting treasure,
Constant faith, fair hope, long leisure,
Days of ease, and nights of pleasure;
    Sacred *Hymen!* these are thine.

Lines on Curll

So when Curll's Stomach the strong Drench o'ercame,
(Infus'd in Vengeance of insulted Fame)
Th' Avenger sees, with a delighted Eye,
His long Jaws open, and his Colour fly;
And while his Guts the keen Emeticks urge,   5
Smiles on the Vomit, and enjoys the Purge.

From the title-page of Pope's *A Full and True Account of a Horrid and Barbarous Revenge by Poison on the Body of Mr. Edmund Curll, Bookseller* (1716).

To Mr. John Moore, Author of the Celebrated Worm-Powder

[written 1716; published (piratically) 1716]

How much, egregious *Moor*, are we
Deceiv'd by Shews and Forms!
Whate'er we think, whate'er we see,
All Humankind are Worms.

Title] Moore's advertisements are familiar to readers of contemporary newspapers. He died in 1737.

Man is a very Worm by Birth,   5
   Vile Reptile, weak, and vain!
A while he crawls upon the Earth,
   Then shrinks to Earth again.

That Woman is a Worm we find,
   E'er since our Grandame's Evil;   10
She first convers'd with her own Kind,
   That antient Worm, the Devil.

The Learn'd themselves we Book-Worms name;
   The Blockhead is a Slow-worm;
The Nymph whose Tail is all on Flame   15
   Is aptly term'd a Glow-worm:

The Fops are painted Butterflies,
   That flutter for a Day;
First from a Worm they take their Rise,
   And in a Worm decay: 20

The Flatterer an Earwig grows;
   Thus Worms suit all Conditions;
Misers are Muckworms, Silk-worms Beaus,
   And Death-watches Physicians.

That Statesmen have the Worm, is seen   25
   By all their winding Play;
Their Conscience is a Worm within,
   That gnaws them Night and Day.

Ah *Moore!* thy Skill were well employ'd,
   And greater Gain would rise,   30
If thou could'st make the Courtier void
   The Worm that never dies!

O learned Friend of *Abchurch-Lane,*
   Who sett'st our Entrails free!
Vain is thy Art, thy Powder vain,   35
   Since Worms shall eat ev'n thee.

Our Fate thou only can'st adjourn
   Some few short Years, no more!
Ev'n *Button*'s Wits to Worms shall turn,
   Who Maggots were before.   40

33. Moore's shop was at the Pestle and Mortar in Abchurch Lane.

A Roman Catholick Version of the First Psalm

FOR THE USE OF A YOUNG LADY

[written c. 1716; published (piratically) 1716]

The Maid is Blest that will not hear
   Of Masquerading Tricks,
Nor lends to Wanton Songs an Ear,
   Nor Sighs for Coach and Six.

To Please her shall her Husband strive   5
   With all his Main and Might,
And in her Love shall Exercise
   Himself both Day and Night.

She shall bring forth most Pleasant Fruit,
   He Flourish still and Stand,   10
Ev'n so all Things shall prosper well,
   That this Maid takes in Hand.

No wicked Whores shall have such Luck
   Who follow their own Wills,
But Purg'd shall be to Skin and Bone,   15
   With *Mercury* and *Pills*.

For why? the Pure and Cleanly Maids
   Shall All, good Husbands gain:
But filthy and uncleanly Jades
   Shall Rot in *Drury-Lane*.   20

A burlesque of Sternhold's version of Psalm 1.
20. *Drury-Lane*.] Notorious as the haunt of prostitutes in Pope's day.

Epitaph. On Sir William Trumbull

One of the Principal Secretaries of State to King William III, *who having resigned his Place, died in his Retirement at* Easthamsted *in* Berkshire, 1716.

[written 1716; published, *Works*, 1717]

A pleasing form, a firm, yet cautious mind,
Sincere, tho' prudent, constant, yet resign'd;

Honour unchang'd, a principle profest,
Fix'd to one side, but mod'rate to the rest;
An honest Courtier, yet a Patriot too,   5
Just to his Prince, yet to his Country true;
Fill'd with the sense of age, the fire of youth;
A scorn of wrangling, yet a zeal for truth;
A gen'rous faith, from superstition free,
A love to peace, and hate of tyranny;   10
Such this man was; who now, from earth remov'd,
At length enjoys that liberty he lov'd.

Sandys's Ghost: Or a Proper New Ballad
on the New Ovid's Metamorphosis

AS IT WAS INTENDED TO BE
TRANSLATED BY PERSONS OF QUALITY

[written c. 1717; published, *PSM*, 1727]

Ye Lords and Commons, Men of Wit
    And Pleasure about Town;
Read this, e'er you translate one Bit
    Of Books of high Renown.

Beware of *Latin* Authors all!   5
    Nor think your Verses Sterling,
Tho' with a Golden Pen you scrawl,
    And scribble in a *Berlin*:

For not the Desk with silver Nails,
    Nor *Bureau* of Expence,   10
Nor Standish well japan'd, avails
    To writing of good Sense.

Hear how a Ghost in dead of Night,
    With saucer Eyes of Fire,
In woful wise did sore affright   15
    A Wit and courtly 'Squire.

Title: *Sandys*] George Sandys (1578–1644), poet; published a translation of Ovid's *Metamorphoses*, 1621–6.
8. *Berlin*] A four-wheeled covered carriage with a hooded seat behind.
11. *Standish*] inkstand.

Rare Imp of *Phœbus*, hopeful Youth!
   Like Puppy tame that uses
To fetch and carry, in his Mouth,
   The Works of all the Muses.   20

Ah! why did he write Poetry,
   That hereto was so civil;
And sell his Soul for Vanity,
   To Rhyming and the Devil?

A Desk he had of curious Work,   25
   With glitt'ring Studs about;
Within the same did *Sandys* lurk,
   Tho' *Ovid* lay without.

Now as he scratch'd to fetch up Thought,
   Forth popp'd the *Sprite* so thin;   30
And from the Key-Hole bolted out,
   All upright as a Pin,

With Whiskers, Band, and Pantaloon,
   And Ruff compos'd most duly;
This 'Squire he dropp'd his Pen full soon,   35
   While as the Light burnt bluely.

Ho! Master *Sam*, quoth *Sandys*' Sprite,
   Write on, nor let me scare ye;
Forsooth, if Rhymes fall in not right,
   To *Budgel* seek, or *Carey*.   40

I hear the Beat of *Jacob*'s Drums,
   Poor *Ovid* finds no Quarter!
See first the merry *P——* comes
   In haste, without his Garter.

Then Lords and Lordings, 'Squires and Knights,
   Wits, Witlings, Prigs and Peers;   46
Garth at *St James*'s, and at *White*'s,
   Beats up for Volunteers.

37. *Master Sam*] Samuel Molyneux, the astronomer (see p. 479, l. 21*n*).
  41. *Jacob*] Jacob Tonson the publisher, who is drumming up volunteers
for the translation of Ovid.
  43. *P—*] Pelham, Thomas, Duke of Newcastle.
  47. *Garth*] Sir Samuel Garth, the editor of this translation.

What *Fenton* will not do, nor *Gay*,
  Nor *Congreve*, *Rowe*, nor *Stanyan*, 50
Tom B—n—t or *Tom D'Urfy* may,
  John Dunton, *Steel*, or any one.

If Justice *Philip*'s costive Head
  Some frigid Rhymes disburses;
They shall like *Persian* Tales be read, 55
  And glad both Babes and Nurses.

Let *W—rw—k*'s Muse with *Ash—t* join,
  And *Ozel*'s with Lord *Hervey*'s:
Tickell and *Addison* combine.
  And *P—pe* translate with *Jervis*. 60

L—— himself, that lively Lord
  Who bows to ev'ry Lady,
Shall join with *F——* in one Accord,
  And be like *Tate* and *Brady*.

Ye *Ladies* too draw forth your Pen, 65
  I pray where can the Hurt lie?
Since you have Brains as well as Men,
  As witness Lady *W—l-y*.

Now, *Tonson*, list thy Forces all,
  Review them, and tell Noses; 70
For to poor *Ovid* shall befal
  A strange *Metamorphosis*.

A *Metamorphosis* more strange
  Than all his Books can vapour;
'To what, (quoth 'Squire) shall *Ovid* change?' 75
  Quoth *Sandys*: *To Waste-Paper*.

50. *Stanyan*] Temple Stanyan (d. 1752), author and politician, who contributed to Book XII of the *Metamorphoses*.
52. *John Dunton*] Eccentric bookseller and satirist (1659–1733).
61. *L——*] Richard Lumley, second Earl of Scarbrough (1688?–1740).
63. *F——*] Probably Philip Frowde (see p. 245).
64. *Tate and Brady*] The rather pedestrian versifiers of the Psalms, 1696.
68. *W—l-y*] Lady Mary Wortley Montagu.

Epigram. On the Toasts of the Kit-Cat Club,

ANNO 1716

[published, *PSM*, 1732]

> Whence deathless *Kit-Cat* took its Name,
>   Few Criticks can unriddle;
> Some say from *Pastry Cook* it came,
>   And some from *Cat* and *Fiddle*.
> From no trim Beau's its Name it boasts,   5
>   Gray Statesman, or green Wits;
> But from this Pell-mell Pack of Toasts,
>   Of old *Cats* and young *Kits*.

Prologue to The Three Hours after Marriage
[written 1717; published 1717]

Authors are judg'd by strange capricious Rules,
The Great Ones are thought mad, the Small Ones Fools:
Yet sure the Best are most severely fated,
For Fools are only laugh'd at, Wits are hated.
Blockheads with Reason Men of Sense abhor;   5
But Fool 'gainst Fool, is barb'rous Civil War.
Why on all Authors then should Criticks fall?
Since some have writ, and shewn no Wit at all.
Condemn a Play of theirs, and they evade it,
Cry, damn not us, but damn the *French* who made it,   10
By running Goods, these graceless Owlers gain,
Theirs are the Rules of *France*, the Plots of *Spain*:
But Wit, like Wine, from happier Climates brought,
Dash'd by these Rogues, turns *English* common Draught:
They pall *Moliere*'s and *Lopez* sprightly strain,   15
And teach dull *Harlequins* to grin in vain.
How shall our Author hope a gentler Fate,
Who dares most impudently—not translate.
It had been civil in these ticklish Times,
To fetch his Fools and Knaves from foreign Climes;   20
Spaniard and *French* abuse to the World's End,
But spare old *England*, lest you hurt a Friend.

Title] A comedy by Pope, Gay, and Arbuthnot.
   11. *Owlers*] Smugglers, whose exploits were much in the papers about
this time.
   15. *Lopez*] Lopez de Vega (1562–1635), the famous Spanish dramatist.

If any Fool is by our Satyr bit,
Let him hiss loud, to show you all—he's hit.
Poets make Characters, as *Salesmen* Cloaths,   25
We take no Measure of your Fops and Beaus;
But here all Sizes and all Shapes you meet,
And fit your selves—like Chaps in *Monmouth-Street.*
  Gallants look here, this *Fool's-Cap has an Air—
Goodly and smart,—with Ears of *Issachar.*   30
Let no One Fool engross it, or confine:
A common Blessing! now 'tis yours, now mine.
But Poets in all Ages, had the Care
To keep this Cap, for such as will, to wear;
Our Author has it now, for ev'ry Wit   35
Of Course resign'd it to the next that writ:
And thus upon the Stage 'tis fairly †thrown,
Let him that takes it, wear it as his own.

28 *Chaps*] Chapmen, cheap salesmen.
  Monmouth-Street] The famous second-hand clothes market.
29. **Fool's-Cap*] *Shews a Cap with Ears. [Stage direction]
37. *fairly* †*thrown*] †Flings down the Cap and *Exit.* [Stage direction]

The Court Ballad

[written 1717; published (piratically?) 1717]

To the Tune of 'To all you Ladies now at Land,' &c.

> To one fair Lady out of court
>   And two fair Ladies in
> Who think the Turk and Pope a sport
>   And Wit and Love no Sin,
> Come these soft lines with nothing Stiff in   5
> To Bellenden Lepell and Griffin
>   With a fa.
>
> What passes in the dark third row
>   And what behind the Scene,
> Couches and crippled Chairs I know,   10
>   And Garrets hung with green;
> I know the Swing of sinful Hack,
> Where many a Damsel cries oh lack.
>   With a fa.

3. *The Turk*] Ulric, the little Turk, who belonged to George I.
6. Ladies in waiting to Princess Caroline.

Then why to court should I repair   15
    Where's such ado with Townsend.
To hear each mortal stamp and swear
    And ev'ry speech in Z—nds end,
To hear 'em rail at honest Sunderland
And rashly blame the realm of Blunderland.   20
                    With a fa.

Alas, like Shutz I cannot pun
    Like Clayton court the Germans
Tell Pickenburg how slim she's grown
    Like Meadows run to sermons,   25
To court ambitious men may roam,
But I and Marlbro' stay at home.
                    With a fa.

In truth by what I can discern,
    Of Courtiers from you Three,   30
Some Wit you have and more may learn,
    From Court than Gay or me,
Perhaps in time you'll leave High Diet,
And Sup with us on Mirth or Quiet,
                    With a fa.   35

In Leister fields, in house full nigh,
    With door all painted green,
Where Ribbans wave upon the tye,
    (A Milliner's I ween)
There may you meet us, three to three,   40
For Gay can well make two of me.
                    With a fa.

But shou'd you catch the Prudish itch,
    And each become a coward,

16. An allusion to Townshend's dismissal from the office of Secretary
of State.

19. Lord Sunderland had helped to turn Townshend out of office.

20. *Blunderland*] Ireland.

22. Perhaps an allusion to Augustus Schutz, equerry to the Prince of
Wales.

23-5. Mrs. Clayton, Lady Bucquenbourg, Miss Meadows, ladies of the
court.

27. *M—o*'] The Duke of Marlborough had a paralytic stroke and fell
into senile decay in 1716.

36. *Leister fields*] Now Leicester Square, where the Prince of Wales
lived.

Bring sometimes with you Lady Rich   45
    And sometimes Mistress Howard,
For Virgins, to keep chaste, must go
Abroad with such as are not so.
                    With a fa.

And thus fair Maids, my ballad ends,   50
    God send the King safe landing,
And make all honest ladies friends,
    To Armies that are Standing.
Preserve the Limits of these nations,
And take off Ladies Limitations.   55
                    With a fa.

45. Lady Rich, wife of Field-Marshal Sir Robert Rich.
46. Mrs. Howard, Countess of Suffolk, mistress of George II.

Epigrams,
Occasion'd by An Invitation to Court
[written 1717; published (piratically) 1717]

I

In the *Lines* that you sent, are the *Muses* and *Graces*;
You have the *Nine* in your *Wit*, and *Three* in your *Faces.*

II

They may talk of the *Goddesses* in *Ida* Vales,
But *you* show your *Wit*, whereas *they* show'd their *Tails.*

III

You *Bellendene, Griffin,* and little *La Pell,*
By G—d you all lie like the D—l in Hell;
To say that at Court there's a Dearth of all Wit,
And send what *Argyle,* would he *write,* might have writ.

IV

Adam had fallen twice, if for an apple
The D—l had brought him *Bellendene* and *La Pell.*

These epigrams were intended to form a pendant to *The Court Ballad.*

V

On Sunday at Six, in the Street that's call'd *Gerrard*,
You may meet the *Two Champions* who are no Lord *S—d.*

VI

They say *Argyll*'s a Wit, for what?
For writing? no,—for writing not.

Epistle to a Lady

In this strange Town a different Course we take,
Refine ourselves to Spirit, for your Sake.
For Want of you, we spend our random Wit on
The first we find with Needham, Brooks, or Briton.
Hackney'd in Sin, we beat about the Town,   5
And like sure Spaniels, at first Scent lie down.
Were Virtue's self in Silks,—faith keep away!
Or Virtue's Virtue scarce would last a Day.

Thus, Madam, most Men talk, and some Men do:
The rest is told you in a Line or two.   10
Some strangely wonder you're not fond to marry—
A double Jest still pleases sweet Sir Harry—
Small-Pox is rife, and *Gay* in dreadful fear—
The good Priests whisper—Where's the Chevalier?
Much in your Absence B—'s Heart endures,   15
And if poor *Pope* is cl–pt, the Fault is yours.

Originally published as a suppressed conclusion of *To a Young Lady,
on leaving the Town after the Coronation.* More probably related to *The
Court Ballad* and the preceding epigrams. See *Rev. of Eng. Stud.* (1958)
IX 146–51.
4. Mother Needham kept a brothel. Nothing is known of Brooks and
Briton.

Occasion'd by some Verses of his Grace the
Duke of Buckingham

[written 1717; published, *Works*, 1717]

Muse, 'tis enough: at length thy labour ends,
And thou shalt live; for *Buckingham* commends.

Let crowds of criticks now my verse assail,
Let *Dennis* write, and nameless numbers rail:
This more than pays whole years of thankless pain; 5
Time, health, and fortune, are not lost in vain.
Sheffield approves, consenting *Phœbus* bends,
And I and Malice from this hour are friends.

Verses Sent to Mrs. T. B. with his Works

BY AN AUTHOR

[written 1717; published 1721]

This Book, which, like its Author, You
By the bare Outside only knew,
(Whatever was in either Good,
Not look'd in, or, not understood)
Comes, as the Writer did too long, 5
To be about you, right or wrong;
Neglected on your Chair to lie,
Nor raise a Thought, nor draw an Eye;
In peevish Fits to have you say,
See there! you're always in my Way! 10
Or, if your Slave you think to bless,
I like this Colour, I profess!
That Red is charming all will hold,
I ever lov'd it—next to Gold.

Can Book, or Man, more Praise obtain? 15
What more could *G—ge* or *S—te* gain?

Sillier than *Gildon* coud'st thou be,
Nay, did all *Jacob* breath in thee,
She keeps thee, Book! I'll lay my Head,
What? throw away a *Fool in Red*: 20
No, trust the Sex's sacred Rule;
The gaudy Dress will save the Fool.

Title: *Mrs. T. B.*] Probably Mistress Teresa Blount.
16. *G—ge or S—te*] Perhaps 'George or Senate'.
17. *G–ld–d*] Charles Gildon, see p. 369, l. 250*n.*
18. *J–c–b*] Giles Jacob (1686–1744). Compiler of *The Poetical Register*,
1720.

A Hymn Written in Windsor Forest
[written 1717; published 1831]

All hail! once pleasing, once inspiring Shade,
  Scene of my youthful Loves, and happier hours!
Where the kind Muses met me as I stray'd,
  And gently pressd my hand, and said, Be Ours!—
Take all thou e're shalt have, a constant Muse: 5
  At Court thou may'st be lik'd, but nothing gain;
Stocks thou may'st buy and sell, but always lose;
  And love the brightest eyes, but love in vain!

Poems 1718-1729

Epistle to Robert Earl of Oxford, and Earl Mortimer

[written 1721; published, Parnell's *Poems*, 1722]

Such were the Notes, thy once-lov'd Poet sung,
'Till Death untimely stop'd his tuneful Tongue.
   Oh just beheld, and lost! admir'd, and mourn'd!
With softest Manners, gentlest Arts, adorn'd!
Blest in each Science, blest in ev'ry Strain!   5
Dear to the Muse, to HARLEY dear——in vain!
   For him, thou oft hast bid the World attend,
Fond to forget the Statesman in the Friend;
For *Swift* and him, despis'd the Farce of State,
The sober Follies of the Wise and Great;   10
Dextrous, the craving, fawning Crowd to quit,
And pleas'd to 'scape from Flattery to Wit.
   Absent or dead, still let a Friend be dear,
(A Sigh the Absent claims, the Dead a Tear)
Recall those Nights that clos'd thy toilsom Days,   15
Still hear thy *Parnell* in his living Lays:
Who careless, now, of Int'rest, Fame, or Fate,
Perhaps forgets that OXFORD e'er was Great;
Or deeming meanest what we greatest call,
Beholds thee glorious only in thy Fall,   20
   And sure if ought below the Seats Divine
Can touch Immortals, 'tis a Soul like thine:
A Soul supreme, in each hard Instance try'd,
Above all Pain, all Passion, and all Pride,
The Rage of Pow'r, the Blast of publick Breath,   25
The Lust of Lucre, and the Dread of Death.
   In vain to Desarts thy Retreat is made;
The Muse attends thee to the silent Shade:
'Tis hers, the brave Man's latest Steps to trace,
Re-judge his Acts, and dignify Disgrace.   30
When Int'rest calls off all her sneaking Train,
And all th' Oblig'd desert, and all the Vain;
She waits, or to the Scaffold, or the Cell,
When the last ling'ring Friend has bid farewel.
Ev'n now she shades thy Evening Walk with Bays,   35

Title] This Epistle was sent to the Earl of Oxford with Dr. Parnelle's
Poems published by our Author, after the said Earl's Imprisonment in the
Tower and Retreat into the Country, in the year, 1721. [P]
  27. *Desarts*] i.e. his family seat at Brampton-Bryan in Herefordshire.

(No Hireling she, no Prostitute to Praise)
Ev'n now, observant of the parting Ray,
Eyes the calm Sun-set of thy Various Day,
Thro' Fortune's Cloud One truly Great can see,
Nor fears to tell, that MORTIMER is He.   40

To Mrs. M. B. on her Birth-day

[written 1723; published 1724]

Oh be thou blest with all that Heav'n can send,
Long Health, long Youth, long Pleasure, and a Friend:
Not with those Toys the female world admire,
Riches that vex, and Vanities that tire.
With added years if Life bring nothing new,   5
But like a Sieve let ev'ry blessing thro',
Some joy still lost, as each vain year runs o'er,
And all we gain, some sad Reflection more;
Is that a Birth-day? 'tis alas! too clear,
'Tis but the Fun'ral of the former year.   10
   Let Joy or Ease, let Affluence or Content,
And the gay Conscience of a life well spent,
Calm ev'ry thought, inspirit ev'ry Grace,
Glow in thy heart, and smile upon thy face.
Let day improve on day, and year on year,   15
Without a Pain, a Trouble, or a Fear;
Till Death unfelt that tender frame destroy,
In some soft Dream, or Extasy of joy:
Peaceful sleep out the Sabbath of the Tomb,
And wake to Raptures in a Life to come.   20

Title: *Mrs. M. B.*] i.e. Martha Blount (see p. 559, *n*).

The Dunciad Variorum

━━━━━━━━━━━━ ✸ ━━━━━━━━━━━━

WITH THE PROLEGOMENA
OF SCRIBLERUS

[written ?1719–28; published 1728; as
Variorum, 1729]

ADVERTISEMENT

*It will be sufficient to say of this Edition, that the reader has here a
much more correct and compleat copy of the* DUNCIAD, *than has
hitherto appeared: I cannot answer but some mistakes may have slipt
into it, but a vast number of others will be prevented, by the Names
being now not only set at length, but justified by the authorities and
reasons given. I make no doubt, the Author's own motive to use real
rather than feign'd names, was his care to preserve the Innocent from
any false Applications; whereas in the former editions which had no
more than the Initial letters, he was made, by Keys printed here, to hurt
the inoffensive; and (what was worse) to abuse his friends, by an impression at* Dublin.

*The Commentary which attends the Poem, was sent me from
several hands, and consequently must be unequally written; yet will it
have one advantage over most commentaries, that it is not made upon
conjectures, or a remote distance of time: and the reader cannot but
derive one pleasure from the very Obscurity of the persons it treats of,
that it partakes of the nature of a* Secret, *which most people love to
be let into, tho' the Men or the Things be ever so inconsiderable or
trivial.*

Of the Persons *it was judg'd proper to give some account: for since
it is only in this monument that they must expect to survive, (and here
survive they will, as long as the English tongue shall remain such as it
was in the reigns of Queen* ANNE *and King* GEORGE) *it seem'd but
humanity to bestow a word or two upon each, just to tell what he was,
what he writ, when he liv'd, or when he dy'd.*

*If a word or two more are added upon the chief Offenders; 'tis only as
a paper pinn'd upon the breast, to mark the Enormities for which they
suffer'd; lest the Correction only should be remember'd, and the Crime
forgotten.*

In some Articles, it was thought sufficient barely to transcribe from
Jacob, Curl, *and other writers of their own rank, who were much*

better acquainted with them than any of the Authors of this Comment can pretend to be. Most of them had drawn each other's Characters on certain occasions; but the few here inserted, are all that could be saved from the general destruction of such Works.

Of the part of Scriblerus *I need say nothing: his Manner is well enough known, and approv'd by all but those who are too much concern'd to be judges.*

The Imitations *of the Ancients are added, to gratify those who either never read, or may have forgotten them; together with some of the Parodies, and Allusions to the most excellent of the Moderns. If any man from the frequency of the former, may think the Poem too much a* Cento; *our Poet will but appear to have done the same thing in jest, which* Boileau *did in earnest; and upon which* Vida, Fracastorius, *and many of the most eminent Latin Poets professedly valued themselves.*

A Letter to the Publisher

OCCASIONED BY THE PRESENT
EDITION OF THE DUNCIAD

It is with pleasure I hear that you have procured a correct Edition of the DUNCIAD, which the many surreptitious ones have rendered so necessary; and it is yet with more, that I am informed it will be attended with a COMMENTARY: a work so necessary, that I cannot think the Author himself would have omitted it, had he approv'd of the first appearance of this Poem.

Such Notes as have occurr'd to me I herewith send you; you will oblige me by inserting them amongst those which are, or will be, transmitted to you by others: since not only the Author's friends, but even strangers, appear ingag'd by humanity, to some care of an orphan of so much genius and spirit, which its parent seems to have abandoned from the very beginning, and suffered to step into the world naked, unguarded, and unattended.

It was upon reading some of the abusive papers lately publish'd, that my great regard to a person whose friendship I shall ever esteem as one of the chief honours of my life, and a much greater respect to Truth than to him or any man living, ingag'd me in Enquiries, of which the inclos'd Notes are the fruit.

I perceiv'd that most of these authors had been (doubtless very wisely) the first Aggressors: they had try'd till they were weary, what was to be got by railing at each other; no body was either concern'd, or surpriz'd, if this or that Scribler was prov'd a Dunce:

but every one was curious to read what could be said to prove Mr. POPE one, and was ready to pay something for such a discovery: A stratagem which wou'd they fairly own, might not only reconcile them to me, but screen them from the resentment of their lawful superiors, whom they daily abuse, only (as I charitably hope) to get that by them, which they cannot get from them.

I found this was not all: ill success in that had transported them to personal abuse, either of himself, or (what I think he could less forgive) of his friends. They had call'd men of virtue and honour Bad Men, long before he had either leisure or inclination to call them Bad Writers: and some had been such old offenders, that he had quite forgotten their persons as well as their slanders, till they were pleas'd to revive them.

Now what had Mr. POPE done before to incense them? He had published those works which are in the hands of every body, in which not the least mention is made of any of them: And what has he done since? He has laugh'd and written the DUNCIAD. What has that said of them? a very serious truth which the publick had said before, that they were dull: and what it had no sooner said, but they themselves were at great pains to procure or even purchase room in the prints, to testify under their hands to the truth of it.

I should still have been silent, if either I had seen any inclination in my friend to be serious with such accusers, or if they had only attack'd his writings: since whoever publishes, puts himself on his tryal by his country. But when his moral character was attack'd, and in a manner from which neither Truth nor Virtue can secure the most Innocent, in a manner which though it annihilates the credit of the accusation with the just and impartial, yet aggravates very much the guilt of the accuser, (I mean by authors without Names:) Then I thought, since the danger is common to all, the concern ought to be so; and that it was an act of justice to detect the Authors, not only on this account, but as many of them are the same, who for several years past, have made free with the greatest Names in Church and State, expos'd to the world the private misfortunes of Families, abus'd all even to Women, and whose prostituted papers (for one or other Party, in the unhappy Divisions of their Country) have insulted the Fallen, the Friendless, the Exil'd, and the Dead.

Besides this, which I take to be a publick concern, I have already confess'd I had a private one. I am one of that number who have long lov'd and esteem'd Mr. POPE, and had often declared it was not his Capacity or Writings (which we ever thought the least valuable part of his character) but the honest, open, and beneficent

Man, that we most esteem'd and lov'd in him. Now if what these people say were believ'd, I must appear to all my friends either a fool or a knave, either impos'd on my self, or imposing on them: So that I am as much interested in the confutation of these calumnies, as he is himself.

I am no Author, and consequently not to be suspected either of jealousy or resentment against any of the men, of whom scarce one is known to me by sight; and as for their writings, I have sought them (on this one occasion) in vain, in the closets and libraries of all my acquaintance. I had still been in the dark, if a Gentleman[1] had not procur'd me (I suppose from some of themselves, for they are generally much more dangerous friends than enemies) the passages I send you. I solemnly protest I have added nothing to the malice or absurdity of them, which it behoves me to declare, since the vouchers themselves will be so soon and so irrecoverably lost. You may in some measure prevent it, by preserving at least their* Titles, and discovering (as far as you can depend on the truth of your information) the names of the conceal'd authors.

The first objection I have heard made to the Poem is, that the persons are too obscure for Satyre. The persons themselves, rather than allow the objection, would forgive the Satyre; and if one could be tempted to afford it a serious answer, were not all assassinates,[2] popular insurrections, the insolence of the rabble without doors and of domesticks within, most wrongfully chastized, if the Meanness of offenders indemnified them from punishment? On the contrary, obscurity renders them more dangerous, as less thought of: Law can pronounce judgment only on open Facts, Morality alone can pass censure on Intentions of mischief; so that for secret calumny or the arrow flying in the dark, there is no publick punishment left, but what a good writer inflicts.

The next objection is, that these sort of authors are Poor. That might be pleaded as an excuse at the Old Baily for lesser crimes than defamation, for 'tis the case of almost all who are try'd there; but sure it can here be none, since no man will pretend that the robbing another of his reputation supplies the want of it in himself. I question not but such authors are poor, and heartily wish the objection were removed by any honest livelihood. But Poverty here is the accident, not the subject: he who describes malice and villany to be pale and meagre, expresses not the least anger against paleness or leanness, but against malice and villany. The apothecary in ROMEO and JULIET is poor, but is he therefore justified in

---

[1] *a Gentleman* ⟨Probably Richard Savage.⟩
* Which we have done in a List in the *Appendix*, No. 2.
[2] *assassinates* ⟨i.e. assassins.⟩

vending poison? Not but poverty itself becomes a just subject of satyre, when it is the consequence of vice, prodigality, or neglect of one's lawful calling; for then it increases the publick burden, fills the streets and high-ways with Robbers, and the garrets with Clippers, Coiners, and Weekly Journalists.

But admitting that two or three of these, offend less in their morals, than in their writings; must poverty make nonsense sacred? If so, the fame of bad authors would be much better taken care of, than that of all the good ones in the world; and not one of a hundred had ever been call'd by his right name.

They mistake the whole matter: It is not charity to encourage them in the way they follow, but to get 'em out of it: For men are not bunglers because they are poor, but they are poor because they are bunglers.

Is it not pleasant enough to hear our authors crying out on the one hand, as if their persons and characters were too sacred for Satyre; and the publick objecting on the other, that they are too mean even for Ridicule? But whether bread or fame be their end, it must be allow'd, our author by and in this poem, has mercifully given 'em a little of both.

There are two or three,[1] who by their rank and fortune have no benefit from the former objections (supposing them good) and these I was sorry to see in such company. But if without any provocation, two or three gentlemen will fall upon one, in an affair wherein his interest and reputation are equally embark'd; they cannot certainly, after they had been content to print themselves his enemies, complain of being put into the number of them?

Others, I'm told, pretend to have been once his Friends[2]; surely they are their enemies who say so, since nothing can be more odious than to treat a friend as they have done: but of this I can't persuade my self, when I consider the constant and eternal aversion of all bad writers to a good one.

Such as claim a merit from being his Admirers, I wou'd gladly ask, if it lays him under any personal obligation? at that rate he would be the most oblig'd humble servant in the world. I dare swear, for these in particular, he never desir'd them to be his Admirers, nor promis'd in return to be theirs; that had truly been a sign he was of their acquaintance; but wou'd not the malicious world have suspected such an approbation of some motive worse than ignorance, in the Author of the ESSAY on CRITICISM? Be it as it will, the reasons of their Admiration and of his Contempt are

---

[1] *two or three* ⟨e.g. Thomas Burnet, George Duckett, Sir Richard Blackmore.⟩

[2] *Friends* ⟨e.g. James Moore Smythe. Cf. *Ep. to Arbuthnot*, 346.⟩

equally subsisting; for His Works and Theirs are the very same that they were.

One therefore of their accusations I believe may be just, 'That he has a contempt for their writings.' And there is another which would probably be sooner allow'd by himself, than by any good judge beside, 'That his own have found too much success with the publick.' But as it cannot consist with his modesty to claim this as a justice, it lies not on him, but entirely on the publick, to defend its own judgment.

There remains what in my opinion might seem a better plea for these people, than any they have made use of. If Obscurity or Poverty were to exempt a man from satyr, much more should Folly or Dulness, which are still more involuntary, nay as much so as personal deformity. But even this will not help them: Deformity becomes the object of ridicule when a man sets up for being hand-some: and so must Dulness when he sets up for a Wit. They are not ridicul'd because Ridicule in itself is or ought to be a pleasure; but because it is just, to undeceive or vindicate the honest and unpre-tending part of mankind from imposition, because particular in-terest ought to yield to general, and a great number who are not naturally Fools ought never to be made so in complaisance to a few who are. Accordingly we find that in all ages, all vain pretenders, were they ever so poor or ever so dull, have been constantly the topicks of the most candid Satyrists, from the Codrus of JUVENAL to the Damon of BOILEAU.

Having mention'd BOILEAU, the greatest Poet and most judi-cious Critic of his age and country, admirable for his talents, and yet perhaps more admirable for his judgment in the proper appli-cation of them; I cannot help remarking the resemblance betwixt Him and our Author in Qualities, Fame, and Fortune; in the dis-tinctions shewn to them by their Superiors, in the general esteem of their Equals, and in their extended reputation amongst For-eigners; in the latter of which ours has met with the better fortune, as he has had for his Translators persons of the most eminent rank and abilities in their respective Nations.* But the resemblance holds in nothing more, than in their being equally abus'd by the ignorant

---

* Essay on Criticism in *French* Verse by General *Hamilton*. The same in Verse also by Monsieur *Roboton*, Counsellor and Privy Secretary to King *George* I.

Rape of the Lock, in *French, Paris*, 1728.

—— —— In *Italian* Verse, by the Abbe *Conti*, a Noble *Venetian*; and by the Marquess *Rangoni*, Envoy Extraordinary from *Modena* to King *George* II.

Others of his Works by *Salvini* of *Florence*, &c.

His Essays and Dissertations on *Homer*, in *French, Paris* 1728.

pretenders to Poetry of their times; of which not the least memory will remain but in their own writings, and in the notes made upon them. What BOILEAU has done in almost all his Poems, our Author has only in this: I dare answer for him he will do it in no more; and on his principle of attacking few but who had slander'd him, he could not have done it at all had he been confin'd from censuring obscure and worthless persons, for scarce any other were his enemies. However, as the parity is so remarkable, I hope it will continue to the last; and if ever he shall give us an edition of this Poem himself, I may see some of 'em treated as gently (on their repentance or better merit) as Perault and Quinault were at last by BOILEAU.[1]

In one point I must be allow'd to think the character of our English Poet the more amiable. He has not been a follower of fortune or success: He has liv'd with the Great without Flattery, been a friend to Men in power without Pensions, from whom as he ask'd, so he receiv'd no favour but what was done Him in his friends. As his Satyrs were the more just for being delay'd, so were his Panegyricks; bestow'd only on such persons as he had familiarly known, only for such virtues as he had long observ'd in them, and only at such times as others cease to praise if not begin to calumniate them, I mean when out of Power or out of Fashion.† A Satyr therefore on writers so notorious for the contrary, became no man so well as himself; as none (it is plain) was so little in Their friendships, or so much in that of those whom they had most abus'd, namely the Greatest and Best of All Parties. Let me add a further reason, that tho' ingag'd in their friendships, he never espous'd their animosities; and can almost singly challenge this honour, not to have written a line of any man, which thro' Guilt, thro' Shame, or thro' Fear, thro' variety of Fortune, or change of Interests, he was ever unwilling to own.

I shall conclude with remarking what a pleasure it must be to every reader of humanity, to see all along, that our Author, in his very laughter, is not indulging his own Ill nature, but only punishing that of others. To his Poem those alone are capable to do Justice, who to use the words of a great Writer, know how hard it is

[1] BOILEAU ⟨See *A Treatise of the Sublime . . . By Mr. Boileau*, 1712, pp. 96–7, 169–78.⟩
† As Mr. *Wycherley*, at the time the Town declaim'd against his Book of Poems: Mr. *Walsh*, after his death: Sir *William Trumbull*, when he had resign'd the Office of Secretary of State; Lord *Bolingbroke* at his leaving *England* after the Queen's death: Lord *Oxford* in his last decline of Life: Mr. Secretary *Craggs* at the end of the South-Sea Year, and after his death: Others, only in *Epitaphs*.

(with regard both to his Subject and his Manner) VETUSTIS
DARE NOVITATEM, OBSOLETIS NITOREM, OBSCURIS LUCEM,
FASTIDITIS GRATIAM.[1] I am,
Your most humble Servant,
WILLIAM CLELAND.[2]

St. *James's*
Dec. 22, 1728.

DENNIS, REM. ON PR. ARTH.

I Cannot but think it the most *reasonable* thing in the world,
to distinguish Good writers, by discouraging the Bad. Nor is it
an *ill-natur'd* thing, in relation even to the very *persons* upon whom
the Reflections are made: It is true, it may deprive them, a little
the sooner, of a *short Profit* and a *transitory Reputation:* But then
it may have a good effect, and oblige them (before it be too late) to
decline that for which they are so very *unfit,* and to have recourse
to *something* in which they may be more successful.

The *Persons* whom *Boileau* has attack'd in his writings, have
been for the most part *Authors,* and most of those Authors, *Poets:*
And the censures he hath pass'd upon them have been *confirm'd*
by all Europe. [Character of Mr. *P.* 1716.]

GILDON, PREF. TO HIS NEW REHEARS.

IT is the common cry of the *Poetasters* of the Town, and their
Fautors, that it is an *Ill-natur'd thing* to expose the *Pretenders* to
Wit and Poetry. The Judges and Magistrates may with full as good
reason be reproach'd with *Ill-nature,* for putting the Laws in exe-
cution against a Thief or Impostor—The same will hold in the
Republick of Letters, if the Criticks and Judges will let every
Ignorant Pretender to Scribling, pass on the World.

THEOBALD, LETT. TO MIST, JUN. 22, 1728

ATTACKS may be levelled, either against *Failures in Genius,* or
against the *Pretensions* of *writing without one.*

---

[1] GRATIAM ⟨Pliny, *Natural History,* Preface § 15.⟩
[2] *CLELAND*] This Gentleman was of Scotland, and bred at the
University of Utrecht, with the Earl of Mar. He served in Spain under
Earl Rivers. After the Peace, he was made one of the Commissioners of
the Customs in Scotland, and then of Taxes in England, in which having
shewn himself for twenty years diligent, punctual, and incorruptible,
though without any other assistance of Fortune, he was suddenly dis-
placed by the Minister in the sixty eighth year of his age; and died two
months after, in 1741. He was a person of Universal Learning, and an
enlarged Conversation; no man had a warmer heart for his Friend, or a
sincerer attachment to the Constitution of his Country. ⟨See p. 810.⟩

CONCANEN, DED. TO THE AUTH. OF THE DUNC.

A *Satyre* upon *Dulness*, is a thing, that has been *used* and *allowed* in *All Ages*.

Out of thine own Mouth will I judge thee, wicked Scribler !

Testimonies of Authors
Concerning our Poet and his Works

M. SCRIBLERUS LECTORI S.

Before we present thee with our exercitations on this most delectable Poem (drawn from the many volumes of our Adversaria on modern Authors) we shall here, according to the laudable usage of editors, collect the various judgments of the Learned concerning our Poet: Various indeed, not only of different authors, but of the same author at different seasons. Nor shall we gather only the Testimonies of such eminent Wits, as would of course descend to posterity, and consequently be read without our collection; but we shall likewise with incredible labour seek out for divers others, which, but for this our diligence, could never at the distance of a few months appear to the eye of the most curious. Hereby thou may'st not only receive the delectation of Variety, but also arrive at a more certain judgment, by a grave and circumspect comparison of the Witnesses with each other, or of each with himself. Hence also thou wilt be enabled to draw reflections, not only of a critical, but a moral nature, by being let into many particulars of the Person as well as Genius, and of the Fortune as well as Merit, of our Author: In which if I relate some things of little concern peradventure to thee, and some of as little even to him; I entreat thee to consider how minutely all true critics and commentators are wont to insist upon such, and how material they seem to themselves, if to none other. Forgive me, gentle reader, if (following learned example) I ever and anon become tedious: allow me to take the same pains to find whether my author were good or bad, well or ill-natured, modest or arrogant; as another, whether his author was fair or brown, short or tall, or whether he wore a coat or a cassock.

We purposed to begin with his Life, Parentage, and Education: But as to these, even his cotemporaries do exceedingly differ. One saith[a], he was educated at home; another[b], that he was bred at St. Omer's by Jesuits; a third[c], not at St. Omer's, but at Oxford; a

[a] Giles Jacob's Lives of Poets, vol. ii. in his Life.
[b] Dennis's Reflect. on the Essay on Crit.
[c] Dunciad dissected, p. 4.

fourth[d], that he had no University education at all. Those who allow him to be bred at home, differ as much concerning his Tutor: One saith[e], he was kept by his father on purpose; a second[f], that he was an itinerant priest; a third[g], that he was a parson; one[h] calleth him a secular clergyman of the Church of Rome; another[i], a monk. As little do they agree about his Father, whom one[k] supposeth, like the Father of Hesiod, a tradesman or merchant; another[l], a husband-man; another[m], a hatter, &c. Nor has an author been wanting to give our Poet such a father as Apuleius hath to Plato, Jamblicus to Pythagoras, and divers to Homer, namely a Dæmon: For thus Mr. Gildon[n]: 'Certain it is, that his original is not from Adam, but the Devil; and that he wanteth nothing but horns and tail to be the exact resemblance of his infernal Father.' Finding, therefore, such contrariety of opinions, and (whatever be ours of this sort of generation) not being fond to enter into controversy, we shall defer writing the life of our Poet, 'till authors can determine among themselves what Parents or Education he had, or whether he had any Education or Parents at all.

Proceed we to what is more certain, his Works, tho' not less uncertain the judgments concerning them; beginning with his ESSAY on CRITICISM, of which hear first the most ancient of Critics,

MR. JOHN DENNIS.

'His precepts are false or trivial, or both; his thoughts are crude and abortive, his expressions absurd, his numbers harsh and un-musical, his rhymes trivial and common;—instead of majesty, we have something that is very mean; instead of gravity, something that is very boyish; and instead of perspicuity and lucid order, we have but too often obscurity and confusion.' And in another place: 'What rare *numbers* are here! Would not one swear that this

[d] Guardian, N° 40. ⟨An essay written by Pope himself.⟩
[e] Jacob's Lives &c. vol. ii.
[f] Dunciad dissected, p. 4.
[g] Farmer P. and his son.
[h] Dunc. dissect.
[i] Characters of the times, p. 45.
[k] Female Dunc. p. ult.
[l] Dunc. dissect.
[m] Roome, Paraphrase on the 4th of Genesis, printed 1729.
[n] Character of Mr. P. and his Writings, in a Letter to a Friend, printed for S. Popping, 1716. p. 10. Curl, in his Key to the Dunciad (first edit. said to be printed for A. Dodd) in the 10th page, declared Gildon to be author of that libel; though in the subsequent editions of his Key he left out this assertion, and affirmed (in the Curliad, p. 4. and 8.) that it was writ by Dennis only.

youngster had espoused some antiquated muse, who had sued out a divorce from some superannuated sinner, upon account of impotence, and who, being poxed by her former spouse, has got the gout in her decrepid age, which makes her *hobble so damnably*[o].' No less peremptory is the censure of our hypercritical Historian

MR. OLDMIXON.

'I dare not say any thing of the Essay on Criticism in verse; but if any more curious reader has discovered in it something *new* which is not in Dryden's prefaces, dedications, and his essay on dramatic poetry, not to mention the French critics, I should be very glad to have the benefit of the discovery[p].'

He is followed (as in fame, so in judgment) by the modest and simple-minded

MR. LEONARD WELSTED;

Who, out of great respect to our poet not naming him, doth yet glance at his Essay, together with the Duke of Buckingham's, and the Criticisms of Dryden, and of Horace, which he more openly taxeth[q]: 'As to the numerous treatises, essays, arts, *&c.* both in verse and prose, that have been written by the moderns on this ground-work, they do but *hackney the same thoughts over again,* making them still more *trite.* Most of their pieces are nothing but a pert, insipid heap of *common place.* Horace has even in his Art of Poetry thrown out several things which plainly shew, he thought an Art of Poetry was of no use, even while he was writing one.'

To all which great authorities, we can only oppose that of

MR. ADDISON.

'[r]The Art of Criticism (saith he) which was published some months since, is a master-piece in its kind. The observations follow one another, like those in Horace's Art of Poetry, without that methodical regularity which would have been requisite in a prose-writer. They are some of them *uncommon,* but such as the reader must assent to, when he sees them explain'd with that ease and perspicuity in which they are delivered. As for those which are the *most known* and the most *receiv'd,* they are placed in so beautiful a light, and illustrated with such apt allusions, that they have in

[o] Reflections critical and satyrical on a Rhapsody called An Essay on Criticism. Printed for Bernard Lintot, octavo.

[p] Essay on Criticism in prose, octavo, 1728. by the author of the Critical History of England.

[q] Preface to his Poems, p. 18, 53.

[r] Spectator, N° 253.

them all the graces of novelty; and make the reader, who was before acquainted with them, still more convinc'd of their truth and solidity. And here give me leave to mention what Monsieur Boileau has so well enlarged upon in the preface to his works: That wit and fine writing doth not consist so much in advancing things that are new, as in giving things that are known an agreeable turn. It is impossible for us who live in the latter ages of the world, to make observations in criticism, morality, or any art or science, which have not been touch'd upon by others; we have little else left us, but to represent the common sense of mankind in more strong, more beautiful, or more uncommon lights. If a reader examines Horace's Art of Poetry, he will find but few precepts in it, which he may not meet with in Aristotle, and which were not commonly known by all the poets of the Augustan age. His way of expressing, and applying them, not his invention of them is what we are chiefly to admire.

'Longinus, in his Reflexions, has given us the same kind of sublime, which he observes in the several passages that occasioned them: I cannot but take notice that our English author has after the same manner exemplify'd several of the precepts in the very precepts themselves.' He then produces some instances of a particular beauty in the numbers, and concludes with saying, that 'there are three poems in our tongue of the same nature, and each a masterpiece in its kind; The Essay on Translated Verse; the Essay on the Art of Poetry; and the Essay on Criticism.' [1]

Of WINDSOR FOREST, positive is the judgment of the affirmative

MR. JOHN DENNIS,

'[B]That it is a wretched rhapsody, impudently writ in emulation of the Cooper's Hill of Sir John Denham: The author of it is obscure, is ambiguous, is affected, is temerarious, is barbarous.'

But the author of the Dispensary

DR. GARTH,[2]

in the preface to his poem of Claremont, differs from this opinion: 'Those who have seen these two excellent poems of Cooper's Hill, and Windsor Forest, the one written by Sir John Denham, the other by Mr. Pope, will shew a great deal of candour if they approve of this.'

Of the Epistle of ELOISA, we are told by the obscure writer of a

---

[1] ⟨By the Earl of Roscommon; by John Sheffield, Duke of Buckingham.⟩

[B] Letter to B. B. ⟨i.e. Barton Booth?⟩ at the end of the Remarks on Pope's Homer, 1717.

[2] *Dr. Garth*] ⟨(1661–1719), physician and poet.⟩

poem called Sawney[t], 'That because Prior's Henry and Emma charm'd the finest tastes, our author writ his Eloise, *in opposition to it*; but forgot innocence and virtue: If you take away her tender thoughts, and her fierce desires, all the rest is of no value.' In which, methinks, his judgment resembleth that of a French taylor on a Villa and gardens by the Thames: All this is very fine, but take away the river, and it is good for nothing.'

But very contrary hereunto was the opinion of

MR. PRIOR

himself, saying in his *Alma*[v],

> O *Abelard!* ill fated youth,
> Thy tale will justify this truth.
> But well I weet thy cruel wrong
> Adorns a nobler Poet's song:
> Dan *Pope*, for thy misfortune griev'd,
> With kind concern and skill has weav'd
> A silken web; and ne'er shall fade
> Its colours: gently has he laid
> The mantle o'er thy sad distress,
> And Venus shall the texture bless, *&c.*

Come we now to his translation of the ILIAD, celebrated by numerous pens, yet shall it suffice to mention the indefatigable

SIR RICHARD BLACKMORE, KT.

Who (tho' otherwise a severe censurer of our author) yet styleth this a 'laudable translation[w].' That ready writer

MR. OLDMIXON,

in his forementioned Essay, frequently commends the same. And the painful

MR. LEWIS THEOBALD

thus extols it[x], 'The spirit of Homer breathes all through this translation.—I am in doubt, whether I should most admire the justness to the original, or the force and beauty of the language, or the sounding variety of the numbers: But when I find all these meet, it puts me in mind of what the poet says of one of his heroes,

---

[t] Printed 1728, p. 12.
[v] Alma, Cant. 2 ⟨287-96⟩.
[w] In his Essays, vol. i. printed for E. Curl.
[x] Censor, vol. ii. n. 33.

That he alone rais'd and flung with ease a weighty stone, that two common men could not lift from the ground; just so, one single person has performed in this translation, what I once despaired to have seen done by the force of several masterly hands.' Indeed the same gentleman appears to have chang'd his sentiment in his Essay on the Art of sinking in reputation, (printed in Mist's Journal, March 30, 1728.) where he says thus: 'In order to sink in reputation, let him take it into his head to descend into Homer (let the world wonder, as it will, how the devil he got there) and pretend to do him into English, so his version denote his neglect of the manner how.' Strange Variation! We are told in

MIST'S JOURNAL, JUNE 8.

'That this translation of the Iliad was not in all respects conformable to the fine taste of his friend Mr. Addison; insomuch that he employed a *younger muse*, in an undertaking of this kind, which he supervised himself.' Whether Mr. Addison did find it conformable to his taste, or not, best appears from his own testimony the year following its publication, in these words:

MR. ADDISON, FREEHOLDER, N° 40.

'When I consider myself as a British freeholder, I am in a particular manner pleased with the labours of those who have improved our language with the translations of old Greek and Latin authors.—We have already most of their Historians in our own tongue, and what is more for the honour of our language, it has been taught to express with elegance the greatest of their Poets in each nation. The illiterate among our own countrymen may learn to judge from Dryden's Virgil of the most perfect Epic performance. And those parts of Homer which have been published already by Mr. Pope, give us reason to think that the Iliad will appear in English with as little disadvantage to that immortal poem.'

As to the rest, there is a slight mistake, for this *younger muse* was an *elder:* Nor was the gentleman (who is a friend of our author) employ'd by Mr. Addison to translate it *after him*, since he saith himself that he did it *before*ʸ. Contrariwise that Mr. Addison engaged our author in this work appeareth by declaration thereof in the preface to the Iliad, printed some time before his death, and by his own letters of October 26, and November 2, 1713. where he declares it is his opinion, that no other person was equal to it.

Next comes his Shakespear on the stage: 'Let him (quoth one, whom I take to be

ʸ Vid. pref. to Mr. Tickel's translation of the first book of the Iliad, 4to.

MR. THEOBALD, MIST'S JOURNAL,
JUNE, 8, 1728.)

'publish such an author as he has least studied, and forget to discharge even the dull duty of an editor. In this project let him lend
the bookseller his name (for a competent sum of money) to promote
the credit of an exorbitant subscription.' Gentle reader, be pleased
to cast thine eye on the *Proposal* below quoted, and on what follows
(some months after the former assertion) in the same Journalist of
June 8. 'The bookseller proposed the book by subscription, and
raised some thousands of pounds for the same: I believe the gentleman did *not* share in the profits of this extravagant subscription.'

'After the Iliad, he undertook (saith

MIST'S JOURNAL, JUNE 8, 1728.)

the sequel of that work, the Odyssey; and having secured the
success by a numerous subscription, he employed some *underlings*
to perform what, according to his proposals, should come from his
own hands.' To which heavy charge we can in truth oppose nothing
but the words of

MR. POPE'S PROPOSAL FOR THE ODYSSEY,
(printed by J. Watts, Jan. 10, 1724.)

'I take this occasion to declare that the subscription for Shakespear
belongs wholly to Mr. Tonson: And that the benefit of *this Proposal*
is not solely for my own use, but for that of *two of my friends*, who
have *assisted me in this work*.' But these very gentlemen are extolled
above our poet himself in another of Mist's Journals, March 30,
1728. saying, 'That he would not advise Mr. Pope to try the
experiment again of getting a great part of a book done by assistants,
lest those extraneous parts should unhappily ascend to the sublime,
and retard the declension of the whole.' Behold! these *Underlings*
are become good writers!

If any say, that before the said Proposals were printed, the subscription was begun without declaration of such assistance; verily
those who set it on foot, or (as their term is) secured it, to wit, the
right honourable the Lord Viscount HARCOURT, were he living,
would testify, and the right honourable the Lord BATHURST, now
living, doth testify the same is a falshood.

Sorry I am, that persons professing to be learned, or of whatever
rank of authors, should either falsely tax, or be falsely taxed. Yet
let us, who are only reporters, be impartial in our citations, and
proceed.

MIST'S JOURNAL, JUNE 8, 1728.

'Mr. Addison raised this author from obscurity, obtained him the
acquaintance and friendship of the *whole body of our nobility*, and
transferred his powerful interests with those great men to this rising
bard, who frequently levied by that means unusual contributions
on the public.' Which surely cannot be, if, as the author of The
Dunciad dissected reporteth; 'Mr. Wycherley had before introduced him into a familiar acquaintance with the *greatest Peers* and
brightest Wits then living.'

'No sooner (saith the same Journalist) was his body lifeless, but
this author, reviving his resentment, libelled the memory of his
departed friend; and, what was still more heinous, made the
scandal public.' Grievous the accusation! unknown the accuser! the
person accused no witness in his own cause; the person, in whose
regard accused, dead! But if there be living any one nobleman
whose friendship, yea any one gentleman whose subscription Mr.
Addison procured to our author; let him stand forth, that truth may
appear! *Amicus Plato, amicus Socrates, sed magis amica veritas.* In
verity, the whole story of the libel is a lye; witness those persons of
integrity, who several years before Mr. Addison's decease, did see
and approve of the said verses, in no wise a libel, but a friendly
rebuke sent privately in our author's own hand to Mr. Addison
himself, and never made public, 'till after their own Journals, and
Curl had printed the same. One name alone, which I am here
authorised to declare, will sufficiently evince this truth, that of the
right honourable the Earl of BURLINGTON.

Next is he taxed with a crime (in the opinion of some authors,
I doubt, more heinous than any in morality) to wit, Plagiarism,
from the inventive and quaint-conceited

JAMES MOORE SMITH GENT.

'[1]Upon reading the third volume of Pope's Miscellanies, I found
five lines which I thought excellent; and happening to praise them,
a gentleman produced a modern comedy (the Rival Modes)
published last year, where were the same verses to a tittle.[1]

'These gentlemen are undoubtedly the first plagiaries, that pretend to make a reputation by stealing from a man's works in his own
life-time, and out of a Public print.' Let us join to this what is
written by the author of the Rival Modes, the said Mr. James
Moore Smith, in a letter to our author himself, who had informed

[1] Daily Journal, March 18, 1728.
[1] *tittle* ⟨They appeared in *Moral Es.* ii 243-8 (p. 568). For James Moore
Smythe see A ii 46.⟩

him, a month before that play was acted, Jan. 27, 172$\frac{6}{7}$, that 'These verses, which he had before given him leave to insert in it, would be known for his, some copies being got abroad. He desires, nevertheless, that, since the lines had been read in his comedy to several, Mr. P. would not deprive it of them,' &c. Surely if we add the testimonies of the Lord BOLINGBROKE, of the Lady[1] to whom the said verses were originally addressed, of Hugh Bethel Esq. and others, who knew them as our author's, long before the said gentleman composed his play; it is hoped, the ingenuous that affect not error, will rectify their opinion by the suffrage of so honourable personages.

And yet followeth another charge, insinuating no less than his enmity both to Church and State, which could come from no other informer than the said

MR. JAMES MOORE SMITH.

'[a]The Memoirs of a Parish clerk was a very dull and unjust abuse of a person[2] who wrote in defence of our Religion and Constitution, and who has been dead many years.' This seemeth also most untrue; it being known to divers that these memoirs were written at the seat of the Lord Harcourt in Oxfordshire, before that excellent person (bishop Burnet's) death, and many years before the appearance of that history, of which they are pretended to be an abuse. Most true it is, that Mr. Moore had such a design, and was himself the man who prest Dr. Arbuthnot and Mr. Pope to assist him therein; and that he borrowed those Memoirs of our author, when that History came forth, with intent to turn them to such abuse. But being able to obtain from our author but one single hint, and either changing his mind, or having more mind than ability, he contented himself to keep the said Memoirs, and read them as his own to all his acquaintance. A noble person there is, into whose company Mr. Pope once chanced to introduce him, who well remembereth the conversation of Mr. Moore to have turned upon the 'Contempt he had for the work of that reverend prelate, and how full he was of a design he declared himself to have of exposing it.' This noble person is the Earl of PETERBOROUGH.

Here in truth should we crave pardon of all the foresaid right honourable and worthy personages, for having mentioned them in the same page with such weekly riff-raff railers and rhymers; but that we had their ever-honoured commands for the same; and that they are introduced not as witnesses in the controversy, but as

---

[1] *Lady* ⟨Martha Blount.⟩
[a] Daily Journal, April 3, 1728.
[2] *person* ⟨Bishop Burnet, who died in 1715.⟩

witnesses that cannot be controverted; not to dispute, but to decide.

Certain it is, that dividing our writers into two classes, of such who were acquaintance, and of such who were strangers, to our author; the former are those who speak well, and the other those who speak evil of him. Of the first class, the most noble

JOHN DUKE OF BUCKINGHAM

sums up his character in these lines:

> '[b]And yet so wond'rous, so sublime a thing,
> As the great Iliad, scarce could make me sing,
> Unless I justly could at once commend
> A *good companion*, and as *firm a friend*;
> One *moral*, or a mere *well-natur'd deed*,
> Can all desert in sciences exceed.'

So also is he decyphered by the honourable

SIMON HARCOURT.

> '[c]Say, wond'rous youth, what column wilt thou chuse,
> What laurel'd arch, for thy triumphant Muse?
> Tho' each great ancient court thee to his shrine,
> Tho' ev'ry laurel thro' the dome be thine,
> Go to the *good* and *just*, an awful train!
> *Thy soul's delight.*——'

Recorded in like manner for his virtuous disposition, and gentle bearing, by the ingenious

MR. WALTER HART,

in this apostrophe:

> '[d]O! ever worthy, ever crown'd with praise!
> Blest in thy *life* and blest in all thy *lays*.
> Add, that the Sisters ev'ry thought refine,
> And ev'n thy *life*, be *faultless* as thy line.
> Yet envy still with fiercer rage pursues,
> Obscures the *virtue*, and defames the Muse.
> A soul like thine, in pain, in grief, resign'd,
> Views with just scorn the malice of mankind.'

The witty and moral satyrist

---

[b] Verses to Mr. P. on his translation of Homer.
[c] Poem prefix'd to his works.
[d] In his Poems, printed for B. Lintot.

DR. EDWARD YOUNG,

wishing some check to the corruption and evil manners of the times, calleth out upon our poet to undertake a task so worthy of his virtue:

> '[e]Why slumbers Pope, who leads the Muse's train,
> Nor hears that *Virtue*, which he *loves*, complain?

MR. MALLET,

In his epistle on Verbal Criticism:

> 'Whose life, severely scan'd, transcends his lays;
> For wit supreme is but his second praise.'

MR. HAMMOND,

That delicate and correct imitator of Tibullus, in his Love Elegies, Elegy xiv.

> 'Now, fir'd by Pope and *Virtue*, leave the age,
>   In low pursuit of self-undoing wrong,
> And trace the author thro' his moral page,
>   Whose blameless life still answers to his song.'

MR. THOMSON,

In his elegant and philosophical poem of the Seasons:

> 'Altho' not sweeter his own Homer sings,
> Yet is his *life* the more endearing song.'[1]

To the same tune also singeth that learned clerk of Suffolk

MR. WILLIAM BROOME.

> '[f]Thus, nobly rising in fair *Virtue*'s cause,
> From thy own *life* transcribe th' *unerring laws*.'

And, to close all, hear the reverend Dean of St. Patrick's:

> 'A Soul with ev'ry virtue fraught,
> By Patriots, Priests, and Poets taught.

---

[e] Universal Passion, Satyr i ⟨35–6⟩.

[1] *endearing song* ⟨*Winter*, ll. 554–5.⟩

[f] In his Poems, and at the end of the Odyssey. ⟨'To Mr. Pope, On his Works,' 1726. The 'learned clerk' was Rector of Oakley Magna, and Vicar of Eye, Suffolk.⟩

Whose filial Piety excells
Whatever Grecian story tells.
A genius for each bus'ness fit,
Whose meanest talent is his Wit,'[1] &c.

Let us now recreate thee by turning to the other side, and shewing his Character drawn by those with whom he never conversed,
and whose countenances he could not know, though turned
against him: First again commencing with the high voiced and never
enough quoted

MR. JOHN DENNIS;

Who, in his Reflections on the Essay on Criticism, thus describeth
him: 'A little affected hypocrite, who has nothing in his mouth but
candour, truth, friendship, good-nature, humanity, and magnanimity. He is so great a lover of falshood, that, whenever he has a
mind to calumniate his cotemporaries, he brands them with some
defect which is just *contrary to some good quality*, for which all their
friends and their acquaintance commend them. He seems to have a
particular pique to *People of Quality*, and authors of that rank.—
He must derive his religion from St. Omer's.'—But in the Character
of Mr. P. and his writings (printed by S. Popping, 1716.) he saith,
'Though he is a professor of the worst religion, yet he *laughs at it*;
but that nevertheless, he is a *virulent Papist*; and yet a *Pillar* for the
Church of England.'
Of both which opinions

MR. LEWIS THEOBALD

seems also to be; declaring, in Mist's Journal of June 22, 1728.
'That, if he is not shrewdly abused, he made it his practice to cackle
to both *parties* in their own sentiments.' But, as to his *pique* against
People of quality, the same Journalist doth not agree, but saith
(May 8, 1728.) 'He had, by some means or other, the *acquaintance*
and *friendship* of the *whole body of our nobility.*'
    However contradictory this may appear, Mr. Dennis and Gildon,
in the character last cited, make it all plain, by assuring us, 'That he
is a creature that reconciles all contradictions; he is a beast, and a
man; a Whig, and a Tory; a writer (at one and the same time) of[g]
Guardians and Examiners; an Assertor of liberty, and of the dis-
pensing power of kings; a Jesuitical professor of truth; a base and
a foul pretender to candour.' So that, upon the whole account, we
must conclude him either to have been a great hypocrite, or a very

[1] *Wit*,' &c. ⟨'A Libel on *D— D—*. And a Certain Great Lord' (1730),
75 ff.⟩
[g] The Names of two weekly Papers.

honest man; a terrible imposer upon both parties, or very moderate to either.

Be it as to the judicious reader shall seem good. Sure it is, he is little favoured of certain authors, whose wrath is perilous: For one declares he ought to have a *price set on his head*, and to be hunted down as a *wild beast*[h]. Another protests that he does not know *what may happen*; advises him to *insure his person*; says he has *bitter enemies*, and expresly declares it will be well if he *escapes with his life*[i]. One desires he would *cut his own throat, or hang himself*[k]. But Pasquin seemed rather inclined it should be done by the Government, representing him engaged in grievous designs with a Lord of Parliament, then under prosecution[l]. Mr. Dennis himself hath written to a *Minister*, that he is one of the most *dangerous persons in this kingdom*[m]; and assureth the public, that he is an *open* and *mortal enemy* to his *country*; a monster, that *will*, one day, shew as *daring a soul* as a *mad Indian*, who runs a *muck* to kill the first Christian he meets[n]. Another gives information of *Treason* discovered in his poem[o]. Mr. Curl boldly supplies an imperfect verse with *Kings* and *Princesses*[p]. And one Matthew Concanen, yet more impudent, publishes at length the Two most SACRED NAMES in this Nation, as members of the Dunciad[q]!

This is prodigious! yet it is almost as strange, that in the midst of these invectives his greatest Enemies have (I know not how) born testimony to some merit in him.

MR. THEOBALD,

in censuring his Shakespear, declares, 'He has so great an *esteem* for Mr. Pope, and so high an *opinion* of his *genius* and *excellencies*; that, notwithstanding he professes a *veneration almost rising to Idolatry* for the writings of this inimitable poet, he would be very loth even to do *him* justice, at the expence of that *other gentleman*'s character[r].'

[h] Theobald, Letter in Mist's Journal, June 22, 1728.

[i] Smedley, Pref. to Gulliveriana, p. 14, 16.

[k] Gulliveriana, p. 332.

[l] Anno 1723.

[m] Anno 1729.

[n] Preface to Rem. on the Rape of the Lock, p. 12. and in the last page of that treatise.

[o] Page 6, 7. of the Preface, by Concanen, to a book intitled A Collection of all the Letters, Essays, Verses, and Advertisements, occasioned by Pope and Swift's Miscellanies. Printed for A. Moore, octavo, 1728.

[p] Key to the Dunciad, 3d edit. p. 18.

[q] A List of Persons, &c. at the end of the forementioned Collection of all the Letters, Essays, &c.

[r] Introduction to his Shakespear restored, in quarto, p. 3.

MR. CHARLES GILDON,

after having violently attacked him in many pieces, at last came to wish from his heart, 'That Mr. Pope would be prevailed upon to give us Ovid's Epistles by his hand, for it is certain we see the original of Sappho to Phaon with much more life and likeness in his version, than in that of Sir Car. Scrope. And this (he adds) is the more to be wished, because in the English tongue we have scarce any thing truly and naturally written upon Love^s.' He also, in taxing Sir Richard Blackmore for his heterodox opinions of Homer, challengeth him to answer what Mr. Pope hath said in his preface to that poet.

MR. OLDMIXON

calls him a great master of our tongue; declares 'the purity and perfection of the English language to be found in his Homer; and, saying there are more good verses in Dryden's Virgil than in any other work, excepts this of our author only^t.'

The Author of a Letter to MR. CIBBER

says, '^vPope *was* so good a versifier [*once*] that his predecessor Mr. Dryden, and his cotemporary Mr. Prior excepted, the harmony of his numbers *is* equal to any body's. And, that he *had* all the merit that a man can have that way.' And

MR. THOMAS COOKE,

after much blemishing our author's Homer, crieth out,

> 'But in his other works what beauties shine!
> While sweetest Music dwells in ev'ry line.
> These he admir'd, on these he stamp'd his praise,
> And bade them live to brighten future days^w.'

So also one who takes the name of

H. STANHOPE,

the maker of certain verses to Duncan Campbell,^x in that poem, which is wholly a satyr on Mr. Pope, confesseth,

> ' 'Tis true, if finest notes alone could show
> (Tun'd justly high, or regularly low)

---

^s Commentary on the Duke of Buckingham's Essay, octavo, 1721, p. 97, 98.

^t In his prose Essay on Criticism.

^v Printed by J. Roberts, 1742. p. 11. ⟨*A Letter to Mr. C—b—r, On his Letter to Mr. P—*. The author was Lord Hervey.⟩

^w Battle of Poets, folio, p. 15.

^x Printed under the title of the Progress of Dulness, duodecimo, 1728.

That we should fame to these mere vocals give;
Pope more than we can offer should receive:
For when some gliding river is his theme,
His lines run smoother than the smoothest stream,' *&c.*

MIST'S JOURNAL, JUNE 8, 1728.

Although he says, 'The smooth numbers of the Dunciad are all that recommend it, nor has it any other merit;' yet that same paper hath these words: 'The author is allowed to be a perfect master of an easy and elegant versification. *In all his works* we find the most *happy turns*, and *natural similes*, wonderfully short and thick sown.'

The Essay on the Dunciad also owns, p. 25. it is very full of *beautiful images*. But the panegyric, which crowns all that can be said on this Poem, is bestowed by our Laureate,

MR. COLLEY CIBBER,

who 'grants it to be a better Poem of its kind than ever was writ;' but adds, 'it was a victory over a parcel of poor wretches, whom it was almost cowardice to conquer.—A man might as well triumph for having killed so many silly flies that offended him. Could he have let them alone, by this time, poor souls! they had all been buried in oblivion[y].' Here we see our excellent Laureate allows the justice of the satyr on every man in it, but *himself*; as the great Mr. Dennis did before him.

The said

MR. DENNIS AND MR. GILDON,

in the most furious of all their works (the forecited Character, p. 5.) do in concert[z] confess, 'That some men of *good understanding* value

[y] Cibber's Letter to Mr. Pope, p. 9, 12.

[z] *In concert*] Hear how Mr. Dennis hath proved our mistake in this place; As to my writing in *concert* with Mr. Gildon, I declare upon the honour and word of a gentleman, that I never wrote so much as one line in *concert* with any one man whatsoever. And these two Letters from Mr. Gildon will plainly shew that we are not writers in *concert* with each other.

Sir,
—*The height of my Ambition is to please Men of the best Judgment; and finding that I have entertained my Master agreeably, I have the extent of the Reward of my Labour.*

Sir,
I had not the opportunity of hearing of your excellent Pamphlet 'till this day. I am infinitely satisfied and pleased with it, and hope you will meet with that encouragement your admirable performance deserves, &c.

CH. GILDON.

'Now is it not plain, that any one who sends such compliments to him for his rhymes.' And (p. 17.) 'That he has got, like Mr. Bays in the Rehearsal, (that is, like Mr. Dryden) a notable knack at rhyming, and writing smooth verse.'

Of his Essay on Man, numerous were the praises bestowed by his avowed enemies, in the imagination that the same was not written by him, as it was printed anonymously.

Thus sang of it even

BEZALEEL MORRIS.

'Auspicious bard! while all admire thy strain,
All but the selfish, ignorant, and vain;
I, whom no bribe to servile flatt'ry drew,
Must pay the tribute to thy merit due:
Thy Muse, sublime, significant, and clear,
Alike informs the Soul, and charms the Ear,' &c.

And

MR. LEONARD WELSTED

thus wrote[a] to the unknown author, on the first publication of the said Essay: 'I must own, after the reception which the vilest and most immoral ribaldry hath lately met with, I was surprised to see what I had long despaired, a performance deserving the name of a poet. Such, Sir, is your work. It is, indeed, above all commendation, and ought to have been published in an age and country more worthy of it: If my testimony be of weight any where, you are sure to have it in the amplest manner,' &c. &c. &c.

Thus we see every one of his works hath been extolled by one or other of his most inveterate Enemies; and to the success of them all they do unanimously give testimony. But it is sufficient, *instar omnium*, to behold the great critic, Mr. Dennis, sorely lamenting it, even from the Essay on Criticism to this day of the Dunciad! 'A most notorious instance (quoth he) of the depravity of genius and taste, the *approbation* this Essay meets with[b]—I can safely affirm, that I never attacked any of these writings, unless they had *success* infinitely beyond their merit.—This, though an empty, has been a *popular* scribler. The epidemic madness of the times has given him *reputation*[c].—If, after the cruel treatment so many extraordinary men (Spencer, Lord Bacon, Ben. Johnson, Milton, Butler, Otway,

---

another, has not been used to write in partnership with him to whom he sends them?' Dennis, Rem. on the Dunc. p. 50. Mr. Dennis is therefore welcome to take this piece to himself.

[a] In a Letter under his hand, dated March 12, 1733.
[b] Dennis, Pref. to his Reflect. on the Essay on Criticism.
[c] Pref. to his Rem. on Homer.

and others) have received from this country, for these last hundred years, I should shift the scene, and shew all that penury changed at once to riot and profuseness; and more squandered away upon *one object*, than would have satisfied the greater part of those extraordinary men;[1] the reader to whom this one creature should be unknown, would fancy him a prodigy of art and nature, would believe that all the great qualities of these persons were centered in him alone.—But if I should venture to assure him, that the PEOPLE of ENGLAND had made such a choice—the reader would either believe me a *malicious enemy*, and *slanderer*; or that the reign of the last (Queen Anne's) *Ministry* was designed by fate to encourage *Fools*[d].'

But it happens, that this our Poet never had any Place, Pension, or Gratuity, in any shape, from the said glorious Queen, or any of her Ministers. All, he owed, in the whole course of his life, to any court, was a subscription, for his Homer, of 200 *l*, from King George I, and 100 *l*. from the prince and princess.

However, lest we imagine our Author's Success was constant and universal, they acquaint us of certain works in a less degree of repute, whereof, although owned by others, yet do they assure us he is the writer. Of this sort Mr. DENNIS[e] ascribes to him *two Farces*, whose names he does not tell, but assures us that *there is not one jest in them:* And an imitation of Horace, whose title he does not mention, but assures us *it is much more execrable than all his works*[f]. The DAILY JOURNAL, May 11, 1728. assures us, 'He is below Tom. Durfey in the Drama, because (as that writer thinks) the Marriage Hater matched, and the Boarding School are better than the What-d'-ye-call-it;' which is not Mr. P.'s, but Mr. Gay's. Mr. GILDON assures us, in his New Rehearsal, p. 48. 'That he was writing a *play* of the Lady Jane Grey;' but it afterwards proved to be Mr. Row's. We are assured by another, 'He wrote a pamphlet called Dr. Andrew Tripe[g];' which proved to be one Dr. Wagstaff's. Mr. THEOBALD assures us, in Mist of the 27th of April, 'That the

---

[1] What this vast sum was Mr. DENNIS himself in another place informs us (pref. to his Remarks on the Rape of the Lock, p. 15) to wit, *a hundred a year*. Whereby we see how great he supposed the moderation of those extraordinary men; even greater than that of his friend Mr. *Giles Jacob*, who said of himself

> *One hundred pounds a year, I think wou'd do*
> *For me, if single—Or if marry'd, two.*

[d] Rem. on Homer, p. 8, 9.
[e] Ibid. p. 8. ⟨The two farces are *The What D'ye Call It*, 1715, and *Three Hours after Marriage*, 1717.⟩
[f] Character of Mr. Pope, p. 7.
[g] Character of Mr. Pope, p. 6.

treatise of the *Profound* is very dull, and that Mr. Pope is the author of it.' The writer of Gulliveriana is of another opinion; and says, 'the whole, or greatest part, of the merit of this treatise must and can only be ascribed to Gulliver[h].' [Here, gentle reader! cannot I but smile at the strange blindness and positiveness of men; knowing the said treatise to appertain to none other but to me, Martinus Scriblerus.]

We are assured, in Mist of June 8, 'That his own *Plays* and *Farces* would better have adorned the Dunciad, than those of Mr. Theobald; for he had neither genius for Tragedy nor Comedy.' Which whether true or not, is not easy to judge; in as much as he hath attempted neither. Unless we will take it for granted, with Mr. Cibber, that his being once very angry at hearing a friend's Play abused, was an infallible proof the Play was his own; the said Mr. Cibber thinking it impossible for a man to be much concerned for any but himself: 'Now let any man judge (saith he) by this concern, who was the true mother of the child[1]?'

But from all that hath been said, the discerning reader will collect, that it little availed our author to have any Candour, since when he declared he did not write for others, it was not credited; as little to have any Modesty, since, when he declined writing in any way himself, the presumption of others was imputed to him. If he singly enterprised one great work, he was taxed of Boldness and Madness to a prodigy[k]: If he took assistants in another, it was complained of, and represented as a great injury to the public[l]. The loftiest heroics, the lowest ballads, treatises against the state or church, satyrs on lords and ladies, raillery on wits and authors, squabbles with book-sellers, or even full and true accounts of monsters, poisons, and murders; of any hereof was there nothing so good, nothing so bad, which hath not at one or other season been to him ascribed. If it bore no author's name, then lay he concealed; if it did, he fathered it upon that author to be yet better concealed: If it resembled any of his styles, then was it evident; if it did not, then disguised he it on set purpose. Yea, even direct oppositions in religion, principles, and politics, have equally been supposed in him inherent. Surely a most rare and singular character! Of which let the reader make what he can.

Doubtless most Commentators would hence take occasion to turn all to their Author's advantage, and from the testimony of his very Enemies would affirm, That his Capacity was boundless, as

[h] Gulliv. p. 336.
[1] Cibber's Letter to Mr. P. p. 19.
[k] Burnet's Homerides, p. 1. of his translation of the Iliad.
[l] The London and Mist's Journals, on his undertaking of the Odyssey.

well as his Imagination; that he was a perfect master of all Styles, and all Arguments; and that there was in those times no other Writer, in any kind, of any degree of excellence, save he himself. But as this is not our own sentiment, we shall determine on nothing; but leave thee, gentle reader, to steer thy judgment equally between various opinions, and to chuse whether thou wilt incline to the Testimonies of Authors avowed, or of Authors concealed; of those who knew him, or of those who knew him not.

Martinus Scriblerus, of the Poem

This Poem, as it celebrateth the most grave and antient of things, Chaos, Night and Dulness, so is it of the most grave and antient kind. *Homer*, (saith *Aristotle*) was the first who gave the *Form*, and (saith *Horace*) who adapted the *Measure*, to heroic poesy. But even before this, may be rationally presumed from what the antients have left written, was a piece by *Homer* composed, of like nature and matter with this of our Poet. For of Epic sort it appeareth to have been, yet of matter surely not unpleasant, witness what is reported of it by the learned Archbishop *Eustathius*, in Odyss. κ. And accordingly *Aristotle* in his poetic, chap. 4. doth further set forth, that as the Iliad and Odyssey gave example to Tragedy, so did this poem to Comedy its first Idæa.

From these authors also it shou'd seem, that the Hero or chief personage of it was no less *obscure*, and his *understanding* and *sentiments* no less quaint and strange (if indeed not more so) than any of the actors in our poem. MARGITES was the name of this personage, whom Antiquity recordeth to have been *Dunce the First*; and surely from what we hear of him, not unworthy to be the root of so spreading a tree, and so numerous a posterity. The poem therefore celebrating him, was properly and absolutely a *Dunciad*; which tho' now unhappily lost, yet is its nature sufficiently known by the infallible tokens aforesaid. And thus it doth appear, that the first Dunciad was the first Epic poem, written by *Homer* himself, and anterior even to the Iliad or Odyssey.

Now forasmuch as our Poet had translated those two famous works of *Homer* which are yet left; he did conceive it in some sort of his duty to imitate that also which was lost: And was therefore induced to bestow on it the same Form which *Homer*'s is reported to have had, namely that of Epic poem, with a title also framed after the antient *Greek* manner, to wit, that of *Dunciad*.

Wonderful it is, that so few of the moderns have been stimulated to attempt some Dunciad! Since in the opinion of the multitude, it might cost less pain and oil, than an imitation of the greater Epic. But possible it is also that on due reflection, the maker might find it easier to paint a *Charlemagne*, a *Brute* or a *Godfry*, with just pomp and dignity heroic, than a *Margites*, a *Codrus*, a *Flecknoe*, or a *Tibbald*.

We shall next declare the occasion and the cause which moved our Poet to this particular work. He lived in those days, when (after providence had permitted the Invention of Printing as a scourge for the Sins of the learned) Paper also became so cheap, and printers so numerous, that a deluge of authors cover'd the land: Whereby not only the peace of the honest unwriting subject was daily molested, but unmerciful demands were made of his applause, yea of his money, by such as would neither earn the one, or deserve the other: At the same time, the Liberty of the Press was so unlimited, that it grew dangerous to refuse them either: For they would forthwith publish slanders unpunish'd, the authors being anonymous; nay the immediate publishers thereof lay sculking under the wings of an Act of Parliament,[1] assuredly intended for better purposes.

[a]Now our author living in those times, did conceive it an endeavour well worthy an honest satyrist, to dissuade the dull and punish the malicious, *the only way that was left*. In that public-spirited view he laid the plan of this Poem, as the greatest service he was capable (without much hurt or being slain) to render his dear country. First, taking things from their original, he considereth the Causes creative of such authors, namely *Dulness* and *Poverty*; the one born with them, the other contracted, by neglect of their proper talent thro' self conceit of greater abilities. This truth he wrapp'd in an *Allegory*[b] (as the constitution of Epic poesy requires) and feigns, that one of these Goddesses had taken up her abode with the other, and that they jointly inspir'd all such writers and such works.[c] He proceedeth to shew the *qualities* they bestow on these authors, and the *effects* they produce: [d]Then the *materials* or *stock*

---

[1] *an Act of Parliament* ⟨By 'An act for laying several duties upon all sope and paper . . .', 10 Anne, C. 19, cxiii, it was laid down, 'That during the [same] term of two and thirty years, no person whatsoever shall sell, or expose to sale, any [such] pamphlet, without the true respective name or names, and place or places of abode, of some known person or persons, by or for whom the same was really printed or published, written or printed thereupon . . .' The law was frequently ignored, either by the device of printing the name of a fictitious publisher on the title-page, or by printing the name of a genuine publisher (e.g. Anne Dodd) without obtaining his or her consent.⟩

[a] Vid. *Bossu, du poeme Epique*, ch. 8.   [b] *Ibid.* ch. 7.
[c] *Book* 1. *Verse* 32, &c.
[d] *Verse* 45 to 52.

with which they furnish them,[e] and (above all) that *self-opinion*[f] which causeth it to seem to themselves vastly greater than it is, and is the prime motive of their setting up in this sad and sorry merchandize. The great power of these Goddesses acting in alliance (whereof as the one is the mother of industry, so is the other of plodding) was to be exemplify'd in some *one, great* and *remarkable action*.[g] And none cou'd be more so than that which our poet hath chosen, the introduction of the lowest diversions of the rabble in *Smithfield* to be the entertainment of the court and town; or in other words, the Action of the Dunciad is the[h] Removal of the Imperial seat of Dulness from the City to the polite world; as that of the Æneid is the Removal of the empire of *Troy* to *Latium*. But as *Homer*, singing only the *Wrath* of *Achilles*, yet includes in his poem the whole history of the *Trojan* war, in like manner our author hath drawn into this single action the whole history of Dulness and her children. To this end she is represented at the very[i] opening of the poem, taking a view of her forces, which are distinguish'd into these three kinds, Party writers, dull poets, and wild criticks.

A *Person* must be fix'd upon to support this action, who (to agree with the said design) must be such an one as is capable of being all three. This *phantom* in the poet's mind, must have a *name*.[k] He seeks for one who hath been concerned in the *Journals*, written bad *Plays* or *Poems*, and published low *Criticisms:* He finds his name to be *Tibbald*, and he becomes of course the Hero of the poem.

The *Fable* being thus according to best example one and entire, as contain'd in the proposition; the *Machinary* is a continued chain of Allegories, setting forth the whole power, ministry, and empire of Dulness, extended thro' her subordinate instruments, in all her various operations.

This is branched into *Episodes*, each of which hath its Moral apart, tho' all conducive to the main end. The crowd assembled in the second book demonstrates the design to be more extensive than to bad poets only, and that we may expect other Episodes, of the Patrons, Encouragers, or Paymasters of such authors, as occasion shall bring them forth. And the third book, if well consider'd, seemeth to embrace the whole world. Each of the Games relateth to some or other vile class of writers. The first concerneth the Plagiary, to whom he giveth the name of *More*; the second the libellous Novellist, whom he styleth *Eliza*; the third the flattering Dedicator; the fourth the bawling Critick or noisy Poet; the fifth the dark

[e] *Verse* 57 to 75.   [f] *Verse* 80.
[g] *Bossu,* ch. 7, 8.   [h] *Verse* 1, 2.
[i] *Verse* 95 to 104.
[k] *Bossu,* ch. 8. Vide *Aristot. Poetic.* c.9.

and dirty Party-writer; and so of the rest, assigning to each some *proper name* or other, such as he cou'd find.

As for the *Characters*, the publick hath already acknowledged how justly they are drawn: The manners are so depicted, and the sentiments so peculiar to those to whom applied, that surely to transfer them to any other, or wiser, personages, wou'd be exceeding difficult. And certain it is, that every person concerned, being consulted apart, will readily own the resemblance of every portrait, his own excepted.

The Descriptions are singular; the Comparisons very quaint; the Narration various, yet of one colour. The purity and chastity of Diction is so preserved, that in the places most suspicious not the *words* but only the *images* have been censured, and yet are those images no other than have been sanctified by antient and classical authority (tho' as was the manner of those good times, not so curiously wrapped up) yea and commented upon by most grave doctors, and approved criticks.

As it beareth the name of Epic, it is thereby subjected to such severe indispensable rules as are laid on all Neotericks,[1] a strict imitation of the antient; insomuch that any deviation accompanied with whatever poetic beauties, hath always been censured by the sound critick. How exact that Imitation hath been in this piece, appeareth not only by its general structure, but by particular allusions infinite, many whereof have escaped both the commentator and poet himself; yea divers by his exceeding diligence are so alter'd and interwoven with the rest, that several have already been, and more will be, by the ignorant abused, as altogether and originally his own.

In a word, the whole poem proveth itself to be the work of our Author when his faculties were in full vigour and perfection: at that exact time of life when years have ripened the judgment, without diminishing the imagination; which by good criticks is held to be punctually at *forty*.[2] For, at that season it was that *Virgil* finished his *Georgics*; and Sir *Richard Blackmore* at the like age composing his *Arthurs*, declared the same to be the very *Acme* and pitch of life for Epic poesy: tho' since he hath altered it to *sixty*,* the year in which he published his *Alfred*. True it is, that the talents for Criticism, namely smartness, quick censure, vivacity of remark, certainty of asseveration, indeed all but acerbity, seem rather the gifts of Youth than of riper age: But it is far otherwise in *Poetry*;

[1] *Neotericks* ⟨i.e. Moderns.⟩

[2] *forty* ⟨Pope was born on May 21, 1688: the *Dunciad* was published on May 18, 1728.⟩

* See his Essay on Heroic poetry.

witness the works of Mr. *Rymer* and Mr. *Dennis,* who beginning with criticism, became afterwards such Poets as no age hath parallel'd. With good reason therefore did our author chuse to write his *Essay* on that subject at twenty, and reserve for his maturer years, this great and wonderful work of the *Dunciad.*

Dunciados Periocha: or, Arguments to the Books

BOOK THE FIRST

The Proposition of the subject. The Invocation, and the Inscription. Then the Original of the great empire of *Dulness,* and cause of the continuance thereof. The beloved seat of the Goddess is described, with her chief attendants and officers, her functions, operations, and effects. Then the poem hasts into the midst of things, presenting her on the evening of a Lord Mayor's day, revolving the long succession of her sons, and the glories past, and to come. She fixes her eye on *Tibbald* to be the instrument of that great event which is the subject of the poem. He is described pensive in his study, giving up the cause, and apprehending the period of her empire from the old age of the present monarch *Settle.* Wherefore debating whether to betake himself to law or politicks, he raises an altar of proper books, and (making first his solemn prayer and declaration) purposes thereon to sacrifice all his unsuccessful writings. As the pyle is kindled, the Goddess beholding the flame from her seat, flies in person and puts it out, by casting upon it the poem of *Thule.* She forthwith reveals her self to him, transports him to her Temple, unfolds all her arts, and initiates him into her mysteries; then announcing the death of *Settle* that night, anoints, and proclaims him Successor.

BOOK THE SECOND

The King being proclaimed, the solemnity is graced with publick Games and sports of various kinds; (not instituted by the Hero, as by *Æneas* in *Virgil,* but for greater honour by the Goddess in person; in like manner as the games *Pythia, Isthmia, &c.* were anciently said to be by the Gods, and as *Thetis* herself appearing according to *Homer* Odyss. 24. proposed the prizes in honour of her son *Achilles.* Hither flock the Poets and Criticks, attended (as is but just) with their Patrons and Book-sellers. The Goddess is first pleased for her disport to propose games to the latter, and setteth up the phantom of a poet which the booksellers contend to over-take. The races described, with their divers accidents: Next, the game for a Poetess: Afterwards the exercises for the *Poets*, of Tick-ling, Vociferating, Diving: the first holds forth the arts and prac-tices of Dedicators, the second of Disputants and fustian poets, the third of profund, dark, and dirty authors. Lastly, for the *Criticks*, the Goddess proposes (with great propriety) an exercise not of their parts but their patience; in hearing the works of two voluminous authors, one in verse and the other in prose, deliber-ately read, without sleeping: The various effects of which, with the several degrees and manners of their operation, are here most lively set forth: Till the whole number, not of criticks only, but of spec-tators, actors, and all present fall fast asleep, which naturally and necessarily ends the games.

BOOK THE THIRD

After the other persons are disposed in their proper places of rest, the Goddess transports the King to her Temple, and there lays him to slumber with his head on her lap; a position of marvellous vir-tue, which causes all the visions of wild enthusiasts, projectors, politicians, inamorato's, castle-builders, chymists and poets. He is immediately carry'd on the wings of fancy to the *Elizian* shade, where on the banks of *Lethe* the souls of the dull are dip'd by *Bavius*, before their entrance into this world. There he is met by the ghost of *Settle*, and by him made acquainted with the wonders of the place, and with those which he is himself destin'd to perform. He takes him to a *Mount of Vision*, from whence he shews him the past triumphs of the empire of Dulness, then the present, and lastly the future. How small a part of the world was ever conquered by *Science*, how soon those conquests were stop'd, and those very nations again reduced to her dominion. Then distinguishing the Island of *Great Britain*, shews by what aids, and by what persons, it shall be forthwith brought to her empire. These he causes to pass in review before his eyes, describing each by his proper figure, charac-ter, and qualifications. On a sudden the Scene shifts, and a vast number of miracles and prodigies appear, utterly surprizing and unknown to the King himself, till they are explained to be the won-ders of his own reign now commencing. On this subject *Settle* breaks into a congratulation, yet not unmix'd with concern, that his own times were but the types of these; He prophecies how first, the nation shall be overrun with farces, opera's, shows; and the throne of Dulness advanced over both the Theatres: Then how her sons shall preside in the seats of arts and sciences, till in conclusion all shall return to their original Chaos: A scene, of which the present Action of the Dunciad is but a Type or Foretaste, giving a Glimpse or *Pisgah-sight* of the promis'd Fulness of her Glory; the Accomplishment whereof will, in all probability, hereafter be the Theme of many other and greater Dunciads.

The Dunciad,* in Three Books
with
Notes Variorum

BOOK THE FIRST

Books and the Man I sing, the first who brings
The Smithfield Muses to the Ear of Kings.
Say great Patricians! (since your selves inspire
These wond'rous works; so Jove and Fate require)

* The *Dunicad, Sic* M.S. It may be well disputed whether this be a right Reading. Ought it not rather to be spelled *Dunceiad,* as the Etymology evidently demands? *Dunce* with an *e,* therefore *Dunceiad* with an *e.* That accurate and punctual Man of Letters, the Restorer of *Shakespeare,* constantly observes the preservation of this very Letter *e,* in spelling the Name of his beloved Author, and not like his common careless Editors, with the omission of one, nay sometimes of two *ee's* [as *Shak'spear*] which is utterly unpardonable. Nor is the neglect of a *Single Letter* so trivial as to some it may appear; the alteration whereof in a learned language is an *Atchivement that brings honour* to the Critick who advances it; and Dr. B⟨entley⟩ will be remembered to posterity for his performances of *this sort,* as long as the world shall have any Esteem for the Remains of *Menander* and *Philemon.* THEOBALD.

I have a just value for the Letter E, and the same affection for the Name of this Poem, as the forecited Critic for that of his Author; yet cannot it induce me to agree with those who would add yet another *e* to it, and call it the *Dunceiade*; which being a French and foreign Termination, is no way proper to a word entirely English, and Vernacular. One *E* therefore in this case is right, and two *E*'s wrong; yet upon the whole I shall follow the Manuscript, and print it without any *E* at all; mov'd thereto by Authority, at all times with Criticks equal if not superior to Reason. In which method of proceeding, I can never enough praise my very good friend, the exact Mr. *Tho. Hearne*; who, if any word occur which to him and all mankind is evidently wrong, yet keeps he it in the Text with due reverence, and only remarks in the Margin, *sic M.S.* In like manner we shall not amend this error in the Title itself, but only note it *obiter,* to evince to the learned that it was not our fault, nor any effect of our own Ignorance or Inattention. SCRIBLERUS.

1. *Books and the Man I sing, etc.*] Wonderful is the stupidity of all the former Criticks and Commentators on this Poem! It breaks forth at the very first line. The Author of the Critique prefix'd to *Sawney,* a Poem,

Say from what cause, in vain decry'd and curst,   5
Still Dunce the second reigns like Dunce the first?
  In eldest time, e'er mortals writ or read,
  E'er Pallas issued from the Thund'rer's head,
  Dulnes o'er all possess'd her antient right,

---

p. 5. hath been so dull as to explain *The Man who brings,* &c. not of the
Hero of the Piece, but of our Poet himself, as if he vaunted that *Kings*
were to be his Readers (an Honour which tho' this Poem hath had, yet
knoweth he how to receive it with more Modesty.) ⟨For James Ralph,
author of *Sawney* (1728), see A iii 159.⟩
  We remit this Ignorant to the first lines of the *Æneid*; assuring him, that
Virgil there speaketh not of himself, but of *Æneas.*

> *Arma virumq; cano, Trojæ qui primus ab oris,*
> *Italiam fato profugus, Lavinaq; venit*
> *Litora: multum ille & terris jactatus et alto &c.*

I cite the whole three verses that I may by the way offer a *Conjectural
Emendation,* purely my own, upon each: First, *oris* should be read *aris,* it
being as we see *Æn.* 2. 513, from the *altar* of *Jupiter Hercæus* that *Æneas*
fled as soon as he saw *Priam* slain. In the second line I would read *flatu*
for *fato,* since it is most clear it was by *Winds* that he arrived at the *Shore*
of *Italy*; *Jactatus* in the third, is surely as improper apply'd to *terris,* as
proper to *alto:* To say a man is *tost on land,* is much at one with saying
he *walks at sea. Risum teneatis amici?* Correct it, as I doubt not it ought
to be, *Vexatus.* SCRIBLERUS.
  This Poem was writ in 1727. In the next year an imperfect Edition was
published at Dublin, and re-printed at London in 12°. Another at Dublin,
and re-printed at London in 8°, and three others in 12° the same year.
But there was no perfect Edition before that of London in 4° 172⅚, which
was attended with the following Notes.   We are willing to
acquaint Posterity that this Poem (as it here stands) was presented to
King George the Second and his Queen, by the hands of Sir R. Walpole,
on the 12th of March 172⅚.
  2. *The* Smithfield-*Muses*] *Smithfield* is the place where Bartholomew
Fair was kept, whose Shews, Machines, and Dramatical Entertainments,
formerly agreeable only to the Taste of the Rabble, were, by the Hero of
this Poem and others of equal Genius, brought to the Theatres of Covent-
Garden, Lincolns-inn-Fields, and the Hay-Market, to be the reigning
Pleasures of the Court and Town. This happened in the Year 1725, and
continued to the Year 1728. See Book 3. Vers. 191, &c.
  3. *Say great* Patricians (*since your selves inspire*

> *These Wond'rous Works*]—Ovid. *Met.* 1⟨2⟩.
>   —*Dii cœptis (nam vos Mutastis & illas).*

6. Alluding to a verse of Mr. *Dryden*'s not in *Mac Flecno* (as it is said
ignorantly in the Key to the *Dunciad, pag.* 1.) but in his verses to Mr.
Congreve ⟨l. 48⟩.

>   *And* Tom *the Second reigns like* Tom *the First.*

⟨Pope is probably glancing at George II, who had succeeded his father
less than a year before the *Dunciad* was published.
  The 'great Patricians' of l. 3 are the Whig aristocracy, who were mainly
responsible for bringing the Hanoverians to England in 1714.⟩

Daughter of Chaos and eternal Night: 10
Fate in their dotage this fair idiot gave,
Gross as her sire, and as her mother grave,
Laborious, heavy, busy, bold, and blind,
She rul'd, in native Anarchy, the mind.
  Still her old empire to confirm, she tries,   15
For born a Goddess, Dulness never dies.
  O thou! whatever Title please thine ear,
Dean, Drapier, Bickerstaff, or Gulliver!
Whether thou chuse Cervantes' serious air,
Or laugh and shake in Rab'lais' easy Chair,   20
Or praise the Court, or magnify Mankind,
Or thy griev'd Country's copper chains unbind;
From thy Bæotia tho' Her Pow'r retires,
Grieve not at ought our sister realm acquires:
Here pleas'd behold her mighty wings out-spread,   25
To hatch a new Saturnian age of Lead.
  Where wave the tatter'd ensigns of Rag-Fair,
A yawning ruin hangs and nods in air;

10. *Daughter of* Chaos, *&c.*] The beauty of this whole Allegory being purely of the Poetical kind, we think it not our proper business as a Scholiast, to meddle with it; but leave it (as we shall in general all such) to the Reader: remarking only, that *Chaos* (according to *Hesiod*, Θεογονία) was the Progenitor of all the Gods. SCRIBL.

18. *Bickerstaff* ⟨Isaac Bickerstaff, a pseudonym used by Swift in some of his lighter satires, e.g. those on Partridge the Astrologer. The name was later adopted by Steele for his *Tatler.*⟩

21. *Or praise the Court, &c.*] *Ironicè*, alluding to *Gulliver's* Representations of both—The next line relates to the Papers of the *Drapier* against the currency of *Wood's* Copper Coin in Ireland, which upon the great discontent of the people, his Majesty was graciously pleased to recal.

23. *From thy* Bæotia] *Bæotia* of old lay under the Raillery of the neighbouring Wits, as *Ireland* does now; tho' each of those nations produced one of the greatest Wits, and greatest Generals, of their age. ⟨The wit produced by Bœotia was Pindar, the general, Epaminondas. Ireland had produced two famous wits in Swift and Congreve; her great general is presumably James Butler, Duke of Ormonde.⟩

24. *Grieve not, my Swift! etc.*] *Ironicè iterum.* The Politicks of *England* and *Ireland* were at this time by some thought to be opposite, or interfering with each other: Dr. *Swift* of course was in the interest of the latter, our Author of the former.

26. *A new* Saturnian *Age of Lead*] The ancient Golden Age is by Poets stiled *Saturnian*; but in the Chymical language, *Saturn* is Lead.

27. Rag-fair] *Rag-fair* is a place near the *Tower* of *London*, where old cloaths and frippery are sold.

28–31. *&c. A yawning ruin &c.*] Hear upon this place the forecited Critick on the *Dunciad.* ⟨i.e. James Ralph⟩ 'These lines (saith he) have no Construction, or are Nonsense. The two shivering Sisters must be the sister Caves of Poverty and Poetry, or the Bed and Cave of Poverty and

Keen, hollow winds howl thro' the bleak recess,
Emblem of Music caus'd by Emptiness: 30
Here in one bed two shiv'ring sisters lye,
The cave of Poverty and Poetry.
This, the Great Mother dearer held than all
The clubs of Quidnunc's, or her own Guild-hall.
Here stood her Opium, here she nurs'd her Owls,   35
And destin'd here th' imperial seat of Fools.
Hence springs each weekly Muse, the living boast
Of Curl's chaste press, and Lintot's rubric post,

Poetry must be the same, (*questionless*) and the two Sisters the Lord knows who?' O the Construction of Grammatical Heads! *Virgil* writeth thus: *Æn.* 1 ⟨166-8⟩—

> *Fronte sub adversa scopulis pendentibus antrum:*
> *Intus aquæ dulces, vivoq; sedilia saxo;*
> *Nympharum domus.——*

May we not say in like manner, "The Nymphs must be the Waters and the Stones, or the Waters and the Stones must be the houses of the Nymphs?' *Insulse!* The second line, *Intus aquæ, &c.* is in a parenthesis (as are the two lines of our Author, *Keen hollow Winds, &c.*) and it is the *Antrum*, and the *yawning Ruin*, in the line before that parenthesis, which are the *Domus*, and the *Cave*.

Let me again, I beseech thee Reader, present thee with another *Conjectural Emendation* on *Virgil's Scopulis pendentibus:* He is here describing a place, whither the weary Mariners of *Æneas* repaired to dress their Dinner.—*Fessi——frugesq; receptas Et torrere parant flammis:* What has *Scopulis pendentibus* here to do? Indeed the *aquæ dulces* and *sedilia* are something; *sweet Waters* to drink, and *Seats* to rest on. The other is surely an error of the Copyists. Restore it, without the least scruple, *Populis prandentibus*.

But for this and a thousand more, expect our Edition of *Virgil*; a Specimen whereof see in the Appendix ⟨IV⟩. SCRIBLERUS.

32. *The cave of Poverty* ⟨In 1714 Theobald had published *The Cave of Poverty, A Poem. Written in Imitation of Shakespeare.*⟩

33. *This the* Great Mother. *&c.*] *Æn.* 1⟨12, 15-18⟩.

> *Urbs antiqua fuit—*
> *Quam Juno fertur terris magis omnibus unam*
> *Posthabita coluisse Samo; hic illius arma,*
> *Hic currus fuit: hoc regnum Dea gentibus esse*
> *(Siqua fata sinant) jam tum tenditq; fovetq;*

33. *The* Great Mother] *Magna mater*, here applyed to *Dulness*. The *Quidnunc's* was a name given to the ancient Members of certain political Clubs, who were constantly enquiring, *Quid nunc?* what news?

38. *Curl's chaste press, and Lintot's rubric post*] Two Booksellers, of whom see Book 2 ⟨49 ff.⟩. The former was fined by the Court of King's-Bench for publishing obscene books; the latter usually adorn'd his shop with Titles in red letters.

Hence hymning Tyburn's elegiac lay,
Hence the soft sing-song on Cecilia's day,   40
Sepulchral lyes our holy walls to grace,
And New-year Odes, and all the Grubstreet race.
    'Twas here in clouded majesty she shone;
Four guardian Virtues, round, support her Throne;
Fierce champion Fortitude, that knows no fears   45
Of hisses, blows, or want, or loss of ears:
Calm Temperance, whose blessings those partake
Who hunger, and who thirst, for scribling sake:

39. *Hence hymning Tyburn—Hence, &c.*]
            —*Genus unde Latinum*
            Albaniq; patres, atq; altæ moenia Romæ.

Virg. ⟨*Aen.* i 6–7⟩.

39. *Hence hymning* Tyburn's *elegiac lay*] It is an ancient English
custom for the Malefactors to sing a Psalm at their Execution at *Tyburn*;
and no less customary to print Elegies on their deaths, at the same time,
or before.

VERSE 40 and 42, Allude to the annual Songs composed to Musick on
St. *Cecilia's* Feast, and those made by the Poet-Laureat for the time being
to be sung at Court, on every New-Years-Day, the words of which are
happily drown'd in the voices and Instruments.

VERSE 41. Is a just Satyr on the Flatteries and Falsehoods admitted tu
be inscribed on the walls of Churches in Epitaphs.

I must not here omit a Reflection, which will occur perpetually through
this Poem, and cannot but greatly endear the Author to every attentive
Observer of it: I mean that *Candour* and *Humanity* which every where
appears in him, to those unhappy Objects of the Ridicule of all mankind,
the bad Poets. He here imputes all scandalous rhimes, scurrilous weekly
papers, lying news, base flatteries, wretched elegies, songs, and verses
(even from those sung at Court, to ballads in the streets) not so much to
Malice or Servility as to Dulness; and not so much to Dulness, as to
Necessity; And thus at the very commencement of his Satyr, makes an
Apology for all that are to be satyrized.

43. *In clouded Majesty she shone*] Milton, ⟨*Par. Lost*, iv 606–7⟩.

            ——*The Moon*
            Rising in clouded Majesty.——

44. *Four guardian Virtues* ⟨The four Cardinal Virtues were a recurring
feature of the pageantry on a Lord Mayor's Day.⟩

45–6. *That knows no fears*] Horat. ⟨*Lib.* II, *Sat.* vii 84⟩.

            Quem neq; pauperies, neq; mors, neq; vincula terrent.

48. *Who hunger, and who thirst*] 'This is an infamous Burlesque on a
Text in Scripture, which shews the Author's delight in Prophaneness,'
(said *Curl* upon this place.) But 'tis very familiar with *Shakespeare* to
allude to Passages of Scripture. Out of a great number I'll select a few, in
which he both alludes to, and quotes the very Texts from holy Writ. In
All's well that ends well, *I am no great* Nebucadnezzar, *I have not much
Skill in Grass.* Ibid. *They are for the flowry Way that leads to the broad
Gate, and the great Fire.* Mat. 7. 13. Much ado about nothing: *All, all,
and* moreover *God saw him when he was hid in the Garden,* Gen. 3. 8. (in

Prudence, whose glass presents th' approaching jayl:
Poetic Justice, with her lifted scale;   50
Where in nice balance, truth with gold she weighs,
And solid pudding against empty praise.
  Here she beholds the Chaos dark and deep,
Where nameless somethings in their causes sleep,
'Till genial Jacob, or a warm Third-day   55
Call forth each mass, a poem or a play.
How Hints, like spawn, scarce quick in embryo lie,
How new-born Nonsense first is taught to cry,
Maggots half-form'd, in rhyme exactly meet,
And learn to crawl upon poetic feet.   60
Here one poor Word a hundred clenches makes,
And ductile dulness new meanders takes;

---

a very jocose Scene.) In Love's Labour lost, he talks of *Sampson*'s carrying
the Gates on his Back; in the Merry Wives of Windsor of *Goliah* and the
Weaver's Beam; and in Henry 4. *Falstaff*'s Soldiers are compared to
Lazarus and the *Prodigal Son*, &c. *The first part of this Note is Mr.*
CURL's: *The rest is Mr.* THEOBALD's. Shakespear Restor'd *Appendix*,
p. 144.

  49. *glass* ⟨The perspective glass through which Prudence was represented in art as gazing.⟩

  53. *Here she beholds, &c.*] That is to say, unformed things, which are
either made into Poems or Plays, as the Booksellers or the Players bid
most. These lines allude to the following in *Garth's Dispensary, Cant.* 6
⟨44-7⟩.

> *Within the chambers of the Globe they spy*
> *The beds where sleeping Vegetables lie,*
> *Till the glad summons of a genial ray*
> *Unbinds the Glebe, and calls them out to day.*

  55. *'Till genial Jacob* ⟨Jacob Tonson (1656?-1736), the leading
publisher of his generation. The third day of a play's run was regularly
set apart for the author's benefit.⟩

  59-60. *Maggots* ⟨Maggot has two senses in this context: (a) grub,
(b) 'a whimsical or perverse fancy'.⟩

  61. *Here one poor* Word *a hundred* clenches *makes*] It may not be amiss
to give an instance or two of these Operations of *Dulness* out of the
Authors celebrated in the Poem. A great Critick formerly held these
Clenches ⟨puns⟩ in such abhorrence, that he declared, 'He that would
Pun, would pick a Pocket.' Yet Mr. *Dennis*'s Works afford us notable
Examples in this kind. '*Alexander* Pope hath sent abroad into the world
as many *Bulls* as his Namesake Pope *Alexander*.'—'Let us take the initial
and final letters of his Surname, *viz.*, A. P——E, and they give you the
Idea of an *Ape*.——*Pope* comes from the Latin word *Popa*, which signifies
a little Wart; or from *Poppysma*, because he was continually *popping* out
squibs of wit, or rather *Po-pysmata*, or *Po-pisms*.' DENNIS. *Daily-
Journal* June 11. 1728.

  62. *And ductile dulness*] A Parody on another in *Garth. Cant.* 1 ⟨26⟩
> *How ductile matter new mæanders takes.*

There motley Images her fancy strike,
Figures ill'pair'd, and Similes unlike.
She sees a Mob of Metaphors advance,   65
Pleas'd with the Madness of the mazy dance:
How Tragedy and Comedy embrace;
How Farce and Epic get a jumbled race;
How Time himself stands still at her command,
Realms shift their place, and Ocean turns to land.   70
Here gay Description Ægypt glads with showers;
Or gives to Zembla fruits, to Barca flowers;
Glitt'ring with ice here hoary hills are seen,
There painted vallies of eternal green,
On cold December fragrant chaplets blow,   75
And heavy harvests nod beneath the snow.
   All these and more, the cloud-compelling Queen
Beholds thro' fogs that magnify the scene:
She, tinsel'd o'er in robes of varying hues,
With self-applause her wild creation views,   80
Sees momentary monsters rise and fall,
And with her own fool's colours gilds them all.
   'Twas on the day, when Thorold, rich and grave,
Like Cimon triumph'd, both on land and wave:

---

68. *How* Farce *and* Epic, &c.] Allude to the Transgressions of the
Unities, in the Plays of such Poets. For the Miracles wrought upon *Time*
and *Place*, and the mixture of Tragedy, Comedy, Farce and Epic, *See*
Pluto *and* Proserpine, Penelope, *&c. as yet extant.* ⟨Theobald wrote *A
Dramatic Entertainment, Call'd Harlequin a Sorcerer: With the Loves of
Pluto and Proserpine* (1725). *Penelope. An English Opera,* by John Mottley,
assisted by Thomas Cooke, was acted at the Haymarket in May, 1728.
For Cooke, see ii 130*n*.⟩

71. Ægypt *glads with Showers*] In the lower *Ægypt* Rain is of no use,
the overflowing of the *Nyle* being sufficient to impregnate the soil.—These
six verses represent the inconsistencies in the description of Poets, who
heap together all glittering and gawdy Images, tho' incompatible in one
season, or in one scene.—*See the* Guardian N° 40. *printed in the* Appendix
⟨V⟩, *Parag.* 6. *See also* Eusden's *whole Works (if to be found.)* It would
not have been unpleasant, to have given Examples of all these Species of
bad writing, from these Authors, but that it is already done in our Treatise
of the *Bathos.* SCRIBL.

77. *The* Cloud-compelling Queen] From *Homer's* Epithet of *Jupiter,*
νεφεληγερέτα Ζεύς.

83. *'Twas on the Day when* Thorold] Sir *George Thorold* Lord Mayor of
London, in the Year 1720. The Procession of a Lord Mayor is made partly
by land, and partly by water. ⟨Thorold, Lord Mayor in 1719, died on
Oct. 29, 1722.⟩—*Cimon* the famous *Athenian* General obtained a Victory
by sea, and another by land, on the same day, over the *Persians* and
Barbarians.

(Pomps without guilt, of bloodless swords and maces,   85
Glad chains, warm furs, broad banners, and broad faces)
Now Night descending, the proud scene was o'er,
But liv'd, in Settle's numbers, one day more.
Now May'rs and Shrieves all hush'd and satiate lay,
Yet eat in dreams the custard of the day;   90
While pensive Poets painful vigils keep,
Sleepless themselves to give their readers sleep.
Much to the mindful Queen the feast recalls,
What City-Swans once sung within the walls;
Much she revolves their arts, their ancient praise,   95
And sure succession down from Heywood's days.

85. *Pomps* ⟨In the sense of πομπή, a procession.⟩

86. *Glad Chains*] The Ignorance of these Moderns! This was altered
in one Edition to *Gold Chains*, shewing more regard to the metal of which
the chains of Aldermen are made, than to the beauty of the Latinism and
Grecism, nay of figurative speech itself.—*Lætas segetes*, glad, for making
glad, *&c.* SCR.

88. *But liv'd in* Settle's *Numbers*] A beautiful manner of speaking,
usual with the Poets in praise of Poetry, in which kind nothing is finer
than those lines of Mr. *Addison* ⟨*A Letter from Italy*, 31–6⟩.

> *Sometimes misguided by the tuneful throng,*
> *I look for streams immortaliz'd in song,*
> *That lost in silence and oblivion lye,*
> *Dumb are their fountains, and their channels dry;*
> *Yet run for ever, by the Muses skill,*
> *And in the smooth description murmur still.*

Settle was alive at this time, and Poet to the City of *London*. His office
was to compose yearly panegyricks upon the Lord Mayors, and Verses to
be spoken in the Pageants: But that part of the shows being by the
frugality of some Lord Mayors at length abolished, the employment of
City Poet ceas'd; so that upon *Settle*'s demise, there was no successor to
that place. ⟨He died in 1724.⟩ This important point of time our Poet
has chosen, as the Crisis of the Kingdom of *Dulness*, who thereupon
decrees to remove her imperial seat from the City, and over-spread the
other parts of the Town: To which great Enterprize all things being now
ripe, she calls the Hero of this Poem.

Mr. *Settle* was once a writer in some vogue, particularly with his Party;
for he was the author or publisher of many noted Pamphlets in the time
of King *Charles* the second. He answered all *Dryden*'s political Poems;
and being cry'd up on one side, succeeded not a little in his Tragedy of
the Empress of Morocco (the first that was ever printed with Cuts.)
'Upon this he grew insolent, the Wits writ against his Play, he replied, and
the Town judged he had the better. In short *Settle* was then thought a
formidable Rival to Mr. *Dryden*; and not only the Town, but the University of *Cambridge*, was divided which to prefer; and in both places the
younger sort inclined to *Elkanah.*' DENNIS. *Pref. to Rem. on* Hom.

For the latter part of his History, see the third Book, verse ⟨281*n*⟩.

96. *John Heywood*] Whose Enterludes were printed in the time of
Henry the eighth. ⟨Pope seems to be confusing John Heywood with the

She saw with joy the line immortal run,
Each sire imprest and glaring in his son;
So watchful Bruin forms with plastic care
Each growing lump, and brings it to a Bear.   100
She saw old Pryn in restless Daniel shine,
And Eusden eke out Blackmore's endless line;
She saw slow Philips creep like Tate's poor page,
And all the Mighty Mad in Dennis rage.

---

later dramatist, Thomas Heywood (d. 1650?), who, like Settle after him, composed the Lord Mayor's pageants for many years.⟩

101. *Old* Prynn *in restless* Daniel] *William Prynn* and *Daniel de Foe* were writers of Verses, as well as of Politicks; as appears by the Poem of the latter *De jure Divino*, and others, and by these lines in *Cowley's* Miscellanies of the former.

> —*One lately did not fear*
> (*Without the Muses leave*) *to plant Verse here.*
> *But it produc'd such base, rough, crabbed hedge-*
> *Rhymes, as e'en set the hearers ears on edge:*
> *Written by* William Prynn Esqui-re, *the*
> Year of our Lord, six hundred thirty three.
> *Brave* Jersey *Muse! and he's for his high stile*
> *Call'd to this day the* Homer *of the Isle.*

Both these Authors had a resemblance in their fates as well as writings, having been a-like sentenc'd to the Pillory. ⟨William Prynne (1600–69) was pilloried for writing *Histrio-mastix* (1633), and had his ears cut off. Defoe stood in the pillory in 1703 for writing *The Shortest Way with the Dissenters.*⟩

Of *Eusden* and *Blackmore*, see ⟨iii 319*n*, ii 258*n*⟩. And *Philips*, ⟨see iii 322*n*⟩.

103. *like Tate's poor page*] *Nahum Tate* ⟨1652–1715⟩ was Poet-Laureate, a cold writer, of no *invention*, but sometimes translated tolerably when befriended by Mr. *Dryden*. In his second part of *Absalom* and *Achitophel* are above two hundred admirable lines together of that great hand, which strongly shine through the insipidity of the rest. Something parallel may be observed of another Author here mention'd.

104. *And all the mighty Mad*] This is by no means to be understood literally, as if Mr. *D.* were really mad; Not that we are ignorant of the *Narrative* of Dr. *R. Norris*, but it deserveth no more regard than the *Pop upon P.* and the like idle Trash, written by *James Moor*, or other young and light Persons, who themselves better deserve to be blooded, scarified, or whipped, for such their ungracious merriment with their Elders. No— it is spoken of that *Excellent* and *Divine Madness*, so often mentioned by *Plato*, that poetical rage and enthusiasm, with which no doubt Mr. *D.* hath, in his time, been highly possessed; and of those *extraordinary hints* and *motions* whereof he himself so feelingly treats in the Preface to Pr. *Arth.* [See Notes on Book 2, verse 256.] SCRIBL. ⟨*The Narrative of Dr. Robert Norris* (1713), which Pope ironically condemns as 'idle trash,' was almost certainly his own. *A Popp upon Pope* (1728) is believed to be the work of Lady Mary Wortley Montagu.⟩

104. *And all the mighty Mad in* Dennis *rage*] This Verse in the sur-reptitious Editions stood thus, *And furious* D—*foam, &c.* which, in that

printed in *Ireland*, was unaccountably filled up with the great name of *Dryden*. Mr. Theobald *in the* Censor, Vol. 2. N° 33. ⟨Jan. 5, 1717⟩ also calls him by the Name of *Furius*. 'The modern *Furius* is to be look'd on as more the object of Pity, than of that which he daily provokes, laughter and contempt. Did we really know how much this *poor Man* (*I wish that reflection on* Poverty *had been spar'd*) suffers by being contradicted, or which is the same thing in effect, by hearing another praised; we should in compassion sometimes attend to him with a silent nod, and let him go away with the triumphs of his ill-nature.' '—*Poor* Furius (*again*) when any of his cotemporaries are spoken well of, quitting the ground of the present dispute steps back a thousand years to call in the succour of the Ancients. His very *Panegyrick* is *spiteful*, and he uses it for the same reason as some Ladies do their commendations of a dead Beauty, who never would have had their good word, but that a living one happened to be mentioned in their company. His applause is not the tribute of his *Heart*, but the sacrifice of his *Revenge*,' *&c.* Indeed his pieces against our Poet are somewhat of an angry character, and as they are now scarce extant, a taste of his stile may be satisfactory to the curious. 'A young squab, short Gentleman, whose outward form though it should be that of downright Monkey, would not differ so much from human shape, as his unthinking immaterial part does from human understanding.—He is as stupid and as venemous as a hunchbacked Toad.—A Book through which folly and ignorance, those bretheren so lame and impotent, do ridiculously look very big, and very dull, and strut, and hobble cheek by jowl, with their arms on kimbo, being led, and supported, and bully-backed by that blind Hector, Impudence.' *Reflect. on the* Essay *on* Crit. Page 26. 29. 30.

It would be unjust not to add his Reasons for this Fury, they are so strong and so coercive. 'I regard him (saith he) as an *Enemy*, not so much to me, as to my King, to my Country, to my Religion, and to that Liberty which has been the sole felicity of my life. A vagary of fortune, who is sometimes pleased to be frolicksome, and the epidemick *Madness of the times*, have given him *Reputation*, and Reputation (as *Hobbs* says) is *Power*, and *that has made him dangerous*. Therefore I look on it as my duty to *King George*, whose faithful subject I am, to my *Country*, of which I have appeared a constant lover; to the *Laws*, under whose protection I have so long lived; and to the *Liberty* of my *Country*, more dear than life to me, of which I have now for forty years been a constant asserter, *&c.* I look upon it as my duty, I say, to do—*you shall see what*—to pull the Lion's skin from this little Ass, which popular error has thrown round him; and to show, that this Author who has been lately so much in vogue, has neither sense in his thoughts, nor english in his expressions. DENNIS, *Rem. on* Hom. *Pref. p. 2. and p.* 91. *&c.*) ⟨Quoted mainly from the Preface. The words '*you shall see what*' are Pope's own.⟩

Besides these publick-spirited reasons, Mr. *D.* had a *private one*; which by his manner of expressing it in page 92, appears to have been equally strong. He was even in bodily fear of his Life, from the machinations of the said Mr. *P.* 'The story (says he) is too long to be told, but who would be acquainted with it, may hear it from Mr. *Curll* my Bookseller.— However, what my reason has suggested to me, that I have with a just *confidence* said, in defiance of his two clandestine weapons, his *Slander* and his *Poyson*'. Which last words of his Book plainly discover, Mr. *D*—his suspicion was that of being *poysoned*, in like manner as Mr. *Curl* had been before him. Of which fact see *A full and true account of a horrid and barbarous revenge by Poyson on the body of* Edmund Curl; printed in 1716, the year antecedent to that wherein these Remarks of Mr. *Dennis* were

In each she marks her image full exprest,   105
But chief, in Tibbald's monster-breeding breast;

---

published. But what puts it beyond all question, is a passage in a very warm treatise in which Mr. *D.* was also concerned, price two pence, called, *A true character of Mr.* Pope *and his writings, printed for S. Popping,* 1716. in the tenth page whereof he is said 'to have insulted people on those calamities and diseases, which he himself gave them by administring *Poyson* to them'; and is called (*p.* 4.) *a lurking waylaying coward, and a stabber in the dark.* Which (with many other things most lively set forth in that piece) must have render'd him a terror, not to Mr. *Dennis* only, but to all Christian People.

For the rest, Mr. *John Dennis* was the Son of a Sadler in *London,* born in 1657. He paid court to Mr. *Dryden*; and having obtained some correspondence with Mr. *Wycherly* and Mr. *Congreve,* he immediately obliged the publick with their Letters. He made himself known to the Government by many admirable Schemes and Projects; which the Ministry, for reasons best known to themselves, constantly kept private. For his character as a writer, it is given us as follows. 'Mr. *Dennis* is excellent at pindarick writings, *perfectly regular* in all his performances, and a person of *sound Learning.* That he is master of a great deal of *Penetration* and *Judgment,* his criticisms (particularly on Prince *Arthur*) do sufficiently demonstrate.' From the same account it also appears, that he writ Plays 'more to get *Reputation* than *Money.*' DENNIS *of himself.* See *Jacob's* Lives of Dram. Poets, page 68. 69. *compared with* page 286.

106. *But chief in* Tibbald] *Lewis Tibbald* (as pronounced) or *Theobald* (as written) was bred an Attorney, and Son to an Attorney (says Mr. *Jacob*) of *Sittenburn* in *Kent.* He was Author of many forgotten Plays, Poems, and other pieces, and of several anonymous Letters in praise of them in *Mist's* Journal. He was concerned in a Paper call'd the *Censor,* and a translation of *Ovid,* as we find from Mr. *Dennis*'s Remarks on *Pope*'s *Homer, p.* 9. 10. 'There is a notorious Ideot, one hight *Whachum,* who from an under-spur-leather to the Law, is become an under-strapper to the Play-house, who has lately burlesqu'd the Metamorphoses of *Ovid* by a vile Translation, *&c.* This Fellow is concerned in an impertinent Paper called the *Censor*'. But notwithstanding this severe character, another Critick says of him 'That he has given us some Pieces which met with approbation; and that *the Cave of Poverty* is an excellent Poem.' *Giles Jacob's Lives of the Poets,* vol. 2. p. 211. He had once a mind to translate the *Odyssey,* the first Book whereof was printed in 1717 by *B. Lintott,* and probably may yet be seen at his Shop. What is still in memory, is a piece now about a year old, it had the arrogant Title of *Shakespear Restored:* Of this he was so proud himself, as to say in one of *Mist's Journals, June* 8. 'That to expose any Errors in it was impracticable.' And in another, *April* 27. 'That whatever care for the future might be taken either by Mr. *P.* or any other assistants, he would still give above 500 Emendations that *shall* escape them *all.*' During the space of two years, while Mr. *Pope* was preparing his Edition of *Shakespear,* and published Advertisements, requesting all lovers of the Author to contribute to a more perfect one; this Restorer (who had then some correspondence with him, and was solliciting favours by Letters) did wholly conceal his design, 'till after its publication (which he was since not asham'd to own, in a *Daily Journal* of *Nov.* 26, 1728.) And then an outcry was made in the Prints, that our Author had joined with the Bookseller to raise an *extravagant subscription*;

Sees Gods with Dæmons in strange league ingage,
And earth, and heav'n, and hell her battles wage.
  She ey'd the Bard, where supperless he sate,
And pin'd, unconscious of his rising fate;   110
Studious he sate, with all his books around,
Sinking from thought to thought, a vast profound!
Plung'd for his sense, but found no bottom there;
Then writ, and flounder'd on, in mere despair.
He roll'd his eyes that witness'd huge dismay,   115
Where yet unpawn'd, much learned lumber lay,
Volumes, whose size the space exactly fill'd;
Or which fond authors were so good to gild;
Or where, by sculpture made for ever known,
The page admires new beauties, not its own.   120

---

in which he had no share, of which he had no knowledge, and against which he had publickly advertised in his own Proposals for *Homer*. Probably that proceeding elevated him to the Dignity he holds in this Poem, which he seems to deserve no other way better than his brethren; unless we impute it to the share he had in the Journals, cited among the *Testimonies of Authors* prefixed to this work.

106. Tibbald'*s monster-breeding breast, Sees Gods with Dæmons*, &c.] This alludes to the extravagancies of the Farces of that author; in which he alone could properly be represented as successor to *Settle*, who had written *Pope Joan, St. George for England*, and other pieces for *Bartlemew-Fair*. ⟨See A iii 281n.⟩ See book 3. vers. 229, &c.

109.—*Supper-less he sate*] It is amazing how the sense of this line hath been mistaken by all the former Commentators, who most idly suppose it to imply, that the Hero of the Poem wanted a supper. In truth a great absurdity! Not that we are ignorant that the Hero of *Homer*'s *Odyssey* is frequently in that circumstance, and therefore it can no way derogate from the grandeur of Epic Poem to represent such Hero under a Calamity, to which the greatest not only of Criticks and Poets, but of Kings and Warriors, have been subject. But much more refin'd, I will venture to say, is the meaning of our author: It was to give us obliquely a curious precept, or what *Bossu* calls a *disguised sentence*, that 'Temperance is the life of Study.' The language of Poesy brings all into Action; and to represent a Critic encompast with books, but without a supper, is a picture which lively expresseth how much the true Critic prefers the diet of the mind to that of the body, one of which he always castigates and often totally neglects, for the greater improvement of the other. SCRIBLERUS.

115. *He roll'd his eyes that witness'd huge dismay*] Milt. ⟨*Par. Lost*, i 56–7⟩.—*Round he throws his eyes. That witness'd huge affliction and dismay*. The progress of a bad Poet in his thoughts being (like the progress of the Devil in *Milton*) thro' a Chaos, might probably suggest this imitation.

120. —*Admires new beauties not its own*. Virg. Geo. 2 ⟨82⟩.
            Miraturq; novas frondes, & non sua poma.

VERSE id. &*c*.] This library is divided into two parts; the one (his polite learning) consists of those books which seem'd to be the models of his poetry, and are preferr'd for one of these three reasons (usual with collectors of Libraries) that they fitted the shelves, or were gilded for

Here swells the shelf with Ogilby the great:
There, stamp'd with arms, Newcastle shines compleat,
Here all his suff'ring brotherhood retire,
And 'scape the martyrdom of jakes and fire;
A Gothic Vatican! of Greece and Rome   125
Well-purg'd, and worthy Withers, Quarles, and Blome.
   But high above, more solid Learning shone,
The Classicks of an Age that heard of none;
There Caxton slept, with Wynkin at his side,
One clasp'd in wood, and one in strong cow-hide.   130

---

shew, or adorned with pictures: The other class our author calls solid
Learning; old bodies of Philosophy, old Commentators, old English
Printers, or old English Translations; all very voluminous, and fit to erect
Altars to Dulness.

121.—Ogilby *the great*] *John Ogilby* ⟨1600–76⟩ was one, who from a
late initiation into literature, made such a progress as might well stile him
the *Prodigy* of his time! sending into the world so many *large Volumes!*
His translations of *Homer* and *Virgil, done to the life,* and with *such
excellent Sculptures!* and (what added great grace to his works) he printed
them all on *special good Paper,* and in a *very good Letter.* WINSTANLY,
Lives of Poets.

122. *There, stamp'd with arms,* Newcastle *shines compleat*] The *Dutchess
of Newcastle* was one who busied herself in the ravishing delights of
Poetry; leaving to posterity in print three *ample Volumes* of her studious
endeavours. WINSTANLY, *ibid. Langbaine* reckons up eight Folio's of her
Grace's; which were usually adorn'd with gilded Covers, and had her
Coat of Arms upon them.

125. *Vatican* ⟨The word was frequently used for the Vatican Library.⟩

126.—*Worthy* Withers, Quarles, *and* Blome] It was printed in the
surreptitious Editions, *W—ly, W—s,* who were Persons eminent for good
life; the one writ the Life of Christ in verse; the other some valuable
pieces in the lyrick kind on pious subjects. The line is here restor'd
according to its Original. ⟨*W—y* is the Rev. Samuel Wesley, 1662–1735.
Pope had probably no grievance against him, and introduced him only as
a poetaster. *W—s* is Isaac Watts (1674–1748), one of the most popular
poets of his day. It was probably his popularity with humble readers that
landed him in the *Dunciad.*⟩

George Withers was a great pretender to poetical zeal against the vices
of the times, and abused the greatest Personages in power, which brought
upon him *frequent correction.* The *Marshalsea* and *Newgate* were no
strangers to him. WINSTANLY. *Quarles* was as dull a writer, but an
honester man. *Blome*'s books are remarkable for their cuts. ⟨In writing
contemptuously of Withers (1588–1667), Pope was following a tradition
already well-established. He was not making an individual or peculiar
judgment. Francis Quarles (1592–1644), the author of *Emblemes* (1635),
was popular with the lower orders, but generally despised by the cultured
reader. Richard Blome (d. 1705) was the publisher, and possibly the compiler, of numerous folios on heraldry, genealogy, geography, etc.⟩

129. *Caxton*] A Printer in the time of *Edw.* 4. *Rich.* 3. and *Henry* 7.
Wynkin de Word, his successor in that of *Henry* 7 and 8. The former
translated into prose *Virgil's Æneis* as a History; of which he speaks in his

There sav'd by spice, like mummies, many a year,
Old Bodies of Philosophy appear.
De Lyra here a dreadful front extends,
And there, the groaning shelves Philemon bends.
 Of these twelve volumes, twelve of amplest size, 135
Redeem'd from tapers and defrauded pyes,
Inspir'd he seizes: These an altar raise:
An hecatomb of pure, unsully'd lays
That altar crowns: A folio Common-place
Founds the whole pyle, of all his works the base; 140
Quarto's, Octavo's, shape the less'ning pyre,
And last, a little Ajax tips the spire.
 Then he. 'Great Tamer of all human art!
First in my care, and nearest at my heart:
Dulness! whose good old cause I yet defend, 145
With whom my Muse began, with whom shall end!
O thou, of business the directing soul,
To human heads like byass to the bowl,
Which as more pond'rous makes their aim more true,
Obliquely wadling to the mark in view. 150
O ever gracious to perplex'd mankind!
Who spread a healing mist before the mind,

Proeme in a very singular manner, as of a book hardly known. *Vid.*
Append. *Tibbald* quotes a rare passage from him in *Mist's Journal* of
March 16, 1728. concerning a *straunge and mervayllouse beaste called*
Sagittarye, which he would have *Shakespear* to mean rather than *Teucer,*
the Archer celebrated by *Homer.* ⟨See Appendix iii, p. 438*n*.⟩

133. *Nich. de Lyra,* or *Harpsfeld,* a very voluminous Commentator,
whose works in five vast Folio's were printed in 1472. ⟨Pope has confused Nicholas de Lyra (d. 1340), the author of the 'five vast Folio's' with
Nicholas Harpsfield (1519?-75), theologian, who wrote *Historia Anglicana*
Ecclesiastica.⟩

134. *Philemon Holland,* Dr. in Physick. He translated *so many books,*
that a man would think he had done *nothing else,* insomuch that he might
be call'd *Translator General of his age.* The books alone of his turning into
English, are sufficient to make a *Country Gentleman a compleat Library.*
WINSTANLY:

138. *hecatomb* ⟨The epithet 'unsully'd' is probably intended to refer to
the sacrifices in classical epic: the purity of the heifers offered on the altar
is often stressed. But Theobald's poems were also 'unsully'd' in the sense
that they had never been thumbed by any reader.⟩

142. *A little* Ajax] In *duodecimo* translated from *Sophocles* by *Tibbald.*
⟨It is doubtful if this translation (1714) was by Theobald.⟩

146. *With whom my Muse began, with whom shall end*] Virg. *Ecl.* 8
⟨11⟩. *A te principium, tibi desinet*—from *Theoc.* ⟨Id. xvii 1.⟩

  'Εκ Διὸς ἀρχώμεσθα καὶ ἐς Δία λήγετε Μοῖσαι.

So *Horace* <Ep. 1 i, i>,
Prima dicte mihi, summa dicende camæna.

And, lest we err by Wit's wild, dancing light,
Secure us kindly in our native night.
Ah! still o'er Britain stretch that peaceful wand,   155
Which lulls th' Helvetian and Batavian land.
Where rebel to thy throne if Science rise,
She does but shew her coward face and dies:
There, thy good Scholiasts with unweary'd pains
Make Horace flat, and humble Maro's strains;   160
Here studious I unlucky moderns save,
Nor sleeps one error in its father's grave,
Old puns restore, lost blunders nicely seek,
And crucify poor Shakespear once a week.
For thee I dim these eyes, and stuff this head,   165
With all such reading as was never read;

162–3. *Nor sleeps one error—Old puns restore, lost blunders, &c.*] As
where he laboured to prove *Shakespear* guilty of terrible *Anacronisms*, or
low *Conundrums*, which Time had cover'd; and conversant in such authors
as *Caxton* and *Wynkin*, rather than in *Homer* or *Chaucer*. Nay so far had
he lost his reverence to this incomparable author, as to say in print, *He
deserved to be whipt.* An insolence which nothing sure can parallel! but
that of *Dennis*, who can be proved to have declared before Company, that
Shakespear was a Rascal. O tempora! O mores! SCRIBLERUS.

164. *And crucify poor* Shakespear *once a week*] For some time, once a
week or fortnight, he printed in *Mist's Journal* a single remark or poor
conjecture on some *word* or *pointing* of *Shakespear*, either in his own name,
or in letters to himself as from others without name. Upon these somebody
made this Epigram,

> '*Tis generous* Tibald! *in thee and thy brothers,*
> *To help us thus to read the works of others:*
> *Never for this can just returns be shown;*
> *For who will help us e'er to read thy own?*

He since publish'd an Edition of Shakespeare with numerous alterations
of the Text, upon bare *Conjectures*, either of his own, or of any others who
sent them to him. To which Mr. *M.* ⟨Mallet⟩ alludes in those Verses of
his very fine poem on that occasion ⟨*On Verbal Criticism*⟩.

> He with low Industry goes gleaning on,
> From good, from bad, from mean, neglecting none:
> His brother Bookworm so, on shelf or stall,
> Will feed alike on *Woolston* or on *Paul* . . .
> Such the grave Bird in Northern Seas is found
> (Whose name a Dutchman only knows to sound)
> Where'er the King of fish moves on before,
> This humble friend attends from shore to shore;
> With eye still earnest, and with bill declin'd,
> He picks up what his Patron drops behind;
> With such choice cates his palate to regale,
> And is the careful Tibbald of a Whale.

166. *With all such reading as was never read*] Such as *Caxton* above-
mentioned, the three destructions of *Troy* by *Wynkin,* and other like
classicks.

For thee supplying, in the worst of days,
Notes to dull books, and prologues to dull plays;
For thee explain a thing till all men doubt it,
And write about it, Goddess, and about it;   170
So spins the silkworm small its slender store,
And labours, 'till it clouds itself all o'er.
Not that my quill to Critiques was confin'd,
My Verse gave ampler lessons to mankind;
So gravest precepts may successless prove,   175
But sad examples never fail to move.
As forc'd from wind-guns, lead itself can fly,
And pond'rous slugs cut swiftly thro' the sky;
As clocks to weight their nimble motion owe,
The wheels above urg'd by the load below;   180
Me, Emptiness and Dulness could inspire,
And were my Elasticity and Fire.
Had heav'n decreed such works a longer date,
Heav'n had decreed to spare the Grubstreet-state.
But see great Settle to the dust descend,   185
And all thy cause and empire at an end!
Cou'd Troy be sav'd by any single hand,
His gray-goose-weapon must have made her stand.
But what can I? my Flaccus cast aside,

168. *Notes to dull books, and prologues to dull plays*] As to *Cook's Hesiod*,
where sometimes a note, and sometimes even *half* a note, are carefully
owned by him: And to *Moore's Comedy* of the *Rival Modes*, and other
authors of the same rank: These were people who writ about the year
1726. ⟨James Moore Smythe's comedy, *The Rival Modes*, was first
performed on Jan. 27, 1727. Thomas Cooke's translation of Hesiod was
published in 1728.⟩

177. *As forc'd from wind-guns*] The Thought of these four verses is
found in a poem of our author's of a very early date (namely writ at
Fourteen Years old and soon after printed, intitled, *To the Author of a
Poem call'd* Successio,) where they stand thus,

> The heaviest Muse the swiftest course has gone,
> As Clocks run fastest when most Lead is on.
> So forc'd from Engines Lead itself can fly,
> And pond'rous Slugs move nimbly thro' the Sky. ⟨p. 7.⟩

183. *Had heav'n decreed such works a longer date*, &c.] Virg. Æn. 2
⟨641-2⟩.

> *Me si cœlicolæ voluissent ducere vitam*
> *Has mihi servassent sedes.—*

187. *Could* Troy *be saved.—His gray-goose-weapon*] *Virg.* ibid. ⟨291-
292⟩.

> *—Si Pergama dextra*
> *Defendi possent, etiam hac defensa fuissent.*

189. *My* Flaccus] A familiar manner of speaking used by modern

Take up th' Attorney's (once my better) Guide?   190
Or rob the Roman geese of all their glories,
And save the state by cackling to the Tories?
Yes, to my Country I my pen consign,
Yes, from this moment, mighty Mist! am thine,
And rival, Curtius! of thy fame and zeal,   195
O'er head and ears plunge for the publick weal.
Adieu my children! better thus expire
Un-stall'd, unsold; thus glorious mount in fire
Fair without spot; than greas'd by grocer's hands,
Or shipp'd with Ward to ape and monkey lands,   200

Cricks of a favourite Author. Mr. *T.* might as justly speak thus of *Horace*, as a French wit did of *Tully* seeing his works in a library, *Ah! mon cher Ciceron! Je le connois bien: c'est le meme que Marc Tulle.*

190. *Take up th'*Attorney's Guide] In allusion to his first profession of an Attorney.

191. *Or rob the* Roman *geese. &c.*] Relates to the well-known story of the geese that saved the Capitol, of which *Virgil, Æn.* 8 ⟨655–6⟩. *Atq; hic auratis volitans argenteus anser Porticibus, Gallos in limine adesse canebat.* A passage I have always suspected. Who sees not the Antithesis of *auratis* and *argenteus* to be unworthy the Virgilian Majesty? and what absurdity to say, a Goose *sings? canebat? Virgil* gives a contrary character of the voice of this silly Bird, in *Ecl.* 9 ⟨36⟩.—*argutos* interstrepere *anser olores.* Read it therefore *adesse strepebat.* And why *auratis porticibus?* Does not the very verse preceding this inform us, *Romuleo recens horrebat regia culmo?* Is this *Thatch* in one line, and *Gold* in another, consistent? I scruple not (*repugnantibus omnibus manuscriptis*) to correct it, *auritis. Horace* uses the same epithet in the same sense ⟨*Od.* 1 xii 11–12⟩,

      —Auritas *fidibus canoris*
      Ducere quercus.

And to say, that *Walls have Ears,* is common even to a proverb. SCRIBL.

194. *Mighty* Mist!] *Nathaniel Mist* was publisher of a famous Tory Paper (see notes on l. ⟨lib.⟩ 3.) in which this Author was sometimes permitted to have a part. ⟨See A iii 28*n.*, 272*n.*, 286*n.*⟩

195. *Curtius* ⟨M. Curtius, the Roman youth who leapt, armed and mounted, into the gulf which had opened in the Forum, *circa* 360 B.C.⟩

197. *Adieu my Children!*] This is a tender and passionate Apostrophe to his own Works which he is going to sacrifice, agreeable to the nature of man in great affliction, and reflecting like a parent, on the many miserable fates to which they would otherwise be subject.

      —*Felix Priameïa virgo!*
      Jussa mori: quæ sortitus non pertulit ullos,
      Nec victoris heri tetigit captiva cubile!
      Nos patriâ incensâ, diversa per æquora vectæ, &c.
        Virg. Æn. 3, ⟨321, 323–5⟩.

200. Ward] *Edward Ward,* a very voluminous Poet in Hudibrastick Verse, but best known by the *London Spy,* in Prose. He has of late Years kept a publick house in the City (but in a genteel way) and with his wit, humour, and good liquor (Ale) afforded his guests a pleasurable entertainment, especially those of the High-Church party. JACOB *Lives of Poets*

Or wafting ginger, round the streets to go,
And visit alehouse where ye first did grow.'
With that, he lifted thrice the sparkling brand,
And thrice he dropt it from his quiv'ring hand:
Then lights the structure, with averted eyes;   205
The rowling smokes involve the sacrifice.
The opening clouds disclose each work by turns,
Now flames old Memnon, now Rodrigo burns,
In one quick flash see Proserpine expire,
And last, his own cold Æschylus took fire.   210

---

vol. 2. p. 225. Great numbers of his works are yearly sold into the
Plantations. He wrote a wretched thing against our Author, call'd *Durgen.*
—Ward in a Book call'd Apollo's Maggot, declar'd this account to be a
great Falsity, protesting that his publick house was not in the City, but in
Moorfields ⟨see p. 428⟩.

   202. *And visit Alehouse*] Waller on the Navy ⟨*To the King on his Navy,*
25–26⟩.

> *Those towers of Oak o'er fertile plains may go,*
> *And visit Mountains where they once did grow.*

   203. *He lifted thrice the sparkling brand, And thrice he dropt it*] Ovid of
Althea on the like occasion, burning her Offspring, Met. 8 ⟨*462–3*⟩.

> *Tum conata quater flammis imponere torrem,*
> *Cæpta quater tenuit.—*

   208. *Now flames old* Memnon, *&c.*] Virg. Æn. 2 ⟨*310–12*⟩.

> *—Jam Deiphobi dedit ampla ruinam*
> *Vulcano superante, domus; jam proximus ardet*
> *Ucalegon.*

   208-9. *Memnon . . . Rodrigo . . . Proserpine*] *Memnon,* a Hero in the
Persian Princess, very apt to take fire, as appears by these lines with which
he begins the Play.

> *By heav'n it fires my frozen blood with rage,*
> *And makes it* scald *my aged Trunk—*

⟨*The Persian Princess* (1717), by Theobald.⟩ *Rodrigo,* the chief personage of the Perfidious Brother, a play written between *T.* and a Watchmaker. ⟨This tragedy was published in 1715 as being 'by Mr. Theobald.'
The following year Henry Meystayer, a watchmaker, published a different
version of the play with a dedication to Theobald, in which he claimed
that the play was substantially his.⟩ The *Rape* of *Proserpine,* one of the
Farces of this Author, in which *Ceres* sets fire to a Corn-field, which
endangered the burning of the Play-house. ⟨At the close of Scene V, the
following stage-direction occurs: 'Ceres here snatches flaming Branches
from her Train, and sets the Corn etc. on Fire.'—This pantomime was
acted at Covent Garden in 1725.⟩

   210. *His own cold* Æschylus] He had been (to use an expression of our
Poet), *about Æschylus* for ten years, and had received Subscriptions for
the same, but then went *about* other Books. The character of this tragic
Poet is Fire and Boldness in a high degree; but our Author supposes it

Then gush'd the tears, as from the Trojan's eyes
When the last blaze sent Ilion to the skies.
   Rowz'd by the light, old Dulness heav'd the head,
Then snatch'd a sheet of Thulè from her bed;
Sudden she flies, and whelms it o'er the pyre: 215
Down sink the flames, and with a hiss expire.
   Her ample presence fills up all the place;
A veil of fogs dilates her awful face;
Great in her charms! as when on Shrieves and May'rs

---

to be very much cooled by the translation; Upon sight of a specimen of it,
was made this Epigram,

> Alas! poor *Æschylus!* unlucky Dog!
> Whom once a *Lobster* kill'd, and now a *Log.*

But this is a grievous error, for *Æschylus* was not slain by the fall of
a Lobster on his head, but of a Tortoise, *teste* Val. Max. l. 9. cap.
12. SCRIBL. ⟨Theobald contracted with Lintot in 1713 to translate
Aeschylus for ten guineas. It never appeared. See also A iii 311*n.*⟩

212. *When the last blaze* . . .] See Virgil, *Aen.* 2, where I would advise
the reader to peruse the story of *Troy*'s destruction, rather than in *Wynkin.*
But I caution him alike in both, to beware of a most grievous error, that
of thinking it was brought about by I know not what *Trojan Horse*; there
never having been any such thing. For first it was not *Trojan*, being made
by the *Greeks*, and secondly it was not a Horse, but a Mare. This is clear
from many verses in *Virgil,*

> Uterum *armato milite complent—*
> *Inclusos* Utero *Danaos—*

Can a horse be said *Utero gerere?* Again,

> Uteroq; *recusso Insonuere cavæ—*
> *Atq;* utero *sonitum quater arma dedere.*

Nay is it not expressly said,

> *Scandit fatalis machina muros*
> Foeta *armis—*

How is it possible the word *fœta* can agree with a horse? and indeed can
it be conceived, that the chaste and Virgin Goddess *Pallas* would employ
her self in forming and fashioning the Male of that species? But this shall
be proved to a Demonstration in our *Virgil Restored.* SCRIBLER.

214. *Thulè*] An unfinished Poem of that name, of which one sheet was
printed fifteen Years ago; by *A. Ph.* a Northern Author. It is an usual
method of putting out a fire, to cast wet sheets upon it. Some Criticks
have been of opinion, that this sheet was of the nature of the *Asbestos,*
which cannot be consumed by fire; but I rather think it only an allegorical
allusion to the coldness and heaviness of the writing. ⟨ < *Thule,* by Ambrose
Philips, was published in the *Freethinker,* No. IX (1718). Philips is called
'a Northern Author' because Pope wishes to suggest that he is a cold
writer. Cf. A i 103*n.* But the phrase makes a punning allusion to *Thule,*
and perhaps to his well-known 'winter-piece,' *An Epistle to the Earl
of Dorset.*⟩

219. *Great in her charms! as when on Shrieves and May'rs
    She looks, and breathes herself into their airs*]

She looks, and breathes her self into their airs.   220
She bids him wait her to the sacred Dome;
Well-pleas'd he enter'd, and confess'd his Home:
So spirits ending their terrestrial race,
Ascend, and recognize their native place:
Raptur'd, he gazes round the dear retreat,   225
And in sweet numbers celebrates the seat.
   Here to her Chosen all her works she shows;
Prose swell'd to verse, Verse loitring into prose;
How random Thoughts now meaning chance to find.
Now leave all memory of sense behind: 230
How Prologues into Prefaces decay,
And these to Notes are fritter'd quite away.
How Index-learning turns no student pale,
Yet holds the Eel of science by the Tail.
How, with less reading than makes felons 'scape,   235
Less human genius than God gives an ape,
Small thanks to France and none to Rome or Greece,
A past, vamp'd, future, old, reviv'd, new piece,
'Twixt Plautus, Fletcher, Congreve, and Corneille,
Can make a Cibber, Johnson, or Ozell.   240

Alma parens confessa Deam; qualisq; videri
Cœlicolis & quanta solet—Virg. Æn. 2.
—*Et lætos oculis afflarat honores.*—Id. Æn. 1 ⟨591⟩.
   221. —*The sacred* Dome] The *Cave of Poverty* above mentioned;
where he no sooner enters, but he Reconnoitres the place of his original;
as *Plato* says the Spirits shall do, at their entrance into the celestial
Regions. His Dialogue of the Immortality of the Soul was translated by
T. in the familiar modern stile of *Prithee Phædo*, and *For God's sake*
Socrates: printed for *B. Lintot*, 1713.
   226. *And in sweet numbers celebrates the seat*] He writ a Poem call'd the
Cave of Poverty, which concludes with a very extraordinary Wish, 'That
some great Genius, or man of distinguished merit may be *starved*, in order
to celebrate her power, and describe her Cave.' It was printed in octavo,
1715.
   235. *makes felons 'scape* ⟨'Benefit of clergy' was still available for
criminals. By an act of 5 Anne c. 6, it was allowed without the traditional
reading test.⟩
   240. *Can make a* Cibber] Mr. *Colly Cibber*, an Author and Actor; of a
good share of wit, and *uncommon vivacity*, which are much improved by
the *conversation* he enjoys, which is of the *best*. J A C O B *Lives of* Dram
Poets. p. 8. Besides 2 Volumes of Plays in 4º, he has made up and translated several others. Mr. *Jacob* omitted to remark, that he is particularly
admirable in Tragedy.
   240. —*Johnson*] *Charles Johnson* ⟨1679-1748⟩, famous for writing a
Play every season, and for being at *Button's* every day. He had probably
thriven better in his Vocation had he been a small matter leaner. He may
justly be called a Martyr to obesity, and to have fallen a victim to the

The Goddess then o'er his anointed head,
With mystic words, the sacred Opium shed;
And lo! her Bird (a monster of a fowl!
Something betwixt a H*** and Owl)
Perch'd on his crown. 'All hail! and hail again,   245
My son! the promis'd land expects thy reign.
Know, Settle, cloy'd with custard and with praise,
Is gather'd to the Dull of antient days,
Safe, where no criticks damn, no duns molest,
Where Gildon, Banks, and high-born Howard rest.   250
I see a King! who leads my chosen sons
To lands, that flow with clenches and with puns:
'Till each fam'd Theatre my empire own,
'Till Albion, as Hibernia, bless my throne!

---

rotundity of his parts. CHA. of the TIMES, printed by CURL, pag. 19.
Some of his Plays are Love in a Forest (*Shakespear*'s As you like it) Wife's
Relief (*Shirley*'s Gamester) The Victim (*Racine*'s Iphigenia) The Sulta-
ness (*Racine*'s Bajazet, the prologue of which abused Dr. *Arbuthnot*, Mr.
Pope, and Mr. *Gay*.) The *Cobler* of *Preston*, his own.

240. —*And* Ozell] Mr. *John Ozell*, if we credit Mr. *Jacob*, did go to
School in '*Leicestershire*, where *somebody* left him *something* to live on,
when he shall retire from business. He was designed to be sent to *Cambridge* in order for Priesthood; but he chose rather to be placed in an
Office of *accounts* in the City, being qualified for the same by his skill in
Arithmetick, and writing the necessary *hands*. He has oblig'd the world
with many translations of French Plays.' JACOB *Lives of* Dram. Poets,
p. 198. ⟨See Pope's 'Errata,' p. 428.⟩

244. *A H—r*] A strange Bird from *Switzerland*. ⟨John James
Heidegger, a Swiss who became manager of the opera-house at Hay-
market.⟩ Here, in the *Dublin* edition, was absurdly inserted the name of
an eminent Lawyer and Member of Parliament, who was a man of wit,
and a friend of the author. ⟨i.e. John Hungerford (d. 1729), who unsuc-
cessfully defended Christopher Layer, the Jacobite, in 1722.⟩

250. *Where* Gildon, Banks, *and high-born* Howard *rest*] *Charles Gildon*
⟨1665–1724⟩, a writer of criticisms and libels of the last age: He
published *Blount*'s blasphemous books against the Divinity of Christ, the
Oracles of reason, &c. ⟨1693⟩. He signalized himself as a Critic, having
written some very bad plays; abused Mr. *P.* very scandalously in an
anonymous Pamphlet of the Life of Mr. *Wycherly* printed by *Curl*, in
another called the New Rehearsal printed in 1714, in a third entitled the
compleat Art of English Poetry, in 2 Volumes, and others.⟩

250. —*Banks*] Was author of the play of the Earl of Essex, Ann
Boleyn, &c. He followed the law as a sollicitor, like *Tibbald*. ⟨John
Banks wrote seven plays between 1677 and 1696.⟩

250. —*Hon.* Edward Howard, Author of the British Princes, and a
great number of wonderful pieces, celebrated by the late Earls of *Dorset*
and *Rochester*, Duke of *Buckingham*, Mr. *Waller*, &c. ⟨Howard, who
was known as 'foolish Ned,' was the author of six plays. *The Brittish
Princes. An Heroick Poem*, published in 1669, was much ridiculed by the
wits.⟩

I see! I see!—' Then rapt, she spoke no more.   255
'God save King Tibbald!' Grubstreet alleys roar.
So when Jove's block descended from on high,
(As sings thy great fore-father, Ogilby,)
Loud thunder to its bottom shook the bog,
And the hoarse nation croak'd, God save King Log!   260

258. *As sings thy great fore-father* Ogilby] See his *Æsop* Fab. ⟨1651⟩ where this excellent hemystic is to be found. Our author shows here and elsewhere, a prodigious Tenderness for a *bad writer*. We see he selects the only good passage perhaps in all that ever *Ogilby* writ; which shows how candid and patient a reader he must have been. What can be more kind and affectionate than these words in the preface to his Poems, 4°. 1717. where he labours to call up all our humanity and forgiveness toward them, by the most moderate representation of their case that has ever been given by any Author? 'Much may be said to extenuate the fault of bad Poets: What we call a *Genius* is hard to be distinguished, by a man himself, from a prevalent inclination: And if it be never so great, he can at first discover it no other way, than by that strong propensity, which renders him the more liable to be mistaken. He has no other method but to make the experiment by writing, and so appealing to the judgment of others: And if he happens to write ill (which is certainly no sin in itself) he is immediately made the Object of Ridicule! I wish we had the humanity to reflect, that even the worst Authors might endeavour to please us, and in that endeavour, deserve something at our hands. We have no cause to quarrel with them, but for their obstinacy in persisting, and even that may admit of alleviating circumstances: For their particular friends may be either ignorant, or unsincere; and the rest of the world too well-bred, to shock them with a truth, which generally their Booksellers are the first that inform them of'.

But how much all Indulgence is lost upon these people may appear from the just Reflection made on their constant Conduct and constant Fate in the following Epigram.

> *Ye little wits, that gleam'd a-while,*
>   *When* P–pe *vouchsaf'd a ray,*
> *Alas! depriv'd of his kind smile,*
>   *How soon ye fade away!*
> *To compass* Phœbus *Car about*
>   *Thus empty Vapours rise;*
> *Each lends his Cloud, to put Him out*
>   *That rear'd him to the Skies.*
> *Alas! those Skies are not your Sphere;*
>   *There, He shall ever burn:*
> *Weep, weep and fall! for Earth ye were,*
>   *And must to Earth return.*

End of the First Book

The Dunciad

BOOK THE SECOND

High on a gorgeous seat, that far outshone
Henley's gilt Tub, or Fleckno's Irish Throne,
Or that, where on her Curlls, the Public pours
All-bounteous, fragrant grains, and golden show'rs;
Great Tibbald sate: The proud Parnassian sneer,   5

Two things there are, upon which the very Basis of all verbal Criticism is founded and supported: The first, that the Author could never fail to use the very best word, on every occasion: The second, that the Critick cannot chuse but know, which it is. This being granted, whenever any doth not fully content us, we take upon us to conclude, first that the author could never have us'd it, And secondly, that he must have used That very one which we conjecture in its stead.

We cannot therefore enough admire the learned *Scriblerus*, for his alteration of the Text in the two last verses of the preceding book, which in all the former editions stood thus

> *Hoarse Thunder to its bottom shook the bog,*
> *And the loud nation croak'd,* God save K. Log!

He has with great judgment transposed these two epithets, putting *hoarse* to the Nation, and *loud* to the Thunder: And this being evidently the true reading, he vouchsafed not so much as to mention the former; For which assertion of the just right of a Critick, he merits the acknowledgement of all sound Commentators.

1. *High on a gorgeous seat*] Parody of *Milton* ⟨*Par. Lost*, ii 1–5⟩,

> *High on a throne of royal state, that far*
> *Outshone the wealth of Ormus and of Ind,*
> *Or where the gorgeous East with richest hand*
> *Show'rs on her Kings barbaric pearl and gold,*
> *Satan exalted sate,——*

2. Henley's *gilt Tub*] The pulpit of a Dissenter is usually called a Tub; but that of Mr. Orator *Henley* was covered with velvet, and adorned with gold. He had also a fair altar, and over it this extraordinary inscription, *The Primitive Eucharist*. See the history of this person, book 3. verse 195.

2. Or Fleckno's *Irish Throne*] *Richard Flecknoe* ⟨d. 1678?⟩ was an Irish Priest, but had laid aside (as himself expressed it) the Mechanick part of Priesthood. He printed some Plays, Poems, Letters and Travels. I doubt not our Author took occasion to mention him in respect to the Poem of Mr. *Dryden*, to which this bears some resemblance; tho' of a character more different from it than that of the *Æneid* from the *Iliad*, or the *Lutrin* of *Boileau* from the *Defaite des Bouts rimeès* of *Sarazin*.

3. *Or that, where on her* Curls *etc.*] *Edm. Curl* stood in the Pillory at *Charing-Cross*, in *March*, 1727–8.

N.B. Mr. *Curl* loudly complain'd of this Note as an Untruth, protesting 'that he stood in the Pillory not in *March* but in *February*'; And of another on Verse 144. Saying, 'he was not tost in a Blanket, but a *Rug.*' *Curliad* in 12°. 1729. *pag.* 19 and 25. ⟨See p. 429.⟩

4. *grains* ⟨The refuse malt left after brewing. By 'golden show'rs' Pope no doubt intends to suggest the yolk of rotten eggs.⟩

The conscious simper, and the jealous leer,
Mix on his look. All eyes direct their rays
On him, and crowds grow foolish as they gaze.
Not with more glee, by hands Pontific crown'd,
With scarlet hats, wide waving, circled round,   10
Rome in her Capitol saw Querno sit,
Thron'd on sev'n hills, the Antichrist of Wit.

    To grace this honour'd day, the Queen proclaims
By herald hawkers, high, heroic Games.
She summons all her sons: An endless band   15
Pours forth, and leaves unpeopled half the land;
A motley mixture! in long wigs, in bags,
In silks, in crapes, in garters, and in rags;
From drawing rooms, from colleges, from garrets,
On horse, on foot, in hacks, and gilded chariots,   20
All who true dunces in her cause appear'd,
And all who knew those dunces to reward.

    Amid that Area wide she took her stand,
Where the tall May-pole once o'erlook'd the Strand;
But now, so ANNE and Piety ordain,   25
A Church collects the saints of Drury-lane.

    With Authors, Stationers obey'd the call,
The field of glory is a field for all;
Glory, and gain, th' industrious tribe provoke;
And gentle Dulness ever loves a joke: 30
A Poet's form she plac'd before their eyes,

11. Querno] *Camillo Querno* was of *Apulia*, who hearing the great
encouragement which *Leo* the tenth gave to Poets, travelled to *Rome* with
a Harp in his hand, and sung to it twenty thousand verses of a Poem called
Alexias. He was introduced as a Buffoon to *Leo*, and promoted to the
honour of the Laurel; a jest, which the Court of *Rome* and the Pope
himself entred into so far, as to hold a solemn Festival on his Coronation,
at which it is recorded the Poet himself was so transported, as to weep for
joy. He was ever after a constant frequenter of the Pope's Table, drank
abundantly, and poured forth verses without number. P A U L U S J O V I U S,
Elog. Vir. doct. ch. 72. Some idea of his Poetry is given us by *Fam. Strada*
in his Prolusions. ⟨For further details about Camillo Querno, see 'Of the
Poet Laureate,' p. 802 f.⟩
    14. *hawkers* ⟨The 'hawker' frequently cried newspapers and news in
the streets.⟩
    17. *bags* ⟨i.e. bag-wigs, in which the hair was enclosed in an orna-
mental bag.⟩
    27. *Stationers* ⟨i.e. booksellers.⟩
    31. *A Poet's Form &c.*] This is what *Juno* does to deceive *Turnus, Æn.*
10 ⟨636-40⟩.

            Tum dea nube cava, tenuem sine viribus umbram,
            In faciem Æneæ (*visu mirabile monstrum*)

And bad the nimblest racer seize the prize;
No meagre, muse-rid mope, adust and thin,
In a dun night-gown of his own loose skin,
But such a bulk as no twelve bards could raise,   35
Twelve starveling bards of these degen'rate days.
All as a partridge plump, full-fed, and fair,
She form'd this image of well-bodied air,
With pert flat eyes she window'd well its head,
A brain of feathers, and a heart of lead,   40
And empty words she gave, and sounding strain,
But senseless, lifeless! Idol void and vain!
Never was dash'd out, at one lucky hit,
A Fool, so just a copy of a Wit;
So like, that criticks said and courtiers swore,   45
A wit it was, and call'd the phantom, More.

Dardaniis ornat telis, clypeumque jubasque
Divini assimilat capitis——Dat inania verba,
Dat sine mente sonum——

The Reader will observe how exactly some of these verses suit with their allegorical application here to a Plagiary. There seems to me a great propriety in this Episode, where such an one is imag'd by a phantom that deludes the grasp of the expecting Bookseller.

33. *adust*] ⟨i.e. atrabilious, sallow.⟩

35. *But such a bulk etc.*] *Virg.* ⟨*Aen.* xii, 899–900⟩
Vix illud lecti bis sex—
Qualia nunc hominum producit corpora tellus.

43. *Never was dash'd out, &c.*] Our author here seems willing to give some account of the possibility of *Dulness* making a *Wit*, (which could be done no other way than by *chance.*) The fiction is the more reconcil'd to probability by the known story of *Apelles*, who being at a loss to express the foam of *Alexander's* horse, dash'd his pencil in despair at the picture, and happen'd to do it by that fortunate stroke.

46. *And call'd the phantom*, More] CURL in his Key to the *Dunciad*, affirm'd this to be *James Moore Smyth*, Esq; and it is probable (considering what is said of him in the Testimonies) that some might fancy our author obliged to represent this gentleman as a Plagiary, or to pass for one himself. His case indeed was like that of a man I have heard of, who as he was sitting in company, perceived his next neighbour had stollen his handkerchief. 'Sir' (said the Thief, finding himself detected) 'do not expose me, I did it for mere want: be so good but to take it privately out of my pocket again, and say nothing.' The honest man did so, but the other cry'd out, 'See Gentlemen! what a Thief we have among us! look, he is stealing my handkerchief'.

Some time before, he had borrowed of Dr. *Arbuthnot* a paper call'd an Historico-physical account of the *South-Sea*; and of Mr. *Pope* the Memoirs of a Parish Clark, which for two years he kept, and read to the Rev. Dr. *Young*, — *Billers*, Esq; and many others, as his own. Being apply'd to for them, he pretended they were lost; but there happening to be another copy of the latter, it came out in *Swift* and *Pope's* Miscellanies. Upon this, it seems he was so far mistaken as to confess his proceeding by

All gaze with ardour: some, a Poet's name,
Others, a sword-knot and lac'd suit inflame.
But lofty Lintot in the circle rose;

---

an endeavour to hide it: unguardedly printing (in the *Daily Journal* of
Apr. 3. 1728.) 'That the contempt which he and others had for those
pieces' (which only himself had shown, and handed about as his own)
'occasion'd their being lost, and for that cause only, not return'd.' A fact,
of which as none but he could be conscious, none but he could be the
publisher of it. The Plagiarisms of this person gave occasion to the
following Epigram

> M—re *always smiles whenever he recites;*
> *He smiles (you think) approving what he writes;*
> *And yet in this no Vanity is shown;*
> *A modest man may like what's not his own.*

This young Gentleman's whole misfortune was too inordinate a passion
to be thought a Wit. Here is a very strong instance, attested by Mr.
Savage son of the late Earl *Rivers*; who having shown some verses of his
in manuscript to Mr. *Moore*, wherein Mr. *Pope* was call'd *first of the
tuneful train*, Mr. *Moore* the next morning sent to Mr. *Savage* to desire
him to give those verses another turn, to wit, 'That *Pope* might now be the
first, because *Moore* had left him unrival'd in turning his style to Comedy.'
This was during the rehearsal of the *Rival Modes*, his first and only work;
the Town condemn'd it in the action, but he printed it in 1726–7 with this
modest Motto,

Hic cæstus, artemque repono.

The smaller pieces which we have heard attributed to this author, are,
An Epigram on the Bridge at *Blenheim*, by Dr. *Evans*; *Cosmelia*, by Mr.
Pit, Mr. *Jones*, &c. The Mock-marriage of a mad Divine, with a Cl— for
a Parson, by Dr. *W.* ⟨i.e. Dr. Wagstaff?⟩. The Saw-pit, a Simile, by a
Friend. ⟨The italics here possibly indicate that Dr. Robert Freind (1667–
1751) is intended.⟩ Certain Physical works on Sir *James Baker*; and
some unown'd Letters, Advertisements and Epigrams against our author
in the *Daily Journal.* ⟨See 'A List of Books, Papers . . .' p. 435. For Sir
James Baker, see below, ii 279*n*.⟩

Nothwithstanding what is here collected of the Person imagin'd by
Curl to be meant in this place, we cannot be of that opinion; since our
Poet had certainly no need of vindicating half a dozen verses to himself
which every reader had done for him; since the name itself is not spell'd
Moore but *More*; and lastly, since the learned *Scriblerus* has so well
prov'd the contrary.

46. *The Phantom,* More] It appears from hence that this is not the
name of a real person, but fictitious; *More* from μωρός, *stultus,* μωρία,
stultitia, to represent the folly of a Plagiary. Thus *Erasmus: Admonuit me*
Mori *cognomen tibi, quod tam ad* Moriæ *vocabulum accedit quam es ipse a
re alienus.* Dedication of *Moriæ Encomion* to Sir *Tho. More*; the Farewell
of which may be our Author's to his Plagiary. *Vale* More! & *Moriam
tuam gnaviter defende. Adieu* More, *and be sure strongly to defend thy own
folly.* Scriblerus.

48. *sword-knot* ⟨A foppish adornment, such as a ribbon or tassel, to
the sword.⟩

49. *But lofty* Lintot] We enter here upon the episode of the Booksellers:
persons, whose names being more known and famous in the learned

'This prize is mine; who tempt it, are my foes: 50
With me began this genius, and shall end.'
He spoke, and who with Lintot shall contend?
    Fear held them mute. Alone untaught to fear,
Stood dauntless Curl, 'Behold that rival here!

---

world than those of the authors in this Poem, do therefore need less explanation. The action of Mr. *Lintot* here imitates that of *Dares* in *Virgil* ⟨*Aen.*, v 381 ff.⟩, rising just in this manner to lay hold on a *Bull*. This eminent Bookseller printed the *Rival Modes* above-mentioned.

54, *&c.*] Something like this is in *Homer, Il.* 10. *ver.* 220. of *Diomed.* Two different manners of the same author in his Similes, are also imitated in the two following; the first of the Bailiff, is short, unadorn'd, and (as the Critics well know) from *familiar life*; the second of the Water-fowl more extended, picturesque, and from *rural life*. The 55th verse is likewise a literal translation of one in *Homer*.

54. *Stood dauntless* Curl, *&c.*] We come now to a character of much respect, that of Mr. *Edmond Curl*. As a plain repetition of great actions is the best praise of them, we shall only say of this eminent man, that he carried the Trade many lengths beyond what it ever before had arrived at, and that he was the envy and admiration of all his profession. He possest himself of a command over all authors whatever; he caus'd them to write what he pleas'd; they could not call their very names their own. He was not only famous among these; he was taken notice of by the *State*, the *Church*, and the *Law*, and received particular marks of distinction from each.

It will be own'd that he is here introduc'd with all possible dignity: he speaks like the intrepid *Diomed*; he runs like the swift-footed *Achilles*; if he falls, 'tis like the beloved *Nisus*; and (what *Homer* makes to be the chief of all praises) he is *favour'd of the Gods:* He says but three words, and his prayer is heard; a Goddess conveys it to the seat of *Jupiter*. Tho' he loses the prize, he gains the victory; the great Mother her self comforts him, she inspires him with expedients, she honours him with an immortal present (such as *Achilles* receives from *Thetis* and *Æneas* from *Venus*) at once instructive and prophetical: After this, he is unrival'd and triumphant.

The tribute our author here pays him, is a grateful return for several unmerited obligations: Many weighty animadversions on the Publick affairs, and many excellent and diverting pieces on Private persons, has he given to his name. If ever he ow'd two verses to any other, he ow'd Mr. *Curl* some thousands. He was every day extending his fame, and inlarging his writings: witness innumerable instances! but it shall suffice only to mention the *Court-Poems*, which he meant to publish as the work of the true writer, a Lady of quality; but being first threaten'd, and afterwards punish'd, for it by Mr. *Pope*, he generously transferr'd it from *her* to *him*, and has now printed it twelve years in his name. The single time that ever he spoke to *C.* was on that affair, and to that happy incident he owes all the favours since received from him. So true is the saying of Dr. *Sydenham*, that 'any one shall be, at some time or other, the better or the worse, for having but *seen* or *spoken* to a good, or a bad man.' ⟨Curll published *Court Poems* on March 23, 1716. In the Advertisement the reader is given to understand that they may be the work either of 'a LADY of Quality' (i.e. Lady Mary Wortley Montagu), or of 'Mr. GAY,' or of 'the Judicious

The race by vigor, not by vaunts is won;   55
So take the hindmost Hell.'—He said, and run.
Swift as a bard the bailiff leaves behind,
He left huge Lintot, and out-stript the wind.
As when a dab-chick waddles thro' the copse,
On feet and wings, and flies, and wades, and hops; 60
So lab'ring on, with shoulders, hands, and head,
Wide as a windmill all his figure spread,
With legs expanded Bernard urg'd the race,
And seem'd to emulate great Jacob's pace.
Full in the middle way there stood a lake,   65
Which Curl's Corinna chanc'd that morn to make,
(Such was her wont, at early dawn to drop
Her evening cates before his neighbour's shop,)
Here fortun'd Curl to slide; loud shout the band,
And Bernard! Bernard! rings thro' all the Strand. 70

Translator of HOMER' (i.e. Pope). The publication was unauthorized. Pope's reply was the famous emetic administered to Curll.⟩
56. *So take the hindmost Hell*] *Horace de Art.* ⟨417⟩.

> *Occupet extremum scabies; mihi turpe relinqui est.*

60. *On feet, and wings, &c.*] Milton ⟨*Par. Lost,* ii 947–50⟩,

> ——*So eagerly the fiend*
> *O'er bog, o'er steep, thro' strait, rough, dense, or rare,*
> *With head, hands, wings, or feet, pursues his way,*
> *And swims, or sinks, or wades, or creeps, or flies.*

66. Curl's Corinna] This name it seems was taken by one Mrs. *T——* ⟨i.e. Thomas⟩, who procured some private Letters of Mr. *Pope*'s, while almost a boy, to Mr. *Cromwell,* and sold them without the consent of either of those gentlemen to *Curl,* who printed them in 12° 1727. He has discover'd her to be the publisher in his *Key,* p. 11. But our Poet had no thought of reflecting on her in this passage; on the contrary, he has been inform'd she is a decent woman and in misfortunes. We only take this opportunity of mentioning the manner in which those Letters got abroad, which the author was asham'd of as very trivial things, full not only of levities, but of wrong judgments of men and books, and only excusable from the youth and inexperience of the writer. ⟨Curll justified his publication of the letters on the grounds that 'Mr. *Cromwell* made a free present of them to the Gentlewoman . . . and when she had an Inclination to dispose of them otherwise, I see no reason she had to ask either Mr. *Cromwell*'s or Mr. *Pope*'s leave for so doing.'⟩

69. *Here fortun'd* Curl *to slide*] *Virg. Æn.* 5. ⟨329–30, 333⟩ of *Nisus.*

> *Labitur infelix, cæsis ut forte juvencis*
> *Fusus humum viridesq; super madefecerat herbas—*
> *Concidit, immundoque fimo, sacroque cruore.*

70. *And* Bernard, Bernard] *Virg.* Ecl. 6. ⟨44⟩
> —*Ut littus, Hyla, Hyla, omne sonaret.*

Obscene with filth the Miscreant lies bewray'd,
Fal'n in the plash his wickedness had lay'd;
Then first (if Poets aught of truth declare)
The caitiff Vaticide conceiv'd a prayer.
   'Hear Jove! whose name my bards and I adore,   75
As much at least as any God's, or more;
And him and his if more devotion warms,
Down with the Bible, up with the Pope's Arms.'
   A place there is, betwixt earth, air and seas,
Where from Ambrosia, Jove retires for ease.   80
There in his seat two spacious Vents appear,
On this he sits, to that he leans his ear,
And hears the various Vows of fond mankind,
Some beg an eastern, some a western wind:
All vain petitions, mounting to the sky,   85
With reams abundant this abode supply;

71. *Obscene with filth,* &c.] Tho' this incident may seem too low and base for the dignity of an Epic Poem, the learned very well know it to be but a copy of *Homer* and *Virgil*; the very words ὄνθος and *Fimus* are used by them, tho' our Poet (in compliance to modern nicety) has remarkably enrich'd and colour'd his language, as well as rais'd the versification, in these two Episodes. Mr. *Dryden* in *Mac-Fleckno* has not scrupled to mention the *Morning Toast* at which the fishes bite in the *Thames, Pissing Ally, Reliques of the Bum, Whipstich, Kiss my* ——, &c. but our author is more grave, and (as a fine writer ⟨Addison⟩ says of *Virgil* in his *Georgics*) *tosses about his* Dung *with an air of Majesty.* If we consider that the Exercises of his *Authors* could with justice be no higher than *Tickling, Chatt'ring, Braying,* or *Diving,* it was no easy matter to invent such Games as were proportion'd to the meaner degree of *Booksellers.* In *Homer* and *Virgil, Ajax* and *Nisus,* the persons drawn in this plight are *Heroes*; whereas here they are such, with whom it had been great impropriety to have join'd any but vile ideas; besides the natural connection there is, between Libellers and common Nusances. Nevertheless I have often heard our author own, that this part of his Poem was (as it frequently happens) what cost him most trouble, and pleas'd him least: but that he hoped 'twas excusable, since levell'd at such as understand no delicate satire: Thus the politest men are sometimes obliged to *swear,* when they happen to have to do with Porters and Oyster-wenches.

74. *Vaticide* ⟨The poet was often called *vates.* Curll was a vaticide because he was a murderer of poets, either by paying them too little, or by producing inaccurate editions of their works.⟩

78. *the* Bible, *the* Pope's Arms] The Bible, *Curl's* sign, the Cross-keys, *Lintot's.*

79. See *Lucian's Icaro-Menippus;* where this Fiction is more extended. *A place there is, betwixt earth, air and seas*] Ovid Met. 12 ⟨39–40⟩.

      Orbe locus medio est, inter terrasq; fretumq;
      Cœlestesq; plagas——

Amus'd he reads, and then returns the bills
Sign'd with that Ichor which from Gods distills.
    In office here fair Cloacina stands,
And ministers to Jove with purest hands;   90
Forth from the heap she pick'd her Vot'ry's pray'r,
And plac'd it next him, a distinction rare!
Oft, as he fish'd her nether realms for wit,
The Goddess favour'd him, and favours yet.
Renew'd by ordure's sympathetic force,   95
As oil'd with magic juices for the course,
Vig'rous he rises; from th' effluvia strong
Imbibes new life, and scours and stinks along,
Re-passes Lintot, vindicates the race,
Nor heeds the brown dishonours of his face.   100
    And now the Victor stretch'd his eager hand
Where the tall Nothing stood, or seem'd to stand;
A shapeless shade! it melted from his sight,
Like forms in clouds, or visions of the night!
To seize his papers, Curl, was next thy care;   105
His papers light, fly diverse, tost in air:
Songs, sonnets, epigrams the winds uplift,

88. Alludes to *Homer, Iliad* 5.
                    —ῥέε δ' ἄμβροτον αἷμα θέοιο,
        'Ιχὼρ οἷος πέρ τε ῥέει μακάρεσσι θεοῖσιν.
        A stream of nectarous humour issuing flow'd,
        Sanguin, such as celestial Spirits may bleed.
                              Milton ⟨*Par. Lost*, vi 332–3⟩.
89. *Cloacina*] The *Roman* Goddess of the Common-shores.
93. *Oft as he fish'd*, &c.] See the Preface to *Swift* and *Pope*'s Miscellanies. ⟨'It has been humourously said, that some have fished the very
Jakes, for Papers left there by Men of Wit . . .' *Miscellanies in Prose and
Verse*, 1727, i 12.⟩
96. *As oil'd with magic juices*] Alluding to the opinion that there are
Ointments us'd by Witches to enable them to fly in the air, &c.
100. *the brown dishonours*] *Virg. Æn.* 5 ⟨357–8⟩.
                    ——*faciem ostentabat, & udo*
        Turpia membra fimo——
103. *A shapeless shade*, &c.] *Virg. Æn.* 6 ⟨701–2⟩.
                    ——*Effugit imago*
        Par levibus ventis, volucrique simillima somno.
105. *To seize his papers* ⟨Cf. Pope's note to ii 66.⟩
106. *His papers light*, &c.] *Virg.* ⟨*Aen.*, vi 74–5⟩ of the Sybil's leaves,
        Carmina—turbata volent rapidis Ludibria Ventis.
The persons mentioned in the next line are some of those, whose Writings, Epigrams or Jests, he had own'd.
107. *sonnets* ⟨i.e. short poems.⟩

And whisk 'em back to Evans, Young, and Swift.
Th' embroider'd Suit, at least, he deem'd his prey;
That suit, an unpaid Taylor snatch'd away!   110
No rag, no scrap, of all the beau, or wit,
That once so flutter'd, and that once so writ.

    Heav'n rings with laughter: Of the laughter vain,
Dulness, good Queen, repeats the jest again.
Three wicked imps of her own Grubstreet Choir   115
She deck'd like Congreve, Addison, and Prior;
Mears, Warner, Wilkins run: Delusive thought!
Breval, Besaleel, Bond, the Varlets caught.

108. *Evans* ⟨Abel Evans (1679–1737) clergyman and minor poet.
110. *An unpaid Taylor*] This line has been loudly complain'd of (in *Mist, June* 8 ⟨1728⟩. *Dedic. to Sawney* ⟨by James Ralph⟩, and others) as a most inhuman satire on the *Poverty* of *Poets*: but it is thought our author would be acquitted by a Jury of *Taylors*. To me this instance seems unluckily chosen; if it be a satire on any body, it must be on a bad PAYMASTER, since the person they have here apply'd it to was a man of Fortune. ⟨Moore Smythe had run through his fortune by 1727, and was unable to meet his creditors. Pope *is*, in fact, sneering at his poverty. The printing of 'PAYMASTER' in capitals is accounted for by the fact that his grandfather, William Smythe, paymaster of the band of Gentlemen-Pensioners, had obtained for him the reversion to this place on condition that he assumed the additional name of Smythe.⟩ Not but Poets may well be jealous of so great a prerogative as *Non-payment:* which Mr. *Dennis* so far asserts as boldly to pronounce, that 'if *Homer* himself was not in debt, it was because no body would trust him.' (*Pref. to Rem. on the Rape of the Lock, p.* 15.)
116. *Like* Congreve, Addison, *and* Prior] These Authors being such whose names will reach posterity, we shall not give any account of them, but proceed to those of whom it is necessary. ——*Besaleel Morris* was author of some Satyrs on the Translators of *Homer* (Mr. *Tickel* and our author) with many other things printed in News-papers.—*Bond* writ a Satyr against Mr. *P.*—Capt. *Breval* was author of *The Confederates*, an ingenious dramatic performance, to expose Mr. *P.* Mr. *Gay*, Dr. *Arb.* and some Ladies of quality. CURL, *Key*, p. 11.
117. *Mears, Warner, Wilkins*] Booksellers and Printers of much anonymous stuff.
118. *Breval, Besaleel, Bond*] I foresee it will be objected from this line, that we were in an error in our assertion on verse 46. of this Book, that *More* was a fictitious name, since these persons are equally represented by the Poet as phantoms. So at first sight it may seem; but be not deceived, Reader! these also are not real persons. 'Tis true *Curl* declares *Breval* a Captain, author of a Libel call'd *The Confederates:* But the same *Curl* first said it was written by *Joseph Gay:* Is his second assertion to be credited any more than his first? He likewise affirms *Bond* to be one who writ a Satire on our Poet; but where is such a Satire to be found? where was such a Writer ever heard of? As for *Besaleel*, it carries Forgery in the very name, nor is it, as the others are, a surname. Thou may'st depend on it no such authors ever lived: All phantoms! SCRIBLERUS.

Curl stretches after Gay, but Gay is gone,
He grasps an empty Joseph for a John!   120
So Proteus, hunted in a nobler shape,
Became when seiz'd, a Puppy, or an Ape.
　　To him the Goddess. 'Son! thy grief lay down,
And turn this whole illusion on the town.
As the sage dame, experienc'd in her trade,   125
By names of Toasts retails each batter'd jade,
(Whence hapless Monsieur much complains at Paris
Of wrongs from Duchesses and Lady Mary's)
Be thine, my stationer! this magic gift;
Cook shall be Prior, and Concanen, Swift;   130

120. *Joseph Gay*, a fictitious name put by *Curl* before several pamphlets, which made them pass with many for Mr. *Gay*'s. ⟨'Joseph Gay' first appeared in 1716, when the name was used to conceal the authorship of a poem, *The Hoop-Petticoat*, by Francis Chute. Later, J. D. Breval's *The Confederates* (1717) was said to be by Joseph Gay; and several other compositions published in 1718-19 were attributed to this imaginary author.⟩

124. *And turn this whole illusion &c.*] It was a common practice of this Bookseller, to publish vile pieces of obscure hands under the names of eminent authors.

127-8. *hapless Monsieur . . . Lady Mary's* ⟨See *Sober Advice*, l. 53*n*, p. 669.⟩

130. Cook *shall be* Prior] The man here specify'd was the son of a *Muggletonian*, who kept a Publick-house at *Braintree* in *Essex*. He writ a thing call'd *The Battle of Poets* ⟨1725⟩, of which *Philips* and *Welsted* were the heroes, and wherein our author attack'd in his moral character, in relation to his *Homer* and *Shakespear:* He writ moreover a Farce of *Penelope*, in the preface of which also he was squinted at: ⟨*Penelope, A Dramatic Opera* (1728) was the joint work of Cooke and John Mottley (1692-1750)⟩ and some malevolent things in the *British, London* and *Daily Journals*. At the same time the honest Gentleman wrote Letters to Mr. *P.* in the strongest terms protesting his innocence. His chief work was a translation of *Hesiod*, to which *Theobald* writ notes, and half-notes, as hath already been said.

And Concanen, Swift] *Matthew Concanen*, an *Irishman*, an anonymous slanderer, and publisher of other men's slanders, particularly on Dr. *Swift* to whom he had obligations, and from whom he had received both in a collection of Poems for his benefit and otherwise, no small assistance; To which *Smedley* (one of his brethren in enmity to *Swift*) alludes in his *Metam.* of *Scriblerus*, p. 7. accusing him of having 'boasted of what he had not written, but others had revis'd and done for him.' He was also author of several scurrilities in the *British* and *London Journals*; and of a pamphlet call'd a *Supplement* to the *Profund*, wherein he deals very unfairly with our Poet, not only frequently blaming Mr. *Broome*'s verses as his, (for which he might indeed seem in some degree accountable, having corrected what that gentleman did) but those of the Duke of *Buckingham*, and others. To this rare piece, some-body humorously caus'd him to take for his motto, *De profundis clamavi.*

He was since a hired Scribler in the *Daily Courant*, where he pour'd

So shall each hostile name become our own,
And we too boast our Garth and Addison.'
   With that she gave him (piteous of his case,
Yet smiling at his ruful length of face)

forth much Billingsgate against the Lord Bolingbroke and others; after
which this man was surprizingly promoted to administer Justice and Law
in Jamaica.

132. *And we too boast our* Garth *and* Addison] Nothing is more remarkable than our author's love of praising good writers. He has celebrated Sir
Isaac Newton, Mr. *Dryden*, Mr. *Congreve*, Mr. *Wycherley*, Dr. *Garth*, Mr.
Walsh, Duke of *Buckingham*, Mr. *Addison*, Lord *Lansdown*; in a word,
almost every man of his time that deserv'd it. It was very difficult to have
that pleasure in a poem on This subject, yet he found means to insert their
panegyrick, and here has made even Dulness out of her own mouth
pronounce it. It must have been particularly agreeable to him to celebrate
Dr. *Garth*; both as his constant friend thro' life, and as he was his predecessor in this kind. of Satire. The *Dispensary* attack'd the whole Body
of Apothecaries, a much more useful one undoubtedly than that of the
bad Poets (if in truth this can be call'd a Body, of which no two members
ever agreed). It also did what *Tibbald* says is unpardonable, drew in *parts
of private character*, and introduced *persons independent of his Subject*.
Much more would *Boileau* have incurr'd his censure, who left all subjects
whatever on all occasions, to fall upon the bad Poets; which it is to be
fear'd wou'd have been more immediately His concern.

But certainly next to commending good Writers, the greatest service to
learning is to expose the bad, who can only that one way be made of any
use to it. This truth is very well set forth in these lines, addrest to our
Author.

> *The craven Rook, and pert Jackdaw,*
>   *(Tho' neither Birds of moral kind)*
> *Yet serve, if hang'd, or stuff'd with straw,*
>   *To show us, which way blows the wind.*
> *Thus dirty Knaves or chatt'ring Fools,*
>   *Strung up by dozens in thy Lay,*
> *Teach more by half than* Dennis' *rules*
>   *And point Instruction ev'ry way.*
> *With* Egypt's *art thy pen may strive*
>   *One potent drop let this but shed,*
> *And ev'ry Rogue that stunk alive*
>   *Becomes a precious Mummy dead.*

133. ——*piteous of his case,*
      Yet smiling at his ruful length of face]

Virg. Æn. 5 ⟨358; 350–1⟩.

> ——*Risit pater optimus illi.*
> *Me liceat casum miserari insontis amici——*
> *Sic fatus, tergum Gætuli immane leonis,* &c.

134. *Ruful length of face*] 'The decrepid person or figure of a man are no
reflections upon his *Genius:* An honest mind will love and esteem a *man
of worth*, tho' he be deform'd or poor. Yet the author of the Dunciad hath
libell'd a person for his *ruful length of face!'* MIST'S JOURN. *June* 8. This
Genius and *man of worth* whom an honest mind should love, is Mr. *Curl*.
True it is, he stood in the Pillory; an accident which will lengthen the face

of any man tho' it were ever so comely, therefore is no reflection on the natural beauty of Mr. *Curl.* But as to reflections on any man's Face, or Figure, Mr. *Dennis* saith excellently; 'Natural deformity comes not by our fault, 'tis often occasioned by calamities and diseases, which a man can no more help, than a monster can his deformity. There is no one misfortune, and no one disease, but what all the rest of men are subject to.——But the deformity of this Author ⟨viz. Pope⟩ is visible, present, lasting, unalterable, and peculiar to himself: it is the mark of God and Nature upon him, to give us warning that we should hold no society with him, as a creature not of our original, nor of our species: And they who have refused to take this warning which God and Nature have given them, and have in spite of it by a senseless presumption, ventur'd to be familiar with him, have severely suffer'd, *&c.* 'Tis certain his original is not from *Adam,* but from the Devil,' *&c.* DENNIS *and* GILDON : *Charact. of Mr.* P. 8°. 1716.

It is admirably observ'd by Mr. *Dennis* against Mr. *Law* ⟨*The Stage Defended,* 1726⟩, p. 33. 'That the language of *Billingsgate* can never be the language of Charity, nor consequently of Christianity.' I should else be tempted to use the language of a Critick: For what is more provoking to a Commentator, than to behold his author thus pourtrayed? Yet I consider it really hurts not *Him*; whereas maliciously to call some *others* dull, might do them prejudice with a world too apt to believe it. Therefore tho' Mr. *D.* may call another a *little ass* or a *young toad,* far be it from us to call him a *toothless lion,* or an *old serpent.* Indeed, had I written these notes (as was once my intent) in the learned language, I might have given him the appellations of *Balatro, Calceatum caput,* or *Scurra in triviis,* being phrases in good esteem, ond frequent usage among the best learned: But in our mother-tongue were I to tax any Gentleman of the Dunciad, surely it should be in wards not to the vulgar intelligible, whereby christian charity, decency, and good accord among authors, might be preserved. SCRIBLERUS.

The good *Scriblerus* here, as on all occasions, eminently shows his Humanity. But it was far otherwise with the Gentlemen of the Dunciad, whose scurrilities were always Personal: They went so far as to libel an eminent Sculptor for making our author's *Busto* in marble, at the request of Mr. *Gibbs* the Architect: which Rhimes had the undeserv'd honour to be answer'd in an *Impromptu* by the Earl of B——

> *Well, Sir, suppose, the* Busto's *a damn'd head,*
> *Suppose, that* Pope's *an Elf;*
> *All he can say for't is, he neither made*
> *The* Busto *nor* Himself.

And by another Person of Quality,

> Rysbrake, *to make a* Pope *of Stone,*
> *Must labour hard and sore;*
> *But it would cost him labour none,*
> *To make a Stone of* Moor.

⟨John Michael Rysbrack (1693–1770) came to England in 1720 from Holland, and soon established himself as a favourite sculptor.—The 'Moor' of the second epigram is James Moore Smythe.⟩ Their Scurrilities were of that nature as provoked every honest man but Mr. *Pope,* yet never to be lamented, since they occasion'd the following amiable Verses ⟨by D. Lewis (1683?–1760).⟩

> *While Malice,* Pope, *denies thy page*
> *It's own celestial Fire;*

A shaggy Tap'stry, worthy to be spread   135
On Codrus' old, or Dunton's modern bed;
Instructive work! whose wry-mouth'd portraiture
Display'd the fates her confessors endure.

While Critics, and while Bards in rage
  Admiring won't admire;

While wayward Pens thy worth assail,
  And envious Tongues decry,
These Times tho' many a Friend bewail,
  These Times bewail not I.

But when the World's loud Praise is thine,
  And Spleen no more shall blame,
When with thy Homer *Thou shalt shine*
  In one establish'd Fame,

When none shall rail, and ev'ry Lay
  Devote a Wreath to Thee;
That Day (for come it will) that Day
  Shall I lament to see.

135. *A shaggy Tap'stry*] A sorry kind of Tapestry frequent in old Inns, made of worsted or some coarser stuff: like that which is spoken of by Doctor *Donne* ⟨Satire iv, 225–6. Cf. also *E. on C.*, 587 (p. 162)⟩— *Faces as frightful as theirs who whip Christ in old hangings.* The imagery woven in it alludes to the mantle of *Cloanthus* in *Æn.* 5. ⟨250–7.⟩

136. *On* Codrus' *old, or* Dunton's *modern bed*] Of *Codrus* the Poet's bed see *Juvenal*, describing his *poverty* very copiously. *Sat.* 3. *v.* 203, *&c.*

  Lectus erat Codro, &c.
  Codrus *had but one bed, so short to boot,*
  That his short Wife's short legs hung dangling out:
  His cupboard's head six earthen pitchers grac'd,
  Beneath them was his trusty tankard plac'd;
  And to support this noble Plate, there lay
  A bending Chiron, cast from honest clay.
  His few Greek *books a rotten chest contain'd,*
  Whose covers much of mouldiness complain'd,
  Where mice and rats devour'd poetic bread,
  And on Heroic Verse luxuriously were fed.
  'Tis true, poor Codrus *nothing had to boast,*
  And yet poor Codrus *all that nothing lost.*
                                                    Dryd.

But Mr. C⟨oncanen⟩ in his dedication of the Letters, Advertisements. *&c.* to the Author of the *Dunciad*, assures us, that '*Juvenal* never satyrized the poverty of *Codrus.*'

John Dunton was a broken Bookseller and abusive scribler: he writ *Neck or Nothing* ⟨1713⟩, a violent satyr on some Ministers of State; *The danger of a death-bed repentance*, a libel on the late Duke of *Devonshire* and on the Rt. Rev. Bishop of *Peterborough.* &c.

138. *confessors* ⟨Accented by Pope, as by Shakespeare, on the first syllable.⟩

Earless on high, stood un-abash'd Defoe,
And Tutchin flagrant from the scourge, below: 140
There Ridpath, Roper, cudgell'd might ye view;
The very worsted still look'd black and blue:
Himself among the storied Chiefs he spies,
As from the blanket high in air he flies,
'And oh! (he cry'd,) what street, what lane, but knows
Our purgings, pumpings, blanketings and blows?   146
In ev'ry loom our labours shall be seen,
And the fresh vomit run for ever green!'
    See in the circle next, Eliza plac'd;

140. Tutchin] *John Tutchin*, author of some vile verses, and of a weekly
paper call'd the *Observator:* He was sentenc'd to be whipp'd thro' several
towns in the west of *England*, upon which he petition'd King *James* II. to
be hanged. When that Prince died in exile, he wrote an invective against
his memory, occasioned by some humane Elegies on his death. He liv'd to
the time of Queen *Anne.* ⟨Tutchin, a stubborn Whig, died in 1707, after
being attacked in the street by ruffians. He published in 1685 *Poems on
several Occasions* (the 'vile verses'), and 1701 the invective to which Pope
alludes: *The British Muse: or Tyranny exposed. A Satire; occasioned by all
the fulsome and lying Poems and Elegies that have been written on the Death
of the late King James.*⟩

141. Ridpath, Roper] Authors of the *Flying-Post* and *Post-Boy*, two
scandalous papers on different sides, for which they equally and alternately were cudgell'd, and deserv'd it. ⟨They died within one day of
each other on Feb. 5 and Feb. 6, 1726. George Ridpath was proprietor of
the Whig *Flying Post*, Abel Roper of the Tory *Post-Boy*⟩.

143. *Himself among the storied chiefs he spies,* &c.] Virg. Æn. 1 ⟨488;
459–60⟩.

> *Se quoq; principibus permixtum agnovit Achivis—*
> *Constitit & lacrymans: Quis jam locus, inquit, Achate!*
> *Quæ regio in terris nostri non plena laboris?*

143. *Himself . . . he spies,* &c.] The history of *Curl's* being toss'd in a
blanket, and whipp'd by the scholars of *Westminster*, is ingeniously and
pathetically related in a poem entituled *Neck or Nothing.* ⟨By Samuel
Wesley the Younger, then head usher of Westminster School. In 1716
Curll had published, without authority, a volume which he called *The
Posthumous Works of Dr. South*, and had included in it a funeral oration
in Latin, spoken by John Barber, Captain of the School, and son of the
famous Alderman Barber, the printer. For this offence he was tossed in a
blanket by the Westminster boys, made to apologize to young Barber, and
finally kicked out of the School Yard amid 'the Huzza's of the Rabble.'⟩
Of his purging and vomiting, see *A full and true account of a horrid
revenge on the body of* Edm. Curl, *&c.* ⟨in the 3d. vol. of Swift and Pope's
Miscellanies.⟩

148. *And the fresh vomit &c.*] A parody on these of a late noble author
⟨Lord Halifax, *Epistle to Lord Dorset*⟩,

> *His bleeding arm had furnish'd all their rooms,*
> *And run for ever purple in the looms.*

149. *See in the circle next,* Eliza *plac'd*] In this game is expos'd in the
most contemptuous manner, the profligate licenciousness of those shame-

I'wo babes of love close clinging to her waste; 150
Fair as before her works she stands confess'd,
In flow'rs and pearls by bounteous Kirkall dress'd.
The Goddess then: 'Who best can send on high
The salient spout, far-streaming to the sky;
His be yon Juno of majestic size, 155
With cow-like-udders, and with ox-like eyes.
This China-Jordan, let the chief o'ercome
Replenish, not ingloriously, at home.'
Chetwood and Curl accept the glorious strife,
(Tho' one his son dissuades, and one his wife) 160

less scriblers (for the most part of That sex, which ought least to be capable of such malice or impudence) who in libellous Memoirs and Novels,
reveal the faults and misfortunes of both sexes, to the ruin or disturbance,
of publick fame or private happiness. Our good Poet, (by the whole cast of
his work being obliged not to take off the Irony) where he cou'd not show
his Indignation, hath shewn his Contempt as much as possible: having
here drawn as vile a picture, as could be represented in the colours of Epic
poesy. SCRIBLERUS.

149. *Eliza Haywood*] This woman was authoress of those most
scandalous books, call'd *The Court of Carimania* ⟨1727⟩, and *The new
Utopia*. ⟨1725.⟩ For the *two Babes of Love*, See CURL, *Key*, p. 12.
But whatever reflection he is pleas'd to throw upon this Lady, surely 'twas
what from him she little deserv'd, who had celebrated his undertakings for
Reformation of Manners, and declared her self 'to be so perfectly acquainted
with the *sweetness of his disposition*, and that *tenderness with which he
consider'd the errors of his fellow-creatures*; that tho' she should find the
little inadvertencies of her *own life* recorded in his papers, she was certain
it would be done in such a manner as she could not but approve,' Mrs.
HAYWOOD, Hist. of *Clar.⟨ina⟩* printed in the *Female Dunciad*, p. 18.
150. *Two babes of love &c.*] Virg. Æn. 5 ⟨285⟩.
Cressa genus, Pholoe, geminique sub ubere nati.
152. *Kirkall*, the Name of a Graver. This Lady's Works were printed
in four Volumes *duod.* with her picture thus dress'd up, before them.
⟨Elisha Kirkall (1682 ?–1742). He introduced a new method of chiaro-
scuro engraving in 1722.⟩
155. ——*This* Juno——
With cow-like udders, and with ox-like eyes]
In allusion to *Homer's* Βοῶπις πότνια Ἥρη.
157. *This* China *Jordan*, &c.] Virg. Æn. 5 ⟨314⟩.
Tertius, Argolica hac galea contentus abito.
This China *Jordan*] In the games of *Homer Il.* 23 ⟨262–5⟩, there are
set together as prizes, a Lady and a Kettle; as in this place Mrs. *Haywood*
and a Jordan. But there the preference in value is given to the *Kettle*, at
which Mad. *Dacier* is justly displeas'd: Mrs. *H.* here is treated with
distinction, and acknowledg'd to be the more valuable of the two.
159. *Chetwood* the name of a Bookseller, whose Wife was said to have
as great an influence over her husband, as *Boileau's Perruquiere*. See
Lutrin. Cant. 2.—*Henry Curl*, the worthy son of his father *Edmund.*

This on his manly confidence relies,
That on his vigor and superior size.
First Chetwood lean'd against his letter'd post;
It rose, and labour'd to a curve at most:
So Jove's bright bow displays its watry round,   165
(Sure sign, that no spectator shall be drown'd).
A second effort brought but new disgrace,
For straining more, it flies in his own face;
Thus the small jett which hasty hands unlock,
Spirts in the gard'ner's eyes who turns the cock.   170
Not so from shameless Curl: Impetuous spread
The stream, and smoaking, flourish'd o'er his head.
So, (fam'd like thee for turbulence and horns,)
Eridanus his humble fountain scorns,
Thro' half the heav'ns he pours th' exalted urn;   175
His rapid waters in their passage burn.

161. *This on his manly confidence relies, That on his vigor*] Virg. Æn. 5
⟨430–1.⟩

> *Ille melior motu, fretusque juventa,*
> *Hic membris & mole valens——*

165. *So* Jove's *bright bow—Sure sign——*] The words of *Homer* of the
Rainbow, in *Iliad* XI ⟨27–8⟩.

> ἅς τε Κρονίων
> 'Εν νέφϊ στήριξε, τέρας μερόπων ἀνθρώπων.

Which Mad. *Dacier* thus renders, *Arcs merveilleux, que le fils de Saturn à
fondez dans les nües, pour etre dans tous les âges un signe à tous les mortels.*

173. *So* (*fam'd like thee for turbulence and horns*) Eridanus] *Virgil* mentions these two qualifications of *Eridanus, Geor.* 4 ⟨371–3⟩.

> *Et gemina auratus taurino* cornua *vultu,*
> *Eridanus, quo non alius per pinguia culta*
> *In mare purpureum* violentior *effluit amnis.*

The Poets fabled of this River *Eridanus,* that it flow'd thro' the skies
Denham, Cooper's Hill ⟨ll. 193–4⟩.

> *Heav'n her* Eridanus *no more shall boast,*
> *Whose Fame like thine in lesser currents lost,*
> *Thy nobler stream shall visit* Jove's *abodes,*
> *To shine among the stars, and bathe the Gods;*

175. *Thro' half the heavens he pours th' exalted urn*] In a manuscript
Dunciad (where are some marginal corrections of some gentlemen some
time deceas'd) I have found another reading of these lines, thus,

> *And lifts his urn thro' half the heav'ns to flow;*
> *His rapid waters in their passage glow.*

This I cannot but think the right: For first, tho' the difference between
burn and *glow* may seem not very material to others, to me I confess the
latter has an elegance, a *Jenesçay quoy,* which is much easier to be conceiv'd than explain'd. Secondly, every reader of our Poet must have
observ'd how frequently he uses this word *glow* in other parts of his
works: To instance only in his *Homer.*

Swift as it mounts, all follow with their eyes;
Still happy Impudence obtains the prize.
Thou triumph'st, victor of the high-wrought day,
And the pleas'd dame soft-smiling leads away.   180
Chetwood, thro' perfect modesty o'ercome,
Crown'd with the Jordan, walks contented home.
    But now for Authors nobler palms remain:
Room for my Lord! three Jockeys in his train;
Six huntsmen with a shout precede his chair;   185
He grins, and looks broad nonsense with a stare.
His honour'd meaning, Dulness thus exprest;
'He wins this Patron who can tickle best.'
    He chinks his purse, and takes his seat of state;
With ready quills the dedicators wait;   190
Now at his head the dext'rous task commence,

(1.) Iliad 9. v. 726.—*With one resentment glows.*
(2.) Iliad 11. v. 626.—*There the battle glows.*
(3.) Ibid. 985.—*The closing flesh that instant ceas'd to glow.*
(4.) Il. 12. v. 55.—*Encompass'd* Hector *glows.*
(5.) Ibid. 475.—*His beating breast with gen'rous ardour glows.*
(6.) Iliad 18. v. 591.—*Another part glow'd with refulgent arms.*
(7.) Ibid. v. 654.—*And curl'd on silver props in order glow.*

I am afraid of growing too luxuriant in examples, or I could stretch this catalogue to a great extent, but these are enough to prove his fondness for this *beautiful word*, which therefore let all future Editions re-place here.

I am aware after all, that *burn* is the proper word to convey an idea of what was said to be Mr. *Curl*'s condition at that time. But from that very reason I infer the direct contrary. For surely every lover of our author will conclude he had more humanity, than to insult a man on such a misfortune or calamity, which could never befal him purely by his *own fault*, but from an unhappy communication with another. *This Note is partly Mr.* THEOBALD, *partly* SCRIBLERUS.

179. *The high-wrought day*] Some affirm, this was originally—*the* well-p—st *day:* but the Poet's decency would not suffer it.

Here the learned Scriblerus manifests great anger: he exclaims against all such *Conjectural Emendations* in this manner. 'Let it suffice, O Pallas! that every noble ancient, Greek or Roman, hath suffer'd the impertinent correction of every Dutch, German, and Switz Schoolmaster! Let our English at least escape, whose intrinsic is scarce of Marble so solid, as not to be impair'd or soil'd by such rude and dirty hands. Suffer them to call their Works their own, and after death at least to find rest and sanctuary from Critics! When these men have ceas'd to rail, let them not begin to do worse, to comment! let them not conjecture into nonsense, correct out of all correctness, and restore into obscurity and confusion. Miserable fate! which can befall only the sprightliest Wits that have written, and befall them only from such dull ones as could never write!' SCRIBLERUS.

188. *tickle* ⟨Tickling with a feather seems to have been a well-understood synonym for flattery.⟩

And instant, fancy feels th' imputed sense;
Now gentle touches wanton o'er his face,
He struts Adonis, and affects grimace:
Rolli the feather to his ear conveys,   195
Then his nice taste directs our Operas:
Welsted his mouth with Classic flatt'ry opes,
And the puff'd Orator bursts out in tropes.
But Oldmixon the Poet's healing balm
Strives to extract from his soft, giving palm;   200
Unlucky Oldmixon! thy lordly master
The more thou ticklest, gripes his fist the faster.
   While thus each hand promotes the pleasing pain,
And quick sensations skip from vein to vein,

195. *Paolo Antonio Rolli*, an *Italian* Poet, and writer of many Operas in that language, which, partly by the help of his genius, prevail'd in *England* near ten years. He taught Italian to some fine Gentlemen who affected to direct the Opera's.

197. *Welsted*] See Note on verse 293 of this Book.

199. *But* Oldmixon, *&c.*] Mr. *John Oldmixon* (next to Mr. *Dennis* the most ancient Critick of our Nation) not so happy as laborious in Poetry, and therefore perhaps characteriz'd by the *Tatler*, Nº. 62. by the name of *Omicron* the *unborn Poet*. CURL, Key to the *D.* p. 13. An unjust censurer of Mr. *Addison*, whom in his imitation of *Bouhours* (call'd the *Arts of Logic and Rhetoric*) he misrepresents in plain matter of fact. In p. 45. he cites the *Spectator* as abusing Dr. *Swift* by name, where there is not the least hint of it: And in p. 304. is so injurious as to suggest, that Mr. *Addison* himself writ that *Tatler* Nº. 43. which says of his *own Simile*, that ''tis as great as ever enter'd into the mind of man.' This person wrote numbers of books which are not come to our knowledge. 'Dramatick works, and a volume of Poetry, consisting of heroic Epistles, *&c.* some whereof are very well done,' saith that great Judge Mr. JACOB. *Lives of Poets, Vol. 2. p. 303.*

I remember a *Pastoral* of his on the *Battle of Blenheim*; a Critical History of *England*; Essay on Criticism, in prose; The Arts of Logic and Rhetoric, in which he frequently reflects on our Author. We find in the *Flying-Post* of *Apr. 13. 1728.* some very flat verses of his against him and Dr. *Sw.* and Mr. *Curl* tells us in the *Curliad*, that he wrote the Ballad called The *Catholic Poet* against the Version of *Homer*, before it appear'd to the public.

But the Top of his Character was a Perverter of History, in that scandalous one of the *Stuarts* in folio, and his Critical History of England, 2 vols. 8º. Being imploy'd by Bishop Kennet in publishing the Historians in his Collection, he falsified Daniel's Chronicle in numberless places. Yet this very man, in the Preface to the first of these, advanc'd a *particular Fact* to charge three Eminent Persons of falsifying the Lord Clarendon's History; which Fact has been disprov'd by the Bishop of Rochester, then the only survivor of them; and the particular part produc'd since, after almost ninety Years, in that noble Author's own Hand. He was all his life a virulent Party-writer for hire, and received his reward in a small place which he yet enjoys.

A youth unknown to Phœbus, in despair,   205
Puts his last refuge all in Heav'n and Pray'r.
What force have pious vows! the Queen of Love
His Sister sends, her vot'ress, from above.
As taught by Venus, Paris learnt the art
To touch Achilles' only tender part;   210
Secure, thro' her, the noble prize to carry,
He marches off, his Grace's Secretary.
  'Now turn to diff'rent sports (the Goddess cries)
And learn, my sons, the wond'rous pow'r of Noise.
To move, to raise, to ravish ev'ry heart,   215
With Shakespear's nature, or with Johnson's art,
Let others aim: 'Tis yours to shake the soul
With thunder rumbling from the mustard-bowl,
With horns and trumpets now to madness swell,
Now sink in sorrows with a tolling Bell.   220
Such happy arts attention can command,
When fancy flags, and sense is at a stand.
Improve we these. Three cat-calls be the bribe
Of him, whose chatt'ring shames the Monkey tribe;
And his this Drum, whose hoarse heroic base   225
Drowns the loud clarion of the braying Ass.'

205. *A youth unknown to* Phœbus, *&c.*] The satire of this Episode being levelled at the base flatteries of authors to worthless wealth or greatness, concludeth here with an excellent lesson to such men; That altho' their pens and praises were as exquisite as they conceit of themselves, yet (even in their own mercenary views) a creature unlettered, who serveth the passions, or pimpeth to the pleasures of such vain, braggart, puft Nobility, shall with those patrons be much more inward, and of them much higher rewarded. SCRIBLERUS.

215. *To move, to raise, &c.—Let others aim—'Tis yours to shake, &c.—*] Virgil, Æn. 6 ⟨847–8, 851–2⟩.

> *Excudent alii spirantia mollius æra,*
> *Credo equidem, vivos ducent de marmore vultus, &c.*
> *Tu, regere imperio populos, Romane, memento,*
> *Hæ tibi erunt artes——*

218. *With Thunder &c.*] The old way of making Thunder and Mustard were the same; but since it is more advantagiously perform'd by troughs of wood with stops in them. Whether Mr. *Dennis* was the inventor of that improvement, I know not; but it is certain, that being once at a Tragedy of a new Author with a friend of his, he fell into a great passion at hearing some, and cry'd, 'S'death! that is *my* Thunder.'

220. *With a tolling Bell*] A mechanical help to the Pathetic, not unuseful to the modern writers of Tragedy.

223. *Three Catcalls*] Certain musical instruments used by one sort of Criticks to confound the Poets of the Theatre. They are of great antiquity, if we may credit *Florent. Christ.* on *Aristophanes* Ἱππεῖς, Act. 1. *Parabasis Chori.*

Now thousand tongues are heard in one loud din:
The Monkey-mimicks rush discordant in.
'Twas chatt'ring, grinning, mouthing, jabb'ring all,
And Noise, and Norton, Brangling, and Breval,   230
Dennis and Dissonance; and captious Art,
And Snip-snap short, and Interruption smart.
'Hold (cry'd the Queen) A Catcall each shall win,
Equal your merits! equal is your din!
But that this well-disputed game may end,   235
Sound forth, my Brayers, and the welkin rend.'
   As when the long-ear'd milky mothers wait
At some sick miser's triple-bolted gate,
For their defrauded, absent foals they make
A moan so loud, that all the Guild awake,   240
Sore sighs Sir G * *, starting at the bray
From dreams of millions, and three groats to pay!
So swells each Windpipe; Ass intones to Ass,
Harmonic twang! of leather, horn, and brass.
Such, as from lab'ring lungs th' Enthusiast blows,   245
High sounds, attempred to the vocal nose.
But far o'er all, sonorous Blackmore's strain,
Walls, steeples, skies, bray back to him again:
In Tot'nam fields, the brethren with amaze
Prick all their ears up, and forget to graze;   250

230. *Norton.* [See verse 383.] *J. Durant Breval,* Author of a very extraordinary Book of Travels, and some Poems. See before, V. 118.
   233. ——*A Catcall each shall win,* &c.] Virg. Ecl. 3 ⟨108-9⟩.
      Non inter nos est tantas componere lites,
      ⟨*Non nostrum inter vos tantas componere lites*⟩
      Et vitula tu dignus, & hic——
   237. milky mothers ⟨See *Ep. to Arbuthnot,* 306n (p. 608).⟩
   237 ff.] A *Simile* with a long tail, in the manner of *Homer.*
   241. *Sir G** ⟨Sir Gilbert Heathcote, who died Jan. 25, 1732-3, was
reputed to be 'worth 700,000 l. very honourably acquired' (see p. 576).⟩
   245. *Enthusiast* ⟨i.e. a man labouring under religious excitement, a
fanatical preacher.⟩
   248. ——*bray back to him again*] A figure of speech taken from *Virgil.*
      Et vox assensu nemorum ingeminata remugit. Geor. 3 ⟨45⟩
      He hears his num'rous herds low o'er the plain,
      While neighb'ring hills low back to them again. Cowley.
   The poet here celebrated, Sir *R. B.* delighted much in the word *Bray,*
which he endeavour'd to ennoble by applying it to the sound of *Armour,*
War, &c. In imitation of him, and strengthen'd by his authority, our
author has here admitted it into Heroic poetry.
   250. *Prick all their ears up, and forget to graze*] Virg. Ecl. 8 ⟨2⟩.
      Immemor herbarum quos est mirata juvenca.
The progress of the sound from place to place, and the scenary here of the

Long Chanc'ry-lane retentive rolls the sound,
And courts to courts return it round and round:
Thames wafts it thence to Rufus' roaring hall,
And Hungerford re-ecchoes, bawl for bawl.
All hail him victor in both gifts of Song,   255
Who sings so loudly, and who sings so long.
This labour past, by Bridewell all descend,

bordering regions, *Tot'nam fields, Chancery-lane,* the *Thames, West-minster-hall,* and *Hungerford-stairs,* are imitated from *Virg. Æn.* 7 ⟨516 ff.⟩ on the sounding the horn of *Alecto.*

> *Audiit & Triviæ longe lacus, audiit amnis*
> *Sulphurea Nar albus aqua, fontesque Velini,* &c.

251. *Long* Chanc'ry-lane] The place where the Courts of Chancery are kept: The long detention of Clients in those Courts, and the difficulty of getting out of them, is humorously allegoriz'd in these lines.

253. *Rufus' roaring hall* ⟨Westminster Hall. It was made noisy partly by the lawyers who disputed there, but even more by the owners of stalls.⟩

254. *Hungerford* ⟨Hungerford Market. It was built in 1680 on the site of what is now Charing Cross Station.⟩

256. *Who sings so loudly, and who sings so long*] A just character of Sir *Richard Blackmore,* Kt. who (as Mr. *Dryden* express'd it) *Writ to the rumbling of his Coach's wheels,* and whose indefatigable Muse produced no less than six Epic poems: *Prince* and *King Arthur,* 20 Books; *Eliza,* 10; *Alfred,* 12; *The Redeemer,* 6: besides *Job* in folio, the whole *Book of Psalms, The Creation,* 7 Books, *Nature of Man,* 3 Books, and many more. 'Tis in this sense he is stiled afterwards, the *Everlasting Blackmore.* Notwithstanding all which, Mr. *Gildon* seems assured, that 'this admirable author did not think himself upon the *same foot* with *Homer.*' *Comp. Art of Poetry,* Vol. i. p. 108.

But how different is the judgment of the author of *Characters of the Times!* p. 25. who says, 'Sir *Richard* is unfortunate in happening to mistake his proper talents, and that he has not for many years been *so much as named,* or even *thought of* among writers.' Even Mr. *Dennis* differs greatly from his friend Mr. *Gildon:* '*Blackmore*'s Action (saith he) has neither unity, nor integrity, nor morality, nor universality; and consequently he can have no *Fable,* and no *Heroic Poem:* His Narration is neither probable, delightful, nor wonderful: His Characters have none of the necessary qualifications.——The things contain'd in his narration are neither in their own nature delightful, nor numerous enough, nor rightly disposed, nor surprising, nor pathetic.——Nay he proceeds so far as to say Sir *Richard* has *no Genius;* first laying down that Genius is caused by a *furious joy* and *pride of soul,* on the conception of an *extraordinary Hint.* Many men (says he) have their *Hints,* without these motions of *fury* and *pride of soul,* because they want fire enough to agitate their spirits; and these we call cold writers: Others who have a great deal of fire, but have not excellent organs, feel the foremention'd *motions,* without the *extraordinary hints;* And these we call fustian writers.' But he declares, that 'Sir *Richard* had neither the *Hints,* nor the *Motions.*' *Remarks on Pr. Arth.* 8°. 1696. *Preface.*

This gentleman in his first works abused the character of Mr. *Dryden,* and in his last of Mr. *Pope,* accusing him in very high and sober terms of

(As morning-pray'r and flagellation end.)
To where Fleet-ditch with disemboguing streams
Rolls the large tribute of dead dogs to Thames,   260
The King of Dykes! than whom, no sluice of mud

---

prophaneness and immorality (*Essay on polite writing*, Vol. 2. p. 270.) on
a meer report from *Edm. Curl*, that he was author of a Travestie on the
first Psalm. ⟨See p. 300.⟩ Mr. *Dennis* took up the same report, but with
the addition of what Sir *Richard* had neglected, an *Argument to prove it;*
which being very curious, we shall here transcribe. (*Remarks on* Homer.
8°. p. 27.) 'It *was* he who burlesqu'd the Psalm of *David*. It is *apparent* to
me that Psalm was burlesqu'd by a *Popish* rhymester. Let rhyming persons who have been brought up *Protestants* be otherwise what they will,
let them be Rakes, let 'em be Scoundrels, let 'em be *Atheists*, yet education has made an invincible impression on them in behalf of the sacred
writings. But a *Popish rhymester* has been brought up with a contempt for
those sacred writings. Now show me another Popish rhymester but he.'
——This manner of argumentation is usual with Mr. *Dennis*; he has
employ'd the same against Sir *Richard* himself in a like charge of *Impiety*
and *Irreligion*. 'All Mr. *Blackmore*'s celestial Machines, as they cannot be
defended so much as by common receiv'd opinion, so are directly contrary
to the doctrine of the Church of *England:* For the visible descent of an
Angel must be a miracle. Now it is the doctrine of the Church of *England*
that miracles had ceas'd a long time before Prince *Arthur* came into the
world. Now if the doctrine of the Church of *England* be true, as we are
oblig'd to believe, then are all the celestial machines in Prince *Arthur*
unsufferable, as wanting not only human but divine probability. But if the
machines are sufferable, that is if they have so much as divine probability,
then it follows of necessity that the doctrine of the Church is false: So I
leave it to every impartial Clergyman to consider, *&c.' Preface to the
Remarks on Prince* Arthur.

It has been suggested in the Character of Mr. *P*. that he had Obligations to Sir *R. B.* He never had any, and never saw him but twice in
his Life.

258. *As morning pray'r and flagellation end*] It is between eleven and
twelve in the morning, after church service, that the criminals are whipp'd
in *Bridewell* ⟨the House of Correction for women⟩.—This is to mark
punctually the Time of the day: *Homer* does it by the circumstance of the
Judges rising from court, or of the Labourer's dinner; our author by one
very proper both to the *Persons* and the *Scene* of his Poem; which we may
remember commenc'd in the evening of the Lord-mayor's day: The first
book passed in that night; the next morning the games begin in the
Strand, thence along *Fleetstreet* (places inhabited by Booksellers) then
they proceed by *Bridewell* toward *Fleetditch*, and lastly thro' *Ludgate* to
the City and the Temple of the Goddess.

259. *The* Diving] This I fancy (says a great Enemy to the Poem) is a
Game which no body could ever think of but the Author: however it is
work'd up admirably well, especially in those lines where he describes
Eusden (he should say *Smedley*) rising up again. ESSAY on the DUNCIAD,
p. 19.

261. *The King of* Dykes, *&c*.] Virg. ⟨*Georg.* i 482, iv 372-3⟩.
    Eridanus, rex fluviorum——
    ——*quo non alius, per pinguia culta,*
    In mare purpureum violentior effluit amnis. ⟨Cf. A ii 173*n*.⟩

With deeper sable blots the silver flood.
'Here strip my children! here at once leap in!
Here prove who best can dash thro' thick and thin,
And who the most in love of dirt excel,   265
Or dark dexterity of groping well.
Who flings most filth, and wide pollutes around
The stream, be his the Weekly Journals, bound.
A pig of lead to him who dives the best.
A peck of coals a-piece shall glad the rest.'   270
    In naked majesty great Dennis stands,

And, Milo-like, surveys his arms and hands,
Then sighing, thus. 'And am I now threescore?
Ah why, ye Gods! should two and two make four?'

264, 265, 266] The three chief qualifications of Party-writers; to stick at nothing, to delight in flinging dirt, and to slander in the dark by guess.

268. *The* Weekly Journals] Papers of news and scandal intermix'd, on different sides and parties and frequently shifting from one side to the other, call'd the *London Journal*, *Mist*'s *Journal*, *British Journal*, *Daily Journal*, &c. the writers of which for some time were *Welsted, Roome, Molloy, Concanen*, and others; persons never seen by our author.

270. *A peck of coals a-piece*] Our indulgent Poet, whenever he has spoken of any dirty or low work, constantly puts us in mind of the Poverty of the offenders, as the only extenuation of such practices. Let any one but remark, when a Thief, a Pickpocket, a Highwayman or a Knight of the Post is spoken of, how much our hatred to those characters is lessen'd, if they add, a *needy* Thief, a *poor* Pickpocket, a *hungry* Highwayman, a *starving* Knight of the Post, &c.

271. *In naked majesty great* Dennis *stands*] The reader, who hath seen in the course of these notes, what a constant attendance Mr. *Dennis* paid to our author, might here expect a particular regard to be shewn him; and consequently may be surprized at his sinking at once, in so few lines, never to rise again! But in truth he looked upon him with some esteem, for having, more generously than the rest, set his *name* to such works. He was not only a formidable Critick who for many years had written against every thing that had success, (the Antagonist of Sir *Richard Blackmore*, Sir *Richard Steele*, Mr. *Addison*, and Mr. *Pope*) but a zealous Politician (not only appearing in his works, where *Poetry* and the *State* are always equally concerned, but in many secret Hints and sage advices given to the Ministers of all reigns.) He is here likened to *Milo*, in allusion to that verse of *Ovid* ⟨*Met*. xv 228–30⟩.

            —*Fletque Milon senior, cum spectat inanes*
            Herculeis similes, fluidos pendere lacertos;
either with regard to his great Age, or because he was undone by trying to pull to pieces an Oak that was too strong for him.

            ——*Remember* Milo's *End,*
            Wedg'd in that timber which he strove to rend.
Lord *Rosc.* ⟨Lord Roscommon, *An Essay on Translated Verse*, 87–8⟩.

273. —*And am I now threescore?*] I shall here, to prove my impartiality, remark a great oversight in our author as to the age of Mr. *Dennis*. He must have been some years above threescore in the Mayoralty of Sir *George Thorold*, which was in 1720, and Mr. *Dennis* was born (as he himself

He said, and climb'd a stranded Lighter's height,   275
Shot to the black abyss, and plung'd down-right.
The Senior's judgment all the crowd admire,
Who but to sink the deeper, rose the higher.
    Next Smedley div'd; slow circles dimpled o'er
The quaking mud, that clos'd, and ope'd no more.   280
All look, all sigh, and call on Smedley lost;
Smedley in vain resounds thro' all the coast.
    Then * * try'd, but hardly snatch'd from sight,
Instant buoys up, and rises into light;
He bears no token of the sabler streams,   285
And mounts far off, among the swans of Thames.
    True to the bottom, see Concanen creep,
A cold, long-winded, native of the deep!
If perseverance gain the Diver's prize,

---

inform'd us in Mr. *Jacob*'s Lives before-mentioned) in 1657; since when
he has happily liv'd eight years more, and is already senior to Mr. *Durfey*,
who hitherto of all our Poets, enjoy'd the longest, bodily, Life. ⟨D'Urfey
had died in 1723, aged seventy. The commas emphasize that D'Urfey's
long life was *bodily* only, and did not extend to his poetic reputation.⟩

279. Smedley] In the surreptitious editions this whole Episode was
apply'd to an initial letter *E—*, by whom if they meant the Laureate,
nothing was more absurd, no part agreeing with his character. The
Allegory evidently demands a person dipp'd in scandal, and deeply
immers'd in dirty work: whereas Mr. *Eusden*'s writings rarely offended
but by their length and multitude, and accordingly are tax'd of nothing
else in book 1. verse 102. But the person here mention'd, an *Irishman*,
was author and publisher of many scurrilous pieces, a weekly *Whitehall
Journal* in the year 1722, in the name of Sir *James Baker*, and particularly
whole Volumes of Billingsgate against Dr. *Swift* and Mr. *Pope*, call'd
Gulliveriana and *Alexand⟨e⟩riana*, printed in 8°. 1728.

281. ——*and call on* Smedley *lost*, &c.] Lord *Roscommon*'s translation
of *Virgil*'s 6th Eclog. ⟨43-4⟩.

Alcides *wept in vain for* Hylas *lost*,
Hylas *in vain resounds thro' all the coast.*

283. *Then * * try'd*] This is an instance of the Tenderness of our author.
The person here intended writ an angry preface against him, grounded on
a Mistake, which he afterwards honourably acknowledg'd in another
printed preface. Since when, he fell under a second mistake, and abus'd
both him and his Friend.

He is a writer of Genius and Spirit, tho' in his youth he was guilty of
some pieces bordering upon bombast. Our Poet here gives him a Panegyric instead of a Satire, being edify'd beyond measure, at this only
instance he ever met with in his life, of one who was much a Poet, con-
fessing himself in an Error: And has supprest his name, as thinking
him capable of a second repentance. ⟨i.e. Aaron Hill.⟩

287. *Concanen*] In the former editions there were only Asterisks in this
place; this name was since inserted merely to fill up the verse, and give
ease to the ear of the reader.

Not everlasting Blackmore this denies: 290
No noise, no stir, no motion can'st thou make,
Th' unconscious flood sleeps o'er thee like a lake.
    Not Welsted so: drawn endlong by his scull,
Furious he sinks; precipitately dull.
Whirlpools and storms his circling arm invest,   295
With all the Might of gravitation blest.
No crab more active in the dirty dance,
Downward to climb, and backward to advance;
He brings up half the bottom on his head,
And boldly claims the Journals and the Lead.   300
    Sudden, a burst of thunder shook the flood.
Lo Smedley rose, in majesty of mud!
Shaking the horrors of his ample brows,
And each ferocious feature grim with ooze.
Greater he looks, and more than mortal stares;   305

290. *Not everlasting* Blackmore] Virg. Æn. 5 ⟨541.⟩
        Nec bonus Eurytion prælato invidit honori, &c.

293. *Welsted*] *Leonard Welsted*, author of the *Triumvirate*, or a Letter
in verse from *Palæmon* to *Celia* at *Bath*, which was meant for a Satire on
Mr. *P.* and some of his friends about the year 1718 ⟨i.e. 1717. It satirized
Pope, Gay, and Arbuthnot for their farce, *Three Hours after Marriage*⟩.
The strength of the metaphors in this passage is to express the great
scurrility and fury of this writer, which may be seen, One day, in a Piece
of his, call'd (as I think) *Labeo.* He writ other things which we cannot
remember. *Smedley* in his *Metam.* of *Scrib.* mentions one, the *Hymn* of a
Gentleman to the *Creator:* and there was another in praise either of a
Cellar or a *Garret. L. W.* characteris'd in the treatise περὶ βάθους or the
Art of sinking as a *Didapper*, and after as an *Eel*, is said to be this person,
by DENNIS *Daily Journal* of *May* 11, 1728. He is mentioned again in
book 3. ⟨163⟩. The foresaid dark anonymous Writers are characterized
also under another animal, a *Mole*, by the author of the ensuing Simile,
which was handed about, at the same time.

> *Dear* W—d, *mark, in dirty hole*
> *That painful animal, a Mole:*
> *Above ground never born to go,*
> *What mighty stir it keeps below!*
> *To make a Molehill, all this strife!*
> *It digs, pokes, undermines, for life;*
> *How proud, a little Dirt to spread!*
> *Conscious of nothing o'er its head:*
> *Till, lab'ring on for want of eyes,*
> *It blunders into Light—and dies.*

302. ——*in Majesty of mud*] Milton ⟨*Par. Lost*, ii 266⟩,
        ——*in majesty of darkness round*
        Circled——⟨*Covers his throne*⟩.

305. *Greater he looks, and more than mortal stares*] Virg. ⟨*Aen.* vi 49–
50⟩ of the Sybil.
        ——*majorque videri*
        Nec mortale sonans——

Then thus the wonders of the Deep declares.
First he relates, how sinking to the chin,
Smit with his mien, the Mud-nymphs suck'd him in:
How young Lutetia, softer than the down,
Nigrina black, and Merdamante brown,   310
Vy'd for his love in jetty bow'rs below;
As Hylas fair was ravish'd long ago.
Then sung, how shown him by the nutbrown maids,
A branch of Styx here rises from the Shades,
That tinctur'd as it runs, with Lethe's streams,   315
And wafting vapours from the Land of Dreams,
(As under seas Alphæus' secret sluice
Bears Pisa's offerings to his Arethuse)
Pours into Thames: Each city-bowl is full
Of the mixt wave, and all who drink grow dull.   320
How to the banks where bards departed doze,
They led him soft; how all the bards arose;

309 f. ⟨'Lutetia' is the classical name for the modern Paris. The name
was thought to be derived from 'its dirty situation.' Lutum = clay, mud.
'Merdamante' = filth-loving.⟩

312. *As* Hylas *fair*] Who was ravish'd by the water-nymphs and drawn
into the river. The story is told at large by *Valerius Flaccus, Lib.* 3. *Argon.*
See *Virg. Ecl.* 6 ⟨43–8⟩.

314. &c. A branch of Styx, &c.] Homer, Il. 2. Catal. ⟨751–5⟩.

> Οἵ τ' ἀμφ' ἱμερτὸν Τιταρησσὸν ἔργ' ἐνέμοντο,
> Ὅς ῥ' ἐς Πηνειὸν προΐει καλλίρροον ὕδωρ,
> Οὐδ' ὅ γε Πηνειῷ συμμίσγεται ἀργυροδίνῃ,
> Ἀλλά τέ μιν καθύπερθεν ἐπιρρέει ἠΰτ' ἔλαιον.
> Ὅρκου γὰρ δεινοῦ Στυγὸς ὕδατός ἐστιν ἀπορρώξ.

Of the land of Dreams in the same region, he makes mention, *Odyss.*
24 ⟨12⟩. See also *Lucian*'s true History. *Lethe* and the *Land of Dreams*
allegorically represent the *Stupefaction* and *visionary Madness* of Poets
equally dull and extravagant. Of *Alphæus* his waters gliding secretly under
the sea of *Pisa*, to mix with those of *Arethuse* in *Sicily, vid. Moschus Idyl.* 8.
Virg. Ecl. 10 ⟨4–5⟩,

> Sic tibi, cum fluctus subter labere Sicanos,
> Doris amara suam non intermisceat undam.

And again, *Æn.* 3 ⟨694–6⟩.

> —Alphæum, fama est, huc Elidis amnem
> Occultas egisse vias, subter mare, qui nunc
> Ore, Arethusa, tuo Siculis confunditur undis.

321. *How to the banks,* &c.] Virg. Ecl. 6 ⟨64, 66–70⟩.

> Tum canit errantem Permessi ad flumina Gallum,
> Utque viro Phœbi chorus assurexerit omnis;
> Ut Linus hæc illi divino carmine pastor,
> Floribus atque apio crines ornatus amaro,
> Dixerit, Hos tibi dant calamos, en accipe, Musæ,
> Ascræo quos ante seni———— &c.

Taylor, sweet bird of Thames, majestic bows,
And Shadwell nods the poppy on his brows;
While Milbourn there, deputed by the rest,   325
Gave him the cassock, surcingle, and vest;
And 'Take (he said) these robes which once were mine,
Dulness is sacred in a sound Divine.'
　　He ceas'd, and show'd the robe; the crowd confess
The rev'rend Flamen in his lengthen'd dress.   330
Slow moves the Goddess from the sable flood,
(Her Priest preceding) thro' the gates of Lud.
Her Criticks there she summons, and proclaims
A gentler exercise to close the games.
'Hear you! in whose grave heads, as equal scales,   335
I weigh what author's heaviness prevails,
Which most conduce to sooth the soul in slumbers,
My Henley's periods, or my Blackmore's numbers?
Attend the trial we propose to make:
If there be man who o'er such works can wake,   340

323. Taylor, *sweet bird of* Thames] *John Taylor* the Water Poet, an honest man, who owns he learn'd not so much as his *Accidence:* a rare example of modesty in a Poet!

> *I must confess I do want eloquence,*
> *And never scarce did learn my Accidence,*
> *For having got from* Possum *to* Posset,
> *I there was gravell'd, could no farther get.*

He wrote fourscore books in the reign of *James* I. and *Charles* I. and afterwards (like Mr. *Ward*) kept a Publick-house in *Long Acre.* He died in 1654.

324. *And* Shadwell *nods the poppy*] *Shadwell* took Opium for many years, and died of too large a dose of it, in the year 1692.

325. Milbourn] *Luke Milbourn* ⟨1649–1720⟩ a Clergyman, the fairest of Criticks; who when he wrote against Mr. *Dryden's Virgil* ⟨1698⟩, did him justice, in printing at the same time his own translations of him, which were intolerable. His manner of writing has a great resemblance with that of the Gentlemen of the *Dunciad* against our author, as will be seen in the Parallel of Mr. *Dryden* and him. *Append.* ⟨vi⟩.

326. *surcingle* ⟨a girdle or belt which confines the cassock.⟩

332. *Gates of* Lud] 'King *Lud* repairing the City, call'd it after his own name, *Lud's* Town; the strong gate which he built in the West part, he likewise for his own honour named *Ludgate.* In the year 1260, this gate was beautified with images of *Lud* and other Kings. Those images in the reign of *Edward* VI. had their heads smitten off, and were otherwise defaced by unadvised folks. Queen *Mary* did set new heads on their old bodies again. The 28th of Q. *Eliz.* the same gate was clean taken down, and newly and beautifully builded with images of *Lud* and others as afore.' STOW's Survey of *London.*

338. *My Henley's periods* ⟨i.e. John ('Orator') Henley, for whom see iii 195*n.*⟩

Sleep's all-subduing charm who dares defy,
And boasts Ulysses' ear with Argus' eye;
To him we grant our amplest pow'rs to sit
Judge of all present, past, and future wit,
To cavil, censure, dictate, right or wrong,   345
Full, and eternal privilege of tongue.'
   Three Cambridge Sophs and three pert Templars came,
The same their talents, and their tastes the same,
Each prompt to query, answer, and debate,
And smit with love of Poesy and Prate.   350
The pond'rous books two gentle readers bring;
The heroes sit; the vulgar form a ring.
The clam'rous crowd is hush'd with mugs of Mum,
'Till all tun'd equal, send a gen'ral hum.
Then mount the clerks; and in one lazy tone,   355
Thro' the long, heavy, painful page, drawl on;
Soft, creeping, words on words, the sense compose,
At ev'ry line, they stretch, they yawn, they doze.
As to soft gales top-heavy pines bow low
Their heads, and lift them as they cease to blow,   360
Thus oft they rear, and oft the head decline,
As breathe, or pause, by fits, the airs divine:
And now to this side, now to that, they nod,
As verse, or prose, infuse the drowzy God.
Thrice Budgel aim'd to speak, but thrice supprest   365

342] See *Hom. Odyss.* 12 ⟨192⟩. *Ovid, Met.* 1 ⟨625⟩.
347. *Sophs* ⟨students in their second or third year.⟩
348. *The same their talents——Each prompt to query*, &c.] Virg. Ecl. 7 ⟨4–5⟩.
    Ambo florentes ætatibus, Arcades ambo,
    Et cantare pares, & respondere parati.
350.] *Smit with the love of sacred song*—Milton ⟨*Par. Lost,* iii 29⟩.
352. *The heroes sit;* &c.] Ovid, M⟨et.⟩ 13 ⟨1⟩.
    Consedere duces, & vulgi stante corona.
353. *Mum* ⟨A kind of beer originally brewed in Brunswick.⟩
 356. *Thro' the long, heavy, painful page,* &c.] All these lines very well
imitate the slow drowziness with which they proceed. It is impossible for
any one who has a poetical ear to read them, without perceiving the
heaviness that lags in the verse to imitate the action it describes. The
Simile of the Pines is very just and well adapted to the subject. ESSAY on
the DUNC. p. 21.
 365. *Thrice* Budgel *aim'd to speak*] Famous for his speeches on many
occasions about the *South Sea* Scheme, &c. 'He is a very ingenious
gentleman, and hath written some excellent Epilogues to Plays, and *one
small* piece on Love, which is very pretty.' JACOB Lives of Poets, vol. 2.
p. 289. But this Gentleman has since made himself much more eminent,
and personally well-known to the greatest statesmen of all parties in this
nation.

By potent Arthur, knock'd his chin and breast.
Toland and Tindal, prompt at Priests to jeer,
Yet silent bow'd to Christ's No kingdom here.
Who sate the nearest, by the words o'ercome
Slept first, the distant nodded to the hum.   370
Then down are roll'd the books; stretch'd o'er 'em lies
Each gentle clerk, and mutt'ring seals his eyes.
As what a Dutchman plumps into the lakes,
One circle first, and then a second makes,
What Dulness dropt among her sons imprest   375
Like motion, from one circle to the rest;
So from the mid-most the nutation spreads
Round, and more round, o'er all the sea of heads.
At last Centlivre felt her voice to fail,
Old James himself unfinish'd left his tale,   380
Boyer the State, and Law the Stage gave o'er,

366. *Arthur* ⟨Blackmore's *Prince Arthur; an heroick poem*, appeared in 1695, and was followed in 1697 by his *King Arthur, An Heroick Poem*. Both were 'pond'rous books' in folio⟩.

367. Toland *and* Tindal] Two persons not so happy as to be obscure, who writ against the Religion of their Country. The surreptitious editions placed here the name of a Gentleman, who, tho' no great friend to the Clergy is a person of Morals and Ingenuity ⟨i.e., Anthony Collins, the deist (1676–1729).⟩ *Tindal* was Author of the *Rights of the Christian Church* ⟨1706⟩: He also wrote an abusive pamphlet against Earl *Stanhope*, which was suppress'd while yet in manuscript by an eminent Person then out of the Ministry, to whom he show'd it expecting his approbation. This Doctor afterwards publish'd the same piece, *mutatis mutandis*, against that very Person when he came into the Administration.

368. *Christ's No kingdom* &c.] This is scandalously said by C U R L, Key to *Dunc.* to allude to a Sermon of a reverend Bishop. ⟨Bishop Hoadly's famous discourse on 'The Nature of the Kingdom or Church of Christ', which occasioned the Bangorian controversy (1717)⟩.

378. *o'er all the sea of heads*] Blackm. Job.
> *A waving sea of heads was round me spread,*
> *And still fresh streams the gazing deluge fed.*

379. *Centlivre*] Mrs. *Susanna Centlivre* ⟨1667 ?–1723⟩, wife to Mr. *Centlivre*, Yeoman of the Mouth to his Majesty. She writ many Plays, and a song (says Mr. *Jacob*, vol. 1, p. 32.) before she was seven years old. She also writ a Ballad against Mr. *Pope's Homer* before he begun it. ⟨See ii 199*n*.⟩

380. *Old James* ⟨Perhaps James Pitt, who was already writing as 'Publicola' in *The London Journal*, and who was later characterized by Pope as 'the eldest and gravest' of the newspaper writers. See *Dunciad* B, ii 312 (p. 747).⟩

381. Boyer *the State, and* Law *the Stage gave o'er*] *A. Boyer*, a voluminous compiler of Annals, Political Collections, *&c.*——⟨Abel Boyer (1667–1729) wrote and compiled *The Political State of Great Britain* from 1711 till his death. He had been forced by the hostility of booksellers to give up his monthly account of Parliamentary Proceedings.⟩ *William*

Nor Motteux talk'd, nor Naso whisper'd more;
Norton, from Daniel and Ostrœa sprung,
Blest with his father's front, and mother's tongue,
Hung silent down his never-blushing head;   385
And all was hush'd, as Folly's self lay dead.
  Thus the soft gifts of Sleep conclude the day,
And stretch'd on bulks, as usual, Poets lay.
Why shou'd I sing what bards the nightly Muse
Did slumbring visit, and convey to stews?   390
Who prouder march'd, with magistrates in state,
To some fam'd round-house, ever open gate!
How Laurus lay inspir'd beside a sink,

Law, A. M. ⟨1686-1761, author of *A Serious Call*⟩ wrote with great
zeal against the Stage, Mr. *Dennis* answer'd with as great. Their books
were printed in 1726. Mr. *Law* affirm'd that 'the Playhouse is the Temple
of the Devil, the peculiar pleasure of the Devil, where all they who go,
yield to the Devil, where all the Laughter is a laughter among Devils, and
that all who are there are hearing Musick in the very Porch of Hell.' To
which Mr. *Dennis* replied, that 'there is every jot as much difference
between a true Play, and one made by a Poetaster, as between *Two
religious books*, the *Bible* and the *Alcoran*.' Then he demonstrates that 'all
those who had written against the Stage were *Jacobites* and *Nonjurors*, and
did it always at a time when something was to be done for the *Pretender*.
Mr. *Collier* publish'd his *Short View* when *France* declar'd for the
Chevalier; and his *Dissuasive* just at the *great Storm*, when the devastation
which that Hurricane wrought had amazed and astonished the minds of
men, and made them obnoxious to melancholy and desponding thoughts.
Mr. *Law* took the opportunity to attack the Stage upon the great prepara-
tions he heard were making abroad, and which the *Jacobites* flatter'd
themselves were design'd in their favour. And as for Mr. *Bedford*'s
Serious Remonstrance, tho' I know nothing of the time of publishing it,
yet I dare to lay odds it was either upon the Duke *D'Aumont*'s being at
Somerset-house, or upon the *late Rebellion*.' DENNIS, Stage defended
against Mr. *Law*, pag. *ult*.

382. *Motteux . . . Naso* ⟨See *Imit. Donne* iv 50, p. 681.⟩

383. Norton] *Norton de Foe*, said to be the natural offspring of the
famous *Daniel* ⟨Defoe⟩. *Fortes creantur fortibus*. One of the authors of
the *Flying-Post*, in which well-bred work Mr. *P*. had sometime the honour
to be abus'd with his betters, and of many hired scurrilities and daily
papers to which he never set his name, in a due fear of Laws and Cudgels.
He is now writing the *Life of Colonel* Charteris. ⟨See p. 571.

'Ostrœa: that is, an oyster wench: hence, in the next verse, *his mother's
tongue*.'⟩

386. *And all was hush'd*, &c.] Alludes to *Dryden*'s verse in the *Indian
Emperor* ⟨III ii 1⟩,

        All things are hush'd, as Nature's self lay dead.

392. *round-house* ⟨a lock-up.⟩

393. *sink* ⟨a cess-pool, a conduit for carrying away dirty water or
sewage. Laurus was lying drunk in the street.⟩

393. *How* Laurus *lay* inspir'd, &c.] This line presents us with an excel-

And to mere mortals seem'd a Priest in drink?
While others timely, to the neighbouring Fleet   395
(Haunt of the Muses) made their safe retreat.

lent Moral, that we are never to pass judgment merely by *appearances*; a Lesson to all men who may happen to see a reverend person in the like situation, not to determine too rashly, since not only the Poets frequently describe a Bard inspir'd in this posture,

(*On* Cam's *fair bank where* Chaucer *lay inspir'd,*

and the like) but an eminent Casuist tells us, that if a Priest be seen in any indecent action, we ought to account it a deception of sight, or illusion of the Devil, who sometimes takes upon him the shape of Holy men on purpose to cause scandal. How little the prophane author of the *Characters of the Times* printed 8°. 1728. regarded this admonition, appears from these words pag. 26. (speaking of the reverend Mr. *Laurence Eusden*) 'A most worthy successor of *Tate* in the Laureatship, a man of insuperable modesty, since certainly it was not his Ambition that led him to seek this illustrious post, but his affection to the Perquisite of *Sack*.' A reflection as mean as it is scandalous! SCRIBLERUS. ⟨Laurus is Eusden, the poet laureate. See iii 31; *Ep. to Arbuthnot* 15*n*, p. 598.⟩

395. *Fleet*] A Prison for insolvent Debtors on the bank of the Ditch.

End of the Second Book

The Dunciad

BOOK THE THIRD

But in her Temple's last recess inclos'd,
On Dulness lap th' Anointed head repos'd.
Him close she curtain'd round with vapors blue,
And soft besprinkled with Cimmerian dew.
Then raptures high the seat of sense o'erflow,   5
Which only heads, refin'd from reason, know.
Hence, from the straw where Bedlam's Prophet nods,
He hears loud Oracles, and talks with Gods.

5, 6, &*c.*] Hereby is intimated that the following Vision is no more than the Chimera of the Dreamer's brain, and not a real or intended satire on the Present Age, doubtless more learned, more inlighten'd, and more abounding with great Genius's in Divinity, Politics, and whatever Arts and Sciences, than all the preceding. For fear of any such mistake of our Poet's honest meaning, he hath again at the end of this Vision, repeated this monition, saying that it all past thro' the *Ivory gate*, which (according to the Ancients) denoteth Falsity. SCRIBLERUS.

8.   *He hears loud Oracles, and talks with Gods.*

Virg. Æn. 7 ⟨90–1⟩.

Et varias audit voces, fruiturque deorum
Colloquio———

Hence the Fool's paradise, the Statesman's scheme,
The air-built Castle, and the golden Dream,   10
The Maid's romantic wish, the Chymist's flame,
And Poet's vision of eternal fame.
And now, on Fancy's easy wing convey'd,
The King descended to th' Elyzian shade.
There, in a dusky vale where Lethe rolls,   15
Old Bavius sits, to dip poetic souls,
And blunt the sense, and fit it for a scull
Of solid proof, impenetrably dull.
Instant when dipt, away they wing their flight,
Where Brown and Mears unbar the gates of Light,   20

15. *There in a dusky vale,* &c.] Virg. Æn. 6 ⟨703 ff.⟩.
> ——*Videt Æneas in valle reducta*
> *˙Seclusum nemus*——
> *Lethæumque domos placidas qui prænatat amnem.*
> *Hunc circum innumeræ gentes,* &c.

16. *Old* Bavius *sits, &c.*] Alluding to the story of *Thetis* dipping *Achilles* to render him impenetrable.
> *At pater Anchises penitus convalle virenti*
> *Inclusas animas, superumque ad lumen ituras,*
> *Lustrabat*——   Virg. Æn. 6.

16. *Old* Bavius *sits*] *Bavius* was an ancient Poet, celebrated by *Virgil* for the like cause as *Tibbald* by our author, tho' in less christian-like manner: For heathenishly it is declared by *Virgil* of *Bavius*, that he ought to be *hated* and *detested* for his evil works; *Qui Bavium non* odit——Whereas we have often had occasion to observe our Poet's great good nature and mercifulness, thro' the whole course of this Poem.

Mr. *Dennis* warmly contends that *Bavius* was no inconsiderable author; nay, that 'he and *Mævius* had (even in *Augustus*'s days) a very formidable Party at *Rome*, who thought them much superior to *Virgil* and *Horace:* For (saith he) I cannot believe they would have fix'd that eternal brand upon them, if they had not been coxcombs in more than ordinary credit.' An argument which (if this Poem should last) will conduce to the honour of the Gentlemen of the *Dunciad.* In like manner he tells us of Mr. *Settle*, that 'he was once a formidable Rival to Mr. *Dryden*, and that in the University of *Cambridge* there were those who gave him the *preference.*' Mr. *Welsted* goes yet farther in his behalf. 'Poor *Settle* was formerly the *Mighty Rival* of *Dryden*: nay, *for many years*, bore his Reputation *above* him.' [*Pref. to his Poems*, 8°. *p.* 51.] And Mr. *Milbourn* cry'd out, 'How little was *Dryden* able, even when his blood run high, to defend himself against Mr. *Settle!*' *Notes on* Dryd. Virg. *p.* 175. These are comfortable opinions! and no wonder some authors indulge them. SCRIBLERUS. ⟨Bavius was probably intended for Shadwell.⟩

20. Brown *and* Mears] Booksellers, Printers for *Tibbald*, Mrs. *Haywood*, or any body.—The Allegory of the souls of the Dull coming forth in the form of Books, and being let abroad in vast numbers by Booksellers, is sufficiently intelligible.

20. *Unbar the gates of Light*] Milton ⟨*Par. Lost*, vi 4⟩.

Demand new bodies, and in Calf's array
Rush to the world, impatient for the day.
Millions and millions on these banks he views,
Thick as the stars of night, or morning dews,
As thick as bees o'er vernal blossoms fly,   25
As thick as eggs at Ward in Pillory.
Wond'ring he gaz'd: When lo! a Sage appears,
By his broad shoulders known, and length of ears,

23–5. *Millions and millions—Thick as the Stars,* &c.] Virg. ⟨*Aen.* vi 309 ff.⟩.

> *Quam multa in sylvis autumni frigore primo*
> *Lapsa cadunt folia, aut ad terram gurgite ab alto*
> *Quam multæ glomerantur aves,* &c.

26. Ward *in Pillory*] *John Ward* of *Hackney,* Esq.; Member of Parliament, being convicted of Forgery, was first expelled the House, and then sentenc'd to the Pillory on the 17th of *Febr.* 1727. Mr. *Curl* looks upon the mention of such a Gentleman in a Satire, as a *great act of Barbarity. Key to the* Dunc. 3*d Edit. p.* 16. And another Author ⟨Ned Ward⟩ thus reasons upon it. *Durgen,* 8°. pag. 11, 12. 'How unworthy is it of *Christian Charity* to animate the *rabble* to abuse a *worthy man* in such a situation? It was in vain! he had no *Eggs* thrown at him; his *Merit* preserv'd him. What cou'd move the Poet thus to mention a *brave Sufferer,* a *gallant Prisoner,* expos'd to the view of all mankind! It was laying aside his *Senses,* it was committing a *Crime* for which the *Law is deficient* not to punish him! nay a Crime which *Man can scarce forgive,* nor *Time efface!* Nothing surely could have induced him but being bribed to it by a great Lady,' (to whom this brave, honest, worthy Gentleman was guilty of no offence but Forgery proved in open Court, &*c.*). But it is evident this verse cou'd not be meant of him; it being notorious that no *Eggs* were thrown at that Gentleman: Perhaps therefore it might be intended of Mr. *Edward Ward* the Poet. ⟨For Edward Ward, see i 200. He had been pilloried in 1705. The 'great Lady' was Katherine, Duchess of Buckinghamshire. (See Pope's note to *Moral Essays,* iii 20, p. 571.)⟩

28. *And length of Ears*] This is a *sophisticated* reading. I think I may venture to affirm all the Copyists are mistaken here: I believe I may say the same of the Cricks; *Dennis, Oldmixon, Welsted,* have pass'd it in silence: I have always stumbled at it, and wonder'd how an error so manifest could escape such accurate persons. I dare assert it proceeded originally from the inadvertency of some Transcriber whose head run on the *Pillory* mention'd two lines before: It is therefore amazing that Mr. *Curl* himself should overlook it! ⟨Pope is punning on Curll's own acquaintance with the pillory. In eighteenth-century slang a man in the pillory was an 'overseer.'⟩ Yet that *Scholiast* takes not the least notice hereof. That the learned *Mist* also read it thus, is plain, from his ranging this passage among those in which our Author was blamed for *personal Satire* on a *Man*'s *Face* (whereof doubtless he might take the *Ear* to be a part;) So likewise *Concanen, Ralph,* the *Flying-Post,* and all the Herd of Commentators.—*Tota armenta sequuntur.*

A very little Sagacity (which all these Gentlemen therefore wanted) will restore to us the true sense of the Poet, thus,

> *By his broad shoulders known, and length of years.*

Known by the band and suit which Settle wore,
(His only suit) for twice three years before: 30
All as the vest, appear'd the wearer's frame,
Old in new state, another yet the same.
Bland and familiar as in life, begun
Thus the great Father to the greater Son.
    'Oh born to see what none can see awake!   35
Behold the wonders of th' Oblivious Lake.
Thou, yet unborn, hast touch'd this sacred shore;
The hand of Bavius drench'd thee o'er and o'er.

But blind to former, as to future Fate,
What mortal knows his pre-existent state?   40
Who knows how long thy transmigrating soul
Did from Bœotian to Bœotian roll?
How many Dutchmen she vouchsaf'd to thrid?
How many stages thro' old Monks she rid?
And all who since, in mild benighted days,   45
Mix'd the Owl's ivy with the Poet's bays?
As man's mæanders to the vital spring
Roll all their tydes, then back their circles bring;
Or whirligigs, twirl'd round by skilful swain,
Suck the thread in, then yield it out again: 50
All nonsense thus, of old or modern date,
Shall in thee centre, from thee circulate.
For this, our Queen unfolds to vision true
Thy mental eye, for thou hast much to view:
Old scenes of glory, times long cast behind,   55
Shall first recall'd, rush forward to thy mind;
Then stretch thy sight o'er all her rising reign,
And let the past and future fire thy brain.

See how easy a change! of one single letter! That Mr. *Settle* was old is
most certain, but he was (happily) a stranger to the Pillory. *This Note
partly Mr.* THEOBALD, *partly* SCRIBLERUS.
    42. *Did from* Bœotian, &*c.*] See the Remark on Book 1. V. 23.
    46. *Mix'd the Owl's Ivy with the Poet's Bays*] Virg. Ec. 8 ⟨12–13⟩.
                ——*sine tempora circum*
            Inter victrices Hederam tibi serpere laurus.
    49. *whirligigs* ⟨The toy was probably one 'consisting of a small spindle
turned by means of string.'⟩
    53. *For this, our Queen* &*c.*] This has a resemblance to that passage in
Milton ⟨*Par. Lost,* xi 411–13⟩, where the Angel,
            To nobler sights from Adam's *eye remov'd
            The film; then purg'd with Euphrasie and Rue
            The visual nerve*—For he had much to see.
There is a general allusion in what follows to that whole passage.

'Ascend this hill, whose cloudy point commands
Her boundless Empire over seas and lands.   60
See round the Poles where keener spangles shine,
Where spices smoke beneath the burning Line,
(Earth's wide extreams) her sable flag display'd;
And all the nations cover'd in her shade!

'Far Eastward cast thine eye, from whence the Sun   65
And orient Science at a birth begun.
One man immortal all that pride confounds,
He, whose long Wall the wand'ring Tartar bounds.
Heav'ns! what a pyle! whole ages perish there:
And one bright blaze turns Learning into air.   70
'Thence to the South extend thy gladden'd eyes;

There rival flames with equal glory rise,
From shelves to shelves see greedy Vulcan roll,
And lick up all their Physick of the Soul.

'How little, mark! that portion of the ball,   75
Where, faint at best, the beams of Science fall.
Soon as they dawn, from Hyperborean skies,
Embody'd dark, what clouds of Vandals rise!
Lo where Mœotis sleeps, and hardly flows
The freezing Tanais thro' a waste of Snows,   80
The North by myriads pours her mighty sons,
Great nurse of Goths, of Alans, and of Huns.
See Alaric's stern port, the martial frame
Of Genseric! and Attila's dread name!
See, the bold Ostrogoths on Latium fall;   85
See, the fierce Visigoths on Spain and Gaul.
See, where the Morning gilds the palmy shore,
(The soil that arts and infant letters bore)
His conqu'ring tribes th' Arabian prophet draws,
And saving Ignorance enthrones by Laws.   90

61, 62. *See round the Poles*, &c.] Almost the whole Southern and Northern Continent wrapt in Ignorance.

65.] Our Author favours the opinion that all Sciences came from the Eastern nations.

66. *Science* ⟨In its earlier sense of knowledge acquired by study.⟩

69.] *Chi Ho-am-ti*, Emperor of *China*, the same who built the great wall between *China* and *Tartary*, destroyed all the books and learned men of that empire.

73, 74.] The *Caliph, Omar* I. having conquer'd *Ægypt*, caus'd his General to burn the *Ptolomæan* library, on the gates of which was this inscription, *Medicina Animæ, The Physick of the Soul.*

88. *The Soil that arts and infant letters bore*] *Phœnicia, Syria*, &c. where *Letters* are said to have been invented. In these Countries *Mahomet* began his Conquests.

See Christians, Jews, one heavy sabbath keep;
And all the Western World believe and sleep.
'Lo Rome herself, proud mistress now no more
Of arts, but thund'ring against Heathen lore;
Her gray-hair'd Synods damning books unread,   95
And Bacon trembling for his brazen head:
Padua with sighs beholds her Livy burn;
And ev'n th' Antipodes Vigilius mourn.
See, the Cirque falls! th' unpillar'd Temple nods!
Streets pav'd with Heroes, Tyber choak'd with Gods!   100
Till Peter's Keys some christen'd Jove adorn,
And Pan to Moses lends his Pagan horn;

---

94. *Thund'ring against Heathen lore*] A strong instance of this pious rage
is plac'd to Pope *Gregory*'s account. *John of Salisbury* gives a very odd
Encomium to this Pope, at the same time that he mentions one of the
strangest effects of this excess of zeal in him. *Doctor sanctissimus ille
Gregorius, qui melleo prædicationis imbre totam rigavit & inebriavit
ecclesiam, non modo* Mathesin *jussit ab aulâ; sed, ut traditur a majoribus,
incendio dedit* probatæ lectionis scripta, *Palatinus quæcunque tenebat
Apollo.* And in another place: *Fertur beatus Gregorius bibliothecam com-
bussisse gentilem; quo divinæ paginæ gratior esset locus, & major authoritas,
& diligentia studiosior. Desiderius* Archbishop of *Vienna* was sharply
reproved by him for teaching Grammar and Literature, and explaining
the Poets; Because (says this Pope) *in uno se ore cum Jovis laudibus, Christi
laudes non capiunt: Et quam grave nefandumque sit, Episcopis canere quod
nec Laico religioso conveniat, ipse considera.* He is said, among the rest, to
have burn'd *Livy; Quia in superstitionibus & sacris Romanorum perpetuò
versatur.* The same Pope is accused by *Vossiüs* and others of having
caus'd the noble monuments of the old *Roman* magnificence to be
destroyed, lest those who came to *Rome* shou'd give more attention to
Triumphal Arches, &c. than to Holy Things. BAYLE, *Dict.*

96. *And Bacon, &c.* ⟨Roger Bacon (1214?-94), the medieval philosopher who was vulgarly supposed to have constructed a brazen head that
could speak. He is represented as trembling *because* he had made it, i.e.
he was likely to incur the displeasure of the Church.⟩

98. *Vigilius* ⟨Vigilius, or Virgilius, an eighth-century Bishop of Salz-
burg, was publicly censured by the Archbishop of Mainz for professing
his belief in the existence of the Antipodes.⟩

99. *Cirque* ⟨probably the Coliseum at Rome.⟩

101. '*Till* Peter's *Keys*, &c.] After the Government of *Rome* devolved
to the Popes, their zeal was for some time exerted in demolishing the
Heathen Temples and Statues, so that the *Goths* scarce destroyed more
Monuments of Antiquity out of Rage, than these out of Devotion. At
length they spar'd some of the Temples by converting them to Churches,
and some of the Statues, by modifying them into Images of Saints. In
much later times, it was thought necessary to change the Statues of *Apollo*
and *Pallas* on the tomb of *Sannazarius*, into *David* and *Judith*; the Lyre
easily became a Harp, and the Gorgon's Head turn'd to that of *Holofernes.*

102. *Moses* ⟨'The medieval belief was that Moses, after descending
from Sinai, had horns on his head.'⟩

See graceless Venus to a Virgin turn'd,
Or Phidias broken, and Apelles burn'd.
　'Behold yon' Isle, by Palmers, Pilgrims trod,　　　105
Men bearded, bald, cowl'd, uncowl'd, shod, unshod,
Peel'd, patch'd, and pyebald, linsey-woolsey brothers,
Grave mummers! sleeveless some, and shirtless others.
That once was Britain—Happy! had she seen
No fiercer sons, had Easter never been.　　　　　110
In peace, great Goddess! ever be ador'd;
How keen the war, if Dulness draw the sword!
Thus visit not thy own! on this blest age
Oh spread thy Influence, but restrain thy Rage!
　'And see! my son, the hour is on its way,　　　115
That lifts our Goddess to imperial sway:
This fav'rite Isle, long sever'd from her reign,
Dove-like, she gathers to her wings again.
Now look thro' Fate! behold the scene she draws!
What aids, what armies, to assert her cause!　　　120
See all her progeny, illustrious sight!
Behold, and count them, as they rise to light.
As Berecynthia, while her offspring vye
In homage, to the mother of the sky,
Surveys around her in the blest abode　　　　　125
A hundred sons, and ev'ry son a God:
Not with less glory mighty Dulness crown'd,
Shall take thro' Grubstreet her triumphant round,
And Her Parnassus glancing o'er at once,
Behold a hundred sons, and each a dunce.　　　　130

107. *linsey-woolsey*
⟨'Linsey-Woolsey: a textile material, woven from a mixture of wool and flax. Hence, adjectivally, 'being neither one thing nor the other.'⟩
110. *Happy—had* Easter *never been*] Virg. Ecl. 6 ⟨45⟩.
　　　　　Et fortunatam, si nunquam armenta fuissent.
110. *Happy—had* Easter *never been*] Wars in *England* anciently, about the right time of celebrating *Easter.*
119, 121. *Now look thro' Fate* &c.] Virg. Æn. 6 ⟨756 ff.⟩.
　　　　　Nunc age, Dardaniam prolem quæ deinde sequatur
　　　　　Gloria, qui maneant Itala de gente nepotes,
　　　　　Illustres animas, nostrumque in nomen ituras,
　　　　　Expediam——.
119. *draws* ⟨i.e. discloses, as when a stage-curtain is 'drawn.'⟩
123. *As* Berecynthia, *&c.*] Virg. ib. ⟨784 ff.⟩
　　　　　Felix prole virum, qualis Berecynthia mater
　　　　　Invehitur curru Phrygias turrita per urbes,
　　　　　Læta deum partu, centum complexa nepotes,
　　　　　Omnes cœlicolas, omnes supera alta tenentes.

'Mark first the youth who takes the foremost place,
And thrusts his person full into your face.
With all thy Father's virtues blest, be born!
And a new Cibber shall the Stage adorn.

'A second see, by meeker manners known,   135
And modest as the maid that sips alone:
From the strong fate of drams if thou get free,
Another Durfey, Ward! shall sing in thee.
Thee shall each Ale-house, thee each Gill-house mourn,
And answ'ring Gin-shops sowrer sighs return!   140

'Lo next two slip-shod Muses traipse along,
In lofty madness, meditating song,
With tresses staring from poetic dreams,
And never wash'd, but in Castalia's streams:
Haywood, Centlivre, Glories of their race!   145
Lo Horneck's fierce, and Roome's funereal face;

131. *Mark first the youth*, &c.] Virg. Æn. 6 ⟨760–1⟩.
> *Ille vides, pura juvenis qui nititur hasta*
> *Proxima sorte tenet lucis loca.—*

133. *With all thy Father's virtues, &c.*] A manner of expression used by
Virgil ⟨Ecl. viii 17⟩,
> *Nascere! præque diem veniens, age Lucifer——*

As also that of *Patriis virtutibus.* Ecl. 4 ⟨17⟩.

134. *a new Cibber* ⟨Theophilus Cibber (1703–58), who was following
his father's profession, and had been appearing on the stage since 1721.⟩

137. *From the strong fate of drams*, &c.] Virg. Æn. 6 ⟨882–3⟩.
> *——si qua fata aspera rumpas,*
> *Tu Marcellus eris!——*

138. Ward] *Vid.* Book 1. Ver. 200.

139. *Thee shall each Ale-house*, &c.] Æn. 7 ⟨759–60⟩.
> *Te nemus Angitiae, vitrea te Fucinus unda,*
> *Te liquidi flevere lacus.*

Virgil again, *Ecl.* 10 ⟨13⟩.
> *Illum etiam lauri, illum flevere myricæ*, &c.

Gill-house ⟨Johnson defines gill as 'a malt liquor medicated with
ground-ivy.'⟩

143. *staring* ⟨standing up, bristling.⟩

145. *Haywood, Centlivre*] See book 2. ⟨149, 379.⟩

146. *Lo* Horneck's *fierce and* Roome's *funereal face*] This stood in one
edition *And* M—'s *ruful face.* But the person who suppos'd himself meant
applying to our author in a modest manner, and with declarations of his
innocence, he removed the occasion of his uneasiness. At the same time
promising to 'do the like to any other who could give him the same
assurance, of having never writ scurrilously against him.'

Horneck *and* Roome] These two are worthily coupled, being both
virulent Party-writers; and one wou'd think prophetically, since immediately after the publishing of this Piece the former dying, the latter suc-

THE DUNCIAD VARIORUM: BOOK III   409

Lo sneering G * * de, half malice and half whim,
A Fiend in glee, ridiculously grim.
Jacob, the Scourge of Grammar, mark with awe,
Nor less revere him, Blunderbuss of Law.   150
Lo Bond and Foxton, ev'ry nameless name,
All crowd, who foremost shall be damn'd to Fame?
Some strain in rhyme; the Muses, on their racks,
Scream, like the winding of ten thousand Jacks:
Some free from rhyme or reason, rule or check,   155
Break Priscian's head, and Pegasus's neck;
Down, down they larum, with impetuous whirl,
The Pindars, and the Miltons, of a Curl.
    'Silence, ye Wolves! while Ralph to Cynthia howls,
And makes Night hideous—Answer him ye Owls!   160

---

ceeded him in *Honour* and *Employment*. ⟨Horneck died Oct. 1728, and
Edward Roome succeeded him as Solicitor to the Treasury.⟩ The first
was *Philip Horneck*, Author of a Billingsgate paper call'd *The High
German Doctor*, in the 2d Vol. of which Nº. 14. you may see the regard
he had for Mr. *P.*—*Edward Roome*, Son of an Undertaker for Funerals in
Fleet-street, writ some of the papers call'd *Pasquin*, and Mr. *Ducket* others,
where by malicious Innuendos, it was endeavour'd to represent him guilty
of malevolent practices with a great man then under prosecution of
Parliament. He since reflected on his, and Dr. Swift's Miscellanies, in his
paper call'd the *Senator*. Of this Man was made the following Epigram.

> *You ask why R— diverts you with his jokes,*
> *Yet, if he writes, is dull as other folks?*
> *You wonder at it—This Sir is the case,*
> *The Jest is lost, unless he prints his Face.*

147. *G**de*] An ill-natur'd Critick who writ a Satire on our Author, yet
unprinted, call'd *The mock Æsop*. and many anonymous Libels in News-
papers for Hire. ⟨Barnham Goode (1674–1739), master at Eton College,
and hack journalist.⟩

149. Jacob] This *Gentleman* is Son of a *considerable Malster* of *Romsey*
in *Southamptonshire*, and bred to the Law under a *very eminent Attorney*:
who, between his *more laborious* Studies, has *diverted* himself with Poetry.
He is a great admirer of Poets and their works, which has occasion'd him
to try his genius that way—He has writ in prose the *Lives* of the *Poets*,
Essays, and a great many Law-Books, *The Accomplish'd Conveyancer*,
Modern Justice, &c. GILES JACOB of himself, *Lives* of Poets, Vol. 1. He
very grossly, and unprovok'd, abused in that book the Author's Friend
Mr. *Gay*. ⟨See p. 429.⟩

150.] Virg. Æn. 6 ⟨842–3⟩.

> ———*duo fulmina belli*
> *Scipiadas, cladem Lybiæ!*———

151. Bond *and* Foxton] Two inoffensive offenders against our poet;
persons unknown, but by being mention'd by Mr. *Curl.*

159. *Ralph*] A name inserted after the first Editions, not known to our
Author till he writ a Swearing-piece call'd *Sawney*, very abusive of Dr.
Swift, Mr. *Gay*, and himself. These lines allude to a thing of his, intituled

'Sense, speech, and measure, living tongues and dead,
Let all give way—and Durgen may be read.
'Flow Welsted, flow! like thine inspirer, Beer,
Tho' stale, not ripe; tho' thin, yet never clear;
So, sweetly mawkish, and so smoothly dull;   165
Heady, not strong, and foaming tho' not full.
'Ah Dennis! Gildon ah! what ill-starr'd rage
Divides a friendship, long confirm'd by age?

Night a *Poem*. Shakespear, Hamlet ⟨1 iv 53–4⟩.
              —*Visit thus the glimpses of the Moon,*
              Making Night hideous—
This low writer constantly attended his own works with Panegyricks in
the Journals, and once in particular prais'd himself highly above Mr.
Addison, in wretched remarks upon that Author's Account of English
Poets, printed in a *London Journal*, Sept. 1728. He was wholly illiterate,
and knew no Language not even *French*: Being advised to read the Rules
of Dramatick Poetry before he began a Play, he smiled and reply'd,
Shakespear writ without Rules. He ended at last in the common Sink of
all such writers, a Political News-paper, to which he was recommended
by his Friend Arnal, and receiv'd a small pittance for pay.

162. *Durgen*] A ridiculous thing of *Ward*'s. ⟨Durgen is explained in
Kersey's *Dictionary* as 'a little thick and short Person: a Dwarf.'⟩

163. *Flow*, Welsted, *flow!* &c.] Parody on *Denham, Cooper's Hill*
⟨188–91⟩.
              O could I flow like thee, and make thy stream
              My great example, as it is my theme.
              Tho' deep, yet clear; tho' gentle, yet not dull;
              Strong, without rage; without o'erflowing, full.
Of this Author see the Remark on Book ii. v. 293. But (to be impartial)
add to it the following different character of him.
Mr. *Welsted* had, in his Youth, rais'd so great Expectations of his
future Genius, that there was a *kind of struggle* between the most eminent
in the two Universities, *which* shou'd have the Honour of his Education.
To *compound* this, he (*civilly*) became a Member of both, and after having
pass'd some time at the One, he removed to the Other. From thence he
return'd to Town, where he became the *darling Expectation* of *all the*
polite Writers, whose encouragement he acknowledg'd in his occasional
Poems, in a manner that *will make no small part of the Fame* of his Pro-
tectors. It also appears, from his *Works*, that he was happy in the Patronage of the most illustrious Characters of the present Age—Incourag'd by
such a *Combination* in his favour, he—publish'd a book of Poems, some
in the *Ovidian*, some in the *Horatian* manner, in both which the most
exquisit Judges pronounce, he even *rival'd his masters*—His Love verses
have rescued that way of writing from Contempt—In his Translations, he
has given us the very soul and spirit of his author. His Ode—his Epistle—
his Verses—his Love-tale—all, are the most perfect things in all Poetry,
etc. WELSTED of *Himself*. Char. of the Times, 8º. 1728. pag. 23, 24.

167. *Ah Dennis*, &c.] The reader, who has seen thro' the course of these
notes, what a constant attendance Mr. *Dennis* paid to our Author and all
his works. may perhaps wonder he should be mention'd but twice, and so

Blockheads with reason wicked wits abhor,
But fool with fool is barb'rous civil war.   170
Embrace, embrace my Sons! be foes no more!
Nor glad vile Poets with true Criticks' gore.
    'Behold yon pair, in strict embraces join'd;
How like their manners, and how like their mind!
Fam'd for good-nature, B * * and for truth;   175

---

slightly touch'd, in this poem. But in truth he look'd upon him with some esteem, for having (more generously than all the rest) *set his Name* to such writings. He was also a very old man at this time. By his own account of himself in Mr. *Jacob's Lives*, he must have been above three score in the mayoralty of Sir *George Thorold* in 1720, and hath since happily lived ten years more. So that he is already senior to Mr. *Durfey*, who hitherto of all our Poets enjoy'd the longest Bodily life. ⟨Cf. ii 273*n.*⟩

171. *Embrace, embrace my Sons! be foes no more*] Virg. Æn. 6 ⟨832 ff.⟩.

> ——*Ne tanta animis assuescite bella,*
> *Neu patriæ validas in viscera vertite vires:*
> *Tuq; prior, tu parce*——*sanguis meus!*——

173. *Behold yon pair, in strict embraces join'd*] Virg. Æn. 6 ⟨826–7⟩.

> *Illæ autem paribus quas fulgere cernis in armis,*
> *Concordes animæ*——

And in the fifth ⟨i.e. *Aen.* v 295–6⟩,

> *Euryalus, forma insignis viridique juventa,*
> *Nisus amore pio pueri.*

175–6. *Fam'd for good nature* B * *, &c.*
    D * *, for pious passion to the youth*]

The first of these was Son of the late Bishop of *S.* ⟨i.e. Gilbert Burnet, Bishop of Salisbury⟩. Author of a weekly paper called *The Grumbler*, as the other was concern'd in another call'd *Pasquin*, in which Mr. *Pope* was abused (particularly with the late Duke of *Buckingham* and Bishop of *Rochester*.) They also join'd in a piece against his first undertaking to translate the *Iliad*, intituled *Homerides*, by Sir *Iliad Dogrel*, printed by *Wilkins* 1715. And Mr. *D.* writ an Epilogue for *Powel's* Puppet-show, reflecting on the same work. Mr. *Curl* gives us this further account of Mr. *B.* 'He did *himself write* a Letter to the E. of *Halifax, informing his Lordship* (as he tells him) *of what he knew much better before:* And he *publish'd in his own name* several political pamphlets, A certain information of a certain discourse, A second Tale of a Tub, *&c. All which* it is strongly affirmed *were written by* Colonel *Ducket.*' Curl, Key, p. 17. But the author of the *Characters of the Times* tells us, these political pieces were not approv'd of by his *own Father*, the Reverend Bishop.

Of the other works of these Gentlemen, the world has heard no more, than it wou'd of Mr. *Pope's*, had their united laudable endeavours discourag'd him from his undertakings. How few good works had ever appear'd (since men of true merit are always the least presuming) had there been always such champions to stifle them in their conception! And were it not better for the publick, that a million of monsters came into the world, than that the Serpents should have strangled one *Hercules* in

D * * for pious passion to the youth,
Equal in wit, and equally polite,
Shall this a Pasquin, that a Grumbler write;
Like are their merits, like rewards they share,
That shines a Consul, this Commissioner.   180
    'But who is he, in closet close y-pent,
Of sober face, with learned dust besprent?
Right well mine eyes arede the myster wight,

---

his cradle? The Union of these two Authors gave occasion to this
Epigram.

> Burnet *and* Duckit, *friends in spite,*
> *Came hissing forth in Verse;*
> *Both were so forward, each wou'd write,*
> *So dull, each hung an A——*
> *Thus* Amphisbœna (*I have read*)
> *At either end assails;*
> *None knows which leads, or which is led,*
> *For both Heads are but Tails.*

176. —— *for pious passion to the youth*] The verse is a literal translation
of *Virgil*, Nisus amore pio pueri ⟨*Aeneid*, v 296⟩——and here, as in the
original, apply'd to Friendship: That between *Nisus* and *Euryalus* is
allow'd to make one of the most amiable Episodes in the world, and surely
was never interpreted in a perverse sense: But it will astonish the Reader
to hear, that on no other occasion than this line, a Dedication was written
to this Gentleman to induce him to think something farther. 'Sir, you are
known to have all that affection for the beautiful part of the creation which
God and Nature design'd.—Sir, you have a very fine Lady—and, Sir, you
have eight very fine Children.'—*&c.* [*Dedic.* to Dennis *Rem. on the Rape
of the Lock.*] The truth is, the poor Dedicator's brain was turn'd upon this
article; he had taken into his head that ever since some *Books* were written
against the *Stage*, and since the *Italian Opera* had prevail'd, the nation
was infected with a vice not fit to be nam'd. He went so far as to print
upon this subject, and concludes his argument with this remark, 'that
he cannot help thinking the Obscenity of Plays excusable at this juncture,
since, when that execrable sin is spread so wide, it may be of use to the
reducing men's minds to the natural desire of women.' DENNIS, *Stage
defended* against Mr. *Law*, p. 20. Our author has solemnly declared to me,
he never heard any creature but the Dedicator mention that Vice and this
Gentleman together.

181. *But who is he*, &c.] Virg. Æn. 6 ⟨808 ff.⟩ questions and answers
in this manner, of *Numa*,

> *Quis procul ille autem ramis insignis olivæ*
> *Sacra ferens?—nosco crines, incanaq; menta, &c.*

183. AREDE] *Read* or *peruse;* tho' sometimes used for *counsel*, 'READE
THY READ, *take thy counsaile. Thomas Sternholde* in his translation of the
first Psalm into *English* metre, hath *wisely* made use of this word,

> *The man is blest that hath not bent*
> *To wicked* READ *his ear.*

But in the last spurious editions of the Singing Psalms the word READ is
changed into *men.* I say spurious editions, because not only here, but quite

On parchment scraps y-fed, and Wormius hight.
To future ages may thy dulness last,   185
As thou preserv'st the dulness of the past!
    'There, dim in clouds, the poreing Scholiasts mark,
Wits, who like Owls see only in the dark,

---

throughout the whole book of Psalms, are strange alterations, all for the
worse! And yet the title-page stands as it us'd to do! and all (which is
abominable in any book, much more in a sacred work) is ascribed to
Thomas Sternhold, John Hopkins, and others! I am confident, were *Sternhold* and *Hopkins* now living, they would proceed against the innovators
as cheats——A liberty which, to say no more of their intolerable alterations, ought by no means to be permitted or approved of, by such as are
for *Uniformity*, and have any regard for the old *English Saxon* tongue.'
HERNE, *Gloss. on* Rob. *of* Gloc. *Art.* rede.
    I do herein agree with Mr. *H*. Little is it of avail to object that such
words are become *unintelligible*. Since they are *Truly English*, Men *ought*
to understand them; and such as are for *Uniformity* should think all
alterations in a Language, *strange, abominable*, and *unwarrantable*. Rightly
therefore, I say again, hath our Poet used ancient words, and poured them
forth, as a precious ointment, upon good old *Wormius* in this place.
SCRIBLERUS.
    Myster wight] Uncouth mortal.
    184. Wormius *hight*] Let not this name, purely fictitious, be conceited
to mean the learned *Olaus Wormius*; much less (as it was unwarrantably
foisted into the surreptitious editions) our own Antiquary Mr. *Thomas
Herne*, who had no way aggrieved our Poet, but on the contrary published
many curious tracts which he hath to his great contentment perused.
    Most rightly are ancient words here imployed in speaking of such who
so greatly delight in the same: We may say not only rightly, but *wisely*, yea
excellently, inasmuch as for the like practise the like praise is given to
Hopkins and *Sternhold* by Mr. *Herne* himself. *Artic.* BEHETT; others say
BEHIGHT, '*promised*, and so it is used *excellently well* by *Tho. Norton* in
his translation into metre of the 116th Psalm, verse 14.

> *I to the Lord will pay my vows,*
>   *That I to him* BEHIGHT.

Where the modern innovators, not understanding the propriety of the
word (which is *Truly English*, from the *Saxon*) have most *unwarrantably*
alter'd it thus,
> *I to the Lord will pay my vows,*
>   *With joy and great* delight.'

    VERSE ibid.—HIGHT] 'In *Cumberland* they say to *hight*, for to *promise*
or *vow*; but HIGHT usually signifies *was call'd:* and so it does in the North
even to this day, notwithstanding what is done in *Cumberland*.' HERNE,
ibid.
    188. *Wits, who like Owls*, &c.] These few lines exactly describe the
right verbal Critick: He is to his Author as a Quack to his Patients, the
more they suffer and complain, the better he is pleas'd; like the famous
Doctor of that sort, who put up in his bills, *He delighted in matters of
difficulty*. Some-body said well of these men, that their heads were
Libraries out of order.

A Lumberhouse of Books in ev'ry head,
For ever reading, never to be read.   190
    'But, where each Science lifts its modern Type,
Hist'ry her Pot, Divinity his Pipe,
While proud Philosophy repines to show
Dishonest sight! his breeches rent below;
Imbrown'd with native Bronze, lo Henley stands,   195
Tuning his voice, and balancing his hands.
How fluent nonsense trickles from his tongue!
How sweet the periods, neither said nor sung!
Still break the benches, Henley! with thy strain,

195. ——*Lo!* Henley *stands, &c*] *J. Henley*, the Orator; he preach'd on
the Sundays Theological matters, and on the Wednesdays upon all other
sciences. Each Auditor paid one shilling. He declaim'd some years unpunish'd against the greatest persons, and occasionally did our author that
honour. WELSTED, in Oratory Transactions, N° 1. publish'd by *Henley*
himself, gives the following account of him. 'He was born at *Melton
Mowbry* in *Leicestershire*. From his own Parish school he went to St. *John's*
College in *Cambridge*. He began there to be uneasy; for it *shock'd* him to
find he was *commanded to believe* against his judgment in points of Religion,
Philosophy, *&c.* for his genius leading him freely to *dispute all propositions*, and *call all points to account*, he was impatient under those fetters of
the free-born mind.——Being admitted to Priest's orders, he found the
examination very short and superficial, and that it was *not necessary to
conform to the Christian Religion* in order either to *Deaconship* or *Priesthood.*' He came to Town, and after having for some years been a writer for
Booksellers he had an ambition to be so for Ministers of State. The only
reason he did not rise in the Church we are told 'was the envy of others,
and a disrelish entertain'd of him, because *he was not qualify'd to be a
compleat Spaniel.*' However he offer'd the service of his pen, in one
morning, to two Great men of opinions and interests directly opposite;
by both of whom being rejected, he set up a new Project, and stiled himself the *Restorer of ancient Eloquence.* He thought 'it as lawful to take a
licence from the King and Parliament at one place, as another; at *Hick's*
Hall, as at Doctors Commons; so set up his Oratory in *Newport*-Market,
Butcher-Row. There (says his friend) he had the *assurance* to form a Plan
which no mortal ever thought of; he had success against all opposition;
challenged his adversaries to fair disputations, and *none would dispute with
him*; writ, read and studied twelve hours a day; compos'd three dissertations a week on all subjects; undertook to teach in *one year* what Schools
and Universities teach in *five*; was not terrify'd by menaces, insults or
satyrs, but still proceeded, matured his bol d scheme, and put the *Church*
and *all that*, in *danger*.' WELSTED, *Narrative*, in *Orat. Transact.* N°. 1.
    After having stood some Prosecutions, he turned his Rhetorick to
Buffoonry upon all publick and private occur rences. All this passed in the
same room; where sometimes he broke Jests, and sometimes that Bread
which he call'd the *Primitive Eucharist.*——This wonderful person struck
Medals, which he dispersed as Tickets to his subscribers: The device, a
Star rising to the Meridian, with this Motto, AD SUMMA; and below,
INVENIAM VIAM AUT FACIAM.

While K ★ ★, B ★ ★, W ★ ★, preach in vain.   200
Oh great Restorer of the good old Stage,
Preacher at once, and Zany of thy Age!
Oh worthy thou of Ægypt's wise abodes,
A decent Priest, where monkeys were the Gods!
But Fate with Butchers plac'd thy priestly Stall,   205
Meek modern faith to murder, hack, and mawl;
And bade thee live, to crown Britannia's praise,
In Toland's, Tindal's, and in Woolston's days.
   'Thou too, great Woolston! here exalt thy throne,
And prove, no Miracles can match thy own.   210
   'Yet oh my sons! a father's words attend:
(So may the fates preserve the ears you lend)
'Tis yours, a Bacon, or a Locke to blame,
A Newton's Genius, or a Seraph's flame:
But O! with one, immortal One dispense,   215
The source of Newton's Light, of Bacon's Sense!
Content, each Emanation of his fires
That beams on earth, each Virtue he inspires,
Each Art he prompts, each Charm he can create,
What-e'er he gives, are giv'n for You to hate.   220
Persist, by all divine in Man un-aw'd,
But learn, ye Dunces! not to scorn your GOD.'
   Thus he, for then a ray of Reason stole
Half thro' the solid darkness of his soul;
But soon the Cloud return'd—and thus the Sire: 225
'See now, what Dulness and her sons admire;
See! what the charms, that smite the simple heart
Not touch'd by Nature, and not reach'd by Art.'

200. *K★★*, *B★★*, *W★★* ⟨i.e. White Kennett (1660–1728), Bishop of
Peterborough; Rev. James Bramston (1694?–1744), a minor poet of some
distinction; and possibly Dr. Robert Warren, whose sermons in three
volumes were published in 1723. It would be rash to assume that Pope
intends to praise any of them. The line may be read as an encomium of
fine preaching thrown away on unappreciative congregations, or a
criticism of the ineffectiveness of their sermons. See *Dunciad B*, iii 204*n*.⟩

208. Of *Toland* and *Tindal*, see book 2 ⟨l. 367⟩. *Tho. Woolston*, an
impious madman, who wrote in a most insolent style against the Miracles
of the Gospel; in the years 1726, 27, &*c*.

213. *blame* ⟨perhaps 'to bring into disrepute, to discredit.'⟩

216. *Newton's Light* ⟨i.e. his enlightenment. But Pope probably intended a secondary reference to Newton's famous researches on Optics.
Cf. his epigram on Newton, p. 808.⟩

222. *But learn, ye Dunces! not to scorn your God*] Virg. Æn. 6. ⟨620⟩
puts this precept into the mouth of a wicked man ⟨Phlegyas⟩, as here
of a stupid one,
         Discite justitiam moniti, & non temnere divos!

He look'd, and saw a sable Sorc'rer rise,
Swift to whose hand a winged volume flies: 230
All sudden, Gorgons hiss, and Dragons glare,
And ten-horn'd fiends and Giants rush to war.
Hell rises, Heav'n descends, and dance on Earth,
Gods, imps, and monsters, music, rage, and mirth,
A fire, a jig, a battle, and a ball,   235
Till one wide Conflagration swallows all.
     Thence a new world, to Nature's laws unknown,
Breaks out refulgent, with a heav'n its own:
Another Cynthia her new journey runs,
And other planets circle other suns: 240
The forests dance, the rivers upward rise,
Whales sport in woods, and dolphins in the skies,
And last, to give the whole creation grace,
Lo! one vast Egg produces human race.
     Joy fills his soul, joy innocent of thought: 245
'What pow'r,' he cries, 'what pow'r these wonders
     wrought?'
'Son! what thou seek'st is in thee. Look, and find
Each monster meets his likeness in thy mind.
Yet would'st thou more? In yonder cloud, behold!
Whose sarcenet skirts are edg'd with flamy gold,   250
A matchless youth: His nod these worlds controuls,
Wings the red lightning, and the thunder rolls.

229. ——*a sable Sorc'rer*] Dr. *Faustus*, the subject of a set of Farces
which lasted in vogue two or three seasons, in which both Play-houses
strove to outdo each other in the years 1726, 27. All the extravagancies in
the sixteen lines following were introduced on the Stage, and frequented
by persons of the first quality in *England* to the twentieth and thirtieth
time.

233. *Hell rises, &c.*] This monstrous absurdity was actually represented
in *Tibbald's Rape of Proserpine.*

240. *And other planets*] Virg. Æn. 6 ⟨641⟩.
          ——*solemque suum, sua sydera norunt.*

242. *Whales sport in woods, &c.*] Hor. ⟨*De Arte Poetica*, 30⟩
          Delphinum sylvis appingit, fluctibus aprum.

244. *Lo! one vast Egg*] In another of these Farces *Harlequin* is hatch'd
upon the Stage, out of a large Egg.

247. *Son! what thou seek'st is in thee*]
          Quod petis in te est——
          Ne te quæsiveris extra. Pers. ⟨*Sat.* i 7⟩.

252. *Wings the red lightning*, &c.] Like *Salmoneus* in *Æn.* 6 ⟨586,
590-1⟩.
          Dum flammas Jovis, & sonitus imitatur Olympi,
          —*Nimbos, & non imitabile fulmen,*
          Ære & cornipedum cursu simularat æquorum.

Angel of Dulness, sent to scatter round
Her magic charms o'er all unclassic ground:
Yon stars, yon suns, he rears at pleasure higher,   255
Illumes their light, and sets their flames on fire.
Immortal Rich! how calm he sits at ease
Mid snows of paper, and fierce hail of pease;
And proud his mistress' orders to perform,
Rides in the whirlwind, and directs the storm.   260
 'But lo! to dark encounter in mid air
New wizards rise: here Booth, and Cibber there:
Booth in his cloudy tabernacle shrin'd,
On grinning dragons Cibber mounts the wind:
Dire is the conflict, dismal is the din,   265
Here shouts all Drury, there all Lincoln's-Inn;
Contending Theatres our empire raise,
Alike their labours, and alike their praise.
 'And are these wonders, Son, to thee unknown?
Unknown to thee? These wonders are thy own.   270
For works like these let deathless Journals tell,
"None but Thy self can be thy parallel."

254. ——*o'er all unclassic ground*] alludes to Mr. *Addison*'s verse in the
praises of *Italy* ⟨i.e. *A Letter from Italy*, 11–12⟩,

> *Poetic fields incompass me around,* /
> *And still I seem to tread on Classic ground.*

As verse ⟨259 and⟩ 260 is a Parody on a noble one of the same Author
in the *Campaign* ⟨291–2⟩; and verse 255, 256, on two sublime verses
of Dr. Y. ⟨*An Epistle to the Right Hon. George Lord Lansdowne*, by
Edward Young, 467–8:

> Who the Sun's height can raise at pleasure higher,
> His lamp illumine, set his flames on fire.⟩

257. *Immortal* Rich] Mr. *John Rich*, Master of the Theatre in *Lincolns-
Inn-Fields*, was the first that excell'd this way.

262. *Booth* and *Cibber*, two of the managers of the Theatre in *Drury-
Lane*.

272. *None but thy self can be thy parallel*] A marvellous line of *Theobald*;
unless the Play call'd the *Double Falshood* be, (as he would have it
believed) *Shakespear*'s: But whether this line be his or not, he proves
Shakespear to have written as bad, (which methinks in an author for
whom he has a Veneration almost *rising to idolatry*, might have been
concealed) as for example,

> Try what *Repentance* can: What can it not?
> But what can it, when one cannot *repent*?
> ——For *Cogitation*
> Resides not in the Man who does not *think. &c.*
> MIST'S JOURN.

It is granted they are all of a piece, and no man doubts but herein he is
able to imitate *Shakespear*.

272. The former Annotator seeming to be of opinion that the *Double*

Falshood is not *Shakespear*'s; it is but justice to give Mr. *Theobald's* Arguments to the contrary: First that the MS. was above sixty years old; secondly, that once Mr. *Betterton* had it, or he hath heard so; thirdly, that some-body told him the author gave it to a bastard-daughter of his: But fourthly and above all, 'that he has a *great mind* every thing that is good in our tongue *should be* Shakespeare's.' I allow these reasons to be truly critical; but what I am infinitely concern'd at is, that so many Errors have escaped the learned Editor: a few whereof we shall here amend, out of a much greater number, as an instance of our regard to this *dear Relick.*

ACT 1. SCENE 1.

> I have his letters of a modern date,
> Wherein by *Julio, good Camillo*'s son
> (Who as he says, [ ] shall follow hard upon,
> And whom I with the growing hour [ ] expect)
> He doth sollicit the return of gold,
> To purchase certain horse that *like him well.*

This place is corrupted: the epithet *good* is a meer insignificant expletive, but the alteration of that single word restores a clear light to the whole context, thus,

> I have his letters of a modern date,
> Wherein, by *July,* (by *Camillo*'s son,
> Who, as he *saith,* shall follow hard upon,
> And whom I with the growing hours expect)
> He doth sollicit the return of gold.

Here you have not only the *Person* specify'd, by whose hands the return was to be made, but the most necessary part, the *Time,* by which it was required. *Camillo*'s son was to follow hard upon—What? Why upon *July.* —*Horse* that *like him well,* is very absurd: Read it, without contradiction,

> ——Horse, that *he likes well.*

ACT 1. at the end.

> ——I must stoop to gain her,
> Throw all my gay *Comparisons* aside,
> And turn my proud additions out of service:

saith *Henriquez* of a maiden of low condition, objecting his high quality: What have his *Comparisons* here to do? Correct it boldly,

> Throw all my gay *Caparisons* aside,
> And turn my proud additions out of service.

ACT 2. SCENE 1.

All the verse of this Scene is confounded with prose.

> ——O that a man
> Could reason down this *Feaver* of the blood,
> Or sooth with *words* the tumult in his heart!
> Then *Julio,* I might be *indeed* thy friend.

Read——this *fervor* of the blood,

> Then *Julio* I might be in *deed* thy friend.

marking the just opposition of deeds and words.

These, Fate reserv'd to grace thy reign divine,
Foreseen by me, but ah! with-held from mine.
In Lud's old walls, tho' long I rul'd renown'd,   275
Far, as loud Bow's stupendous bells resound;
Tho' my own Aldermen conferr'd my bays,
To me committing their eternal praise,
Their full-fed Heroes, their pacific May'rs,
Their annual trophies, and their monthly wars.   280
Tho' long my Party built on me their hopes,
For writing pamphlets, and for burning Popes;

ACT 4. SCENE 1.

How his eyes *shake* fire!—said by *Violante*,
observing how the lustful shepherd looks at her. It must be, as the sense
plainly demands,

——How his eyes *take* fire!
And measure every piece of youth about me!

Ibid. That, tho' I *wore disguises* for some *ends*.
She had but one disguise, and wore it but for one end. Restore it, with the
alteration but of two letters,

That, tho' I *were disguised* for some *end*.

ACT 4. SCENE 2.

—To oaths no more give credit,
To tears, to vows; false *both!*—

False Grammar I'm sure. *Both* can relate but to *two* things: And see! how
easy a change sets it right!

To tears, to vows, false *troth*—

I could shew you that very word troth, in *Shakespear* a hundred times.

Ib. For there is nothing left thee now to look for,
That can bring *comfort*, but a *quiet grave.*

This I fear is of a piece with *None but itself can be its parallel:* for the
grave *puts an end* to all sorrow, it can then need no *comfort.* Yet let us
vindicate *Shakespear* where we can: I make no doubt he wrote thus,

For there is nothing left thee now to look for,
Nothing that can bring *quiet*, but the grave.

Which reduplication of the word gives a much stronger emphasis to
Violante's concern. This figure is called *Anadyplosis.* I could shew you a
hundred just such in him, if I had nothing else to do. SCRIBLERUS.

⟨The reference to *Anadyplosis* is a satirical thrust at Theobald's
pedantry: he had mentioned this figure in *Shakespeare Restored*, p. 13.
The whole note is a parody of Theobald's editorial method and idiom.⟩

280. Annual trophies, on the *Lord Mayor's Day*; and monthly wars, in
the *Artillery Ground.*

281. *Tho' long my Party*] *Settle*, like most Party-writers, was very
uncertain in his political principles. He was employ'd to hold the pen in
the *Character* of a *Popish successor* ⟨1681⟩, but afterwards printed his
Narrative ⟨1683⟩ on the contrary side. He had managed the Ceremony
of a famous Pope-burning on *Nov.* 17, 1680: then became a Trooper of

P.A.P.—P

(Diff'rent our parties, but with equal grace
The Goddess smiles on Whig and Tory race,
'Tis the same rope at sev'ral ends they twist,   285
To Dulness, Ridpath is as dear as Mist.)
Yet lo! in me what authors have to brag on!
Reduc'd at last to hiss in my own dragon.
Avert it, heav'n! that thou or Cibber e'er
Should wag two serpent tails in Smithfield fair.   290
Like the vile straw that's blown about the streets
The needy Poet sticks to all he meets,
Coach'd, carted, trod upon, now loose, now fast,
In the Dog's tail his progress ends at last.
Happier thy fortunes! like a rolling stone,   295
Thy giddy dulness still shall lumber on,
Safe in its heaviness, can never stray,
And licks up every blockhead in the way.
Thy dragons Magistrates and Peers shall taste,
And from each show rise duller than the last: 300
Till rais'd from Booths to Theatre, to Court,
Her seat imperial, Dulness shall transport.
Already, Opera prepares the way,
The sure fore-runner of her gentle sway.
To aid her cause, if heav'n thou can'st not bend,   305

King *James*'s army at *Hounslow-heath*: After the Revolution he kept a
Booth at *Bartlemew-fair*, where in his Droll call'd St. *George for England*,
he acted in his old age in a Dragon of green leather of his own invention.
He was at last taken into the Charterhouse, and there dyed, aged about
60 years.

283–84.   ——*With equal grace*
                    Our Goddess smiles on Whig and Tory race]
Virg. Æn. 10 ⟨108, 112⟩,
                    Tros Rutulusve fuat, nullo discrimine habebo.
                    ——*Rex Jupiter omnibus idem.*

286. *To Dulness*, Ridpath *is as dear as* Mist] *George Ridpath*, author for
several years of the *Flying-Post*, a Whig-paper; *Nathaniel Mist*, publisher
of the Weekly Journal, a Tory-paper. ⟨For Ridpath, see ii 141*n*.; for
Mist, see i 194*n*.⟩

299. *Magistrates and Peers*] It stood in the first edition with blanks,
Thy dragons * * *and* * * *. *Concanen* was sure, 'they must needs mean no-
body but the *King* and *Queen*, and said he would insist it was so, till the
Poet clear'd himself by filling up the blanks otherwise agreeably to the
context, and consistent with his *allegiance*.' [Pref. to a Collection of Verses,
Essays, Letters, *&c.* against Mr. *P*. printed for *A. Moore*, pag. 6.]

303. *Opera* ⟨See *Dunciad B*, iv 45–70 (p. 769).⟩

305. ——*If heav'n thou canst not bend, &c.*]
Virg. Æn. 7 ⟨312⟩.
                    Flectere si nequeo superos, Acheronta movebo.

Hell thou shalt move; for Faustus is thy friend:
Pluto with Cato thou for her shalt join,
And link the Mourning-Bride to Proserpine.
Grubstreet! thy fall should men and Gods conspire,
Thy stage shall stand, ensure it but from Fire.   310
Another Æschylus appears! prepare
For new Abortions, all ye pregnant Fair!
In flames, like Semeles, be brought to bed,
While opening Hell spouts wild-fire at your head.
    'Now Bavius, take the poppy from thy brow,   31ζ
And place it here! here all ye Heroes bow!
This, this is He, foretold by ancient rhymes,
Th' Augustus born to bring Saturnian times:
Beneath his reign, shall Eusden wear the bays,

307. —*Faustus is thy friend*, Pluto *with* Cato, &c.] Names of miserable Farces of *Tibbald* and others, which it was their custom to get acted at the end of the best Tragedies, to spoil the digestion of the audience. ⟨Congreve's *The Mourning Bride*, 1697; Addison's *Cato*, 1713. See iii **229n.**⟩

310. ——*ensure it but from fire*] In *Tibbald's* Farce of *Proserpine* a Cornfield was set on fire; whereupon the other Playhouse had a Barn burnt down for the recreation of the spectators. They also rival'd each other in showing the Burnings of Hell-fire, in Dr. *Faustus.* ⟨Cf. i **208n.**⟩

311. *Another Æschylus appears!* &c.] It is reported of *Æschylus*, that when his Tragedy of the *Furies* was acted, the audience were so terrify'd that the children fell into fits, and the big-bellied women miscarried. *Tibbald* is translating this author: he printed a specimen of him many years ago, of which I only remember that the first Note contains some comparison between *Prometheus* and *Christ crucify'd.*

313. ——*Like Semeles*——] See *Ovid, Met.* 3.

317. *This, this is he, &c.*] Virg. Æn. 6 ⟨791-4⟩.

> Hic vir, hic est! tibi quem promitti sæpius audis,
> Augustus Cæsar, divum genus; aurea condet
> Sæcula qui rursus Latio, regnata per arva
> Saturno quondam——

Saturnian here relates to the age of *Lead*, mention'd book 1. ver. 26.

319. Eusden *wear the bays*] *Laurence Eusden*, Poet-Laureate: Mr. *Jacob* gives a catalogue of some few only of his works, which were very numerous. Mr. *Cook* in his *Battle of Poets* saith of him,

> Eusden, *a laurel'd Bard, by fortune rais'd,*
> *By very few was read, by fewer prais'd.*

Mr. *Oldmixon* in his Arts of Logic and Rhetoric, p. 413, 414. affirms, 'That of all the Galimatia's he ever met with, none comes up to some verses of this Poet, which have as much of the Ridiculum and the Fustian in 'em as can well be jumbled together, and are of that sort of nonsense which so perfectly confounds all Ideas, that there is no distinct one left in the mind. Further he says of him, that he hath prophesy'd his own poetry shall be sweeter than *Catullus, Ovid*, and *Tibullus*, but we have little hope of the accomplishment of it from what he hath lately publish'd.' Upon which Mr. *Oldmixon* has not spar'd a reflection, 'That the putting

Cibber preside Lord-Chancellor of Plays,   320
B * * sole Judge of Architecture sit,
And Namby Pamby be prefer'd for Wit!

---

the Laurel on the head of one who writ such verses, will give futurity a
very lively idea of the Judgment and Justice of those who bestow'd it.'
Ibid. p. 417. But the well-known learning of that Noble Person who was
then Lord Chamberlain, might have screen'd him from this unmannerly
reflection. ⟨Eusden's appointment (Dec. 24, 1718) was due to the Duke
of Newcastle, then Lord Chamberlain.⟩ Mr. *Eusden* was made *Laureate*
for the same reason that Mr. *Tibbald* was made *Hero* of This Poem,
because there was *no better to be had*. Nor ought Mr. *Oldmixon* to complain, so long after, that the Laurel would better have become his own
brows, or any other's: It were decent to acquiesce in the opinion of the
Duke of *Buckingham* upon this matter.

> —*In rush'd* Eusden, *and cry'd, Who shall have it,*
> *But I the true Laureate to whom the King gave it?*
> Apollo *begg'd pardon, and granted his claim,*
> *But vow'd, that till then he ne'er heard of his name.*
>   Session of Poets.

I have before observ'd something like Prophesy in our Author. Eusden,
whom he here couples with Cibber, no sooner died but his place of
Laureate was supply'd by Cibber, in the year 1730, on which was made
the ensuing Epigram.

> In merry old England it once was a rule,
> The King had his Poet, and also his Fool:
> But now we're so frugal, I'd have you to know it,
> That C**r can serve both for Fool and for Poet.

320. *Lord-Chancellor of Plays* ⟨As one of the three patentees of Drury
Lane, Cibber was in a position to accept or refuse new plays submitted
for performance.⟩

321. B** *sole judge of Architecture*] W——m B—ns—n (late Surveyor of
the Buildings to his Majesty King *George* I.) gave in a report to the *Lords*,
that Their House and the Painted Chamber adjoining were in immediate
danger of falling. Whereupon the Lords met in a Committee to appoint
some other place to sit in, while the House should be taken down. But it
being proposed to cause some other Builders first to inspect it, they found
it in very good condition. The Lords, upon this, were going upon an
address to the King against *B—ns—n*, for such a misrepresentation; but
the Earl of *Sunderland*, then Secretary, gave them an assurance that his
Majesty would remove him, which was done accordingly. In favour of
this man, the famous Sir *Christopher Wren*, who had been Architect to
the Crown for above fifty years, who laid the first stone of St. *Paul*'s, and
lived to finish it, had been displac'd from his employment at the age of
near ninety years. ⟨For Benson, see *Dunciad B*, iv 110 (p. 772).⟩

322. *And* Namby Pamby] An author ⟨i.e. Ambrose Philips⟩ whose
eminence in the Infantine stile obtain'd him this name. He was (saith Mr.
JACOB) 'one of the Wits at *Button*'s, and a Justice of the Peace.' But since
he hath met with higher preferment, in *Ireland:* and a much greater
character we have of him in Mr. GILDON's Compleat Art of Poetry,
vol. 1. p. 157. 'Indeed he confesses, he dares not set him *quite on the same
foot* with *Virgil*, lest it should *seem* Flattery: but he is much mistaken if

While naked mourns the Dormitory wall,
And Jones' and Boyle's united labours fall,
While Wren with sorrow to the grave descends,   325
Gay dies un-pension'd with a hundred Friends,

posterity does not afford him a *greater esteem* then he *at present enjoys*.'
This is said of his Pastorals, of which see in the Appendix the *Guardian*,
at large. He endeavour'd to create some mis-understanding between our
author and Mr. *Addison*, whom also soon after he abused as much. His
constant cry was, that Mr. *P.* was an Enemy to the government; and in
particular he was the avowed author of a report very industriously spread,
that he had a hand in a Party-paper call'd the *Examiner*: A falshood well
known to those yet living, who had the direction and publication of it.

> *Qui meprise* Cotin, *n'estime point son* Roy,
> *Et n'a, (selon* Cotin,) *ni* Dieu, *ni* Foy, *ni* Loy.

323. *Dormitory wall*] The Dormitory in *Westminster* was a building
intended for the lodging of the King's Scholars; toward which a sum was
left by Dr. *Edw. Hannes*, the rest was raised by contributions procured
from several eminent persons by the interest of *Francis* late Bishop of
Rochester, and Dean of *Westminster*. He requested the Earl of *Burlington*
to be the Architect, who carry'd on the work till the Bill against that
learned Prelate was brought in, which ended in his banishment. The shell
being finished according to his Lordship's design, the succeeding Dean
and Chapter employ'd a common builder to do the inside, which is
perform'd *accordingly*.

324. Jones' *and* Boyle's *united labours*] At the time when this Poem was
written, the Banquetting-house of *Whitehall*, the Church and Piazza of
Covent-garden, and the Palace and Chappel of *Somerset-house*, the works
of the famous *Inigo Jones*, had been for many years so neglected, as to be
in danger of ruin. The Portico of *Covent-garden* Church had been just
then ⟨1727⟩ restored and beautify'd at the expence of *Richard* ⟨Boyle⟩
Earl of *Burlington*; who, at the same time, by his publication of the
designs of that great Master and *Palladio*, as well as by many noble
buildings of his own, revived the true Taste of Architecture in this
Kingdom. ⟨In 1727 William Kent (1684–1748) published, with the assistance of Burlington, *Designs of Inigo Jones*. This work included one design
by Palladio, and a few by Burlington. In 1730 Burlington brought out an
edition of Palladio's *Fabbriche Antiche*.⟩

326. Gay *dies un-pension'd*, &c.] See Mr. *Gay's* Fable of the *Hare* and
Many Friends. This gentleman was early in the friendship of our author,
which has continued many years. He wrote several works of humour with
great success, the *Shepherd's Week, Trivia*, the *What d'ye call it*, &c.
(printed together in 4°. by *J. Tonson*) *Fables*; and lastly, the celebrated
Beggar's Opera; a piece of Satire which hit all tastes and degrees of men,
from those of the highest Quality to the very Rabble: That verse of
Horace ⟨Sat. II i 69⟩

Primores populi arripuit, populumque tributim,

could never be so justly applied as to this. The vast success of it was
unprecedented, and almost incredible: What is related of the wonderful
effects of the ancient Music or Tragedy hardly came up to it: *Sophocles*
and *Euripides* were less follow'd and famous. It was acted in *London* sixty-
three days, uninterrupted; and renew'd the next season with equal

Hibernian Politicks, O Swift, thy doom,
And Pope's, translating three whole years with Broome.
  'Proceed great days! till Learning fly the shore,
Till Birch shall blush with noble blood no more,   330
Till Thames see Eton's sons for ever play,
Till Westminster's whole year be holiday;
Till Isis' Elders reel, their Pupils' sport;
And Alma Mater lye dissolv'd in Port!
  'Signs following signs lead on the Mighty Year;   335
See! the dull stars roll round and re-appear.
She comes! the Cloud-compelling Pow'r, behold!
With Night Primæval, and with Chaos old.

---

applauses. It spread into all the great towns of *England*, was play'd in
many places to the 30th, and 40th time, at *Bath* and *Bristol* 50, *&c.* It
made its progress into *Wales, Scotland*, and *Ireland*, where it was performed 24 days together. It was lastly acted in *Minorca*. The fame of it
was not confin'd to the author only; the Ladies carry'd about with 'em the
favourite songs of it in Fans; and houses were furnish'd with it in Screens.
The person who acted *Polly*, till then obscure, became all at once the
favourite of the town; her *Pictures* were ingraved and sold in great
numbers; her *Life* written; books of *Letters* and *Verses* to her publish'd;
and pamphlets made even of her *Sayings* and *Jests*. ⟨Lavinia Fenton
(1708–60), the actress who played the part of Polly, became the mistress,
and, in 1751, the wife, of Charles Paulet, third Duke of Bolton.⟩
  Furthermore, it drove out of *England* the *Italian Opera*, which had
carry'd all before it for ten years: That Idol of the Nobility and the people,
which the great Critick Mr. *Dennis* by the labours and outcries of a whole
life could not overthrow, was demolish'd in one winter by a single stroke
of this gentleman's pen. This remarkable period happen'd in the year
1728. Yet so great was his modesty, that he constantly prefixed to all the
editions of it this Motto, *Nos hæc novimus esse nihil.*
  327. Hibernian *politicks*] The Politicks of *England* and *Ireland* at this
time were thought by some to be opposite or interfering with each other.
Dr. *Swift* of course was in the interests of the latter. ⟨The 'Drapier
Letters' were published in 1724. Cf. i 24*n*.⟩
  328. *And* Pope's, *translating*] He concludes his Irony with a stroke upon
himself: For whoever imagines this a sarcasm on the other ingenious
person is greatly mistaken. The opinion our author had of him was
sufficiently shown, by his joining him in the undertaking of the *Odyssey:*
in which Mr. *Broome* having ingaged without any previous agreement,
discharged his part so much to Mr. *Pope's* satisfaction, that he gratified
him with the full sum of *Five hundred pounds*, and a present of all those
books for which his own interest could procure him Subscribers, to the
value of *One hundred more*. The author only seems to lament, that he was
imploy'd in Translation at all.
  329. *Proceed great days*] Virg. Ecl. 4 ⟨12⟩,
      ——*Incipient magni procedere menses*
  337, &c. *She comes! the Cloud-compelling pow'r, behold!* &c.] Here the
Muse, like *Jove's* Eagle, after a sudden stoop at ignoble game, soareth
again to the skies. As Prophecy hath ever been one of the chief provinces

Lo! the great Anarch's ancient reign restor'd,
Light dies before her uncreating word: 340
As one by one, at dread Medæa's strain,
The sick'ning Stars fade off th' æthereal plain;
As Argus' eyes, by Hermes' wand opprest,
Clos'd one by one to everlasting rest:
Thus at her felt approach, and secret might,   345
Art after Art goes out, and all is Night.
See sculking Truth in her old cavern lye,
Secur'd by mountains of heap'd casuistry:
Philosophy, that touch'd the Heavens before,
Shrinks to her hidden cause, and is no more: 350
See Physic beg the Stagyrite's defence!
See Metaphysic call for aid on Sence!
See Mystery to Mathematicks fly!
In vain! they gaze, turn giddy, rave, and die.
Thy hand great Dulness! lets the curtain fall,   355
And universal Darkness covers all.'

---

of Poesy, our poet here foretells from what we feel, what we are to fear;
and in the style of other Prophets, hath used the future tense for the
preterit: since what he says shall be, is already to be seen, in the writings
of some even of our most adored authors, in Divinity, Philosophy,
Physics, Metaphysics, &c. (who are too good indeed to be named in such
company.) Do not gentle reader, rest too secure in thy contempt of the
Instruments for such a revolution in learning, or despise such weak agents
as have been described in our poem, but remember what the *Dutch* stories
somewhere relate, that a great part of their Provinces was once overflow'd,
by a small opening made in one of their dykes by a single *Water-Rat*.

However, that such is not seriously the judgment of our Poet, but that
he conceiveth better hopes from the diligence of our Schools, from the
regularity of our Universities, the discernment of our Great men, the
encouragement of our Patrons, and the genius of our Writers in all kinds,
(notwithstanding some few exceptions in each) may plainly be seen from
his conclusion; where by causing all this Vision to pass thro' the *Ivory
Gate*, he expressly in the language of poesy declares all such imaginations
to be wild, ungrounded, and fictitious.

SCRIBLERUS.

343. *As* Argus' *eyes &c.*] Ovid Met. 1 ⟨686-7; 713-14⟩.
    Et quamvis sopor est oculorum parte receptus,
    Parte tamen vigilat—Vidit Cyllenius omnes
    Succubuisse oculos, &c. ibid.

347. *Truth in her old cavern lye*] Alludes to the saying of *Democritus,*
that Truth lay at the bottom of a deep well.

351. *See Physic &c.* ⟨Physic = natural science.⟩

353. *Mystery* ⟨In its theological sense: 'a religious truth known only
from divine revelation; usually a doctrine of the faith involving difficulties
which human reason is incapable of solving.'⟩

'Enough! enough!' the raptur'd Monarch cries;
And thro' the Ivory Gate the Vision flies.

358. *And thro' the Ivory Gate the Vision flies*] Virg. Æn. 6 ⟨893–6⟩
Sunt geminæ somni portæ; quarum altera fertur
Cornea, qua veris facilis datur exitus umbris;
Altera, candenti perfecta nitens elephanto,
Sed falsa ad cœlum mittunt insomnia manes.

M. Scriblerus Lectori

The *Errata* of this Edition we thought (gentle reader) to have
trusted to thy candor and benignity, to correct with thy pen, as
accidental Faults escaped the press: But seeing that certain Cen-
sors do give to such the name of *Corruptions of the Text* and *false
Readings*, charge them on the Editor, and judge that correcting the
same is to be called *Restoring*, and an *Atchievement that brings Honour to the Critic*; we have in like manner taken it upon ourselves.

Book i. Verse 8. *E'er Pallas issu'd from the Thund'rers head. E'er*
is the contraction of *ever*, but that is by no means the sense in this
place: Correct it, without the least scruple, *E're*, the contraction of
or-ere, an old *English* word for *before*. What Ignorance of our
mother tongue!

Verse 6. *Still Dunce* [ ] *second reigns like Dunce the first.* Read
infallibly, still Dunce *the* second—Want of knowledge in the very
Measure!

Verse 23, 24.——*tho' her power* retires,
    Grieve not at ought our sister realms acquire.
Read,—*our sister* realm acquires. Want of Ear even in Rhime!

Verse 38.——Lintot's *rubric's post*. Read, *rubric post*. I am aware,
there is such a Substantive as *Rubric, The Rubric*; but here (I can
assure the Editor) it is an Adjective.

Verse 189. Remarks. *C'est le mem quem* Mare ⟨Marc⟩ Tulle. Correct it boldly, *le meme que* Mare ⟨Marc⟩ Tulle. Ignorance in the
French!

Book ii. verse 79. Imitations.—Terrasque *fretamque*. Read
fretumque, Neut. Unskilfulness in *Latin!*

Ibid. verse 88.—ῥέε δ' Ἀμβροτον, correct the Accents thus,
ῥέε δ' Ἄμβροτον—πέργε, Corr. πέρ τε. Want of understanding
in *Greek!*

Book i. verse 258. Rem. Tenderness for *a bad writer*, read *the bad
writers*. Plur. False *English:* No Relative!

Verse 197. Rem. *Incensa* [. ,] make it a plain Comma; [,] a strange
sort of Punctuation this, [. ,] invented sure by the Editor!

Verse 208. Imit. *Uc, alegon.* Monstrous Division! away with that Comma!

Book ii. verse 369. Leave out these words—*When he came into the Administration;* For these Gentlemen never write against any man *in power.* This betrays great want of knowledge in Authors!

After so shameful ignorance in *Greek, Latin, French, English,* Quantity, Accent, Rhyme, Grammar, we cannot wonder at such Errors as the following. Book i. verse 101. *Rem.* for 254, read 258. and for 300, read 281.——Book ii. verse 75, for *Here* r. *Hear,* Verse 118. Rem. col. 2. for *Libel,* read *silly book,* it deserves not the name of a Libel. Verse 251, for *Courts* of *Chancery* r. *Offices,* for *those Courts* r. *that Court,* and for *them* r. *it.* Verse 317. for *sacred* r. *secret.* Book iii. verse 46. Imit. for *hedæram* r. *hederam.* Verse 56. for *run forward* r. *rush forward.* We must also observe the careless manner of spelling sometimes *Satyr,* sometimes *Satire,* in the Notes, probably from the different Orthography of the various Annotators; however no excuse for the Editor, who ought constantly to have spelled it *Satire.*

In our Prolegomena likewise, pag. 12. line 6. where it is said, certain Verses were *never made publick till by Curl their own Bookseller;* Correct and strengthen the passage thus, *never made publick till in* their own Journals, *and by Curl* their own Bookseller, *&c.* But this, gentle reader, be so candid as to believe the Error only of the Printer.

Vale & fruere.

Errata

We should think (gentle Reader) that we but ill perform'd our Part, if we corrected not as well *our own Errours* now, as formerly those of the *Printer.* Since what moved us to this Work, was solely the Love of *Truth,* not in the least any Vain-glory, or Desire to contend with *Great Authors.* And farther, our Mistakes we conceive will the rather be pardoned, as scarce possible to be avoided in writing of such Persons and Works as do ever shun the Light. However, that we may not any way soften or extenuate the same, we give them thee in the very Words of our Antagonists: not defending, but retracting them from our heart, and craving excuse of the Parties offended: For surely in this Work, it hath been above all things our desire, *to provoke no Man.*

ERROUR I. *Testimonies,* page 35 ⟨p. 339⟩. Mr. Gildon *and* Dennis *in their* Character of Mr. P—*&c.*] Hear how Mr. *Dennis* hath

prov'd our Mistake in this place. 'As to my writing *in concert* with
Mr. *Gildon*, I declare upon the word and honour of a *Gentleman*,
that I never wrote so much as one Line *in concert with any one Man
whatsoever*; and these two Letters from Mr. *Gildon* will plainly
show, that we are not Writers *in concert* with each other.

*Sir,—The height of my Ambition is to please Men of the best
Judgment; and finding that I have entertain'd my Master agreeably, I
have the Extent of the Reward of my Labour*, &c.

*Sir, I had not the opportunity of hearing your excellent Pamphlet
'till this Day; I am infinitely satisfied and pleas'd with it, and hope you
will meet with that Encouragement which your admirable Performance
deserves*, &c.
                                                    CH. GILDON.

'Now is it not plain, that any one who sends such Compliments
to another, has not been us'd to write in *Partnership* with him to
whom he sends them ?' [Dennis's *Remarks on the* Dunciad, *pag.* 50.]
Mr. *Dennis* is therefore welcome to take this Piece to himself.

ERROUR II. Book I. Note on Verse 200. Edward Ward *has of
late kept a publick House in the City*.] The said *Edward Ward*
declares this to be a great Falsity; protesting, that 'He selleth *Port*;
neither is his publick House in the *City*, but in *Moor-Fields*.'
[Ward *in the Notes on* Apollo's Maggot, 8vo.]

ERROUR III. Book I. Verse 240. Ozell.] Mr. *Jacob's* Character
of Mr. *Ozell*, seems vastly short of his Merits; and he ought to have
further Justice done him, having since fully confuted all Sarcasms
on his Learning and Genius, by an Advertisement of *Sept.* 20, 1729.
in a Paper call'd the *Weekly Medley*, &c. 'As to my *Learning*, this
envious Wretch knew, and every body knows, that the *whole
Bench of Bishops*, not long ago, were pleas'd to give me a *Purse of
Guineas*, for discovering the erroneous Translations of the Com-
mon-Prayer in *Portuguese, Spanish, French, Italian*, &c. As for my
Genius, let Mr. *Cleland* shew better Verses in all *Pope's* Works than
Ozell's Version of *Boileau's Lutrin*, which the late Lord *Halifax*
was so pleas'd with, that he complimented him with Leave to
dedicate it to him, *&c. &c*. Let him show better and truer Poetry
in the *Rape of the Locke*, than in *Ozell's Rape of the Bucket, (la
Secchia rapita)* which, because an ingenious Author happen'd to
mention in the same breath with *Pope's*, viz. *Let* Ozell *sing the
Bucket*, Pope *the Lock*, the little Gentleman had like to run mad.—
And Mr. *Toland* and Mr. *Gildon* publickly declar'd, *Ozell's* Translation of *Homer* to be, as it was *prior*, so likewise *superior* to *Pope's*.—
Surely, surely, every Man is free to deserve well of his Country!
                                                    JOHN OZELL.'

We cannot but subscribe to such Reverend Testimonies, as those of the *Bench of Bishops*, Mr. *Toland*, and Mr. *Gildon*.

ERROUR IV. Book 2. Note on Verse 3. Edm. Curll *stood in the Pillory at* Charing-Cross, *in* March 172$\frac{7}{8}$.] 'This, saith *Edm. Curll*, is a false Assertion,—'I had indeed the Corporal punishment of what the Gentlemen of the Long Robe are pleas'd jocosely to call, *mounting the Rostrum*, for one Hour: but that *Scene of Action* was not in the Month of *March*, but in *February*.' [*Curliad* 12°. *pag.* 19.]

ERROUR V. Book 2. Note on Verse 143. *The History of* Curl's *being tost in a Blanket.*] 'Here, quoth *Curl, ibid.* pag. 25. *Scriblerus!* Thou leesest in what thou assertest, concerning a Blanket: It was not a *Blanket*, but a *Rug*.'

ERROUR VI. Book 3. Note on Verse 147. Goode *writ a Satyr on our Author, call'd the* Mock Æsop.] '*Bar. Goode* maketh Oath, with most solemn Protestation, that herein he is greatly wronged; and wisheth the most heavy Curses to fall on himself and his Family, if ever he wrote any such thing.

Jurat. coram nos,

J. Dennis, D. Mallet, R. Savage.'

We find this to be true; for the Satyr he writ, was call'd not Mock Esop, *but* Mack Esop.

ERROUR VII. Book 3. Ver. 149.

Jacob, *The Scourge of Grammar, mark with awe;*

Nor less revere him Blunderbuss of Law.]

There may seem some Error in these Verses, Mr. *Jacob* having proved our Author to have a Respect for him, by this undeniable Argument. 'He had once a *Regard* for my *Judgment*; otherwise he would never have subscribed Two Guineas to me, for one small Book in *Octavo*.' [Jacob's *Letter* to Dennis, *in his Remarks on the* Dunciad, pag. 49.] Therefore I should think the Appellation of *Blunderbuss* to Mr. *Jacob*, like that of *Thunderbolt* to *Scipio*, was meant in his Honour.

Mr. *Dennis* argues the same way. 'My Writings having made great Impression on the Minds of all sensible Men, Mr. *P*— *repented*, and to *give proof of his Repentance*, subscribed to my Two Volumes of select Works—and afterwards to my Two Volumes of Letters.' [*Ibid.* pag. 40.] We should hence believe, the Name of Mr. *Dennis* hath also crept into this Poem by some Mistake. From hence, gentle Reader! thou may'st beware, when thou givest to such Authors, not to flatter thy self that thy Motives are Good Nature or Charity. But whereas Mr. *Dennis* adds, that a Letter which our Author writ to him, was also *in acknowledgment of that Repentance,*

in this surely he erreth; for the said Letter was but a civil Answer
to one of his own, whereby it should seem that he himself was first
touch'd with Repentance, and with some Guineas.

    SIR,   April 29, 1721.
*As you have subscrib'd for two of my Books, I have order'd them to be
left for you at Mr. Congreve's Lodgings: As most of those Letters were
writ during the Time that I was so unhappy as to be in a State of War
with you, I was forced to maim and mangle at least ten of them, that no
Footsteps might remain of that Quarrel. I particularly left out about
half the Letter which was writ upon publishing the Paper call'd the*
Guardian.

I am, SIR,
Your most obedient,
Humble Servant,
JOHN DENNIS.

Appendix

I. PREFACE PREFIX'D TO THE FIVE IMPERFECT EDITIONS OF THE DUNCIAD, PRINTED AT DUBLIN AND LONDON, IN OCTAVO & DUOD

(*a*) THE PUBLISHER TO THE READER

It will be found a true observation, tho' somewhat surprizing, that
when any scandal is vented against a man of the highest distinction
and character, either in the State or in Literature, the publick in
general afford it a most quiet reception; and the larger part accept

    (*a*) *The Publisher*] Who he was is uncertain; but *Edward Ward* tells us
in his Preface to *Durgen*, that 'most Judges are of opinion this Preface is
not of *English* Extraction but *Hibernian*, &c.' He means Dr. *Swift*, who
whether Publisher or not, may be said in a sort to be Author of the Poem:
For when He, together with Mr. *Pope*, (for reasons specify'd in their
Preface to the Miscellanies) determin'd to own the most trifling pieces in
which they had any hand, and to destroy all that remain'd in their power,
the first sketch of this poem was snatch'd from the fire by Dr. *Swift*, who
persuaded his friend to proceed in it, and to him it was therefore Inscribed. But the occasion of printing it was as follows. There was publish'd
in those Miscellanies, a Treatise of the *Bathos*, or *Art of Sinking in Poetry*,
in which was a Chapter, where the Species of bad Writers were rang'd in
Classes, and initial Letters of Names prefix'd, for the most part at random.
But such was the number of Poets eminent in that Art, that some one or
other took every Letter to himself. All fell into so violent a fury, that for
half a year or more the common News-Papers (in most of which they had
some Property, as being hired Writers) were filled with the most abusive
Falshoods and Scurrilities they could possibly devise: A Liberty in no
way to be wonder'd at in those People, and in those Papers, that, for many
years during the uncontrolled License of the Press, had aspersed almost

it as favourably as if it were some kindness done to themselves: Whereas if a known scoundrel or blockhead chance but to be touch'd upon, a whole legion is up in arms, and it becomes the common cause of all Scriblers, Booksellers, and Printers whatsoever.

Not to search too deeply into the *Reason* hereof, I will only observe as a *Fact*, that every week for these two Months past, the town has been persecuted with (*b*) Pamphlets, Advertisements, Letters, and weekly Essays, not only against the Wit and Writings, but against the Character and Person of Mr. *Pope*. And that of all those men who have received pleasure from his Writings (which by modest computation may be about a (*c*) hundred thousand in these Kingdoms of *England* and *Ireland*, not to mention, *Jersey*, *Guernsey*, the *Orcades*, those in the *New world*, and *Foreigners* who have translated him into their languages) of all this number, not a man hath stood up to say one word in his defence.

The only exception is the (*d*) Author of the following Poem, who doubtless had either a better insight into the grounds of this clamour, or a better opinion of Mr. *Pope*'s integrity, join'd with a greater personal love for him, than any other of his numerous friends and admirers.

Further, that he was in his peculiar intimacy, appears from the knowledge he manifests of the most *private* Authors of all the

all the great Characters of the Age, and this with Impunity, their own Persons and Names being utterly secret and obscure. This gave Mr. Pope the Thought, that he had now some Opportunity of doing good, by detecting and dragging into light these common Enemies of Mankind; since to invalidate this universal Slander, it sufficed to shew what contemptible Men were the Authors of it. He was not without hopes, that by manifesting the Dullness of those who had only Malice to recommend them, either the Booksellers would not find their Account in employing them, or the Men themselves, when discovered, want Courage to proceed in so unlawful an occupation. This it was that gave birth to the Dunciad, and he thought it an happiness, that by the late Flood of Slander on himself, he had acquired such a peculiar right over their Names as was necessary to his Design.

(*b*) *Pamphlets, Advertisements*, &c.] See the List of these anonymous papers with their dates and Authors thereunto annexed N° 2.

(*c*) *About a hundred thousand*] It is surprizing with what stupidity this Preface, which is almost a continued Irony, was taken by these Authors. This passage among others they understood to be serious. Hear the Laureate (Letter to Mr. Pope, p. 9). 'Though I grant the Dunciad a better Poem of its kind than ever was writ; yet, when I read it with those *vainglorious* encumbrances of Notes and Remarks upon it, &c.—it is amazing, that you, who have writ with such masterly spirit upon the ruling Passion, should be so blind a slave to your own, as not to see how far a *low avarice of Praise*, &c. (taking it for granted that the notes of Scriblerus and others, were the author's own.)

(*d*) *The Author of the following Poem*, &c.] A very plain Irony, speaking of Mr. *Pope* himself.

anonymous pieces against him, and from his having in this Poem attacked (*e*) no man living, who had not before printed or published some scandal against this particular Gentleman.

How I became possest of it, is of no concern to the Reader; but it would have been a wrong to him, had I detain'd this publication: since those *Names* which are its chief ornaments, die off daily so fast, as must render it too soon unintelligible. If it provoke the Author to give us a more perfect edition, I have my end.

Who he is, I cannot say, and (which is great pity) there is certainly (*f*) nothing in his style and manner of writing, which can distinguish, or discover him. For if it bears any resemblance to that of Mr. *P.* 'tis not improbable but it might be done on purpose, with a view to have it pass for his. But by the frequency of his allusions to *Virgil*, and a *labor'd* (not to say *affected*) *shortness* in imitation of him, I should think him more an admirer of the *Roman* Poet than of the *Grecian*, and in that not of the same taste with his Friend.

I have been well inform'd, that this work was the labour of full (*g*) *six* years of his life, and that he retired himself entirely from all the avocations and pleasures of the world, to attend diligently to its correction and perfection; and six years more he intended to bestow upon it, as it should seem by this verse of *Statius*, which was cited at the head of his manuscript.

> *Oh mihi bissenos multum vigilata per annos,*
> (*h*) *Duncia!*

(*e*) The Publisher in these words went a little too far: but it is certain whatever Names the Reader finds that are unknown to him, are of such: and the exception is only of two or three, whose dulness or scurrility all mankind agree to have justly entitled them to a place in the Dunciad.

(*f*) *There is certainly nothing in his Style,* &c.] This Irony had small effect in concealing the Author. The Dunciad, imperfect as it was, had not been publish'd two days, but the whole Town gave it to Mr. *Pope*.

(*g*) *The Labour of full* six *years,* &c.] This also was honestly and seriously believ'd, by divers of the Gentlemen of the Dunciad. *J. Ralph*, Pref. to *Sawney*, 'We are told it was the labour of *six years*, with the utmost *assiduity* and *application:* It is no great compliment to the Author's sense, to have employed so *large a part* of his *Life,* &c.' So also *Ward*, Pref. to *Durg*. 'The Dunciad, as the Publisher very *wisely* confesses, cost the Author *six years retirement from all the pleasures of life,* to but half finish his abusive undertaking—tho' it is somewhat difficult to conceive, from either its Bulk or Beauty, that it cou'd be so long in hatching, *&c.* But the *length of time* and *closeness of application* were mentioned to prepossess the reader with a good opinion of it.'

Nevertheless the Prefacer to Mr. *Curl's Key* (a great Critick) was of a different sentiment, and thought it might be written in *six days*.

It is to be hoped they will as well understand, and write as gravely upon what *Scriblerus* hath said of this Poem.

(*h*) The same learned Prefacer took this word to be really in *Statius*.

Hence also we learn the true *Title* of the Poem; which with the same certainty as we call that of *Homer* the *Iliad*, of *Virgil* the *Æneid*, of *Camoens* the *Lusiad*, of *Voltaire* the *Henriad* (i), we may pronounce could have been, and can be no other, than

THE DUNCIAD.

It is styled *Heroic*, as being *doubly* so; not only with respect to its nature, which according to the Best Rules of the Ancients and strictest ideas of the Moderns, is critically such; but also with regard to the Heroical disposition and high courage of the Writer, who dar'd to stir up such a formidable, irritable, and implacable race of mortals.

The time and date of the Action is evidently in the last reign, when the office of City Poet expir'd upon the death of *Elkanah Settle*, and he has fix'd it to the Mayoralty of Sir *Geo. Thorold*.[1] But there may arise some obscurity in Chronology from the *Names* in the Poem, by the inevitable removal of some Authors, and insertion of others, in their Niches. For whoever will consider the Unity of the whole design, will be sensible, that the *Poem was not made for these Authors, but these Authors for the Poem:* And I should judge they were clapp'd in as they rose, fresh and fresh, and chang'd from day to day, in like manner as when the old boughs wither, we thrust new ones into a chimney.

I would not have the reader too much troubled or anxious, if he cannot decypher them; since when he shall have found them out, he will probably know no more of the Persons than before.

Yet we judg'd it better to preserve them as they are, than to change them for *fictitious names*, by which the Satyr would only be multiplied, and applied to many instead of one. Had the Hero, for instance, been called *Codrus*, how many would have affirm'd him to be Mr. *W——* Mr. *D——* Sir *R——* *B——*, &c. but now, all that unjust scandal is saved, by calling him *Theobald*, which by good luck happens to be the name of a real person.

I am indeed aware, that this name may to some appear too *mean*, for the Hero of an Epic Poem: but it is hoped, they will alter that opinion, when they find, that an Author no less eminent than *la Bruyere* has thought him worthy a place in his Characters.

Voudriez vous, THEOBALDE, *que je crusse que vous êtes baisse? que vous n'êtes plus Poete, ni bel esprit? que vous êtes presentement*

'By a quibble on the word *Duncia*, the Dunciad is formed,' *pag.* 3. Mr. *Ward* also follows him in the same opinion.

(i) *The Henriad*] The French Poem of Monsieur *Voltaire*, entitled *La Henriade*, had been publish'd at *London* the year before.

[1] *Thorold* ⟨Cf. A i 88n., 83n.⟩

*aussi mauvais Juge de tout genre d'Ouvrage, que mechant Auteur?
Votre air libre & presumptueux me rassure, & me persuade tout le
contraire, &c.* Characteres, Vol. I. *de la Societe & de la Conversation, pag.* 176. Edit. Amst. 1720.

II. A LIST OF BOOKS, PAPERS, AND VERSES, IN
WHICH OUR AUTHOR WAS ABUSED, PRINTED
BEFORE THE PUBLICATION OF THE DUNCIAD:
WITH THE TRUE NAMES OF THE AUTHORS

Reflections Critical and Satyrical on a late Rhapsody called an
Essay on Criticism. By Mr. *Dennis.* Printed for *B. Lintot.* Price 6*d.*

A New Rehearsal, or Bays the Younger, Containing an Examen
of Mr. *Rowe*'s Plays, and a word or two upon Mr. *Pope*'s Rape of
the Locke. Anon. [*Charles Gildon.*] Printed for *J. Roberts,* 1714.
Price 1*s.*

Homerides, or a Letter to Mr. *Pope,* occasion'd by his intended
Translation of Homer. By Sir *Iliad Doggrel.* [*T. Burnet* and *G.
Ducket* Esquires] Printed for *W. Wilkins,* 1715, Price 6*d.*

Æsop at the Bear-garden. A Vision in imitation of the Temple of
Fame. By Mr. *Preston.* Sold by *John Morphew,* 1715. Price 6*d.*

The Catholic Poet, or Protestant Barnaby's sorrowful Lamentation, a Ballad about Homer's Iliad [by Mrs. *Centlivre* and others]
1715. Price 1*d.*

An Epilogue to a Puppet-show at Bath, concerning the said
Iliad, by *George Ducket* Esq; Printed by *E. Curl.*

A compleat Key to the What-d'ye-call-it, Anon. [Mr. *Th—*]
Printed for *J. Roberts,* 1715.

A true character of Mr. *Pope* and his Writings, in a Letter to a
Friend, Anon. [Messieurs *Gildon* and *Dennis.*] Printed for *S. Popping,* 1716. Price 3*d.*

The Confederates, a Farce. By *Joseph Gay* [*J. D. Breval.*] Printed
for *R. Burleigh,* 1717. Price 1*s.*

Remarks upon Mr. *Pope*'s Translation of Homer, with two
Letters concerning the Windsor Forrest and the Temple of Fame.
By Mr. *Dennis.* Printed for *E. Curl,* 1717. Price 1*s.* 6*d.*

Satires on the Translators of Homer, Mr. *P.* and Mr. *T.* Anon.
[*Bez. Morris*] 1717. Price 6*d.*

The Triumvirate, or a Letter from Palæmon to Celia at Bath.
Anon. [*Leonard Welsted.*] Price 1*s.* 1718. Folio.

The Battle of Poets, a Heroic Poem. [By *Tho. Cooke*] Printed for
J. Roberts. Folio. 1725.

Memoirs of Lilliput, Anon. [Mrs. *Eliz. Haywood.*] 8°. Printed
1727.

An Essay on Criticism, in Prose, by the Author of the Critical History of England [*J. Oldmixon*] 8° 1728.

Gulliveriana, and Alexandriana. With an ample Preface and Critique on *Swift* and *Pope*'s Miscellanies [By *Jonathan Smedley.*] Printed for *J. Roberts* 8° 1728. Advertised before the publication of the Dunciad in the Daily Journal, *April* 13. 1728.

Characters of the Times, or an Account of the Writings, Characters, *&c.* of several Gentlemen libell'd by *S*— and *P*— in a late Miscellany, 8° 1728. [*C*—*l* and *W*—*d.*]¹

Remarks on Mr. *Pope*'s Rape of the Lock, in Letters to a Friend. [By Mr. *Dennis.*] Written in 1714, tho' not printed till 1728. 8°.

Verses, Letters, Essays, or Advertisements in the publick Prints

British Journal, *Nov.* 25, 1727. A Letter on *Swift* and *Pope*'s Miscellanies. [Writ ·by *Concanen.*]

Daily Journal, *March* 18, 1728. A Letter by *Philomauri.* [*James Moore Smyth.*]

Id. *March* 29. A Letter about *Thersites* and accusing the Author of Disaffection to the Government. [*James Moore Smyth.*]

Mist's Weekly Journal, *March* 30. An Essay on the Arts of a Poets sinking in reputation, Or a supplement to the Art of sinking in Poetry [supposed by Mr. *Theobald.*]

Daily Journal, *April* 3. A Letter under the name of *Philo-ditto* [by *James Moore Smyth.*]

Flying-Post, *April* 4. A Letter against *Gulliver* and Mr. *P.* [Mr. *Oldmixon.*]

Daily Journal, *April* 5. An Auction of Goods at *Twickenham*, [by *J. Moore Smyth.*]

Flying-Post. *April* 6. A Fragment of a Treatise upon *Swift* and *Pope*, [by Mr. *Oldmixon.*]

The Senator, *April* 9. On the same, [by *Edward Roome.*]

Daily Journal, *April* 8. Advertisement [by *James Moore Smyth.*]

Daily Journal, *April* 9. Letter and Verses against Dr. *Swift*, [by ** Esq;]

Flying-Post, *April* 13. Verses against the same, and against Mr. *P*—'s *Homer*, [by *J. Oldmixon.*]

Daily Journal, *April* 16. Verses on Mr. *P.* [by ** Esq;.]

Id. *April* 23. Letter about a Translation of the character of *Thersites* in *Homer*, [*J*—*D*—, &c.]

Mist's Weekly Journal, *April* 27. A Letter of *Lewis Theobald.*

Daily Journal, *May* 11. A Letter against Mr. *P.* at large, Anon. [*John Dennis.*]

---

¹ ⟨i.e. Curll and Welsted. See A i 240 and iii 163*n*, pp. 369, 410.⟩

All these were afterwards reprinted in a Pamphlet entitled, A collection of all the Verses, Essays, Letters and Advertisements occasion'd by *Pope* and *Swift*'s Miscellanies. Prefaced by *Concanen*, Anonymous. 8°. Printed for *A. Moore*, 1728. Price 1s. Others of an elder date, having layn as waste paper many years, were upon the publication of the Dunciad brought out, and their Authors betrayed by the mercenary Booksellers (in hope of some possibility of vending a few) by advertising them in this manner— *The Confederates*, a Farce by Capt. *Breval*, (for which he is *put into the Dunciad*.) An *Epilogue to Powel's Puppetshow*, by Col. *Ducket*, (for which he is *put into the Dunciad*.) Essays, *&c*. by Sir *Rich. Blackmore. N.B.* It is for a passage in pag. — of this book that Sir *Richard* was *put into the Dunciad*.) And so of others.

AFTER THE DUNCIAD, 1728

An Essay on the Dunciad, 8°. Printed for *J. Roberts*. [In this book, *pag*. 9. it was formally declared 'That the complaint of the aforesaid Pieces, Libels, and Advertisements, was forged and untrue, that all mouths had been silent except in Mr. *Pope*'s praise, and nothing against him publish'd, but, by Mr. THEOBALD.' *Price 6d.*

Sawney, in blank Verse, occasion'd by the Dunciad, with a Critique on that Poem. [By *J. Ralph*, a person never mention'd in it at first, but inserted after this.] Printed for *J. Roberts*. 8°. Price 1s.

A compleat Key to the Dunciad, by *E. Curl.* 12°. Price 6d.

A second and third Edition of the same, with Additions. 12°.

The Popiad, by *E. Curl*, extracted from *J. Dennis*, Sir *R. Blackmore*, &c. 12°. Price 6d.

The Curliad, by the same E. Curl.

The Female Dunciad, collected by the same Mr. *Curl.* 12°. Price 6d. With the Metamorphosis of *P*— into a stinging Nettle, [by Mr. *Foxton*.] 12°.

The Metamorphosis of *Scriblerus* into *Snarlerus*, [by *J. Smedley*.] Printed for *A. Moore*. Folio. Price 6d.

The Dunciad dissected, or Farmer *P.* and his Son, by *Curl.* 12°.

An Essay on the Taste and Writings of the present times, said to be writ by a Gentleman of C. C. C. *Oxon*. Printed for *J. Roberts*, 8°.

The Arts of Logic and Rhetorick, partly taken from *Bouhours*, with new Reflections, *&c*. [by *John Oldmixon*.] 8°.

Remarks on the Dunciad, by Mr. Dennis, Dedicated to Mr. Theobald. 8°.

A Supplement to the Profund, Anon. [By *Matthew Concanen*.] 8⁰.

Mist's Weekly Journal, June 8. A long Letter sign'd *W. A.* [*Dennis, Theobald*, and others.]

Daily Journal, *June* II. A Letter sign'd *Philoscriblerus*, on the name of *Pope.*—Letter to Mr. *Theobald* in Verse, sign'd *B. M.* against Mr. *P.*—Many other little Epigrams about this time in the same papers, [by *James Moore* and others.]

Mist's Journal, *June* 22. A Letter by *Lewis Theobald*.

Flying-Post, *August* 8. Letter on *Pope* and *Swift*.

Daily Journal, *August* 8. Letter charging the Author of the Dunciad with Treason.

Durgen, A plain Satyr on a pompous Satyrist. [By *Edw. Ward*, with a little of *James Moore*.]

Apollo's Maggot in his Cups, by E. Ward.

Labeo, [A Paper of Verses written by *Leonard Welsted*.] which after came into *One Epistle*, and was publish'd by James Moore, 4ᵗᵒ. 1730. Another part of it came out in Welsted's own name in 1731, under the just Title of *Dulness and Scandal*, fol.

Gulliveriana Secunda, Being a collection of many of the Libels in the News papers, like the former Volume under the same title, by *Smedley*. Advertised in the Craftsman *November* 9, 1728. with this remarkable promise, that '*any thing* which *any body* shou'd send as Mr. *Pope*'s or Dr. *Swift*'s, shou'd be inserted and published as Theirs.'

Pope Alexander's Supremacy and Infallibility examin'd *&c.* 4ᵗᵒ. By Geo. Ducket and John Dennis.

Dean Jonathan's Paraphrase on the 4ᵗʰ Chapter of Genesis. Writ by E. Room, fol. 1729.

Verses on the Imitator of *Horace* by a Lady [or between a Lady, a Lord, and a Court Squire] Printed for *J. Roberts*, fol. 1733.

An Epistle from a Nobleman to a Dr. of Divinity, from *Hampton Court* [Lord *H—y*] Printed for *J. Roberts* also, fol. 1733.

A Letter from Mr. Cibber to Mr. Pope. Printed for W. Lewis in Covent Garden, octavo.

III. A COPY OF CAXTON'S PREFACE TO HIS
TRANSLATION OF VIRGIL.[1]

After dyuerse Werkes, made translated and achieued, hauyng noo
werke in hande I sittyng in my studye where as laye many dyuerse
paunflettes and bookys. happened that to my hande cam a lytyl
booke in frenshe. whiche late was translated oute of latyn by some
noble clerke of fraunce whiche booke is named *Eneydos* (made in
latyn by that noble poete & grete clerke *Vyrgyle*) whiche booke I
sawe over and redde therein. How after the generall destruccyon of
the grete *Troye*, *Eneas* departe dberynge his olde fader *anchises* upon
his sholdres, his lytyl son *yolas* on his hande. his wyfe wyth moche
other people followynge, and how he shipped and departed wyth
alle thystorye of his aduentures that he had *er he cam to the atchieue-
ment of his conquest of ytalye* as all a longe shall be shewed in this
present boke. In whiche booke I had grete playsyr. by cause of the
fayr and honest termes & wordes in frenshe Whyche I neuer sawe
to fore lyke. ne none so playsaunt ne so wel ordred. whiche booke
as me semed sholde be moche requysyte to noble men to see as wel
for the eloquence as the historyes. How wel that many hondred
yerys passed was the sayd booke of *Eneydos* wyth other workes
made and lerned dayly in scolis specyally in *ytalye* and other places,
whiche historye the sayd *Vyrgyle* made in metre, And whan I had
aduysed me in this sayd booke. *I delybered and concluded* to translate it in to englyshe. And forthwyth toke a penne and ynke and
wrote a leef or tweyne, whyche I ouersawe agayn to corecte it, And
whan I sawe the fayr & straunge termes therein, I doubted that it
sholde not please some gentylmen whiche late blamed me sayeng
that in my translacyons I had ouer curyous termes whiche coude
not be vnderstande of comyn peple, and desired me to vse olde and
homely termes in my translacyons. and fayn wolde I satysfye
euery man, and so to doo toke an olde boke and redde therein, and
certaynly the englyshe was so rude and brood that I coude not wele
vnderstande it. And also my lorde *Abbot* of *Westmynster* ded do
shewe to me late certayn euydences wryton in olde englyshe. for to
reduce it in to our englyshe now vsid, And certaynly it was wryton
in suche wyse that it was more lyke to dutche than englyshe. I coude

---

[1] ⟨In *Mist's Journal*, March 16, 1728, Theobald had cited Caxton to
clear up a passage in *Troilus and Cressida*, v v 14: 'The dreadfull Sagittary
Appauls our numbers.' Pope had assumed that the Sagittary was Teucer;
but Theobald (with the help of Caxton) was able to show that it was 'a
mervayllouse beste'; in fact, a Centaur. The mistake probably rankled,
and Pope took refuge once again in ridicule; but the joke at Caxton's
expense amounts to no more than laughing at a man because his clothes
are old-fashioned.⟩

not reduce ne brynge it to be vnderstonden, And certaynly our langage now vsed varyeth ferre from that whiche was vsed and spoken whan I was borne, For we englyshe men, ben borne vnder the domynacyon of the mone. whiche is neuer stedfaste, but euer wauerynge, wexynge one season, and waneth & dyscreaseth another season, And that comyn englyshe that is spoken in one shyre varyeth from another. In so moche that in my dayes happened that certayn marchants were in a ship in Tamyse for to haue sayled ouer the see into Zelande, and for lacke of wynde thei taryed atte forlond. and wente to lande for to refreshe them And one of theym named *Sheffelde* a mercer cam in to an hows and axed for mete, and specyally he axyd after eggys. And the goode wyf answerde. that she coude speke no frenshe. And the merchant was angry. for he also coude speke no frenshe. but wolde haue hadde egges, and she vnderstode hym not, And thenne at laste another sayd that he wolde haue eyren, then the good wyf sayd that she vnderstod hym wel, Loo what sholde a man in thyse dayes now wryte. egges or eyren, certaynly it is harde to playse euery man, by cause of dyuersite & change of langage. For in these dayes euery man that is in ony reputacyon in his contre. wyll vtter his comyny-cacyon and maters in suche maners & termes, that fewe men shall vnderstonde theym, And som honest and grete clerkes haue ben wyth me and desired me to wryte the moste curyous termes that I coude fynde, And thus bytwene playn rude, & curyous I stande abashed. but in my Judgemente, the comyn termes that be dayli vsed ben lyghter to be vnderstonde than the olde and ancyent englyshe, And for as moche as this present booke is not *for a rude vplondyshe man* to laboure therein, ne rede it, but onely for a clerke & a noble gentylman that feleth and vnderstondeth in faytes of armes in loue & in noble chyualrye, Therefore in a meane be-twene bothe I haue reduced & translated this sayd booke in to our englyshe not ouer rude ne curyous but in suche termes as shall be vnderstanden by goddys grace accordynge to my copye. And yf ony man wyll enter mete in redyng of hit and fyndeth suche termes that he can not vnderstande late hym goo rede and lerne *Vyrgyll*, or the pystles of *Ouyde*, and ther he shall see and vnderstonde lyghtly all, Yf he haue a good redar & enformer, For this booke is not for euery rude and vnconnynge man to see, but to clerkys & very gentylmen that understande gentylnes and scyence. Thenne I praye alle theym that shall rede in this lytyl treatys to holde me for excused for the translatynge of hit. For I knowleche my selfe ignorant of connynge to enpryse on me so hie and noble a werke, But I praye Mayster *John Skelton* late created poete laureate in the vnyuersite of *Oxenforde* to ouersee and correcte this sayd booke.

And t'addresse and expowne where as shall be founde faulte to
theym that shall requyre it. For hym I knowe for suffycyent to
expowne and englyshe euery dyffyculte that is therein, For he hath
late translated the epystlys of *Tulle*, and the boke of *Dyodorus
Syculus*. and diuerse others werkes oute of latyn in to englyshe
not in rude and olde langage. but in *polysshed and ornate termes*
craftely, as he that hath redde *Vyrgyle*, *Ouyde*, *Tullye*, and all the
other noble poetes and oratours, to me unknown: And also he hath
redde the ix muses and vnderstande theyr musicalle scyences. and
to whom of theym eche scyence is appropred. I suppose he hath
dronken of Elycons well. Then I praye hym & suche other to correcte adde or mynysshe where as he or they shall fynde faulte, For
I haue but folowed my copye in frenche as nygh as me is possyble,
And yf ony worde be sayd therein well, I am glad. and yf otherwyse
I submytte my sayd boke to theyr correctyon, Whiche boke I
presente vnto the hye born my *tocomynge* naturall & souerayn lord
Arthur by the grace of God Prynce of *Walys*, Duke of *Cornewayll*.
& Erle of *Chester* first bygoten Son and heyer vnto our most dradde
naturall & souerayn lorde & most crysten kynge, *Henry* the vij. by
the grace of God kynge of *Englonde* and of *Fraunce* & lord of
Irelonde, byseeching his noble grace to receyve it in thanke of me his
moste humble subget & seruant, And I shall praye vnto almyghty
God for his prosperous encreasyng in vertue, wysedom, and hu-
manyte that he may be egal wyth the most renômed of alle his noble
progenytours. And so to lyue in this present lyf, that after this
transitorye lyfe he and we alle may come to everlastynge lyf in
heuen, *Amen:*

At the end of the Book.

Here fynyssheth the boke of *Eneydos*, compyled by *Vyrgyle*,
whiche hathe be translated out of *latyne* in to *frenshe*, and out of
frenshe reduced in to *Englysshe* by me *Wyllm. Caxton*, the xxij daye
of *Juyn*. the yere of our lorde. M. iiij C lxxxx. The fythe yere of the
Regne of kyng *Henry* the seuenth.

IV. VIRGILIUS RESTAURATUS:[1] SEU MARTINI
SCRIBLERI SUMMI CRITICI CASTIGATIONUM IN
ÆNEIDEM SPECIMEN:

ÆNEIDEM totam, Amice Lector, innumerabilibus pœne mendis
scaturientem, ad pristinum sensum revocabimus. In singulis
ferè versibus spuriæ occurrunt lectiones, in omnibus quos un-
quam vidi codicibus aut vulgatis aut ineditis, ad opprobrium

[1] ⟨The title is intended to ridicule Theobald's *Shakespeare Restored*.⟩

usque Criticorum, in hunc diem existentes. Interea adverte oculos, & his paucis fruere. At si quæ sint in hisce castigationibus de quibus non satis liquet, syllabarum quantitates, προλεγόμενα nostra Libro ipsi præfigenda, ut consulas, moneo.

I. SPECIMEN LIBRI PRIMI, VERS. I. (a)

Arma Virumque cano, Trojæ qui primus ab *oris*
Italiam, *fato* profugus, Lavinaque venit
Litora: multum ille & terris *jactatus* & alto,
Vi superum———

II. VERS. 52. (b)

—Et quisquis *Numen* Junonis adoret?

III. VERS. 86. (c)

—Venti velut *agmine facto*
Qua data porta ruunt—

IV. VERS. 117. (d)

Fidumque vehebat *Orontem.*

V. VERS. 119. (e)

Excutitur, pronusque *magister*
Volvitur in caput———

(a) Arma Virumque cano, Trojæ qui primus ab *Aris*
    Italiam, *flatu* profugus, *Latinaque* venit
    Litora: multum ille & terris *vexatus*, & alto,
    Vi superum———
Ab *aris*, nempe Hercæi Jovis, vide lib. 2. vers. 512, 550.—*Flatu*, ventorum Æoli, ut sequitur—*Latina* certè littora cum Æneas aderat, *Lavina* non nisi postea ab ipso nominata, Lib. 12. vers. 193—*Jactatus*, *terris* non convenit.

(b) ——Et quisquis *Nomen* Junonis adoret?
Longè melius, quam ut antea, *Numen.*
Et Procul dubio sic Virgilius.

(c) —Venti velut *aggere fracto*
Qua data porta ruunt——
Sic corrige, meo periculo.

(d) *Fortemque* vehebat *Orontem:*
Non *fidum*, quia Epitheton *Achatæ* notissimum,
Oronti nunquam datur.

(e) —Excutitur: pronusque magis tèr
Volvitur in caput——
    Aio Virgilium aliter non scripsisse, quod planè confirmatur ex sequentibus—*Ast illum* ter *fluctus ibidem Torquet*——

VI. VERS. 122. (*f*)

Apparent rari nantes in gurgite vasto
Arma virùm——

VII. VERS. 151 (*g*)

Atque rotis *summas* leviter perlabitur *undas.*

VIII. VERS. 154. (*h*)

Jamque *faces* & saxa volant, *furor arma ministrat.*

IX. VERS. 170. (*i*)

Fronte sub adversa *scopulis pendentibus* antrum,
Intus aquæ dulces, vivoque sedilia saxo.

X. VERS. 188. (*k*)

——Tres littore *cervos*
Prospicit errantes: hos *tota armenta* sequuntur
A tergo——

XI. VERS. 748.

Arcturum pluviasque Hyades, *geminosque Triones;*
Error gravissimus. Corrige,—*septemque Triones.*

(*f*) *Armi hominum:* Ridicule anteà *Arma virum* quæ ex ferro conflata,
quomodo possunt *natare?*
   (*g*) Atque rotis *spumas* leviter perlabitur *udas. Summas,* & *leviter perlabi,*
pleonasmus est: Mirificè altera lectio Neptuni agilitatem & celeritatem
exprimit; simili modo Noster de Camilla, Æn. 11.—*intactæ segetis per
summa volaret,* &c. hyperbolicè.
   (*h*) Jam *fæces* & saxa volant, *fugiuntque Ministri:* Uti solent, instanti
periculo.—*Fæces, facibus* longe præstant, quid enim nisi fæces jactarent
vulgus sordidum?
   (*i*) Fronte sub adversa *populis prandentibus* antrum.
Sic malim, longe potiùs quam *scopulis pendentibus:* Nugæ! Nonne vides
versu sequenti *dulces aquas* ad potandum & sedilia ad discubendum dari?
In quorum usum? prandentium.
   (*k*) ——Tres litore *corvos*
Aspicit errantes: hos *agmina tota* sequuntur
A tergo—*Cervi,* lectio vulgata, absurditas notissima: hæc animalia in
   Africa non inveniri, quis nescit? At motus & ambulandi ritus Cor-
   vorum, quis non agnovit hoc loco? Litore, locus ubi errant Corvi, uti
   Noster alibi,
Et sola secum sicca spaciatur arena.
Omen præclarissimum, immo et *agminibus* Militum frequentèr observa-
   tum, ut patet ex Historicis.

XII. VERS. 631. (*l*)

Quare agite O juvenes, *tectis* succedite nostris.

LIBER SECUNDUS. VERS. I. (*a*)

Conticuere omnes, intentique ora tenebant,
Inde toro *Pater* Æneas sic orsus ab alto:

VERS. 3. (*b*)

Infandum Regina jubes renovare dolorem.

VERS. 4. (*c*)

Trojanas ut *opes*, & lamentabile regnum.

VERS. 5. (*d*)

Eruerint Danai, Quæque ipse *miserrima vidi*
Et quorum pars magna fui.

(*l*) Quare agite O Juvenes, *tectis* succedite nostris.
Lectis potius dicebat Dido, polita magis oratione, & quæ unica voce et
    Torum & Mensam exprimebat: Hanc lectionem probe confirmat
    appellatio O *Juvenes!* Duplicem hunc sensum alibi etiam Maro lepidè
    innuit,
Æn. 4. vers. 19. Huic uni forsan potui succumbere *culpæ*:
                Anna! fatebor enim—
Corrige, *Huic uni* [*Viro* scil.] potui succumbere; Culpas
Anna? fatebor enim, *&c.* Vox *succumbere* quam eleganter ambigua!

LIB. II. VERS. I. *&c.*

(*a*) *Concubuere* omnes, intentèque ora tenebant;
Inde toro *satur* Æneas sic orsus ab alto.
Concubuere, quia toro Æneam vidimus accumbentem: quin & altera
ratio, scil. *Conticuere & ora tenebant*, tautologicè dictum. In Manuscripto
perquam rarissimo in Patris Musæo, legitur *ore gemebant*; sed magis
ingeniosè quam verè. *Satur* Æneas, quippe qui jam-jam a prandio sur-
rexit: *Pater* nihil ad rem attinet.
    (*b*) *Infantum* regina jubes renovare dolorem. Sic haud dubito veterrimis
codicibus scriptum fuisse: hoc satis constat ex perantiqua illa Brittan-
norum Cantilena vocata *Chevy-Chace*, cujus autor hunc locum sibi ascivit
in hæc verba,
            The Child may rue that is unborn.
    (*c*) Trojanas ut *Oves* & lamentabile regnum *Diruerint*—Mallem *oves*
potius quam *opes*, quoniam in antiquissimis illis temporibus oves &
armenta divitiæ regum fuere. Vel fortasse *Oves Paridis* innuit, quas super
Idam nuperrime pascebat, & jam in vindictam pro Helenæ raptu, a
Menelao, Ajace aliisque ducibus, meritò occisas.
    (*d*) —Quœque ipse *miserrimus audi*,
Et quorum pars magna fui——
Omnia tam *audita* quam *visa* recta distinctione enarrare hic Æneas
profitetur: Multa quorum nox ea fatalis sola conscia fuit, Vir probus &
pius tanquam *visa* referre non potuit.

VERS. 7. (*e*)

—Quis talia *fando*
Temperet *a* lacrymis ?

VERS. 9. (*f*)

Et jam nox *humida* cœlo
Præcipitat, suadentque *cadentia* sydera somnos.
Sed si tantus amor *casus* cognoscere *nostros*, (*g*)
Et *breviter* Trojæ *supremum* audire laborem,
Quanquam animus meminisse horret, *luctuque refugit*, (*h*)
Incipiam.

VERS. 13. (*i*)

Fracti bello, fatisque repulsi,
Ductores Danaûm, tot jam labentibus annis,
Instar montis *Equum*, divina Palladis arte,
Ædificant——*&c.*

(*e*)——Quis talia *flendo,*
Temperet *in* lachrymis?——Major enim doloris indicatio, absque modo
lachrymare, quam solummodo *a* lachrymis non temperare?
(*f*) Et jam nox *lumina* cœlo
Præcipitat, suadentque *latentia* sydera somnos.
Lectio, *humida*, vespertinum rorem solum innuere videtur: magis mi
arridet *Lumina*, quæ *latentia* postquam *præcipitantur*, Auroræ adventum
annunciant.
(*g*) Sed si tantus amor *curas* cognoscere *noctis,*
Et *brevì ter* Trojæ, *superumque* audire *labores.*
Curæ Noctis (scilicet Noctis Excidii Trojani) magis compendiosè (vel
ut dixit ipse *breviter*) totam Belli catastrophen denotat, quam diffusa illa
& indeterminata lectio, *casus nostros. Ter* audire gratum esse Didoni,
patet ex libro quarto, ubi dicitur, *Iliacosque iterum demens audire labores
Exposcit: Ter* enim pro *sæpe* usurpatur. *Trojæ, superumque labores,* rectè,
quia non tantum homines sed & Dii sese his laboribus immiscuerunt.
Vide Æn. 2. vers. 610, *&c.*
(*h*) Quamquam animus meminisse horret, *luctusque resurgit. Resurgit*
multò proprius dolorem renascentem notat, quam ut hactenus, *refugit.*
(*i*) *Tracti* bello, fatisque repulsi.
Tracti & *Repulsi*, Antithesis perpulcra!
Fracti frigidè & vulgaritèr.
Equum jam *Trojanum*, (ut vulgus loquitur) adeamus; quem si *Equam
Græcam* vocabis Lector, minimè pecces : Solæ enim femellæ utero gestant.
Uterumque *armato milite complent*—Uteroque *recusso Insonuere cavæ*——
Atque utero *sonitum quater arma dedere.*—*Inclusos utero Danaos* &c. Vox
fæta non convenit maribus,—*Scandit fatalis machina muros, Foeta armis*
——Palladem Virginem, Equo mari fabricando invigilare decuisse quis
putat? Incredibile prorsus! Quamobrem existimo veram *Equæ* lectionem
passim restituendam, nisi ubi forte metri caussa, *Equum* potius quam
Equam, Genus pro *Sexu,* dixit Maro. Vale! dum hæc paucula corriges,
majus opus moveo.

V. A CONTINUATION OF THE GUARDIAN: ON THE SUBJECT OF PASTORALS

Compulerantque greges Corydon & Thyrsis in unum.
Ex illo Corydon, Corydon est tempore nobis
⟨VIRG. Ecl. vii⟩

Monday, April 27, 1713 ⟨No. 40⟩

1. I Designed to have troubled the Reader with no farther Discourses of *Pastorals*, but being informed that I am taxed of Partiality in not mentioning an Author whose Eclogues are published in the same Volume with Mr. *Philips*'s; I shall employ this Paper in Observations upon him, written in the *free Spirit of Criticism*, and without apprehension of offending that Gentleman, whose character it is that he takes the greatest care of his Works before they are published, and has the least concern for them afterwards.

2. I have laid it down as the first rule of Pastoral, that its Idea should be taken from the manners of the *Golden Age*, and the Moral form'd upon the representation of *Innocence*; 'tis therefore plain that any Deviations from that design degrade a Poem from being true Pastoral. In this view it will appear that *Virgil* can only have *two* of his Eclogues allowed to be such: His first and ninth must be rejected, because they describe the ravages of Armies, and oppressions of the Innocent; *Corydon*'s criminal Passion for *Alexis* throws out the second; the calumny and railing in the third are not proper to that state of Concord; the eighth represents unlawful ways of procuring Love by Inchantments, and introduces a Shepherd whom an inviting Precipice tempts to Self-Murder. As to the fourth, sixth, and tenth, they are given up by (*a*) *Heinsius, Salmasius, Rapin*, and the Criticks in general. They likewise observe that but *eleven* of all the *Idyllia* of *Theocritus* are to be admitted as Pastorals; and even out of that number the greater part will be excluded for *one* or *other* of the *Reasons abovementioned*. So that when I remark'd in a former paper, that *Virgil*'s Eclogues taken all together are rather *select Poems* than *Pastorals*; I might have said the same thing with no less truth of *Theocritus*. The reason of this I take to be yet unobserved by the Criticks, *viz. They never meant them all for Pastorals*.

Now it is plain *Philips* hath done this, and *in that Particular* excelled both *Theocritus* and *Virgil*.

3. As *Simplicity* is the distinguishing Characteristick of Pastoral, *Virgil* hath been thought guilty of too courtly a Stile; his Language is *perfectly pure*, and he often forgets he is among Peasants. I have

(*a*) *See* Rapin *de* Carm. Past. *pars* 3.

frequently wonder'd, that since he was so conversant in the writings of *Ennius*, he had not imitated the *Rusticity* of the *Doric*, as well by the help of the *old obsolete Roman* Language, as *Philips* hath by the *antiquated English*: for example, might he not have said *Quoi* instead of *Cui*; *quoijum* for *cujum*; *volt* for *vult*, &c. as well as our Modern hath *Welladay* for *Alas*, *whilome* for *of old*, *make mock* for *deride*, and *witless Younglings* for *simple Lambs*, &c. by which means he had attained as much of the Air of *Theocritus*, as *Philips* hath of *Spencer*?

4. Mr. *Pope* hath fallen into the *same error with Virgil*. His Clowns do not converse in *all the Simplicity* proper to the Country: His names are borrow'd from *Theocritus* and *Virgil*, which are improper to the Scene of his Pastorals. He introduces *Daphnis*, *Alexis* and *Thyrsis* on *British* Plains, as *Virgil* had done before him on the *Mantuan:* Whereas *Philips*, who hath the strictest regard to Propriety, makes choice of names *peculiar to the Country*, and more agreeable to a Reader of *Delicacy*; such as *Hobbinol, Lobbin, Cuddy*, and *Colin Clout*.

5. So easie as Pastoral Writing may seem, (in the *Simplicity* we have described it) yet it requires great *Reading*, both of the *Ancients* and *Moderns*, to be a master of it. *Philips* hath given us manifest proofs of his *Knowledge of Books:* It must be confessed his competitor hath imitated some *single thoughts* of the Ancients well enough, (if we consider he had not the happiness of an University Education) but he hath dispersed them, *here* and *there*, without that order and method which Mr. *Philips* observes, whose *whole* third Pastoral is an instance how well he hath studied the fifth of *Virgil*, and how judiciously *reduced Virgil*'s thoughts to the standard of Pastoral; as his contention of *Colin Clout* and the *Nightingale* shows with what *exactness* he hath imitated *every line* in *Strada*.

6. When I remarked it as a principal fault, to introduce *Fruits* and *Flowers* of a *Foreign growth*, in descriptions where the Scene lies in our *own Country*, I did not design that observation should extend also to *Animals*, or the *sensitive Life*; for *Philips* hath with great judgment described *Wolves* in *England* in his first Pastoral. Nor would I have a Poet slavishly confine himself (as Mr. *Pope* hath done) to one particular *season* of the Year, one certain *time* of the *day*, and one *unbroken Scene* in each Eclogue. 'Tis plain *Spencer* neglected this Pedantry, who in his Pastoral of *November* mentions the mournful song of the *Nightingale:*

Sad Philomel *her song in Tears doth steep.*

And Mr. *Philips*, by a poetical Creation, hath raised up finer beds of Flowers than the most industrious Gardiner; his Roses,

Endives, Lillies, Kingcups and Daffadils blow *all in the same season*.

7. But the better to discover the merits of our two contemporary Pastoral Writers, I shall endeavour to draw a Parallel of them, by setting several of their particular thoughts in the same light, whereby it will be obvious how much *Philips* hath the advantage. With what Simplicity he introduces two Shepherds singing alternately!

Hobb.   *Come, Rosalind, O come, for without thee*
        What Pleasure can the Country have for me:
        Come, Rosalind, O come; my brinded Kine,
        My snowy Sheep, my Farm, and all, is thine.

Lanq.   *Come Rosalind, O come; here shady Bowers*
        Here are cool Fountains, and here springing Flow'rs.
        Come, Rosalind; Here ever let us stay,
        And sweetly wast our live-long time away.

Our other Pastoral Writer, in expressing the same thought, deviates into *downright Poetry*.

Streph. *In Spring the Fields, in Autumn Hills I love,*
         At Morn the Plains, at Noon the shady Grove,
         But Delia always; forc'd from Delia's sight,
         Nor Plains at Morn, nor Groves at Noon delight.

Daph.   *Sylvia's like Autumn ripe, yet mild as May,*
         More bright than Noon, yet fresh as early Day;
         Ev'n Spring displeases, when she shines not here,
         But blest with her, 'tis Spring throughout the Year.

In the first of these Authors, two Shepherds thus *innocently* describe the Behaviour of their Mistresses.

Hobb.   *As Marian bath'd, by chance I passed by,*
        She blush'd, and at me cast a side-long Eye:
        Then swift beneath the crystal Wave she try'd
        Her beauteous Form, but all in vain, to hide.

Lanq.   *As I to cool me bath'd one sultry day,*
        Fond Lydia lurking in the Sedges lay.
        The wanton laugh'd, and seem'd in haste to fly;
        Yet often stopp'd, and often turn'd her Eye.

The other Modern (who it must be confessed hath a *knack of versifying*) hath it as follows.

Streph.   *Me gentle* Delia *beckons from the Plain,*
           Then, hid in Shades, eludes her eager Swain;
           But feigns a Laugh, to see me search around,
           And by that Laugh the willing Fair is found.

Daph.   *The sprightly* Sylvia *trips along the Green,*
           She runs, but hopes she does not run unseen;
           While a kind glance at her Pursuer flyes,
           How much at variance are her Feet and Eyes!

There is nothing the Writers of this kind of Poetry are fonder of, than descriptions of Pastoral Presents. *Philips* says thus of a Sheep-hook.

           Of season'd Elm; where studs of Brass appear,
           To speak the Giver's name, the month and year.
           The hook of polish'd Steel, the handle turn'd,
           And richly by the Graver's skill adorn'd.

The other of a Bowl embossed with Figures.

           ———*where wanton Ivy twines,*
           And swelling Clusters bend the curling Vines;
           Four Figures rising from the work appear,
           The various Seasons of the rolling year;
           And What is that which binds the radiant Sky,
           Where twelve bright Signs in beauteous order lie?

The simplicity of the Swain in this place, who forgets the name of the *Zodiack*, is no ill imitation of *Virgil*; but how much more plainly and unaffectedly would *Philips* have dressed this Thought in his *Doric?*

           And what that hight, which girds the Welkin sheen,
           Where twelve gay Signs in meet array are seen?

If the Reader would indulge his curiosity any farther in the comparison of Particulars, he may read the first Pastoral of *Philips* with the second of his Contemporary, and the fourth and sixth of the former with the fourth and first of the latter; where several parallel places will occur to every one.

Having now shown some parts, in which these two Writers may be compared, it is a justice I owe to Mr. *Philips*, to discover those in which *no man can compare with him*. First, That *beautiful Rusticity*, of which I shall only produce two Instances, out of a hundred not yet quoted.

> *O woful day ! O day of Woe, quoth he,*
> *And woful I, who live the day to see !*

The simplicity of Diction, the melancholy flowing of the Numbers, the solemnity of the Sound, and the easie turn of the Words, in this *Dirge*, (to make use of our Author's Expression) are extreamly elegant.

In another of his Pastorals, a Shepherd utters a *Dirge* not much inferior to the former, in the following lines.

> *Ah me the while ! ah me ! the luckless day,*
> *Ah luckless Lad ! the rather might I say;*
> *Ah silly I ! more silly than my Sheep,*
> *Which on the flowry Plains I once did keep.*

How he still charms the ear with these *artful Repetitions* of the Epithets; and how *significant* is the last verse! I defy the most common Reader to repeat them, without feeling some *motions of compassion*.

In the next place I shall rank his *Proverbs*, in which I formerly observed he excells: for example,

> *A* rolling Stone *is ever bare of* Moss;
> *And to their cost,* green years old proverbs *cross.*
> —*He that* late lyes down, *as* late will rise,
> *And Sluggard-like, till noon-day snoaring lyes.*
>   *Against* Ill-Luck *all cunning* Fore-sight *fails;*
> *Whether we sleep or wake, it nought avails.*
> —*Nor fear, from* upright *Sentence,* wrong.

Lastly, his *elegant Dialect,* which alone might prove him the eldest born of *Spencer,* and our only true *Arcadian.* I should think it proper for the several writers of Pastoral, to confine themselves to their several *Counties. Spencer* seems to have been of this opinion: for he hath laid the scene of one of his Pastorals in *Wales,* where with all the Simplicity natural to that part of our Island, one Shepherd bids the other *good morrow* in an unusual and elegant manner.

> Diggon Davy, *I bid hur God-day:*
> *Or* Diggon *hur is, or I mis-say.*

Diggon answers,

> *Hur was hur, while it was day-light;*
> *But now hur is a most wretched wight,* &c.

But the most beautiful example of this kind that I ever met with, is in a very valuable Piece, which I chanced to find among some old Manuscripts, entituled, *A Pastoral Ballad:* which I think, for its nature and simplicity, may (notwithstanding the modesty of the Title) be allowed a perfect Pastoral: It is composed in the *Somersetshire* Dialect, and the names such as are proper to the Country People. It may be observed, as a further beauty of this Pastoral, the words *Nymph, Dryad, Naiad, Fawn, Cupid,* or *Satyr,* are not once mentioned through the whole. I shall make no Apology for inserting some few lines of this excellent Piece. *Cicily* breaks thus into the subject, as she is going a Milking:

Cicily.   Rager *go vetch tha (b) Kee, or else tha Zun*
           Will quite be go, be vore c'have half a don.

Roger.   *Thou shouldst not ax ma tweece, but I've a be*
           To dreave our Bull to bull tha Parson's Kee.

It is to be observed, that this whole Dialogue is formed upon the *Passion of Jealousie*; and his mentioning the Parson's Kine naturally revives the Jealousie of the Shepherdess *Cicily,* which she expresses as follows:

Cicily.   *Ah* Rager, Rager, *chez was zore avraid*
           When in yond Vield you kiss'd tha Parson's Maid:
           Is this tha Love that once to me you zed,
           When from tha Wake thou brought'st me Gingerbread?

Roger.   Cicily *thou charg'st me valse,—I'll zwear to thee,*
           Tha Parson's Maid is still a Maid for me.

In which Answer of his are express'd at once that *Spirit of Religion,* and that *Innocence of the Golden Age,* so necessary to be observed by all Writers of Pastoral.

At the conclusion of this piece, the Author reconciles the Lovers, and ends the Eclogue the most *simply* in the world.

                So Rager *parted vor to vetch tha Kee,*
                And vor her Bucket in went Cicily.

I am loath to show my fondness for Antiquity so far as to prefer this ancient *British* Author to our present *English* Writers of Pastoral; but I cannot avoid making this obvious Remark, that *Philips* hath hit into the *same Road* with this old *West Country* Bard of ours.

(*b*) That is, the *Kine* or *Cows.*

After all that hath been said, I hope none can think it any Injustice to Mr. *Pope*, that I forbore to mention him as a Pastoral Writer; since upon the whole, he is of the same class with *Moschus* and *Bion*, whom we have excluded that rank; and of whose Eclogues, as well as some of *Virgil*'s, it may be said, that (according to the description we have given of this sort of Poetry) they are by no means *Pastorals*, but *something better*.

VI. A PARALLEL OF THE CHARACTERS OF MR. DRYDEN AND MR. POPE, AS DRAWN BY CERTAIN OF THEIR CONTEMPORARIES

MR. DRYDEN. HIS POLITICKS, RELIGION, MORALS

Mr. *Dryden* is a mere Renegado from *Monarchy*, *Poetry*, and *good Sense*. (*a*) A true *Republican* Son of a *monarchical* Church. (*b*) A Republican *Atheist* (*c*) *Dryden* was from the beginning an ἀλλοπρόσαλλος, and I doubt not will continue so to the last. (*d*)

In the Poem call'd *Absalom and Achitophel* are notoriously traduced, The KING, the QUEEN, the LORDS and GENTLE-MEN, not only their Honourable Persons exposed, but the WHOLE NATION and its REPRESENTATIVES notoriously libell'd; It is *Scandalum Magnatum*, yea of MAJESTY itself. (*e*)

He looks upon *God's Gospel* as a *foolish Fable*, like the *Pope*, to whom he is a pitiful Purveyor. (*f*) His very *Christianity* may be questioned. (*g*) He ought to expect more Severity than other men, as he is *most unmerciful* in his own *Reflections* on others. (*h*) With as good right as his *Holiness*, he sets up for *Poetical Infallibility*. (*i*)

MR. DRYDEN ONLY A VERSIFYER

His whole Libel is all *bad matter*, beautify'd (which is *all* that can be said of it) with *good metre*. (*k*) Mr. *Dryden*'s Genius did not appear in any thing more than his *Versification*, and whether he is to be ennobled for *that only*, is a question. (*l*)

MR. DRYDEN'S VIRGIL

Tonson calls it *Dryden*'s *Virgil*, to show that this is not that *Virgil* so admired in the Augustæan age, but a *Virgil* of another stamp, a *silly, impertinent, nonsensical* Writer. (*m*) None but a *Bavius*, a *Mævius*, or a *Bathyllus* carp'd at *Virgil*, and none but such unthinking Vermin *admire* his Translator. (*n*) It is true, *soft and easy*

(*a*) *Milbourn on Dryden's Virgil*, 8° 1698. *p.* 6.
(*b*) *pag.* 38.   (*c*) *pag.* 192.   (*d*) *pag.* 8.
(*e*) *Whip and Key*, 4°, *printed for R. Janeway* 1682. *Preface.*
(*f*) *ibid.*   (*g*) *Milbourn, p.* 9.
(*h*) *ibid. p.* 175.   (*i*) *pag.* 39.
(*k*) *Whip and Key, pref.*
(*l*) *Oldmixon, Essay on Criticism*, p. 84.
(*m*) *Milbourn*, pag. 4.   (*n*) Pag. 35.

VI. A PARALLEL OF THE CHARACTERS OF
MR. DRYDEN AND MR. POPE

MR. POPE. HIS POLITICKS, RELIGION, MORALS

Mr. *Pope* is an open and mortal *Enemy* to his *Country*, and the *Commonwealth* of *Learning*. (*a*) Some call him a Popish *Whig*, which is directly inconsistent. (*b*) *Pope* as a Papist must be a *Tory* and *High-flyer*. (*c*) He is *both* a *Whig* and a *Tory*. (*d*) He hath made it his custom to cackle to more than one Party in their own Sentiments. (*e*)

In his *Miscellanies*, the Persons abused are, The KING, the QUEEN, His late MAJESTY, both Houses of PARLIAMENT, the *Privy-Council*, the Bench of *Bishops*, the Establish'd CHURCH, the present MINISTRY, &*c*. To make sense of some passages, they must be constru'd into ROYAL SCANDAL. (*f*)

He is a *Popish* Rhymester, bred up with a *Contempt* of the *Sacred Writings*. (*g*) His *Religion* allows him to *destroy Hereticks*, not only with his pen, but with fire and sword; and such were all those *unhappy Wits* whom he sacrificed to his *accursed Popish Principles*. (*h*) It deserved Vengeance to suggest, that Mr. *Pope* had less *Infallibility* than his *Namesake at Rome*. (*i*)

MR. POPE ONLY A VERSIFYER

The *smooth numbers* of the Dunciad are *all* that recommend it, nor has it *any other merit*. (*k*) It must be own'd that he hath got a notable *Knack* of rhymeing, and writing *smooth verse*. (*l*)

MR. POPE'S HOMER

The *Homer* which *Lintot* prints, does not talk like *Homer*, but like *Pope*; and he who translated him one wou'd swear had a Hill in *Tipperary* for his *Parnassus*, and a puddle in some Bog for his *Hippocrene*. (*m*) He has no *Admirers* among those that can distinguish, discern, and judge. (*n*)

(*a*) *Dennis*, Remarks on the Rape of the Lock, pref. p. 12.
(*b*) Dunciad dissected.   (*c*) Preface to *Gulliveriana*.
(*d*) *Denn.* and *Gild.* Character of Mr. *P.*
(*e*) *Theobald*, Letter in *Mist*'s Journal, *June* 22, 1728.
(*f*) List, at the end of a Collection of Verses, Letters, Advertisements, 8°. Printed for *A. Moore*, 1728. and the Preface to it, pag. 6.
(*g*) *Dennis*'s Remarks on *Homer*, p. 27.
(*h*) Preface to *Gulliveriana*, p. 11.
(*i*) Dedication to the Collection of Verses, Letters, pag. 9.
(*k*) *Mist*'s *Journal, of June* 8, 1728.
(*l*) *Character of Mr.* P. and *Dennis on Homer*.
(*m*) *Dennis*'s Remarks on *Pope*'s *Homer*, pag. 12.   (*n*) Ibid.

POEMS: 1718–1729

lines might become *Ovid*'s Epistles or Art of Love—But *Virgil* who is all great and majestic, *&c.* requires strength of lines, weight of words, and closeness of expressions, not an *ambling Muse* running on a Carpet-ground, and shod as lightly as a *Newmarket* racer.— He has numberless faults in his *English*, in *Sense*, in his *Author's meaning*, and in propriety of *Expression*. (*o*)

MR. DRYDEN UNDERSTOOD NO GREEK OR LATIN

Mr. *Dryden* was *once*, I have heard, at *Westminster School:* Dr. *Busby* wou'd have *whipt him* for so childish a Paraphrase. (*p*) The meanest Pedant in *England* wou'd *whip a Lubber* of twelve for *construing so absurdly*. (*q*) The Translator is *mad, every line* betrays his Stupidity. (*r*) The faults are innumerable, and convince me that Mr. *Dryden* did not, or would not *understand his Author*. (*s*) This shows how fit Mr. *D.* may be to *translate Homer !* A mistake in a single letter might fall on the *Printer* well enough, but Εἴχωρ for Ἴχωρ must be the error of the *Author:* Nor had he art enough to correct it at the Press. (*t*) Mr. *Dryden* writes for the *Court Ladies*—He writes for the *Ladies*, and not for use. (*u*)

The Translator puts in a little *Burlesque* now and then into *Virgil*, for a Ragout to his *cheated Subscribers*. (*w*)

MR. DRYDEN TRICK'D HIS SUBSCRIBERS

I wonder that any man who cou'd not but be conscious of his own *unfitness* for it, shou'd go to amuse the learned world with such an *Undertaking !* A man ought to value his *Reputation* more than *Money*; and not to hope that those who can read for themselves, will be *Imposed upon*, merely by a *partially and unseasonably-celebrated Name*. (*x*) *Poetis quidlibet audendi* shall be Mr. *Dryden*'s Motto, tho' it should extend to *Picking of Pockets*. (*y*)

NAMES BESTOW'D ON MR. DRYDEN

An APE.] A crafty *Ape* drest up in a gaudy Gown—Whips put into an *Ape*'s paw, to play pranks with—None but *Apish* and *Papish* Brats will heed him. *Whip and Key, Pref.*

An ASS.] A Camel will take upon him no more burden than is sufficient for his strength, but there is *another Beast* that crouches under all: Mr. *Dryden*, &c. *Milb.* p. 105.

(*o*) Pag. 22, and 192.　　　　(*p*) *Milbourn*, pag. 72.
(*q*) Pag. 203.　　　(*r*) Pag. 78.　　　(*s*) Pag. 206.
(*t*) Pag. 19.　　　(*u*) Pag. 124, 190.　　　(*w*) Pag. 67.
(*x*) *Milbourn*, p. 192.　　　(*y*) *Ibid.* p. 125.

He hath a knack at *smooth verse*, but without either *Genius* or good *Sense*, or any tolerable knowledge of *English*. The qualities which distinguish *Homer* are the beauties of his Diction and the *harmony of his Versification*——But this little Author who is so much in vogue, has neither *Sense* in his *Thoughts*, nor *English* in his *Expressions*. (*o*)

MR. POPE UNDERSTOOD NO GREEK

He hath undertaken to translate *Homer* from the *Greek*, of which he knows not *one word*, into *English*, of which he understands ⟨almost⟩ *as little*. (*p*) I wonder how this Gentleman wou'd look should it be discover'd, that he has not translated *ten verses* together in any book of *Homer* with justice to the Poet, and yet he dares reproach his fellow-writers with *not understanding Greek*. (*q*) He has stuck so little to his Original, as to have his *knowledge in Greek* called in question. (*r*) I should be glad to know which it is of all *Homer*'s Excellencies, which has so delighted the *Ladies*, and the Gentlemen who judge like *Ladies*. (*s*)

But he has a notable talent at *Burlesque*; his genius slides so naturally into it, that he hath burlesqu'd *Homer* without designing it. (*t*)

MR. POPE TRICK'D HIS SUBSCRIBERS

'Tis indeed somewhat *bold*, and almost *prodigious*, for a *single man* to undertake such a work! But 'tis too late to dissuade by demonstrating the *madness* of your Project: The Subscribers' expectations have been rais'd, in proportion to what their *Pockets have been drain'd of*. (*u*) *Pope* has been concern'd in Jobbs, and hired out his *Name* to Booksellers. (*x*)

NAMES BESTOW'D ON MR. POPE

An APE.] Let us take the initial letter of his christian name, and the initial and final letters of his surname, *viz.* A. P. E. and they give you the same Idea of an *Ape*, as his face, *&c. Dennis*, Daily Journal, *May* 11, 1728.

An ASS.] It is my duty to pull off the Lion's skin from this little *Ass. Dennis*'s Rem. on *Homer*, pref.

(*o*) Character of Mr. *P.* pag. 17. and Remarks on *Homer*, p. 91.
(*p*) *Dennis*'s Remarks on *Homer*, p. 12.
(*q*) Daily Journal of *April* 23, 1728.
(*r*) Supplement to the Profund. Pref. ⟨p. v⟩.
(*s*) *Oldmixon*, Essay on Criticism, p. 66.
(*t*) *Dennis*'s Remarks, p. 28.   (*u*) *Burnet, Homerides. p.* 1, &c.
(*x*) *British Journal, Nov.* 25, 1727.

A FROG.] Poet *Squab* indued with Poet *Maro*'s Spirit! an ugly, *croaking* kind of *Vermine*, which would swell to the bulk of an *Oxe*. Pag. 11.

A COWARD.] A *Clinias* or a *Damætas*, or a man of Mr. *Dryden*'s *own Courage*. Pag. 176.

A KNAVE.] Mr. *Dryden* has heard of *Paul, the Knave of Jesus Christ:* And if I mistake not, I've read somewhere of *John Dryden Servant to his Majesty*. Pag. 57.

A FOOL.] Had he not been such a self-conceited *Fool—Whip and Key, pref*. Some great Poets are positive *Blockheads. Milbourn,* p. 34.

A THING.] So little a *Thing* as Mr. *Dryden. Ibid.* pag. 35.

A FROG.] A *squab* short Gentleman—a little creature that like the *Frog* in the Fable, swells and is angry that it is not allow'd *to be as big as an Oxe. Dennis's Remarks on the Rape of the Lock, pref. p. 9.*

A COWARD.] A lurking, way-laying *Coward. Char. of Mr. P. pag. 3.*

A KNAVE.] He is one whom God and nature have mark'd for *want* of common *honesty. Ibid.*

A FOOL.] Great *Fools* will be christen'd by the names of great Poets, and *Pope* will be called *Homer. Dennis's* Rem. on *Homer, p. 37.*

A THING.] A little, abject, *Thing. Ibid. p. 8.*

VII. A LIST OF ALL OUR AUTHOR'S GENUINE WORKS

The Works of Mr. ALEXANDER POPE, in quarto and folio. Printed for *Jacob Tonson* and *Bernard Lintot*, in the year 1717. This Edition contains whatsoever is his, except these few following, which have been written since that time.

INSCRIPTION to Dr. *Parnel*'s Poems; To the Right Honourable ROBERT Earl of OXFORD and Earl MORTIMER.

VERSES on Mr. ADDISON'S Treatise of *Medals,* first printed after his death in Mr. *Tickel*'s Edition of his Works.

EPITAPHS: On the Honourable *Simon Harcourt:* on the Honourable *Robert Digby:* on Mrs. *Corbett*; and another intended for Mr. *Rowe.*

The WHOLE ILIAD of HOMER, with the PREFACE, and the NOTES, (except the *Extracts from Eustathius* in the four last volumes, made by Mr. *Broome*; and the *Essay* on the *Life* and *Writings of Homer,* which tho' collected by our Author, was put together by Dr. *Parnell.*)

TWELVE BOOKS of the ODYSSEY, with some parts of other Books; and the *Dissertation* by way of *Postscript* at the end.

The *Preface* to Mr. *Tonson*'s Edition of SHAKESPEAR.

MISCELLANIES by Dr. *Swift* and our Author, *&c.* Printed for *B. Motte.*

And some *Spectators* and *Guardians.*

By the Author a Declaration

Whereas certain Haberdashers of Points and Particles, being instigated by the spirit of Pride, and assuming to themselves the name of Critics and Restorers, have taken upon them to adulterate the common and current sense of our Glorious Ancestors, Poets of this Realm, by clipping, coining, defacing the images, mixing their own base allay, or otherwise falsifying the same; which they publish, utter, and vend as genuine: The said haberdashers having no right thereto, as neither heirs, executors, administrators, assigns, or in any sort related to such Poets, to all or any of them: Now We, having carefully revised this our Dunciad,[a] beginning with the word Books, and ending with the words buries all, containing the entire sum of one thousand and twelve Lines, do declare every word, figure, point, and comma of this impression to be authentic: And do therefore strictly enjoin and forbid any person or persons whatsoever, to erase, reverse, put between hooks,[1] or by any other means directly or indirectly change or mangle any of them. And we do hereby earnestly exhort all our brethren to follow this our example, which we heartily wish our Great Predecessors had heretofore set, as a remedy and prevention of all such abuses. Provided always, that nothing in this Declaration shall be construed to limit the lawful and undoubted right of every subject of this Realm, to judge, censure, or condemn, in the whole or in part, any Poem or Poet whatsoever.

> Given under our hand at London, this third day of January, in the year of our Lord One thousand, seven hundred, thirty and two.

Declarat' cor' me,

JOHN BARBER, Mayor.

[a] Read thus confidently, instead of 'beginning with the word *Books*, and ending with the word *flies*,' as formerly it stood ; Read also 'containing the entire sum of *one thousand, seven hundred, and fifty four* verses,' instead of '*one thousand and twelve* lines;' such being the initial and final words, and such the true and entire contents, of this Poem.

Thou art to know, reader! that the first Edition thereof, like that of Milton, was never seen by the Author (though living and not blind;) The Editor himself confest as much in his Preface: And no two poems were ever published in so arbitrary a manner. The Editor of this, had as boldly suppressed whole Passages, yea the entire last book; as the Editor of Paradise lost, added and augmented. Milton himself gave but *ten* books, his editor *twelve*; this Author gave *four* books, his Editor only *three*. But we have happily done justice to both; and presume we shall live, in this our last labour, as long as in any of our others. BENTLEY.

[1] *hooks* ⟨Bentley's word for the brackets by which he indicated the passages in *Paradise Lost* that he considered spurious. Cf. iv 194*n*, p. 776.⟩

Minor Verse 1718–1729

―――――――――――❈―――――――――――

Lines on Mr. Hatton's Clocks
[written 1718; published 1871]

From hour to hour melodiously they chime
With silver sounds, and sweetly tune out time.

Lines to Lord Bathurst
[written 1718; published 1843]

A wood? quoth Lewis; and with that,
He laughd, and shook his Sides so fat:
His tongue (with Eye that markd his cunning)
Thus fell a reas'ning, not a running.
   Woods are (not to be too prolix)   5
Collective Bodies of strait Sticks.
It is, my Lord, a meer Conundrum
To call things Woods, for what grows und'r 'em.
For Shrubs, when nothing else at top is,
Can only constitute a Coppice.   10
But if you will not take my word,
See Anno quart. of Edward, third.
And that they're Coppice calld, when dock'd,
Witness Ann. prim. of Henry Oct.
   If this a Wood you will maintain   15
Meerly because it is no Plain;
Holland (for all that I can see)
Might e'en as well be termed the Sea;
And C—by be fair harangu'd
An honest Man, because not hang'd.   20

――――――――――――――――――

Title: *Lord Bathurst*] Allen, Earl Bathurst (1684–1775), to whom Pope addressed his third *Moral Essay* (p.570), and in whose plantations at Cirencester he took an interest.
   1. *Lewis*] Erasmus Lewis (1670–1754), friend of Pope, Swift, Bathurst, and Lord Oxford's devoted political servant.
   19. *C—by*] Thomas, Earl Coningsby, see p. 496.

Verses in the Scriblerian Manner

TO THE RT. HONBLE. THE EARL OF OXFORD

[written 1718; published 1950]

One★ that should be a Saint,
    and one★ that's a Sinner,
And one★ that pays reckning
    but ne'r eats a Dinner,
In short Pope and Gay (as   5
    you'l see in the margin)
Who saw you in Tower, and since
    your enlarging,
And Parnell who saw you not since
    you did treat him,   10
Will venture it now—you have
    no Stick to beat him—
Since these for your Jury, good
    and true men, vous-avez;
Pray grant Us Admittance,   15
    and shut out Miles Davies.

7. *in Tower*] Oxford was confined in the Tower from July 1715 until
July 1717.
16. *Miles Davies*] Bibliographer (1662-1719?).

Three Epitaphs on
John Hewet and Sarah Drew

[written 1718; published 1737, 1718, 1950]

I

When Eastern lovers feed the fun'ral fire,
On the same pile the faithful fair expire;
Here pitying heav'n that virtue mutual found,
And blasted both, that it might neither wound.
Hearts so sincere th' Almighty saw well pleas'd,   5
Sent his own lightning, and the Victims seiz'd.

II. EPITAPH ON JOHN HEWET AND SARAH DREW
IN THE CHURCHYARD AT STANTON HARCOURT

NEAR THIS PLACE LIE THE BODIES OF
JOHN HEWET AND SARAH DREW
AN INDUSTRIOUS YOUNG MAN, AND
VIRTUOUS MAIDEN OF THIS PARISH;
CONTRACTED IN MARRIAGE
WHO BEING WITH MANY OTHERS AT HARVEST
WORK, WERE BOTH IN AN INSTANT KILLED
BY LIGHTNING ON THE LAST DAY OF JULY
1718

Think not by rigorous judgment seiz'd,
A pair so faithful could expire;
Victims so pure Heav'n saw well pleas'd
And snatch'd them in Cœlestial fire.

Live well and fear no sudden fate; 5
When God calls Virtue to the grave,
Alike tis Justice, soon or late,
Mercy alike to kill or save.

Virtue unmov'd can hear the Call,
And face the Flash that melts the Ball. 10

III. EPITAPH ON THE STANTON-HARCOURT
LOVERS

Here lye two poor Lovers, who had the mishap
Tho very chaste people, to die of a Clap.

Answer to Mrs. Howe

[written c. 1718; published 1718]

What is PRUDERY?
'Tis a Beldam,
Seen with Wit and Beauty seldom.
'Tis a fear that starts at shadows.
'Tis, (no, 'tisn't) like Miss *Meadows*.

The original title ran as follows: '*Mrs. Lepell, and Mrs. How, two Maids
of Honour to the Princess, ask'd Mr. Pope what* Prudery *is.* (*He making Use
of that Expression in Conversation.*) *His Answer.*'
4. *Miss Meadows*] A Maid of Honour known for her grave demeanour.

'Tis a Virgin hard of Feature,   5
Old, and void of all good-nature;
Lean and fretful; would seem wise;
Yet plays the fool before she dies.
'Tis an ugly envious Shrew,
That rails at dear *Lepell* and You.   10

Epitaph. Intended for Mr. Rowe
in Westminster Abbey

[written 1718; published, Lintot's
Miscellany, 1720]

Thy reliques, *Rowe*, to this fair urn we trust,
And sacred, place by *Dryden*'s awful dust:
Beneath a rude and nameless stone he lies,
To which thy tomb shall guide inquiring eyes.
Peace to thy gentle shade, and endless Rest!   5
Blest in thy genius, in thy love too blest!
One grateful woman to thy fame supplies
What a whole thankless land to his denies.

3. *a rude and nameless stone*] The Tomb of Mr. *Dryden* was erected upon
this hint by the Duke of *Buckingham*; to which was originally intended
this Epitaph . . . ⟨see below.⟩ Which the author since chang'd into the
plain Inscription now upon it, being only the name of that Great Poet,

DRYDEN.

Natus Aug. 9. 1631.
Mortuus Maij 1. 1701.
Johannes Sheffield, Dux Buckinghamiensis, fecit. [P]

Epitaph. designed for Mr. Dryden's
Monument

[written 1718; published, Lintot's
Miscellany, 1726]

This *SHEFFIELD* rais'd. The sacred Dust below
Was *DRYDEN* once: The rest who does not know?

Epistle to James Craggs, Esq;
Secretary of State

[written 1718? published, *Works*, 1735]

A soul as full of Worth, as void of Pride,
Which nothing seeks to show, or needs to hide,
Which nor to Guilt, nor Fear, its Caution owes,
And boasts a Warmth that from no Passion flows;
A Face untaught to feign! a judging Eye,   5
That darts severe upon a rising Lye,
And strikes a blush thro' frontless Flattery.
All this thou wert; and being this before,
Know, Kings and Fortune cannot make thee more.
Then scorn to gain a Friend by servile ways,   10
Nor wish to lose a Foe these Virtues raise;
But candid, free, sincere, as you began,
Proceed—a Minister, but still a Man;
Be not (exalted to whate'er degree)
Asham'd of any Friend, not ev'n of Me.   15
The Patriot's plain, but untrod path pursue;
If not, 'tis I must be ashamed of You.

A Dialogue

[written c. 1718; published 1775]

Pope.   Since my old Friend is grown so great,
        As to be Minister of State,
        I'm told (but 'tis not true I hope)
        That *Craggs* will be asham'd of *Pope*.

Craggs. Alas! if I am such a Creature,   5
        To grow the worse for growing greater;
        Why Faith, in Spite of all my Brags,
        'Tis *Pope* must be asham'd of *Craggs*.

On Lady Mary Wortley Montagu's Portrait

[written 1719; published 1803]

The play full smiles around the dimpled mouth
That happy air of Majesty and Youth.

So would I draw (but oh, 'tis vain to try
My narrow Genius does the power deny)
The Equal Lustre of the Heavenly mind   5
Where every grace with every Virtue's join'd
Learning not vain, and wisdom not severe.
With Greatness easy, and with wit sincere.
With Just Description shew the Soul Divine
And the whole Princess in my work should shine.   10

To Sir Godfrey Kneller, On his painting for me the Statues of Apollo, Venus and Hercules

[written c. 1719; published, Steele's
Miscellanies, 1727]

What God, what Genius did the Pencil move
    When KNELLER painted These?
Twas Friendship—warm as *Phœbus*, kind as Love,
    And strong as *Hercules*.

In behalf of Mr. Southerne. To the Duke of Argyle

EPIGRAM

[written 1719; published 1721]

Argyle his Praise, when *Southerne* wrote,
First struck out this, and then that Thought;
Said *this* was Flatt'ry, *that* a Fault.
    How shall your Bard contrive?

My Lord, consider what you do,   5
He'll lose his Pains and Verses too;
For if these Praises fit not You,
    They'll fit no Man alive.

Lines from Acis and Galatea

[written c. 1719; published 1732]

I. AIR

The Flocks shall leave the Mountains,
The Woods the Turtle-Dove,

The Nymphs forsake the Fountains
Ere I forsake my Love.

Not Showers to Larks so pleasing,
  Nor Sunshine to the Bee;
Nor Sleep to Toil so easing
  As these dear Smiles to me.

II. CHORUS

Wretched Lovers, Fate has past
This sad Decree, no Joy shall last.
Wretched Lovers, quit your Dream,
Behold the Monster, *Polypheme*.
See what ample Strides he takes,   5
The Mountain nods, the Forest shakes,
The Waves run frighted to the Shores.
Hark! how the thund'ring Giant roars.

The words for Handel's masque, *Acis and Galatea*, are claimed to have been translated from the Italian 'by Mr. Pope, Dr. Arbuthnot, and Mr. Gay'. The extent of Pope's contribution to the book is unknown, but these two pieces unmistakably derive from him.

Duke upon Duke

AN EXCELLENT NEW BALLAD. TO THE TUNE OF CHEVY CHASE

[written c. 1719; published 1720]

To Lordings proud I tune my Lay,
  Who feast in Bower or Hall:
Though Dukes they be, to Dukes I say,
  That Pride will have a Fall.

Now, that this same it is right sooth,   5
  Full plainly doth appear,
From what befel *John* Duke of *Guise*,
  And *Nic.* of *Lancastere*.

Sir John Guise (*c.* 1677–1732) was M.P. for Gloucestershire 1705–10 and for Marlow 1722–7. His sister was married to Pope's friend, Edward Blount. The other disputant, Lechmere, Chancellor of the Duchy of Lancaster, was notoriously so overbearing in manner, hot-tempered, and violent, as to be a fair target for ridicule.

When *Richard Cœur de Lyon* reign'd,
  (Which means a Lion's Heart)   10
Like him his Barons rag'd and roar'd,
  Each play'd a Lion's Part.

A Word and Blow was then enough,
  (Such Honour did them prick)
If you but turn'd your Cheek, a Cuff,   15
  And if your A—se, a Kick.

Look in their Face, they tweak'd your Nose,
  At ev'ry Turn fell to 't;
Come near, they trod upon your Toes;
  They fought from Head to Foot.   20

Of these, the Duke of *Lancastere*
  Stood Paramount in Pride;
He kick'd, and cuff'd, and tweak'd, and trod
  His Foes, and Friends beside.

Firm on his Front his Beaver sate,   25
  So broad, it hid his Chin;
For why? he deem'd no Man his Mate,
  And fear'd to tan his Skin.

With *Spanish* Wool he dy'd his Cheek,
  With Essence oil'd his Hair;   30
No Vixen Civet-Cat so sweet,
  Nor could so scratch and tear.

Right tall he made himself to show,
  Though made full short by G—d:
And when all other Dukes did bow,   35
  This Duke did only nod.

Yet courteous, blithe, and debonair,
  To *Guise*'s Duke was he;
Was never such a loving Pair,
  How could they disagree?   40

Oh, thus it was. He lov'd him dear,
  And cast how to requite him:
And having no Friend left but this,
  He deem'd it meet to fight him.

Forthwith he drench'd his desp'rate Quill; 45
   And thus he did indite:
'This Eve at Whisk ourself will play,
   Sir Duke! be here to Night.'

Ah no, ah no, the guileless *Guise*
   Demurely did reply, 50
I cannot go, nor yet can stand,
   So sore the Gout have I.

The Duke in Wrath call'd for his Steeds,
   And fiercely drove them on;
Lord! Lord! how rattl'd then thy Stones, 55
   Oh Kingly *Kensington*!

All in a Trice he rush'd on *Guise*,
   Thrust out his Lady dear,
He tweak'd his Nose, trod on his Toes,
   And smote him on the Ear. 60

But mark, how 'midst of Victory,
   Fate plays her old Dog Trick!
Up leap'd Duke *John*, and knock'd him down,
   And so down fell Duke *Nic*.

Alas, oh *Nic*! Oh *Nic*. alas! 65
   Right did thy Gossip call thee:
As who should say, alas the Day,
   When *John* of *Guise* shall maul thee.

For on thee did he clap his Chair,
   And on that Chair did sit; 70
And look'd, as if he meant therein
   To do—what was not fit.

Up didst thou look, oh woeful Duke!
   Thy Mouth yet durst not ope,
Certes for fear, of finding there 75
   A T—d instead of Trope.

'Lye there, thou Caitiff vile! quoth *Guise*,
   No *Sheet* is here to save thee:
The Casement it is shut likewise;
   Beneath my Feet I have thee. 80

'If thou hast ought to speak, speak out.'
  Then *Lancastere* did cry,
'Know'st thou not me, nor yet thy self?
  Who thou, and whom am I?

'Know'st thou not me, who (God be prais'd)   85
  Have brawl'd, and quarrel'd more,
Than all the Line of *Lancastere*
  That battl'd heretofore?

'In Senates fam'd for many a Speech,
  And (what some awe must give ye,   90
Tho' laid thus low beneath thy breech,)
  Still of the Council Privy.

'Still of the *Dutchy* Chancellor,
  Durante Life I have it;
And turn, as now thou dost on me,   95
  Mine A—e on them that gave it.'

But now the Servants they rush'd in;
  And Duke *Nic.* up leap'd he:
I will not cope against such odds,
  But, *Guise*! I'll fight with thee: 100

To-morrow with thee will I fight
  Under the Greenwood Tree;
'No, not to-morrow, but to night
  (Quoth *Guise*) I'll fight with thee.'

And now the Sun declining low   105
  Bestreak'd with Blood the Skies;
When, with his Sword at Saddle Bow,
  Rode forth the valiant *Guise*;

Full gently praunch'd he o'er the Lawn;
  Oft' roll'd his Eyes around,   110
And from the Stirrup stretch'd, to find
  Who was not to be found.

Long brandish'd he the Blade in Air,
  Long look'd the Field all o'er:
At length he spy'd the Merry-men brown,   115
  And eke the Coach and four.

From out the Boot bold *Nicholas*
  Did wave his Wand so white,
As pointing out the gloomy Glade
  Wherein he meant to fight.   120

All in that dreadful Hour, so calm
  Was *Lancastere* to see,
As if he meant to take the Air,
  Or only take a Fee.

And so he did—for to *New Court*   125
  His rowling Wheels did run:
Not that he shunn'd the doubtful Strife,
  But *Bus'ness* must be done.

Back in the Dark, by *Brompton* Park,
  He turn'd up through the Gore;   130
So slunk to *Cambden* House so high,
  All in his Coach and four.

Mean while Duke *Guise* did fret and fume,
  A Sight it was to see;
Benumm'd beneath the Evening Dew,   135
  Under the Greenwood Tree.

Then, wet and weary, home he far'd,
  Sore mutt'ring all the way,
'The Day I meet him, *Nic.* shall rue
  The Cudgel of that Day.   140

'Mean Time on every Pissing-Post
  Paste we this Recreant's Name,
So that each Pisser-by shall read,
  And piss against the same.'

Now God preserve our gracious King!   145
  And grant, his Nobles all
May learn this Lesson from Duke *Nic.*
  That *Pride will have a Fall.*

An Inscription upon a Punch-Bowl, in the South-Sea Year for a Club, chas'd with Jupiter placing Callista in the Skies & Europa with the Bull

[written 1720; published 1831]

Come, fill the South-Sea Goblet full;
    The Gods shall of our Stock take care:
Europa pleas'd accepts the *Bull*,
    And Jove with Joy puts off the *Bear*.

To Mr. Gay,

WHO WROTE HIM A CONGRATULATORY LETTER ON THE FINISHING HIS HOUSE

[written 1720; published, 1-6, 1803; 7-14, 1737]

Ah friend, 'tis true—this truth you lovers know—
In vain my structures rise, my gardens grow,
In vain fair Thames reflects the double scenes
Of hanging mountains, and of sloping greens:
Joy lives not here; to happier seats it flies,   5
And only dwells where WORTLEY casts her eyes.

What are the gay parterre, the chequer'd shade,
The morning bower, the ev'ning colonade,
But soft recesses of uneasy minds,
To sigh unheard in, to the passing winds?   10

So the struck deer in some sequester'd part
Lies down to die, the arrow at his heart;
There, stretch'd unseen in coverts hid from day,
Bleeds drop by drop, and pants his life away.

6. *Wortley*] Lady Mary Wortley Montagu.

Epitaph. On the Honble. Simon Harcourt, Only Son of the Lord Chancellor Harcourt

AT THE CHURCH OF STANTON-HARCOURT IN
OXFORDSHIRE, 1720

[written 1722; published 1724]

To this sad Shrine, who'er thou art, draw near,
Here lies the Friend most lov'd, the Son most dear:
Who ne'er knew Joy, but Friendship might divide,
Or gave his Father grief, but when he dy'd.

How vain is Reason, Eloquence how weak,   5
If *Pope* must tell what *HARCOURT* cannot speak?
Oh let thy once-lov'd Friend inscribe thy Stone,
And with a Father's Sorrows mix his own!

Verses to Mrs. Judith Cowper

[written 1722; published 1769]

Tho' sprightly Sappho force our love and praise,
A softer wonder my pleas'd soul surveys,
The mild Erinna, blushing in her bays.
So while the sun's broad beam yet strikes the sight,
All mild appears the moon's more sober light,   5
Serene, in virgin majesty, she shines;
And, un-observed, the glaring sun declines.

Compare *Moral Essay* II ll. 253-6, p. 568.

Lines to Bolingbroke

[written 1724; published 1871]

What pleasing Phrensy steals away my Soul?
    Thro' thy blest Shades (La Source) I seem to rove
I see thy fountains fall, thy waters roll
    And breath the Zephyrs that refresh thy Grove
I hear whatever can delight inspire   5
Villete's soft Voice and St John's silver Lyre.

A version of Horace, *Od.* III IV 5-8, complimenting Lady Bolingbroke,
Marquise of Villette. Their residence, La Source, near Orleans, was at
the source of the Loiret; hence the pun in l. 6.

Inscription

[written 1725; published, *Letters*, 1735]

Nymph of the Grot, these sacred Springs I keep,`
And to the Murmur of these Waters sleep;
Ah spare my Slumbers, gently tread the Cave!
And drink in silence, or in silence lave!

A version of a popular Latin epigram.

> *Hujus Nympha loci, sacri custodia fontis*
> *Dormio, dum blandæ sentio murmur aquæ.*
> *Parce meum, quisquis tangis cava marmora, somnum*
> *Rumpere, sive bibas, sive lavare, tace.*

Epitaph. On Lady Kneller

[written 1725; published 1838]

One day I mean to Fill Sir Godfry's tomb,
If for my body all this Church has room.
Down with more Monuments! More room! (she cryd)
For I am very large, and very wide.

A protest against Lady Kneller's proposal to replace a wall tablet in Twickenham church commemorating Pope's father with a monument to her husband.

On a certain Lady at Court

[written c. 1725; published, *PSM*, 1732]

I know the thing that's most uncommon;
   (Envy be silent and attend!)
I know a Reasonable Woman,
   Handsome and witty, yet a Friend.

Not warp'd by Passion, aw'd by Rumour,   5
   Not grave thro' Pride, or gay thro' Folly,
An equal Mixture of good Humour,
   And sensible soft Melancholy.

'Has she no Faults then (Envy says) Sir?'
   Yes she has one, I must aver: 10
When all the World conspires to praise her,
   The Woman's deaf, and does not hear.

On Mrs Howard, afterwards Countess of Suffolk, mistress of George II.

Lines On Swift's Ancestors
[written 1726; published 1814]

> Jonathan Swift
> Had the gift,
> By fatherige, motherige,
> And by brotherige,
> To come from Gutherige,   5
> But now is spoil'd clean,
> And an Irish Dean.
> In this church he has put
> A stone of two foot;
> With a cup and a can, Sir,   10
> In respect to his grandsire;
> So Ireland change thy tone,
> And cry, O hone! O hone!
> For England hath its own.

Swift put up a plain monument to his grandfather, and also presented a cup to the church of Goodrich, or Gotheridge.

Receipt to make Soup

FOR THE USE OF DEAN SWIFT

[written 1726; published ? 1726]

> Take a knuckle of Veal
> (You may buy it, or steal),
> In a few peices cut it,
> In a Stewing pan put it,
> Salt, pepper and mace   5
> Must season this knuckle,

Shortly after Swift's return to Ireland in August 1726, Pope met with an accident. One night in early September, the coach in which Boling-broke was sending him home overturned while crossing a stream, and he was rescued from drowning in it only at the cost of severe cuts sustained in his right hand when one of the footmen 'pulled him out through the window'. As the news of the accident spread, Pope's friends gathered round, and Twickenham became the centre of much hospitality. One day, a dish of stewed veal was prepared according to a recipe from Pulteney's cook, Monsieur Devaux, which was greatly 'approved of at one of our Twickenham entertainments'. It was probably on this occasion that Pope suggested sending Swift a composite letter, in the production of which he was joined by Gay, Bolingbroke, Mrs. Howard, and Pulteney. Pope's own contribution to this letter was a rhymed version of the recipe.

Then what's join'd to a place,
With other Herbs muckle;
That which killed King Will,
And what never stands still,   10
Some sprigs of that bed
Where Children are bred,
Which much you will mend, if
Both Spinage and Endive,
And Lettuce and Beet,   15
With Marygold meet;
Put no water at all;
For it maketh things small;
Which, lest it should happen,
A close cover clap on;   20
Put this pot of Wood's mettle
In a hot boiling kettle,
And there let it be,
(Mark the Doctrine I teach)
About——let me see,——   25
Thrice as long as you preach.
So skimming the fat off,
Say Grace, with your hat off
O then, with what rapture
Will it fill Dean and Chapter!   30

7. I.e. Celery.
9. I.e. Sorrell; the supposed name of King William III's horse which
indirectly caused his death by stumbling.
10. I.e. Thyme.
11 f. Parsley.

Presentation Verses to Nathaniel Pigott

[published 1948]

The Muse this one Verse to learn'd Pigot addresses,
    In whose Heart, like his Writings, was never found flaw;
Whom Pope prov'd his Friend in his two chief distresses,
    Once in danger of Death, once in danger of Law.

                                        Sept. 23. 1726.

Nathaniel Pigott (1661–1737), a Barrister at Law, lived at Whitton near
Twickenham, and it was evidently to his house that Pope was carried after
the accident in which his coach was upset when crossing the river Crane
on a dark night in September 1726.

The Capon's Tale

TO A LADY WHO FATHER'D HER LAMPOONS
UPON HER ACQUAINTANCE
[written c. 1726; published, *PSM*, 1727]

In *Yorkshire* dwelt a sober Yeoman,
Whose Wife, a clean, pains-taking Woman,
Fed num'rous Poultry in her Pens,
And saw her Cocks well serve her Hens.

A Hen she had, whose tuneful Clocks   5
Drew after her a Train of Cocks:
With Eyes so piercing, yet so pleasant,
You would have sworn this Hen a Pheasant.
All the plum'd Beau-monde round her gathers;

Lord! what a Brustling up of Feathers!   10
Morning from Noon there was no knowing,
There was such Flutt'ring, Chuckling, Crowing:
Each forward Bird must thrust his head in,
And not a Cock but would be treading.

Yet tender was this Hen so fair,   15
And hatch'd more Chicks than she could rear.

Our prudent Dame bethought her then
Of some Dry-Nurse to save her Hen;
She made a Capon drunk: In fine
He eat the Sops, she sipp'd the Wine: 20
His Rump well pluck'd with Nettles stings,
And claps the Brood beneath his Wings.

The feather'd Dupe awakes content,
O'erjoy'd to see what God had sent.
Thinks he's the Hen, clocks, keeps a Pother,   25
A foolish Foster-Father-Mother.

Such, Lady *Mary*, are your Tricks;
But since you hatch, pray own your Chicks:
You should be better skill'd in Nocks,
Nor like your Capons, serve your Cocks.   30

The Discovery: or, The Squire turn'd Ferret

AN EXCELLENT NEW BALLAD

To the Tune of *High Boys! up go we*; *Chevy Chase*;
Or what you please.

[written 1726; published 1726]

Most true it is, I dare to say,
  E'er since the Days of *Eve*,
The weakest Woman sometimes may
  The wisest Man deceive.

For *D——nt* circumspect, sedate,   5
  A *Machiavel* by Trade,
Arriv'd Express, with News of Weight,
  And thus, at Court, he said.

At *Godliman*, hard by the *Bull*,
  A Woman, long thought barren,   10
Bears *Rabbits*,—Gad! so plentiful,
  You'd take her for a Warren.

These Eyes, quoth He, beheld them clear:
  What, do ye doubt my View?
Behold this Narrative that's here;   15
  Why, Zounds! and Blood! 'tis true!

Mary Toft (or Tofts) of Godalming was said to have given birth from time to time to a (variously specified) number of rabbits. *The Whitehall Evening-Post* of 26 November printed an 'Extract of Letter from Mr. John Howard, Surgeon and Man-Midwife at Guildford, to a near Relation . . . dated 22 November 1726,' in which he reported the delivery of the seventeenth rabbit, and then went on to say that 'last Tuesday' [15 November] Mr. St. André, his Majesty's Anatomist, who had been present and had assisted Howard, was 'satisfied in the Truth of the wondrous Delivery: As was Mr. Molineaux, Secretary to the Prince, who was also here . . .' The affair created the greatest excitement. Not only doctors were interested, but 'Great Numbers of the Nobility have been to see her' (*London Journal*, 3 December). The woman confessed to the fraud on 7 December, and was 'ordered to be prosecuted . . . for being a vile Cheat and Imposter'.

5. *D—nt*] 'Mr. Davenant', who wrote the first account of the supposed delivery.

Some said that *D—gl—s* sent should be,
   Some talk'd of *W—lk—r*'s Merit,
But most held, in this Midwifery,
   No Doctor like a FERRET.   20

But *M–l–n–x*, who heard this told,
   (Right wary He and wise)
Cry'd sagely, 'Tis not safe, I hold,
   To trust to *D——nt*'s Eyes.

A Vow to God He then did make   25
   He would himself go down,
St. A–d–re too, the Scale to take
   Of that *Phœnomenon.*

He order'd then his Coach and Four;
   (The Coach was quickly got 'em)   30
Resolv'd this *Secret* to explore,
   And search it to the *Bottom.*

At *Godliman* they now arrive,
   For Haste they made exceeding;
As Courtiers should, whene'er they strive   35
   To be inform'd of Breeding.

The good Wife to the Surgeon sent,
   And said to him, Good Neighbour,
'Tis pity that two Squires so Gent—
   Should come and lose their Labour.   40

The Surgeon with a *Rabbit* came,
   And first in Pieces cut it;
Then slyly thrust it up *that same*,
   As far as Man could put it.

(Ye *Guildford* Inn-keepers take heed   45
   You dress not such a *Rabbit*
Ye Poult'rers eke, destroy the Breed,
   'Tis so unsav'ry a-Bit.)

17. *D–gl–s*] James Douglas (1675–1742) Physician and Obstetrist, Physician to Queen Caroline, present at Mary Toft's confession.
18. *W–lk–r*] Perhaps Dr. Middleton Walker, 'an eminent Man-mid-wife', d. 1732.
21. *M–l–n–x*] Samuel Molyneux (1689–1728). Astronomer; Secretary to the Prince of Wales.

But hold! says *Molly*, first let's **try**,
   Now that her Legs are ope,   50
If ought within we may descry
   By Help of Telescope.

The Instrument himself did make,
   He rais'd and level'd right,
But all about was so opake,   55
   It could not aid his Sight.

On Tiptoe then the Squire he stood,
   (But first He gave Her Money)
Then reach'd as high as e'er He cou'd,
   And cry'd, I feel a C O N Y.   60

Is it alive? *St. A–d–re* cry'd;
   It is; I feel it stir.
Is it full grown? The Squire reply'd,
   It is; see here's the F U R.

And now two Legs *St. A–d–re* got,   65
   And then came two Legs more;
Now fell the Head to *Molly*'s Lot,
   And so the Work was o'er.

The Woman, thus being brought to Bed,
   Said, to reward your Pains,   70
St. A–d–re shall dissect the Head,
   And thou shalt have the Brains.

He lap'd it in a Linnen Rag,
   Then thank'd Her for Her Kindness;
And cram'd it in the Velvet Bag   75
   That serves his R—l H——

That Bag—which *Jenny*, wanton Slut,
   First brought to foul Disgrace;
Stealing the Papers thence she put
   Veal-Cutlets in their Place.   80

O! happy would it be, I ween,
   Could they these *Rabbits* smother;
Molly had ne'er a Midwife been,
   Nor she a shameful Mother.

Why has the Proverb falsly said   85
   Better two Heads than one;
Could *Molly* hide this *Rabbit*'s Head,
   He still might shew his own.

Epigram, in a Maid of Honour's Prayer-Book

[written 1726; published (piratically) 1727]

When *Israel*'s Daughters mourn'd their past Offences,
They dealt in *Sackcloth*, and turn'd *Cynder-Wenches*:
But *Richmond*'s Fair-ones never spoil their Locks,
They use white Powder, and wear Holland-Smocks.
O comely Church! where Females find *clean Linen*   5
As decent to *repent* in, as to *sin* in.

3. *Richmond's Fair-ones*] The maids of honour at the court of the Prince
and Princess of Wales.

Verses on Gulliver's Travels

[written 1727; published 1727]

I. TO QUINBUS FLESTRIN, THE MAN-MOUNTAIN
A LILLIPUTIAN ODE

    In Amaze
    Lost, I gaze!
    Can our Eyes
    Reach thy Size?
    May my Lays   5
    Swell with Praise
    Worthy thee!
    Worthy me!
    Muse inspire,
    All thy Fire!   10
    Bards of old
    Of him told,
    When they said
    Atlas Head
    Propt the Skies: 15
See! and believe your Eyes!

    See him stride
    Vallies wide:

Over Woods,
Over Floods.   20
When he treads,
Mountains Heads
Groan and shake;
Armies quake,
Lest his Spurn   25
Overturn
Man and Steed:
Troops take Heed!
Left and Right,
Speed your Flight!   30
Lest an Host
Beneath his Foot be lost.

Turn'd aside
From his Hide,
Safe from Wound   35
Darts rebound.
From his Nose
Clouds he blows;
When he speaks,
Thunder breaks!   40
When he eats,
Famine threats;
When he drinks,
Neptune shrinks!
Nigh thy Ear,   45
In Mid Air,
On thy Hand
Let me stand,
So shall I,
Lofty Poet! touch the Sky.   50

II. THE LAMENTATION OF GLUMDALCLITCH,
FOR THE LOSS OF GRILDRIG

A PASTORAL

Soon as *Glumdalclitch* mist her pleasing Care,
She wept, she blubber'd, and she tore her Hair.
No *British* Miss sincerer Grief has known,
Her Squirrel missing, or her Sparrow flown.

She furl'd her Sampler, and hawl'd in her Thread,   5
And stuck her Needle into *Grildrig*'s Bed;
Then spread her Hands, and with a Bounce let fall
Her Baby, like the Giant in *Guild-hall*.
In Peals of Thunder now she roars, and now
She gently whimpers like a lowing Cow.   10
Yet lovely in her Sorrow still appears:
Her Locks dishevell'd, and her Flood of Tears
Seem like the lofty Barn of some rich Swain,
When from the Thatch drips fast a Show'r of Rain.

In vain she search'd each Cranny of the House,   15
Each gaping Chink impervious to a Mouse.
'Was it for this (she cry'd) with daily Care
Within thy Reach I set the Vinegar?
And fill'd the Cruet with the Acid Tide,
While Pepper-Water-Worms thy Bait supply'd;   20
Where twin'd the Silver Eel around thy Hook,
And all the little Monsters of the Brook.
Sure in that Lake he dropt—My *Grilly*'s drown'd'—
She dragg'd the Cruet, but no *Grildrig* found.
'Vain is thy Courage, *Grilly*, vain thy Boast;   25
But little Creatures enterprise the most.
Trembling, I've seen thee dare the Kitten's Paw;
Nay, mix with Children, as they play'd at Taw;
Nor fear the Marbles, as they bounding flew:
Marbles to them, but rolling Rocks to you.   30

'Why did I trust thee with that giddy Youth?
Who from a *Page* can ever learn the Truth?
Vers'd in Court Tricks, that Money-loving Boy
To some Lord's Daughter sold the living Toy;
Or rent him Limb from Limb in cruel Play,   35
As Children tear the Wings of Flies away;
From Place to Place o'er *Brobdingnag* I'll roam,
And never will return, or bring thee home.
But who hath Eyes to trace the passing Wind,
How then thy fairy Footsteps can I find?   40
Dost thou bewilder'd wander all alone,
In the green Thicket of a Mossy Stone,
Or tumbled from the Toadstool's slipp'ry Round,
Perhaps all maim'd, lie grov'ling on the Ground?
Dost thou, inbosom'd in the lovely Rose,   45
Or sunk within the Peach's Down, repose?

Within the King-Cup if thy Limbs are spread,
Or in the golden Cowslip's Velvet Head;
O show me, *Flora*, 'midst those Sweets, the Flow'r
Where sleeps my *Grildrig* in his fragrant Bow'r!   50
  'But ah! I fear thy little Fancy roves
On little Females, and on little Loves;
Thy Pigmy Children, and thy tiny Spouse,
The Baby Play-things that adorn thy House,
Doors, Windows, Chimnies, and the spacious Rooms,   55
Equal in Size to Cells of Honeycombs.
Hast thou for these now ventur'd from the Shore,
Thy Bark a Bean-shell, and a Straw thy Oar?
Or in thy Box, now bounding on the Main?
Shall I ne'er bear thy self and House again?   60
And shall I set thee on my Hand no more,
To see thee leap the Lines, and traverse o'er
My spacious Palm? Of Stature scarce a Span,
Mimick the Actions of a real Man?
No more behold thee turn my Watches Key,   65
As Seamen at a Capstern Anchors weigh?
How wert thou wont to walk with cautious Tread,
A Dish of Tea like Milk-Pail on thy Head?
How chase the Mite that bore thy Cheese away,
And keep the rolling Maggot at a Bay?'   70

  She said, but broken Accents stopt her Voice,
Soft as the Speaking Trumpet's mellow Noise:
She sobb'd a Storm, and wip'd her flowing Eyes,
Which seem'd like two broad Suns in misty Skies:
O squander not thy Grief, those Tears command   75
To weep upon our Cod in *Newfound-land*:
The plenteous Pickle shall preserve the Fish,
And *Europe* taste thy Sorrows in a Dish.

III. TO MR. LEMUEL GULLIVER, THE GRATEFUL ADDRESS OF THE UNHAPPY HOUYHNHNMS, NOW IN SLAVERY AND BONDAGE IN ENGLAND

  To thee, we Wretches of the *Houyhnhnm* Band,
Condemn'd to labour in a barb'rous Land,
Return our Thanks. Accept our humble Lays,
And let each grateful *Houyhnhnm* neigh thy Praise.

O happy *Yahoo*, purg'd from human Crimes,   5
By thy sweet Sojourn in those virtuous Climes,
Where reign our Sires! There, to thy Countrey's Shame,
Reason, you found, and Virtue were the same.
Their Precepts raz'd the Prejudice of Youth,
And even a *Yahoo* learn'd the Love of Truth.   10

Art thou the first who did the Coast explore;
Did never *Yahoo* tread that Ground before?
Yes, Thousands. But in Pity to their Kind,
Or sway'd by Envy, or through Pride of Mind,
They hid their Knowledge of a nobler Race,   15
Which own'd, would all their Sires and Sons disgrace.

You, like the *Samian*, visit Lands unknown,
And by their wiser Morals mend your own.
Thus *Orpheus* travell'd to reform his Kind,
Came back, and tam'd the Brutes he left behind.   20

You went, you saw, you heard: With Virtue fraught,
Then spread those Morals which the *Houyhnhnms* taught.
Our Labours here must touch thy gen'rous Heart,
To see us strain before the Coach and Cart;
Compell'd to run each knavish Jockey's Heat!   25
Subservient to *New-market*'s annual cheat!
With what Reluctance do we Lawyers bear,
To fleece their Countrey Clients twice a Year?
Or manag'd in your Schools, for Fops to ride,
How foam, how fret beneath a Load of Pride!   30
Yes, we are slaves—but yet, by Reason's Force,
Have learnt to bear Misfortune, like a Horse.

O would the Stars, to ease my Bonds, ordain,
That gentle *Gulliver* might guide my Rein!
Safe would I bear him to his Journey's End,   35
For 'tis a Pleasure to support a Friend.
But if my Life be doom'd to serve the Bad,
O! may'st thou never want an easy Pad!
                                        Houyhnhnm.

IV. MARY GULLIVER TO CAPTAIN LEMUEL
GULLIVER

ARGUMENT. *The Captain, some Time after his Return, being retired
to Mr.* Sympson's *in the Country, Mrs.* Gulliver, *apprehending
from his late Behaviour some Estrangement of his Affections,
writes him the following expostulating, soothing, and tenderly-
complaining Epistle.*

Welcome, thrice welcome to thy native Place!
——What, touch me not? what, shun a Wife's Embrace?
Have I for this thy tedious Absence born,
And wak'd and wish'd whole Nights for thy Return?
In five long Years I took no second Spouse;   5
What *Redriff* Wife so long hath kept her Vows?
Your Eyes, your Nose, Inconstancy betray;
Your Nose you stop, your Eyes you turn away.
'Tis said, that thou shouldst cleave unto thy Wife;
Once *thou* didst cleave, and *I* could cleave for Life.   10
Hear and relent! hark, how thy Children moan;
Be kind at least to these, they are thy own:
Behold, and count them all; secure to find
The honest Number that you left behind.
See how they pat thee with their pretty Paws: 15
Why start you? are they Snakes? or have they Claws?
Thy Christian Seed, our mutual Flesh and Bone:
Be kind at least to these, they are thy own.

Biddel, like thee, might farthest *India* rove;
He chang'd his Country, but retain'd his Love.   20
There's Captain *Pennel*, absent half his Life,
Comes back, and is the kinder to his Wife.
Yet *Pennel*'s Wife is brown, compar'd to me;
And Mistress *Biddel* sure is Fifty three.

Not touch me! never Neighbour call'd me Slut!   25
Was *Flimnap*'s Dame more sweet in *Lilliput*?
I've no red Hair to breathe an odious Fume;
At least thy Consort's cleaner than thy *Groom*.
Why then that dirty Stable-boy thy Care?
What mean those Visits to the *Sorrel Mare*?   30
Say, by what Witchcraft, or what Dæmon led,
Preferr'st thou *Litter* to the Marriage Bed?

Some say the Dev'l himself is in that *Mare*:
If so, our *Dean* shall drive him forth by Pray'r.
Some think you mad, some think you are possest   35
That *Bedlam* and clean Straw will suit you best:
Vain Means, alas, this Frenzy to appease!
That *Straw*, that *Straw* would heighten the Disease.

My Bed, (the Scene of all our former Joys,
Witness two lovely Girls, two lovely Boys)   40
Alone I press; in Dreams I call my Dear,
I stretch my Hand, no *Gulliver* is there!
I wake, I rise, and shiv'ring with the Frost,
Search all the House; my *Gulliver* is lost!
Forth in the Street I rush with frantick Cries: 45
The Windows open; all the Neighbours rise:
Where sleeps my Gulliver? *O tell me where*?
The Neighbours answer, *With the Sorrel Mare.*

At early Morn, I to the Market haste,
(Studious in ev'ry Thing to please thy Taste)   50
A curious *Fowl* and *Sparagrass* I chose,
(For I remember you were fond of those,)
Three Shillings cost the first, the last sev'n Groats;
Sullen you turn from both, and call for *Oats.*

Others bring Goods and Treasure to their Houses,   55
Something to deck their pretty Babes and Spouses;
My *only* Token was a Cup like Horn,
That's made of nothing but a Lady's *Corn.*
'Tis not for that I grieve; no, 'tis to see
The *Groom* and *Sorrel Mare* preferr'd to me!   60

These, for some Moments when you deign to quit,
And (at due distance) sweet Discourse admit,
'Tis all my Pleasure thy past Toil to know,
For pleas'd Remembrance builds Delight on Woe.
At ev'ry Danger pants thy Consort's Breast,   65
And gaping Infants squawle to hear the rest.
How did I tremble, when by thousands bound,
I saw thee stretch'd on *Lilliputian* Ground;
When scaling Armies climb'd up ev'ry Part,
Each Step they trod, I felt upon my Heart.   70
But when thy Torrent quench'd the dreadful Blaze,
King, Queen and Nation, staring with Amaze,

Full in my View how all my Husband came,
And what extinguish'd theirs, encreas'd my Flame.
Those *Spectacles*, ordain'd thine Eyes to save,   75
Were once my Present; *Love* that Armour gave.
How did I mourn at *Bolgolam*'s Decree!
For when he sign'd thy Death, he sentenc'd me.

When folks might see thee all the Country round
For Six-pence, I'd have giv'n a thousand Pound.   80
Lord! when the *Giant-Babe* that Head of thine
Got in his Mouth, my Heart was up in mine!
When in the *Marrow-Bone* I see thee ramm'd;
Or on the House-top by the *Monkey* cramm'd;
The Piteous Images renew my Pain,   85
And all thy Dangers I weep o'er again!
But on the *Maiden*'s *Nipple* when you rid,
Pray Heav'n, 'twas all a wanton Maiden did!
Glumdalclitch too!—with thee I mourn her Case.
Heav'n guard the gentle Girl from all Disgrace!   90
O may the King that one Neglect forgive,
And pardon her the Fault by which I live!
Was there no other Way to set him free?
My Life, alas! I fear prov'd Death to Thee!

O teach me, Dear, new Words to speak my Flame;   95
Teach me to wooe thee by thy best-lov'd Name!
Whether the Style of *Grildrig* please thee most,
So call'd on *Brobdingnag*'s stupendous Coast,
When on the Monarch's ample Hand you sate,
And hollow'd in his Ear Intrigues of State: 100
Or *Quinbus Flestrin* more Endearment brings,
When like a Mountain you look'd down on Kings:
If Ducal *Nardac*, *Lilliputian* Peer,
Or *Glumglum*'s humbler Title sooth thy Ear:
Nay, wou'd kind *Jove* my Organs so dispose,   105
To hymn harmonious *Houyhnhnm* thro' the Nose,
I'd call thee *Houyhnhnm*, that high sounding Name,
Thy Children's Noses all should twang the same.
So might I find my loving Spouse of course
Endu'd with all the *Virtues* of a *Horse*.   110

V. THE WORDS OF THE KING OF BROBDINGNAG,
AS HE HELD CAPTAIN GULLIVER BETWEEN HIS
FINGER AND THUMB FOR THE INSPECTION OF
THE SAGES AND LEARNED MEN OF THE COURT

In Miniature see *Nature*'s Power appear;
Which wings the Sun-born Insects of the Air,
Which frames the Harvest-bug, too small for Sight,
And forms the Bones and Muscles of the Mite!
Here view him stretch'd. The Microscope explains,   5
That the Blood, circling, flows in human Veins;
See, in the Tube he pants, and sprawling lies,
Stretches his little Hands, and rolls his Eyes!

Smit with his Countrey's Love, I've heard him prate
Of Laws and Manners in his Pigmy State.   10
By Travel, generous Souls enlarge the Mind,
Which home-bred Prepossession had confin'd;
Yet will he boast of many Regions known,
But still, with partial Love, extol his own.
He talks of Senates, and of Courtly Tribes,   15
Admires their Ardour, but forgets their Bribes;
Of hireling Lawyers tells the just Decrees,
Applauds their Eloquence, but sinks their Fees.
Yet who his Countrey's partial Love can blame?
'Tis sure some Virtue to conceal its Shame.   20

The World's the native City of the Wise;
He sees his *Britain* with a Mother's Eyes;
Softens Defects, and heightens all its Charms,
Calls it the Seat of Empire, Arts and Arms!
Fond of his Hillock Isle, his narrow Mind   25
Thinks Worth, Wit, Learning, to that Spot confin'd;
Thus Ants, who for a Grain employ their Cares,
Think all the Business of the Earth is theirs.
Thus Honey-combs seem Palaces to Bees;
And Mites imagine all the World a Cheese.   30

When Pride in such contemptuous Beings lies,
In Beetles, Britons, Bugs and Butterflies,
Shall we, like Reptiles, glory in Conceit?
Humility's the Virtue of the Great.

Epitaph. On James Craggs, Esq.;
In Westminster-Abbey

JACOBUS CRAGGS
REGI MAGNÆ BRITANNIÆ A SECRETIS
ET CONSILIIS SANCTIORIBUS,
PRINCIPIS PARITER AC POPULI AMOR & DELICIÆ:
VIXIT TITULIS ET INVIDIA MAJOR,
ANNOS HEU PAUCOS, XXXV.
OB. FEB. XVI. M DCC XX.

[written 1720; revised and published 1727]

Statesman, yet Friend to Truth! of Soul sincere,
In Action faithful, and in Honour clear!
Who broke no promise, serv'd no private end,
Who gain'd no Title, and who lost no Friend,
Ennobled by Himself, by All approv'd,   5
Prais'd, wept, and honour'd, by the Muse he lov'd.

Fragment of a Satire
[written c. 1727; published, *PSM*, 1727]

If meagre *Gildon* draws his venal Quill,
I wish the Man a Dinner, and sit still.
If dreadful *Dennis* raves in furious Fret,
I'll answer *Dennis* when I am in Debt.
'Tis Hunger, and not Malice, makes them print,   5
And who'll wage War with *Bedlam* or the *Mint*?
    Should some more sober Criticks come abroad,
If wrong, I smile; if right, I kiss the Rod.
Pains, Reading, Study, are their just Pretence,
And all they want is Spirit, Taste, and Sense.   10
Commas and *Points* they set exactly right;
And 'twere a Sin to rob them of their *Mite*.
Yet ne'er one Sprig of Laurel grac'd those Ribbalds,
From slashing *B—y* down to pidling *Tibbalds*:

An expansion of the original poem (see p. 293,) later to be incorporated
in the *Ep. to Arbuthnot* (1735), p. 603.
    14. *slashing B—y*] Richard Bentley, scholar and Master of Trinity
College, Cambridge.

Who thinks he *reads* when he but *scans* and *spells*, 15
A Word-catcher, that lives on Syllables.
Yet ev'n this Creature may some Notice claim,
Wrapt round and sanctify'd with *Shakespear*'s Name;
Pretty, in Amber to observe the forms
Of Hairs, or Straws, or Dirt, or Grubs, or Worms: 20
The *Thing*, we know, is neither rich nor rare,
But wonder how the Devil it got there.
  Are others angry? I excuse them too,
Well may they rage; I give them *but* their Due.
Each Man's true Merit 'tis not hard to find; 25
But each Man's secret Standard in his Mind,
That casting Weight, Pride adds to Emptiness;
This, who can *gratify*? For who can *guess*?
The Wretch whom pilfer'd Pastorals renown,
Who turns a *Persian* Tale for half a Crown, 30
Just writes to make his Barrenness appear,
And strains, from hard bound Brains, six Lines a Year;
In Sense still wanting, tho' he lives on Theft,
Steals much, spends little, yet has nothing left:
Johnson, who now to Sense, now Nonsense leaning, 35
Means not, but blunders round about a Meaning;
And he, whose Fustian's so sublimely bad,
It is not Poetry, but Prose run mad:
Should modest Satire bid all these *translate*,
And own that nine such Poets make a *Tate*; 40
How would they fume, and stamp, and roar, and chafe!
How would they swear, not *Congreve*'s self was safe!
  Peace to all such! but were there one, whose Fires
Apollo kindled, and fair *Fame* inspires,
Blest with each Talent, and each Art to please, 45
And born to write, converse, and live with ease;
Should such a Man, too fond to rule alone,
Bear, like the *Turk*, no Brother near the Throne;
View him with scornful, yet with fearful eyes,
And hate for Arts that caus'd himself to rise; 50
Damn with faint Praise, assent with civil Leer,
And without sneering, teach the rest to sneer;
Wishing to wound, and yet afraid to strike,
Just hint a Fault, and hesitate Dislike;

29–30. *The Wretch . . . Crown*] Ambrose Philips. See p. 285.
  35. *Johnson*] Author of the *Victim*, and Cobler of *Preston* [P]. His dishonourable mention was probably earned by his attack on Gay's *Three Hours after Marriage*.

Alike reserv'd to blame, or to commend,   55
A tim'rous Foe, and a suspicious Friend,
Dreading ev'n Fools, by Flatterers besieg'd,
And so obliging that he ne'er oblig'd:
Who, if two Wits on rival Themes contest,
Approves of each, but likes the worst the best;   60
Like *Cato* gives his *little Senate* Laws,
And sits attentive to his own Applause;
While Wits and Templars ev'ry Sentence raise,
And wonder with a foolish Face of Praise.
What Pity, Heav'n! if such a Man there be.   65
Who would not weep, if *A—n* were he?

Sylvia, a Fragment
[written ?; published, *PSM*, 1727]

Sylvia my Heart in wond'rous wise alarm'd,
Aw'd without Sense, and without Beauty charm'd,
But some odd Graces and fine Flights she had,
Was just not ugly, and was just not mad;
Her Tongue still run, on credit from her Eyes,   5
More pert than witty, more a Wit than wise.
Good Nature, she declar'd it, was her Scorn,
Tho' 'twas by that alone she could be born.
Affronting all, yet fond of a good Name,
A Fool to Pleasure, yet a Slave to Fame;   10
Now coy and studious in no Point to fall,
Now all agog for *D—y* at a Ball:
Now deep in *Taylor* and the *Book of Martyrs*,
Now drinking Citron with his *Gr—* and *Ch—*

Men, some to Business, some to Pleasure take,   15
But ev'ry Woman's in her Soul a Rake.
Frail, fev'rish Sex! their Fit now chills, now burns;
Atheism and Superstition rule by Turns;
And the meer Heathen in her carnal Part,
Is still a sad good Christian at her Heart.   20

This sketch was incorporated in 1735 in the *Epistle to a Lady. Of the
Characters of Women.* See pp. 561–7, ll. 45–50, 59–68, 215–16.
  14. *his Gr—and C—*] Philip, Duke of Wharton and the notorious **rake**,
Francis Chartres.

Lines from the Art of Sinking

[written c. 1727; published, *PSM*, 1727]

WHO KNOCKS AT THE DOOR?

For whom thus rudely pleads my loud-tongu'd Gate,
That he may enter?——

SHUT THE DOOR

The wooden Guardian of our Privacy
Quick on its Axle turn.——

BRING MY CLOATHS

Bring me what Nature, Taylor to the *Bear*,
To *Man* himself deny'd: She gave me Cold,
But would not give me Cloaths.——

LIGHT THE FIRE

Bring forth some Remnant of *Promethean* theft,
Quick to expand th' inclement Air congeal'd
By *Boreas*'s rude breath.——

SNUFF THE CANDLE

Yon Luminary Amputation needs,
Thus shall you save its half-extinguish'd Life.

UNCORK THE BOTTLE AND CHIP THE BREAD

Apply thine Engine to the spungy Door,
Set *Bacchus* from his glassy Prison free,
And strip white *Ceres* of her nut-brown Coat.

These six examples of the 'Cumbrous' and 'Buskin' styles of writing
have all the appearance of having been concocted specially for the comic
illustration of those styles.

Verses to be placed under
the Picture of England's Arch-Poet

CONTAINING A COMPLEAT CATALOGUE OF
HIS WORKS

[written c. 1727; published, *PSM*, 1732]

See who ne'er was or will be half read!
Who first sung *Arthur*, then sung *Alfred*,
Prais'd great *Eliza* in God's anger,
Till all true *Englishmen* cry'd, hang her!
Made *William*'s Virtues wipe the bare A——   5
And hang'd up *Marlborough* in *Arras*:

Then hiss'd from Earth, grew Heav'nly quite;
Made ev'ry Reader curse the *Light*;
Maul'd human *Wit* in one thick Satyr,
Next in three Books, sunk human *Nature*,   10
Un-did *Creation* at a Jerk,
And of *Redemption* made damn'd Work.

Then took his Muse at once, and dipt her
Full in the middle of the Scripture.
What Wonders there the Man grown old, did!   15
Sternhold himself he *out-Sternholded*,
Made *David* seem so mad and freakish,
All thought him just what thought King *Achiz*.
No Mortal read his *Salomon*,
But judg'd *Roboam* his own Son.   20

An attack on Sir Richard Blackmore.
   2. *Arthur*] Two Heroick Poems in Folio, twenty Books [P]; i.e. *Prince Arthur*, 1695, and *King Arthur*, 1697.
   Alfred] Heroick Poem in twelve Books [P].
   3. *Eliza*] Heroick Poem in Folio, ten Books [P].
   6. *Marlborough . . . Arras*] Instructions to *Vanderbank* a Tapestry-Weaver [P].
   8. *Light*] Hymn to the *Light* [P].
   9. *Wit*] Satyr against *Wit* [P].
   10. *Nature*] Of the *Nature* of Man [P].
   11. *Creation*] *Creation*, a Poem in seven Books [P].
   12. *Redemption*] The *Redeemer*, another Heroick Poem in six Books [P].
   16. *Sternhold*] The Elizabethan versifier of the Psalms, often derided by Pope.
   17. *David*] Translation of all the *Psalms* [P].
   19. *Salomon*] *Canticles* and *Ecclesiast* [P].

Moses he serv'd as *Moses Pharaoh*,
And *Deborah*, as She *Sise-rah*:
Made *Jeremy* full sore to cry,
And *Job* himself curse God and die.

What Punishment all this must follow?   25
Shall *Arthur* use him like King *Tollo*,
Shall *David* as *Uriah* slay him,
Or dext'rous *Deb'rah Sisera*-him?
Or shall *Eliza* lay a Plot,
To treat him like her Sister *Scot*,   30
Shall *William* dub his better End,
Or *Marlb'rough* serve him like a Friend?
No, none of these—Heav'n spare his Life!
But send him, honest *Job*, thy *Wife*.

21. *Moses . . . Deborah*] Paraphrase of the Canticles of *Moses* and *Deborah*, &c. [P].
23. *Jeremy*] The *Lamentations* [P].
24. *Job*] The whole Book of *Job*, a Poem in Folio [P].
30. *Sister Scot*] Mary, Queen of Scots.
31. *better End*] Kick him on the Breech, not Knight him on the Shoulder [P]. Blackmore was knighted in 1697.

To the Right Honourable the Earl of Oxford

UPON A PIECE OF NEWS IN MIST, THAT THE
REV. MR. W. REFUS'D TO WRITE AGAINST
MR. POPE BECAUSE HIS BEST PATRON HAD A
FRIENDSHIP FOR THE SAID P.

[written 1728; published 1809]

Wesley, if Wesley 'tis they mean,
They say, on Pope would fall
Would his best Patron let his Pen
Discharge his inward Gall.

What Patron this, a doubt must be   5
Which none but you can clear,
Or Father Francis cross the sea,
Or else Earl Edward here.

The 'piece of News in Mist' appeared in *Mist's Weekly Journal* on 8 June 1728 as an epistle purporting to defend Pope from the attacks which followed the publication of the *Dunciad* in the previous month.
7. *Father Francis*] Francis Atterbury, the exiled bishop of Rochester.
8. *Earl Edward*] Edward Harley, second Earl of Oxford.

That both were good must be confest,
And much to both he owes;   10
But which to Him will be the best
The Lord of Oxford knows.

Epitaph. On G——

[written 1728; published, *PSM*, 1732]

Well then, poor G—— lies under ground!
So there's an end of honest *Jack.*
So little Justice here he found,
'Tis ten to one he'll ne'er come back.

When his opera, *Polly*, was banned, Gay was deprived of his apartments in Whitehall. Writing to Pope, he remarked that he had 'no continuing city here. I begin to look upon myself as one already dead, and
desire . . . that you will . . . see these words put upon [my grave-stone]:

Life's a jest, and all things show it,
I thought so once, but now I know it,

with what more you may think proper.' Pope's response, it is practically
certain, was this mock epitaph on Gay's 'court' death.

Epitaphs from the Latin on the Count of Mirandula

[written c. 1729; published, *PSM*, 1732]

*Joannes jacet hic Mirandula—cætera norunt
Et Tagus & Ganges—forsan & Antipodes.*

I. LORD CONINGSBY'S EPITAPH

Here lies Lord Coningsby—be civil,
The rest God knows—so does the Devil.

II. APPLIED TO F. C.

Here *Francis Ch—s* lies—Be civil!
The rest God knows—perhaps the Devil.

I. 1. *Coningsby*] Thomas Lord Coningsby (1656?–1729). A Whig peer,
once suspected of peculation; was forward in the impeachment of Pope's
friend, Lord Oxford, 1715.
II. 1. *Ch—s*] The notorious rake, Francis Chartres.

Lines

[published, *Works*, 1741]

I. IN CONCLUSION OF A SATIRE

But what avails to lay down rules for sense?
In ——'s Reign these fruitless lines were writ,
When Ambrose Philips was preferr'd for Wit!

II. INSCRIPTIO

And thou! whose sense, whose humour, and whose rage,
At once can teach, delight, and lash the age,
Whether thou choose Cervantes' serious air,
Or laugh and shake in Rab'lais' easy chair,
Praise courts, and monarchs, or extol mankind,   5
Or thy grieved country's copper chains unbind;
Attend whatever title please thine ear,
Dean, Drapier, Bickerstaff, or Gulliver.
From thy Bœotia, lo! the fog retires,
Yet grieve not thou at what our Isle acquires;   10
Here dulness reigns, with mighty wings outspread,
And brings the true Saturnian age of lead.

I. From a letter to Swift (15 October 1725), quoting 'the conclusion of one of my Satires'. No poem of Pope's as printed ends in this way; but the last line, practically unaltered, appeared in the first edition of the *Dunciad* (A, III 322).

II. From a letter (January, 1729) to Swift, enclosing, not the poem on Dulness, but 'what most nearly relates to yourself, the inscription to it'.

Epitaph. on Sir Godfrey Kneller
In Westminster-Abby 1723

[written c. 1729; published 1730]

Kneller, by Heav'n and not a Master taught,
Whose Art was Nature, and whose Pictures thought;
Now for two ages having snatch'd from fate
Whate'er was Beauteous, or whate'er was Great,
Lies crown'd with Princes Honours, Poets Lays,   5
Due to his Merit, and brave Thirst of Praise.

Living, great Nature fear'd he might outvie
Her works; and dying, fears herself may die.

7-8. Imitated from the famous Epitaph on Raphael:
———*Raphael, timuit quo sospite, vinci*
Rerum magna parens, & moriente, mori. [P]

Epitaph. On the Monument of the Honble. Robert Digby, and of his Sister Mary, erected by their Father the Lord Digby, in the Church of Sherborne in Dorsetshire, 1727

[written 1727-30? published, Lewis's
Miscellany, 1730]

Go! fair Example of untainted youth,
Of modest wisdom, and pacifick truth:
Compos'd in suff'rings, and in joy sedate,
Good without noise, without pretension great.
Just of thy word, in ev'ry thought sincere,   5
Who knew no wish but what the world might hear:
Of softest manners, unaffected mind,
Lover of peace, and friend of human kind:
Go live! for heav'ns Eternal year is thine,
Go, and exalt thy Moral to Divine.   10
    And thou blest Maid! attendant on his doom,
Pensive hast follow'd to the silent tomb,
Steer'd the same course to the same quiet shore,
Not parted long, and now to part no more!
Go then, where only bliss sincere is known!   15
Go, where to love and to enjoy are one!
    Yet take these tears, Mortality's relief,
And till we share your joys, forgive our grief;
These little rites, a Stone, a Verse, receive,
'Tis all a Father, all a Friend can give!   20

Poems 1730-1744

An Essay on Man

OR THE FIRST BOOK OF ETHIC EPISTLES TO H. ST. JOHN L. BOLINGBROKE

[written 1730–32; published 1733–34]

TO THE READER

As the Epistolary Way of Writing hath prevailed much of late, we have ventured to publish this Piece composed some Time since, and whose Author chose this Manner, notwithstanding his Subject was high and of dignity, because of its being mixt with Argument, *which of its Nature approacheth to Prose. This, which we first give the Reader, treats of the* Nature and State of MAN, *with Respect to the* UNIVERSAL SYSTEM; *the rest will treat of him with Respect to* his OWN SYSTEM, *as an* Individual, *and as a* Member of Society; *under one or other of which Heads all Ethicks are included.*

As he imitates no Man, *so he would be thought to vye with no Man in these Epistles, particularly with the noted Author of* TWO *lately published*[1]: *But this he may most surely say, that the Matter of them is such, as is of* Importance *to* all in general, *and of* Offence *to* none in particular.

TO THE READER

The Author was induced to publish these Epistles separately for two Reasons, The one, that he might not impose upon the Publick too much at once of what he thought incorrect; The other, that by this Method he might profit of its Judgement on the Parts, in order to make the Whole less unworthy.

THE DESIGN

Having proposed to write some pieces on Human Life and Manners, such as (to use my lord Bacon's expression) *come home to Men's Business and Bosoms,* I thought it more satisfactory to begin with considering *Man* in the abstract, his *Nature* and his *State:* since, to prove any moral duty, to enforce any moral precept, or to examine

[1] I.e. Pope's own acknowledged poems: *Mor. Ess.*, III, and *Imit. Hor., Sat.*, II i.

the perfection or imperfection of any creature whatsoever, it is necessary first to know what *condition* and *relation* it is placed in, and what is the proper *end* and *purpose* of its *being*.

The science of Human Nature is, like all other sciences, reduced to a *few clear points*: There are not *many certain truths* in this world. It is therefore in the Anatomy of the Mind as in that of the Body; more good will accrue to mankind by attending to the large, open, and perceptible parts, than by studying too much such finer nerves and vessels, the conformations and uses of which will for ever escape our observation. The *disputes* are all upon these last, and, I will venture to say, they have less sharpened the *wits* than the *hearts* of men against each other, and have diminished the practice, more than advanced the theory, of Morality. If I could flatter myself that this Essay has any merit, it is in steering betwixt the extremes of doctrines seemingly opposite, in passing over terms utterly unintelligible, and in forming a *temperate* yet not *inconsistent*, and a *short* yet not *imperfect* system of Ethics.

This I might have done in prose; but I chose verse, and even rhyme, for two reasons. The one will appear obvious; that principles, maxims, or precepts so written, both strike the reader more strongly at first, and are more easily retained by him afterwards: The other may seem odd, but is true, I found I could express them more *shortly* this way than in prose itself; and nothing is more certain, than that much of the *force* as well as *grace* of arguments or instructions, depends on their *conciseness*. I was unable to treat this part of my subject more in detail, without becoming dry and tedious; or more *poetically*, without sacrificing perspicuity to ornament, without wandring from the precision, or breaking the chain of reasoning: If any man can unite all these without diminution of any of them, I freely confess he will compass a thing above my capacity.

What is now published, is only to be considered as a *general Map* of MAN, marking out no more than the *greater parts*, their *extent*, their *limits*, and their *connection*, but leaving the particular to be more fully delineated in the charts which are to follow. Consequently, these Epistles in their progress (if I have health and leisure to make any progress) will be less dry, and more susceptible of poetical ornament. I am here only opening the *fountains*, and clearing the passage. To deduce the *rivers*, to follow them in their course, and to observe their effects, may be a task more agreeable.

ARGUMENT OF THE FIRST EPISTLE

Of the Nature and State of Man, with respect to the UNIVERSE.

Of Man *in the abstract.*—I. *That we can judge only with regard to* our own system, *being ignorant of the* relations *of systems and things*, VER. 17, &c. II. *That Man is not to be deemed* imperfect, *but a Being suited to his* place *and* rank *in the creation, agreeable to the* general Order *of things, and conformable to* Ends *and* Relations *to him unknown*, VER. 35, &c. III. *That it is partly upon his* ignorance *of future events, and partly upon the* hope *of a future state, that all his happiness in the present depends*, VER. 77, &c. IV. *The* pride *of aiming at more knowledge, and pretending to more Perfection, the cause of Man's error and misery. The* impiety *of putting himself in the place of* God, *and judging of the fitness or unfitness, perfection or imperfection, justice or injustice of his dispensations*, VER. 113, &c. V. *The* absurdity *of conceiting himself the* final cause *of the creation, or expecting that perfection in the* moral *world, which is not in the* natural, VER. 131, &c. VI. *The* unreasonableness *of his complaints against* Providence, *while on the one hand he demands the Perfections of the Angels, and on the other the bodily qualifications of the Brutes; though, to possess any of the* sensitive faculties *in a higher degree, would render him miserable*, VER. 173, &c. VII. *That throughout the whole visible world, an* universal order *and* gradation *in the sensual and mental faculties is observed, which causes a* subordination *of creature to creature, and of all creatures to Man. The gradations of* sense, instinct, thought, reflection, reason; *that Reason alone countervails all the other faculties*, VER. 207. VIII. *How much farther this order and* subordination *of living creatures may extend, above and below us; were any part of which broken, not that part only, but the whole connected* creation *must be destroyed*. VER. 233. IX. *The* extravagance, madness, *and* pride *of such a desire*, VER. 259. X. *The consequence of all the* absolute submission *due to Providence, both as to our present and* future state, VER. 281, &c. *to the end.*

Awake, my ST. JOHN! leave all meaner things
To low ambition, and the pride of Kings.
Let us (since Life can little more supply
Than just to look about us and to die)
Expatiate free o'er all this scene of Man;   5

Epistle I. Of the NATURE and STATE of MAN with respect to the UNIVERSE. [P]
1. *meaner*] Meaner than philosophy.

A mighty maze! but not without a plan;
A Wild, where weeds and flow'rs promiscuous shoot,
Or Garden, tempting with forbidden fruit.
Together let us beat this ample field,
Try what the open, what the covert yield;   10
The latent tracts, the giddy heights explore
Of all who blindly creep, or sightless soar;
Eye Nature's walks, shoot Folly as it flies,
And catch the Manners living as they rise;
Laugh where we must, be candid where we can;   15
But vindicate the ways of God to Man.
   1. Say first, of God above, or Man below,
What can we reason, but from what we know?
Of Man what see we, but his station here,
From which to reason, or to which refer?   20

6–16. 'The 6th, 7th, and 8th lines allude to the Subjects of This Book,
the General Order and Design of Providence; the Constitution of the
human Mind, whose Passions cultivated are Virtues, neg[lected], Vices;
the Temptations of misapplyd Selflove and wrong pursuits of Power,
Pleasure and false Happiness. The 10th, 11th, 12th, etc. allude to the
[sub]jects of the following books; the [various?] characters and capacities
of Men, of Learning and Ignorance, [the?] Knowledge of mankind and
the Manners [of the age?]. The last line sums up the moral and main Drift
of the whole, [the?]]ustification of the Ways of Provi[dence].' P's MS
note.

6–14. Cf. *The Explicator* (vol. 1, no. 2, Nov. 1942): 'as the seeming
planlessness of the garden is planned . . ., so it might be with Man and
his World; as the natural garden exhibits a wide range of diversity and
prolific growth, so does the system of creation'.

8–16. *Par. Lost*, I 1–2, 26. Pope emphasizes the connection between his
poem and Milton's.

12. There is a mode of motion appropriate to man, which is neither
creeping nor soaring: 'those who *blindly creep* are the ignorant and
indifferent; those who *sightless soar* are the presumptuous, who endeavour
to transcend the bounds prescribed to the intellect of man'.

13. *walks*] Cf. besides the garden sense of this term its hunting sense as
the haunt or resort of game.

15. *candid*] H. More, *Enchir. Eth.* 'Candor is that which guides us to
interpret with Benignity the Words and Actions of all Men: But when
they are such as cannot well be borne; then, with an honest and decent
Liberty, to check and reprehend them.'

17 ff. *He can reason only from* Things known, *and judge only with regard
to his* own System. [P]

17–18. 'The principle of analogical reasoning in theology is the assumption that the universe being regulated by uniform laws, those laws which
we can trace in that part of it which falls under our observation, extend
also to that part of it which we cannot see. Cf. Milton, *Par. Lost*, V 174.'

19. *station*] Perhaps an astronomical term, but chiefly a military and
hierarchical one, which stresses man's limitedness of purview.

Thro' worlds unnumber'd tho' the God be known,
'Tis ours to trace him only in our own.
He, who thro' vast immensity can pierce,
See worlds on worlds compose one universe,
Observe how system into system runs, 25
What other planets circle other suns,
What vary'd being peoples ev'ry star,
May tell why Heav'n has made us as we are.
But of this frame the bearings, and the ties,
The strong connections, nice dependencies, 30
Gradations just, has thy pervading soul
Look'd thro'? or can a part contain the whole?
  Is the great chain, that draws all to agree,
And drawn supports, upheld by God, or thee? 34
  II. Presumptuous Man! the reason wouldst thou find,
Why form'd so weak, so little, and so blind!
First, if thou canst, the harder reason guess,
Why form'd no weaker, blinder, and no less!
Ask of thy mother earth, why oaks are made
Taller or stronger than the weeds they shade? 40
Or ask of yonder argent fields above,
Why JOVE'S Satellites are less than JOVE?
  Of Systems possible, if 'tis confest
That Wisdom infinite must form the best,

23. A reply to Lucretius's celebration of Epicurus as a mortal whose mind, defying religion, did pierce through vast immensity and beyond the universe to reach a godlike knowledge of why we are as we are.

27. A favourite hypothesis of scientists, divines, and poets, frequently used to humble human self-esteem.

29–31. A figure blended of architectural, hierarchical, and astronomical allusions. *Connexions, dependencies, gradations* were key terms of the new sciences with respect to the hierarchies both of being and the stellar systems.

33–4. Zeus's golden chain in the Iliad—'Whose strong Embrace holds Heav'n, and Earth, and Main' (Pope's *Il.*, VIII 26)—became identified with the chain of being.

35 ff. *He is not therefore a Judge of his own perfection or imperfection, but is certainly such a Being as is suited to his* Place *and* Rank *in the Creation* [P].

37. *harder*] In being a less congenial question for pride to resolve.

42. *Satellites*] Here used as plural of the Latin *satelles* and syllabicated accordingly.

43–50. The function of this passage is evidently to summarize a set of propositions: (1) that a God of infinite wisdom exists; (2) that such a God will necessarily have chosen to create, out of all possible systems, the best; (3) that the best will necessarily have been that which actualizes the maximum number of possible modes of being, and so is 'full' of existents —a *plenum formarum*—'cohering' because actualization of all the possibles leaves no gaps; (4) that the *plenum's* structure is hierarchical, a ladder of

Where all must full or not coherent be,   45
And all that rises, rise in due degree;
Then, in the scale of reas'ning life, 'tis plain
There must be, somewhere, such a rank as Man;
And all the question (wrangle e'er so long)
Is only this, if God has plac'd him wrong?   50
  Respecting Man, whatever wrong we call,
May, must be right, as relative to all.
In human works, tho' labour'd on with pain,
A thousand movements scarce one purpose gain;
In God's, one single can its end produce;   55
Yet serves to second too some other use.
So Man, who here seems principal alone,
Perhaps acts second to some sphere unknown,
Touches some wheel, or verges to some goal;
'Tis but a part we see, and not a whole.   60
  When the proud steed shall know why Man restrains
His fiery course, or drives him o'er the plains;
When the dull Ox, why now he breaks the clod,
Is now a victim, and now Ægypt's God:
Then shall Man's pride and dulness comprehend   65
His actions', passions', being's, use and end;
Why doing, suff'ring, check'd, impell'd; and why

---

beings of greater and greater complexity of faculties, rising by even steps
(*due degrees*) from nothingness to God. The conclusion is that in the part
of the ladder which embraces rational existents (e.g. man and angel) there
could no more be a gap than elsewhere: there had to be a creature which
combined the rational nature with an animal one, for such a creature
(besides being an empirical fact) was certainly one of the conceivable
possibles. The argument then settles down to the important issue (49–50):
whether the powers of this hybrid creature are suited to the terrestrial and
mortal state assigned him. The epistle then tries to show, (1) that they must
be right with respect to the whole system of things, both *ex hypothesi* and
on the analogy that all visible creatures including man have a function
though not necessarily one known to them; (2) that they are right with
respect to man himself, since they contribute to his well-being, which any
alteration in them would disturb. A hint of humour may lurk in l. 48.

53–4. *works . . . movements*] Metaphorical as well as literal (cf. *wheel*,
59). Work: 'a set of parts forming a machine or piece of mechanism'
(*OED*); movement: 'a particular part or group of parts in a mechanism,
serving some special purpose' (*OED*).

60. Cf. 1 Cor. XIII 12: 'For now we see through a glass, darkly; but then
face to face: now I know in part; but then shall I know even as also I am
known.' The idea is fundamental to theodicy.

64. *Ægypt's God*] The sacred Memphian bull, worshipped under the
name of Apis.

67. The pairs of verbs pick up, respectively, the ideas in 63–4, 61–2,
and suggest the duality of man's status in their active and passive forms.

This hour a slave, the next a deity.
   Then say not Man's imperfect, Heav'n in fault;
Say rather, Man's as perfect as he ought;   70
His knowledge measur'd to his state and place,
His time a moment, and a point his space.
If to be perfect in a certain sphere,
What matter, soon or late, or here or there?
The blest today is as completely so,   75
As who began a thousand years ago.
   III. Heav'n from all creatures hides the book of Fate,
All but the page prescrib'd, their present state;
From brutes what men, from men what spirits know:
Or who could suffer Being here below?   80
The lamb thy riot dooms to bleed to-day,
Had he thy Reason, would he skip and play?
Pleas'd to the last, he crops the flow'ry food,
And licks the hand just rais'd to shed his blood.
Oh blindness to the future! kindly giv'n,   85
That each may fill the circle mark'd by Heav'n;
Who sees with equal eye, as God of all,
A hero perish, or a sparrow fall,
Atoms or systems into ruin hurl'd,
And now a bubble burst, and now a world.   90

69–71. Received opinions in apologetic thought.

73–4. Cf. Pope's letter to Caryll, 8 March 1733: 'Nothing is so plain as that he [the author of the *Essay on Man*, as yet anonymous] quits his proper subject, this present world, to assert his belief of a future state, and yet there is an *if* instead of a *since* that would overthrow his meaning.' But Pope could not have changed *if* to *since* without appealing to Revelation, which, as his remark to Caryll shows, he was determined not to do, and which lay outside the terms of his poem.

75–6. Once transferred to beatitude in eternity, man loses nothing by not having been transferred there earlier, eternity being all 'instant'.

77 ff. *His happiness depends on his* Ignorance *to a certain degree* [P].

79 ff. See this pursued in Epist. 3. Vers. 66, &c. 79, &c. [P].

81–90. Man is presented as the middle and least attractive term in the ratio: lamb is to man as man is to God. In his status as an inferior, man lacks the lamb's trustfulness; in his status as a superior, he lacks God's impartial thoughtfulness.

87. God's vision (equal in its attention to all) has been placed in contrast with his creatures' blindness. *Equal* may also carry something of its Latin sense: *aequus* = propitious, benign.

87–90. Matt., X 29–31: 'Are not two sparrows sold for a farthing? and one of them shall not fall on the ground without your Father. But the very hairs of your head are all numbered. Fear ye not, therefore, ye are of more value than many sparrows.' Pope says that God's providence embraces both sparrow and man.

Hope humbly then; with trembling pinions soar;
Wait the great teacher Death, and God adore!
What future bliss, he gives not thee to know,
But gives that Hope to be thy blessing now.
Hope springs eternal in the human breast: 95
Man never Is, but always To be blest:
The soul, uneasy and confin'd from home,
Rests and expatiates in a life to come.
   Lo! the poor Indian, whose untutor'd mind
Sees God in clouds, or hears him in the wind;   100
His soul proud Science never taught to stray
Far as the solar walk, or milky way;
Yet simple Nature to his hope has giv'n,
Behind the cloud-topt hill, an humbler heav'n;
Some safer world in depth of woods embrac'd,   105
Some happier island in the watry waste,
Where slaves once more their native land behold,
No fiends torment, no Christians thirst for gold!
To Be, contents his natural desire,
He asks no Angel's wing, no Seraph's fire;   110
But thinks, admitted to that equal sky,
His faithful dog shall bear him company,
   IV. Go, wiser thou! and in thy scale of sense
Weigh thy Opinion against Providence;
Call Imperfection what thou fancy'st such,   115
Say, here he gives too little, there too much;

91 ff. *And on his* Hope *of a* Relation *to a future State* [P]. As faith is
belief in the unproved, so hope is expectation of the unknown.

94. Further open'd in Epist. 2. Vers. 283. Epist. 3. Vers. 74. Epist. 4.
Vers. 346 &c. [P].

99 ff. There is irony directed against the Indian (cf. the naive material-
ism of his after-life, and *Ess.*, IV 177–8) as well as against proud Science.
Both (being human) are incapable of understanding God's ways, though
the Indian surpasses proud Science in trusting them.

110–12. Cf. I 125–8. Simple nature shows its humility both in not
aspiring to higher orders and in not excluding those lower.

110. *Seraph's fire*] An attribute traditionally assigned, owing to the
'presumed derivation of the word from a Hebrew root sāraph to burn'
(*OED*). Cf. *Ess.*, I 278.

111. *equal*] Cf. above, 87.

113 ff. *The* Pride *of aiming at more Knowledge and Perfection, and the*
Impiety *of pretending to judge of the Dispensations of Providence, the causes
of his* Error *and* Misery [P].

113–15. *sense . . . Opinion . . . fancy'st*] The three terms stress the
contrast of man's mind with God's: unlike God, man is dependent on
sense, subject to opinion, and likely to be misled by fancy.

Destroy all creatures for thy sport or gust,
Yet cry, If Man's unhappy, God's unjust;
If Man alone ingross not Heav'n's high care,
Alone made perfect here, immortal there: 120
Snatch from his hand the balance and the rod,
Re-judge his justice, be the GOD of GOD!
   In Pride, in reas'ning Pride, our error lies;
All quit their sphere, and rush into the skies.
Pride still is aiming at the blest abodes,   125
Men would be Angels, Angels would be Gods.
Aspiring to be Gods, if Angels fell,
Aspiring to be Angels, Men rebel;
And who but wishes to invert the laws
Of ORDER, sins against th' Eternal Cause.   130
   v. Ask for what end the heav'nly bodies shine,
Earth for whose use? Pride answers, ' 'Tis for mine:
For me kind Nature wakes her genial pow'r,
Suckles each herb, and spreads out ev'ry flow'r;
Annual for me, the grape, the rose renew   135
The juice nectareous, and the balmy dew;
For me, the mine a thousand treasures brings;
For me, health gushes from a thousand springs;
Seas roll to waft me, suns to light me rise;
My foot-stool earth, my canopy the skies.'   140
   But errs not Nature from this gracious end,
From burning suns when livid deaths descend,
When earthquakes swallow, or when tempests sweep
Towns to one grave, whole nations to the deep?
'No ('tis reply'd) the first Almighty Cause   145
Acts not by partial, but by gen'ral laws;

117. *gust*] To please the palate.
128. So Satan plans to destroy Adam and Eve (*Par. Lost*, IV 524–7) by persuading them to reject

> Envious commands, invented with design
> To keep them low, whom knowledge might exalt
> Equal with gods. Aspiring to be such,
> They taste and die.

131 ff. *The* Absurdity *of conceiting himself the* Final Cause *of the Creation, or expecting that Perfection in the* moral *world which is not in the* natural [P].
133. *genial*] Generative, as in *Par. Lost.* VII 282.
140. *canopy*] The canopy of a throne.
142. *livid*] The observed colour of plague victims.
145–8. A highly elliptical passage, impacting in the mouth of the anthropocentrist stock explanations of physical evils: (1) that God's laws are calculated for general good, not that of the part, though they may

Th' exceptions few; some change since all began,
And what created perfect?'—Why then Man?
If the great end be human Happiness,
Then Nature deviates; and can Man do less?   150
As much that end a constant course requires
Of show'rs and sun-shine, as of Man's desires;
As much eternal springs and cloudless skies,
As Men for ever temp'rate, calm, and wise.
If plagues or earthquakes break not Heav'n's design, 155
Why then a Borgia, or a Catiline?
Who knows but he, whose hand the light'ning forms,
Who heaves old Ocean, and who wings the storms,
Pours fierce Ambition in a Cæsar's mind,
Or turns young Ammon loose to scourge mankind? 160
From pride, from pride, our very reas'ning springs;
Account for moral as for nat'ral things:
Why charge we Heav'n in those, in these acquit?
In both, to reason right is to submit.
   Better for Us, perhaps, it might appear,   165
Were there all harmony, all virtue here;
That never air or ocean felt the wind;
That never passion discompos'd the mind:
But ALL subsists by elemental strife;
And Passions are the elements of Life.   170
The gen'ral ORDER, since the whole began,
Is kept in Nature, and is kept in Man.

---

perhaps, on rare occasions, be suspended in the interest of the part; (2) that deteriorations in the system may account for the intrusion of some evils; (3) that the Creation, as a thing created, is by definition imperfect, God alone being perfect. Pope's point (ll. 148–72) is that the anthropocentrist has implicitly abandoned his position in the arguments used to explain physical evils; ought to abandon it altogether; and if he does so, will see that God's dispositions in the moral realm (likewise calculated for general good) are as readily justified as His dispositions in the natural.

147. *some . . . began*] This may refer either to Newton's belief that irregularities were gradually accruing in the system, or to the traditional theory that the world was less perfect since the Fall; or to both.

152. *desires*] I.e. passions.

155-6. As God has established general laws for the larger good of the whole which sometimes bring about natural evils in particular instances, so God has given man passions which sometimes result in moral evils—a reply to the contention that a good God would have made man incapable of sinning.

160. *young Ammon*] Alexander the Great.

170. See this subject extended in Epist. 2 from Vers. 100, to 122, 165, &c. [P].

VI. What would this Man? Now upward will he soar,
And little less than Angel, would be more;
Now looking downwards, just as griev'd appears 175
To want the strength of bulls, the fur of bears.
Made for his use all creatures if he call,
Say what their use, had he the pow'rs of all?
Nature to these, without profusion kind,
The proper organs, proper pow'rs assign'd; 180
Each seeming want compensated of course,
Here with degrees of swiftness, there of force;
All in exact proportion to the state;
Nothing to add, and nothing to abate.
Each beast, each insect, happy in its own; 185
Is Heav'n unkind to Man, and Man alone?
Shall he alone, whom rational we call,
Be pleas'd with nothing, if not bless'd with all?
   The bliss of Man (could Pride that blessing find)
Is not to act or think beyond mankind; 190
No pow'rs of body or of soul to share,
But what his nature and his state can bear.
Why has not Man a microscopic eye?
For this plain reason, Man is not a Fly.
Say what the use, were finer optics giv'n, 195
T' inspect a mite, not comprehend the heav'n?
Or touch, if tremblingly alive all o'er,
To smart and agonize at ev'ry pore?
Or quick effluvia darting thro' the brain,
Die of a rose in aromatic pain? 200

173 ff. *The Unreasonableness of the Complaints* ⟨by Lucretius, Pliny and others⟩ *against Providence, and that to possess more Faculties would make us miserable* [P].

181. *of course*] In the normal course of events.

182. It is a certain Axiom in the Anatomy of Creatures, that in proportion as they are form'd for Strength, their Swiftness is lessen'd; or as they are form'd for Swiftness, their Strength is abated [P].

185. Vid. Epist. 3 Vers. 79, &c. and 110, &c. [P].

193–206. It was a point of constant emphasis in Pope's day that man's sensory powers had 'that Degree of Perfection, which is most fit and suitable to our Estate and Condition'. Locke observed that if man had 'microscopical Eyes', 'he would not make any great Advantage by the Change.'

194. *Man . . . Fly*] The fly's eye was supposed to have microscopic powers.

195–6. Cf. *Dunc.* B, IV 453 ff. and note (p. 788).

196. Note the common symbolical belief that man's sight, unlike the animals', was formed to look upwards.

199. *effluvia*] Streams of invisible particles by which Epicurus and others believed that odours communicated themselves to the brain.

If nature thunder'd in his op'ning ears,
And stunn'd him with the music of the spheres,
How would he wish that Heav'n had left him still
The whisp'ring Zephyr, and the purling rill?
Who finds not Providence all good and wise,   205
Alike in what it gives, and what denies?

    VII. Far as Creation's ample range extends,
The scale of sensual, mental pow'rs ascends:
Mark how it mounts, to Man's imperial race,
From the green myriads in the peopled grass: 210
What modes of sight betwixt each wide extreme,
The mole's dim curtain, and the lynx's beam:
Of smell, the headlong lioness between,
And hound sagacious on the tainted green:
Of hearing, from the life that fills the flood,   215
To that which warbles thro' the vernal wood:
The spider's touch, how exquisitely fine!
Feels at each thread, and lives along the line:
In the nice bee, what sense so subtly true
From pois'nous herbs extracts the healing dew: 220
How Instinct varies in the grov'ling swine,
Compar'd, half-reas'ning elephant, with thine:

201–2. Pope closes his instances with a comparison at the opposite end of the scale—between man and angel (cf. man and fly, above)—alluding to the belief that it was given to angels but not to mortals to hear the music of the spheres.

207 ff. *There is an universal* ORDER *and* GRADATION *thro' the whole visible world, of the* sensible *and* mental *Faculties, which causes the* Subordination *of Creature to Creature, and of all Creatures to Man, whose* Reason *alone countervails all the other Faculties.* The Extent, Limits, and Use of *Human Reason* and *Science,* the Author design'd as the subject of his next Book of Ethic Epistles. [P]

212. *beam*] Alluding to the old theory that sight depended on emission of rays from the eye.

213. The manner of the Lions hunting their Prey in the Deserts of Africa is this; at their first going out in the night-time they set up a loud Roar, and then listen to the Noise made by the Beasts in their Flight, pursuing them by the Ear, and not by the Nostril. It is probable, the story of the Jackall's hunting for the Lion was occasion'd by observation of the Defect of Scent in that terrible Animal. [P]

Allusions to the lion's relatively imperfect smell and sight are found in Buffon's *Natural History,* but the source of the curious misinformation that lions hunt by ear has not been discovered.

214. *sagacious*] 'Acute in perception, esp. by the sense of smell'.

   tainted] Imbued with the scent of an animal (usually a hunted animal).

220. *healing dew*] The phrase reflects the common medicinal use of honey in Pope's day and the ancient belief that honey was a dew that fell on flowers.

'Twixt that, and Reason, what a nice barrier;
For ever sep'rate, yet for ever near!
Remembrance and Reflection how ally'd;   225
What thin partitions Sense from Thought divide:
And Middle natures, how they long to join,
Yet never pass th' insuperable line!
Without this just gradation, could they be
Subjected these to those, or all to thee?   230
The pow'rs of all subdu'd by thee alone,
Is not thy Reason all these pow'rs in one?
    VIII. See, thro' this air, this ocean, and this earth,
All matter quick, and bursting into birth.
Above, how high progressive life may go!   235
Around, how wide! how deep extend below!
Vast chain of being, which from God began,
Natures æthereal, human, angel, man,
Beast, bird, fish, insect! what no eye can see,
No glass can reach! from Infinite to thee,   240
From thee to Nothing!—On superior pow'rs
Were we to press, inferior might on ours:
Or in the full creation leave a void,
Where, one step broken, the great scale's destoy'd:
From Nature's chain whatever link you strike,   245
Tenth or ten thousandth, breaks the chain alike.
    And if each system in gradation roll,
Alike essential to th' amazing whole;
The least confusion but in one, not all
That system only, but the whole must fall.   250
Let Earth unbalanc'd from her orbit fly,
Planets and Suns run lawless thro' the sky,

223–4. Pope adopts regularly in the *Essay* (cf. III 83 ff.) the orthodox position, opposed by Montaigne and others, that man differs from animal in kind, not merely in degree.

223. *barrier*] Johnson, *Dict.* (1755): 'It is sometimes pronounced with the accent on the last syllable, but it is placed more properly upon the first.'

224. The faculty allotted to beasts was simple memory.

227. *Middle natures*] Natures transitional between the main steps of the scale.

233 ff. *How much farther this* Gradation *and* Subordination *may extend? were any part of which broken, the* whole connected Creation *must be destroy'd.* [P]

233. *this air . . . earth*] The traditional classification of forms of life according to the three inhabited elements: cf. *Ess.*, III 116–20.

251. *unbalanc'd*] The antithesis of God's act of creation in *Par. Lost*, VII 242, whereby 'Earth, self-balanc'd, on her centre hung.'

Let ruling Angels from their spheres be hurl'd,
Being on being wreck'd, and world on world,
Heav'n's whole foundations to their centre nod,   255
And Nature tremble to the throne of God:
All this dread ORDER break—for whom? for thee?
Vile worm!—oh Madness, Pride, Impiety!
    IX. What if the foot, ordain'd the dust to tread,
Or hand to toil, aspir'd to be the head?   260
What if the head, the eye, or ear repin'd
To serve mere engines to the ruling Mind?
Just as absurd for any part to claim
To be another, in this gen'ral frame:
Just as absurd, to mourn the tasks or pains   265
The great directing MIND of ALL ordains.
    All are but parts of one stupendous whole,
Whose body, Nature is, and God the soul;
That, chang'd thro' all, and yet in all the same,
Great in the earth, as in th' æthereal frame,   270
Warms in the sun, refreshes in the breeze,
Glows in the stars, and blossoms in the trees,
Lives thro' all life, extends thro' all extent,
Spreads undivided, operates unspent,
Breathes in our soul, informs our mortal part,   275
As full, as perfect, in a hair as heart;
As full, as perfect, in vile Man that mourns,
As the rapt Seraph that adores and burns;
To him no high, no low, no great, no small;
He fills, he bounds, connects, and equals all.   280

253. *ruling Angels*] According to Aquinas, the shaking of the ruling
angels from their spheres is to be a sign of the end of the world.
    258. *The Extravagance, Impiety, and Pride of such a desire.* [P]
    263–6. A favourite position in moral philosophy from the Stoics down.
    265. Vid. the prosecution and application of this in Epist. 4. Ver.
162 [P].
    269. So Augustine speaks of God as 'immutabilis, mutans omnia'
(*Conf.*, I iv).
    274. Standard predications of God in catholic theology.
    276. Cf. Aquinas's argument that the soul is wholly in the whole body
and at the same time wholly in each part of the body.
    278. Above, I 110n. Aquinas says that 'The first and highest [of the
angels] are called Seraphim, i.e. fiery or setting on fire, because fire is
used to designate intensity of love or desire.'
    280. The four verbs epitomize much of the argument of *Ess.*, I, III,
and IV. On *fills*, see the preceding lines and III 21–6, IV 61–2; on *bounds*,
III 110 and 79 ff; on *connects*, III 23 and 111 ff; on *equals*, IV 53–62, esp.
61–2 and 326.

x. Cease then, nor ORDER Imperfection name:
Our proper bliss depends on what we blame.
Know thy own point: This kind, this due degree
Of blindness, weakness, Heav'n bestows on thee.
Submit—In this, or any other sphere,   285
Secure to be as blest as thou canst bear:
Safe in the hand of one disposing Pow'r,
Or in the natal, or the mortal hour.
All Nature is but Art, unknown to thee;
All Chance, Direction, which thou canst not see;   290
All Discord, Harmony, not understood;
All partial Evil, universal Good:
And, spite of Pride, in erring Reason's spite,
One truth is clear, 'Whatever IS, is RIGHT.'

281 ff. *The Consequence of all, the* absolute Submission *due to Providence, both as to our* present *and* future *State* [P].

281–4. *Par. Lost*, VIII 167–84, is the best commentary on this passage, and comes close to summarizing the argument of this Epistle.

289. A traditional conception in both pagan and Christian thought (like the four which follow it).

290. A favourite topic of the Stoics; the theme of Boethius's *De cons. phil.*, and cf. Matt., x 29–30, and Christian writing in general.

ARGUMENT OF THE SECOND EPISTLE

Of the Nature and State of Man, *with respect to* Himself, *as an Individual.* I. The *business of Man not to pry into* God, *but to study* himself. *His* Middle Nature; *his Powers and Frailties,* VER. 1 to 18. *The Limits of his* Capacity, VER. 19, &c. II. *The two Principles of Man,* Self-love *and* Reason, *both necessary,* VER. 53, &c. Self-love *the stronger, and why,* VER. 67, &c. *Their end the same,* VER. 81, &c. III. *The* PASSIONS, *and their use,* VER. 93 to 130. *The* predominant Passion, *and its force,* VER. 131 to 160. *Its Necessity, in directing Men to different purposes,* VER. 165, &c. *Its providential Use, in fixing our Principle, and ascertaining our Virtue,* VER. 177. IV. Virtue *and* Vice *joined in our* mixed Nature; *the limits near, yet the things* separate *and* evident: *What is the office of* Reason, VER. 203 to 216. V. *How odious* Vice *in itself, and how we deceive ourselves into it,* VER. 217. VI. *That, however, the* Ends *of* Providence *and* general Good *are answered in our Passions and Imperfections,* VER. 238, &c. *How usefully these are distributed to all* Orders of Men, VER. 242. *How useful they are to* Society, VER. 249. *And to the* Individuals, VER. 261. *In every* state, *and every* age *of life,* VER. 271, &c.

Know then thyself, presume not God to scan;
The proper study of Mankind is Man.
Plac'd on this isthmus of a middle state,
A being darkly wise, and rudely great:
With too much knowledge for the Sceptic side,   5
With too much weakness for the Stoic's pride,
He hangs between; in doubt to act, or rest,
In doubt to deem himself a God, or Beast;
In doubt his Mind or Body to prefer,
Born but to die, and reas'ning but to err;   10
Alike in ignorance, his reason such,
Whether he thinks too little, or too much:
Chaos of Thought and Passion, all confus'd;
Still by himself abus'd, or disabus'd;
Created half to rise, and half to fall;   15
Great lord of all things, yet a prey to all;
Sole judge of Truth, in endless Error hurl'd:
The glory, jest, and riddle of the world!
  Go, wond'rous creature! mount where Science guides,
Go, measure earth, weigh air, and state the tides;   20
Instruct the planets in what orbs to run,
Correct old Time, and regulate the Sun;

Epistle II. *Of the* NATURE *and* STATE *of* MAN *as an* INDIVIDUAL [P].
  1 ff. *The business of Man not to pry into God, but to study himself. His*
Middle Nature, *his* Powers, Frailties, *and the* Limits *of his* Capacity [P].
  1. *scan*] Often misread to imply the total exclusion of knowledge about
God. Pope's point is that God's dispensations are not to be presumptu-
ously pried into and carped at by human reason.
  6. *Stoic's pride*] The traditional charge against the Stoics because of
their belief that men could extirpate their passions and attain to impas-
sivity, like God's.
  7. *in . . . rest*] The contrast in this line and the next is between Stoic
and Epicurean alternatives: cf. *Ess.*, IV 21-4. *Rest* is Stoic apathy, and *act*
is apparently Epicurean hedonism.
  11-12. I.e. man's proper reasoning should fall between these extremes
in the direction of self-knowledge, as in the remainder of this epistle.
  20. *measure earth*] Many calculations of the earth's measurements were
being made in Pope's time and earlier.
  weigh air] Alluding to the experiments of Torricelli, Boyle, and others.
  state . . . tides] With reference to the work of Newton, continued in
Pope's time by Euler, Bernouilli, and others, to determine the causes and
operations of the tides.
  21. Cf. the determinations of planetary motions by Newton, Halley,
Flamsteed, Cassini, etc.
  22. *Correct . . . Time*] Pope may refer to some such 'correction' as
Newton describes in *Principia*: 'Absolute time, in Astronomy, is distinguish'd from Relative, by the Equation or correction of vulgar time.

Go, soar with Plato to th' empyreal sphere,
To the first good, first perfect, and first fair;
Or tread the mazy round his follow'rs trod,   25
And quitting sense call imitating God;
As Eastern priests in giddy circles run,
And turn their heads to imitate the Sun.
Go, teach Eternal Wisdom how to rule—
Then drop into thyself, and be a fool!   30
    Superior beings, when of late they saw
A mortal Man unfold all Nature's law,
Admir'd such wisdom in an earthly shape,
And shew'd a NEWTON as we shew an Ape.
    Could he, whose rules the rapid Comet bind,   35
Describe or fix one movement of his Mind?
Who saw its fires here rise, and there descend,
Explain his own beginning, or his end?
Alas what wonder! Man's superior part
Uncheck'd may rise, and climb from art to art: 40
But when his own great work is but begun,
What Reason weaves, by Passion is undone.
    Trace Science then, with Modesty thy guide;
First strip off all her equipage of Pride,
Deduct what is but Vanity, or Dress,   45
Or Learning's Luxury, or Idleness;
Or tricks to shew the stretch of human brain,
Mere curious pleasure, or ingenious pain:
Expunge the whole, or lop th' excrescent parts
Of all, our Vices have created Arts: 50
Then see how little the remaining sum,
Which serv'd the past, and must the times to come!
    II. Two Principles in human nature reign;

For the natural days are truly unequal, though they are commonly consider'd as equal, and used for a measure of time: Astronomers correct this
inequality for their more accurate deducing of the celestial motions.'
    23. *empyreal sphere*] The outermost sphere of the universe, abode of
God and (for Pope) of Plato's archetypes of Ideas.
    26. Referring to the soul's leaving behind the body ('sense') for neo-
platonic trances, such as Plotinus is said to have enjoyed, and to the
characteristic teaching of neo-platonists that 'he that dares soar above the
gross impediments of flesh, to converse with divine objects, will become
little less than a God'.
    46. 'I.e. what is done by learning after a fashion intended to make a
show or to save trouble'.
    53 ff. *The* TWO PRINCIPLES *of* MAN, SELF-LOVE *and* REASON,

Self-love, to urge, and Reason, to restrain;
Nor this a good, nor that a bad we call,   55
Each works its end, to move or govern all:
And to their proper operation still,
Ascribe all Good; to their improper, Ill.
　Self-love, the spring of motion, acts the soul;
Reason's comparing balance rules the whole.   60
Man, but for that, no action could attend,
And, but for this, were active to no end;
Fix'd like a plant on his peculiar spot,
To draw nutrition, propagate, and rot;
Or, meteor-like, flame lawless thro' the void,   65
Destroying others, by himself destroy'd.
　Most strength the moving principle requires;
Active its task, it prompts, impels, inspires.
Sedate and quiet the comparing lies,
Form'd but to check, delib'rate, and advise.   70
Self-love still stronger, as its objects nigh;
Reason's at distance, and in prospect lie:
That sees immediate good by present sense;
Reason, the future and the consequence.
Thicker than arguments, temptations throng,   75
At best more watchful this, but that more strong.
The action of the stronger to suspend
Reason still use, to Reason still attend:
Attention, habit and experience gains,
Each strengthens Reason, and Self-love restrains.   80
　Let subtle schoolmen teach these friends to fight,
More studious to divide than to unite,
And Grace and Virtue, Sense and Reason split,
With all the rash dexterity of Wit:
Wits, just like fools, at war about a Name,   85
Have full as oft no meaning, or the same.

---

both necessary, 59. *Self-love the* stronger, *and why?*, 67. *their* End *the same*, 81. [P]
　53. Alluding to the fundamental antithesis, in all the traditional psychologies, between regulatory and appetitive elements in man's nature, usually connected in one way or another with the doctrine of his two souls, rational and sensitive.
　54. *Self-love*] I.e. self-maintenance or self-fulfilment; each natural being strives to keep going with its own particular go.
　59. *acts*] activates.
　62, 65–6. Self-love is likened to the tendency of heavenly bodies to keep moving, and reason to the force of gravitation that is necessary to hold them in their orbits.

Self-love and Reason to one end aspire,
Pain their aversion, Pleasure their desire;
But greedy that its object would devour,
This taste the honey, and not wound the flow'r: 90
Pleasure, or wrong or rightly understood,
Our greatest evil, or our greatest good.
   III. Modes of Self-love the Passions we may call;
'Tis real good, or seeming, moves them all;
But since not every good we can divide,   95
And Reason bids us for our own provide;
Passions, tho' selfish, if their means be fair,
List under Reason, and deserve her care;
Those, that imparted, court a nobler aim,
Exalt their kind, and take some Virtue's name.   100
   In lazy Apathy let Stoics boast
Their Virtue fix'd; 'tis fix'd as in a frost,
Contracted all, retiring to the breast;
But strength of mind is Exercise, not Rest:
The rising tempest puts in act the soul,   105
Parts it may ravage, but preserves the whole.
On life's vast ocean diversely we sail,
Reason the card, but Passion is the gale;
Nor God alone in the still calm we find,
He mounts the storm, and walks upon the wind.   110
   Passions, like Elements, tho' born to fight,
Yet, mix'd and soften'd, in his work unite:
These 'tis enough to temper and employ;
But what composes Man, can Man destroy?
Suffice that Reason keep to Nature's road,   115
Subject, compound them, follow her and God.

93 ff. *The* PASSIONS, *and their* Use [P].
98. *List*] Enlist.
99. *Those, that imparted*] I.e. the passions when reason is imparted
to them.
108. *card*] The mariner's chart or map.
109–10. Cf. the 'great calm' of Matt. VIII 26.
111–22. A further comparison between man and the exterior universe
to emphasize the importance of utilizing his whole nature—in keeping
with the implications in the preceding passage that the world outside man
is inclusive, not exclusive: tempests are as necessary as calms, gales as
necessary as compasses or maps. Man's duty is to achieve by creative skill
an inner harmony of all his powers, imposing order on the *chaos* indicated
in II 13.
111–12. The traditional conception of personality as a blending of the
four humours or elements in man, the application of which to the passions was regularly made.

Love, Hope, and Joy, fair pleasure's smiling train,
Hate, Fear, and Grief, the family of pain;
These mix'd with art, and to due bounds confin'd,
Make and maintain the balance of the mind: 120
The lights and shades, whose well accorded strife
Gives all the strength and colour of our life.
   Pleasures are ever in our hands or eyes,
And when in act they cease, in prospect rise;
Present to grasp, and future still to find,   125
The whole employ of body and of mind.
All spread their charms, but charm not all alike;
On diff'rent senses diff'rent objects strike;
Hence diff'rent Passions more or less inflame,
As strong or weak, the organs of the frame;   130
And hence one master Passion in the breast,
Like Aaron's serpent, swallows up the rest.
   As Man, perhaps, the moment of his breath,
Receives the lurking principle of death;
The young disease, that must subdue at length,   135
Grows with his growth, and strengthens with his strength:
So, cast and mingled with his very frame,
The Mind's disease, its ruling Passion came;
Each vital humour which should feed the whole,
Soon flows to this, in body and in soul.   140
Whatever warms the heart, or fills the head,
As the mind opens, and its functions spread,
Imagination plies her dang'rous art,
And pours it all upon the peccant part.
   Nature its mother, Habit is its nurse;   145
Wit, Spirit, Faculties, but make it worse;
Reason itself but gives it edge and pow'r;
As Heav'n's blest beam turns vinegar more sowr;

133 ff. *The* PREDOMINANT PASSION, *and its* Force. The Use of this
doctrine, as apply'd to the Knowledge of mankind, is one of the subjects
of the second book [P].

139. *vital humour*] The several sorts of 'spirits'—natural, vital, animal
—that in the old physiology were credited with nourishing the powers of
body and soul.

142. I.e. as the individual matures from infancy into manhood.

143-4. The traditional view of the dangerous force of imagination in
man's moral life.

144. *peccant*] An epithet given to the humours of the body, when they
are either morbid, or in too great abundance.

146. *Faculties*] three sorts—natural, vital, and animal, corresponding to
the kinds of spirits.

We, wretched subjects tho' to lawful sway,
In this weak queen, some fav'rite still obey.   150
Ah! if she lend not arms, as well as rules,
What can she more than tell us we are fools?
Teach us to mourn our Nature, not to mend,
A sharp accuser, but a helpless friend!
Or from a judge turn pleader, to persuade   155
The choice we make, or justify it made;
Proud of an easy conquest all along,
She but removes weak passions for the strong:
So, when small humors gather to a gout,
The doctor fancies he has driv'n them out.   160
    Yes, Nature's road must ever be prefer'd;
Reason is here no guide, but still a guard:
'Tis hers to rectify, not overthrow,
And treat this passion more as friend than foe:
A mightier Pow'r the strong direction sends,   165
And sev'ral Men impels to sev'ral ends.
Like varying winds, by other passions tost,
This drives them constant to a certain coast.
Let pow'r or knowledge, gold or glory, please,
Or (oft more strong than all) the love of ease;   170
Thro' life 'tis followed, ev'n at life's expence;
The merchant's toil, the sage's indolence,
The monk's humility, the hero's pride,
All, all alike, find Reason on their side.
    Th' Eternal Art educing good from ill,   175
Grafts on this Passion our best principle:
'Tis thus the Mercury of Man is fix'd,
Strong grows the Virtue with his nature mix'd;

159. Gout was thought to arise from 'a redundancy of humours' and was 'considered as a . . . paroxysm, tending to free the body of an offensive . . . matter, by throwing it upon the extremities'.

165 ff. *Its* Necessity, *in directing men to different purposes.* The particular application of this to the *several Pursuits* of Men, and the *General Good* resulting thence, falls also into the succeeding books [P].

165–6. The traditional view that God ensures the variety of dispositions and inclinations by which the world's work is enabled to be carried on.

175 ff. *Its* providential Use, *in fixing our* PRINCIPLE, *and ascertaining our* VIRTUE [P].

177. *Mercury . . . fix'd*] I.e. the dominion of a ruling passion 'sets' or determines the otherwise infinite variableness of man's emotional nature, as various 'sulphurs' (according to the metallurgy of Pope's time) 'fix', in the metallic substances as we know them, the primal mercury of which all of them are composed. The term *mercury* was frequently applied to volatility of character.

The dross cements what else were too refin'd,
And in one interest body acts with mind.   180
　　As fruits ungrateful to the planter's care
On savage stocks inserted learn to bear;
The surest Virtues thus from Passions shoot,
Wild Nature's vigor working at the root.
What crops of wit and honesty appear   185
From spleen, from obstinacy, hate, or fear!
See anger, zeal and fortitude supply;
Ev'n av'rice, prudence; sloth, philosophy;
Lust, thro' some certain strainers well refin'd,
Is gentle love, and charms all womankind: 190
Envy, to which th' ignoble mind's a slave,
Is emulation in the learn'd or brave:
Nor Virtue, male or female, can we name,
But what will grow on Pride, or grow on Shame.
　　Thus Nature gives us (let it check our pride)   195
The virtue nearest to our vice ally'd;
Reason the byass turns to good from ill,
And Nero reigns a Titus, if he will.
The fiery soul abhor'd in Catiline,
In Decius charms, in Curtius is divine.   200
The same ambition can destroy or save,
And make a patriot as it makes a knave.
　　IV. This light and darkness in our chaos join'd,
What shall divide? The God within the mind.
　　Extremes in Nature equal ends produce,   205
In Man they join to some mysterious use;
Tho' each by turns the other's bound invade,
As, in some well-wrought picture, light and shade,

180. Pope's point is analogous to Donne's in *The Extasie*: neither body
nor soul is dispensable.

181. *fruits*] Equivalent, as used here, to 'grafts' or 'scions'.

195 ff. VIRTUE *and* VICE *join'd in our* Mixt Nature; *the Limits* near, *yet
the things* separate, *and* evident. *The Office of* Reason [P].

195-6. An epigrammatic way of saying (in contradistinction to theories
that real virtue is the result of pure reason or pure grace) that we are
indebted to nature for a passional force that can be turned as readily into
a characteristic virtue as a characteristic vice.

198. *will*] Both 'if he chooses' and 'if he performs an act of will'.

200. *Decius . . . Curtius*] Examples of patriotic self-abnegation.

203-4. Alludes to the creative act of God which man is to imitate in
ordering his own 'chaos'.

205. *Extremes in Nature*] Evidently the 'reconciled extremes' of drought
and rain, seedtime and harvest, life and death, chance and permanence,
to which Pope refers in *Mor. Ess.*, iii 161 ff. and on which, in the traditional view, the well-being of the world is founded.

And oft so mix, the diff'rence is too nice
Where ends the Virtue, or begins the Vice.   210
   Fools! who from hence into the notion fall,
That Vice or Virtue there is none at all.
If white and black blend, soften, and unite
A thousand ways, is there no black or white?
Ask your own heart, and nothing is so plain;   215
'Tis to mistake them, costs the time and pain.
   v. Vice is a monster of so frightful mien,
As, to be hated, needs but to be seen;
Yet seen too oft, familiar with her face,
We first endure, then pity, then embrace.   220
But where th' Extreme of Vice, was ne'er agreed:
Ask where's the North? at York, 'tis on the Tweed;
In Scotland, at the Orcades; and there,
At Greenland, Zembla, or the Lord knows where:
No creature owns it in the first degree,   225
But thinks his neighbour farther gone than he.
Ev'n those who dwell beneath its very zone,
Or never feel the rage, or never own;
What happier natures shrink at with affright,
The hard inhabitant contends is right.   230
   vi. Virtuous and vicious ev'ry Man must be,
Few in th' extreme, but all in the degree;
The rogue and fool by fits is fair and wise,
And ev'n the best, by fits, what they despise.
'Tis but by parts we follow good or ill,   235
For, Vice or Virtue, Self directs it still;
Each individual seeks a sev'ral goal;
But HEAV'N'S great view is One, and that the Whole:
That counter-works each folly and caprice;
That disappoints th' effect of ev'ry vice: 240
That happy frailties to all ranks apply'd,
Shame to the virgin, to the matron pride,

211–15. I.e. good and evil are absolutes, and known intuitively. Pope is making the point of the Cambridge Platonists.

217 ff. VICE *odious in itself, and how we* deceive *ourselves into it* [P].

225. *degree*] An equivoque, sustaining both the usual sense and Pope's geographical image: cf. *zone* in 227.

230. *hard*] The man who lives in an atmosphere of vice becomes hardened to it, as the native of Greenland or Nova Zembla (l. 224) to cold.

231 ff. *The* ENDS *of* PROVIDENCE *and* General Good *answer'd in our* Passions *and* Imperfections. *How usefully these are distributed to all* Orders of men [P].

Fear to the statesman, rashness to the chief,
To kings presumption, and to crowds belief,
That Virtue's ends from Vanity can raise,   245
Which seeks no int'rest, no reward but praise;
And build on wants, and on defects of mind,
The joy, the peace, the glory of Mankind.
   Heav'n forming each on other to depend,
A master, or a servant, or a friend,   250
Bids each on other for assistance call,
'Till one Man's weakness grows the strength of all.
Wants, frailties, passions, closer still ally
The common int'rest, or endear the tie:
To these we owe true friendship, love sincere,   255
Each home-felt joy that life inherits here:
Yet from the same we learn, in its decline,
Those joys, those loves, those int'rests to resign:
Taught half by Reason, half by mere decay,
To welcome death, and calmly pass away.   260
   Whate'er the Passion, knowledge, fame, or pelf,
Not one will change his neighbor with himself.
The learn'd is happy nature to explore,
The fool is happy that he knows no more;
The rich is happy in the plenty giv'n,   265
The poor contents him with the care of Heav'n.
See the blind beggar dance, the cripple sing.
The sot a hero, lunatic a king;
The starving chemist in his golden views
Supremely blest, the poet in his muse.   270
   See some strange comfort ev'ry state attend,
And Pride bestow'd on all, a common friend;
See some fit Passion ev'ry age supply,
Hope travels thro', nor quits us when we die.
   Behold the child, by Nature's kindly law,   275
Pleas'd with a rattle, tickled with a straw:
Some livelier play-thing gives his youth delight,
A little louder, but as empty quite:
Scarfs, garters, gold, amuse his riper stage;
And beads and pray'r-books are the toys of age: 280

---

249 ff. *How useful these are to* SOCIETY *in general, and to* INDIVIDUALS
in particular, in every STATE, 261, *and ev'ry* AGE *of Life*, 271 [P].
249–52. A favourite thesis of traditional political theory.
255. *sincere*] Cf. IV 15*n* (p. 536).
273. A standard conception in the theory of passions.
279. *Scarfs*] The badge of doctors of divinity.

Pleas'd with this bauble still, as that before;
'Till tir'd he sleeps, and Life's poor play is o'er!
  Mean-while Opinion gilds with varying rays
Those painted clouds that beautify our days;
Each want of happiness by Hope supply'd,   285
And each vacuity of sense by Pride:
These build as fast as knowledge can destroy;
In Folly's cup still laughs the bubble, joy;
One prospect lost, another still we gain;
And not a vanity is giv'n in vain;   290
Ev'n mean Self-love becomes, by force divine,
The scale to measure others wants by thine.
See! and confess, one comfort still must rise,
'Tis this, Tho' Man's a fool, yet GOD IS WISE.

288. *bubble*] The word takes on additional meaning from its common early senses—'deceptive show' and 'dupe'.
291-2. See farther of the Use of this *Principle* in Man. Epist. 3. Ver. 121, 124, 134, 144, 199, &c. And Epist. 4. Ver. 358, and 368 [P].

ARGUMENT OF THE THIRD EPISTLE

Of the Nature and State of Man, *with respect to* Society. I. The *whole Universe one system of Society,* VER. 7, &c. *Nothing made wholly for itself, nor yet wholly for* another, VER. 27. *The happiness of* Animals *mutual,* VER. 49. II. Reason *or* Instinct *operate alike to the good of each individual,* VER. 79. Reason *or* Instinct *operate also to Society, in all animals,* VER. 109. III. *How far* Society *carried by Instinct,* VER. 115. *How much farther by Reason,* VER. 131. IV. *Of that which is called the* State of Nature, VER. 147. *Reason instructed by Instinct in the invention of* Arts, VER. 171, *and in the Forms of* Society, VER. 179. V. *Origin of Political Societies,* VER. 199. *Origin of Monarchy,* VER. 209. *Patriarchal government,* VER. 215. VI. *Origin of true Religion and Government, from the same principle, of Love,* VER. 231, &c. *Origin of Superstition and Tyranny, from the same principle, of Fear,* VER. 241, &c. *The Influence of Self-love operating to the* social *and* public Good, VER. 269. *Restoration of true Religion and Government on their first principle,* VER. 283. *Mixt Government,* VER. 294. *Various Forms of each, and the true end of all,* VER. 303, &c.

Here then we rest: 'The Universal Cause
Acts to one end, but acts by various laws.'
In all the madness of superfluous health,
The trim of pride, the impudence of wealth,
Let this great truth be present night and day;   5
But most be present, if we preach or pray.
   Look round our World; behold the chain of Love
Combining all below and all above.
See plastic Nature working to this end,
The single atoms each to other tend,   10
Attract, attracted to, the next in place
Form'd and impell'd its neighbour to embrace.
See Matter next, with various life endu'd,
Press to one centre still, the gen'ral Good.
See dying vegetables life sustain,   15
See life dissolving vegetate again:
All forms that perish other forms supply,
(By turns we catch the vital breath, and die)
Like bubbles on the sea of Matter born,
They rise, they break, and to that sea return.   20
Nothing is foreign: Parts relate to whole;
One all-extending all-preserving Soul
Connects each being, greatest with the least;
Made Beast in aid of Man, and Man of Beast;
All serv'd, all serving! nothing stands alone;   25
The chain holds on, and where it ends, unknown.
   Has God, thou fool! work'd solely for thy good,
Thy joy, thy pastime, thy attire, thy food?
Who for thy table feeds the wanton fawn,
For him as kindly spread the flow'ry lawn.   30

Epistle III. Of the NATURE and STATE of Man with respect to SOCIETY [P].

1 ff. The whole Universe one System of Society [P].

2. *one end*] The 'gen'ral good', as in 14, below.

7–26. An influential group of concepts in traditional 'poetic' metaphysics.

9. *plastic Nature*] The informing and forming power of God, as manifested in the creativity of nature: cf. the *natura naturans* of the Schools.

12. *neighbour . . . embrace*] A locution emphasizing unity through love at the inanimate level.

14. *Press . . . centre*] Alluding to the supposed movement of matter to earth's centre.

18. I.e. man is also subject to vicissitude.

27 ff. Nothing made wholly for *Itself*, nor yet wholly for *another*, but the Happiness of all animals *mutual* [P]. Pope's argument is both that man is made for the animals as well as the animals for man, and that animals are made for themselves as well as for men.

Is it for thee the lark ascends and sings?
Joy tunes his voice, joy elevates his wings:
Is it for thee the linnet pours his throat?
Loves of his own and raptures swell the note:
The bounding steed you pompously bestride,   35
Shares with his lord the pleasure and the pride:
Is thine alone the seed that strews the plain?
The birds of heav'n shall vindicate their grain:
Thine the full harvest of the golden year?
Part pays, and justly, the deserving steer: 40
The hog, that plows not nor obeys thy call,
Lives on the labours of this lord of all.
   Know, Nature's children all divide her care;
The fur that warms a monarch, warm'd a bear.
While Man exclaims, 'See all things for my use!'   45
'See man for mine!' replies a pamper'd goose;
And just as short of Reason he must fall,
Who thinks all made for one, not one for all.
   Grant that the pow'rful still the weak controul,
Be Man the Wit and Tyrant of the whole: 50
Nature that Tyrant checks; he only knows,
And helps, another creature's wants and woes.
Say, will the falcon, stooping from above,
Smit with her varying plumage, spare the dove?
Admires the jay the insect's gilded wings?   55
Or hears the hawk when Philomela sings?
Man cares for all: to birds he gives his woods,
To beasts his pastures, and to fish his floods;
For some his Int'rest prompts him to provide,
For more his pleasure, yet for more his pride;   60
All feed on one vain Patron, and enjoy
Th'extensive blessing of his luxury.
That very life his learned hunger craves,
He saves from famine, from the savage saves;
Nay, feasts the animal he dooms his feast,   65
And, 'till he ends the being, makes it blest;
Which sees no more the stroke, or feels the pain,
Than favour'd Man by touch etherial slain.
The creature had his feast of life before;
Thou too must perish, when thy feast is o'er!   70

50. *Wit*] The only intellectual being in the terrestrial system.
53–6. The traditional belief that man alone has sense of beauty.
64. *savage*] Cf. III 168*n*.

To each unthinking being, Heav'n a friend,
Gives not the useless knowledge of its end:
To Man imparts it; but with such a view
As, while he dreads it, makes him hope it too:
The hour conceal'd, and so remote the fear,   75
Death still draws nearer, never seeming near.
Great standing miracle! that Heav'n assign'd
Its only thinking thing this turn of mind.
    II. Whether with Reason, or with Instinct blest,
Know, all enjoy that pow'r which suits them best;   80
To bliss alike by that direction tend,
And find the means proportion'd to their end.
Say, where full Instinct is th'unerring guide,
What Pope or Council can they need beside?
Reason, however able, cool at best,   85
Cares not for service, or but serves when prest,
Stays 'till we call, and then not often near;
But honest Instinct comes a volunteer;
Sure never to o'er-shoot, but just to hit,
While still too wide or short is human Wit;   90
Sure by quick Nature happiness to gain,
Which heavier Reason labours at in vain.
This too serves always, Reason never long;
One must go right, the other may go wrong.
See then the acting and comparing pow'rs   95
One in their nature, which are two in ours,
And Reason raise o'er Instinct as you can,
In this 'tis God directs, in that 'tis Man.
    Who taught the nations of the field and wood
To shun their poison, and to chuse their food?   100

77. I.e. *miracle*] that while man is the only animal whose faculties enable
him to apprehend the certain approach of death, his action is not paralysed
by it.

79 ff. *Reason* or *Instinct* alike operate for the good of each *Individual*,
and they operate also to SOCIETY, in *all Animals* [P].

79. I.e. whether man or animal.

83–98. Pope throughout adopts the orthodox view of instinct as the
direct power of God acting in animals, and therefore superior in its
accuracy to reason.

84. *Council*] The Roman Catholic council, which claims to be infallible.

99–108. The effects of animal instinct may be employed as evidence
either of a contriving mind, or of a providential care, in the Creator. They
are here adduced in neither point of view, but to show the equable
distribution of the means by which the great end of the universe is
attained; that means being, reason in man, instinct in animals.

Prescient, the tides or tempests to withstand,
Build on the wave, or arch beneath the sand?
Who made the spider parallels design,
Sure as De-moivre, without rule or line?
Who bid the stork, Columbus-like, explore   105
Heav'ns not his own, and worlds unknown before?
Who calls the council, states the certain day,
Who forms the phalanx, and who points the way?
   III. God, in the nature of each being, founds
Its proper bliss, and sets its proper bounds: 110
But as he fram'd a Whole, the Whole to bless,
On mutual Wants built mutual Happiness:
So from the first eternal ORDER ran,
And creature link'd to creature, man to man.
Whate'er of life all-quick'ning æther keeps,   115
Or breathes thro' air, or shoots beneath the deeps,
Or pours profuse on earth; one nature feeds
The vital flame, and swells the genial seeds.
Not Man alone, but all that roam the wood,
Or wing the sky, or roll along the flood,   120
Each loves itself, but not itself alone,
Each sex desires alike, 'till two are one.
Nor ends the pleasure with the fierce embrace;
They love themselves, a third time, in their race.
Thus beast and bird their common charge attend,   125
The mothers nurse it, and the sires defend;
The young dismiss'd to wander earth or air,
There stops the Instinct, and there ends the care;
The link dissolves, each seeks a fresh embrace,
Another love succeeds, another race.   130

101–2. Evidently an allusion, in the first instance, to the supposed nesting habits of the halcyon, 'on the wave', and in the second, to the reported nesting habits, 'beneath the sand', of the kingfisher, with which the halcyon was usually identified.

104. *De-moivre*] Demoivre, *an eminent Mathematician* [P] (1667–1754), a French Protestant who settled in London, propounded what is to-day known as 'De Moivre's Theorem' in trigonometry, and contributed significantly to the theory of probability.

115 ff. How far SOCIETY carry'd by INSTINCT [P].

115. *æther*] 'the element breathed by the Gods' (*OED*).

118. *The . . . flame*] 'A fine warm, igneous substance, supposed to reside in the hearts of animals, as necessary to life, or rather, as that which constitutes life itself.'

genial] Above, I 133*n*.

119–20. Creatures classified by the element they inhabit, as in I 233.

123. *embrace*] Cf. III 12*n*.

A longer care Man's helpless kind demands;
That longer care contracts more lasting bands:
Reflection, Reason, still the ties improve,
At once extend the int'rest, and the love;
With choice we fix, with sympathy we burn;   135
Each Virtue in each Passion takes its turn;
And still new needs, new helps, new habits rise,
That graft benevolence on charities.
Still as one brood, and as another rose,
These nat'ral love maintain'd, habitual those: 140
The last, scarce ripen'd into perfect Man,
Saw helpless him from whom their life began:
Mem'ry and fore-cast just returns engage,
That pointed back to youth, this on to age:
While pleasure, gratitude, and hope, combin'd,   145
Still spread the int'rest, and preserv'd the kind.
    IV. Nor think, in NATURE'S STATE they blindly trod;
The state of Nature was the reign of God:
Self-love and Social at her birth began,
Union the bond of all things, and of Man.   150
Pride then was not; nor arts, that Pride to aid;
Man walk'd with beast, joint tenant of the shade;
The same his table, and the same his bed;
No murder cloath'd him, and no murder fed.
In the same temple, the resounding wood,   155
All vocal beings hymn'd their equal God.
The shrine with gore unstain'd, with gold undrest,
Unbrib'd, unbloody, stood the blameless priest:
Heav'n's attribute was Universal Care,
And Man's prerogative to rule, but spare.   160
Ah! how unlike the man of times to come!
Of half that live the butcher and the tomb;
Who, foe to Nature, hears the gen'ral groan,
Murders their species, and betrays his own.
But just disease to luxury succeeds,   165

131 ff. How much farther SOCIETY is carry'd by REASON [P].
135–46. Pope's point is that marriage ramifies into all the characteristic
human relationships, affections, and hence virtues.
138. I.e. a general virtuous habit of mind on concrete natural affections.
147 ff. Of the STATE of NATURE: That it was SOCIAL [P].
147–50. I.e. the state of nature was not a state of war, like Hobbes's,
and not without society and law, like Lucretius's, but much more like
Locke's, which 'approximates . . . the Golden Age of the Poets'.
147, 148. State] With a play on the political meaning; cf. reign.
156. equal] Cf. I 87n.

And ev'ry death its own avenger breeds;
The Fury-passions from that blood began,
And turn'd on Man a fiercer savage, Man.
　　See him from Nature rising slow to Art!
To copy Instinct then was Reason's part;   170
Thus then to Man the voice of Nature spake—
'Go, from the Creatures thy instructions take:
Learn from the birds what food the thickets yield;
Learn from the beasts the physic of the field;
Thy arts of building from the bee receive;   175
Learn of the mole to plow, the worm to weave;
Learn of the little Nautilus to sail,
Spread the thin oar, and catch the driving gale.
Here too all forms of social union find,
And hence let Reason, late, instruct Mankind: 180
Here subterranean works and cities see;
There towns aerial on the waving tree.
Learn each small People's genius, policies,
The Ant's republic, and the realm of Bees;
How those in common all their wealth bestow,   185
And Anarchy without confusion know;
And these for ever, tho' a Monarch reign,
Their sep'rate cells and properties maintain.
Mark what unvary'd laws preserve each state,
Laws wise as Nature, and as fix'd as Fate.   190
In vain thy Reason finer webs shall draw,
Entangle Justice in her net of Law,
And right, too rigid, harden into wrong;
Still for the strong too weak, the weak too strong.
Yet go! and thus o'er all the creatures sway,   195
Thus let the wiser make the rest obey,
And for those Arts mere Instinct could afford,
Be crown'd as Monarchs, or as Gods ador'd.'
　　v. Great Nature spoke; observant Men obey'd;
Cities were built, Societies were made: 200

168. *Savage* here means wild animal, as in III 64.
169 ff. *Reason* instructed by *Instinct* in the Invention of ARTS, and in the FORMS of *Society* [P].
177–8. Oppian, Halieut. Lib. I. describes this Fish in the following manner. They swim on the surface of the Sea, on the back of their Shells, which exactly resemble the Hulk of a Ship; they raise two Feet like Masts, and extend a Membrane between which serves as a Sail; the other two Feet they employ as Oars at the side. They are usually seen in the Mediterranean [P].
181–2. Referring especially to ant-hills and bee-hives.
199 ff. Origine of POLITICAL SOCIETIES [P].

Here rose one little state; another near
Grew by like means, and join'd, thro' love or fear.
Did here the trees with ruddier burdens bend,
And there the streams in purer rills descend?
What War could ravish, Commerce could bestow,   205
And he return'd a friend, who came a foe.
Converse and Love mankind might strongly draw,
When Love was Liberty, and Nature Law.
Thus States were form'd; the name of King unknown,
'Till common int'rest plac'd the sway in one.   210
'Twas VIRTUE ONLY (or in arts or arms,
Diffusing blessings, or averting harms)
The same which in a Sire the Sons obey'd,
A Prince the Father of a People made.
  VI. 'Till then, by Nature crown'd, each Patriarch sate, 215
King, priest, and parent of his growing state;
On him, their second Providence, they hung,
Their law his eye, their oracle his tongue.
He from the wond'ring furrow call'd the food,
Taught to command the fire, controul the flood,   220
Draw forth the monsters of th'abyss profound,
Or fetch th'aerial eagle to the ground.
'Till drooping, sick'ning, dying, they began
Whom they rever'd as God to mourn as Man:
Then, looking up from sire to sire, explor'd   225
One great first father, and that first ador'd.
Or plain tradition that this All begun,
Convey'd unbroken faith from sire to son,
The worker from the work distinct was known,
And simple Reason never sought but one: 230
Ere Wit oblique had broke that steddy light,
Man, like his Maker, saw that all was right,
To Virtue, in the paths of Pleasure, trod,
And own'd a Father when he own'd a God.
LOVE all the faith, and all th'allegiance then;   235

210 ff. Origine of MONARCHY [P].

215 ff. ⟨Origin⟩ of PATRIARCHIAL GOVERNMENT [P].

217–24. Like Locke, Temple, and other writers, Pope finds the origins of patriarchal authority in filial habit and the natural veneration of the offspring for their instructor and provider.

235 ff. Origine of TRUE RELIGION and GOVERNMENT from the Principle of LOVE: and of SUPERSTITION and TYRANNY, from that of FEAR [P].

235. In Stoic political theory, tyranny was said to operate on the principle of fear, proper rule on the principle of confidence and love.

For Nature knew no right divine in Men,
No ill could fear in God; and understood
A sov'reign being but a sov'reign good.
True faith, true policy, united ran,
That was but love of God, and this of Man.   240
    Who first taught souls enslav'd, and realms undone,
Th' enormous faith of many made for one;
That proud exception to all Nature's laws,
T'invert the world, and counter-work its Cause?
Force first made Conquest, and that conquest, Law;   245
'Till Superstition taught the tyrant awe,
Then shar'd the Tyranny, then lent it aid,
And Gods of Conqu'rors, Slaves of Subjects made:
She, 'midst the light'ning's blaze, and thunder's sound,
When rock'd the mountains, and when groan'd the ground,
She taught the weak to bend, the proud to pray,   251
To Pow'r unseen, and mightier far than they:
She, from the rending earth and bursting skies,
Saw Gods descend, and fiends infernal rise:
Here fix'd the dreadful, there the blest abodes;   255
Fear made her Devils, and weak Hope her Gods;
Gods partial, changeful, passionate, unjust,
Whose attributes were Rage, Revenge, or Lust;
Such as the souls of cowards might conceive,
And, form'd like tyrants, tyrants would believe.   260
Zeal then, not charity, became the guide,
And hell was built on spite, and heav'n on pride.
Then sacred seem'd th'etherial vault no more;
Altars grew marble then, and reek'd with gore:
Then first the Flamen tasted living food;   265
Next his grim idol smear'd with human blood;
With Heav'n's own thunders shook the world below,
And play'd the God an engine on his foe.
    So drives Self-love, thro' just and thro' unjust,
To one Man's pow'r, ambition, lucre, lust: 270
The same Self-love, in all, becomes the cause
Of what restrains him, Government and Laws.
For, what one likes if others like as well,
What serves one will, when many wills rebel?

236. Locke's thesis throughout his *Civil Govt.*
241–82. The usual account of the corruption of the state of nature,
which finally drove men to formal government and laws.
242. *enormous*] 'Deviating from ordinary rule or type; monstrous'.
269 ff. The Influence of SELF-LOVE operating to the SOCIAL and
Public Good [P].

How shall he keep, what, sleeping or awake,   275
A weaker may surprise, a stronger take?
His safety must his liberty restrain:
All join to guard what each desires to gain.
Forc'd into virtue thus by Self-defence,
Ev'n Kings learn'd justice and benevolence: 280
Self-love forsook the path it first pursu'd,
And found the private in the public good.
    'Twas then, the studious head or gen'rous mind,
Follow'r of God or friend of human-kind,
Poet or Patriot, rose but to restore   285
The Faith and Moral, Nature gave before;
Re-lum'd her ancient light, not kindled new;
If not God's image, yet his shadow drew:
Taught Pow'r's due use to People and to Kings,
Taught nor to slack, nor strain its tender strings,   290
The less, or greater, set so justly true,
That touching one must strike the other too;
'Till jarring int'rests of themselves create
Th'according music of a well-mix'd State.
Such is the World's great harmony, that springs   295
From Order, Union, full Consent of things!
Where small and great, where weak and mighty, made
To serve, not suffer, strengthen, not invade,
More pow'rful each as needful to the rest,
And, in proportion as it blesses, blest,   300
Draw to one point, and to one centre bring
Beast, Man, or Angel, Servant, Lord, or King.
    For Forms of Government let fools contest;
Whate'er is best administer'd is best:

283 ff. Restoration of *True Religion* and *Government* on their first
Principle. *Mixt* Governments; with the various Forms of each, and the
TRUE USE OF ALL. The Deduction and Application of the foregoing
Principles, with the *Use* or *Abuse* of *Civil* and *Ecclesiastical Policy*, was
intended for the subject of the third book [P].

286. *Moral*] Equivalent to 'ethical principles'.

292. *strike*] I.e. cause to sound.

297-300. A common theme in moral and sermon literature, often with
implied or stated reference to 1 Cor., XII.

303-4. Essentially the doctrine of Aristotle in the *Politics*, where he
argues that forms of government are to be judged according to their
effectiveness in procuring the aim of every good state, which is that the
inhabitants of it should be happy. Warburton notes that the lines were
misinterpreted in a contemporary pamphlet (as they were later by others),
with the consequence that Pope jotted down in the offending book: 'The
author of these lines [Pope] was far from meaning that no one Form of
Government is, in itself, better yn another . . . but that no form of

For Modes of Faith, let graceless zealots fight;   305
His can't be wrong whose life is in the right:
In Faith and Hope the world will disagree,
But all Mankind's concern is Charity:
All must be false that thwart this One great End,
And all of God, that bless Mankind or mend.   310
    Man, like the gen'rous vine, supported lives;
The strength he gains is from th'embrace he gives.
On their own Axis as the Planets run,
Yet make at once their circle round the Sun:
So two consistent motions act the Soul;   315
And one regards Itself, and one the Whole.
    Thus God and Nature link'd the gen'ral frame,
And bade Self-love and Social be the same.

Government, however excellent or preferable in itself, can be sufficient
to make a People happy, unless it be administerd with Integrity. On ye
contrary, the Best sort of Governmt, when ye Form of it is preserved, and
ye *administration* corrupt, is most dangerous.'

305–10. The position of the Cambridge Platonists.

305. *graceless*] An equivoque.

311–16. Pope closes the epistle (cf. its beginning) with two figures
relating to the love that binds the universe. The love of the vine and elm
was often cited in this connection, and Newton's principle of attractive
force holding the planets in their orbits was assimilated in Pope's time to
older ideas of the diffusive love of God.

318. The central theme of much ethical writing in Pope's time and
before.

ARGUMENT OF THE FOURTH EPISTLE

Of the Nature and State of Man, *with respect to* Happiness. I. False
Notions of Happiness, Philosophical and Popular, answered from
VER. 19 to 76. II. *It is the End of all Men, and attainable by all,*
VER. 29. *God intends Happiness to be* equal; *and to be so, it must be*
social, *since all particular Happiness depends on general, and since
he governs by* general, *not* particular Laws, VER. 35. *As it is
necessary for* Order, *and the peace and welfare of* Society, *that*
external goods *should be* unequal, *Happiness is not made to consist
in these,* VER. 49. *But, notwithstanding the inequality, the* balance *of Happiness among Mankind is kept even by Providence, by
the two Passions of* Hope *and* Fear, VER. 67. III. *What the
Happiness of* Individuals *is, as far as is consistent with the constitution of this world; and that the* good Man *has here the advantage,*
VER. 77. *The error of imputing to* Virtue *what are only the calamities of* Nature, *or of* Fortune, VER. 93. IV. *The folly of expecting
that God should alter his general Laws in favour of particulars,*

VER. III. V. *That we are not judges who are good; but that who-*
ever they are, they must be happiest, VER. 131, &c. VI. *That*
external goods *are not the proper rewards, but often inconsistent*
with, or destructive of Virtue, VER. 167. *That even these can make*
no Man happy without Virtue: Instanced in Riches, VER. 185.
Honours, VER. 193. Nobility, VER. 205. Greatness, VER. 217.
Fame, VER. 237. Superior Talents, VER. 259. *With pictures of*
human Infelicity in Men possest of them all, VER. 269, &c. VII.
That Virtue only *constitutes a Happiness, whose object is* universal,
and whose prospect eternal, VER. 309, &c. *That the* perfection *of*
Virtue *and* Happiness *consists in a* conformity *to the* ORDER *of*
PROVIDENCE *here, and a* Resignation *to it here and hereafter,*
VER. 325, &c.

Oh Happiness! our being's end and aim!
Good, Pleasure, Ease, Content! whate'er thy name:
That something still which prompts th' eternal sigh,
For which we bear to live, or dare to die,
Which still so near us, yet beyond us lies,   5
O'er-look'd, seen double, by the fool, and wise.
Plant of celestial seed! if dropt below,
Say, in what mortal soil thou deign'st to grow?
Fair op'ning to some Court's propitious shine,
Or deep with di'monds in the flaming mine?   10
Twin'd with the wreaths Parnassian lawrels yield,
Or reap'd in iron harvests of the field?
Where grows?—where grows it not?—If vain our toil,
We ought to blame the culture, not the soil:
Fix'd to no spot is Happiness sincere,   15
'Tis no where to be found, or ev'ry where;
'Tis never to be bought, but always free,
And fled from Monarchs, ST. JOHN! dwells with thee.
    Ask of the Learn'd the way, the Learn'd are blind,
This bids to serve, and that to shun mankind;   20
Some place the bliss in action, some in ease,
Those call it Pleasure, and Contentment these;
Some sunk to Beasts, find pleasure end in pain;

Epistle IV. Of the NATURE and STATE of MAN, with respect to
HAPPINESS [P].
    8. *mortal*] The epithet is important. Where amongst human beings?
    10. Appropriate to the plant figure, on the old belief that minerals were
organisms ripened by the sun's rays.
    15. *sincere*] Unmixed, pure, as perhaps at II 255.

Some swell'd to Gods, confess ev'n Virtue vain;
Or indolent, to each extreme they fall,   25
To trust in ev'ry thing, or doubt of all.
   Who thus define it, say they more or less
Than this, that Happiness is Happiness?
   II. Take Nature's path, and mad Opinion's leave,
All states can reach it, and all heads conceive;   30
Obvious her goods, in no extreme they dwell,
There needs but thinking right, and meaning well;
And mourn our various portions as we please,
Equal is Common Sense, and Common Ease.
   Remember, Man, 'the Universal Cause   35
Acts not by partial, but by gen'ral laws;'
And makes what Happiness we justly call
Subsist not in the good of one, but all.
There's not a blessing Individuals find,
But some way leans and hearkens to the kind.   40
No Bandit fierce, no Tyrant mad with pride,
No cavern'd Hermit, rests self-satisfy'd.
Who most to shun or hate Mankind pretend,
Seek an admirer, or would fix a friend.
Abstract what others feel, what others think,   45
All pleasures sicken, and all glories sink;
Each has his share; and who would more obtain,
Shall find, the pleasure pays not half the pain.
   ORDER is Heav'n's first law; and this confest,
Some are, and must be, greater than the rest,   50
More rich, more wise; but who infers from hence
That such are happier, shocks all common sense.
Heav'n to Mankind impartial we confess,
If all are equal in their Happiness:
But mutual wants this Happiness increase,   55
All Nature's diff'rence keeps all Nature's peace.
Condition, circumstance is not the thing;
Bliss is the same in subject or in king,
In who obtain defence, or who defend,
In him who is, or him who finds a friend: 60

29 ff. HAPPINESS the END of all Men, and attainable by all [P].
The accepted view, in traditional ethics.

35 ff. GOD governs by *general* not *particular* Laws: intends Happiness
to be *equal*, and to be so, it must be *social*, since all perfect Happiness
depends on general [P].

49 ff. It is necessary for ORDER and the common Peace, that *External
Goods* be *unequal*, therefore Happiness is not constituted in these [P].

Heav'n breaths thro' ev'ry member of the whole
One common blessing, as one common soul.
But Fortune's gifts if each alike possest,
And each were equal, must not all contest?
If then to all Men Happiness was meant,   65
God in Externals could not place Content.
 Fortune her gifts may variously dispose,
And these be happy call'd, unhappy those;
But Heav'n's just balance equal will appear,
While those are plac'd in Hope, and these in Fear: 70
Not present good or ill, the joy or curse,
But future views of better, or of worse.
 Oh sons of earth! attempt ye still to rise,
By mountains pil'd on mountains, to the skies?
Heav'n still with laughter the vain toil surveys,   75
And buries madmen in the heaps they raise.
 III. Know, all the good that individuals find,
Or God and Nature meant to mere Mankind;
Reason's whole pleasure, all the joys of Sense,
Lie in three words, Health, Peace, and Competence.   80
But Health consists with Temperance alone,
And Peace, oh Virtue! Peace is all thy own.
The good or bad the gifts of Fortune gain,
But these less taste them, as they worse obtain.
Say, in pursuit of profit or delight,   85
Who risk the most, that take wrong means, or right?
Of Vice or Virtue, whether blest or curst,
Which meets contempt, or which compassion first?
Count all th'advantage prosp'rous Vice attains,
'Tis but what Virtue flies from and disdains: 90
And grant the bad what happiness they wou'd,
One they must want, which is, to pass for good.
 Oh blind to truth, and God's whole scheme below,
Who fancy Bliss to Vice, to Virtue Woe!
Who sees and follows that great scheme the best,   95
Best knows the blessing, and will most be blest.

67 ff. The balance of human happiness kept equal (notwithstanding *Externals*) by HOPE and FEAR. The Exemplification of this Truth, by a view of the *Equality* of *Happiness* in the several particular *Stations* of Life, were [was] design'd for the subject of a future Epistle [P].

77 ff. In what the Happiness of *Individuals* consists, and that the GOOD MAN has the advantage, even in this world [P].

84. *worse*] Adverbial.

93 ff. That no man is unhappy thro' VIRTUE [P].

But fools the Good alone unhappy call,
For ills or accidents that chance to all.
See FALKLAND dies, the virtuous and the just!
See god-like TURENNE prostrate on the dust!　　100
See SIDNEY bleeds amid the martial strife!
Was this their Virtue, or Contempt of Life?
Say, was it Virtue, more tho' Heav'n ne'er gave,
Lamented DIGBY! sunk thee to the grave?
Tell me, if Virtue made the Son expire,　　105
Why, full of days and honour, lives the Sire?
Why drew Marseille's good bishop purer breath,
When Nature sicken'd, and each gale was death?
Or why so long (in life if long can be)
Lent Heav'n a parent to the poor and me?　　110
　IV. What makes all physical or moral ill?
There deviates Nature, and here wanders Will.
God sends not ill; if rightly understood,
Or partial Ill is universal Good,
Or Change admits, or Nature lets it fall,　　115
Short and but rare, 'till Man improv'd it all.
We just as wisely might of Heav'n complain,
That righteous Abel was destroy'd by Cain;
As that the virtuous son is ill at ease,
When his lewd father gave the dire disease.　　120
Think we, like some weak Prince, th'Eternal Cause,
Prone for his fav'rites to reverse his laws?
　Shall burning Ætna, if a sage requires,
Forget to thunder, and recall her fires?

99. Falkland was killed at the battle of Newbury, 20 Sept. 1643. Clarendon refers to his 'prodigious parts', 'inimitable sweetness and delight', 'flowing and obliging . . . goodness to mankind', and 'simplicity and integrity of life'.

100. Turenne was slain 27 July 1675 at Sassbach in Baden. He was called 'the Support of the Throne, the Father of his Soldiers, the Delight of his Countrymen, and An Honour to Human Kind'.

101. Sidney was fatally wounded at Zutphen, 22 Sept. 1586.

103–6. Robert Digby died, aged 40, in 1726. His father, Lord Digby, was 74 when this fourth epistle was published. For Pope's epitaph on the son see p. 498.

107–8. Though most of the doctors and clergy who did not flee from Marseilles in 1720 fell victim to the plague, Belsunce survived.

110. Pope's mother died, aged 91, 7 June 1733.

116. 'till . . . all] E.g. in his fall and its consequences.

123–4. Empedocles was variously reported to have fallen into the crater of Aetna while trying to conceal himself, to have been the victim of an eruption which he was seeking to observe scientifically, or to have thrown

On air or sea new motions be imprest,   125
Oh blameless Bethel! to relieve thy breast?
When the loose mountain trembles from on high,
Shall gravitation cease, if you go by?
Or some old temple, nodding to its fall,
For Chartres' head reserve the hanging wall?   130
   v. But still this world (so fitted for the knave)
Contents us not. A better shall we have?
A kingdom of the Just then let it be:
But first consider how those Just agree.
The good must merit God's peculiar care;   135
But who, but God, can tell us who they are?
One thinks on Calvin Heav'n's own spirit fell,
Another deems him instrument of hell;
If Calvin feel Heav'n's blessing, or its rod,
This cries there is, and that, there is no God.   140
What shocks one part will edify the rest,
Nor with one system can they all be blest.
The very best will variously incline,
And what rewards your Virtue, punish mine.
'Whatever IS, is RIGHT.'—This world, 'tis true,   145
Was made for Cæsar—but for Titus too:
And which more blest? who chain'd his country, say,
Or he whose Virtue sigh'd to lose a day?
   'But sometimes Virtue starves, while Vice is fed.'
What then? Is the reward of Virtue bread?   150
That, Vice may merit; 'tis the price of toil;
The knave deserves it, when he tills the soil,
The knave deserves it when he tempts the main,

---

himself into the volcano to confirm reports that he had become a God.
Pope's lines fit best the second version.

125-6. Hugh Bethel (d. 1748), one of Pope's oldest and firmest friends.

130. Francis Chartres, a notorious scoundrel, lately dead. See Pope's
note to *Moral. Ess.*, III 20 (p. 571).

133. *kingdom . . . Just*] I.e. of the righteous in the sight of God.

141-4. I.e. the very best men will differ in their judgement, with the
result that what you take to be a reward of what you call virtue will seem
to me a punishment of what I call virtue.

145-6. *This . . . Caesar*] Alluding to the complaint of Cato in Addison's tragedy, IV iv 23-4:

        Justice gives way to force: the conquer'd world
        Is *Caesar's: Cato* has no business in it—

148. Alluding to the anecdote told of the Emperor Titus, that when
he lost a day, he sighed at night.

151. *That*] I.e. bread.

Where Folly fights for kings, or dives for gain.
The good man may be weak, be indolent,   155
Nor is his claim to plenty, but content.
But grant him Riches, your demand is o'er?
'No—shall the good want Health, the good want Pow'r?'
Add Health and Pow'r, and ev'ry earthly thing;
'Why bounded Pow'r? why private? why no king?'   160
Nay, why external for internal giv'n?
Why is not Man a God, and Earth a Heav'n?
Who ask and reason thus, will scarce conceive
God gives enough, while he has more to give:
Immense that pow'r, immense were the demand;   165
Say, at what part of nature will they stand?
    VI. What nothing earthly gives, or can destroy,
The soul's calm sun-shine, and the heart-felt joy,
Is Virtue's prize: A better would you fix?
Then give Humility a coach and six,   170
Justice a Conq'ror's sword, or Truth a gown,
Or Public Spirit its great cure, a Crown.
Weak, foolish man! will Heav'n reward us there
With the same trash mad mortals wish for here?
The Boy and Man an individual makes,   175
Yet sigh'st thou now for apples and for cakes?
Go, like the Indian, in another life
Expect thy dog, thy bottle, and thy wife:
As well as dream such trifles are assign'd,
As toys and empires, for a god-like mind.   180
Rewards, that either would to Virtue bring
No joy, or be destructive of the thing:
How oft by these at sixty are undone
The virtues of a saint at twenty-one!
    To whom can Riches give Repute, or Trust,   185
Content, or Pleasure, but the Good and Just?
Judges and Senates have been bought for gold,
Esteem and Love were never to be sold.
Oh fool! to think God hates the worthy mind,
The lover and the love of human-kind,   190
Whose life is healthful, and whose conscience clear;
Because he wants a thousand pounds a year.

160. I.e. why a private citizen?
169 ff. That *External Goods* are not the proper rewards of *Virtue*, often inconsistent with, or destructive of it; but that all these can make no man happy without *Virtue*. Instanced in each of them [P].
185 ff. 1. RICHES [P].

> Honour and shame from no Condition rise;
> Act well your part, there all the honour lies.
> Fortune in Men has some small diff'rence made,   195
> One flaunts in rags, one flutters in brocade,
> The cobler apron'd, and the parson gown'd,
> The friar hooded, and the monarch crown'd.
> 'What differ more (you cry) than crown and cowl?'
> I'll tell you, friend! a Wise man and a Fool.   200
> You'll find, if once the monarch acts the monk,
>
> Or, cobler-like, the parson will be drunk,
> Worth makes the man, and want of it, the fellow;
> The rest is all but leather or prunella.
>   Stuck o'er with titles and hung round with strings,   205
> That thou may'st be by kings, or whores of kings.
> Boast the pure blood of an illustrious race,
> In quiet flow from Lucrece to Lucrece;
> But by your father's worth if yours you rate,
> Count me those only who were good and great.   210
> Go! if your ancient, but ignoble blood
> Has crept thro' scoundrels ever since the flood,
> Go! and pretend your family is young;
> Nor own, your fathers have been fools so long.
> What can ennoble sots, or slaves, or cowards?   215
> Alas! not all the blood of all the HOWARDS.
>   Look next on Greatness; say where Greatness lies?
> 'Where, but among the Heroes and the Wise?'
> Heroes are much the same, the point's agreed,
> From Macedonia's madman to the Swede;   220
> The whole strange purpose of their lives, to find
> Or make, an enemy of all mankind!
> Not one looks backward, onward still he goes,
> Yet ne'er looks forward farther than his nose.
> No less alike the Politic and Wise,   225

193 ff. 2. HONOURS [P].

194. The central maxim (along with that which opens Epistle II) of traditional ethics.

204. I.e. dress: the cobbler's apron of leather, the clergyman's gown of prunella.

205-6. 3. TITLES [P].

205. A contemptuous image of carcasses dressed for the table (or for sacrifice) may be relevant here. For *Strings*, see p. 631, l. 14*n*.

207 ff. 4. BIRTH [P].

217 ff. 5. GREATNESS [P].

220. *Macedonia's madman*] Alexander the Great.

the Swede] Charles XII (1682–1718). 'His behavior at *Bender* shews him rather fitted for Bedlam than to govern a Nation.'

All sly slow things, with circumspective eyes:
Men in their loose unguarded hours they take,
Not that themselves are wise, but others weak.
But grant that those can conquer, these can cheat,
'Tis phrase absurd to call a Villain Great: 230
Who wickedly is wise, or madly brave,
Is but the more a fool, the more a knave.
Who noble ends by noble means obtains,
Or failing, smiles in exile or in chains,
Like good Aurelius let him reign, or bleed   235
Like Socrates, that Man is great indeed.
What's Fame? a fancy'd life in others breath,
A thing beyond us, ev'n before our death.
Just what you hear, you have, and what's unknown
The same (my Lord) if Tully's or your own.   240
All that we feel of it begins and ends
In the small circle of our foes or friends;
To all beside as much an empty shade,
An Eugene living, as a Cæsar dead,
Alike or when, or where, they shone, or shine,   245
Or on the Rubicon, or on the Rhine.
A Wit's a feather, and a Chief a rod;
An honest Man's the noblest work of God.
Fame but from death a villain's name can save,
As Justice tears his body from the grave,   250
When what t'oblivion better were resign'd,
Is hung on high, to poison half mankind.
All fame is foreign, but of true desert,
Plays round the head, but comes not to the heart:
One self-approving hour whole years out-weighs   255
Of stupid starers, and of loud huzzas;
And more true joy Marcellus exil'd feels,
Than Cæsar with a senate at his heels.
     In Parts superior what advantage lies?
Tell (for You can) what is it to be wise?   260

237 ff. 6. FAME [P].
243-4. *as much . . . dead*] I.e. a Eugene living is as much an empty
shade as a Caesar dead.
244. *Eugene*] Prince Eugene of Savoy (1663–1736), the commander of
the Imperial armies in the War of the Spanish Succession and the joint
hero with Marlborough of Blenheim and Malplaquet.
247. Alluding to the pen with which the wit writes, and the truncheon
of the general.
259 ff. 7. SUPERIOR PARTS [P].
260. *You*] I.e. Bolingbroke.

'Tis but to know how little can be known;
To see all others faults, and feel our own:
Condemn'd in bus'ness or in arts to drudge
Without a second, or without a judge:
Truths would you teach, or save a sinking land?   265
All fear, none aid you, and few understand.
Painful preheminence! yourself to view
Above life's weakness, and its comforts too.
  Bring then these blessings to a strict account,
Make fair deductions, see to what they mount.   270
How much of other each is sure to cost;
How each for other oft is wholly lost;
How inconsistent greater goods with these;
How sometimes life is risq'd, and always ease:
Think, and if still the things thy envy call,   275
Say, would'st thou be the Man to whom they fall?
To sigh for ribbands if thou art so silly,
Mark how they grace Lord Umbra, or Sir Billy:
Is yellow dirt the passion of thy life?
Look but on Gripus, or on Gripus' wife: 280
If Parts allure thee, think how Bacon shin'd,
The wisest, brightest, meanest of mankind:
Or ravish'd with the whistling of a Name,
See Cromwell, damn'd to everlasting fame!
If all, united, thy ambition call,   285
From ancient story learn to scorn them all.
There, in the rich, the honour'd, fam'd and great,
See the false scale of Happiness complete!
In hearts of Kings, or arms of Queens who lay,
How happy! those to ruin, these betray,   290
Mark by what wretched steps their glory grows,
From dirt and sea-weed as proud Venice rose;
In each how guilt and greatness equal ran,
And all that rais'd the Hero, sunk the Man.
Now Europe's laurels on their brows behold,   295
But stain'd with blood, or ill exchang'd for gold,
Then see them broke with toils, or sunk in ease,
Or infamous for plunder'd provinces.

277. *ribbands*] Cf. IV 205.
285. *all*] The worldly goods dealt with separately above, 185 ff. 275 ff.
288. *scale*] Ladder: cf. *steps* in 291.
290. I.e. what a form their happiness took, consisting in ruining the kings who trusted and betraying the queens who loved them.

Oh wealth ill-fated! which no act of fame
E'er taught to shine, or sanctify'd from shame!   300
What greater bliss attends their close of life?
Some greedy minion, or imperious wife,
The trophy'd arches, story'd halls invade,
And haunt their slumbers in the pompous shade.
Alas! not dazzled with their noon-tide ray,   305
Compute the morn and ev'ning to the day;
The whole amount of that enormous fame,
A Tale, that blends their glory with their shame!
    VII. Know then this truth (enough for Man to know)
'Virtue alone is Happiness below.'   310
The only point where human bliss stands still,
And tastes the good without the fall to ill,
Where only Merit constant pay receives,
Is blest in what it takes, and what it gives;
The joy unequal'd, if its end it gain,   315
And if it lose, attended with no pain:
Without satiety, tho' e'er so blest,
And but more relish'd as the more distress'd:
The broadest mirth unfeeling Folly wears,
Less pleasing far than Virtue's very tears.   320
Good, from each object, from each place acquir'd,
For ever exercis'd, yet never tir'd;
Never elated, while one man's oppress'd;
Never dejected, while another's bless'd;
And where no wants, no wishes can remain,   325
Since but to wish more Virtue, is to gain.
    See! the sole bliss Heav'n could on all bestow;
Which who but feels can taste, but thinks can know:
Yet poor with fortune, and with learning blind,
The bad must miss; the good, untaught, will find;   330

307. *enormous*] Cf. III 242.

308. *Tale*] 'Tally', as well as 'story': cf. 'compute' in 306.

309 ff. That VIRTUE only constitutes a Happiness, whose Object is *Universal*, and whose Prospect *Eternal* [P].

310. *Virtue*] Regularly identified with benevolence.

311. The allusion here seems to be to the pole, or central point, of a spherical body: which, during the rotatory motion of every other part, continues immovable and at rest.

313–14. I.e. the only point where merit uninterruptedly receives its reward, in the recipient bringing the happiness of receiving, in the giver the happiness of giving.

327 ff. That the *Perfection of Happiness* consists in a *Conformity* to the *Order* of *Providence* here, and a *Resignation* to it, here and hereafter [P].

Slave to no sect, who takes no private road,
But looks thro' Nature, up to Nature's God;
Pursues that Chain which links th'immense design,
Joins heav'n and earth, and mortal and divine;
Sees, that no being any bliss can know,   335
But touches some above, and some below;
Learns, from this union of the rising Whole,
The first, last purpose of the human soul;
And knows where Faith, Law, Morals, all began,
All end, in LOVE of GOD, and LOVE of MAN.   340
    For him alone, Hope leads from goal to goal,
And opens still, and opens on his soul,
'Till lengthen'd on to Faith, and unconfin'd,
It pours the bliss that fills up all the mind.
He sees, why Nature plants in Man alone   345
Hope of known bliss, and Faith in bliss unknown:
(Nature, whose dictates to no other kind
Are giv'n in vain, but what they seek they find)
Wise is her present; she connects in this
His greatest Virtue with his greatest Bliss,   350
At once his own bright prospect to be blest,
And strongest motive to assist the rest.
    Self-love thus push'd to social, to divine,
Gives thee to make thy neighbour's blessing thine.
Is this too little for the boundless heart?   355
Extend it, let thy enemies have part:
Grasp the whole worlds of Reason, Life, and Sense,
In one close system of Benevolence:
Happier as kinder, in whate'er degree,
And height of Bliss but height of Charity.   360
    God loves from Whole to Parts: but human soul
Must rise from Individual to the Whole.
Self-love but serves the virtuous mind to wake,
As the small pebble stirs the peaceful lake;
The centre mov'd, a circle strait succeeds,   365
Another still, and still another spreads,
Friend, parent, neighbour, first it will embrace,
His country next, and next all human race,

341. I.e. from such objectives as are represented in Ep. II and III
(through the extension of self-love into *caritas*) to those represented here:
cf. II 274, 285, III 145, with I 91 ff. and this passage.
    347-8. A traditional argument for immortality based ultimately on the
axiom, *Natura nihil facit frustra.*
    357. I.e. creatures with life only; creatures with feeling or 'sense'—as
animals; and creatures with reason—as men and angels.

Wide and more wide, th'o'erflowings of the mind
Take ev'ry creature in, of ev'ry kind;   370
Earth smiles around, with boundless bounty blest,
And Heav'n beholds its image in his breast.
   Come then, my Friend, my Genius, come along,
Oh master of the poet, and the song!
And while the Muse now stoops, or now ascends,   375
To Man's low passions, or their glorious ends,
Teach me, like thee, in various nature wise,
To fall with dignity, with temper rise;
Form'd by thy converse, happily to steer
From grave to gay, from lively to severe;   380
Correct with spirit, eloquent with ease,
Intent to reason, or polite to please.
Oh! while along the stream of Time thy name
Expanded flies, and gathers all its fame,
Say, shall my little bark attendant sail,   385
Pursue the triumph, and partake the gale?
When statesmen, heroes, kings, in dust repose,
Whose sons shall blush their fathers were thy foes,
Shall then this verse to future age pretend
Thou wert my guide, philosopher, and friend?   390
That urg'd by thee, I turn'd the tuneful art
From sounds to things, from fancy to the heart;
For Wit's false mirror held up Nature's light;
Shew'd erring Pride, WHATEVER IS, IS RIGHT;
That REASON, PASSION, answer one great aim;   395
That true SELF-LOVE and SOCIAL are the same;
That VIRTUE only makes our Bliss below;
And all our Knowledge is, OURSELVES TO KNOW.

389. *pretend*] In the Latin sense: stretch out before, i.e. proclaim.

Moral Essays

[Epistles to Several Persons]

Est brevitate opus, ut currat sententia, neu se
Impediat verbis lassas onerantibus aures:
Et sermone opus est modo tristi, sæpe jocoso,
Defendente vicem modo Rhetoris atque Poetæ,
Interdum urbani, parcentis viribus, atque
Extenuantis eas consultò.

HOR. [*Sat.* I. X. 9-14]

❀

Epistle I. To Richard Temple, Viscount Cobham

[written 1730-33; published Jan. 1734]

ARGUMENT OF THE FIRST EPISTLE

Of the Knowledge *and* Characters *of* Men. *That it is not sufficient for this knowledge to consider Man in the* Abstract: Books *will not serve the purpose, nor yet our own* Experience *singly,* v. 1. *General maxims, unless they be formed upon* both, *will be but notional,* v. 10. *Some Peculiarity in every man, characteristic to himself, yet varying from himself,* v. 15. *The further difficulty of separating and fixing this, arising from our own Passions, Fancies, Faculties,* &c. v. 23. *The shortness of Life, to observe in, and the uncertainty of the* Principles of Action *in men, to observe by,* v. 29, &c. *Our own Principle of action often hid from ourselves* v. 41. *No judging of the* Motives *from the actions; the same actions proceeding from contrary Motives, and the same Motives influencing contrary actions,* v. 51. *Yet to form* Characters, *we can only take the* strongest actions *of a man's life, and try to make them* agree: *The utter uncertainty of this, from* Nature *itself, and from* Policy, v. 71. Characters *given according to the* rank *of men in the world,* v. 87. *And some reason for it,* v. 92. Education *alters the* Nature, *or at*

Heading] First printed in 1733 [P]. Sir Richard Temple (1675–1749), Whig politician and soldier, raised to the peerage as Viscount Cobham on the Hanoverian succession, became a Field Marshal in 1742. He opposed the Government in the debates on the Excise Bill (1733) and thereafter was one of the Opposition Whigs. He lived at Stowe, where he entertained his friends and erected monuments and temples to their memories in the elaborate landscape gardens.

least Character *of many,* v. 101. *Some few Characters plain, but in general confounded, dissembled, or inconsistent,* v. 122. *The same man utterly different in different places and seasons,* v. 130. *Unimaginable weaknesses in the greatest,* v. 140, &c. *Nothing constant and certain but* God *and* Nature, v. 154. Actions, Passions, Opinions, Manners, Humours, *or* Principles *all subject to change. No judging by* Nature, *from* v. 158 to 173. *It only remains to find (if we can) his* RULING PASSION: *That will certainly influence all the rest, and can reconcile the seeming or real inconsistency of all his actions,* v. 174. *Instanced in the extraordinary character of* Wharton, v. 179. *A caution against mistaking* second qualities *for* first, *which will destroy all possibility of the knowledge of mankind,* v. 210. *Examples of the strength of the* Ruling Passion, *and its continuation to the last breath,* v. 222, &c.

Yes, you despise the man to Books confin'd,
Who from his study rails at human kind;
Tho' what he learns, he speaks and may advance
Some gen'ral maxims, or be right by chance.
The coxcomb bird, so talkative and grave,   5
That from his cage cries Cuckold, Whore, and Knave,
Tho' many a passenger he rightly call,
You hold him no Philosopher at all.
  And yet the fate of all extremes is such,
Men may be read, as well as Books too much.   10
To Observations which ourselves we make,
We grow more partial for th' observer's sake;
To written Wisdom, as another's, less:
Maxims are drawn from Notions, these from Guess.
  There's some Peculiar in each leaf and grain,   15
Some unmark'd fibre, or some varying vein:
Shall only Man be taken in the gross?
Grant but as many sorts of Mind as Moss.
  That each from other differs, first confess;
Next, that he varies from himself no less: 20
Add Nature's, Custom's, Reason's, Passion's strife,
And all Opinion's colours cast on life.
  Yet more; the diff'rence is as great between

14. *Notions*] Defined by Locke as complex ideas, with 'their original and constant existence more in the thoughts of men than in the reality of things'.
  these] i.e. observations. The general sceptical argument developed in the first half of the Epistle derives from Montaigne.
  18. There are above 300 sorts of Moss observed by Naturalists [P].

The optics seeing, as the objects seen.
All Manners take a tincture from our own,   25
Or come discolour'd thro' our Passions shown.
Or Fancy's beam enlarges, multiplies,
Contracts, inverts, and gives ten thousand dyes.
　　Our depths who fathoms, or our shallows finds,
Quick whirls, and shifting eddies, of our minds?   30
Life's stream for Observation will not stay,
It hurries all too fast to mark their way.
In vain sedate reflections we would make,
When half our knowledge we must snatch, not take.
On human actions reason tho' you can,   35
It may be reason, but it is not man:
His Principle of action once explore,
That instant 'tis his Principle no more.
Like following life thro' creatures you dissect,
You lose it in the moment you detect.   40
　　Oft in the Passions' wild rotation tost,
Our spring of action to ourselves is lost:
Tir'd, not determin'd, to the last we yield,
And what comes then is master of the field.
As the last image of that troubled heap,   45
When Sense subsides, and Fancy sports in sleep,
(Tho' past the recollection of the thought)
Becomes the stuff of which our dream is wrought:
Something as dim to our internal view,
Is thus, perhaps, the cause of most we do.   50
　　In vain the Sage, with retrospective eye,
Would from th' apparent What conclude the Why,
Infer the Motive from the Deed, and show,
That what we chanc'd was what we meant to do.
Behold! If Fortune or a Mistress frowns,   55
Some plunge in bus'ness, others shave their crowns:
To ease the Soul of one oppressive weight,
This quits an Empire, that embroils a State:
The same adust complexion has impell'd

39. Stephen Hales the physiologist was a neighbour and friend of
Pope's. See *Moral Es*. ii, 198*n*, p. 566.

46. *Sense*] consciousness.

56. *shave their crowns*] become monks.

59. *adust complexion*] originally a medical term; 'characterized by dryness of the body, heat, thirst, burnt colour of the blood and little serum
in it' (*OED*).

impell'd] The rhyme with *field* appears to be one of the very few false
rhymes in Pope.

Charles to the Convent, Philip to the Field.   60
    Not always Actions show the man: we find
Who does a kindness, is not therefore kind;
Perhaps Prosperity becalm'd his breast,
Perhaps the Wind just shifted from the east:
Not therefore humble he who seeks retreat,   65
Pride guides his steps, and bids him shun the great:
Who combats bravely is not therefore brave,
He dreads a death-bed like the meanest slave:
Who reasons wisely is not therefore wise,
His pride in Reas'ning, not in Acting lies.   70
    But grant that Actions best discover man;
Take the most strong, and sort them as you can.
The few that glare each character must mark,
You balance not the many in the dark.
What will you do with such as disagree?   75
Suppress them half, or call them Policy?
Must then at once (the character to save)
The plain rough Hero turn a crafty Knave?
Alas! in truth the man but chang'd his mind,
Perhaps was sick, in love, or had not din'd.   80
Ask why from Britain Cæsar would retreat?
Cæsar himself might whisper he was beat.
Why risk the world's great empire for a Punk?
Cæsar perhaps might answer he was drunk.
But, sage historians! 'tis your task to prove   85
One action Conduct; one, heroic Love.
    'Tis from high Life high Characters are drawn;
A Saint in Crape is twice a Saint in Lawn;
A Judge is just, a Chanc'lor juster still;
A Gownman, learn'd; a Bishop, what you will;   90
Wise, if a Minister; but, if a King,
More wise, more learn'd, more just, more ev'rything.
Court-virtues bear, like Gems, the highest rate,
Born where Heav'n's influence scarce can penetrate:
In life's low vale, the soil the virtues like,   95
They please as Beauties, here as Wonders strike.

60. Charles V. ⟨and⟩ Philip II [P].

83-4. The substitution of Caesar for Peter the Great in 1744 has
landed Pope in a historical mis-statement. Drunkenness was never one of
Caesar's vices. And 'Punk'—though perhaps the right word for the
Lithuanian peasant girl who was successively Peter's lover, consort, and
successor (as Catherine I)—does not seem to suit Cleopatra.

88. *Lawn* is the fine linen used for the sleeves of bishops; *crape* is the
thin worsted that the inferior clergy generally wore.

Tho' the same Sun with all-diffusive rays
Blush in the Rose, and in the Diamond blaze,
We prize the stronger effort of his pow'r,
And justly set the Gem above the Flow'r.   100
  'Tis Education forms the common mind,
Just as the Twig is bent, the Tree's inclin'd.
Boastful and rough, your first son is a 'Squire;
The next a Tradesman, meek, and much a lyar;
Tom struts a Soldier, open, bold, and brave;   105
Will sneaks a Scriv'ner, an exceeding knave:
Is he a Churchman? then he's fond of pow'r: ⎫
A Quaker? sly: A Presbyterian? sow'r: ⎬
A smart Free-thinker? all things in an hour. ⎭
  True, some are open, and to all men known;   110
Others so very close, they're hid from none;
(So Darkness strikes the sense no less than Light)
Thus gracious CHANDOS is belov'd at sight,
And ev'ry child hates Shylock, tho' his soul
Still sits at squat, and peeps not from its hole.   115
At half mankind when gen'rous Manly raves,
All know 'tis Virtue, for he thinks them knaves:
When universal homage Umbra pays,
All see 'tis Vice, and itch of vulgar praise.
When Flatt'ry glares, all hate it in a Queen,   120
While one there is who charms us with his Spleen.
  But these plain Characters we rarely find;
Tho' strong the bent, yet quick the turns of mind:

101–9. Pope is satirizing the vulgar error and prevalent neo-classic notion that all members of a single profession share the same characteristics.

106. *Scriv'ner*] Notary; and consequently one who 'received money to place out at interest, and who supplied those who wanted to raise money on security' (*OED*).

109. *Free-thinker*] A 'society' Deist or atheist. See also ll. 162–5.

113. James Brydges, first Duke of Chandos (1673–1744). Whig million-aire. Chandos was a lavish patron of all the arts and his mansion at Cannons, near Edgware, was one of the most magnificent in England. Pope and his friends were irritated and distressed by a whispering campaign which identified the character of Timon (*Moral Es.* iv, ll. 99–176) with Chandos. The compliment here was apparently intended to remove the impression that Pope had satirized the Duke as Timon.

115. Cf.   him there they found
                 Squat like a Toad.
Par. Lost, iv 799–800. Another reminiscence of this passage is in *Epistle to Arbuthnot*, 319, p. 608.

116. *Manly*] The 'plain dealer' in Wycherley's comedy (1676).

121. *his Spleen*] His misanthropy. The compliment appears to be intended for Swift.

Or puzzling Contraries confound the whole,
Or Affectations quite reverse the soul.   125
Or Falshood serves the dull for policy,
And in the Cunning, Truth itself's a lye:
Unthought-of Frailties cheat us in the Wise,
The Fool lies hid in inconsistencies.
　　See the same man, in vigour, in the gout;   130
Alone, in company; in place, or out;
Early at Bus'ness, and at Hazard late;
Mad at a Fox-chace, wise at a Debate;
Drunk at a Borough, civil at a Ball,
Friendly at Hackney, faithless at Whitehall.   135
　　Catius is ever moral, ever grave,
Thinks who endures a knave, is next a knave,
Save just at dinner—then prefers, no doubt,
A Rogue with Ven'son to a Saint without.
　　Who would not praise Patritio's high desert,   140
His hand unstain'd, his uncorrupted heart,
His comprehensive head! all Int'rests weigh'd,
All Europe sav'd, yet Britain not betray'd.
He thanks you not, his pride is in Picquette,
New-market-fame, and judgment at a Bett.   145
　　What made (say Montagne, or more sage Charron!)
Otho a warrior, Cromwell a buffoon?
A perjur'd Prince a leaden Saint revere,

126. I.e. *flat falsehood* is often, if unexpectedly, to be met with in the stupid.

135. I.e. full of professions, when a candidate for a seat in Parliament (the Middlesex members were nominated at Hackney) and faithless to those professions when the object of them is secure.

136. *Catius*] The epicure in Horace, *Sat.*, II iv.

140. *Patritio*] Sidney, first Earl of Godolphin (1645–1712).

143. *Britain not betray'd*] The Tories had accused Marlborough of prolonging the war against France to serve his own interest.

146. 'Charron was an admirer of Montagne; had contracted a strict friendship with him; and has transferred an infinite number of his thoughts into his famous book *De la Sagesse*; but his moderating everywhere the extravagant Pyrrhonism of his friend, is the reason why the poet calls him *more sage Charron*' [Warburton].

147. M. Salvius Otho, Roman emperor from January to April 69, had been a companion of Nero in his debaucheries. On the news of the revolt of Vitellius reaching Rome, Otho is said by Tacitus to have led his army against the enemy in person and on foot. Cromwell's buffooneries are a relic of royalist prejudice.

148. Louis XI of France wore in his Hat a leaden image of the Virgin Mary, which when he swore by, he feared to break his oath [P].

A godless Regent tremble at a Star?
The throne a Bigot keep, a Genius quit,   150
Faithless thro' Piety, and dup'd thro' Wit?
Europe a Woman, Child, or Dotard rule,
And just her wisest monarch made a fool?
　Know, God and Nature only are the same:
In Man, the judgment shoots at flying game,   155
A bird of passage! gone as soon as found,
Now in the Moon perhaps, now under ground.
　Ask men's Opinions: Scoto now shall tell
How Trade increases, and the World goes well;
Strike off his Pension, by the setting sun,   160
And Britain, if not Europe, is undone.
　That gay Free-thinker, a fine talker once,
What turns him now a stupid silent dunce?
Some God, or Spirit he has lately found,
Or chanc'd to meet a Minister that frown'd.   165
　Manners with Fortunes, Humours turn with Climes,
Tenets with Books, and Principles with Times.
　Judge we by Nature? Habit can efface,
Int'rest o'ercome, or Policy take place:
By Actions? those Uncertainty divides: 170
By Passions? these Dissimulation hides:
Opinions? they still take a wider range:
Find, if you can, in what you cannot change.
　Search then the Ruling Passion: There alone,
The Wild are constant, and the Cunning known;   175
The Fool consistent, and the False sincere;
Priests, Princes, Women, no dissemblers here.

149. Philip Duke of Orleans, Regent of France in the minority of
Louis XV. superstitious in judicial astrology, tho' an unbeliever in all
religion. [P]
　150-1. Philip V of Spain ⟨d. 1746⟩, who, after renouncing the throne
for Religion, resum'd it to gratify his Queen; and Victor Amadeus II.
King of Sardinia ⟨d. 1732⟩, who resign'd the crown, and trying to reas-
sume it, was imprisoned till his death [P].
　152-3. The 'Child' is Louis XV, the 'wisest monarch' no doubt Victor
Amadeus II, the 'Woman' probably the Czarina Anna Ivanovna (Empress
1730-40) and the 'Dotard' Clement XII (Pope 1730-41).
　158-61. James Johnston (1655-1737), a Twickenham neighbour of
Pope's, Secretary of State for Scotland, 1692-6. Johnston's 'Pension' was
the grant of £5,000, received in 1697 and paid out of the annual tithes in
the rents of the nonjuring Scotch bishops. Johnston was a Whig and a
great favourite of Queen Caroline.
　162. *Free-thinker*] See l. 109*n*, above.

This clue once found, unravels all the rest,
The prospect clears, and Wharton stands confest.
Wharton, the scorn and wonder of our days,   180
Whose ruling Passion was the Lust of Praise;
Born with whate'er could win it from the Wise,
Women and Fools must like him or he dies;
Tho' wond'ring Senates hung on all he spoke,
The Club must hail him master of the joke.   185
Shall parts so various aim at nothing new?
He'll shine a Tully and a Wilmot too.
Then turns repentant, and his God adores
With the same spirit that he drinks and whores;
Enough if all around him but admire,   190
And now the Punk applaud, and now the Fryer.
Thus with each gift of nature and of art,
And wanting nothing but an honest heart;
Grown all to all, from no one vice exempt,
And most contemptible, to shun contempt;   195
His Passion still, to covet gen'ral praise,
His Life, to forfeit it a thousand ways;
A constant Bounty which no friend has made;
An angel Tongue, which no man can persuade;
A Fool, with more of Wit than half mankind,   200
Too quick for Thought, for Action too refin'd;
A Tyrant to the wife his heart approves;

179. *Wharton*] Philip, Duke of Wharton (1698–1731), visited Old Pretender at Avignon and Marie Beatrix at St. Germain, 1716; created Duke of Wharton 1718, to retain him in the Whig interest; adopted in 1726 the cause of 'James III', urging a Spanish invasion of England, and became a Roman Catholic; served against Gibraltar, 1727, and outlawed, 1729; died in Catalonia.

184. His most dazzling parliamentary performance was his defence of Pope's friend Atterbury in the House of Lords in May 1723.

185. He was president of one of the short-lived Hell-Fire Clubs.

187. *Wilmot*] John Willmot, Earl of Rochester, famous for his Wit and Extravagancies in the time of Charles the Second [P].

188–9. 'He has public devotions twice a day, and assists at them in person with exemplary devotion; and there is nothing pleasanter than the remarks of some pious ladies on the conversion of so great a sinner' (Lady Mary Wortley Montagu).

191. *Fryer*] Wharton became a Roman Catholic in 1726 and entered a convent for a brief period in 1729.

198. One beneficiary of Wharton's 'Bounty' was Pope's friend Edward Young, who dedicated his tragedy *The Revenge* (1721) to the Duke and was said to have received £2,000 for the compliment.

202. His first wife (by a Fleet marriage in 1715, when Wharton was only sixteen) was Martha Holmes (d. 1726). Although he abandoned or

A Rebel to the very king he loves;
He dies, sad out-cast of each church and state,
And (harder still) flagitious, yet not great!   205
Ask you why Wharton broke thro' ev'ry rule?
'Twas all for fear the Knaves should call him Fool.
    Nature well known, no prodigies remain,
Comets are regular, and Wharton plain.
    Yet, in this search, the wisest may mistake,   210
If second qualities for first they take,
When Catiline by rapine swell'd his store,
When Cæsar made a noble dame a whore,
In this the Lust, in that the Avarice
Were means, not ends; Ambition was the vice.   215
That very Cæsar, born in Scipio's days,
Had aim'd, like him, by Chastity at praise.
Lucullus, when Frugality could charm,
Had roasted turnips in the Sabin farm.
In vain th' observer eyes the builder's toil,   220
But quite mistakes the scaffold for the pile.
    In this one Passion man can strength enjoy,
As Fits give vigour, just when they destroy.
Time, that on all things lays his lenient hand,
Yet tames not this; it sticks to our last sand.   225
Consistent in our follies and our sins,
Here honest Nature ends as she begins.

---

neglected her for most of their married life, he had occasional fits of affection. His second wife, Maria Theresa O'Byrne, seems to have been better treated.

203. A bill of indictment was preferred against him for High Treason. He had been aide-de-camp to the Conde de los Torres at the unsuccessful siege of Gibraltar by the Spanish in 1727. He was outlawed by a resolution of the House of Lords on 3 April 1729.

204. This is an overstatement. Wharton died a member of the Church of Rome, in a Franciscan convent at Poblet in Catalonia, and attired in the habit of the Order.

209. The study of comets had been notably advanced in Pope's time by Newton (*De Systemate Mundi*, 1687) and Halley (*Synopsis Astronomiae Cometicae*, 1705).

212. *Catiline*] L. Sergius Catilina, the notorious conspirator.

213. *noble dame*] Servilia, the sister of Cato and mother of Brutus.

216. *Scipio*] P. Cornelius Scipio Africanus Major, the conqueror of Hannibal.

218. *Lucullus*] L. Licinius Lucullus, the conqueror of Mithridates, devoted his retirement to the exploitation of a natural genius for luxury.

224. *lenient*] softening.

Behold a rev'rend sire, whom want of grace
Has made the father of a nameless race,
Shov'd from the wall perhaps, or rudely press'd   230
By his own son, that passes by unbless'd;
Still to his wench he crawls on knocking knees,
And envies ev'ry sparrow that he sees.

A salmon's belly, Helluo, was thy fate,
The doctor call'd, declares all help too late.   235
Mercy! cries Helluo, mercy on my soul!
Is there no hope? Alas!—then bring the jowl.

The frugal Crone, whom praying priests attend,
Still tries to save the hallow'd taper's end,
Collects her breath, as ebbing life retires,   240
For one puff more, and in that puff expires.

'Odious! in woollen! 'twould a Saint provoke,
(Were the last words that poor Narcissa spoke)
No, let a charming Chintz, and Brussels lace
Wrap my cold limbs, and shade my lifeless face: 245
One would not, sure, be frightful when one's dead—
And—Betty—give this Cheek a little Red.'

Old Politicians chew on wisdom past,
And totter on in bus'ness to the last;
As weak, as earnest, and as gravely out,   250

228–33. Perhaps intended for Lancelot Blackburne (1658–1743), the
disreputable Archbishop of York. See also *1740*, l. 58 (p. 829), and *Sob.
Adv.*, ll. 43–4 (p. 669).
234–7. 'When *Philoxenus* the *Epicure* had fallen desperately sick upon
glutting himself on a delicate and costly fish, perceiving he was to die, he
calls for the remainder of his fish, and eats it up, and dies a true Martyr to
his belly' (Hales, *Golden Remains*).
242. *Odious*] Like *frightful* (l. 246) this was fashionable feminine slang.
Congreve's Millamant uses both words. See also *Moral Es.* ii, l. 40,
p. 561.
242–7. This story, as well as the others, is founded on fact, tho' the
author had the goodness not to mention the names. Several attribute this
in particular to a very celebrated Actress, who, in detestation of the
thought of being buried in woollen, gave these her last orders with her
dying breath. [P] The actress was Anne Oldfield (1683–1730), who is
attacked, perhaps because she was Cibber's ally, more than once by Pope.
(See *Sober Advice*, ll. 4–5, *Imit. Hor.*, *Ep.*, ii i 331.) Narcissa, the heroine
of Cibber's *Love's Last Shift*, was one of her stock parts. A series of Acts
of Parliament making it illegal to bury the dead in anything but woollens
had been passed from 1666 onwards as a protective measure against
foreign linen.
247. *Betty*] A generic name in the eighteenth century for the lady's
maid. Compare *Rape of Lock*, 1 148 (p. 223).
249. *bus'ness*] in the conduct of public affairs.

As sober Lanesb'row dancing in the gout.
  The Courtier smooth, who forty years had shin'd
An humble servant to all human kind,
Just brought out this, when scarce his tongue could stir,
'If—where I'm going—I could serve you, Sir?'   255
  'I give and I devise, (old Euclio said,
And sigh'd) My lands and tenements to Ned.'
Your money, Sir? 'My money, Sir, what all?
Why,—if I must—(then wept) I give it Paul.'
The Manor, Sir?—'The Manor! hold,' he cry'd,   260
'Not that,—I cannot part with that'—and dy'd.
  And you! brave COBHAM, to the latest breath
Shall feel your ruling passion strong in death:
Such in those moments as in all the past,
'Oh, save my Country, Heav'n!' shall be your last.   265

251. *Lanesb'row*] An ancient Nobleman, who continued this practice long after his legs were disabled by the gout. Upon the death of Prince George of Denmark, he demanded an audience of the Queen, to advise her to preserve her health and dispel her grief by *Dancing* [P]. James Lane, second Viscount Lanesborough (1650–1724).
256–61. Euclio is the miser in Plautus' *Aulularia*.

Epistle II. To a Lady

OF THE CHARACTERS OF WOMEN[1]

[written 1732–34; published 1735]

ARGUMENT

Of the Characters of *Women* (consider'd only as contradistin-guished from the other Sex.) That these are yet more inconsistent and incomprehensible than those of Men, of which Instances are given even from such Characters as are plainest, and most strongly mark'd; as in the *Affected*, Ver. 7, &c. The *Soft-natur'd*. 29. the *Cunning*, 45. the *Whimsical*, 53. the *Wits and Refiners*, 87. the *Stupid* and *Silly*, 101. How Contrarieties run thro' them all.
  But tho' the *Particular Characters* of this Sex are more various than those of Men, the *General Characteristick*, as to the *Ruling Passion*, is more uniform and confin'd. In what That lies, and

[1] Of the CHARACTERS of WOMEN, *treating of this Sex only as con-tradistinguished from the other* [P]. The lady was Martha Blount ('Patty'; 1690–1763), a Catholic and almost certainly Pope's mistress, to whom his devotion remained unbroken. By his will he left her £1,000, all his goods and chattels and a life-interest in the rest of his estate.

whence it *proceeds*, 207, *&c.* Men are best known in publick
Life, Women in private, 199. What are the *Aims*, and the *Fate* of
the Sex, both as to *Power* and *Pleasure?* 219, 231, &c. Advice for
their true Interest, 249. The Picture of an esteemable Woman,
made up of the best kind of Contrarieties, 269, *&c.*

Nothing so true as what you once let fall,
'Most Women have no Characters at all'.
Matter too soft a lasting mark to bear,
And best distinguish'd by black, brown, or fair.
  How many pictures of one Nymph we view,   5
All how unlike each other, all how true!
Arcadia's Countess, here, in ermin'd pride,
Is there, Pastora by a fountain side:
Here Fannia, leering on her own good man,
Is there, a naked Leda with a Swan.   10
Let then the Fair one beautifully cry,
In Magdalen's loose hair and lifted eye,
Or drest in smiles of sweet Cecilia shine,
With simp'ring Angels, Palms, and Harps divine;
Whether the Charmer sinner it, or saint it,   15
If Folly grows romantic, I must paint it.
  Come then, the colours and the ground prepare!
Dip in the Rainbow, trick her off in Air,
Chuse a firm Cloud, before it fall, and in it
Catch, ere she change, the Cynthia of this minute.   20

1. That their particular Characters are not so strongly mark'd as those
of Men, seldom so fixed, and still more inconsistent with themselves [P].
  7–13. Attitudes in which several ladies affected to be drawn, and sometimes one lady in them all.—The poet's politeness and complaisance to
the sex is observable in this instance, amongst others, that, whereas in the
Characters of Men he has sometimes made use of real names, in the
Characters of Women always fictitious [P].
  Arcadia's Countess] The full title of Sir Philip Sidney's romance was
(in compliment to his sister Mary) *The Countesse of Pembrokes Arcadia*
(1590). Pope's countess may have been Margaret, first wife of the eighth
Earl of Pembroke, whose portrait with a lamb is still at Wilton. This
would explain 'Pastora'. The other 'attitudes' may be due to a confused
recollection by Pope of two fine double portraits of a husband and wife
(Fannia), a version of Leonardo's 'Leda and the Swan', and two Mary
Magdalens which are also at Wilton.
  16. *romantic*] extravagant.
  17–18. Note the technical terms from painting. To dip is to immerse
in a colouring solution; to trick is to sketch in outline.

Rufa, whose eye quick-glancing o'er the Park,
Attracts each light gay meteor of a Spark,
Agrees as ill with Rufa studying Locke,
As Sappho's diamonds with her dirty smock,
Or Sappho at her toilet's greazy task,　　　　25
With Sappho fragrant at an ev'ning Mask:
So morning Insects that in muck begun,
Shine, buzz, and fly-blow in the setting-sun.
　　How soft is Silia! fearful to offend,
The Frail one's advocate, the Weak one's friend:　30
To her, Calista prov'd her conduct nice,
And good Simplicius asks of her advice.
Sudden, she storms! she raves! You tip the wink,
But spare your censure; Silia does not drink.
All eyes may see from what the change arose,　　35
All eyes may see—a Pimple on her nose.
　　Papillia, wedded to her doating spark,
Sighs for the shades—'How charming is a Park!'
A Park is purchas'd, but the Fair he sees
All bath'd in tears—'Oh odious, odious Trees!'　40
　　Ladies, like variegated Tulips, show,

'Tis to their Changes that their charms they owe;
Their happy Spots the nice admirer take,
Fine by defect, and delicately weak.
'Twas thus Calypso once each heart alarm'd,　　45
Aw'd without Virtue, without Beauty charm'd;
Her Tongue bewitch'd as odly as her Eyes,
Less Wit than Mimic, more a Wit than wise:
Strange graces still, and stranger flights she had,
Was just not ugly, and was just not mad;　　　50
Yet ne'er so sure our passion to create,

21. Instances of contrarieties given even from such Characters as are most strongly mark'd and seemingly therefore most consistent. As I. In the *Affected*, v. 21 &c. [P].

Rufa] Red-head, popularly deemed lubricious.

24. *Sappho*] Lady Mary Wortley Montagu.

29–40. Contrarieties in the *Soft-natured* [P].

31. *Calista*] Calista was the guilty heroine of Rowe's *The Fair Penitent* (1703).

nice] Punctilious, though with a flavour of contempt.

32. *Simplicius*] The historical Simplicius was a sixth-century neo-platonist.

37. *Papillia*] *Papilio* is Latin for butterfly.

45–52. III. Contrarieties in the *Cunning* and *Artful* [P]. Calypso represents a rewriting of the opening lines of 'Sylvia, a Fragment', p. 492.

As when she touch'd the brink of all we hate.
  Narcissa's nature, tolerably mild,
To make a wash, would hardly stew a child,
Has ev'n been prov'd to grant a Lover's pray'r,   55
And paid a Tradesman once to make him stare,
Gave alms at Easter, in a Christian trim,
And made a Widow happy, for a whim.
Why then declare Good-nature is her scorn,
When 'tis by that alone she can be born?   60
Why pique all mortals, yet affect a name?
A fool to Pleasure, and a slave to Fame:
Now deep in Taylor and the Book of Martyrs,
Now drinking citron with his Grace and Chartres.
Now Conscience chills her, and now Passion burns;   65
And Atheism and Religion take their turns;
A very Heathen in the carnal part,
Yet still a sad, good Christian at her heart.
  See Sin in State, majestically drunk,
Proud as a Peeress, prouder as a Punk;   70
Chaste to her Husband, frank to all beside,
A teeming Mistress, but a barren Bride.
What then? let Blood and Body bear the fault,
Her Head's untouch'd, that noble Seat of Thought:
Such this day's doctrine—in another fit   75
She sins with Poets thro' pure Love of Wit.
What has not fir'd her bosom or her brain?
Cæsar and Tall-boy, Charles and Charlema'ne.
As Helluo, late Dictator of the Feast,

53–68. IV. In the *Whimsical* [P]. Narcissa, like Calypso, has been made
up from the *disjecta membra* of 'Sylvia, a Fragment'.

54. *wash*] Washes for the hair or the skin were normally home-made in
the eighteenth century.

63. *Taylor*] Jeremy Taylor's *Holy Living and Holy Dying* had reached
its twenty-fourth edition in 1727.

Book of Martyrs] John Foxe's martyrology, *Actes and Monuments*
(1563) reached a ninth edition in 1684.

64. *citron*] Citron-water, brandy flavoured with citron- or lemon-peel.
his Grace] Philip Duke of Wharton (see note to *Moral Es.* i, 179, p. 556).
Chartres] See *To Bathurst*, 20n, p. 571.

69–87. V. In the *Lewd* and *Vicious* [P]. The lines and note were not
added until the 1744 edition, presumably because the character was of a
contemporary, though her identity remains uncertain.

73. *fault*] Pope regularly rhymes 'fault' with such words as 'taught' (see
l. 212), 'brought' (*Dunciad*, 1 226), 'ought' (*Eloisa to Abelard*, 184).

78. *Tall-boy*] The booby young lover in Richard Brome's comedy *The
Jovial Crew* (1641), which was still a stock piece in the eighteenth century.
Charles] Used generically for the typical footman.

79. *Helluo*] Glutton, in Latin.

The Nose of Hautgout, and the Tip of Taste, 80
Critick'd your wine, and analyz'd your meat,
Yet on plain Pudding deign'd at-home to eat;
So Philomedé, lect'ring all mankind
On the soft Passion, and the Taste refin'd,
Th' Address, the Delicacy—stoops at once, 85
And makes her hearty meal upon a Dunce.
  Flavia's a Wit, has too much sense to Pray,
To Toast our wants and wishes, is her way;
Nor asks of God, but of her Stars to give
The mighty blessing, 'while we live, to live.' 90
Then all for Death, that Opiate of the soul!
Lucretia's dagger, Rosamonda's bowl.
Say, what can cause such impotence of mind?
A Spark too fickle, or a Spouse too kind.
Wise Wretch! with Pleasures too refin'd to please, 95
With too much Spirit to be e'er at ease,
With too much Quickness ever to be taught,
With too much Thinking to have common Thought:
Who purchase Pain with all that Joy can give,
And die of nothing but a Rage to live. 100
  Turn then from Wits; and look on Simo's Mate,
No Ass so meek, no Ass so obstinate:
Or her, that owns her Faults, but never mends,
Because she's honest, and the best of Friends:
Or her, whose life the Church and Scandal share, 105
For ever in a Passion, or a Pray'r:
Or her, who laughs at Hell, but (like her Grace)
Cries, 'Ah! how charming if there's no such place!'
Or who in sweet vicissitude appears
Of Mirth and Opium, Ratafie and Tears, 110
The daily Anodyne, and nightly Draught,
To kill those foes to Fair ones, Time and Thought.
Woman and Fool are two hard things to hit,
For true No-meaning puzzles more than Wit.
  But what are these to great Atossa's mind? 115

80. *Hautgout*] 'Anything with a strong relish or strong scent, as over-
kept venison or game' (Johnson).
  87–100. VI. Contrarieties in the Witty and Refin'd [P].
  98. *common thought*] Common sense.
  108. *charming*] Feminine slang, like *odious* (l. 140).
  110. *Ratafie*] A sort of cherry brandy made with peach and apricot
stones.
  115. *Atossa*] This character first appeared in the 1744 edition. Though

Scarce once herself, by turns all Womankind!
Who, with herself, or others, from her birth
Finds all her life one warfare upon earth:
Shines, in exposing Knaves, and painting Fools,
Yet is, whate'er she hates and ridicules.   120
No Thought advances, but her Eddy Brain
Whisks it about, and down it goes again.
Full sixty years the World has been her Trade,
The wisest Fool much Time has ever made.
From loveless youth to unrespected age,   125
No Passion gratify'd except her Rage.
So much the Fury still out-ran the Wit,
The Pleasure miss'd her, and the Scandal hit.
Who breaks with her, provokes Revenge from Hell,
But he's a bolder man who dares be well: 130
Her ev'ry turn with Violence pursu'd,
Nor more a storm her Hate than Gratitude.
To that each Passion turns, or soon or late;
Love, if it makes her yield, must make her hate:
Superiors ? death! and Equals ? what a curse!   135
But an Inferior not dependant ? worse.
Offend her, and she knows not to forgive;
Oblige her, and she'll hate you while you live:

---

some details are more applicable to Sarah, Duchess of Marlborough, the
character is clearly based on Katherine, Duchess of Buckinghamshire
(1682?-1743). The name is well chosen. The historical Atossa was the
daughter of Cyrus and the sister of Cambyses, the Duchess of Buckinghamshire was a natural daughter of James II and a half-sister of the Old
Pretender. The Duke had been one of the earliest to salute Pope's genius
(see Epistle to Arbuthnot, 139) and Pope edited his posthumous Works
(1723). Pope would seem to have been on friendly terms with the Duchess
until 1729, when his revision of a character she had written of herself led
to a quarrel. The first draft of Atossa was probably written at this period.
In 1735 there was a reconciliation and Pope wrote an epitaph on her
'Booby Son' the second Duke (see pp. 698, 822). The Duchess's will
irritated Pope since all her private papers were left in the hands of Lord
Hervey, his enemy. Perhaps prompted by this, Pope put the final touches
to the character. The Duchess was an arrogant, quarrelsome, eccentric
woman, but was not without energy, intelligence, and public spirit.
    118. The Duchess was engaged in constant law-suits with the Duke's
natural children.
    121-2. The Duchess, always eccentric, finally became insane.
    125. Her first husband was James, third Earl of Anglesey. She obtained
a separation from him by an Act of Parliament in 1701 because of his
brutality to her. In her old age she became one of the town's jokes.
    126. Pope later attributed her eventual insanity to the violence of her
rages.
    138. Pope had obliged her more than once in editing the Duke's works,

But die, and she'll adore you—Then the Bust
And Temple rise—then fall again to dust.   140
Last night, her Lord was all that's good and great,
A Knave this morning, and his Will a Cheat.
Strange! by the Means defeated of the Ends,
By Spirit robb'd of Pow'r, by Warmth of Friends,
By Wealth of Follow'rs! without one distress   145
Sick of herself thro' very selfishness!
Atossa, curs'd with ev'ry granted pray'r,
Childless with all her Children, wants an Heir.
To Heirs unknown descends th' unguarded store
Or wanders, Heav'n-directed, to the Poor.   150
   Pictures like these, dear Madam, to design,
Asks no firm hand, and no unerring line;
Some wand'ring touch, or some reflected light,
Some flying stroke alone can hit 'em right:
For how should equal Colours do the knack?   155
Chameleons who can paint in white and black?
   'Yet Cloe sure was form'd without a spot—'
Nature in her then err'd not, but forgot.
'With ev'ry pleasing, ev'ry prudent part,
Say, what can Cloe want?'—she wants a Heart.   160
She speaks, behaves, and acts just as she ought;
But never, never, reach'd one gen'rous Thought.
Virtue she finds too painful an endeavour,
Content to dwell in Decencies for ever.
So very reasonable, so unmov'd,   165
As never yet to love, or to be lov'd.
She, while her Lover pants upon her breast,
Can mark the figures on an Indian chest;

---

but it was his attempt (made at her request) to revise the character she
had written of herself that precipitated the explosion. After the quarrel
the Duchess tried to liquidate her obligations to him by sending him a
note for £100. Pope refused the money.

   139–40. The Duchess erected elaborate and expensive monuments to
her husband and her son.

   142. The disputes with the Duke's illegitimate children were over his
will.

   148–50. Her five children by the Duke all predeceased her and at her
death there was 'a trial at bar to prove who was heir-at-law' to the Duke.
Some distant Irish connections called Walsh were at last found to be his
heirs.

   157–80. The character of Cloe was probably a last-minute addition.
Some features seem to be derived from Henrietta Hobart, later Mrs.
Howard, later Countess of Suffolk (1681–1767), an intimate friend of
Pope, Swift, and Martha Blount.

And when she sees her Friend in deep despair,
Observes how much a Chintz exceeds Mohair.		170
Forbid it Heav'n, a Favour or a Debt
She e'er should cancel—but she may forget.
Safe is your Secret still in Cloe's ear;
But none of Cloe's shall you ever hear.
Of all her Dears she never slander'd one,		175
But cares not if a thousand are undone.
Would Cloe know if you're alive or dead?
She bids her Footman put it in her head.
Cloe is prudent—would you too be wise?
Then never break your heart when Cloe dies.		180
　　One certain Portrait may (I grant) be seen,
Which Heav'n has varnish'd out, and made a *Queen*:
The same for ever! and describ'd by all
With Truth and Goodness, as with Crown and Ball:
Poets heap Virtues, Painters Gems at will,		185
And show their zeal, and hide their want of skill.
'Tis well—but, Artists! who can paint or write,
To draw the Naked is your true delight:
That Robe of Quality so struts and swells,
None see what Parts of Nature it conceals.		190
Th' exactest traits of Body or of Mind,
We owe to models of an humble kind.
If QUEENSBERRY to strip there's no compelling,
'Tis from a Handmaid we must take a Helen.
From Peer or Bishop 'tis no easy thing		195
To draw the man who loves his God, or King:
Alas! I copy (or my draught would fail)
From honest Mah'met, or plain Parson Hale.

170. Mohair was a fine material made from the hair of the Angora goat.
182. *varnish'd out*] i.e. completed, and a coat of varnish applied.
a Queen] Queen Caroline (1683-1737). A firm supporter of Walpole. Pope's antipathy to her was political, though politics may have been reinforced by his dislike of her Vice-Chamberlain and confidant Lord Hervey and his affection for the King's mistress, Mrs. Howard.
193. Catherine Hyde, Duchess of Queensberry (1700-77), the friend and protectress of Gay, and one of the most beautiful women of the eighteenth century.
197. *draught*] Drawing, sketch or picture.
198. *Mah'met*] Servant to the late king, said to be the son of a Turkish Bassa, whom he took at the siege of Buda, and constantly kept about his person [P].
Parson Hale] Dr. Stephen Hales (1677-1761), the perpetual curate of Teddington and a famous physiologist, witnessed Pope's will. His vivisections distressed Pope.

But grant, in Public Men sometimes are shown,
A Woman's seen in Private life alone: 200
Our bolder Talents in full light display'd,
Your Virtues open fairest in the shade.
Bred to disguise, in Public 'tis you hide;
There, none distinguish 'twixt your Shame or Pride,
Weakness or Delicacy; all so nice, 205
That each may seem a Virtue, or a Vice.

In Men, we various Ruling Passions find,
In Women, two almost divide the kind;
Those, only fix'd, they first or last obey,
The Love of Pleasure, and the Love of Sway. 210

That, Nature gives; and where the lesson taught
Is but to please, can Pleasure seem a fault?
Experience, this; by Man's oppression curst,
They seek the second not to lose the first.

Men, some to Bus'ness, some to Pleasure take; 215
But ev'ry Woman is at heart a Rake:
Men, some to Quiet, some to public Strife;
But ev'ry Lady would be Queen for life.

Yet mark the fate of a whole Sex of Queens!
Pow'r all their end, but Beauty all the means. 220
In Youth they conquer, with so wild a rage,
As leaves them scarce a Subject in their Age:
For foreign glory, foreign joy, they roam;
No thought of Peace or Happiness at home.
But Wisdom's Triumph is well-tim'd Retreat, 225
As hard a science to the Fair as Great!
Beauties, like Tyrants, old and friendless grown,
Yet hate to rest, and dread to be alone,

199. In the former Editions, between this and the foregoing lines, a want of Connection might be perceived, occasioned by the omission of certain *Examples* and *Illustrations* to the Maxims laid down; and tho' some of these have since been found, viz. the Characters of *Philomedé*, *Atossa*, *Cloe*, and some verses following, others are still wanting, nor can we answer that these are exactly inserted. [P]

207. The former part having shewn, that the *particular Characters* of Women are more various than those of Men, it is nevertheless observ'd, that the *general* Characteristic of the sex, as to the *ruling Passion*, is more uniform [P]. For Pope's theory of the Ruling Passion see *E. on Man*, II 133 ff. (p. 520).

211. This is occasioned partly by their *Nature*, partly by their *Education*, and in some degree by *Necessity* [P].

212. *fault*] For the rhyme see note to l. 73.

215–26. This couplet, like the characters of Calypso and Narcissa, derives from Pope's 'Sylvia, a Fragment' (p. 492).

219. What are the *Aims* and the *Fate* of this Sex?—I. As to *Power* [P].

Worn out in public, weary ev'ry eye,
Nor leave one sigh behind them when they die.   230
   Pleasures the sex, as children Birds, pursue,
Still out of reach, yet never out of view,
Sure, if they catch, to spoil the Toy at most,
To covet flying, and regret when lost:
At last, to follies Youth could scarce defend,   235
'Tis half their Age's prudence to pretend;
Asham'd to own they gave delight before,
Reduc'd to feign it, when they give no more:
As Hags hold Sabbaths, less for joy than spight,
So these their merry, miserable Night;   240
Still round and round the Ghosts of Beauty glide,
And haunt the places where their Honour dy'd.
   See how the World its Veterans rewards!
A Youth of frolicks, an old Age of Cards,
Fair to no purpose, artful to no end,   245
Young without Lovers, old without a Friend,
A Fop their Passion, but their Prize a Sot,
Alive, ridiculous, and dead, forgot!
   Ah Friend! to dazzle let the Vain design,   249
To raise the Thought and touch the Heart, be thine!
That Charm shall grow, while what fatigues the Ring
Flaunts and goes down, an unregarded thing.
So when the Sun's broad beam has tir'd the sight,
All mild ascends the Moon's more sober light,
Serene in Virgin Modesty she shines,   255
And unobserv'd the glaring Orb declines.
   Oh! blest with Temper, whose unclouded ray
Can make to morrow chearful as to day;
She, who can love a Sister's charms, or hear
Sighs for a Daughter with unwounded ear;   260
She, who ne'er answers till a Husband cools,
Or, if she rules him, never shows she rules;

231. II. As to *Pleasure* [P].
231–2. This couplet derives from 'Stanzas. From the french of Malherbe' (p. 114).
240. *Night*] Visiting night.
241–2. These two lines derive from 'Epigram' (p. 808).
243–8. These lines had already appeared as 5–10 of 'To Mrs. *M.B.* on Her Birth-day' (p. 315).
249. Advice for their true Interest [P].
251. *the Ring*] A clump of trees in Hyde Park, round which the carriages of the fashionable world used to drive.
253–6. Transferred from verses to Mrs. Judith Cowper (p. 473).

Charms by accepting, by submitting sways,
Yet has her humour most, when she obeys;
Lets Fops or Fortune fly which way they will;   265
Disdains all loss of Tickets, or Codille;
Spleen, Vapours, or Small-pox, above them all,
And Mistress of herself, tho' China fall.
    And yet, believe me, good as well as ill,
Woman's at best a Contradiction still.   270
Heav'n, when it strives to polish all it can
Its last best work, but forms a softer Man;
Picks from each sex, to make its Fav'rite blest,
Your love of Pleasure, our desire of Rest,
Blends, in exception to all gen'ral rules,   275
Your Taste of Follies, with our Scorn of Fools,
Reserve with Frankness, Art with Truth ally'd,
Courage with Softness, Modesty with Pride,
Fix'd Principles, with Fancy ever new;
Shakes all together, and produces—You.   280
    Be this a Woman's Fame: with this unblest,
Toasts live a scorn, and Queens may die a jest.
This Phœbus promis'd (I forget the year)
When those blue eyes first open'd on the sphere;
Ascendant Phœbus watch'd that hour with care,   285
Averted half your Parents simple Pray'r,
And gave you Beauty, but deny'd the Pelf
Which buys your sex a Tyrant o'er itself.
The gen'rous God, who Wit and Gold refines,
And ripens Spirits as he ripens Mines,   290
Kept Dross for Duchesses, the world shall know it,
To you gave Sense, Good-humour, and a Poet.

266. *Tickets*] Lottery tickets.
Codille] A term in the fashionable card game *ombre*.
267. *Small-pox*] Martha Blount had had small-pox in 1714.
269. The Picture of an estimable Woman, with the best kinds of contrarieties [P].
283. Martha Blount was forty-four when the Epistle was published in 1735.
286. *half your Parents simple Pray'r*] An allusion to *Aeneid*, II 794 f.—which Dryden had translated,

      Apollo heard, and granting half his Pray'r,
      Shuffled in Winds the rest, and toss'd in empty Air.

289. *Wit and Gold refines*] Phoebus refined wit as god of poetry, gold as the god of the sun—in accordance with the vulgar error that it was created by the sun's rays.
292. *Good-humour*] Martha's sunny disposition particularly endeared her to Pope. He had already sung the praises of good humour in *Rape of Lock*, V 29–32 (p. 238), and *Ep. to Miss Blount*, 61 ff. (p. 170).

Epistle III. To Allen Lord Bathurst

[written 1730-32; published 1733]

ARGUMENT

Of the Use *of* Riches. *That it is known to few, most falling into one of the extremes,* Avarice *or* Profusion, v. 1, &c. *The Point discuss'd, whether the invention of Money has been more commodious, or pernicious to Mankind,* v. 21 to 78. *That Riches, either to the* Avaricious *or the* Prodigal, *cannot afford Happiness, scarcely Necessaries,* v. 81 to 108. *That Avarice is an absolute Frenzy, without an End or Purpose,* v. 109 &c. *Conjectures about the Motives of Avaricious men,* v. 113 to 152. *That the conduct of men, with respect to Riches, can only be accounted for by the* ORDER OF PROVIDENCE, *which works the general Good out of Extremes, and brings all to its great End by perpetual Revolutions,* v. 161 to 178. *How a* Miser *acts upon Principles which appear to him reasonable,* v. 179. *How a* Prodigal *does the same,* v. 199. *The due Medium, and true use of Riches,* v. 219. *The* Man *of* Ross, v. 250. *The fate of the* Profuse *and the* Covetous, *in two examples; both miserable in Life and in Death,* v. 301, &c. *The Story of Sir* Balaam, v. 341 to the end.

> Who shall decide, when Doctors disagree,
> And soundest Casuists doubt, like you and me?
> You hold the word, from Jove to Momus giv'n,
> That Man was made the standing jest of Heav'n;
> And Gold but sent to keep the fools in play,   5
> For some to heap, and some to throw away.
>   But I, who think more highly of our kind,
> (And surely, Heav'n and I are of a mind)
> Opine, that Nature, as in duty bound,
> Deep hid the shining mischief under ground: 10
> But when by Man's audacious labour won,
> Flam'd forth this rival to, its Sire, the Sun,

Heading] Allen Bathurst (1685-1775), Tory M.P. for Cirencester from 1705 till he was raised to the peerage as Baron Bathurst (1712). His easy morals were notorious, but the philosophy does not seem to have amounted to much more than worldly wisdom. Bathurst was a lifelong friend of Congreve, Prior, and Swift as well as Pope. He was an enthusiastic landscape gardener at both his country houses (Cirencester and Riskins, *recte* Richings, near Slough, where 'Pope's Walk' is still preserved).
    3. *Momus*] Derisive blame; personified as a god in the *Theogony* of Hesiod.

Then careful Heav'n supply'd two sorts of Men,
To squander these, and those to hide agen.
  Like Doctors thus, when much dispute has past, 15
We find our tenets just the same at last.
Both fairly owning, Riches in effect
No grace of Heav'n or token of th' Elect;
Giv'n to the Fool, the Mad, the Vain, the Evil,
To Ward, to Waters, Chartres, and the Devil. 20

20. JOHN WARD, of Hackney, Esq.; Member of Parliament, being
prosecuted by the Duchess of Buckingham, and convicted of Forgery,
was first expelled the House, and then stood in the Pillory on the 17th of
March 1727. He was suspected of joining in a conveyance with Sir John
Blunt, to secrete fifty thousand pounds of that Director's Estate, forfeited
to the South Sea Company by Act of Parliament. The Company recovered
the fifty thousand pounds against Ward; but he set up prior conveyances
of his real estate to his brother and son, and conceal'd all his personal,
which was computed to be one hundred and fifty thousand pounds: These
conveyances being also set aside by a bill in Chancery, Ward was
imprisoned, and hazarded the forfeiture of his life, by not giving in his
effects till the last day, which was that of his examination. During his
confinement, his amusement was to give poison to dogs and cats, and see
them expire by slower or quicker torments. To sum up the *worth* of this
gentleman, at the several æra's of his life; at his standing in the Pillory he
was *worth above two hundred thousand pounds;* at his commitment to
Prison, he was *worth one hundred and fifty thousand,* but has been since so
far diminished in his reputation, as to be thought a *worse man* by *fifty or
sixty thousand.* [P]
  FR. CHARTRES ⟨1675-1732⟩, a man infamous for all manner of vices.
When he was an ensign in the army, he was drumm'd out of the regiment
for a cheat; he was next banish'd Brussels, and drumm'd out of Ghent on
the same account. After a hundred tricks at the gaming-tables, he took to
lending of money at exorbitant interest and on great penalties, accumulating premium, interest, and capital into a new capital, and seizing to a
minute when the payments became due; in a word, by a constant attention to the vices, wants, and follies of mankind, he acquired an immense
fortune. His house was a perpetual bawdy-house. He was twice condemn'd for rapes, and pardoned: but the last time not without imprisonment in Newgate, and large confiscation. He died in Scotland in 1731,
aged 62. The populace at his funeral rais'd a great riot, almost tore the
body out of the coffin, and cast dead dogs, &c. into the grave along with it.
The following Epitaph contains his character very justly drawn by Dr.
Arbuthnot:

HERE continueth to rot
The Body of FRANCIS CHARTRES,
Who with an INFLEXIBLE CONSTANCY,
and INIMITABLE UNIFORMITY of Life,
PERSISTED,
In spite of AGE and INFIRMITIES,
In the Practice of EVERY HUMAN VICE;
Excepting PRODIGALITY and HYPOCRISY:
His insatiable AVARICE exempted him from the
first,

What Nature wants, commodious Gold bestows,
'Tis thus we eat the bread another sows:
But how unequal it bestows, observe,
'Tis thus we riot, while who sow it, starve.
What Nature wants (a phrase I much distrust)   25
Extends to Luxury, extends to Lust:
And if we count among the Needs of life
Another's Toil, why not another's Wife?
Useful, I grant, it serves what life requires,
But dreadful too, the dark Assassin hires: 30
Trade it may help, Society extend;
But lures the Pyrate, and corrupts the Friend:
It raises Armies in a Nation's aid,
But bribes a Senate, and the Land's betray'd.
Oh! that such bulky Bribes as all might see,   35

His matchless IMPUDENCE from the second.
Nor was he more singular
in the undeviating *Pravity* of his *Manners*
Than successful
in *Accumulating* WEALTH.
For, without TRADE or PROFESSION,
Without TRUST of PUBLIC MONEY,
And without BRIBE-WORTHY Service,
He acquired, or more properly created,
A MINISTERIAL ESTATE.
He was the only Person of his Time,
Who cou'd CHEAT without the Mask of HONESTY,
Retain his Primeval MEANNESS
When possess'd of TEN THOUSAND a YEAR,
And having daily deserved the GIBBET for what
he *did*,
Was at last condemn'd to it for what he *could*
not *do*.
Oh Indignant Reader!
Think not his Life useless to Mankind!
PROVIDENCE conniv'd at his execrable Designs,
To give to After-ages
A conspicuous PROOF and EXAMPLE,
Of how small Estimation is EXORBITANT WEALTH
in the Sight of GOD,
By his bestowing it on the most UNWORTHY of
ALL MORTALS.

This Gentleman was *worth seven thousand pounds a year* estate in Land, and about *one hundred thousand in Money*. [P]

Mr. WATERS, the third of these worthies, was a man no way resembling the former in his military, but extremely so in his civil capacity; his great fortune having been rais'd by the like diligent attendance on the necessities of others. But this gentleman's history must be deferred till his death, when his *worth* may be known more certainly. [P] See l. 125n.

Still, as of old, incumber'd Villainy!
In vain may Heroes fight, and Patriots rave;
If secret Gold saps on from knave to knave.
Could France or Rome divert our brave designs,
With all their brandies or with all their wines ?   40
What could they more than Knights and Squires confound,
Or water all the Quorum ten miles round ?
A Statesman's slumbers how this speech would spoil!
'Sir, Spain has sent a thousand jars of oil;
Huge bales of British cloth blockade the door;   45
A hundred oxen at your levee roar.'
    Poor Avarice one torment more would find;
Nor could Profusion squander all in kind.
Astride his cheese Sir Morgan might we meet,
And Worldly crying coals from street to street,   50
(Whom with a wig so wild, and mien so maz'd,
Pity mistakes for some poor tradesman craz'd).
Had Colepepper's whole wealth been hops and hogs,
Could he himself have sent it to the dogs ?
His Grace will game: to White's a Bull be led,   55
With spurning heels and with a butting head.
To White's be carried, as to ancient games,
Fair Coursers, Vases, and alluring Dames.

38. *saps*] A military metaphor; 'undermines the position'.
39. *Rome*] The Pretender's headquarters.
42. *water*] I.e. treat.
Quorum] Justices of the Peace.
50. Some Misers of great wealth, proprietors of the coal-mines, had enter'd at this time into an association to keep up coals to an extravagant price, whereby the poor were reduced almost to starve, till one of them taking the advantage of underselling the rest, defeated the design. One of these Misers was *worth ten thousand*, another *seven thousand* a year. [P]
Worldly is Lady Mary's penurious husband Edward Wortley Montagu (1681–1761).
53. Sir WILLIAM COLEPEPPER, Bart. ⟨1668–1740⟩ a person of an ancient family, and ample fortune, without one other quality of a Gentleman, who, after ruining himself at the Gaming-table, past the rest of his days in sitting there to see the ruin of others; preferring to subsist upon borrowing and begging, rather than to enter into any reputable method of life, and refusing a post in the army which was offer'd him. [P]
55. *His Grace*] The allusion is no doubt to Wriothesley Russell, third Duke of Bedford (1708–32), who on 27 November 1731 lost £3,800 at White's to Henry Jansen. The episode is commemorated in *Imit. Donne*, II 88 (q.v., p. 678).
White's] A chocolate-house established in St. James's Street about 1699 and converted into a club about 1730 to exclude the professional sharpers. White's was notorious for the high play.

Shall then Uxorio, if the stakes he sweep,
Bear home six Whores, and make his Lady weep?   60
Or soft Adonis, so perfum'd and fine,
Drive to St. James's a whole herd of swine?
Oh filthy check on all industrious skill,
To spoil the nation's last great trade, Quadrille!
　　Once, we confess, beneath the Patriot's cloak,   65
From the crack'd bag the dropping Guinea spoke,
And gingling down the back-stairs, told the crew,
'Old Cato is as great a Rogue as you.'
Blest paper-credit! last and best supply!
That lends Corruption lighter wings to fly!   70
Gold imp'd by thee, can compass hardest things,
Can pocket States, can fetch or carry Kings;
A single leaf shall waft an Army o'er,
Or ship off Senates to a distant Shore;
A leaf, like Sibyl's, scatter to and fro   75
Our fates and fortunes, as the winds shall blow:
Pregnant with thousands flits the Scrap unseen,
And silent sells a King, or buys a Queen.

　　59. *Uxorio*] John Hervey, first Earl of Bristol (1665–1751), passionately fond of his wife and a great sportsman.
　　61. *Adonis*] Apparently Lord Bristol's son John, Baron Hervey (1696–1743), who as Vice-Chamberlain had official apartments in St. James's Palace, and whose effeminate appearance was continually satirized by Pope.
　　63. *filthy*] Feminine slang.
　　64. Quadrille was the fashionable card-game.
　　65–8. This is a true story, which happened in the reign of William III, to an unsuspected old Patriot ⟨Sir Christopher Musgrave, 1632?–1704⟩, who coming out at the back-door from having been closeted by the King, where he had received a large bag of Guineas, the bursting of the bag discovered his business there. [P]
　　71. *imp'd*] A term of falconry, meaning to insert a feather into a hawk's damaged wing, so as to increase its power of flight.
　　72. In our author's time, many Princes had been sent about the world, and great changes of Kings projected in Europe. The partition-treaty ⟨1700⟩ had dispos'd of Spain; France had set up a King of England ⟨1701⟩, who was sent to Scotland, and back again ⟨1715⟩; King Stanislaus was sent to Poland ⟨1704 and 1733⟩, and back again ⟨1709 and 1733⟩; the Duke of Anjou was sent to Spain ⟨1700⟩, and Don Carlos to Italy ⟨1731⟩. [P]
　　74. Alludes to several Ministers, Counsellors, and Patriots banished in our times to Siberia, and to that MORE GLORIOUS FATE of the PARLIA-MENT OF PARIS, banished to Pontoise in the year 1720. [P]
　　75. *A Leaf like Sybils.*—Virg. Aen. 6. [P] Cf. VI 116, in Dryden's version:
　　　　But, oh! commit not thy prophetic mind
　　　　To flitting leaves, and sport of every wind.
　　78. *buys a Queen*] An allusion to the rumour that Queen Caroline had accepted a large present from Robert Knight, the cashier of the South Sea Company.

Since then, my Lord, on such a World we fall,
What say you ? 'Say ? Why take it, Gold and all.'   80
What Riches give us let us then enquire:
Meat, Fire, and Cloaths. What more ? Meat, Cloaths, and
    Fire.
Is this too little ? would you more than live ?
Alas! 'tis more than Turner finds they give.
Alas! 'tis more than (all his Visions past)   85
Unhappy Wharton, waking, found at last!
What can they give ? to dying Hopkins Heirs;
To Chartres, Vigour; Japhet, Nose and Ears ?
Can they, in gems bid pallid Hippia glow,
In Fulvia's buckle ease the throbs below,   90
Or heal, old Narses, thy obscener ail,
With all th' embroid'ry plaister'd at thy tail ?

84. *Turner*] One, who, being possessed of three hundred thousand
pounds, laid down his Coach, because Interest was reduced from five to
four *per cent.* and then put seventy thousand into the Charitable Corporation for better interest; which sum having lost, he took it so much to
heart, that he kept his chamber ever after. It is thought he would not have
outliv'd it, but that he was heir to another considerable estate, which he
daily expected, and that by this course of life he sav'd both cloaths and all
other expences. [P]
86. *Wharton*] A Nobleman of great qualities, but as unfortunate in the
application of them, as if they had been vices and follies. See his Character in the first Epistle. [P] For the career of Philip Duke of Wharton see
the notes to *Moral Es.* i, 179–209 (pp. 556–7).
87. *Hopkins*] A Citizen, whose rapacity obtained him the name of
Vultur Hopkins. He lived worthless, but died *worth three hundred thousand
pounds*, which he would give to no person living, but left it so as not to be
inherited till after the second generation. His counsel representing to him
how many years it must be, before this could take effect, and that his
money could only lie at interest all that time, he expressed great joy thereat,
and said, 'They would then be as long in spending, as he had been in
getting it.' But the Chancery afterwards set aside the will, and gave it to
the heir at law. [P]
88. *Chartres*] See l. 20n.
Japhet, Nose and Ears] JAPHET CROOK ⟨1662–1734⟩, alias Sir *Peter
Stranger*, was punished with the loss of those parts, for having forged a
conveyance of an Estate to himself, upon which he took up several
thousand pounds. He was at the same time sued in Chancery for having
fraudulently obtain'd a Will by which he possess'd another considerable
Estate, in wrong of the brother of the deceas'd. By these means he was
worth a great sum, which (in reward for the small loss of his ears) he
enjoy'd in prison till his death, and quietly left to his executor. [P]
89. *Hippia*] Hippia's name and complexion both derive from a fashionable abbreviation of *hypochondria*.
91. *old Narses*] William, first Earl Cadogan (1675–1726), a dis-.
tinguished soldier.

They might (were Harpax not too wise to spend)
Give Harpax self the blessing of a Friend;
Or find some Doctor that would save the life   95
Of wretched Shylock, spite of Shylock's Wife:
But thousands die, without or this or that,
Die, and endow a College, or a Cat:
To some, indeed, Heav'n grants the happier fate,
T' enrich a Bastard, or a Son they hate.   100
  Perhaps you think the Poor might have their part?
Bond damns the Poor, and hates them from his heart:
The grave Sir Gilbert holds it for a rule,
That 'every man in want is knave or fool:'
'God cannot love (says Blunt, with tearless eyes)   105
The wretch he starves'—and piously denies:

93–4. Harpax (Greek for 'robber') is perhaps an ideal figure.

96. *Shylock*] Probably a further reference to Wortley Montagu (see l. 50*n*) and Pope's old enemy Lady Mary (see *Moral Es.* ii, 24*n*).

98. A famous Dutchess of R. in her last will left considerable legacies and annuities to her Cats [P]. 'La Belle Stuart', Frances Theresa Stuart, Duchess of Richmond (1647–1702).

102. This epistle was written in the year 1730, when a corporation was established to hand money to the poor upon pledges, by the name of the *Charitable Corporation*; It was under the direction of the Right Honourable Sir R. S., Sir Arch. Grant, Mr. Denis Bond, Mr. Burroughs, &c., but the whole was turned only to an iniquitous method of enriching particular people, to the ruin of such numbers, that it became a parliamentary concern to endeavour the relief of those unhappy sufferers, and three of the managers, who were members of the house, were expelled. By the report of the committee, appointed to enquire into that iniquitous affair, it appears, that when it was objected to the intended removal of the office, that the Poor, for those use it was erected, would be hurt by it, Bond, one of the Directors, replied, Damn the Poor. That 'God hates the poor,' and, 'That every man in want is knave or fool,' &c. were the genuine apothegms of some of the persons here mentioned. [P] 'The Charitable Corporation, for Relief of Industrious Poor, by assisting them with small Sums upon Pledges at legal Interest' was incorporated in 1707, but only became active in 1725. By 1732 its subscribed capital amounted to £353,817. A large proportion of the capital found its way into the pockets of John Thomson, the chief warehouse-keeper, and his tools, but Thomson's depredations were only made possible by the active connivance of most of the eight directors of the company. Three of the directors were M.P.s and were all expelled the House of Commons.

103. *Sir Gilbert*] Sir Gilbert Heathcote (1652–1733), one of the founders, and later Governor, of the Bank of England; he was reputed to be the richest commoner in England. His reputation for meanness arose from a dispute with the parson of his parish over his brother's funeral fees; his objection, however, was for paying fees for the same corpse in two places.

105. *Blunt*] Sir John Blunt. See l. 135*n*.

But the good Bishop, with a meeker air,
Admits, and leaves them Providence's care.
  Yet, to be just to these poor men of pelf,
Each does but hate his Neighbour as himself: 110
Damn'd to the Mines, an equal fate betides
The Slave that digs it, and the Slave that hides.
Who suffer thus, mere Charity should own,
Must act on motives pow'rful, tho' unknown:
Some War, some Plague, or Famine they foresee,   115
Some Revelation hid from you and me.
Why Shylock wants a meal, the cause is found,
He thinks a Loaf will rise to fifty pound.
What made Directors cheat in South-sea year?
To live on Ven'son when it sold so dear.   120
Ask you why Phryne the whole Auction buys?
Phryne foresees a general Excise.
Why she and Sappho raise that monstrous sum?
Alas! they fear a man will cost a plum.
  Wise Peter sees the World's respect for Gold,   125
And therefore hopes this Nation may be sold:
Glorious Ambition! Peter, swell thy store,
And be what Rome's great Didius was before.

120. In the extravagance and luxury of the South-sea year, the price of
a haunch of Venison was from three to five pounds [P].

121–2. Many people about the year 1733, had a conceit that such a
thing was intended, of which it is not improbable this lady might have
some intimation. [P] Walpole's Excise Bill of 1733 was a warehousing
scheme designed to make England a storehouse for the temporary deposit
of goods, and London a free port. The Opposition interpreted it as a
general excise, which so much alarmed the public that Walpole decided
to withdraw the measure. Phryne was probably Maria Skerret (1702?–38),
Walpole's mistress and his second wife. The historical Phryne was an
Athenian hetaira of humble origin, but of great beauty and wealth.

124. *plum*] Eighteenth-century slang for £100,000.

125. PETER WALTER ⟨1664?–1746⟩, a person not only eminent in the
wisdom of his profession, as a dextrous attorney, but allow'd to be a good,
if not a safe, conveyancer; extremely respected by the Nobility of this
land, tho' free from all manner of luxury and ostentation: his Wealth was
never seen, and his bounty never heard of, except to his own son, for
whom he procured an employment of considerable profit, of which he
gave him as much as was *necessary*. Therefore the taxing of this gentleman
with any Ambition, is certainly a great wrong to him. [P] His activities as
moneylender-in-chief to the aristocracy brought him much notoriety. See
also l. 20, *Imit. Hor.*, *Sat.*, II i 3, 40, II ii 168, *Ep.*, II i 197, *Imit. Donne*,
II 66 f., *Epilogue to Satires*, I 121, II 58, and *1740*, 26(?).

128. A Roman Lawyer, so rich as to purchase the Empire when it was
set to sale upon the death of Pertinax. [P]

The Crown of Poland, venal twice an age,
To just three millions stinted modest Gage.   130
But nobler scenes Maria's dreams unfold,
Hereditary Realms, and worlds of Gold.
Congenial souls! whose life one Av'rice joins,
And one fate buries in th' Asturian Mines.
    Much injur'd Blunt! why bears he Britain's hate? 135
A wizard told him in these words our fate:
'At length Corruption, like a gen'ral flood,
(So long by watchful Ministers withstood)
Shall deluge all; and Av'rice creeping on,
Spread like a low-born mist, and blot the Sun;   140
Statesman and Patriot ply alike the stocks,
Peeress and Butler share alike the Box,
And Judges job, and Bishops bite the town,
And mighty Dukes pack cards for half a crown.

129. The Polish throne became vacant in 1696 with the death of John
Sobieski, in 1707, at the abdication of Augustus II, in 1709 at the abdication of Stanislas I, and in 1733 on the death of Augustus II. The Polish
nobility, who were the electors to the crown, were unblushingly venal.
    130-4. The two persons here mentioned were of Quality, each of whom
in the Missisippi despis'd to realize above *three hundred thousand pounds*;
the Gentleman with a view to the purchase of the Crown of Poland, the
Lady on a vision of the like royal nature. They since retired into Spain,
where they are still in search of gold in the mines of the Asturies. [P]
Joseph Gage (1678?-1753?) acquired Mississippi stock representing the
value of 13,000,000 l. and offered Augustus, king of Poland, 3,000,000 l.
for the crown, which was declined. Gage obtained from the King of
Spain a grant for working and draining all the gold mines in Old Spain.
The Asturian gold-mines were not very profitable, but in 1741 the King
give him a silver mine of great value. His second wife was Lady Mary
Herbert (1700?-70?), of whom Horace Walpole reports that she made a
'prodigious fortune in the Mississippi, & refused the Duke of Bouillon,
being determined to marry nobody but a Sovereign Prince; but refusing
to realise, lost the whole, & met Gage in the Asturian mines.'
    132. *Hereditary Realms*] Lady Mary Herbert's mother is said to have
been the illegitimate daughter of James II.
    135. Sir JOHN BLUNT ⟨1665-1733⟩, originally a scrivener, was one of
the first projectors of the South-sea company, and afterwards one of the
directors of the famous scheme in 1720. He was also one of those who
suffer'd most severely by the bill of pains and penalties on the said
directors. He was a Dissenter of a most religious deportment, and profess'd to be a great believer. Whether he did really credit the prophecy
here mentioned is not certain, but it was constantly in this very style he
declaimed against the corruption and luxury of the age, the partiality of
Parliaments, and the misery of party-spirit. He was particularly eloquent
against *Avarice* in great and noble persons, of which he had indeed liv'd
to see many miserable examples. He died in the year 1732. [P]
    143. *job*] Deal in stocks; *bite*] swindle.
    144. *pack*] Cheat at.

See Britain sunk in lucre's sordid charms,   145
And France reveng'd of ANNE's and EDWARD's arms!'
No mean Court-badge, great Scriv'ner! fir'd thy brain,
Nor lordly Luxury, nor City Gain:
No, 'twas thy righteous end, asham'd to see
Senates degen'rate, Patriots disagree,   150
And nobly wishing Party-rage to cease,
To buy both sides, and give thy Country peace.
   'All this is madness,' cries a sober sage:
But who, my friend, has reason in his rage?
   'The ruling Passion, be it what it will,   155
The ruling Passion conquers Reason still.'
Less mad the wildest whimsey we can frame,
Than ev'n that Passion, if it has no Aim;
For tho' such motives Folly you may call,
The Folly's greater to have none at all.   160
   Hear then the truth: ' 'Tis Heav'n each Passion sends,
And diff'rent men directs to diff'rent ends.
Extremes in Nature equal good produce,
Extremes in Man concur to gen'ral use.'
Ask we what makes one keep, and one bestow?   165
That POW'R who bids the Ocean ebb and flow,
Bids seed-time, harvest, equal course maintain,
Thro' reconcil'd extremes of drought and rain,
Builds Life on Death, on Change Duration founds,
And gives th' eternal wheels to know their rounds.   170
   Riches, like insects, when conceal'd they lie,
Wait but for wings, and in their season, fly.
Who sees pale Mammon pine amidst his store,
Sees but a backward steward for the Poor;
This year a Reservoir, to keep and spare,   175
The next a Fountain, spouting thro' his Heir,
In lavish streams to quench a Country's thirst,
And men and dogs shall drink him 'till they burst.

---

150. *Patriots disagree*] Walpole owed his long tenure of power at least in part to the divisions within the Opposition.

152. The South Sea Company offered to take over the National Debt; and since members of every political party rushed to buy stock, Blunt might be said to have bought both sides.

155–6. For the Ruling Passion see *Moral Es.* i (especially ll. 174 f.) and *E. on Man*, II 123–44.

163–4. See *E. on Man*, II 205–6, where the emphasis is on man the individual, and the paradox is the co-operation between vice and virtue in a particular person. Here Pope is thinking in terms of society, e.g. that the spendthrift is balanced by the miser.

Old Cotta sham'd his fortune and his birth,
Yet was not Cotta void of wit or worth: 180
What tho' (the use of barb'rous spits forgot)
His kitchen vy'd in coolness with his grot?
His court with nettles, moats with cresses stor'd,
With soups unbought and sallads blest his board.
If Cotta liv'd on pulse, it was no more   185
Than Bramins, Saints, and Sages did before;
To cram the Rich was prodigal expence,
And who would take the Poor from Providence?
Like some lone Chartreux stands the good old Hall,
Silence without, and Fasts within the wall;   190
No rafter'd roofs with dance and tabor sound,
No noontide-bell invites the country round;
Tenants with sighs the smoakless tow'rs survey,
And turn th' unwilling steeds another way:
Benighted wanderers, the forest o'er,   195
Curse the sav'd candle, and unop'ning door;
While the gaunt mastiff growling at the gate,
Affrights the beggar whom he longs to eat.
    Not so his Son, he mark'd this oversight,
And then mistook reverse of wrong for right.   200
(For what to shun will no great knowledge need,
But what to follow, is a task indeed.)
What slaughter'd hecatombs, what floods of wine,
Fill the capacious Squire, and deep Divine!
Yet no mean motive this profusion draws,   205
His oxen perish in his country's cause;
'Tis GEORGE and LIBERTY that crowns the cup,
And Zeal for that great House which eats him up.
The woods recede around the naked seat,
The Sylvans groan—no matter—for the Fleet: 210
Next goes his Wool—to clothe our valiant bands,
Last, for his Country's love, he sells his Lands.
To town he comes, completes the nation's hope,
And heads the bold Train-bands, and burns a Pope.
And shall not Britain now reward his toils,   215
Britain, that pays her Patriots with her Spoils?

179. *Old Cotta*] Sir John Cutler (see l. 315*n*).
184. —dapidus mensas onerabat inemptis. VIRG. [P] *Georg.*, IV 133.
199. Cutler's son-in-law, Charles Bodvile Robartes, second Earl of
Radnor (1660–1723).
214. *Train-bands*] The London militia.

In vain at Court the Bankrupt pleads his cause,
His thankless Country leaves him to her Laws.
   The Sense to value Riches, with the Art
T'enjoy them, and the Virtue to impart,   220
Not meanly, nor ambitiously pursu'd,
Not sunk by sloth, nor rais'd by servitude;
To balance Fortune by a just expence,
Join with Oeconomy, Magnificence;
With Splendour, Charity; with Plenty, Health;   225
Oh teach us, BATHURST! yet unspoil'd by wealth!
That secret rare, between th' extremes to move
Of mad Good-nature, and of mean Self-love.
   To Want or Worth well-weigh'd, be Bounty giv'n,
And ease, or emulate, the care of Heav'n,   230
Whose measure full o'erflows on human race;
Mend Fortune's fault, and justify her grace.
Wealth in the gross is death, but life diffus'd,
As Poison heals, in just proportion us'd:
In heaps, like Ambergrise, a stink it lies,   235
But well-dispers'd, is Incense to the Skies.
   Who starves by Nobles, or with Nobles eats?
The Wretch that trusts them, and the Rogue that cheats.
Is there a Lord, who knows a cheerful noon
Without a Fiddler, Flatt'rer, or Buffoon?   240
Whose table, Wit, or modest Merit share,
Un-elbow'd by a Gamester, Pimp, or Play'r?
Who copies Your's, or OXFORD's better part,
To ease th' oppress'd, and raise the sinking heart?
Where-e'er he shines, oh Fortune, gild the scene,   245
And Angels guard him in the golden Mean!
There, English Bounty yet a-while may stand,
And Honour linger ere it leaves the land.
   But all our praises why should Lords engross?
Rise, honest Muse! and sing the MAN of ROSS: 250

243. *Oxford's*] Edward Harley, Earl of Oxford ⟨1689–1741⟩. The son of
Robert, created Earl of Oxford and Earl Mortimer by Queen Anne. This
Nobleman died regretted by all men of letters, great numbers of whom
had experienc'd his benefits. He left behind him one of the most noble
Libraries in Europe. [P]

250. MAN of ROSS] The person here celebrated, who with a small
Estate actually performed all these good works, and whose true name was
almost lost (partly by the title of the *Man of Ross* given him by way of
eminence, and partly by being buried without so much as an inscription)
was called Mr. John Kyrle. He died in the year 1724, aged 90, and lies
interr'd in the chancel of the church of Ross in Herefordshire. [P]

Pleas'd Vaga echoes thro' her winding bounds,
And rapid Severn hoarse applause resounds.
Who hung with woods yon mountain's sultry brow?
From the dry rock who bade the waters flow?
Not to the skies in useless columns tost,   255
Or in proud falls magnificently lost,
But clear and artless, pouring thro' the plain
Health to the sick, and solace to the swain.
Whose Cause-way parts the vale with shady rows?
Whose Seats the weary Traveller repose?   260
Who taught that heav'n-directed spire to rise?
The MAN of ROSS, each lisping babe replies.
Behold the Market-place with poor o'erspread!
The MAN of ROSS divides the weekly bread:
Behold yon Alms-house, neat, but void of state,   265
Where Age and Want sit smiling at the gate:
Him portion'd maids, apprentic'd orphans blest,
The young who labour, and the old who rest.
Is any sick? the MAN of ROSS relieves,
Prescribes, attends, the med'cine makes, and gives.   270
Is there a variance? enter but his door,
Balk'd are the Courts, and contest is no more.
Despairing Quacks with curses fled the place,
And vile Attornies, now an useless race.
     'Thrice happy man! enabled to pursue   275
What all so wish, but want the pow'r to do!
Oh say, what sums that gen'rous hand supply?
What mines, to swell that boundless charity?'
     Of Debts, and Taxes, Wife and Children clear,
This man possest—five hundred pounds a year.   280
Blush, Grandeur, blush! proud Courts, withdraw your
Ye little Stars! hide your diminish'd rays.   [blaze!
     'And what? no monument, inscription, stone?
His race, his form, his name almost unknown?'
Who builds a Church to God, and not to Fame,   285
Will never mark the marble with his Name:
Go, search it there, where to be born and die,
Of rich and poor makes all the history;
Enough, that Virtue fill'd the space between;
Prov'd, by the ends of being, to have been.   290
When Hopkins dies, a thousand lights attend

251. *Vaga*] The Wye.
287. The Parish-register [P].
291–2. See l. 87*n*.

The wretch, who living sav'd a candle's end:
Should'ring God's altar a vile image stands,
Belies his features, nay extends his hands;
That live-long wig which Gorgon's self might own,   295
Eternal buckle takes in Parian stone.
Behold what blessings Wealth to life can lend!
And see, what comfort it affords our end.
　　In the worst inn's worst room, with mat half-hung,
The floors of plaister, and the walls of dung,   300
On once a flock-bed, but repair'd with straw,
With tape-ty'd curtains, never meant to draw,
The George and Garter dangling from that bed
Where tawdry yellow strove with dirty red,
Great Villers lies—alas! how chang'd from him,   305
That life of pleasure, and that soul of whim!
Gallant and gay, in Cliveden's proud alcove,
The bow'r of wanton Shrewsbury and love;
Or just as gay, at Council, in a ring
Of mimick'd Statesmen, and their merry King.   310
No Wit to flatter, left of all his store!
No Fool to laugh at, which he valu'd more.
There, Victor of his health, of fortune, friends,
And fame; this lord of useless thousands ends.
　　His Grace's fate sage Cutler could foresee,   315
And well (he thought) advis'd him, 'Live like me.'

293–6. The poet ridicules the wretched taste of carving large perriwigs on Busto's, of which there are several vile examples in the tombs at Westminster and elsewhere [P].

299–314. This Lord, yet more famous for his vices than his misfortunes, after having been possess'd of about 50,000 pound a year, and past thro' many of the highest posts in the kingdom, died in the year 1687, in a remote inn in Yorkshire, reduc'd to the utmost misery. [P] Though poetically effective Pope's lines are not historically inaccurate. Buckingham did die in Yorkshire in 1687, but not in an inn or in poverty. The legend was already in existence a few days after Buckingham died.

301. Flock-beds were only used by the middle classes; the aristocracy had feather-beds.

307. A delightful palace, on the banks of the Thames, built by the Duke of Buckingham [P].

308. The Countess of Shrewsbury, a woman abandon'd to gallantries. The Earl her husband was kill'd by the Duke of Buckingham in a duel; and it has been said, that during the combat she held the Duke's horses in the habit of a page. [P]

315. Cutler] Sir John Cutler (1608?–1693) was a rich London merchant, who promoted the subscriptions raised by the City for Charles II. He received both a knighthood and a baronetcy in 1660. Although he was a generous benefactor of the Grocers' Company, Gresham's College, the

As well his Grace reply'd, 'Like you, Sir John?
That I can do, when all I have is gone.'
Resolve me, Reason, which of these is worse,
Want with a full, or with an empty purse?   320
Thy life more wretched, Cutler, was confess'd,
Arise, and tell me, was thy death more bless'd?
Cutler saw tenants break, and houses fall,
For very want; he could not build a wall.
His only daughter in a stranger's pow'r,   325
For very want; he could not pay a dow'r.
A few grey hairs his rev'rend temples crown'd,
'Twas very want that sold them for two pound.
What ev'n deny'd a cordial at his end,
Banish'd the doctor, and expell'd the friend?   330
What but a want, which you perhaps think mad,
Yet numbers feel, the want of what he had.
Cutler and Brutus, dying both exclaim,
'Virtue! and Wealth! what are ye but a name!'
    Say, for such worth are other worlds prepar'd?   335
Or are they both, in this their own reward?
A knotty point! to which we now proceed.
But you are tir'd—I'll tell a tale. 'Agreed.'
    Where London's column, pointing at the skies,
Like a tall bully, lifts the head, and lyes;   340
There dwelt a Citizen of sober fame,
A plain good man, and Balaam was his name;
Religious, punctual, frugal, and so forth;
His word would pass for more than he was worth.
One solid dish his week-day meal affords,   345
An added pudding solemniz'd the Lord's:
Constant at Church, and Change; his gains were sure,
His givings rare, save farthings to the poor.
    The Dev'l was piqu'd such saintship to behold,
And long'd to tempt him like good Job of old: 350
But Satan now is wiser than of yore,

College of Physicians, and the parish of St. Margaret's, Westminster, his
personal parsimony earned for him an undeserved notoriety, which by
Pope's time had become legendary. Pope's account is quite unhistorical.
    339. The Monument, built in memory of the fire of London, with a
inscription, importing that city to have been burnt by the Papists [P].
    342. *Balaam*] Perhaps modelled on Thomas Pitt (1653-1726), grand-
father of the statesman, who had made a great deal of money in underhand
ways, was remarkably pious, owned an estate in Cornwall, and bought and
represented the rotten borough of Old Sarum.

And tempts by making rich, not making poor.
   Rouz'd by the Prince of Air, the whirlwinds sweep
The surge, and plunge his Father in the deep;
Then full against his Cornish lands they roar,   355
And two rich ship-wrecks bless the lucky shore.
   Sir Balaam now, he lives like other folks,
He takes his chirping pint, and cracks his jokes:
'Live like yourself,' was soon my Lady's word;
And lo! two puddings smoak'd upon the board.   360
   Asleep and naked as an Indian lay,
An honest factor stole a Gem away:
He pledg'd it to the knight; the knight had wit,
So kept the Diamond, and the rogue was bit.
Some scruple rose, but thus he eas'd his thought,   365
'I'll now give six-pence where I gave a groat,
Where once I went to church, I'll now go twice—
And am so clear too of all other vice.'
   The Tempter saw his time; the work he ply'd;
Stocks and Subscriptions pour on ev'ry side,   370
'Till all the Dæmon makes his full descent,
In one abundant show'r of Cent. per Cent.,
Sinks deep within him, and possesses whole,
Then dubs Director, and secures his soul.
   Behold Sir Balaam, now a man of spirit,   375
Ascribes his gettings to his parts and merit,
What late he call'd a Blessing, now was Wit,
And God's good Providence, a lucky Hit.
Things change their titles, as our manners turn:
His Compting-house employ'd the Sunday-morn;   380
Seldom at Church ('twas such a busy life)
But duly sent his family and wife.
There (so the Dev'l ordain'd) one Christmas-tide
My good old Lady catch'd a cold, and dy'd.
   A Nymph of Quality admires our Knight;   385
He marries, bows at Court, and grows polite:

355. The author has placed the scene of these shipwrecks in Cornwall,
not only from their frequency on that coast, but from the inhumanity of
the inhabitants to those to whom that misfortune arrives: When a ship
happens to be stranded there, they have been known to bore holes in it,
to prevent its getting off; to plunder, and sometimes even to massacre the
people: Nor has the Parliament of England been yet able wholly to
suppress these barbarities. [P]

361–4. Pitt bought the celebrated Pitt diamond for £20,400 when he
was Governor of Fort St. George, Madras. Later he sold it for over six
times as much to the Duke of Orleans.

Leaves the dull Cits, and joins (to please the fair)
The well-bred cuckolds in St. James's air:
First, for his Son a gay Commission buys,
Who drinks, whores, fights, and in a duel dies: 390
His daughter flaunts a Viscount's tawdry wife;
She bears a Coronet and P–x for life.
In Britain's Senate he a seat obtains,
And one more Pensioner St. Stephen gains.
My Lady falls to play; so bad her chance,   395
He must repair it; takes a bribe from France;
The House impeach him; Coningsby harangues;
The Court forsake him, and Sir Balaam hangs:
Wife, son, and daughter, Satan, are thy own,
His wealth, yet dearer, forfeit to the Crown: 400
The Devil and the King divide the prize,
And sad Sir Balaam curses God and dies.

394. —atque unum civem donare *Sibyllæ*. J U V. [P] Juvenal, III 3.
397. *Coningsby*] Thomas, Earl Coningsby (1645?-1729), appointed in
1715 a commissioner to investigate the intrigue leading up to the Peace
of Utrecht, and to impeach Harley. See his satirical epitaph, p. 496.

Epistle IV. To Richard Boyle, Earl of Burlington

[written 1730-31; published 1731]

ARGUMENT

Of the Use *of* Riches. *The Vanity of Expence in People of Wealth and
Quality. The abuse of the word* Taste, v. 13. *That the first principle
and foundation, in this as in every thing else, is* Good Sense, v. 40.
The chief proof of it is to follow *Nature, even in works of mere
Luxury and Elegance. Instanced in* Architecture *and* Gardening,
where all must be adapted to the Genius *and* Use *of the Place, and
the Beauties not forced into it, but resulting from it,* v. 50. *How men
are disappointed in their most expensive undertakings, for want of
this true Foundation, without which nothing can please* long, *if at*

Heading] Richard Boyle, third Earl of Burlington and fourth Earl of
Cork (1695-1753), an enthusiastic Palladian who was largely responsible
for the exclusion of baroque and rococo influences from Georgian
architecture. He reconstructed Burlington House, Piccadilly, on classical
lines c. 1716, and added to his country house at Chiswick a villa (1727-36)
modelled on one of Palladio's own. Pope was on friendly terms with him
by 1716 or earlier.

all; *and the best* Examples *and* Rules *will but be perverted into something* burdensome *or ridiculous*, v. 65, &c. to 92. *A description of the* false Taste *of* Magnificence; *the first grand Error of which is to imagine that* Greatness *consists in the* Size *and* Dimension, *instead of the* Proportion *and* Harmony *of the* whole, v. 97, *and the second, either in joining together* Parts incoherent, *or too* minutely resembling, *or in the* Repetition *of the* same *too frequently*, v. 105, &c. *A word or two of false Taste in* Books, *in* Music, *in* Painting, *even in* Preaching *and* Prayer, *and lastly in* Entertainments, v. 133, &c. *Yet* PROVIDENCE *is justified in giving Wealth to be squandered in this manner, since it is dispersed to the Poor and Laborious part of mankind*, v. 169. [*Recurring to what is laid down in the first book, Ep.* ii, *and in the Epistle preceding this*, v. 159, &c.] *What are the* proper Objects *of Magnificence, and a proper field for the Expence of* Great Men, v. 177, &c., *and finally, the* Great and Public Works *which become a* Prince, v. 191, *to the end.*

MY LORD,

The Clamour rais'd about this Epistle could not give me so much pain, as I receiv'd pleasure in seeing the general Zeal of the World in the cause of a Great Man who is Beneficent, and the particular Warmth of your Lordship in that of a private Man who is innocent.

It was not the Poem *that deserv'd this from you; for as I had the Honour to be your friend, I cou'd not treat you quite like a Poet: but sure the* Writer *deserv'd more Candor even from those who knew him not, than to promote a Report which in regard to that Noble Person, was* Impertinent; *in regard to me*, Villainous. *Yet I had no great Cause to wonder, that a Character belonging to* twenty *shou'd be applied to* one; *since, by that means*, nineteen *wou'd escape the Ridicule.*

I was too well content with my Knowledge of that Noble Person's Opinion in this Affair, to trouble the publick about it. But since Malice and Mistake are so long a dying, I take the opportunity of this third Edition to declare His Belief, not only of My Innocence, but of Their Malignity, of the former of which my own Heart is as conscious, as I fear some of theirs must be of the latter. His Humanity feels a Concern for the Injury done to Me, *while His Greatness of Mind can bear with Indifference the Insult offer'd to* Himself.

However, my Lord, I own, that Critics of this Sort can intimidate me, nay half incline me to write no more: It wou'd be making the Town a Compliment which I think it deserves, and which some, I am sure, wou'd take very kindly. This way of Satire is dangerous, as long as Slander rais'd by Fools of the lowest Rank, can find any Countenance from those of a Higher. Even from the Conduct shewn on this occasion,

I have learnt there are some who wou'd rather be wicked *than*
ridiculous; *and therefore it may be safer to attack* Vices *than* Follies.
I will leave my Betters in the quiet Possession of their Idols, *their*
Groves, *and their* High-Places; *and change my Subject from their*
Pride *to their* Meanness, *from their* Vanities *to their* Miseries: *And
as the only certain way to avoid Misconstruction, to lessen Offence, and
not to multiply ill-natur'd Applications, I may probably in my next
make use of* Real *Names and not of Fictitious Ones.* I am,
My Lord,
Your Faithful,
Affectionate Servant,
A. POPE.

'Tis strange, the Miser should his Cares employ,
To gain those Riches he can ne'er enjoy:
Is it less strange, the Prodigal should wast
His wealth, to purchase what he ne'er can taste?
Not for himself he sees, or hears, or eats;   5
Artists must chuse his Pictures, Music, Meats:
He buys for Topham, Drawings and Designs,
For Pembroke Statues, dirty Gods, and Coins;
Rare monkish Manuscripts for Hearne alone,
And Books for Mead, and Butterflies for Sloane.   10
Think we all these are for himself? no more
Than his fine Wife, alas! or finer Whore.
    For what has Virro painted, built, and planted?
Only to show, how many Tastes he wanted.
What brought Sir Visto's ill got wealth to waste?   15
Some Dæmon whisper'd, 'Visto! have a Taste.'

6. *Artists*] Experts, connoisseurs.
    7. *Topham*] A Gentleman famous for a judicious collection of Draw-
ings. [P] Richard Topham (d. 1735), Keeper of the Records in the Tower.
His valuable collection of drawings, portraits, and engravings was
bequeathed with his books to Eton College Library.
    8. Thomas Herbert, eighth Earl of Pembroke (1656–1733), Whig
politician who devoted his leisure to collecting statues, pictures, and coins.
    9. Thomas Hearne (1678–1735), the most eminent medievalist of
Pope's generation.
    10. *Mead . . . Sloane*] Two eminent Physicians; the one had an excel-
lent Library, the other the finest collection in Europe of natural curiosities; both men of great learning and humanity [P]. Richard Mead (1673–
1754) was Physician in Ordinary to George II and Queen Caroline. His
collection of books numbered some thirty thousand volumes. Sir Hans
Sloane (1660–1753) was First Physician to George II and President of the
Royal College of Physicians, 1719–35. His collections were bought by the
nation after his death and formed the nucleus of the British Museum.

Heav'n visits with a Taste the wealthy fool,
And needs no Rod but Ripley with a Rule.
See! sportive fate, to punish aukward pride,
Bids Bubo build, and sends him such a Guide: 20
A standing sermon, at each year's expense,
That never Coxcomb reach'd Magnificence!
  You show us, Rome was glorious, not profuse,
And pompous buildings once were things of Use.
Yet shall (my Lord) your just, your noble rules   25
Fill half the land with Imitating Fools;
Who random drawings from your sheets shall take,
And of one beauty many blunders make;
Load some vain Church with old Theatric state,
Turn Arcs of triumph to a Garden-gate;   30
Reverse your Ornaments, and hang them all
On some patch'd dog-hole ek'd with ends of wall,
Then clap four slices of Pilaster on't,
That, lac'd with bits of rustic, makes a Front.
Or call the winds thro' long Arcades to roar,   35
Proud to catch cold at a Venetian door;
Conscious they act a true Palladian part,
And if they starve, they starve by rules of art.
  Oft have you hinted to your brother Peer,
A certain truth, which many buy too dear: 40
Something there is more needful than Expence,
And something previous ev'n to Taste—'tis Sense:

18. *Ripley*] This man was a carpenter, employ'd by a first Minister, who rais'd him to an Architect, without any genius in the art; and after some wretched proofs of his insufficiency in public Buildings, made him Comptroller of the Board of works [P].

20. *Bubo*] George Bubb, who later took the name Dodington and finally became Baron Melcombe (1691–1762), satirized as 'Bubo' (Latin for owl) and 'Bufo' (Latin for toad) in *Epistle to Arbuthnot*, ll. 230, 280 (pp. 605–7). See also *Epilogue to Satires I*, 12, 68 (pp. 688–90). He completed the mansion at Eastbury, Dorset. The architect was Vanbrugh, for whose abilities Pope shared Swift's ignorant contempt.

23. The Earl of Burlington was then publishing the Designs of Inigo Jones, and the Antiquities of Rome by Palladio [P]. *The Designs of Inigo Jones, consisting of Plans and Elevations for Public and Private Buildings*, 2 vols., 1727, (published in Kent's name) and *Fabriche antiche disegnate da Andrea Palladio Vicentino*, 1730.

32. *dog-hole*] 'A vile hole; a mean habitation' (Johnson).

33. *Pilaster*] 'A square column sometimes insulated, but often set within a wall' (Johnson).

34. *rustic*] 'Characterized by a surface artificially roughened or left rough-hewn' (*OED*).

36. *Venetian door*] A Door or Window, so called, from being much practised at Venice, by Palladio and others [P].

Good Sense, which only is the gift of Heav'n,
And tho' no science, fairly worth the sev'n:
A Light, which in yourself you must perceive;   45
Jones and Le Nôtre have it not to give.
 To build, to plant, whatever you intend,
To rear the Column, or the Arch to bend,
To swell the Terras, or to sink the Grot;
In all, let Nature never be forgot.   50
But treat the Goddess like a modest fair,
Nor over-dress, nor leave her wholly bare;
Let not each beauty ev'ry where be spy'd,
Where half the skill is decently to hide.
He gains all points, who pleasingly confounds,   55
Surprizes, varies, and conceals the Bounds.
 Consult the Genius of the Place in all;
That tells the Waters or to rise, or fall,
Or helps th' ambitious Hill the heav'n to scale,
Or scoops in circling theatres the Vale,   60
Calls in the Country, catches opening glades,
Joins willing woods, and varies shades from shades,
Now breaks or now directs, th' intending Lines;
Paints as you plant, and, as you work, designs.
 Still follow Sense, of ev'ry Art the Soul,   65
Parts answ'ring parts shall slide into a whole,
Spontaneous beauties all around advance,
Start ev'n from Difficulty, strike from Chance;
Nature shall join you, Time shall make it grow
A Work to wonder at—perhaps a STOW.   70
 Without it, proud Versailles! thy glory falls;
And Nero's Terraces desert their walls:
The vast Parterres a thousand hands shall make,
Lo! COBHAM comes, and floats them with a Lake:

46. *Inigo Jones* the celebrated Architect, and M. *Le Nôtre*, the designer
of the best Gardens of France [P]. André Le Nôtre (1613–1700) laid out
the gardens at Versailles and Fontainebleau.
 63. *th' intending lines*] Those which lead the eye forward.
 70. STOW] The seat and gardens of the Lord Viscount Cobham in
Buckinghamshire [P]. Bridgman began the process of blending the landscape with the garden, and Gibbs, Vanbrugh, and Kent dotted temples,
columns, and arches about. Bridgman was succeeded by Kent, on whose
death the ruralizing of the place continued under 'Capability' Brown.
 71. Until the advent of the landscape gardeners Le Nôtre's gardens at
Versailles were considered the best in Europe.
 72. Probably referring to the Golden House of Nero.
 74. *floats*] (= flood, inundate) a technical agricultural term.

Or cut wide views thro' Mountains to the Plain,   75
You'll wish your hill or shelter'd seat again.
Ev'n in an ornament its place remark,
Nor in an Hermitage set Dr. Clarke.
    Behold Villario's ten-years toil compleat;
His Quincunx darkens, his Espaliers meet,   80
The Wood supports the Plain, the parts unite,
And strength of Shade contends with strength of Light;
A waving Glow his bloomy beds display,
Blushing in bright diversities of day,
With silver-quiv'ring rills mæander'd o'er—   85
Enjoy them, you! Villario can no more;
Tir'd of the scene Parterres and Fountains yield,
He finds at last he better likes a Field.
    Thro' his young Woods how pleas'd Sabinus stray'd,
Or sat delighted in the thick'ning shade   90
With annual joy the red'ning shoots to greet,
Or see the stretching branches long to meet!
His Son's fine Taste an op'ner Vista loves,
Foe to the Dryads of his Father's groves,
One boundless Green, or flourish'd Carpet views,   95
With all the mournful family of Yews;
The thriving plants ignoble broomsticks made,
Now sweep those Alleys they were born to shade.

75–6. This was done in Hertfordshire, by a wealthy citizen, at the expence of above 5000 l. by which means (merely to overlook a dead plain) he let in the north-wind upon his house and parterre, which were before adorned and defended by beautiful woods [P]. At Moor Park, Rickmansworth.

78. Dr. S. Clarke's busto placed by the Queen in the Hermitage, while the Dr. duely frequented the Court [P]. The Hermitage was one of the ornamental features in Richmond Park. In 1732, busts of Boyle, Locke, Newton, and Wollaston by Rysbrack and of Samuel Clarke by Guelfi were installed there. Samuel Clarke (1675–1729) was the most distinguished English philosopher between Locke and Berkeley.

80. *Quincunx*] A group of five trees, four planted in a square or rectangle (one at each corner) and the fifth in the centre. For Pope's own quincunx see *Imit. Hor.*, *Sat.*, ii i 130 (p. 618).

84. See 'The Garden', ll. 7–8, p. 12.

95. The two extremes in parterres, which are equally faulty; a *boundless Green*, large and naked as a field, or a *flourished Carpet*, where the greatness and nobleness of the piece is lessened by being divided into too many parts, with scroll'd works and beds, of which the examples are frequent [P].

96. Touches upon the ill taste of those who are so fond of Ever-greens (particularly Yews, which are the most tonsile) as to destroy the nobler Forest-trees, to make way for such little ornaments as Pyramids of dark-green, continually repeated, not unlike a Funeral procession [P].

At Timon's Villa let us pass a day,
Where all cry out, 'What sums are thrown away!' 100
So proud, so grand, of that stupendous air,
Soft and Agreeable come never there.
Greatness, with Timon, dwells in such a draught
As brings all Brobdignag before your thought.
To compass this, his building is a Town, 105
His pond an Ocean, his parterre a Down:
Who but must laugh, the Master when he sees,
A puny insect, shiv'ring at a breeze!
Lo, what huge heaps of littleness around!
The whole, a labour'd Quarry above ground. 110
Two Cupids squirt before: a Lake behind
Improves the keenness of the Northern wind.
His Gardens next your admiration call,
On ev'ry side you look, behold the Wall!
No pleasing Intricacies intervene, 115
No artful wildness to perplex the scene;
Grove nods at grove, each Alley has a brother,
And half the platform just reflects the other.
The suff'ring eye inverted Nature sees,
Trees cut to Statues, Statues thick as trees, 120
With here a Fountain, never to be play'd,
And there a Summer-house, that knows no shade;
Here Amphitrite sails thro' myrtle bow'rs;
There Gladiators fight, or die, in flow'rs;
Un-water'd see the drooping sea-horse mourn, 125
And swallows roost in Nilus' dusty Urn.
    My Lord advances with majestic mien,
Smit with the mighty pleasure, to be seen:
But soft—by regular approach—not yet—
First thro' the length of yon hot Terrace sweat, 130
And when up ten steep slopes you've dragg'd your thighs,
Just at his Study-door he'll bless your eyes.

99. *At Timon's Villa*] This description is intended to comprize the
principles of a false Taste of Magnificence, and to exemplify what was
said before, that nothing but Good Sense can attain it [P]. Timon is
almost certainly nobody in particular, a personification of aristocratic
pride; but many of the details of the grounds and house derive from
actual offences against taste committed by Pope's contemporaries.
    124. The two Statues of the *Gladiator pugnans* and *Gladiator moriens*
[P].
    130. The *Approaches* and *Communications* of house with garden, or of
one part with another, ill judged and inconvienient [P].

His Study! with what Authors is it stor'd?
In Books, not Authors, curious is my Lord;
To all their dated Backs he turns you round,   135
These Aldus printed, those Du Suëil has bound.
Lo some are Vellom, and the rest as good
For all his Lordship knows, but they are Wood.
For Locke or Milton 'tis in vain to look,
These shelves admit not any modern book.   140
    And now the Chapel's silver bell you hear,
That summons you to all the Pride of Pray'r:
Light quirks of Musick, broken and uneven,
Make the soul dance upon a Jig to Heaven.
On painted Cielings you devoutly stare,   145
Where sprawl the Saints of Verrio or Laguerre,
On gilded clouds in fair expansion lie,
And bring all Paradise before your eye.
To rest, the Cushion and soft Dean invite,
Who never mentions Hell to ears polite.   150
    But hark! the chiming Clocks to dinner call;
A hundred footsteps scrape the marble Hall:
The rich Buffet well-colour'd Serpents grace,
And gaping Tritons spew to wash your face.

133. The false Taste in Books; a satyr on the vanity in collecting them, more frequent in men of Fortune than the study to understand them. Many delight chiefly in the elegance of the print, or of the binding: some have carried it so far, as to cause the upper shelves to be filled with painted books of wood; others pique themselves so much upon books in a language they do not understand as to exclude the most useful in one they do. [P]

136. Aldo Manutio, the Renaissance Venetian printer, and the Abbé Du Sueil, a famous Paris binder of the early eighteenth century.

143. The false Taste in *Music*, improper to the subjects, as of light airs in Churches, often practised by the organists, *&c.* [P].

145. —And in *Painting* ⟨i.e. false taste in⟩ (from which even Italy is not free) of naked figures in Churches, *&c.* which has obliged some Popes to put draperies on some of those of the best masters [P].

146. *Verrio or Laguerre*] Verrio (Antonio) ⟨1639–1707⟩ painted many cielings, &c. at Windsor, Hampton-court, &c. and Laguerre ⟨1663–1721⟩ at Blenheim-castle, and other places [P]. See *Windsor-Forest*, 303–10*n*.

150. This is a fact; a reverend Dean preaching at Court, threatned the sinner with punishment in 'a place which he thought it not decent to name in so polite an assembly' [P]. Knightly Chetwood (1650–1720), Dean of Gloucester.

153. Taxes the incongruity of *Ornaments* (tho' sometimes practised by the ancients) where an open mouth ejects the water into a fountain, or where the shocking images of serpents, &c. are introduced in Grottos or Buffets [P].

Is this a dinner? this a Genial room?   155
No, 'tis a Temple, and a Hecatomb.
A solemn Sacrifice, perform'd in state,
You drink by measure, and to minutes eat.
So quick retires each flying course, you'd swear
Sancho's dread Doctor and his Wand were there.   160
Between each Act the trembling salvers ring,
From soup to sweet-wine, and God bless the King.
In plenty starving, tantaliz'd in state,
And complaisantly help'd to all I hate,
Treated, caress'd, and tir'd, I take my leave,   165
Sick of his civil Pride from Morn to Eve;
I curse such lavish cost, and little skill,
And swear no Day was ever past so ill.
    Yet hence the Poor are cloath'd, the Hungry fed;
Health to himself, and to his Infants bread   170
The Lab'rer bears: What his hard Heart denies,
His charitable Vanity supplies.
    Another age shall see the golden Ear
Imbrown the Slope, and nod on the Parterre,
Deep Harvests bury all his pride has plann'd,   175
And laughing Ceres re-assume the land.
    Who then shall grace, or who improve the Soil?
Who plants like BATHURST, or who builds like BOYLE.
'Tis Use alone that sanctifies Expence,
And Splendor borrows all her rays from Sense.   180
    His Father's Acres who enjoys in peace,
Or makes his Neighbours glad, if he encrease;
Whose chearful Tenants bless their yearly toil,
Yet to their Lord owe more than to the soil;
Whose ample Lawns are not asham'd to feed   185

155. The proud Festivals of some men are here set forth to ridicule,
where pride destroys the ease, and formal regularity all the pleasurable
enjoyment of the entertainment [P].

155. *Genial*] 'Of or pertaining to a feast' (*OED*).

160. *Sancho's dread Doctor*] See Don Quixote, chap. xlvii [P].

169. The *Moral* of the whole, where PROVIDENCE is justified in giving
Wealth to those who squander it in this manner. A bad Taste employs
more hands and diffuses Expence more than a good one. This recurs to
what is laid down in Book i. Epist. II v. 230-7 (p. 523), and in the Epistle
preceding this, v. 161 &c. [P]

174. *Slope*] A technical term for the artificial banks used by landscape
gardeners.

176. *laughing Ceres*] The smiling scene that a cornfield exhibits.

178. For Allen, Lord Bathurst see p. 570 above. 'Boyle' is Richard
Boyle, Earl of Burlington, the poem's dedicatee.

The milky heifer and deserving steed;
Whose rising Forests, not for pride or show,
But future Buildings, future Navies grow:
Let his plantations stretch from down to down,
First shade a Country, and then raise a Town.   190
    You too proceed! make falling Arts your care,
Erect new wonders, and the old repair,
Jones and Palladio to themselves restore,
And be whate'er Vitruvius was before:
Till Kings call forth th' Idea's of your mind,   195
Proud to accomplish what such hands design'd,
Bid Harbors open, public Ways extend,
Bid Temples, worthier of the God, ascend;
Bid the broad Arch the dang'rous Flood contain,
The Mole projected break the roaring Main;   200
Back to his bounds their subject Sea command,
And roll obedient Rivers thro' the Land;
These Honours, Peace to happy Britain brings,
These are Imperial Works, and worthy Kings.

190. *Country*] A tract or district owned by the same proprietor.
194. M. Vitruvius Pollio (born c. 88 B.C.), author of *De Architectura*.
195–204. The poet after having touched upon the proper objects of
Magnificence and Expence, in the private works of great men, comes to
those great and public works which become a Prince. This Poem was
published in the year 1732, when some of the new-built Churches, by the
Act of Queen Anne, were ready to fall, being founded in boggy land
(which is satirically alluded to in our author's imitation of Horace Lib. ii.
Sat. 2 ⟨l. 119⟩.

Shall half the new-built Churches round thee fall)
others were vilely executed, thro' fraudulent cabals between undertakers,
officers, &c. Dagenham-breach had done very great mischiefs; many of
the Highways throughout England were hardly passable, and most of
those which were repaired by Turnpikes were made jobs for private lucre,
and infamously executed, even to the entrances of London itself: The
proposal of building a Bridge at Westminster had been petition'd against
and rejected; but in two years after the publication of this poem, an Act
for building a Bridge past thro' both houses. After many debates in the
committee, the execution was left to the carpenter above-mentioned ⟨l.
18⟩, who would have made it a wooden one; to which our author alludes
in these lines,

Who builds a Bridge that never drove a pile?
Should Ripley venture, all the world would smile.

See the notes on that place ⟨*Imit. Hor., Ep.*, II i 186⟩. [P] See the note to
Imit. Hor., Sat., II ii 119, p. 622. Dagenham Breach was the result of a
storm in 1707 which broke through a sluice in the bank of the Thames,
costing over £40,000 to repair and not completed until 1723. An Act for
the construction of Westminster Bridge was passed in 1736, and Burlington was (from 1737) one of the Commissioners appointed to superintend
the work. The first stone was laid in 1739 and it was opened in 1750.

An Epistle from Mr. Pope, to Dr. Arbuthnot

[written 1731–4; published 1735]

Neque sermonibus Vulgi *dederis te, nec in* Præmiis *humanis spem posueris rerum tuarum: suis te oportet illecebris* ipsa Virtus *trahat ad verum decus. Quid de te alii loquantur, ipsi videant, sed loquentur tamen.*

TULLY [*De Re Publica,* Lib. VI, cap. XXIII].

ADVERTISEMENT

This Paper is a Sort of Bill of Complaint, begun many years since, and drawn up by snatches, as the several Occasions offer'd. I had no thoughts of publishing it, till it pleas'd some Persons of Rank and Fortune [the Authors[1] *of* Verses to the Imitator of Horace, *and of an* Epistle to a Doctor of Divinity from a Nobleman at Hampton Court,] *to attack in a very extraordinary manner, not only my Writings* (*of which being publick the Publick judge*) *but my* Person, Morals, *and* Family, *whereof to those who know me not, a truer Information may be requisite. Being divided between the Necessity to say something of* Myself, *and my own Laziness to undertake so awkward a Task, I thought it the shortest way to put the last hand to this Epistle. If it have any thing pleasing, it will be That by which I am most desirous to please, the* Truth *and the* Sentiment; *and if any thing offensive, it will be only to those I am least sorry to offend, the* Vicious *or* the Ungenerous.

Many will know their own Pictures in it, there being not a Circumstance but what is true; but I have, for the most part spar'd their Names, *and they may escape being laugh'd at, if they please.*

I would have some of them know, it was owing to the Request of the learned and candid Friend to whom it is inscribed, that I make not as free use of theirs as they have done of mine. However I shall have this Advantage, and Honour, on my side, that whereas by their proceeding, any Abuse may be directed at any man, no Injury can possibly be done by mine, since a Nameless Character can never be found out, but by its Truth *and* Likeness.

> Shut, shut the door, good *John !* fatigu'd I said,
> Tye up the knocker, say I'm sick, I'm dead,

---

[1] *Authors*] Lord Hervey and Lady Mary Wortley Montagu.
1. *good John*] Pope's servant, John Serle.

The Dog-star rages! nay 'tis past a doubt,
All *Bedlam*, or *Parnassus*, is let out:
Fire in each eye, and Papers in each hand,   5
They rave, recite, and madden round the land.
   What Walls can guard me, or what Shades can hide?
They pierce my Thickets, thro' my Grot they glide,
By land, by water, they renew the charge,
They stop the Chariot, and they board the Barge.   10
No place is sacred, not the Church is free,
Ev'n *Sunday* shines no *Sabbath-day* to me:
Then from the *Mint* walks forth the Man of Ryme,
Happy! to catch me, just at Dinner-time.
   Is there a Parson, much be-mus'd in Beer,   15
A maudlin Poetess, a ryming Peer,
A Clerk, foredoom'd his Father's soul to cross,
Who pens a Stanza when he should *engross*?
Is there, who lock'd from Ink and Paper, scrawls
With desp'rate Charcoal round his darken'd walls?   20
All fly to *Twit'nam*, and in humble strain
Apply to me, to keep them mad or vain.
Arthur, whose giddy Son neglects the Laws,
Imputes to me and my damn'd works the cause:
Poor *Cornus* sees his frantic Wife elope,   25
And curses Wit, and Poetry, and *Pope*.
   Friend to my Life, (which did not you prolong,
The World had wanted many an idle Song)
What *Drop* or *Nostrum* can this Plague remove?
Or which must end me, a Fool's Wrath or Love?   30
A dire Dilemma! either way I'm sped,
If Foes, they write, if Friends, they read me dead.
Seiz'd and ty'd down to judge, how wretched I!
Who can't be silent, and who will not lye;

3. *The Dog-star rages*] Sirius reappears in late summer, the customary
time of rehearsing poetry in Ancient Rome.

8. *my Grot*] see *Sat.* II i 124*n*, p. 617.

10. *the Barge*] Pope employed a waterman to convey him between
London and Twickenham.

13. *the Mint*] see *Sat.* II i 99*n*, p. 616.

15. A reference to the late poet laureate, Laurence Eusden—the word
bemus'd echoes his name—a type of the Drunken Poet.

23. *Arthur . . . Son*] Arthur Moore a politician, and James Moore
Smythe, who had given offence by refusing to remove some of Pope's
unpublished verses from his comedy *The Rival Modes*, 1727.

33. *ty'd down*] Contemporary readers would recall the scene in
Wycherley's *Plain Dealer* (v. 3), where Oldfox gags and ties down the
Widow, to hear his well-penned stanzas.

To laugh, were want of Goodness and of Grace,   35
And to be grave, exceeds all Pow'r of Face.
I sit with sad Civility, I read
With honest anguish, and an aking head;
And drop at last, but in unwilling ears,
This saving counsel, 'Keep your Piece nine years.'   40
   Nine years! cries he, who high in *Drury-lane*
Lull'd by soft Zephyrs thro' the broken Pane,
Rymes e're he wakes, and prints before *Term* ends,
Oblig'd by hunger and Request of friends:
'The Piece you think is incorrect: why take it,   45
I'm all submission, what you'd have it, make it.'
   Three things another's modest wishes bound,
My Friendship, and a Prologue, and ten Pound.
   Pitholeon sends to me: 'You know his Grace,
I want a Patron; ask him for a Place.'   50
Pitholeon libell'd me—'but here's a Letter
Informs you Sir, 'twas when he knew no better.
Dare you refuse him? *Curl* invites to dine,
He'll write a *Journal*, or he'll turn *Divine*.'
   Bless me! a Packet.—' 'Tis a stranger sues,   55
A Virgin Tragedy, an Orphan Muse.'
If I dislike it, 'Furies, death and rage!'
If I approve, 'Commend it to the Stage.'
There (thank my Stars) my whole Commission ends,
The Play'rs and I are, luckily, no friends.   60

40. *Keep . . . nine years*] the famous counsel of Horace, *Ars Poetica* 388, nonumque prematur in annum, Membranis intus positis.

41. *high*] i.e. in a garret.
Drury-lane] In Pope's time the abode of harlots and other disreputable characters.

43. *before Term ends*] i.e. the legal terms, with which the publishing 'seasons' synchronized.

49. *Pitholeon*] The name taken from a foolish Poet at *Rhodes*, who pretended much to *Greek*. Schol. in Horat. lib. i. Dr. Bentley pretends, that this Pitholeon libelled Caesar also. See notes on Hor. Sat. x l. 1 ⟨v. 22⟩ [P]. The MS shows that Leonard Welsted was intended, a poet and critic of ability; for his quarrel with P, see l. 375*n*. But 'Pitholeon' also fits Thomas Cooke, the translator of Hesiod (1728), who had written to P. in apology for 'libelling' him.

53. Edmund Curll, a bookseller of infamous reputation, who specialized in publishing scandalous biographies and private papers not meant for the press. P had suffered from his attentions since 1714, and had revenged himself by administering an emetic. He also manoeuvred Curll into publishing an unauthorized edition of his *Letters*.

Fir'd that the House reject him, ' 'Sdeath I'll print it
And shame the Fools—your Int'rest, Sir, with *Lintot*.'
Lintot, dull rogue! will think your price too much.
'Not Sir, if you revise it, and retouch.'
All my demurrs but double his attacks,   65
At last he whispers 'Do, and we go snacks.'
Glad of a quarrel, strait I clap the door,
Sir, let me see your works and you no more.
  'Tis sung, when *Midas*' Ears began to spring,
(*Midas*, a sacred Person and a King)   70
His very Minister who spy'd them first,
(Some say his Queen) was forc'd to speak, or burst.
And is not mine, my Friend, a sorer case,
When ev'ry Coxcomb perks them in my face?
'Good friend forbear! you deal in dang'rous things,   75
I'd never name Queens, Ministers, or Kings;
Keep close to Ears, and those let Asses prick,
Tis nothing'—Nothing? if they bite and kick?
Out with it, *Dunciad!* let the secret pass,
That Secret to each Fool, that he's an Ass: 80
The truth once told, (and wherefore shou'd we lie?)
The Queen of *Midas* slept, and so may I.
  You think this cruel? take it for a rule,
No creature smarts so little as a Fool.
Let Peals of Laughter, *Codrus!* round thee break,   85
Thou unconcern'd canst hear the mighty Crack.
Pit, Box and Gall'ry in convulsions hurl'd,
Thou stand'st unshook amidst a bursting World.

62. Bernard Lintot, the bookseller who had published P's Homer.
  72. *his Queen*] The Story is told by some ⟨Ovid *Met*. xi 146 and
Persius *Sat*. i 121⟩ of his Barber, but by *Chaucer* of his Queen. See Wife
of Bath's Tale in *Dryden's* Fables ⟨ll. 157–200⟩. [P]
  76. A reflection upon the political alliance of Walpole and Queen
Caroline.
  80. I.e. that his ears (his marks of folly) are visible.
  85. *Codrus*] The name of a poet ridiculed by Virgil and Juvenal.
  86–8. Alluding to Horace ⟨*Ode* III iii 7, 8⟩

              Si fractus illabatur orbis,
              Impavidum ferient ruinæ. [P]

But P alludes more particularly to Addison's rendering:

         Should the whole frame of nature round him break,
         In ruine and confusion hurl'd,
         He, unconcern'd, would hear the mighty crack,
         And stand secure amidst a falling world.

P had quoted the first and third lines in Ch. xii of *Peri Bathous* to show
how 'Sometimes a single *Word* [crack] will vulgarize a poetical idea.'

EPISTLE TO DR. ARBUTHNOT

Who shames a Scribler? break one cobweb thro',
He spins the slight, self-pleasing thread anew;   90
Destroy his Fib, or Sophistry; in vain,
The Creature's at his dirty work again;
Thron'd in the Centre of his thin designs;
Proud of a vast Extent of flimzy lines.
Whom have I hurt? has Poet yet, or Peer,   95
Lost the arch'd eye-brow, or *Parnassian* sneer?
And has not *Colly* still his Lord, and Whore?
His Butchers *Henley*, his Free-masons *Moor?*
Does not one Table *Bavius* still admit?
Still to one Bishop *Philips* seem a Wit?   100
Still *Sapho*—'Hold! for God-sake—you'll offend:
No Names—be calm—learn Prudence of a Friend:
I too could write, and I am twice as tall,
But Foes like these!'—One Flatt'rer's worse than all;
Of all mad Creatures, if the Learn'd are right,   105
It is the Slaver kills, and not the Bite.
A Fool quite angry is quite innocent;
Alas! 'tis ten times worse when they *repent*.

One dedicates, in high Heroic prose,
And ridicules beyond a hundred foes;   110
One from all *Grubstreet* will my fame defend,
And, more abusive, calls himself my friend.
This prints my Letters, that expects a Bribe,
And others roar aloud, 'Subscribe, subscribe.'
There are, who to my Person pay their court,   115
I cough like *Horace*, and tho' lean, am short,

96. *Parnassian sneer*] Cf. *Dunciad* A ii 5 p. 371.

97. *Colly*] Cibber, comic actor, dramatist, and since 1730, poet laureate.
He had aroused P's animosity by his treatment of P and his friends in
plays and as actor-manager; but the quarrel did not grow acute until C
attacked P in *A Letter . . . to Mr. Pope* (1742) and P retaliated by dis-
placing Theobald with C in *The Dunciad* (1743).

98. *His Butchers Henley*] A mountebank preacher in government pay
who had frequently attacked P. See p. 414n. On Easter Day, 1729, he
delivered a sermon purporting to display the religious History and Use of
the Butchers Calling.

his Free-masons Moor] Moore-Smythe (l. 23n).

99. *Bavius*] Bavius and Maevius were two poetasters who owe their
immortality to the enmity which they displayed towards Virgil and
Horace.

100. *to one Bishop*] Ambrose Philips, P's rival in pastoral poetry, had
gone to Ireland as secretary to Archbishop Boulter.

113. *Letters*] Some of P's letters had been surreptitiously printed by
Curll in 1726.

Ammon's great Son one shoulder had too high,
Such *Ovid*'s nose, and 'Sir! you have an *Eye*—'
Go on, obliging Creatures, make me see
All that disgrac'd my Betters, met in me: 120
Say for my comfort, languishing in bed,
'Just so immortal *Maro* held his head:'
And when I die, be sure you let me know
Great *Homer* dy'd three thousand years ago.

Why did I write? what sin to me unknown   125
Dipt me in Ink, my Parents', or my own?
As yet a Child, nor yet a Fool to Fame,
I lisp'd in Numbers, for the Numbers came.
I left no Calling for this idle trade,
No Duty broke, no Father dis-obey'd.   130
The Muse but serv'd to ease some Friend, not Wife,
To help me thro' this long Disease, my Life,
To second, ARBUTHNOT! thy Art and Care,
And teach, the Being you preserv'd, to bear.

But why then publish? *Granville* the polite,   135
And knowing *Walsh*, would tell me I could write;
Well-natur'd *Garth* inflam'd with early praise,
And *Congreve* lov'd, and *Swift* endur'd my Lays;
The Courtly *Talbot, Somers, Sheffield* read,
Ev'n mitred *Rochester* would nod the head,   140
And *St. John*'s self (great *Dryden*'s friends before)
With open arms receiv'd one Poet more.

117. *Ammon's great Son*] Alexander the Great; see *Temple of Fame*, 152n (p. 178).

130. *no Father dis-obey'd*] a reference to Moore-Smythe; see l. 23.

140. *Rochester*] Atterbury.

141. *Dryden's friends*] All these were Patrons or Admirers of Mr. *Dryden*, tho' a scandalous Libel against him, entituled, *Dryden's Satyr to his Muse*, has been printed in the Name of the Lord *Somers*, of which he was wholly ignorant.

These are the persons to whose account the Author charges the publication of his first pieces: Persons with whom he was conversant (and he adds belov'd) at 16 or 17 years of age; an early period for such acquaintance! The catalogue might be made yet more illustrious, had he not confined it to that time when he writ the *Pastorals* and *Windsor Forest*, on which he passes a sort of Censure in the lines following,

   While pure Description held the place of Sense, &c
                [P]

135-41. Granville, Walsh, and Garth were poets; Talbot, Duke of Shrewsbury, Lord Somers and Sheffield, Duke of Buckingham were statesmen and patrons. Sheffield's poems were edited by Pope.

Happy my Studies, when by these approv'd!
Happier their Author, when by these belov'd!
From these the world will judge of Men and Books,   145
Not from the *Burnets*, *Oldmixons*, and *Cooks*.
    Soft were my Numbers, who could take offence
While pure Description held the place of Sense?
Like gentle *Fanny*'s was my flow'ry Theme,
A painted Mistress, or a purling Stream.   150
Yet then did *Gildon* draw his venal quill;
I wish'd the man a dinner, and sate still:
Yet then did *Dennis* rave in furious fret;
I never answer'd, I was not in debt:
If want provok'd, or madness made them print,   155
I wag'd no war with *Bedlam* or the *Mint*.
    Did some more sober Critic come abroad?
If wrong, I smil'd; if right, I kiss'd the rod.
Pains, reading, study, are their just pretence,
And all they want is spirit, taste, and sense.   160
Comma's and points they set exactly right,
And 'twere a sin to rob them of their Mite.
Yet ne'r one sprig of Laurel grac'd these ribalds,
From slashing *Bentley* down to pidling *Tibalds*.
Each Wight who reads not, and but scans and spells,   165
Each Word-catcher that lives on syllables,
Ev'n such small Critics some regard may claim,
Preserv'd in *Milton*'s or in *Shakespear*'s name.
Pretty! in Amber to observe the forms
Of hairs, or straws, or dirt, or grubs, or worms;   170
The things, we know, are neither rich nor rare,
But wonder how the Devil they got there?

146. Authors of secret and scandalous History [P]. Thomas Burnet is
believed to have written *Pope Alexander's Supremacy* (1729), a severe
attack upon P. John Oldmixon had criticized his work in the *Arts of
Logick and Rhetorick* (1728). For Cooke, see l. 49*n*.
    150. *A painted Meadow, or a purling stream* is a Verse of Mr. *Addison*
[P].
    A Letter from Italy ll. 165-6.
    151-92. A version of these lines originally introduced the character of
Addison (Atticus), see p. 490. Gildon had *The Rape of the Lock* censured
in *A New Rehearsal* (1714) and Dennis in *The Progress of Dulness* (1728).
    156. *the Mint*] see *Sat.* II i 99*n*.
    157-72. These lines first appeared in *Miscellanies* (1727) as an expan-
sion of the character of Addison. See p. 490.
    164. *slashing Bentley*] Bentley had attempted to restore the true text of
Par. Lost (1732) on the assumption that the blind Milton was at the mercy
of an amanuensis.

Were others angry? I excus'd them too;
Well might they rage; I gave them but their due.
A man's true merit 'tis not hard to find,   175
But each man's secret standard in his mind,
That Casting-weight Pride adds to Emptiness,
This, who can gratify? for who can *guess*?
The Bard whom pilf'red Pastorals renown,
Who turns a *Persian* Tale for half a crown,   180
Just writes to make his barrenness appear,
And strains from hard-bound brains eight lines a-year:
He, who still wanting tho' he lives on theft,
Steals much, spends little, yet has nothing left:
And he, who now to sense, now nonsense leaning,   185
Means not, but blunders round about a meaning:
And he, whose Fustian's so sublimely bad,
It is not Poetry, but Prose run mad:
All these, my modest Satire bad *translate*,
And own'd, that nine such Poets made a *Tate*.   190
How did they fume, and stamp, and roar, and chafe?
And swear, not *Addison* himself was safe.
    Peace to all such! but were there One whose fires
True Genius kindles, and fair Fame inspires,
Blest with each Talent and each Art to please,   195
And born to write, converse, and live with ease:
Shou'd such a man, too fond to rule alone,
Bear, like the *Turk*, no brother near the throne,
View him with scornful, yet with jealous eyes,
And hate for Arts that caus'd himself to rise;   200
Damn with faint praise, assent with civil leer,
And without sneering, teach the rest to sneer;
Willing to wound, and yet afraid to strike,
Just hint a fault, and hesitate dislike;
Alike reserv'd to blame, or to commend,   205
A tim'rous foe, and a suspicious friend,
Dreading ev'n fools, by Flatterers besieg'd,
And so obliging that he ne'er oblig'd;
Like *Cato*, give his little Senate laws,
And sit attentive to his own applause;   210

180. *a Persian tale*] Amb. Philips translated a Book called the *Persian Tales*. [P] Half a crown was the prostitute's customary charge.
    193-214. For earlier versions of the character of Atticus (Addison), see pp. 293, 490.
    205. The ideal critic, like Walsh (*E. on C.* 730), 'justly knew to blame or to commend.'
    209. Cf. P's prologue to Addison's *Cato* (1713) l. 23, p. 211.

While Wits and Templers ev'ry sentence raise,
And wonder with a foolish face of praise.
Who but must laugh, if such a man there be?
Who would not weep, if *Atticus* were he!
    What tho' my Name stood rubric on the walls?   215
Or plaister'd posts, with Claps in capitals?
Or smoaking forth, a hundred Hawkers load,
On Wings of Winds came flying all abroad?
I sought no homage from the Race that write;
I kept, like *Asian* Monarchs, from their sight: 220
Poems I heeded (now be-rym'd so long)
No more than Thou, great GEORGE! a Birth-day Song.
I ne'r with Wits or Witlings past my days,
To spread about the Itch of Verse and Praise;
Nor like a Puppy daggled thro' the Town,   225
To fetch and carry Sing-song up and down;
Nor at Rehearsals sweat, and mouth'd, and cry'd,
With Handkerchief and Orange at my side:
But sick of Fops, and Poetry, and Prate,
To *Bufo* left the whole *Castalian* State.   230
    Proud, as *Apollo* on his forked hill,
Sate full-blown *Bufo*, puff'd by ev'ry quill;
Fed with soft Dedication all day long,
Horace and he went hand in hand in song.
His Library, (where Busts of Poets dead   235
And a true *Pindar* stood without a head)
Receiv'd of Wits an undistinguish'd race,
Who first his Judgment ask'd, and then a Place:
Much they extoll'd his Pictures, much his Seat,
And flatter'd ev'ry day, and some days eat: 240

214. *Atticus*] It was a great Falshood which some of the Libels reported, that this Character was written after the Gentleman's ⟨*Addison's*⟩ death, which see refuted in the Testimonies prefix'd to the Dunciad. But the occasion of writing it was such, as he would not make publick in regard to his memory; and all that could further be done was to omit the Name, in the Editions of his Works. [P]
215–16. *stood rubric*] Books were advertised by 'clapping' copies of title-pages to boards or posts in front of booksellers' shops. Pope's former publisher Lintot, was especially fond of red-letter title pages.
218. Hopkins, in the 104th Psalm [P].
232. *Bufo*] A Theophrastan character of a Patron, composed of certain traits, which Pope had observed in Bubb Dodington (l. 280n.) and the Earl of Halifax.
236. *Pindar*] ridicules the affectation of Antiquaries, who frequently exhibit the headless *Trunks* and *Terms* of Statues, for Plato, Homer, Pindar, &c. Vide *Fulv.*, *Ursin*, &c. [P]

Till grown more frugal in his riper days,
He pay'd some Bards with Port, and some with Praise,
To some a dry Rehearsal was assign'd,
And others (harder still) he pay'd in kind.
Dryden alone (what wonder?) came not nigh,   245
Dryden alone escap'd this judging eye:
But still the Great have kindness in reserve,
He help'd to bury whom he help'd to starve.
   May some choice Patron bless each gray goose quill!
May ev'ry *Bavius* have his *Bufo* still!   250
So, when a Statesman wants a Day's defence,
Or Envy holds a whole Week's war with Sense,
Or simple Pride for Flatt'ry makes demands;
May Dunce by Dunce be whistled off my hands!
Blest be the *Great!* for those they take away,   255
And those they left me—For they left me GAY,
Left me to see neglected Genius bloom,
Neglected die! and tell it on his Tomb;
Of all thy blameless Life the sole Return
My Verse, and QUEENSB'RY weeping o'er thy Urn!   260
Oh let me live my own! and die so too!
('To live and die is all I have to do:')
Maintain a Poet's Dignity and Ease,
And see what friends, and read what books I please.
Above a Patron, tho' I condescend   265
Sometimes to call a Minister my Friend:
I was not born for Courts or great Affairs,
I pay my Debts, believe, and say my Pray'rs,
Can sleep without a Poem in my head,
Nor know, if *Dennis* be alive or dead.   270
   Why am I ask'd, what next shall see the light?
Heav'ns! was I born for nothing but to write?
Has Life no Joys for me? or (to be grave)
Have I no Friend to serve, no Soul to save?
'I found him close with *Swift*'—'Indeed? no doubt'   275
(Cries prating *Balbus*) 'something will come out.'
'Tis all in vain, deny it as I will.

248. *help'd to bury*] Mr. Dryden, after having liv'd in Exigencies, had
a magnificent Funeral bestow'd upon him by the contribution of several
Persons of Quality [P].

260. *Queensb'ry*] During Gay's last years, he was taken under the
protection of the Duke and Duchess of Queensberry, who erected his
monument in Westminster Abbey.

262. From Denham's *Of Prudence*, ll. 93, 4.

'No, such a Genius never can lye still,'
And then for mine obligingly mistakes
The first Lampoon Sir *Will.* or *Bubo* makes.   280
Poor guiltless I! and can I chuse but smile,
When ev'ry Coxcomb knows me by my *Style?*
    Curst be the Verse, how well soe'er it flow,
That tends to make one worthy Man my foe,
Give Virtue scandal, Innocence a fear,   285
Or from the soft-ey'd Virgin steal a tear!
But he, who hurts a harmless neighbour's peace,
Insults fal'n Worth, or Beauty in distress,
Who loves a Lye, lame slander helps about,
Who writes a Libel, or who copies out: 290
That Fop whose pride affects a Patron's name,
Yet absent, wounds an Author's honest fame;
Who can your Merit selfishly approve,
And show the Sense of it, without the Love;
Who has the Vanity to call you Friend,   295
Yet wants the Honour injur'd to defend;
Who tells whate'er you think, whate'er you say,
And, if he lye not, must at least betray:
Who to the *Dean* and *silver Bell* can swear,
And sees at *Cannons* what was never there: 300
Who reads but with a Lust to mis-apply,
Make Satire a Lampoon, and Fiction, Lye.
A Lash like mine no honest man shall dread,
But all such babling blockheads in his stead.
    Let *Sporus* tremble—'What? that Thing of silk,   305

279 ff. Boileau had suffered in the same way (*Ep.* VI 69 ff.).

280. Easily recognizable type figures. Sir William Yonge was a parliamentary tool of Walpole's, ready to speak agreeably by the hour on nothing. Bubb Dodington was an obvious mark for satire owing to his political improbity, tactless extravagance, and affectation of patronage. See also p. 589, l. 20*n.*

282. *Style*] 'There is nothing more foolish than to pretend to be sure of knowing a great writer by his style.' Pope recorded by Spence.

289–304. An abbreviated version of these lines had appeared in a newspaper in January 1732 as a paraphrase of Horace, *Sat.* 4. *Lib.* 1 p. 814.

299. *Dean*] See the Epistle to the Earl of *Burlington* [P]. *Moral Es.* iv 141–50, p. 593.

305. *Sporus*] It was originally *Paris*, but that Name having been, as we conceive, the only reason that so contemptible a Character could be applied to a Noble and Beautiful Person, the Author changed it to this of *Sporus*, as a Name which has never yet been so mis-applied [P].

A passage in Suetonius (*Nero*, XXVIII i) accounts for the change. This is a character of Lord Hervey, who had been collaborating with Lady M. W. Montagu in attacks upon Pope.

Sporus, that mere white Curd of Ass's milk?
Satire or Sense alas! can *Sporus* feel?
Who breaks a Butterfly upon a Wheel?'
Yet let me flap this Bug with gilded wings,
This painted Child of Dirt that stinks and stings;   310
Whose Buzz the Witty and the Fair annoys,
Yet Wit ne'er tastes, and Beauty ne'er enjoys,
So well-bred Spaniels civilly delight
In mumbling of the Game they dare not bite.
Eternal Smiles his Emptiness betray,   315
As shallow streams run dimpling all the way.
Whether in florid Impotence he speaks,
And, as the Prompter breathes, the Puppet squeaks;
Or at the Ear of *Eve*, familiar Toad,
Half Froth, half Venom, spits himself abroad,   320
In Puns, or Politicks, or Tales, or Lyes,
Or Spite, or Smut, or Rymes, or Blasphemies.
His Wit all see-saw between *that* and *this*,
Now high, now low, now Master up, now Miss,
And he himself one vile Antithesis.   325
Amphibious Thing! that acting either Part,
The trifling Head, or the corrupted Heart!
Fop at the Toilet, Flatt'rer at the Board,
Now trips a Lady, and now struts a Lord.
Eve's Tempter thus the Rabbins have exprest,   330
A Cherub's face, a Reptile all the rest;
Beauty that shocks you, Parts that none will trust,
Wit that can creep, and Pride that licks the dust.
   Not Fortune's Worshipper, nor Fashion's Fool,
Not Lucre's Madman, nor Ambition's Tool,   335
Not proud, nor servile, be one Poet's praise
That, if he pleas'd, he pleas'd by manly ways;
That Flatt'ry, ev'n to Kings, he held a shame,
And thought a Lye in Verse or Prose the same:
That not in Fancy's Maze he wander'd long,   340
But stoop'd to Truth, and moraliz'd his song:

---

306. *Ass's milk*] Ass's milk was commonly prescribed as a tonic 'in all
weakly Constitutions as being more thin, light, and easier of Digestion'
than cow's milk.
   319. In the fourth Book of *Milton* ⟨l. 800⟩, the Devil is represented in
this Posture. It is but justice to own that the Hint of *Eve* and the *Serpent*
was taken from the *Verses on the Imitator of* Horace. [P] Eve is Queen
Caroline.
   341. *stoop'd to Truth*] The poet 'stoops' to Truth as a falcon to its lure,

That not for Fame, but Virtue's better end,
He stood the furious Foe, the timid Friend,
The damning Critic, half-approving Wit,
The Coxcomb hit, or fearing to be hit;   345
Laugh'd at the loss of Friends he never had,
The dull, the proud, the wicked, and the mad;
The distant Threats of Vengeance on his head,
The Blow unfelt, the Tear he never shed;
The Tale reviv'd, the Lye so oft o'erthrown;   350
Th' imputed Trash, and Dulness not his own;
The Morals blacken'd when the Writings scape;
The libel'd Person, and the pictur'd Shape;
Abuse on all he lov'd, or lov'd him, spread,
A Friend in Exile, or a Father, dead;   355
The Whisper that to Greatness still too near,
Perhaps, yet vibrates on his SOVEREIGN's Ear—
Welcome for thee, fair Virtue! all the past:
For thee, fair Virtue! welcome ev'n the *last!*
          'But why insult the Poor, affront the Great?'   360
A Knave's a Knave, to me, in ev'ry State,
Alike my scorn, if he succeed or fail,
Sporus at Court, or *Japhet* in a Jayl,

---

or Browne's 'haggard and unreclaimed Reason' to 'the lure of Faith'
(*Rel. Med.* 1 x).

moraliz'd his song] cf. *E. on Man* iv 391–3, p. 547. The phrase is found
in *Faerie Queene*, I invoc. l. 9.

349. *The Blow unfelt*] Alluding to a fictitious account of an assault
committed on Pope in 1728.

350. *Lye*] That he set his Name to Mr. *Broom*'s Verses, that he
receiv'd Subscriptions for *Shakespear*, &c. which tho' publickly disprov'd
were nevertheless shamelessly repeated in the Libels, and even in the
Paper call'd, *The Nobleman's Epistle* [P]. Hervey's *Nobleman's Epistle*
mentions only that he 'sold *Broome*'s Labours printed with *P—pe*'s Name.'

351. *Trash*] Profane *Psalms, Court Poems*, and many Libellous Things
in his Name, printed by *Curl*, &c. [P].

His version of the first psalm (see p. 300) and *Court Poems*, the work
of Gay and Lady Mary, were printed in 1716.

353. *the pictur'd Shape*] An illustration in *Pope Alexander's Supremacy
and Infallibility Examin'd* (1729) represents Pope as a hunchbacked ape
squatting on a pedestal and leaning on a pile of books.

354. *Abuse*] Namely on the Duke of *Buckingham*, Earl of *Burlington*,
Lord *Bathurst*, Lord *Bolingbroke*, Bishop *Atterbury*, Dr. *Swift*, Mr. *Gay*,
Dr. *Arbuthnot*, his Friends, his Parents, and his very *Nurse*, aspers'd in
printed Papers by *James Moore* and *G. Ducket*, Esquires, *Welsted, Tho.
Bentley*, and other obscure persons. [P]

355. *Friend in Exile*] Atterbury.

356. *The Whisper*] I.e. from Hervey (cf. l. 319).

Japhet] Japhet Crook, the forger. See *Moral Es.* iii 88n, p. 575.

A hireling Scribler, or a hireling Peer,
Knight of the Post corrupt, or of the Shire,   365
If on a Pillory, or near a Throne,
He gain his Prince's Ear, or lose his own.
　　Yet soft by Nature, more a Dupe than Wit,
Sapho can tell you how this Man was bit
This dreaded Sat'rist *Dennis* will confess   370
Foe to his Pride, but Friend to his Distress:
So humble, he has knock'd at *Tibbald*'s door,
Has drunk with *Cibber*, nay has rym'd for *Moor*.
Full ten years slander'd, did he once reply?
Three thousand Suns went down on *Welsted*'s Lye: 375
To please a *Mistress*, One aspers'd his life;
He lash'd him not, but let her be his *Wife*:
Let *Budgel* charge low *Grubstreet* on his quill,
And write whate'er he pleas'd, except his *Will*;
Let the *Two Curls* of Town and Court, abuse   380
His Father, Mother, Body, Soul, and Muse.

365. *Knight of the Post*] One who got his living by giving false evidence.
366. *Pillory . . . lose his own*] Pope writes with Japhet Crook's fate in mind.
371. *Friend to his Distress*] Pope had tried to promote (1731) a subscription edition of some of Dennis's Works.
374. *ten years*] It was so long, after many libels, before the Author of the *Dunciad* published that Poem, till when, he never writ a word in answer to the many Scurrilities and Falsehoods concerning him. [P]
375. *Welsted's Lye*] This Man had the Impudence to tell in print, that Mr. *P.* had occasion'd a *Lady's death*, and to *name* a person he never heard of. He also publish'd that he had libell'd the Duke of *Chandos*; with whom (it was added) that he had liv'd in familiarity, and receiv'd from him a Present of *five hundred pounds:* The Falsehood of which is known to his Grace. Mr. *P.* never receiv'd any Present farther than the Subscription for *Homer*, from him, or from Any Great Man whatsoever. [P]
376. William Windham is believed to have collaborated with Lady Mary and Hervey in *Verses to the Imitator of Horace*. His mistress was the Countess of Deloraine, the 'Delia' of *Sat.* II i 81, p. 616.
378. *Budgel*] *Budgel* in a Weekly Pamphlet call'd the *Bee*, bestow'd much abuse on him, in the imagination that he writ some things about the *Last Will* of Dr. *Tindal*, in the *Grubstreet Journal; a Paper* wherein he never had the *least Hand, Direction*, or *Supervisal*, nor the *least knowledge of its author*. [P] Pope's connection with the *Journal* is still a matter of conjecture. Budgell (see p. 285) almost certainly forged Tindal's will, by means of which he excluded the next heir and obtained the greater part of the estate.
380. The Court *Curll* was Hervey.
381. In some of *Curl's* and other Pamphlets, Mr. *Pope's* Father was said to be a Mechanic, a Hatter, a Farmer, nay a Bankrupt. But, what is stranger, a *Nobleman* ⟨Hervey⟩ (if such a Reflection can be thought to

Yet why? that Father held it for a rule
It was a Sin to call our Neighbour Fool,
That harmless Mother thought no Wife a Whore,—
Hear this! and spare his Family, *James More!* 385
Unspotted Names! and memorable long,
If there be Force in Virtue, or in Song.
    Of gentle Blood (part shed in Honour's Cause,
While yet in *Britain* Honour had Applause)
Each Parent sprung—'What Fortune, pray?'—
    Their own, 390
And better got than *Bestia*'s from the Throne.
Born to no Pride, inheriting no Strife,
Nor marrying Discord in a Noble Wife,
Stranger to Civil and Religious Rage,
The good Man walk'd innoxious thro' his Age. 395
No Courts he saw, no Suits would ever try,
Nor dar'd an Oath, nor hazarded a Lye:
Un-learn'd, he knew no Schoolman's subtle Art,
No Language, but the Language of the Heart.
By Nature honest, by Experience wise, 400
Healthy by Temp'rance and by Exercise:

---

come from a Nobleman) has dropt an Allusion to this pitiful Untruth, in
his *Epistle to a Doctor of Divinity:* And the following line,

    Hard as thy Heart, and as thy Birth Obscure,

had fallen from a like Courtly pen, in the *Verses to the Imitator of Horace.*
Mr. *Pope*'s Father was of a Gentleman's Family in *Oxfordshire*, the Head
of which was the Earl of *Downe*, whose sole Heiress married the Earl of
Lindsey.—His Mother was the Daughter of *William Turnor*, Esq; of
York: She had three Brothers, one of whom was kill'd, another died in
the Service of King *Charles*, the eldest following his Fortunes, and
becoming a General Officer in *Spain*, left her what Estate remain'd after
the Sequestrations and Forfeitures of her Family—Mr. *Pope* died in
1717, aged 75; She in 1733, aged 93, a very few Weeks after this Poem
was finished. The following Inscription was placed by their Son on their
Monument, in the Parish of Twickenham, in Middlesex.

D.O.M.
ALEXANDRO POPE, VIRO INNOCUO,
PROBO, PIO, QUI VIXIT ANNOS LXXV, OB. MDCCXVII.
ET EDITHÆ CONJUGI INCULPABILI, PIENTISSIMÆ,
QUÆ VIXIT ANNOS XCIII, OB. MDCCXXXIII.
PARENTIBUS BENEMERENTIBUS FILIUS FECIT, ET SIBI.
[P]

391. *Bestia*] L. Calpurnius Bestia, who here seems to signify Marlborough was a Roman Consul, bribed by Jugurtha into a dishonourable
peace.

His Life, tho' long, to sickness past unknown,
His Death was instant, and without a groan.
Oh grant me thus to live, and thus to die!
Who sprung from Kings shall know less joy than I.   405
  O Friend! may each Domestick Bliss be thine!
Be no unpleasing Melancholy mine:
Me, let the tender Office long engage
To rock the Cradle of reposing Age,
With lenient Arts extend a Mother's breath,   410
Make Languor smile, and smooth the Bed of Death,
Explore the Thought, explain the asking Eye,
And keep a while one Parent from the Sky!
On Cares like these if Length of days attend,
May Heav'n, to bless those days, preserve my Friend,   415
Preserve him social, chearful, and serene,
And just as rich as when he serv'd a QUEEN!
Whether that Blessing be deny'd, or giv'n,
Thus far was right, the rest belongs to Heav'n.

405. cf. Hor., *Sat.* I iii 142: Privatusque magis vivam te rege beatus.
406–19. Pope sent a version of these lines to Aaron Hill on Sept. 3,
1731, informing him of Mrs. Pope's illness. See p. 812.

Imitations of Horace

————————————————— ❊ —————————————————

The First Satire of the Second Book
of Horace Imitated
[written 1733; published 1733]

ADVERTISEMENT

The Occasion of publishing these Imitations *was the Clamour raised on
some of my* Epistles. *An Answer from* Horace *was both more full, and
of more Dignity, than any I cou'd have made in my own person; and
the Example of much greater Freedom in so eminent a Divine as* Dr.
Donne, *seem'd a proof with what Indignation and Contempt a Christian may treat Vice or Folly, in ever so low, or ever so high, a Station.
Both these Authors were acceptable to the Princes and Ministers under
whom they lived: The Satires of Dr.* Donne *I versify'd at the Desire
of the Earl of* Oxford *while he was Lord Treasurer, and of the Duke
of* Shrewsbury *who had been Secretary of State; neither of whom
look'd upon a Satire on Vicious Courts as any Reflection on those they
serv'd in. And indeed there is not in the world a greater Error, than
that which Fools are so apt to fall into, and Knaves with good reason
to incourage, the mistaking a* Satyrist *for a* Libeller; *whereas to a
true* Satyrist *nothing is so odious as a* Libeller, *for the same reason as
to a man truly* Virtuous *nothing is so hateful as a* Hypocrite.

—Uni aequus Virtuti atque ejus Amicis. [P]

> *P.* There are (I scarce can think it, but am told)
> There are to whom my Satire seems too bold,
> Scarce to wise *Peter* complaisant enough,
> And something said of *Chartres* much too rough.
> The Lines are weak, another's pleas'd to say,   5
> Lord *Fanny* spins a thousand such a Day.
> Tim'rous by Nature, of the Rich in awe,
> I come to Council learned in the Law.

3, 4. Referring to *Moral Es.* iii 125, 20, 88; pp. 577, 571, 575.
6. *Lord Fanny*] Pope first used this *soubriquet*, presumably for Hervey,
in *The Master Key to Popery* (1732).
8. His friend, William Fortescue, later Master of the Rolls.

613

You'll give me, like a Friend both sage and free,
Advice; and (as you use) without a Fee.   10
F. I'd write no more.
                    P. Not write? but then I *think*,
And for my Soul I cannot sleep a wink.
I nod in Company, I wake at Night,
Fools rush into my Head, and so I write.

  F. You could not do a worse thing for your Life.   15
Why, if the Nights seem tedious—take a Wife;
Or rather truly, if your Point be Rest,
Lettuce and Cowslip Wine; *Probatum est.*
But talk with *Celsus, Celsus* will advise
Hartshorn, or something that shall close your Eyes.   20
Or if you needs must write, write CÆSAR's Praise:
You'll gain at least a *Knighthood*, or the *Bays.*
  P. What? like Sir *Richard*, rumbling, rough and fierce,
With ARMS, and GEORGE, and BRUNSWICK crowd the
     Verse?
Rend with tremendous Sound your ears asunder,   25
With Gun, Drum, Trumpet, Blunderbuss & Thunder?
Or nobly wild, with *Budgell's* Fire and Force,
Paint Angels trembling round his *falling Horse?*
  F. Then all your Muse's softer Art display,
Let *Carolina* smooth the tuneful Lay,   30
Lull with *Amelia's* liquid Name the Nine,
And sweetly flow through all the Royal Line.
  P. Alas! few Verses touch their nicer Ear;
They scarce can bear their *Laureate* twice a Year:
And justly CÆSAR scorns the Poet's Lays,   35
It is to *History* he trusts for Praise.
  F. Better be *Cibber*, I'll maintain it still,
Than ridicule all *Taste*, blaspheme *Quadrille,*

19. *Celsus*] The chief Roman writer on medicine.
20. *Hartshorn*] A pleasantry on the novelty of the prescription.
23. *Sir Richard*] Blackmore, physician and poet.
27. Referring to Budgell's ludicrous *Poem upon His Majesty's Late
Journey to Cambridge and Newmarket,* 1728, in which the fate of
George II's illustrious steed, shot under him at the battle of Oudenarde,
is sung. The trembling angels are Pope's invention.
34. *twice a Year*] The poet laureate's duties were to celebrate with odes
the New Year and the King's Birthday. At this time the office was held
by Colley Cibber.
38. *ridicule all Taste*] See *Moral Es.* IV *passim.*
blaspheme Quadrille] Referring to *Moral Es.* iii 64, p. 574.

Abuse the City's best good Men in Metre,
And laugh at Peers that put their Trust in *Peter*.   40
Ev'n those you touch not, hate you.
                                    P. What should ail 'em?
    F. A hundred smart in *Timon* and in *Balaam*:
The fewer still you name, you wound the more;
Bond is but one, but *Harpax* is a Score.
    P. Each Mortal has his Pleasure: None deny   45
Scarsdale his Bottle, *Darty* his Ham-Pye;
Ridotta sips and dances, till she see
The doubling Lustres dance as fast as she;
F— loves the *Senate*, *Hockley-Hole* his Brother
Like in all else, as one Egg to another.   50
I love to pour out all myself, as plain
As downright *Shippen*, or as old *Montagne*.
In them, as certain to be lov'd as seen,
The Soul stood forth, nor kept a Thought within;
In me what Spots (for Spots I have) appear,   55
Will prove at least the Medium must be clear.
In this impartial Glass, my Muse intends
Fair to expose myself, my Foes, my Friends;
Publish the present Age, but where my Text
Is Vice too high, reserve it for the next: 60
My Foes shall wish my Life a longer date,
And ev'ry Friend the less lament my Fate.
    My Head and Heart thus flowing thro' my Quill,
Verse-man or Prose-man, term me which you will,
Papist or Protestant, or both between,   65
Like good *Erasmus* in an honest Mean,
In Moderation placing all my Glory,
While Tories call me Whig, and Whigs a Tory.
    Satire's my Weapon, but I'm too discreet
To run a Muck, and tilt at all I meet;   70

---

39. Referring to *Moral Es.* iii 103.
    42. *Timon . . . Balaam*] Referring to *Moral Es.* iv ll. 99 ff. (p. 592), and
Moral Es. iii ll. 339–402 (p. 584).
    44. *Bond . . . Harpax*] Referring to *Moral Es.* iii 102, 93.
    47. *Ridotta*] A name for a type of Society woman: from the Italian,
ridotto, a social assembly consisting of music and dancing, introduced
into England in 1722 [*OED*].
    49. *F—*] Stephen Fox. His more famous brother Henry is credited by
Chesterfield with spending 'a fair younger brother's portion . . . in the
common vices of youth, gaming included'.
    Hockley-Hole] A Bear-garden near Clerkenwell Green.

I only wear it in a Land of Hectors,
Thieves, Supercargoes, Sharpers, and Directors.
Save but our *Army*! and let *Jove* incrust
Swords, Pikes, and Guns, with everlasting Rust!
Peace is my dear Delight—not *Fleury*'s more: 75
But touch me, and no Minister so sore.
Who-e'er offends, at some unlucky Time
Slides into Verse, and hitches in a Rhyme,
Sacred to Ridicule! his whole Life long,
And the sad Burthen of some merry Song.   80
    Slander or Poyson, dread from *Delia*'s Rage,
Hard Words or Hanging, if your Judge be *Page*.
From furious *Sappho* scarce a milder Fate,
P—x'd by her Love, or libell'd by her Hate:
Its proper Pow'r to hurt, each Creature feels,   85
Bulls aim their horns, and Asses lift their heels,
'Tis a Bear's Talent not to kick, but hug,
And no man wonders he's not stung by Pug:
So drink with *Waters*, or with *Chartres* eat,
They'll never poison you, they'll only cheat.   90
    Then learned Sir (to cut the Matter short)
What-e'er my Fate, or well or ill at Court,
Whether old Age, with faint, but chearful Ray,
Attends to gild the Evening of my Day,
Or Death's black Wing already be display'd   95
To wrap me in the Universal Shade;
Whether the darken'd Room to muse invite,
Or whiten'd Wall provoke the Skew'r to write,
In Durance, Exile, Bedlam, or the Mint,
Like *Lee* or *Budgell*, I will Rhyme and Print.   100

71. *Hectors*] the name given to a group of dissolute young gentlemen in the second half of the seventeenth century, who swaggered 'by night about [London], breaking windows, upsetting sedans, beating quiet men, and offering rude caresses to pretty women'. Here, perhaps less specifically, 'bullies'.

72. *Supercargoes*] Officers on board merchant ships whose business it was to superintend the cargo and commercial transactions of the voyage. Supercargoes were proverbial for their wealth.

Directors] South-Sea Company directors.

73. 'The maintenance of a standing army at the command of the sovereign had, since the revolution, been declaimed against by the tories as a constant menace to English liberty'.

83. *Sappho*] Lady Mary Wortley Montagu.

88. *Pug*] A common nickname for a pet dog.

99 *the Mint*] A sanctuary for insolvent debtors and others in Southwark.

100. Lee, tragic dramatist, spent five years in Bedlam, and was reported

F. Alas young Man! your Days can ne'r be long,
In Flow'r of Age you perish for a Song!
Plums, and Directors, *Shylock* and his Wife,
Will club their Testers, now, to take your Life!
    P. What? arm'd for *Virtue* when I point the Pen,   105
Brand the bold Front of shameless, guilty Men,
Dash the proud Gamester in his gilded Car,
Bare the mean Heart that lurks beneath a Star;
Can there be wanting to defend Her Cause,
Lights of the Church, or Guardians of the Laws?   110
Could pension'd *Boileau* lash in honest Strain
Flatt'rers and Bigots ev'n in *Louis*' Reign?
Could Laureate *Dryden* Pimp and Fry'r engage,
Yet neither *Charles* nor *James* be in a Rage?
And I not strip the Gilding off a Knave,   115
Un-plac'd, un-pension'd, no Man's Heir, or Slave?
I will, or perish in the gen'rous Cause.
Hear this, and tremble! you, who 'scape the Laws.
Yes, while I live, no rich or noble knave
Shall walk the World, in credit, to his grave.   120
To VIRTUE ONLY and HER FRIENDS, A FRIEND
The World beside may murmur, or commend.
Know, all the distant Din that World can keep
Rolls o'er my *Grotto*, and but sooths my Sleep.
There, my Retreat the best Companions grace,   125
Chiefs, out of War, and Statesmen, out of Place.
There *St. John* mingles with my friendly Bowl,
The Feast of Reason and the Flow of Soul:
And He, whose Lightning pierc'd th' *Iberian* Lines,

---

to have written a twenty-five act play there. Budgell, who was to commit suicide in 1737, was a miscellaneous writer of unstable mind.

103. *Plums*] 'A "plum" is no temptation to [an honest man]. He likes and loves himself too well to change hearts with one of those corrupt miscreants, who amongst them gave that name to a round sum of money gained by rapine and plunder of the commonwealth' (Shaftesbury's *Characteristics*).

Directors . . . Wife] Referring to *Moral Es.* iii 119, 96.

112. *Flatt'rers and Bigots*] in *Le Lutrin*.

113. *Pimp and Fry'r engage*] united in the character of Friar Dominick in *The Spanish Friar* (1680).

124. *my Grotto*] Pope's grounds at Twickenham were divided by the main road from London to Hampton Court. To avoid crossing it, Pope built an underground passage which also led to a stone arbour or temple, adorned with a large number of rare stones given to Pope by his friends. Here he was accustomed to sit.

129. *He*] *Charles Mordaunt* Earl of Peterborough, who in the Year 1705

Now, forms my Quincunx, and now ranks my Vines,   130
Or tames the Genius of the stubborn Plain,
Almost as quickly, as he conquer'd *Spain*.
  Envy must own, I live among the Great,
No Pimp of Pleasure, and no Spy of State,
With Eyes that pry not, Tongue that ne'er repeats,   135
Fond to spread Friendships, but to cover Heats,
To help who want, to forward who excel;
This, all who know me, know; who love me, tell;
And who unknown defame me, let them be
Scriblers or Peers, alike are *Mob* to me.   140
This is my Plea, on this I rest my Cause—
What saith my Council learned in the Laws ?
  F. Your Plea is good. But still I say, beware!
Laws are explain'd by Men—so have a care.
It stands on record that in *Richard*'s Times   145
A Man was hang'd for very honest Rhymes.
Consult the Statute: *quart.* I think it is,
Edwardi Sext. or *prim. & quint, Eliz:*
See *Libels, Satires*—here you have it—read.
  P. Libels and *Satires !* lawless Things indeed!   150
But grave *Epistles*, bringing Vice to light,
Such as a *King* might read, a *Bishop* write,
Such as Sir *Robert* would approve—
                          F. Indeed ?
The Case is alter'd—you may then proceed.
In such a Cause the Plaintiff will be hiss'd,   155
My Lords the Judges laugh, and you're dismiss'd.

---

took *Barcelona*, and in the Winter following with only 280 Horse and
900 foot enterprized, and accomplished the capture of *Valentia* [P].
  130. *Quincunx*] A disposition of five trees by which four are placed at
the corners, the fifth at the centre, of a square.
  140. *Mob*] A popular abbreviation of *mobile vulgus*, against which Swift
had exclaimed in *Tatler* 230.
  146. The Man was the poet Collingbourne, the King was Richard III,
and the very honest Rhymes were
          The Cat, the Rat, and Lovel our Dog,
          Do rule al England, vnder a Hog.
See *A Mirror for Magistrates*, 1563, tragedy 23.
  147. 3 and 4 Edward VI c. 15 is 'An Acte against fonde and fantasticall
Prophesies': 1 Eliz. c. 6 is 'An Acte for the explanation of the Statute
[1 Ph. and Mary c. 3] of sedytyous Woordes and Rumours:' 5 Eliz. c. 15
deals with the same subject as 3 and 4 Edward VI c. 15. The maximum
penalty allowed was imprisonment for life and loss of goods on the
second offence.
  153. *Sir Robert*] Walpole.

The Second Satire of the Second Book of Horace Paraphrased

[written 1733; published 1734]

What, and how great, the Virtue and the Art
To live on little with a chearful heart,
(A Doctrine sage, but truly none of mine)
Lets talk, my friends, but talk before we dine:
Not when a gilt Buffet's reflected pride   5
Turns you from sound Philosophy aside;
Not when from Plate to Plate your eyeballs roll,
And the brain dances to the mantling bowl.
  Hear Bethel's Sermon, one not vers'd in schools,
But strong in sense, and wise without the rules.   10
  Go work, hunt, exercise! (he thus began)
Then scorn a homely dinner, if you can.
Your wine lock'd up, your Butler stroll'd abroad,
Or fish deny'd, (the River yet un-thaw'd)
If then plain Bread and milk will do the feat,   15
The pleasure lies in *you*, and not the meat.
Preach as I please, I doubt our curious men
Will chuse a *Pheasant* still before a *Hen*;
Yet Hens of *Guinea* full as good I hold,
Except you eat the feathers, green and gold.   20
Of *Carps* and *Mullets* why prefer the *great*,
(Tho' cut in pieces e'er my Lord can eat)
Yet for *small Turbots* such esteem profess?
Because God made these large, the other less.
  Oldfield, with more than Harpy throat endu'd,   25
Cries, 'Send me, Gods! a whole Hog *barbecu'd!*'
Oh blast it, South-winds! till a stench exhale,
Rank as the ripeness of a Rabbit's tail.
By what *Criterion* do ye eat, d'ye think,
If this is priz'd for *sweetness*, that for *stink?*   30
When the tir'd Glutton labours thro' a Treat,
He finds no relish in the sweetest Meat;

8. *mantling*] sparkling.
  9. *Bethel*] See *E. on Man*, IV 125–6n (p. 540).
  25. *Oldfield*] This eminent Glutton ran thro' a fortune of fifteen
hundred pounds a year in the simple luxury of good eating. [Warburton].
He is mentioned again in *Ep.* II ii 87.
  26. *barbecu'd*] A *West-Indian* Term of Gluttony, a Hog roasted whole,
stuff'd with Spice, and basted with *Madera* Wine [P].

He calls for something bitter, something sour,
And the rich feast concludes extremely poor:
Cheap eggs, and herbs, and olives still we see,   35
Thus much is left of old Simplicity!
  The *Robin-red-breast* till of late had rest,
And children sacred held a *Martin*'s nest,
Till *Becca-ficos* sold so dev'lish dear
To one that was, or would have been a Peer.   40
Let me extoll a *Cat* on Oysters fed,
I'll have a Party at the *Bedford Head*,
Or ev'n to crack live *Crawfish* recommend,
I'd never doubt at Court to make a Friend.
  'Tis yet in vain, I own, to keep a pother   45
About one Vice, and fall into the other:
Between Excess and Famine lies a mean,
Plain, but not sordid, tho' not splendid, clean.
Avidien or his Wife (no matter which,
For him you'll call a dog, and her a bitch)   50
Sell their presented Partridges, and Fruits,
And humbly live on rabbits and on roots:
One half-pint bottle serves them both to dine,
And is at once their vinegar and wine.
But on some lucky day (as when they found   55
A lost Bank-bill, or heard their Son was drown'd)
At such a feast old vinegar to spare,
Is what two souls so gen'rous cannot bear;
Oyl, tho' it stink, they drop by drop impart,
But sowse the Cabbidge with a bounteous heart.   60
  He knows to live, who keeps the middle state,
And neither leans on this side, nor on that:
Nor stops, for one bad Cork, his Butler's pay,
Swears, like Albutius, a good Cook away;
Nor lets, like Nævius, ev'ry error pass,   65
The musty wine, foul cloth, or greasy glass.

37. *The Robin-red-breast*] A. Hayward (*Art of Dining*, 1883, p. 37) reports that the robin is 'remarkable for a delicate bitter flavour.'

39. *Becca-ficos*] A name given in Italy to small migratory birds of the genus Sylvia much esteemed as dainties: identical with the British Petty-chaps and Blackcaps [*OED*].

42. *Bedford Head*] A famous Eating-house [and Tavern] [P]. In Southampton Street, Covent Garden. See *Sob. Adv.* l. 150 (p. 672).

49. *Avidien . . . his Wife*] Generally recognized as a portrait of Wortley Montagu and Lady Mary.

51. *Sell . . . Partridges*] i.e. sell the presents which had been given to them. But compare *Ep.* II ii 234 (p. 656).

56. *their Son*] E. W. Montagu (1713-76), who was notoriously unstable.

Now hear what blessings Temperance can bring:
(Thus said our Friend, and what he said I sing.)
First Health: The stomach (cram'd from ev'ry dish,
A Tomb of boil'd, and roast, and flesh, and fish,   70
Where Bile, and wind, and phlegm, and acid jar,
And all the Man is one intestine war)
Remembers oft the School-boy's simple fare,
The temp'rate sleeps, and spirits light as air!
    How pale, each Worshipful and rev'rend Guest   75
Rise from a Clergy, or a City, feast!
What life in all that ample Body say,
What heav'nly Particle inspires the clay?
The Soul subsides; and wickedly inclines
To seem but mortal, ev'n in sound Divines.   80
On morning wings how active springs the Mind,
That leaves the load of yesterday behind?
How easy ev'ry labour it pursues?
How coming to the Poet ev'ry Muse?
Not but we may exceed, some Holy time,   85
Or tir'd in search of Truth, or search of Rhyme.
Ill Health some just indulgence may engage,
And more, the Sickness of long Life, Old-age:
For fainting Age what cordial drop remains,
If our intemp'rate Youth the Vessel drains?   90

    Our Fathers prais'd rank Ven'son. You suppose
Perhaps, young men! our Fathers had no nose?
Not so: a Buck was then a week's repast,
And 'twas their point, I ween, to make it last:
More pleas'd to keep it till their friends could come,   95
Than eat the sweetest by themselves at home.
Why had not I in those good times my birth,
E're Coxcomb-pyes or Coxcombs were on earth?
    Unworthy He, the voice of Fame to hear,
(That sweetest Music to an honest ear;   100
For 'faith Lord Fanny! you are in the wrong,
The World's good word is better than a Song)
Who has not learn'd, fresh Sturgeon and Ham-pye
Are no rewards for Want, and Infamy!
When Luxury has lick'd up all thy pelf,   105
Curs'd by thy neighbours, thy Trustees, thy self,
To friends, to fortune, to mankind a shame,
Think how Posterity will treat thy name;

101. *Lord Fanny*] Lord Hervey.

And buy a Rope, that future times may tell
Thou hast at least bestow'd one penny well.   110
   'Right, cries his Lordship, for a Rogue in need
To have a Taste, is Insolence indeed:
In me 'tis noble, suits my birth and state,
My wealth unwieldy, and my heap too great.'
Then, like the Sun, let Bounty spread her ray,   115
And shine that Superfluity away.
Oh Impudence of wealth! with all thy store,
How dar'st thou let one worthy man be poor?
Shall half the new-built Churches round thee fall?
Make Keys, build Bridges, or repair White-hall: 120
Or to thy Country let that heap be lent,
As M**o's was, but not at five *per Cent.*
   Who thinks that Fortune cannot change her mind,
Prepares a dreadful Jest for all mankind!
And who stands safest, tell me? is it he   125
That spreads and swells in puff'd Prosperity,
Or blest with little, whose preventing care
In Peace provides fit arms against a War?
   Thus Bethel spoke, who always speaks his thought,
And always thinks the very thing he ought: 130
His equal mind I copy what I can,
And as I love, would imitate the Man.
In *South-sea* days not happier, when surmis'd
The Lord of thousands, than if now *Excis'd*;

119 f. Pope recurs once more to favourite projects. cf. *Windsor Forest*,
ll. 375 ff. (p. 208), *Moral Es.* IV 191–204 (p. 595).

119. Churches in London and Westminster built under the acts of
9 and 10 Anne and 1 Geo. I. St. John's, Smith Square, and St. Anne's,
Limehouse, were giving cause for concern.

120. *Make Keys*] Pope refers to the need of an embankment on the
river front at Whitehall.

build Bridges] The Thames at this time was crossed by London Bridge
only, in the London area; but an Act was passed in 1736, in spite of
opposition, for the construction of Westminster Bridge.

repair White-hall] Whitehall had been the King's palace since the time
of Henry VIII. All but the banqueting hall was destroyed by fire in 1691
and 1698, and was never rebuilt, the ruins being allowed to cumber the
ground for many years. See *Dunciad* A iii 324 (p. 423).

122. The Duchess of Marlborough's own account (1737) reads: 'From
the beginning of the reduction of the interest I lent such sums to the
government as reduced the interest from 6 *per cent* to 4 *per cent.*; thinking
it would have a good effect for the security of the nation' (*Opinions*, 1788,
p. 49).

133. *South-sea days*] The South Sea Bubble broke in the latter half of
1720.

134. *Excis'd*] The excise was originally 'a commodity tax paid indirectly

In Forest planted by a Father's hand,   135
Than in five acres now of rented land.
Content with little, I can piddle here
On Broccoli and mutton, round the year;
But ancient friends, (tho' poor, or out of play)
That touch my Bell, I cannot turn away.   140
'Tis true, no Turbots dignify my boards,
But gudgeons, flounders, what my Thames affords.
To Hounslow-heath I point, and Bansted-down,
Thence comes your mutton, and these chicks my own:
From yon old wallnut-tree a show'r shall fall;   145
And grapes, long-lingring on my only wall,
And figs, from standard and Espalier join:
The dev'l is in you if you cannot dine.
Then chearful healths (your Mistress shall have place)
And, what's more rare, a Poet shall say *Grace*.   150
Fortune not much of humbling me can boast;
Tho' double-tax'd, how little have I lost?
My Life's amusements have been just the same,
Before, and after Standing Armies came.
My lands are sold, my Father's house is gone;   155
I'll hire another's, is not that my own,
And yours my friends? thro' whose free-opening gate
None comes too early, none departs too late;
(For I, who hold sage Homer's rule the best,
Welcome the coming, speed the going guest.)   160

---

by consumers as a contribution to the expenses of national defence'
(Ashley, *Finan. and Commer. Policy under the Cromwellian Protectorate*,
1934, p. 62). But Walpole's Excise Bill of 1733 was a warehousing scheme
designed to make England a storehouse for the temporary deposit of
goods, and London a free port. The Opposition interpreted it as a general
excise, which so much alarmed the public that Walpole decided to withdraw the measure.

135. *In Forest*] Binfield, in Windsor Forest, where the elder Pope had
retired about 1700.

136. *five acres*] at Twickenham, which Pope leased, with a house, from
Thomas Vernon in 1718.

137. *piddle*] i.e. to toy with one's food [*OED*]. Pope speaks of piddling
with his translation of Homer, and also applies the word to Theobald
(*Ep. to Arbuthnot*, l. 164).

143. *Bansted-down*] Banstead Downs, four miles from Epsom, are still
noted for their sheep pasturage.

147. *Espalier*] A fruit-tree trained on a lattice [*OED*].

154. *Standing Armies*] see *Sat.* II i 73*n* (p. 616).

159. *sage Homer's rule*] *Odyssey*, xv 83–4. Translated by Pope,

> True friendship's laws are by this rule exprest,
> Welcome the coming, speed the parting guest.

'Pray heav'n it last! (cries Swift) as you go on;
I wish to God this house had been your own:
Pity! to build, without a son or wife:
Why, you'll enjoy it only all your life.'—
Well, if the Use be mine, can it concern one   165
Whether the Name belong to Pope or Vernon?
What's *Property*? dear Swift! you see it alter
From you to me, from me to Peter Walter,
Or, in a mortgage, prove a Lawyer's share,
Or, in a jointure, vanish from the Heir,   170
Or in pure Equity (the Case not clear)
The Chanc'ry takes your rents for twenty year:
At best, it falls to some ungracious Son
Who cries, my father's damn'd, and all's my own.
Shades, that to Bacon could retreat afford,   175
Become the portion of a booby Lord;
And Hemsley once proud Buckingham's delight,
Slides to a Scriv'ner or a City Knight.
Let Lands and Houses have what Lords they will,
Let Us be fix'd, and our own Masters still.   180

164. Referring to Swift's *Imit. Hor., Sat.* II vi 1-10, printed below at p. 659.

166. *Vernon*] Pope's landlord.

168. *Peter Walter*] a notorious money-lender. See p. 577, l. 125*n.*

175. *Shades*] Sir Nicholas Bacon, father of Sir Francis, had built a mansion at Gorhambury near St. Albans, which was finished in 1568. From the Bacon family it passed to the Meautis family, from whom it was purchased by Sir Harbottle Grimston, whose son left it at his death in 1700 to his great-nephew, William Luckyn. Luckyn took the name of Grimston and was raised to the peerage in 1719. His reputation as a 'booby Lord' is based on his play *The Lawyer's Fortune, or Love in a Hollow Tree*, 1705, which was reprinted in 1736 with derisive notes and a frontispiece in the foreground of which is an ass, wearing a coronet.

177. *proud Buckingham's delight*] Villers, Duke of Buckingham [P]. Helmsley, in the North Riding of Yorkshire, came into the Duke's possession in 1657 on his marrying the daughter of Lord Fairfax, who then owned it. The house and estates were sold in 1692 to Sir Charles Duncombe, a London banker, for the sum of (it is said) £90,000.

The First Epistle of the First Book of Horace Imitated

[written c. 1737; published 1738]

St. John, whose love indulg'd my labours past
Matures my present, and shall bound my last!

Why will you break the Sabbath of my days?
Now sick alike of Envy and of Praise.
Publick too long, ah let me hide my Age! 5
See modest Cibber now has left the Stage:
Our Gen'rals now, retir'd to their Estates,
Hang their old Trophies o'er the Garden gates,

In Life's cool evening satiate of applause,
Nor fond of bleeding, ev'n in BRUNSWICK's cause. 10
   A Voice there is, that whispers in my ear,
('Tis Reason's voice, which sometimes one can hear)
'Friend Pope! be prudent, let your Muse take breath,
And never gallop Pegasus to death;
Lest stiff, and stately, void of fire, or force, 15
You limp, like Blackmore, on a Lord Mayor's horse.'
   Farewell then Verse, and Love, and ev'ry Toy,
The rhymes and rattles of the Man or Boy:
What right, what true, what fit, we justly call,
Let this be all my care—for this is All: 20
To lay this harvest up, and hoard with haste
What ev'ry day will want, and most, the last.
   But ask not, to what Doctors I apply?
Sworn to no Master, of no Sect am I:
As drives the storm, at any door I knock, 25
And house with Montagne now, or now with Lock.
Sometimes a Patriot, active in debate,
Mix with the World, and battle for the State,
Free as young Lyttleton, her cause pursue,
Still true to Virtue, and as warm as true: 30
Sometimes, with Aristippus, or St. Paul,
Indulge my Candor, and grow all to all;

16. *Blackmore*] The fame of this heavy Poet, however problematical elsewhere, was universally received in the City of London. His versification is here exactly described: stiff, and not strong; stately and yet dull, like the sober and slow-paced Animal generally employed to mount the Lord Mayor: and therefore here humourously opposed to Pegasus [P].

26. *Montagne . . . Lock*] i.e. now with a loose, now with a regular way of thinking.

27. *Patriot*] A member of the Opposition. See *Dia.* i 24*n* (p. 689).

31. Omnis Aristippum decuit color, & status, & res [P]. (Horace, *Ep.* I xvii 23.) Aristippus founded the Cyrenaic school of Philosophers, who held that, since the present only can be experienced, momentary pleasure is the chief good. He was Bolingbroke's favourite philosopher.

St. Paul] cf. 'I am made all things to all men' (1 Cor. ix 22); 'Even as I please all men in all things . . . [that they may be saved]' (1 Cor. x 33); 'Let your moderation be known unto all men' (Phil. iv 5).

32. *Candor*] i.e. Impartiality.

Back to my native Moderation slide,
And win my way by yielding to the tyde.
   Long, as to him who works for debt, the Day;   35
Long as the Night to her whose love's away;
Long as the Year's dull circle seems to run,
When the brisk Minor pants for twenty-one;
So slow th' unprofitable Moments roll,
That lock up all the Functions of my soul;   40
That keep me from Myself; and still delay
Life's instant business to a future day:
That task, which as we follow, or despise,
The eldest is a fool, the youngest wise;
Which done, the poorest can no wants endure,   45
And which not done, the richest must be poor.
   Late as it is, I put my self to school,
And feel some comfort, not to be a fool.
Weak tho' I am of limb, and short of sight,
Far from a Lynx, and not a Giant quite,   50
I'll do what MEAD and CHESELDEN advise,
To keep these limbs, and to preserve these eyes.
Not to go back, is somewhat to advance,
And men must walk at least before they dance.
   Say, does thy blood rebel, thy bosom move   55
With wretched Av'rice, or as wretched Love?
Know, there are Words, and Spells, which can controll
(Between the Fits) this Fever of the soul:
Know, there are Rhymes, which (fresh and fresh apply'd)
Will cure the arrant'st Puppy of his Pride.   60
Be furious, envious, slothful, mad or drunk,
Slave to a Wife or Vassal to a Punk,
A Switz, a High-dutch, or a Low-dutch Bear—
All that we ask is but a patient Ear.
   'Tis the first Virtue, Vices to abhor;   65
And the first Wisdom, to be Fool no more.
But to the world, no bugbear is so great,
As want of figure, and a small Estate.
To either India see the Merchant fly,
Scar'd at the spectre of pale Poverty!   70
See him, with pains of body, pangs of soul,
Burn through the Tropic, freeze beneath the Pole!

45. *can . . . endure*] i.e. can want nothing.
51. Mead was the most famous physician of his day, and Cheselden the
most famous surgeon.
52. *these eyes*] Towards the end of his life, Pope suffered from cataract.

Wilt thou do nothing for a nobler end,
Nothing, to make Philosophy thy friend?
To stop thy foolish views, thy long desires,   75
And ease thy heart of all that it admires?
　　Here, Wisdom calls: 'Seek Virtue first! be bold!
As Gold to Silver, Virtue is to Gold.'
There, London's voice: 'Get Mony, Mony still!
And then let Virtue follow, if she will.'   80
This, this the saving doctrine, preach'd to all,
From low St. James's up to high St. Paul;
From him whose quills stand quiver'd at his ear,
To him who notches Sticks at Westminster.
　　BARNARD in spirit, sense, and truth abounds.   85
'Pray then what wants he?' fourscore thousand pounds,
A Pension, or such Harness for a slave
As Bug now has, and Dorimant would have.
BARNARD, thou art a *Cit*, with all thy worth;
But wretched Bug, his *Honour*, and so forth.   90
　　Yet every child another song will sing,
'Virtue, brave boys! 'tis Virtue makes a King.'
True, conscious Honour is to feel no sin,
He's arm'd without that's innocent within;
Be this thy Screen, and this thy Wall of Brass;   95
Compar'd to this, a Minister's an Ass.
　　And say, to which shall our applause belong,
This new Court jargon, or the good old song?
The modern language of corrupted Peers,
Or what was spoke at CRESSY and POITIERS?   100

82. The Dean of St. Paul's, Francis Hare, had shown his High-Churchmanship by attacking the Bishop of Bangor's views in a pamphlet entitled *Church Authority Vindicated*, 1719. The Rector of St. James's, Westminster was Secker, whose Whig politics must have associated him in Pope's mind with the Low Church party.

84. *Sticks*] Exchequer tallies; i.e. sticks cut into two parts, on each of which is marked with notches, what is due between debtor and creditor.

87. *Harness*] the order of the Garter, which 'Bug' had been given in 1712.

88. *Bug*] the nickname of Henry de Grey, Duke of Kent. Its origin is suggested in a note of the Earl of Dartmouth to Burnet's *History of his Own Times*: 'The Earl of Kent was strong in nothing but money and smell, the latter to a high degree.'

Dorimant] a fop in Etherege's *Man of Mode*.

89. *Cit*] Short for *citizen*.

95. *Screen*] Warburton quotes from Dacier's note on *murus aheneus:* ' "an *old veteran*, armed cap-à-pie in *brass*, and *placed to cover his Fellow*." Our Poet has happily served himself of this impertinence to convey a fine stroke of Satire.' See *Dia.* i 22*n* (p. 689).

Who counsels best? who whispers, 'Be but Great,
With Praise or Infamy, leave that to fate;
Get Place and Wealth, if possible, with Grace;
If not, by any means get Wealth and Place.'
For what? to have a Box where Eunuchs sing,   105
And foremost in the Circle eye a King.
Or he, who bids thee face with steddy view
Proud Fortune, and look shallow Greatness thro':
And, while he bids thee, sets th' Example too?
If such a Doctrine, in St. James's air,   110
Shou'd chance to make the well-drest Rabble stare;
If honest S*z take scandal at a spark,
That less admires the Palace than the Park,
Faith I shall give the answer Reynard gave,
'I cannot like, Dread Sir! your Royal Cave;   115
Because I see by all the Tracks about,
Full many a Beast goes in, but none comes out.'
Adieu to Virtue if you're once a Slave:
Send her to Court, you send her to her Grave.

Well, if a King's a Lion, at the least   120
The People are a many-headed Beast:
Can they direct what measures to pursue,
Who know themselves so little what to do?
Alike in nothing but one Lust of Gold,
Just half the land would buy, and half be sold: 125
Their Country's wealth our mightier Misers drain,
Or cross, to plunder Provinces, the Main:
The rest, some farm the Poor-box, some the Pews;
Some keep Assemblies, and wou'd keep the Stews;
Some with fat Bucks on childless Dotards fawn;   130
Some win rich Widows by their Chine and Brawn;
While with the silent growth of ten per Cent,
In Dirt and darkness hundreds stink content.

Of all these ways, if each pursues his own,
Satire be kind, and let the wretch alone.   135

---

106. *a King*] George II was an enthusiastic patron of Handel's operas.
112. *S*z*] Augustus Schutz, Keeper of the Privy Purse, noted for his gravity of demeanour.
127. *to plunder Provinces*] A reference to Marlborough, 'infamous for plunder'd provinces' (*E. on Man*, iv 298).
128. *farm the Poor-box*] alluding to the officers who embezzled the funds of the Charitable Corporation. See *Moral Es.* iii 102n (p. 576).
129. *keep Assemblies*] e.g. Beau Nash, who had ruled at Bath since about 1705.

But show me one, who has it in his pow'r
To act consistent with himself an hour.
Sir Job sail'd forth, the evening bright and still,
'No place on earth (he cry'd) like Greenwich hill!'
Up starts a Palace, lo! th' obedient base   140
Slopes at its foot, the woods its sides embrace,
The silver Thames reflects its marble face.
Now let some whimzy, or that Dev'l within
Which guides all those who know not what they mean
But give the Knight (or give his Lady) spleen;   145
'Away, away! take all your scaffolds down,
For Snug's the word: My dear! we'll live in Town.'
    At am'rous Flavio is the Stocking thrown?
That very night he longs to lye alone.
The Fool whose Wife elopes some thrice a quarter,   150
For matrimonial Solace dies a martyr.
Did ever Proteus, Merlin, any Witch,
Transform themselves so strangely as the Rich?
'Well, but the Poor'—the Poor have the same itch:
They change their weekly Barber, weekly News,   155
Prefer a new Japanner to their shoes,
Discharge their Garrets, move their Beds, and run
(They know not whither) in a Chaise and one;
They hire their Sculler, and when once aboard,
Grow sick, and damn the Climate—like a Lord.   160
    You laugh, half Beau half Sloven if I stand,
My Wig all powder, and all snuff my Band;
You laugh, if Coat and Breeches strangely vary,
White Gloves, and Linnen worthy Lady Mary!
But when no Prelate's Lawn with Hair-shirt lin'd,   165
Is half so incoherent as my Mind,
When (each Opinion with the next at strife,
One ebb and flow of follies all my Life)
I plant, root up, I build, and then confound,
Turn round to square, and square again to round;   170

148. An old custom according to which on the wedding night the bride's stocking was thrown among the guests; it was supposed that the person hit by it would be the first of the company to be married [*OED*].

152. *Proteus*] a sea-god who had the power of assuming any form he pleased.

156. *Japanner*] Shoe-black. A new 'art', according to Gay, *Trivia*, ii 166.

164. Lady Mary Wortley Montague seems to have been a bye-word for slovenliness.

You never change one muscle of your face,
You think this Madness but a common case,
Nor once to Chanc'ry, nor to Hales apply;
Yet hang your lip, to see a Seam awry!
Careless how ill I with myself agree;   175
Kind to my dress, my figure, not to Me.
Is this my Guide, Philosopher, and Friend?
This, He who loves me, and who ought to mend?
Who ought to make me (what he can, or none,)
That Man divine whom Wisdom calls her own,   180
Great without Title, without Fortune bless'd,
Rich ev'n when plunder'd, honour'd while oppress'd,
Lov'd without youth, and follow'd without power,
At home tho' exil'd, free, tho' in the Tower.
In short, that reas'ning, high, immortal Thing,   185
Just less than Jove, and much above a King,
Nay half in Heav'n—except (what's mighty odd)
A Fit of Vapours clouds this Demi-god.

173. *Hales*] The Doctor of Bedlam [P]. But he had died in 1728.
177. *Guide, Philosopher, and Friend*] Pope had addressed Bolingbroke
by these titles in *E. on Man*, iv 390.

The Sixth Epistle of the First Book
of Horace Imitated

[written c. 1737; published 1738]

'Not to Admire, is all the Art I know,
To make men happy, and to keep them so.'
[Plain Truth, dear MURRAY, needs no flow'rs of speech,
So take it in the very words of *Creech*.]
    This Vault of Air, this congregated Ball,   5
Self-centred Sun, and Stars that rise and fall,
There are, my Friend! whose philosophic eyes
Look thro', and trust the Ruler with his Skies,

4. *Creech*] From whose Translation of *Horace* ⟨1684⟩ the two first lines
are taken [P]. Creech's version runs:

                    Not to admire, as most are wont to do,
                    It is the only method that I know,
                    To make Men happy, and to keep 'em so.

To him commit the hour, the day, the year,
And view this dreadful All without a fear.   10
  Admire we then what Earth's low entrails hold, ⎫
Arabian shores, or Indian seas infold?   ⎬
All the mad trade of Fools and Slaves for Gold? ⎭
Or Popularity, or Stars and Strings?
The Mob's applauses, or the gifts of Kings?   15
Say with what eyes we ought at Courts to gaze,
And pay the Great our homage of Amaze?
  If weak the pleasure that from these can spring,
The fear to want them is as weak a thing:
Whether we dread, or whether we desire,   20
In either case, believe me, we admire;
Whether we joy or grieve, the same the curse,
Surpriz'd at better, or surpriz'd at worse.
Thus good, or bad, to one extreme betray
Th' unbalanc'd Mind, and snatch the Man away;   25
For Vertue's self may too much Zeal be had;
The worst of Madmen is a Saint run mad.
  Go then, and if you can, admire the state
Of beaming diamonds, and reflected plate;
Procure a *Taste* to double the surprize,   30
And gaze on Parian Charms with learned eyes:
Be struck with bright Brocade, or Tyrian Dye,
Our Birth-day Nobles splendid Livery:
If not so pleas'd, at Council-board rejoyce,
To see their Judgments hang upon thy Voice;   35
From morn to night, at Senate, Rolls, and Hall,
Plead much, read more, dine late, or not at all.
But wherefore all this labour, all this strife?
For Fame, for Riches, for a noble Wife?
Shall One whom Nature, Learning, Birth, conspir'd   40
To form, not to admire, but be admir'd,
Sigh, while his Chloë, blind to Wit and Worth,
Weds the rich Dulness of some Son of earth?
Yet Time ennobles, or degrades each Line;
It brighten'd CRAGS's, and may darken thine: 45
And what is Fame? the Meanest have their day,
The Greatest can but blaze, and pass away.

14. *Strings*] the ribbons of the knightly Orders. Cf. *E. on Man*, iv 205.
33. Cf. *Rape*, i 23, *Ep.* II i 332.
36. I.e. in Parliament, the Court of Chancery, and the High Court of
Justice.

Grac'd as thou art, with all the Pow'r of Words,
So known, so honour'd, at the House of Lords;
Conspicuous Scene! another yet is nigh,   50
(More silent far) where Kings and Poets lye;
Where MURRAY (long enough his Country's pride)
Shall be no more than TULLY, or than HYDE!
   Rack'd with Sciatics, martyr'd with the Stone,
Will any mortal let himself alone?   55
See Ward by batter'd Beaus invited over,
And desp'rate Misery lays hold on Dover.
The case is easier in the Mind's disease;
There, all Men may be cur'd, whene'er they please.
Would ye be blest? despise low Joys, low Gains; ⎫   60
Disdain whatever CORNBURY disdains;   ⎬
Be Virtuous, and be happy for your pains.   ⎭
   But art thou one, whom new opinions sway,
One, who believes as Tindal leads the way,
Who Virtue and a Church alike disowns,   65
Thinks that but words, and this but brick and stones?
Fly then, on all the wings of wild desire!
Admire whate'er the maddest can admire.
Is Wealth thy passion? Hence! from Pole to Pole,
Where winds can carry, or where waves can roll,   70
For Indian spices, for Peruvian gold,
Prevent the greedy, and out-bid the bold:
Advance thy golden Mountain to the skies;
On the broad base of fifty thousand rise,
Add one round hundred, and (if that's not fair)   75
Add fifty more, and bring it to a square.
For, mark th' advantage; just so many score
Will gain a Wife with half as many more,
Procure her beauty, make that beauty chaste,
And then such Friends—as cannot fail to last.   80
A Man of wealth is dubb'd a Man of worth,
Venus shall give him Form, and Anstis Birth.
(Believe me, many a German Prince is worse,
Who proud of Pedigree, is poor of Purse)

50. *another*] He was buried in Westminster Abbey.
   53. *Hyde*] First Earl of Clarendon. Charles II's chief adviser and Lord
Chancellor.
   56. Joshua Ward, the quack doctor; see Ep. II i 182*n* (p. 642).
   57. *Dover*] Thomas Dover (1660–1742), physician, extravagantly fond
of prescribing quicksilver.
   61. Henry Hyde, Viscount Cornbury (1710–53), a political opponent
of Walpole.

His Wealth brave Timon gloriously confounds;   85
Ask'd for a groat, he gives a hundred pounds;
Or if three Ladies like a luckless Play,
Takes the whole House upon the Poet's day.
Now, in such exigencies not to need,
Upon my word, you must be rich indeed;   90
A noble superfluity it craves,
Not for your self, but for your Fools and Knaves;
Something, which for your Honour they may cheat,
And which it much becomes you to forget.
If Wealth alone then make and keep us blest,   95
Still, still be getting, never, never rest.
  But if to Pow'r and Place your Passion lye,
If in the Pomp of Life consist the Joy;
Then hire a Slave, (or if you will, a Lord)
To do the Honours, and to give the Word;   100
Tell at your Levee, as the Crouds approach,
To whom to nod, whom take into your Coach,
Whom honour with your hand: to make remarks,
Who rules in Cornwall, or who rules in Berks;
'This may be troublesome, is near the Chair;   105
That makes three Members, this can chuse a May'r.'
Instructed thus, you bow, embrace, protest,   ⎫
Adopt him Son, or Cozen at the least,   ⎬
Then turn about, and laugh at your own Jest.   ⎭
  Or if your life be one continu'd Treat,   110
If to live well means nothing but to eat;
Up, up! cries Gluttony, 'tis break of day,
Go drive the Deer, and drag the finny-prey;
With hounds and horns go hunt an Appetite—
So Russel did, but could not eat at night,   115

85. *Timon*] see *Moral Es.* iv 99 ff (p. 592).
104. *Who rules in Cornwall*] A matter of great importance since the county and its boroughs returned forty-four members to parliament. Corruption was notoriously rife there.
Berks] Pope may be hinting at court influence upon the Windsor seats; or he may have been in need of a rhyme.
115. *Russel*] 'There was a Lord Russell who, by living too luxuriously, had quite spoiled his constitution. He did not love sport, but used to go out with his dogs every day, only to hunt for an appetite. If he felt anything of that, he would cry out, "Oh, I have found it!" turn short round and ride home again, though they were in the midst of the finest chase.— It was this Lord, who, when he met a beggar, and was entreated by him to give him something because he was almost famished with hunger, called him "a happy dog!" and envied him too much to relieve him.—P' (Spence, p. 291).

Call'd happy Dog! the Beggar at his door,
And envy'd Thirst and Hunger to the Poor.
　Or shall we ev'ry Decency confound,
Thro' Taverns, Stews, and Bagnio's take our round,
Go dine with Chartres, in each Vice out-do   120
K—l's lewd Cargo, or Ty—y's Crew,
From Latian Syrens, French Circæan Feasts,
Return well travell'd, and transform'd to Beasts,
Or for a Titled Punk, or Foreign Flame,
Renounce our Country, and degrade our Name?   125
　If, after all, we must with Wilmot own,
The Cordial Drop of Life is Love alone,
And Swift cry wisely, 'Vive la Bagatelle!'
The Man that loves and laughs, must sure do well.
Adieu—if this advice appear the worst,   130
E'en take the Counsel which I gave you first:
Or better Precepts if you can impart,
Why do, I'll follow them with all my heart.

121. *K—l's . . . Ty—y's*] George Hay, Earl of Kinnoull, and James
O'Hara, Baron Tyrawley, ambassadors at Constantinople and Lisbon.
Kinnoull behaved notoriously badly to his wife, Lord Oxford's daughter;
Tyrawley's seraglio was equally notorious.

127. *The Cordial Drop*] Rochester's *Letter from Artemisa, in the town,
to Cloe in the country*, ll. 40-5:

> Love, . . .
> That Cordial-drop Heav'n in our cup has thrown,
> To make the nauseous Draught of Life go down.

The First Epistle of the Second Book
of Horace Imitated

TO AUGUSTUS

[written c. 1736; published 1737]

Ne Rubeam, pingui donatus Munere!
HOR. [*Ep. II. i. 267*]

ADVERTISEMENT

The Reflections of Horace, *and the Judgments past in his Epistle to*
Augustus, *seem'd so seasonable to the present Times, that I could not
help applying them to the use of my own Country. The Author thought*

them considerable enough to address them to His Prince[1]*; whom he paints with all the great and good Qualities of a Monarch, upon whom the* Romans *depended for the Encrease of an* Absolute Empire. *But to make the Poem entirely English, I was willing to add one or two of those Virtues which contribute to the Happiness of a* Free People, *and are more consistent with the Welfare of* our Neighbours.

This Epistle will show the learned World to have fallen into two mistakes; one, that Augustus *was a Patron of Poets in general; whereas he not only prohibited all but the Best Writers to name him, but recommended that Care even to the Civil Magistrate:* Admonebat[2] Prætores, ne paterentur Nomen suum obsolefieri, &c. *The other, that this Piece was only a* general Discourse of Poetry; *whereas it was an* Apology for the Poets, *in order to render* Augustus *more their Patron.* Horace *here pleads the Cause of his Cotemporaries, first against the Taste of the Town, whose humour it was to magnify the Authors of the preceding Age; secondly against the Court and Nobility, who encouraged only the Writers for the Theatre; and lastly against the Emperor himself, who had conceived them of little use to the Government. He shews (by a view of the Progress of Learning, and the Change of Taste among the* Romans) *that the Introduction of the Polite Arts of* Greece *had given the Writers of his Time great advantages over their Predecessors, that their* Morals *were much improved, and the Licence of those ancient Poets restrained: that* Satire *and* Comedy *were become more just and useful; that whatever extravagancies were left on the Stage, were owing to the Ill Taste of the Nobility; that Poets, under due Regulations, were in many respects useful to the* State; *and concludes, that it was upon them the Emperor himself must depend, for his Fame with Posterity.*

We may farther learn from this Epistle, that Horace *made his Court to this Great Prince, by writing with a decent Freedom toward him, with a just Contempt of his low Flatterers, and with a manly Regard to his own Character.*

> While You, great Patron of Mankind, sustain
> The balanc'd World, and open all the Main;

---

[1] This poem is addressed to George II, also christened Augustus; but since the king was openly contemptuous of letters, and Pope (and the Opposition for whom he is speaking) disliked the Court, the compliments, imitated from those sincerely paid by Horace to Augustus, are to be construed ironically.

[2] *Admonebat* &c.] from Suetonius, *Augustus*, sect. 89.

1. *sustain . . . World*] Pope seems to imply that Walpole's pacific policy prevented England from taking her full part in foreign affairs.

2. *open*] To render available for trade, used ironically. Complaints of Spanish attacks upon English merchantmen were frequent.

Your Country, chief, in Arms abroad defend,
At home, with Morals, Arts, and Laws amend;
How shall the Muse, from such a Monarch, steal   5
An hour, and not defraud the Publick Weal?
  Edward and Henry, now the Boast of Fame,
And virtuous Alfred, a more sacred Name,
After a Life of gen'rous Toils endur'd,
The Gaul subdu'd, or Property secur'd,   10
Ambition humbled, mighty Cities storm'd,
Or Laws establish'd, and the World reform'd;
Clos'd their long Glories with a sigh, to find
Th' unwilling Gratitude of base mankind!
All human Virtue to its latest breath   15
Finds Envy never conquer'd, but by Death.
The great Alcides, ev'ry Labour past,
Had still this Monster to subdue at last.
Sure fate of all, beneath whose rising ray
Each Star of meaner merit fades away;   20
Oppress'd we feel the Beam directly beat,
Those Suns of Glory please not till they set.
  To Thee, the World its present homage pays,
The Harvest early, but mature the Praise:
Great Friend of LIBERTY! in *Kings* a Name   25
Above all Greek, above all Roman Fame:
Whose Word is Truth, as sacred and rever'd,
As Heav'n's own Oracles from Altars heard.
Wonder of Kings! like whom, to mortal eyes
None e'er has risen, and none e'er shall rise.   30
  Just in one instance, be it yet confest
Your People, Sir, are partial in the rest.
Foes to all living worth except your own,
And Advocates for Folly dead and gone.
Authors, like Coins, grow dear as they grow old;   35
It is the rust we value, not the gold.
Chaucer's worst ribaldry is learn'd by rote,
And beastly Skelton Heads of Houses quote:

3. See l. 397n. Written before George II's exploits at the battle of
Dettingen.
  abroad] This poem was published soon after the King's return from a
prolonged visit to Hanover.
  7. Edward III and Henry V.
  36. *rust we value*] cf. *Ep. to Addison* (p. 216) l. 36.
  38. *beastly Skelton*] Poet Laureat to Hen. 8. a Volume of whose Verses
has been lately reprinted, consisting almost wholly of Ribaldry, Obscenity,

One likes no language but the Faery Queen;
A Scot will fight for Christ's Kirk o' the Green;   40
And each true Briton is to Ben so civil,
He swears the Muses met him at the Devil.
    Tho' justly Greece her eldest sons admires,
Why should not we be wiser than our Sires?
In ev'ry publick Virtue we excell,   45
We build, we paint, we sing, we dance as well,
And learned Athens to our Art must stoop,
Could she behold us tumbling thro' a hoop.
    If Time improve our Wit as well as Wine,
Say at what age a Poet grows divine?   50
Shall we, or shall we not, account him so,
Who dy'd, perhaps, an hundred years ago?
End all dispute; and fix the year precise
When British bards begin t'Immortalize?
    'Who lasts a Century can have no flaw,   55
I hold that Wit a Classick, good in law.'
    Suppose he wants a year, will you compound?
And shall we deem him Ancient, right and sound,
Or damn to all Eternity at once,
At ninety nine, a Modern, and a Dunce?   60
    'We shall not quarrel for a year or two;
By Courtesy of England, he may do.'
    Then, by the rule that made the Horse-tail bare,
I pluck out year by year, as hair by hair,
And melt down Ancients like a heap of snow: 65
While you, to measure merits, look in Stowe,
And estimating Authors by the year,
Bestow a Garland only on a Bier.

---

and Scurrilous Language [P]. Skelton's works were reprinted in 1736 for the first time since 1568.
    40. *Christ's Kirk o' the Green*] A Ballad made by a King of Scotland [P]. Variously attributed to James I and James V. The poem had been reprinted frequently in Pope's life-time.
    42. The Devil Tavern, where Ben. Johnson held his Poetical Club [P].
    48. A reference to the contemporary popularity of pantomime.
    62. *Courtesy of England*] A legal term signifying the custom by which a husband, after his wife's death, holds certain kinds of property which she has inherited. The husband will not be disturbed in his tenure of property, nor the poet in his tenure of fame, in spite of their being unable to make out a prescriptive title.
    66. *Stowe*] 'The most accurate and businesslike of the Elizabethan chroniclers' (*DNB*). His *Summarie of Englyshe Chronicles* was published in 1565 and his *Annales* in 1580.

Shakespear, (whom you and ev'ry Play-house bill
Style the divine, the matchless, what you will)   70
For gain, not glory, wing'd his roving flight,
And grew Immortal in his own despight.
Ben, old and poor, as little seem'd to heed
The Life to come, in ev'ry Poet's Creed.
Who now reads Cowley ? if he pleases yet,   75
His moral pleases . not his pointed wit;
Forgot his Epic, nay Pindaric Art,
But still I love the language of his Heart.
    'Yet surely, surely, these were famous men!
What Boy but hears the sayings of old Ben ?   80
In all debates where Criticks bear a part,
Not one but nods, and talks of Johnson's Art,
Of Shakespear's Nature, and of Cowley's Wit;
How Beaumont's Judgment check'd what Fletcher writ;
How Shadwell hasty, Wycherly was slow;   85
But, for the Passions, Southern sure and Rowe.
These, only these, support the crouded stage,
From eldest Heywood down to Cibber's age.'
    All this may be; the People's Voice is odd,
It is, and it is not, the voice of God.   90

69. Shakespear and Ben. Johnson may truly be said not much to have
thought of this Immortality, the one in many pieces composed in haste
for the Stage; the other in his Latter works in general, which *Dryden*
call'd his *Dotages* [P].

75. Cowley's reputation declined with the turn of the century, when
'correctness' of versification and restraint of expression came to be valued.
His wit had been adversely criticized by Dryden in the *Preface to the
Fables*, and by Addison in *Spectator* 62; Gildon and others had published
their disapproval of his epic, the *Davideis*; and the taste for Pindarique
imitations was going out.

77. *Pindaric Art*] which has much more merit than his *Epic:* but very
unlike the Character, as well as Numbers, of Pindar [P].

82-3. *Art . . . Nature*] e.g. Dryden's *Essay of Dramatic Poesy.* cf.
Dunciad A ii 216 (p. 389).

85. *Shadwell . . . Wycherly*] Nothing was less true than this particular:
But the whole Paragraph has a mixture of Irony, and must not altogether
be taken for Horace's own Judgment, only the common Chatt of the pretenders to Criticism; in some things right, in others wrong: as he tells us
in his answer,

Interdum vulgus rectum videt, est ubi peccat. [P]

86. *Southern . . . Rowe*] The principal followers of Otway in senti-
mental tragedy.

88. John Heywood (1497?-1580?) was the author of several interludes,
amongst them *The Four P's* and *The Pardoner and the Friar*. See *Dunciad,
A i 96. Eldest* distinguishes him from the Jacobean dramatist, Thomas
Heywood.

IMITATIONS OF HORACE: EP. II i 639

To Gammer Gurton if it give the bays,
And yet deny the Careless Husband praise,
Or say our fathers never broke a rule;
Why then I say, the Publick is a fool.
But let them own, that greater faults than we   95
They had, and greater Virtues, I'll agree.
Spenser himself affects the obsolete,
And Sydney's verse halts ill on Roman feet:
Milton's strong pinion now not Heav'n can bound,
Now serpent-like, in prose he sweeps the ground,   100
In Quibbles, Angel and Archangel join,
And God the Father turns a School-Divine.
Not that I'd lop the Beauties from his book,
Like slashing Bentley with his desp'rate Hook;
Or damn all Shakespear, like th' affected fool   105
At Court, who hates whate'er he read at School.
    But for the Wits of either Charles's days,
The Mob of Gentlemen who wrote with Ease;
Sprat, Carew, Sedley, and a hundred more,

91. *Gammer Gurton*, a piece of very low humour, one of the first printed
Plays in English, and therefore much valued by some Antiquaries [P]. It
was reprinted in 1661.
92. *the Careless Husband*] A successful comedy by Cibber, first produced in 1704.
97. *Spenser . . . obsolete*] Particularly in the Shepherd's Calendar,
where he imitates the unequal Measures, as well as the Language, of
Chaucer [P]. Pope is quoting from Ben Jonson's *Discoveries*: '*Spencer*, in
affecting the Ancients writ no Language.'
98. *on Roman feet*] Specimens of Sidney's elegiacs and sapphics are
found in the *Arcadia*, Book I. His works had been reprinted by Curll and
others in 1725.
101. *Quibbles*] e.g. *Par. Lost*, vi 609-28.
102. *School-Divine*] e.g. *ibid.* iii 80-134.
104. *Like slashing Bentley*] See *Ep. to Arbuthnot*, l. 164*n* (p. 603).
Hook] In a note to *Dunciad*, B iv 194, Pope, mimicking Bentley, uses
the word to designate the square brackets within which Bentley enclosed
passages which he considered spurious. The metaphor from hedging is
also apparent.
106. Pope refers to Hervey's *Epistle from a Nobleman to a Doctor of
Divinity*, 1733:
                . . . That all I learn'd from *Doctor Freind* at School,
                By *Gradus*, *Lexicon*, or Grammar-Rule . . .
                Has quite deserted this poor *John-Trot* Head,
                And left plain native *English* in its stead.
109. *Sprat*] Thomas Sprat (1635-1713); Bishop of Rochester, 1684.
'A worse Cowley,' Pope thought him.
    Carew] Thomas Carew (1595?-1639?), lyric poet. Pope called him 'a
bad Waller'.
    Sedley] Sir Charles Sedley (1639-1701), lyric poet. 'Sedley is a very

(Like twinkling Stars the Miscellanies o'er)   110
One Simile, that solitary shines
In the dry Desert of a thousand lines,
Or lengthen'd Thought that gleams thro' many a page,
Has sanctify'd whole Poems for an age.

    I lose my patience, and I own it too,   115
When works are censur'd, not as bad, but new;
While if our Elders break all Reason's laws,
These fools demand not Pardon, but Applause.

    On Avon's bank, where flow'rs eternal blow,
If I but ask, if any weed can grow?   120
One Tragic sentence if I dare deride
Which Betterton's grave Action dignify'd,
Or well-mouth'd Booth with emphasis proclaims,
(Tho' but, perhaps, a muster-roll of Names)
How will our Fathers rise up in a rage,   125
And swear, all shame is lost in George's Age!
You'd think no Fools disgrac'd the former Reign,
Did not some grave Examples yet remain,
Who scorn a Lad should teach his Father skill,
And, having once been wrong, will be so still.   130
He, who to seem more deep than you or I,
Extols old Bards, or Merlin's Prophecy,
Mistake him not; he envies, not admires,
And to debase the Sons, exalts the Sires.
Had ancient Times conspir'd to dis-allow   135
What then was new, what had been ancient now?
Or what remain'd, so worthy to be read
By learned Criticks, of the mighty Dead?

    In Days of Ease, when now the weary Sword
Was sheath'd, and *Luxury* with *Charles* restor'd;   140
In every Taste of foreign Courts improv'd,
'All by the King's Example, liv'd and lov'd.'
Then Peers grew proud in Horsemanship t' excell,

---

insipid writer;' Pope told Spence, 'except in some few of his little love-verses'.

    124. An absurd Custom of several Actors, to pronounce with Emphasis the meer *Proper Names* of Greeks or Romans, which (as they call it) *fill the mouth* of the Player [P].

    132. *Merlin's Prophecy*] Translated from the Welsh by Geoffrey of Monmouth and embodied in his *Historia Regum Britanniæ* (Book vii), an English translation of which was made by Aaron Thompson (1718).

    139 ff. Cf. *E. on C.* ll. 534–59.

    142. *A Verse of the Lord* Lansdown [P]. From *The Progress of Beauty*.

    143. *Horsemanship . . . Romance*] The Duke of Newcastle's Book of

New-market's Glory rose, as Britain's fell;
The Soldier breath'd the Gallantries of France,   145
And ev'ry flow'ry Courtier writ Romance.
Then Marble soften'd into life grew warm,
And yielding Metal flow'd to human form:
Lely on animated Canvas stole
The sleepy Eye, that spoke the melting soul.   150
No wonder then, when all was Love and Sport,
The willing Muses were debauch'd at Court;
On each enervate string they taught the Note
To pant, or tremble thro' an Eunuch's throat.
But Britain, changeful as a Child at play,   155
Now calls in Princes, and now turns away.
Now Whig, now Tory, what we lov'd we hate;
Now all for Pleasure, now for Church and State;
Now for Prerogative, and now for Laws;
Effects unhappy! from a Noble Cause.   160
    Time was, a sober Englishman wou'd knock
His servants up, and rise by five a clock,
Instruct his Family in ev'ry rule,
And send his Wife to Church, his Son to school.
To worship like his Fathers was his care;   165
To teach their frugal Virtues to his Heir;
To prove, that Luxury could never hold;
And place, on good Security, his Gold.
Now Times are chang'd, and one Poetick Itch
Has seiz'd the Court and City, Poor and Rich: 170
Sons, Sires, and Grandsires, all will wear the Bays,
Our Wives read Milton, and our Daughters Plays,
To Theatres, and to Rehearsals throng,
And all our Grace at Table is a Song.
I, who so oft renounce the Muses, lye,   175
Not —'s self e'er tells more *Fibs* than I;
When, sick of Muse, our follies we deplore,
And promise our best Friends to ryme no more;

Horsemanship: the Romance of *Parthenissa* ⟨1654⟩, by the Earl of Orrery,
and most of the French Romances translated by *Persons of Quality* [P].
    The Duke of Newcastle wrote two books on Horsemanship, *Methode
et Invention Nouvelle de Dresser les Chevaux* (Antwerp, 1658) and *A New
Method and Extraordinary Invention to Dress Horses* (1667).
    149. Sir Peter Lely (1618–80), a Dutchman, came to England in 1641
and established a reputation as a portrait-painter, but his greatest fame
and prosperity was gained after the Restoration.
    153. The Siege of Rhodes ⟨1656⟩ by Sir William Davenant, the first
Opera sung in England [P].

We wake next morning in a raging Fit,
And call for Pen and Ink to show our Wit.   180
    He serv'd a 'Prenticeship, who sets up shop;
Ward try'd on Puppies, and the Poor, his Drop;
Ev'n Radcliff's Doctors travel first to France,
Nor dare to practise till they've learn'd to dance.
Who builds a Bridge that never drove a pyle?   185
(Should Ripley venture, all the World would smile)
But those who cannot write, and those who can,
All ryme, and scrawl, and scribble, to a man.
    Yet Sir, reflect, the mischief is not great;
These Madmen never hurt the Church or State: 190
Sometimes the Folly benefits mankind;
And rarely Av'rice taints the tuneful mind.
'Allow him but his Play-thing of a Pen,
He ne'er rebels, or plots, like other men:
Flight of Cashiers, or Mobs, he'll never mind;   195
And knows no losses while the Muse is kind.
To cheat a Friend, or Ward, he leaves to Peter;
The good man heaps up nothing but mere metre,
Enjoys his Garden and his Book in quiet;
And then—a perfect Hermit in his Diet.   200
Of little use the Man you may suppose,
Who says in verse what others say in prose;
Yet let me show, a Poet's of some weight,
And (tho' no Soldier) useful to the State.

182. *Ward*] A famous Empirick, whose Pill and Drop had several surprizing effects, and were one of the principal subjects of Writing and Conversation at this time [P].

183. Sir John Radcliffe (1653–1714), physician, left money to endow medical travelling fellowships. From his estate the Radcliffe Library, Infirmary, and Observatory at Oxford were built and endowed.

186. Thomas Ripley (d. 1758), architect, who owed his advancement to Walpole.

195. *Flight of Cashiers*] Robert Knight, cashier of the South Sea Company, fled to France, after being found guilty of notorious breach of trust by the House of Lords.

197. *Peter*] i.e. Peter Walter. See *Sat.* II ii 168*n* (p. 624) and p. 577, l. 125*n*.

204. Horace had not acquitted himself much to his credit in this capacity; (*non bene relicta parmula*, ⟨*Od.* II vii 10⟩) in the battle of Philippi. It is manifest he alludes to himself in this whole account of a Poet's character; but with an intermixture of Irony: *Vivit siliquis & pane secundo* has a relation to his Epicurism; *Os tenerum pueri*, is ridicule: The nobler office of a Poet follows, *Torquet ab obscœnis—Mox etiam pectus—Rectè facta refert, &c.* which the Imitator has apply'd where he thinks it more due than to himself. He hopes to be pardoned, if, as he is sincerely

What will a Child learn sooner than a song?   205
What better teach a Foreigner the tongue?
What's long or short, each accent where to place,
And speak in publick with some sort of grace.
I scarce can think him such a worthless thing,
Unless he praise some monster of a King,   210
Or Virtue, or Religion turn to sport,
To please a lewd, or un-believing Court.
Unhappy Dryden!—In all Charles's days,
Roscommon only boasts unspotted Bays;
And in our own (excuse some Courtly stains)   215
No whiter page than Addison remains.
He, from the taste obscene reclaims our Youth,
And sets the Passions on the side of Truth;
Forms the soft bosom with the gentlest art,
And pours each human Virtue in the heart.   220
Let Ireland tell, how Wit upheld her cause,
Her Trade supported, and supply'd her Laws;
And leave on SWIFT this grateful verse ingrav'd,
The Rights a Court attack'd, a Poet sav'd.
Behold the hand that wrought a Nation's cure,   225
Stretch'd to relieve the Idiot and the Poor,
Proud Vice to brand, or injur'd Worth adorn,
And stretch the Ray to Ages yet unborn.
Not but there are, who merit other palms;
Hopkins and Sternhold glad the heart with Psalms;   230
The Boys and Girls whom Charity maintains,
Implore your help in these pathetic strains:
How could Devotion touch the country pews,
Unless the Gods bestow'd a proper Muse?
Verse chears their leisure, Verse assists their work,   235

---

inclined to praise what deserves to be praised, he arraigns what deserves
to be arraigned, in the 210, 211, and 212th Verses [P].

214. *Roscommon*] Wentworth Dillon, fourth Earl of Roscommon
(1633?–1685), whose *Essay on Translated Verse* was published in 1684.
See *E. on C.* ll. 725–6.

222. *Trade supported*] He refers to Swift's *Proposal for the Universal Use
of Irish Manufacture* (1720).

supply'd] i.e. made up for the deficiences of her laws.

226. *the Idiot and the Poor*] A Foundation for the maintenance of Idiots,
and a Fund for assisting the Poor, by lending small sums of Money on
demand [P].

230. Sternhold's metrical version of the Psalms, begun in 1549, was
completed by Hopkins and others in 1562.

Verse prays for Peace, or sings down Pope and Turk.
The silenc'd Preacher yields to potent strain,
And feels that grace his pray'r besought in vain,
The blessing thrills thro' all the lab'ring throng,
And Heav'n is won by violence of Song.   240
    Our rural Ancestors, with little blest,
Patient of labour when the end was rest,
Indulg'd the day that hous'd their annual grain,
With feasts, and off'rings, and a thankful strain:
The joy their wives, their sons, and servants share,   245
Ease of their toil, and part'ners of their care:
The laugh, the jest, attendants on the bowl,
Smooth'd ev'ry brow, and open'd ev'ry soul:
With growing years the pleasing Licence grew,
And Taunts alternate innocently flew.   250
But Times corrupt, and Nature, ill-inclin'd,
Produc'd the point that left a sting behind;
Till friend with friend, and families at strife,
Triumphant Malice rag'd thro' private life.
Who felt the wrong, or fear'd it, took th' alarm,   255
Appeal'd to Law, and Justice lent her arm.
At length, by wholesom dread of statutes bound,
The Poets learn'd to please, and not to wound:
Most warp'd to Flatt'ry's side; but some, more nice,
Preserv'd the freedom, and forbore the vice.   260
Hence Satire rose, that just the medium hit,
And heals with Morals what it hurts with Wit.
    We conquer'd France, but felt our captive's charms;
Her Arts victorious triumph'd o'er our Arms:
Britain to soft refinements less a foe,   265
Wit grew polite, and Numbers learn'd to flow.
Waller was smooth; but Dryden taught to join ⎫
The varying verse, the full resounding line,   ⎬
The long majestic march, and energy divine.   ⎭

236. *sings . . . Turk*] 'My name is as bad a one as yours, and hated by
all bad poets, from Hopkins and Sternhold to Gildon and Cibber. The
first prayed against me joined with the Turk . . .' (Pope to Swift, Oct. 15,
1725). The allusion is to a line in the prayer at the end of the metrical
psalms: 'From Pope and Turk defend us, Lord'.
    257. *statutes*] See *Sat.* II i 147*n* (p. 618).
    267. Mr. Waller about this time ⟨1664⟩, with the E. of Dorset, Mr.
Godolphin, and others, translated the Pompey of Corneille; and the more
correct French Poets began to be in reputation [P].
    268. 'Energy' as a critical term denoting vigour of expression is derived
from an imperfect understanding of Aristotle's use of ἐνέργεια for the

Tho' still some traces of our rustic vein   270
And splay-foot verse, remain'd, and will remain.
Late, very late, correctness grew our care,
When the tir'd nation breath'd from civil war.
Exact Racine, and Corneille's noble fire
Show'd us that France had something to admire.   275
Not but the Tragic spirit was our own,
And full in Shakespear, fair in Otway shone:
But Otway fail'd to polish or refine,
And fluent Shakespear scarce effac'd a line.
Ev'n copious Dryden, wanted, or forgot,   280
The last and greatest Art, the Art to blot.
　　Some doubt, if equal pains or equal fire
The humbler Muse of Comedy require?
But in known Images of life I guess
The labour greater, as th' Indulgence less.   285
Observe how seldom ev'n the best succeed:
Tell me if Congreve's Fools are Fools indeed?
What pert low Dialogue has Farqu'ar writ!
How Van wants grace, who never wanted wit!
The stage how loosely does Astræa tread,   290
Who fairly puts all Characters to bed:
And idle Cibber, how he breaks the laws,
To make poor Pinky eat with vast applause!
But fill their purse, our Poet's work is done,

---

species of metaphor which calls up a mental picture of something 'acting'
or moving (*OED*).

278. Thomas Otway (1652–1685), tragic dramatist; author of *The
Orphan*, 1680, and *Venice Preserved*, 1682.

287. *Congreve's Fools*] Pope probably refers to Brisk, the 'pert Coxcomb' in *The Double Dealer*, and more particularly to Witwoud, whose
character Congreve mentions in the epistle dedicatory to *The Way of the
World*, as intended for an unusual type of fool, who 'should appear
ridiculous, not so much through a natural folly . . . as through an affected
wit.'

288. *Farqu'ar*] George Farquhar (1677–1707), author of *The Beaux
Stratagem* (1707) and other comedies.

289. *Van*] Sir John Vanbrugh (1664–1726), comic dramatist and
architect. Author of *The Confederacy* (1705) and other plays.

290. *Astræa*] A Name taken by Mrs. Afra Behn, Authoress of
several obscene Plays, &c. [P].

B. 1640, d. 1689. Astræa was the goddess of justice. Hence the use of
'fairly' in l. 291.

293. cf. *The Tatler* (No. 188). '*Penkethman* devours a cold Chick with
great Applause.' As Don Lewis in Cibber's *Love Makes a Man* (1700)
(Act IV) Penkethman ate two chickens in three seconds.

Alike to them, by Pathos or by Pun. 295
　　O you! whom Vanity's light bark conveys
On Fame's mad voyage by the wind of Praise;
With what a shifting gale your course you ply;
For ever sunk too low, or born too high!
Who pants for glory finds but short repose, 300
A breath revives him, or a breath o'erthrows!
Farewel the stage! if just as thrives the Play,
The silly bard grows fat, or falls away.
　　There still remains to mortify a Wit,
The many-headed Monster of the Pit: 305
A sense-less, worth-less, and unhonour'd crowd;
Who to disturb their betters mighty proud,
Clatt'ring their sticks, before ten lines are spoke,
Call for the Farce, the Bear, or the Black-joke.
What dear delight to Britons Farce affords! 310
Farce once the taste of Mobs, but now of Lords;
(For Taste, eternal wanderer, now flies
From heads to ears, and now from ears to eyes.)
The Play stands still; damn action and discourse,
Back fly the scenes, and enter foot and horse; 315
Pageants on pageants, in long order drawn,
Peers, Heralds, Bishops, Ermin, Gold, and Lawn;
The Champion too! and, to complete the jest,
Old Edward's Armour beams on Cibber's breast!
With laughter sure Democritus had dy'd, 320
Had he beheld an Audience gape so wide.
Let Bear or Elephant be e'er so white,
The people, sure, the people are the sight!
Ah luckless Poet! stretch thy lungs and roar,
That Bear or Elephant shall heed thee more 325
While all its throats the Gallery extends,
And all the Thunder of the Pit ascends!

309. *Black-joke*] A popular air.
313. From Plays to Operas, and from Operas to Pantomimes.
315. *scenes*] The flats which met in the centre to form a painted scene, and were drawn apart to reveal the inner stage.
319. The Coronation of Henry the Eighth and Queen Anne Boleyn, in which the Playhouses vied with each other to represent all the pomp of a Coronation. In this noble contention, the Armour of one of the Kings of England was borrowed from the Tower, to dress the Champion [P].
George II was crowned on Oct. 11, 1727. On Oct. 26, Shakespeare's *Henry VIII* was performed at Drury Lane with Booth as Henry, Cibber as Wolsey, Wilks as Buckingham, and Mrs. Porter as Queen Catherine. Special attention was paid to the coronation of Anne Boleyn, which alone cost the managers £1,000.

Loud as the Wolves on Orcas' stormy steep,
Howl to the roarings of the Northern deep.
Such is the shout, the long-applauding note,   330
At Quin's high plume, or Oldfield's petticoat,
Or when from Court a birth-day suit bestow'd
Sinks the lost Actor in the tawdry load.
Booth enters—hark! the Universal Peal!
'But has he spoken?' Not a syllable.   335
'What shook the stage, and made the people stare?'
Cato's long Wig, flowr'd gown, and lacquer'd chair.
    Yet lest you think I railly more than teach,
Or praise malignly Arts I cannot reach,
Let me for once presume t'instruct the times,   340
To know the Poet from the Man of Rymes:
'Tis He, who gives my breast a thousand pains,
Can make me feel each Passion that he feigns,
Inrage, compose, with more than magic Art,
With Pity, and with Terror, tear my heart;   345
And snatch me, o'er the earth, or thro' the air,
To Thebes, to Athens, when he will, and where.
    But not this part of the poetic state
Alone, deserves the favour of the Great:
Think of those Authors, Sir, who would rely   350
More on a Reader's sense, than Gazer's eye.
Or who shall wander where the Muses sing?
Who climb their Mountain, or who taste their spring?
How shall we fill a Library with Wit,
When Merlin's Cave is half unfurnish'd yet?   355
    My Liege! why Writers little claim your thought,

328. *Orcas*] The farthest Northern Promontory of Scotland, opposite
to the Orcades [P].
    331. *Quin's high plume*] Addison remarks (*Spect.* 42) that 'the ordinary
method of making an Hero, is to clap a huge Plume of feathers upon his
head.'
    Oldfield's petticoat] 'A Princess generally receives her grandeur from
. . . the broad sweeping train that follows her in all her motions, and finds
constant employment for a boy who stands behind her to open and spread
it to advantage' (Addison, op. cit.). Mrs. Townley (Mrs. Oldfield) hides
her lover Plotwell under her petticoat in *Three Hours after Marriage*
(1717), Act II, by Pope, Gay, and Arbuthnot.
    332. *birth-day suit*] one of the magnificent suits worn at royal birthday
celebrations. See *Ep.* I vi 33, *Rape*, i 23; *Imit. Donne*, iv 218–25.
    337. See Addison's *Cato* (1713) V i, where the initial stage direction
reads 'CATO solus, *sitting in a thoughtful posture* . . .'
    355. *Merlin's Cave*] A Building ⟨by Kent, 1735⟩ in the Royal Gardens
of Richmond, where is a small, but choice Collection of Books [P].

I guess; and, with their leave, will tell the fault:
We Poets are (upon a Poet's word)
Of all mankind, the creatures most absurd:
The season, when to come, and when to go,   360
To sing, or cease to sing, we never know;
And if we will recite nine hours in ten,
You lose your patience, just like other men.
Then too we hurt our selves, when to defend
A single verse, we quarrel with a friend;   365
Repeat unask'd; lament, the Wit's too fine
For vulgar eyes, and point out ev'ry line.
But most, when straining with too weak a wing,
We needs will write Epistles to the King;
And from the moment we oblige the town,   370
Expect a Place, or Pension from the Crown;
Or dubb'd Historians by express command,
T' enroll your triumphs o'er the seas and land;
Be call'd to Court, to plan some work divine,
As once for LOUIS, Boileau and Racine.   375
    Yet think great Sir! (so many Virtues shown)
Ah think, what Poet best may make them known?
Or chuse at least some Minister of Grace,
Fit to bestow the Laureat's weighty place.
    Charles, to late times to be transmitted fair,   380
Assign'd his figure to Bernini's care;
And great Nassau to Kneller's hand decreed
To fix him graceful on the bounding Steed:
So well in paint and stone they judg'd of merit:
But Kings in Wit may want discerning spirit.   385
The Hero William, and the Martyr Charles,
One knighted Blackmore, and one pension'd Quarles;

372. Dryden and Shadwell had held the office of historiographer royal
(recreated in 1661) with the laureateship.

375. Boileau and Racine were appointed historiographers to Louis XIV
in 1677.

378. *some Minister*] Walpole appointed Cibber poet laureate in 1730.

381. Bernini was the architect who designed the great colonnade of
St. Peter's. His bust of Charles I, made in Rome in 1636-7, perished in
the fire at Whitehall in 1696.

382. Kneller's equestrian portrait of William III with allegorical
figures, now at Hampton Court, was painted in 1701 to commemorate
William's return to England after signing the peace of Ryswick in 1697.

387-9. Blackmore was knighted for his services as court physician, not
for his poetry. Nothing is known of Quarles's pension or Jonson's reference to it. The meaning of ll. 388-9 still awaits explanation.

Which made old Ben, and surly Dennis swear,
'No Lord's anointed, but a Russian Bear.'

Not with such Majesty, such bold relief,   390
The Forms august of King, or conqu'ring Chief,
E'er swell'd on Marble; as in Verse have shin'd
(In polish'd Verse) the Manners and the Mind.
Oh! could I mount on the Mæonian wing,
Your Arms, your Actions, your Repose to sing!   395
What seas you travers'd! and what fields you fought!
Your Country's Peace, how oft, how dearly bought!
How barb'rous rage subsided at your word,
And Nations wonder'd while they dropp'd the sword!
How, when you nodded, o'er the land and deep,   400
Peace stole her wing, and wrapt the world in sleep;
Till Earth's extremes your mediation own,
And Asia's Tyrants tremble at your Throne—
But Verse alas! your Majesty disdains;
And I'm not us'd to Panegyric strains: 405
The Zeal of Fools offends at any time,
But most of all, the Zeal of Fools in ryme.
Besides, a fate attends on all I write,
That when I aim at praise, they say I bite.
A vile Encomium doubly ridicules;   410
There's nothing blackens like the ink of fools;
If true, a woful likeness, and if lyes,
'Praise undeserv'd is scandal in disguise:'
Well may he blush, who gives it, or receives;
And when I flatter, let my dirty leaves   415
(Like Journals, Odes, and such forgotten things
As Eusden, Philips, Settle, writ of Kings)
Cloath spice, line trunks, or flutt'ring in a row,
Befringe the rails of Bedlam and Sohoe.

394. Homer was thought to have been an inhabitant of Maeonia.
    397. Walpole's pacific policy, reluctantly adopted by George II, was
becoming increasingly unpopular. *Dearly* is especially ironical. cf. *Dia.* i
151–160 (p. 694).
    417. For Eusden and Philips, see *Ep. to Arbuthnot*, 15*n*, 100*n*. Elkanah
Settle (1648–1724) wrote birthday odes for George I and the Prince of
Wales, 1717.

The Second Epistle of the Second Book
of Horace Imitated by Mr. Pope

[written c. 1736; published 1737]

Ludentis speciem dabit & torquebitur—
[HOR. *Ep. II. ii. 124.*]

Dear Col'nel! *Cobham*'s and your Country's Friend!
You love a Verse, take such as I can send.
A Frenchman comes, presents you with his Boy,
Bows and begins.—'This Lad, Sir, is of Blois:
Observe his Shape how clean! his Locks how curl'd!   5
My only Son, I'd have him see the World:
His French is pure; his Voice too—you shall hear—
Sir, he's your Slave, for twenty pound a year.
Mere Wax as yet, you fashion him with ease,
Your Barber, Cook, Upholst'rer, what you please.   10
A perfect Genius at an Opera-Song—
To say too much, might do my Honour wrong:
Take him with all his Virtues, on my word;
His whole Ambition was to serve a Lord,

But Sir, to you, with what wou'd I not part?   15
Tho' faith, I fear 'twill break his Mother's heart.
Once, (and but once) I caught him in a Lye,
And then, unwhipp'd, he had the grace to cry:
The Fault he has I fairly shall reveal,
(Cou'd you o'erlook but that)—it is, to steal.'   20
    If, after this, you took the graceless Lad,
Cou'd you complain, my Friend, he prov'd so bad?
Faith, in such case, if you should prosecute,
I think Sir Godfry should decide the Suit;
Who sent the Thief that stole the Cash, away,   25
And punish'd him that put it in his way.
    Consider then, and judge me in this light;
I told you when I went, I could not write;

---

1. Colonel Anthony Browne of Abscourt farm, near Walton-on-Thames.
    4. *Blois*] A town in which French was reputed to be spoken with exceptional purity.
    24. *Sir Godfry*] An eminent Justice of Peace, who decided much in the manner of Sancho Pança [P]. Sir Godfrey Kneller. This alluded to his dismissing a soldier who had stolen a joint of meat, and accused the butcher of having tempted him by it.

You said the same; and are you discontent
With Laws, to which you gave your own assent?   30
Nay worse, to ask for Verse at such a time!
D'ye think me good for nothing but to rhime?
  In ANNA's Wars, a Soldier poor and old,
Had dearly earn'd a little purse of Gold:
Tir'd with a tedious March, one luckless night,   35
He slept, poor Dog! and lost it, to a doit.
This put the Man in such a desp'rate Mind,   ⎫
Between Revenge, and Grief, and Hunger join'd,   ⎬
Against the Foe, himself, and all Mankind,   ⎭
He leapt the Trenches, scal'd a Castle-Wall,   40
Tore down a Standard, took the Fort and all.
'Prodigious well!' his great Commander cry'd,
Gave him much Praise, and some Reward beside.
Next pleas'd his Excellence a Town to batter;
(Its Name I know not, and it's no great matter)   45
'Go on, my Friend (he cry'd) see yonder Walls!
Advance and conquer! go where Glory calls!
More Honours, more Rewards, attend the Brave'—

Don't you remember what Reply he gave?
'D'ye think me, noble Gen'ral, such a Sot?
Let him take Castles who has ne'er a Groat.'   50
  Bred up at home, full early I begun
To read in Greek, the Wrath of Peleus' Son.
Besides, my Father taught me from a Lad,
The better Art to know the good from bad: 55
(And little sure imported to remove,
To hunt for Truth in *Maudlin*'s learned Grove.)
But knottier Points we knew not half so well,
Depriv'd us soon of our Paternal Cell;
And certain Laws, by Suff'rers thought unjust,   60
Deny'd all Posts of Profit or of Trust:
Hopes after Hopes of pious Papists fail'd,
While mighty WILLIAM's thundring Arm prevail'd.
For Right Hereditary tax'd and fin'd,
He stuck to Poverty with Peace of Mind;   65
And me, the Muses help'd to undergo it;
Convict a Papist He, and I a Poet.
But (thanks to *Homer*) since I live and thrive,
Indebted to no Prince or Peer alive,

43. *some Reward*] a departure from the Latin in order to reflect upon Marlborough's avarice.

Sure I should want the Care of ten *Monroes*,   70
If I would scribble, rather than repose.
   Years foll'wing Years, steal something ev'ry day,
At last they steal us from our selves away;
In one our Frolicks, one Amusements end,
In one a Mistress drops, in one a Friend: 75
This subtle Thief of Life, this paltry Time,
What will it leave me, if it snatch my Rhime?
If ev'ry Wheel of that unweary'd Mill
That turn'd ten thousand Verses, now stands still.
   But after all, what wou'd you have me do?   80
When out of twenty I can please not two;
When this Heroicks only deigns to praise,
Sharp Satire that, and that Pindaric lays?
One likes the Pheasant's wing, and one the leg;
The Vulgar boil, the Learned roast an Egg;   85
Hard Task! to hit the Palate of such Guests,
When Oldfield loves, what Dartineuf detests.
   But grant I may relapse, for want of Grace,
Again to rhime, can *London* be the Place?
Who there his Muse, or Self, or Soul attends?   90
In Crouds and Courts, Law, Business, Feasts and Friends?
My Counsel sends to execute a Deed:
A Poet begs me, I will hear him read:
In Palace-Yard at Nine you'll find me there—
At Ten for certain, Sir, in Bloomsb'ry-Square—   95
Before the Lords at Twelve my Cause comes on—
There's a Rehearsal, Sir, exact at One.—
'Oh but a Wit can study in the Streets,
And raise his Mind above the Mob he meets.'
Not quite so well however as one ought;   100
A Hackney-Coach may chance to spoil a Thought,
And then a nodding Beam, or Pig of Lead,
God knows, may hurt the very ablest Head.
Have you not seen at Guild-hall's narrow Pass,
Two Aldermen dispute it with an Ass?   105
And Peers give way, exalted as they are,
Ev'n to their own S-r-v--nce in a Carr?

---

70. *Monroes*] *Dr.* MONROE, *Physician to Bedlam Hospital* [P].
87. *Oldfield*] See *Sat.* II ii 25. Dartineuf, another celebrated epicure,
appears in *Sat.* II i 46.
107. *S—r—v—nce*] Sir-reverence, i.e. human excrement.
Carr] A word normally used in the sense of 'triumphal chariot'.

Go, lofty Poet! and in such a Croud,
Sing thy sonorous Verse—but not aloud.
Alas! to Grotto's and to Groves we run,   110
To Ease and Silence, ev'ry Muse's Son:
Blackmore himself, for any grand Effort,
Would drink and doze at *Tooting* or *Earl's-Court.*
How shall I rhime in this eternal Roar?
How match the Bards whom none e'er match'd before? 115
The Man, who stretch'd in Isis' calm Retreat
To Books and Study gives sev'n years compleat,
See! strow'd with learned dust, his Night-cap on,
He walks, an Object new beneath the Sun!
The Boys flock round him, and the People stare: ⎫   120
So stiff, so mute! some Statue, you would swear, ⎬
Stept from its Pedestal to take the Air.   ⎭
And here, while Town, and Court, and City roars,
With Mobs, and Duns, and Soldiers, at their doors;
Shall I, in *London*, act this idle part?   125
Composing Songs, for Fools to get by heart?
    The *Temple* late two Brother Sergeants saw,
Who deem'd each other Oracles of Law;
With equal Talents, these congenial Souls
One lull'd th' *Exchequer*, and one stunn'd the *Rolls;* 130
Each had a Gravity wou'd make you split,
And shook his head at *Murray*, as a Wit.
'Twas, 'Sir your Law'—and 'Sir, your Eloquence'—
'Yours *Cowper*'s Manner—and yours *Talbot*'s Sense.'
    Thus we dispose of all poetic Merit,   135
Yours *Milton*'s Genius, and mine *Homer*'s Spirit.
Call *Tibbald Shakespear*, and he'll swear the Nine
Dear *Cibber!* never match'd one Ode of thine.
Lord! how we strut thro' *Merlin*'s Cave, to see
No Poets there, but *Stephen*, you, and me.   140
Walk with respect behind, while we at ease
Weave Laurel Crowns, and take what Names we please.
'My dear *Tibullus!*' if that will not do,
'Let me be *Horace*, and be *Ovid* you.

113. *Tooting or Earl's-Court*] Two Villages within a few Miles of
London [P].
    117. *sev'n years*] the term for completing the M.A. degree.
    134. *Cowper . . . Talbot*] Two Lord Chancellors.
Merlin's Cave] See *Ep.* II i 355*n* (p. 647).
    140. *Stephen*] Stephen Duck, the Thresher Poet, was Library Keeper
at Merlin's Cave. See p. 802 and note.

Or, I'm content, allow me *Dryden*'s strains,   145
And you shall rise up *Otway* for your pains.'
Much do I suffer, much, to keep in peace
This jealous, waspish, wrong-head, rhiming Race;
And much must flatter, if the Whim should bite
To court applause by printing what I write: 150
But let the Fit pass o'er, I'm wise enough,
To stop my ears to their confounded stuff.
　In vain, bad Rhimers all mankind reject,
They treat themselves with most profound respect;
'Tis to small purpose that you hold your tongue,   155
Each prais'd within, is happy all day long.
But how severely with themselves proceed
The Men, who write such Verse as we can read?

Their own strict Judges, not a word they spare
That wants or Force, or Light, or Weight, or Care,   160
Howe'er unwillingly it quits its place,
Nay tho' at Court (perhaps) it may find grace:
Such they'll degrade; and sometimes, in its stead,
In downright Charity revive the dead;
Mark where a bold expressive Phrase appears,   165
Bright thro' the rubbish of some hundred years;
Command old words that long have slept, to wake,
Words, that wise *Bacon*, or brave *Raleigh* spake;
Or bid the new be *English*, Ages hence,
(For Use will father what's begot by Sense)   170
Pour the full Tide of Eloquence along, ⎫
Serenely pure, and yet divinely strong, ⎬
Rich with the Treasures of each foreign Tongue; ⎭
Prune the luxuriant, the uncouth refine,
But show no mercy to an empty line;   175
Then polish all, with so much life and ease,
You think 'tis Nature, and a knack to please:
'But Ease in writing flows from Art, not Chance,
As those move easiest who have learn'd to dance.'
　If such the Plague and pains to write by rule,   180
Better (say I) be pleas'd, and play the fool;
Call, if you will, bad Rhiming a disease,
It gives men happiness, or leaves them ease.

---

168. When talking over the design of a standard English Dictionary
with Warburton, Pope accepted Bacon as an authority but rejected
Raleigh as 'too affected'.
178-9. Slightly altered from *E. on C.*, ll. 362-3.

There liv'd, *in primo Georgii* (they record)
A worthy Member, no small Fool, a Lord;   185
Who, tho' the House was up, delighted sate,
Heard, noted, answer'd, as in full Debate:

In all but this, a man of sober Life,
Fond of his Friend, and civil to his Wife,
Not quite a Mad-man, tho' a Pasty fell,   190
And much too wise to walk into a Well:
Him, the damn'd Doctors and his Friends immur'd,
They bled, they cupp'd, they purg'd; in short, they cur'd:
Whereat the Gentleman began to stare—
My Friends? he cry'd, p—x take you for your care!   195
That from a Patriot of distinguish'd note,
Have bled and purg'd me to a simple *Vote*.
    Well, on the whole, *plain* Prose must be my fate:
Wisdom (curse on it) will come soon or late.
There is a time when Poets will grow dull: 200
I'll e'en leave Verses to the Boys at school:
To Rules of Poetry no more confin'd,
I learn to smooth and harmonize my Mind,
Teach ev'ry Thought within its bounds to roll,
And keep the equal Measure of the Soul.   205
    Soon as I enter at my Country door,
My Mind resumes the thread it dropt before;
Thoughts, which at Hyde-Park-Corner I forgot,
Meet and rejoin me, in the pensive Grott.
There all alone, and Compliments apart,   210
I ask these sober questions of my Heart.
    If, when the more you drink, the more you crave,
You tell the Doctor; when the more you have,
The more you want, why not with equal ease
Confess as well your Folly, as Disease?   215
The Heart resolves this matter in a trice,
'Men only feel the Smart, but not the Vice.'
    When golden Angels cease to cure the Evil,
You give all royal Witchcraft to the Devil:
When servile Chaplains cry, that Birth and Place   220
Indue a Peer with Honour, Truth, and Grace,
Look in that Breast, most dirty Duke! be fair,
Say, can you find out one such Lodger there?

218. It was generally believed as late as Stuart times that King's Evil
(i.e. Scrofula) could be cured by the royal touch. Queen Anne 'touched',
but the power was not claimed for George I or subsequent kings. The
angel was a gold coin presented by the king to each patient.

Yet still, not heeding what your Heart can teach,
You go to Church to hear these Flatt'rers preach.　　225
　　Indeed, could Wealth bestow or Wit or Merit,
A grain of Courage, or a spark of Spirit,
The wisest Man might blush, I must agree,
If vile Van-muck lov'd Sixpence, more than he.
　　If there be truth in Law, and *Use* can give　　230
A *Property*, that's yours on which you live.
Delightful *Abs-court*, if its Fields afford
Their Fruits to you, confesses you its Lord:
All Worldly's Hens, nay Partridge, sold to town,
His Ven'son too, a Guinea makes your own:　　235
He bought at thousands, what with better wit
You purchase as you want, and bit by bit;
Now, or long since, what diff'rence will be found?
You pay a Penny, and he paid a Pound.
　　Heathcote himself, and such large-acred Men,　　240
Lords of fat *E'sham*, or of Lincoln Fen,
Buy every stick of Wood that lends them heat,
Buy every Pullet they afford to eat.
Yet these are Wights, who fondly call their own
Half that the Dev'l o'erlooks from Lincoln Town.　　245
The Laws of God, as well as of the Land,
Abhor, a *Perpetuity* should stand:
Estates have wings, and hang in Fortune's pow'r
Loose on the point of ev'ry wav'ring Hour;
Ready, by force, or of your own accord,　　250
By sale, at least by death, to change their Lord.
Man? and *for ever?* Wretch! what wou'dst thou have?
Heir urges Heir, like Wave impelling Wave:
All vast Possessions (just the same the case
Whether you call them Villa, Park, or Chace)　　255

229. *vile Van-muck*] Joshua [?] Vanneck, a Dutch merchant in London, who in the autumn of 1738 had offered to buy Dawley Farm from Boling-broke at a price which proved unacceptable.

232. The estate of Apps-Court, near Walton-on-Thames, was leased by Lord Halifax to Anthony Browne.

234. *Worldly*] i.e. Wortley Montagu. cf. *Sat.* II ii 51 and *Moral Es.* iii 50.

245. An oblique way of saying that they envy their neighbours' estates.

247. *Perpetuity*] 'Unlimited duration; exemption from intermission or ceasing, where, though all who have interest should join in a covenant, they could not bar or pass the estate. It is odious in law, destructive to the commonwealth, and an impediment to commerce, by preventing the wholesome circulation of property.'

Alas, my BATHURST! what will they avail?
Join *Cotswold* Hills to *Saperton*'s fair Dale,
Let rising Granaries and Temples here,
There mingled Farms and Pyramids appear,
Link Towns to Towns with Avenues of Oak,   260
Enclose whole Downs in Walls, 'tis all a joke!
Inexorable Death shall level all,
And Trees, and Stones, and Farms, and Farmer fall.
    Gold, Silver, Iv'ry, Vases sculptur'd high,
Paint, Marble, Gems, and Robes of *Persian* Dye,   265
There are who have not—and thank Heav'n there are
Who, if they have not, think not worth their care.
    Talk what you will of Taste, my Friend, you'll find,
Two of a Face, as soon as of a Mind.
Why, of two Brothers, rich and restless one   270
Ploughs, burns, manures, and toils from Sun to Sun;
The other slights, for Women, Sports, and Wines,
All *Townshend*'s Turnips, and all *Grovenor*'s Mines:
Why one like *Bu*— with Pay and Scorn content,
Bows and votes on, in Court and Parliament;   275
One, driv'n by strong Benevolence of Soul,
Shall fly, like *Oglethorp*, from Pole to Pole:
Is known alone to that Directing Pow'r,
Who forms the Genius in the natal Hour;
That God of Nature, who, within us still,   280
Inclines our Action, not constrains our Will;
Various of Temper, as of Face or Frame,
Each Individual: His great End the same.
    Yes, Sir, how small soever be my heap,
A part I will enjoy, as well as keep.   285
My Heir may sigh, and think it want of Grace
A man so poor wou'd live without a *Place*:
But sure no Statute in his favour says,
How free, or frugal, I shall pass my days:
I, who at some times spend, at others spare,   290
Divided between Carelesness and Care.
'Tis one thing madly to disperse my store,
Another, not to heed to treasure more;

273. The Grosvenors had owned coal mines in N. Wales since the
sixteenth century. Townshend, the retired Whig statesman, was cultivating his Norfolk estates. His large-scale turnip-culture permitted subsequent development in breeding stock.
274. *Bu*—] Bubb Dodington.

Glad, like a Boy, to snatch the first good day,
And pleas'd, if sordid Want be far away.   295
   What is't to me (a Passenger God wot)
Whether my Vessel be first-rate or not?
The Ship it self may make a better figure,
But I that sail, am neither less nor bigger.
I neither strut with ev'ry fav'ring breath,   300
Nor strive with all the Tempest in my teeth.
In Pow'r, Wit, Figure, Virtue, Fortune, plac'd
Behind the foremost, and before the last.
   'But why all this of Av'rice? I have none.'
I wish you joy, Sir, of a Tyrant gone;   305
But does no other lord it at this hour,
As wild and mad? the Avarice of Pow'r?
Does neither Rage inflame, nor Fear appall?
Not the black Fear of Death, that saddens all?
With Terrors round can Reason hold her throne,   310
Despise the known, nor tremble at th' unknown?
Survey both Worlds, intrepid and entire,
In spight of Witches, Devils, Dreams, and Fire?
Pleas'd to look forward, pleas'd to look behind,
And count each Birth-day with a grateful mind?   315
Has Life no sourness, drawn so near its end?
Can'st thou endure a Foe, forgive a Friend?
Has Age but melted the rough parts away,
As Winter-fruits grow mild e'er they decay?
Or will you think, my Friend, your business done,   320
When, of a hundred thorns, you pull out one?
   Learn to live well, or fairly make your Will;
You've play'd, and lov'd, and eat, and drank your fill:
Walk sober off; before a sprightlier Age
Comes titt'ring on, and shoves you from the stage: 325
Leave such to trifle with more grace and ease,
Whom Folly pleases, and whose Follies please.

300. *strut*] swell, or protrude. Pope contrasts the picture of a man
swaggering along, with that of a man forcing his way, head forward,
against a strong wind.

An Imitation of the Sixth Satire of
the Second Book of Horace

[written c. 1737; published 1738]

ADVERTISEMENT

The World may be assured, this Publication is no way meant to interfere with the *Imitations* of *Horace* by Mr. *Pope*: His Manner, and that of Dr. *Swift* are so entirely different, that they can admit of no Invidious Comparison. The Design of the one being to sharpen the Satire, and open the Sense of the Poet; of the other to rend[er] his native *Ease* and *Familiarity* yet more easy and familiar.

> I've often wish'd that I had clear
> For life, six hundred pounds a year,
> A handsome House to lodge a Friend,
> A River at my garden's end,
> A Terras-walk, and half a Rood   5
> Of Land, set out to plant a Wood.
>   Well, now I have all this and more,
> I ask not to increase my store;
> But here a Grievance seems to lie,
> All this is mine but till I die;   10
> I can't but think 'twould sound more clever,
> To me and to my Heirs for ever.
>   If I ne'er got, or lost a groat,
> By any *Trick*, or any *Fault;*
> And if I pray by Reason's rules,   15
> And not like forty other Fools:
> As thus, 'Vouchsafe, oh gracious Maker!
> To grant me this and t' other Acre:
> Or if it be thy Will and Pleasure
> Direct my Plow to find a Treasure:'   20
> But only what my Station fits,
> And to be kept in my right wits.
> Preserve, Almighty Providence!
> Just what you gave me, Competence:
> And let me in these Shades compose   25
> Something in Verse as true as Prose;
> Remov'd from all th' ambitious Scene,
> Nor puff'd by Pride, nor sunk by Spleen.

This poem was written by Swift in 1714 and published in 1727. It was reprinted in 1738 with additions by Pope; lines 9–28 are possibly his, ll. 133–221 certainly his.

In short, I'm perfectly content,
Let me but live on this side *Trent*:   30
Nor cross the Channel twice a year,
To spend six months with Statesmen here.
  I must by all means come to town,
'Tis for the Service of the Crown,
'Lewis, the Dean will be of use,   35
Send for him up, take no excuse.'
The toil, the danger of the Seas;
Great Ministers ne'er think of these;
Or let it cost five hundred pound,
No matter where the money's found;   40
It is but so much more in debt,
And that they ne'er consider'd yet.
'Good Mr. Dean go change your gown,
Let my Lord know you've come to town.'
I hurry me in haste away,   45
Not thinking it is Levee-day;
And find his Honour in a Pound,
Hemm'd by a triple Circle round,
Chequer'd with Ribbons blue and green;
How should I thrust my self between?   50
Some Wag observes me thus perplext,
And smiling, whispers to the next,
'I thought the Dean had been too proud,
To justle here among a croud.'
Another in a surly fit,   55
Tells me I have more Zeal than Wit,
'So eager to express your love,
You ne'er consider whom you shove,
But rudely press before a Duke.'
I own, I'm pleas'd with this rebuke,   60
And take it kindly meant to show
What I desire the World should know.
  I get a whisper, and withdraw;
When twenty Fools I never saw
Come with Petitions fairly penn'd,   65
Desiring I would stand their friend.
  This, humbly offers me his Case—
That, begs my int'rest for a Place—
A hundred other Men's affairs
Like Bees are humming in my ears.   70

49. *Ribbons*] the insignia of the Orders of the Garter and the Thistle.

'Tomorrow my Appeal comes on,
Without your help the Cause is gone'—
'The Duke expects my Lord and you,
About some great Affair, at Two—'
'Put my Lord Bolingbroke in mind,   75
To get my Warrant quickly sign'd:
Consider, 'tis my first request.'—
Be satisfy'd, I'll do my best:—
Then presently he falls to teize,
'You may for certain, if you please;   80
I doubt not, if his Lordship knew—
And, Mr. Dean, one word from you'—
    'Tis (let me see) three years and more,
(October next it will be four)
Since HARLEY bid me first attend,   85
And chose me for an humble friend;
Wou'd take me in his Coach to chat,
And question me of this and that;
As, 'What's o'clock?' And, 'How's the Wind?'
'Who's Chariot's that we left behind?'   90
Or gravely try to read the lines
Writ underneath the Country Signs;
Or, 'Have you nothing new to-day
From Pope, from Parnel, or from Gay?'
Such tattle often entertains   95
My Lord and me as far as Stains,
As once a week we travel down
To Windsor, and again to Town,
Where all that passes, *inter nos*,
Might be proclaim'd at Charing-Cross.   100
    Yet some I know with envy swell,
Because they see me us'd so well:
'How think you of our Friend the Dean?
I wonder what some people mean;
My Lord and he are grown so great,   105
Always together, *tête à tête*,
What, they admire him for his jokes—
See but the fortune of some Folks!'
There flies about a strange report
Of some Express arriv'd at Court,   110
I'm stopp'd by all the fools I meet,

84. Swift was first introduced to Harley on Oct. 4, 1710.
94. Three of Swift's fellow-members of the Scriblerus Club.
100. *Charing-cross*] where Royal Proclamations are read.

And catechis'd in ev'ry street.
'You, Mr. Dean, frequent the great;
Inform us, will the Emp'ror treat?
Or do the Prints and Papers lye?'   115
Faith, Sir, you know as much as I.
'Ah Doctor, how you love to jest?
'Tis now no secret'—I protest

'Tis one to me—'Then tell us, pray,
When are the Troops to have their pay?'   120
And, tho' I solemnly declare
I know no more than my Lord Mayor,
They stand amaz'd, and think me grown
The closest mortal ever known.
     Thus in a sea of folly toss'd,   125
My choicest Hours of life are lost;
Yet always wishing to retreat,
Oh, could I see my Country Seat!
There, leaning near a gentle Brook,
Sleep, or peruse some ancient Book,   130
And there in sweet oblivion drown
Those Cares that haunt the Court and Town.
     O charming Noons! and Nights divine!
Or when I sup, or when I dine,
My Friends above, my Folks below,   135
Chatting and laughing all-a-row,
The Beans and Bacon set before 'em,
The Grace-cup serv'd with all decorum:
Each willing to be pleas'd, and please,
And even the very Dogs at ease!   140
Here no man prates of idle things,
How this or that Italian sings,
A Neighbour's Madness, or his Spouse's,
Or what's in either of the *Houses:*
But something much more our concern,   145
And quite a scandal not to learn:
Which is the happier, or the wiser,
A man of Merit, or a Miser?
Whether we ought to chuse our Friends,
For their own Worth, or our own Ends?   150
What good, or better, we may call,
And what, the very best of all?

114. The Emperor was the only allied power who refused to make
peace with France in 1713 on terms especially favourable to England.

Our Friend Dan *Prior* told, (you know)
A Tale extreamly *a propos:*
Name a Town Life, and in a trice,   155
He had a Story of *two Mice.*
  Once on a time (so runs the Fable)
A Country Mouse, right hospitable,
Receiv'd a Town Mouse at his Board,
Just as a Farmer might a Lord.   160
A frugal Mouse upon the whole,
Yet lov'd his Friend, and had a Soul;
Knew what was handsome, and wou'd do't,
On just occasion, *coute qui coute.*
He brought him Bacon (nothing lean)   165
Pudding, that might have pleas'd a Dean;
Cheese, such as men in Suffolk make,
But wish'd it Stilton for his sake;
Yet to his Guest tho' no way sparing,
He eat himself the Rind and paring.   170
Our Courtier scarce could touch a bit,
But show'd his Breeding, and his Wit,
He did his best to seem to eat,
And cry'd, 'I vow you're mighty neat.
As sweet a Cave as one shall see!   175
A most Romantic hollow Tree!
A pretty kind of savage Scene!
But come, for God's sake, live with Men:
Consider, Mice, like Men, must die,
Both small and great, both you and I: 180
Then spend your life in Joy and Sport,
(This doctrine, Friend, I learnt at Court.)'
  The veriest Hermit in the Nation
May yield, God knows, to strong Temptation.
Away they come, thro thick and thin,   185
To a tall house near Lincoln's-Inn:
('Twas on the night of a Debate,
When all their Lordships had sate late.)
  Behold the place, where if a Poet
Shin'd in Description, he might show it,   190
Tell how the Moon-beam trembling falls
And tips with silver all the walls:
Palladian walls, Venetian doors,
Grotesco roofs, and Stucco floors:

167. 'I found my wife vexed at her people for grumbling to eate
Suffolk cheese, which I also am vexed at.' Pepys's *Diary*, Oct. 4, 1661.

But let it (in a word) be said,   195
The Moon was up, and Men a-bed,
The Napkins white, the Carpet red:
The Guests withdrawn had left the Treat,
And down the Mice sate, *tête à tête.*

   Our Courtier walks from dish to dish,   200
Tastes for his Friend of Fowl and Fish;
Tells all their names, lays down the law,
'*Que ça est bon! Ah goutez ça!*
That Jelly's rich, this Malmsey healing,
Pray dip your Whiskers and your Tail in'.   205
Was ever such a happy Swain?
He stuffs and swills, and stuffs again.
'I'm quite asham'd—'tis mighty rude
To eat so much—but all's so good.

I have a thousand thanks to give—   210
My Lord alone knows how to live'.
   No sooner said, but from the Hall
Rush Chaplain, Butler, Dogs and all:
'A Rat, a Rat! clap to the door'—
The Cat comes bouncing on the floor.   215
O for the Heart of Homer's Mice,
Or Gods to save them in a trice!
(It was by Providence, they think,
For your damn'd Stucco has no chink)
'An't please your Honour, quoth the Peasant,   220
This same Dessert is not so pleasant:
Give me again my hollow Tree!
A Crust of Bread, and Liberty.'

The Seventh Epistle of
the First Book of Horace

IMITATED IN THE MANNER OF DR. SWIFT

[written c. 1738; published, *Works*, 1739]

'Tis true, my Lord, I gave my word,
I would be with you, June the third;
Chang'd it to August, and (in short)
Have kept it—as you do at Court.
You humour me when I am sick,   5
Why not when I am splenatick?

In town, what Objects could I meet?
The shops shut up in every street,
And Fun'rals black'ning all the Doors,
And yet more melancholy Whores: 10
And what a dust in ev'ry place!
And a thin Court that wants your Face,
And Fevers raging up and down,
And P—x and P* both in town!
    'The Dog-days are no more the case.'   15
'Tis true, but Winter comes apace:
Then southward let your Bard retire,
Hold out some months 'twixt Sun and Fire,
And you shall see, the first warm Weather,
Me and the Butterflies together.   20
    My lord, your Favours well I know;
'Tis with Distinction you bestow;
And not to every one that comes,
Just as a Scotsman does his Plumbs.
'Pray take them, Sir,—Enough's a Feast: 25
Eat some, and pocket up the rest—'
What rob your Boys? those pretty rogues!—
'No Sir, you'll leave them to the *Hogs*.'
Thus Fools with Compliments besiege ye,
Contriving never to oblige ye.   30
Scatter your Favours on a Fop,
Ingratitude's the certain crop;
And 'tis but just, I'll tell you wherefore,
You give the things you never care for.
A wise man always is or should   35
Be mighty ready to do good;
But makes a diff'rence in his thought
Betwixt a Guinea and a Groat.
    Now this I'll say, you'll find in me
A safe Companion, and a free;   40
But if you'd have me always near—
A word, pray, in your Honour's ear.
I hope it is your Resolution
To give me back my Constitution!
The sprightly Wit, the lively Eye,   45
Th' engaging Smile, the Gaiety,
That laugh'd down many a Summer's Sun,
And kept you up so oft till one;
And all that voluntary Vein,

49. *voluntary*] growing wild or naturally; of spontaneous growth.

As when Belinda rais'd my Strain.   50
  A Weasel once made shift to slink
In at a Corn-loft thro' a Chink;
But having amply stuff'd his skin,
Cou'd not get out as he got in:
Which one belonging to the House   55
('Twas not a Man, it was a Mouse)
Observing, cry'd, 'You scape not so,
Lean as you came, Sir, you must go.'
  Sir, you may spare your Application
I'm no such Beast, nor his Relation;   60
Nor one that Temperance advance,
Cramm'd to the throat with Ortolans:
Extremely ready to resign
All that may make me none of mine.
South-sea Subscriptions take who please,   65
Leave me but Liberty and Ease.
'Twas what I said to Craggs and Child,
Who prais'd my Modesty, and smil'd.
Give me, I cry'd (enough for me)
My Bread, and Independency!   70
So bought an Annual Rent or two.
And liv'd—just as you see I do;
Near fifty, and without a Wife,
I trust that sinking Fund, my Life.
Can I retrench? Yes, mighty well,   75
Shrink back to my Paternal Cell,
A little House, with Trees a-row,
And like its Master, very low,
There dy'd my Father, no man's Debtor,
And there I'll die, nor worse nor better.   80
  To set this matter full before you,
Our old Friend Swift will tell his Story.
'Harley, the Nation's great Support,'—
But you may read it, I stop short.

67. Craggs had given him some South-sea subscriptions, of which
he neglected to make any benefit. Child was head of the famous banking
firm.
  79. Pope's father died at Chiswick in 1717.

Sober Advice from Horace, to the Young Gentlemen about Town

AS DELIVER'D IN HIS SECOND SERMON
IMITATED IN THE MANNER OF MR. POPE

Together with the ORIGINAL TEXT, *as restored by the Rev^d* R. BENTLEY, *Doctor of Divinity. And some Remarks on the* VERSION.

[written c. 1734; published 1734]

TO ALEXANDER POPE, Esq;

SIR,

I have so great a Trust in your Indulgence toward me, as to believe you cannot but Patronize this Imitation, so much in your own Manner, and whose Birth I may truly say is owing to you. In that Confidence, I would not suppress the Criticisms made upon it by the *Reverend Doctor*, the rather, since he has promised to *mend the Faults* in the next Edition, with the same Goodness he has practised to *Milton*. I hope you will believe that while I express my Regard for you, it is only out of Modesty I conceal my Name; since, tho' perhaps, I may not profess myself your Admirer so much as some others, I cannot but be, with as much inward Respect, Good-will, and Zeal as any Man,

> *Dear Sir,*
> *Your most Affectionate*
> AND
> *Faithful Servant.*

> The Tribe of Templars, Play'rs, Apothecaries,
> Pimps, Poets, Wits, Lord *Fanny*'s, Lady *Mary*'s,
> And all the Court in Tears, and half the Town,
> Lament dear charming *Oldfield*, dead and gone!
> Engaging *Oldfield!* who, with Grace and Ease,   5
> Could joyn the Arts, to ruin, and to please.

[NOTÆ BENTLEIANÆ.] *Imitated.* Why Imitated? Why not translated? *Odi Imitatores!* A Metaphrast had not turned *Tigellius*, and *Fufidius*, *Malchinus* and *Gargonius* (for I say *Malchinus*, not *Malthinus*, and *Gargonius*, not *Gorgonius*) into so many LADIES. *Benignus, hic, hunc*, &c. all of the Masculine Gender: Every School-boy knows more than our Imitator. [P]. Notes on the Latin attributed to Bentley are omitted from this edition.

2. *Lord Fanny's, Lady Mary's*] Lord Hervey and Lady M. Wortley Montagu.

Not so, who of Ten Thousand gull'd her Knight,
Then ask'd Ten Thousand for a second Night:
The Gallant too, to whom she pay'd it down,
Liv'd to refuse that Mistress half a Crown.   10
  Con. Philips cries, 'A sneaking Dog I hate.'
That's all three Lovers have for their Estate!
'Treat on, treat on,' is her eternal Note,
And Lands and Tenements go down her Throat.
Some damn the Jade, and some the Cullies blame,   15
But not Sir *H—t*, for he does the same.
  With all a Woman's Virtues but the P—x,
Fufidia thrives in Money, Land, and Stocks:
For Int'rest, ten *per Cent.* her constant Rate is;
Her Body? hopeful Heirs may have it *gratis*.   20
She turns her very Sister to a Job,
And, in the Happy Minute, picks your Fob:
Yet starves herself, so little her own Friend,
And thirsts and hungers only at one End:
A Self-Tormentor, worse than (in the Play)   25
The Wretch, whose Av'rice drove his *Son* away.

  But why all this? I'll tell ye, 'tis my Theme:
'Women and Fools are always in Extreme.'
Rufa's at either end a Common-Shoar,
Sweet *Moll* and *Jack* are Civet-Cat and Boar: 30
Nothing in Nature is so lewd as *Peg*,
Yet, for the World, she would not shew her Leg!
While bashful *Jenny*, ev'n at Morning-Prayer,
Spreads her Fore-Buttocks to the Navel bare.
But diff'rent Taste in diff'rent Men prevails,   35
And one is fired by Heads, and one by Tails;
Some feel no Flames but at the *Court* or *Ball*,
And others hunt white Aprons in the *Mall*.
  My Lord of *L—n*, chancing to remark
A *noted Dean* much busy'd in the Park,   40

11. *Con. Philips*] Teresia Constantia Phillips, well-known courtesan.
18. *Fufidia*] Lady Mary Wortley Montagu.
25. *Play*] *See* My *Terence, Heautontimorumenos:* There is nothing in Dr. *Hare's*. BENT. [P]. Hare's edition of Terence (1724) is the object of censure in Bentley's edition (1726) from the first page to the last.
29. *Rufa*] She appears again in *Moral Es.* ii 21.
Common-Shoar] common sewer.
34. *A Verse taken from Mr.* Pope [P]. *Dunciad* (1728) ii 141.
39. *L—n*] i.e. Edmund Gibson, Bishop of London.
40. *noted Dean*] Thomas Sawbridge, Dean of Ferns and Leighlin, who had been indicted for rape in 1730.

'Proceed (he cry'd) proceed, my Reverend Brother,
'Tis *Fornicatio simplex*, and no other:
Better than lust for Boys, with *Pope* and *Turk*,
Or others Spouses, like my Lord of —'
 May no such Praise (cries *J—s*) e'er be mine! 45
J—s, who bows at *Hi—sb—w*'s *hoary Shrine*.
 All you, who think the *City* ne'er can thrive,
Till ev'ry Cuckold-maker's flea'd alive;
Attend, while I their Miseries explain,
And pity Men of Pleasure still in Pain! 50
Survey the Pangs they bear, the Risques they run,
Where the most lucky are but last undone.
See wretched *Monsieur* flies to save his Throat,
And quits his Mistress, Money, Ring, and Note!
See good Sir *George* of ragged Livery stript, 55
By worthier Footmen pist upon and whipt!
Plunder'd by Thieves, or Lawyers which is worse,
One bleeds in Person, and one bleeds in Purse;
This meets a Blanket, and that meets a Cudgel—
And all applaud the Justice—All, but *Budgel*. 60
 How much more safe, dear Countrymen! his State,
Who trades in Frigates of the second Rate?
And yet some Care of *S—st* should be had,
Nothing so mean for which he can't run mad;
His Wit confirms him but a Slave the more, 65
And makes a Princess whom he found a Whore.

44. *my Lord of—*] *Others read* Lord-Mayor [P]. The blank should be filled by *York*—alluding to Archbishop Blackburne, who was popularly believed to have kept more than one mistress.

45. *J—s*] One Jefferies, co-respondent in a divorce bill brought by Lord Hillsborough in 1735 against his wife, then aged 51.

53. *wretched Monsieur*] One Rémond, who pestered Lady Mary with letters wherein gallantry was tempered by requests for financial advice. At her suggestion he bought South Sea stock and later sold it advantageously. Pleased with the success he brought her £900 and begged her to reinvest it. After some demur Lady Mary consented, and put the money back in South Sea stock just before the collapse. She retrieved £400 and sent him the news, to which he replied that he knew her tricks, was convinced that she had all his money untouched, and that he would print her letters unless she returned it. See *Dunciad* A, ii 127, and *Dia.* i 112.

55. *Sir George*] Presumably Sir G. Oxenden, Lord of the Treasury, and seducer.

60. *Budgel*] A Gentleman as celebrated for his Gallantries as his Politicks; an Entertaining History of which may be published, without the least Scandal on the Ladies. E. CURL. [P]

63. *S—st*] Bolingbroke.

The Youth might save much Trouble and Expence,
Were he a Dupe of only common Sense.
But here's his point; 'A Wench (he cries) for me!
I never touch a Dame of Quality.'   70
    To *Palmer*'s Bed no Actress comes amiss,
He courts the whole *Personæ Dramatis:*
He too can say, 'With Wives I never sin.'
But Singing-Girls and Mimicks draw him in.
Sure, worthy Sir, the Diff'rence is not great,   75
With *whom* you lose your Credit and Estate?
This, or that Person, what avails to shun?
What's wrong is wrong, wherever it be done:
The Ease, Support, and Lustre of your Life,
Destroy'd alike with Strumpet, Maid, or Wife.   80
    What push'd poor *Ellis* on th' Imperial Whore?
'Twas but to be where CHARLES had been before.
The fatal Steel unjustly was apply'd,
When not his Lust offended, but his Pride:
Too hard a Penance for defeated Sin,   85
Himself shut out, and *Jacob Hall* let in.
    Suppose that honest Part that rules us all,
Should rise, and say— 'Sir *Robert!* or Sir *Paul!*
Did I demand, in my most vig'rous hour,
A Thing descended from the Conqueror?   90
Or when my pulse beat highest, ask for any
Such Nicety, as Lady or Lord *Fanny?*'—
What would you answer? Could you have the Face,⎤
When the poor Suff'rer humbly mourn'd his Case, ⎬
To cry 'You weep the Favours of her GRACE?' ⎦   95
    Hath not indulgent Nature spread a Feast,
And giv'n enough for Man, enough for Beast?
But Man corrupt, perverse in all his ways,
In search of Vanities from Nature strays:

86. 'Jacob Hall, the famous rope-dancer, was fashionable in London at
that time [*c.* 1668]. His nimbleness and his strength greatly delighted his
audience in public; so much so, that a desire arose to see what he was in
private . . . This acrobat by no means disappointed conjectures which
had been ventured on this subject by Lady Castlemaine—at least if the
conjectures of the general public were to be believed, and the burden of
innumerable street-ballads which did the dancer more honour than the
Countess.'
95. Spoken not of one particular Dutchess, but of divers Dutchesses [P].
96. The original Manuscript has it,
                    —*Spread a Feast*
        Of—enough for Man, enough for Beast:
but we prefer the present, as the purer Diction [P].

Yea, tho' the Blessing's more than he can use,   100
Shuns the permitted, the forbid pursues!
Weigh well the Cause from whence these Evils spring,

'Tis in thyself, and not in God's good Thing:
Then, lest Repentence punish such a Life,
Never, ah, never! kiss thy Neighbour's Wife.   105
  First, Silks and Diamonds veil no finer Shape,
Or plumper Thigh, than lurk in humble Crape:
And *secondly*, how innocent a *Belle*
Is she who shows what Ware she has to sell;
Not Lady-like, displays a milk-white Breast,   110
And hides in sacred Sluttishness the rest.
  Our ancient Kings (and sure those Kings were wise,
Who judg'd themselves, and saw with their own Eyes)
A War-horse never for the Service chose,
But ey'd him round, and stript off all the Cloaths;   115
For well they knew, proud Trappings serve to hide
A heavy Chest, thick Neck, or heaving Side.
But Fools are ready Chaps, agog to buy,
Let but a comely Fore-hand strike the Eye:
No Eagle sharper, every Charm to find,   120
To all defects, *Ty—y* not so blind:
Goose-rump'd, Hawk-nos'd, Swan-footed, is my Dear?
They'l praise her *Elbow*, *Heel*, or *Tip o' th' Ear*.
  A Lady's Face is all you see undress'd;
(For none but Lady M— shows the Rest)   125
But if to Charms more latent you pretend,
What Lines encompass, and what Works defend!
Dangers on Dangers! obstacles by dozens!
Spies, Guardians, Guests, old Women, Aunts, and
        Cozens!
Could you directly to her Person go,   ⎫   130
Stays will obstruct above, and Hoops below, ⎬
And if the Dame says yes, the Dress says no. ⎭
Not thus at *N—dh—m*'s; your judicious Eye
May measure there the Breast, the Hip, the Thigh!
And will you run to Perils, Sword, and Law,   135
All for a Thing you ne're so much as *saw*?

118. *Chaps*] Abbreviation of *chapmen*.
  121. *Ty—y*] Lady Tyrawley (d. 1733) seems to have been notoriously
short-sighted.
  129. *Cozens*] There is a famous Stay-maker of this name, which stiffens
the *double entendre* here meant [Curll].
  133. *N—dh—m*] Mother Needham kept a notorious brothel in Park
Place, St. James's.

'The Hare once seiz'd the Hunter heeds no more
The little Scut he so pursu'd before,
Love follows flying Game (as *Sucklyn* sings)
And 'tis for that the wanton Boy has Wings.'   140
Why let him Sing—but when you're in the Wrong,
Think ye to cure the Mischief with a Song?
Has Nature set no bounds to wild Desire?
No Sense to guide, no Reason to enquire,
What solid Happiness, what empty Pride?   145
And what is best indulg'd, or best deny'd?
If neither Gems adorn, nor Silver tip
The flowing Bowl, will you not wet your Lip?
When sharp with Hunger, scorn you to be fed,
Except on *Pea-Chicks*, at the *Bedford-head*?   150
Or, when a tight, neat Girl, will serve the Turn,
In errant Pride continue stiff, and burn?
I'm a plain Man, whose Maxim is profest,
'The Thing at hand is of all Things the *best*.'
But Her who will, and then will not comply,   155
Whose Word is *If*, *Perhaps*, and *By-and-By*,
Z—ds! let some Eunuch or Platonic take—
So *B—t* cries, Philosopher and Rake!
Who asks no more (right reasonable Peer)
Than not to wait too long, nor pay too dear.   160
Give me a willing Nymph! 'tis all I care,
Extremely clean, and tolerably fair,
Her Shape her own, whatever Shape she have,
And just that White and Red which Nature gave.
Her I transported touch, transported view,   165
And call her *Angel! Goddess! Montague!*
No furious Husband thunders at the Door;

No barking Dog, no Household in a Roar;
From gleaming Swords no shrieking Women run;
No wretched Wife cries out, *Undone! Undone!*   170
Seiz'd in the Fact, and in her Cuckold's Pow'r,
She kneels, she weeps, and worse! resigns her Dow'r.
Me, naked me, to Posts, to Pumps they draw,
To Shame eternal, or eternal Law.

138. *Scut*] a hare's tail.
139. There is nothing resembling these lines in Suckling, but they are
akin to him in philosophy.
150. *Bedford-head*] See *Sat.* II   42*n*, p. 620.
158. B—t] Bathurst

Oh Love! be deep Tranquility my Luck!   175
No Mistress *H—ysh—m* near, no Lady *B—ck!*
For, to be taken, is the Dev'll in Hell;
This Truth, let *L—l, J—ys, O—w* tell.

176. Mrs. Heysham and Lady Buck appear to have witnessed the in-
fidelity of Lady Hillsborough (see l. 45*n*) with Jefferies (see l. 178).
178. *L—l*] Richard Liddel, against whom his friend, Lord Abergavenny, brought an action in 1729 for criminal conversation with Lady
Abergavenny.
O—w] History has dealt kindly with the reputation of the Onslows.
Endeavours to discover what underlay this reference have failed.

The First Ode of
the Fourth Book of Horace

TO VENUS

[written c. 1736; published 1737]

Again? new Tumults in my Breast?
Ah spare me, Venus! let me, let me rest!
    I am not now, alas! the man
As in the gentle Reign of My Queen *Anne.*
      Ah sound no more thy soft alarms,   5
Nor circle sober fifty with thy Charms.
    Mother too fierce of dear Desires!
Turn, turn to willing Hearts your wanton fires.
      To *Number five* direct your Doves,
There spread round MURRAY all your blooming Loves;
    Noble and young, who strikes the heart   11
With every sprightly, every decent part;
    Equal, the injur'd to defend,
To charm the Mistress, or to fix the Friend.
      He, with a hundred Arts refin'd,   15
Shall stretch thy Conquests over half the kind:
    To him each Rival shall submit,
Make but his riches equal to his Wit.
      Then shall thy Form the Marble grace,
(Thy Græcian Form) and Chloe lend the Face: 20
    His House, embosom'd in the Grove,
Sacred to social Life and social Love,

6. *sober fifty*] Pope was born in 1688.
9. *Number five*] Murray's lodgings in King's Bench Walk. He was
thirty-two when this poem was published. Lord Chief Justice, 1756–88.

Shall glitter o'er the pendent green,
Where Thames reflects the visionary Scene.
    Thither, the silver-sounding Lyres   25
Shall call the smiling Loves, and young Desires;
    There, every Grace and Muse shall throng,
Exalt the Dance, or animate the Song;
    There, Youths and Nymphs, in consort gay,
Shall hail the rising, close the parting day.   30
    With me, alas! those joys are o'er;
For me, the vernal Garlands bloom no more.
    Adieu! fond hope of mutual fire,
The still-believing, still-renew'd desire;
    Adieu! the heart-expanding bowl,   35
And all the kind Deceivers of the soul!
    —But why? ah tell me, ah too dear!
Steals down my cheek th' involuntary Tear?
    Why words so flowing, thoughts so free,
Stop, or turn nonsense at one glance of Thee?   40
    Thee, drest in Fancy's airy beam,
Absent I follow thro' th' extended Dream,
    Now, now I seize, I clasp thy charms,
And now you burst, (ah cruel!) from my arms,
    And swiftly shoot along the Mall,   45
    Or softly glide by the Canal,
    Now shown by Cynthia's silver Ray,
And now, on rolling Waters snatch'd away.

Part of the Ninth Ode
of the Fourth Book of Horace
[written 1737? published 1751]

Lest you should think that Verse shall die,
    Which sounds the Silver Thames along,
Taught on the Wings of Truth, to fly
    Above the reach of vulgar Song;

Tho' daring Milton sits Sublime,   5
    In Spencer native Muses play;
Nor yet shall Waller yield to time,
    Nor pensive Cowley's moral Lay.

Sages and Chiefs long since had birth
    E're Cæsar was, or Newton nam'd,   10

These rais'd new Empires o'er the Earth,
   And Those new Heav'ns and Systems fram'd;

Vain was the chief's and sage's pride
   They had no Poet and they dyd!
In vain they schem'd, in vain they bled   15
   They had no Poet and are dead!

The Second Satire of Dr. John Donne, Dean of St. Paul's, Versifyed

[written 1713; revised 1733? published,
Works, 1735]

Quid vetat, ut nosmet Lucili scripta legentes
Quærere, num illius, num rerum dura negarit
Versiculos natura magis factos, & euntes
Mollius?   HOR. [*Sat.* I x 56–9]

Yes; thank my stars! as early as I knew
This Town, I had the sense to hate it too:
Yet here, as ev'n in Hell, there must be still
One Giant-Vice, so excellently ill,
That all beside one pities, not abhors;   5
As who knows Sapho, smiles at other whores.
    I grant that Poetry's a crying sin;
It brought (no doubt) th' *Excise* and *Army* in:
Catch'd like the plague, or love, the Lord knows how,
But that the cure is starving, all allow.   10
Yet like the Papists is the Poets state,
Poor and disarm'd, and hardly worth your hate.
    Here a lean Bard, whose wit could never give
Himself a dinner, makes an Actor live:
The Thief condemn'd, in law already dead,   15
So prompts, and saves a Rogue who cannot read.
Thus as the pipes of some carv'd Organ move,
The gilded Puppets dance and mount above,
Heav'd by the breath th' inspiring Bellows blow;
Th' inspiring Bellows lie and pant below.   20
    One sings the Fair; but Songs no longer move,
No Rat is rhym'd to death, nor Maid to love:
In Love's, in Nature's spite, the siege they hold,
And scorn the Flesh, the Dev'l, and all but Gold.
    These write to Lords, some mean reward to get,   25
As needy Beggars sing at doors for meat.
Those write because all write, and so have still
Excuse for writing, and for writing ill.
    Wretched indeed! but far more wretched yet
Is he who makes his meal on others wit: 30
'Tis chang'd no doubt from what it was before,
His rank digestion makes it wit no more:

8. *th' Excise and Army*] See *Sat.* II i 73*n* and *Sat.* II ii 134*n*.
12. *Poor and disarm'd*] Cf. *Sat.* II ii 151–4, and *Ep.* II ii 67.

Sense, past thro' him, no longer is the same,
For food digested takes another name.
  I pass o'er all those Confessors and Martyrs   35
Who live like S—tt—n, or who die like Chartres,
Out-cant old Esdras, or out-drink his Heir,
Out-usure Jews, or Irishmen out-swear;
Wicked as Pages, who in early years
Act Sins which Prisca's Confessor scarce hears: 40
Ev'n those I pardon, for whose sinful sake
Schoolmen new tenements in Hell must make;
Of whose strange crimes no Canonist can tell
In what Commandment's large contents they dwell.
  One, one man only breeds my just offence;   45
Whom Crimes gave wealth, and wealth gave impudence:
Time, that at last matures a Clap to Pox,
Whose gentle progress makes a Calf an Ox,
And brings all natural events to pass,
Hath made him an Attorney of an Ass.   50
No young Divine, new-benefic'd, can be
More pert, more proud, more positive than he.
What further could I wish the Fop to do,
But turn a Wit, and scribble verses too?
Pierce the soft lab'rinth of a Lady's ear   55
With rhymes of this *per Cent.* and that *per Year?*
Or court a Wife, spread out his wily parts,
Like nets or lime-twigs, for rich Widows hearts?
Call himself Barrister to ev'ry wench,
And wooe in language of the Pleas and Bench?   60
Language, which Boreas might to Auster hold,
More rough than forty Germans when they scold.
  Curs'd be the Wretch! so venal and so vain;
Paltry and proud, as drabs in Drury-lane.
'Tis such a bounty as was never known,   65
If Peter deigns to help you to your *own:*
What thanks, what praise, if Peter but supplies!
And what a solemn face if he denies!
Grave, as when Pris'ners shake the head, and swear
'Twas only Suretyship that brought 'em there.   70

36. *S—tt—n*] General Richard Sutton, a debauched supporter of Walpole.
40 *Prisca*] i.e. a sinner of a bygone generation.
64. *Drury-lane*] See *Ep. to Arbuthnot*, 41*n* (p. 599).
66. *Peter*] Peter Walter, once more.
70. *Suretyship*] responsibility taken by one person on behalf of another, as for payment of a debt.

His *Office* keeps your Parchment-Fates entire,
He starves with cold to save them from the Fire;
For you, he walks the streets thro' rain or dust,
For not in Chariots Peter puts his trust;
For you he sweats and labours at the Laws,   75
Takes God to witness he affects your Cause,
And lyes to every Lord in every thing,
Like a King's Favourite—or like a King.
    These are the talents that adorn them all,
From wicked Waters ev'n to godly —   80
Not more of Simony beneath black Gowns,
Nor more of Bastardy in heirs to Crowns.
In shillings and in pence at first they deal,
And steal so little, few perceive they steal;
Till like the Sea, they compass all the land,   85
From Scots to Wight, from Mount to Dover strand.
And when rank Widows purchase luscious nights,
Or when a Duke to Jansen punts at White's,
Or City heir in mortgage melts away,
Satan himself feels far less joy than they.   90
Piecemeal they win this Acre first, then that,
Glean on, and gather up the whole Estate:
Then strongly fencing ill-got wealth by law,
Indentures, Cov'nants, Articles they draw;
Large as the Fields themselves, and larger far   95
Than Civil Codes, with all their glosses, are:
So vast, our new Divines, we must confess,
Are Fathers of the Church for writing less.
But let them write for You, each Rogue impairs
The Deeds, and dextrously omits, *ses Heires:*   100
No Commentator can more slily pass
O'er a learn'd, unintelligible place;
Or, in Quotation, shrewd Divines leave out
Those words, that would against them clear the doubt.
    So Luther thought the Paternoster long,   105

80. *Waters*] i.e. Peter Walter. See p. 577, l. 125*n.*
godly—] Paul Foley, according to Lord Orrery. Macaulay describes
him as a lawyer of 'spotless integrity and munificent charity'. But can
Pope have had in mind a man who died so far back as 1699?
88. *a Duke*] Wriothesley Russell, third Duke of Bedford who on
Nov. 27, 1731 lost £3,800 to Jansen after playing for twenty-five hours
running.
White's] A chocolate-house in St. James's Street converted into a
private club, and notorious as a gaming-house: a resort of 'infamous
sharpers and noble cullies'. See further *Moral Es.* iii 55, *Dunciad*, B i 203.

When doom'd to say his Beads and Evensong:
But having cast his Cowle, and left those laws,
Adds to Christ's prayer, the *Pow'r and Glory* clause.
  The Lands are bought; but where are to be found
Those ancient Woods, that shaded all the ground?   110
We see no new-built Palaces aspire,
No Kitchens emulate the Vestal Fire.
Where are those Troops of poor, that throng'd of yore
The good old Landlord's hospitable door?
Well, I could wish, that still in lordly domes   115
Some beasts were kill'd, tho' not whole hecatombs,
That both Extremes were banish'd from their walls,
Carthusian Fasts, and fulsome Bacchanals;
And all mankind might that just mean observe,
In which none e'er could surfeit, none could starve.   120
These, as good works 'tis true we all allow;
But oh! these works are not in fashion now:
Like rich old Wardrobes, things extremely rare,
Extremely fine, but what no man will wear.
  Thus much I've said, I trust without offence;   125
Let no Court-Sycophant pervert my sense,
Nor sly Informer watch these words to draw
Within the reach of Treason, or the Law.

108. *Pow'r and Glory clause*] The 'power and glory clause', which is not
found in the Vulgate, was taken by Erasmus (1516) from all the Greek
codices, and passed into Luther's (1521) and most Reformed versions.

The Fourth Satire of Dr. John Donne,
Dean of St. Paul's, Versifyed

[written 1713? revised and published 1733]

*Quid vetat, ut nosmet Lucili scripta legentes
Quærere, num illius, num rerum dura negarit
Versiculos natura magis factos, & euntes
Mollius?*   HOR. [*Sat.* I x 56–9]

Well, if it be my time to quit the Stage,
Adieu to all the Follies of the Age!
I die in Charity with Fool and Knave,
Secure of Peace at least beyond the Grave.
I've had my *Purgatory* here betimes,   5
And paid for all my Satires, all my Rhymes:

The Poet's Hell, its Tortures, Fiends and Flames,
To this were Trifles, Toys, and empty Names.
  With foolish *Pride* my Heart was never fir'd,
Nor the vain Itch *t'admire*, or *be admir'd*;   10
I hop'd for no *Commission* from his Grace;
I bought no *Benefice*, I begg'd no *Place*;
Had no *new Verses*, or *new Suit* to show;
Yet went to COURT!—the Dev'l wou'd have it so.
But, as the Fool, that in reforming Days   15
Wou'd go to Mass in jest, (as Story says)
Could not but think, to pay his *Fine* was odd,
Since 'twas no form'd Design of serving God:
So was I punish'd, as if full as *proud*,
As prone to *Ill*, as negligent of *Good*,   20
As deep in *Debt*, without a thought to pay, ⎫
As *vain*, as *idle*, and as *false*, as they   ⎬
Who *live* at *Court*, for going once that Way! ⎭
  Scarce was I enter'd, when behold! there came
A Thing which *Adam* had been pos'd to name;   25
Noah had refus'd it lodging in his Ark,
Where all the Race of *Reptiles* might embark:
A verier Monster than on *Africk*'s Shore
The Sun e're got, or slimy *Nilus* bore,
Or *Sloane*, or *Woodward*'s wondrous Shelves contain;   30
Nay, all that lying Travellers can feign.
The Watch would hardly let him pass at noon,
At night, wou'd swear him dropt out of the moon,
One whom the mob, when next we find or make
A Popish plot, shall for a Jesuit take;   35
And the wise Justice starting from his chair
Cry, by your Priesthood tell me what you are?
  Such was the Wight: Th' apparel on his back
Tho' coarse was rev'rend, and tho' bare, was black.
The suit, if by the fashion one might guess,   40
Was velvet in the youth of good Queen *Bess*,
But mere tuff-taffety what now remained;
So Time, that changes all things, had ordain'd!
Our sons shall see it leisurely decay,
First turn plain rash, then vanish quite away.   45
  This Thing has *travell'd*, speaks each Language too,

30. The two rival collections of natural curiosities. Sloane's is now in the custody of the British Museum, Woodward's forms the nucleus of the Woodwardian Museum at Cambridge.
45. *rash*] a smooth textile fabric made of silk or worsted.

And knows what's fit for ev'ry State to do;
Of whose best Phrase and courtly Accent join'd,
He forms one Tongue exotic and refin'd.
Talkers, I've learn'd to bear; *Motteux* I knew,   50
Henley himself I've heard, nay *Budgel* too:
The Doctor's Wormwood Style, the Hash of Tongues,
A Pedant makes; the Storm of *Gonson*'s Lungs,
The whole Artill'ry of the Terms of War,
And (all those Plagues in one) the bawling Bar;   55
These I cou'd bear; but not a Rogue so civil,
Whose Tongue can complement you to the Devil.
A Tongue that can cheat Widows, cancel Scores,
Make *Scots* speak Treason, cozen subtlest Whores,
With Royal Favourites in Flatt'ry vie,   60
And *Oldmixon* and *Burnet* both out-lie.
   He spies me out. I whisper, gracious God!
What Sin of mine cou'd merit such a Rod?
That all the Shot of Dulness now must be
From this thy Blunderbuss discharg'd on me!   65
'Permit (he cries) no stranger to your fame
To crave your sentiment, if —'s your name.
What *Speech* esteem you most?'—'The *King*'s,' said I,
'But the best *Words*?'—'O Sir, the *Dictionary*.'
'You miss my aim; I mean the most acute   70
And perfect *Speaker*?'—'*Onslow*, past dispute.'
'But Sir, of Writers?'—'*Swift*, for closer Style,
And *Ho—y* for a Period of a Mile.'
'Why yes, 'tis granted, these indeed may pass
Good common Linguists, and so *Panurge* was: 75
Nay troth, th'*Apostles*, (tho' perhaps too rough)
Had once a pretty Gift of Tongues enough.
Yet these were all *poor Gentlemen*! I dare
Affirm, 'twas *Travel* made them what they were.'
   Thus others Talents having nicely shown,   80
He came by sure Transition to his own:
Till I cry'd out, 'You prove yourself so able,
Pity! you was not Druggerman at *Babel*:

61. See *Ep. to Arbuthnot*, 146*n*. But perhaps Burnet, in this context, is
the Bishop of Salisbury whose *History of his own Times* had given offence.
72. *closer*] i.e. more concise.
73. As a controversial writer Bishop Hoadly possessed uncommon
talents; but he extended his periods to a disagreeable length. See also
Dunciad A ii 368 (Pope's note, p. 399).
75. For Panurge's fluency in languages see Rabelais, Book ii, Ch. ix.
83. *Druggerman*] A variant of *dragoman*, an interpreter.

For had they found a Linguist half so good,
I make no question but the *Tow'r* had stood.'   85
    'Obliging Sir! for Courts you sure were made:
Why then for ever buried in the shade?
Spirits like you, believe me, shou'd be seen,
The King would smile on you—at least the Queen?'
'Ah gentle Sir! you Courtiers so cajol us—   90
But *Tully* has it, *Nunquam minus solus*:
But as for *Courts*, forgive me if I say,
No Lessons now are taught the *Spartan* way:
Tho' in his Pictures Lust be full display'd,
Few are the Converts *Aretine* has made;   95
And tho' the Court show *Vice* exceeding clear,
None shou'd, by my Advice, learn *Virtue* there.'
    At this, entranc'd, he lifts his Hands and Eyes,
Squeaks like a high-stretch'd Lutestring, and replies:
'Oh 'tis the sweetest of all earthly things   100
To gaze on Princes, and to talk of Kings!'
'Then happy Man who shows the Tombs!' said I,
'He dwells amidst the Royal Family;
He, ev'ry Day, from *King* to *King* can walk,
Of all our *Harries*, all our *Edwards* talk,   105
And get by speaking Truth of Monarchs dead,
What few can of the living, *Ease* and *Bread*.'
'Lord! Sir, a meer *Mechanick*! strangely low,
And coarse of Phrase—your *English* all are so.
How elegant your *Frenchman*?'—'Mine, d'ye mean?   110
I have but one, I hope the Fellow's clean.'
'Oh! Sir, politely so! nay, let me dye,
Your only wearing is your *Padua-soy*.'
'Not Sir, my only—I have better still,
And this, you see, is but my Dishabille—'   115
Wild to get loose, his Patience I provoke,
Mistake, confound, object, at all he spoke.
But as coarse Iron, sharpen'd, mangles more,
And Itch most hurts, when anger'd to a Sore;
So when you plague a Fool, 'tis still the Curse,   120
You only make the Matter worse and worse.
    He past it o'er; affects an easy Smile
At all my Peevishness, and turns his Style.
He asks, 'What *News*?' I tell him of new Plays,

95. Pietro Aretino wrote some lascivious sonnets (1523) to accompany
drawings by Giulio Romano.
113. *Padua-soy*] A strong corded silk fabric.

New Eunuchs, Harlequins, and Operas.   125
He hears; and as a Still, with Simples in it,
Between each Drop it gives, stays half a Minute;
Loth to enrich me with too quick Replies,
By little, and by little, drops his Lies.
Meer *Houshold Trash!* of Birth-Nights, Balls and Shows,
More than ten *Holingsheds*, or *Halls*, or *Stows*.   131
When the *Queen* frown'd, or smil'd, he knows; and what
A subtle Minister may make of that?
Who sins with whom? who got his Pension *Rug*,
Or quicken'd a Reversion by a *Drug?*   135
Whose Place is *quarter'd out*, three Parts in four,
And whether to a Bishop, or a Whore?
Who, having lost his Credit, pawn'd his Rent,
Is therefore fit to have a *Government?*
Who in the *Secret*, deals in Stocks secure,   140
And cheats th'unknowing Widow, and the Poor?
Who makes a *Trust*, or *Charity*, a Job,
And gets an Act of Parliament to rob?
Why *Turnpikes* rise, and now no Cit, nor Clown
Can *gratis* see the *Country*, or the *Town?*   145
Shortly no Lad shall *chuck*, or Lady *vole*,
But some excising Courtier will have Toll.
He tells what Strumpet Places sells for Life,
What 'Squire his Lands, what Citizen his Wife?
And last (which proves him wiser still than all)   150
What Lady's Face is not a whited Wall?

125. *Eunuchs*] see *Ep.* 1 i 105. *Harlequins*] a part in eighteenth-century
pantomime, frequently played at this time by Rich, the theatrical
impresario.
    130. *Birth-Nights*] the splendid celebrations on royal birthdays.
    131. Holinshed's *Chronicles* was published in 1578, Hall's in 1542; for
Stow see *Ep.* II i 66n (p. 637). They chronicle trifling events along with
events of greater importance.
    132. *the Queen*] Donne referred to the reigning monarch; but Pope in
following him implied that though George II reigned, it was Queen
Caroline who ruled.
    134. *Rug*] i.e. safe.
    142. Pope refers to the scandal of the Charitable Corporation, founded
in 1730 to lend money to the Poor. Complaints began to be made in 1731,
and in 1732 the directors were found guilty of embezzlement. See Pope's
note to *Moral Es.* iii 102 (p. 576).
    144. The turnpike system of exacting toll from travellers for road
repairs was started in Charles II's reign, but it made little headway against
popular feeling until the middle of the eighteenth century.
    146. *chuck*] play at chuck-farthing.
    vole] win all the tricks at ombre or quadrille.
    147. *excising*] see *Sat.* II ii 134n (p. 622).

As one of *Woodward*'s Patients, sick and sore,
I puke, I nauseate,—yet he thrusts in more;
Trims *Europe*'s Balance, tops the Statesman's part,
And talks *Gazettes* and *Post-Boys* o'er by heart.　155
Like a big Wife at sight of loathsome Meat,
Ready to cast, I yawn, I sigh, and sweat:
Then as a licens'd Spy, whom nothing can
Silence, or hurt, he libels the *Great Man*;
Swears every *Place entail'd* for Years to come,　160
In *sure Succession* to the Day of Doom:
He names the *Price* for ev'ry *Office* paid,
And says our *Wars thrive ill*, because *delay'd*;
Nay hints, 'tis by Connivance of the Court,
That *Spain* robs on, and *Dunkirk*'s still a Port.　165
Not more Amazement seiz'd on *Circe*'s Guests,
To see themselves fall endlong into Beasts,
Than mine, to find a Subject staid and wise,
Already half turn'd Traytor by surprize.
I fear'd th'Infection slide from him to me,　170
As in the Pox, some give it, to get free;
And quick to swallow me, methought I saw
One of our Giant *Statutes* ope its Jaw!
In that nice Moment, as another Lye
Stood just a-tilt, the *Minister* came by.　175
Away he flies. He bows, and bows again;
And close as *Umbra* joins the dirty Train.
Not *Fannius* self more impudently near.

152. Woodward's practice of administering emetics to his patients was a fruitful source of contemporary jest and controversy.

155. *The London Gazette* has been in circulation since 1665; *The Post Boy* started in 1695, and continued as *The Daily Post Boy* from 1728 till 1735.

159. *the Great Man*] Walpole. See *Dia.* i 26n. The courtier confirms all the charges brought against Walpole's government by the opposition.

162. It was common knowledge that Walpole bribed extensively.

163. Walpole's policy of avoiding European wars was constantly criticized by the Opposition, who feared that the unchecked growth of French power would be a menace to English liberties.

165. Complaints at the seizure of English merchant ships by Spanish guarda-costas which led to the War of Jenkin's Ear (1739). See *Dia.* i 18n.

Dunkirk] Under the Treaty of Utrecht (1712) France was to demolish the fortifications of Dunkirk, a port from which privateers attacked English shipping. The harbour was believed to be under repair at this time.

175. A cask full of his lies is tilted up, and one is ready to flow over.
178. *Fannius self*] Lord Hervey. Cf. *Ep. to Arbuthnot*, ll. 319, 356.

When half his Nose is in his Patron's Ear.
I quak'd at heart; and still afraid to see   180
All the Court fill'd with stranger things than he,
Ran out as fast, as one that pays his Bail,
And dreads more Actions, hurries from a Jail.

Bear me, some God! oh quickly bear me hence
To wholesome Solitude, the Nurse of Sense: 185
Where Contemplation prunes her ruffled Wings,
And the free Soul looks down to pity Kings.
There sober Thought pursu'd th'amusing theme
Till Fancy colour'd it, and form'd a Dream.
A *Vision* Hermits can to Hell transport,   190
And force ev'n me to see the Damn'd at Court.
Not *Dante* dreaming all th' Infernal State,
Beheld such Scenes of *Envy*, *Sin*, and *Hate*.
Base Fear becomes the Guilty, not the Free;
Suits Tyrants, Plunderers, but suits not me.   195
Shall I, the Terror of this sinful Town,
Care, if a livery'd Lord or smile or frown?
Who cannot flatter, and detest who can,
Tremble before a *noble Serving-Man?*
O my fair Mistress, *Truth*! Shall I quit thee,   200
For huffing, braggart, puft *Nobility?*
Thou, who since Yesterday, hast roll'd o'er all
The busy, idle Blockheads of the Ball,
Hast thou, O *Sun*! beheld an emptier sort,
Than such as swell this Bladder of a Court?   205
Now pox on those who shew a *Court in Wax!*
It ought to bring all Courtiers on their backs.
Such painted Puppets, such a varnish'd Race
Of hollow Gewgaws, only Dress and Face,
Such waxen Noses, stately, staring things,   210
No wonder some Folks bow, and think them *Kings*.
    See! where the *British* Youth, engag'd no more
At *Fig*'s at *White*'s, with *Felons*, or a *Whore*,
Pay their last Duty to the *Court*, and come
All fresh and fragrant, to the *Drawing-Room*:   215

206. A famous Show of the COURT of FRANCE in Waxwork. [P]
  213. *Fig's*, a Prize-fighter's Academy, where the young Nobility
receiv'd instruction in those days: *White's* was a noted gaming-house. It
was also customary for the nobility and gentry to visit the condemned
criminals in Newgate. [P] For White's see *Imit. Donne*, ii 88n.

In Hues as gay, and Odours as divine,
As the fair Fields they sold to look so fine.
'That's *Velvet* for a *King*!' the Flattr'er swears;
'Tis true, for ten days hence 'twill be *King Lear*'s.
Our Court may justly to our Stage give Rules,   220
That helps it both to *Fool's-Coats* and to *Fools*.
And why not Players strut in Courtiers Cloaths?
For these are Actors too, as well as those:
Wants reach all States; they beg but better drest,
And all is *splendid Poverty* at best.   225
    Painted for sight, and essenc'd for the smell,
Like Frigates fraught with Spice and Cochine'l,
Sail in the *Ladies*: How each Pyrate eyes
So weak a Vessel, and so rich a Prize!
Top-gallant he, and she in all her Trim,   230
He boarding her, she striking sail to him.
'*Dear Countess*! you have Charms all Hearts to hit!'
And '*sweet Sir Fopling*! you have so much wit!'
Such Wits and Beauties are not prais'd for nought,
For both the Beauty and the Wit are *bought*.   235
'Twou'd burst ev'n *Heraclitus* with the Spleen,
To see those Anticks, *Fopling* and *Courtin*:
The *Presence* seems, with things so richly odd,
The Mosque of *Mahound*, or some queer *Pa-god*.
See them survey their Limbs by *Durer*'s Rules,   240
Of all Beau-kind the best proportion'd Fools!
Adjust their Cloaths, and to Confession draw
Those venial sins, an Atom, or a Straw:
But oh! what Terrors must distract the Soul,
Convicted of that mortal Crime, a Hole!   245
Or should one Pound of Powder less bespread
Those Monkey-Tails that wag behind their Head!
Thus finish'd and corrected to a hair,
They march, to prate their Hour before the Fair,
So first to preach a white-glov'd Chaplain goes,   250
With Band of Lily, and with Cheek of Rose,
Sweeter than *Sharon*, in immaculate trim,
Neatness itself impertinent in him.

219. Cf. *Ep*. II i 332.
233. Sir Fopling Flutter appears in Etherege's *The Man of Mode* (1676).
236. Even Heraclitus, 'the weeping philosopher', would burst his
spleen with laughter (a common expression) at these antics.
238. *Presence*] presence-chamber.
240. *Durer's Rules*] Dürer's *Vier bücher von menschlicher Proportion*
(1528).

Let but the Ladies smile, and they are blest;
Prodigious! how the Things *Protest*, *Protest*:   255
Peace, Fools! or *Gonson* will for Papists seize you,
If once he catch you at your *Jesu! Jesu!*
　　Nature made ev'ry Fop to plague his Brother,
Just as one Beauty mortifies another.
But here's the *Captain*, that will plague them both,   260
Whose Air cries Arm! whose very Look's an Oath:
Tho' his Soul's Bullet, and his Body Buff!
Damn him, he's honest, Sir,—and that's enuff.
He spits fore-right; his haughty Chest before,
Like batt'ring Rams, beats open ev'ry Door;   265
And with a Face as red, and as awry,
As *Herod*'s Hang-dogs in old Tapestry,
Scarecrow to Boys, the breeding Woman's curse;
Has yet a strange Ambition to *look worse*:
Confounds the Civil, keeps the Rude in awe,   270
Jests like a licens'd Fool, commands like Law.
Frighted, I quit the Room, but leave it so,
As Men from Jayls to Execution go;
For hung with *Deadly Sins* I see the Wall,
And lin'd with *Giants*, deadlier than 'em all: 275
Each Man an *Ascapart*, of Strength to toss
For Quoits, both *Temple-Bar* and *Charing-Cross*.
Scar'd at the grizly Forms, I sweat, I fly,
And shake all o'er, like a discover'd Spy.
Courts are too much for Wits so weak as mine;   280
Charge them with Heav'n's Artill'ry, bold *Divine!*
From such alone the Great Rebukes endure,
Whose *Satyr*'s *sacred*, and whose Rage *secure*.
'Tis mine to wash a few slight Stains; but theirs
To deluge Sin, and drown a Court in Tears.   285
Howe'er, what's now *Apocrypha*, my Wit,
In time to come, may pass for *Holy Writ*.

267. Cf. *E. on C.* l. 587.
275. The Room hung with Tapestry, now very antient, representing
the *Seven Deadly Sins* [P]. Pope refers to the early sixteenth-century
Flemish tapestries, bought by Wolsey for the 'Legate's chaumbre at
Hampton Courte' in 1522, which now hang in the Great Watching
Chamber there.
276. *Ascapart*] A Giant famous in Romances. [P] He was said to have
been defeated by Sir Bevis of Southampton.

Epilogue to the Satires

Written in 1738
[published 1738]

DIALOGUE I

Fr. Not twice a twelvemonth you appear in **Print**,
And when it comes, the Court see nothing in't.
You grow *correct* that once with Rapture writ,
And are, besides, too *Moral* for a Wit.
Decay of Parts, alas! we all must feel—   5
Why now, this moment, don't I see you steal?
'Tis all from *Horace: Horace* long before ye
Said, 'Tories call'd him Whig, and Whigs a Tory.'
And taught his Romans, in much better metre,
'To laugh at Fools who put their trust in *Peter*.'   10
    But *Horace*, Sir, was delicate, was nice;
Bubo observes, he lash'd no sort of *Vice:*
Horace would say, *Sir* Billy *serv'd the Crown*,
Blunt *could do Bus'ness*, H—ggins *knew the Town*,
In *Sappho* touch the *Failings of the Sex*,   15
In rev'rend Bishops note some *small Neglects*,
And own, the *Spaniard* did a *waggish thing*,
Who cropt our Ears, and sent them to the King.
His sly, polite, insinuating stile
Could please at Court, and make AUGUSTUS smile: 20

1 ff. These two lines are from Horace ⟨*Sat.* II iii 1–4⟩; and the only lines
that are so in the whole Poem; being meant to give a handle to that which
follows in the character of an impertinent Censurer,
                        '*Tis all from Horace; etc.* [P]
    8. Quoted from *Sat.* II i 68.
    10. Quoted with a slight alteration from *Sat.* II i 40.
    12. *Bubo*] Some guilty person very fond of making such an observation
[P] Bubb Dodington; see l. 68 and *Ep. to Arbuthnot*, 280 (p. 607).
    13. *Sir Billy*] Yonge. See *Ep. to Arbuthnot*, 280n.
    14. *Blunt*] Director of the South Sea Company. See *Moral Es.* iii 135*n*.
H—ggins] Formerly Jaylor of the Fleet prison, enriched himself by
many exactions, for which he was tried and expelled [P]. During his
trial Huggins called several gentry to testify to his character, thus showing
that he 'knew the town'.
    15. *Sappho*] see *Sat.* II i 83.
    18. *cropt our Ears*] Said to be executed by the Captain of a Spanish
ship on one Jenkins a Captain of an English one. He cut off his ears, and
bid him carry them to the King his master [P].
    Jenkins's ear was said to have been cut off on April 9, 1731; but it was
not until March, 1737-8, two months before this poem was published,
that Jenkins appeared before the House of Commons.

An artful Manager, that crept between
His Friend and Shame, and was a kind of *Screen*.
But 'faith your very Friends will soon be sore;
Patriots there are, who wish you'd jest no more—
And where's the Glory ? 'twill be only thought   25
The Great man never offer'd you a Groat.
Go see Sir ROBERT—
                                    P. See Sir ROBERT !—hum—
And never laugh—for all my life to come ?
Seen him I have, but in his happier hour
Of Social Pleasure, ill-exchang'd for Pow'r;   30
Seen him, uncumber'd with the Venal tribe,
Smile without Art, and win without a Bribe.
Would he oblige me ? let me only find,
He does not think me what he thinks mankind.
Come, come, at all I laugh He laughs, no doubt,   35
The only diff'rence is, I dare laugh out.

F. Why yes: with *Scripture* still you may be free;
A Horse-laugh, if you please, at *Honesty*;
A Joke on JEKYL, or some odd *Old Whig*,
Who never chang'd his Principle, or Wig: 40

22. *His Friend &c.*]
          Omne vafer vitium ridenti Flaccus amico
          Tangit, & admissus circum præcordia ludit.
⟨Persius, *Sat.* i 116⟩. [P]
Screen] A metaphor peculiarly appropriated to a certain person in power [P]. A reference to Walpole's policy of opposing all Parliamentary enquiries into public frauds.

24. *Patriots*] This appelation was generally given to those in opposition to the Court. Though some of them (which our author hints at) had views too mean and interested to deserve that name [P].

26. *The Great man*] A phrase, by common use, appropriated to the first minister [P].

27–36. Walpole owed this back-handed compliment to his having used his influence with Fleury to procure an Abbey at Avignon for Southcote, who had been the means of saving Pope's life when he was a young man.

31. These two verses were originally in the poem, though omitted in all the first editions [P].

34. Alluding to the political maxim attributed to him, *All men have their price*, a perversion of his comment upon certain declamatory 'patriots': *All those men have their price*.

39. *Jekyl*] Sir Joseph Jekyl, Master of the Rolls, a true Whig in his principles, and a man of the utmost probity. He sometimes voted against the Court, which drew upon him the laugh here described of ONE ⟨Walpole⟩ who bestowed it equally upon Religion and Honesty. He died a few months after the publication of this poem. [P]

40. *or Wig*] Alluding to the change of fashion in periwigs from full-bottomed to tie-wigs.

A Patriot is a Fool in ev'ry age,
Whom all Lord Chamberlains allow the Stage:
These nothing hurts; they keep their Fashion still,
And wear their strange old Virtue as they will.

If any ask you, 'Who's the Man, so near   45
His Prince, that writes in Verse, and has his Ear?'
Why answer LYTTELTON, and I'll engage
The worthy Youth shall ne'er be in a rage:
But were his Verses vile, his Whisper base,
You'd quickly find him in Lord *Fanny*'s case.   50
Sejanus, Wolsey, hurt not honest FLEURY,
But well may put some Statesmen in a fury.

Laugh then at any, but at Fools or Foes;
These you but anger, and you mend not those:
Laugh at your Friends, and if your Friends are sore,   55
So much the better, you may laugh the more.
To Vice and Folly to confine the jest,
Sets half the World, God knows, against the rest;
Did not the Sneer of more impartial men
At Sense and Virtue, balance all agen.   60
Judicious Wits spread wide the Ridicule,
And charitably comfort Knave and Fool.

P. Dear Sir, forgive the Prejudice of Youth:
Adieu Distinction, Satire, Warmth, and Truth!
Come harmless *Characters* that no one hit,   65
Come *Henley*'s Oratory, *Osborn*'s Wit!
The Honey dropping from *Favonio*'s tongue,
The Flow'rs of *Bubo*, and the Flow of *Y—ng !*

42. This reflects upon the act carried in the previous year (1737), which
provided that no play could be publicly acted without the licence of the
Lord Chamberlain.
47. George Lyttelton, Secretary to the Prince of Wales, distinguished
both for his writings and speeches in the spirit of Liberty [P].
50. *Lord Fanny*] Hervey. See *Ep. to Arbuthnot*, ll. 319, 356, 357.
51. *Sejanus, Wolsey*] The one the wicked minister of Tiberius; the
other, of Henry VIII. The writers against the Court usually bestowed
these and other odious names on the Minister, without distinction, and in
the most injurious manner. See *Dial.* II v 137 [P].
Fleury] Cardinal: and Minister to Louis XV. It was a Patriot-fashion,
at that time, to cry up his wisdom and honesty [P].
66. *Henley . . . Osborn*] See them in their places in the Dunciad ⟨B iii
199, ii 312, pp. 759, 747 [P]⟩.
68. Bubb Dodington and Sir W. Yonge. Cf. *Ep. to Arbuthnot*, l. 280.

The gracious Dew of Pulpit Eloquence;
And all the well-whipt Cream of Courtly Sense,   70
That first was *H—vy's, F—*'s next, and then
The *S—*te's, and then *H—vy's* once agen.
O come, that easy *Ciceronian* stile,
So *Latin*, yet so *English* all the while,
As, tho' the Pride of *Middleton* and *Bland*,   75
All Boys may read, and Girls may understand!
Then might I sing without the least Offence,
And all I sung should be the *Nation's Sense:*
Or teach the melancholy Muse to mourn,
Hang the sad Verse on CAROLINA's Urn,   80
And hail her passage to the Realms of Rest,
All Parts perform'd, and *all* her Children blest!
So—Satire is no more—I feel it die—
No *Gazeteer* more innocent than I!
And let, a God's-name, ev'ry Fool and Knave   85
Be grac'd thro' Life, and flatter'd in his Grave.

F. Why so? if Satire know its Time and Place,
You still may lash the Greatest—in Disgrace:
For Merit will by turns forsake them all;
Would you know when? exactly when they fall.   90
But let all Satire in all Changes spare
Immortal *S—k*, and grave *De—re!*

69. Alludes to some court sermons, and florid panegyrical speeches;
particularly one very full of puerilities and flatteries; which afterwards got
into an address in the same pretty style; and was lastly served up in an
Epitaph, between Latin and English, published by its author [P]. Henry
Fox moved the address of condolence on the Queen's death sent by the
Commons to the King on January 24, 1737-8. Pope evidently believed
(l. 71) that Hervey wrote Fox's speech. It became 'The Se[na]te's' on its
acceptance by the Commons. It was afterwards served up again in
Hervey's Latin epitaph.
73-5. Pope refers to Hervey's Latin epitaph on the Queen, and hints
that Middleton, author of the *Life of Cicero*, and Bland, Provost of Eton,
collaborated to write it for him.
78. *Nation's Sense*] The cant of politics at that time.
80. *Carolina*] Queen consort to King George II. She died in 1737. Her
death gave occasion, as is observed above, to many indiscreet and mean
performances unworthy of her memory, whose last moments manifested
the utmost courage and resolution [P].
82. Contemporary gossip reported that the Queen had died without
taking the last sacrament and without being reconciled to the Prince of
Wales.
84. *Gazeteer*] a journalist appointed and paid by the government.
92. *S—k . . . De—re*] A title given *that* Lord ⟨Selkirk⟩ by King
James II. He was of the Bedchamber to King William; he was so to King

Silent and soft, as Saints remove to Heav'n,
All Tyes dissolv'd, and ev'ry Sin forgiv'n,
These, may some gentle, ministerial Wing   95
Receive, and place for ever near a King!
There, where no Passion, Pride, or Shame transport,
Lull'd with the sweet *Nepenthe* of a Court;
There, where no Father's Brother's, Friend's Disgrace
Once break their Rest, or stir them from their Place;   100
But past the Sense of human Miseries,
All Tears are wip'd for ever from all Eyes;
No Cheek is known to blush, no Heart to throb,
Save when they lose a Question, or a Job.

P. Good Heav'n forbid, that I shou'd blast their Glory,
Who know how like Whig-Ministers to Tory,   106
And when three Sov'reigns dy'd, could scarce be vext,
Consid'ring what a Gracious Prince was next.
Have I in silent wonder seen such things
As Pride in Slaves, and Avarice in Kings,   110
And at a Peer, or Peeress shall I fret,
Who starves a Sister, or forswears a Debt?
Virtue, I grant you, is an empty boast;
But shall the Dignity of *Vice* be lost?
Ye Gods! shall *Cibber*'s Son, without rebuke   115
Swear like a Lord? or *Rich* out-whore a Duke?
A Fav'rite's *Porter* with his Master vie,
Be brib'd as often, and as often lie?
Shall *Ward* draw Contracts with a Statesman's skill?
Or *Japhet* pocket, like his Grace, a Will?   120
Is it for *Bond* or *Peter* (paltry Things!)
To pay their Debts or keep their Faith like Kings?
If *Blount* dispatch'd himself, he play'd the man,

George I, he was so to King George II. *This* Lord ⟨De La Warr⟩ was very
skilful in all the forms of the House, in which he discharged himself with
great gravity [P].
     104. *lose a Question*] i.e. when they have a motion or proposal rejected
by parliament.
     112. Lady Mary. See *Sob. Adv.* 21, 53*n* (pp. 668-9).
     115. *Cibber's Son . . . Rich*] Two Players: look for them in the Dunciad
⟨B̲III 142, 261, pp. 756, 761⟩. [P]
     119-21. *Ward . . . Japhet . . . Bond . . . Peter*] See *Moral Es.* iii 20,
88, 102, 125.
     120. *pocket . . . Will*] Pope alludes here and in l. 122 to Archbishop
Wake's action in handing George I's will to his son, who suppressed it.
     123. *Blount*] Author of an impious and foolish Book called The Oracles

And so may'st Thou, Illustrious *Passeran!*
But shall a *Printer*, weary of his life,   125
Learn from their Books to hang himself and Wife?
This, this, my friend, I cannot, must not bear;
Vice thus abus'd, demands a Nation's care;
This calls the Church to deprecate our Sin,
And hurls the Thunder of the Laws on *Gin*.   130

     Let modest *Foster*, if he will, excell
Ten Metropolitans in preaching well;
A simple Quaker, or a Quaker's Wife,
Out-do *Landaffe*, in Doctrine—yea, in Life;
Let humble ALLEN, with an aukward Shame,   135
Do good by stealth, and blush to find it Fame.
Virtue may chuse the high or low Degree,
'Tis just alike to Virtue, and to me;
Dwell in a Monk, or light upon a King,
She's still the same, belov'd, contented thing.   140
Vice is undone, if she forgets her Birth,
And stoops from Angels to the Dregs of Earth:
But 'tis the *Fall* degrades her to a Whore;
Let *Greatness* own her, and she's mean no more:
Her Birth, her Beauty, Crowds and Courts confess,   145
Chaste Matrons praise her, and grave Bishops bless:
In golden Chains the willing World she draws,
And hers the Gospel is, and hers the Laws:
Mounts the Tribunal, lifts her scarlet head,

---

of Reason, who being in love with a near kinswoman of his, and rejected, gave himself a stab in the arm, as pretending to kill himself, of the consequence of which he really died [P].

124. *Passeran*] Author of another, called a Philosophical Discourse on Death [P].

125. *a Printer*] A Fact that happened in London a few years past. The unhappy man left behind him a paper justifying his action by the reasonings of some of these authors [P].

130. *Gin*] A spirituous liquor, the exorbitant use of which had almost destroyed the lowest rank of the People till it was restrained by an act of Parliament in 1736 [P].

131. James Foster (1697–1753), a popular Anabaptist preacher.

133. *a Quaker's Wife*] Mary Drummond, sister, not wife, of George Drummond, the able Lord Provost of Edinburgh.

134. *Landaffe*] A poor Bishoprick in Wales, as poorly supplied [P]. The bishop was John Harris. In 1699 the see of Llandaff was worth £230 p.a.

141 ff. An elaborate allusion to Molly Skerrett, long the mistress of Walpole, who married her in 1738.

And sees pale Virtue carted in her stead!   150
Lo! at the Wheels of her Triumphal Car,
Old *England*'s Genius, rough with many a Scar,
Dragg'd in the Dust! his Arms hang idly round,
His Flag inverted trails along the ground!
Our Youth, all liv'ry'd o'er with foreign Gold,   155
Before her dance; behind her crawl the Old!
See thronging Millions to the Pagod run,
And offer Country, Parent, Wife, or Son!
Hear her black Trumpet thro' the Land proclaim,
That 'Not to be corrupted is the Shame.'   160
In Soldier, Churchman, Patriot, Man in Pow'r,
'Tis Av'rice all, Ambition is no more!
See, all our Nobles begging to be Slaves!
See, all our Fools aspiring to be Knaves!
The Wit of Cheats, the Courage of a Whore,   165
Are what ten thousand envy and adore.
All, all look up, with reverential Awe,
On Crimes that scape, or triumph o'er the Law:
While Truth, Worth, Wisdom, daily they decry—
'Nothing is Sacred now but Villany.'   170

Yet may this Verse (if such a Verse remain)
Show there was one who held it in disdain.

150. *carted*] Carting, or exhibiting from a cart, was a punishment of
prostitutes and procuresses.
154. A sneer at Walpole's policy of peace at any price.

Epilogue to the Satires

Written in 1738
[published 1738]

DIALOGUE II

Fr. Tis all a Libel—*Paxton* (Sir) will say.
P. Not yet, my Friend! to-morrow 'faith it may;
And for that very cause I print to day.
How shou'd I fret, to mangle ev'ry line,
In rev'rence to the Sins of *Thirty-nine!*   5
Vice with such Giant-strides comes on amain,

1. Paxton (d. 1744) was the Treasury Solicitor, and was employed to
read all new publications and report libels on the government to the
Secretaries of State.
2. Perhaps an allusion to the Playhouse Act (see *Dia.* i 42*n*) believed by
the Opposition to be tending towards a restraint on the liberty of the press.

Invention strives to be before in vain;
Feign what I will, and paint it e'er so strong,
Some rising Genius sins up to my Song.
   F. Yet none but you by Name the Guilty lash;   10
Ev'n *Guthry* saves half *Newgate* by a Dash.
Spare then the Person, and expose the Vice.
   P. How Sir! not damn the Sharper, but the Dice?
Come on then Satire! gen'ral, unconfin'd,
Spread thy broad wing, and sowze on all the Kind.   15
Ye Statesmen, Priests, of one Religion all!
Ye Tradesmen vile, in Army, Court, or Hall!
Ye Rev'rend Atheists!—*F.* Scandal! name them, Who?
   P. Why that's the thing you bid me not to do.
Who starv'd a Sister, who forswore a Debt,   20
I never nam'd—the Town's enquiring yet.
The pois'ning Dame—*Fr.* You mean—*P.* I don't.—*Fr.*
   You do.
   P. See! now I keep the Secret, and not you.
The bribing Statesman—*Fr.* Hold! too high you go.
   P. The brib'd Elector—*Fr.* There you stoop too low. 25
   P. I fain wou'd please you, if I knew with what:
Tell me, which Knave is lawful Game, which not?
Must great Offenders, once escap'd the Crown,
Like Royal Harts, be never more run down?
Admit your Law to spare the Knight requires;   30
As Beasts of Nature may we hunt the Squires?
Suppose I censure—you know what I mean—
To save a Bishop, may I name a Dean?
   Fr. A Dean, Sir? no: his Fortune is not made,
You hurt a man that's rising in the Trade.   35

   10. *by Name*] 'I would indeed [manifest my disdain and abhorrence of vice in my writings] with more restrictions, and less personally; it is more agreeable to my nature, which those who know it not are greatly mistaken in: But General Satire in Times of General Vice has no force, and is no Punishment: People have ceas'd to be ashamed of it when so many are join'd with them; and tis only by hunting One or two from the Herd that any Examples can be made. If a man writ all his Life against the Collective Body of the Banditti, or against Lawyers, would it do the least Good, or lessen the Body? But if some are hung up, or pilloryed, it may prevent others. And in my low Station, with no other Power than this, I hope to deter, if not to reform.' Pope to Arbuthnot, Aug. 2, 1734.
   11. *Guthry*] The Ordinary of *Newgate*, who publishes the Memoirs of the Malefactors, and is often prevailed upon to be so tender of their reputation, as to set down no more than the initials of their name [P].
   15. *sowze*] used of a hawk, swooping down upon its prey.
   20. Referring to *Dia.* i 112.
   22. *The pois'ning Dame*] A reference to *Sat.* ii i 81?

 P. If not the Tradesman who set up to day,
Much less the 'Prentice who to morrow may.
Down, down, proud Satire! tho' a Realm be spoil'd,
Arraign no mightier Thief than wretched *Wild*,
Or if a Court or Country's made a Job,   40
Go drench a Pick-pocket, and join the Mob.
 But Sir, I beg you, for the Love of Vice!
The matter's weighty, pray consider twice:
Have you less Pity for the needy Cheat,
The poor and friendless Villain, than the Great? 45
Alas! the small Discredit of a Bribe
Scarce hurts the Lawyer, but undoes the Scribe.
Then better sure it Charity becomes
To tax Directors, who (thank God) have Plums;
Still better, Ministers; or if the thing   50
May pinch ev'n there—why lay it on a King.
 Fr. Stop! stop!
      P. Must Satire, then, nor *rise* nor *fall?*
Speak out, and bid me blame no Rogues at all.
 Fr. Yes, strike that *Wild*, I'll justify the blow.
 P. Strike? why the man was hang'd ten years ago: 55
Who now that obsolete Example fears?
Ev'n *Peter* trembles only for his Ears.
 Fr. What always *Peter? Peter* thinks you mad,
You make men desp'rate if they once are bad:
Else might he take to Virtue some years hence— 60
 P. As *S—k*, if he lives, will love the PRINCE.
 Fr. Strange spleen to *S—k!*
      P. Do I wrong the Man?
God knows, I praise a Courtier where I can.
When I confess, there *is* who feels for Fame,
And melts to Goodness, need I SCARBROW name? 65

39. Jonathan Wild, a famous Thief, and Thief-Impeacher, who was at
last caught in his own train and hanged ⟨1725⟩ [P]. Wild had become
synonymous with Walpole in political journalism.
 41. *drench a Pick-pocket*] Pickpockets were sometimes ducked and
sometimes pumped upon.
 49. *Plums*] see *Sat.* II i 103*n* (p. 617).
 57. Peter ⟨Walter⟩ had, the year before this, narrowly escaped the
Pillory for forgery: and got off with a severe rebuke only from the
bench [P].
 61. Lord Selkirk. See Pope's note to *Dia.* i 92.
 Much as Selkirk hates the Prince now, he will love him when the Prince
succeeds to the throne, because then it will pay him. Similarly, not until
it pays him will Peter love virtue.
 65. *Scarbrow*] Earl of; and Knight of the Garter, whose personal

Pleas'd let me own, in *Esher*'s peaceful Grove
(Where *Kent* and Nature vye for PELHAM's Love)
The Scene, the Master, opening to my view,
I sit and dream I see my CRAGS anew!
　Ev'n in a Bishop I can spy Desert;   70
Secker is decent, *Rundel* has a Heart,
Manners with Candour are to *Benson* giv'n,
To *Berkley*, ev'ry Virtue under Heav'n.
　But does the Court a worthy Man remove?
That instant, I declare, he has my Love: 75
I shun his Zenith, court his mild Decline;
Thus SOMMERS once, and HALIFAX were mine.
Oft in the clear, still Mirrour of Retreat,
I study'd SHREWSBURY, the wise and great:
CARLETON's calm Sense, and STANHOPE's noble Flame, 80
Compar'd, and knew their gen'rous End the same:
How pleasing ATTERBURY's softer hour!
How shin'd the Soul, unconquer'd in the Tow'r!

---

attachments to the king appeared from his steddy adherence to the royal
interest, after his resignation of his great employment of Master of the
Horse; and whose known honour and virtue made him esteemed by all
parties [P].
　66. The House and Gardens of *Esher* in *Surrey*, ⟨designed by Kent⟩
belonging to the Honourable Mr. Pelham, Brother of the Duke of Newcastle. The author could not have given a more amiable idea of his
Character than in comparing him to Mr. Craggs [P].
　71. *decent*] Pope intended to commend Secker's moderation, the most
conspicuous trait in his character. Secker was Bishop of Oxford, Rundle
of Derry, Benson of Gloucester, and Berkeley (the philosopher) of Cloyne.
　77. *Sommers*] John Lord Sommers died in 1716. He had been Lord
Keeper in the reign of William III. who took from him the seals in 1700.
The author had the honour of knowing him in 1706. A faithful, able, and
incorrupt minister; who, to the qualities of a consummate statesman,
added those of a man of Learning and Politeness [P].
　Halifax] A peer, no less distinguished by his love of letters than his
abilities in Parliament. He was disgraced in 1710, on the Change of
Q. Anne's ministry [P].
　79. *Shrewsbury*] Charles Talbot, Duke of Shrewsbury, had been
Secretary of state, Embassador in France, Lord Lieutenant of Ireland,
Lord Chamberlain, and Lord Treasurer. He several times quitted his
employments, and was often recalled. He died in 1718 [P].
　80. *Carleton*] Hen. Boyle, Lord Carleton (nephew of the famous Robert
Boyle) who was Secretary of state under William III. and President of the
Council under Q. Anne [P]. Pope's memory played him false about
Carleton's official posts.
　Stanhope] James Earl Stanhope. A Nobleman of equal courage, spirit,
and learning. General in Spain, and Secretary of state [P].
　83. Bishop Atterbury was imprisoned in the Tower for treasonable
correspondence with the Pretender. Pope gave evidence at his trial (1723).

How can I PULT'NEY, CHESTERFIELD forget,
While *Roman* Spirit charms, and *Attic* Wit: 85
ARGYLE, the State's whole Thunder born to wield,
And shake alike the Senate and the Field:
Or WYNDHAM, just to Freedom and the Throne,
The Master of our Passions, and his own.
Names, which I long have lov'd, nor lov'd in vain,   90
Rank'd with their Friends, not number'd with their
        Train;
And if yet higher the proud List should end,
Still let me say! No Follower, but a Friend.

    Yet think not Friendship only prompts my Lays;
I follow *Virtue*, where she shines, I praise,   95
Point she to Priest or Elder, Whig or Tory,
Or round a Quaker's Beaver cast a Glory.
I never (to my sorrow I declare)
Din'd with the MAN of ROSS, or my LORD MAY'R.
Some, in their choice of Friends (nay, look not grave) 100
Have still a secret Byass to a Knave:
To find an honest man, I beat about,
And love him, court him, praise him, in or out.
    Fr. Then why so few commended?
                                    P. Not so fierce;
Find you the Virtue, and I'll find the Verse.   105
But random Praise—the Task can ne'er be done,
Each Mother asks it for her Booby Son,
Each Widow asks it for the Best of Men,
For him she weeps, and him she weds agen.

84. Two prominent members of the Parliamentary opposition.
88. Sir William Wyndham, Chancellor of the Exchequer under Queen
Anne, made early a considerable figure; but since a much greater both by
his ability and eloquence, joined with the utmost judgment and temper
[P].
92. *yet higher*] An allusion to his friendship with Frederick, Prince of
Wales.
99. *The Man of Ross*] John Kyrle, the philanthropist, previously commended in *Moral Es.* iii 250 ff. (p. 581).
My Lord May'r] Sir John Barnard [P]. He was regarded as one of
the greatest examples of private and public virtues that the age had produced.
107. Perhaps a reference to the Duchess of Buckingham's request for
an epitaph on her son. See p. 564.
108. *Each Widow*] Perhaps a reference to Mrs. John Knight who
begged an epitaph for her husband. See p. 823.

Praise cannot stoop, like Satire, to the Ground;   110
The Number may be hang'd, but not be crown'd.
Enough for half the Greatest of these days
To 'scape my Censure, not expect my Praise:
Are they not rich? what more can they pretend?
Dare they to hope a Poet for their Friend?   115
What RICHELIEU wanted, LOUIS scarce could gain,
And what young AMMON wish'd, but wish'd in vain.
No Pow'r the Muse's Friendship can command;
No Pow'r, when Virtue claims it, can withstand:
To *Cato*, *Virgil* pay'd one honest line;   120
O let my Country's Friends illumin mine!
—What are you thinking? *Fr.* Faith, the thought's no Sin,
I think your Friends are out, and would be in.
   P. If merely to come in, Sir, they go out,
The way they take is strangely round about.   125
   Fr. They too may be corrupted, you'll allow?
   P. I only call those Knaves who are so now.
   Is that too little? Come then, I'll comply—
Spirit of *Arnall!* aid me while I lye.
COBHAM's a Coward, POLWARTH is a Slave,   130
And LYTTLETON a dark, designing Knave,
St. JOHN has ever been a wealthy Fool—
But let me add, Sir ROBERT's mighty dull,
Has never made a Friend in private life,
And was, besides, a Tyrant to his Wife.   135
   But pray, when others praise him, do I blame?
Call *Verres*, *Wolsey*, any odious name?
Why rail they then, if but a Wreath of mine
Oh All-accomplish'd St. JOHN! deck thy Shrine?
   What? shall each spur-gall'd Hackney of the Day,   140
When *Paxton* gives him double Pots and Pay,

110. *stoop*] For the metaphor, see p. 608, l. 341*n.*
111. *The Number*] Lat. *numerus*, those who count as population and nothing beyond.
120. *one honest line*] *Aen.* viii 670.
130. *Polwarth*] The Hon. Hugh Hume, Son of Alexander Earl of Marchmont, Grandson of Patric Earl of Marchmont, and distinguished, like them, in the cause of Liberty [P].
135. Ironical. Walpole paid no regard to his wife's infidelities.
137. See *Dia.* i 51.
138. *Why rail they*] *The Daily Gazetteer*, the Government's paper, had complained, after the publication of *Ep.* 1 i, that only Bolingbroke and other 'avowed Enemies to their Country are thought worthy of his Panegyrics'.

Or each new-pension'd Sycophant, pretend
To break my Windows, if I treat a Friend;
Then wisely plead, to me they meant no hurt,
But 'twas my Guest at whom they threw the dirt?   145
Sure, if I spare the Minister, no rules
Of Honour bind me, not to maul his Tools;
Sure, if they cannot cut, it may be said
His Saws are toothless, and his Hatchets Lead.
   It anger'd TURENNE, once upon a day.   150
To see a Footman kick'd that took his pay:
But when he heard th' Affront the Fellow gave,
Knew one a Man of Honour, one a Knave;
The prudent Gen'ral turn'd it to a jest,
And begg'd, he'd take the pains to kick the rest.   155
Which not at present having time to do—
   Fr. Hold Sir! for God's-sake, where's th' Affront to you?
Against your worship when had *S—k* writ?
Or *P—ge* pour'd forth the Torrent of his Wit?
Or grant, the Bard whose Distich all commend,   160
[*In Pow'r a Servant, out of Pow'r a Friend.*]
To *W—le* guilty of some venial Sin,
What's that to you, who ne'er was out nor in?
   The Priest whose Flattery be-dropt the Crown,
How hurt he you? he only stain'd the Gown.   165
And how did, pray, the Florid Youth offend.
Whose Speech you took, and gave it to a Friend?
   P. Faith it imports not much from whom it came
Whoever borrow'd, could not be to blame,
Since the whole House did afterwards the same: 170
Let Courtly Wits to Wits afford supply,
As Hog to Hog in Huts of *Westphaly*;

143. *break my Windows*] Which was done when Bolingbroke and
Bathurst were one day dining with him at Twickenham.
   150. Viscomte de Turenne (1611-1675), Marshal of France. The story
is told by A. M. de Ramsay in his *Histoire*.
   158. Lord Selkirk. See *Dia.* i 92n.
   159. *P—ge*] Judge Page; see *Sat.* II i 82.
   160. *the Bard*] A verse taken out of a poem by ⟨Dodington⟩ to Sir
R. W. [P].
   164. Spoken not of any particular priest, but of many priests [P].
Spoken originally of Dr. Alured Clarke, a protégé of Queen Caroline,
who published *An Essay Towards the Character of Her Late Majesty*, but
Pope may have added this note on reflecting that the lines would also
apply to Dr. Gilbert, later Archbishop of York, who wept in the pulpit
when preaching about the Queen by the King's command.
   166. This seems to allude to a complaint made v. 71 of the preceding
Dialogue [P]

If one, thro' Nature's Bounty or his Lord's,
Has what the frugal, dirty soil affords,
From him the next receives it, thick or thin,   175
As pure a Mess almost as it came in;
The blessed Benefit, not there confin'd,
Drops to the third who nuzzles close behind;
From tail to mouth, they feed, and they carouse;
The last, full fairly gives it to the *House*.   180
   Fr. This filthy Simile, this beastly Line,
Quite turns my Stomach—*P.* So does Flatt'ry mine;
And all your Courtly Civet-Cats can vent,
Perfume to you, to me is Excrement.
   But hear me further.—*Japhet*, 'tis agreed,   185
Writ not, and *Chartres* scarce could write or read,
In all the Courts of *Pindus* guiltless quite;
But Pens can forge, my Friend, that cannot write.
And must no Egg in *Japhet*'s Face be thrown,
Because the Deed he forg'd was not my own?   190
Must never Patriot then declaim at Gin,
Unless, good man! he has been fairly in?
No zealous Pastor blame a failing Spouse,
Without a staring Reason on his Brows?
And each Blasphemer quite escape the Rod,   195
Because the insult's not on Man, but God?
   Ask you what Provocation I have had?
The strong Antipathy of Good to Bad.
When Truth or Virtue an Affront endures,
Th' Affront is mine, my Friend, and should be yours.   200
Mine, as a Foe profess'd to false Pretence,
Who think a Coxcomb's Honour like his Sense;
Mine, as a Friend to ev'ry worthy mind;
And mine as Man, who feel for all mankind.
   Fr. You're strangely proud.
                P. So proud, I am no Slave: ⎤   205
So impudent, I own myself no Knave: ⎬
So odd, my Country's Ruin makes me grave. ⎦
Yes, I am proud; I must be proud to see
Men not afraid of God, afraid of me:

185. *Japhet—Chartres*] See the Epistle to Lord Bathurst [P]. *Moral Es.*
iii 88, 20.
  187. *Pindus*] a mountain in Thessaly associated with the Muses.
  191. See *Dia.* i 130*n*.
  204. From Terence: 'Homo sum: humani nihil a me alienum puto' [P].
Heautontimorumenos, l. 77.

Safe from the Bar, the Pulpit, and the Throne,   210
Yet touch'd and sham'd by *Ridicule* alone.
    O sacred Weapon! left for Truth's defence,
Sole Dread of Folly, Vice, and Insolence!
To all but Heav'n-directed hands deny'd,
The Muse may give thee, but the Gods must guide.   215
Rev'rent I touch thee! but with honest zeal;
To rowze the Watchmen of the Publick Weal,
To Virtue's Work provoke the tardy Hall,
And goad the Prelate slumb'ring in his Stall.
    Ye tinsel Insects! whom a Court maintains,   220
That counts your Beauties only by your Stains,
Spin all your Cobwebs o'er the Eye of Day!
The Muse's wing shall brush you all away:
All his Grace preaches, all his Lordship sings,
All that makes Saints of Queens, and Gods of Kings,   225
All, all but Truth, drops dead-born from the Press,
Like the last Gazette, or the last Address.
    When black Ambition stains a Publick Cause,
A Monarch's sword when mad Vain-glory draws,
Not *Waller*'s Wreath can hide the Nation's Scar,   230
Nor *Boileau* turn the Feather to a Star.
    Not so, when diadem'd, with Rays divine,
Touch'd with the Flame that breaks from Virtue's Shrine.
Her Priestess Muse forbids the Good to dye,
And ope's the Temple of Eternity;   235
There other *Trophies* deck the truly Brave,
Than such as *Anstis* casts into the Grave;
Far other *Stars* than ★ and ★★ wear,

218. *the tardy Hall*] i.e. Westminster Hall, formerly the seat of the High
Court of Justice; hence, the administration of Justice [*OED*].
222. *Cobwebs*] Weak and slight sophistry against virtue and honour.
Thin colours over vice, as unable to hide the light of Truth, as cobwebs
to shade the sun [P].
227. *Address*] the formal reply of the Lords or of the Commons to the
King's Speech at the opening of parliament.
228. The case of Cromwell in the civil war of England; and (v 229) of
Louis XIV. in his conquest of the Low Countries [P].
230. Pope is referring to *Upon the late Storme, and of the death of his
Highnesse Ensuing the same* (1659).
231. See his Ode on *Namur;* where (to use his own words) *il a fait un
Astre de la Plume blanche qui le Roy porte ordinairement à son Chapeau, &
qui est en effet une espèce de Comete, fatale à nos ennemis* [P].
237. The chief Herald at Arms. It is the custom, at the funeral of great
peers, to cast into the grave the broken staves and ensigns of honour [P].
238. Perhaps 'George' and 'Frederick'.

And may descend to *Mordington* from *Stair:*
Such as on HOUGH'S unsully'd Mitre shine,   240
Or beam, good DIGBY! from a Heart like thine.
Let Envy howl while Heav'n's whole Chorus sings,
And bark at Honour not confer'd by Kings;
Let Flatt'ry sickening see the Incense rise,
Sweet to the World, and grateful to the Skies: 245
Truth guards the Poet, sanctifies the line,
And makes Immortal, Verse as mean as mine.
   Yes, the last Pen for Freedom let me draw,
When Truth stands trembling on the edge of Law:
Here, Last of *Britons!* let your Names be read;   250
Are none, none living? let me praise the Dead,
And for that Cause which made your Fathers shine,
Fall, by the Votes of their degen'rate Line!
   Fr. Alas! alas! pray end what you began,
And write next winter more *Essays on Man.*   255

239. *Stair*] John Dalrymple Earl of Stair, Knight of the Thistle; served in all the wars under the Duke of Marlborough; and afterwards as Embassador in France [P]. Nothing is known of Lord Mordington except that his wife kept a public gaming house in Covent Garden.

240. Dr. John *Hough* Bishop of *Worcester*, and the Lord Digby. The one an assertor of the Church of England in opposition to the false measures of King James II. The other as firmly attached to the cause of that King. Both acting out of principle, and equally men of honour and virtue [P].

245. Quoted from *Temple of Fame*, 377.

249. An allusion to the threatened censorship of the press.

VER. *ult.*] This was the last poem of the kind printed by our author, with a resolution to publish no more; but to enter thus, in the most plain and solemn manner he could, a sort of PROTEST against that insuperable corruption and depravity of manners, which he had been so unhappy as to live to see. Could he have hoped to have amended any, he had continued those attacks; but bad men were grown so shameless and so powerful, that Ridicule was become as unsafe as it was ineffectual. The Poem raised him, as he knew it would, some enemies; but he had reason to be satisfied with the approbation of good men, and the testimony of his own conscience [P].

On receiving from the Right Hon. the Lady Frances Shirley a Standish and Two Pens

[written c. 1739; published 1751]

Yes, I beheld th' Athenian Queen
    Descend in all her sober charms;
'And take (she said, and smil'd serene)
    Take at this hand celestial arms:

'Secure the radiant weapons wield;   5
    This golden lance shall guard Desert,
And if a Vice dares keep the field,
    This steel shall stab it to the heart.'

Aw'd, on my bended knees I fell,
    Receiv'd the weapons of the sky;   10
And dipt them in the sable Well,
    The fount of Fame or Infamy.

'What *well?* what *weapon?* (Flavia cries)
    A standish, steel and golden pen;
It came from Bertrand's, not the skies;   15
    I gave it you to write again.

'But, Friend, take heed whom you attack;
    You'll bring a House (I mean of Peers)
Red, Blue, and Green, nay white and black,
    L . . . . . . and all about your ears.   20

Warburton published this poem as an appendix to the *Epilogue to the Satires*, for which Pope had been threatened with prosecution in the House of Lords. 'On which', Warburton continues, 'with great resentment against his enemies, for not being willing to distinguish between

Grave Epistles bringing Vice to light

and licentious Libels, he began a *third Dialogue*, more severe and sublime than the first and second; which being no secret, matters were soon compromised. His enemies agreed to drop the prosecution, and he promised to leave the third Dialogue unfinished and suppressed. This affair occasioned this little beautiful poem, to which it alludes throughout, but more especially in the four last stanzas.'

Title: *Lady Frances Shirley*] (c. 1706–78). Daughter of Lord Ferrers, whose widow was Pope's neighbour at Twickenham.

14. *standish*] an inkstand.

15. *Bertrand's*] A famous toy-shop at Bath.

19. *Red, Blue and Green*] The ribbons of the orders of the Bath, the Garter, and the Thistle respectively.

'You'd write as smooth again on glass,
    And run, on ivory, so glib,
As not to stick at fool or ass,
    Nor stop at Flattery or Fib.

'*Athenian Queen!* and *sober charms!*   25
    I tell ye, fool, there's nothing in't:
'Tis Venus, Venus gives these arms;
    In Dryden's Virgil see the print.

'Come, if you'll be a quiet soul,
    That dares tell neither Truth nor Lies,   30
I'll list you in the harmless roll
    Of those that sing of these poor eyes.'

---

19. *white and black*] The spiritual Peers, who might have taken offence at *Epil. to Sat.*, 11 70.

20. *L . . .*] Carruthers conjectures 'Lambeth', and refers to the offence given by the allusion to Archbishop Wake in *Epil. to Sat.*, 1 120.

28. When she delivers Æneas a suit of heavenly armour. Dryden's *Virgil*, plate 79.

On lying in the Earl of Rochester's Bed at Atterbury

[written c. 1739; published 1739]

With no poetick ardors fir'd,
  I press the bed where *Wilmot* lay:
That here he lov'd, or here expir'd,
  Begets no numbers grave or gay.

But 'neath thy roof, *Argyle*, are bred   5
  Such thoughts, as prompt the brave to lie,
Stretch'd forth in honour's nobler bed,
  Beneath a nobler roof, the sky.

Such flames, as high in patriots burn,
  Yet stoop to bless a child or wife: 10
And such as wicked kings may mourn,
  When freedom is more dear than life.

Title: *Rochester*] John Wilmot, second Earl of Rochester (1647–80), the Restoration poet.

5. *Argyle*] The original footnote ran: 'Atterbury [now Adderbury] House formerly belonged to the witty Earl of Rochester, but is now a Country Seat belonging to his Grace the Duke of Argyle.'

Verses on a Grotto by the River Thames at Twickenham, composed of Marbles, Spars, and Minerals

[written 1740; published 1741]

Thou who shalt stop, where *Thames*' translucent Wave
Shines a broad Mirrour thro' the shadowy Cave;
Where lingering Drops from Mineral Roofs distill,
And pointed Crystals break the sparkling Rill,
Unpolish'd Gemms no Ray on Pride bestow,   5
And latent Metals innocently glow:
Approach. Great NATURE studiously behold!
And eye the Mine without a Wish for Gold.
Approach: But aweful! Lo th' *Ægerian* Grott,
Where, nobly-pensive, ST. JOHN sate and thought;   10
Where *British* Sighs from dying WYNDHAM stole,
And the bright Flame was shot thro' MARCHMONT's Soul.
Let such, such only, tread this sacred Floor,
Who dare to love their Country, and be poor.

9. *Ægerian Grott*] Egeria was one of the goddesses of prophecy who instructed Numa Pompilius.

11. Sir William Wyndham, the leader of the Hanover Tories, died on 17 July 1740.

12. Hugh Hume, Lord Polwarth, a prominent member of the Whig opposition to Walpole's government, had succeeded to his father's title as Earl of Marchmont on 27 February 1739/40.

The Dunciad

IN FOUR BOOKS

———————————❧———————————

PRINTED ACCORDING TO THE COMPLETE
COPY FOUND IN THE YEAR 1742
WITH THE PROLEGOMENA OF SCRIBLERUS,
AND NOTES VARIORUM
To which are added
SEVERAL NOTES NOW FIRST PUBLISH'D,
THE HYPERCRITICS OF ARISTARCHUS,
AND HIS DISSERTATION ON
THE HERO OF THE POEM

Tandem Phœbus adest, morsusque inferre parantem
Congelat, et patulos, ut erant, indurat hiatus
OVID.

[Book 4, written c. 1741; published 1742]
[Books 1–3, revised c. 1741; published 1743]

ADVERTISEMENT TO THE READER

I have long had a design of giving some sort of Notes on the Works of this Poet. Before I had the happiness of his acquaintance, I had written a Commentary on his Essay on Man, *and have since finished another on the* Essay on Criticism. *There was one already on the* Dunciad, *which had met with general approbation: but I still thought some additions were wanting (of a more serious kind) to the humorous Notes of* Scriblerus, *and even to those written by Mr.* Cleland, Dr. Arbuthnot, *and others. I had lately the pleasure to pass some months with the Author in the Country, where I prevailed upon him to do what I had long desired, and favour me with his explanation of several passages in his Works. It happen'd, that just at that juncture was published a ridiculous book[1] against him, full of Personal Reflections which furnished him with a lucky opportunity of improving* This Poem, *by giving it the only thing it wanted,* a more considerable Hero. *He was always sensible of its defect in that particular, and owned he had let it pass with the Hero it had, purely for want of a better; not entertaining the least expectation that such an one was reserved for*

[1] ⟨*A Letter from Mr. Cibber to Mr. Pope,* 1742.⟩

this Post, as has since obtained the Laurel: *But since that had happened, he could no longer deny this justice either to* him *or the* Dunciad.

*And yet I will venture to say, there was another motive which had
still more weight with our Author: This person was one, who from every
Folly (not to say Vice) of which another would be ashamed, has constantly derived a* Vanity; *and therefore was the* man in the world
who would least be hurt by it.

W. W.[1]

BY AUTHORITY.

𝕭𝔂 𝖇𝖎𝖗𝖙𝖚𝖊 𝖔𝖋 𝖙𝖍𝖊 𝕬𝖚𝖙𝖍𝖔𝖗𝖎𝖙𝖞 𝖎𝖓 𝖀𝖘 𝖇𝖊𝖘𝖙𝖊𝖉 𝖇𝖞 𝖙𝖍𝖊 Act for subjecting
Poets to the power of a Licenser, 𝖜𝖊 𝖍𝖆𝖛𝖊 𝖗𝖊𝖛𝖎𝖘𝖊𝖉 𝖙𝖍𝖎𝖘 𝕻𝖎𝖊𝖈𝖊;
𝖜𝖍𝖊𝖗𝖊 𝖋𝖎𝖓𝖉𝖎𝖓𝖌 𝖙𝖍𝖊 𝖘𝖙𝖞𝖑𝖊 𝖆𝖓𝖉 𝖆𝖕𝖕𝖊𝖑𝖑𝖆𝖙𝖎𝖔𝖓 𝖔𝖋 KING to 𝖍𝖆𝖛𝖊 𝖇𝖊𝖊𝖓
𝖌𝖎𝖛𝖊𝖓 𝖙𝖔 𝖆 𝖈𝖊𝖗𝖙𝖆𝖎𝖓 Pretender, Pseudo-Poet, 𝖔𝖗 Phantom, 𝖔𝖋 𝖙𝖍𝖊
𝖓𝖆𝖒𝖊 𝖔𝖋 TIBBALD; 𝖆𝖓𝖉 𝖆𝖕𝖕𝖗𝖊𝖍𝖊𝖓𝖉𝖎𝖓𝖌 𝖙𝖍𝖊 𝖘𝖆𝖒𝖊 𝖒𝖆𝖞 𝖇𝖊 𝖉𝖊𝖊𝖒𝖊𝖉
𝖎𝖓 𝖘𝖔𝖒𝖊 𝖘𝖔𝖗𝖙 𝖆 𝕽𝖊𝖋𝖑𝖊𝖈𝖙𝖎𝖔𝖓 𝖔𝖓 Majesty, 𝖔𝖗 𝖆𝖙 𝖑𝖊𝖆𝖘𝖙 𝖆𝖓 𝖎𝖓𝖘𝖚𝖑𝖙
𝖔𝖓 𝖙𝖍𝖆𝖙 𝕷𝖊𝖌𝖆𝖑 𝕬𝖚𝖙𝖍𝖔𝖗𝖎𝖙𝖞 𝖜𝖍𝖎𝖈𝖍 𝖍𝖆𝖘 𝖇𝖊𝖘𝖙𝖔𝖜𝖊𝖉 𝖔𝖓 𝖆𝖓𝖔𝖙𝖍𝖊𝖗 𝖕𝖊𝖗𝖘𝖔𝖓
𝖙𝖍𝖊 Crown of Poesy: 𝖂𝖊 𝖍𝖆𝖛𝖊 𝖔𝖗𝖉𝖊𝖗𝖊𝖉 𝖙𝖍𝖊 𝖘𝖆𝖎𝖉 Pretender, Pseudo-
Poet, 𝖔𝖗 Phantom, 𝖚𝖙𝖙𝖊𝖗𝖑𝖞 to vanish, 𝖆𝖓𝖉 evaporate 𝖔𝖚𝖙 𝖔𝖋 𝖙𝖍𝖎𝖘
𝖜𝖔𝖗𝖐:[2] 𝕬𝖓𝖉 𝖉𝖔 𝖉𝖊𝖈𝖑𝖆𝖗𝖊 𝖙𝖍𝖊 𝖘𝖆𝖎𝖉 𝕿𝖍𝖗𝖔𝖓𝖊 𝖔𝖋 𝕻𝖔𝖊𝖘𝖞 𝖋𝖗𝖔𝖒 𝖍𝖊𝖓𝖈𝖊𝖋𝖔𝖗𝖙𝖍
to be 𝖆𝖇𝖉𝖎𝖈𝖆𝖙𝖊𝖉 𝖆𝖓𝖉 𝖛𝖆𝖈𝖆𝖓𝖙, 𝖚𝖓𝖑𝖊𝖘𝖘 𝖉𝖚𝖑𝖞 𝖆𝖓𝖉 𝖑𝖆𝖜𝖋𝖚𝖑𝖑𝖞 𝖘𝖚𝖕𝖕𝖑𝖎𝖊𝖉 𝖇𝖞
𝖙𝖍𝖊 LAUREATE himself. 𝕬𝖓𝖉 𝖎𝖙 𝖎𝖘 𝖍𝖊𝖗𝖊𝖇𝖞 𝖊𝖓𝖆𝖈𝖙𝖊𝖉, 𝖙𝖍𝖆𝖙 𝖓𝖔 𝖔𝖙𝖍𝖊𝖗
𝖕𝖊𝖗𝖘𝖔𝖓 𝖉𝖔 𝖕𝖗𝖊𝖘𝖚𝖒𝖊 𝖙𝖔 𝖋𝖎𝖑𝖑 𝖙𝖍𝖊 𝖘𝖆𝖒𝖊.

ƆC. Ch.[3]

[1] ⟨Though Warburton, Pope's friend and literary executor, initialled
this Advertisement, it was probably written by Pope.⟩

[2] ⟨Theobald still appears, however, at i 133, 286, and in several of
the notes.⟩

[3] ⟨Intended to suggest the monogram of the Lord Chamberlain,
Charles, second Duke of Grafton.⟩

Martinus Scriblerus
his
Prolegomena and Illustrations
to the
Dunciad:

WITH THE
HYPER-CRITICS OF ARISTARCHUS

DENNIS, REMARKS ON PR. ARTHUR
⟨See p. 324.⟩

A LETTER TO THE PUBLISHER,
OCCASIONED BY THE FIRST CORRECT
EDITION OF THE DUNCIAD
⟨See pp. 318–324.⟩

TESTIMONIES OF AUTHORS
CONCERNING OUR POET AND HIS WORKS
⟨See pp. 325–343.⟩

MARTINUS SCRIBLERUS
OF THE POEM
⟨See pp. 343–349.⟩

Ricardus Aristarchus of the Hero of the Poem

Of the Nature of *Dunciad* in general, whence derived, and on what authority founded, as well as of the art and conduct of this our poem in particular, the learned and laborious Scriblerus hath, according to his manner, and with tolerable share of judgment, dissertated. But when he cometh to speak of the *Person* of the *Hero* fitted for such poem, in truth he miserably halts and hallucinates. For, misled by one Monsieur Bossu, a Gallic critic, he prateth of I cannot tell what *Phantom of a Hero*, only raised up to support the Fable. A putid conceit! As if Homer and Virgil, like modern Undertakers, who first build their house and then seek out for a tenant, had contrived the story of a War and a Wandering, before they once thought either of Achilles or Æneas. We shall therefore set our good brother and the world also right in this particular, by giving our word, that in the *greater Epic*, the prime intention of the Muse is to exalt Heroic Virtue, in order to propagate the love of it among the children of men; and consequently that the Poet's first thought must needs be turned upon a real subject meet for laud and celebration; not one whom he is to make, but one whom he may find, truly illustrious. This is the *primum mobile* of his poetic world, whence every thing is to receive life and motion. For this subject being found, he is immediately ordained, or rather acknowledged, an *Hero*, and put upon such action as befitteth the dignity of his character.

But the Muse ceases not here her Eagle-flight. Sometimes, satiated with the contemplation of these *Suns* of glory, she turneth downward on her wing, and darts like lightning on the *Goose* and *Serpent* kind. For we may apply to the Muse in her various moods, what an ancient master of Wisdom affirmeth of the Gods in general: *Si Dii non irascuntur impiis et injustis, nec pios utique justosque diligunt. In rebus enim diversis, aut in utramque partem moveri necesse est, aut in neutram. Itaque qui bonos diligit, & malos odit; & qui malos non odit, nec bonos diligit. Quia & diligere bonos ex odio malorum venit; & malos odisse ex bonorum caritate descendit.* Which in the vernacular idiom may be thus interpreted: 'If the Gods be not provoked at evil men, neither are they delighted with the good and just. For contrary objects must either excite contrary affections, or no affections at all. So that he who loveth good men, must at the same time hate the bad; and he who hateth not bad men, cannot love the good; because to love good men proceedeth from an aversion to evil, and to hate evil men from a tenderness to the good.' From this delicacy of the Muse arose the *little Epic*, (more lively and choleric than her elder sister, whose bulk and complexion incline her to the flegmatic) and for this some notorious Vehicle of vice and folly was sought out, to make thereof an example. An early instance of which (nor could it escape the accurate Scriblerus) the Father of Epic poem himself affordeth us. From him the practice descended to the Greek Dramatic poets, his offspring; who in the composition of their *Tetralogy*, or set of four pieces, were wont to make the last a *Satyric Tragedy*. Happily one of these ancient *Dunciads* (as we may well term it) is come down to us amongst the Tragedies of Euripides. And what doth the reader think may be the subject? Why truly, and it is worth his observation, the unequal Contention of an *old, dull, debauched, buffoon Cyclops*, with the heaven-directed *Favourite of* Minerva; who after having quietly born all the monster's obscene and impious ribaldry, endeth the farce in punishing him with the mark of an indelible brand in his *forehead*. May we not then be excused, if for the future we consider the Epics of Homer, Virgil, and Milton, together with this our poem, as a complete *Tetralogy*, in which the last worthily holdeth the place or station of the *satyric* piece?

Proceed we therefore in our subject. It hath been long, and alas for pity! still remaineth a question, whether the Hero of the *greater Epic* should be an *honest man?* or, as the French critics express it, *un honnête homme*[a]; but it never admitted of any doubt that the Hero of the *little Epic* should *not* be so. Hence, to the advantage of our *Dunciad*, we may observe how much juster the *Moral* of that Poem must needs be, where so important a question is previously decided.

But then it is not every Knave, nor (let me add) Fool, that is a fit subject for a Dunciad. There must still exist some Analogy, if not Resemblance of Qualities, between the Heroes of the two Poems; and this in order to admit what Neoteric critics call the *Parody*, one of the liveliest graces of the little Epic. Thus it being agreed that the constituent qualities of the greater Epic Hero, are *Wisdom, Bravery,* and *Love,* from whence springeth *heroic Virtue*; it followeth that those of the lesser Epic Hero, should be *Vanity, Impudence,* and *Debauchery,* from which happy assemblage resulteth *heroic Dulness,* the never-dying subject of this our Poem.

This being confessed, come we now to particulars. It is the character of true *Wisdom,* to seek its chief support and confidence within itself; and to place that support in the resources which proceed from a conscious rectitude of Will.—And are the advantages of *Vanity,* when arising to the heroic standard, at all short of this self-complacence? Nay, are they not, in the opinion of the enamoured owner, far beyond it? 'Let the world' (will such an one say) 'impute to me what Folly or weakness they please; but till *Wisdom* can give me something that will make me more heartily happy, I am content to be GAZED AT[b].' This we see is *Vanity* according to the *heroic* gage or measure; not that low and ignoble species which pretendeth to *Virtues* we *have not,* but the laudable ambition of being *gazed at* for glorying in those *Vices* which all the world know *we have.* 'The world may ask (says he) why I make my follies publick? Why not? I have passed my time very pleasantly with them[c].' In short, there is no sort of Vanity such a Hero would scruple, but that which might go near to degrade him from his high station in this our Dunciad; namely, 'Whether it would not be *Vanity* in him, to take shame to himself for *not being a wise man*[d]?'

Bravery, the second attribute of the true Hero, is Courage manifesting itself in every limb; while, in its correspondent virtue in the mock Hero, that Courage is all collected into the *Face.* And

---

[a] Si un Heros Poëtique doit être un honnête homme. Bossu, du Poême Epique, lib. v. ch. 5.
[b] Dedication to the Life of C.C.   [c] Life, p. 2. octavo Ed.
[d] Life, ibid.

as Power when drawn together, must needs be more strong than when dispersed, we generally find this kind of courage in so high and heroic a degree, that it insults not only Men, but Gods. Mezentius is without doubt the bravest character in all the Æneis; but how? His bravery, we know, was an high courage of blasphemy. And can we say less of this brave man's, who having told us that he placed 'his *Summum bonum* in those follies, which he was not content barely to possess but would likewise glory in,' adds, '*If I am misguided,* 'TIS NATURE'S FAULT, *and I follow* HER[e].' Nor can we be mistaken in making this happy quality a species of *Courage,* when we consider those illustrious marks of it, which made his *Face* 'more known (as he justly boasteth) than most in the kingdom,' and his *Language* to consist of what we must allow to be the most *daring* Figure of Speech, that which is taken from the *Name of God.*

Gentle Love, the next ingredient in the true Hero's composition, is a mere bird of passage, or (as Shakespear calls it) *summerteeming Lust,* and evaporates in the heat of *Youth;* doubtless by that refinement it suffers in passing through those *certain strainers* which our Poet somewhere speaketh of. But when it is let alone to work upon the *Lees,* it acquireth strength by *Old age;* and becometh a standing ornament to the little Epic. It is true indeed, there is one objection to its fitness for such an use: For not only the Ignorant may think it *common,* but it is admitted to be so, even by Him who best knoweth its nature. 'Don't you think (saith he) to say only *a man has his Whore,* ought to go for little or nothing? Because *defendit numerus,* take the first ten thousand men you meet, and I believe you would be no loser if you betted ten to one, that every single sinner of them, one with another, had been guilty of the same frailty[f].' But here he seemeth not to have done himself justice: The man is sure enough a Hero, who has his Lady at fourscore. How doth his Modesty herein lessen the merit of a *whole wellspent* Life: not taking to himself the commendation (which *Horace* accounted the greatest in a theatrical character) of continuing to the very *dregs,* the same he was from the beginning,

> —— *Servetur ad* IMUM
> *Qualis ab incepto processerat* ——

But let us farther remark, that the calling her *his* whore, implieth she was *his own,* and not his *neighbour*'s. Truly a commendable Continence! and such as Scipio himself must have applauded. For how much Self-denial was necessary not to covet his Neighbour's whore? and what disorders must the coveting her have occasioned,

---

[•] Life, p. 23 octavo.   [f] Letter to Mr. P. p. 46.

in that Society, where (according to this Political Calculator) *nine* in *ten* of all ages have their *concubines?*

We have now, as briefly as we could devise, gone through the three constituent Qualities of either Hero. But it is not in any, or all of these, that Heroism properly or essentially resideth. It is a lucky result rather from the collision of these lively Qualities against one another. Thus, as from Wisdom, Bravery, and Love, ariseth *Magnanimity*, the object of *Admiration*, which is the aim of the greater Epic; so from Vanity, Impudence, and Debauchery springeth *Buffoonry*, the source of *Ridicule*, that 'laughing ornament,' as he well termeth itᵍ, of the little Epic.

He is not ashamed (God forbid he ever should be ashamed!) of this Character; who deemeth, that not *Reason* but *Risibility* distinguisheth the human species from the brutal. 'As Nature (saith this profound Philosopher) distinguished our species from the mute creation by our Risibility, her design MUST have been by *that faculty* as evidently to raise our HAPPINESS, as by OUR *os sublime* (OUR ERECTED FACES) to lift the dignity of our FORM above themʰ.' All this considered, how complete a Hero must he be, as well as how *happy* a Man, whose Risibility lieth not barely in his *muscles* as in the common sort, but (as himself informeth us) in his very *spirits?* And whose *Os sublime* is not simply an *erect face*, but a Brazen head, as should seem by his comparing it with one of Iron, said to belong to the late king of Swedenⁱ!

But whatever personal qualities a Hero may have, the examples of Achilles and Æneas shew us, that all those are of small avail, without the constant *assistance of the* GODS: for the subversion and erection of Empires have never been judged the work of Man. How greatly soever then we may esteem of his high talents, we can hardly conceive his personal prowess alone sufficient to restore the decayed empire of Dulness. So weighty an atchievement must require the particular favour and protection of the GREAT: who being the natural patrons and supporters of *Letters*, as the ancient Gods were of *Troy*, must first be drawn off and engaged in another Interest, before the total subversion of them can be accomplished. To surmount, therefore, this last and greatest difficulty, we have in this excellent man a professed Favourite and Intimado of the Great. And look of what force ancient Piety was to draw the Gods into the party of Æneas, that, and much stronger is modern Incense, to engage the Great in the party of Dulness.

Thus have we essayed to pourtray or shadow out this noble Imp of Fame. But now the impatient reader will be apt to say, if so many

ᵍ Letter to Mr. P. p. 31.
ʰ Life, p. 23, 24.   ⁱ Letter, p. 8.

and various graces go to the making up a Hero, what mortal shall suffice to bear this character? Ill hath he read, who sees not in every trace of this picture, that *individual*, ALL-ACCOMPLISHED PERSON, in whom these rare virtues and lucky circumstances have agreed to meet and concentre with the strongest lustre and fullest harmony.

The good Scriblerus indeed, nay the World itself might be imposed on in the late spurious editions, by I can't tell what *Sham-hero*, or *Phantom:* But it was not so easy to impose on HIM whom this egregious error most of all concerned. For no sooner had the fourth book laid open the high and swelling scene, but he recognized his own heroic Acts: And when he came to the words,

Soft on her lap her Laureat son reclines,

(though *Laureat* imply no more than *one crowned with laurel*, as befitteth any Associate or Consort in Empire) he ROAR'D (like a Lion) and VINDICATED HIS RIGHT OF FAME: Indeed not without cause, he being there represented as *fast asleep*; so unbeseeming the eye of Empire, which, like that of Providence, should never slumber. 'Hah! (saith he) fast asleep it seems! that's a little too strong. Pert and dull at least you might have allowed me, but as seldom asleep as any fool[k].' However, the injured Hero may comfort himself with this reflexion, that tho' it be *sleep*, yet it is not the *sleep of death*, but of *immortality*. Here he will[l] *live* at least, tho' not *awake*; and in no worse condition than many an enchanted Warrior before him. The famous *Durandarte*, for instance, was, like him, cast into a long slumber by *Merlin* the *British Bard* and Necromancer: and his example, for submitting to it with so good a grace, might be of use to our Hero. For this disastrous knight being sorely pressed or driven to make his answer by several *persons of quality*, only replied with a sigh, *Patience, and shuffle the cards*[m].

But now, as nothing in this world, no not the most sacred or perfect things either of Religion or Government, can escape the teeth or tongue of Envy, methinks I already hear these carpers objecting to the clear title of our Hero.

'It would never (say they) have been esteemed sufficient to make an Hero for the Iliad or Æneis, that Achilles was brave enough to overturn one Empire, or Æneas pious enough to raise another, had they not been Goddess-born, and Princes bred. What then did this Author mean, by erecting a Player instead of one of his Patrons, (a person never a hero even on the Stage[n]) to this dignity of Collegue in the empire of Dulness, and Atchiever of a work

[k] Letter, p. 53.   [l] Letter, p. 1.
[m] Don Quixote, Part ii. Book ii. ch. 22.   [n] See Life, p. 148.

that neither old Omar, Attila, nor John of Leiden could entirely compass ?'

To all this we have, as we conceive, a sufficient answer from the Roman historian, *Fabrum esse suæ quemque fortunæ: Every man is the* Smith *of his own fortune*. The politic Florentine Nicholas Machiavel goeth still farther, and affirms that a man needs but to *believe himself a Hero* to be one of the best. 'Let him (saith he) but fancy himself capable of the highest things, and he will of course be able to atchieve them.' Laying this down as a principle, it will certainly and incontestably follow, that, if ever Hero *was* such a character, OURS *is:* For if ever man *thought* himself such, OURS *doth*. Hear how he constantly paragons himself, at one time to ALEXANDER the Great and CHARLES the XII. of SWEDEN, for the excess and delicacy of his Ambition[o]; to HENRY the IV. of FRANCE, for honest Policy[p]; to the first BRUTUS, for love of Liberty[q]; and to Sir ROBERT WALPOLE, for good Government while in power[r]: At another time, to the godlike SOCRATES, for his diversions and amusements[s]; to HORACE, MONTAIGNE, and Sir WILLIAM TEMPLE, for an elegant Vanity that makes them for ever read and admired[t]; to TWO Lord CHANCELLORS, for Law, from whom, when confederate against him at the bar, he carried away the prize of Eloquence[v]; and, to say all in a word, to the right reverend the Lord BISHOP of LONDON himself, in the art of writing *pastoral letters*[w].

Nor did his *Actions* fall short of the sublimity of his Conceptions. In his early youth he *met the Revolution* at Nottingham[x] face to face, at a time when his betters contented themselves with *following* her. [It was here he got acquainted with *Old Battle-array*,[1] of whom he hath made so honourable mention in one of his immortal Odes.] But he shone in Courts as well as Camps: He was *called up* when *the nation fell in labour* of this *Revolution*[y]*:* and was a gossip at her christening, with the Bishop and the ladies.[z]

As to his *Birth*, it is true he pretendeth no relation either to Heathen God or Goddess; but, what is as good, he was descended from a *Maker* of both[a]. And that he did not pass himself on the world for a Hero, as well by birth as education, was his own fault: For, his

[o] Life, p. 149.   [p] P. 424.   [q] P. 366.   [r] P. 457.
[s] P. 18.   [t] P. 425.   [v] P. 436, 437.   [w] P. 52.   [x] P. 47.
[1] *Battle-array* ⟨'*Old Battle-array*' is a gibe at Cibber's New-Year ode for 1733 (*Gent. Mag.* iii 40). He had allowed himself to write:

> As freedom the jewel of life is,
> 'Twas bought by old battle-array.⟩

[y] P. 57.   [z] P. 58, 59.
[a] A Statuary. ⟨I.e. Caius Gabriel Cibber, 1630–1700. He executed a Pallas and an Apollo for the first Duke of Devonshire.⟩

lineage he bringeth into his life as an Anecdote, and is sensible he had it in his power *to be thought no body's son at all*[b]*:* And what is that but coming into the world a Hero?

[But be it, (the punctilious Laws of Epic Poesy so requiring) that a Hero of more than mortal birth must needs be had, even for this we have a remedy. We can easily derive our Hero's Pedigree from a Goddess of no small power and authority amongst men; and legitimate and install him after the right classical and authentic fashion: For, like as the ancient Sages found a Son of Mars in a mighty warrior; a Son of Neptune in a skilful Seaman; a Son of Phœbus in a harmonious Poet; so have we here, if need be, a Son of FORTUNE in an artful *Gamester*. And who fitter than the Off-spring of *Chance*, to assist in restoring the Empire of *Night* and *Chaos* ?]

There is in truth another objection of greater weight, namely, 'That this Hero still existeth, and hath not yet finished his earthly course. For if Solon said well, that no man could be called happy till his death, surely much less can any one, till then, be pronounced a Hero: this species of men being far more subject than others to the caprices of Fortune and Humour.' But to this also we have an answer, that will be deemed (we hope) decisive. It cometh from *himself*, who, to cut this dispute short, hath solemnly protested that *he will never change or amend.*

With regard to his *Vanity*, he declareth that nothing shall ever part them. 'Nature (saith he) hath amply supplied me in Vanity; a pleasure which neither the pertness of Wit, nor the gravity of Wisdom, will ever persuade me to part with[c].' Our poet had charitably endeavoured to administer a cure to it: But he telleth us plainly, 'My superiors perhaps may be mended by him; but for my part I own myself incorrigible. I look upon my Follies as the best part of my Fortune[d].' And with good reason: We see to what they have brought him!

Secondly, as to *Buffoonry*, 'Is it (saith he) a time of day for me to leave off these fooleries, and set up a new character? I can no more put off my Follies than my Skin; I have often tried, but they stick too close to me; nor am I sure my friends are displeased with them, for in this light I afford them frequent matter of mirth, *&c. &c.*[e].' Having then so publickly declared himself *incorrigible*, he is become *dead in law*, (I mean the *law Epopœian*) and descendeth to the Poet as his property: who may take him, and deal with him, as if he had been dead as long as an old Egyptian hero; that is to say, *embowel* and *embalm him for posterity.*

Nothing therefore (we conceive) remains to hinder his own

[b] Life, p. 6.   [c] P. 424.   [d] P. 19.   [e] P. 17.

Prophecy of himself from taking immediate effect. A rare felicity! and what few prophets have had the satisfaction to see, alive! Nor can we conclude better than with that extraordinary one of his, which is conceived in these Oraculous words, MY DULNESS WILL FIND SOMEBODY TO DO IT RIGHT*.

> [*Tandem Phœbus adest, morsusque inferre parantem*
> *Congeleat, et patulos, ut erant, INDURAT hiatus.*]⁸

* Ibid. p. 243. octavo edit.
⁸ [*Ovid*, of the serpent biting at Orpheus's head.]

ARGUMENT TO BOOK THE FIRST

The Proposition, the Invocation, and the Inscription. Then the Original of the great Empire of Dulness, and cause of the continuance thereof. The College of the Goddess in the City, with her private Academy for Poets in particular; the Governors of it, and the four Cardinal Virtues. Then the Poem hastes into the midst of things, presenting her, on the evening of a Lord Mayor's day, revolving the long succession of her Sons, and the glories past and to come. She fixes her eye on Bays to be the Instrument of that great Event which is the Subject of the Poem. He is described pensive among his Books, giving up the Cause, and apprehending the Period of her Empire: After debating whether to betake himself to the Church, or to Gaming, or to Party-writing, he raises an Altar of proper books, and (making first his solemn prayer and declaration) purposes thereon to sacrifice all his unsuccessful writings. As the pile is kindled, the Goddess beholding the flame from her seat, flies and puts it out by casting upon it the poem of Thulé. She forthwith reveals herself to him, transports him to her Temple, unfolds her Arts, and initiates him into her Mysteries; then announcing the death of Eusden the Poet Laureate, anoints him, carries him to Court, and proclaims him Successor.

> The Mighty Mother, and her Son who brings
> The Smithfield Muses to the ear of Kings,

The DUNCIAD, sic. MS. It may well be disputed whether this be a right reading: Ought it not rather to be spelled *Dunceiad*, as the Etymology evidently demands? *Dunce* with an *e*, therefore *Dunceiad* with an *e*. That accurate and punctual Man of Letters, the Restorer of *Shakespeare*, constantly observes the preservation of this very Letter *e*, in spelling the Name of his beloved Author, and not like his common careless Editors, with the omission of one, nay sometimes of two *ee*'s, [as *Shakspear*] which is utterly unpardonable. 'Nor is the neglect of a *Single Letter* so trivial as to some it may appear; the alteration whereof in a learned language is an

Atchievement that brings honour to the Critic who advances it; and Dr. Bentley will be remembered to posterity for his performances of this sort as long as the world shall have any esteem for the remains of Menander and Philemon.' THEOBALD. ⟨Cf. A i i *n*.⟩

This is surely a slip in the learned author of the foregoing note; there having been since produced by an accurate Antiquary, an *Autograph* of *Shakspeare* himself, whereby it appears that he spelled his own name without the first *e*. And upon this authority it was, that those most Critical Curators of his Monument in Westminster Abby erased the former wrong reading, and restored the true spelling on a new piece of old Ægyptian Granite. Nor for this only do they deserve our thanks, but for exhibiting on the same Monument the first Specimen of an *Edition* of an author in *Marble*; where (as may be seen on comparing the Tomb with the Book) in the space of five lines, two Words and a whole Verse are changed, and it is to be hoped will there stand, and outlast whatever hath been hitherto done in Paper; as for the future, our Learned Sister University (the other Eye of England) is taking care to perpetuate a *Total new Shakespear*, at the Clarendon press. BENTL.

It is to be noted, that this great Critic also has omitted one circumstance; which is, that the Inscription with the Name of Shakspeare was intended to be placed on the Marble Scroll to which he points with his hand; instead of which it is now placed behind his back, and that Specimen of an Edition is put on the Scroll, which indeed Shakspeare hath great reason to point at. ANON.

Though I have as just a value for the letter *E* . . . SCRIBLERUS ⟨A i i⟩.

This Poem was written in the year 1726 . . . SCHOL. VET. ⟨A i i⟩.

It was expresly confessed in the Preface to the first edition, that this Poem was not published by the Author himself. It was printed originally in a foreign Country. And what foreign Country? Why, one notorious for blunders; where finding blanks only instead of proper names, these blunderers filled them up at their pleasure.

The very *Hero* of the Poem hath been mistaken to this hour; so that we are obliged to open our Notes with a discovery who he really was. We learn from the former Editor, that this Piece was presented by the Hands of Sir Robert Walpole to King George II. Now the author directly tells us, his Hero is the Man

————*who brings*
The Smithfield Muses to the ear of Kings.

And it is notorious who was the person on whom this Prince conferred the honour of the *Laurel*.

It appears as plainly from the *Apostrophe* to the *Great* in the third verse, that Tibbald could not be the person, who was never an Author in fashion, or caressed by the Great; whereas this single characteristic is sufficient to point out the true Hero; who, above all other Poets of his time, was the *Peculiar Delight* and *Chosen Companion* of the Nobility of England; and wrote, as he himself tells us, certain of his Works at the *earnest Desire* of *Persons of Quality*.

Lastly, The sixth verse affords full proof; this Poet being the only one who was universally known to have had a *Son* ⟨Theophilus Cibber.⟩ so exactly like him, in his poetical, theatrical, political, and moral Capacities, that it could justly be said of him

Still Dunce the second reign'd like Dunce the first.

BENTL.

I sing. Say you, her instruments the Great!
Call'd to this work by Dulness, Jove, and Fate;
You by whose care, in vain decry'd and curst,   5
Still Dunce the second reigns like Dunce the first;
Say how the Goddess bade Britannia sleep,
And pour'd her Spirit o'er the land and deep.

In eldest time, e'er mortals writ or read,
E'er Pallas issu'd from the Thund'rer's head,   10
Dulness o'er all possess'd her ancient right,
Daughter of Chaos and eternal Night:
Fate in their dotage this fair Ideot gave,
Gross as her sire, and as her mother grave,
Laborious, heavy, busy, bold, and blind,   15
She rul'd, in native Anarchy, the mind.

Still her old Empire to restore she tries,
For, born a Goddess, Dulness never dies.

O Thou! whatever title please thine ear,
Dean, Drapier, Bickerstaff, or Gulliver!   20
Whether thou chuse Cervantes' serious air,
Or laugh and shake in Rab'lais' easy chair,
Or praise the Court, or magnify Mankind,

---

1. *her Son who brings, &c.*] Wonderful is the stupidity . . . SCRIBLERUS ⟨A 1 i⟩.

2. *The Smithfield Muses*] *Smithfield* is the place . . . Court and Town ⟨A i 2⟩. This happened in the Reigns of King George I, and II. See Book 3.

12. *Daughter of Chaos, &c.* ⟨A i 10⟩.

15. *Laborious, heavy, busy, bold, &c.*] I wonder the learned Scriblerus has omitted to advertise the Reader, at the opening of this Poem, that Dulness here is not to be taken contractedly for mere Stupidity, but in the enlarged sense of the word, for all Slowness of Apprehension, Shortness of Sight, or imperfect Sense of things. It includes (as we see by the Poet's own words) Labour, Industry, and some degree of Activity and Boldness: a ruling principle not inert, but turning topsy-turvy the Understanding, and inducing an Anarchy or confused State of Mind. This remark ought to be carried along with the reader throughout the work; and without this caution he will be apt to mistake the Importance of many of the Characters, as well as of the Design of the Poet. Hence it is that some have complained he chuses too mean a subject, and imagined he employs himself, like Domitian, in killing flies; whereas those who have the true key will find he sports with nobler quarry, and embraces a larger compass; or (as one saith, on a like occasion)

> *Will see his Work, like Jacob's ladder, rise,*
> *Its foot in dirt, its head amid the skies.*

BENTL.

17. *Still her old Empire to restore*] This Restoration makes the Completion of the Poem. *Vide* Book 4.

23. *Or praise the Court, &c.* ⟨A i 21⟩.

Or thy griev'd Country's copper chains unbind;
From thy Bœotia tho' her Pow'r retires,   25
Mourn not, my SWIFT, at ought our Realm acquires,
Here pleas'd behold her mighty wings out-spread
To hatch a new Saturnian age of Lead.
  Close to those walls where Folly holds her throne,
And laughs to think Monroe would take her down,   30
Where o'er the gates, by his fam'd father's hand
Great Cibber's brazen, brainless brothers stand;
One Cell there is, conceal'd from vulgar eye,
The Cave of Poverty and Poetry.
Keen, hollow winds howl thro' the bleak recess,   35
Emblem of Music caus'd by Emptiness.
Hence Bards, like Proteus long in vain ty'd down,
Escape·in Monsters, and amaze the town.
Hence Miscellanies spring, the weekly boast
Of Curl's chaste press, and Lintot's rubric post: 40
Hence hymning Tyburn's elegiac lines,
Hence Journals, Medleys, Merc'ries, Magazines:

28. *To hatch a new Saturnian age of Lead*] The ancient . . . Lead
⟨A i 26⟩. She is said here only to be spreading her wings to hatch this
age; which is not produced completely till the fourth book.

30. *Monroe* ⟨James Monro, M.D., 1680–1752, physician to Bethlehem
Hospital for the insane—the place 'where Folly holds her throne' (l. 29).⟩

31. *By his fam'd father's hand*] Mr. Caius-Gabriel Cibber, father of the
Poet Laureate. The two Statues of the Lunatics over the gates of Bedlam-
hospital were done by him, and (as the son justly says of them) are no ill
monuments of his fame as an Artist.

34. *Poverty and Poetry*] I cannot here omit a remark that will greatly
endear our Author to every one, who shall attentively observe that
Humanity and Candor, which every where appears in him towards those
unhappy objects of the ridicule of all mankind, the bad Poets. He here
imputes . . . to be satyrized ⟨A i 41⟩.

37. *Hence Bards, like Proteus*]

> *Sunt quibus in plures jus est transire figuras:*
> *Ut tibi, complexi terram maris incola, Proteu;*
> *Nunc* violentus aper, *nunc quem tetigisse timerent,*
> Anguis *eras, modo te faciebant* cornua Taurum,
> *Sæpe* Lapis *poteras.*
>   Ovid. Met. viii ⟨730 ff.⟩.

40. *Curl's chaste press, &c.* ⟨A i 38⟩.

41, 42. *Hence hymning Tyburn's* ⟨A i 39⟩.

41. *Hence hymning Tyburn's elegiac lines*] It is an ancient English
custom . . . before ⟨A i 39⟩.

42. *Magazines*] Miscellanies in prose and verse, in which at some times

> ——*new-born nonsense first is taught to cry;*

at others, dead-born Dulness appears in a thousand shapes. These were
thrown out weekly and monthly by every miserable scribler; or picked up

Sepulchral Lyes, our holy walls to grace,
And New-year Odes, and all the Grub-street race.
  In clouded Majesty here Dulness shone; 45
Four guardian Virtues, round, support her throne:
Fierce champion Fortitude, that knows no fears
Of hisses, blows, or want, or loss of ears:
Calm Temperance, whose blessings those partake
Who hunger, and who thirst for scribling sake: 50
Prudence, whose glass presents th' approaching jayl:
Poetic Justice, with her lifted scale,
Where, in nice balance, truth with gold she weighs,
And solid pudding against empty praise.
  Here she beholds the Chaos dark and deep, 55
Where nameless Somethings in their causes sleep,
'Till genial Jacob, or a warm Third day,
Call forth each mass, a Poem, or a Play:
How hints, like spawn, scarce quick in embryo lie,
How new-born nonsense first is taught to cry, 60
Maggots half-form'd in rhyme exactly meet,
And learn to crawl upon poetic feet.
Here one poor word an hundred clenches makes,
And ductile dulness new meanders takes;
There motley Images her fancy strike, 65
Figures ill pair'd, and Similies unlike.
She sees a Mob of Metaphors advance,
Pleas'd with the madness of the mazy dance:
How Tragedy and Comedy embrace;
How Farce and Epic get a jumbled race; 70

---

piece-meal and stolen from any body, under the title of Papers, Essays, Queries, Verses, Epigrams, Riddles, &c. equally the disgrace of human Wit, Morality, and Decency. P. W.

  43. *Sepulchral Lyes* ⟨A i 41⟩.
  44. *New-year Odes*] Made by the Poet Laureate for the time being, to be sung at Court on every New-year's day, the words of which are happily drowned in the voices and instruments. ⟨Cf. A i 40.⟩ The *New-year Odes* of the Hero of this work were of a cast distinguished from all that preceded him, and made a conspicuous part of his character as a writer, which doubtless induced our Author to mention them here so particularly.
  45. *In clouded Majesty* ⟨A i 43⟩.
  47. ——*that knows no fears, &c.* ⟨A i 45–6⟩.
  50. *Who hunger, and who thirst, &c.* ⟨A i 48⟩.
  55. *Here she beholds, &c.* ⟨A i 53⟩.
  63. *Here one poor word, &c.* ⟨A i 61⟩.
  64. *And ductile Dulness, &c.* ⟨A i 62⟩.
  70, *&c. How Farce and Epic, &c.* ⟨A i 68⟩.

How Time himself stands still at her command,
Realms shift their place, and Ocean turns to land.
Here gay Description Ægypt glads with show'rs,
Or gives to Zembla fruits, to Barca flow'rs;
Glitt'ring with ice here hoary hills are seen,　　　　75
There painted vallies of eternal green,
In cold December fragrant chaplets blow,
And heavy harvests nod beneath the snow.
　　All these, and more, the cloud-compelling Queen
Beholds thro' fogs, that magnify the scene.　　　　80
She, tinsel'd o'er in robes of varying hues,
With self-applause her wild creation views;
Sees momentary monsters rise and fall,
And with her own fools-colours gilds them all.
　　'Twas on the day, when * * rich and grave,　　　　85
Like Cimon, triumph'd both on land and wave:
(Pomps without guilt, of bloodless swords and maces,
Glad chains, warm furs, broad banners, and broad faces)
Now Night descending, the proud scene was o'er,
But liv'd, in Settle's numbers, one day more.　　　　90
Now May'rs and Shrieves all hush'd and satiate lay,
Yet eat, in dreams, the custard of the day;
While pensive Poets painful vigils keep,
Sleepless themselves, to give their readers sleep.
Much to the mindful Queen the feast recalls　　　　95
What City Swans once sung within the walls;
Much she revolves their arts, their ancient praise,
And sure succession down from Heywood's days.
She saw, with joy, the line immortal run,
Each sire imprest and glaring in his son:　　　　100
So watchful Bruin forms, with plastic care,
Each growing lump, and brings it to a Bear.
She saw old Pryn in restless Daniel shine,

73. *Ægypt glads with show'rs* ⟨A i 71⟩.
79. *The cloud-compelling Queen* ⟨A i 77⟩.
85, 86. *'Twas on the Day, when * * rich and grave, Like Cimon, triumph'd*]
Viz. a Lord Mayor's Day; his name the author had left in blanks, but most
certainly could never be that which the Editor foisted in formerly, and
which no way agrees with the chronology of the poem. BENTL.
　The Procession . . . Barbarians ⟨A i 83⟩.
88. *Glad chains* ⟨A i 86⟩.
90. *But liv'd, in Settle's numbers* ⟨A i 88⟩.
　Ibid. *But liv'd, in Settle's numbers, one day more*] Settle was poet to the
City of London. His office . . . that place ⟨A i 88⟩.
98. *Heywood* ⟨A i 96⟩.
103. *Old Pryn, &c.* ⟨A i 101⟩.

And Eusden eke out Blackmore's endless line;
She saw slow Philips creep like Tate's poor page,   105
And all the mighty Mad in Dennis rage.
   In each she marks her Image full exprest,
But chief in BAYS's monster-breeding breast;
Bays, form'd by nature Stage and Town to bless,
And act, and be, a Coxcomb with success.   110
Dulness with transport eyes the lively Dunce,
Remembring she herself was Pertness once.
Now (shame to Fortune!) an ill Run at Play
Blank'd his bold visage, and a thin Third day:

104. *And Eusden eke out, &c.*] Laurence Eusden . . . reflection ⟨A iii 319⟩. Nor ought Mr. Oldmixon to complain, so long after, that the Laurel would have better become his own brows, or any other's: It were more decent to acquiesce in the opinion of the Duke of *Buckingham* upon this matter:

> ——*In rush'd Eusden, and cry'd, Who shall have it,*
> *But I, the true Laureate, to whom the King gave it?*
> *Apollo beg'd pardon, and granted his claim,*
> *But vow'd that 'till then he ne'er heard of his name.*
> Session of Poets

The same plea might also serve for his successor, Mr. Cibber; and is further strengthened in the following Epigram, made on that occasion:

> *In merry old England it once was a rule,*
> *The King had his Poet, and also his Fool:*
> *But now we're so frugal, I'd have you to know it,*
> *That Cibber can serve both for Fool and for Poet.*

Of Blackmore, see Book 2. Of Philips, Book 1, ver. 258. and Book 3. *prope fin.*

Nahum Tate . . . mentioned ⟨A i 103⟩.

106. *And all the mighty Mad* ⟨A i 104⟩.

106. *And all the mighty Mad in Dennis rage*] Mr. Theobald, in the Censor . . . p. 286 ⟨A i 104⟩.

109. *Bays, formd by Nature, &c.*] It is hoped the poet here hath done full justice to his Hero's Character, which it were a great mistake to imagine was wholly sunk in stupidity; he is allowed to have supported it with a wonderful mixture of Vivacity. This character is heightened according to his own desire, in a Letter he wrote to our author. 'Pert and dull at least you might have allowed me. What! am I only to be dull, and dull still, and again, and for ever?' He then solemnly appealed to his own conscience, that 'he could not think himself so, nor believe that our poet did; but that he spoke worse of him than he could possibly think; and concluded it must be merely to shew his *Wit*, or for some *Profit* or *Lucre* to himself.' Life of C. C. chap. vii. and Letter to Mr. P. pag. 15. 40. 53.

113. *shame to Fortune!*] Because she usually shews favour to persons of this Character, who have a three-fold pretence to it.

114. *Blank'd* ⟨Either to whiten, make pale; or, to put out of countenance.⟩

Third day ⟨Cf. A i 55n.⟩

Swearing and supperless the Hero sate,   115
Blasphem'd his Gods, the Dice, and damn'd his Fate.
Then gnaw'd his pen, then dash'd it on the ground,
Sinking from thought to thought, a vast profound!
Plung'd for his sense, but found no bottom there,
Yet wrote and flounder'd on, in mere despair.   120
Round him much Embryo, much Abortion lay,
Much future Ode, and abdicated Play;
Nonsense precipitate, like running Lead,
That slip'd thro' Cracks and Zig-zags of the Head;
All that on Folly Frenzy could beget,   125
Fruits of dull Heat, and Sooterkins of Wit.
Next, o'er his Books his eyes began to roll,
In pleasing memory of all he stole,
How here he sipp'd, how there he plunder'd snug
And suck'd all o'er, like an industrious Bug.   130
Here lay poor Fletcher's half-eat scenes, and here
The Frippery of crucify'd Molière;
There hapless Shakespear, yet of Tibbald sore,

115. *supperless the Hero sate*] It is amazing . . . SCRIBL. ⟨A i 109⟩.
But since the discovery of the true Hero of the poem, may we not add
that nothing was so natural, after so great a loss of Money at Dice, or of
Reputation by his Play, as that the Poet should have no great stomach
to eat a supper? Besides, how well has the Poet consulted his Heroic
Character, in adding that he *swore* all the time! BENTL.

122. *abdicated* ⟨Possibly, to disown. But Pope appears to be thinking
of half-written plays which Cibber had given up in disgust or despair.⟩

123. *precipitate* ⟨Perhaps in its adjectival sense only of 'violently
hurried'.⟩

126. *Sooterkins of Wit* ⟨'Sooterkin: A joke upon the Dutch women,
supposing that by their constant use of stoves, which they place under
their petticoats, they breed a kind of small animal in their bodies, called a
sooterkin, of the size of a mouse, which when mature slips out.'—Grose,
A Classical Dictionary of the Vulgar Tongue.⟩

131. *poor Fletcher's half-eat scenes*] A great number of them taken out
to patch up his Plays.

132. *The Frippery*] 'When I fitted up an old play, it was as a good
housewife will mend old linnen, when she had not better employment.'
Life, p. 217. octavo. ⟨For Molière, see Pope's note to B i 253.⟩

133. *hapless Shakespear, &c.*] It is not to be doubted but Bays was a
subscriber to Tibbald's Shakespear. He was frequently liberal this way;
and, as he tells us, 'subscribed to Mr. Pope's Homer, out of pure
Generosity and Civility; but when Mr. Pope did so to his Nonjuror, he
concluded it could be nothing but a joke.' Letter to Mr. P. p. 24.
This Tibbald, or Theobald, published an edition of Shakespear, of
which he was so proud himself as to say, in one of Mist's Journals, June 8,
'That to expose any Errors in it was impracticable.' And in another,
April 27, 'That whatever care might for the future be taken by any other
Editor, he would still give above five hundred Emendations, that *shall*
escape them all.'

Wish'd he had blotted for himself before.
The rest on Out-side merit but presume,   135
Or serve (like other Fools) to fill a room;
Such with their shelves as due proportion hold,
Or their fond Parents drest in red and gold;
Or where the pictures for the page attone,
And Quarles is sav'd by Beauties not his own.   140
Here swells the shelf with Ogilby the great;
There, stamp'd with arms, Newcastle shines complete:
Here all his suff'ring brotherhood retire,
And 'scape the martyrdom of jakes and fire:
A Gothic Library! of Greece and Rome   145
Well purg'd, and worthy Settle, Banks, and Broome.
    But, high above, more solid Learning shone,
The Classics of an Age that heard of none;

134. *Wish'd he had blotted*] It was a ridiculous praise which the Players gave to Shakespear, 'that he never blotted a line'. Ben Johnson honestly wished he had blotted a thousand; and Shakespear would certainly have wished the same, if he had lived to see those alterations in his works, which, not the Actors only (and especially the daring Hero of this poem) have made on the *Stage*, but the presumptuous Critics of our days in their *Editions*.

135. *The rest on Out-side merit, &c.*] This Library is divided into three parts; the first consists of those authors from whom he stole, and whose works he mangled; the second, of such as fitted the shelves, or were gilded for shew, or adorned with pictures; the third class our author calls solid learning, old bodies of Divinity, old Commentaries, old English Printers, or old English Translations; all very voluminous, and fit to erect altars to Dulness. ⟨Cf. A i 120.⟩

140. *Quarles is saved* ⟨The quaint illustrations to Francis Quarles's *Emblemes*. (1635) were executed by William Marshall. Cf. A i 126*n*.⟩

141. *Ogilby the great* ⟨A i 121⟩.

142. *Newcastle shines complete* ⟨A i 122⟩.

146. *Worthy Settle, Banks, and Broome*] The Poet has mentioned these three authors in particular, as they are parallel to our Hero in his three capacities: 1. Settle was his Brother Laureate; only indeed upon half-pay, for the City instead of the Court; but equally famous for unintelligible flights in his poems on public occasions, such as Shows, Birth-days, &c. 2. Banks was his Rival in *Tragedy* (tho' more successful in one of his Tragedies, the *Earl of Essex*, which is yet alive: *Anna Boleyn*, the *Queen of Scots*, and *Cyrus the Great*, are dead and gone. These he drest in a sort of *Beggars Velvet*, or a happy mixture of the *thick Fustian* and *thin Prosaic*; exactly imitated in *Perolla and Isidora*, *Cæsar in Ægypt*, and the *Heroic Daughter*. 3. Broome was a serving-man of Ben. Johnson, who once picked up a *Comedy* from his Betters, or from some cast scenes of his Master, not entirely contemptible. ⟨For Settle and Banks, see A i 88*n*., iii 281*n*., and i 250*n*. The three plays in which Banks is 'exactly imitated' are by Cibber.—Richard Brome (d. 1652?) was author or part-author of more than twenty plays.⟩

147. *More solid Learning*] Some have objected, that books of this sort

There Caxton slept, with Wynkyn at his side,
One clasp'd in wood, and one in strong cow-hide;   150
There, sav'd by spice, like Mummies, many a year,
Dry Bodies of Divinity appear:
De Lyra there a dreadful front extends,
And here the groaning shelves Philemon bends.
  Of these twelve volumes, twelve of amplest size,   155
Redeem'd from tapers and defrauded pies,
Inspir'd he seizes: These an altar raise:
An hecatomb of pure, unsully'd lays
That altar crowns: A folio Common-place
Founds the whole pile, of all his works the base: 160
Quartos, octavos, shape the less'ning pyre;
A twisted Birth-day Ode completes the spire.
  Then he: 'Great Tamer of all human art!
First in my care, and ever at my heart;
Dulness! whose good old cause I yet defend,   165
With whom my Muse began, with whom shall end;
E'er since Sir Fopling's Periwig was Praise,
To the last honours of the Butt and Bays:

---

suit not so well the library of our Bays, which they imagine consisted of
Novels, Plays, and obscene books; but they are to consider, that he
furnished his shelves only for ornament, and read these books no more
than the *Dry bodies of Divinity*, which, no doubt, were purchased by his
Father when he designed him for the Gown. See the note on v. 200.

149. *Caxton*] A Printer . . . hardly known ⟨A i 129⟩. 'Happened that
to my hande . . . Vyrgyle made in metre' ⟨A i 129⟩.

153. *De Lyra* ⟨A i 133⟩.

154. *Philemon* ⟨A i 134⟩.

166. *With whom my Muse began, &c.* ⟨A i 146⟩.

167. *Sir Fopling's Periwig*] The first visible cause of the passion of the
Town for our Hero, was a fair flaxen full-bottom'd Periwig, which, he
tells us, he wore in his first play of the *Fool in fashion* ⟨1696⟩. It
attracted, in a particular manner, the Friendship of Col. Brett, who
wanted to purchase it. 'Whatever contempt (says he) Philosophers may
have for a fine Periwig, my friend, who was not to despise the world but
to live in it, knew very well that so material an article of dress upon the
head of a man of sense, if it became him, could never fail of drawing to
him a more partial Regard and Benevolence, than could possibly be hoped
for in an ill-made one. This perhaps, may soften the grave censure which
so youthful a purchase might otherwise have laid upon him. In a word,
he made his attack upon this Periwig, as your young fellows generally do
upon a lady of pleasure, first by a few familiar praises of her person, and
then a civil enquiry into the price of it; and we finished our bargain that
night over a bottle.' See Life, octavo p. 303. This remarkable Periwig
usually made its entrance upon the stage in a sedan, brought in by two
chairmen, with infinite approbation of the audience.

168. *the Butt and Bays* ⟨i.e. the laureate's butt of sack and his laurel
crown.⟩

O thou! of Bus'ness the directing soul!
To this our head like byass to the bowl,   170
Which, as more pond'rous, made its aim more true,
Obliquely wadling to the mark in view:
O! ever gracious to perplex'd mankind,
Still spread a healing mist before the mind;
And lest we err by Wit's wild dancing light,   175
Secure us kindly in our native night.
Or, if to Wit a coxcomb make pretence,
Guard the sure barrier between that and Sense;
Or quite unravel all the reas'ning thread,
And hang some curious cobweb in its stead!   180
As, forc'd from wind-guns, lead itself can fly,
And pond'rous slugs cut swiftly thro the sky;
As clocks to weight their nimble motion owe,
The wheels above urg'd by the load below:
Me Emptiness, and Dulness could inspire,   185
And were my Elasticity, and Fire.
Some Dæmon stole my pen (forgive th' offence)
And once betray'd me into common sense:
Else all my Prose and Verse were much the same;
This, prose on stilts; that, poetry fall'n lame.   190
Did on the stage my Fops appear confin'd?
My Life gave ampler lessons to mankind.
Did the dead Letter unsuccessful prove?
The brisk Example never fail'd to move.
Yet sure had Heav'n decreed to save the State,   195
Heav'n had decreed these works a longer date.
Could Troy be sav'd by any single hand,
This grey-goose weapon must have made her stand.
What can I now? my Fletcher cast aside,
Take up the Bible, once my better guide?   200

188. *And once betray'd me* ⟨in *The Careless Husband*. Cf. *Ep.* II i 92.⟩
195. *Had Heav'n decreed, &c.* ⟨A i 183⟩.
197, 198. *Could Troy be sav'd—This grey-goose weapon* ⟨A i 187⟩.
    199. *my Fletcher*] A familiar manner of speaking, used by modern Critics, of a favourite author. Bays might as justly speak thus of Fletcher, as a French Wit did of Tully, seeing his works in a library, 'Ah! mon cher Ciceron! je le connois bien; c'est le même que Marc Tulle.' But he had a better title to call Fletcher *his own*, having made so free with him. ⟨Cf. A i 189.⟩
    200. *Take up the Bible*] When, according to his Father's intention, he had been a *Clergyman*, or (as he thinks himself) a *Bishop* of the Church of England. Hear his own words: 'At the time that the fate of King James, the Prince of Orange and Myself, were on the anvil, Providence thought fit to postpone mine, 'till theirs were determined: But had my father

Or tread the path by vent'rous Heroes trod,
This Box my Thunder, this right hand my God?
Or chair'd at White's amidst the Doctors sit,
Teach Oaths to Gamesters, and to Nobles Wit?
Or bidst thou rather Party to embrace?   205
(A friend to Party thou, and all her race;
'Tis the same rope at different ends they twist;
To Dulness Ridpath is as dear as Mist.)
Shall I, like Curtius, desp'rate in my zeal,
O'er head and ears plunge for the Commonweal?   210
Or rob Rome's ancient geese of all their glories,
And cackling save the Monarchy of Tories?
Hold—to the Minister I more incline;
To serve his cause, O Queen! is serving thine.
And see! thy very Gazetteers give o'er,   215
Ev'n Ralph repents, and Henly writes no more.
What then remains? Ourself. Still, still remain
Cibberian forehead, and Cibberian brain.
This brazen Brightness, to the 'Squire so dear;
This polish'd Hardness, that reflects the Peer;   220
This arch Absurd, that wit and fool delights;
This Mess, toss'd up of Hockley-hole and White's;
Where Dukes and Butchers join to wreathe my crown,
At once the Bear and Fiddle of the town.

---

carried me a month sooner to the University, who knows but that purer
fountain might have washed my Imperfections into a capacity of writing,
instead of Plays and annual *Odes*, Sermons and *Pastoral Letters?*' Apology
for his Life, chap. iii ⟨Cf. A i 190.⟩

202. *This Box my Thunder, this Right hand my God*]

    Dextra mihi Deus, & telum quod missile libro.

Virgil ⟨*Aen.* x 773⟩ of the Gods of Mezentius.
⟨Box = dice-box.⟩

208. *Ridpath—Mist*] George Ridpath, author of a Whig paper, called
the Flying post; Nathanael Mist, of a famous Tory Journal.

211. *Or rob Rome's ancient geese* ⟨A i 191⟩.

213. *the Minister* ⟨i.e. Walpole.⟩

214. *O Queen!* ⟨i.e. Dullness. But Pope was probably thinking too of
Queen Caroline, whose understanding with Walpole was complete. To
serve Walpole was to serve Queen Caroline.⟩

215. *Gazetteers*] A band of ministerial writers, hired at the price mentioned in the note on book ii. ver. 316, who on the very day their Patron
quitted his post, laid down their paper, and declared they would never
more meddle in Politics.

222. *Hockley-hole* ⟨see p. 615.⟩

224. *Bear and Fiddle* ⟨Cibber is at once the person baited and the
jester. 'Bear' and 'Fiddle' are associated through bear-baiting, at which
playing on the fiddle seems to have been a preliminary.⟩

'O born in sin, and forth in folly brought!   225
Works damn'd, or to be damn'd! (your father's fault)
Go, purify'd by flames ascend the sky,
My better and more christian progeny!
Unstain'd, untouch'd, and yet in maiden sheets;
While all your smutty sisters walk the streets.   230
Ye shall not beg, like gratis-given Bland,
Sent with a Pass, and vagrant thro' the land;
Not sail, with Ward, to Ape-and-monkey climes,
Where vile Mundungus trucks for viler rhymes;
Not sulphur-tipt, emblaze an Ale-house fire;   235
Not wrap up Oranges, to pelt your sire!
O! pass more innocent, in infant state,
To the mild Limbo of our Father Tate:
Or peaceably forgot, at once be blest
In Shadwell's bosom with eternal Rest!   240
Soon to that mass of Nonsense to return,
Where things destroy'd are swept to things unborn.'
    With that, a Tear (portentous sign of Grace!)
Stole from the Master of the sev'nfold Face:
And thrice he lifted high the Birth-day brand,   245
And thrice he dropt it from his quiv'ring hand;
Then lights the structure, with averted eyes:
The rowling smokes involve the sacrifice.
The op'ning clouds disclose each work by turns,
Now flames the Cid, and now Perolla burns;   250

225. *O born in sin, &c.* ⟨A i 197⟩.
228. *My better and more christian progeny*] 'It may be observable, that
my muse and my spouse were equally prolific; that the one was seldom
the mother of a Child, but in the same year the other made me the father
of a Play. I think we had a dozen of each sort between us; of both which
kinds some *died* in their *Infancy*,' *&c.* Life of C. C. p. 217. 8vo edit.
229. *Unstain'd, untouch'd, &c.* ⟨A i 197⟩.
231. *gratis-given Bland—Sent with a Pass*] It was a practice so to give
the Daily Gazetteer and ministerial pamphlets (in which this B. was a
writer) and to send them *Post-free* to all the Towns in the kingdom.
233. *Ward* ⟨A i 200⟩.
234. *vile Mundungus* ⟨i.e. tobacco of poor quality.⟩
236. *Oranges* ⟨Oranges were regularly sold in the theatres, and were
occasionally used for pelting the actors when they or the play failed to
give satisfaction.⟩
238, 240. *Tate—Shadwell*] Two of his predecessors in the Laurel.
⟨See A i 103, and A ii 324.⟩
241. *And thrice he lifted, &c.* ⟨A i 203⟩.
244. *the sev'nfold Face* ⟨The phrase describes Cibber's impenetrable
assurance, but also suggests the mobile face of the born actor.⟩
250. *Now flames the Cid, &c.* ⟨A i 208⟩.
250. *Now flames the Cid, &c.*] In the first notes on the Dunciad

Great Cæsar roars, and hisses in the fires;
King John in silence modestly expires:
No merit now the dear Nonjuror claims,
Molière's old stubble in a moment flames.
Tears gush'd again, as from pale Priam's eyes   255
When the last blaze sent Ilion to the skies.
   Rowz'd by the light, old Dulness heav'd the head;
Then snatch'd a sheet of Thulè from her bed,
Sudden she flies, and whelms it o'er the pyre;
Down sink the flames, and with a hiss expire.   260
   Her ample presence fills up all the place;
A veil of fogs dilates her awful face:
Great in her charms! as when on Shrieves and May'rs
She looks, and breathes herself into their airs.
She bids him wait her to her sacred Dome: 265
Well pleas'd he enter'd, and confess'd his home.
So Spirits ending their terrestrial race,
Ascend, and recognize their Native Place.
This the Great Mother dearer held than all
The clubs of Quidnuncs, or her own Guild-hall: 270
Here stood her Opium, here she nurs'd her Owls,
And here she plann'd th' Imperial seat of Fools.
   Here to her Chosen all her works she shews;
Prose swell'd to verse, verse loit'ring into prose:

⟨A i 240⟩ it was said, that this Author was particularly excellent at Tragedy. 'This (says he) is as unjust as to say I could not dance on a Rope.' But certain it is that he had attempted to dance on this Rope, and fell most shamefully, having produced no less than four Tragedies (the names of which the Poet preserves in these few lines) the three first of them were fairly printed, acted, and damned; the fourth suppressed, in fear of the like treatment.

253. *the dear Nonjuror—Molière's old stubble*] A Comedy threshed out of Molière's Tartuffe, and so much the Translator's favourite, that he assures us all our author's dislike to it could only arise from *disaffection to the Government*;

> *Qui meprise Cotin, n'estime point son Roi,*
> *Et n'a, selon Cotin, ni Dieu, ni foi, ni loi.*
>
> Boil. ⟨Satire ix⟩.

He assures us, that 'when he had the honour to kiss his Majesty's hand upon presenting his dedication of it, he was graciously pleased, out of his Royal bounty, to order him two hundred pounds for it. And this he doubts not *grieved* Mr. P.'

256. *When the last blaze, &c.* ⟨A i 212⟩.
258. *Thulè* ⟨A i 214⟩.
263. *Great in her charms! &c.* ⟨A i 219⟩.
265. *sacred Dome*] Where he no sooner enters . . . regions ⟨A i 221⟩.
269. *This the Great Mother, &c.* ⟨A i 33⟩.
269. *Great Mother* ⟨A i 33⟩.

How random thoughts now meaning chance to find,   275
Now leave all memory of sense behind:
How Prologues into Prefaces decay,
And these to Notes are fritter'd quite away:
How Index-learning turns no student pale,
Yet holds the eel of science by the tail: 280
How, with less reading than makes felons scape,
Less human genius than God gives an ape,
Small thanks to France, and none to Rome or Greece,
A past, vamp'd, future, old, reviv'd, new piece,
'Twixt Plautus, Fletcher, Shakespear, and Corneille,   285
Can make a Cibber, Tibbald, or Ozell.
  The Goddess then, o'er his anointed head,
With mystic words, the sacred Opium shed.
And lo! her bird, (a monster of a fowl,
Something betwixt a Heideggre and owl,)   290
Perch'd on his crown. 'All hail! and hail again,
My son! the promis'd land expects thy reign.
Know, Eusden thirsts no more for sack or praise;
He sleeps among the dull of ancient days;
Safe, where no Critics damn, no duns molest,   295
Where wretched Withers, Ward, and Gildon rest,
And high-born Howard, more majestic sire,
With Fool of Quality compleats the quire.
Thou Cibber! thou, his Laurel shalt support,
Folly, my son, has still a Friend at Court.   300
Lift up your gates, ye Princes, see him come!
Sound, sound ye Viols, be the Cat-call dumb!

286. *Tibbald*] Lewis Tibbald (as pronounced) or Theobald (as written) was bred an Attorney, and son to an Attorney (says Mr. Jacob) of Sittenburn in Kent. He was Author of some forgotten Plays, Translations, and other pieces. He was concerned in a paper called the Censor, and a Translation of Ovid. 'There is a notorious Idiot, one hight Whachum, who, from an under-spur-leather to the Law, is become an understrapper to the Play-house, who hath lately burlesqued the Metamorphoses of Ovid by a vile Translation, &c. This fellow is concerned in an impertinent paper called the Censor.' DENNIS Rem. on Pope's Hom. p. 9, 10. ⟨Cf. A i 106.⟩
  Ibid. *Ozell* ⟨A i 240, and Errata, p. 428.⟩
  290. *A Heideggre* ⟨A i 244⟩.
  293. *Eusden* ⟨He died in 1730. Cf. A ii 393.⟩
  296. *Withers* ⟨A i 126⟩.   Ibid. *Gildon* ⟨A i 250⟩.
  296. *Ward, and Gildon* ⟨Ward had died in 1731; Gildon, in 1724.⟩
  297. *Howard* ⟨A i 250⟩.
  298. *Fool of Quality* ⟨i.e. Lord Hervey. The death of Hervey, August 5, 1743, enabled Pope to make this last-minute change in the text.⟩

Bring, bring the madding Bay, the drunken Vine;
The creeping, dirty, courtly Ivy join.
And thou! his Aid de camp, lead on my sons,   305
Light-arm'd with Points, Antitheses, and Puns.
Let Bawdry, Bilingsgate, my daughters dear,
Support his front, and Oaths bring up the rear:
And under his, and under Archer's wing,
Gaming and Grub-street skulk behind the King.   310
   'O! when shall rise a Monarch all our own,
And I, a Nursing-mother, rock the throne,
'Twixt Prince and People close the Curtain draw,
Shade him from Light, and cover him from Law;
Fatten the Courtier, starve the learned band,   315
And suckle Armies, and dry-nurse the land:
'Till Senates nod to Lullabies divine,
And all be sleep, as at an Ode of thine.'

        She ceas'd, Then swells the Chapel-royal throat:
        'God save king Cibber!' mounts in ev'ry note.   320

304. *The creeping . . . Ivy* ⟨See p. 167, l. 706n, and below, 'Of the
Poet Laureate', p. 801⟩.

309, 310. *Under Archer's wing,—Gaming, &c.*] When the Statute
against Gaming was drawn up, it was represented, that the King, by
ancient custom, plays at Hazard, one night in the year ⟨i.e. Twelfth
Night⟩; and therefore a clause was inserted, with an exception as to that
particular. Under this pretence, the Groom-porter had a Room appropriated to Gaming all the summer the Court was at Kensington, which
his Majesty accidentally being acquainted of, with a just indignation
prohibited. It is reported, the same practice is yet continued wherever the
Court resides, and the Hazard Table there open to all the professed
Gamesters in town.

> Greatest *and* justest SOV'REIGN! *know you this?*
> *Alas! no more, than* Thames' *calm* head *can know*
> *Whose meads his* arms *drown, or whose corn o'erflow.*
>   Donne to Queen Eliz.

⟨*Satire* v 28–30.⟩

311. *O when shall rise a Monarch, &c.*] Boileau, Lutrin, Chant. 2
⟨51–6⟩.

> *Helas! qu'est devenu ce tems, cet heureux tems,*
> *Où les Rois s'honoroient du nom de Faineans:*
> *S'endormoient sur le trone, & me servant sans honte,*
> *Laissoient leur sceptre au mains ou d'un mair, ou d'un comte:*
> *Aucun soin n'approchoit de leur paisible cour,*
> *On reposoit la nuit, on dormoit tout le jour, &c.*

319. *Chapel-royal*] The Voices and Instruments used in the service of
the Chapel-royal being also employed in the performance of the Birth-day
and New-year Odes.

Familiar White's, 'God save King Colley!' cries;
'God save king Colley!' Drury-lane replies:
To Needham's quick the voice triumphal rode,
But pious Needham dropt the name of God;
Back to the Devil the last echoes roll,   325
And 'Coll!' each Butcher roars at Hockley-hole.
    So when Jove's block descended from on high
(As sings thy great forefather Ogilby)
Loud thunder to its bottom shook the bog,
And the hoarse nation croak'd, 'God save King Log!'

324. *Needham*] A Matron of great fame, and very religious in her way; whose constant prayer it was, that she might 'get enough by her profession to leave it off in time, and make her peace with God'. But her fate was not so happy; for being convicted, and set in the pillory, she was (to the lasting shame of all her great Friends and Votaries) so ill used by the populace, that it put an end to her days.

325. *Back to the Devil*] The Devil Tavern in Fleet-street, where these Odes are usually rehearsed before they are performed at Court. Upon which a Wit of those times made this epigram:

> When Laureates make Odes, do you ask of what sort?
>   Do you ask if they're good, or are evil?
> You may judge—from the Devil they come to the Court,
>   And go from the Court to the Devil.

328. *—Ogilby)—God save king Log!*] ⟨A i 258.⟩

The End of the First Book

BOOK THE SECOND

ARGUMENT

The King being proclaimed, the solemnity is graced with public Games *and sports of various kinds; not instituted by the Hero, as by Æneas in Virgil, but for greater honour by the* Goddess *in person (in like manner as the games Pythia, Isthmia, &c. were anciently said to be ordained by the Gods, and as Thetis herself appearing, according to Homer, Odyss. 24. proposed the prizes in honour of her son Achilles.) Hither flock the Poets and Critics, attended, as is but just, with their Patrons and Booksellers. The Goddess is first pleased, for her disport, to propose games to the* Booksellers, *and setteth up the Phantom of a Poet, which they contend to overtake. The Races described, with their divers accidents. Next, the game for a* Poetess. *Then follow the Exercises for the* Poets, *of tickling, vociferating, diving: The first holds forth the arts and practices of* Dedicators, *the second of* Disputants *and* fustian Poets, *the third of* profound, dark, *and* dirty Party-writers. *Lastly, for the* Critics, *the Goddess proposes (with great propriety) an Exercise, not of their parts, but their patience, in hearing the works of two voluminous Authors, one in* verse, *and the other in* prose, *deliberately read, without sleeping: The various effects of which, with the several degrees and manners of their operation, are here set forth; 'till the whole number, not of Critics only, but of spectators, actors, and all present, fall fast asleep; which naturally and necessarily ends the games.*

High on a gorgeous seat, that far out-shone
Henley's gilt tub, or Fleckno's Irish throne,
Or that where on her Curls the Public pours,
All-bounteous, fragrant Grains and Golden show'rs,
Great Cibber sate: The proud Parnassian sneer,   5
The conscious simper, and the jealous leer,
Mix on his look: All eyes direct their rays
On him, and crowds turn Coxcombs as they gaze.
His Peers shine round him with reflected grace,
New edge their dulness, and new bronze their face.   10
So from the Sun's broad beam, in shallow urns
Heav'ns twinkling Sparks draw light, and point their
        horns.
    Not with more glee, by hands Pontific crown'd,
With scarlet hats wide-waving circled round,
Rome in her Capitol saw Querno sit,   15
Thron'd on sev'n hills, the Antichrist of wit.
    And now the Queen, to glad her sons, proclaims
By herald Hawkers, high heroic Games.

Two things there are . . . all sound Commentators ⟨A ii⟩.
1. *High on a gorgeous seat* ⟨A ii 1⟩.
2. *Henley's gilt tub* ⟨A ii 2⟩.
Ibid. *or Fleckno's Irish throne*] Richard Fleckno . . . Sarazin ⟨A ii 2⟩.
    It may be just worth mentioning, that the Eminence from whence the ancient Sophists entertained their auditors, was called by the pompous name of a Throne;—ἐπὶ θρόνου τινὸς ὑψηλοῦ μάλα σοφιστικῶς καὶ σοβαρῶς. Themistius, Orat. i.
    3. *Or that where on her Curls, &c.*] Edmund Curl . . . p. 19, 25 ⟨A ii 3⟩. Much in the same manner Mr. Cibber remonstrated that his Brothers at Bedlam, mentioned Book i. were not *Brazen*, but *Blocks*; yet our author let it pass unaltered, as a trifle, that no way lessened the Relationship.
    9. *Peers* ⟨Cibber's 'peers' are his brother dunces of the pen, but also those among the English nobility who delighted in his society. Cf. B i 220.⟩
    15. *Querno*] Camillo Querno . . . Prolusions. ⟨A ii 11.⟩

They summon all her Race: An endless band
Pours forth, and leaves unpeopled half the land.   20
A motley mixture! in long wigs, in bags,
In silks, in crapes, in Garters, and in rags,
From drawing rooms, from colleges, from garrets,
On horse, on foot, in hacks, and gilded chariots:
All who true Dunces in her cause appear'd,   25
And all who knew those Dunces to reward.
     Amid that area wide they took their stand,
Where the tall may-pole once o'er-look'd the Strand;
But now (so ANNE and Piety ordain)
A Church collects the saints of Drury-lane.   30
     With Authors, Stationers obey'd the call,
(The field of glory is a field for all.)
Glory, and gain, th' industrious tribe provoke;
And gentle Dulness ever loves a joke.
A Poet's form she plac'd before their eyes,   35
And bade the nimblest racer seize the prize;
No meagre, muse-rid mope, adust and thin,
In a dun night-gown of his own loose skin;
But such a bulk as no twelve bards could raise,
Twelve starv'ling bards of these degen'rate days.   40
All as a partridge plump, full-fed, and fair,
She form'd this image of well-body'd air;
With pert flat eyes she window'd well its head;
A brain of feathers, and a heart of lead;
And empty words she gave, and sounding strain,   45
But senseless, lifeless! idol void and vain!
Never was dash'd out, at one lucky hit,
A fool, so just a copy of a wit;
So like, that critics said, and courtiers swore,
A Wit it was, and call'd the phantom More.   50
     All gaze with ardour: Some a poet's name,
Others a sword-knot and lac'd suit inflame.
But lofty Lintot in the circle rose:
'This prize is mine; who tempt it are my foes;

35. *A Poet's form, &c.* ⟨A ii 31⟩.
39. *But such a bulk, &c.* ⟨A ii 35⟩.
47. *Never was dash'd out, &c.* ⟨A ii 43⟩.
   50. *and call'd the phantom More*] CURL, in his Key . . . handkerchief!'
⟨A ii 46⟩.
   The plagiarisms . . . *repono* ⟨A ii 46⟩.
   50. *the phantom More* ⟨A ii 46⟩.
   53. *But lofty Lintot* ⟨A ii 49⟩.

With me began this genius, and shall end.' 55
He spoke: and who with Lintot shall contend?
   Fear held them mute. Alone, untaught to fear,
Stood dauntless Curl; 'Behold that rival here!
The race by vigour, not by vaunts is won;
So take the hindmost, Hell.'—He said, and run. 60
Swift as a bard the bailiff leaves behind,
He left huge Lintot, and out-strip'd the wind.
As when a dab-chick waddles thro' the copse
On feet and wings, and flies, and wades, and hops;
So lab'ring on, with shoulders, hands, and head, 65
Wide as a wind-mill all his figures spread,
With arms expanded Bernard rows his state,
And left-legg'd Jacob seems to emulate.
Full in the middle way there stood a lake,
Which Curl's Corinna chanc'd that morn to make: 70
(Such was her wont, at early dawn to drop
Her evening cates before his neighbour's shop,)
Here fortun'd Curl to slide; loud shout the band,
And Bernard! Bernard! rings thro' all the Strand.
Obscene with filth the miscreant lies bewray'd, 75
Fal'n in the plash his wickedness had laid:
Then first (if Poets aught of truth declare)
The caitiff Vaticide conceiv'd a pray'r.
   Hear Jove! whose name my bards and I adore,
As much at least as any God's, or more; 80
And him and his, if more devotion warms,
Down with the Bible, up with the Pope's Arms.
   A place there is, betwixt earth, air, and seas,
Where, from Ambrosia, Jove retires for ease.

58. *Stood dauntless Curl* ⟨A ii 54⟩.
60. *So take the hindmost, Hell* ⟨A ii 56⟩.
61. *&c.* ⟨A ii 54⟩.
64, 65. *On feet and wings, &c.* ⟨A ii 60⟩.
67, 68. *With arms expanded, Bernard rows his state,*
     And left-legg'd Jacob seems to emulate]
Milton, of the motion of the Swan ⟨*Par. Lost*, vii 440⟩,
       ———*rows*
     His state with oary feet.
And Dryden, of another's,—*With two left legs*—⟨Cf. A ii 64*n*.⟩
70. *Curl's Corinna* ⟨A ii 66⟩.
73. *Here fortun'd Curl to slide* ⟨A ii 69⟩.
74. *And Bernard! Bernard!* ⟨A ii 70⟩.
75. *Obscene with filth, &c.* ⟨A ii 71⟩.
82. *the Bible . . . the Pope's Arms* ⟨A ii 78⟩.
83. ⟨A ii 79⟩. Ibid. *A place there is, &c.* ⟨A ii 79⟩.

There in his seat two spacious vents appear,   85
On this he sits, to that he leans his ear,
And hears the various vows of fond mankind:
Some beg an eastern, some a western wind
All vain petitions, mounting to the sky,
With reams abundant this abode supply,   90
Amus'd he reads, and then returns the bills
Sign'd with that Ichor which from Gods distils.
　　In office here fair Cloacina stands,
And ministers to Jove with purest hands.
Forth from the heap she pick'd her Vot'ry's pray'r,   95
And plac'd it next him, a distinction rare!
Oft had the Goddess heard her servant's call,
From her black grottos near the Temple-wall,
List'ning delighted to the jest unclean
Of link-boys vile, and watermen obscene;   100
Where as he fish'd her nether realms for Wit,
She oft had favour'd him, and favours yet.
Renew'd by ordure's sympathetic force,
As oil'd with magic juices for the course,
Vig'rous he rises; from th' effluvia strong   105
Imbibes new life, and scours and stinks along;
Re-passes Lintot, vindicates the race,
Nor heeds the brown dishonours of his face.
　　And now the victor stretch'd his eager hand
Where the tall Nothing stood, or seem'd to stand;   110
A shapeless shade, it melted from his sight,
Like forms in clouds, or visions of the night.
To seize his papers, Curl, was next thy care;
His papers light, fly diverse, tost in air;
Songs, sonnets, epigrams the winds uplift,   115
And whisk 'em back to Evans, Young, and Swift.
Th' embroider'd suit at least he deem'd his prey;
That suit an unpay'd taylor snatch'd away.

92. ⟨A ii 88⟩.
93. *Cloacina* ⟨A ii 89⟩.
98. *black grottos* ⟨Coal wharves on the Thames, or in Fleet Ditch⟩.
101. *Where as he fish'd, &c.* ⟨A ii 93⟩.
104. *As oil'd with magic juices* ⟨A ii 96⟩.
108. *the brown dishonours* ⟨A ii 100⟩.
111. *A shapeless shade, &c.* ⟨A ii 103⟩.
114. *His papers light, &c.* ⟨A ii 106⟩.
116. *Evans, Young, and Swift*] Some of those persons whose writings, epigrams, or jests he had owned. See Note on ver. 50.
118. *an unpay'd taylor* ⟨A ii 111⟩.

No rag, no scrap, of all the beau, or wit,
That once so flutter'd, and that once so writ.　　120
　　Heav'n rings with laughter: Of the laughter vain,
Dulness, good Queen, repeats the jest again.
Three wicked imps, of her own Grubstreet choir,
She deck'd like Congreve, Addison, and Prior;
Mears, Warner, Wilkins run: delusive thought!　　125
Breval, Bond, Besaleel, the varlets caught.
Curl stretches after Gay, but Gay is gone,
He grasps an empty Joseph for a John:
So Proteus, hunted in a nobler shape,
Became, when seiz'd, a puppy, or an ape.　　130
　　To him the Goddess: 'Son! thy grief lay down,
And turn this whole illusion on the town:
As the sage dame, experienc'd in her trade,
By names of Toasts retails each batter'd jade;
(Whence hapless Monsieur much complains at Paris　　135
Of wrongs from Duchesses and Lady Maries;)
Be thine, my stationer! this magic gift;
Cook shall be Prior, and Concanen, Swift:
So shall each hostile name become our own,
And we too boast our Garth and Addison.'　　140
　　With that she gave him (piteous of his case,
Yet smiling at his rueful length of face)
A shaggy Tap'stry, worthy to be spread
On Codrus' old, or Dunton's modern bed;

124. *like Congreve, Addison, and Prior* ⟨A ii 116⟩.
125. *Mears, Warner, Wilkins* ⟨A ii 117⟩.
126. *Breval, Bond, Besaleel* ⟨A ii 118⟩.
128. *Gay* ⟨A ii 120⟩.
132. *And turn this whole illusion, &c.* ⟨A ii 124⟩.
138. *Cook shall be Prior* ⟨A ii 130⟩.
138. *and Concanen, Swift* ⟨A ii 287⟩.
140. *And we too boast our Garth and Addison*] Nothing . . . Mr. Addison; ⟨A ii 132⟩ in a word, almost every man of his time that deserved it; even Cibber himself (presuming him to be author of the Careless Husband.) It was very difficult . . . *dead.* ⟨A ii 132.⟩
141, 142. ——*piteous of his case, &c.* ⟨A ii 133⟩.
142. *rueful length of face* ⟨A ii 134⟩.
The good Scriblerus here, as on all occasions, eminently shews his humanity. But it was far otherwise with the gentlemen of the Dunciad, whose scurrilities were always personal, and of that nature which provoked every honest man but Mr. Pope; yet never to be lamented . . . *to see* ⟨A ii 134⟩.
143. *A shaggy Tap'stry* ⟨A ii 135⟩.
144. *On Codrus' old, or Dunton's modern bed* ⟨A ii 136⟩.

Instructive work! whose wry-mouth'd portraiture   145
Display'd the fates her confessors endure.
Earless on high, stood unabash'd De Foe,
And Tutchin flagrant from the scourge below.
There Ridpath, Roper, cudgell'd might ye view,
The very worsted still look'd black and blue.   150
Himself among the story'd chiefs he spies,
As from the blanket high in air he flies,
'And oh! (he cry'd) what street, what lane but knows,
Our purgings, pumpings, blankettings, and blows?
In ev'ry loom our labours shall be seen,   155
And the fresh vomit run for ever green!'
    See in the circle next, Eliza plac'd,
Two babes of love close clinging to her waist;
Fair as before her works she stands confess'd,
In flow'rs and pearls by bounteous Kirkall dress'd.   160
The Goddess then: 'Who best can send on high
The salient spout, far-streaming to the sky;
His be yon Juno of majestic size,
With cow-like udders, and with ox-like eyes.
This China Jordan let the chief o'ercome   165
Replenish, not ingloriously, at home.'
Osborne and Curl accept the glorious strife,
(Tho' this his Son dissuades, and that his Wife.)

148. *Tutchin* ⟨A ii 140⟩.
149. *Ridpath, Roper*] Authors of the Flying-post and Post-boy, two
scandalous papers on different sides, for which they equally and alternately deserved to be cudgelled, and were so ⟨Cf. A ii 141⟩.
151. *Himself . . . he spies* ⟨A ii 143⟩.
151. *Himself . . . he spies*] The history of Curl's being tossed in a
blanket, and whipped by the scholars of Westminster, is well known. Of
his purging . . . in Swift and Pope's Miscell. ⟨A ii 143⟩.
156. *And the fresh vomit, &c.* ⟨A ii 148⟩.
157. *See in the circle next* ⟨A ii 149⟩.
Ibid. *Eliza Haywood* ⟨A ii 149⟩.
158. *Two babes of love. &c.* ⟨A ii 150⟩.
160. *Kirkall* ⟨A ii 152⟩.
163. *yon Juno, &c.* ⟨A ii 155⟩.
165. *This China Jordan* ⟨A ii 157⟩.
167. *Osborne*] A Bookseller in Grays-Inn, very well qualified by his
impudence to act this part; and therefore placed here instead of a less
deserving Predecessor. This man published advertisements for a year
together, pretending to sell Mr. Pope's Subscription books of Homer's
Iliad at half the price: Of which books he had none, but cut to the size
of them (which was Quarto) the common books in folio, without Copper-
plates, on a worse paper, and never above half the value.
    Upon this Advertisement the Gazetteer harangued thus, July 6, 1739.
'How melancholy must it be to a Writer to be so unhappy as to see his

One on his manly confidence relies,
One on his vigour and superior size.   170
First Osborne lean'd against his letter'd post;
It rose, and labour'd to a curve at most.
So Jove's bright bow displays its wat'ry round,
(Sure sign, that no spectator shall be drown'd)
A second effort brought but new disgrace,   175
The wild Meander wash'd the Artist's face:
Thus the small jett, which hasty hands unlock,
Spirts in the gard'ner's eyes who turns the cock.
Not so from shameless Curl; impetuous spread
The stream, and smoking flourish'd o'er his head.   180
So (fam'd like thee for turbulence and horns)
Eridanus his humble fountain scorns;
Thro' half the heav'ns he pours th' exalted urn;
His rapid waters in their passage burn.

  Swift as it mounts, all follow with their eyes: 185
Still happy Impudence obtains the prize.
Thou triumph'st, Victor of the high-wrought day,
And the pleas'd dame, soft-smiling, lead'st away.
Osborne, thro' perfect modesty o'ercome,
Crown'd with the Jordan, walks contented home.   190
  But now for Authors nobler palms remain;
Room for my Lord! three jockeys in his train;
Six huntsmen with a shout precede his chair:
He grins, and looks broad nonsense with a stare.
His Honour's meaning Dulness thus exprest,   195
'He wins this Patron, who can tickle best.'
  He chinks his purse, and takes his seat of state:
With ready quills the Dedicators wait;
Now at his head the dextrous task commence,
And, instant, fancy feels th' imputed sense;   200

---

works hawked for sale in a manner so fatal to his fame! How, with
Honour to your self, and Justice to your Subscribers, can this be done?
What an Ingratitude to be charged on the *Only honest Poet* that lived in
1738! and than whom *Virtue* has not had a *shriller Trumpeter* for many
ages! That you were once *generally admired and esteemed* can be denied
by none; but that you and your works are now despised, is verified by *this
fact:*' which being utterly false, did not indeed much humble the Author,
but drew this just chastisement on the Bookseller.

  169, 170. *One on his manly confidence, &c.* ⟨A ii 161⟩.
  173, 174. *So Jove's bright bow, &c.* ⟨A ii 165⟩.
  181, 182. *So (fam'd like thee, &c.* ⟨A ii 173⟩.
  183. *Thro' half the heav'ns, &c.* ⟨A ii 175⟩.
  187. *the high-wrought day* ⟨A ii 179⟩.

Now gentle touches wanton o'er his face,
He struts Adonis, and affects grimace:
Rolli the feather to his ear conveys,
Then his nice taste directs our Operas:
Bentley his mouth with classic flatt'ry opes,   205
And the puff'd orator bursts out in tropes.
But Welsted most the Poet's healing balm
Strives to extract from his soft, giving palm;
Unlucky Welsted! thy unfeeling master,
The more thou ticklest, gripes his fist the faster.   210
    While thus each hand promotes the pleasing pain,
And quick sensations skip from vein to vein;
A youth unknown to Phœbus, in despair,
Puts his last refuge all in heav'n and pray'r.
What force have pious vows! The Queen of Love   215
His sister sends, her vot'ress, from above.

203. *Paolo Antonio Rolli* ⟨A ii 195⟩.
205. *Bentley his mouth, &c.*] Not spoken of the famous Dr. Richard
Bentley, but of one Thom. Bentley, a small critic, who aped his uncle in
a *little Horace*. The great one was intended to be dedicated to the Lord
Hallifax, but (on a change of the Ministry) was given to the Earl of Oxford;
for which reason the little one was dedicated to his son the Lord Harley.
A taste of this *Classic Elocution* may be seen in his following Panegyric on
the Peace of Utrecht. *Cupimus Patrem tuum, fulgentissimum illud Orbis
Anglicani jubar,* adorare. *O ingens* Reipublicæ *nostræ columen! O fortunatam tanto* Heroe *Britanniam! Illi tali tantoque viro* DEUM *per* Omnia
adfuisse, manumque ejus & mentem direxisse, CERTISSIMUM EST. Hujus
enim Unius *ferme opera,* æquissimis & perhonorificis conditionibus,
*diuturno, heu nimium! bello, finem impositum videmus. O Diem æterna
memoria dignissimam! qua terrores Patriæ omnes excidit,* Pacemque *diu
exoptatam toti fere Europæ restituit, ille Populi Anglicani Amor, Harleius.*
Thus critically (that is verbally) translated:
'Thy Father, that most refulgent star of the Anglican Orb, we much
desire to *adore!* Oh mighty Column of our *Republic!* Oh Britain, fortunate
in such an *Hero!* That to such and so great a Man GOD was ever present,
in *every thing,* and all along directed both his hand and his heart, is a *Most
Absolute Certainty!* For it is in a manner by the operation of this *Man
alone,* that we behold a *War* (alas! how much too long an one!) brought
at length to an end, *on the most just and most honourable Conditions.* Oh
Day eternally to be memorated! wherein All the Terrors of his Country
were ended, and a PEACE (long wish'd for by *almost all Europe*) was
restored by HARLEY, the Love and Delight of the People of England.'
    But that this Gentleman can write in a different style, may be seen in a
letter he printed to Mr. Pope, wherein several Noble Lords are treated in
a most extraordinary language, particularly the Lord Bolingbroke abused
for that very PEACE which he here makes the *single work* of the Earl of
Oxford, directed by *God Almighty.*
207. *Welsted* ⟨A ii 293⟩.
213. *A youth unknown to Phœbus, &c.* ⟨A ii 205⟩.

As taught by Venus, Paris learnt the art
To touch Achilles' only tender part;
Secure, thro' her, the noble prize to carry,
He marches off, his Grace's Secretary.   220
    'Now turn to diff'rent sports (the Goddess cries)
And learn, my sons, the wond'rous pow'r of Noise.
To move, to raise, to ravish ev'ry heart,
With Shakespear's nature, or with Johnson's art,
Let others aim: 'Tis yours to shake the soul   225
With Thunder rumbling from the mustard bowl,
With horns and trumpets now to madness swell,
Now sink in sorrows with a tolling bell;
Such happy arts attention can command,
When fancy flags, and sense is at a stand.   230
Improve we these. Three Cat-calls be the bribe
Of him, whose chatt'ring shames the Monkey tribe:
And his this Drum, whose hoarse heroic base
Drowns the loud clarion of the braying Ass.'
    Now thousand tongues are heard in one loud din: 235
The Monkey-mimics rush discordant in;
'Twas chatt'ring, grinning, mouthing, jabb'ring all,
And Noise and Norton, Brangling and Breval,
Dennis and Dissonance, and captious Art,
And Snip-snap short, and Interruption smart,   240
And Demonstration thin, and Theses thick,
And Major, Minor, and Conclusion quick.
'Hold (cry'd the Queen) a Cat-call each shall win;
Equal your merits! equal is your din!
But that this well-disputed game may end,   245
Sound forth my Brayers, and the welkin rend.'
    As when the long-ear'd milky mothers wait
At some sick miser's triple-bolted gate,
For their defrauded, absent foals they make
A moan so loud, that all the guild awake;   250
Sore sighs Sir Gilbert, starting at the bray,
From dreams of millions, and three groats to pay.

223, 225. *To move, to raise, &c.* ⟨A ii 215⟩.
226. *With Thunder, &c.* ⟨A ii 218⟩.
228. *—with a tolling bell* ⟨A ii 220⟩.
231. *Three Cat-calls* ⟨A ii 223⟩.
238. *Norton*] See ver. 417.—*J. Durant Breval,* Author of a very extraordinary Book of Travels, and some Poems. See before, Note on ver. 126
⟨A ii 230⟩.
243. *a Cat-call, &c.* ⟨A ii 233⟩.
247. *As when the, &c.* ⟨A ii 239⟩.

So swells each wind-pipe; Ass intones to Ass,
Harmonic twang! of leather, horn, and brass;
Such as from lab'ring lungs th' Enthusiast blows,   255
High Sound, attemp'red to the vocal nose;
Or such as bellow from the deep Divine;
There Webster! peal'd thy voice, and Whitfield! thine.
But far o'er all, sonorous Blackmore's strain;
Walls, steeples, skies, bray back to him again.   260
In Tot'nam fields, the brethren, with amaze,
Prick all their ears up, and forget to graze;
Long Chanc'ry-lane retentive rolls the sound,
And courts to courts return it round and round;
Thames wafts it thence to Rufus' roaring hall,   265
And Hungerford re-echoes bawl for bawl.
All hail him victor in both gifts of song,
Who sings so loudly, and who sings so long.
    This labour past, by Bridewell all descend,
(As morning pray'r, and flagellation end)   270
To where Fleet-ditch with disemboguing streams
Rolls the large tribute of dead dogs to Thames,
The King of dykes! than whom no sluice of mud
With deeper sable blots the silver flood.
'Here strip, my children! here at once leap in,   275
Here prove who best can dash thro' thick and thin,
And who the most in love of dirt excel,
Or dark dexterity of groping well.
Who flings most filth, and wide pollutes around
The stream, be his the Weekly Journals bound,   280
A pig of lead to him who dives the best;
A peck of coals a-piece shall glad the rest.'

258. *Webster—and Whitfield*] The one the writer of a News-paper called the Weekly Miscellany, the other a Field-preacher. This thought the only means of advancing Christianity was by the New-birth of religious madness; That, by the old death of fire and faggot: And therefore they agree in this, though in no other earthly thing, to abuse all the sober Clergy.
    260. *bray back to him again* ⟨A ii 248⟩.
    262. *Prick all their ears up, &c.* ⟨A ii 250⟩.
    263. *Long Chanc'ry-Lane* ⟨A ii 251⟩.
    268. *Who sings so loudly, &c.* ⟨A ii 256⟩.
    270. *As morning pray'r, &c.* ⟨A ii 258⟩.
    273. *The King of dykes! &c.* ⟨A ii 261⟩.
    276, 277, 278. ⟨A ii 264⟩.
    280. *the Weekly Journals* ⟨A ii 268⟩.
    282. '*A peck of coals a-piece*' ⟨A ii 270⟩.

In naked majesty Oldmixon stands,
And Milo-like surveys his arms and hands;
Then sighing, thus, 'And am I now three-score?   285
Ah why, ye Gods! should two and two make four?'
He said, and clim'd a stranded lighter's height,
Shot to the black abyss, and plung'd down-right.
The Senior's judgment all the crowd admire,
Who but to sink the deeper, rose the higher.   290
　　Next Smedley div'd; slow circles dimpled o'er
The quaking mud, that clos'd, and op'd no more.
All look, all sigh, and call on Smedley lost;
Smedley in vain resounds thro' all the coast.
　　Then * essay'd; scarce vanish'd out of sight,   295
He buoys up instant, and returns to light:
He bears no token of the sabler streams,
And mounts far off among the Swans of Thames.
　　True to the bottom, see Concanen creep,
A cold, long-winded, native of the deep: 300
If perseverance gain the Diver's prize,
Not everlasting Blackmore this denies:
No noise, no stir, no motion can'st thou make,
Th' unconscious stream sleeps o'er thee like a lake.
　　Next plung'd a feeble, but a desp'rate pack,   305
With each a sickly brother at his back:
Sons of a Day! just buoyant on the flood,
Then number'd with the puppies in the mud.
Ask ye their names? I could as soon disclose
The names of these blind puppies as of those.   310
Fast by, like Niobe (her children gone)

283. *Oldmixon*] Mr. JOHN OLDMIXON . . . vol. ii. p. 303 ⟨A ii 199⟩.
In his Essay on Criticism . . . death ⟨A ii 199⟩.
He is here likened to Milo . . . Lord Rosc. ⟨A ii 271⟩.
　291. *Smedley*] The person here mentioned . . . in octavo, 1728 ⟨A ii 279⟩.
　293. *and call on Smedley lost; &c.* ⟨A ii 281⟩.
　295. *Then * essay'd* ⟨See A ii 283*n*.⟩.
　299. *Concanen*] MATTHEW CONCANEN, an Irishman, bred to the law. Smedley (one of his brethren in enmity to Swift) in his Metamorphosis of Scriblerus, p. 7. accuses him of 'having boasted . . . Jamaica ⟨A ii 130⟩.
　302. *Not everlasting Blackmore* ⟨A ii 290⟩.
　306, 307. *With each a sickly brother, &c.*] These were daily Papers, a number of which, to lessen the expence, were printed one on the back of another.
　311. *like Niobe*] See the story in Ovid, Met. vii. where the miserable Petrefaction of this old Lady is pathetically described.

Sits Mother Osborne, stupify'd to stone!
And Monumental Brass this record bears,
'These are,—ah no! these were, the Gazetteers!'
    Not so bold Arnall; with a weight of skull,   315
Furious he dives, precipitately dull.

312. *Osborne*] A name assumed by the eldest and gravest of these writers, who at last being ashamed of his Pupils, gave his paper over, and in his age remained silent. ⟨James Pitt, 'formerly a country School-Master, conducted the *London Journal* under the name of *Fr. Osborne*; which the Country Writers, from the Heaviness of the Style, converted into *Mother Osborne*.'⟩

314. *Gazetteers*] We ought not to suppress that a modern Critic here taxeth the Poet with an Anachronism, affirming these Gazetteers not to have lived within the time of his poem, and challenging us to produce any such paper of that date. But we may with equal assurance assert, these Gazetteers not to have lived since, and challenge all the learned world to produce one such paper at this day. Surely therefore, where the point is so obscure, our author ought not to be censured too rashly. SCRIBL.

Notwithstanding this affected ignorance of the good Scriblerus, the *Daily Gazetteer* was a title given very properly to certain papers, each of which lasted but a day. Into this, as a common sink, was received all the trash, which had been before dispersed in several Journals, and circulated at the public expence of the nation. The authors were the same obscure men; though sometimes relieved by occasional essays from Statesmen, Courtiers, Bishops, Deans, and Doctors. The meaner sort were rewarded with Money; others with Places or Benefices, from an hundred to a thousand a year. It appears from the *Report* of the *Secret Committee* for enquiring into the Conduct of R. Earl of O. ⟨*Robert Earl of Orford*⟩ 'That no less than *fifty-thousand, seventy-seven pounds, eighteen shillings*, were paid to Authors and Printers of News-papers, such as Free-Britons, Daily-Courants, Corn-Cutter's Journals, Gazetteers, and other political papers, between Feb. 10, 1731, and Feb. 10, 1741.' Which shews the Benevolence of One Minister to have expended, for the current dulness of ten years in Britain, double the sum which gained Louis XIV. so much honour, in annual Pensions to Learned men all over Europe. In which, and in a much longer time, not a Pension at Court, nor Preferment in the Church or Universities, of any Consideration, was bestowed on any man distinguished for his Learning separately from Party-merit, or Pamphlet-writing.

It is worth a reflection, that of all the Panegyrics bestowed by these writers on this great Minister, not one is at this day extant or remembred; nor even so much credit done to his Personal character by all they have written, as by one short occasional compliment of our Author.

> *Seen him I have; but in his* happier hour
> *Of* social pleasure, *ill exchang'd for* Pow'r!
> *Seen him, uncumber'd by the Venal Tribe,*
> Smile *without* Art, *and* win *without a* Bribe.

⟨*Epilogue to the Satires*, i 29–32.⟩

315. *Arnall*] WILLIAM ARNALL, bred an Attorney, was a perfect Genius in this sort of work. He began under twenty with furious Party-papers; then succeeded Concanen in the British Journal. At the first publication of the Dunciad, he prevailed on the Author not to give him his due place in it, by a letter professing his detestation of such practices

Whirlpools and storms his circling arm invest,
With all the might of gravitation blest.
No crab more active in the dirty dance,
Downward to climb, and backward to advance.   320
He brings up half the bottom on his head,
And loudly claims the Journals and the Lead.
    The plunging Prelate, and his pond'rous Grace,
With holy envy gave one Layman place.
When lo! a burst of thunder shook the flood.   325
Slow rose a form, in majesty of Mud;
Shaking the horrors of his sable brows,
And each ferocious feature grim with ooze.
Greater he looks, and more than mortal stares:
Then thus the wonders of the deep declares.   330
    First he relates, how sinking to the chin,
Smit with his mien, the Mud-nymphs suck'd him in:
How young Lutetia, softer than the down,
Nigrina black, and Merdamante brown,
Vy'd for his love in jetty bow'rs below,   335
As Hylas fair was ravish'd long ago.
Then sung, how shown him by the Nut-brown maids
A branch of Styx here rises from the Shades,
That tinctur'd as it runs with Lethe's streams,
And wafting Vapours from the Land of dreams,   340
(As under seas Alphæus' secret sluice
Bears Pisa's off'rings to his Arethuse)
Pours into Thames: and hence the mingled wave
Intoxicates the pert, and lulls the grave:

---

as his Predecessor's. But since, by the most unexampled insolence, and
personal abuse of several great men, the Poet's particular friends, he most
amply deserved a niche in the Temple of Infamy: Witness a paper, called
the Free Briton, a Dedication intituled To the Genuine Blunderer, 1732,
and many others. He writ for hire, and valued himself upon it; not indeed
without cause, it appearing by the aforesaid REPORT, that he received
'for Free Britons, and other writings, in the space of *four years*, no less
than *ten thousand nine hundred and ninety-seven pounds, six shillings, and
eight pence*, out of the Treasury.'
    323. *The plunging Prelate, &c.* ⟨Sir Robert Walpole used to relate an
anecdote of Sherlock, Bishop of London, who was his contemporary at
Eton, 'that when some of the Scholars, going to bathe in the Thames,
stood shivering on the Bank, Sherlock plunged in immediately over his
head and ears'. By 'his pond'rous Grace', Pope most probably intended
John Potter (1674?-1747), Archbishop of Canterbury.⟩
    329. *Greater he looks, &c.* ⟨A ii 305⟩.
    336. *As Hylas fair* ⟨A ii 312⟩.
    338. *A branch of Styx, &c.* ⟨A ii 314⟩.

Here brisker vapours o'er the Temple creep,   345
There, all from Paul's to Aldgate drink and sleep.
   Thence to the banks where rev'rend Bards repose,
They led him soft; each rev'rend Bard arose;
And Milbourn chief, deputed by the rest,
Gave him the cassock, surcingle, and vest.   350
'Receive (he said) these robes which once were mine,
Dulness is sacred in a sound divine.'
   He ceas'd, and spread the robe; the crowd confess
The rev'rend Flamen in his lengthen'd dress.
Around him wide a sable Army stand,   355
A low-born, cell-bred, selfish, servile band,
Prompt or to guard or stab, to saint or damn,
Heav'n's Swiss, who fight for any God, or Man.
   Thro' Lud's fam'd gates, along the well-known Fleet
Rolls the black troop, and overshades the street,   360
'Till show'rs of Sermons, Characters, Essays,
In circling fleeces whiten all the ways:
So clouds replenish'd from some bog below,
Mount in dark volumes, and descend in snow.
Here stopt the Goddess; and in pomp proclaims   365
A gentler exercise to close the games.
   'Ye Critics! in whose heads, as equal scales,
I weigh what author's heaviness prevails;
Which most conduce to sooth the soul in slumbers,
My H—ley's periods, or my Blackmore's numbers;   370
Attend the trial we propose to make:
If there be man, who o'er such works can wake,
Sleep's all-subduing charms who dares defy,
And boasts Ulysses' ear with Argus' eye;
To him we grant our amplest pow'rs to sit   375
Judge of all present, past, and future wit;
To cavil, censure, dictate, right or wrong,
Full and eternal privilege of tongue.'
   Three College Sophs, and three pert Templars came,
The same their talents, and their tastes the same;   380

347. *Thence to the banks,* &c. ⟨A ii 321.⟩
349. *Milbourn* ⟨A ii 325⟩.
356. *cell-bred* ⟨i.e. bred in ignorance of the world⟩.
357. *to saint* ⟨to canonize, endow with saintly attributes⟩.
358. *Swiss* ⟨The Swiss mercenary soldiers, and hence, a term of contempt for a hireling supporter. Pope seems to be thinking more particularly here of the clerical journalists, such as Hoadly, Bland, Henley.⟩
359. *Lud's fam'd gates* ⟨A ii 332⟩.   374. ⟨A ii 342⟩.
380, 381. *The same their talents,* &c. ⟨A ii 348⟩.

Each prompt to query, answer, and debate,
And smit with love of Poesy and Prate.
The pond'rous books two gentle readers bring;
The heroes sit, the vulgar form a ring
The clam'rous crowd is hush'd with mugs of Mum,   385
'Till all tun'd equal, send a gen'ral hum.
Then mount the Clerks, and in one lazy tone
Thro' the long, heavy, painful page drawl on;
Soft creeping, words on words, the sense compose,
At ev'ry line they stretch, they yawn, they doze.   390
As to soft gales top-heavy pines bow low
Their heads, and lift them as they cease to blow:
Thus oft they rear, and oft the head decline,
As breathe, or pause, by fits, the airs divine.
And now to this side, now to that they nod,   395
As verse, or prose, infuse the drowzy God.
Thrice Budgel aim'd to speak, but thrice supprest
By potent Arthur, knock'd his chin and breast.
Toland and Tindal, prompt at priests to jeer,
Yet silent bow'd to Christ's No kingdom here.   400
Who sate the nearest, by the words o'ercome,
Slept first; the distant nodded to the hum.
Then down are roll'd the books; stretch'd o'er 'em lies
Each gentle clerk, and mutt'ring seals his eyes.
As what a Dutchman plumps into the lakes,   405
One circle first, and then a second makes;
What Dulness dropt among her sons imprest
Like motion from one circle to the rest;
So from the mid-most the nutation spreads
Round and more round, o'er all the sea of heads.   410
At last Centlivre felt her voice to fail,
Motteux himself unfinish'd left his tale,
Boyer the State, and Law the Stage gave o'er,

382. *And smit with love, &c.* ⟨A ii 350⟩.
384. *The heroes sit, &c.* ⟨A ii 352⟩.
388. *Thro' the long, heavy, painful page, &c.* ⟨A ii 356⟩.
397. *Thrice Budgel aim'd to speak* ⟨A ii 365⟩.
399. *Toland and Tindal*] Two persons, not so happy as to be obscure, who writ against the Religion of their Country. ⟨Cf. A ii 367.⟩
400. *Christ's No kingdom, &c.*] This is said by Curl, Key to Dunc. to allude to a sermon of a reverend Bishop. ⟨Cf. A ii 368.⟩
410. *O'er all the sea of heads* ⟨A ii 378⟩.
411. *Centlivre* ⟨A ii 379⟩.
413. *Boyer the State, and Law the Stage gave o'er* ⟨A ii 381⟩.

Morgan and Mandevil could prate no more;
Norton, from Daniel and Ostrœa sprung, 415
Bless'd with his father's front, and mother's tongue,
Hung silent down his never-blushing head;
And all was hush'd, as Folly's self lay dead.
  Thus the soft gifts of Sleep conclude the day,
And stretch'd on bulks, as usual, Poets lay. 420
Why should I sing what bards the nightly Muse
Did slumb'ring visit, and convey to stews;
Who prouder march'd, with magistrates in state,
To some fam'd round-house, ever open gate!
How Henley lay inspir'd beside a sink, 425
And to mere mortals seem'd a Priest in drink:
While others, timely, to the neighb'ring Fleet
(Haunt of the Muses) made their safe retreat.

414. *Morgan*] A writer against Religion, distinguished no otherwise from the rabble of his tribe than by the pompousness of his Title; for having stolen his Morality from Tindal, and his Philosophy from Spinoza, he calls himself, by the courtesy of England, a *Moral Philosopher*. W.

Ibid. *Mandevil*] This writer, who prided himself as much in the reputation of an *Immoral Philosopher*, was author of a famous book called the Fable of the Bees ⟨1714, 1729⟩; which may seem written to prove, that Moral Virtue is the invention of knaves, and Christian Virtue the imposition of fools; and that Vice is necessary, and alone sufficient to render Society flourishing and happy. W.

415. *Norton*] Norton De Foe . . . his name ⟨A ii 383⟩.

418. *And all was hush'd, &c.* ⟨A ii 386⟩.

426. *And to mere mortals, &c.*] This line presents . . . to cause scandal.' SCRIBL. ⟨A ii 393⟩.

427. *Fleet* ⟨A ii 395⟩.

The End of the Second Book

ARGUMENT TO BOOK THE THIRD

After the other persons are disposed in their proper places of rest, the Goddess transports the King to her Temple, and there lays him to slumber with his head on her lap; a position of marvellous virtue, which causes all the Visions of wild enthusiasts, projectors, politicians, inamoratos, castle-builders, chemists, and poets. He is immediately carried on the wings of Fancy, and led by a mad Poetical Sibyl, to the Elysian *shade; where, on the banks of* Lethe, *the souls of the dull are dipped by* Bavius, *before their entrance into this world. There he is met by the ghost of* Settle, *and by him made acquainted with the wonders of the place, and with those which he himself is destined to perform. He takes him to a* Mount *of Vision, from whence he shews him the past triumphs of the Empire of Dulness, then the present, and lastly the future: how small a part of the world was ever conquered by Science, how soon those conquests were stopped, and those very nations again reduced to her dominion. Then distinguishing the Island of* Great-Britain, *shews by what aids, by what persons, and by what degrees it shall be brought to her Empire. Some of the persons he causes to pass in review before his eyes, describing each by his proper figure, character, and qualifications. On a sudden the Scene shifts, and a vast number of miracles and prodigies appear, utterly surprising and unknown to the King himself, 'till they are explained to be the wonders of his own reign now commencing. On this Subject* Settle *breaks into a congratulation, yet not unmixed with concern, that his own times were but the types of these. He prophesies how first the nation shall be over-run with* Farces, Operas, *and* Shows; *how the throne of Dulness shall be advanced over the* Theatres, *and set up even at* Court: *then how her Sons shall preside in the seats of* Arts *and* Sciences: *giving a glimpse, or Pisgah-sight of the future Fulness of her Glory, the accomplishment whereof is the subject of the fourth and last book.*

But in her Temple's last recess inclos'd,
On Dulness' lap th' Anointed head repos'd.
Him close she curtains round with Vapours blue,
And soft besprinkles with Cimmerian dew.
Then raptures high the seat of Sense o'erflow,   5
Which only heads refin'd from Reason know.
Hence, from the straw where Bedlam's Prophet nods,
He hears loud Oracles, and talks with Gods:
Hence the Fool's Paradise, the Statesman's Scheme,
The air-built Castle, and the golden Dream,   10
The Maid's romantic wish, the Chemist's flame,
And Poet's vision of eternal Fame.
    And now, on Fancy's easy wing convey'd,
The King descending, views th' Elysian Shade.
A slip-shod Sibyl led his steps along,   15
In lofty madness meditating song;
Her tresses staring from Poetic dreams,
And never wash'd, but in Castalia's streams.
Taylor, their better Charon, lends an oar,

5, 6, &c. ⟨A iii 5, 6⟩.
How much the good Scriblerus was mistaken, may be seen from the Fourth book, which, it is plain from hence, he had never seen. BENT.
7, 8. *Hence, from the straw, &c.* ⟨A iii 8⟩.
19. *Taylor* ⟨A ii 323⟩.

(Once swan of Thames, tho' now he sings no more.)   20
Benlowes, propitious still to blockheads, bows;
And Shadwell nods the Poppy on his brows.
Here, in a dusky vale where Lethe rolls,
Old Bavius sits, to dip poetic souls,
And blunt the sense, and fit it for a skull   25
Of solid proof, impenetrably dull:
Instant, when dipt, away they wing their flight,
Where Brown and Mears unbar the gates of Light,
Demand new bodies, and in Calf's array,
Rush to the world, impatient for the day.   30
Millions and millions on these banks he views,
Thick as the stars of night, or morning dews,
As thick as bees o'er vernal blossoms fly,
As thick as eggs at Ward in Pillory.
   Wond'ring he gaz'd: When lo! a Sage appears,   35
By his broad shoulders known, and length of ears,
Known by the band and suit which Settle wore
(His only suit) for twice three years before:
All as the vest, appear'd the wearer's frame,
Old in new state, another yet the same.   40
Bland and familiar as in life, begun

21. *Benlowes*] A country gentleman, famous for his own bad Poetry, and for patronizing bad Poets, as may be seen from many Dedications of Quarles and others to him. Some of these anagram'd his name, *Benlowes* into *Benevolus:* to verify which, he spent his whole estate upon them. ⟨(1602–76), author of *Theophila, or Love's Sacrifice* and other works.⟩

22. *Shadwell* ⟨A ii 324⟩.

23. *Here in a dusky vale, &c.* ⟨A iii 15⟩.

24. *Old Bavius sits* ⟨A iii 16⟩.

24. *Old Bavius sits*] Bavius . . . the gentlemen of the Dunciad ⟨A iii 16⟩.

28. *unbar the gates of Light* ⟨A iii 20⟩.

28. *Brown and Mears*] Booksellers, Printers for any body.—The allegory . . . intelligible ⟨A iii 20⟩.

31, 32. *Millions and millions—Thick as the stars, &c.* ⟨A iii 23⟩.

34. *Ward in Pillory* ⟨A iii 26⟩.

36. *and length of ears* ⟨A iii 28⟩.

37. *Settle*] Elkanah Settle was once a Writer in vogue, as well as Cibber, both for Dramatic Poetry and Politics. Mr. Dennis tells us that 'he was a formidable rival to Mr. Dryden, and that in the University of Cambridge there were those who gave him the *preference*'. Mr. Welsted goes yet farther in his behalf: 'Poor Settle was formerly the *Mighty rival* of Dryden; nay, for *many years*, bore his reputation *above* him.' Pref. to his Poems, 8vo. p. 31. And Mr. Milbourn cried out, 'How little was Dryden able, even when his blood run high, to defend himself against Mr. Settle!' Notes on Dryd. Virg. p. 175. These are comfortable opinions! and no wonder some authors indulge them.

He was author or publisher . . . *Rem. on* Hom. ⟨A i 88⟩.

Thus the great Father to the greater Son.
  'Oh born to see what none can see awake!
Behold the wonders of th' oblivious Lake.
Thou, yet unborn, hast touch'd this sacred shore;   45
The hand of Bavius drench'd thee o'er and o'er.
But blind to former as to future fate,
What mortal knows his pre-existent state?
Who knows how long thy transmigrating soul
Might from Bœotian to Bœotian roll?   50
How many Dutchmen she vouchsaf'd to thrid?
How many stages thro' old Monks she rid?
And all who since, in mild benighted days,
Mix'd the Owl's ivy with the Poet's bays?
As man's Mæanders to the vital spring   55
Roll all their tides, then back their circles bring;
Or whirligigs, twirl'd round by skilful swain,
Suck the thread in, then yield it out again:
All nonsense thus, of old or modern date,
Shall in thee centre, from thee circulate.   60
For this, our Queen unfolds to vision true
Thy mental eye, for thou hast much to view:
Old scenes of glory, times long cast behind
Shall, first recall'd, rush forward to thy mind:
Then stretch thy sight o'er all her rising reign,   65
And let the past and future fire thy brain.
  'Ascend this hill, whose cloudy point commands
Her boundless empire over seas and lands.
See, round the Poles where keener spangles shine,
Where spices smoke beneath the burning Line,   70
(Earth's wide extremes) her sable flag display'd,
And all the nations cover'd in her shade!
  'Far eastward cast thine eye, from whence the Sun
And orient Science their bright course begun:
One god-like Monarch all that pride confounds,   75
He, whose long wall the wand'ring Tartar bounds;
Heav'ns! what a pile! whole ages perish there,

50. *Might from Bœotian, &c.*] Bœotia lay under the ridicule of the Wits
formerly, as Ireland does now; tho' it produced one of the greatest Poets
and one of the greatest Generals of Greece:

Bœotum crasso jurares aere natum.
HORAT.

54. *Mix'd the Owl's ivy* ⟨A iii 46⟩.
61, 62. *For this, our Queen, &c.* ⟨A iii 53⟩.
69. *See, round the Poles, &c.* ⟨A iii 61, 62⟩.
73. ⟨A iii 65⟩.   75. ⟨A iii 69⟩.

And one bright blaze turns Learning into air.
   'Thence to the south extend thy gladden'd eyes;
There rival flames with equal glory rise,   80
From shelves to shelves see greedy Vulcan roll,
And lick up all their Physic of the Soul.
   'How little, mark! that portion of the ball,
Where, faint at best, the beams of Science fall:
Soon as they dawn, from Hyperborean skies   85
Embody'd dark, what clouds of Vandals rise!
Lo! where Mæotis sleeps, and hardly flows
The freezing Tanais thro' a waste of snows,
The North by myriads pours her mighty sons,
Great nurse of Goths, of Alans, and of Huns!   90
See Alaric's stern port! the martial frame
Of Genseric! and Attila's dread name!
See the bold Ostrogoths on Latium fall;
See the fierce Visigoths on Spain and Gaul!
See, where the morning gilds the palmy shore   95
(The soil that arts and infant letters bore)
His conqu'ring tribes th' Arabian prophet draws,
And saving Ignorance enthrones by Laws.
See Christians, Jews, one heavy sabbath keep,
And all the western world believe and sleep.   100
   'Lo! Rome herself, proud mistress now no more
Of arts, but thund'ring against heathen lore;
Her grey-hair'd Synods damning books unread,
And Bacon trembling for his brazen head.
Padua, with sighs, beholds her Livy burn,   105
And ev'n th' Antipodes Vigilius mourn.
See, the Cirque falls, th' unpillar'd Temple nods,
Streets pav'd with Heroes, Tyber choak'd with Gods:
'Till Peter's keys some christ'ned Jove adorn,
And Pan to Moses lends his pagan horn;   110
See graceless Venus to a Virgin turn'd,
Or Phidias broken, and Apelles burn'd.
   'Behold yon' Isle, by Palmers, Pilgrims trod,
Men bearded, bald, cowl'd, uncowl'd, shod, unshod,
Peel'd, patch'd, and pyebald, linsey-wolsey brothers,   115
Grave Mummers! sleeveless some, and shirtless others.
That once was Britain—Happy! had she seen

81, 82. ⟨A iii 73, 74⟩.   96. ⟨A iii 88⟩.
102. *thund'ring against heathen lore* ⟨A iii 94⟩.
109. *'Till Peter's keys, &c.* ⟨A iii 101⟩.
117, 118. *Happy!—had Easter never been!* ⟨A iii 110⟩.

No fiercer sons, had Easter never been.
In peace, great Goddess, ever be ador'd;
How keen the war, if Dulness draw the sword!   120
Thus visit not thy own! on this blest age
Oh spread thy Influence, but restrain thy Rage.
   'And see, my son! the hour is on its way,
That lifts our Goddess to imperial sway;
This fav'rite Isle, long sever'd from her reign,   125
Dove-like, she gathers to her wings again.
Now look thro' Fate! behold the scene she draws!
What aids, what armies to assert her cause!
See all her progeny, illustrious sight!
Behold, and count them, as they rise to light.   130
As Berecynthia, while her offspring vye
In homage to the Mother of the sky,
Surveys around her, in the blest abode,
An hundred sons, and ev'ry son a God:
Not with less glory mighty Dulness crown'd,   135
Shall take thro' Grub-street her triumphant round;
And her Parnassus glancing o'er at once,
Behold an hundred sons, and each a Dunce.
   'Mark first that Youth who takes the foremost place,
And thrusts his person full into your face.   140
With all thy Father's virtues blest, be born!
And a new Cibber shall the stage adorn.
   'A second see, by meeker manners known,
And modest as the maid that sips alone;
From the strong fate of drams if thou get free,   145
Another Durfey, Ward! shall sing in thee.
Thee shall each ale-house, thee each gill-house mourn,
And answ'ring gin-shops sowrer sighs return.

126. *Dove-like, she gathers*] This is fulfilled in the fourth book.
127, 129. *Now look thro' Fate! &c.* ⟨A iii 119⟩.
131. *As Berecynthia, &c.* ⟨A iii 123⟩.
139. *Mark first that Youth, &c.* ⟨A iii 131⟩.
141. *With all thy Father's virtues, &c.*] A manner of expression . . .
Ecl. iv. ⟨A iii 133⟩.
It was very natural to shew to the Hero, before all others, his own Son,
who had already begun to emulate him in his theatrical, poetical, and even
political capacities. By the attitude in which he here presents himself, the
reader may be cautioned against ascribing wholly to the Father the merit
of the epithet *Cibberian*, which is equally to be understood with an eye to
the Son.
145. *From the strong fate of drams* ⟨A iii 137⟩.
147. *Thee shall each ale-house, &c.* ⟨A iii 139⟩.

'Jacob, the scourge of Grammar, mark with awe,
Nor less revere him, blunderbuss of Law.   150
Lo P--p--le's brow, tremendous to the town,
Horneck's fierce eye, and Roome's funereal Frown.
Lo sneering Goode, half malice and half whim,
A Fiend in glee, ridiculously grim.
Each Cygnet sweet of Bath and Tunbridge race,   155
Whose tuneful whistling makes the waters pass:
Each Songster, Riddler, ev'ry nameless name,
All crowd, who foremost shall be damn'd to Fame.
Some strain in rhyme; the Muses, on their racks,
Scream like the winding of ten thousand jacks: 160
Some free from rhyme or reason, rule or check,
Break Priscian's head, and Pegasus's neck;
Down, down they larum, with impetuous whirl,
The Pindars, and the Miltons of a Curl.
     'Silence, ye Wolves! while Ralph to Cynthia howls,   165
And makes Night hideous—Answer him, ye Owls!
     'Sense, speech, and measure, living tongues and dead,
Let all give way—and Morris may be read.
     'Flow Welsted, flow! like thine inspirer, Beer,
Tho' stale, not ripe; tho' thin, yet never clear;   170

149. *Jacob* ⟨A iii 149⟩.
149, 150. There may seem some error . . . Charity. ⟨As in 'Errata',
p. 429.⟩
150. ⟨A iii 150⟩.
152. *Horneck and Roome*] These two were virulent Party-writers,
worthily coupled together, and one would think prophetically, since, after
the publishing of this piece, the former dying, the latter succeeded him in
Honour and *Employment*. The first was Philip Horneck, Author of a
Billingsgate paper call'd The High German Doctor. Edward Roome was
son of an Undertaker for Funerals in Fleetstreet, and writ some of the
papers call'd Pasquin, where by malicious Innuendos he endeavoured to
represent our Author guilty of malevolent practices with a great man then
under prosecution of Parliament. P⟨opp⟩le was the author of some vile
Plays and Pamphlets. He published abuses on our author in a Paper called
the Prompter. ⟨Cf. A iii 146.⟩
153. *Goode* ⟨A iii 147⟩.
156. *Whose tuneful whistling makes the waters pass*] There were several
successions of these sort of minor poets, at Tunbridge, Bath, &c. singing
the praise of the Annuals flourishing for that season; whose names indeed
would be nameless, and therefore the Poet slurs them over with others
in general.
165. *Ralph*] James Ralph . . . Sept. 1728 ⟨A iii 159⟩. He ended at
last . . . a small pittance for pay ⟨A iii 159⟩.
168. *Morris*] *Besaleel*, see Book 2 ⟨126⟩.
169. *Flow Welsted, flow! &c.* ⟨A iii 163⟩.
169. *Flow* Welsted, *&c.*] Of this Author . . . *pag.* 23, 24 ⟨A iii 163⟩.
It should not be forgot to his honour, that he received at one time the sum

So sweetly mawkish, and so smoothly dull;
Heady, not strong; o'erflowing, tho' not full.
    'Ah Dennis! Gildon ah! what ill-starr'd rage
Divides a friendship long confirm'd by age?
Blockheads with reason wicked wits abhor,   175
But fool with fool is barb'rous civil war.
Embrace, embrace my sons! be foes no more!
Nor glad vile Poets with true Critic's gore.
    'Behold yon Pair, in strict embraces join'd;
How like in manners, and how like in mind!   180
Equal in wit, and equally polite,
Shall this a Pasquin, that a Grumbler write;
Like are their merits, like rewards they share,
That shines a consul, this Commissioner.'
    'But who is he, in closet close y-pent,   185
Of sober face, with learned dust besprent?'
'Right well mine eyes arede the myster wight,
On parchment scraps y-fed, and Wormius hight.
To future ages may thy dulness last,
As thou preserv'st the dulness of the past!   190
    'There, dim in clouds, the poring Scholiasts mark,
Wits, who like owls, see only in the dark,

---

of 500 pounds for secret service, among the other excellent authors hired
to write anonymously for the Ministry. See Report of the Secret Committee, &c. in 1742.
    173. *Ah Dennis, &c.*] The reader . . . at this time ⟨A iii 167⟩. By his
own account of himself in Mr. *Jacob's Lives*, he must have been above
threescore, and happily lived many years after. So that he was senior to
Mr. *Durfey*, who hitherto of all our Poets enjoy'd the longest Bodily life.
⟨Cf. A ii 273*n*.⟩
    177. *Embrace, embrace my sons!* ⟨A iii 171⟩.
    179. *Behold yon Pair, &c.* ⟨A iii 173⟩.
    179. *Behold yon Pair, &c.*] One of these . . . 1715 ⟨A iii 175⟩.
Of the other works of these Gentlemen the world has heard no more,
than it would of Mr. *Pope's*, had their united laudable endeavours discourag'd him from pursuing his studies . . . Cradle? C. ⟨A iii 175⟩.
    After many Editions of this poem, the Author thought fit to omit the
names of these two persons, whose injury to him was of so old a date. In
the verses he omitted, it was said that one of them had a *pious passion* for
the other. It was a literal translation of *Virgil, Nisus amore pio pueri*—and
there, as in the original, applied to Friendship: That between *Nisus* . . .
Gentleman together ⟨A iii 176⟩.
    184. *That shines a* Consul, *this* Commissioner] Such places were given
at this time to such sort of Writers.
    185. *But who is he, &c* ⟨A iii 181⟩.
    187. *arede* ⟨A iii 183⟩.   Ibid. *myster wight* ⟨A iii 183⟩.
    188. Wormius *hight* ⟨A iii 184⟩.   188. *hight* ⟨A iii 184⟩.
    192. *Wits, who, like owls, &c.* ⟨A iii 188⟩.

A Lumberhouse of books in ev'ry head,
For ever reading, never to be read!
    'But, where each Science lifts its modern type,   195
Hist'ry her Pot, Divinity his Pipe,
While proud Philosophy repines to show,
Dishonest sight! his breeches rent below;
Imbrown'd with native bronze, lo! Henley stands,
Tuning his voice, and balancing his hands.   200
How fluent nonsense trickles from his tongue!
How sweet the periods, neither said, nor sung!
Still break the benches, Henley! with thy strain,
While Sherlock, Hare, and Gibson preach in vain.
Oh great Restorer of the good old Stage,   205
Preacher at once, and Zany of thy age!
Oh worthy thou of Ægypt's wise abodes,
A decent priest, where monkeys were the gods!
But fate with butchers plac'd thy priestly stall,
Meek modern faith to murder, hack, and mawl;   210
And bade thee live, to crown Britannia's praise,
In Toland's, Tindal's, and in Woolston's days.
    'Yet oh, my sons! a father's words attend:
(So may the fates preserve the ears you lend)
'Tis yours, a Bacon or a Locke to blame,   215
A Newton's genius, or a Milton's flame:
But oh! with One, immortal one dispense,
The source of Newton's Light, of Bacon's Sense!
Content, each Emanation of his fires
That beams on earth, each Virtue he inspires,   220
Each Art he prompts, each Charm he can create,
Whate'er he gives, are giv'n for you to hate.
Persist, by all divine in Man unaw'd,
But, "Learn, ye DUNCES! not to scorn your GOD." '
    Thus he, for then a ray of Reason stole   225
Half thro' the solid darkness of his soul;
But soon the cloud return'd—and thus the Sire:
'See now, what Dulness and her sons admire!

199. *lo! Henley stands. &c.*] J. Henley the Orator . . . FACIAM ⟨A iii 195⟩. This man had an hundred pounds a year given him for the secret service of a weekly paper of unintelligible nonsense, called the Hyp-Doctor.
    204. *Sherlock, Hare, Gibson*] Bishops of Salisbury, Chichester, and London.
    212. ⟨A iii 208⟩.
    224. *But, 'Learn, ye Dunces! not to scorn your God'* ⟨A iii 222⟩.
    Ibid. *'not to scorn your God'*] See this subject pursued in Book 4.

See what the charms, that smite the simple heart
Not touch'd by Nature, and not reach'd by Art.'   230
    His never-blushing head he turn'd aside,
(Not half so pleas'd when Goodman prophesy'd)
And look'd, and saw a sable Sorc'rer rise,
Swift to whose hand a winged volume flies:
All sudden, Gorgons hiss, and Dragons glare,   235
And ten-horn'd fiends and Giants rush to war.
Hell rises, Heav'n descends, and dance on Earth:
Gods, imps, and monsters, music, rage, and mirth,
A fire, a jigg, a battle, and a ball,
'Till one wide conflagration swallows all.   240
    Thence a new world to Nature's laws unknown,
Breaks out refulgent, with a heav'n its own:
Another Cynthia her new journey runs,
And other planets circle other suns.
The forests dance, the rivers upward rise,   245
Whales sport in woods, and dolphins in the skies;
And last, to give the whole creation grace,
Lo! one vast Egg produces human race.
    Joy fills his soul, joy innocent of thought;
'What pow'r, he cries, what pow'r these wonders   250
          wrought?'
'Son; what thou seek'st is in thee! Look, and find
Each Monster meets his likeness in thy mind.
Yet would'st thou more? In yonder cloud behold,
Whose sarsenet skirts are edg'd with flamy gold,
A matchless Youth! his nod these worlds controuls,   255
Wings the red lightning, and the thunder rolls.
Angel of Dulness, sent to scatter round
Her magic charms o'er all unclassic ground:

---

232. (*Not half so pleas'd when Goodman prophesy'd*)] Mr. Cibber tells
us, in his Life, p. 149. that Goodman being at the rehearsal of a play, in
which he had a part, clapped him on the shoulder, and cried, 'If he does
not make a good actor, I'll be d—d—' 'And (says Mr. Cibber) I make it
a question, whether Alexander himself, or Charles the twelfth of Sweden,
when at the head of their first victorious armies, could feel a greater
transport in their bosoms than I did in mine.'
    237. *Hell rises, &c.* ⟨A iii 233⟩.
    244. *And other planets* ⟨A iii 240⟩.
    246. *Whales sport in woods, &c.* ⟨A iii 242⟩.
    248. *Lo! one vast Egg &c.* ⟨A iii 244⟩.
    251. *Son; what thou seek'st, &c.* ⟨A iii 247⟩.
    256. *Wings the red light'ning, &c.* ⟨A iii 252⟩.
    258. —*o'er all unclassic ground* ⟨A iii 254⟩.

Yon stars, yon suns, he rears at pleasure higher,
Illumes their light, and sets their flames on fire.   260
Immortal Rich! how calm he sits at ease
'Mid snows of paper, and fierce hail of pease;
And proud his Mistress' orders to perform,
Rides in the whirlwind, and directs the storm.
  'But lo! to dark encounter in mid air   265
New wizards rise; I see my Cibber there!
Booth in his cloudy tabernacle shrin'd,
On grinning dragons thou shalt mount the wind.
Dire is the conflict, dismal is the din,
Here shouts all Drury, there all Lincoln's-inn;   270
Contending Theatres our empire raise,
Alike their labours, and alike their praise.
  'And are these wonders, Son, to thee unknown?
Unknown to thee? These wonders are thy own.
These Fate reserv'd to grace thy reign divine,   275
Foreseen by me, but ah! with-held from mine.
In Lud's old walls tho' long I rul'd, renown'd
Far as loud Bow's stupendous bells resound;
Tho' my own Aldermen confer'd the bays,
To me committing their eternal praise,   280
Their full-fed Heroes, their pacific May'rs,
Their annual trophies, and their monthly wars:

261. *Immortal Rich!* ⟨A iii 257⟩.

266. *I see my Cibber there!*] The history of the foregoing absurdities is
verified by himself, in these words (Life, chap, xv.) 'Then sprung forth
that succession of monstrous medleys that have so long infested the stage,
which arose upon one another alternately at both houses, out-vying each
other in expence.' He then proceeds to excuse his own part in them, as
follows: 'If I am asked why I assented? I have no better excuse for my
error than to confess I did it against my conscience, and had not virtue
enough to starve. Had Henry IV. of France a better for changing his
Religion? I was still in my heart, as much as he could be, on the side of
Truth and Sense; but with this difference, that I had their leave to quit
them when they could not support me.—But let the question go which
way it will, Harry IVth has *always been allowed a great man*'. This must
be confest a full answer, only the question still seems to be, 1. How the
doing a thing against one's conscience is an excuse for it? and, 2dly, It
will be hard to prove how he got the leave of Truth and Sense to quit
their service, unless he can produce a Certificate that he ever was in it.

266, 267. *Booth* and *Cibber* were joint managers of the Theatre in
Drury-lane.

268. *On grinning dragons, &c.*] In his Letter to Mr. P. Mr. C. solemnly
declares this not to be *literally true*. We hope therefore the reader will
understand it *allegorically* only.

282. ⟨A iii 280⟩.

Tho' long my Party built on me their hopes,
For writing Pamphlets, and for roasting Popes;
Yet lo! in me what authors have to brag on!　285
Reduc'd at last to hiss in my own dragon.
Avert it Heav'n! that thou, my Cibber, e'er
Should'st wag a serpent-tail in Smithfield fair!
Like the vile straw that's blown about the streets,
The needy Poet sticks to all he meets,　290
Coach'd, carted, trod upon, now loose, now fast,
And carry'd off in some Dog's tail at last.
Happier thy fortunes! like a rolling stone,
Thy giddy dulness still shall lumber on,
Safe in its heaviness, shall never stray,　295
But lick up ev'ry blockhead in the way.
Thee shall the Patriot, thee the Courtier taste,
And ev'ry year be duller than the last.
'Till rais'd from booths, to Theatre, to Court,
Her seat imperial Dulness shall transport.　300
Already Opera prepares the way,
The sure fore-runner of her gentle sway:
Let her thy heart, next Drabs and Dice, engage,
The third mad passion of thy doting age.
Teach thou the warb'ling Polypheme to roar,　305
And scream thyself as none e'er scream'd before!
To aid our cause, if Heav'n thou can'st not bend,
Hell thou shalt move; for Faustus is our friend:
Pluto with Cato thou for this shalt join,
And link the Mourning Bride to Proserpine.　310
Grubstreet! thy fall should men and Gods conspire,
Thy stage shall stand, ensure it but from Fire.

283. *Tho' long my Party* ⟨A iii 281⟩.
297. *Thee shall the Patriot, &c.* ⟨A iii 299⟩.
305. *Polypheme*] He translated the Italian Opera of Polifemo; but unfortunately lost the whole jest of the story. The Cyclops asks Ulysses his *name*, who tells him his name is *Noman*: After his eye is put out, he roars and calls the Brother Cyclops to his aid: They enquire *who has hurt him?* he answers *Noman*; whereupon they all go away again. Our ingenious Translator made Ulysses answer, *I take no name*, whereby all that follow'd became unintelligible. Hence it appears that Mr. Cibber (who values himself on subscribing to the English Translation of Homer's Iliad) had not that merit with respect to the Odyssey, or he might have been better instructed in the Greek *Pun-nology.*
308, 309. *Faustus, Pluto, &c.*] Names of miserable Farces which ... audience ⟨A iii 307⟩.
312. *ensure it but from Fire* ⟨A iii 310⟩.

Another Æschylus appears! prepare
For new abortions, all ye pregnant fair!
In flames, like Semele's, be brought to bed,   315
While op'ning Hell spouts wild-fire at your head.
  'Now Bavius take the poppy from thy brow,
And place it here! here all ye Heroes bow!
This, this is he, foretold by ancient rhymes:
Th' Augustus born to bring Saturnian times.   320
Signs following signs lead on the mighty year!
See! the dull stars roll round and re-appear.
See, see, our own true Phœbus wears the bays!
Our Midas sits Lord Chancellor of Plays!
On Poets' Tombs see Benson's titles writ!   325
Lo! Ambrose Philips is prefer'd for Wit!
See under Ripley rise a new White-hall,
While Jones' and Boyle's united labours fall:
While Wren with sorrow to the grave descends,
Gay dies unpension'd with a hundred friends,   330
Hibernian Politics, O Swift! thy fate;
  And Pope's, ten years to comment and translate.
  'Proceed, great days! 'till Learning fly the shore,
'Till Birch shall blush with noble blood no more,
'Till Thames see Eaton's sons for ever play,   335
'Till Westminster's whole year be holiday,

313. *Another Æschylus appears!*] It is reported . . . miscarried ⟨A iii 311⟩.

315. *like Semele's* ⟨A iii 313⟩.

319, 320. *This, this is he, &c.* ⟨A iii 317⟩.

323. *Phœbus* ⟨See iv 61n., 93n.⟩

324. *Midas* ⟨i.e. Cibber is as bad a judge of poetry as Midas, who, called upon to judge between Apollo and Pan, awarded the prize to Pan. There may be a secondary suggestion that Cibber was coining money for himself from the theatre.⟩

325. *Benson's titles writ* ⟨A iii 321. Cf. iv 110n.⟩

326. *Ambrose Philips*] He was (saith Mr. JACOB) . . . *enjoys'* ⟨A iii 322⟩. He endeavour'd . . . of it ⟨A iii 322⟩.

327. *a new White-hall* ⟨Pope probably means the Admiralty building planned by Ripley, 1724–6.⟩

328. *Jones' and Boyle's united labours* ⟨A iii 324⟩.

330. *Gay dies unpension'd, &c.* ⟨A iii 326⟩.

331. *Hibernian Politics*] See book I. ver. 26.

332. *And Pope's . . . to comment and translate* ⟨A iii 328n.⟩

333. *Proceed, great days! &c.*] It may perhaps seem incredible, that so great a Revolution in Learning as is here prophesied, should be brought about by such *weak Instruments* as have been [hitherto] described in our poem: But do not thou, gentle reader, rest too secure in thy contempt of these Instruments. Remember what the Dutch stories . . . SCRIBL. ⟨A iii 337⟩.

'Till Isis' Elders reel, their pupils' sport,
And Alma mater lie dissolv'd in Port!'
    'Enough! enough!' the raptur'd Monarch cries;
And thro' the Iv'ry Gate the Vision flies.   340

340. *And thro' the Iv'ry Gate, &c.* ⟨A iii 358⟩.

The End of the Third Book

BOOK THE FOURTH

ARGUMENT

The Poet being, in this Book, to declare the Completion *of the* Prophecies *mention'd at the end of the former, makes a new* Invocation; *as the greater Poets are wont, when some high and worthy matter is to be sung. He shews the Goddess coming in her Majesty, to destroy* Order *and* Science, *and to substitute the* Kingdom *of the* Dull *upon earth. How she leads captive the* Sciences, *and silenceth the* Muses; *and what they be who succeed in their stead. All her Children, by a wonderful attraction, are drawn about her; and bear along with them divers others, who promote her Empire by connivance, weak resistance, or discouragement of Arts; such as Half-wits, tasteless Admirers, vain Pretenders, the Flatterers of Dunces, or the Patrons of them. All these crowd round her; one of them offering to approach her, is driven back by a Rival, but she commends and encourages both. The first who speak in form are the* Genius's *of the* Schools, *who assure her of their care to advance her Cause, by confining Youth to* Words, *and keeping them out of the way of real Knowledge. Their Address, and her gracious Answer; with her Charge to them and the Universities. The* Universities *appear by their proper Deputies, and assure her that the same method is observ'd in the progress of* Education; *The speech of* Aristarchus *on this subject. They are driven off by a band of young Gentlemen return'd from* Travel *with their* Tutors; *one of whom delivers to the Goddess, in a polite oration, an account of the whole Conduct and Fruits of their* Travels: *presenting to her at the same time a young Nobleman perfectly accomplished. She receives him graciously, and indues him with the happy quality of* Want of Shame. *She sees loitering about her a number of* Indolent Persons *abandoning all business and duty, and dying with laziness: To these approaches the Antiquary* Annius, *intreating her to make them* Virtuosos, *and assign them over to him: But* Mummius, *another Antiquary, complaining of his fraudulent proceeding, she finds a method to reconcile their difference. Then enter a Troop of people fantastically adorn'd, offering her strange and exotic presents: Amongst them, one stands forth and demands justice on another, who had deprived him of one of the greatest Curiosities in nature: but he justifies himself so well, that the Goddess gives them both her approbation. She recommends to them to find proper employment for the* Indolents *before-mentioned, in the study of* Butterflies, Shells, Birds-nests, Moss, &c. *but with particular caution, not to proceed beyond* Trifles, *to any useful or extensive views of Nature, or of the Author of Nature. Against the last of these apprehensions, she is secured by a hearty Address from the* Minute Philosophers *and* Freethinkers, *one of whom speaks in the name of the rest. The Youth thus instructed and principled, are delivered to her in a body, by the hands of* Silenus; *and then admitted to taste the Cup of the* Magus *her High Priest, which causes a total oblivion of all Obligations, divine, civil, moral, or rational. To these her Adepts she sends* Priests, Attendants, *and* Comforters, *of various kinds; confers on them* Orders *and* Degrees; *and then dismissing them with a speech, confirming to each his* Privileges *and telling what she expects from each, concludes with a* Yawn *of extraordinary virtue: The Progress and Effects whereof on all Orders of men, and the Consummation of all, in the Restoration of* Night *and* Chaos, *conclude the Poem.*

        Yet, yet a moment, one dim Ray of Light
        Indulge, dread Chaos, and eternal Night!
        Of darkness visible so much be lent,
        As half to shew, half veil the deep Intent.

The DUNCIAD, Book IV.] This Book may properly be distinguished from the former, by the Name of the GREATER DUNCIAD, not so indeed in Size, but in Subject; and so far contrary to the distinction anciently made of the *Greater* and *Lesser Iliad*. But much are they mistaken who imagine this Work in any wise inferior to the former, or of any other hand than of our Poet; of which I am much more certain than that the *Iliad* itself was the Work of *Solomon*, or the *Batrachomuomachia* of *Homer*, as *Barnes* hath affirmed. BENT. P. W. ⟨Joshua Barnes, 1654–1712, editor of Homer.⟩

1, &c.] This is an Invocation of much Piety. The Poet willing to approve himself a genuine Son, beginneth by shewing (what is ever agreeable to *Dulness*) his high respect for *Antiquity* and a *Great Family*, how dull, or dark soever: Next declareth his love for *Mystery* and *Obscurity*; and lastly his Impatience to be *re-united* to her. SCRIBL. P.W.

2. *dread Chaos, and eternal Night*] Invoked, as the Restoration of their Empire is the Action of the Poem. P.W.

4. *half to shew, half veil*] This is a great propriety, for a dull Poet can never express himself otherwise than by *halves*, or imperfectly. SCRIBL. P.W.

I understand it very differently; the Author in this work had indeed a

Ye Pow'rs! whose Mysteries restor'd I sing,   5
To whom Time bears me on his rapid wing,
Suspend a while your Force inertly strong,
Then take at once the Poet and the Song.
  Now flam'd the Dog-star's unpropitious ray,
Smote ev'ry Brain, and wither'd ev'ry Bay;   10
Sick was the Sun, the Owl forsook his bow'r,
The moon-struck Prophet felt the madding hour:
Then rose the Seed of Chaos, and of Night,
To blot out Order, and extinguish Light,
Of dull and venal a new World to mold,   15
And bring Saturnian days of Lead and Gold.

---

deep Intent; there were in it *Mysteries* or ἀπόρρητα which he durst not fully reveal, and doubtless in divers verses (according to *Milton*)

—— *more is meant than meets the ear* ⟨*Il Penseroso*, l. 120⟩.

BENT. P.W.

6. *To whom Time bears me*] Fair and softly, good Poet! (cries the gentle *Scriblerus* on this place.) For sure in spite of his unusual modesty, he shall not travel so fast toward Oblivion, as divers others of more Confidence have done: For when I revolve in my mind the Catalogue of those who have the most boldly promised to themselves Immortality, *viz. Pindar, Luis Gongora, Ronsard, Oldham,* Lyrics; *Lycophron, Statius, Chapman, Blackmore,* Heroics; I find the one half to be already dead, and the other in utter darkness. But it becometh not us, who have taken upon us the office of Commentator, to suffer our Poet thus prodigally to cast away his Life; contrariwise, the more hidden and abstruse is his work, and the more remote its beauties from common Understanding, the more is it our duty to draw forth and exalt the same, in the face of Men and Angels. Herein shall we imitate the laudable Spirit of those, who have (for this very reason) delighted to comment on the Fragments of *dark* and *uncouth* Authors, preferred *Ennius* to *Virgil*, and chosen to turn the dark Lanthorn of *Lycophron*, rather than to trim the everlasting Lamp of *Homer*. SCRIBL. P.W.

7. *Force inertly strong*] Alluding to the *Vis inertiæ of Matter*, which, tho' it really be no Power, is yet the Foundation of all the Qualities and Attributes of that sluggish Substance. P.W.

14. *To blot out* Order, *and extinguish* Light] The two great Ends of her Mission; the one in quality of Daughter of *Chaos*, the other as Daughter of *Night. Order* here is to be understood extensively, both as Civil and Moral, the distinctions between high and low in Society, and true and false in Individuals: *Light*, as Intellectual only, Wit, Science, Arts. P.W.

15. *Of dull and venal*] The Allegory continued: *dull* referring to the extinction of Light or Science, *venal* to the destruction of Order, or the Truth of Things. P.W.

Ibid. *a new World*] In allusion to the Epicurean opinion, that from the Dissolution of the natural World into Night and Chaos, a new one should arise; this the Poet alluding to, in the Production of a new moral World, makes it partake of its original Principles. P.W.

16. Lead *and* Gold] *i.e.* dull and venal. P.W.

　　She mounts the Throne: her head a Cloud conceal'd,
In broad Effulgence all below reveal'd,
('Tis thus aspiring Dulness ever shines)
Soft on her lap her Laureat son reclines.　　　　　　　20
　　Beneath her foot-stool, *Science* groans in Chains,
And *Wit* dreads Exile, Penalties and Pains.
There foam'd rebellious *Logic*, gagg'd and bound,
There, stript, fair *Rhet'ric* languish'd on the ground;
His blunted Arms by *Sophistry* are born,　　　　　　　25
And shameless *Billingsgate* her Robes adorn.

　　18. *all below reveal'd*] Vet. Adag. 𝕿𝖍𝖊 𝖍𝖎𝖌𝖍𝖊𝖗 𝖞𝖔𝖚 𝖈𝖑𝖎𝖒𝖇, 𝖙𝖍𝖊 𝖒𝖔𝖗𝖊 𝖞𝖔𝖚
𝖘𝖍𝖊𝖂 𝖞𝖔𝖚𝖗 𝕬——. Verified in no instance more than in Dulness aspiring.
Emblematized also by an Ape climbing and exposing his posteriors.
SCRIBL. P.W.
　　20. *her Laureat son reclines*] With great judgment it is imagined by the
Poet, that such a Collegue as Dulness had elected, should sleep on the
Throne, and have very little share in the Action of the Poem. Accordingly
he hath done little or nothing from the day of his Anointing; having past
through the second book without taking part in any thing that was
transacted about him, and thro' the third in profound Sleep. Nor ought
this, well considered, to seem strange in our days, when so many *King-
consorts* have done the like. SCRIBL.
　　This verse our excellent Laureate took so to heart, that he appealed to
all mankind, 'if he was not as *seldom asleep as any fool?*' But it is hoped the
Poet hath not injured him, but rather verified his Prophecy (p. 243. of
his own Life, 8vo. ch. ix.) where he says '*the Reader will be as much
pleased to find me a* Dunce *in my* Old age, *as he was to prove me a* brisk
blockhead *in my* Youth'. Wherever there was any room for Briskness, or
Alacrity of any sort, *even in sinking*, he hath had it allowed him; but here,
where there is nothing for him to do but to take his natural rest, he must
permit his Historian to be silent. It is from their *actions* only that Princes
have their character, and Poets from their *works:* And if in *those* he be *as
much asleep as any fool*, the Poet must leave him and them to *sleep to all
eternity.* BENT.
　　Ibid. *her Laureat*] 'When I find my Name in the satyrical works of this
Poet, I never look upon it as any malice meant to me, but PROFIT to
himself. For he considers that *my Face* is more *known* than most in the
nation; and therefore *a Lick at the Laureate* will be a sure bait *ad
captandum vulgus*, to catch little readers.' Life of Colley Cibber, chap. ii.
　　Now if it be certain, that the works of our Poet have owed their success
to this ingenious expedient, we hence derive an unanswerable Argument,
that this Fourth DUNCIAD, as well as the former three, hath had the
Author's last hand, and was by him intended for the Press: Or else to
what purpose hath he crowned it, as we see, by this finishing stroke, the
profitable *Lick* at the *Laureate?* BENT.
　　21, 22. *Beneath her footstool, &c.*] We are next presented with the
pictures of those whom the Goddess leads in Captivity. *Science* is only
depressed and confined so as to be rendered useless; but *Wit* or *Genius*,
as a more dangerous and active enemy, punished, or driven away: *Dulness*
being often reconciled in some degree with Learning, but never upon any
terms with Wit. And accordingly it will be seen that she admits something
like each Science, as Casuistry, Sophistry, &c. P.W.

Morality, by her false Guardians drawn,
Chicane in Furs, and *Casuistry* in Lawn,
Gasps, as they straiten at each end the cord,
And dies, when Dulness gives her Page the word.   30
Mad *Mathesis* alone was unconfin'd,
Too mad for mere material chains to bind,
Now to pure Space lifts her extatic stare,
Now running round the Circle, finds it square.
But held in ten-fold bonds the *Muses* lie,   35
Watch'd both by Envy's and by Flatt'ry's eye:
There to her heart sad Tragedy addrest
The dagger wont to pierce the Tyrant's breast;
But sober History restrain'd her rage,
And promis'd Vengeance on a barb'rous age.   40
There sunk Thalia, nerveless, cold, and dead,
Had not her Sister Satyr held her head:
Nor cou'd'st thou, CHESTERFIELD! a tear refuse,
Thou wept'st, and with thee wept each gentle Muse.

28. *in* Furs . . . *in* Lawn ⟨i.e. in the Law . . . in the Church. The 'Furs' are the ermine robes of the judges. 'Lawn' is the fine linen used for the sleeves of a bishop.⟩

30. *gives her* Page *the word*] There was a Judge of this name ⟨see p. 616, l. 82⟩, always ready to hang any man, of which he was suffered to give a hundred miserable examples during a long life, even to his dotage. Tho' the candid *Scriblerus* imagined *Page* here to mean no more than a *Page* or *Mute*, and to allude to the custom of strangling State Criminals in *Turkey* by Mutes or Pages. A practice more decent than that of *our Page*, who before he hanged any person, loaded him with reproachful language. SCRIBL.

31. *Mad* Mathesis] Alluding to the strange Conclusions some Mathematicians have deduced from their principles concerning the *real Quantity of Matter*, the *Reality of Space*, &c.

34. *finds it square*] Regards the wild and fruitless attempts of *squaring the Circle*. P.W.

36. *Watch'd both by* Envy's *and by* Flatt'ry's *eye*] One of the misfortunes falling on Authors, from the *Act* for subjecting *Plays* to the power of a *Licenser*, being the false representations to which they were expos'd, from such as either gratify'd their Envy to Merit, or made their Court to Greatness, by perverting general Reflections against Vice into Libels on particular Persons.

43. *Nor cou'd'st thou, &c.*] This Noble Person in the year 1737, when the Act aforesaid was brought into the House of Lords, opposed it in an excellent speech (says Mr. *Cibber*) 'with a lively spirit, and uncommon eloquence'. This speech had the honour to be answered by the said Mr. *Cibber*, with a lively spirit also, and in a manner very uncommon, in the 8th Chapter of his *Life and Manners*. And here, gentle Reader, would I gladly insert the other speech, whereby thou mightest judge between them: but I must defer it on account of some differences not yet adjusted between the noble Author and myself, concerning the *True Reading* of certain passages. SCRIBL.

When lo! a Harlot form soft sliding by,   45
With mincing step, small voice, and languid eye;
Foreign her air, her robe's discordant pride
In patch-work flutt'ring, and her head aside.
By singing Peers up-held on either hand,
She tripp'd and laugh'd, too pretty much to stand; 50
Cast on the prostrate Nine a scornful look,
Then thus in quaint Recitativo spoke.
   'O *Cara! Cara!* silence all that train:
Joy to great Chaos! let Division reign:
Chromatic tortures soon shall drive them hence,   55
Break all their nerves, and fritter all their sense:
One Trill shall harmonize joy, grief, and rage,
Wake the dull Church, and lull the ranting Stage;
To the same notes thy sons shall hum, or snore,
And all thy yawning daughters cry, *encore.*   60
Another Phœbus, thy own Phœbus, reigns,
Joys in my jiggs, and dances in my chains.
But soon, ah soon Rebellion will commence.

45. *When lo! a Harlot form*] Every Reader will see, that from this verse to the 68th is a detach'd piece. We suppose it rightly inserted here, from what is said of her casting a scornful look on the *prostrate Muses*: but if any one can show us a properer place we shall be obliged to him. The Attitude given to this Phantom represents the nature and genius of the *Italian* Opera; its affected airs, its effeminate sounds, and the practice of patching up these Operas with favourite Songs, incoherently put together. These things were supported by the subscriptions of the Nobility. This circumstance that Opera should prepare for the opening of the grand Sessions, was prophesied of in Book 3. ver. 304.
> *Already Opera prepares the way,*
> *The sure fore-runner of her gentle sway.*

54. *let Division reign*] Alluding to the false taste of playing tricks in Music with numberless divisions, to the neglect of that harmony which conforms to the Sense, and applies to the Passions. Mr. *Handel* had introduced a great number of Hands, and more variety of Instruments into the Orchestra, and employed even Drums and Cannon to make a fuller Chorus; which prov'd so much too manly for the fine Gentlemen of his age, that he was obliged to remove his Music into *Ireland.* After which they were reduced, for want of Composers, to practise the patch-work above mentioned. ⟨Senesino was particularly celebrated for his 'divisions', i.e. breaking up each of a succession of long notes into a number of short ones, and so dwelling on a single syllable of the word he was singing.⟩

61. *thy own* Phœbus *reigns*]
> *Tuus jam regnat Apollo.* Virg. ⟨Ecl. iv 10.⟩

Not the ancient *Phœbus*, the God of Harmony, but a modern *Phœbus* of *French* extraction, married to the Princess *Galimathia*, one of the handmaids of Dulness, and an assistant to Opera. Of whom see *Bouhours*, and other Critics of that nation. SCRIBL. P.W.

If Music meanly borrows aid from Sense:
Strong in new Arms, lo! Giant Handel stands,   65
Like bold Briareus, with a hundred hands;
To stir, to rouze, to shake the Soul he comes,
And Jove's own Thunders follow Mars's Drums.
Arrest him, Empress; or you sleep no more'—
She heard, and drove him to th' Hibernian shore.   70
    And now had Fame's posterior Trumpet blown,
And all the Nations summon'd to the Throne.
The young, the old, who feel her inward sway,
One instinct seizes, and transports away.
None need a guide, by sure Attraction led,   75
And strong impulsive gravity of Head:

64. *Music meanly borrows aid, &c.* ⟨Pope appears to be referring to
Handel's oratorios.⟩
71. *Fame's posterior Trumpet*] *Posterior*, viz. her *second* or *more certain*
Report: unless we imagine this word *posterior* to relate to the position of
one of her Trumpets, according to *Hudibras:*

> She blows not both with the same Wind,
> But one before and one behind;
> And therefore modern Authors name
> One good, and t'other evil Fame.
>   ⟨Pt. II, Canto i, 71-2, 75-6.⟩ P.W.

75. *None need a* guide, &c.] The sons of Dulness want no instructors
in study, nor guides in life: they are their own masters in all Sciences, and
their own Heralds and Introducers into all places. P.W.
76 to 101.] It ought to be observed that here are three classes in this
assembly. The first of men absolutely and avowedly dull, who naturally
adhere to the Goddess, and are imagined in the simile of the Bees about
their Queen. The second involuntarily drawn to her, tho' not caring to
own her influence; from ver. 81 to 90. The third of such, as, tho' not
members of her state, yet advance her service by flattering Dulness,
cultivating mistaken talents, patronizing vile scriblers, discouraging living
merit, or setting up for wits, and Men of taste in arts they understand not;
from ver. 91 to 101. In this new world of Dulness each of these three
classes hath its appointed station, as best suits its nature, and concurs to
the harmony of the System. The *first* drawn only by the strong and simple
impulse of Attraction, are represented as falling directly down into her;
as conglobed into her substance, and resting in her centre.

> —— *All their centre found,*
> *Hung to the Goddess, and coher'd around.*

The *second*, tho' within the sphere of her attraction, yet having at the
same time a different motion, they are carried, by the composition of
these two, in planetary revolutions round her centre, some nearer to it,
some further off:

> *Who gently drawn, and struggling less and less,*
> *Roll in her Vortex, and her pow'r confess.*

The *third* are properly *excentrical*, and no constant members of her state
or system: sometimes at an immense distance from her influence, and

None want a place, for all their Centre found,
Hung to the Goddess, and coher'd around.
Not closer, orb in orb, conglob'd are seen
The buzzing Bees about their dusky Queen.   80
   The gath'ring number, as it moves along,
Involves a vast involuntary throng,
Who gently drawn, and struggling less and less,
Roll in her Vortex, and her pow'r confess.
Not those alone who passive own her laws,   85
But who, weak rebels, more advance her cause.
Whate'er of dunce in College or in Town
Sneers at another, in toupee or gown;
Whate'er of mungril no one class admits,
A wit with dunces, and a dunce with wits.   90
   Nor absent they, no members of her state,
Who pay her homage in her sons, the Great;
Who false to Phœbus, bow the knee to Baal;
Or impious, preach his Word without a call.
Patrons, who sneak from living worth to dead,   95
With-hold the pension, and set up the head;
Or vest dull Flatt'ry in the sacred Gown;
Or give from fool to fool the Laurel crown.
And (last and worst) with all the cant of wit,
Without the soul, the Muse's Hypocrit.   100
   There march'd the bard and blockhead, side by side,
Who rhym'd for hire, and patroniz'd for pride.
Narcissus, prais'd with all a Parson's pow'r,
Look'd a white lilly sunk beneath a show'r.
There mov'd Montalto with superior air;   105

---

sometimes again almost on the surface of her *broad effulgence*. Their use
in their Perihelion, or nearest approach to Dulness, is the same in the
moral World, as that of *Comets* in the natural, namely to refresh and
recreate the Dryness and decays of the system; in the manner marked out
from ver. 91 to 98. P.W.

88. *toupee* ⟨'A curl or artificial lock of hair on the top of the head, esp.
as a crowning feature of the periwig; a periwig in which the front hair was
combed up, over a pad, into such a top-knot'.⟩

93. *false to* Phœbus] Spoken of the ancient and true *Phœbus*, not the
French Phœbus, who hath no chosen Priests or Poets, but equally inspires
any man that pleaseth to sing or preach. SCRIBL.

103–4. *Narcissus* ⟨Lord Hervey, to whom Dr. Conyers Middleton
dedicated his *Life of Cicero* in 1741. Hervey was an epileptic, and had a
noticeably white face.⟩

105. *Montalto* ⟨The 'decent Knight' of l. 113, i.e. Sir Thomas
Hanmer.⟩

His stretch'd-out arm display'd a Volume fair;
Courtiers and Patriots in two ranks divide,
Thro' both he pass'd, and bow'd from side to side:
But as in graceful act, with awful eye
Compos'd he stood, bold Benson thrust him by: 110
On two unequal crutches propt he came,
Milton's on this, on that one Johnston's name.
The decent Knight retir'd with sober rage,
Withdrew his hand, and clos'd the pompous page.
[But (happy for him as the times went then)   115
Appear'd Apollo's May'r and Aldermen,
On whom three hundred gold-capt youths await,
To lug the pond'rous volume off in state.]
    When Dulness, smiling—'Thus revive the Wits!

106. *a Volume* ⟨i.e. his edition of Shakespeare. See l. 113.⟩
107. *Courtiers and Patriots* ⟨The 'Courtiers' are the Court party, the supporters of the administration. By the 'Patriots' Pope probably intends the Opposition of Whigs led by Pulteney, and of Tories led by Bolingbroke and (till his death in 1740) by Wyndham.⟩
108. *bow'd from side to side* ⟨As being of no *one* party.⟩
110. *bold* Benson] This man endeavoured to raise himself to Fame by erecting monuments, striking coins, setting up heads, and procuring translations, of *Milton*; and afterwards by a great passion for *Arthur Johnston*, a *Scotch* physician's Version of the Psalms, of which he printed many fine Editions. See more of him, Book 3. ver. 325. P.W. ⟨Benson's admiration for Milton resulted in his setting up a monument to him in the Abbey (1737). See p. 834. He had a bust of Johnston executed by Rysbrach.—Arthur Johnston, M.D. (1587–1641), a Scots physician and writer of Latin verse.⟩
113. *The decent* Knight] An eminent person, who was about to publish a very pompous Edition of a great Author, *at his own expence.* P.W. ⟨Hanmer's edition of Shakespeare appeared in 1743-4.⟩
115–18. ⟨'These four lines were printed in a separate leaf by Mr. Pope in the last edition, which he himself gave, of the Dunciad, with directions to the printer, to put this leaf into its place as soon as Sir T. H.'s Shakespear should be published. B.'⟩
116. *Apollo's May'r and Aldermen* ⟨In the context this appears to be the Vice-Chancellor of Oxford University, and the Heads of the various colleges. The Clarendon Press was about to publish Hanmer's *Shakespeare*; but Pope had a quarrel with Oxford of a more serious kind. In the summer of 1741 both Pope and Warburton had been unofficially approached to discover whether they would be willing to accept a Doctor's degree from the University of Oxford. Both men were willing, but unhappily for Warburton his enemies in Oxford succeeded in having the proposal, so far as it related to him, outvoted. Pope thereupon told Warburton: 'I will be doctored with you, or not at all,' and refused to accept the degree offered to him.⟩
117. *gold-capt* ⟨The Gentleman-Commoner at Oxford wore a gold tassel on his cap.⟩
119. *'Thus revive, &c.*] The Goddess applauds the practice of tacking the obscure names of Persons not eminent in any branch of learning, to

But murder first, and mince them all to bits;   120
As erst Medea (cruel, so to save!)
A new Edition of old Æson gave,
Let standard-Authors, thus, like trophies born,
Appear more glorious as more hack'd and torn,
And you, my Critics! in the chequer'd shade,   125
Admire new light thro' holes yourselves have made.
    'Leave not a foot of verse, a foot of stone,
A Page, a Grave, that they can call their own;
But spread, my sons, your glory thin or thick,
On passive paper, or on solid brick.   130
So by each Bard an Alderman shall sit,
A heavy Lord shall hang at ev'ry Wit,
And while on Fame's triumphal Car they ride,
Some Slave of mine be pinion'd to their side.'
    Now crowds on crowds around the Goddess press,   135
Each eager to present the first Address.
Dunce scorning Dunce beholds the next advance,
But Fop shews Fop superior complaisance.
When lo! a Spectre rose, whose index-hand
Held forth the Virtue of the dreadful wand;   140
His beaver'd brow a birchen garland wears,
Dropping with Infant's blood, and Mother's tears.

---

those of the most distinguished Writers; either by printing *Editions* of
their works with impertinent alterations of their Text, as in the former
instances, or by setting up *Monuments* disgraced with their own vile
names and inscriptions, as in the latter. P.W.
    122. *old Æson*] Of whom Ovid (very applicable to these restored
authors)
            Æson *miratur*,
            Dissimilemque animum *subiit*—— ⟨Met. vii.⟩
                                                P.W.

    128. *A Page, a Grave*] For what less than a Grave can be granted to a
dead author? or what less than a Page can be allow'd a living one? P.W.
    Ibid. *A Page*] *Pagina*, not *Pedissequus*. A Page of a Book, not a Servant,
Follower, or Attendant; no Poet having had a *Page* since the death of Mr.
Thomas Durfey. SCRIBL. P.W.
    131. *So by each Bard and Alderman, &c.*] Vide the *Tombs of the Poets*,
Editio Westmonasteriensis. P.W. ⟨Alluding to the monument erected
for Butler by Alderman Barber. See p. 834.⟩
    134. *Some Slave of mine* ⟨In allusion to the custom in ancient Rome
of placing a chained slave beside a victorious general as he rode through
the city.⟩
    139. *a Spectre* ⟨The ghost of Dr. Busby, the famous headmaster of
Westminster School.⟩
    140. *the dreadful wand*] A Cane usually born by Schoolmasters, which
drives the poor Souls about like the wand of Mercury. SCRIBL. P.W.

O'er ev'ry vein a shudd'ring horror runs;
Eton and Winton shake thro' all their Sons.
All Flesh is humbled, Westminster's bold race   145
Shrink, and confess the Genius of the place:
The pale Boy-Senator yet tingling stands,
And holds his breeches close with both his hands.
    Then thus. 'Since Man from beast by Words is known,
Words are Man's province, Words we teach alone.   150
When Reason doubtful, like the Samian letter,
Points him two ways, the narrower is the better.
Plac'd at the door of Learning, youth to guide,
We never suffer it to stand too wide.
To ask, to guess, to know, as they commence,   155
As Fancy opens the quick springs of Sense,
We ply the Memory, we load the brain,
Bind rebel Wit, and double chain on chain,
Confine the thought, to exercise the breath;
And keep them in the pale of Words till death.   160
Whate'er the talents, or howe'er design'd,
We hang one jingling padlock on the mind:
A Poet the first day, he dips his quill;
And what the last ? a very Poet still.
Pity! the charm works only in our wall,   165
Lost, lost too soon in yonder House or Hall.

148. *And holds his breeches*] An effect of Fear somewhat like this, is
described in the 7th Æneid ⟨515, 518⟩,

> *Contremuit nemus——*
> *Et trepidæ matres pressere ad pectora natos.*

nothing being so natural in any apprehension, as to lay close hold on
whatever is suppos'd to be most in danger. But let it not be imagined the
author would insinuate these youthful Senators (tho' so lately come from
school) to be under the undue influence of any *Master.* SCRIBL. P.W.
    151. *like the Samian letter*] The letter Y, used by Pythagoras ⟨a native
of Samos⟩ as an emblem of the different roads of Virtue and Vice.

> *Et tibi quae Samios diduxit litera ramos.*
> Persius ⟨Sat. iii 56⟩. P.W.

153. *Plac'd at the door, &c.*] This circumstance of the *Genius Loci* (with
that of the Index-hand before) seems to be an allusion to the *Table of
Cebes*, where the Genius of human Nature points out the road to be
pursued by those entering into life. Ὁ δὲ γέρων ὁ ἄνω ἐστηκὼς ἔχων χάρτην
τινὰ ἐν τῇ χειρί, καὶ τῇ ἑτέρᾳ ὥσπερ δεικνύων τι οὗτος Δαίμων καλεῖται &c. P.W.
    159. *to exercise the breath*] By obliging them to get the classic poets by
heart, which furnishes them with endless matter for Conversation, and
Verbal amusement for their whole lives. P.W.
    165. *our wall* ⟨Busby is speaking. He refers to the 'Dormitory wall'
mentioned in A iii 323n.⟩
    166. *in yonder* House *or* Hall] Westminster-hall and the House of
Commons.

There truant WYNDHAM ev'ry Muse gave o'er,
There TALBOT sunk, and was a Wit no more!
How sweet an Ovid, MURRAY was our boast!
How many Martials were in PULT'NEY lost!   170
Else sure some Bard, to our eternal praise,
In twice ten thousand rhyming nights and days,
Had reach'd the Work, the All that mortal can;
And South beheld that Master-piece of Man.'
'Oh (cry'd the Goddess) for some pedant Reign!   175
Some gentle JAMES, to bless the land again;
To stick the Doctor's Chair into the Throne,
Give law to Words, or war with Words alone,
Senates and Courts with Greek and Latin rule,
And turn the Council to a Grammar School!   180
For sure, if Dulness sees a grateful Day,
'Tis in the shade of Arbitrary Sway.

174. *that Master-piece of Man*] viz. an *Epigram*. The famous Dr. *South* declared a perfect Epigram to be as difficult a performance as an Epic Poem. And the Critics say, 'an Epic Poem is the greatest work human nature is capable of'. P.W.

176. *Some gentle* JAMES, *&c.*] Wilson tells us that this King, *James* the first, took upon himself to teach the Latin tongue to Car, Earl of Somerset; and that Gondomar the Spanish Ambassador wou'd speak false Latin to him, on purpose to give him the pleasure of correcting it, whereby he wrought himself into his good graces.

This great Prince was the first who assumed the title of *Sacred Majesty*, which his loyal Clergy transfer'd from *God* to *Him*. 'The principles of Passive Obedience and Non-resistance (says the Author ⟨Bolingbroke⟩ of the Dissertation on Parties, Letter 8.) which before his time had skulk'd perhaps in some old Homily, were talk'd, written, and preach'd into vogue in that inglorious reign.' P.W.

181, 182. *if Dulness sees, &c.*] And grateful it is in Dulness to make this confession. I will not say she alludes to that celebrated verse of Claudian ⟨*De Consulatu Stilichonis*, iii 113⟩,

> ——*nunquam* Libertas *gratior exstat*
> *Quam sub* Rege pio——

But this I will say, that the words *Liberty* and *Monarchy* have been frequently confounded and mistaken one for the other by the gravest authors. I should therefore conjecture, that the genuine reading of the forecited verse was thus,

> ——*nunquam* Libertas *gratior exstat*
> *Quam sub* Lege *pia*——

and that *Rege* was the reading only of Dulness herself: And therefore she might allude to it. SCRIBL.

I judge quite otherwise of this passage: The genuine reading is *Libertas*, and *Rege*: So Claudian gave it. But the error lies in the first verse: It should be *Exit*, not *Exstat*, and then the meaning will be, that Liberty was never *lost*, or *went away* with so good a grace, as under a good King: it being without doubt a tenfold shame to lose it under a bad one.

This farther leads me to animadvert upon a most grievous piece of

O! if my sons may learn one earthly thing,
Teach but that one, sufficient for a King;
That which my Priests, and mine alone, maintain,   185
Which as it dies, or lives, we fall, or reign·
May you, may Cam, and Isis preach it long!
"The RIGHT DIVINE of Kings to govern wrong." '
    Prompt at the call, around the Goddess roll
Broad hats, and hoods, and caps, a sable shoal: 190
Thick and more thick the black blockade extends,
A hundred head of Aristotle's friends.
Nor wert thou, Isis! wanting to the day,
    [Tho' Christ-church long kept prudishly away.]
Each staunch Polemic, stubborn as a rock,   195
Each fierce Logician, still expelling Locke,
Came whip and spur, and dash'd thro' thin and thick
On German Crouzaz, and Dutch Burgersdyck.

---

nonsense to be found in all the Editions of the Author of the Dunciad
himself. A most capital one it is, and owing to the confusion above mentioned by Scriblerus, of the two words *Liberty* and *Monarchy*. Essay on
Crit. ⟨90-1⟩.

> *Nature, like* Monarchy, *is but restrain'd*
> *By the same Laws herself at first ordain'd.*

Who sees not, it should be, *Nature like* Liberty? Correct it therefore
repugnantibus omnibus (even tho' the Author himself should oppugn) in all
the impressions which have been, or shall be, made of his works. BENTL.
P.W.
    187. *Cam, and Isis* ⟨The two Universities were still preaching the
doctrine of passive obedience. Oxford in particular remained very cool to
the Hanoverians, and correspondingly sympathetic to the Jacobites and
to Nonjurors.⟩
    190. *shoal* ⟨i.e. school. The word is applied to fish, frogs, seals, etc.⟩
    194. [*Tho' Christ-church*] This line is doubtless spurious, and foisted
in by the impertinence of the Editor; and accordingly we have put it
between Hooks. For I affirm this College came as early as any other, by
its *proper Deputies*; nor did any College pay homage to Dulness in its
whole body. BENTL. P.W. ⟨In the Preface to his edition of *Paradise Lost*
Bentley explained that those passages in the poem which he believed to
have been 'foisted in' by Milton's 'editor', he had put 'between two
Hooks'. Cf. *Ep.* II i 104*n.*, p. 639.⟩
    196. *still expelling* Locke] In the year 1703 there was a meeting of the
heads of the University of Oxford to censure Mr. Locke's Essay on
Human Understanding, and to forbid the reading it. See his Letters in
the last Edit.
    197. *thin and thick* ⟨Cf. A ii 264*n.*⟩
    198. *On German* Crouzaz *and Dutch* Burgersdyck] There seems to be
an improbability that the Doctors and Heads of Houses should ride on
horseback, who of late days, being gouty or unwieldy, have kept their
coaches. But these are horses of great strength, and fit to carry any weight,
as their German and Dutch extraction may manifest; and very famous we

THE DUNCIAD: BOOK IV

As many quit the streams that murm'ring fall

As many quit the streams that murm'ring fall
To lull the sons of Marg'ret and Clare-hall,   200
Where Bentley late tempestuous wont to sport
In troubled waters, but now sleeps in Port.
Before them march'd that awful Aristarch;
Plow'd was his front with many a deep Remark:
His Hat, which never vail'd to human pride,   205
Walker with rev'rence took, and lay'd aside.
Low bow'd the rest: He, kingly, did but nod;
So upright Quakers please both Man and God.
'Mistress! dismiss that rabble from your throne:
Avaunt——is Aristarchus yet unknown?   210

---

may conclude, being honour'd with *Names*, as were the horses Pegasus
and Bucephalus. SCRIBL. P.W. ⟨Jean Pierre de Crousaz, (1663–1748),
Swiss philosopher, published (1737) a confutation of the religious views
he found in the *Essay on Man*. Francis Burgersdyck (1590–1629) was
Professor of Logic and Philosophy at Leyden.⟩

199. *the streams*] The River Cam, running by the walls of these Col-
leges, which are particularly famous for their skill in Disputation. P.W.
⟨'Marg'ret' is St. John's College, Cambridge, founded by the will of
Lady Margaret Beaufort.⟩

202. *sleeps in Port*] viz. 'now retired into harbour, after the tempests
that had long agitated his society.' ⟨i.e. Trinity College, Cambridge.
Bentley's long quarrel with the Fellows ended in 1738.⟩ So *Scriblerus*.
But the learned *Scipio Maffei* understands it of a certain Wine called *Port*,
from *Oporto* a city of Portugal, of which this Professor invited him to
drink abundantly. SCIP. MAFF. *de Compotationibus Academicis*. P.W.
⟨Port was, in fact, Bentley's favourite wine. His comment on claret was
that it 'would be Port if it could'. The *De Compotationibus Academicis* is
a Pope-Warburton joke, and may possibly refer to some occasion at
Cambridge when Maffei was too hospitably entertained by Bentley.⟩

204. *Remark* ⟨Used with special reference to such titles as Bentley's
Remarks upon a late Discourse of Free Thinking, 1713.⟩

205–8. *His Hat, &c.*] The Hat-worship, as the Quakers call it, is an
abomination to that sect: yet, where it is necessary to pay that respect to
man (as in the Courts of Justice and Houses of Parliament) they have, to
avoid offence, and yet not violate their conscience, permitted other people
to uncover them. P.W.

206. *Walker* ⟨Dr. Richard Walker, Vice-Master of Trinity College
and Bentley's chief ally. See iv 273.⟩

207. — *He, kingly, did but nod*] Milton ⟨*Par. Lost*, xi 249–50⟩,
                    — *He, kingly, from his State
                    Declin'd not* ——

210. — *is* Aristarchus *yet unknown?*]
          —— *Sic notus* Ulysses? Virg. ⟨*Aeneid*, ii 44⟩.
          Dost thou not feel me, Rome? Ben. Johnson ⟨*Catiline*, 1 i 1⟩.

210. *Aristarchus*] A famous Commentator, and Corrector of Homer,
whose name has been frequently used to signify a complete Critic. The
Compliment paid by our author to this eminent Professor, in applying to

Thy mighty Scholiast, whose unweary'd pains
Made Horace dull, and humbled Milton's strains.
Turn what they will to Verse, their toil is vain,
Critics like me shall make it Prose again.
Roman and Greek Grammarians! know your Better: 215
Author of something yet more great than Letter;
While tow'ring o'er your Alphabet, like Saul,
Stands our Digamma, and o'er-tops them all.
'Tis true, on Words is still our whole debate,
Disputes of *Me* or *Te*, of *aut* or *at*,   220
To sound or sink in *cano*, O or A,
Or give up Cicero to C or K.
Let Freind affect to speak as Terence spoke,
And Alsop never but like Horace joke:
For me, what Virgil, Pliny may deny,   225
Manilius or Solinus shall supply:
For Attic Phrase in Plato let them seek,
I poach in Suidas for unlicens'd Greek.

---

him so great a Name, was the reason that he hath omitted to comment on
this part which contains his own praises. We shall therefore supply that
loss to our best ability. SCRIBL. P.W.

212. *Made Horace dull, &c.* ⟨In his edition of Horace, 1711, and of
Paradise Lost, 1732.⟩

215. *Roman and Greek* Grammarians, *&c.*] Imitated from Propertiu
⟨Bk. II, Eleg. xxv 65–6⟩ speaking of the Æneid.

> *Cedite*, Romani *scriptores, cedite* Graii!
> Nescio quid majus *nascitur Iliade.*

217, 218. *While tow'ring o'er your Alphabet, &c.*] Alludes to the boasted
restoration of the Æolic Digamma, in his long projected Edition of
Homer. He calls it *something more than Letter*, from the enormous figure
it would make among the other letters, being one Gamma set upon the
shoulders of another. P.W.

223, 224. *Freind, — Alsop*] Dr. Robert Freind, master of Westminster-
school, and canon of Christ-church—Dr. Anthony Alsop, a happy
imitator of the Horatian style. P.W.

226. *Manilius or Solinus*] Some Critics having had it in their choice to
comment either on Virgil or Manilius, Pliny or Solinus, have chosen the
worse author, the more freely to display their critical capacity. P.W.
⟨Bentley's edition of Manilius was published in 1739.—Gaius Julius
Solinus was the compiler of a work entitled *Collectanea rerum memora-
bilium*, consisting mainly of historical and geographical observations. He
owed a great deal to Pliny.⟩

228, *&c. Suidas, Gellius, Stobæus*] The first a Dictionary-writer, a
collector of impertinent facts and barbarous words; the second a minute
Critic; the third an author, who gave his Common-place book to the
public, where we happen to find much Mince-meat of old books. P.W.
⟨Suidas flourished A.D. 1100. He was edited by Ludolph Küster (see iv
237), with the assistance of Bentley. Aulus Gellius, the Roman grammarian,

In ancient Sense if any needs will deal,
Be sure I give them Fragments, not a Meal;   230
What Gellius or Stobæus hash'd before,
Or chew'd by blind old Scholiasts o'er and o'er.
The critic Eye, that microscope of Wit,
Sees hairs and pores, examines bit by bit:
How parts relate to parts, or they to whole,   235
The body's harmony, the beaming soul,
Are things which Kuster, Burman, Wasse shall see,
When Man's whole frame is obvious to a *Flea*.
    'Ah, think not, Mistress! more true Dulness lies
In Folly's Cap, than Wisdom's grave disguise.   240
Like buoys, that never sink into the flood,
On Learning's surface we but lie and nod.
Thine is the genuine head of many a house,
And much Divinity without a *Νοῦς*.
Nor could a BARROW work on ev'ry block,   245
Nor has one ATTERBURY spoil'd the flock.
See! still thy own, the heavy Canon roll,
And Metaphysic smokes involve the Pole.

---

circa 130 A.D., compiled a work called *Noctes Atticae*, containing many fragments of ancient writers.--Stobæus, a Greek writer, circa 400 A.D., also preserved in his work valuable fragments of ancient literature.⟩

232. *Or chew'd by blind old Scholiasts*] These taking the same things eternally from the mouth of one another. P.W.

237. *Kuster, Burman, Wasse* ⟨For Kuster see iv 228*n*.; Burman, a Dutch scholar, published Bentley's emendations to the fragments of Menander; Wasse published an edition of Sallust.⟩

244. *And much Divinity without a Νοῦς*] A word much affected by the learned Aristarchus ⟨i.e. Bentley⟩ in common conversation, to signify *Genius* or natural *acumen*. But this passage has a farther view: *Νοῦς* was the Platonic term for *Mind*, or the *first Cause*, and that system of Divinity is here hinted at which terminates in blind Nature without a *Νοῦς*: such as the Poet afterwards describes (speaking of the dreams of one of these later Platonists)

> *Or that* bright Image *to our Fancy draw,*
> *Which* Theocles *in raptur'd Vision saw,*
> *That* Nature — *&c.* P.W.

⟨See below, iv 486.⟩

245, 246. *Barrow, Atterbury*] Isaac Barrow ⟨1630–77⟩ Master of Trinity, Francis Atterbury Dean of Christ-church, both great Genius's and eloquent Preachers; one more conversant in the sublime Geometry, the other in classical Learning; but who equally made it their care to advance the polite Arts in their several Societies. P.W.

245. *block* ⟨In the double sense of a block of stone waiting to be worked by the sculptor, and a blockhead.⟩

247. *the heavy Canon*] Canon here, if spoken of *Artillery*, is in the plural number; if of the *Canons of the House*, in the singular, and meant

For thee we dim the eyes, and stuff the head
With all such reading as was never read: 250
For thee explain a thing till all men doubt it,
And write about it, Goddess, and about it:
So spins the silk-worm small its slender store,
And labours till it clouds itself all o'er.

  'What tho' we let some better sort of fool   255
Thrid ev'ry science, run thro' ev'ry school?
Never by tumbler thro' the hoops was shown
Such skill in passing all, and touching none.
He may indeed (if sober all this time)
Plague with Dispute, or persecute with Rhyme.   260
We only furnish what he cannot use,
Or wed to what he must divorce, a Muse:
Full in the midst of Euclid dip at once,
And petrify a Genius to a Dunce:
Or set on Metaphysic ground to prance,   265
Show all his paces, not a step advance.
With the same Cement, ever sure to bind,
We bring to one dead level ev'ry mind.
Then take him to devellop, if you can,
And hew the Block off, and get out the Man.   270
But wherefore waste I words? I see advance
Whore, Pupil, and lac'd Governor from France.

---

only of *one:* in which case I suspect the *Pole* to be a false reading, and that
it should be the *Poll*, or *Head* of that Canon. It may be objected, that this
is a mere *Paranomasia* or *Pun.* But what of that? Is any figure of Speech
more apposite to our gentle Goddess, or more frequently used by her,
and her Children, especially of the University? Doubtless it better suits
the Character of Dulness, yea of a Doctor, than that of an Angel; yet
Milton fear'd not to put a considerable quantity into the mouths of his.
It hath indeed been observed, that they were the Devil's Angels, as if he
did it to suggest the Devil was the Author as well of false Wit, as of false
Religion, and that the Father of Lies was also the Father of Puns. But this
is idle: It must be own'd a Christian practice, used in the primitive times
by some of the Fathers, and in later by most of the Sons of the Church;
till the debauch'd reign of Charles the second, when the shameful Passion
for *Wit* overthrew every thing: and even then the best Writers admitted it,
provided it was obscene, under the name of the *Double entendre.* SCRIBL.
P.W.

264. *petrify a Genius*] Those who have no Genius, employ'd in works
of imagination; those who have, in abstract sciences. P.W.

270. *And hew the Block off*] A notion of Aristotle, that there was
originally in every block of marble, a Statue, which would appear on the
removal of the superfluous parts. P.W.

272. *lac'd Governor*] Why *lac'd*? Because Gold and Silver are necessary
trimming to denote the dress of a person of rank, and the Governor must

Walker! our hat'—nor more he deign'd to say,
But, stern as Ajax' spectre, strode away.
   In flow'd at once a gay embroider'd race,   275
And titt'ring push'd the Pedants off the place:
Some would have spoken, but the voice was drown'd
By the French horn, or by the op'ning hound.
The first came forwards, with as easy mien,
As if he saw St. James's and the Queen.   280
When thus th' attendant Orator begun.
'Receive, great Empress! thy accomplish'd Son:
Thine from the birth, and sacred from the rod,
A dauntless infant! never scar'd with God.
The Sire saw, one by one, his Virtues wake: 285
The Mother begg'd the blessing of a Rake.
Thou gav'st that Ripeness, which so soon began,
And ceas'd so soon, he ne'er was Boy, nor Man.

---

be supposed so in foreign countries, to be admitted into Courts and other places of fair reception. But how comes Aristarchus to know by sight that this Governor came from France? Why, by the laced coat. SCRIBL. P.W.

   Ibid. *Whore, Pupil, and lac'd Governor*] Some Critics have objected to the order here, being of opinion that the Governor should have the precedence before the Whore, if not before the Pupil. But were he so placed, it might be thought to insinuate that the Governor led the Pupil to the Whore: and were the Pupil placed first, he might be supposed to lead the Governor to her. But our impartial Poet, as he is drawing their Picture, represents them in the order in which they are generally seen; namely, the Pupil between the Whore and the Governor; but placeth the Whore first, as she usually governs both the other. P.W.

   276. *And titt'ring push'd, &c.*] Hor. ⟨*Ep.* II ii 216⟩.
        Rideat & pulset lasciva decentiùs ætas.

P.W. ⟨Cf. *Ep.* II ii 324–5.⟩
   278. *op'ning* ⟨i.e. giving tongue. There is an almost identical usage at l. 403.⟩
   280. *As if he saw St.* James's] Reflecting on the disrespectful and indecent Behaviour of several forward young Persons in the Presence, so offensive to all serious men, and to none more than the good Scriblerus. P.W.
   281. *th'attendant Orator*] The Governor above said. The Poet gives him no particular name; being unwilling, I presume, to offend or do injustice to any, by celebrating one only with whom this character agrees, in preference to so many who equally deserve it. SCRIBL. P.W.
   282–334. *Receive, great Empress! &c.* ⟨'If I may judge myself, I think the travelling Governor's Speech one of the best things in my new editions [i.e. additions?] to the Dunciad.'—Pope to Spence, *Anecdotes*, p. 264.⟩
   284. *A dauntless Infant! &c.* Hor. ⟨Bk. III, Ode iv 20⟩.
        — ⟨*Non*⟩ *sine Dis Animosus Infans.*

   286. *the blessing of a Rake* ⟨i.e. that she might be blessed by her son becoming a rake.⟩

Thro' School and College, thy kind cloud o'ercast,
Safe and unseen the young Æneas past: 290
Thence bursting glorious, all at once let down,
Stunn'd with his giddy Larum half the town.
Intrepid then, o'er seas and lands he flew:
Europe he saw, and Europe saw him too.
There all thy gifts and graces we display,   295
Thou, only thou, directing all our way!
To where the Seine, obsequious as she runs,
Pours at great Bourbon's feet her silken sons;
Or Tyber, now no longer Roman, rolls,
Vain of Italian Arts, Italian Souls: 300
To happy Convents, bosom'd deep in vines,
Where slumber Abbots, purple as their wines:
To Isles of fragrance, lilly-silver'd vales,
Diffusing languor in the panting gales:
To lands of singing, or of dancing slaves,   305
Love-whisp'ring woods, and lute-resounding waves.
But chief her shrine where naked Venus keeps,
And Cupids ride the Lyon of the Deeps;
Where, eas'd of Fleets, the Adriatic main
Wafts the smooth Eunuch and enamour'd swain.   310
Led by my hand, he saunter'd Europe round,
And gather'd ev'ry Vice on Christian ground;
Saw ev'ry Court, heard ev'ry King declare
His royal Sense, of Op'ra's or the Fair;
The Stews and Palace equally explor'd,   315
Intrigu'd with glory, and with spirit whor'd;
Try'd all *hors-d'œuvres*, all *liqueurs* defin'd,
Judicious drank, and greatly-daring din'd;

290. *unseen the young* Æneas *past: Thence bursting glorious*] See Virg.
Æn. 1 〈411-14〉,

> *At Venus obscuro gradientes aëre sepsit,*
> *Et multo nebulæ circum Dea fudit amictu,*
> *Cernere ne quis eos;*—1. *neu quis contingere possit;*
> 2. *Molirive moram;—aut* 3. *veniendi poscere causas.*

Where he enumerates the causes why his mother took this care of him:
to wit, 1. that no-body might touch or correct him: 2. might stop or detain
him: 3. examine him about the progress he had made, or so much as guess
why he came there. P.W.

303. *Lilly-silver'd vales*] Tuberoses.

308. *the Lyon of the Deeps*] The winged Lyon, the Arms of Venice.
This Republic heretofore the most considerable in Europe, for her Naval
Force and the extent of her Commerce; now illustrious for her *Carnivals*.
P.W.

318. *greatly-daring din'd*] It being indeed no small risque to eat thro'

Dropt the dull lumber of the Latin store,
Spoil'd his own language, and acquir'd no more;   320
All Classic learning lost on Classic ground;
And last turn'd *Air*, the Echo of a Sound!
See now, half-cur'd, and perfectly well-bred,
With nothing but a Solo in his head;
As much Estate, and Principle, and Wit,   325
As Jansen, Fleetwood, Cibber shall think fit;
Stol'n from a Duel, follow'd by a Nun,
And, if a Borough chuse him, not undone;
See, to my country happy I restore
This glorious Youth, and add one Venus more.   330
Her too receive (for her my soul adores)
So may the sons of sons of sons of whores,
Prop thine, O Empress! like each neighbour Throne,
And make a long Posterity thy own.'
      Pleas'd, she accepts the Hero, and the Dame,   335
Wraps in her Veil, and frees from sense of Shame.

---

those extraordinary compositions, whose disguis'd ingredients are generally unknown to the guests, and highly inflammatory and unwholesome.
P.W. ⟨Cf. ll. 553-4.⟩

324. *With nothing but a* Solo *in his head*] Wi.h nothing but a *Solo*?
Why, if it be a *Solo*, how should there be any thing else? Palpable
Tautology! Read boldly an *Opera*, which is enough of conscience for such
a head as has lost all its Latin. BENTL. P.W.

326. *Jansen, Fleetwood, Cibber*] Three very eminent persons, all Managers of *Plays*; who, tho' not Governors by profession, had, each in his
way, concern'd themselves in the Education of Youth; and regulated their
Wits, their Morals, or their Finances, at that period of their age which is
the most important, their entrance into the polite world. Of the last of
these, and his Talents for this end, see Book I. ver. 199, *&c*. P.W. ⟨The
note is ironical throughout. Cibber and Fleetwood were 'managers of
plays' at Drury Lane, and were also notorious gamblers. Sir Henry Jansen
(d. 1766) managed his play at gaming-tables. See *Donne* ii 88*n*., p. 678.⟩

328. *And, if a Borough, &c*. ⟨Members of Parliament were immune
from arrest for debt.⟩

331. *Her too receive, &c*.] This confirms what the learned Scriblerus
advanced in his Note on ver. 272, that the Governor, as well as the Pupil,
had a particular interest in this lady. P.W.

332. *So may the sons of sons, &c*.] Virg.

        Et nati natorum, et qui nascentur ab illis. Æn. iii ⟨98⟩.

⟨The 'sons of whores' may possibly be a thrust at the Duke of Grafton,
who, as Lord Chamberlain, had given Cibber the laureateship in 1730
and so had 'propped the throne' of dullness. His father, the first Duke, as
the natural son of Barbara Villiers, Duchess of Cleveland, qualified for
Pope's contemptuous phrase; the second Duke was accordingly one of
the 'sons of sons of whores'.⟩

Then look'd, and saw a lazy, lolling sort,
Unseen at Church, at Senate, or at Court,
Of ever-listless Loit'rers, that attend
No cause, no Trust, no Duty, and no Friend.   340
Thee too, my Paridel! she mark'd thee there,
Stretch'd on the rack of a too easy chair,
And heard thy everlasting yawn confess
The Pains and Penalties of Idleness.
She pity'd! but her Pity only shed   345
Benigner influence on thy nodding head.
   But Annius, crafty Seer, with ebon wand,
And well dissembled em'rald on his hand,
False as his Gems, and canker'd as his Coins,
Came, cramm'd with capon, from where Pollio dines. 350
Soft, as the wily Fox is seen to creep,
Where bask on sunny banks the simple sheep,
Walk round and round, now prying here, now there;
So he; but pious, whisper'd first his pray'r.
   'Grant, gracious Goddess! grant me still to cheat, 355
O may thy cloud still cover the deceit!
Thy choicer mists on this assembly shed,
But pour them thickest on the noble head.
So shall each youth, assisted by our eyes,
See other Cæsars, other Homers rise;   360

341. *Thee too, my* Paridel!] The Poet seems to speak of this young gentleman with great affection. The name is taken from Spenser, who gives it to a *wandering Courtly 'Squire*, that travell'd about for the same reason, for which many young Squires are now fond of travelling, and especially to *Paris.* P.W.

342. *&c. Stretch'd on the rack &c.*] Virg. Æn. vi ⟨617⟩.

> *Sedet*, æternumque sedebit,
> *Infelix Theseus, Phlegyasque* miserrimus *omnes*
> *Admonet*—

347. *Annius*] The name taken from Annius the Monk of Viterbo, famous for many Impositions and Forgeries of ancient manuscripts and inscriptions, which he was prompted to by mere Vanity, but our Annius had a more substantial motive. P.W. ⟨Perhaps Sir Andrew Fountaine, purchaser of antiques for the museums of the wealthy.⟩

355. *grant me still to cheat! &c.*] Hor. ⟨Bk. 1, Ep. xvi 60–2⟩.

> —— *Da, pulchra Laverna,*
> *Da mihi fallere* ——
> *Noctem peccati & fraudibus objice nubem.*

Ibid. *still to cheat*] Some read *skill*, but that is frivolous, for Annius hath that skill already; or if he had not, *skill* were not wanting to cheat such persons. BENTL. P.W.

Thro' twilight ages hunt th' Athenian fowl,
Which Chalcis Gods, and mortals call an Owl,
Now see an Attys, now a Cecrops clear,
Nay, Mahomet! the Pigeon at thine ear;
Be rich in ancient brass, tho' not in gold,   365
And keep his Lares, tho' his house be sold;
To headless Phœbe his fair bride postpone,
Honour a Syrian Prince above his own;
Lord of an Otho, if I vouch it true;
Blest in one Niger, till he knows of two.'   370
    Mummius o'erheard him; Mummius, Fool-renown'd,
Who like his Cheops stinks above the ground,
Fierce as a startled Adder, swell'd, and said,
Rattling an ancient Sistrum at his head.
    'Speak'st thou of Syrian Princes? Traitor base!   375

361. *hunt th' Athenian fowl*] The Owl stamp'd on the reverse of the ancient money of Athens.

    Which Chalcis *Gods, and Mortals call an* Owl

is the verse by which Hobbes renders that of Homer ⟨*Iliad*, xiv 291⟩,
    Χαλκίδα κικλήσκουσι θεοὶ, ἄνδρες δε Κύμινδιν.   P.W.

363. *Cecrops*] The first King of Athens, of whom it is hard to suppose any Coins are extant; but not so improbable as what follows, that there should be any of Mahomet, who forbad all Images. Nevertheless one of these Annius's made a counterfeit one, now in the collection of a learned Nobleman. P.W.

369, 370. *Otho . . . Niger* ⟨See *To Mr. Addison*, ll. 39*f*, p. 216.⟩

371. *Mummius*] This name is not merely an allusion to the Mummies he was so fond of, but probably referred to the Roman General of that name, who burn'd Corinth, and committed the curious Statues to the Captain of a Ship, assuring him, 'that if any were lost or broken, he should procure others to be made in their stead:' by which it should seem (whatever may be pretended) that Mummius was no Virtuoso. P.W. ⟨Perhaps Lord Sandwich, virtuoso and President of the Egyptian Club.⟩

372. *Cheops*] A King of Egypt, whose body was certainly to be known, as being buried alone in his Pyramid, and is therefore more genuine than any of the Cleopatra's. This Royal Mummy, being stolen by a wild Arab, was purchas'd by the Consul of Alexandria, and transmitted to the Museum of Mummius; for proof of which he brings a passage in Sandys's *Travels*, where that accurate and learned Voyager assures us that he saw the Sepulchre empty, which agrees exactly (saith he) with the time of the theft above mention'd. But he omits to observe that Herodotus tells the same thing of it in his time. P.W.

374. *Sistrum* ⟨A musical instrument originally peculiar to Egypt and the worship of Isis. At meetings of the Egyptian Club, founded about 1740, a sistrum was laid before the President, Lord Sandwich.⟩

375. *Speak'st thou of Syrian Princes? &c.*] The strange story following which may be taken for a fiction of the Poet, is justified by a true relation in Spon's *Voyages*. Vaillant (who wrote the History of the Syrian Kings as it is to be found on medals) coming from the Levant, where he had been

Mine, Goddess! mine is all the horned race.
True, he had wit, to make their value rise;
From foolish Greeks to steal them, was as wise;
More glorious yet, from barb'rous hands to keep,
When Sallee Rovers chac'd him on the deep.   380
Then taught by Hermes, and divinely bold,
Down his own throat he risqu'd the Grecian gold;
Receiv'd each Demi-God, with pious care,
Deep in his Entrails—I rever'd them there,
I bought them, shrouded in that living shrine,   385
And, at their second birth, they issue mine.'
    'Witness great Ammon! by whose horns I swore,
(Reply'd soft Annius) this our paunch before
Still bears them, faithful; and that thus I eat,
Is to refund the Medals with the meat.   390
To prove me, Goddess! clear of all design,
Bid me with Pollio sup, as well as dine:
There all the Learn'd shall at the labour stand,
And Douglas lend his soft, obstetric hand.'
    The Goddess smiling seem'd to give consent;   395
So back to Pollio, hand in hand, they went.
    Then thick as Locusts black'ning all the ground,
A tribe, with weeds and shells fantastic crown'd,
Each with some wond'rous gift approach'd the Pow'r,
A Nest, a Toad, a Fungus, or a Flow'r.   400
But far the foremost, two, with earnest zeal,
And aspect ardent to the Throne appeal.

---

collecting various Coins, and being pursued by a Corsaire of Sallee,
swallowed down twenty gold medals. A sudden Bourasque freed him
from the Rover, and he got to land with them in his belly. On his road
to Avignon he met two Physicians, of whom he demanded assistance. One
advis'd Purgations, the other Vomits. In this uncertainty he took neither,
but pursued his way to Lyons, where he found his ancient friend, the
famous Physician and Antiquary Dufour, to whom he related his adven-
tures. Dufour first ask'd him *whether the Medals were of the higher
Empire?* He assur'd him they were. Dufour was ravish'd with the hope of
possessing such a treasure, he bargain'd with him on the spot for the
most curious of them, and was to recover them at his own expence. P.W.
    376. *horned race* ⟨See 387n.⟩
    383. *each* Demi-God] They are called Θεῖοι on their Coins. P.W.
    387. *Witness great* Ammon!] Jupiter Ammon is call'd to witness, as the
father of Alexander, to whom those Kings succeeded in the division of the
Macedonian Empire, and whose *Horns* they wore on their Medals.
    394. *Douglas*] A Physician of great Learning and no less Taste; above
all curious in what related to *Horace*, of whom he collected every Edition,
Translation, and Comment, to the number of several hundred volumes.
P.W. ⟨James Douglas, M.D., 1675-1742, a celebrated obstetrician.⟩

The first thus open'd: 'Hear thy suppliant's call,
Great Queen, and common Mother of us all!
Fair from its humble bed I rear'd this Flow'r,   405
Suckled, and chear'd, with air, and sun, and show'r,
Soft on the paper ruff its leaves I spread,
Bright with the gilded button tipt its head,
Then thron'd in glass, and nam'd it CAROLINE:
Each Maid cry'd, charming! and each Youth, divine!   410
Did Nature's pencil ever blend such rays,
Such vary'd light in one promiscuous blaze?
Now prostrate! dead! behold that Caroline:
No Maid cries, charming! and no Youth, divine!
And lo the wretch! whose vile, whose insect lust   415
Lay'd this gay daughter of the Spring in dust.
Oh punish him, or to th' Elysian shades
Dismiss my soul, where no Carnation fades.'
    He ceas'd, and wept. With innocence of mien,
Th' Accus'd stood forth, and thus address'd the Queen.

    'Of all th' enamel'd race, whose silv'ry wing   421
Waves to the tepid Zephyrs of the spring,
Or swims along the fluid atmosphere,
Once brightest shin'd this child of Heat and Air.
I saw, and started from its vernal bow'r   425
The rising game, and chac'd from flow'r to flow'r.

405, &c. *Fair from its humble bed, &c.—nam'd it* Caroline:
              Each Maid cry'd, charming! *and each Youth,* divine!
              Now prostrate! dead! behold that Caroline
              No Maid cries, charming! *and no Youth,* divine!
These Verses are translated from Catullus, Epith. ⟨42–7⟩.

              Ut flos in septis secretus nascitur hortis,
              Quem mulcent auræ, firmat Sol, educat imber,
              Multi illum pueri, multæ optavere puellæ:
              Idem quum tenui carptus defloruit ungui,
              Nulli illum pueri, nullæ optavere puellæ, &c.

407–9. *Soft on the paper ruff, &c.* ⟨A reference to measures taken by the eighteenth-century gardener to produce the perfect carnation.⟩

409. *and nam'd it* Caroline] It is a compliment which the Florists usually pay to Princes and great persons, to give their names to the most curious Flowers of their raising: Some have been very jealous of vindicating this honour, but none more than that ambitious Gardiner at Hammersmith, who caused his Favourite to be painted on his Sign, with this inscription, *This is* My *Queen Caroline.* P.W.

421. *Of all th'enamel'd race*] The poet seems to have an eye to Spenser, Muiopotmos ⟨ll. 17–18⟩.

              Of all the race of silver-winged Flies
              Which do possess the Empire of the Air.

It fled, I follow'd; now in hope, now pain;
It stopt, I stopt; it mov'd, I mov'd again.
At last it fix'd, 'twas on what plant it pleas'd,
And where it fix'd, the beauteous bird I seiz'd: 430
Rose or Carnation was below by care;
I meddle, Goddess! only in my sphere.
I tell the naked fact without disguise,
And, to excuse it, need but shew the prize;
Whose spoils this paper offers to your eye,   435
Fair ev'n in death! this peerless *Butterfly*.'
　　'My sons! (she answer'd) both have done your parts:
Live happy both, and long promote our arts.
But hear a Mother, when she recommends
To your fraternal care, our sleeping friends.   440
The common Soul, of Heav'n's more frugal make,
Serves but to keep fools pert, and knaves awake:
A drowzy Watchman, that just gives a knock,
And breaks our rest, to tell us what's a clock.
Yet by some object ev'ry brain is stirr'd;   445
The dull may waken to a Humming-bird;
The most recluse, discreetly open'd find
Congenial matter in the Cockle-kind;
The mind, in Metaphysics at a loss,
May wander in a wilderness of Moss;   450
The head that turns at super-lunar things,
Poiz'd with a tail, may steer on Wilkins' wings.
　　'O! would the Sons of Men once think their Eyes

427, 428. *It fled, I follow'd, &c.*]
　　　　　　　—I started back,
　　It started back; but pleas'd I soon return'd,
　　Pleas'd it return'd as soon—Milton ⟨*Par. Lost*, iv 402-3⟩.

440. *our sleeping friends*] Of whom see ver. 345 above.

450. *a wilderness of Moss*] Of which the Naturalists count I can't tell
how many hundred species. P.W.

452. Wilkins' *wings*] One of the first Projectors of the Royal Society,
who, among many enlarged and useful notions, entertain'd the extravagant hope of a possibility to fly to the Moon; which has put some
volatile Genius's upon making wings for that purpose. P.W. ⟨Wilkins
(1614-72), was Bishop of Chester, one of the founders of the Royal
Society, and its first secretary.⟩

453. *O! would the Sons of men, &c.*] This is the third speech of the
Goddess to her Suppliants, and completes the whole of what she had to
give in instruction on this important occasion, concerning Learning, Civil
Society, and Religion. In the first speech, ver. 119, to her Editors and
conceited Critics, she directs how to deprave Wit and discredit fine
Writers. In her second, ver. 175, to the Educators of Youth, she shews

And Reason giv'n them but to study *Flies!*
See Nature in some partial narrow shape,   455
And let the Author of the Whole escape:
Learn but to trifle; or, who most observe,
To wonder at their Maker, not to serve.'
    'Be that my task (replies a gloomy Clerk,
Sworn foe to Myst'ry, yet divinely dark;   460
Whose pious hope aspires to see the day
When Moral Evidence shall quite decay,
And damns implicit faith, and holy lies,
Prompt to impose, and fond to dogmatize:)
Let others creep by timid steps, and slow,   465
On plain Experience lay foundations low,
By common sense to common knowledge bred,
And last, to Nature's Cause thro' Nature led.
All-seeing in thy mists, we want no guide,
Mother of Arrogance, and Source of Pride!   470
We nobly take the high Priori Road,
And reason downward, till we doubt of God:

---

them how all Civil Duties may be extinguish'd, in that one doctrine of
divine Hereditary Right. And in this third, she charges the Investigators
of Nature to amuse themselves in Trifles, and rest in Second causes, with
a total disregard of the First. This being all that Dulness can wish, is all
she needs to say; and we may apply to her (as the Poet hath manag'd it)
what hath been said of true Wit, that *She neither says too little, nor too
much.* P.W.

459. *a gloomy Clerk*] The Epithet gloomy in this line may seem the
same with that of dark in the next. But *gloomy* relates to the uncomfort-
able and disastrous condition of an irreligious Sceptic, whereas *dark*
alludes only to his puzzled and embroiled Systems. P.W. ⟨The 'sworn
foe to Myst'ry' is perhaps Dr. Samuel Clarke (1675–1729). See 471n. By
'Myst'ry' is meant religious truth known only through divine revelation.⟩

462. *When Moral Evidence shall quite decay*] Alluding to a ridiculous
and absurd way of some Mathematicians, in calculating the gradual decay
of Moral Evidence by mathematical proportions: according to which
calculation, in about fifty years it will be no longer probable that Julius
Cæsar was in Gaul, or died in the Senate House. See *Craig's Theologiæ
Christianæ Principia Mathematica.* But as it seems evident, that facts of a
thousand years old, for instance, are now as probable as they were five
hundred years ago; it is plain that if in fifty more they quite disappear,
it must be owing, not to their Arguments, but to the extraordinary Power
of our Goddess; for whose help therefore they have reason to pray. P.W.

471. *the high Priori Road*] Those who, from the effects in this Visible
world, deduce the Eternal Power and Godhead of the First Cause tho'
they cannot attain to an adequate idea of the Deity, yet discover so much
of him, as enables them to see the End of their Creation, and the Means
of their Happiness: whereas they who take this high Priori Road (such as
Hobbs, Spinoza, Des Cartes, and some better Reasoners) for one that
goes right, ten lose themselves in Mists, or ramble after Visions which

Make Nature still incroach upon his plan;
And shove him off as far as e'er we can:
Thrust some Mechanic Cause into his place;   475
Or bind in Matter, or diffuse in Space.
Or, at one bound o'er-leaping all his laws,
Make God Man's Image, Man the final Cause,
Find Virtue local, all Relation scorn,
See all in *Self*, and but for self be born: 480
Of nought so certain as our *Reason* still,

---

deprive them of all sight of their End, and mislead them in the choice of
wrong means. P.W. ⟨'He alludes to Dr. Clarke's famous Demonstrations
of the Attributes of God, a book which Bolingbroke, who hated Clarke
because he was a favourite of Queen Caroline, impotently attacked.'⟩

473. *Make Nature still*] This relates to such as being ashamed to assert
a mere Mechanic Cause, and yet unwilling to forsake it intirely, have had
recourse to a certain *Plastic Nature, Elastic Fluid, Subtile Matter, &c.*
P.W. ⟨'Plastic nature'—Cudworth's phrase for a life-force which, he
held, accounted for natural processes without the interference of God.
Berkeley scoffs at it in *Alciphron*. 'Subtile matter' [materia subtilis] was a
term coined by Descartes to describe a material which he supposed to fill
the whole of space. It was by such philosophical refinements that God
was 'shoved off'.⟩

475-6.   *Thrust some* Mechanic Cause *into his place,*
            Or bind in Matter, *or diffuse* in Space.]
The first of these Follies is that of Des Cartes, the second of Hobbs, the
third of some succeeding Philosophers. P.W. ⟨The 'folly' of Descartes
was his explanation of celestial motions by his hypothesis of vortices.
Hobbes had suggested that God might be composed of a subtle or refined
matter: he would not admit existence to anything immaterial. The philosophers who 'diffuse God in space' may include Henry More who, in his
anxiety to rescue spirit from being a mere abstraction, claimed extension
for it while distinguishing it still from matter.⟩

478, &c. *Make God Man's Image, Man the final Cause,*
            Find Virtue local, *all* Relation *scorn,*
            See all in Self—
Here the Poet, from the errors relating to a Deity in Natural Philosophy,
descends to those in Moral. Man was made according to *God's Image*; this
false Theology, measuring his Attributes by ours, makes God after *Man's
Image.* This proceeds from the imperfection of his *Reason.* The next, of
imagining himself the Final Cause, is the effect of his *Pride:* as the making
Virtue and Vice arbitrary, and Morality the imposition of the Magistrate,
is of the *Corruption* of his *heart.* Hence he centers every thing in *himself.*
The Progress of Dulness herein differing from that of Madness; one ends
in *seeing all in God*, the other in *seeing all in Self.* P.W. ⟨Bolingbroke had
ridiculed those anthropomorphic divines who made God after man's
image. Hobbes may fairly be said to be among those philosophers who
'find Virtue local', and to 'see all in *Self*'; but perhaps Mandeville is the
writer in Pope's mind here. Those who make 'Man the final Cause' are
presumably the atheists.⟩

481. *Of nought so certain as our* Reason *still*] Of which we have most

Of nought so doubtful as of *Soul* and *Will*.
Oh hide the God still more! and make us see
Such as Lucretius drew, a God like Thee:
Wrapt up in Self, a God without a Thought,   485
Regardless of our merit or default.
Or that bright Image to our fancy draw,
Which Theocles in raptur'd vision saw,
While thro' Poetic scenes the Genius roves,

---

cause to be diffident. *Of nought so doubtful as of* Soul *and* Will: two things
the most self-evident, the Existence of our Soul, and the Freedom of our
Will. P.W.

484. *Such as Lucretius drew*] Lib. 1 ver. 57.

> *Omnis enim per se Divom natura necesse'st*
> *Immortali ævo* summa cum pace *fruatur,*
> Semota *ab nostris rebus,* summotaque *longe—*
> *Nec bene pro* meritis *capitur, nec tangitur* ira.

From whence the two verses following are translated, and wonderfully
agree with the character of our Goddess. SCRIBL. P.W.

488. *Which* Theocles *in raptur'd Vision saw*] Thus this Philosopher
⟨Theocles, in Shaftesbury's dialogue, *The Moralists, a Philosophical
Rhapsody*⟩ calls upon his Friend, to partake with him in these Visions:

> "To-morrow, when the Eastern Sun
> With his first Beams adorns the front
> Of yonder Hill, if you're content
> To wander with me in the Woods you see,
> We will pursue those Loves of ours,
> By favour of the Sylvan Nymphs:

and invoking first the *Genius* of the *Place*, we'll try to obtain at least some
faint and distant view of the *Sovereign Genius* and *first Beauty.*' *Charact.*
Vol. 2. pag. 245.

This *Genius* is thus apostrophized (pag. 345.) by the same Philosopher:

> '—O glorious *Nature!*
> Supremely fair, and sovereignly good!
> All-loving, and all-lovely! all divine!
> Wise Substitute of Providence! *impower'd*
> *Creatress!* or *impow'ring Deity,*
> *Supreme Creator!*
> Thee I invoke, and thee alone adore.'

Sir *Isaac Newton* distinguishes between these two in a very different
manner. [Princ. Schol. gen. sub fin.]—*Hunc cognoscimus solummodo per
proprietates suas & attributa, & per sapientissimas & optimas rerum
structuras, & causas finales; veneramur autem & colimus ob dominium.
Deus etenim sine dominio, providentia, & causis finalibus, nihil aliud est
quam* Fatum & Natura. P.W.

489. *roves,—Or wanders wild in Academic Groves*] 'Above all things I
lov'd *Ease,* and of all Philosophers those who reason'd most *at their Ease,*
and were never angry or disturb'd, as those call'd *Sceptics* never were. I
look'd upon this kind of Philosophy as the *prettiest, agreeablest, roving
Exercise of the Mind,* possible to be imagined.' ⟨*Characteristics*⟩ Vol. 2.
p. 206. P.W.

Or wanders wild in Academic Groves;   490
That NATURE our Society adores,
Where Tindal dictates, and Silenus snores.'
 Rous'd at his name, up rose the bowzy Sire,
And shook from out his Pipe the seeds of fire;
Then snapt his box, and strok'd his belly down: 495
Rosy and rev'rend, tho' without a Gown.
Bland and familiar to the throne he came,
Led up the Youth, and call'd the Goddess *Dame*.
Then thus. 'From Priest-craft happily set free,
Lo! ev'ry finish'd Son returns to thee: 500
First slave to Words, then vassal to a Name,
Then dupe to Party; child and man the same;
Bounded by Nature, narrow'd still by Art,
A trifling head, and a contracted heart.
Thus bred, thus taught, how many have I seen,   505
Smiling on all, and smil'd on by a Queen.
Mark'd out for Honours, honour'd for their Birth,
To thee the most rebellious things on earth:
Now to thy gentle shadow all are shrunk,
All melted down, in Pension, or in Punk!   510
So K ⋆ so B ⋆ ⋆ sneak'd into the grave,
A Monarch's half, and half a Harlot's slave.

492. *Silenus*] Silenus was an Epicurean Philosopher, as appears from
Virgil, Eclog. 6. where he sings the Principles of that Philosophy in his
drink. P.W. ⟨Thomas Gordon, the translator of Tacitus, called Silenus
because he was a Commissioner of the Wine Licences, an appointment
which was made in recognition of his journalistic services to the
government⟩.

494. *seeds of Fire*] The Epicurean language, *Semina rerum*, or Atoms.
Virg. Eclog. 6 ⟨31 ff.⟩, *Semina ignis—semina flammæ*—P.W.

495. *his box* ⟨snuff-box.⟩

501. *First slave to Words, &c.*] A Recapitulation of the whole Course
of Modern Education describ'd in this book, which confines Youth to the
study of *Words* only in Schools, subjects them to the authority of *Systems*
in the Universities, and deludes them with the names of *Party-distinctions*
in the World. All equally concurring to narrow the Understanding, and
establish Slavery and Error in Literature, Philosophy, and ⸢Politics. The
whole finished in modern Free-thinking; the completion of whatever is
vain, wrong, and destructive to the happiness of mankind, as it establishes
Self-love for the sole Principle of Action. P.W.

510. *Punk* ⟨whore.⟩

511. *So K⋆ so B⋆⋆* ⟨Henry de Grey, Duke of Kent (1671-1740), see
p. 627, and James, third Earl of Berkeley (1680-1736), First Lord of the
Admiralty under George I. The reference to a 'Harlot's slave' indicates
that they must have owed their places to the influence of one of George I's
mistresses.⟩

Poor W * * nipt in Folly's broadest bloom,
Who praises now? his Chaplain on his Tomb.
Then take them all, oh take them to thy breast!   515
Thy *Magus*, Goddess! shall perform the rest.'
    With that, a WIZARD OLD his *Cup* extends;
Which who so tastes, forgets his former friends,
Sire, Ancestors, Himself. One casts his eyes
Up to a *Star*, and like Endymion dies: 520
A *Feather* shooting from another's head,
Extracts his brain, and Principle is fled,
Lost is his God, his Country, ev'ry thing;
And nothing left but Homage to a King!
The vulgar herd turn off to roll with Hogs,   525
To run with Horses, or to hunt with Dogs;
But, sad example! never to escape
Their Infamy, still keep the human shape.
    But she, good Goddess, sent to ev'ry child
Firm Impudence, or Stupefaction mild;   530
And strait succeeded, leaving shame no room,

513. *Poor W** ⟨Perhaps the dissipated young Earl of Warwick.⟩

517. *With that a Wizard old, &c.*] ⟨Almost certainly Walpole. In the lines that follow, Pope is probably thinking in particular of William Pulteney. Though he was not made Earl of Bath till 1742, Pulteney had been growing steadily more lukewarm in opposition, and rumours that he was willing to be silenced by a peerage had been circulating for some years.⟩

517. *his Cup, &c.*] The *Cup* of *Self-love*, which causes a total oblivion of the obligations of Friendship, or Honour, and of the Service of God or our Country; all sacrificed to Vain-glory, Court-worship, or yet meaner considerations of Lucre and brutal Pleasures. From ver. 520 to 528. P.W.

518. *Which whoso tastes, forgets his former friends,—Sire, &c.*] Homer of the Nepenthe, Odyss. 4 ⟨220–1⟩.

    Αὐτίκ' ἄρ' εἰς οἶνον βάλε φάρμακον, ἔνθεν ἔπινον
    Νηπενθές τ' ἄχολόν τε, κακῶν ἐπίληθον ἁπάντων.

520. *a Star* ⟨Worn by Knights of the Garter or Knights of the Bath.⟩

521. *Feather* ⟨Worn by Knights of the Garter in their caps.⟩

523, 524. *Lost is his God, &c.*] So strange as this must seem to a mere English reader, the famous Mons. de la Bruyere declares it to be the character of every good Subject in a Monarchy: 'Where (says he) *there is no such thing as Love of our Country*, the Interest, the Glory and Service of the *Prince* supply its place.' *De la Republique*, Chap. 10. P.W.

529. *But she, good Goddess, &c.*] The only comfort such people can receive, must be owing in some shape or other to Dulness; which makes some stupid, others impudent, gives Self-conceit to some, upon the Flatteries of their dependants, presents the false colours of Interest to others, and busies or amuses the rest with idle Pleasures or Sensuality, till they become easy under any infamy. Each of which species is here shadowed under Allegorical persons. P.W.

Cibberian forehead, or Cimmerian gloom.
   Kind Self-conceit to some her glass applies,
Which no one looks in with another's eyes:
But as the Flatt'rer or Dependant paint,   535
Beholds himself a Patriot, Chief, or Saint.
   On others Int'rest her gay liv'ry flings,
Int'rest, that waves on Party-colour'd wings:
Turn'd to the Sun, she casts a thousand dyes,
And, as she turns, the colours fall or rise.   540
   Others the Syren Sisters warble round,
And empty heads console with empty sound.
No more, alas! the voice of Fame they hear,
The balm of Dulness trickling in their ear.
Great C * *, H * *, P * *, R * *, K *,   545
Why all your Toils? your Sons have learn'd to sing.
How quick Ambition hastes to ridicule!
The Sire is made a Peer, the Son a Fool.
   On some, a Priest succinct in amice white
Attends; all flesh is nothing in his sight!   550
Beeves, at his touch, at once to jelly turn,
And the huge Boar is shrunk into an Urn:
The board with specious miracles he loads,

541. *the Syren Sisters* ⟨The Muses of Opera⟩.
545. *Great C* * &c.* ⟨William Cowper, first Earl Cowper, Simon Harcourt, first Viscount Harcourt, Thomas Parker, first Earl of Maccles-field, and Peter King, first Baron King of Ockham, were at different times Lord Chancellor; Sir Robert Raymond, first Baron Raymond, was Lord Chief Justice. Their sons (in Harcourt's case, grandson) were undistinguished, and, as Pope's line implies, patrons of the opera.⟩
549. *amice* ⟨An oblong piece of white linen, used in the Western Church in conjunction with the alb, now generally folded so as to lie round the neck and shoulders. Pope's priest is a chef; the amice is presumably his cap.⟩
553. *The board with* specious Miracles he loads, *&c*] Scriblerus seems at a loss in this place. *Speciosa miracula* (says he) according to Horace ⟨*Ars Poetica*, 144-5⟩, were the monstrous Fables of the Cyclops, Læstrygons, Scylla, *&c*. What relation have these to the transformation of Hares into Larks, or of Pigeons into Toads? I shall tell thee. The Læstrygons spitted Men upon Spears, as we do Larks upon Skewers: and the fair Pigeon turn'd to a Toad is similar to the fair Virgin Scylla ending in a filthy beast. But here is the difficulty, why Pigeons in so shocking a shape should be brought to a Table. Hares indeed might be cut into Larks at a second dressing, out of frugality: Yet that seems no probable motive, when we consider the extravagance before mention'd, of dissolving whole Oxen and Boars into a small vial of Jelly; nay it is expresly said, that *all Flesh is nothing in his sight*. I have searched in Apicius, Pliny, and the Feast of Trimalchio, in vain: I can only resolve it into some mysterious superstitious Rite, as it is said to be done by a *Priest*, and soon after called

Turns Hares to Larks, and Pigeons into Toads.
Another (for in all what one can shine?)   555
Explains the *Seve* and *Verdeur* of the Vine.
What cannot copious Sacrifice attone?
Thy Treufles, Perigord! thy Hams, Bayonne!
With French Libation, and Italian Strain,
Wash Bladen white, and expiate Hays's stain.   560
Knight lifts the head, for what are crowds undone
To three essential Partriges in one?
Gone ev'ry blush, and silent all reproach,
Contending Princes mount them in their Coach.
    Next bidding all draw near on bended knees,   565
The Queen confers her *Titles* and *Degrees*.
Her children first of more distinguish'd sort,
Who study Shakespeare at the Inns of Court,
Impale a Glow-worm, or Vertù profess,
Shine in the dignity of F. R. S.   570
Some, deep Free-Masons, join the silent race
Worthy to fill Pythagoras's place:

---

a *Sacrifice*, attended (as all ancient sacrifices were) with *Libation* and *Song*. SCRIBL.

This good Scholiast, not being acquainted with modern Luxury, was ignorant that these were only the miracles of *French Cookery*, and that particularly *Pigeons en crapeau* were a common dish. P.W.

555. *in all what one can shine?*] Alludes to that of Virgil, Ecl. 8. ⟨63⟩

        ——*non omnia possumus omnes.*

556. Seve *and* Verdeur] French Terms relating to Wines. ⟨Seve: the fineness and strength of flavour proper to any particular wine. Verdeur: briskness.⟩ St. Evremont has a very pathetic Letter to a *Nobleman in disgrace*, advising him to seek Comfort in a *good Table*, and particularly to be attentive to *these Qualities* in his Champaigne. P.W.

560. *Bladen—Hays*] Names of Gamesters. Bladen is a black man. Robert Knight Cashier of the South-sea Company, who fled from England in 1720, (afterwards pardoned in 1742.)—These lived with the utmost magnificence at Paris, and kept open Tables frequented by persons of the first Quality of England, and even by Princes of the Blood of France. P.W.

Ibid. *Bladen, &c.*] The former Note of *Bladen is a black man*, is very absurd. The Manuscript here is partly obliterated, and doubtless could only have been, *Wash Blackmoors white*, alluding to a known Proverb. SCRIBL. P.W.

562. *three essential Partriges in one*] i.e. two dissolved into Quintessence to make sauce for the third. The honour of this invention belongs to France, yet has it been excell'd by our native luxury, an hundred squab Turkeys being not unfrequently deposited in one Pye in the Bishopric of Durham: to which our Author alludes in ver. 593 of this work.

571. *Some, deep Free-Masons, join the silent race*] The Poet all along expresses a very particular concern for this silent Race: He has here

Some Botanists, or Florists at the least,
Or issue Members of an Annual feast.
Nor past the meanest unregarded, one   575
Rose a Gregorian, one a Gormogon.
The last, not least in honour or applause,
Isis and Cam made Doctors of her Laws.
  Then blessing all, 'Go Children of my care!
To Practice now from Theory repair.   580
All my commands are easy, short and full:
My Sons! be proud, be selfish, and be dull.
Guard my Prerogative, assert my Throne:
This Nod confirms each Privilege your own.
The Cap and Switch be sacred to his Grace;   585
With Staff and Pumps the Marquis lead the Race;
From Stage to Stage the licens'd Earl may run,
Pair'd with his Fellow-Charioteer the Sun;
The learned Baron Butterflies design,
Or draw to silk Arachne's subtile line;   590

---

provided, that in case they will not waken or open (as was before proposed) to a *Humming-Bird* or *Cockle*, yet at worst they may be made Free-
Masons; where *Taciturnity* is the *only* essential Qualification, as it was the
chief of the disciples of Pythagoras. P.W.

  576. *a Gregorian, one a Gormogon*] A sort of Lay-brothers, *Slips* from
the Root of the Free-Masons. P.W. ⟨The Gregorians and Gormogons
were both founded in the early eighteenth century in ridicule of the
Freemasons.⟩

  584. *each* Privilege *your own, &c.*] This speech of Dulness to her Sons
at parting may possibly fall short of the Reader's expectation; who may
imagine the Goddess might give them a Charge of more consequence,
and, from such a Theory as is before delivered, incite them to the practice
of something more extraordinary, than to personate Running-Footmen,
Jockeys, Stage Coachmen, &c.
  But if it be well consider'd, that whatever inclination they might have
to do mischief, her sons are generally render'd harmless by their Inability;
and that it is the common effect of Dulness (even in her greatest efforts)
to defeat her own design; the Poet, I am persuaded, will be justified, and
it will be allow'd that these worthy persons, in their several ranks, do as
much as can be expected from them. P.W.

  585. *The Cap and Switch, &c.* ⟨i.e. the cap and switch of a jockey.⟩
  586. *With Staff and Pumps, &c.* ⟨Running-footmen wore 'pumps' (a
sort of shoe without heels), and carried a long staff, when accompanying
their master's coach.⟩
  587-8. *the licens'd Earl* ⟨'Earl of Salisbury who took the property of
a Stage Coach and drove it himself.'⟩
  589. *The learned Baron* ⟨'Baron Charles de Geer, a friend and pupil
of Linnæus, and a celebrated entomologist.'⟩
  590. *Arachne's subtile line*] This is one of the most ingenious employments assign'd, and therefore recommended only to Peers of Learning.
Of weaving Stockings of the Webs of Spiders, see the Phil. Trans. P.W.

The Judge to dance his brother Sergeant call;
The Senator at Cricket urge the Ball;
The Bishop stow (Pontific Luxury!)
An hundred Souls of Turkeys in a pye;
The sturdy Squire to Gallic masters stoop,   595
And drown his Lands and Manors in a Soupe.
Others import yet nobler arts from France,
Teach Kings to fiddle, and make Senates dance.
Perhaps more high some daring son may soar,
Proud to my list to add one Monarch more;   600
And nobly conscious, Princes are but things
Born for First Ministers, as Slaves for Kings,
Tyrant supreme! shall three Estates command,
And MAKE ONE MIGHTY DUNCIAD OF THE LAND!'
    More she had spoke, but yawn'd—All Nature nods: 605
What Mortal can resist the Yawn of Gods?
Churches and Chapels instantly it reach'd;

591. *The Judge to dance his brother Serjeant call*] Alluding perhaps to that ancient and solemn *Dance* intitled *A Call of Sergeants*. P.W. ⟨At a call of sergeants certain ancient ceremonies were observed which had some resemblance to a country dance.⟩

592. *The Senator at Cricket, &c.* ⟨Several peers were noted at this time for their interest in cricket, a game which gave offence to many because it encouraged lords and gentlemen to associate with 'butchers and cobblers'.⟩

593–4. *The Bishop stow, &c.* ⟨See iv 562*n*.⟩

598. *Teach Kings to fiddle*] An ancient amusement of Sovereign Princes, (viz.) Achilles, Alexander, Nero; tho' despised by Themistocles, who was a Republican.—*Make Senates dance*, either after their Prince, or to Pontoise, or Siberia. P.W. ⟨See *Moral Es.*, iii 72*n*; The Parliament of Paris was banished by Dubois to Pontoise, 1720.⟩

599–604. *Perhaps more high, &c.* ⟨In these daring lines Pope is attacking Walpole's long ascendancy as First Minister. He had been virtual ruler of the country since 1721. He fell at last in Jan. 1742—two months before this attack was made upon him in *The New Dunciad*.⟩

606. *What Mortal can resist the Yawn of Gods*] This verse is truly Homerical; as is the conclusion of the Action, where the great Mother composes all, in the same manner as Minerva at the period of the Odyssey. —It may indeed seem a very singular Epitasis of a Poem, to end as this does, with a *Great Yawn*; but we must consider it as the *Yawn of a God*, and of powerful effects. It is not out of Nature, most long and grave counsels concluding in this very manner: Nor without Authority, the incomparable Spencer having ended one of the most considerable of his works with a *Roar*, but then it is the *Roar of a Lion*, the effects whereof are described as the Catastrophe of his Poem. P.W. ⟨See *Mother Hubberds Tale*, ll. 1337 ff.⟩

607. *Churches and Chapels, &c.*] The Progress of this Yawn is judicious, natural, and worthy to be noted. First it seizeth the Churches and Chapels; then catcheth the Schools, where, tho' the boys be unwilling to sleep, the Masters are not: Next Westminster-hall, much more hard

(St. James's first, for leaden Gilbert preach'd)
Then catch'd the Schools; the Hall scarce kept awake;
The Convocation gap'd, but could not speak: 610
Lost was the Nation's Sense, nor could be found,
While the long solemn Unison went round:
Wide, and more wide, it spread o'er all the realm;
Ev'n Palinurus nodded at the Helm:
The Vapour mild o'er each Committee crept;   615
Unfinish'd Treaties in each Office slept;
And Chiefless Armies doz'd out the Campaign;
And Navies yawn'd for Orders on the Main.
    O Muse! relate (for you can tell alone,
Wits have short Memories, and Dunces none)   620
Relate, who first, who last resign'd to rest;
Whose Heads she partly, whose completely blest;

---

indeed to subdue, and not totally put to silence even by the Goddess:
Then the Convocation, which tho' extremely desirous to speak, yet cannot: Even the House of Commons, justly called the Sense of the Nation
⟨cf. *Dia. I*, p. 691, l. 78n.⟩, is *lost* (that is to say *suspended*) during the
Yawn (far be it from our Author to suggest it could be lost any longer!)
but it spreadeth at large over all the rest of the Kingdom, to such a
degree, that Palinurus himself (tho' as incapable of sleeping as Jupiter)
yet noddeth for a moment: the effect of which, tho' ever so momentary,
could not but cause some Relaxation, for the time, in all public affairs.
SCRIBL. P.W.

    608. *leaden*] An Epithet from the *Age* she had just then restored,
according to that sublime custom of the Easterns, in calling new-born
Princes after some great and recent Event. SCRIBL. ⟨The preacher is
Dr. John Gilbert, afterwards Archbishop of York.⟩

    610. *The Convocation gap'd, but could not speak*] ⟨The Lower House
of Convocation of the Clergy had been prorogued in 1717, and did not
again receive the royal licence to transact business till 1861.⟩

    614. *Ev'n Palinurus nodded, &c.* ⟨Walpole, the pilot of the Ship of
State.⟩

    615-8.] These Verses were written many years ago, and may be found
in the State Poems of that time. So that Scriblerus is mistaken, or whoever else have imagined this Poem of a fresher date. P.W. ⟨Pope is
referring to the delay in fitting out two expeditions to Spanish America
in 1740. One, under the command of Sir Charles Ogle, sailed at the
end of October to join Admiral Vernon at Jamaica; the other, after
considerable mismanagement, had sailed under Anson for Peru on
Sept. 18. The reference to 'unfinish'd Treaties' may be intended to glance
at the Convention which was signed by England and Spain on Jan. 14,
1739. It was 'unfinished' in the sense that it was inconclusive, and left
several important points unsettled. By 'chiefless Armies' Pope may be
alluding to the troops sent out to the West Indies under Lord Cathcart,
who died from the effects of the climate.⟩

    620. *Wits have short Memories*] This seems to be the reason why the
Poets, whenever they give us a Catalogue, constantly call for help on the

What Charms could Faction, what Ambition lull,
The Venal quiet, and intrance the Dull;
'Till drown'd was Sense, and Shame, and Right, and
   Wrong—   625
O sing, and hush the Nations with thy Song!

     ★   ★   ★   ★   ★   ★

  In vain, in vain,—the all-composing Hour
Resistless falls: The Muse obeys the Pow'r.
She comes! she comes! the sable Throne behold
Of *Night* Primæval, and of *Chaos* old!   630
Before her, *Fancy*'s gilded clouds decay,
And all its varying Rain-bows die away.
Wit shoots in vain its momentary fires,
The meteor drops, and in a flash expires.
As one by one, at dread Medea's strain,   635
The sick'ning stars fade off th' ethereal plain;
As Argus' eyes by Hermes' wand opprest,
Clos'd one by one to everlasting rest;
Thus at her felt approach, and secret might,
Art after *Art* goes out, and all is Night.   640

Muses, who, as the Daughters of *Memory*, are obliged not to forget any
thing. So Homer, Iliad 2 ⟨488, 491–2⟩,

    Πληθὺν δ' οὐκ ἂν ἐγὼ μυθήσομαι, οὐδ' ὀνομήνω,
    Εἰ μὴ 'Ολυμπιάδες Μοῦσαι, Διὸς αἰγιόχοιο
    Θυγατέρες, μνησαίαθ'—

And Virgil, Æn. 7 ⟨645–6⟩,
    Et meministis enim, Divæ, & memorare potestis:
    Ad nos vix tenuis famæ perlabitur aura.
But our Poet had yet another reason for putting this Task upon the Muse,
that all besides being *asleep*, she only could relate what passed. SCRIBL.
P.W.
  626. ⟨To the couplet with which Pope closed *The New Dunciad* of
1742 the following note was added:
  o'er the Land and Deep] It was but necessary for the Poet to say this
expressly, that Britain might not be suppos'd to be in this condition
alone, but in company with all other Nations of Europe. It had been a
monstrous impropriety, in such a case, to have made any Nation keep
awake, except *France*. But our Poet, tho' a Satyrist, is an utter enemy to
all National Reflections. SCRIBL.
  It is impossible to lament sufficiently the loss of the rest of this Poem,
just at the opening of so fair a scene as the Invocation seems to promise.
It is to be hop'd however that the Poet compleated it, and that it will not
be lost to posterity, if we may trust to a Hint given in one of his Satires
[*Sat.* II i 59].
    Publish the present Age, but where the Text
    Is Vice too high, reserve it for the next.⟩

  637. *As Argus eyes, &c.* ⟨A iii 343.⟩

See skulking *Truth* to her old Cavern fled,
Mountains of Casuistry heap'd o'er her head!
Philosophy, that lean'd on Heav'n before,
Shrinks to her second cause, and is no more.
Physic of *Metaphysic* begs defence,   645
And *Metaphysic* calls for aid on *Sense!*
See *Mystery* to *Mathematics* fly!
In vain! they gaze, turn giddy, rave, and die.
Religion blushing veils her sacred fires,
And unawares *Morality* expires.   650
Nor *public* Flame, nor *private*, dares to shine;
Nor *human* Spark is left, nor Glimpse *divine!*
Lo! thy dread Empire, CHAOS! is restor'd;
Light dies before thy uncreating word:
Thy hand, great Anarch! lets the curtain fall;   655
And Universal Darkness buries All.

APPENDIX

I. PREFACE

Prefixed to the five first imperfect Editions of the
DUNCIAD, in three books, printed at DUBLIN and
LONDON, in octavo and duodecimo, 1727

⟨See p. 430⟩

II. A LIST OF BOOKS, PAPERS, AND VERSES

In which our Author was abused, before the
Publication of the DUNCIAD; with the true Names
of the Authors

⟨See p. 434⟩

III. ADVERTISEMENT

To the FIRST EDITION with Notes, in Quarto, 1729

⟨See p. 317⟩

IV. ADVERTISEMENT TO THE FIRST EDITION

separate, of the FOURTH BOOK of the DUNCIAD

We apprehend it can be deemed no injury to the author of the three
first books of the Dunciad, that we publish this Fourth. It was
found merely by accident, in taking a survey of the *Library* of a late

eminent nobleman; but in so blotted a condition, and in so many detach'd pieces, as plainly shewed it to be not only *incorrect*, but *unfinished*. That the author of the three first books had a design to extend and complete his poem in this manner, appears from the dissertation prefixt to it, where it is said, that *the design is more extensive, and that we may expect other episodes to complete it:* And from the declaration in the argument to the third book, that *the accomplishment of the prophecies therein, would be the theme hereafter of a greater Dunciad.* But whether or no he be the author of this, we declare ourselves ignorant. If he be, we are no more to be blamed for the publication of it, than Tucca and Varius for that of the last six books of the Æneid, tho' perhaps inferior to the former.

If any person be possessed of a more perfect copy of this work, or of any other fragments of it, and will communicate them to the publisher, we shall make the next edition more complete: In which, we also promise to insert any *Criticisms* that shall be published (if at all to the purpose) with the *Names* of the *Authors*; or any letters sent us (tho' not to the purpose) shall yet be printed under the title of *Epistolæ Obscurorum Virorum*; which, together with some others of the same kind formerly laid by for that end, may make no unpleasant addition to the future impressions of this poem.

V. THE GUARDIAN

Being a continuation of some former Papers on the subject of PASTORALS.

⟨See p. 445⟩

VI. OF THE POET LAUREATE

November 19, 1729

The time of the election of a Poet Laureate being now at hand, it may be proper to give some account of the *rites* and *ceremonies* anciently used at that Solemnity, and only discontinued through the neglect and degeneracy of later times. These we have extracted from an historian of undoubted credit, a reverend bishop, the learned Paulus Jovius; and are the same that were practised under the pontificate of Leo X, the great restorer of learning.

As we now see an *age* and a *court*, that for the encouragement of poetry rivals, if not exceeds, that of this famous Pope, we cannot but wish a restoration of all its *honours* to *poesy*; the rather, since there are so many parallel circumstances in the *person* who was then honoured with the laurel, and in *him*, who (in all probability) is now to wear it.

I shall translate my author exactly as I find it in the 82d chapter of his Elogia Vir. Doct. He begins with the character of the poet himself, who was the original and father of all Laureates, and called Camillo. He was a plain country-man of Apulia, whether a *shepherd* or *thresher*,[1] is not material. 'This man (says Jovius) excited by the fame of the great encouragement given to poets at court, and the high honour in which they were held, came to the city, bringing with him a strange kind of lyre in his hand, and at least some *twenty thousand of verses*. All the wits and critics of the court flock'd about him, delighted to see a *clown*, with a ruddy, hale complexion, and in his own long hair, so top full of poetry; and at the first sight of him all agreed he was born to be *Poet Laureate*[a]. He had a most hearty welcome in an *island* of the river Tiber (an agreeable place, not unlike our Richmond[2]) where he was first made to *eat* and *drink plentifully*, and *to repeat his verses to every body*. Then they adorn'd him with a new and elegant garland, composed of *vine-leaves*, *laurel*, and *brassica* (a sort of cabbage) so composed, says my author, emblematically, *ut tam sales, quam lepide ejus temulentia, Brassicæ remedio cohibenda, notaretur*. He was then saluted by common consent with the title of *archi-poeta*, or *arch-poet*, in the style of those days, in ours, *Poet Laureate*. This honour the poor man received with the most sensible demonstrations of joy, his eyes drunk with tears and gladness[b]. Next the public acclamation was expressed in a *canticle*, which is transmitted to us, as follows:

> '*Salve, brassicea virens corona,*
> *Et lauro, archipoeta, pampinoque !*
> *Dignus principis auribus Leonis.*'

> *All hail, arch-poet without peer !*
> *Vine, bay, or cabbage fit to wear,*
> *And worthy of the* prince's ear.

From hence he was conducted in pomp to the *Capitol* of Rome, mounted on an *elephant*, thro' the shouts of the populace, where the ceremony ended.

The historian tells us farther, 'That at his introduction to Leo, he

---

[1] *thresher* ⟨The satire which follows is directed against Stephen Duck (1705–56), the agricultural labourer and poet patronized by Queen Caroline. On Nov. 19, 1730, Swift told Gay that he heard Duck was to be the new laureate, in succession to Eusden.⟩

[a] Apulus præpingui vultu alacer, & prolixe comatus, omnino dignus festa laurea videretur.

[2] *Richmond* ⟨Among Queen Caroline's gifts to Duck was 'a Small House at Richmond in Surrey⟩.'

[b] Manantibus præ gaudio oculis.

not only poured forth verses innumerable, like a torrent, but also *sung* them with *open mouth*. Nor was he only *once* introduced, or on *stated* days (like our Laureates) but made a *companion* to his *master*, and entertained as one of the instruments of his *most elegant pleasures*. When the prince was at table, the poet had his place at the window. When the prince had⁰ half eaten his meat, he gave with his own hands the rest to the poet. When the poet drank, it was out of the prince's own flaggon, insomuch (says the historian) that thro' so great good eating and drinking he contracted a most terrible gout.' Sorry I am to relate what follows, but that I cannot leave my reader's curiosity unsatisfied in the catastrophe of this extraordinary man. To use my author's words, which are remarkable, *mortuo Leone, profligatisque poetis, &c.* 'When Leo died, and poets were no more' (for I would not understand *profligatis* literally, as if poets then were *profligate*) this unhappy Laureate was forthwith reduced to return to his country, where, oppress'd with *old age* and *want*, he miserably perish'd in a *common hospital*.

We see from this sad conclusion (which may be of example to the poets of our time) that it were happier to meet with no encouragement at all, to remain at the plough, or other lawful occupation, than to be elevated above their condition, and taken out of the common means of life, without a surer support than the *temporary*, or, at best, *mortal* favours of the great. It was doubtless for this consideration, that when the Royal Bounty[1] was lately extended to a *rural genius*, care was taken to *settle it upon him for life*. And it hath been the practice of our Princes, never to remove from the station of Poet Laureate any man who hath once been chosen, tho' never so much greater Genius's might arise in his time. A noble instance, how much the *charity* of our monarchs hath exceeded their *love of fame*.

To come now to the intent of this paper. We have here the whole ancient *ceremonial* of the Laureate. In the first place the crown is to be mix'd with *vine-leaves*, as the vine is the plant of Bacchus, and full as essential to the honour, as the *butt of sack* to the salary.

Secondly, the *brassica* must be made use of as a qualifier of the former. It seems the *cabbage* was anciently accounted a remedy for *drunkenness*; a power the French now ascribe to the onion, and style a soupe made of it, *soupe d'Yvronge*. I would recommend a large mixture of the *brassica* if Mr. Dennis be chosen;[2] but if

---

⁰ Semesis opsoniis.

[1] *Royal Bounty* ⟨Queen Caroline allowed Duck a salary of £30 per annum, which was later raised to £80.⟩

[2] *be chosen* ⟨The gibe here is directed at the poetical intoxication of Dennis.⟩

Mr. Tibbald, it is not so necessary, unless the cabbage be supposed to signify the same thing with respect to *poets* as to *taylors,* viz. *stealing.*[1] I should judge it not amiss to add another plant to this garland, to wit, *ivy:* Not only as it anciently belonged to poets in general; but as it is emblematical of the three virtues of a court poet in particular; it is *creeping, dirty,* and *dangling.*[2]

In the next place, a *canticle* must be composed and sung in laud and praise of the new poet. If Mr. CIBBER be laureated, it is my opinion no man can *write* this but himself: And no man, I am sure, can *sing* it so affectingly.[3] But what this canticle should be, either in his or the other candidates' case, I shall not pretend to determine.

Thirdly, there ought to be a *public show,* or entry of the poet: To settle the order or procession of which, Mr. Anstis[4] and Mr. DENNIS ought to have a conference. I apprehend here two difficulties: One, of procuring an *elephant*; the other of teaching the poet to ride him: Therefore I should imagine the next animal in size or dignity would do best; either a *mule* or a large *ass*; particularly if that noble one could be had, whose portraiture makes so great an ornament of the *Dunciad,* and which (unless I am misinform'd) is yet in the park of a nobleman near this city[5]:——Unless Mr. CIBBER be the man; who may, with great propriety and beauty, ride on a *dragon,* if he goes by land; or if he chuse the water, upon one of his own *swans* from *Cæsar in Egypt.*[6]

We have spoken sufficiently of the *ceremony*; let us now speak of the *qualifications* and *privileges* of the Laureate. First, we see he must be able to make verses *extempore,* and to pour forth innumerable, if requir'd. In this I doubt Mr. TIBBALD. Secondly, he ought to *sing,* and intrepidly, *patulo ore*: Here, I confess the excellency of Mr. CIBBER. Thirdly, he ought to carry a *lyre* about with him: If a large one be thought too cumbersome, a small one may be contrived to hang about the neck, like an order, and be very much a grace to the person. Fourthly, he ought to have a good *stomach,* to eat and drink whatever his betters think fit; and there-

[1] *stealing* ⟨'Cabbage: Shreds (or larger pieces) of cloth cut off by tailors in the process of cutting out clothes, and appropriated by them as a perquisite'.⟩

[2] *dangling* ⟨Cf. B i 304.⟩

[3] *affectingly* ⟨For Cibber's squeaky voice, cf. B iii 306*n.*⟩

[4] *Anstis* ⟨John Anstis (1669–1744), Garter King-of-Arms, and author of several heraldic works. One of the duties of his office was to regulate public processions.⟩

[5] *city* ⟨The nobleman is perhaps Lord Hervey, whose regimen of ass's milk was well known. Cf. *Ep. to Arbuthnot,* 306*n.*⟩

[6] *Egypt* ⟨For his *Caesar in Egypt* (1724) the stage carpenter had made pasteboard swans to swim on an imaginary Nile. When drawn across the stage, they occasioned some ridicule among the audience.⟩

fore it is in this high office as in many others, no puny constitution can discharge it. I do not think CIBBER or TIBBALD here so happy: but rather a stanch, vigorous, season'd, and dry *old gentleman*,[1] whom I have in my eye.

I could also wish at this juncture, such a person as is truly jealous of the *honour* and *dignity* of *poetry*; no joker, or trifler; but a bard in *good earnest*; nay, not amiss if a critic, and the better if a little *obstinate*. For when we consider what great privileges have been lost from this office (as we see from the forecited authentic record of Jovius) namely those of *feeding* from the *prince's table, drinking* out of his *own flaggon*, becoming even his *domestic* and *companion*; it requires a man warm and resolute, to be able to claim and obtain the restoring of these high honours. I have cause to fear the most of the candidates would be liable, either through the influence of ministers, or for rewards or favours, to give up the glorious rights of the Laureate: Yet I am not without hopes, there is *one*, from whom a *serious* and *steddy* assertion of these privileges may be expected; and, if there be such a one, I must do him the justice to say, it is Mr. DENNIS the worthy president of our society.[2]

VII. ADVERTISEMENT

Printed in the JOURNALS, 1730

Whereas, upon occasion of certain Pieces relating to the Gentlemen of the Dunciad, some have been willing to suggest, as if they looked upon them as an *abuse:* we can do no less than own, it is our opinion, that to call these Gentlemen *bad authors* is no sort of *abuse*, but a great *truth*. We cannot alter this opinion without some reason; but we promise to do it in respect to every person who thinks it an injury to be represented as no *Wit*, or *Poet*, provided he procures a Certificate of his being really such, from any *three of his companions* in the Dunciad, or from Mr. *Dennis singly*, who is esteemed equal to any three of the number.

VIII. A PARALLEL OF THE CHARACTERS OF MR. DRYDEN AND MR. POPE

As drawn by certain of their Contemporaries

⟨See p. 452⟩

BY THE AUTHOR: A DECLARATION

⟨See p. 458⟩

[1] *gentleman* ⟨Dennis, at this time over seventy, is intended.⟩
[2] *society* ⟨i.e. the Grub-Street Society.⟩

Minor Verse 1730–1744

Prologue to Sophonisba

BY A FRIEND

[written 1730; published 1730]

When learning, after the long *Gothic* night,
Fair, o'er the western world, renew'd his light,
With arts arising *Sophonisba* rose:
The tragic muse, returning, wept her woes.
With her th' *Italian* scene first learnt to glow;   5
And the first tears for her were taught to flow.
Her charms the *Gallic* muses next inspir'd:
Corneille himself saw, wonder'd, and was fir'd.
    What foreign theatres with pride have shewn,
Britain, by juster title, makes her own.   10
When freedom is the cause, 'tis hers to fight;
And hers, when freedom is the theme, to write.
For this, a *British Author* bids again
The heroine rise, to grace the *British* scene.
Here, as in life, she breathes her genuine flame: 15
She asks what bosom has not felt the same?
Asks of the *British Youth*—Is silence there?
She dares to ask it of the *British Fair.*
    To night, our home-spun author would be true,
At once, to nature, history, and you.   20
Well-pleas'd to give our neighbours due applause,
He owns their learning, but disdains their laws.
Not to his patient touch, or happy flame,
'Tis to his *British* heart he trusts for fame.
If *France* excel him in one free-born thought,   25
The man, as well as poet, is in fault.
    [*Nature*! informer of the poet's art,
Whose force alone can raise or melt the heart,
Thou art his guide; each passion, every line,
Whate'er he draws to please, must all be thine.   30
Be thou his judge: in every candid breast,
Thy silent whisper is the sacred test.]

27–32. This concluding paragraph was probably the work of Mallet.

Epigram
[written 1730; published, Lewis's
Miscellany, 1730]

When other Ladies to the Groves go down,
Corinna still, and *Fulvia* stay in Town;
Those Ghosts of Beauty ling'ring here reside,
And haunt the Places where their Honour dy'd.

The second couplet was later incorporated in *Epistle to a Lady. Of the
Characters of Women*, p. 568, ll. 241–2.

Epitaph. Intended for Sir Isaac Newton, In Westminster-Abbey
[written c. 1730; published 1730]

ISAACUS NEWTONIUS

Quem Immortalem,
Testantur Tempus, Natura, Cœlum:
Mortalem
Hoc Marmor fatetur.

Nature, and Nature's Laws lay hid in Night.
God said, *Let Newton be !* and All was *Light.*

Epitaph. On Mr. Elijah Fenton, At Easthamsted in Berks, 1730
[written 1730; published 1730]

This modest Stone what few vain Marbles can
May truly say, here lies an honest Man.
A Poet, blest beyond the Poet's fate,
Whom Heav'n kept sacred from the Proud and Great.
Foe to loud Praise, and Friend to learned Ease,   5
Content with Science in the Vale of Peace.
Calmly he look'd on either Life, and here
Saw nothing to regret, or there to fear;
From Nature's temp'rate feast rose satisfy'd,
Thank'd Heav'n that he had liv'd, and that he dy'd.   10

Epitaph. On General Henry Withers,
In Westminster-Abbey, 1729
[written c. 1730; published 1730]

Here WITHERS rest! thou bravest, gentlest mind,
Thy Country's friend, but more of Human kind.
Oh born to Arms! O Worth in Youth approv'd!
O soft Humanity, in Age belov'd!
For thee the hardy Vet'ran drops a tear, 5
And the gay Courtier feels the sigh sincere.
WITHERS adieu! yet not with thee remove
Thy Martial spirit, or thy Social love!
Amidst corruption, luxury, and rage,
Still leave some ancient virtues to our age: 10
Nor let us say, (those English glories gone)
The last true Briton lies beneath this stone.

When first printed, these lines were preceded by a prose epitaph which
appears on the monument and is believed to be Pope's also:

HENRY WITHERS, Lieutenant General, descended from a military
stock, and bred in arms, in Britain, Dunkirk, and Tangier. Thro' the
whole course of the two last wars of England with France, he served in
Ireland, in the Low Countries, and in Germany; was present in every
battle, and at every siege; and distinguished in all by an activity, a
valour, and zeal, which nature gave and honour improved. A love of
glory and of his country, animated and raised him above that spirit
which the trade of war inspires; a desire of acquiring riches and
honours by the miseries of mankind. His temper was humane, his
benevolence universal, and among all those ancient virtues, which he
preserved in practice and in credit, none was more remarkable than his
hospitality. He died at the age of 78 years, on the 11th of November
MDCCXXIX. To whom this Monument is erected by his Companion
in the wars, and his friend thro' life, HENRY DISNEY.

Disney and Withers were both old friends of Pope.

Epitaph. On Mrs. Corbet, Who dyed of
a Cancer in her Breast
[written 1730?; published 1730]

Here rests a Woman, good without pretence,
Blest with plain Reason and with sober Sense;

The lady commemorated was Elizabeth, daughter of Sir Uvedale
Corbett, of Longnor, Shropshire. She died at Paris, 1 March 1724/5.

No Conquests she, but o'er herself desir'd,
No Arts essay'd, but not to be admir'd.
Passion and Pride were to her soul unknown,   5
Convinc'd, that Virtue only is our own.
So unaffected, so compos'd a mind,
So firm yet soft, so strong yet so refin'd,
Heav'n, as its purest Gold, by Tortures try'd;
The Saint sustain'd it, but the Woman dy'd.   10

To Mr. C

ST. JAMES'S PLACE. LONDON, OCTOBER 22

[written 1730?; published 1774]

Few words are best; I wish you well:
   Bethel, I'm told, will soon be here:
Some morning-walks along the Mall,
   And evening-friends will end the year.

If, in this interval, between   5
   The falling leaf and coming frost,
You please to see, on Twit'nam green,
   Your friend, your poet, and your host;

For three whole days you here may rest
   From office, business, news, and strife: 10
And (what most folks would think a jest)
   Want nothing else, except your wife.

Addressed to William Cleland (1673–1741), of the *Dunciad* and the
Timon-Chandos controversies (see p. 324).
  2. *Bethel*] Hugh Bethel (see p. 540.)

Epigrams from The Grub-Street Journal
1730–1731

I. ON J. M. S. GENT.

To prove himself no Plagiary, MOORE,
Has writ such stuff, as none e'er writ before.
Thy prudence, MOORE, is like that Irish Wit,
Who shew'd his breech, to prove 'twas not besh—

II. ON MR. M—RE'S GOING TO LAW WITH
MR. GILLIVER
INSCRIB'D TO ATTORNEY TIBBALD

Once in his Life M—RE judges right:
  His Sword and Pen not worth a Straw,
An *Author* that cou'd never *write*,
A *Gentleman* that dares not *fight*,
  Has but one way to teaze—by *Law*.   5

This suit dear TIBBALD kindly hatch;
  Thus thou may'st help the sneaking Elf:
And sure a *Printer* is his Match,
  Who's but a *Publisher* himself.

III. ON J. M. S. GENT.

A gold watch found on Cinder Whore,
Or a good verse on *J*—*my M*—*e*,
Proves but what either shou'd conceal,
Not that they're rich, but that they steal.

IV. EPITAPH. ON JAMES MOORE SMYTHE

Here lyes what had nor *Birth*, nor *Shape*, nor *Fame*;
No *Gentleman!* no *man!* no-*thing!* no *name!*
For *Jammie* ne'er grew *James*; and what they call
More, shrunk to *Smith*—and Smith's no name at all.
Yet dye thou can'st not, Phantom, oddly fated: 5
For how can no-thing be annihilated?
        Ex nihilo nihil fit.

V. ON THE CANDIDATES FOR THE LAUREL

Shall Royal praise be rhym'd by such a ribald,
As fopling C——R, or Attorney T——D?
Let's rather wait one year for better luck;
One year may make a singing Swan of *Duck*.
Great G——! such servants since thou well can'st lack, 5
Oh! save the Salary, and drink the Sack!

VI. ON THE SAME

Behold! ambitious of the *British* bays,
C——R and DUCK contend in rival lays:
But, gentle COLLEY, should thy verse prevail,
Thou hast no fence, alas! against his flail:

Wherefore thy claim resign, allow his right;   5
For DUCK can *thresh*, you know, as well as *write*.

VII. ON DENNIS

Shou'd D——s print how once you robb'd your Brother,
Traduc'd your Monarch, and debauch'd your Mother;
Say what revenge on D—— can be had;
Too dull for laughter, for reply too mad?
Of one so poor you cannot take the law;   5
On one so old your sword you scorn to draw.
    Uncag'd then let the harmless Monster rage,
Secure in dullness, madness, want, and age.

VIII. OCCASION'D BY SEEING SOME SHEETS OF DR. B–TL–Y'S EDITION OF MILTON'S PARADISE LOST

Did MILTON'S Prose, O CHARLES, thy Death defend?
A furious Foe unconscious proves a Friend.
On MILTON'S Verse does B—t—ly comment?—Know
A weak officious Friend becomes a Foe.
While he but sought his Author's Fame to further,   5
The murd'rous Critic has aveng'd thy Murder.

I. 'An Epigram Occasioned by some scurrilous Verses on Pope and Swift, privately handed about, and written by J[ame]s M[oo]re Sm[y]th.'
    II. This piece continues the attack on Moore Smythe. Gilliver was Pope's principal publisher.
    IV. Cf. *Dunciad* A, II 46 (p. 373).
    V. On the death of the Poet Laureate, Eusden, on 27 September 1730, the names of possible successors were much canvassed in the papers. Cibber was appointed on 3 December, but Stephen Duck, the 'thresher poet', was just then being taken up by Queen Caroline (see pp. 802–5).
    2. *C—r*, . . . *T—d*] Cibber, . . . Tibbald.
    4. *Duck*] Stephen Duck.
    5. *G—*] George II.

Lines to a Friend

WRITTEN AT HIS MOTHER'S BEDSIDE

[written 1731; published 1751]

While ev'ry Joy, successful Youth! is thine,
Be no unpleasing Melancholy mine.

These Lines, later to be used as the conclusion of *An Epistle to Dr. Arbuthnot* (1734), are found in a letter to Aaron Hill (3 September 1731).

Me long, ah long! may these soft Cares engage;
To rock the Cradle of reposing Age,
With lenient Arts prolong a Parent's Breath,   5
Make Languor smile, and smooth the Bed of Death.
Me, when the Cares my better Years have shown
Another's Age, shall hasten on my own;
Shall some kind Hand, like *B****'s or thine,
Lead gently down, and favour the Decline?   10
In Wants, in Sickness, shall a *Friend* be nigh,
Explore my *Thought*, and watch my asking *Eye*?
Whether that Blessing be deny'd, or giv'n,
Thus far, is right; the rest belongs to Heav'n.

9. *B***'s*] Bolingbroke's.

Epitaph. On Charles Earl of Dorset, In the Church of Withyham in Sussex

[written 1731?; published, *Works*, 1735]

Dorset, the Grace of Courts, the Muses Pride,
Patron of Arts, and Judge of Nature, dy'd!
The Scourge of Pride, tho' sanctify'd or great,
Of Fops in Learning, and of Knaves in State:
Yet soft his Nature, tho' severe his Lay,   5
His Anger moral, and his Wisdom gay.
Blest Satyrist! who touch'd the Mean so true,
As show'd, Vice had his Hate and Pity too.
Blest Courtier! who could King and Country please,
Yet sacred keep his Friendships, and his Ease.   10
Blest Peer! his great Forefathers ev'ry Grace
Reflecting, and reflected in his Race;
Where other Buckhursts, other Dorsets shine,
And Patriots still, or Poets, deck the Line.

1. Charles Sackville, sixth Earl of Dorset (1638–1706). Pope considered Dorset 'the best of the Restoration wits.
11. *his great Forefathers*] particularly the first Earl, author of the Induction to *A Mirror for Magistrates*, and part-author of *Gorboduc*.

On the Countess of Burlington cutting Paper

[written 1732; published, *PSM*, 1732]

Pallas grew vap'rish once and odd,
She would not do the least right thing,

Either for Goddess or for God,
   Nor work, nor play, nor paint, nor sing.

Jove frown'd, and 'Use (he cry'd) those Eyes   5
   So skilful and those Hands so taper;
Do something exquisite, and wise—'
   She bow'd, obey'd him, and cut Paper.

This vexing him who gave her Birth,
   Thought by all Heav'n a burning Shame;   10
What does she next, but bids on Earth
   Her *B—l—n* do just the same.

Pallas, you give yourself strange Airs;
   But sure you'll find it hard to spoil
The Sense and Taste of one that bears   15
   The Name of *Savil* and of *Boyle*.

Alas! one bad Example shown,
   How quickly all the Sex pursue!
See Madam! see, the Arts o'erthrown,
   Between *John Overton* and *You*.   20

8. *cut Paper*] i.e. into shapes of flowers, etc.
16. Lady Burlington was a Savile, and her husband a Boyle.
20. *John Overton*] Doubtless a member of the family of print-sellers and engravers.

Horace, Satyr 4. Lib. 1. Paraphrased

INSCRIBED TO THE HONORABLE MR——

[written 1731; published 1732]

[1] Absentem qui rodit Amicum [2] Qui non *defendit*, alio culpante: [3] Solutos Qui captat *Risus* hominum, *Famamque dicacis*: [4] Fingere qui *Non Visa* potest: [5] *Commissa tacere* Qui nequit:—Hic Niger est: Hunc, tu Romane, caveto

1. The *Fop*, whose Pride affects a *Patron*'s name,
   Yet *absent*, wounds an author's honest fame:
2. That more abusive Fool, who calls me *Friend*,
   Yet wants the honour, injur'd to defend:

This sketch of a Fop, later incorporated in the *Epistle to Dr. Arbuthnot*, (p. 607, ll. 291-304), was occasioned by gossip which immediately followed the publication of *Of Taste*, on 13 December 1731.

3. Who spreads a *Tale*, a *Libel* hands about,   5
   Enjoys the *Jest*, and copies *Scandal* out:
4. Who to the *Dean* and *Silver Bell* can swear,
   And sees at C—*n*—*ons* what was never there;
5. Who tells you all I *mean*, and all I *say*;
   And, if he *lyes* not, must at least *betray*:   10
   —Tis not the *sober Satyrist* you should dread,
   But such a *babling Coxcomb* in his stead.

7. *the Dean and Silver Bell*] Quoted from the description of 'Timon's
Villa' in *Of Taste*, ll. 141, 149–50 (p. 593).
8. *C–n–ns*] Canons, the Duke of Chandos's seat near Edgware.

Wrote by Mr. P. in a Volume of Evelyn on Coins, presented to a painter by a parson

[written c. 1732; published 1735]

T–m W—*d* of *Ch–sw–c*, deep divine,
To painter *K*—*t* presents his *coin*;
'Tis the first time I dare to say,
That *Churchman* e'er gave coin to *Lay*.

Title: *Evelyn on Coins*] Numismata. A Discourse of Medals, Antient
and Modern. By John Evelyn. 1697.
1. *T–m W–d*] Thomas Wood, vicar of Chiswick, 1716–32.
2. *K–t*] William Kent, architect and painter.

The Six Maidens

[written c. 1732; published 1949]

A tower there is, where six Maidens do dwell;
This Tow'r it belongs to the Dev'l of Hell;
And sure of all Devils this must be the best,
Who by six such fair Maidens at once is possest.

So bright are their beauties, so charming their eyes,   5
As in spite of his Fall, might make Lucifer rise;
But then they're so blithe and so buxome withall,
As, tho ten Devils rose, they could make them to fall.

A squib on the Prince of Wales and his intrigues with the six maids of
honour to Queen Caroline.
1. *A Tower*] Windsor Castle.

Ah why, good Lord Grantham, were you so uncivil
To send at a dash all these Nymphs to the Devil?   10
And yet why, Madam Dives, at your lot should you stare?
'Tis known all the Dives's ever went there.

There, Mordaunt, Fitzwilliams, &c. remain;
(I promis'd I never would mention Miss Vane.)
Ev'n Cart'ret and Meadows, so pure of desires,   15
Are lump'd with the rest of these charming Hell fires.

O! sure to King George 'tis a dismal disaster,
To see his own Maids serve a new Lord and Master.
Yet this, like their old one, for nothing will spare,
And treateth them all, like a Prince of the Air.   20

Who climbs these High Seats oh his joy shall be great!
Tho strait be the passage, and narrow the Gate;
And who now of his Court, to this place would not go,
Prepard for the Devil and his Angells also?

9. *Lord Grantham*] Henry d'Auverquerque, Earl of Grantham (*c.* 1672–
1754). Lord Chamberlain to Princess (later Queen) Caroline, 1716–37.
16. *Hell fires*] A term for reckless young people, derived from the Hell-
fire Club, 1720.

Epitaph. For Dr. Francis Atterbury, Bishop of Rochester, Who died in Exile at Paris, in 1732

[His only Daughter having expired in his arms,
immediately after she arrived in France to see him.]

[written 1732; published 1751]

DIALOGUE

SHE

Yes, we have liv'd—one pang, and then we part!
May Heav'n, dear Father! now, have *all* thy Heart.
Yet ah! how once we lov'd, remember still,
Till you are Dust like me.

HE

Dear Shade! I will:
Then mix this Dust with thine—O spotless Ghost!   5
O more than Fortune, Friends, or Country lost!
Is there on earth one Care, one Wish beside?
Yes—*Save my Country, Heav'n,*
—He said, and dy'd.

Poems from Miscellanies. The Third Volume.
1732

I. EPITAPH [OF BY-WORDS]

Here lies a round Woman, who thought *mighty odd*
Every Word she e'er heard in this Church about God.
To convince her of *God* the good Dean did indeavour,
But still in her Heart she held *Nature* more *clever*.
Tho' he talk'd much of Virtue, her Head always run   5
Upon something or other, she found better *Fun*.
For the Dame, by her Skill in Affairs Astronomical,
Imagin'd, to live in the Clouds was but *comical*.
In this World, she despis'd every Soul she met here,
And now she's in t'other, she thinks it but *Queer*.   10

II. EPIGRAM FROM THE FRENCH

Sir, I admit your gen'ral Rule
That every Poet is a Fool:
But you yourself may serve to show it,
That every Fool is not a Poet.

III

You beat your Pate, and fancy Wit will come:
Knock as you please, there's no body at home.

IV. EPIGRAM

Peter complains, that God has given
To his poor Babe a Life so short:
Consider *Peter*, he's in Heaven;
'Tis good to have a Friend at Court.

Epitaph. On Mr. Gay. In Westminster-Abbey
1732
[written 1733; published 1733]

Of Manners gentle, of Affections mild;
In Wit, a Man; Simplicity, a Child;
With native Humour temp'ring virtuous Rage,
Form'd to delight at once and lash the age;
Above Temptation, in a low Estate,   5
And uncorrupted, ev'n among the Great;
A safe Companion, and an easy Friend,
Unblam'd thro' Life, lamented in thy End.
These are Thy Honours! not that here thy Bust
Is mix'd with Heroes, or with Kings thy dust;   10
But that the Worthy and the Good shall say,
Striking their pensive bosoms—*Here* lies GAY.

The Crux-Easton Epigrams
[written 1733; published 1750]

I. ON SEEING THE LADIES AT CRUX-EASTON
WALK IN THE WOODS BY THE GROTTO

Extempore by Mr. POPE

Authors the world and their dull brains have trac'd,
To fix the ground where paradise was plac'd.
Mind not their learned whims and idle talk,
Here, here's the place, where these bright angels walk.

II. INSCRIPTION ON A GROTTO OF SHELLS AT
CRUX-EASTON THE WORK OF NINE YOUNG
LADIES

Here shunning idleness at once and praise
This radiant pile nine rural sisters raise;
The glitt'ring emblem of each spotless dame,
Clear as her soul, and shining as her frame;

The Misses Lisle of Crux-Easton are reported to have amused themselves 'by standing on niches in the Grotto as the Nine Muses; Pope
being placed in the midst, as Apollo'.

Beauty which Nature only can impart, 5
And such a polish as disgraces Art;
But Fate dispos'd them in this humble sort,
And hid in desarts what wou'd charm a court.

Prologue, For the Benefit of Mr. Dennis, 1733

[written 1733; published 1733]

As when that Hero, who in each Campaign
Had brav'd the *Goth*, and many a *Vandal* slain,
Lay Fortune-struck, a Spectacle of Woe!
Wept by each Friend, forgiv'n by ev'ry Foe:
Was there a gen'rous, a reflecting Mind, 5
But pities *Belisarius*, Old and Blind?
Was there a Chief, but melted at the Sight?
A common Soldier, but who clubb'd his *Mite*?
Such, such Emotions should in *Britons* rise,
When prest by Want and Weakness, *Dennis* lies; 10
Dennis, who long had warr'd with modern *Huns*,
Their Quibbles routed, and defy'd their Puns;
A desp'rate Bulwark, sturdy, firm, and fierce,
Against the *Gothick* Sons of frozen Verse;
How chang'd from him, who made the Boxes groan, 15
And shook the Stage with Thunders all his own!
Stood up to dash each vain Pretender's Hope,
Maul the *French* Tyrant, or pull down the Pope!
If there's a *Briton*, then, true bred and born,
Who holds Dragoons and Wooden-Shoes in scorn; 20
If there's a Critick of distinguish'd Rage;
If there's a Senior, who contemns this Age;
Let him to Night his just Assistance lend,
And be the Critick's, *Briton*'s, Old-man's Friend.

A performance of *The Provoked Husband* was given for Dennis's benefit at the Haymarket Theatre on 18 December 1733. The evidence suggests that if Pope's prologue was in fact spoken on this occasion, its authorship was not revealed.

16. *Thunders all his own*] Dennis was said to have invented an improved method of making stage-thunder for his play, *Appius and Virginia*, 1709. The play failed, but the thunder was a success.

18. *French Tyrant*] Dennis wrote a play against the French, *Liberty Asserted*, in 1704, which (so the tale went) so offended the French king 'that he never would make Peace with England, unless the delivering up Mr. Dennis, was one of the Articles of it'.

To the Earl of Burlington asking who writ the Libels against him
[written c. 1733; published 1736]

You wonder Who this Thing has writ,
So full of Fibs, so void of Wit?
Lord! never ask who thus could serve ye?
Who can it be but Fibster H—y.

Lord Hervey's anonymous attack on Pope, entitled *An Epistle to a Doctor of Divinity from a Nobleman at Hampton Court*, was reported by Hervey to have put Pope 'in a most violent fury'.

To Ld. Hervey & Lady Mary Wortley
[written c. 1733; published 1950]

When I but call a flagrant Whore unsound,
Or have a Pimp or Flaterer in the Wind,
Sapho enrag'd crys out your Back is round,
Adonis screams—Ah! Foe to all Mankind!

Thanks, dirty Pair! you teach me what to say,   5
When you attack my Morals, Sense, or Truth,
I answer thus—poor Sapho you grow grey,
And sweet Adonis—you have lost a Tooth.

References to Sappho and Lord Fanny in the first *Imitation of Horace* provoked Lord Hervey and Lady Mary Wortley Montagu to collaborate in *Verses Addressed to the Imitator of Horace*. This epigram anticipates the retort in *An Epistle to Dr. Arbuthnot*.

[A Character]
[written c. 1734; published 1871]

Mark by what wretched steps Great * * grows,
From dirt and sea-weed as proud Venice rose;
One equal course how Guilt and Greatness ran,
And all that rais'd the Hero sunk the Man.
Now Europe's Lawrels on his brows behold,   5
But stain'd with Blood, or ill exchang'd for Gold.
What wonder tryumphs never turn'd his brain

A character of the Duke of Marlborough. It is a manuscript revision and expansion of *Essay on Man*, IV 291–308 probably designed for a revised edition, but suppressed. Lines from the *Essay on Man* are printed in italic.

Fill'd with mean fear to lose mean joy to gain.
Hence see him modest free from pride or shew
Some Vices were too high but none too low   10
Go then indulge thy age in Wealth and ease
Stretch'd on the spoils of plunder'd palaces
Alas what *wealth*, which no one act of fame
E'er taught to shine, or sanctified from shame
Alas what *ease* those furies of thy life   15
Ambition Av'rice and th' imperious Wife.
The trophy'd Arches, story'd Halls invade,
And haunt his slumbers in the pompous Shade.
No joy no pleasure from successes past
Timid and therefore treacherous to the last   20
Hear him in accents of a pining Ghost
Sigh, with his Captive for his ofspring lost
Behold him loaded with unreverend years
Bath'd in unmeaning unrepentant tears
Dead, by regardless Vet'rans born on high   25
Dry pomps and Obsequies without a sigh.
Who now his fame or fortune shall prolong
In vain his consort bribes for venal song
No son nor Grandson shall the line sustain
The husband toils the Adulterer sweats in vain: 30
In vain a nations zeal a senate's cares
'Madness and lust' (said God) 'be you his heirs
'O'er his vast heaps in drunkenness of pride
Go wallow Harpyes and your prey divide'
Alas! not dazzled with his Noontide ray,   35
Compute the Morn and Evening of his Day:
The whole amount of that enormous Fame
A Tale! that blends the Glory with the Shame!

38. *Tale*] 'Tally', as well as 'story': cf. 'compute', l. 36

Epigrams Occasioned by Cibber's Verses in Praise of Nash

[written c. 1735; published 1928]

I

O Nash! more blest in ev'ry other thing,
But in thy Poet wretched as a King!

I. 1. Richard ('Beau') Nash (1674–1762), Arbiter Elegantiarum at Bath,
c. 1705–c. 1745.

Thy Realm disarm'd of each offensive Tool,
Ah! leave not this, this Weapon to a Fool.
Thy happy Reign all other Discord quells;   5
Oh doe but silence Cibber, and the Bells.
Apollo's genuine Sons thy fame shall raise
And all Mankind, but Cibber, sing thy praise.

II

Cibber! write all thy Verses upon Glasses,
The only way to save 'em from our A—s.

3. '. . . it was thought necessary to forbid the wearing of swords at
Bath, as they often tore the ladies' clothes, and frighted them, by sometimes appearing upon trifling occasions.' Goldsmith, *Life of Nash*.
6. *the Bells*] 'Upon a stranger's arrival at Bath he is welcomed by a peal
of the Abbey bells', *ibid.*

Epigram. On One who made long Epitaphs

[written 1736; published, *Works*, 1738]

Friend! for your Epitaphs I'm griev'd,
    Where still so much is said,
One half will never be believ'd,
    The other never read.

Epitaph. On Edmund Duke of Buckingham, who died in the Nineteenth Year of his Age,

1735

[written c. 1736; published, *Works*, 1738]

If modest Youth, with cool Reflection crown'd,
And ev'ry opening Virtue blooming round,
Could save a Mother's justest Pride from fate,
Or add one Patriot to a sinking state;
This weeping marble had not ask'd thy Tear,   5
Or sadly told, how many Hopes lie here!
The living Virtue now had shone approv'd,
The Senate heard him, and his Country lov'd.
Yet softer Honours, and less noisy Fame
Attend the shade of gentle *Buckingham*:   10

In whom a Race, for Courage fam'd and Art,
Ends in the milder Merit of the Heart;
And Chiefs or Sages long to Britain giv'n,
Pays the last Tribute of a Saint to Heav'n.

Epitaph. On John Knight

[written 1736; published 1736]

JOANNI KNIGHT

De *Goss-field* Com. *Essex*. Armig.
Qui obiit *Oct*. 2. 1733. Æt. 50.

ANNA CRAGGS,

JACOBI CRAGGS, Regi GEORGIO I A Secretis, Soror,
MEMORIÆ & AMORI SACRUM
Conjugi suo Charissimo H.S.P.

O fairest Pattern to a failing Age!
Whose Publick Virtue knew no Party rage:
Whose Private Name all Titles recommend,
The pious Son, fond Husband, faithful Friend:
In Manners plain, in Sense alone refind,   5
Good without Show, and without weakness kind:
To Reason's equal dictates ever true,
Calm to resolve, and constant to pursue.
In Life, with ev'ry social Grace adorn'd,
In Death, by Friendship, Honour, Virtue; mourn'd.   10

Bounce to Fop

AN HEROICK EPISTLE
FROM A DOG AT TWICKENHAM TO
A DOG AT COURT

[written 1727–36?; published 1736]

To thee, sweet *Fop*, these Lines I send,
Who, tho' no Spaniel, am a Friend.
Tho, once my Tail in wanton play,
Now frisking this, and then that way,

Bounce was a bitch belonging to Pope; Fop seems to have been Lady
Suffolk's dog.

Chanc'd, with a Touch of just the Tip,   5
To hurt your Lady-lap-dog-ship;
Yet thence to think I'd bite your Head off!
Sure *Bounce* is one you never read of.

FOP! you can dance, and make a Leg,
Can fetch and carry, cringe and beg,   10
And (what's the Top of all your Tricks)
Can stoop to pick up *Strings* and *Sticks*.
We Country Dogs love nobler Sport,
And scorn the Pranks of Dogs at Court.
Fye, naughty Fop! where e'er you come   15
To f—t and p—ss about the Room,
To lay your Head in every Lap,
And, when they think not of you—snap!
The worst that Envy, or that Spite
E'er said of me, is, I can bite: 20
That sturdy Vagrants, Rogues in Rags,
Who poke at me, can make no Brags;
And that to towze such Things as *flutter*,
To honest *Bounce* is Bread and Butter.

While you, and every courtly Fop,   25
Fawn on the Devil for a Chop,
I've the Humanity to hate
A Butcher, tho' he brings me Meat;
And let me tell you, have a Nose,
(Whatever stinking Fops suppose)   30
That under Cloth of Gold or Tissue,
Can smell a Plaister, or an Issue.

Your pilf'ring Lord, with simple Pride,
May wear a Pick-lock at his Side;
My Master wants no Key of State,   35
For *Bounce* can keep his House and Gate.

When all such Dogs have had their Days,
As knavish *Pams*, and fawning *Trays*;
When pamper'd *Cupids*, bestly *Veni*'s,
And motly, squinting *Harvequini*'s,   40

10. *fetch and carry*] Cf. *Ep. to Arbuthnot*, ll. 225 f, p. 605.
12. Cf. 'Voyage to Lilliput', chap. III § 4; *Ess. on Man*, IV 205, p. 542;
Imit. Hor., *Ep.* I vi 14, p. 631.

Shall lick no more their Lady's Br—,
But die of Looseness, Claps, or Itch;
Fair *Thames* from either ecchoing Shoare
Shall hear, and dread my manly Roar.

See *Bounce*, like *Berecynthia*, crown'd   45
With thund'ring Offspring all around,
Beneath, beside me, and a top,
A hundred Sons! and not one *Fop*.

Before my Children set your Beef,
Not one true *Bounce* will be a Thief;   50
Not one without Permission feed,
(Tho' some of *J*—'s hungry Breed)
But whatsoe'er the Father's Race,
From me they suck a little Grace.
While your fine Whelps learn all to steal,   55
Bred up by Hand on Chick and Veal.

My Eldest-born resides not far,
Where shines great *Strafford*'s glittering Star:
My second (Child of Fortune!) waits
At *Burlington*'s Palladian Gates: 60
A third majestically stalks
(Happiest of Dogs!) in *Cobham*'s Walks:
One ushers Friends to *Bathurst*'s Door;
One fawns, at *Oxford*'s, on the Poor.

Nobles, whom Arms or Arts adorn,   65
Wait for my Infants yet unborn.
None but a Peer of Wit and Grace,
Can hope a Puppy of my Race.

And O! wou'd Fate the Bliss decree
To mine (a Bliss too great for me)   70
That two, my tallest Sons, might grace
Attending each with stately Pace,
Iülus' Side, as erst *Evander*'s,
To keep off Flatt'rers, Spies, and Panders,
To let no noble Slave come near,   75
And scare Lord *Fannys* from his Ear:
Then might a Royal Youth, and true,
Enjoy at least a Friend—or two:

73. *Iülus*] Son of Æneas; reference to the Prince of Wales [P].
76. Cf. *Ep. to Arbuthnot*, l. 319, p. 608.

A Treasure, which, of Royal kind,
Few but Himself deserve to find.   80

Then *Bounce* ('tis all that *Bounce* can crave)
Shall wag her Tail within the Grave.

And tho' no Doctors, Whig, or Tory ones,
Except the Sect of *Pythagoreans*,
Have Immortality assign'd   85
To any Beast, but *Dryden*'s Hind:
Yet Master *Pope*, whom Truth and Sense
Shall call their Friend some Ages hence,
Tho' now on loftier Themes he sings
Than to bestow a Word on *Kings*,   90
Has sworn by *Sticks* (the Poet's Oath,
And Dread of Dogs and Poets both)
Man and his Works he'll soon renounce,
And roar in Numbers worthy *Bounce*.

86. A Milk-white Hind, immortal and unchang'd. Ver. I. Of the *Hind*
and *Panther*. [P]

Epigram. Engraved on the Collar of a Dog which I gave to his Royal Highness

[written c. 1737; published, *Works*, 1738]

I am his Highness' Dog at *Kew*;
Pray tell me Sir, whose Dog are you?

Sonnet Written upon Occasion of the Plague, and found on a Glass-Window at Chalfont

(IN IMITATION OF MILTON)

[written 1737; published, *Milton's Works*, 1738]

Fair Mirrour of foul Times! whose fragile Sheene
Shall as it blazeth, break; while Providence
(Aye watching o'er his Saints with Eye unseen,)
Spreads the red Rod of angry Pestilence,
To sweep the wicked and their Counsels hence;   5

This appears to have been intended as a hoax to catch the connoisseurs.

Yea al¹ to break the Pride of lustful Kings,
  Who Heaven's Lore reject for brutish Sense;
As erst he scourg'd *Jessides'* Sin of yore
  For the fair *Hittite*, when on Seraph's Wings
He sent him War, or Plague, or Famine sore.   10

Epitaph. For One who would not be buried in Westminster-Abbey

[written 1738?; published, *Works*, 1738]

HEROES, and KINGS! your distance keep:
In peace let one poor Poet sleep,
Who never flatter'd Folks like you:
Let Horace blush, and Virgil too.

Epitaph. On Himself

[written 1741?; published 1741]

Under this Marble, or under this Sill,
Or under this Turf, or e'en what they will;
Whatever an Heir, or a Friend in his stead,
Or any good Creature shall lay o'er my Head;
Lies He who ne'er car'd, and still cares not a Pin,
What they said, or may say of the Mortal within.
But who living and dying, serene still and free,
Trusts in God, that as well as he was, he shall be.

One Thousand Seven Hundred and Forty

A POEM

[written 1740; published 1797]

O wretched B—, jealous now of all,
What God, what mortal, shall prevent thy fall?
Turn, turn thy eyes from wicked men in place,
And see what succour from the Patriot Race.
C—, his own proud dupe, thinks Monarchs things   5
Made just for him, as other fools for Kings;

1. *B*—] Britain.
4. *Patriot Race*] The Opposition. See Pope's note to *Dia.* i 24.
5. Carteret. His policy was to displace Walpole in royal favour.

Controls, decides, insults thee every hour,
And antedates the hatred due to Pow'r.
   Thro' Clouds of Passion P—'s views are clear,
He foams a Patriot to subside a Peer;   10
Impatient sees his country bought and sold,
And damns the market where he takes no gold.
   Grave, righteous S— joggs on till, past belief,
He finds himself companion with a thief.
   To purge and let thee blood, with fire and sword,   15
Is all the help stern S— wou'd afford.
   That those who bind and rob thee, would not kill,
Good C— hopes, and candidly sits still.
   Of Ch—s W— who speaks at all,
No more than of Sir Har—y or Sir P—.   20
Whose names once up, they thought it was not wrong
To lie in bed, but sure they lay too long.
   G—r, C—m, B—t, pay thee due regards,
Unless the ladies bid them mind their cards.
         with wit that must
And C—d who speaks so well and writes,   25
Whom (saving W.) every S. *harper bites*,
         must needs
Whose wit and   equally provoke one,
Finds thee, at best, the butt to crack his joke on.
   As for the rest, each winter up they run,
And all are clear, that something must be done.   30
Then urg'd by C—t, or by C—t stopt,
Inflam'd by P—, or by P— dropt;
They follow rev'rently each wond'rous wight,
Amaz'd that one can read, that one can write:
So geese to gander prone obedience keep,   35
Hiss if he hiss, and if he slumber, sleep.

  9. *P—'s*] William Pulteney. See *Dia.* i 24*n* (p. 689).
  10. He was not created Earl of Bath till 1742, but rumours that he could
be bought with a peerage had been persistent in 1737.
  13. Perhaps Sandys, a prominent member of the Opposition.
  16. Perhaps Shippen, the Jacobite leader.
  18. *C—*] Perhaps Lord Cornbury. See *Ep. I vi 61* (p. 632).
  19. *Ch—s W—*] Perhaps 'Chandos, Winchilsea'.
  20. I do not recognize Sir Harry. Sir P— is evidently Sir Paul Methuen.
  23. Gower, Cobham, Bathurst.
  25. *C—d*] Chesterfield.
  26. *W*] Perhaps Peter Walter.
  29. The country gentlemen of the Tory Opposition, who 'run up' to
attend sessions of Parliament.
  31. *C—t*] Carteret.   32. *P—*] Pulteney.

Till having done whate'er was fit or fine,
Utter'd a speech, and ask'd their friends to dine;
Each hurries back to his paternal ground,
Content but for five shillings in the pound,   40
Yearly defeated, yearly hopes they give,
And all agree, Sir Robert cannot live.
   Rise, rise, great W — fated to appear,
Spite of thyself a glorious minister!
Speak the loud language Princes . . .   45
And treat with half the . . .
At length to B— kind, as to thy . . .
Espouse the nation, you . . .
   What can thy H . . .
Dress in Dutch . . .   50
Tho' still he travels on no bad pretence,
To shew . . .
   Or those foul copies of thy face and tongue,
Veracious W— and frontless Young;
Sagacious Bub, so late a friend, and there   55
So late a foe, yet more sagacious H—?
Hervey and Hervey's school, F— H—y, H—n,
Yea, moral Ebor, or religious Winton.
How! what can O—w, what can D—
The wisdom of the one and other chair,   60

40 The country gentlemen's grievance was the land-tax,—increased to four shillings in the pound in 1740—which Walpole had designed to ease by means of his Excise Bill, defeated in 1733. See *Sat.* II ii 134*n* (p. 622).

42. *Sir Robert*] Walpole.

43. *W*—] Walpole.

47. Croker completed the couplet:

> At length to Britain kind, as to thy whore,
> Espouse the nation, you debauched before.

Walpole married Maria Skerrett, whom he had kept for ten years, in 1738. See p. 693, l. 141*n*.

49. *thy H*] Walpole's brother, Horace, ambassador at the Hague (1733–40).

54. *W*—] Winnington.

55. *Bub*] Dodington.

56. Bishop Hare of Chichester, although a staunch Whig, had opposed the government on the Quaker Bill in 1736 but returned to his allegiance soon after.

57. Fox (i.e. Stephen Fox), Harry (i.e. Harry Fox), Hinton (i.e. John Poulett, Lord Hinton); all political protégés of Lord Hervey.

58. Archbishop Blackburne of York (see p. 669), and Bishop Hoadly of Winchester. The epithets are ironical.

59. Onslow and Lord De la Warr, Speakers of the House of Commons and of the House of Lords respectively.

N— laugh, or D—s sager
Or thy dread truncheon M.'s mighty peer?
What help from J—s opiates canst thou draw
Or H—k's quibbles voted into law?
   C. that Roman in his nose alone,   65
Who hears all causes, B—, but thy own,
Or those proud fools whom nature, rank, and fate
Made fit companions for the Sword of State.
   Can the light packhorse, or the heavy steer,
The sowzing Prelate, or the sweating Peer,   70
Drag out with all its dirt and all its weight,
The lumb'ring carriage of thy broken State?
Alas! the people curse, the carman swears,
The drivers quarrel, and the master stares.
   The plague is on thee, Britain, and who tries   75
To save thee in th' infectious office *dies*.
The first firm P—y soon resign'd his breath,
Brave S—w lov'd thee, and was ly'd to death.
Good M—m—t's fate tore P—th from thy side,
And thy last sigh was heard when W—m died.   80
   Thy Nobles Sl—s, thy Se—s bought with gold,

61. Newcastle . . . Dorset. The word *sneer* would complete the line.
62. The Duke of Marlborough had deserted the Opposition in 1738 and had been rewarded with a court appointment.
63. *J—s*] Probably Sir Joseph Jekyll.
64. *H—k*] Hardwicke, the Lord Chancellor. Perhaps a reference to Hardwick's objections to certain clauses in the smuggling Bill (1736), which were modified because of his opposition.
65. *C.*] Spencer Compton, Earl of Wilmington, whose nose, Pope wrote to Marchmont, was all that could be found remarkable to set on his monument.
66. *B—*] Britain.
67-8. Alluding to the Lord High Chamberlain's privilege of disposing of the Sword of State to be carried by any peer he may select, at the opening or closing of a parliamentary session.
70. *sowzing*] i.e. powerful.
77. Daniel Pulteney's undeviating hostility to Walpole provided a valuable satiric contrast to his cousin's vacillation (l. 9).
78. Lord Scarbrough committed suicide on Jan. 29, 1740. His action was attributed to his wishing to avoid marriage with the Dowager Duchess of Manchester, but Pope seems to have believed that he was too sensitive to malicious interpretation of his political behaviour.
79. Lord Marchmont had died on Feb. 27, 1740. His son, Lord Polwarth, by succeeding to the title, was incapacitated from sitting in the House of Commons, and was not elected as a representative of the Scottish Peers until 1750.
80. Sir William Wyndham, the leader of the Hanoverian Tories, died on June 17, 1740.
81. Perhaps 'Thy Nobles Slaves, thy Senates bought with gold'.

Thy Clergy perjur'd, thy whole People sold.
An atheist ⌣ a ⊕ ''''s ad . . .
Blotch thee all o'er, and sink . . .
    Alas! on one alone our all relies,   85
Let him be honest, and he must be wise,
Let him no trifler from his   school,
Nor like his . . . still a . . .
Be but a man! unministered, alone,
And free at once the Senate and the Throne;   90
Esteem the public love his best supply,
A ☉'s true glory his integrity;
Rich *with* his . . . *in* his . . . strong,
Affect no conquest, but endure no wrong.
Whatever his religion or his blood,   95
His public virtue makes his title good.
Europe's just balance and our own may stand,
And one man's honesty redeem the land.

83. Perhaps
    'An Atheist court, a thief's administration,
    Blotch thee all o'er, and sink thee to damnation.'
85. Frederick, Prince of Wales.
92. Perhaps *King's*.
93 ff. Probably the lines were intended to run:
    Rich *with* his Britain, *in* his Britain strong
    Affect no conquest, &c.
The allusion in that case would be to George II's preference for Hanover.
The Patriot King would 'affect no conquest' on the Continent, but he
would 'endure no wrong' from Spain. He would be rich enough with
Britain, and strong in her love.
95. *Whatever his religion*] Pope is expressing his personal opinion.
Though a professing Catholic at a time when anti-Catholic legislation
made life unpleasant for the faithful, Pope was open-minded in religious
matters. See *Sat.* II i 64–6.

Epigram. [*On lopping Trees in his Garden.*]
[written c. 1740; published 1741]

My Ld. complains, that *P*— (stark mad with Gardens)
Has lopp'd three Trees, the Value of three Farthings:
But he's my Neighbour, cries the Peer polite,
And if he'll visit me, I'll wave my Right.
What? on Compulsion? and against my Will   5
A Lord's Acquaintance?—Let him file his *Bill.*

Verbatim from Boileau

Un jour, dit un Auteur, &c. EPISTLE II

[written c. 1740; published 1741]

Once (says an Author, where, I need not say)
Two Trav'lers found an Oyster in their Way;
Both fierce, both hungry, the Dispute grew strong,
While, Scale in Hand, Dame *Justice* past along.
Before her each with Clamour pleads the Laws,   5
Explain'd the Matter, and would win the Cause;
Dame *Justice*, weighing long the doubtful Right,
Takes, opens, swallows it, before their Sight.
The Cause of Strife remov'd so rarely well,
There, take (says *Justice*) take ye each a *Shell*.   10
We thrive at *Westminster* on Fools like you,
'Twas a fat Oyster——Live in Peace——Adieu.

On the Benefactions in the late Frost, 1740

[written 1740; published 1740]

Yes, 'tis the time! I cry'd, impose the chain!
  Destin'd and due to wretches self-enslav'd!
But when I saw such Charity remain,
  I half could wish this people might be sav'd.
Faith lost, and Hope, their Charity begins;   5
  And 'tis a wise design on pitying heav'n,
If this can cover multitudes of sins,
  To take the only way to be forgiven.

Epigrams 1738-1741

I. ON QUEEN CAROLINE'S DEATH-BED

Here lies wrapt up in forty thousand towels
The only proof that C*** had bowels.

II ON A PICTURE OF QUEEN CAROLINE, DRAWN BY LADY BURLINGTON

Alas! what room for Flattry, or for Pride!
She's dead!—but thus she lookd the hour she dy'd,
Peace, blubbring Bishop! peace thou flattring Dean!
This single Crayon, Madam, saints the Queen.

III. LINES ON MINISTERS

—But Ministers like Gladiators live;
Tis half their business, Blows to ward, or give,
The good their Virtue might effect, or sense,
Dies between Exigents, and self defence.

III. These verses from MS Egerton 1950 are written on the back of some notes about the *Essay on Criticism* and the *Essay on Man*. Their subject suggests that they were drafted when Pope was at work on the later *Imitations of Horace*.

IV. COUPLET

May THESE put Money in your Purse,
For I assure you, I've read worse.

A. P.

IV. To the concluding lines of a poem entitled 'The Author's Picture: A Fourth Epistle to Mr. Pope' which read:

The most I seriously would hope,
Is, just to read the Words, A. POPE,
Writ, without Sneer, or Shew of Banter,
Beneath your friendly *Imprimantur*.

the author, John Bancks, has appended a footnote stating:

A copy of these Epistles having been sent to Mr. Pope, he was pleased to return them with Subscriptions for two Sets of the Author's Works, and the following Couplet . . .

V. ON DR. ALURED CLARKE

Let Clarke make half his life the poor's support,
But let him give the other half to court.

V. Spence reports Pope as saying that this couplet was in the manuscript for *Dunciad* IV. 'But I believe I shall omit it; though, if rightly understood, it has more of commendation than satire in it.' Alured Clarke (1696–1742) had been a prebendary of Winchester and Westminster before being appointed Dean of Exeter.

VI. COUPLET FROM HORACE

In unambitious silence be my lot,
Yet ne'er a friend forgetting, till forgot.

VI. Pope wrote to Lord Marchmont, 10 January 1739: 'I am learning Horace's verse [*Epist.* 1 xi 9]—"Oblitusque meorum, obliviscendus et illis;" but I learn it (what I think the best way) backwards,' and appended the couplet above.

VII. COUPLET ON HIS GROTTO

And life itself can nothing more supply
Than just to plan our projects, and to die.

VIII. LINES TO KING GEORGE II

O all-accomplish'd Cæsar! on thy Shelf
Is room for all Pope's Works—and Pope himself:

'Tis true Great Bard, thou on my shelf shall lye
With Oxford, Cowper, Noble Strafford by:
But for thy Windsor, a New Fabric Raise   5
And There Triumphant Sing Thy Soverain's Praise.

VIII. Elwin glosses the last four lines: 'the king answers that he permits the "bard's" works to have a place in a library adorned with portraits of Oxford, Cowper, and Strafford—all politicians whom he honours more than authors,—but that he has no desire to see Pope in person, and his Windsor must be a second poetical fabric of his own raising, similar to the Windsor Forest in which he sang the praises of Queen Anne.'

IX. [ON SHAKESPEAR'S MONUMENT]

After an hundred and thirty years' nap,
Enter Shakespear, with a loud clap.

X. [ON SHAKESPEAR'S MONUMENT]

Thus Britain lov'd me; and preserv'd my Fame,
Clear from a *Barber*'s or a *Benson*'s Name.

Mock inscriptions for the blank scroll on Shakespeare's monument in Westminster Abbey.

Alderman John Barber (1675–1740) erected a monument to Samuel Butler in Westminster Abbey. At the end of the Latin inscription appear the words:

Hoc tandem, posito Marmore, curavit
Johannes Barber, Civis Londinensis, 1721.

William Benson (1682–1754), Surveyor-General of Works, erected a monument to Milton in Westminster Abbey in 1737.

Epigram. On Cibber's Declaration that he will have the Last Word with Mr. Pope

[written 1742; published 1742]

Quoth *Cibber* to *Pope*, tho' in Verse you foreclose,
I'll have the last Word, for by G—d I'll write Prose.
Poor *Colley*, thy Reas'ning is none of the strongest,
For know, the last Word is the Word that lasts longest.

Tom Southerne's Birth-day Dinner at Ld. Orrery's

[written 1742; published 1742]

Resign'd to live, prepar'd to die,
With not one sin but poetry,
This day TOM's fair account has run
(Without a blot) to eighty one.
Kind *Boyle* before his poet lays   5
A table with a cloth of bays;
And *Ireland*, mother of sweet singers,
Presents her harp still to his fingers,
The feast, his towring genius marks
In yonder wildgoose, and the larks!   10
The mushrooms shew his wit was sudden!
And for his judgment lo a pudden!
Roast beef, tho' old, proclaims him stout,
And grace, altho' a bard, devout.
May TOM, whom heav'n sent down to raise   15
The price of prologues and of plays,
Be ev'ry birth-day more a winner,
Digest his thirty-thousandth dinner;
Walk to his grave without reproach,
And scorn a rascal and a coach!   20

Epigram [On Bishop Hough]

[written c. 1742; published 1742]

A bishop by his Neighbours hated
Has Cause to wish himself translated.

For Pope's opinion of Hough see *Epil. to Sat.*, II 240, p. 703.

But why shou'd *Hough* desire Translation,
Lov'd and esteem'd by all the Nation?
   Yet if it be the old Man's Case,   5
I'll lay my Life, I know the Place:
'Tis where God sent some that adore him,
And whither *Enoch* went before him.

Epitaph on Mr. Rowe

IN WESTMINSTER-ABBEY

[written 1743?; published 1743]

Thy Reliques, *Rowe*! to this sad Shrine we trust,
And near thy *Shakespear* place thy honour'd Bust,
Oh next him skill'd to draw the tender Tear,
For never Heart felt Passion more sincere:
To nobler Sentiment to fire the Brave,   5
For never *Briton* more disdain'd a Slave!
Peace to thy gentle Shade, and endless Rest,
Blest in thy Genius, in thy Love too blest;
And blest, that timely from Our Scene remov'd
Thy Soul enjoys that Liberty it lov'd.   10

To these, so mourn'd in Death, so lov'd in Life!
The childless Parent and the widow'd Wife
With tears inscribes this monumental Stone,
That holds their Ashes and expects her own.

2. *thy Shakespear*] Rowe was Shakespeare's first editor (1709).
   11. *these*] I.e. Rowe and his daughter Charlotte Fane, whose death
(1739) is recorded on the pedestal of Rowe's bust.

Fragment of Brutus, an Epic

[written 1743; published 1954]

The Patient Chief, who lab'ring long, arriv'd
On Britains Shore and brought with fav'ring Gods
Arts Arms and Honour to her Ancient Sons:
Daughter of Memory! from elder Time
Recall; and me, with Britains Glory fir'd,   5
Me, far from meaner Care or meaner Song,
Snatch to thy Holy Hill of Spotless Bay,
My Countrys Poet, to record her Fame.

Lines on Bounce

[written 1744; published 1872]

> Ah Bounce! ah gentle Beast! why wouldst thou dye,
> When thou had'st Meat enough, and Orrery?

Pope's dog, Bounce, had been entrusted to Lord Orrery, under whose care she died. On 10 April 1744, he wrote to Orrery:

I dread to enquire into the particulars of ye Fate of Bounce. Perhaps you conceald them, as Heav'n often does Unhappy Events, in pity to the Survivors, or not to hasten on my End by Sorrow. I doubt not how much Bounce was lamented: They might say as the Athenians did to Arcite, in Chaucer,

> Ah Arcite! gentle Knight! why would'st thou die,
> When thou had'st Gold enough, and Emilye?

The couplet which follows was probably the last he ever wrote.

Index of Titles

Acis and Galatea, Lines from   *page* 466
Adriani Morientis ad Animam   116
Alcander   265
Alley, The   10
Answer to Mrs. Howe   463
Argus   75
Arrival of Ulysses in Ithaca, The   69
Art of Sinking in Poetry, Lines from The   493
Artimesia   13
Atticus   293, 490

Balance of Europe, The   279
Boetius, de cons. Philos., From   115
Bounce to Fop   823
Brutus   836

Capon's Tale, The   477
Challenge, The; see Court Ballad, The
Character, A   820
Characters of Men, The   549
Characters of Women, The   559
Chaucer, Imitation of   9
Chorus's to the Tragedy of Brutus, Two   296
Cleopatra; see On the Statue of Cleopatra
Couplet from Horace   833
Couplet on his Grotto   834
Couplets on Wit   295
Court Ballad, The   305
Critical Specimen, Lines from The   277

Dialogue, A   465
Discovery, The   478
Dryope, The Fable of   26
Duke upon Duke   467
Dunciad in Four Books, The   709
Dunciad Variorum, The   317
Dying Christian to his Soul, The   116

Elegy to the Memory of an Unfortunate Lady   262
Eloisa to Abelard   252
Epigram, Engraved on the Collar of a Dog, 826; *from the French,*
    817; in a Maid of Honour's Prayer-Book, 481; *occasion'd by Ozell's*
    Translation of Boileau's Lutrin, 271; *on Authors and Booksellers,*
    276; on Bishop Hough, 835; *on Cibber's Declaration that he will*
    have the Last Word with Mr. Pope, 835; *on lopping Trees in his*

Epigram, (contd.)

    Garden, 831; *on One who made long Epitaphs*, 822; *on Poets*, 276; *on seeing the Ladies at Crux-Easton*, 818; *on the Balance of Europe*, 279; *on the Toasts of the Kit-Cat Club*, 304; '*Peter complains*', 817; '*When other Ladies* . . .', 808; '*You beat your Pate*', 817

Epigrams from Private Letters   *page* 276

Epigrams from The Grub-street Journal   810

Epigrams, Occasion'd by an Invitation to Court   307

Epigrams occasioned by Cibber's verses in praise of Nash   821

Epigrams on Shakespear's Monument   834

Epilogue to Jane Shore   213

Epilogue to the Satires   688

Episode of Sarpedon, The   60

Epistle to Dr. Arbuthnot, An   597

Epistle to Allen Lord Bathurst   570

Epistle to Miss Blount, with the Works of Voiture   169

Epistle to Miss Blount . . . after the Coronation   243

Epistle to Richard Boyle, Earl of Burlington   586

Epistle to James Craggs, Esq;   465

Epistle to Henry Cromwell, Esq; An   267

Epistle to Mr. Jervas   249

Epistle to a Lady   308, 559

Epistle to Robert, Earl of Oxford   313

Epitaph, for Dr. Francis Atterbury, 816; *on Edmund Duke of Buckingham*, 822; *Of By-Words*, 817; *on John Lord Caryll*, 278; *on Mrs. Corbet*, 809; *on James Craggs, Esq.*, 490; *on . . . Robert Digby, and . . . his Sister Mary*, 498; *on Charles Earl of Dorset*, 813; *designed for Mr. Dryden's Monument*, 464; *on Mr. Elijah Fenton*, 808; *on G—*, 496; *on Mr. Gay*, 818; *on the Honble. Simon Harcourt*, 473; *on Himself*, 827; *on Sir Godfrey Kneller*, 497; *on Lady Kneller*, 474; *on John Knight*, 813; *intended for Sir Isaac Newton*, 808; *on P. P. Clerk of the Parish*, 294; *intended for Mr. Rowe*, 464; *on Mr. Rowe*, 836; *on Sir William Trumbull*, 300; *for One who would not be buried in Westminster Abbey*, 827; *on General Henry Withers*, 809

Epitaphs from the Latin on the Count of Mirandula, 496; *on John Hewet and Sarah Drew, Three*, 462

Essay on Criticism, An   143

Essay on Man, An   501

Fable of Dryope, The   26

Fable of Vertumnus and Pomona, The   22

Farewell to London, A   245

Fragment of a Satire; see *Atticus*

Garden, The   12

Gardens of Alcinous, The   59

Gulliver's Travels, Verses on   481

Happy Life of a Country Parson, The	*page* 15
Homer, Translations of	59, 60, 69, 75
Horace, Satyr 4. Lib. I. Paraphrased	814
Hymn of St. Francis Xavier	115
Hymn Written in Windsor Forest, A	310

Imitation of Martial   117
Imitations of English Poets   3
Imitations of Horace, Sat. II. i, 613; *Sat. II. ii,* 619; *Ep. I. i.* 624; *Ep. I. vi,* 630; *Ep. II. i,* 634; *Ep. II. ii,* 650; *Sat. II. vi,* 659; *Ep. I. vii,* 664; *Sat. I. ii,* 667; *Od. IV. i,* 673; *Od. IV. ix,* 674
Impertinent, The; see *Satires of Donne Versifyed*
Impromptu, to Lady Winchelsea   288
In behalf of Mr. Southerne   466
Inscriptio   497
Inscription, Martha Blount; A: P: 283; 'Nymph of the Grot', 474; *on a Grotto of Shells at Crux-Easton,* 818; *upon a Punch-Bowl, An,* 472

January and May   76

Key to the Lock, Four Poems from A   289

Letter to Cromwell   271
Lines, added to Wycherley's poems, 272; *from The Critical Specimen,* 277; *in Conclusion of a Satire,* 497; *on Bounce,* 837; *on Coffee,* 278; *on Curll,* 298; *on Dulness,* 272; *on Ministers,* 833; *on Mr. Hatton's Clocks,* 461; *on Swift's Ancestors,* 475; *on Writing a Tragedy,* 278; *Fatis agimur,* 276; *My Pylades,* 276; *to Lord Bathurst,* 461; *to Bolingbroke,* 473; *to a Friend,* 812; *to King George II,* 834

Macer   290
Messiah   189
Moral Essays; see *Characters of Men, The; Characters of Women, The; Epistle to Allen Lord Bathurst; Epistle to . . . Richard, Earl of Burlington*

Occasion'd by some Verses of . . . the Duke of Buckingham   308
Ode for Musick, on St. Cecilia's Day   139
Ode on Solitude   265
Odyssey; see *Homer*
Of a Lady singing to her Lute   3
Of her Picture   4
Of her Sickness   4
Of her Sighing   5
Of her walking in a Garden after a Shower   4
Of the Lady who could not sleep in a stormy Night   3
Of the Use of Riches; see *Epistle to Allen Lord Bathurst*

On a certain Lady at Court   page 474
On a Fan   12
On a Lady who P—st at the Tragedy of Cato   283
On a Picture of Queen Caroline drawn by Lady Burlington   832
On Dr. Alured Clarke   833
On Lady Mary Wortley Montagu's Portrait   465
On lying in the Earl of Rochester's Bed at Atterbury   706
On Queen Caroline's Death-bed   832
On receiving from the Right Hon. the Lady Frances Shirley a Standish
    and two Pens,   704
On Silence   8
On the Benefactions in the late Frost   832
On the Countess of Burlington cutting Paper   813
On the Statue of Cleopatra   111
One Thousand Seven Hundred and Forty   827

Paraphrase on Thomas a Kempis, A   17
Pastorals   119
Phryne   14
Polyphemus and Acis   18
Prayer of Brutus, The,   118
Presentation Verses to Nathaniel Pigott   476
Presenting a Lark   6
Prologue, Design'd for Mr. Durfey's last Play, 212; for the Benefit of
    Mr. Dennis, 819; to Cato, 211; to Sophonisba, 807; to The Three
    Hours after Marriage, 304
Psalm xci   113

Rape of the Lock, The   217
Receipt to make a Cuckold, A   283
Receipt to make Soup   475
River, The   6
Roman Catholick Version of the First Psalm, A   300
Rondeau   111

Sandys's Ghost   301
Sapho to Phaon   29
Satires of Donne Versifyed   676, 679
Scriblerian Invitations   285, 462
Six Maidens, The   815
Sober Advice from Horace   667
Sonnet written upon Occasion of the Plague   826
Stanzas from . . . Malherbe   114
Statius his Thebais, The First Book of   35
Successio; see To the Author of a Poem, intitled, Successio
Sylvia, a fragment   492

Temple of Fame, The   172
Three Gentle Shepherds, The   285

To a Lady with the Temple of Fame *page* 289
To Belinda on the Rape of the Lock 284
To Mr. Addison, Occasioned by his Dialogues on Medals 215
To Mrs. M. B. on her Birth-day 315
To Eustace Budgell, Esq. On his Translation of . . . Theophrastus 288
To Mr. C 810
To Mr. Gay 472
To Lord Hervey and Lady Mary Wortley 820
To Mr. John Moore, Author of the celebrated Worm-Powder 298
To Sir Godfrey Kneller 466
To the Author of a Poem, intitled, Successio 7
To the Earl of Burlington asking who writ the Libels against him, 820
To the Earl of Oxford . . . upon a piece of News in Mist 495
Tom Southerne's Birth-day Dinner 835
Two or Three 283

Umbra 293
Unfortunate Lady; see *Elegy to the Memory of*
Universal Prayer, The 247
Upon a Girl of Seven Years Old 284

Verbatim from Boileau 832
Verses in Imitation of Cowley 5
Verses occasion'd by an &c. at the End of Mr. D'Urfy's Name in the
  Title to one of his Plays 280
Verses on a Grotto . . . at Twickenham 707
Verses on Gulliver's Travels 481
Verses sent to Mrs. T. B. with his Works 309
Verses to be placed under the Picture of England's Arch-Poet 494
Verses to be prefix'd before Bernard Lintot's new Miscellany 279
Verses to Mrs. Judith Cowper 473
Vertumnus and Pomona, The Fable of 22

Weeping 5
Wife of Bath her Prologue, The 98
Windsor-Forest 195
Winter Piece, A 283
Written over a Study; out of Maynard 118
Wrote by Mr. P. in a Volume of Evelyn on Coins 815

Index of First Lines

A Bishop by his Neighbours hated | *page* 835
A gold watch found on Cinder Whore | 811
A manly Form; a bold, yet modest mind | 278
A pleasing form, a firm, yet cautious mind | 300
A Pox of all Senders | 287
A Shepherd's Boy (he seeks no better Name) | 129
A Soul as full of Worth, as void of Pride | 465
A Tower there is, where six Maidens do dwell | 815
A Wood? quoth Lewis; and with that | 461
Adam had fallen twice, if for an apple | 307
After an hundred and thirty years' nap | 834
Again? new Tumults in my Breast? | 673
Ah Bounce! ah gentle Beast! why wouldst thou dye | 837
Ah fleeting Spirit! wand'ring Fire | 116
Ah, friend! 'tis true—this truth you lovers know | 472
Ah *Serenissa*, from our arms | 4
Alas! poor *Æschylus*! unlucky Dog! | 367
Alas! what room for Flattry; or for Pride | 832
All hail, arch poet without peer! | 802
All hail! once pleasing, once inspiring Shade | 310
And life itself can nothing more supply | 834
And thou! whose sense, whose humour, and whose rage | 497
Apply thine Engine to the spungy Door | 493
Argyle his Praise, when *Southerne* wrote | 466
As gods sometimes descend from heav'n and deign | 3
As long as Moco's happy Tree shall grow | 278
As man's meanders to the vital spring | 266
As some fond virgin, whom her mother's care | 243
As when that Hero, who in each Campaign | 819
As when the freezing blasts of Boreas blow | 283
At length, my Friend (while Time, with still career | 117
At length, my soul! thy fruitless hopes give o'er | 114
At length the Board, in loose disjointed Chat | 275
Authors are judg'd by strange capricious Rules | 304
Authors the world and their dull brains have trac'd | 818
Awake, my *St. John*! leave all meaner things | 503

Barrels conceal the Liquor they contain | 290
Begone ye Criticks, and restrain your Spite | 7
Behold a Scene of Misery and Woe! | 267
Behold! ambitious of the *British* bays | 811
Behold the Woes of Matrimonial Life | 98
Beneath the Shade a spreading Beech displays | 132
Books and the Man I sing, the first who brings | 349
Bring forth some Remnant of *Promethean* theft | 493
Bring me what Nature, Taylor to the *Bear* | 493

Burnet and *Duckit*, friends in spite   *page* 412
But if to Solitude we turn our Eyes   274
But Ministers like Gladiators live   833
But our Great Turks in wit must reign alone   295
But what avails to lay down rules for sense?   497

Cibber! write all thy Verses upon Glasses   822
Close to the best known Author, *Umbra* sits   293
Close to the gates a spacious garden lies   59
Come, fill the South-Sea Goblet full   472
Come, gentle Air! th'*Æolian* Shepherd said   12

Damnation follows Death in other Men   276
Dear Col'nel! *Cobham's* and your Country's Friend!   650
Dear, damn'd, distracting Town, farewell!   245
Dear Mr. Cromwell, May it please ye!   267
Descend ye Nine! descend and sing   139
Did Milton's Prose, O Charles, thy Death defend?   812
Dorset, the Grace of Courts, the Muses Pride   813

Each pretty Carecter with pleasing Smart   283

Fain would my Muse the flow'ry Treasures sing   12
Fair charmer cease, nor make your voice's prize   3
Fair Mirrour of foul Times! whose fragile Sheene   826
Father of All! in every Age   247
Fatis agimur, cedite fatis!   276
Few words are best; I wish you well   810
First in these Fields I try the Sylvan Strains   123
Fly *Pegasæan* Steed, thy Rider bear   277
For whom thus rudely pleads my loud-tongu'd Gate   493
Fraternal Rage, the guilty *Thebes* Alarms   36
Friend! for your Epitaphs I'm griev'd   822
From fair Symæthis and her Faunus came   18
From hour to hour melodiously they chime   461

Go! fair Example of untainted youth   498
Go tuneful bird, forbear to soar   6
Goddess of Woods, tremendous in the chase   118
Grown old in Rhyme, 'twere barbarous to discard   212

Hail, dear Collegiate, Fellow-Operator   290
Hail sacred spring, whose fruitful stream   6
Happy the man, whose wish and care   265
He who beneath thy shelt'ring wing resides   113
Here *Francis Ch—s* lies—Be civil!   496
Here lies a round Woman, who thought *mighty odd*   817
Here lies Lord Coningsby—be civil   496

Here lies wrapt up in forty thousand towels *page* 832
Here lye two poor Lovers, who had the mishap 463
Here lyes what had nor *Birth*, nor *Shape*, nor *Fame* 811
Here rests a Woman, good without pretence 809
Here, shunning idleness at once and praise 818
Here, stopt by hasty Death, Alexis lies 117
Here Withers rest! thou bravest, gentlest mind 809
Heroes, and Kings! your distance keep 827
His Eye-Balls burn, he wounds the smoaking Plain 267
Honour and Wealth, the Joys we seek, deny 274
How foolish Men on Expeditions goe! 288
How much, egregious *Moor*, are we 298

I am his Highness' Dog at *Kew* 826
I know the thing that's most uncommon 474
I'd call them Mountains, but can't call them so 267
If meagre Gildon draws his venal quill 293, 490
If modest Youth, with cool Reflection crown'd 822
In Amaze 481
In ev'ry Town, where *Thamis* rolls his Tyde 10
In merry old England it once was a rule 422
In Miniature see *Nature's* Power appear 489
In that soft Season when descending Showers 173
In the *Lines* that you sent, are the *Muses* and *Graces* 307
In these deep solitudes and awful cells 252
In these gay Thoughts the Loves and Graces shine 169
In this strange Town a different Course we take 308
In unambitious silence be my lot 833
In vain you boast Poetic Names of yore 288
In *Yorkshire* dwelt a sober Yeoman 477
I've often wish'd that I had clear 659

Jonathan Swift 475
Jove call'd before him t'other Day 280
Jove was alike to *Latian* and to *Phrygian* 278

Kneller, by Heav'n and not a Master taught 497

Lac'd in her *Cosins* new appear'd the Bride 266
Lest you should think that Verse shall die 674
Let Clarke make half his life the poor's support 833
Let not the whigs our tory club rebuke 287

Mark by what wretched steps Great * * grows 820
May THESE put Money in your Purse 833
More always smiles whenever he recites 374
Most true it is, I dare to say 478
Muse, 'tis enough: at length thy labour ends 308
My Ld. complains, that *P—* (stark mad with Gardens) 831

My Lord, forsake your Politick Utopians *page* 286
My *Pylades*! what *Juv'nal* says, no Jest is 276

Nature, and Nature's Laws lay hid in Night 808
Nothing so true as what you once let fall 560
'Not to Admire, is all the Art I know 630
Not twice a twelve month you appear in Print 688
Now *Europe's* balanc'd, neither Side prevails 279
Now wits gain praise by copying other wits 295
Nymph of the Grot, these sacred Springs I keep 474

O all-accomplish'd Cæsar! on thy Shelf 834
O fairest Pattern to a failing Age! 823
O Nash! more blest in ev'ry other thing 821
O Reader, if that thou canst read 294
O Thou, whose all-creating hands sustain 115
O wretched B—, jealous now of all 827
Of *gentle Philips* will I ever sing 285
Of Manners gentle, of Affections mild 818
Oh be thou blest with all that Heav'n can send 315
Oh tyrant Love! hast thou possest 152
On Sunday at Six, in the Street that's call'd *Gerrard* 308
Once in his Life M—re judges right 811
Once (says an Author, where, I need not say) 832
One day I mean to Fill Sir Godfry's tomb 474
One that should be a Saint 462
Ozell, at *Sanger's* Call, invok'd his Muse 271

Pallas grew vap'rish once and odd 813
Parson, these Things in thy possessing 15
Peter complains, that God has given 817
Phryne had Talents for Mankind 14
Pleas'd in these lines, *Belinda*, you may view 284
Prodigious this! the Frail one of our Play 213

Quoth *Cibber* to *Pope*, tho' in Verse you foreclose 835

Resign'd to live, prepar'd to die 835

St. John, whose love indulg'd my labours past 835
Say, lovely Youth, that dost my Heart command 29
Says *Cibber* to *Pope* . . . (*see* Quoth *Cibber* to *Pope* . . .)
See how the sun in dusky skies 4
See the wild Waste of all-devouring years! 215
See who ne'er was or will be half read! 494
Shall Royal praise be rhym'd by such a ribald 811
She drinks! She drinks! Behold the matchless Dame! 266

She said, and for her lost *Galanthis* sighs   page 26
Shields, helms, and swords all jangle as they hang   265
Shou'd *D—s* print how once you robb'd your Brother   812
Shut, shut the door, good *John*! fatigu'd I said   597
Silence! Coœval with Eternity   8
Since my old Friend is grown so great   465
Sir, I admit your gen'ral Rule   817
Sir,—This Letter greets you from the Shades   271
So Clocks to Lead their nimble Motions owe   273
So on *Mæotis'* Marsh, (where Reeds and Rushes   277
So swift,—this moment here, the next 'tis gone   266
So Waters putrifie with Rest, and lose   274
So when Curll's Stomach the strong Drench o'ercame   298
Some *Colinæus* praise, some *Bleau*   279
Some, over each Orac'lous Glass, fore-doom   275
Some who grow dull religious strait commence   295
Soon as *Glumdalclitch* mist her pleasing Care   482
Speak, Gracious Lord, oh speak; thy Servant hears   17
Statesman, yet Friend to Truth! of Soul sincere   490
Such were the Notes, thy once-lov'd Poet sung   313
Sylvia my Heart in wond'rous wise alarm'd   492

Take a knuckle of Veal   475
Tell me, by all the melting joys of Love   278
The Doctor and Dean, Pope, Parnell and Gay   286
The Fair Pomona flourish'd in his Reign   22
The Flocks shall leave the Mountains   466
The *Fop*, whose Pride affects a *Patron's* name   814
The Maid is Blest that will not hear   300
The Mighty Mother, and her Son who brings   719
The Muse this one Verse to learn'd Pigot addresses   476
The nymph her graces here express'd may find   4
The Patient Chief, who lab'ring long, arriv'd   836
The play full smiles around the dimpled mouth   465
The Poize of Dulness to the heavy Skull   273
The Sun descending, the *Phæacian* Train   69
The *Spaniard* hides his Ponyard in his Cloke   291
The Tribe of Templars, Play'rs, Apothecaries   667
The wooden Guardian of our Privacy   493
There are (I scarce can think it, but am told)   613
There liv'd in *Lombardy*, as Authors write   76
They may talk of the *Goddesses* in *Ida* Vales   307
They say *Argyll*'s a Wit, for what?   308
Think not by rigorous judgment seiz'd   463
This Book, which, like its Author, You   309
This Letter greets you from the Shades   271
This modest Stone what few vain Marbles can   808
This *Sheffield* rais'd. The sacred Dust below   464
This verse be thine, my friend, nor thou refuse   249

Tho' *Artimesia* talks, by Fits   *page* 14
Tho' many a Wit from time to time has rose   290
Tho' sprightly Sappho force our love and praise   473
Tho the Dean has run from us in manner uncivil   286
Thou art my God, sole object of my love   115
Thou who shalt stop, where *Thames*' translucent
    Wave   707
Thus Britain lov'd me; and preserv'd my Fame   834
Thus Dulness, the safe Opiate of the Mind   272
Thus either Men in private useless Ease   273
Thus have I *seen*, in *Araby* the blest   267
Thus *Hector*, great in Arms, contends in vain   61
Thy Forests, *Windsor!* and thy green Retreats   195
Thy reliques, *Rowe*, to this fair urn we trust   464
Thy Reliques, *Rowe*! to this sad Shrine we trust   836
Thyrsis, the Musick of that murm'ring Spring   135
Tir'd with vain hopes, and with complaints as vain   118
'Tis all a Libel—*Paxton* (Sir) will say   694
'Tis gen'rous, *Tibald!* in thee and thy brothers   363
'Tis hard to say, if greater Want of Skill   144
'Tis rumour'd, *Budgell* on a time   288
'Tis strange, the Miser should his Cares employ   588
'Tis true, my Lord, I gave my word   664
To Lordings proud I tune my Lay   467
To one fair Lady out of court   305
To prove himself no Plagiary, Moore   810
To thee, sweet *Fop*, these Lines I send   823
To thee, we Wretches of the *Houyhnhnm* Band   484
To this sad Shrine, who'er thou art, draw near   473
To wake the soul by tender strokes of art   211
Tom Wood of *Chiswic*, deep divine   815
Two or *Three* Visits, with *Two* or *Three* Bows   283

Under this Marble, or under this Sill   827

Venus beheld her, 'midst her Crowd of Slaves   266
Vital spark of heav'nly flame   116

Welcome, thrice welcome to thy native Place!   486
Well, if it be my time to quit the Stage   679
Well, Sir, suppose the *Busto*'s a damn'd head   382
Well then, poor *G*—— lies under ground!   496
Wesley, if Wesley 'tis they mean   495
What, and how great, the Virtue and the Art   619
What Authors lose, their Booksellers have won   276
What beck'ning ghost, along the moonlight shade   262
What dire Offence from am'rous Causes springs   218
What God, what Genius did the Pencil move   466
What is Prudery? 'Tis a Beldam   463

What pleasing Phrensy steals away my Soul?   *page* 473
What wonder tryumphs never turn'd his brain   820
What's Fame with Men, by Custom of the Nation   289
When Eastern lovers feed the fun'ral fire   462
When I but call a flagrant Whore unsound   820
When *Israel*'s Daughters mourn'd their past Offences   481
When learning, after the long *Gothic* night   807
When love would strike th'offending fair   5
When other Ladies to the Groves go down   808
When simple *Macer*, now of high Renown   292
When wise *Ulysses*, from his native coast   75
Whence deathless *Kit-Cat* took its Name   304
While *Celia's* tears make sorrow bright   5
While ev'ry Joy, successful Youth! is thine   812
While maudlin Whigs deplor'd their *Cato*'s Fate   283
While You, great Patron of Mankind, sustain   635
Who shall decide, when Doctors disagree   570
Whoe're thou art whom this fair statue charms   III
Whose honours with increase of ages grow   266
Wit is like faith by such warm Fools profest   295
With no poetick ardors fir'd   706
Wit's Queen, (if what the Poets sing be true)   284
Wits starve as useless to a Common weal   295
Women ben full of Ragerie   9
Woud you your writings to some Palates fit   295
Wretched Lovers, Fate has past   467

Ye Lords and Commons, Men of Wit   301
Ye Nymphs of *Solyma!* begin the Song   189
Ye shades, where sacred truth is sought   296
Yes, I beheld th' Athenian Queen   704
Yes; thank my stars! as early as I knew   676
Yes, 'tis the time! I cry'd, impose the chain!   832
Yes, we have liv'd—one pang, and then we part!   816
Yes, you despise the man to Books confin'd   550
Yon Luminary Amputation needs   493
You ask why *Roome* diverts you with his jokes   409
You beat your Pate, and fancy Wit will come   817
You *Bellenden, Griffin,* and little *La Pell*   307
You know where you did despise   III
You who shall stop where . . . (*See*—Thou who shalt stop . . .)
You wonder Who this Thing has writ   820